时代教育·国外高校优秀教材精选

线性代数引论

(英文版·原书第5版)

Introduction to Linear Algebra

李 W. 约翰逊(Lee W. Johnson)
(美)R. 迪安 里斯(R. Dean Riess) 著
吉米 T. 阿诺德(Jimmy T. Arnold)

机械工业出版社

图书在版编目(CIP)数据

线性代数引论 = Introduction to Linear Algebra:第 5 版/（美）约翰逊（Johnson, L. W.）等著. —北京：机械工业出版社，2002.7（2008.3 重印）
（时代教育·国外高校优秀教材精选）
ISBN 978-7-111-10628-9

Ⅰ.线… Ⅱ.约… Ⅲ.线性代数-高等学校-教材-英文 Ⅳ.0151.2

中国版本图书馆 CIP 数据核字(2002)第 053677 号

机械工业出版社(北京市百万庄大街 22 号　邮政编码 100037)
责任编辑:刘小慧　封面设计:鞠　杨　责任印制:李　妍
北京蓝海印刷有限公司印刷
2008 年 3 月第 1 版·第 5 次印刷
184mm×260mm ·38.5 印张·2 插页·967 千字
标准书号:ISBN 978-7-111-10628-9
定价:36.00 元

凡购本书，如有缺页、倒页、脱页，由本社发行部调换
销售服务热线电话:(010) 68326294
购书热线电话:(010) 88379639 88379641 88379643
编辑热线电话:(010) 88379711
封面无防伪标均为盗版

国外高校优秀教材审定委员会

序

本书是由约翰逊、里斯、阿诺德编著的《线性代数引论》第5版，出版于2002年。

线性代数是学习自然科学、工程和社会科学的学生的一门重要的基础课程，其核心内容包括矩阵理论以及向量空间理论。这些概念和理论不仅为各个专业领域提出相关问题时提供了准确的数学表达语言，而且也为解决问题提供了有力的工具。本书的主要内容有矩阵与线性方程组、二维和三维空间、向量空间 R^n、特征值问题、向量空间和线性变换、行列式、特征值及其应用等。

作为线性代数课程的教材，本书有如下特点：

1. 内容覆盖了我国现行理工科大学线性代数课程的全部内容，与我国现行的线性代数教学大纲和教材体系比较接近，但比国内现有教材的内容更为丰富，且更有深度。

2. 本书的编写采取了模块式的结构，便于使用者取舍。线性代数的核心内容主要由三部分组成，它们是矩阵理论与线性方程组、向量空间的基本概念以及特征值问题，作者将它们分别列入第1章、第3章、第4章。这样，对于学时较少，要求相对较低的专业和读者，可以只选这三章，用30学时左右就可以掌握线性代数的最基本的知识，对于学时充裕、要求较高的专业可以从容地增加其它章节。

3. 在内容处理上，及早引进一些重要的概念，例如在第1章就引入线性组合和线性无关的概念，从而帮助学生很快地从用一般方法解线性方程组过渡到用基、生成系等概念来处理和解决相应的问题。又如在第3章及时建立向量空间 R^n 的概念和从 R^n 到 R^m 的线性变换，那么在第4章一开始简单地引入行列式概念后，就可以比较深入地讨论特征值问题。

4. 向量空间的概念是线性代数学习中的一个难点，为了分散难点，使学生能更平稳地、逐步地接受这个抽象概念，本书作了一系列的铺垫。例如第1章先引入线性无关的概念，然后在第2章讨论二维空间和三维空间，这是两个非常形象，又是学生很熟悉的空间，在这个基础上推广到 R^n 这个 n 维空间，实现了从感性思维到理性思维的第一个飞跃。最后再进入完全抽象的一般线性空间。

5. 线性代数是一门既严谨又抽象的课程，为了使学生既易于入门，又能领会数学抽象的威力，作者通过许多有实际背景的例子，从具体计算入手，自然地、逐步地建立抽象的概念和理论。

6. 21世纪是信息的时代，现代教学手段促进了教学改革的步伐，为进一步提高教学质量提供了有利的教学环境。本书通过例子介绍了在科技工作者中非常流行的数学软件Matlab在线性代数中的应用，并且每章结尾都附有专门用Matlab做的练习题，这对于培养学生运用现代数学软件学习线性代数和应用代数知识解决实际问题能起到很好的作用。

总之，本书系统新颖、内容丰富、联系实际、语言通畅，且结合数学软件提供了一个现代化的学习环境，相对于国内现行教学大纲，教师便于取舍内容组织教学，不失为一本很好的教科书和教学参考书。

本书可供理工科、经济管理各专业学生作为学习线性代数的教科书或教学参考书，也可供科技人员和自学者参考。

俞正光

清华大学数学科学系

出版说明

随着我国加入 WTO，国际间的竞争越来越激烈，而国际间的竞争实际上也就是人才的竞争、教育的竞争。为了加快培养具有国际竞争力的高水平技术人才，加快我国教育改革的步伐，国家教育部近来出台了一系列倡导高校开展双语教学、引进原版教材的政策。以此为契机，机械工业出版社近期推出了一系列国外影印版教材，其内容涉及高等学校公共基础课，以及机、电、信息领域的专业基础课和专业课。

引进国外优秀原版教材，在有条件的学校推动开展英语授课或双语教学，自然也引进了先进的教学思想和教学方法，这对提高我国自编教材的水平，加强学生的英语实际应用能力，使我国的高等教育尽快与国际接轨，必将起到积极的推动作用。

为了做好教材的引进工作，机械工业出版社特别成立了由著名专家组成的国外高校优秀教材审定委员会。这些专家对实施双语教学做了深入细致的调查研究，对引进原版教材提出许多建设性意见，并慎重地对每一本将要引进的原版教材一审再审，精选再精选，确认教材本身的质量水平，以及权威性和先进性，以期所引进的原版教材能适应我国学生的外语水平和学习特点。在引进工作中，审定委员会还结合我国高校教学课程体系的设置和要求，对原版教材的教学思想和方法的先进性、科学性严格把关。同时尽量考虑原版教材的系统性和经济性。

这套教材出版后，我们将根据各高校的双语教学计划，举办原版教材的教师培训，及时地将其推荐给各高校选用。希望高校师生在使用教材后及时反馈意见和建议，使我们更好地为教学改革服务。

机械工业出版社
高等教育分社

PREFACE

Linear algebra is an important component of undergraduate mathematics, particularly for students majoring in the scientific, engineering, and social science disciplines. At the practical level, matrix theory and the related vector-space concepts provide a language and a powerful computational framework for posing and solving important problems. Beyond this, elementary linear algebra is a valuable introduction to mathematical abstraction and logical reasoning because the theoretical development is self-contained, consistent, and accessible to most students.

Therefore, this book stresses both practical computation and theoretical principles and centers on the principal topics of the first four chapters:

matrix theory and systems of linear equations,

elementary vector-space concepts, and

the eigenvalue problem.

This core material can be used for a brief (10-week) course at the late-freshman/sophomore level. There is enough additional material in Chapters 5–7 either for a more advanced or a more leisurely paced course.

FEATURES

Our experience teaching freshman and sophomore linear algebra has led us to carefully choose the features of this text. Our approach is based on the way students learn *and* on the tools they need to be successful in linear algebra as well as in related courses.

We have found that students learn more effectively when the material has a consistent level of difficulty. Therefore, in Chapter 1, we provide early and meaningful coverage of topics such as linear combinations and linear independence. This approach helps the student negotiate what is usually a dramatic jump in level from solving systems of linear equations to working with concepts such as basis and spanning set.

TOOLS STUDENTS NEED (WHEN THEY NEED THEM)

The following examples illustrate how we provide students with the tools they need for success.

An early introduction to eigenvalues. In Chapter 3, elementary vector-space ideas (subspace, basis, dimension, and so on) are introduced in the familiar setting of R^n. Therefore, it is possible to cover the eigenvalue problem very early and in much greater depth than is usually possible. A brief introduction to determinants is given in Section 4.2 to facilitate the early treatment of eigenvalues.

An early introduction to linear combinations. In Section 1.5, we observe that the matrix-vector product $A\mathbf{x}$ can be expressed as a linear combination of the columns of

A, $A\mathbf{x} = x_1\mathbf{A}_1 + x_2\mathbf{A}_2 + \cdots + x_n\mathbf{A}_n$. This viewpoint leads to a simple and natural development for the theory associated with systems of linear equations. For instance, the equation $A\mathbf{x} = \mathbf{b}$ is consistent if and only if $\mathbf{b}$ is expressible as a linear combination of the columns of A. Similarly, a consistent equation $A\mathbf{x} = \mathbf{b}$ has a unique solution if and only if the columns of A are linearly independent. This approach gives some early motivation for the vector-space concepts (introduced in Chapter 3) such as subspace, basis, and dimension. The approach also simplifies ideas such as rank and nullity (which are then naturally given in terms of dimension of appropriate subspaces).

Applications to different fields of study. Some applications are drawn from difference equations and differential equations. Other applications involve interpolation of data and least-squares approximations. In particular, students from a wide variety of disciplines have encountered problems of drawing curves that fit experimental or empirical data. Hence, they can appreciate techniques from linear algebra that can be applied to such problems.

Computer awareness. The increased accessibility of computers (especially personal computers) is beginning to affect linear algebra courses in much the same way as it has calculus courses. Accordingly, this text has somewhat of a numerical flavor, and (when it is appropriate) we comment on various aspects of solving linear algebra problems in a computer environment.

A Comfort in the Storm

We have attempted to provide the type of student support that will encourage success in linear algebra—one of the most important undergraduate mathematics courses that students take.

A gradual increase in the level of difficulty. In a typical linear algebra course, the students find the techniques of Gaussian elimination and matrix operations fairly easy. Then, the ensuing material relating to vector spaces is suddenly much harder. We do three things to lessen this abrupt midterm jump in difficulty:

1. We introduce linear independence early in Section 1.7.
2. We include a new Chapter 2, "Vectors in 2-Space and 3-Space."
3. We first study vector space concepts such as subspace, basis, and dimension in Chapter 3, in the familiar geometrical setting of R^n.

Clarity of exposition. For many students, linear algebra is the most rigorous and abstract mathematical course they have taken since high-school geometry. We have tried to write the text so that it is accessible, but also so that it reveals something of the power of mathematical abstraction. To this end, the topics have been organized so that they flow logically and naturally from the concrete and computational to the more abstract. Numerous examples, many presented in extreme detail, have been included in order to illustrate the concepts. The sections are divided into subsections with boldface headings. This device allows the reader to develop a mental outline of the material and to see how the pieces fit together.

Extensive exercise sets. We have provided a large number of exercises, ranging from routine drill exercises to interesting applications and exercises of a theoretical nature. The more difficult theoretical exercises have fairly substantial hints. The computational exercises are written using workable numbers that do not obscure the point with a mass of cumbersome arithmetic details.

Trustworthy answer key. Except for the theoretical exercises, solutions to the odd-numbered exercises are given at the back of the text. We have expended considerable effort to ensure that these solutions are correct.

Spiraling exercises. Many sections contain a few exercises that hint at ideas that will be developed later. Such exercises help to get the student involved in thinking about extensions of the material that has just been covered. Thus the student can anticipate a bit of the shape of things to come. This feature helps to lend unity and cohesion to the material.

Historical notes. We have a number of historical notes. These assist the student in gaining a historical and mathematical perspective of the ideas and concepts of linear algebra.

Supplementary exercises. We include, at the end of each chapter, a set of supplementary exercises. These exercises, some of which are true–false questions, are designed to test the student's understanding of important concepts. They often require the student to use ideas from several different sections.

Integration of MATLAB. We have included a collection of MATLAB projects at the end of each chapter. For the student who is interested in computation, these projects provide hands-on experience with MATLAB.

A short MATLAB appendix. Many students are not familiar with MATLAB. Therefore, we include a *very* brief appendix that is sufficient to get the student comfortable with using MATLAB for problems that typically arise in linear algebra.

The vector form for the general solution. To provide an additional early introduction to linear combinations and spanning sets, in Section 1.5 we introduce the idea of the vector form for the general solution of $A\mathbf{x} = \mathbf{b}$.

SUPPLEMENTS

Solutions Manuals

An Instructor's Solutions Manual and a Student's Solutions Manual are available. The odd-numbered computational exercises have answers at the back of the book. The student's solutions manual (ISBN 0-201-65860-7) includes detailed solutions for these exercises. The instructor's solutions manual (ISBN 0-201-75814-8) contains solutions to all the exercises.

New Technology Resource Manual. This manual was designed to assist in the teaching of the MATLAB, Maple, and Mathematica programs in the context of linear algebra. This manual is available from Addison-Wesley (ISBN 0-201-75812-1) or via [our website,] http://www.aw.com/jra.

Organization

To provide greater flexibility, Chapters 4, 5, and 6 are essentially independent. These chapters can be taken in any order once Chapters 1 and 3 are covered. Chapter 7 is a mélange of topics related to the eigenvalue problem: quadratic forms, differential equations, QR factorizations, Householder transformations, generalized eigenvectors, and so on. The sections in Chapter 7 can be covered in various orders. A schematic diagram illustrating the chapter dependencies is given below. Note that Chapter 2, "Vectors in 2-Space and 3-Space," can be omitted with no loss of continuity.

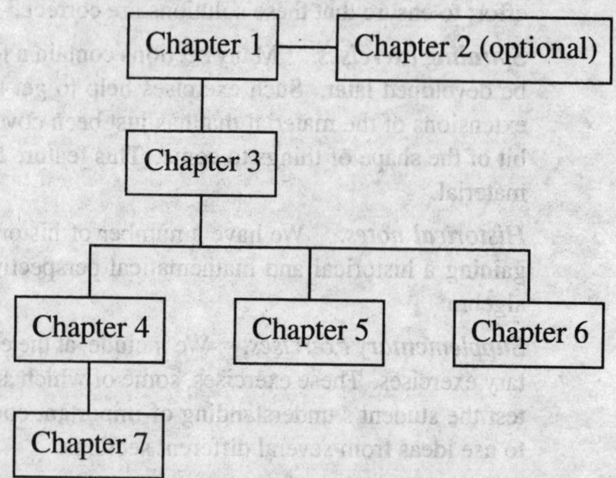

We especially note that Chapter 6 (Determinants) can be covered before Chapter 4 (Eigenvalues). However, Chapter 4 contains a brief introduction to determinants that should prove sufficient to users who do not wish to cover Chapter 6.

A very short but useful course at the beginning level can be built around the following sections:

Section 1.1–1.3, 1.5–1.7, 1.9

Sections 3.1–3.6

Sections 4.1–4.2, 4.4–4.5

A syllabus that integrates abstract vector spaces. Chapter 3 introduces elementary vector-space ideas in the familiar setting of R^n. We designed Chapter 3 in this way so that it is possible to cover the eigenvalue problem much earlier and in greater depth than is generally possible. Many instructors, however, prefer an integrated approach to vector spaces, one that combines R^n and abstract vector spaces. The following syllabus, similar to ones used successfully at several universities, allows for a course that integrates abstract vector spaces into Chapter 3. This syllabus also allows for a detailed treatment of determinants:

Sections 1.1–1.3, 1.5–1.7, 1.9

Sections 3.1–3.3, 5.1–5.3, 3.4–3.5, 5.4–5.5

Sections 4.1–4.3, 6.4–6.5, 4.4–4.7

Augmenting the core sections. As time and interest permit, the core of Sections 1.1–1.3, 1.5–1.7, 1.9, 3.1–3.6, 4.1–4.2, and 4.4–4.5 can be augmented by including various combinations of the following sections:

(a) *Data fitting and approximation:* 1.8, 3.8–3.9, 7.5–7.6.

(b) *Eigenvalue applications:* 4.8, 7.1–7.2.

(c) *More depth in vector space theory:* 3.7, Chapter 5.

(d) *More depth in eigenvalue theory:* 4.6–4.7, 7.3–7.4, 7.7–7.8.

(e) *Determinant theory:* Chapter 6.

To allow the possibility of getting quickly to eigenvalues, Chapter 4 contains a brief introduction to determinants. If the time is available and if it is desirable, Chapter 6 (Determinants) can be taken after Chapter 3. In such a course, Section 4.1 can be covered quickly and Sections 4.2–4.3 can be skipped.

Finally, in the interest of developing the student's mathematical sophistication, we have provided proofs for almost every theorem. However, some of the more technical proofs (such as the demonstration that $\det(AB) = \det(A)\det(B)$) are deferred to the end of the sections. As always, constraints of time and class maturity will dictate which proofs should be omitted.

ACKNOWLEDGMENTS

A great many valuable contributions to the Fifth Edition were made by those who reviewed the manuscript as it developed through various stages:

Idris Assani, University of North Carolina, Chapel Hill

Satish Bhatnagar, University of Nevada, Las Vegas

Richard Daquila, Muskingum College

Robert Dobrow, Clarkson University

Branko Grunbaum, University of Washington

Isom Herron, Rennsselaer Polytechnic Institute

Diane Hoffoss, Rice University

Richard Kubelka, San Jose State University

Tong Li, University of Iowa

David K. Neal, Western Kentucky University

Eileen Shugart, Virginia Institute of Technology

Nader Vakil, Western Illinios University

Tarynn Witten, Trinity University

Christos Xenophontos, Clarkson University

In addition, we wish to thank Michael A. Jones, Montclair State University and Isom Herron, Rennsselaer Polytech Institute for their careful work in accuracy checking this edition.

Blacksburg, Virginia

L.W.J.
R.D.R.
J.T.A.

CONTENTS

序 iv

出版说明 vi

1 MATRICES AND SYSTEMS OF LINEAR EQUATIONS 1

1.1 Introduction to Matrices and Systems of Linear Equations 2
1.2 Echelon Form and Gauss–Jordan Elimination 14
1.3 Consistent Systems of Linear Equations 28
1.4 Applications (Optional) 39
1.5 Matrix Operations 46
1.6 Algebraic Properties of Matrix Operations 61
1.7 Linear Independence and Nonsingular Matrices 71
1.8 Data Fitting, Numerical Integration, and Numerical Differentiation (Optional) 80
1.9 Matrix Inverses and Their Properties 92

2 VECTORS IN 2-SPACE AND 3-SPACE 113

2.1 Vectors in the Plane 114
2.2 Vectors in Space 128
2.3 The Dot Product and the Cross Product 135
2.4 Lines and Planes in Space 148

3 THE VECTOR SPACE R^n 163

3.1 Introduction 164
3.2 Vector Space Properties of R^n 167
3.3 Examples of Subspaces 176
3.4 Bases for Subspaces 188
3.5 Dimension 202
3.6 Orthogonal Bases for Subspaces 214
3.7 Linear Transformations from R^n to R^m 225
3.8 Least-Squares Solutions to Inconsistent Systems, with Applications to Data Fitting 243
3.9 Theory and Practice of Least Squares 255

4 **THE EIGENVALUE PROBLEM** 275

4.1 The Eigenvalue Problem for (2 × 2) Matrices 276
4.2 Determinants and the Eigenvalue Problem 280
4.3 Elementary Operations and Determinants (Optional) 290
4.4 Eigenvalues and the Characteristic Polynomial 298
4.5 Eigenvectors and Eigenspaces 307
4.6 Complex Eigenvalues and Eigenvectors 315
4.7 Similarity Transformations and Diagonalization 325
4.8 Difference Equations; Markov Chains; Systems of Differential Equations (Optional) 338

5 **VECTOR SPACES AND LINEAR TRANSFORMATIONS** 357

5.1 Introduction 358
5.2 Vector Spaces 360
5.3 Subspaces 368
5.4 Linear Independence, Bases, and Coordinates 375
5.5 Dimension 388
5.6 Inner-Product Spaces, Orthogonal Bases, and Projections (Optional) 392
5.7 Linear Transformations 403
5.8 Operations with Linear Transformations 411
5.9 Matrix Representations for Linear Transformations 419
5.10 Change of Basis and Diagonalization 431

6 **DETERMINANTS** 447

6.1 Introduction 448
6.2 Cofactor Expansions of Determinants 448
6.3 Elementary Operations and Determinants 455
6.4 Cramer's Rule 465
6.5 Applications of Determinants: Inverses and Wronksians 471

7 **EIGENVALUES AND APPLICATIONS** 483

7.1 Quadratic Forms 484
7.2 Systems of Differential Equations 493
7.3 Transformation to Hessenberg Form 502

7.4 Eigenvalues of Hessenberg Matrices 510
7.5 Householder Transformations 519
7.6 The *QR* Factorization and Least-Squares Solutions 531
7.7 Matrix Polynomials and the Cayley–Hamilton Theorem 540
7.8 Generalized Eigenvectors and Solutions of Systems of Differential Equations 546

APPENDIX: AN INTRODUCTION TO MATLAB AP1

ANSWERS TO SELECTED ODD-NUMBERED EXERCISES AN1

INDEX I1

教师反馈表

Matrices and Systems of Linear Equations

1

Overview

In this chapter we discuss systems of linear equations and methods (such as Gauss-Jordan elimination) for solving these systems. We introduce matrices as a convenient language for describing systems and the Gauss-Jordan solution method.

We next introduce the operations of addition and multiplication for matrices and show how these operations enable us to express a linear system in matrix-vector terms as

$$A\mathbf{x} = \mathbf{b}.$$

Representing the matrix A in column form as $A = [\mathbf{A}_1, \mathbf{A}_2, \ldots, \mathbf{A}_n]$, we then show that the equation $A\mathbf{x} = \mathbf{b}$ is equivalent to

$$x_1\mathbf{A}_1 + x_2\mathbf{A}_2 + \cdots + x_n\mathbf{A}_n = \mathbf{b}.$$

The equation above leads naturally to the concepts of linear combination and linear independence. In turn, those ideas allow us to address questions of existence and uniqueness for solutions of $A\mathbf{x} = \mathbf{b}$ and to introduce the idea of an inverse matrix.

Core Sections

1.1 *Introduction to Matrices and Systems of Linear Equations*
1.2 *Echelon Form and Gauss-Jordan Elimination*
1.3 *Consistent Systems of Linear Equations*
1.5 *Matrix Operations*
1.6 *Algebraic Properties of Matrix Operations*
1.7 *Linear Independence and Nonsingular Matrices*
1.9 *Matrix Inverses and Their Properties*

INTRODUCTION TO MATRICES AND SYSTEMS OF LINEAR EQUATIONS

In the real world, problems are seldom so simple that they depend on a single input variable. For example, a manufacturer's profit clearly depends on the cost of materials, but it also depends on other input variables such as labor costs, transportation costs, and plant overhead. A realistic expression for profit would involve all these variables. Using mathematical language, we say that profit is a *function of several variables*.

In linear algebra we study the simplest functions of several variables, the ones that are *linear*. We begin our study by considering linear equations. By way of illustration, the equation

$$x_1 + 2x_2 + x_3 = 1$$

is an example of a linear equation, and $x_1 = 2, x_2 = 1, x_3 = -3$ is one solution for the equation. In general a ***linear equation*** in n unknowns is an equation that can be put in the form

$$a_1x_1 + a_2x_2 + \cdots + a_nx_n = b. \tag{1}$$

In (1), the coefficients $a_1, a_2, \ldots, a_n$ and the constant b are known, and $x_1, x_2, \ldots, x_n$ denote the unknowns. A ***solution*** to Eq. (1) is any sequence $s_1, s_2, \ldots, s_n$ of numbers such that the substitution $x_1 = s_1, x_2 = s_2, \ldots, x_n = s_n$ satisfies the equation.

Equation (1) is called linear because each term has degree one in the variables $x_1, x_2, \ldots, x_n$. (Also, see Exercise 37.)

EXAMPLE 1 Determine which of the following equations are linear.

(i) $x_1 + 2x_1x_2 + 3x_2 = 4$

(ii) $x_1^{1/2} + 3x_2 = 4$

(iii) $2x_1^{-1} + \sin x_2 = 0$

(iv) $3x_1 - x_2 = x_3 + 1$

Solution Only Eq. (iv) is linear. The terms x_1x_2, $x_1^{1/2}$, x_1^{-1}, and $\sin x_2$ are all nonlinear.

Linear Systems

Our objective is to obtain simultaneous solutions to a system (that is, a set) of one or more linear equations. Here are three examples of systems of linear equations.

(a)
$$\begin{aligned} x_1 + x_2 &= 3 \\ x_1 - x_2 &= 1 \end{aligned}$$

(b)
$$\begin{aligned} x_1 - 2x_2 - 3x_3 &= -11 \\ -x_1 + 3x_2 + 5x_3 &= 15 \end{aligned}$$

(c)
$$\begin{aligned} 3x_1 - 2x_2 &= 1 \\ 6x_1 - 4x_2 &= 6 \end{aligned}$$

In terms of solutions, it is easy to check that $x_1 = 2, x_2 = 1$ is one solution to system (a). Indeed, it can be shown that this is the *only* solution to the system.

On the other hand, $x_1 = -4$, $x_2 = 2$, $x_3 = 1$ and $x_1 = -2$, $x_2 = 6$, $x_3 = -1$ are both solutions to system (b). In fact, it can be verified by substitution that $x_1 = -3 - x_3$ and $x_2 = 4 - 2x_3$ yields a solution to system (b) for any choice of x_3. Thus, this system has infinitely many solutions.

Finally, note that the equations given in (c) can be viewed as representing two parallel lines in the plane. Therefore, system (c) has no solution. (Another way to see that (c) has no solution is to observe that the second equation in (c), when divided by 2, reduces to $3x_1 - 2x_2 = 3$. Because the first equation requires $3x_1 - 2x_2 = 1$, there is no way that both equations can be satisfied.)

In general, an **$(m \times n)$ *system of linear equations*** is a set of equations of the form:

$$\begin{aligned} a_{11}x_1 + a_{12}x_2 + \cdots + a_{1n}x_n &= b_1 \\ a_{21}x_1 + a_{22}x_2 + \cdots + a_{2n}x_n &= b_2 \\ \vdots \qquad\qquad\qquad \vdots \quad &\quad \vdots \\ a_{m1}x_1 + a_{m2}x_2 + \cdots + a_{mn}x_n &= b_m. \end{aligned} \qquad (2)^*$$

For example, the general form of a (3×3) system of linear equations is

$$\begin{aligned} a_{11}x_1 + a_{12}x_2 + a_{13}x_3 &= b_1 \\ a_{21}x_1 + a_{22}x_2 + a_{23}x_3 &= b_2 \\ a_{31}x_1 + a_{32}x_2 + a_{33}x_3 &= b_3. \end{aligned}$$

A ***solution*** to system (2) is a sequence $s_1, \ldots, s_n$ of numbers that is simultaneously a solution for each equation in the system. The double subscript notation used for the coefficients is necessary to provide an "address" for each coefficient. For example, a_{32} appears in the third equation as the coefficient of x_2.

EXAMPLE 2

(a) Display the system of equations with coefficients $a_{11} = 2$, $a_{12} = -1$, $a_{13} = -3$, $a_{21} = -2$, $a_{22} = 2$, and $a_{23} = 5$, and with constants $b_1 = -1$ and $b_2 = 3$.

(b) Verify that $x_1 = 1$, $x_2 = 0$, $x_3 = 1$ is a solution for the system.

Solution

(a) The system is

$$\begin{aligned} 2x_1 - x_2 - 3x_3 &= -1 \\ -2x_1 + 2x_2 + 5x_3 &= 3. \end{aligned}$$

(b) Substituting $x_1 = 1$, $x_2 = 0$, and $x_3 = 1$ yields

$$\begin{aligned} 2(1) - (0) - 3(1) &= -1 \\ -2(1) + 2(0) + 5(1) &= 3. \end{aligned}$$

*For clarity of presentation, we assume throughout the chapter that the constants a_{ij} and b_i are real numbers, although all statements are equally valid for complex constants. When we consider eigenvalue problems, we will occasionally encounter linear systems having complex coefficients, but the solution technique is no different. In Chapter 4 we will discuss the technical details of solving systems that have complex coefficients.

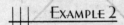

Geometric Interpretations of Solution Sets

We can use geometric examples to get an initial impression about the nature of solution sets for linear systems. For example, consider a general (2×2) system of linear equations

$$a_{11}x_1 + a_{12}x_2 = b_1 \quad (a_{11}, a_{12} \text{ not both zero})$$
$$a_{21}x_1 + a_{22}x_2 = b_2 \quad (a_{21}, a_{22} \text{ not both zero}).$$

Geometrically, the solution set for each of these equations can be represented as a line in the plane. A solution for the system, therefore, corresponds to a point (x_1, x_2) where the lines intersect. From this geometric interpretation, it follows that there are exactly three possibilities:

1. The two lines are coincident (the same line), so there are infinitely many solutions.
2. The two lines are parallel (never meet), so there are no solutions.
3. The two lines intersect at a single point, so there is a unique solution.

The three possibilities are illustrated in Fig. 1.1 and in Example 3.

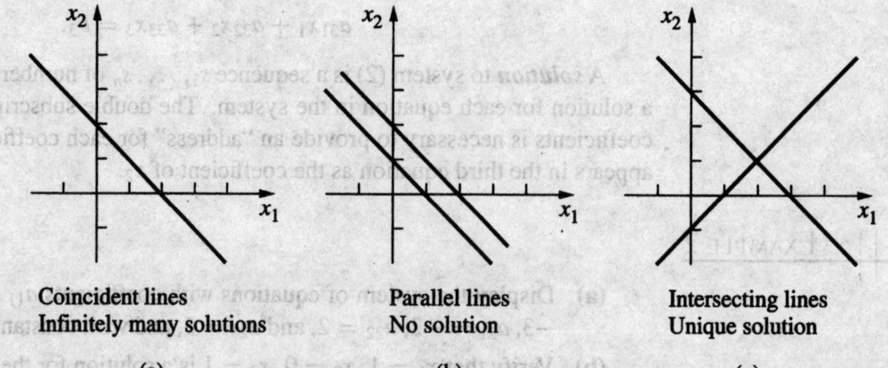

Figure 1.1 The three possibilities for the solution set of a (2×2) system.

EXAMPLE 3 Give a geometric representation for each of the following systems of equations.

(a) $x_1 + x_2 = 2$
$2x_1 + 2x_2 = 4$

(b) $x_1 + x_2 = 2$
$x_1 + x_2 = 1$

(c) $x_1 + x_2 = 3$
$x_1 - x_2 = 1$

Solution The representations are displayed in Fig. 1.1. ■

The graph of a linear equation in three variables, $ax_1+bx_2+cx_3=d$, is a plane in three-dimensional space (as long as one of a, b, or c is nonzero). So, as another example, let us consider the general (2×3) system:

$$a_{11}x_1 + a_{12}x_2 + a_{13}x_3 = b_1$$
$$a_{21}x_1 + a_{22}x_2 + a_{23}x_3 = b_2.$$

Because the solution set for each equation can be represented by a plane, there are two possibilities:

1. The two planes might be coincident, or they might intersect in a line. In either case, the system has infinitely many solutions.
2. The two planes might be parallel. In this case, the system has no solution.

Note, for the case of the general (2×3) system, that the possibility of a unique solution has been ruled out.

As a final example, consider a general (3×3) system:

$$a_{11}x_1 + a_{12}x_2 + a_{13}x_3 = b_1$$
$$a_{21}x_1 + a_{22}x_2 + a_{23}x_3 = b_2$$
$$a_{31}x_1 + a_{32}x_2 + a_{33}x_3 = b_3.$$

If we view this (3×3) system as representing three planes, it is easy to see from the geometric perspective that there are three possible outcomes: infinitely many solutions, no solution, or a unique solution (see Fig. 1.2). Note that Fig. 1.2(b) does not illustrate every possible case of a (3×3) system that has no solution. For example, if just two of three planes are parallel, then the system has no solution even though the third plane might intersect each of the two parallel planes.

We conclude this subsection with the following remark, which we will state formally in Section 1.3 (see Corollary to Theorem 3). This remark says that the possible outcomes suggested by the geometric interpretations shown in Figs. 1.1 and 1.2 are typical for any system of linear equations.

Remark An $(m \times n)$ system of linear equations has either infinitely many solutions, no solution, or a unique solution.

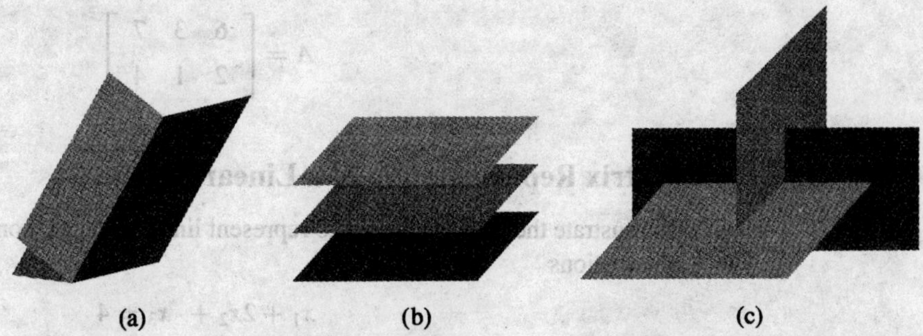

(a) (b) (c)

Figure 1.2 The general (3×3) system may have (a) infinitely many solutions, (b) no solution, or (c) a unique solution.

In general, a system of equations is called ***consistent*** if it has at least one solution, and the system is called ***inconsistent*** if it has no solution. By the preceding remark, a consistent system has either one solution or an infinite number of solutions; it is not possible for a linear system to have, for example, exactly five solutions.

Matrices

We begin our introduction to matrix theory by relating matrices to the problem of solving systems of linear equations. Initially we show that matrix theory provides a convenient and natural symbolic language to describe linear systems. Later we show that matrix theory is also an appropriate and powerful framework within which to analyze and solve more general linear problems, such as least-squares approximations, representations of linear operations, and eigenvalue problems.

The rectangular array

$$\begin{bmatrix} 1 & 3 & -1 & 2 \\ 4 & 2 & 1 & -3 \\ 0 & 2 & 0 & 3 \end{bmatrix}$$

is an example of a matrix. More generally, an $(m \times n)$ ***matrix*** is a rectangular array of numbers of the form

$$A = \begin{bmatrix} a_{11} & a_{12} & \cdots & a_{1n} \\ a_{21} & a_{22} & \cdots & a_{2n} \\ \vdots & & & \vdots \\ a_{m1} & a_{m2} & \cdots & a_{mn} \end{bmatrix}.$$

Thus an $(m \times n)$ matrix has m rows and n columns. The subscripts for the entry a_{ij} indicate that the number appears in the ith row and jth column of A. For example, a_{32} is the entry in the third row and second column of A. We will frequently use the notation $A = (a_{ij})$ to denote a matrix A with entries a_{ij}.

EXAMPLE 4 Display the (2×3) matrix $A = (a_{ij})$, where $a_{11} = 6$, $a_{12} = 3$, $a_{13} = 7$, $a_{21} = 2$, $a_{22} = 1$, and $a_{23} = 4$.

Solution

$$A = \begin{bmatrix} 6 & 3 & 7 \\ 2 & 1 & 4 \end{bmatrix}$$

Matrix Representation of a Linear System

To illustrate the use of matrices to represent linear systems, consider the (3×3) system of equations

$$\begin{aligned} x_1 + 2x_2 + x_3 &= 4 \\ 2x_1 - x_2 - x_3 &= 1 \\ x_1 + x_2 + 3x_3 &= 0. \end{aligned}$$

If we display the coefficients and constants for this system in matrix form,

$$B = \begin{bmatrix} 1 & 2 & 1 & 4 \\ 2 & -1 & -1 & 1 \\ 1 & 1 & 3 & 0 \end{bmatrix},$$

then we have expressed compactly and naturally all the essential information. The matrix B is called the *augmented matrix* for the system.

In general, with the $(m \times n)$ system of linear equations

$$\begin{aligned} a_{11}x_1 + a_{12}x_2 + \cdots + a_{1n}x_n &= b_1 \\ a_{21}x_1 + a_{22}x_2 + \cdots + a_{2n}x_n &= b_2 \\ \vdots \qquad\qquad & \quad \vdots \\ a_{m1}x_1 + a_{m2}x_2 + \cdots + a_{mn}x_n &= b_m, \end{aligned} \tag{3}$$

we associate two matrices. The ***coefficient matrix*** for system (3) is the $(m \times n)$ matrix A where

$$A = \begin{bmatrix} a_{11} & a_{12} & \cdots & a_{1n} \\ a_{21} & a_{22} & \cdots & a_{2n} \\ \vdots & & & \vdots \\ a_{m1} & a_{m2} & \cdots & a_{mn} \end{bmatrix}.$$

The ***augmented matrix*** for system (3) is the $[m \times (n+1)]$ matrix B where

$$B = \begin{bmatrix} a_{11} & a_{12} & \cdots & a_{1n} & b_1 \\ a_{21} & a_{22} & \cdots & a_{2n} & b_2 \\ \vdots & & & \vdots & \vdots \\ a_{m1} & a_{m2} & \cdots & a_{mn} & b_m \end{bmatrix}.$$

Note that B is nothing more than the coefficient matrix A augmented with an extra column; the extra column is the right-hand side of system (3).

The augmented matrix B is usually denoted as $[A \mid \mathbf{b}]$, where A is the coefficient matrix and

$$\mathbf{b} = \begin{bmatrix} b_1 \\ b_2 \\ \vdots \\ b_m \end{bmatrix}.$$

EXAMPLE 5 Display the coefficient matrix A and the augmented matrix B for the system

$$\begin{aligned} x_1 - 2x_2 + x_3 &= 2 \\ 2x_1 + x_2 - x_3 &= 1 \\ -3x_1 + x_2 - 2x_3 &= -5. \end{aligned}$$

Solution The coefficient matrix A and the augmented matrix $[A \mid \mathbf{b}]$ are given by

$$A = \begin{bmatrix} 1 & -2 & 1 \\ 2 & 1 & -1 \\ -3 & 1 & -2 \end{bmatrix} \quad \text{and} \quad [A \mid \mathbf{b}] = \begin{bmatrix} 1 & -2 & 1 & 2 \\ 2 & 1 & -1 & 1 \\ -3 & 1 & -2 & -5 \end{bmatrix}.$$

Elementary Operations

As we shall see, there are two steps involved in solving an $(m \times n)$ system of equations. The steps are:

1. Reduction of the system (that is, the elimination of variables).
2. Description of the set of solutions.

The details of both steps will be left to the next section. For the remainder of this section, we will concentrate on giving an overview of the reduction step.

The goal of the reduction process is to simplify the given system by eliminating unknowns. It is, of course, essential that the reduced system of equations have the same set of solutions as the original system.

DEFINITION 1 **Two systems of linear equations in n unknowns are *equivalent* provided that they have the same set of solutions.**

Thus the reduction procedure must yield an equivalent system of equations. The following theorem provides three operations, called ***elementary operations***, that can be used in reduction.

THEOREM 1 If one of the following elementary operations is applied to a system of linear equations, then the resulting system is equivalent to the original system.

1. Interchange two equations.
2. Multiply an equation by a nonzero scalar.
3. Add a constant multiple of one equation to another.

(In part 2 of Theorem 1, the term ***scalar*** means a constant; that is, a number.) The proof of Theorem 1 is included in Exercise 41 of Section 1.1.

To facilitate the use of the elementary operations listed above, we adopt the following notation:

Notation	***Elementary Operation Performed***
$E_i \leftrightarrow E_j$	The ith and jth equations are interchanged.
kE_i	The ith equation is multiplied by the nonzero scalar k.
$E_i + kE_j$	k times the jth equation is added to the ith equation.

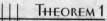

The following simple example illustrates the use of elementary operations to solve a (2×2) system. (The complete solution process for a general $(m \times n)$ system is described in detail in the next section.)

EXAMPLE 6 Use elementary operations to solve the system

$$\begin{aligned} x_1 + \ x_2 &= 5 \\ -x_1 + 2x_2 &= 4. \end{aligned}$$

Solution The elementary operation $E_2 + E_1$ produces the following equivalent system:

$$\begin{aligned} x_1 + \ x_2 &= 5 \\ 3x_2 &= 9. \end{aligned}$$

The operation $\frac{1}{3}E_2$ then leads to

$$\begin{aligned} x_1 + x_2 &= 5 \\ x_2 &= 3. \end{aligned}$$

Finally, using the operation $E_1 - E_2$, we obtain

$$\begin{aligned} x_1 \quad &= 2 \\ x_2 &= 3. \end{aligned}$$

By Theorem 1, the system above is equivalent to the original system. Hence the solution to the original system is also $x_1 = 2$, $x_2 = 3$.

(***Note:*** Example 6 illustrates a *systematic* method for solving a system of linear equations. This method is called ***Gauss-Jordan elimination*** and is described fully in the next section.)

Row Operations

As noted earlier, we want to use an augmented matrix as a shorthand notation for a system of equations. Because equations become translated to rows in the augmented matrix, we want to perform elementary operations on the rows of a matrix. Toward that end, we introduce the following terminology.

DEFINITION 2 The following operations, performed on the rows of a matrix, are called ***elementary row operations:***

1. Interchange two rows.
2. Multiply a row by a nonzero scalar.
3. Add a constant multiple of one row to another.

As before, we adopt the following notation:

Notation	***Elementary Row Operation***
$R_i \leftrightarrow R_j$	The ith and jth rows are interchanged.
kR_i	The ith row is multiplied by the nonzero scalar k.
$R_i + kR_j$	k times the jth row is added to the ith row.

We say that two $(m \times n)$ matrices, B and C, are ***row equivalent*** if one can be obtained from the other by a sequence of elementary row operations. Now if B is the augmented matrix for a system of linear equations and if C is row equivalent to B, then C is the augmented matrix for an equivalent system. This observation follows because the elementary row operations for matrices exactly duplicate the elementary operations for equations.

Thus, we can solve a linear system with the following steps:

1. Form the augmented matrix B for the system.
2. Use elementary row operations to transform B to a row equivalent matrix C which represents a "simpler" system.
3. Solve the simpler system that is represented by C.

We will specify what we mean by a simpler system in the next section. For now, we illustrate in Example 7 how using elementary row operations to reduce an augmented matrix is exactly parallel to using elementary operations to reduce the corresponding system of equations.

EXAMPLE 7 Consider the (3×3) system of equations

$$\begin{aligned} 2x_2 + x_3 &= -2 \\ 3x_1 + 5x_2 - 5x_3 &= 1 \\ 2x_1 + 4x_2 - 2x_3 &= 2. \end{aligned}$$

Use elementary operations on equations to reduce the following system. Simultaneously use elementary row operations to reduce the augmented matrix for the system.

Solution In the left-hand column of the following table, we will reduce the given system of equations using elementary operations. In the right-hand column we will perform the analogous elementary row operations on the augmented matrix. (***Note:*** At each step of the process, the system of equations obtained in the left-hand column is equivalent to the original system. The corresponding matrix in the right-hand column is the augmented matrix for the system in the left-hand column.)

Our initial goal is to have x_1 appear in the first equation with coefficient 1, and then to eliminate x_1 from the remaining equations. This can be accomplished by the following steps:

System: ***Augmented Matrix:***

$$\begin{aligned} 2x_2 + x_3 &= -2 \\ 3x_1 + 5x_2 - 5x_3 &= 1 \\ 2x_1 + 4x_2 - 2x_3 &= 2 \end{aligned} \qquad \begin{bmatrix} 0 & 2 & 1 & -2 \\ 3 & 5 & -5 & 1 \\ 2 & 4 & -2 & 2 \end{bmatrix}$$

$E_1 \leftrightarrow E_3$: $R_1 \leftrightarrow R_3$:

$$\begin{aligned} 2x_1 + 4x_2 - 2x_3 &= 2 \\ 3x_1 + 5x_2 - 5x_3 &= 1 \\ 2x_2 + x_3 &= -2 \end{aligned} \qquad \begin{bmatrix} 2 & 4 & -2 & 2 \\ 3 & 5 & -5 & 1 \\ 0 & 2 & 1 & -2 \end{bmatrix}$$

$(1/2)E_1$: $(1/2)R_1$:

$$\begin{aligned} x_1 + 2x_2 - x_3 &= 1 \\ 3x_1 + 5x_2 - 5x_3 &= 1 \\ 2x_2 + x_3 &= -2 \end{aligned} \qquad \begin{bmatrix} 1 & 2 & -1 & 1 \\ 3 & 5 & -5 & 1 \\ 0 & 2 & 1 & -2 \end{bmatrix}$$

$E_2 - 3E_1$: $R_2 - 3R_1$:

$$\begin{aligned} x_1 + 2x_2 - x_3 &= 1 \\ -x_2 - 2x_3 &= -2 \\ 2x_2 + x_3 &= -2 \end{aligned} \qquad \begin{bmatrix} 1 & 2 & -1 & 1 \\ 0 & -1 & -2 & -2 \\ 0 & 2 & 1 & -2 \end{bmatrix}$$

The variable x_1 has now been eliminated from the second and third equations. Next, we eliminate x_2 from the first and third equations and leave x_2, with coefficient 1, in the second equation. We continue the reduction process with the following operations:

$(-1)E_2$: $(-1)R_2$:

$$\begin{aligned} x_1 + 2x_2 - x_3 &= 1 \\ x_2 + 2x_3 &= 2 \\ 2x_2 + x_3 &= -2 \end{aligned} \qquad \begin{bmatrix} 1 & 2 & -1 & 1 \\ 0 & 1 & 2 & 2 \\ 0 & 2 & 1 & -2 \end{bmatrix}$$

$E_1 - 2E_2$: $R_1 - 2R_2$:

$$\begin{aligned} x_1 \qquad - 5x_3 &= -3 \\ x_2 + 2x_3 &= 2 \\ 2x_2 + x_3 &= -2 \end{aligned} \qquad \begin{bmatrix} 1 & 0 & -5 & -3 \\ 0 & 1 & 2 & 2 \\ 0 & 2 & 1 & -2 \end{bmatrix}$$

$E_3 - 2E_2$: $R_3 - 2R_2$:

$$\begin{aligned} x_1 \qquad - 5x_3 &= -3 \\ x_2 + 2x_3 &= 2 \\ -3x_3 &= -6 \end{aligned} \qquad \begin{bmatrix} 1 & 0 & -5 & -3 \\ 0 & 1 & 2 & 2 \\ 0 & 0 & -3 & -6 \end{bmatrix}$$

The variable x_2 has now been eliminated from the first and third equations. Next, we eliminate x_3 from the first and second equations and leave x_3, with coefficient 1, in the third equation:

System: ***Augmented Matrix:***

$(-1/3)E_3$: $(-1/3)R_3$:

$$\begin{aligned} x_1 \qquad - 5x_3 &= -3 \\ x_2 + 2x_3 &= \ \ 2 \\ x_3 &= \ \ 2 \end{aligned} \qquad \begin{bmatrix} 1 & 0 & -5 & -3 \\ 0 & 1 & 2 & 2 \\ 0 & 0 & 1 & 2 \end{bmatrix}$$

$E_1 + 5E_3$: $R_1 + 5R_3$:

$$\begin{aligned} x_1 \qquad\qquad &= 7 \\ x_2 + 2x_3 &= 2 \\ x_3 &= 2 \end{aligned} \qquad \begin{bmatrix} 1 & 0 & 0 & 7 \\ 0 & 1 & 2 & 2 \\ 0 & 0 & 1 & 2 \end{bmatrix}$$

$E_2 - 2E_3$: $R_2 - 2R_3$:

$$\begin{aligned} x_1 \qquad\qquad &= \ \ 7 \\ x_2 \qquad &= -2 \\ x_3 &= \ \ 2 \end{aligned} \qquad \begin{bmatrix} 1 & 0 & 0 & 7 \\ 0 & 1 & 0 & -2 \\ 0 & 0 & 1 & 2 \end{bmatrix}$$

The last system above clearly has a unique solution given by $x_1 = 7$, $x_2 = -2$, and $x_3 = 2$. Because the final system is equivalent to the original given system, both systems have the same solution. ■

The reduction process used in the preceding example is known as ***Gauss-Jordan elimination*** and will be explained in Section 1.2. Note the advantage of the shorthand notation provided by matrices. Because we do not need to list the variables, the sequence of steps in the right-hand column is easier to perform and record.

Example 7 illustrates that row equivalent augmented matrices represent equivalent systems of equations. The following corollary to Theorem 1 states this in mathematical terms.

COROLLARY Suppose $[A \mid \mathbf{b}]$ and $[C \mid \mathbf{d}]$ are augmented matrices, each representing a different $(m \times n)$ system of linear equations. If $[A \mid \mathbf{b}]$ and $[C \mid \mathbf{d}]$ are row equivalent matrices, then the two systems are also equivalent. ■

1.1 EXERCISES

Which of the equations in Exercises 1–6 are linear?

1. $x_1 + 2x_3 = 3$

2. $x_1x_2 + x_2 = 1$

3. $x_1 - x_2 = \sin^2 x_1 + \cos^2 x_1$

4. $x_1 - x_2 = \sin^2 x_1 + \cos^2 x_2$

5. $|x_1| - |x_2| = 0$

6. $\pi x_1 + \sqrt{7}x_2 = \sqrt{3}$

In Exercises 7–10, coefficients are given for a system of the form (2). Display the system and verify that the given values constitute a solution.

7. $a_{11} = 1$, $a_{12} = 3$, $a_{21} = 4$, $a_{22} = -1$, $b_1 = 7$, $b_2 = 2$; $x_1 = 1$, $x_2 = 2$

8. $a_{11} = 6,\quad a_{12} = -1,\quad a_{13} = 1,\quad a_{21} = 1,$
$a_{22} = 2,\quad a_{23} = 4,\quad b_1 = 14,\quad b_2 = 4;$
$x_1 = 2,\quad x_2 = -1,\quad x_3 = 1$

9. $a_{11} = 1,\quad a_{12} = 1,\quad a_{21} = 3,\quad a_{22} = 4,$
$a_{31} = -1,\quad a_{32} = 2,\quad b_1 = 0,\quad b_2 = -1,$
$b_3 = -3;\quad x_1 = 1,\quad x_2 = -1$

10. $a_{11} = 0,\quad a_{12} = 3,\quad a_{21} = 4,\quad a_{22} = 0,$
$b_1 = 9,\quad b_2 = 8;\quad x_1 = 2,\quad x_2 = 3$

In Exercises 11–14, sketch a graph for each equation to determine whether the system has a unique solution, no solution, or infinitely many solutions.

11. $\begin{aligned} 2x + y &= 5 \\ x - y &= 1 \end{aligned}$

12. $\begin{aligned} 2x - y &= -1 \\ 2x - y &= 2 \end{aligned}$

13. $\begin{aligned} 3x + 2y &= 6 \\ -6x - 4y &= -12 \end{aligned}$

14. $\begin{aligned} 2x + y &= 5 \\ x - y &= 1 \\ x + 3y &= 9 \end{aligned}$

15. The (2×3) system of linear equations

$$\begin{aligned} a_1x + b_1y + c_1z &= d_1 \\ a_2x + b_2y + c_2z &= d_2 \end{aligned}$$

is represented geometrically by two planes. How are the planes related when:

a) The system has no solution?

b) The system has infinitely many solutions?

Is it possible for the system to have a unique solution? Explain.

In Exercises 16–18, determine whether the given (2×3) system of linear equations represents coincident planes (that is, the same plane), two parallel planes, or two planes whose intersection is a line. In the latter case, give the parametric equations for the line; that is, give equations of the form $x = at + b$, $y = ct + d$, $z = et + f$.

16. $\begin{aligned} 2x_1 + x_2 + x_3 &= 3 \\ -2x_1 + x_2 - x_3 &= 1 \end{aligned}$

17. $\begin{aligned} x_1 + 2x_2 - x_3 &= 2 \\ x_1 + x_2 + x_3 &= 3 \end{aligned}$

18. $\begin{aligned} x_1 + 3x_2 - 2x_3 &= -1 \\ 2x_1 + 6x_2 - 4x_3 &= -2 \end{aligned}$

19. Display the (2×3) matrix $A = (a_{ij})$, where $a_{11} = 2$, $a_{12} = 1$, $a_{13} = 6$, $a_{21} = 4$, $a_{22} = 3$, and $a_{23} = 8$.

20. Display the (2×4) matrix $C = (c_{ij})$, where $c_{23} = 4$, $c_{12} = 2$, $c_{21} = 2$, $c_{14} = 1$, $c_{22} = 2$, $c_{24} = 3$, $c_{11} = 1$, and $c_{13} = 7$.

21. Display the (3×3) matrix $Q = (q_{ij})$, where $q_{23} = 1$, $q_{32} = 2$, $q_{11} = 1$, $q_{13} = -3$, $q_{22} = 1$, $q_{33} = 1$, $q_{21} = 2$, $q_{12} = 4$, and $q_{31} = 3$.

22. Suppose the matrix C in Exercise 20 is the augmented matrix for a system of linear equations. Display the system.

23. Repeat Exercise 22 for the matrices in Exercises 19 and 21.

In Exercises 24–29, display the coefficient matrix A and the augmented matrix B for the given system.

24. $\begin{aligned} x_1 - x_2 &= -1 \\ x_1 + x_2 &= 3 \end{aligned}$

25. $\begin{aligned} x_1 + x_2 - x_3 &= 2 \\ 2x_1 \qquad - x_3 &= 1 \end{aligned}$

26. $\begin{aligned} x_1 + 3x_2 - x_3 &= 1 \\ 2x_1 + 5x_2 + x_3 &= 5 \\ x_1 + x_2 + x_3 &= 3 \end{aligned}$

27. $\begin{aligned} x_1 + x_2 + 2x_3 &= 6 \\ 3x_1 + 4x_2 - x_3 &= 5 \\ -x_1 + x_2 + x_3 &= 2 \end{aligned}$

28. $\begin{aligned} x_1 + x_2 - 3x_3 &= -1 \\ x_1 + 2x_2 - 5x_3 &= -2 \\ -x_1 - 3x_2 + 7x_3 &= 3 \end{aligned}$

29. $\begin{aligned} x_1 + x_2 + x_3 &= 1 \\ 2x_1 + 3x_2 + x_3 &= 2 \\ x_1 - x_2 + 3x_3 &= 2 \end{aligned}$

In Exercises 30–36, display the augmented matrix for the given system. Use elementary operations on equations to obtain an equivalent system of equations in which x_1 appears in the first equation with coefficient one and has been eliminated from the remaining equations. Simultaneously, perform the corresponding elementary row operations on the augmented matrix.

30. $\begin{aligned} 2x_1 + 3x_2 &= 6 \\ 4x_1 - x_2 &= 7 \end{aligned}$

31. $\begin{aligned} x_1 + 2x_2 - x_3 &= 1 \\ x_1 + x_2 + 2x_3 &= 2 \\ -2x_1 + x_2 \qquad &= 4 \end{aligned}$

32. $\begin{aligned} x_2 + x_3 &= 4 \\ x_1 - x_2 + 2x_3 &= 1 \\ 2x_1 + x_2 - x_3 &= 6 \end{aligned}$

33. $\begin{aligned} x_1 + x_2 &= 9 \\ x_1 - x_2 &= 7 \\ 3x_1 + x_2 &= 6 \end{aligned}$

34. $\begin{aligned} x_1 + x_2 + x_3 - x_4 &= 1 \\ -x_1 + x_2 - x_3 + x_4 &= 3 \\ -2x_1 + x_2 + x_3 - x_4 &= 2 \end{aligned}$

35. $\begin{aligned} x_2 + x_3 - x_4 &= 3 \\ x_1 + 2x_2 - x_3 + x_4 &= 1 \\ -x_1 + x_2 + 7x_3 - x_4 &= 0 \end{aligned}$

36. $\begin{aligned} x_1 + x_2 &= 0 \\ x_1 - x_2 &= 0 \\ 3x_1 + x_2 &= 0 \end{aligned}$

37. Consider the equation $2x_1 - 3x_2 + x_3 - x_4 = 3$.

a) In the six different possible combinations, set any two of the variables equal to 1 and graph the equation in terms of the other two.

b) What type of graph do you always get when you set two of the variables equal to two fixed constants?

c) What is one possible reason the equation in formula (1) is called *linear*?

38. Consider the (2×2) system

$$a_{11}x_1 + a_{12}x_2 = b_1$$
$$a_{21}x_1 + a_{22}x_2 = b_2.$$

Show that if $a_{11}a_{22} - a_{12}a_{21} \neq 0$, then this system is equivalent to a system of the form

$$c_{11}x_1 + c_{12}x_2 = d_1$$
$$c_{22}x_2 = d_2,$$

where $c_{11} \neq 0$ and $c_{22} \neq 0$. Note that the second system always has a solution. [*Hint:* First suppose that $a_{11} \neq 0$, and then consider the special case in which $a_{11} = 0$.]

39. In the following (2×2) linear systems (A) and (B), c is a nonzero scalar. Prove that any solution, $x_1 = s_1$, $x_2 = s_2$, for (A) is also a solution for (B). Conversely, show that any solution, $x_1 = t_1$, $x_2 = t_2$, for (B) is also a solution for (A). Where is the assumption that c is nonzero required?

(A) $$\begin{aligned} a_{11}x_1 + a_{12}x_2 &= b_1 \\ a_{21}x_1 + a_{22}x_2 &= b_2 \end{aligned}$$

(B) $$\begin{aligned} a_{11}x_1 + a_{12}x_2 &= b_1 \\ ca_{21}x_1 + ca_{22}x_2 &= cb_2 \end{aligned}$$

40. In the (2×2) linear systems that follow, the system (B) is obtained from (A) by performing the elementary operation $E_2 + cE_1$. Prove that any solution, $x_1 = s_1$, $x_2 = s_2$, for (A) is a solution for (B). Similarly, prove that any solution, $x_1 = t_1$, $x_2 = t_2$, for (B) is a solution for (A).

(A) $$\begin{aligned} a_{11}x_1 + a_{12}x_2 &= b_1 \\ a_{21}x_1 + a_{22}x_2 &= b_2 \end{aligned}$$

(B) $$\begin{aligned} a_{11}x_1 + a_{12}x_2 &= b_1 \\ (a_{21} + ca_{11})x_1 + (a_{22} + ca_{12})x_2 &= b_2 + cb_1 \end{aligned}$$

41. Prove that any of the elementary operations in Theorem 1 applied to system (2) produces an equivalent system. [*Hint:* To simplify this proof, represent the ith equation in system (2) as $f_i(x_1, x_2, \ldots, x_n) = b_i$; so

$$f_i(x_1, x_2, \ldots, x_n) = a_{i1}x_1 + a_{i2}x_2 + \cdots + a_{in}x_n$$

for $i = 1, 2, \ldots, m$. With this notation, system (2) has the form of (A), which follows. Next, for example, if a multiple of c times the jth equation is added to the kth equation, a new system of the form (B) is produced:

(A)	(B)
$f_1(x_1, x_2, \ldots, x_n) = b_1$	$f_1(x_1, x_2, \ldots, x_n) = b_1$
$\vdots$	$\vdots$
$f_j(x_1, x_2, \ldots, x_n) = b_j$	$f_j(x_1, x_2, \ldots, x_n) = b_j$
$\vdots$	$\vdots$
$f_k(x_1, x_2, \ldots, x_n) = b_k$	$g(x_1, x_2, \ldots, x_n) = r$
$\vdots$	$\vdots$
$f_m(x_1, x_2, \ldots, x_n) = b_m$	$f_m(x_1, x_2, \ldots, x_n) = b_m$

where $g(x_1, x_2, \ldots, x_n) = f_k(x_1, x_2, \ldots, x_n) + cf_j(x_1, x_2, \ldots, x_n)$, and $r = b_k + cb_j$. To show that the operation gives an equivalent system, show that any solution for (A) is a solution for (B), and vice versa.]

42. Solve the system of two nonlinear equations in two unknowns

$$\begin{aligned} x_1^2 - 2x_1 + x_2^2 &= 3 \\ x_1^2 \quad\quad - x_2^2 &= 1. \end{aligned}$$

1.2 ECHELON FORM AND GAUSS-JORDAN ELIMINATION

As we noted in the previous section, our method for solving a system of linear equations will be to pass to the augmented matrix, use elementary row operations to reduce the augmented matrix, and then solve the simpler but equivalent system represented by the reduced matrix. This procedure is illustrated in Fig. 1.3.

The objective of the Gauss-Jordan reduction process (represented by the middle block in Fig. 1.3) is to obtain a system of equations simplified to the point where we

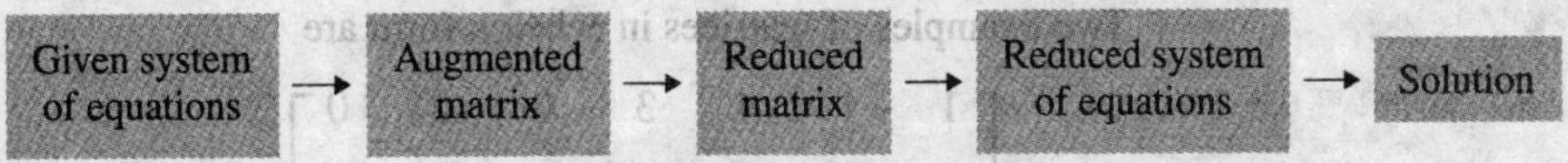

Figure 1.3 Procedure for solving a system of linear equations

can immediately describe the solution. See, for example, Examples 6 and 7 in Section 1.1. We turn now to the question of how to describe this objective in mathematical terms—that is, how do we know when the system has been simplified as much as it can be? The answer is: The system has been simplified as much as possible when it is in reduced echelon form.

Echelon Form

When an augmented matrix is reduced to the form known as *echelon form*, it is easy to solve the linear system represented by the reduced matrix. The formal description of echelon form is given in Definition 3. Then, in Definition 4, we describe an even simpler form known as *reduced echelon form.*

DEFINITION 3

An $(m \times n)$ matrix B is in ***echelon form*** if:

1. All rows that consist entirely of zeros are grouped together at the bottom of the matrix.
2. In every nonzero row, the first nonzero entry (counting from left to right) is a 1.
3. If the $(i + 1)$-st row contains nonzero entries, then the first nonzero entry is in a column to the right of the first nonzero entry in the ith row.

Put informally, a matrix A is in echelon form if the nonzero entries in A form a staircase-like pattern, such as the four examples shown in Fig. 1.4. (***Note:*** Exercise 46 shows that there are exactly seven different types of echelon form for a (3×3) matrix. Figure 1.4 illustrates four of the possible patterns. In Fig. 1.4, the entries marked $*$ can be zero or nonzero.)

$$A=\begin{bmatrix}1 & * & * \\ 0 & 1 & * \\ 0 & 0 & 1\end{bmatrix} \quad A=\begin{bmatrix}1 & * & * \\ 0 & 1 & * \\ 0 & 0 & 0\end{bmatrix} \quad A=\begin{bmatrix}1 & * & * \\ 0 & 0 & 1 \\ 0 & 0 & 0\end{bmatrix} \quad A=\begin{bmatrix}0 & 1 & * \\ 0 & 0 & 1 \\ 0 & 0 & 0\end{bmatrix}$$

Figure 1.4 Patterns for four of the seven possible types of (3×3) matrices in echelon form. Entries marked $*$ can be either zero or nonzero.

Two examples of matrices in echelon form are

$$A = \begin{bmatrix} 1 & -1 & 4 & 3 & 0 & 2 & 0 \\ 0 & 0 & 1 & 8 & -4 & 3 & 2 \\ 0 & 0 & 0 & 1 & 2 & 1 & 2 \\ 0 & 0 & 0 & 0 & 0 & 1 & 3 \\ 0 & 0 & 0 & 0 & 0 & 0 & 0 \end{bmatrix} \quad B = \begin{bmatrix} 0 & 1 & -1 & 4 & 3 \\ 0 & 0 & 1 & 6 & -5 \\ 0 & 0 & 0 & 0 & 1 \end{bmatrix}.$$

We show later that every matrix can be transformed to echelon form with elementary row operations. It turns out, however, that echelon form is not unique. In order to guarantee uniqueness, we therefore add one more constraint and define a form known as *reduced echelon form*. As noted in Theorem 2, reduced echelon form is unique.

DEFINITION 4 A matrix that is in echelon form is in ***reduced echelon form*** provided that the first nonzero entry in any row is the only nonzero entry in its column.

Figure 1.5 gives four examples (corresponding to the examples in Fig. 1.4) of matrices in reduced echelon form.

$$A = \begin{bmatrix} 1 & 0 & 0 \\ 0 & 1 & 0 \\ 0 & 0 & 1 \end{bmatrix} \quad A = \begin{bmatrix} 1 & 0 & * \\ 0 & 1 & * \\ 0 & 0 & 0 \end{bmatrix} \quad A = \begin{bmatrix} 1 & * & 0 \\ 0 & 0 & 1 \\ 0 & 0 & 0 \end{bmatrix} \quad A = \begin{bmatrix} 0 & 1 & 0 \\ 0 & 0 & 1 \\ 0 & 0 & 0 \end{bmatrix}$$

Figure 1.5 Patterns for four of the seven possible types of (3×3) matrices in reduced echelon form. Entries marked $*$ can be either zero or nonzero.

Two examples of matrices in reduced echelon form are

$$A = \begin{bmatrix} 1 & 0 & 0 & 2 \\ 0 & 1 & 0 & -1 \\ 0 & 0 & 1 & 3 \end{bmatrix} \quad B = \begin{bmatrix} 1 & 2 & 0 & 1 & -1 \\ 0 & 0 & 1 & 3 & 4 \\ 0 & 0 & 0 & 0 & 0 \end{bmatrix}.$$

As can be seen from these examples and from Figs. 1.4 and 1.5, the feature that distinguishes reduced echelon form from echelon form is that the leading 1 in each nonzero row has only 0's above and below it.

EXAMPLE 1 For each matrix shown, choose one of the following phrases to describe the matrix.

(a) The matrix is not in echelon form.

(b) The matrix is in echelon form, but not in reduced echelon form.

(c) The matrix is in reduced echelon form.

$$A = \begin{bmatrix} 1 & 0 & 0 \\ 2 & 1 & 0 \\ 3 & -4 & 1 \end{bmatrix}, \qquad B = \begin{bmatrix} 1 & 3 & 2 \\ 0 & -1 & 1 \\ 0 & 0 & 1 \end{bmatrix},$$

$$C = \begin{bmatrix} 0 & 1 & -1 & 0 \\ 0 & 0 & 0 & 1 \\ 0 & 0 & 0 & 0 \end{bmatrix}, \quad D = \begin{bmatrix} 1 & 2 & 3 & 4 & 5 \\ 0 & 0 & 1 & 2 & 3 \\ 0 & 0 & 0 & 1 & 0 \end{bmatrix}, \quad E = \begin{bmatrix} 1 \\ 0 \\ 0 \end{bmatrix},$$

$$F = \begin{bmatrix} 0 \\ 0 \\ 1 \end{bmatrix}, \qquad G = [1 \;\; 0 \;\; 0], \qquad H = [0 \;\; 0 \;\; 1].$$

Solution A, B, and F are not in echelon form; D is in echelon form but not in reduced echelon form; C, E, G, and H are in reduced echelon form. ■

Solving a Linear System Whose Augmented Matrix Is in Reduced Echelon Form

Software packages that can solve systems of equations typically include a command that produces the reduced echelon form of a matrix. Thus, to solve a linear system on a machine, we first enter the augmented matrix for the system and then apply the machine's reduce command. Once we get the machine output (that is, the reduced echelon form for the original augmented matrix), we have to interpret the output in order to find the solution. The next example illustrates this interpretation process.

EXAMPLE 2 Each of the following matrices is in reduced echelon form and is the augmented matrix for a system of linear equations. In each case, give the system of equations and describe the solution.

$$B = \begin{bmatrix} 1 & 0 & 0 & 3 \\ 0 & 1 & 0 & -2 \\ 0 & 0 & 1 & 7 \\ 0 & 0 & 0 & 0 \end{bmatrix}, \qquad C = \begin{bmatrix} 1 & 0 & -1 & 0 \\ 0 & 1 & 3 & 0 \\ 0 & 0 & 0 & 1 \end{bmatrix},$$

$$D = \begin{bmatrix} 1 & -3 & 0 & 4 & 2 \\ 0 & 0 & 1 & -5 & 1 \\ 0 & 0 & 0 & 0 & 0 \end{bmatrix}, \quad E = \begin{bmatrix} 1 & 2 & 0 & 5 \\ 0 & 0 & 1 & 0 \\ 0 & 0 & 0 & 0 \end{bmatrix}.$$

Solution

Matrix B: Matrix B is the augmented matrix for the following system:

$$\begin{aligned} x_1 \qquad\qquad &= 3 \\ x_2 \qquad &= -2 \\ x_3 &= \;\;7. \end{aligned}$$

Therefore, the system has the unique solution $x_1 = 3$, $x_2 = -2$, and $x_3 = 7$.

Matrix C: Matrix C is the augmented matrix for the following system

$$\begin{aligned} x_1 \qquad\quad -x_3 &= 0 \\ x_2 + 3x_3 &= 0 \\ 0x_1 + 0x_2 + 0x_3 &= 1. \end{aligned}$$

Because no values for x_1, x_2, or x_3 can satisfy the third equation, the system is inconsistent.

Matrix D: Matrix D is the augmented matrix for the following system

$$\begin{aligned} x_1 - 3x_2 \qquad + 4x_4 &= 2 \\ x_3 - 5x_4 &= 1. \end{aligned}$$

We solve each equation for the leading variable in its row, finding

$$\begin{aligned} x_1 &= 2 + 3x_2 - 4x_4 \\ x_3 &= 1 + 5x_4. \end{aligned}$$

In this case, x_1 and x_3 are the dependent (or constrained) variables whereas x_2 and x_4 are the independent (or unconstrained) variables. The system has infinitely many solutions, and particular solutions can be obtained by assigning values to x_2 and x_4. For example, setting $x_2 = 1$ and $x_4 = 2$ yields the solution $x_1 = -3$, $x_2 = 1$, $x_3 = 11$, and $x_4 = 2$.

Matrix E: The second row of matrix E sometimes leads students to conclude erroneously that the system of equations is inconsistent. Note the critical difference between the third row of matrix C (which did represent an inconsistent system) and the second row of matrix E. In particular, if we write the system corresponding to E, we find

$$\begin{aligned} x_1 + 2x_2 \quad &= 5 \\ x_3 &= 0. \end{aligned}$$

Thus, the system has infinitely many solutions described by

$$\begin{aligned} x_1 &= 5 - 2x_2 \\ x_3 &= 0 \end{aligned}$$

where x_2 is an independent variable.

As we noted in Example 2, if an augmented matrix has a row of zeros, we sometimes jump to the conclusion (an *erroneous* conclusion) that the corresponding system of equations is inconsistent (see the discussion of matrix E in Example 2). Similar confusion can arise when the augmented matrix has a column of zeros. For example, consider the matrix

$$\begin{bmatrix} 1 & 0 & 0 & -2 & 0 & 3 \\ 0 & 0 & 1 & -4 & 0 & 1 \\ 0 & 0 & 0 & 0 & 1 & 2 \end{bmatrix},$$

where F is the augmented matrix for a system of 3 equations in 5 unknowns. Thus, F represents the system

$$\begin{aligned} x_1 \quad - 2x_4 \quad &= 3 \\ x_3 - 4x_4 \quad &= 2 \\ x_5 &= 2. \end{aligned}$$

The solution of this system is $x_1 = 3 + 2x_4$, $x_3 = 1 + 4x_4$, $x_5 = 2$, and x_4 is arbitrary. Note that the equations place no constraint whatsoever on the variable x_2. That does not mean that x_2 must be zero; instead, it means that x_2 is also arbitrary.

Recognizing an Inconsistent System

Suppose $[A \mid \mathbf{b}]$ is the augmented matrix for an $(m \times n)$ linear system of equations. If $[A \mid \mathbf{b}]$ is in reduced echelon form, you should be able to tell at a glance whether the linear system has any solutions. The idea was illustrated by matrix C in Example 2.

In particular, we can show that if the last nonzero row of $[A \mid \mathbf{b}]$ has its leading 1 in the last column, then the linear system has no solution. To see why this is true, suppose the last nonzero row of $[A \mid \mathbf{b}]$ has the form

$$[0, 0, 0, \ldots, 0, 1].$$

This row, then, represents the equation

$$0x_1 + 0x_2 + 0x_3 + \cdots + 0x_n = 1.$$

Because this equation cannot be satisfied, it follows that the linear system represented by $[A \mid \mathbf{b}]$ is inconsistent. We list this observation formally in the following remark.

Remark Let $[A \mid \mathbf{b}]$ be the augmented matrix for an $(m \times n)$ linear system of equations, and let $[A \mid \mathbf{b}]$ be in reduced echelon form. If the last nonzero row of $[A \mid \mathbf{b}]$ has its leading 1 in the last column, then the system of equations has no solution.

When you are carrying out the reduction of $[A \mid \mathbf{b}]$ to echelon form by hand, you might encounter a row that consists entirely of zeros except for a nonzero entry in the last column. In such a case, there is no reason to continue the reduction process since you have found an equation in an equivalent system that has no solution; that is, the system represented by $[A \mid \mathbf{b}]$ is inconsistent.

Reduction to Echelon Form

The following theorem guarantees that every matrix can be transformed to one and only one matrix that is in reduced echelon form.

THEOREM 2 Let B be an $(m \times n)$ matrix. There is a unique $(m \times n)$ matrix C such that:

(a) C is in reduced echelon form

and

(b) C is row equivalent to B.

Suppose B is the augmented matrix for an $(m \times n)$ system of linear equations. One important consequence of this theorem is that it shows we can always transform B by a series of elementary row operations into a matrix C which is in reduced echelon form. Then, because C is in reduced echelon form, it is easy to solve the equivalent linear system represented by C (recall Example 2).

The following steps show how to transform a given matrix B to reduced echelon form. As such, this list of steps constitutes an informal proof of the existence portion of Theorem 2. We do not prove the uniqueness portion of Theorem 2. The steps listed assume that B has at least one nonzero entry (because if B has only zero entries, then B is already in reduced row echelon form).

Reduction to Reduced Echelon Form for an $(m \times n)$ Matrix

Step 1. Locate the first (left-most) column that contains a nonzero entry.

Step 2. If necessary, interchange the first row with another row so that the first nonzero column has a nonzero entry in the first row.

Step 3. If a denotes the leading nonzero entry in row one, multiply each entry in row one by $1/a$. (Thus, the leading nonzero entry in row one is a 1.)

Step 4. Add appropriate multiples of row one to each of the remaining rows so that every entry below the leading 1 in row one is a 0.

Step 5. Temporarily ignore the first row of this matrix and repeat Steps 1–4 on the submatrix that remains. Stop the process when the resulting matrix is in echelon form.

Step 6. Having reached echelon form in Step 5, continue on to reduced echelon form as follows: Proceeding upward, add multiples of each nonzero row to the rows above in order to zero all entries above the leading 1.

The next example illustrates an application of the six-step process just described. When doing a small problem by hand, however, it is customary to alter the steps slightly—instead of going all the way to echelon form (sweeping from left to right) and then going from echelon to reduced echelon form (sweeping from bottom to top), it is customary to make a single pass (moving from left to right) introducing 0's above and below the leading 1. Example 3 demonstrates this single-pass variation.

EXAMPLE 3 Use elementary row operations to transform the following matrix to reduced echelon form

$$A = \begin{bmatrix} 0 & 0 & 0 & 0 & 2 & 8 & 4 \\ 0 & 0 & 0 & 1 & 3 & 11 & 9 \\ 0 & 3 & -12 & -3 & -9 & -24 & -33 \\ 0 & -2 & 8 & 1 & 6 & 17 & 21 \end{bmatrix}.$$

Solution The following row operations will transform A to reduced echelon form.

$R_1 \leftrightarrow R_3, (1/3)R_1$: Introduce a leading 1 into the first row of the first nonzero column.

$$\begin{bmatrix} 0 & 1 & -4 & -1 & -3 & -8 & -11 \\ 0 & 0 & 0 & 1 & 3 & 11 & 9 \\ 0 & 0 & 0 & 0 & 2 & 8 & 4 \\ 0 & -2 & 8 & 1 & 6 & 17 & 21 \end{bmatrix}$$

$R_4 + 2R_1$: Introduce 0's below the leading 1 in row 1.

$$\begin{bmatrix} 0 & 1 & -4 & -1 & -3 & -8 & -11 \\ 0 & 0 & 0 & 1 & 3 & 11 & 9 \\ 0 & 0 & 0 & 0 & 2 & 8 & 4 \\ 0 & 0 & 0 & -1 & 0 & 1 & -1 \end{bmatrix}$$

$R_1 + R_2, R_4 + R_2$: Introduce 0's above and below the leading 1 in row 2.

$$\begin{bmatrix} 0 & 1 & -4 & 0 & 0 & 3 & -2 \\ 0 & 0 & 0 & 1 & 3 & 11 & 9 \\ 0 & 0 & 0 & 0 & 2 & 8 & 4 \\ 0 & 0 & 0 & 0 & 3 & 12 & 8 \end{bmatrix}$$

$(1/2)R_3$: Introduce a leading 1 into row 3.

$$\begin{bmatrix} 0 & 1 & -4 & 0 & 0 & 3 & -2 \\ 0 & 0 & 0 & 1 & 3 & 11 & 9 \\ 0 & 0 & 0 & 0 & 1 & 4 & 2 \\ 0 & 0 & 0 & 0 & 3 & 12 & 8 \end{bmatrix}$$

$R_2 - 3R_3, R_4 - 3R_3$: Introduce 0's above and below the leading 1 in row 3.

$$\begin{bmatrix} 0 & 1 & -4 & 0 & 0 & 3 & -2 \\ 0 & 0 & 0 & 1 & 0 & -1 & 3 \\ 0 & 0 & 0 & 0 & 1 & 4 & 2 \\ 0 & 0 & 0 & 0 & 0 & 0 & 2 \end{bmatrix}$$

$(1/2)R_4$: Introduce a leading 1 into row 4.

$$\begin{bmatrix} 0 & 1 & -4 & 0 & 0 & 3 & -2 \\ 0 & 0 & 0 & 1 & 0 & -1 & 3 \\ 0 & 0 & 0 & 0 & 1 & 4 & 2 \\ 0 & 0 & 0 & 0 & 0 & 0 & 1 \end{bmatrix}$$

$R_1 + 2R_4, R_2 - 3R_4, R_3 - 2R_4$: Introduce 0's above the leading 1 in row 4.

$$\begin{bmatrix} 0 & 1 & -4 & 0 & 0 & 3 & 0 \\ 0 & 0 & 0 & 1 & 0 & -1 & 0 \\ 0 & 0 & 0 & 0 & 1 & 4 & 0 \\ 0 & 0 & 0 & 0 & 0 & 0 & 1 \end{bmatrix}$$

■

Having provided this example of how to transform a matrix to reduced echelon form, we can be more specific about the procedure for solving a system of equations that is diagrammed in Fig. 1.3.

> ### Solving a System of Equations
>
> Given a system of equations:
>
> ***Step 1.*** Create the augmented matrix for the system.
>
> ***Step 2.*** Transform the matrix in Step 1 to reduced echelon form.
>
> ***Step 3.*** Decode the reduced matrix found in Step 2 to obtain its associated system of equations. (This system is equivalent to the original system.)
>
> ***Step 4.*** By examining the reduced system in Step 3, describe the solution set for the original system.

The next example illustrates the complete process.

EXAMPLE 4 Solve the following system of equations:

$$\begin{aligned} 2x_1 - 4x_2 + 3x_3 - 4x_4 - 11x_5 &= 28 \\ -x_1 + 2x_2 - x_3 + 2x_4 + 5x_5 &= -13 \\ -3x_3 + x_4 + 6x_5 &= -10 \\ 3x_1 - 6x_2 + 10x_3 - 8x_4 - 28x_5 &= 61. \end{aligned}$$

Solution We first create the augmented matrix and then transform it to reduced echelon form. The augmented matrix is

$$\begin{bmatrix} 2 & -4 & 3 & -4 & -11 & 28 \\ -1 & 2 & -1 & 2 & 5 & -13 \\ 0 & 0 & -3 & 1 & 6 & -10 \\ 3 & -6 & 10 & -8 & -28 & 61 \end{bmatrix}.$$

The first step is to introduce a leading 1 into row 1. We can introduce the leading 1 if we multiply row 1 by 1/2, but that would create fractions that are undesirable for hand work. As an alternative, we can add row 2 to row 1 and avoid fractions.

$R_1 + R_2$:
$$\begin{bmatrix} 1 & -2 & 2 & -2 & -6 & 15 \\ -1 & 2 & -1 & 2 & 5 & -13 \\ 0 & 0 & -3 & 1 & 6 & -10 \\ 3 & -6 & 10 & -8 & -28 & 61 \end{bmatrix}$$

$R_2 + R_1, R_4 - 3R_1$: Introduce 0's below the leading 1 in row 1.

$$\begin{bmatrix} 1 & -2 & 2 & -2 & -6 & 15 \\ 0 & 0 & 1 & 0 & -1 & 2 \\ 0 & 0 & -3 & 1 & 6 & -10 \\ 0 & 0 & 4 & -2 & -10 & 16 \end{bmatrix}$$

$R_1 - 2R_2, R_3 + 3R_2, R_4 - 4R_2$: Introduce 0's above and below the leading 1 in row 2.

$$\begin{bmatrix} 1 & -2 & 0 & -2 & -4 & 11 \\ 0 & 0 & 1 & 0 & -1 & 2 \\ 0 & 0 & 0 & 1 & 3 & -4 \\ 0 & 0 & 0 & -2 & -6 & 8 \end{bmatrix}$$

$R_1 + 2R_3, R_4 + 2R_3$: Introduce 0's above and below the leading 1 in row 3.

$$\begin{bmatrix} 1 & -2 & 0 & 0 & 2 & 3 \\ 0 & 0 & 1 & 0 & -1 & 2 \\ 0 & 0 & 0 & 1 & 3 & -4 \\ 0 & 0 & 0 & 0 & 0 & 0 \end{bmatrix}$$

The matrix above represents the system of equations

$$\begin{aligned} x_1 - 2x_2 \qquad\qquad + 2x_5 &= 3 \\ x_3 \qquad - x_5 &= 2 \\ x_4 + 3x_5 &= -4. \end{aligned}$$

Solving the preceding system, we find:

$$\begin{aligned} x_1 &= 3 + 2x_2 - 2x_5 \\ x_3 &= 2 \qquad\quad + x_5 \\ x_4 &= -4 \qquad\; - 3x_5 \end{aligned} \tag{1}$$

In Eq. (1) we have a nice description of all of the infinitely many solutions to the original system—it is called the ***general solution*** for the system. For this example, x_2 and x_5 are viewed as independent (or unconstrained) variables and can be assigned values arbitrarily. The variables x_1, x_3, and x_4 are dependent (or constrained) variables, and their values are determined by the values assigned to x_2 and x_5. For example, in Eq. (1), setting $x_2 = 1$ and $x_5 = -1$ yields a ***particular solution*** given by $x_1 = 7$, $x_2 = 1$, $x_3 = 1$, $x_4 = -1$, and $x_5 = -1$.

Electronic Aids and Software

One testimony to the practical importance of linear algebra is the wide variety of electronic aids available for linear algebra computations. For instance, many scientific calculators can solve systems of linear equations and perform simple matrix operations. For computers there are general-purpose computer algebra systems such as Derive, Mathematica, and Maple that have extensive computational capabilities. Special-purpose linear algebra software such as MATLAB is very easy to use and can perform virtually any type of matrix calculation.

In the following example, we illustrate the use of MATLAB. From time to time, as appropriate, we will include other examples that illustrate the use of electronic aids.

EXAMPLE 5 In certain applications, it is necessary to evaluate sums of powers of integers such as

$$1+2+3+\cdots+n,$$
$$1^2+2^2+3^2+\cdots+n^2,$$
$$1^3+2^3+3^3+\cdots+n^3, \quad \text{and so on.}$$

Interestingly, it is possible to derive simple formulas for such sums. For instance, you might be familiar with the formula

$$1+2+3+\cdots+n=\frac{n(n+1)}{2}.$$

Such formulas can be derived using the following result: If n and r are positive integers, then there are constants $a_1, a_2, \ldots, a_{r+1}$ such that

$$1^r+2^r+3^r+\cdots+n^r=a_1n+a_2n^2+a_3n^3+\cdots+a_{r+1}n^{r+1}. \tag{2}$$

Use Eq. (2) to find the formula for $1^3+2^3+3^3+\cdots+n^3$. (***Note:*** Eq. (2) can be derived from the theory of linear difference equations.)

Solution From Eq. (2) there are constants a_1, a_2, a_3, and a_4 such that

$$1^3+2^3+3^3+\cdots+n^3=a_1n+a_2n^2+a_3n^3+a_4n^4.$$

If we evaluate the formula just given for $n=1$, $n=2$, $n=3$, and $n=4$, we obtain four equations for a_1, a_2, a_3, and a_4:

$$\begin{array}{rrrrrl}
a_1+ & a_2+ & a_3+ & a_4= & 1 & (n=1)\\
2a_1+ & 4a_2+ & 8a_3+ & 16a_4= & 9 & (n=2)\\
3a_1+ & 9a_2+ & 27a_3+ & 81a_4= & 36 & (n=3)\\
4a_1+ & 16a_2+ & 64a_3+ & 256a_4= & 100. & (n=4)
\end{array}$$

The augmented matrix for this system is

$$A=\begin{bmatrix} 1 & 1 & 1 & 1 & 1\\ 2 & 4 & 8 & 16 & 9\\ 3 & 9 & 27 & 81 & 36\\ 4 & 16 & 64 & 256 & 100 \end{bmatrix}.$$

We used MATLAB to solve the system by transforming A to reduced echelon form. The steps, as they appear on a computer screen, are shown in Fig. 1.6. The symbol >> is a prompt from MATLAB. At the first prompt, we entered the augmented matrix A

```
>>A=[1,1,1,1,1;2,4,8,16,9;3,9,27,81,36;4,16,64,256,100]

A=
     1     1     1     1     1
     2     4     8    16     9
     3     9    27    81    36
     4    16    64   256   100

>>C=rref(A)

C=
    1.0000         0         0         0         0
         0    1.0000         0         0    0.2500
         0         0    1.0000         0    0.5000
         0         0         0    1.0000    0.2500

>>C

C=
     1     0     0     0     0
     0     1     0     0   1/4
     0     0     1     0   1/2
     0     0     0     1   1/4
```

Figure 1.6 Using MATLAB in Example 5 to row reduce the matrix A to the matrix C.

and then MATLAB displayed A. At the second prompt, we entered the MATLAB row-reduction command, `C = rref(A)`. The new matrix C, as displayed by MATLAB, is the result of transforming A to reduced echelon form.

MATLAB normally displays results in decimal form. To obtain a rational form for the reduced matrix C, from the submenu *numerical form* we selected *rat* and entered C, finding

$$C = \begin{bmatrix} 1 & 0 & 0 & 0 & 0 \\ 0 & 1 & 0 & 0 & 1/4 \\ 0 & 0 & 1 & 0 & 1/2 \\ 0 & 0 & 0 & 1 & 1/4 \end{bmatrix}.$$

From this, we have $a_1 = 0$, $a_2 = 1/4$, $a_3 = 1/2$, and $a_4 = 1/4$. Therefore, the formula for the sum of the first n cubes is

$$1^3 + 2^3 + 3^3 + \cdots + n^3 = \frac{1}{4}n^2 + \frac{1}{2}n^3 + \frac{1}{4}n^4$$

or, after simplification,

$$1^3 + 2^3 + 3^3 + \cdots + n^3 = \frac{n^2(n+1)^2}{4}.$$ ∎

ADDING INTEGERS Mathematical folklore has it that Gauss discovered the formula $1+2+3+\cdots+n = n(n+1)/2$ when he was only ten years old. To occupy time, his teacher asked the students to add the integers from 1 to 100. Gauss immediately wrote an answer and turned his slate over. To his teacher's amazement, Gauss had the only correct answer in the class. Young Gauss had recognized that the numbers could be put in 50 sets of pairs such that the sum of each pair was 101:

$$(50+51)+(49+52)+(48+53)+\cdots+(1+100) = 50(101) = 5050.$$

Soon his brilliance was brought to the attention of the Duke of Brunswick, who thereafter sponsored the education of Gauss.

1.2 EXERCISES

Consider the matrices in Exercises 1–10.

a) Either state that the matrix is in echelon form or use elementary row operations to transform it to echelon form.

b) If the matrix is in echelon form, transform it to reduced echelon form.

1. $\begin{bmatrix} 1 & 2 \\ 0 & 1 \end{bmatrix}$ **2.** $\begin{bmatrix} 1 & 2 & -1 \\ 0 & 1 & 3 \end{bmatrix}$

3. $\begin{bmatrix} 2 & 3 & 1 \\ 4 & 1 & 0 \end{bmatrix}$ **4.** $\begin{bmatrix} 0 & 1 & 1 \\ 1 & 2 & 3 \end{bmatrix}$

5. $\begin{bmatrix} 0 & 0 & 2 & 3 \\ 2 & 0 & 1 & 4 \end{bmatrix}$ **6.** $\begin{bmatrix} 2 & 0 & 3 & 1 \\ 0 & 0 & 1 & 2 \end{bmatrix}$

7. $\begin{bmatrix} 1 & 3 & 2 & 1 \\ 0 & 1 & 4 & 2 \\ 0 & 0 & 1 & 1 \end{bmatrix}$ **8.** $\begin{bmatrix} 2 & -1 & 3 \\ 0 & 1 & 1 \\ 0 & 0 & -3 \end{bmatrix}$

9. $\begin{bmatrix} 1 & 2 & -1 & -2 \\ 0 & 2 & -2 & -3 \\ 0 & 0 & 0 & 1 \end{bmatrix}$

10. $\begin{bmatrix} -1 & 4 & -3 & 4 & 6 \\ 0 & 2 & 1 & -3 & -3 \\ 0 & 0 & 0 & 1 & 2 \end{bmatrix}$

In Exercises 11–21, each of the given matrices represents the augmented matrix for a system of linear equations. In each exercise, display the solution set or state that the system is inconsistent.

11. $\begin{bmatrix} 1 & 1 & 0 \\ 0 & 1 & 0 \end{bmatrix}$ **12.** $\begin{bmatrix} 1 & 1 & 0 \\ 0 & 0 & 2 \end{bmatrix}$

13. $\begin{bmatrix} 1 & 2 & 1 & 0 \\ 0 & 1 & 3 & 1 \end{bmatrix}$ **14.** $\begin{bmatrix} 1 & 2 & 2 & 1 \\ 0 & 1 & 0 & 0 \end{bmatrix}$

15. $\begin{bmatrix} 1 & 1 & 1 & 0 \\ 0 & 1 & 0 & 0 \\ 0 & 0 & 0 & 1 \end{bmatrix}$ **16.** $\begin{bmatrix} 1 & 2 & 0 & 1 \\ 0 & 1 & 1 & 0 \\ 0 & 0 & 2 & 0 \end{bmatrix}$

17. $\begin{bmatrix} 1 & 0 & 1 & 0 & 0 \\ 0 & 0 & 1 & 1 & 0 \\ 0 & 0 & 0 & 1 & 0 \end{bmatrix}$ **18.** $\begin{bmatrix} 1 & 2 & 1 & 3 \\ 0 & 0 & 0 & 2 \\ 0 & 0 & 0 & 0 \end{bmatrix}$

19. $\begin{bmatrix} 1 & 0 & 0 & 1 \\ 0 & 1 & 0 & 1 \\ 0 & 0 & 0 & 1 \end{bmatrix}$

20. $\begin{bmatrix} 1 & 1 & 2 & 0 & 2 & 0 \\ 0 & 1 & 1 & 1 & 0 & 0 \\ 0 & 0 & 1 & 2 & 1 & 2 \end{bmatrix}$

21. $\begin{bmatrix} 2 & 1 & 3 & 2 & 0 & 1 \\ 0 & 0 & 1 & 1 & 2 & 1 \\ 0 & 0 & 0 & 0 & 3 & 0 \end{bmatrix}$

In Exercises 22–35, solve the system by transforming the augmented matrix to reduced echelon form.

22. $\begin{aligned} 2x_1 - 3x_2 &= 5 \\ -4x_1 + 6x_2 &= -10 \end{aligned}$

23. $\begin{aligned} x_1 - 2x_2 &= 3 \\ 2x_1 - 4x_2 &= 1 \end{aligned}$

24. $\begin{aligned} x_1 - x_2 + x_3 &= 3 \\ 2x_1 + x_2 - 4x_3 &= -3 \end{aligned}$

25. $\begin{aligned} x_1 + x_2 &= 2 \\ 3x_1 + 3x_2 &= 6 \end{aligned}$

26. $\begin{aligned} x_1 - x_2 + x_3 &= 4 \\ 2x_1 - 2x_2 + 3x_3 &= 2 \end{aligned}$

27. $\begin{aligned} x_1 + x_2 - x_3 &= 2 \\ -3x_1 - 3x_2 + 3x_3 &= -6 \end{aligned}$

28. $\begin{aligned} 2x_1 + 3x_2 - 4x_3 &= 3 \\ x_1 - 2x_2 - 2x_3 &= -2 \\ -x_1 + 16x_2 + 2x_3 &= 16 \end{aligned}$

29. $\begin{aligned} x_1 + x_2 - x_3 &= 1 \\ 2x_1 - x_2 + 7x_3 &= 8 \\ -x_1 + x_2 - 5x_3 &= -5 \end{aligned}$

30. $\begin{aligned} x_1 + x_2 \qquad\qquad\quad - x_5 &= 1 \\ x_2 + 2x_3 + x_4 + 3x_5 &= 1 \\ x_1 \qquad - x_3 + x_4 + x_5 &= 0 \end{aligned}$

31. $\begin{aligned} x_1 \qquad + x_3 + x_4 - 2x_5 &= 1 \\ 2x_1 + x_2 + 3x_3 - x_4 + x_5 &= 0 \\ 3x_1 - x_2 + 4x_3 + x_4 + x_5 &= 1 \end{aligned}$

32. $\begin{aligned} x_1 + x_2 &= 1 \\ x_1 - x_2 &= 3 \\ 2x_1 + x_2 &= 3 \end{aligned}$

33. $\begin{aligned} x_1 + x_2 &= 1 \\ x_1 - x_2 &= 3 \\ 2x_1 + x_2 &= 2 \end{aligned}$

34. $\begin{aligned} x_1 + 2x_2 &= 1 \\ 2x_1 + 4x_2 &= 2 \\ -x_1 - 2x_2 &= -1 \end{aligned}$

35. $\begin{aligned} x_1 - x_2 - x_3 &= 1 \\ x_1 \qquad + x_3 &= 2 \\ x_2 + 2x_3 &= 3 \end{aligned}$

In Exercises 36–40, find all values a for which the system has no solution.

36. $\begin{aligned} x_1 + 2x_2 &= -3 \\ ax_1 - 2x_2 &= 5 \end{aligned}$

37. $\begin{aligned} x_1 + 3x_2 &= 4 \\ 2x_1 + 6x_2 &= a \end{aligned}$

38. $\begin{aligned} 2x_1 + 4x_2 &= a \\ 3x_1 + 6x_2 &= 5 \end{aligned}$

39. $\begin{aligned} 3x_1 + ax_2 &= 3 \\ ax_1 + 3x_2 &= 5 \end{aligned}$

40. $\begin{aligned} x_1 + ax_2 &= 6 \\ ax_1 + 2ax_2 &= 4 \end{aligned}$

In Exercises 41 and 42, find all values α and β where $0 \le \alpha \le 2\pi$ and $0 \le \beta \le 2\pi$.

41. $\begin{aligned} 2\cos\alpha + 4\sin\beta &= 3 \\ 3\cos\alpha - 5\sin\beta &= -1 \end{aligned}$

42. $\begin{aligned} 2\cos^2\alpha - \sin^2\beta &= 1 \\ 12\cos^2\alpha + 8\sin^2\beta &= 13 \end{aligned}$

43. Describe the solution set of the following system in terms of x_3:

$$\begin{aligned} x_1 + x_2 + x_3 &= 3 \\ x_1 + 2x_2 \qquad &= 5. \end{aligned}$$

For x_1, x_2, x_3 in the solution set:

a) Find the maximum value of x_3 such that $x_1 \ge 0$ and $x_2 \ge 0$.

b) Find the maximum value of $y = 2x_1 - 4x_2 + x_3$ subject to $x_1 \ge 0$ and $x_2 \ge 0$.

c) Find the minimum value of $y = (x_1 - 1)^2 + (x_2 + 3)^2 + (x_3 + 1)^2$ with no restriction on x_1 or x_2. [*Hint:* Regard y as a function of x_3 and set the derivative equal to 0; then apply the second-derivative test to verify that you have found a minimum.]

44. Let A and I be as follows:

$$A = \begin{bmatrix} 1 & d \\ c & b \end{bmatrix}, \qquad I = \begin{bmatrix} 1 & 0 \\ 0 & 1 \end{bmatrix}.$$

Prove that if $b - cd \ne 0$, then A is row equivalent to I.

45. As in Fig. 1.4, display all the possible configurations for a (2×3) matrix that is in echelon form. [*Hint:* There are seven such configurations. Consider the various positions that can be occupied by one, two, or none of the symbols.]

46. Repeat Exercise 45 for a (3×2) matrix, for a (3×3) matrix, and for a (3×4) matrix.

47. Consider the matrices B and C:

$$B = \begin{bmatrix} 1 & 2 \\ 2 & 3 \end{bmatrix}, \qquad C = \begin{bmatrix} 1 & 2 \\ 3 & 4 \end{bmatrix}.$$

By Exercise 44, B and C are both row equivalent to matrix I in Exercise 44. Determine elementary row operations that demonstrate that B is row equivalent to C.

48. Repeat Exercise 47 for the matrices

$$B = \begin{bmatrix} 1 & 4 \\ 3 & 7 \end{bmatrix}, \qquad C = \begin{bmatrix} 1 & 2 \\ 2 & 1 \end{bmatrix}.$$

49. A certain three-digit number N equals fifteen times the sum of its digits. If its digits are reversed, the resulting number exceeds N by 396. The one's digit is one larger than the sum of the other two. Give a linear system of three equations whose three unknowns are the digits of N. Solve the system and find N.

50. Find the equation of the parabola, $y = ax^2 + bx + c$, that passes through the points $(-1, 6)$, $(1, 4)$, and $(2, 9)$. [*Hint:* For each point, give a linear equation in a, b, and c.]

51. Three people play a game in which there are always two winners and one loser. They have the understanding that the loser gives each winner an amount equal to what the winner already has. After three games, each has lost just once and each has \$24. With how much money did each begin?

52. Find three numbers whose sum is 34 when the sum of the first and second is 7, and the sum of the second and third is 22.

53. A zoo charges \$6 for adults, \$3 for students, and \$.50 for children. One morning 79 people enter and pay a total of \$207. Determine the possible numbers of adults, students, and children.

54. Find a cubic polynomial, $p(x) = a+bx+cx^2+dx^3$, such that $p(1) = 5$, $p'(1) = 5$, $p(2) = 17$, and $p'(2) = 21$.

In Exercises 55–58, use Eq. (2) to find the formula for the sum. If available, use linear algebra software for Exercises 57 and 58.

55. $1 + 2 + 3 + \cdots + n$

56. $1^2 + 2^2 + 3^2 + \cdots + n^2$

57. $1^4 + 2^4 + 3^4 + \cdots + n^4$

58. $1^5 + 2^5 + 3^5 + \cdots + n^5$

1.3 CONSISTENT SYSTEMS OF LINEAR EQUATIONS

We saw in Section 1.1 that a system of linear equations may have a unique solution, infinitely many solutions, or no solution. In this section and in later sections, it will be shown that with certain added bits of information we can, without solving the system, either eliminate one of the three possible outcomes or determine precisely what the outcome will be. This will be important later when situations will arise in which we are not interested in obtaining a specific solution, but we need to know only how many solutions there are.

To illustrate, consider the general (2×3) linear system

$$\begin{aligned} a_{11}x_1 + a_{12}x_2 + a_{13}x_3 &= b_1 \\ a_{21}x_1 + a_{22}x_2 + a_{23}x_3 &= b_2. \end{aligned}$$

Geometrically, the system is represented by two planes, and a solution corresponds to a point in the intersection of the planes. The two planes may be parallel, they may be coincident (the same plane), or they may intersect in a line. Thus the system is either inconsistent or has infinitely many solutions; the existence of a unique solution is impossible.

Solution Possibilities for a Consistent Linear System

We begin our analysis by considering the $(m \times n)$ system of linear equations

$$\begin{aligned} a_{11}x_1 + a_{12}x_2 + \cdots + a_{1n}x_n &= b_1 \\ a_{21}x_1 + a_{22}x_2 + \cdots + a_{2n}x_n &= b_2 \\ \vdots \qquad\qquad\qquad & \quad \vdots \\ a_{m1}x_1 + a_{m2}x_2 + \cdots + a_{mn}x_n &= b_m. \end{aligned} \tag{1}$$

Our goal is to deduce as much information as possible about the solution set of system (1) without actually solving the system.

To that end, let $[A \mid \mathbf{b}]$ denote the augmented matrix for system (1). We know we can use row operations to transform the $[m \times (n+1)]$ matrix $[A \mid \mathbf{b}]$ to a row equivalent matrix $[C \mid \mathbf{d}]$ where $[C \mid \mathbf{d}]$ is in reduced echelon form. Hence, instead of trying to deduce the various possibilities for the solution set of (1), we will focus on the simpler problem of analyzing the solution possibilities for the *equivalent* system represented by the matrix $[C \mid \mathbf{d}]$.

We begin by making four remarks about an $[m \times (n+1)]$ matrix $[C \mid \mathbf{d}]$ that is in reduced echelon form. Our first remark recalls an observation made in Section 1.2.

Remark 1: The system represented by the matrix $[C \mid \mathbf{d}]$ is inconsistent if and only if $[C \mid \mathbf{d}]$ has a row of the form $[0, 0, 0, \ldots, 0, 1]$.

Our second remark also follows because $[C \mid \mathbf{d}]$ is in reduced echelon form. In particular, we know every nonzero row of $[C \mid \mathbf{d}]$ has a leading 1. We also know there are no other nonzero entries in a column of $[C \mid \mathbf{d}]$ that contains a leading 1. Thus, if x_k is the variable corresponding to a leading 1, then x_k can be expressed in terms of other variables that do not correspond to any leading ones in $[C \mid \mathbf{d}]$. Therefore, we obtain

Remark 2: Every variable corresponding to a leading 1 in $[C \mid \mathbf{d}]$ is a dependent variable. (That is, each "leading-one variable" can be expressed in terms of the independent or "nonleading-one variables.")

We illustrate Remark 2 with the following example.

EXAMPLE 1 Consider the matrix $[C \mid \mathbf{d}]$ given by

$$[C \mid \mathbf{d}] = \begin{bmatrix} 1 & 2 & 0 & 3 & 0 & 4 & 1 \\ 0 & 0 & 1 & 2 & 0 & 3 & 2 \\ 0 & 0 & 0 & 0 & 1 & 1 & 2 \\ 0 & 0 & 0 & 0 & 0 & 0 & 0 \\ 0 & 0 & 0 & 0 & 0 & 0 & 0 \end{bmatrix}.$$

The matrix $[C \mid \mathbf{d}]$ is in reduced echelon form and represents the consistent system

$$\begin{aligned} x_1 + 2x_2 + \quad 3x_4 + \quad + 4x_6 &= 1 \\ x_3 + 2x_4 + \quad + 3x_6 &= 2 \\ x_5 + x_6 &= 2. \end{aligned}$$

The dependent variables (corresponding to the leading 1's) are x_1, x_3, and x_5. They can be expressed in terms of the other (independent) variables as follows:

$$\begin{aligned} x_1 &= 1 - 2x_2 - 3x_4 - 4x_6 \\ x_3 &= 2 \qquad\quad - 2x_4 - 3x_6 \\ x_5 &= 2 \qquad\qquad\quad - x_6. \end{aligned}$$

Our third remark gives a bound on the number of nonzero rows in $[C \mid \mathbf{d}]$. Let r denote the number of nonzero rows in $[C \mid \mathbf{d}]$. (Later we will see that the number r is called the "rank" of C.) Since every nonzero row contains a leading 1, the number r is equal to the number of leading 1's. Because the matrix is in echelon form, there cannot be more leading 1's in $[C \mid \mathbf{d}]$ than there are columns. Since the matrix $[C \mid \mathbf{d}]$ has $n+1$ columns, we conclude:

Remark 3: Let r denote the number of nonzero rows in $[C \mid \mathbf{d}]$. Then, $r \le n + 1$.

Our fourth remark is a consequence of Remark 1 and Remark 3. Let r denote the number of nonzero rows in $[C \mid \mathbf{d}]$. If $r = n+1$, then $[C \mid \mathbf{d}]$ has a row of the form $[0, 0, \ldots, 0, 1]$ and hence the system represented by $[C \mid \mathbf{d}]$ must be inconsistent. Therefore, if the system is consistent, we need to have $r < n+1$. This observation leads to:

Remark 4: Let r denote the number of nonzero rows in $[C \mid \mathbf{d}]$. If the system represented by $[C \mid \mathbf{d}]$ is consistent, then $r \le n$.

In general, let $[C \mid \mathbf{d}]$ be an $[m \times (n+1)]$ matrix in reduced echelon form where $[C \mid \mathbf{d}]$ represents a consistent system. According to Remark 2, if $[C \mid \mathbf{d}]$ has r nonzero rows, then there are r dependent (constrained) variables in the solution of the system corresponding to $[C \mid \mathbf{d}]$. In addition, by Remark 4, we know $r \le n$. Since there are n variables altogether in this $(m \times n)$ system, the remaining $n-r$ variables are independent (or unconstrained) variables. See Theorem 3.

THEOREM 3 Let $[C \mid \mathbf{d}]$ be an $[m \times (n+1)]$ matrix in reduced echelon form, where $[C \mid \mathbf{d}]$ represents a consistent system. Let $[C \mid \mathbf{d}]$ have r nonzero rows. Then $r \le n$ and in the solution of the system there are $n - r$ variables that can be assigned arbitrary values. ■

Theorem 3 is illustrated below in Example 2.

EXAMPLE 2 Illustrate Theorem 3 using the results of Example 1.

Solution The augmented matrix $[C \mid \mathbf{d}]$ in Example 1 is (5×6) and represents a consistent system since it does not have a row of the form $[0, 0, 0, 0, 0, 1]$. The matrix has $r = 3$ nonzero rows and hence must have $n - r = 6 - 3 = 3$ independent variables. The 3 dependent variables and 3 independent variables are displayed in Example 1. ■

The remark in Section 1.1 that a system of linear equations has either infinitely many solutions, no solution, or a unique solution is an immediate consequence of Theorem 3. To see why, let $[A \mid \mathbf{b}]$ denote the augmented matrix for a system of m equations in n unknowns. Then $[A \mid \mathbf{b}]$ is row equivalent to a matrix $[C \mid \mathbf{d}]$ that is in reduced echelon form. Since the two augmented matrices represent equivalent systems, both of the systems have the same solution set. By Theorem 3, we know the only possibilities for the system represented by $[C \mid \mathbf{d}]$ (and hence for the system represented by $[A \mid \mathbf{b}]$) are:

1. The system is inconsistent.
2. The system is consistent and, in the notation of Theorem 3, $r < n$. In this case there are $n - r$ unconstrained variables, so the system has infinitely many solutions.
3. The system is consistent and $r = n$. In this case there are no unconstrained variables, so the system has a unique solution.

We can also use Theorem 3 to draw some conclusions about a general $(m \times n)$ system of linear equations in the case where $m < n$. These conclusions are given in the following corollary. Note that the hypotheses do not require the augmented matrix for the system to be in echelon form. Nor do the hypotheses require the system to be consistent.

COROLLARY Consider an $(m \times n)$ system of linear equations. If $m < n$, then either the system is inconsistent or it has infinitely many solutions.

Proof Consider an $(m \times n)$ system of linear equations where $m < n$. If the system is inconsistent, there is nothing to prove. If the system is consistent, then Theorem 3 applies. For a consistent system, suppose that the augmented matrix $[A \mid \mathbf{b}]$ is row equivalent to a matrix $[C \mid \mathbf{d}]$ that is in echelon form and has r nonzero rows. Because the given system has m equations, the augmented matrix $[A \mid \mathbf{b}]$ has m rows. Therefore the matrix $[C \mid \mathbf{d}]$ also has m rows. Because r is the number of nonzero rows for $[C \mid \mathbf{d}]$, it is clear that $r \leq m$. But $m < n$, so it follows that $r < n$. By Theorem 3, there are $n - r$ independent variables. Because $n - r > 0$, the system has infinitely many solutions. ∎

EXAMPLE 3 What are the possibilities for the solution set of a (3×4) system of linear equations? If the system is consistent, what are the possibilities for the number of independent variables?

Solution By the corollary to Theorem 3, the system either has no solution or has infinitely many solutions. If the system reduces to a system with r equations, then $r \leq 3$. Thus r must be 1, 2, or 3. (The case $r = 0$ can occur only when the original system is the trivial system in which all coefficients and all constants are zero.) If the system is consistent, the number of free parameters is $4 - r$, so the possibilities are 3, 2, and 1. ∎

EXAMPLE 4 What are the possibilities for the solution set of the following (3×4) system?

$$\begin{aligned} 2x_1 - x_2 + x_3 - 3x_4 &= 0 \\ x_1 + 3x_2 - 2x_3 + x_4 &= 0 \\ -x_1 - 2x_2 + 4x_3 - x_4 &= 0 \end{aligned}$$

Solution First note that $x_1 = x_2 = x_3 = x_4 = 0$ is a solution, so the system is consistent. By the corollary to Theorem 3, the system must have infinitely many solutions. That is, $m = 3$ and $n = 4$, so $m < n$. ∎

Homogeneous Systems

The system in Example 4 is an example of a homogeneous system of equations. More generally, the $(m \times n)$ system of linear equations given in (2) is called a ***homogeneous*** system of linear equations:

$$\begin{aligned} a_{11}x_1 + a_{12}x_2 + \cdots + a_{1n}x_n &= 0 \\ a_{21}x_1 + a_{22}x_2 + \cdots + a_{2n}x_n &= 0 \\ \vdots \qquad\qquad\qquad & \;\;\vdots \\ a_{m1}x_1 + a_{m2}x_2 + \cdots + a_{mn}x_n &= 0. \end{aligned} \tag{2}$$

Thus system (2) is the special case of the general $(m \times n)$ system (1) given earlier in which $b_1 = b_2 = \cdots = b_m = 0$. Note that a homogeneous system is always consistent, because $x_1 = x_2 = \cdots = x_n = 0$ is a solution to system (2). This solution is called the ***trivial solution*** or ***zero solution***, and any other solution is called a ***nontrivial solution.*** A homogeneous system of equations, therefore, either has the trivial solution as the unique solution or also has nontrivial (and hence infinitely many) solutions. With these observations, the following important theorem is an immediate consequence of the corollary to Theorem 3.

THEOREM 4 A homogeneous ($m \times n$) system of linear equations always has infinitely many nontrivial solutions when $m < n$.

EXAMPLE 5 What are the possibilities for the solution set of

$$\begin{aligned} x_1 + 2x_2 + x_3 + 3x_4 &= 0 \\ 2x_1 + 4x_2 + 3x_3 + x_4 &= 0 \\ 3x_1 + 6x_2 + 6x_3 + 2x_4 &= 0? \end{aligned}$$

Solve the system.

Solution By Theorem 4, the system has infinitely many nontrivial solutions. We solve by reducing the augmented matrix:

$$\begin{bmatrix} 1 & 2 & 1 & 3 & 0 \\ 2 & 4 & 3 & 1 & 0 \\ 3 & 6 & 6 & 2 & 0 \end{bmatrix}.$$

$R_2 - 2R_1, R_3 - 3R_1$:

$$\begin{bmatrix} 1 & 2 & 1 & 3 & 0 \\ 0 & 0 & 1 & -5 & 0 \\ 0 & 0 & 3 & -7 & 0 \end{bmatrix}$$

$R_3 - 3R_2, R_1 - R_2$:

$$\begin{bmatrix} 1 & 2 & 0 & 8 & 0 \\ 0 & 0 & 1 & -5 & 0 \\ 0 & 0 & 0 & 8 & 0 \end{bmatrix}$$

$(1/8)R_3, R_1 - 8R_3, R_2 + 5R_3$:

$$\begin{bmatrix} 1 & 2 & 0 & 0 & 0 \\ 0 & 0 & 1 & 0 & 0 \\ 0 & 0 & 0 & 1 & 0 \end{bmatrix}.$$

Note that the last column of zeros is maintained under elementary row operations, so the given system is equivalent to the homogeneous system

$$\begin{aligned} x_1 + 2x_2 &= 0 \\ x_3 &= 0 \\ x_4 &= 0. \end{aligned}$$

Therefore, we obtain

$$\begin{aligned} x_1 &= -2x_2 \\ x_3 &= 0 \\ x_4 &= 0 \end{aligned}$$

as the solution.

EXAMPLE 6 What are the possibilities for the solution set of

$$\begin{aligned} 2x_1 + 4x_2 + 2x_3 &= 0 \\ -2x_1 - 2x_2 + 2x_3 &= 0 \\ 2x_1 + 6x_2 + 9x_3 &= 0? \end{aligned}$$

Solve the system.

Solution Theorem 4 no longer applies because $m = n = 3$. However, because the system is homogeneous, either the trivial solution is the unique solution or there are infinitely many nontrivial solutions. To solve, we reduce the augmented matrix

$$\begin{bmatrix} 2 & 4 & 2 & 0 \\ -2 & -2 & 2 & 0 \\ 2 & 6 & 9 & 0 \end{bmatrix}.$$

$(1/2)R_1, R_2 + 2R_1, R_3 - 2R_1$:

$$\begin{bmatrix} 1 & 2 & 1 & 0 \\ 0 & 2 & 4 & 0 \\ 0 & 2 & 7 & 0 \end{bmatrix}$$

$(1/2)R_2, R_1 - 2R_2, R_3 - 2R_2$:

$$\begin{bmatrix} 1 & 0 & -3 & 0 \\ 0 & 1 & 2 & 0 \\ 0 & 0 & 3 & 0 \end{bmatrix}$$

$(1/3)R_3, R_1 + 3R_3, R_2 - 2R_3$:

$$\begin{bmatrix} 1 & 0 & 0 & 0 \\ 0 & 1 & 0 & 0 \\ 0 & 0 & 1 & 0 \end{bmatrix}.$$

Therefore, we find $x_1 = 0$, $x_2 = 0$, and $x_3 = 0$ is the only solution to the system. ■

EXAMPLE 7 For the system of equations

$$\begin{aligned} x_1 - 2x_2 + 3x_3 &= b_1 \\ 2x_1 - 3x_2 + 2x_3 &= b_2 \\ -x_1 \qquad + 5x_3 &= b_3, \end{aligned}$$

determine conditions on b_1, b_2, and b_3 that are necessary and sufficient for the system to be consistent.

Solution The augmented matrix is

$$\begin{bmatrix} 1 & -2 & 3 & b_1 \\ 2 & -3 & 2 & b_2 \\ -1 & 0 & 5 & b_3 \end{bmatrix}.$$

The augmented matrix reduces to

$$\begin{bmatrix} 1 & 0 & -5 & -3b_1 + 2b_2 \\ 0 & 1 & -4 & -2b_1 + b_2 \\ 0 & 0 & 0 & -3b_1 + 2b_2 + b_3 \end{bmatrix}.$$

If $-3b_1+2b_2+b_3 \neq 0$ the system is inconsistent. On the other hand, if $-3b_1+2b_2+b_3 = 0$, then the system has general solution

$$\begin{aligned} x_1 &= -3b_1 + 2b_2 + 5x_3 \\ x_2 &= -2b_1 + b_2 + 4x_3. \end{aligned}$$

Thus, the given system is consistent if and only if $-3b_1 + 2b_2 + b_3 = 0$. ■

Conic Sections and Quadric Surfaces

An interesting application of homogeneous equations involves the quadratic equation in two variables:

$$ax^2 + bxy + cy^2 + dx + ey + f = 0. \tag{3}$$

If Eq. (3) has real solutions, then the graph is a curve in the xy-plane. If at least one of a, b, or c is nonzero, the resulting graph is known as a ***conic section.*** Conic sections include such familiar plane figures as parabolas, ellipses, hyperbolas, and (as well) certain degenerate forms such as points and lines. Objects as diverse as planets, comets, man-made satellites, and electrons follow trajectories in space that correspond to conic sections. The earth, for instance, travels in an elliptical path about the sun, with the sun at one focus of the ellipse.

In this subsection we consider an important data-fitting problem associated with Eq. (3), namely:

Suppose we are given several points in the xy-plane, (x_1, y_1), (x_2, y_2), $\ldots$, (x_n, y_n). *Can we find coefficients* $a, b, \ldots, f$ *so that the graph of Eq. (3) passes through the given points?*

For example, if we know an object is moving along an ellipse, can we make a few observations of the object's position and then determine its complete orbit? As we will see, the answer is yes. In fact, if an object follows a trajectory that corresponds to the graph of Eq. (3), then five or fewer observations are sufficient to determine the complete trajectory.

The following example introduces the data-fitting technique. As you will see, Example 8 describes a method for finding the equation of the line passing through two points in the plane. This is a simple and familiar problem, but its very simplicity is a virtue because it suggests methods we can use for solving more complicated problems.

EXAMPLE 8 The general equation of a line is $dx + ey + f = 0$. Find the equation of the line through the points $(1, 2)$ and $(3, 7)$.

Solution In an analytic geometry course, we would probably find the equation of the line by first calculating the slope of the line. In this example, however, we are interested in developing methods that can be used to find equations for more complicated curves; and we do not want to use special purpose techniques, such as slopes, that apply only to lines.

Since the points (1, 2) and (3, 7) lie on the line defined by $dx + ey + f = 0$, we insert these values into the equation and find the following conditions on the coefficients d, e, and f:

$$\begin{aligned} d + 2e + f &= 0 \\ 3d + 7e + f &= 0. \end{aligned}$$

We are guaranteed from Theorem 4 that the preceding homogeneous linear system has nontrivial solutions; that is, we can find a line passing through the two given points. To find the equation of the line, we need to solve the system. We begin by forming the associated augmented matrix

$$\begin{bmatrix} 1 & 2 & 1 & 0 \\ 3 & 7 & 1 & 0 \end{bmatrix}.$$

The preceding matrix can be transformed to reduced echelon form, yielding

$$\begin{bmatrix} 1 & 0 & 5 & 0 \\ 0 & 1 & -2 & 0 \end{bmatrix}.$$

It follows that the solution is $d = -5f$, $e = 2f$, and hence the equation of the line is

$$-5fx + 2fy + f = 0.$$

Canceling the parameter f, we obtain an equation for the line:

$$-5x + 2y + 1 = 0.$$ ■

Example 8 suggests how we might determine the equation of a conic that passes through a given set of points in the *xy*-plane. In particular, see Eq. (3); the general conic has six coefficients, $a, b, \ldots, f$. So, given any five points (x_i, y_i) we can insert these five points into Eq. (3) and the result will be a homogeneous system of five equations for the six unknown coefficients that define the conic section. By Theorem 4, the resulting system is guaranteed to have a nontrivial solution—that is, we can guarantee that any five points in the plane lie on the graph of an equation of the form (3). Example 9 illustrates this point.

EXAMPLE 9 Find the equation of the conic section passing through the five points $(-1, 0)$, $(0, 1)$, $(2, 2)$, $(2, -1)$, $(0, -3)$. Display the graph of the conic.

Solution The augmented matrix for the corresponding homogeneous system of five equations in six unknowns is listed below. In creating the augmented matrix, we formed the rows in the same order the points were listed and formed columns using the same order the unknowns were listed in Eq. (3). For example, the third row of the augmented matrix arises from inserting (2, 2) into Eq. (3):

$$4a + 4b + 4c + 2d + 2e + f = 0.$$

In particular, the augmented matrix is

$$\begin{bmatrix} 1 & 0 & 0 & -1 & 0 & 1 & 0 \\ 0 & 0 & 1 & 0 & 1 & 1 & 0 \\ 4 & 4 & 4 & 2 & 2 & 1 & 0 \\ 4 & -2 & 1 & 2 & -1 & 1 & 0 \\ 0 & 0 & 9 & 0 & -3 & 1 & 0 \end{bmatrix}.$$

We used MATLAB to transform the augmented matrix to reduced echelon form, finding

$$\begin{bmatrix} 1 & 0 & 0 & 0 & 0 & 7/18 & 0 \\ 0 & 1 & 0 & 0 & 0 & -1/2 & 0 \\ 0 & 0 & 1 & 0 & 0 & 1/3 & 0 \\ 0 & 0 & 0 & 1 & 0 & -11/18 & 0 \\ 0 & 0 & 0 & 0 & 1 & 2/3 & 0 \end{bmatrix}.$$

Thus, the coefficients of the conic through these five points are given by

$$a = -7f/18, b = f/2, c = -f/3, d = 11f/18, e = -2f/3.$$

Setting $f = 18$, we obtain a version of Eq. (3) with integer coefficients:

$$-7x^2 + 9xy - 6y^2 + 11x - 12y + 18 = 0.$$

The graph of this equation is an ellipse and is shown in Fig. 1.7. The graph was drawn using the contour command from MATLAB. Contour plots and other features of MATLAB graphics are described in the Appendix. ■

Finally, it should be noted that the ideas discussed above are not limited to the xy-plane. For example, consider the quadratic equation in three variables:

$$ax^2 + by^2 + cz^2 + dxy + exz + fyz + gx + hy + iz + j = 0. \tag{4}$$

The graph of Eq. (4) is a surface in three-space; the surface is known as a ***quadric surface***. Counting the coefficients in Eq. (4), we find ten. Thus, given any nine points in three-space, we can find a quadric surface passing through the nine points (see Exercises 30–31).

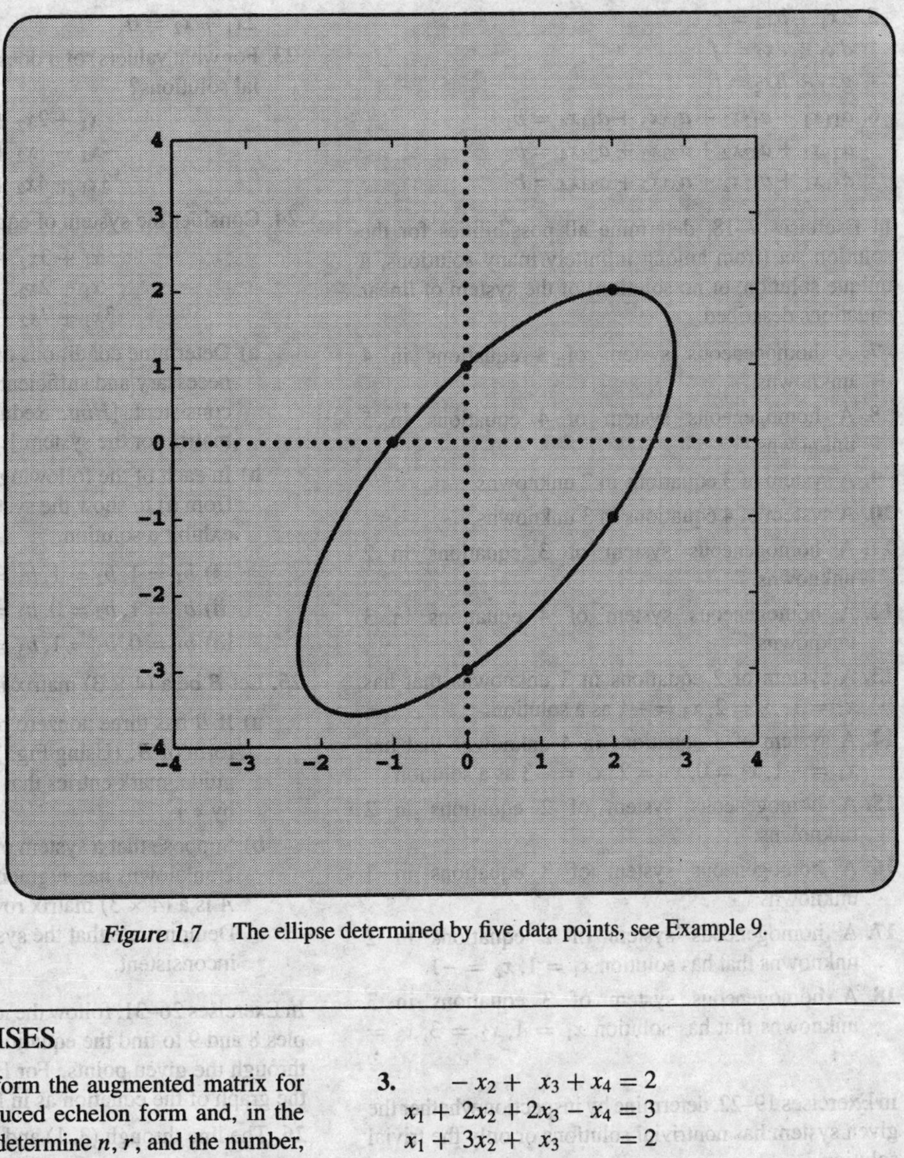

Figure 1.7 The ellipse determined by five data points, see Example 9.

1.3 EXERCISES

In Exercises 1–4, transform the augmented matrix for the given system to reduced echelon form and, in the notation of Theorem 3, determine n, r, and the number, $n - r$, of independent variables. If $n - r > 0$, then identify $n - r$ independent variables.

1.
$$\begin{aligned} 2x_1 + 2x_2 - x_3 &= 1 \\ -2x_1 - 2x_2 + 4x_3 &= 1 \\ 2x_1 + 2x_2 + 5x_3 &= 5 \\ -2x_1 - 2x_2 - 2x_3 &= -3 \end{aligned}$$

2.
$$\begin{aligned} 2x_1 + 2x_2 &= 1 \\ 4x_1 + 5x_2 &= 4 \\ 4x_1 + 2x_2 &= -2 \end{aligned}$$

3.
$$\begin{aligned} -x_2 + x_3 + x_4 &= 2 \\ x_1 + 2x_2 + 2x_3 - x_4 &= 3 \\ x_1 + 3x_2 + x_3 \phantom{{}+x_4} &= 2 \end{aligned}$$

4.
$$\begin{aligned} x_1 + 2x_2 + 3x_3 + 2x_4 &= 1 \\ x_1 + 2x_2 + 3x_3 + 5x_4 &= 2 \\ 2x_1 + 4x_2 + 6x_3 + x_4 &= 1 \\ -x_1 - 2x_2 - 3x_3 + 7x_4 &= 2 \end{aligned}$$

In Exercises 5 and 6, assume that the given system is consistent. For each system determine, in the notation of Theorem 3, all possibilities for the number, r of nonzero rows and the number, $n - r$, of unconstrained variables. Can the system have a unique solution?

5. $ax_1 + bx_2 = c$
$dx_1 + ex_2 = f$
$gx_1 + hx_2 = i$

6. $a_{11}x_1 + a_{12}x_2 + a_{13}x_3 + a_{14}x_4 = b_1$
$a_{21}x_1 + a_{22}x_2 + a_{23}x_3 + a_{24}x_4 = b_2$
$a_{31}x_1 + a_{32}x_2 + a_{33}x_3 + a_{34}x_4 = b_3$

In Exercises 7–18, determine all possibilities for the solution set (from among infinitely many solutions, a unique solution, or no solution) of the system of linear equations described.

7. A homogeneous system of 3 equations in 4 unknowns.

8. A homogeneous system of 4 equations in 5 unknowns.

9. A system of 3 equations in 2 unknowns.

10. A system of 4 equations in 3 unknowns.

11. A homogeneous system of 3 equations in 2 unknowns.

12. A homogeneous system of 4 equations in 3 unknowns.

13. A system of 2 equations in 3 unknowns that has $x_1 = 1, x_2 = 2, x_3 = -1$ as a solution.

14. A system of 3 equations in 4 unknowns that has $x_1 = -1, x_2 = 0, x_3 = 2, x_4 = -3$ as a solution.

15. A homogeneous system of 2 equations in 2 unknowns.

16. A homogeneous system of 3 equations in 3 unknowns.

17. A homogeneous system of 2 equations in 2 unknowns that has solution $x_1 = 1, x_2 = -1$.

18. A homogeneous system of 3 equations in 3 unknowns that has solution $x_1 = 1, x_2 = 3, x_3 = -1$.

In Exercises 19–22, determine by inspection whether the given system has nontrivial solutions or only the trivial solution.

19. $2x_1 + 3x_2 - x_3 = 0$
$x_1 - x_2 + 2x_3 = 0$

20. $x_1 + 2x_2 - x_3 + 2x_4 = 0$
$2x_1 + x_2 + x_3 - x_4 = 0$
$3x_1 - x_2 - 2x_3 + 3x_4 = 0$

21. $x_1 + 2x_2 - x_3 = 0$
$x_2 + 2x_3 = 0$
$4x_3 = 0$

22. $x_1 - x_2 = 0$
$3x_1 = 0$
$2x_1 + x_2 = 0$

23. For what value(s) of a does the system have nontrivial solutions?

$$\begin{aligned} x_1 + 2x_2 + x_3 &= 0 \\ -x_1 - x_2 + x_3 &= 0 \\ 3x_1 + 4x_2 + ax_3 &= 0. \end{aligned}$$

24. Consider the system of equations

$$\begin{aligned} x_1 + 3x_2 - x_3 &= b_1 \\ x_1 + 2x_2 \quad\;\; &= b_2 \\ 3x_1 + 7x_2 - x_3 &= b_3. \end{aligned}$$

a) Determine conditions on b_1, b_2, and b_3 that are necessary and sufficient for the system to be consistent. [*Hint:* Reduce the augmented matrix for the system.]

b) In each of the following, either use your answer from **a)** to show the system is inconsistent or exhibit a solution.

i) $b_1 = 1, b_2 = 1, b_3 = 3$
ii) $b_1 = 1, b_2 = 0, b_3 = -1$
iii) $b_1 = 0, b_2 = 1, b_3 = 2$

25. Let B be a (4×3) matrix in reduced echelon form.

a) If B has three nonzero rows, then determine the form of B. (Using Fig. 1.5 of Section 1.2 as a guide, mark entries that may or may not be zero by $*$.)

b) Suppose that a system of 4 linear equations in 2 unknowns has augmented matrix A, where A is a (4×3) matrix row equivalent to B. Demonstrate that the system of equations is inconsistent.

In Exercises 26–31, follow the ideas illustrated in Examples 8 and 9 to find the equation of the curve or surface through the given points. For Exercises 28–29, display the graph of the equation as in Fig. 1.7.

26. The line through (3, 1) and (7, 2).

27. The line through (2, 8) and (4, 1).

28. The conic through (−4, 0), (−2, −2), (0, 3), (1, 1), and (4, 0).

29. The conic through (−4, 1), (−1, 2), (3, 2), (5, 1), and (7, −1).

30. The quadric surface through (0, 0, 1), (1, 0, 1), (0, 1, 0), (3, 1, 0), (2, 0, 4), (1, 1, 2), (1, 2, 1), (2, 2, 3), (2, 2, 1).

31. The quadric surface through (1, 2, 3), (2, 1, 0), (6, 0, 6), (3, 1, 3), (4, 0, 2), (5, 5, 1), (1, 1, 2), (3, 1, 4), (0, 0, 2).

In Exercises 32–33, note that the equation of a circle has the form

$$ax^2 + ay^2 + bx + cy + d = 0.$$

Hence a circle is determined by three points. Find the equation of the circle through the given points.

32. (1, 1), (2, 1), and (3, 2)

33. (4, 3), (1, 2), and (2, 0)

1.4 APPLICATIONS (OPTIONAL)

In this brief section we discuss networks and methods for determining flows in networks. An example of a network is the system of one-way streets shown in Fig. 1.8. A typical problem associated with networks is estimating the flow of traffic through this network of streets. Another example is the electrical network shown in Fig. 1.9. A typical problem consists of determining the currents flowing through the loops of the circuit.

(***Note:*** The network problems we discuss in this section are kept very simple so that the computational details do not obscure the ideas.)

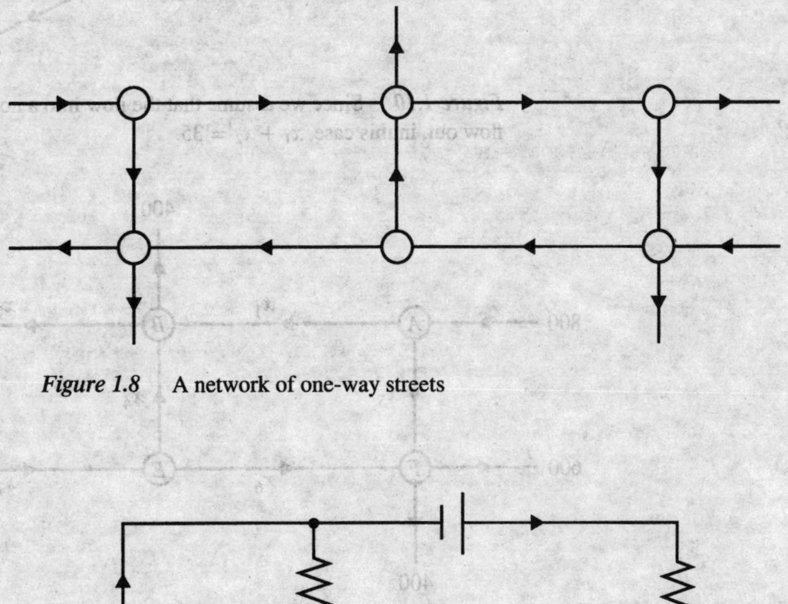

Figure 1.8 A network of one-way streets

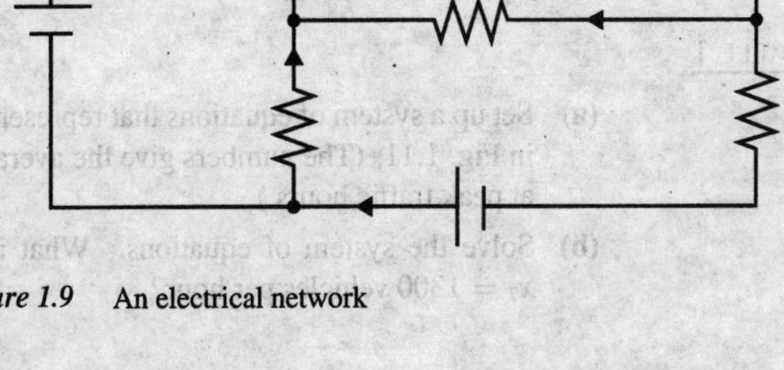

Figure 1.9 An electrical network

Flows in Networks

Networks consist of branches and nodes. For the street network shown in Fig. 1.8, the branches are the streets and the nodes are the intersections. We assume for a network that the total flow into a node is equal to the total flow out of the node. For example, Fig. 1.10 shows a flow of 40 into a node and a total flow of $x_1 + x_2 + 5$ out of the node. Since we assume that the flow into a node is equal to the flow out, it follows that the flows x_1 and x_2 must satisfy the linear equation $40 = x_1 + x_2 + 5$, or equivalently,

$$x_1 + x_2 = 35.$$

As an example of network flow calculations, consider the system of one-way streets in Fig. 1.11, where the flow is given in vehicles per hour. For instance, $x_1 + x_4$ vehicles per hour enter node B, while $x_2 + 400$ vehicles per hour leave.

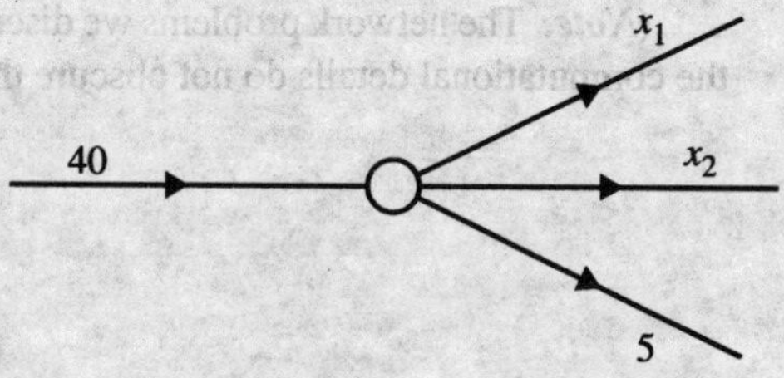

Figure 1.10 Since we assume that the flow into a node is equal to the flow out, in this case, $x_1 + x_2 = 35$.

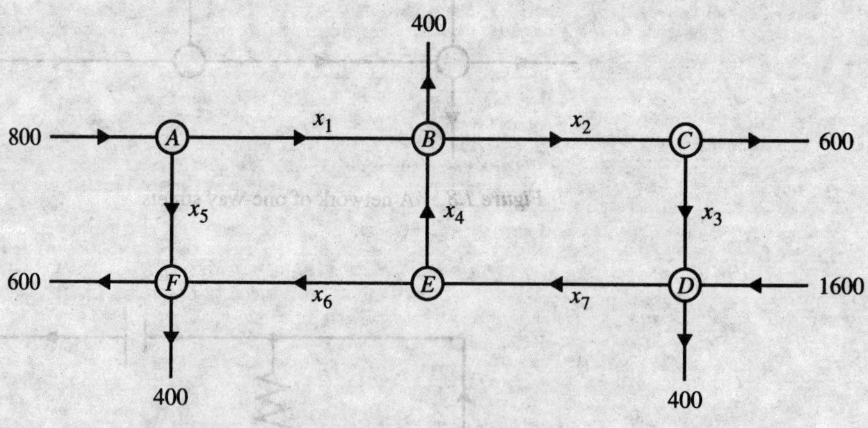

Figure 1.11 The traffic network analyzed in Example 1

EXAMPLE 1

(a) Set up a system of equations that represents traffic flow for the network shown in Fig. 1.11. (The numbers give the average flows into and out of the network at peak traffic hours.)

(b) Solve the system of equations. What is the traffic flow if $x_6 = 300$ and $x_7 = 1300$ vehicles per hour?

Solution

(a) Since the flow into a node is equal to the flow out, we obtain the following system of equations:

$$\begin{aligned} 800 &= x_1 + x_5 && \text{(Node } A\text{)} \\ x_1 + x_4 &= 400 + x_2 && \text{(Node } B\text{)} \\ x_2 &= 600 + x_3 && \text{(Node } C\text{)} \\ 1600 + x_3 &= 400 + x_7 && \text{(Node } D\text{)} \\ x_7 &= x_4 + x_6 && \text{(Node } E\text{)} \\ x_5 + x_6 &= 1000. && \text{(Node } F\text{)} \end{aligned}$$

(b) The augmented matrix for the system above is

$$\begin{bmatrix} 1 & 0 & 0 & 0 & 1 & 0 & 0 & 800 \\ 1 & -1 & 0 & 1 & 0 & 0 & 0 & 400 \\ 0 & 1 & -1 & 0 & 0 & 0 & 0 & 600 \\ 0 & 0 & 1 & 0 & 0 & 0 & -1 & -1200 \\ 0 & 0 & 0 & 1 & 0 & 1 & -1 & 0 \\ 0 & 0 & 0 & 0 & 1 & 1 & 0 & 1000 \end{bmatrix}.$$

Some calculations show that this matrix is row equivalent to

$$\begin{bmatrix} 1 & 0 & 0 & 0 & 0 & -1 & 0 & -200 \\ 0 & 1 & 0 & 0 & 0 & 0 & -1 & -600 \\ 0 & 0 & 1 & 0 & 0 & 0 & -1 & -1200 \\ 0 & 0 & 0 & 1 & 0 & 1 & -1 & 0 \\ 0 & 0 & 0 & 0 & 1 & 1 & 0 & 1000 \\ 0 & 0 & 0 & 0 & 0 & 0 & 0 & 0 \end{bmatrix}.$$

Therefore, the solution is

$$\begin{aligned} x_1 &= x_6 - 200 \\ x_2 &= x_7 - 600 \\ x_3 &= x_7 - 1200 \\ x_4 &= x_7 - x_6 \\ x_5 &= 1000 - x_6. \end{aligned}$$

If $x_6 = 300$ and $x_7 = 1300$, then (in vehicles per hour)

$$x_1 = 100, \quad x_2 = 700, \quad x_3 = 100, \quad x_4 = 1000, \quad x_5 = 700.$$

We normally want the flows in a network to be nonnegative. For instance, consider the traffic network in Fig. 1.11. If x_6 were negative, it would indicate that traffic was flowing from F to E rather than in the prescribed direction from E to F.

EXAMPLE 2 Consider the street network in Example 1 (see Fig. 1.11). Suppose that the streets from A to B and from B to C must be closed (that is, $x_1 = 0$ and $x_2 = 0$). How might the traffic be rerouted?

Solution By Example 1, the flows are

$$\begin{aligned} x_1 &= x_6 - 200 \\ x_2 &= x_7 - 600 \\ x_3 &= x_7 - 1200 \\ x_4 &= x_7 - x_6 \\ x_5 &= 1000 - x_6. \end{aligned}$$

Therefore, if $x_1 = 0$ and $x_2 = 0$, it follows that $x_6 = 200$ and $x_7 = 600$. Using these values, we then obtain $x_3 = -600$, $x_4 = 400$, and $x_5 = 800$. In order to have nonnegative flows, we must reverse directions on the street connecting C and D; this change makes $x_3 = 600$ instead of -600. The network flows are shown in Fig. 1.12. ∎

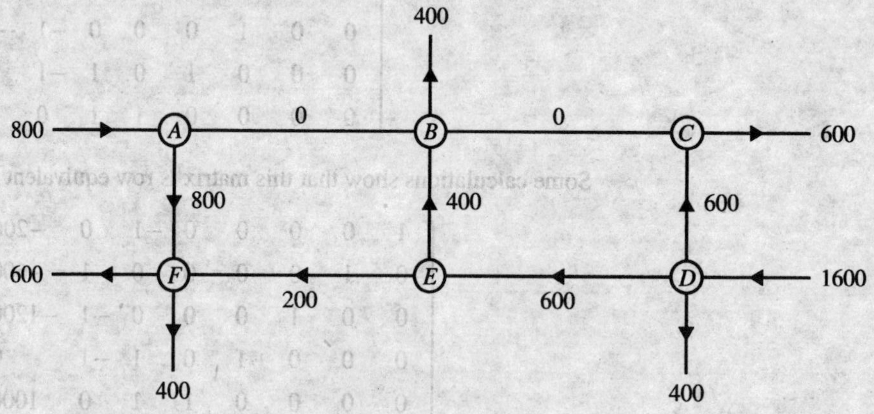

Figure 1.12 The traffic network analyzed in Example 2

Electrical Networks

We now consider current flow in simple electrical networks such as the one illustrated in Fig. 1.13. For such networks, current flow is governed by Ohm's law and Kirchhoff's laws, as follows.

> ***Ohm's Law:*** The voltage drop across a resistor is the product of the current and the resistance.
>
> ***Kirchhoff's First Law:*** The sum of the currents flowing into a node is equal to the sum of the currents flowing out.
>
> ***Kirchhoff's Second Law:*** The algebraic sum of the voltage drops around a closed loop is equal to the total voltage in the loop.

(*Note:* With respect to Kirchhoff's second law, two basic closed loops in Fig. 1.13 are the counterclockwise paths $BDCB$ and $BCAB$. Also, in each branch, we make a tentative

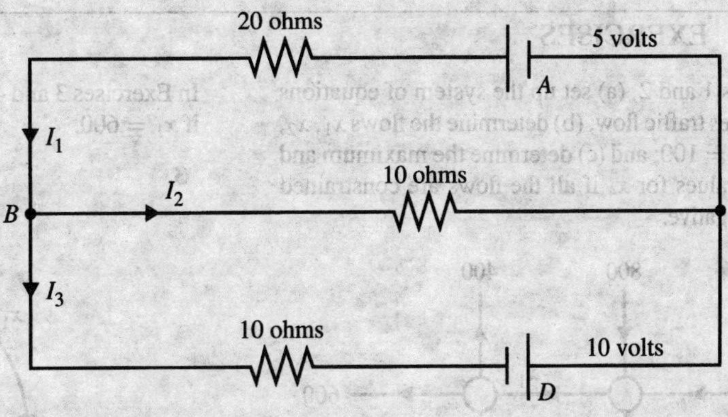

Figure 1.13 The electrical network analyzed in Example 3

assignment for the direction of current flow. If a current turns out to be negative, we then reverse our assignment for that branch.)

EXAMPLE 3 Determine the currents I_1, I_2, and I_3 for the electrical network shown in Fig. 1.13.

Solution Applying Kirchhoff's second law to the loops *BDCB* and *BCAB*, we obtain equations

$$\begin{aligned} -10I_2 + 10I_3 &= 10 \qquad (BDCB) \\ 20I_1 + 10I_2 &= \ \ 5 \qquad (BCAB). \end{aligned}$$

Applying Kirchhoff's first law to either of the nodes B or C, we find $I_1 = I_2 + I_3$. Therefore,

$$I_1 - I_2 - I_3 = 0.$$

The augmented matrix for this system of three equations is

$$\begin{bmatrix} 1 & -1 & -1 & 0 \\ 0 & -10 & 10 & 10 \\ 20 & 10 & 0 & 5 \end{bmatrix}.$$

This matrix can be row reduced to

$$\begin{bmatrix} 1 & 0 & 0 & 0.4 \\ 0 & 1 & 0 & -0.3 \\ 0 & 0 & 1 & 0.7 \end{bmatrix}.$$

Therefore, the currents are

$$I_1 = 0.4, \qquad I_2 = -0.3, \qquad I_3 = 0.7.$$

Since I_2 is negative, the current flow is from C to B rather than from B to C, as tentatively assigned in Fig. 1.13.

1.4 EXERCISES

In Exercises 1 and 2, (a) set up the system of equations that describes traffic flow; (b) determine the flows x_1, x_2, and x_3 if $x_4 = 100$; and (c) determine the maximum and minimum values for x_4 if all the flows are constrained to be nonnegative.

1.

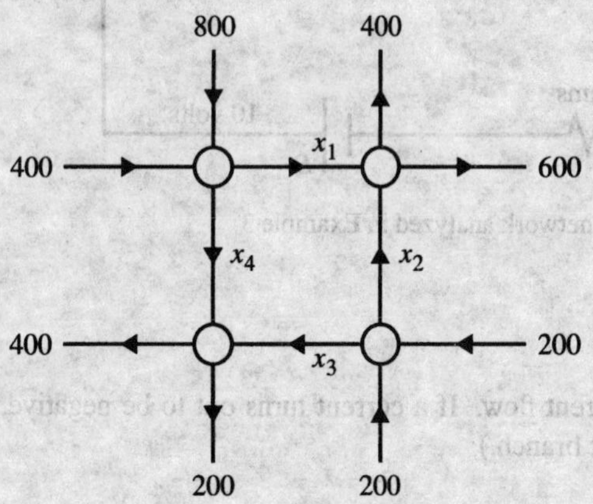

2.

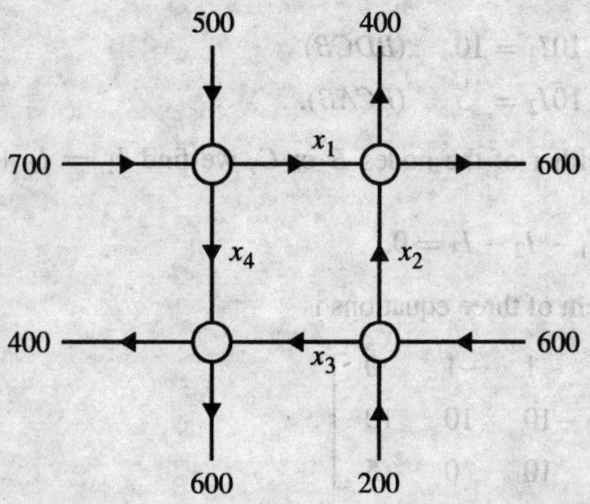

In Exercises 3 and 4, find the flow of traffic in the rotary if $x_1 = 600$.

3.

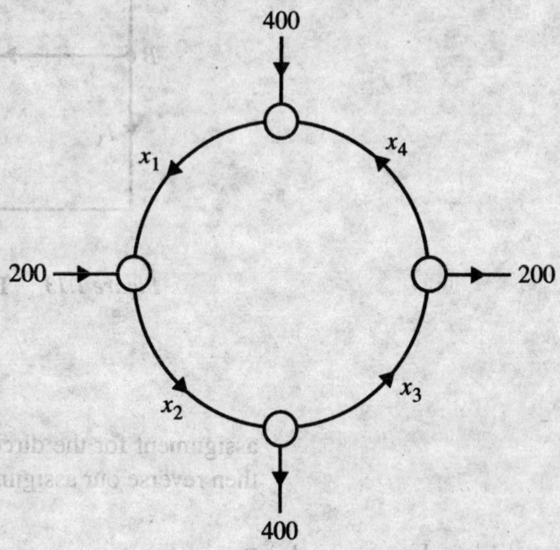

4.

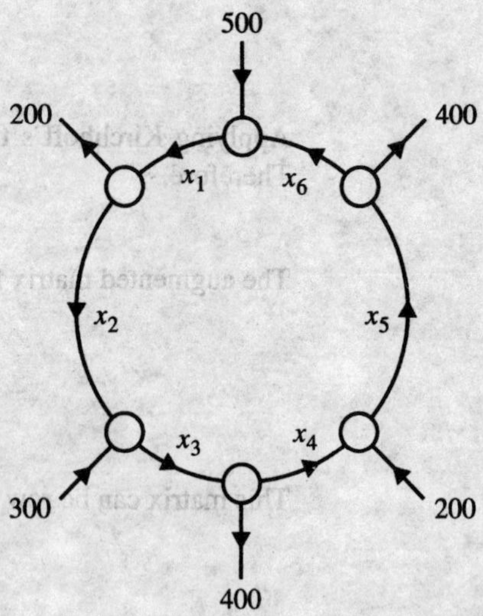

In Exercises 5–8, determine the currents in the various branches.

5.

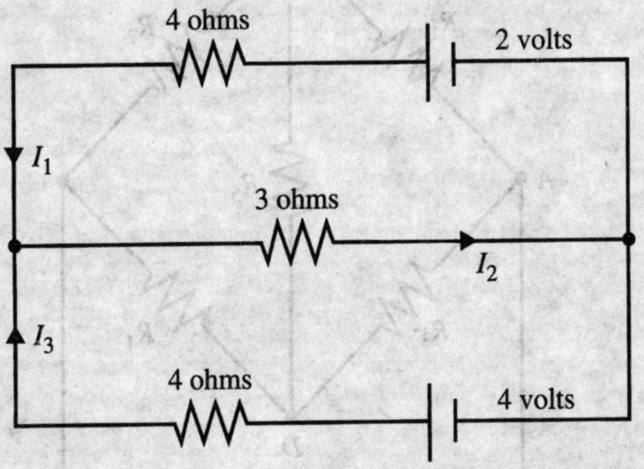

6.

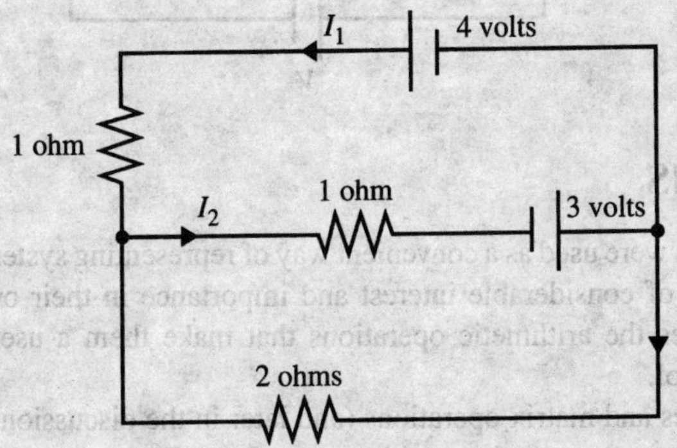

7.

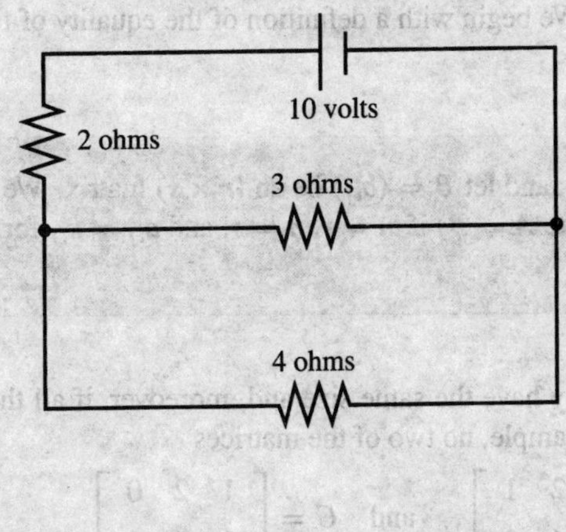

8.

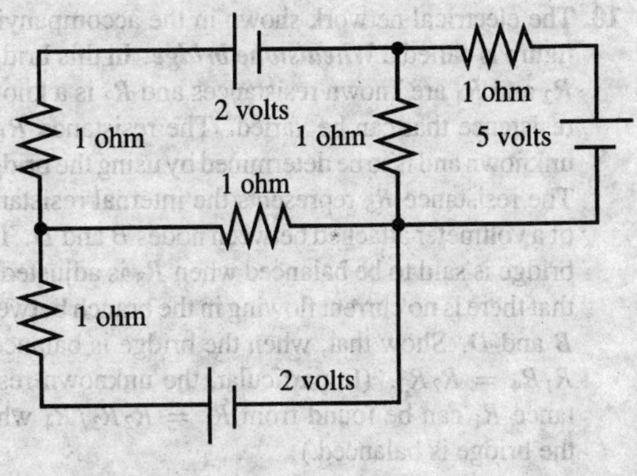

9. a) Set up the system of equations that describes the traffic flow in the accompanying figure.

b) Show that the system is consistent if and only if $a_1 + b_1 + c_1 + d_1 = a_2 + b_2 + c_2 + d_2$.

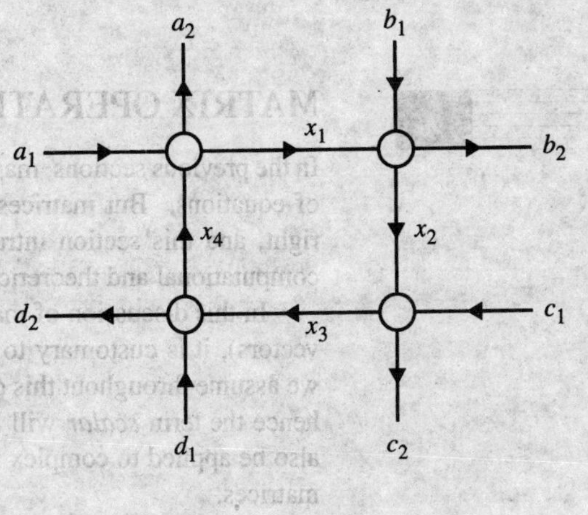

10. The electrical network shown in the accompanying figure is called a ***Wheatstone bridge***. In this bridge, R_2 and R_4 are known resistances and R_3 is a known resistance that can be varied. The resistance R_1 is unknown and is to be determined by using the bridge. The resistance R_5 represents the internal resistance of a voltmeter attached between nodes B and D. The bridge is said to be balanced when R_3 is adjusted so that there is no current flowing in the branch between B and D. Show that, when the bridge is balanced, $R_1R_4 = R_2R_3$. (In particular, the unknown resistance R_1 can be found from $R_1 = R_2R_3/R_4$ when the bridge is balanced.)

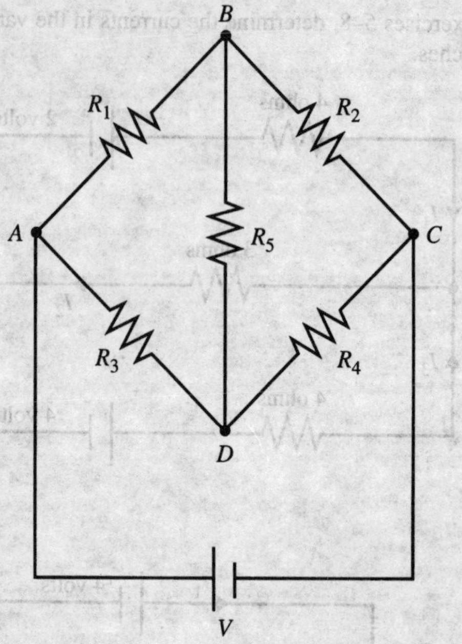

1.5 MATRIX OPERATIONS

In the previous sections, matrices were used as a convenient way of representing systems of equations. But matrices are of considerable interest and importance in their own right, and this section introduces the arithmetic operations that make them a useful computational and theoretical tool.

In this discussion of matrices and matrix operations (and later in the discussion of vectors), it is customary to refer to numerical quantities as ***scalars***. For convenience we assume throughout this chapter that all matrix (and vector) entries are real numbers; hence the term *scalar* will mean a real number. In later chapters the term *scalar* will also be applied to complex numbers. We begin with a definition of the equality of two matrices.

DEFINITION 5 **Let $A = (a_{ij})$ be an $(m \times n)$ matrix, and let $B = (b_{ij})$ be an $(r \times s)$ matrix. We say that A and B are *equal* (and write $A = B$) if $m = r$, $n = s$, and $a_{ij} = b_{ij}$ for all i and j, $1 \le i \le m$, $1 \le j \le n$.**

Thus two matrices are equal if they have the same size and, moreover, if all their corresponding entries are equal. For example, no two of the matrices

$$A = \begin{bmatrix} 1 & 2 \\ 3 & 4 \end{bmatrix}, \quad B = \begin{bmatrix} 2 & 1 \\ 4 & 3 \end{bmatrix}, \quad \text{and} \quad C = \begin{bmatrix} 1 & 2 & 0 \\ 3 & 4 & 0 \end{bmatrix}$$

are equal.

Matrix Addition and Scalar Multiplication

The first two arithmetic operations, matrix addition and the multiplication of a matrix by a scalar, are defined quite naturally. In these definitions we use the notation $(Q)_{ij}$ to denote the ijth entry of a matrix Q.

DEFINITION 6 Let $A = (a_{ij})$ and $B = (b_{ij})$ both be $(m \times n)$ matrices. The ***sum***, $A + B$, is the $(m \times n)$ matrix defined by

$$(A + B)_{ij} = a_{ij} + b_{ij}.$$

Note that this definition requires that A and B have the same size before their sum is defined. Thus if

$$A = \begin{bmatrix} 1 & 2 & -1 \\ 2 & 3 & 0 \end{bmatrix}, \quad B = \begin{bmatrix} -3 & 1 & 2 \\ 0 & -4 & 1 \end{bmatrix}, \quad \text{and} \quad C = \begin{bmatrix} 1 & 2 \\ 3 & 1 \end{bmatrix},$$

then

$$A + B = \begin{bmatrix} -2 & 3 & 1 \\ 2 & -1 & 1 \end{bmatrix},$$

while $A + C$ is undefined.

DEFINITION 7 Let $A = (a_{ij})$ be an $(m \times n)$ matrix, and let r be a scalar. The ***product***, rA, is the $(m \times n)$ matrix defined by

$$(rA)_{ij} = ra_{ij}.$$

For example,

$$2\begin{bmatrix} 1 & 3 \\ 2 & -1 \\ 0 & 3 \end{bmatrix} = \begin{bmatrix} 2 & 6 \\ 4 & -2 \\ 0 & 6 \end{bmatrix}.$$

EXAMPLE 1 Let the matrices A, B, and C be given by

$$A = \begin{bmatrix} 1 & 3 \\ -2 & 7 \end{bmatrix}, \quad B = \begin{bmatrix} 6 & 1 \\ 2 & 4 \end{bmatrix}, \quad \text{and} \quad C = \begin{bmatrix} 1 & 2 & -1 \\ 3 & 0 & 5 \end{bmatrix}.$$

Find each of $A + B$, $A + C$, $B + C$, $3C$, and $A + 2B$, or state that the indicated operation is undefined.

Solution The defined operations yield

$$A+B=\begin{bmatrix}7 & 4\\ 0 & 11\end{bmatrix},\quad 3C=\begin{bmatrix}3 & 6 & -3\\ 9 & 0 & 15\end{bmatrix},\quad \text{and}\quad A+2B=\begin{bmatrix}13 & 5\\ 2 & 15\end{bmatrix},$$

while $A + C$ and $B + C$ are undefined. ∎

Vectors in R^n

Before proceeding with the definition of matrix multiplication, recall that a point in n-dimensional space is represented by an ordered n-tuple of real numbers $\mathbf{x} = (x_1, x_2, \ldots, x_n)$. Such an n-tuple will be called an ***n-dimensional vector*** and will be written in the form of a matrix,

$$\mathbf{x}=\begin{bmatrix}x_1\\ x_2\\ \vdots\\ x_n\end{bmatrix}.$$

For example, an arbitrary three-dimensional vector has the form

$$\mathbf{x}=\begin{bmatrix}x_1\\ x_2\\ x_3\end{bmatrix},$$

and the vectors

$$\mathbf{x}=\begin{bmatrix}1\\ 2\\ 3\end{bmatrix},\quad \mathbf{y}=\begin{bmatrix}3\\ 2\\ 1\end{bmatrix},\quad \text{and}\quad \mathbf{z}=\begin{bmatrix}2\\ 3\\ 1\end{bmatrix}$$

are distinct three-dimensional vectors. The set of all n-dimensional vectors with real components is called ***Euclidean n-space*** and will be denoted by R^n. Vectors in R^n will be denoted by boldface type. Thus R^n is the set defined by

$$R^n = \{\mathbf{x}\colon \mathbf{x}=\begin{bmatrix}x_1\\ x_2\\ \vdots\\ x_n\end{bmatrix} \quad\text{where}\quad x_1, x_2, \ldots, x_n \text{ are real numbers}\}.$$

As the notation suggests, an element of R^n can be viewed as an $(n \times 1)$ real matrix, and conversely an $(n \times 1)$ real matrix can be considered an element of R^n. Thus addition and scalar multiplication of vectors is just a special case of these operations for matrices.

Vector Form of the General Solution

Having defined addition and scalar multiplication for vectors and matrices, we can use these operations to derive a compact expression for the general solution of a consistent system of linear equations. We call this expression the ***vector form for the general solution***.

The idea of the vector form for the general solution is straightforward and is best explained by a few examples.

EXAMPLE 2 The matrix B is the augmented matrix for a homogeneous system of linear equations. Find the general solution for the linear system and express the general solution in terms of vectors

$$B = \left[\begin{array}{cccc|c} 1 & 0 & -1 & -3 & 0 \\ 0 & 1 & 2 & 1 & 0 \end{array}\right].$$

Solution Since B is in reduced echelon form, it is easy to write the general solution:

$$x_1 = x_3 + 3x_4, \qquad x_2 = -2x_3 - x_4.$$

In vector form, therefore, the general solution can be expressed as

$$\mathbf{x} = \begin{bmatrix} x_1 \\ x_2 \\ x_3 \\ x_4 \end{bmatrix} = \begin{bmatrix} x_3 + 3x_4 \\ -2x_3 - x_4 \\ x_3 \\ x_4 \end{bmatrix} = \begin{bmatrix} x_3 \\ -2x_3 \\ x_3 \\ 0 \end{bmatrix} + \begin{bmatrix} 3x_4 \\ -x_4 \\ 0 \\ x_4 \end{bmatrix}$$

$$= x_3 \begin{bmatrix} 1 \\ -2 \\ 1 \\ 0 \end{bmatrix} + x_4 \begin{bmatrix} 3 \\ -1 \\ 0 \\ 1 \end{bmatrix}.$$

This last expression is called the *vector form for the general solution.* ■

In general, the vector form for the general solution of a homogeneous system consists of a sum of well-determined vectors multiplied by the free variables. Such expressions are called "linear combinations" and we will use this concept of a linear combination extensively, beginning in Section 1.7. The next example illustrates the vector form for the general solution of a nonhomogeneous system.

EXAMPLE 3 Let B denote the augmented matrix for a system of linear equations

$$B = \left[\begin{array}{ccccc|c} 1 & -2 & 0 & 0 & 2 & 3 \\ 0 & 0 & 1 & 0 & -1 & 2 \\ 0 & 0 & 0 & 1 & 3 & -4 \end{array}\right].$$

Find the vector form for the general solution of the linear system.

Solution Since B is in reduced echelon form, we readily find the general solution:

$$x_1 = 3 + 2x_2 - 2x_5, x_3 = 2 + x_5, x_4 = -4 - 3x_5.$$

Expressing the general solution in vector form, we obtain

$$\mathbf{x} = \begin{bmatrix} x_1 \\ x_2 \\ x_3 \\ x_4 \\ x_5 \end{bmatrix} = \begin{bmatrix} 3 + 2x_2 - 2x_5 \\ x_2 \\ 2 + x_5 \\ -4 - 3x_5 \\ x_5 \end{bmatrix} = \begin{bmatrix} 3 \\ 0 \\ 2 \\ -4 \\ 0 \end{bmatrix} + \begin{bmatrix} 2x_2 \\ x_2 \\ 0 \\ 0 \\ 0 \end{bmatrix} + \begin{bmatrix} -2x_5 \\ 0 \\ x_5 \\ -3x_5 \\ x_5 \end{bmatrix}$$

$$= \begin{bmatrix} 3 \\ 0 \\ 2 \\ -4 \\ 0 \end{bmatrix} + x_2 \begin{bmatrix} 2 \\ 1 \\ 0 \\ 0 \\ 0 \end{bmatrix} + x_5 \begin{bmatrix} -2 \\ 0 \\ 1 \\ -3 \\ 1 \end{bmatrix}.$$

Thus, the general solution has the form $\mathbf{x} = \mathbf{b} + a\mathbf{u} + b\mathbf{v}$, where $\mathbf{b}$, $\mathbf{u}$, and $\mathbf{v}$ are fixed vectors in R^5. ■

Scalar Product

In vector calculus, the ***scalar product*** (or ***dot product***) of two vectors

$$\mathbf{u} = \begin{bmatrix} u_1 \\ u_2 \\ \vdots \\ u_n \end{bmatrix} \quad \text{and} \quad \mathbf{v} = \begin{bmatrix} v_1 \\ v_2 \\ \vdots \\ v_n \end{bmatrix}$$

in R^n is defined to be the number $u_1v_1 + u_2v_2 + \cdots + u_nv_n = \sum_{i=1}^{n} u_iv_i$. For example, if

$$\mathbf{u} = \begin{bmatrix} 2 \\ 3 \\ -1 \end{bmatrix} \quad \text{and} \quad \mathbf{v} = \begin{bmatrix} -4 \\ 2 \\ 3 \end{bmatrix},$$

then the scalar product of $\mathbf{u}$ and $\mathbf{v}$ is $2(-4) + 3(2) + (-1)3 = -5$. The scalar product of two vectors will be considered further in the following section, and in Chapter 3 the properties of R^n will be more fully developed.

Matrix Multiplication

Matrix multiplication is defined in such a way as to provide a convenient mechanism for describing a linear correspondence between vectors. To illustrate, let the variables $x_1, x_2, \ldots, x_n$ and the variables $y_1, y_2, \ldots, y_m$ be related by the linear equations

$$\begin{aligned} a_{11}x_1 + a_{12}x_2 + \cdots + a_{1n}x_n &= y_1 \\ a_{21}x_1 + a_{22}x_2 + \cdots + a_{2n}x_n &= y_2 \\ \vdots \qquad\qquad\qquad & \quad \vdots \\ a_{m1}x_1 + a_{m2}x_2 + \cdots + a_{mn}x_n &= y_m. \end{aligned} \tag{1}$$

If we set

$$\mathbf{x} = \begin{bmatrix} x_1 \\ x_2 \\ \vdots \\ x_n \end{bmatrix} \quad \text{and} \quad \mathbf{y} = \begin{bmatrix} y_1 \\ y_2 \\ \vdots \\ y_m \end{bmatrix},$$

then (1) defines a correspondence $\mathbf{x} \to \mathbf{y}$ from vectors in R^n to vectors in R^m. The ith equation of (1) is

$$a_{i1}x_1 + a_{i2}x_2 + \cdots + a_{in}x_n = y_i,$$

and this can be written in a briefer form as

$$\sum_{j=1}^{n} a_{ij}x_j = y_i. \tag{2}$$

If A is the coefficient matrix of system (1),

$$A = \begin{bmatrix} a_{11} & a_{12} & \cdots & a_{1n} \\ a_{21} & a_{22} & \cdots & a_{2n} \\ \vdots & & & \vdots \\ a_{m1} & a_{m2} & \cdots & a_{mn} \end{bmatrix},$$

then the left-hand side of Eq. (2) is precisely the scalar product of the ith row of A with the vector $\mathbf{x}$. Thus if we define the product of A and $\mathbf{x}$ to be the $(m \times 1)$ vector $A\mathbf{x}$ whose ith component is the scalar product of the ith row of A with $\mathbf{x}$, then $A\mathbf{x}$ is given by

$$A\mathbf{x} = \begin{bmatrix} \sum_{j=1}^{n} a_{1j}x_j \\ \sum_{j=1}^{n} a_{2j}x_j \\ \vdots \\ \sum_{j=1}^{n} a_{mj}x_j \end{bmatrix}.$$

Using the definition of equality (Definition 5), we see that the simple matrix equation

$$A\mathbf{x} = \mathbf{y} \tag{3}$$

is equivalent to system (1).

In a natural fashion, we can extend the idea of the product of a matrix and a vector to the product, AB, of an $(m \times n)$ matrix A and an $(n \times s)$ matrix B by defining the ijth entry of AB to be the scalar product of the ith row of A with the jth column of B. Formally, we have the following definition.

Definition 8 Let $A = (a_{ij})$ be an $(m \times n)$ matrix, and let $B = (b_{ij})$ be an $(r \times s)$ matrix. If $n = r$, then the ***product*** AB is the $(m \times s)$ matrix defined by

$$(AB)_{ij} = \sum_{k=1}^{n} a_{ik}b_{kj}.$$

If $n \neq r$, then the product AB is not defined.

The definition can be visualized by referring to Fig. 1.14.

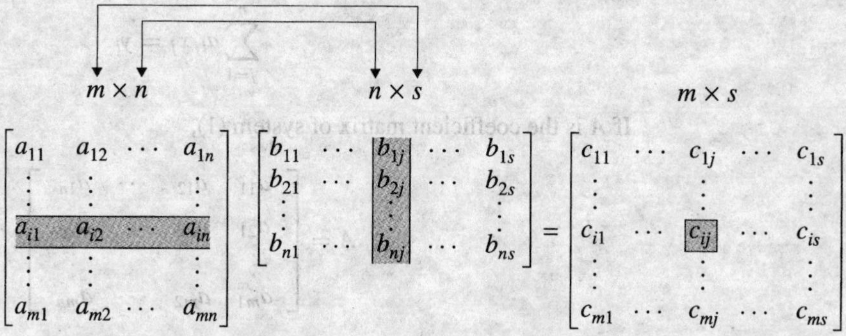

Figure 1.14 The ijth entry of AB is the scalar product of the ith row of A and the jth column of B.

Thus the product AB is defined only when the inside dimensions of A and B are equal. In this case the outside dimensions, m and s, give the size of AB. Furthermore, the ijth entry of AB is the scalar product of the ith row of A with the jth column of B. For example,

$$\begin{bmatrix} 2 & 1 & -3 \\ -2 & 2 & 4 \end{bmatrix} \begin{bmatrix} -1 & 2 \\ 0 & -3 \\ 2 & 1 \end{bmatrix}$$

$$= \begin{bmatrix} 2(-1) + 1(0) + (-3)2 & 2(2) + 1(-3) + (-3)1 \\ (-2)(-1) + 2(0) + 4(2) & (-2)2 + 2(-3) + 4(1) \end{bmatrix} = \begin{bmatrix} -8 & -2 \\ 10 & -6 \end{bmatrix},$$

whereas the product

$$\begin{bmatrix} 2 & 1 & -3 \\ -2 & 2 & 4 \end{bmatrix} \begin{bmatrix} -1 & 0 & 2 \\ 2 & -3 & 1 \end{bmatrix}$$

is undefined.

EXAMPLE 4 Let the matrices A, B, C, and D be given by

$$A = \begin{bmatrix} 1 & 2 \\ 2 & 3 \end{bmatrix}, \quad B = \begin{bmatrix} -3 & 2 \\ 1 & -2 \end{bmatrix},$$

$$C = \begin{bmatrix} 1 & 0 & -2 \\ 0 & 1 & 1 \end{bmatrix}, \text{ and } D = \begin{bmatrix} 3 & 1 \\ -1 & -2 \\ 1 & 1 \end{bmatrix}.$$

Find each of AB, BA, AC, CA, CD, and DC, or state that the indicated product is undefined.

Solution The definition of matrix multiplication yields

$$AB = \begin{bmatrix} -1 & -2 \\ -3 & -2 \end{bmatrix}, \quad BA = \begin{bmatrix} 1 & 0 \\ -3 & -4 \end{bmatrix}, \quad \text{and} \quad AC = \begin{bmatrix} 1 & 2 & 0 \\ 2 & 3 & -1 \end{bmatrix}.$$

The product CA is undefined, and

$$CD = \begin{bmatrix} 1 & -1 \\ 0 & -1 \end{bmatrix} \quad \text{and} \quad DC = \begin{bmatrix} 3 & 1 & -5 \\ -1 & -2 & 0 \\ 1 & 1 & -1 \end{bmatrix}.$$

Example 4 illustrates that matrix multiplication is not commutative; that is, normally AB and BA are different matrices. Indeed, the product AB may be defined while the product BA is undefined, or both may be defined but have different dimensions. Even when AB and BA have the same size, they usually are not equal.

EXAMPLE 5 Express each of the linear systems

$$\begin{aligned} x_1 &= 2y_1 - y_2 \\ x_2 &= -3y_1 + 2y_2 \\ x_3 &= y_1 + 3y_2 \end{aligned} \quad \text{and} \quad \begin{aligned} y_1 &= -4z_1 + 2z_2 \\ y_2 &= 3z_1 + z_2 \end{aligned}$$

as a matrix equation and use matrix multiplication to express x_1, x_2, and x_3 in terms of z_1 and z_2.

Solution We have

$$\begin{bmatrix} x_1 \\ x_2 \\ x_3 \end{bmatrix} = \begin{bmatrix} 2 & -1 \\ -3 & 2 \\ 1 & 3 \end{bmatrix} \begin{bmatrix} y_1 \\ y_2 \end{bmatrix} \quad \text{and} \quad \begin{bmatrix} y_1 \\ y_2 \end{bmatrix} = \begin{bmatrix} -4 & 2 \\ 3 & 1 \end{bmatrix} \begin{bmatrix} z_1 \\ z_2 \end{bmatrix}.$$

Substituting for $\begin{bmatrix} y_1 \\ y_2 \end{bmatrix}$ in the left-hand equation gives

$$\begin{bmatrix} x_1 \\ x_2 \\ x_3 \end{bmatrix} = \begin{bmatrix} 2 & -1 \\ -3 & 2 \\ 1 & 3 \end{bmatrix} \begin{bmatrix} -4 & 2 \\ 3 & 1 \end{bmatrix} \begin{bmatrix} z_1 \\ z_2 \end{bmatrix} = \begin{bmatrix} -11 & 3 \\ 18 & -4 \\ 5 & 5 \end{bmatrix} \begin{bmatrix} z_1 \\ z_2 \end{bmatrix}.$$

Therefore,

$$\begin{aligned} x_1 &= -11z_1 + 3z_2 \\ x_2 &= 18z_1 - 4z_2 \\ x_3 &= 5z_1 + 5z_2. \end{aligned}$$

The use of the matrix equation (3) to represent the linear system (1) provides a convenient notational device for representing the $(m \times n)$ system

$$\begin{aligned} a_{11}x_1 + a_{12}x_2 + \cdots + a_{1n}x_n &= b_1 \\ a_{21}x_1 + a_{22}x_2 + \cdots + a_{2n}x_n &= b_2 \\ \vdots \qquad\quad \vdots \qquad\qquad\quad \vdots \quad &\quad \vdots \\ a_{m1}x_1 + a_{m2}x_2 + \cdots + a_{mn}x_n &= b_m \end{aligned} \tag{4}$$

of linear equations with unknowns $x_1, \ldots, x_n$. Specifically, if $A = (a_{ij})$ is the coefficient matrix of (4), and if the unknown $(n \times 1)$ matrix $\mathbf{x}$ and the constant $(m \times 1)$ matrix $\mathbf{b}$ are defined by

$$\mathbf{x} = \begin{bmatrix} x_1 \\ x_2 \\ \vdots \\ x_n \end{bmatrix} \quad \text{and} \quad \mathbf{b} = \begin{bmatrix} b_1 \\ b_2 \\ \vdots \\ b_m \end{bmatrix},$$

then the system (4) is equivalent to the matrix equation

$$A\mathbf{x} = \mathbf{b}. \tag{5}$$

EXAMPLE 6 Solve the matrix equation $A\mathbf{x} = \mathbf{b}$, where

$$A = \begin{bmatrix} 1 & 3 & -1 \\ 2 & 5 & -1 \\ 2 & 8 & -2 \end{bmatrix}, \quad \mathbf{x} = \begin{bmatrix} x_1 \\ x_2 \\ x_3 \end{bmatrix}, \quad \text{and} \quad \mathbf{b} = \begin{bmatrix} 2 \\ 6 \\ 6 \end{bmatrix}.$$

Solution The matrix equation $A\mathbf{x} = \mathbf{b}$ is equivalent to the (3×3) linear system

$$\begin{aligned} x_1 + 3x_2 - x_3 &= 2 \\ 2x_1 + 5x_2 - x_3 &= 6 \\ 2x_1 + 8x_2 - 2x_3 &= 6. \end{aligned}$$

This system can be solved in the usual way—that is, by reducing the augmented matrix—to obtain $x_1 = 2, x_2 = 1, x_3 = 3$. Therefore,

$$\mathbf{s} = \begin{bmatrix} 2 \\ 1 \\ 3 \end{bmatrix}$$

is the unique solution to $A\mathbf{x} = \mathbf{b}$.

Other Formulations of Matrix Multiplication

It is frequently convenient and useful to express an $(m \times n)$ matrix $A = (a_{ij})$ in the form

$$A = [\mathbf{A}_1, \mathbf{A}_2, \ldots, \mathbf{A}_n], \tag{6}$$

where for each j, $1 \le j \le n$, $\mathbf{A}_j$ denotes the jth column of A. That is, $\mathbf{A}_j$ is the $(m \times 1)$ column vector

$$\mathbf{A}_j = \begin{bmatrix} a_{1j} \\ a_{2j} \\ \vdots \\ a_{mj} \end{bmatrix}.$$

For example, if A is the (2×3) matrix

$$A = \begin{bmatrix} 1 & 3 & 6 \\ 2 & 4 & 0 \end{bmatrix}, \tag{7}$$

then $A = [\mathbf{A}_1, \mathbf{A}_2, \mathbf{A}_3]$, where

$$\mathbf{A}_1 = \begin{bmatrix} 1 \\ 2 \end{bmatrix}, \quad \mathbf{A}_2 = \begin{bmatrix} 3 \\ 4 \end{bmatrix}, \quad \text{and} \quad \mathbf{A}_3 = \begin{bmatrix} 6 \\ 0 \end{bmatrix}.$$

The next two theorems use Eq. (6) to provide alternative ways of expressing the matrix products $A\mathbf{x}$ and AB; these methods will be extremely useful in our later development of matrix theory.

THEOREM 5 Let $A = [\mathbf{A}_1, \mathbf{A}_2, \ldots, \mathbf{A}_n]$ be an $(m \times n)$ matrix whose jth column is $\mathbf{A}_j$, and let $\mathbf{x}$ be the $(n \times 1)$ column vector

$$\mathbf{x} = \begin{bmatrix} x_1 \\ x_2 \\ \vdots \\ x_n \end{bmatrix}.$$

Then the product $A\mathbf{x}$ can be expressed as

$$A\mathbf{x} = x_1\mathbf{A}_1 + x_2\mathbf{A}_2 + \cdots + x_n\mathbf{A}_n.$$

The proof of this theorem is not difficult and uses only Definitions 5, 6, 7, and 8; the proof is left as an exercise for the reader. To illustrate Theorem 5, let A be the matrix

$$A = \begin{bmatrix} 1 & 3 & 6 \\ 2 & 4 & 0 \end{bmatrix},$$

and let $\mathbf{x}$ be the vector in R^3,

$$\mathbf{x} = \begin{bmatrix} x_1 \\ x_2 \\ x_3 \end{bmatrix}.$$

Then

$$A\mathbf{x} = \begin{bmatrix} 1 & 3 & 6 \\ 2 & 4 & 0 \end{bmatrix} \begin{bmatrix} x_1 \\ x_2 \\ x_3 \end{bmatrix}$$
$$= \begin{bmatrix} x_1 + 3x_2 + 6x_3 \\ 2x_1 + 4x_2 + 0x_3 \end{bmatrix}$$
$$= x_1 \begin{bmatrix} 1 \\ 2 \end{bmatrix} + x_2 \begin{bmatrix} 3 \\ 4 \end{bmatrix} + x_3 \begin{bmatrix} 6 \\ 0 \end{bmatrix};$$

so that $A\mathbf{x} = x_1\mathbf{A}_1 + x_2\mathbf{A}_2 + x_3\mathbf{A}_3$. In particular, if we set

$$\mathbf{x} = \begin{bmatrix} 2 \\ 2 \\ -3 \end{bmatrix},$$

then $A\mathbf{x} = 2\mathbf{A}_1 + 2\mathbf{A}_2 - 3\mathbf{A}_3$.

From Theorem 5, we see that the matrix equation $A\mathbf{x} = \mathbf{b}$ corresponding to the $(m \times n)$ system (4) can be expressed as

$$x_1\mathbf{A}_1 + x_2\mathbf{A}_2 + \cdots + x_n\mathbf{A}_n = \mathbf{b}. \tag{8}$$

Thus, Eq. (8) says that solving $A\mathbf{x} = \mathbf{b}$ amounts to showing that $\mathbf{b}$ can be written in terms of the columns of A.

EXAMPLE 7 Solve

$$x_1 \begin{bmatrix} 1 \\ 2 \\ 2 \end{bmatrix} + x_2 \begin{bmatrix} 3 \\ 5 \\ 8 \end{bmatrix} + x_3 \begin{bmatrix} -1 \\ -1 \\ -2 \end{bmatrix} = \begin{bmatrix} 2 \\ 6 \\ 6 \end{bmatrix}.$$

Solution By Theorem 5, the given equation is equivalent to the matrix equation $A\mathbf{x} = \mathbf{b}$, where

$$A = \begin{bmatrix} 1 & 3 & -1 \\ 2 & 5 & -1 \\ 2 & 8 & -2 \end{bmatrix}, \quad \mathbf{x} = \begin{bmatrix} x_1 \\ x_2 \\ x_3 \end{bmatrix}, \quad \text{and} \quad \mathbf{b} = \begin{bmatrix} 2 \\ 6 \\ 6 \end{bmatrix}.$$

This equation was solved in Example 6 giving $x_1 = 2$, $x_2 = 1$, $x_3 = 3$, so we have

$$2 \begin{bmatrix} 1 \\ 2 \\ 2 \end{bmatrix} + \begin{bmatrix} 3 \\ 5 \\ 8 \end{bmatrix} + 3 \begin{bmatrix} -1 \\ -1 \\ -2 \end{bmatrix} = \begin{bmatrix} 2 \\ 6 \\ 6 \end{bmatrix}. \qquad \blacksquare$$

Although Eq. (8) is not particularly efficient as a computational tool, it is useful for understanding how the internal structure of the coefficient matrix affects the possible solutions of the linear system $A\mathbf{x} = \mathbf{b}$.

Another important observation, which we will use later, is an alternative way of expressing the product of two matrices, as given in Theorem 6.

THEOREM 6 Let A be an $(m \times n)$ matrix, and let $B = [\mathbf{B}_1, \mathbf{B}_2, \ldots, \mathbf{B}_s]$ be an $(n \times s)$ matrix whose kth column is $\mathbf{B}_k$. Then the jth column of AB is $A\mathbf{B}_j$, so that

$$AB = [A\mathbf{B}_1, A\mathbf{B}_2, \ldots, A\mathbf{B}_s].$$

Proof If $A = (a_{ij})$ and $B = (b_{ij})$, then the jth column of AB contains the entries

$$\sum_{k=1}^{n} a_{1k}b_{kj}$$
$$\sum_{k=1}^{n} a_{2k}b_{kj}$$
$$\vdots$$
$$\sum_{k=1}^{n} a_{mk}b_{kj};$$

and these are precisely the components of the column vector $A\mathbf{B}_j$, where

$$\mathbf{B}_j = \begin{bmatrix} b_{1j} \\ b_{2j} \\ \vdots \\ b_{nj} \end{bmatrix}.$$

It follows that we can write AB in the form $AB = [A\mathbf{B}_1, A\mathbf{B}_2, \ldots, A\mathbf{B}_s]$. ∎

To illustrate Theorem 6, let A and B be given by

$$A = \begin{bmatrix} 2 & 6 \\ 0 & 4 \\ 1 & 2 \end{bmatrix} \quad \text{and} \quad B = \begin{bmatrix} 1 & 3 & 0 & 1 \\ 4 & 5 & 2 & 3 \end{bmatrix}.$$

Thus the column vectors for B are

$$\mathbf{B}_1 = \begin{bmatrix} 1 \\ 4 \end{bmatrix}, \quad \mathbf{B}_2 = \begin{bmatrix} 3 \\ 5 \end{bmatrix}, \quad \mathbf{B}_3 = \begin{bmatrix} 0 \\ 2 \end{bmatrix}, \quad \text{and} \quad \mathbf{B}_4 = \begin{bmatrix} 1 \\ 3 \end{bmatrix}$$

and

$$A\mathbf{B}_1 = \begin{bmatrix} 26 \\ 16 \\ 9 \end{bmatrix}, \quad A\mathbf{B}_2 = \begin{bmatrix} 36 \\ 20 \\ 13 \end{bmatrix}, \quad A\mathbf{B}_3 = \begin{bmatrix} 12 \\ 8 \\ 4 \end{bmatrix}, \quad \text{and} \quad A\mathbf{B}_4 = \begin{bmatrix} 20 \\ 12 \\ 7 \end{bmatrix}.$$

Calculating AB, we see immediately that AB is a (3×4) matrix with columns $A\mathbf{B}_1$, $A\mathbf{B}_2$, $A\mathbf{B}_3$, and $A\mathbf{B}_4$; that is,

$$AB = \begin{bmatrix} 26 & 36 & 12 & 20 \\ 16 & 20 & 8 & 12 \\ 9 & 13 & 4 & 7 \end{bmatrix}.$$

1.5 EXERCISES

The (2×2) matrices listed in Eq. (9) are used in several of the exercises that follow.

$$A = \begin{bmatrix} 2 & 1 \\ 1 & 3 \end{bmatrix}, \quad B = \begin{bmatrix} 0 & -1 \\ 1 & 3 \end{bmatrix}, \quad C = \begin{bmatrix} -2 & 3 \\ 1 & 1 \end{bmatrix}, \quad Z = \begin{bmatrix} 0 & 0 \\ 0 & 0 \end{bmatrix} \qquad (9)$$

Exercises 1–6 refer to the matrices in Eq. (9).

1. Find (a) $A + B$; (b) $A + C$; (c) $6B$; and (d) $B + 3C$.

2. Find (a) $B + C$; (b) $3A$; (c) $A + 2C$; and (d) $C + 8Z$.

3. Find a matrix D such that $A + D = B$.

4. Find a matrix D such that $A + 2D = C$.

5. Find a matrix D such that $A + 2B + 2D = 3B$.

6. Find a matrix D such that $2A + 5B + D = 2B + 3A$.

The vectors listed in Eq. (10) are used in several of the exercises that follow.

$$\mathbf{r} = \begin{bmatrix} 1 \\ 0 \end{bmatrix}, \quad \mathbf{s} = \begin{bmatrix} 2 \\ -3 \end{bmatrix}, \quad \mathbf{t} = \begin{bmatrix} 1 \\ 4 \end{bmatrix}, \quad \mathbf{u} = \begin{bmatrix} -4 \\ 6 \end{bmatrix} \qquad (10)$$

In Exercises 7–12, perform the indicated computation, using the vectors in Eq. (10) and the matrices in Eq. (9).

7. a) $\mathbf{r} + \mathbf{s}$
b) $2\mathbf{r} + \mathbf{t}$
c) $2\mathbf{s} + \mathbf{u}$

8. a) $\mathbf{t} + \mathbf{s}$
b) $\mathbf{r} + 3\mathbf{u}$
c) $2\mathbf{u} + 3\mathbf{t}$

9. a) $A\mathbf{r}$
b) $B\mathbf{r}$
c) $C(\mathbf{s} + 3\mathbf{t})$

10. a) $B\mathbf{t}$
b) $C(\mathbf{r} + \mathbf{s})$
c) $B(\mathbf{r} + \mathbf{s})$

11. a) $(A + 2B)\mathbf{r}$
b) $(B + C)\mathbf{u}$

12. a) $(A + C)\mathbf{r}$
b) $(2B + 3C)\mathbf{s}$

Exercises 13–20 refer to the vectors in Eq. (10). In each exercise, find scalars a_1 and a_2 that satisfy the given equation, or state that the equation has no solution.

13. $a_1\mathbf{r} + a_2\mathbf{s} = \mathbf{t}$

14. $a_1\mathbf{r} + a_2\mathbf{s} = \mathbf{u}$

15. $a_1\mathbf{s} + a_2\mathbf{t} = \mathbf{u}$

16. $a_1\mathbf{s} + a_2\mathbf{t} = \mathbf{r} + \mathbf{t}$

17. $a_1\mathbf{s} + a_2\mathbf{u} = 2\mathbf{r} + \mathbf{t}$

18. $a_1\mathbf{s} + a_2\mathbf{u} = \mathbf{t}$

19. $a_1\mathbf{t} + a_2\mathbf{u} = 3\mathbf{s} + 4\mathbf{t}$

20. $a_1\mathbf{t} + a_2\mathbf{u} = 3\mathbf{r} + 2\mathbf{s}$

Exercises 21–24 refer to the matrices in Eq. (9) and the vectors in Eq. (10).

21. Find $\mathbf{w}_2$, where $\mathbf{w}_1 = B\mathbf{r}$ and $\mathbf{w}_2 = A\mathbf{w}_1$. Calculate $Q = AB$. Calculate $Q\mathbf{r}$ and verify that $\mathbf{w}_2$ is equal to $Q\mathbf{r}$.

22. Find $\mathbf{w}_2$, where $\mathbf{w}_1 = C\mathbf{s}$ and $\mathbf{w}_2 = A\mathbf{w}_1$. Calculate $Q = AC$. Calculate $Q\mathbf{s}$ and verify that $\mathbf{w}_2$ is equal to $Q\mathbf{s}$.

23. Find $\mathbf{w}_3$, where $\mathbf{w}_1 = C\mathbf{r}$, $\mathbf{w}_2 = B\mathbf{w}_1$, and $\mathbf{w}_3 = A\mathbf{w}_2$. Calculate $Q = A(BC)$ and verify that $\mathbf{w}_3$ is equal to $Q\mathbf{r}$.

24. Find $\mathbf{w}_3$, where $\mathbf{w}_1 = A\mathbf{r}$, $\mathbf{w}_2 = C\mathbf{w}_1$, and $\mathbf{w}_3 = B\mathbf{w}_2$. Calculate $Q = B(CA)$ and verify that $\mathbf{w}_3$ is equal to $Q\mathbf{r}$.

Exercises 25–30 refer to the matrices in Eq. (9). Find each of the following.

25. $(A + B)C$

26. $(A + 2B)A$

27. $(A + C)B$

28. $(B + C)Z$

29. $A(BZ)$

30. $Z(AB)$

The matrices and vectors listed in Eq. (11) are used in several of the exercises that follow.

$$A = \begin{bmatrix} 2 & 3 \\ 1 & 4 \end{bmatrix}, \quad B = \begin{bmatrix} 1 & 2 \\ 1 & 4 \end{bmatrix}, \quad \mathbf{u} = \begin{bmatrix} 1 \\ 3 \end{bmatrix},$$

$$\mathbf{v} = \begin{bmatrix} 2, 4 \end{bmatrix}, \quad C = \begin{bmatrix} 2 & 1 \\ 4 & 0 \\ 8 & -1 \\ 3 & 2 \end{bmatrix}, \qquad (11)$$

$$D = \begin{bmatrix} 2 & 1 & 3 & 6 \\ 2 & 0 & 0 & 4 \\ 1 & -1 & 1 & -1 \\ 1 & 3 & 1 & 2 \end{bmatrix}, \quad \mathbf{w} = \begin{bmatrix} 2 \\ 3 \\ 1 \\ 1 \end{bmatrix}.$$

Exercises 31–41 refer to the matrices and vectors in Eq. (11). Find each of the following.

31. AB and BA

32. DC

33. $A\mathbf{u}$ and $\mathbf{v}A$

34. $\mathbf{uv}$ and $\mathbf{vu}$

35. $\mathbf{v}(B\mathbf{u})$

36. $B\mathbf{u}$

37. CA

38. CB

39. $C(B\mathbf{u})$

40. $(AB)\mathbf{u}$ and $A(B\mathbf{u})$

41. $(BA)\mathbf{u}$ and $B(A\mathbf{u})$

In Exercises 42–49, the given matrix is the augmented matrix for a system of linear equations. Give the vector form for the general solution.

42. $\begin{bmatrix} 1 & 0 & -1 & -2 & 0 \\ 0 & 1 & 2 & 3 & 0 \end{bmatrix}$

43. $\begin{bmatrix} 1 & 0 & -1 & -2 \\ 0 & 1 & 2 & 3 \end{bmatrix}$

44. $\begin{bmatrix} 1 & 0 & -1 & 0 & -1 \\ 0 & 1 & 2 & 0 & 1 \\ 0 & 0 & 0 & 1 & 1 \end{bmatrix}$

45. $\begin{bmatrix} 1 & 0 & -1 & 0 & -1 & 0 \\ 0 & 1 & 2 & 0 & 1 & 0 \\ 0 & 0 & 0 & 1 & 1 & 0 \end{bmatrix}$

46. $\begin{bmatrix} 1 & 0 & -1 & -2 & -3 & 1 \\ 0 & 1 & 2 & 3 & 4 & 0 \end{bmatrix}$

47. $\begin{bmatrix} 1 & 0 & -1 & -2 & -3 & 0 \\ 0 & 1 & 2 & 3 & 4 & 0 \end{bmatrix}$

48. $\begin{bmatrix} 1 & 0 & -1 & 0 & -1 & -2 & 0 \\ 0 & 1 & 2 & 0 & 1 & 2 & 0 \\ 0 & 0 & 0 & 1 & 1 & 1 & 0 \end{bmatrix}$

49. $\begin{bmatrix} 1 & -1 & 0 & -2 & 0 & 0 \\ 0 & 0 & 1 & 2 & 0 & 0 \\ 0 & 0 & 0 & 0 & 1 & 0 \end{bmatrix}$

50. In Exercise 40, the calculations $(AB)\mathbf{u}$ and $A(B\mathbf{u})$ produce the same result. Which calculation requires fewer multiplications of individual matrix entries? (For example, it takes two multiplications to get the (1, 1) entry of AB.)

51. The next section will show that all the following calculations produce the same result:

$$C[A(B\mathbf{u})] = (CA)(B\mathbf{u}) = [C(AB)]\mathbf{u} = C[(AB)\mathbf{u}].$$

Convince yourself that the first expression requires the fewest individual multiplications. [*Hint:* Forming $B\mathbf{u}$ takes four multiplications, and thus $A(B\mathbf{u})$ takes eight multiplications, and so on.] Count the number of multiplications required for each of the four preceding calculations.

52. Refer to the matrices and vectors in Eq. (11).

a) Identify the column vectors in $A = [\mathbf{A}_1, \mathbf{A}_2]$ and $D = [\mathbf{D}_1, \mathbf{D}_2, \mathbf{D}_3, \mathbf{D}_4]$.

b) In part (a), is $\mathbf{A}_1$ in R^2, R^3, or R^4? Is $\mathbf{D}_1$ in R^2, R^3, or R^4?

c) Form the (2×2) matrix with columns $[A\mathbf{B}_1, A\mathbf{B}_2]$, and verify that this matrix is the product AB.

d) Verify that the vector $D\mathbf{w}$ is the same as $2\mathbf{D}_1 + 3\mathbf{D}_2 + \mathbf{D}_3 + \mathbf{D}_4$.

53. Determine whether the following matrix products are defined. When the product is defined, give the size of the product.

a) AB and BA, where A is (2×3) and B is (3×4)

b) AB and BA, where A is (2×3) and B is (2×4)

c) AB and BA, where A is (3×7) and B is (6×3)

d) AB and BA, where A is (2×3) and B is (3×2)

e) AB and BA, where A is (3×3) and B is (3×1)

f) $A(BC)$ and $(AB)C$, where A is (2×3), B is (3×5), and C is (5×4)

g) AB and BA, where A is (4×1) and B is (1×4)

54. What is the size of the product $(AB)(CD)$, where A is (2×3), B is (3×4), C is (4×4), and D is (4×2)? Also calculate the size of $A[B(CD)]$ and $[(AB)C]D$.

55. If A is a matrix, what should the symbol A^2 mean? What restrictions on A are required in order that A^2 be defined?

56. Set

$$O = \begin{bmatrix} 0 & 0 \\ 0 & 0 \end{bmatrix},$$

$$A = \begin{bmatrix} 2 & 0 \\ 0 & 2 \end{bmatrix}, \text{ and}$$

$$B = \begin{bmatrix} 1 & b \\ b^{-1} & 1 \end{bmatrix},$$

where $b \neq 0$. Show that O, A, and B are solutions to the matrix equation $X^2 - 2X = O$. Conclude that this quadratic equation has infinitely many solutions.

57. Two newspapers compete for subscriptions in a region with 300,000 households. Assume that no household subscribes to both newspapers and that the following table gives the probabilities that a household will change its subscription status during the year.

	From **A**	*From* **B**	*From None*
To **A**	.70	.15	.30
To **B**	.20	.80	.20
To None	.10	.05	.50

For example, an interpretation of the first column of the table is that during a given year, newspaper A can expect to keep 70% of its current subscribers while losing 20% to newspaper B and 10% to no subscription.

At the beginning of a particular year, suppose that 150,000 households subscribe to newspaper A, 100,000 subscribe to newspaper B, and 50,000 have no subscription. Let P and $\mathbf{x}$ be defined by

$$P = \begin{bmatrix} .70 & .15 & .30 \\ .20 & .80 & .20 \\ .10 & .05 & .50 \end{bmatrix} \text{ and } \mathbf{x} = \begin{bmatrix} 150{,}000 \\ 100{,}000 \\ 50{,}000 \end{bmatrix}.$$

The vector $\mathbf{x}$ is called the ***state vector*** for the beginning of the year. Calculate $P\mathbf{x}$ and $P^2\mathbf{x}$ and interpret the resulting vectors.

58. Let $A = \begin{bmatrix} 1 & 2 \\ 3 & 4 \end{bmatrix}$.

a) Find all matrices $B = \begin{bmatrix} a & b \\ c & d \end{bmatrix}$ such that $AB = BA$.

b) Use the results of part (a) to exhibit (2×2) matrices B and C such that $AB = BA$ and $AC \neq CA$.

59. Let A and B be matrices such that the product AB is defined and is a square matrix. Argue that the product BA is also defined and is a square matrix.

60. Let A and B be matrices such that the product AB is defined. Use Theorem 6 to prove each of the following.

a) If B has a column of zeros, then so does AB.

b) If B has two identical columns, then so does AB.

61. a) Express each of the linear systems i) and ii) in the form $A\mathbf{x} = \mathbf{b}$.

i) $\begin{aligned} 2x_1 - x_2 &= 3 \\ x_1 + x_2 &= 3 \end{aligned}$ **ii)** $\begin{aligned} x_1 - 3x_2 + x_3 &= 1 \\ x_1 - 2x_2 + x_3 &= 2 \\ x_2 - x_3 &= -1 \end{aligned}$

b) Express systems i) and ii) in the form of Eq. (8).

c) Solve systems i) and ii) by Gaussian elimination. For each system $A\mathbf{x} = \mathbf{b}$, represent $\mathbf{b}$ as a linear combination of the columns of the coefficient matrix.

62. Solve $A\mathbf{x} = \mathbf{b}$, where A and $\mathbf{b}$ are given by

$$A = \begin{bmatrix} 1 & 1 \\ 1 & 2 \end{bmatrix}, \quad \mathbf{b} = \begin{bmatrix} 2 \\ 3 \end{bmatrix}.$$

63. Let A and I be the matrices

$$A = \begin{bmatrix} 1 & 1 \\ 1 & 2 \end{bmatrix}, \quad I = \begin{bmatrix} 1 & 0 \\ 0 & 1 \end{bmatrix}.$$

a) Find a (2×2) matrix B such that $AB = I$. [*Hint:* Use Theorem 6 to determine the column vectors of B.]

b) Show that $AB = BA$ for the matrix B found in part (a).

64. Prove Theorem 5 by showing that the ith component of $A\mathbf{x}$ is equal to the ith component of $x_1\mathbf{A}_1 + x_2\mathbf{A}_2 + \cdots + x_n\mathbf{A}_n$, where $1 \leq i \leq m$.

65. For A and C, which follow, find a matrix B (if possible) such that $AB = C$.

a) $A = \begin{bmatrix} 1 & 3 \\ 1 & 4 \end{bmatrix}, \quad C = \begin{bmatrix} 2 & 6 \\ 3 & 6 \end{bmatrix}$

b) $A = \begin{bmatrix} 1 & 1 & 1 \\ 0 & 2 & 1 \\ 2 & 4 & 3 \end{bmatrix}, \quad C = \begin{bmatrix} 1 & 0 & 0 \\ 1 & 2 & 0 \\ 1 & 3 & 5 \end{bmatrix}$

c) $A = \begin{bmatrix} 1 & 2 \\ 2 & 4 \end{bmatrix}, \quad C = \begin{bmatrix} 0 & 0 \\ 0 & 0 \end{bmatrix},$

where $B \neq C$.

66. A (3×3) matrix $T = (t_{ij})$ is called an ***upper-triangular*** matrix if T has the form

$$T = \begin{bmatrix} t_{11} & t_{12} & t_{13} \\ 0 & t_{22} & t_{23} \\ 0 & 0 & t_{33} \end{bmatrix}.$$

Formally, T is upper triangular if $t_{ij} = 0$ whenever $i > j$. If A and B are upper-triangular (3×3) matrices, verify that the product AB is also upper triangular.

67. An $(n \times n)$ matrix $T = (t_{ij})$ is called upper triangular if $t_{ij} = 0$ whenever $i > j$. Suppose that A and B are $(m \times n)$ upper-triangular matrices. Use Definition 8 to prove that the product AB is upper triangular. That is, show that the ijth entry of AB is zero when $i > j$.

In Exercises 68–70, find the vector form for the general solution.

68. $$\begin{aligned} x_1 + 3x_2 - 3x_3 + 2x_4 - 3x_5 &= -4 \\ 3x_1 + 9x_2 - 10x_3 + 10x_4 - 14x_5 &= 2 \\ 2x_1 + 6x_2 - 10x_3 + 21x_4 - 25x_5 &= 53 \end{aligned}$$

69. $$\begin{aligned} 14x_1 - 8x_2 + 3x_3 - 49x_4 + 29x_5 &= 44 \\ -8x_1 + 5x_2 - 2x_3 + 29x_4 - 16x_5 &= -24 \\ 3x_1 - 2x_2 + x_3 - 11x_4 + 6x_5 &= 9 \end{aligned}$$

70. $$\begin{aligned} 18x_1 + 18x_2 - 10x_3 + 7x_4 + 2x_5 + 50x_6 &= 26 \\ -10x_1 - 10x_2 + 6x_3 - 4x_4 - x_5 - 27x_6 &= -13 \\ 7x_1 + 7x_2 - 4x_3 + 5x_4 + 2x_5 + 30x_6 &= 18 \\ 2x_1 + 2x_2 - x_3 + 2x_4 + x_5 + 12x_6 &= 8 \end{aligned}$$

71. In Exercise 57 we saw that the state vector giving the number of newspaper subscribers in year n could be found by forming $P^n\mathbf{x}$ where $\mathbf{x}$ is the initial state. Later, in Section 3.8, we will see that as n grows larger and larger, the vector $P^n\mathbf{x}$ tends toward a limit. Use MATLAB to calculate $P^n\mathbf{x}$ for $n = 1, 2, \ldots, 30$. For ease of reading, display the results using bank format in the MATLAB numeric options menu. What do you think the steady state distribution of newspapers will be?

1.6 ALGEBRAIC PROPERTIES OF MATRIX OPERATIONS

In the previous section we defined the matrix operations of addition, multiplication, and the multiplication of a matrix by a scalar. For these operations to be useful, the basic rules they obey must be determined. As we will presently see, many of the familiar algebraic properties of real numbers also hold for matrices. There are, however, important exceptions. We have already noted, for example, that matrix multiplication is not commutative. Another property of real numbers that does not carry over to matrices is the cancellation law for multiplication. That is, if a, b, and c are real numbers such that $ab = ac$ and $a \neq 0$, then $b = c$. By contrast, consider the three matrices

$$A = \begin{bmatrix} 1 & 1 \\ 1 & 1 \end{bmatrix}, \quad B = \begin{bmatrix} 1 & 4 \\ 2 & 1 \end{bmatrix}, \quad \text{and} \quad C = \begin{bmatrix} 2 & 2 \\ 1 & 3 \end{bmatrix}.$$

Note that $AB = AC$ but $B \neq C$. This example shows that the familiar cancellation law for real numbers does not apply to matrix multiplication.

Properties of Matrix Operations

The next three theorems list algebraic properties that do hold for matrix operations. In some cases, although the rule seems obvious and the proof simple, certain subtleties should be noted. For example, Theorem 9 asserts that $(r + s)A = rA + sA$, where r and s are scalars and A is an $(m \times n)$ matrix. Although the same addition symbol, $+$, appears on both sides of the equation, two different addition operations are involved; $r + s$ is the sum of two scalars, and $rA + sA$ is the sum of two matrices.

Our first theorem lists some of the properties satisfied by matrix addition.

THEOREM 7 If A, B, and C are $(m \times n)$ matrices, then the following are true:

1. $A + B = B + A$.
2. $(A + B) + C = A + (B + C)$.
3. There exists a unique $(m \times n)$ matrix $\mathcal{O}$ (called the ***zero matrix***) such that $A + \mathcal{O} = A$ for every $(m \times n)$ matrix A.
4. Given an $(m \times n)$ matrix A, there exists a unique $(m \times n)$ matrix P such that $A + P = \mathcal{O}$.

These properties are easily established, and the proofs of 2–4 are left as exercises. Regarding properties 3 and 4, we note that the zero matrix, $\mathcal{O}$, is the $(m \times n)$ matrix, all of whose entries are zero. Also the matrix P of property 4 is usually called the additive inverse for A, and the reader can show that $P = (-1)A$. The matrix $(-1)A$ is also denoted as $-A$, and the notation $A - B$ means $A + (-B)$. Thus property 4 states that $A - A = \mathcal{O}$.

***Proof of Property* 1** If $A = (a_{ij})$ and $B = (b_{ij})$ are $(m \times n)$ matrices, then, by Definition 6,

$$(A + B)_{ij} = a_{ij} + b_{ij}.$$

Similarly, by Definition 6,

$$(B + A)_{ij} = b_{ij} + a_{ij}.$$

Since addition of real numbers is commutative, $a_{ij} + b_{ij}$ and $b_{ij} + a_{ij}$ are equal. Therefore, $A + B = B + A$. ■

Three associative properties involving scalar and matrix multiplication are given in Theorem 8.

THEOREM 8

1. If A, B, and C are $(m \times n)$, $(n \times p)$, and $(p \times q)$ matrices, respectively, then $(AB)C = A(BC)$.
2. If r and s are scalars, then $r(sA) = (rs)A$.
3. $r(AB) = (rA)B = A(rB)$. ■

The proof is again left to the reader, but we will give one example to illustrate the theorem.

EXAMPLE 1 Demonstrate that $(AB)C = A(BC)$, where

$$A = \begin{bmatrix} 1 & 2 \\ -1 & 3 \end{bmatrix}, \quad B = \begin{bmatrix} 2 & -1 & 3 \\ 1 & -1 & 1 \end{bmatrix}, \quad \text{and} \quad C = \begin{bmatrix} 3 & 1 & 2 \\ -2 & 1 & -1 \\ 4 & -2 & -1 \end{bmatrix}.$$

Solution Forming the products AB and BC yields

$$AB = \begin{bmatrix} 4 & -3 & 5 \\ 1 & -2 & 0 \end{bmatrix} \quad \text{and} \quad BC = \begin{bmatrix} 20 & -5 & 2 \\ 9 & -2 & 2 \end{bmatrix}.$$

Therefore, $(AB)C$ is the product of a (2×3) matrix with a (3×3) matrix, whereas $A(BC)$ is the product of a (2×2) matrix with a (2×3) matrix. Forming these products, we find

$$(AB)C = \begin{bmatrix} 38 & -9 & 6 \\ 7 & -1 & 4 \end{bmatrix} \quad \text{and} \quad A(BC) = \begin{bmatrix} 38 & -9 & 6 \\ 7 & -1 & 4 \end{bmatrix}.$$ ■

Finally, the distributive properties connecting addition and multiplication are given in Theorem 9.

THEOREM 9

1. If A and B are $(m \times n)$ matrices and C is an $(n \times p)$ matrix, then $(A+B)C = AC + BC$.
2. If A is an $(m \times n)$ matrix and B and C are $(n \times p)$ matrices, then $A(B+C) = AB + AC$.
3. If r and s are scalars and A is an $(m \times n)$ matrix, then $(r+s)A = rA + sA$.
4. If r is a scalar and A and B are $(m \times n)$ matrices, then $r(A+B) = rA + rB$.

Proof We will prove property 1 and leave the others to the reader. First observe that $(A+B)C$ and $AC + BC$ are both $(m \times p)$ matrices. To show that the components of these two matrices are equal, let $Q = A + B$, where $Q = (q_{ij})$. Then $(A+B)C = QC$, and the rsth component of QC is given by

$$\sum_{k=1}^{n} q_{rk}c_{ks} = \sum_{k=1}^{n} (a_{rk} + b_{rk})c_{ks} = \sum_{k=1}^{n} a_{rk}c_{ks} + \sum_{k=1}^{n} b_{rk}c_{ks}.$$

Because

$$\sum_{k=1}^{n} a_{rk}c_{ks} + \sum_{k=1}^{n} b_{rk}c_{ks}$$

is precisely the rsth entry of $AC + BC$, it follows that $(A+B)C = AC + BC$. ■

The Transpose of a Matrix

The concept of the transpose of a matrix is important in applications. Stated informally, the transpose operation, applied to a matrix A, interchanges the rows and columns of A. The formal definition of transpose is as follows.

DEFINITION 9

If $A = (a_{ij})$ is an $(m \times n)$ matrix, then the ***transpose*** of A, denoted A^T, is the $(n \times m)$ matrix $A^T = (b_{ij})$, where $b_{ij} = a_{ji}$ for all i and j, $1 \le j \le m$, and $1 \le i \le n$.

The following example illustrates the definition of the transpose of a matrix:

EXAMPLE 2 Find the transpose of $A = \begin{bmatrix} 1 & 3 & 7 \\ 2 & 1 & 4 \end{bmatrix}$.

Solution By Definition 9, A^T is the (3×2) matrix

$$A^T = \begin{bmatrix} 1 & 2 \\ 3 & 1 \\ 7 & 4 \end{bmatrix}.$$

■

In the preceding example, note that the first row of A becomes the first column of A^T, and the second row of A becomes the second column of A^T. Similarly, the columns of A become the rows of A^T. Thus A^T is obtained by interchanging the rows and columns of A.

Three important properties of the transpose are given in Theorem 10.

THEOREM 10 If A and B are $(m \times n)$ matrices and C is an $(n \times p)$ matrix, then:

1. $(A+B)^T = A^T + B^T$.
2. $(AC)^T = C^T A^T$.
3. $(A^T)^T = A$.

Proof We will leave properties 1 and 3 to the reader and prove property 2. Note first that $(AC)^T$ and $C^T A^T$ are both $(p \times m)$ matrices, so we have only to show that their corresponding entries are equal. From Definition 9, the ijth entry of $(AC)^T$ is the jith entry of AC. Thus the ijth entry of $(AC)^T$ is given by

$$\sum_{k=1}^{n} a_{jk} c_{ki}.$$

Next the ijth entry of $C^T A^T$ is the scalar product of the ith row of C^T with the jth column of A^T. In particular, the ith row of C^T is $[c_{1i}, c_{2i}, \ldots, c_{ni}]$ (the ith column of C), whereas the jth column of A^T is

$$\begin{bmatrix} a_{j1} \\ a_{j2} \\ \vdots \\ a_{jn} \end{bmatrix}$$

(the jth row of A). Therefore, the ijth entry of $C^T A^T$ is given by

$$c_{1i} a_{j1} + c_{2i} a_{j2} + \cdots + c_{ni} a_{jn} = \sum_{k=1}^{n} c_{ki} a_{jk}.$$

Finally, since

$$\sum_{k=1}^{n} c_{ki} a_{jk} = \sum_{k=1}^{n} a_{jk} c_{ki},$$

the ijth entries of $(AC)^T$ and $C^T A^T$ agree, and the matrices are equal. ∎

The transpose operation is used to define certain important types of matrices, such as positive-definite matrices, normal matrices, and symmetric matrices. We will consider these in detail later and give only the definition of a symmetric matrix in this section.

DEFINITION 10 A matrix A is ***symmetric*** if $A = A^T$.

If A is an $(m \times n)$ matrix, then A^T is an $(n \times m)$ matrix, so we can have $A = A^T$ only if $m = n$. An $(n \times n)$ matrix is called a ***square matrix***; thus if a matrix is symmetric, it must be a square matrix. Furthermore, Definition 9 implies that if $A = (a_{ij})$ is an $(n \times n)$ symmetric matrix, then $a_{ij} = a_{ji}$ for all i and j, $1 \le i, j \le n$. Conversely, if A is square and $a_{ij} = a_{ji}$ for all i and j, then A is symmetric.

Example 3 Determine which of the matrices

$$A = \begin{bmatrix} 1 & 2 \\ 2 & 3 \end{bmatrix}, \quad B = \begin{bmatrix} 1 & 2 \\ 1 & 2 \end{bmatrix}, \quad \text{and} \quad C = \begin{bmatrix} 1 & 6 \\ 3 & 1 \\ 2 & 0 \end{bmatrix}$$

is symmetric. Also show that B^TB and C^TC are symmetric.

Solution By Definition 9,

$$A^T = \begin{bmatrix} 1 & 2 \\ 2 & 3 \end{bmatrix}, \quad B^T = \begin{bmatrix} 1 & 1 \\ 2 & 2 \end{bmatrix}, \quad \text{and} \quad C^T = \begin{bmatrix} 1 & 3 & 2 \\ 6 & 1 & 0 \end{bmatrix}.$$

Thus A is symmetric since $A^T = A$. However, $B^T \neq B$ and $C^T \neq C$. Therefore, B and C are not symmetric. As can be seen, the matrices B^TB and C^TC are symmetric:

$$B^TB = \begin{bmatrix} 2 & 4 \\ 4 & 8 \end{bmatrix} \quad \text{and} \quad C^TC = \begin{bmatrix} 14 & 9 \\ 9 & 37 \end{bmatrix}.$$

In Exercise 49, the reader is asked to show that Q^TQ is *always* a symmetric matrix whether or not Q is symmetric.

In the $(n \times n)$ matrix $A = (a_{ij})$, the entries $a_{11}, a_{22}, \ldots, a_{nn}$ are called the ***main diagonal*** of A. For example, the main diagonal of a (3×3) matrix is illustrated in Fig. 1.15. Since the entries a_{ij} and a_{ji} are symmetric partners relative to the main diagonal, symmetric matrices are easily recognizable as those in which the entries form a symmetric array relative to the main diagonal. For example, if

$$\begin{bmatrix} a_{11} & a_{12} & a_{13} \\ a_{21} & a_{22} & a_{23} \\ a_{31} & a_{32} & a_{33} \end{bmatrix}$$

Figure 1.15
Main diagonal

$$A = \begin{bmatrix} 2 & 3 & -1 \\ 3 & 4 & 2 \\ -1 & 2 & 0 \end{bmatrix} \quad \text{and} \quad B = \begin{bmatrix} 1 & 2 & 2 \\ -1 & 3 & 0 \\ 5 & 2 & 6 \end{bmatrix},$$

then, by inspection, A is symmetric, whereas B is not.

The Identity Matrix

As we will see later, the $(n \times n)$ identity matrix plays an important role in matrix theory. In particular, for each positive integer n, the ***identity matrix*** I_n is defined to be the

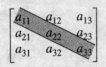

$(n \times n)$ matrix with ones on the main diagonal and zeros elsewhere:

$$I_n = \begin{bmatrix} 1 & 0 & 0 & \cdots & 0 \\ 0 & 1 & 0 & \cdots & 0 \\ 0 & 0 & 1 & \cdots & 0 \\ \vdots & & & & \vdots \\ 0 & 0 & 0 & \cdots & 1 \end{bmatrix}.$$

That is, the ijth entry of I_n is 0 when $i \neq j$, and is 1 when $i = j$. For example, I_2 and I_3 are given by

$$I_2 = \begin{bmatrix} 1 & 0 \\ 0 & 1 \end{bmatrix} \quad \text{and} \quad I_3 = \begin{bmatrix} 1 & 0 & 0 \\ 0 & 1 & 0 \\ 0 & 0 & 1 \end{bmatrix}.$$

The identity matrix is the multiplicative identity for matrix multiplication. Specifically, let A denote an $(n \times n)$ matrix. Then, as in Exercise 62, it is not hard to show that

$$AI_n = A \quad \text{and} \quad I_nA = A.$$

Identity matrices can also be used with rectangular matrices. For example, let B denote a $(p \times q)$ matrix. Then, as in Exercise 62,

$$BI_q = B \quad \text{and} \quad I_pB = B.$$

By way of illustration, consider

$$A = \begin{bmatrix} 1 & 2 & 0 \\ -1 & 3 & 4 \\ 6 & 1 & 8 \end{bmatrix}, \quad B = \begin{bmatrix} 2 & 3 & 1 \\ 1 & 5 & 7 \end{bmatrix}, \quad C = \begin{bmatrix} -2 & 0 \\ 8 & 3 \\ 6 & 1 \end{bmatrix},$$

and

$$\mathbf{x} = \begin{bmatrix} 1 \\ 0 \\ 3 \end{bmatrix}.$$

Note that

$$I_3A = AI_3 = A$$
$$BI_3 = B$$
$$I_3C = C$$
$$I_3\mathbf{x} = \mathbf{x},$$

whereas the products I_3B and CI_3 are not defined.

Usually the dimension of the identity matrix is clear from the context of the problem under consideration, and it is customary to drop the subscript, n, and denote the $(n \times n)$ identity matrix simply as I. So, for example, if A is an $(n \times n)$ matrix, we will write

$IA = AI = A$ instead of $I_n A = AI_n = A$. Note that the identity matrix is a symmetric matrix.

Scalar Products and Vector Norms

The transpose operation can be used to represent scalar products and vector norms. As we will see, a vector norm provides a method for measuring the size of a vector.

To illustrate the connection between transposes and the scalar product, let $\mathbf{x}$ and $\mathbf{y}$ be vectors in R^3 given by

$$\mathbf{x} = \begin{bmatrix} 1 \\ -3 \\ 2 \end{bmatrix} \quad \text{and} \quad \mathbf{y} = \begin{bmatrix} 1 \\ 2 \\ 1 \end{bmatrix}.$$

Then $\mathbf{x}^T$ is the (1×3) vector

$$\mathbf{x}^T = [1, -3, 2],$$

and $\mathbf{x}^T\mathbf{y}$ is the scalar (or (1×1) matrix) given by

$$\mathbf{x}^T\mathbf{y} = [1, -3, 2]\begin{bmatrix} 1 \\ 2 \\ 1 \end{bmatrix} = 1 - 6 + 2 = -3.$$

More generally, if $\mathbf{x}$ and $\mathbf{y}$ are vectors in R^n,

$$\mathbf{x} = \begin{bmatrix} x_1 \\ x_2 \\ \vdots \\ x_n \end{bmatrix}, \quad \mathbf{y} = \begin{bmatrix} y_1 \\ y_2 \\ \vdots \\ y_n \end{bmatrix},$$

then

$$\mathbf{x}^T\mathbf{y} = \sum_{i=1}^{n} x_i y_i;$$

that is, $\mathbf{x}^T\mathbf{y}$ is the scalar product or dot product of $\mathbf{x}$ and $\mathbf{y}$. Also note that $\mathbf{y}^T\mathbf{x} = \sum_{i=1}^{n} y_i x_i = \sum_{i=1}^{n} x_i y_i = \mathbf{x}^T\mathbf{y}$.

One of the basic concepts in computational work is that of the length or norm of a vector. If

$$\mathbf{x} = \begin{bmatrix} a \\ b \end{bmatrix}$$

is in R^2, then $\mathbf{x}$ can be represented geometrically in the plane as the directed line segment $\overrightarrow{OP}$ from the origin O to the point P, which has coordinates (a, b), as illustrated in Fig. 1.16. By the Pythagorean theorem, the length of the line segment $\overrightarrow{OP}$ is $\sqrt{a^2 + b^2}$.

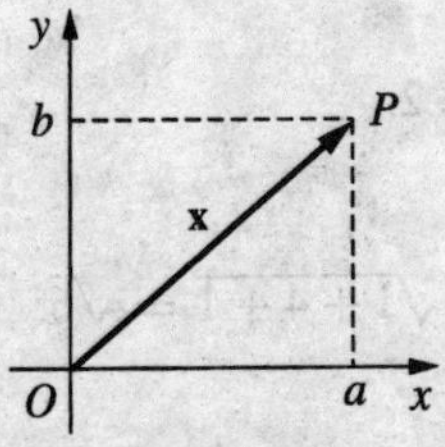

Figure 1.16
Geometric vector in two-space

A similar idea is used in R^n. For a vector $\mathbf{x}$ in R^n,

$$\mathbf{x} = \begin{bmatrix} x_1 \\ x_2 \\ \vdots \\ x_n \end{bmatrix},$$

it is natural to define the ***Euclidean length***, or ***Euclidean norm*** of $\mathbf{x}$, denoted by $\|\mathbf{x}\|$, to be

$$\|\mathbf{x}\| = \sqrt{x_1^2 + x_2^2 + \cdots + x_n^2}.$$

(The quantity $\|\mathbf{x}\|$ gives us a way to measure the size of the vector $\mathbf{x}$.)

Noting that the scalar product of $\mathbf{x}$ with itself is

$$\mathbf{x}^T\mathbf{x} = x_1^2 + x_2^2 + \cdots + x_n^2,$$

we have

$$\|\mathbf{x}\| = \sqrt{\mathbf{x}^T\mathbf{x}}. \tag{1}$$

For vectors $\mathbf{x}$ and $\mathbf{y}$ in R^n, we define the Euclidean distance between $\mathbf{x}$ and $\mathbf{y}$ to be $\|\mathbf{x} - \mathbf{y}\|$. Thus the distance between $\mathbf{x}$ and $\mathbf{y}$ is given by

$$\begin{aligned} \|\mathbf{x} - \mathbf{y}\| &= \sqrt{(\mathbf{x} - \mathbf{y})^T(\mathbf{x} - \mathbf{y})} \\ &= \sqrt{(x_1 - y_1)^2 + (x_2 - y_2)^2 + \cdots + (x_n - y_n)^2}. \end{aligned} \tag{2}$$

EXAMPLE 4 If $\mathbf{x}$ and $\mathbf{y}$ in R^3 are given by

$$\mathbf{x} = \begin{bmatrix} -2 \\ 3 \\ 2 \end{bmatrix} \quad \text{and} \quad \mathbf{y} = \begin{bmatrix} 1 \\ 2 \\ -1 \end{bmatrix},$$

then find $\mathbf{x}^T\mathbf{y}$, $\|\mathbf{x}\|$, $\|\mathbf{y}\|$, and $\|\mathbf{x} - \mathbf{y}\|$.

Solution We have

$$\mathbf{x}^T\mathbf{y} = [\,-2 \quad 3 \quad 2\,] \begin{bmatrix} 1 \\ 2 \\ -1 \end{bmatrix} = -2 + 6 - 2 = 2.$$

Also, $\|\mathbf{x}\| = \sqrt{\mathbf{x}^T\mathbf{x}} = \sqrt{4+9+4} = \sqrt{17}$, and $\|\mathbf{y}\| = \sqrt{\mathbf{y}^T\mathbf{y}} = \sqrt{1+4+1} = \sqrt{6}$. Subtracting $\mathbf{y}$ from $\mathbf{x}$ gives

$$\mathbf{x} - \mathbf{y} = \begin{bmatrix} -3 \\ 1 \\ 3 \end{bmatrix},$$

so $\|\mathbf{x} - \mathbf{y}\| = \sqrt{(\mathbf{x} - \mathbf{y})^T(\mathbf{x} - \mathbf{y})} = \sqrt{9+1+9} = \sqrt{19}$. ■

1.6 EXERCISES

The matrices and vectors listed in Eq. (3) are used in several of the exercises that follow.

$$A = \begin{bmatrix} 3 & 1 \\ 4 & 7 \\ 2 & 6 \end{bmatrix}, \quad B = \begin{bmatrix} 1 & 2 & 1 \\ 7 & 4 & 3 \\ 6 & 0 & 1 \end{bmatrix},$$

$$C = \begin{bmatrix} 2 & 1 & 4 & 0 \\ 6 & 1 & 3 & 5 \\ 2 & 4 & 2 & 0 \end{bmatrix}, \quad D = \begin{bmatrix} 2 & 1 \\ 1 & 4 \end{bmatrix},$$

$$E = \begin{bmatrix} 3 & 6 \\ 2 & 3 \end{bmatrix}, \quad F = \begin{bmatrix} 1 & 1 \\ 1 & 1 \end{bmatrix},$$

$$\mathbf{u} = \begin{bmatrix} 1 \\ -1 \end{bmatrix}, \quad \mathbf{v} = \begin{bmatrix} -3 \\ 3 \end{bmatrix} \qquad (3)$$

Exercises 1–25 refer to the matrices and vectors in Eq. (3). In Exercises 1–6, perform the multiplications to verify the given equality or nonequality.

1. $(DE)F = D(EF)$ **2.** $(FE)D = F(ED)$
3. $DE \neq ED$ **4.** $EF \neq FE$
5. $F\mathbf{u} = F\mathbf{v}$ **6.** $3F\mathbf{u} = 7F\mathbf{v}$

In Exercises 7–12, find the matrices.

7. A^T **8.** D^T **9.** E^TF
10. A^TC **11.** $(F\mathbf{v})^T$ **12.** $(EF)\mathbf{v}$

In Exercises 13–25, calculate the scalars.

13. $\mathbf{u}^T\mathbf{v}$ **14.** $\mathbf{v}^TF\mathbf{u}$ **15.** $\mathbf{v}^TD\mathbf{v}$
16. $\mathbf{v}^TF\mathbf{v}$ **17.** $\mathbf{u}^T\mathbf{u}$ **18.** $\mathbf{v}^T\mathbf{v}$
19. $\|\mathbf{u}\|$ **20.** $\|D\mathbf{v}\|$ **21.** $\|A\mathbf{u}\|$
22. $\|\mathbf{u}-\mathbf{v}\|$ **23.** $\|F\mathbf{u}\|$ **24.** $\|F\mathbf{v}\|$
25. $\|(D-E)\mathbf{u}\|$

26. Let A and B be (2×2) matrices. Prove or find a counterexample for this statement: $(A-B)(A+B) = A^2 - B^2$.

27. Let A and B be (2×2) matrices such that $A^2 = AB$ and $A \neq \mathcal{O}$. Can we assert that, by cancellation, $A = B$? Explain.

28. Let A and B be as in Exercise 27. Find the flaw in the following proof that $A = B$.

Since $A^2 = AB$, $A^2 - AB = \mathcal{O}$. Factoring yields $A(A-B) = \mathcal{O}$. Since $A \neq \mathcal{O}$, it follows that $A - B = \mathcal{O}$. Therefore, $A = B$.

29. Two of the six matrices listed in Eq. (3) are symmetric. Identify these matrices.

30. Find (2×2) matrices A and B such that A and B are symmetric, but AB is not symmetric. [*Hint:* $(AB)^T = B^TA^T = BA$.]

31. Let A and B be $(n \times n)$ symmetric matrices. Give a necessary and sufficient condition for AB to be symmetric. [*Hint:* Recall Exercise 30.]

32. Let G be the (2×2) matrix that follows, and consider any vector $\mathbf{x}$ in R^2 where both entries are not simultaneously zero:

$$G = \begin{bmatrix} 2 & 1 \\ 1 & 1 \end{bmatrix}, \quad \mathbf{x} = \begin{bmatrix} x_1 \\ x_2 \end{bmatrix}; \quad |x_1| + |x_2| > 0.$$

Show that $\mathbf{x}^TG\mathbf{x} > 0$. [*Hint:* Write $\mathbf{x}^TG\mathbf{x}$ as a sum of squares.]

33. Repeat Exercise 32 using the matrix D in Eq. (3) in place of G.

34. For F in Eq. (3), show that $\mathbf{x}^TF\mathbf{x} \geq 0$ for all $\mathbf{x}$ in R^2. Classify those vectors $\mathbf{x}$ such that $\mathbf{x}^TF\mathbf{x} = 0$.

If $\mathbf{x}$ and $\mathbf{y}$ are vectors in R^n, then the product $\mathbf{x}^T\mathbf{y}$ is often called an inner product. Similarly, the product $\mathbf{x}\mathbf{y}^T$ is often called an outer product. Exercises 35–40 concern outer products; the matrices and vectors are given in Eq. (3). In Exercises 35–40, form the outer products.

35. $\mathbf{u}\mathbf{v}^T$ **36.** $\mathbf{u}(F\mathbf{u})^T$ **37.** $\mathbf{v}(E\mathbf{v})^T$
38. $\mathbf{u}(E\mathbf{v})^T$ **39.** $(A\mathbf{u})(A\mathbf{v})^T$ **40.** $(A\mathbf{v})(A\mathbf{u})^T$

41. Let $\mathbf{a}$ and $\mathbf{b}$ be given by

$$\mathbf{a} = \begin{bmatrix} 1 \\ 2 \end{bmatrix} \quad \text{and} \quad \mathbf{b} = \begin{bmatrix} 3 \\ 4 \end{bmatrix}.$$

a) Find $\mathbf{x}$ in R^2 that satisfies both $\mathbf{x}^T\mathbf{a} = 6$ and $\mathbf{x}^T\mathbf{b} = 2$.

b) Find $\mathbf{x}$ in R^2 that satisfies both $\mathbf{x}^T(\mathbf{a}+\mathbf{b}) = 12$ and $\mathbf{x}^T\mathbf{a} = 2$.

42. Let A be a (2×2) matrix, and let B and C be given by

$$B = \begin{bmatrix} 1 & 3 \\ 1 & 4 \end{bmatrix} \quad \text{and} \quad C = \begin{bmatrix} 2 & 3 \\ 4 & 5 \end{bmatrix}.$$

a) If $A^T + B = C$, what is A?

b) If $A^T B = C$, what is A? and

c) Calculate $B\mathbf{C}_1$, $\mathbf{B}_1^T C$, $(B\mathbf{C}_1)^T \mathbf{C}_2$, and $\|C\mathbf{B}_2\|$.

43. Let

$$A = \begin{bmatrix} 4 & -2 & 2 \\ 2 & 4 & -4 \\ 1 & 1 & 0 \end{bmatrix} \quad \text{and} \quad \mathbf{u} = \begin{bmatrix} 1 \\ 3 \\ 2 \end{bmatrix}.$$

a) Verify that $A\mathbf{u} = 2\mathbf{u}$.

b) Without forming A^5, calculate the vector $A^5\mathbf{u}$.

c) Give a formula for $A^n\mathbf{u}$, where n is a positive integer. What property from Theorem 8 is required to derive the formula?

44. Let A, B, and C be $(m \times n)$ matrices such that $A + C = B + C$. The following statements are the steps in a proof that $A = B$. Using Theorem 7, provide justification for each of the assertions.

a) There exists an $(m \times n)$ matrix $\mathcal{O}$ such that $A = A + \mathcal{O}$.

b) There exists an $(m \times n)$ matrix D such that $A = A + (C + D)$.

c) $A = (A + C) + D = (B + C) + D$.

d) $A = B + (C + D)$.

e) $A = B + \mathcal{O}$.

f) $A = B$.

45. Let A, B, C, and D be matrices such that $AB = D$ and $AC = D$. The following statements are steps in a proof that if r and s are scalars, then $A(rB + sC) = (r + s)D$. Use Theorems 8 and 9 to provide reasons for each of the steps.

a) $A(rB + sC) = A(rB) + A(sC)$.

b) $A(rB + sC) = r(AB) + s(AC) = rD + sD$.

c) $A(rB + sC) = (r + s)D$.

46. Let $\mathbf{x}$ and $\mathbf{y}$ be vectors in R^n such that $\|\mathbf{x}\| = \|\mathbf{y}\| = 1$ and $\mathbf{x}^T\mathbf{y} = 0$. Use Eq. (1) to show that $\|\mathbf{x} - \mathbf{y}\| = \sqrt{2}$.

47. Use Theorem 10 to show that $A + A^T$ is symmetric for any square matrix A.

48. Let A be the (2×2) matrix

$$A = \begin{bmatrix} 1 & 2 \\ 3 & 6 \end{bmatrix}.$$

Choose some vector $\mathbf{b}$ in R^2 such that the equation $A\mathbf{x} = \mathbf{b}$ is inconsistent. Verify that the associated equation $A^T A\mathbf{x} = A^T\mathbf{b}$ is consistent for your choice of $\mathbf{b}$. Let $\mathbf{x}^*$ be a solution to $A^T A\mathbf{x} = A^T\mathbf{b}$, and select some vectors $\mathbf{x}$ at random from R^2. Verify that $\|A\mathbf{x}^* - \mathbf{b}\| \le \|A\mathbf{x} - \mathbf{b}\|$ for any of these random choices for $\mathbf{x}$. (In Chapter 3, we will show that $A^T A\mathbf{x} = A^T\mathbf{b}$ is always consistent for any $(m \times n)$ matrix A regardless of whether $A\mathbf{x} = \mathbf{b}$ is consistent or not. We also show that any solution $\mathbf{x}^*$ of $A^T A\mathbf{x} = A^T\mathbf{b}$ satisfies $\|A\mathbf{x}^* - \mathbf{b}\| \le \|A\mathbf{x} - \mathbf{b}\|$ for all $\mathbf{x}$ in R^n; that is, such a vector $\mathbf{x}^*$ minimizes the length of the residual vector $\mathbf{r} = A\mathbf{x} - \mathbf{b}$.)

49. Use Theorem 10 to prove each of the following:

a) If Q is any $(m \times n)$ matrix, then $Q^T Q$ and QQ^T are symmetric.

b) If A, B, and C are matrices such that the product ABC is defined, then $(ABC)^T = C^T B^T A^T$. [*Hint:* Set $BC = D$.]
Note: These proofs can be done quickly without considering the entries in the matrices.

50. Let Q be an $(m \times n)$ matrix and $\mathbf{x}$ any vector in R^n. Prove that $\mathbf{x}^T Q^T Q\mathbf{x} \ge 0$. [*Hint:* Observe that $Q\mathbf{x}$ is a vector in R^m.]

51. Prove properties 2, 3, and 4 of Theorem 7.

52. Prove property 1 of Theorem 8. [*Note:* This is a long exercise, but the proof is similar to the proof of part 2 of Theorem 10.]

53. Prove properties 2 and 3 of Theorem 8.

54. Prove properties 2, 3, and 4 of Theorem 9.

55. Prove properties 1 and 3 of Theorem 10.

In Exercises 56–61, determine n and m so that $I_n A = A$ and $AI_m = A$, where:

56. A is (2×3)

57. A is (5×7)

58. A is (4×4)

59. A is (4×6)

60. A is (4×2)

61. A is (5×5)

62. a) Let A be an $(n \times n)$ matrix. Use the definition of matrix multiplication to show that $AI_n = A$ and $I_n A = A$.

b) Let B be a $(p \times q)$ matrix. Use the definition of matrix multiplication to show that $BI_q = B$ and $I_p B = B$.

1.7 LINEAR INDEPENDENCE AND NONSINGULAR MATRICES

Section 1.5 demonstrated how the general linear system

$$\begin{aligned} a_{11}x_1 + a_{12}x_2 + \cdots + a_{1n}x_n &= b_1 \\ a_{21}x_1 + a_{22}x_2 + \cdots + a_{2n}x_n &= b_2 \\ \vdots \quad\quad \vdots \quad\quad\quad\quad \vdots \quad &\quad \vdots \\ a_{m1}x_1 + a_{m2}x_2 + \cdots + a_{mn}x_n &= b_m \end{aligned} \tag{1}$$

can be expressed as a matrix equation $A\mathbf{x} = \mathbf{b}$. We observed in Section 1.1 that system (1) may have a unique solution, infinitely many solutions, or no solution. The material in Section 1.3 illustrates that, with appropriate additional information, we can know which of the three possibilities will occur. The case in which $m = n$ is of particular interest, and in this and later sections, we determine conditions on the matrix A in order that an $(n \times n)$ system has a unique solution.

Linear Independence

If $A = [\mathbf{A}_1, \mathbf{A}_2, \ldots, \mathbf{A}_n]$, then, by Theorem 5 of Section 1.5, the equation $A\mathbf{x} = \mathbf{b}$ can be written in terms of the columns of A as

$$x_1\mathbf{A}_1 + x_2\mathbf{A}_2 + \cdots + x_n\mathbf{A}_n = \mathbf{b}. \tag{2}$$

From Eq. (2), it follows that system (1) is consistent if, and only if, $\mathbf{b}$ can be written as a sum of scalar multiples of the column vectors of A. We call a sum such as $x_1\mathbf{A}_1 + x_2\mathbf{A}_2 + \cdots + x_n\mathbf{A}_n$ a ***linear combination*** of the vectors $\mathbf{A}_1, \mathbf{A}_2, \ldots, \mathbf{A}_n$. Thus $A\mathbf{x} = \mathbf{b}$ is consistent if, and only if, $\mathbf{b}$ is a linear combination of the columns of A.

EXAMPLE 1 If the vectors $\mathbf{A}_1$, $\mathbf{A}_2$, $\mathbf{A}_3$, $\mathbf{b}_1$, and $\mathbf{b}_2$ are given by

$$\mathbf{A}_1 = \begin{bmatrix} 1 \\ 2 \\ -1 \end{bmatrix}, \quad \mathbf{A}_2 = \begin{bmatrix} 1 \\ 3 \\ 1 \end{bmatrix}, \quad \mathbf{A}_3 = \begin{bmatrix} 1 \\ 4 \\ 3 \end{bmatrix},$$

$$\mathbf{b}_1 = \begin{bmatrix} 3 \\ 8 \\ 1 \end{bmatrix}, \quad \text{and} \quad \mathbf{b}_2 = \begin{bmatrix} 2 \\ 5 \\ -1 \end{bmatrix},$$

then express each of $\mathbf{b}_1$ and $\mathbf{b}_2$ as a linear combination of the vectors $\mathbf{A}_1, \mathbf{A}_2, \mathbf{A}_3$.

Solution If $A = [\mathbf{A}_1, \mathbf{A}_2, \mathbf{A}_3]$, that is,

$$A = \begin{bmatrix} 1 & 1 & 1 \\ 2 & 3 & 4 \\ -1 & 1 & 3 \end{bmatrix},$$

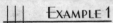

then expressing $\mathbf{b}_1$ as a linear combination of $\mathbf{A}_1, \mathbf{A}_2, \mathbf{A}_3$ is equivalent to solving the (3×3) linear system with matrix equation $A\mathbf{x} = \mathbf{b}_1$. The augmented matrix for the system is

$$\begin{bmatrix} 1 & 1 & 1 & 3 \\ 2 & 3 & 4 & 8 \\ -1 & 1 & 3 & 1 \end{bmatrix},$$

and solving in the usual manner yields

$$\begin{aligned} x_1 &= 1 + x_3 \\ x_2 &= 2 - 2x_3, \end{aligned}$$

where x_3 is an unconstrained variable. Thus $\mathbf{b}_1$ can be expressed as a linear combination of $\mathbf{A}_1, \mathbf{A}_2, \mathbf{A}_3$ in infinitely many ways. Taking $x_3 = 2$, for example, yields $x_1 = 3$, $x_2 = -2$, so

$$3\mathbf{A}_1 - 2\mathbf{A}_2 + 2\mathbf{A}_3 = \mathbf{b}_1;$$

that is,

$$3\begin{bmatrix} 1 \\ 2 \\ -1 \end{bmatrix} - 2\begin{bmatrix} 1 \\ 3 \\ 1 \end{bmatrix} + 2\begin{bmatrix} 1 \\ 4 \\ 3 \end{bmatrix} = \begin{bmatrix} 3 \\ 8 \\ 1 \end{bmatrix}.$$

If we attempt to follow the same procedure to express $\mathbf{b}_2$ as a linear combination of $\mathbf{A}_1, \mathbf{A}_2, \mathbf{A}_3$, we discover that the system of equations $A\mathbf{x} = \mathbf{b}_2$ is inconsistent. Therefore, $\mathbf{b}_2$ cannot be expressed as a linear combination of $\mathbf{A}_1, \mathbf{A}_2, \mathbf{A}_3$. ■

It is convenient at this point to introduce a special symbol, $\boldsymbol{\theta}$, to denote the m-dimensional ***zero vector***. Thus $\boldsymbol{\theta}$ is the vector in R^m, all of whose components are zero:

$$\boldsymbol{\theta} = \begin{bmatrix} 0 \\ 0 \\ \vdots \\ 0 \end{bmatrix}.$$

We will use $\boldsymbol{\theta}$ throughout to designate zero vectors in order to avoid any possible confusion between a zero vector and the scalar zero. With this notation, the $(m \times n)$ homogeneous system

$$\begin{aligned} a_{11}x_1 + a_{12}x_2 + \cdots + a_{1n}x_n &= 0 \\ a_{21}x_1 + a_{22}x_2 + \cdots + a_{2n}x_n &= 0 \\ \vdots \qquad \vdots \qquad\qquad \vdots \quad & \;\; \vdots \\ a_{m1}x_1 + a_{m2}x_2 + \cdots + a_{mn}x_n &= 0 \end{aligned} \tag{3}$$

has the matrix equation $A\mathbf{x} = \boldsymbol{\theta}$, which can be written as

$$x_1\mathbf{A}_1 + x_2\mathbf{A}_2 + \cdots + x_n\mathbf{A}_n = \boldsymbol{\theta}. \tag{4}$$

In Section 1.3, we observed that the homogeneous system (3) always has the trivial solution $x_1 = x_2 = \cdots = x_n = 0$. Thus in Eq. (4), $\boldsymbol{\theta}$ can always be expressed as a linear combination of the columns $\mathbf{A}_1, \mathbf{A}_2, \ldots, \mathbf{A}_n$ of A by taking $x_1 = x_2 = \cdots = x_n = 0$. There could, however, be nontrivial solutions, and this leads to the following definition.

DEFINITION 11 A set of m-dimensional vectors $\{\mathbf{v}_1, \mathbf{v}_2, \ldots, \mathbf{v}_p\}$ is said to be ***linearly independent*** if the only solution to the vector equation

$$a_1\mathbf{v}_1 + a_2\mathbf{v}_2 + \cdots + a_p\mathbf{v}_p = \boldsymbol{\theta}$$

is $a_1 = 0, a_2 = 0, \ldots, a_p = 0$. The set of vectors is said to be ***linearly dependent*** if it is not linearly independent. That is, the set is linearly dependent if we can find a solution to $a_1\mathbf{v}_1 + a_2\mathbf{v}_2 + \cdots + a_p\mathbf{v}_p = \boldsymbol{\theta}$ where not all the a_i are zero.

Any time you need to know whether a set of vectors is linearly independent or linearly dependent, you should start with the dependence equation:

$$a_1\mathbf{v}_1 + a_2\mathbf{v}_2 + \cdots + a_p\mathbf{v}_p = \boldsymbol{\theta} \tag{5}$$

You would then solve Eq. (5). If there are nontrivial solutions, then the set of vectors is linearly dependent. If Eq. (5) has only the trivial solution, then the set of vectors is linearly independent.

We can phrase Eq. (5) in matrix terms. In particular, let V denote the $(m \times p)$ matrix made up from the vectors $\mathbf{v}_1, \mathbf{v}_2, \ldots, \mathbf{v}_p$:

$$V = [\mathbf{v}_1, \mathbf{v}_2, \ldots, \mathbf{v}_p].$$

Then Eq. (5) is equivalent to the matrix equation

$$V\mathbf{x} = \boldsymbol{\theta}. \tag{6}$$

Thus to determine whether the set $\{\mathbf{v}_1, \mathbf{v}_2, \ldots, \mathbf{v}_p\}$ is linearly independent or dependent, we solve the homogeneous system of equations (6) by forming the augmented matrix $[V \mid \boldsymbol{\theta}]$ and reducing $[V \mid \boldsymbol{\theta}]$ to echelon form. If the system has nontrivial solutions, then $\{\mathbf{v}_1, \mathbf{v}_2, \ldots, \mathbf{v}_p\}$ is a linearly dependent set. If the trivial solution is the only solution, then $\{\mathbf{v}_1, \mathbf{v}_2, \ldots, \mathbf{v}_p\}$ is a linearly independent set.

EXAMPLE 2 Determine whether the set $\{\mathbf{v}_1, \mathbf{v}_2, \mathbf{v}_3\}$ is linearly independent or linearly dependent, where

$$\mathbf{v}_1 = \begin{bmatrix} 1 \\ 2 \\ 3 \end{bmatrix}, \quad \mathbf{v}_2 = \begin{bmatrix} 2 \\ -1 \\ 4 \end{bmatrix}, \quad \text{and} \quad \mathbf{v}_3 = \begin{bmatrix} 0 \\ 5 \\ 2 \end{bmatrix}.$$

Solution To determine whether the set is linearly dependent, we must determine whether the vector equation

$$x_1\mathbf{v}_1 + x_2\mathbf{v}_2 + x_3\mathbf{v}_3 = \boldsymbol{\theta} \tag{7}$$

has a nontrivial solution. But Eq. (7) is equivalent to the (3×3) homogeneous system of equations $V\mathbf{x} = \boldsymbol{\theta}$, where $V = [\mathbf{v}_1, \mathbf{v}_2, \mathbf{v}_3]$. The augmented matrix, $[V \mid \boldsymbol{\theta}]$, for this system is

$$\begin{bmatrix} 1 & 2 & 0 & 0 \\ 2 & -1 & 5 & 0 \\ 3 & 4 & 2 & 0 \end{bmatrix}.$$

This matrix reduces to

$$\begin{bmatrix} 1 & 0 & 2 & 0 \\ 0 & 1 & -1 & 0 \\ 0 & 0 & 0 & 0 \end{bmatrix}.$$

Therefore, we find the solution $x_1 = -2x_3$, $x_2 = x_3$, where x_3 is arbitrary. In particular, Eq. (7) has nontrivial solutions, so $\{\mathbf{v}_1, \mathbf{v}_2, \mathbf{v}_3\}$ is a linearly dependent set. Setting $x_3 = 1$, for example, gives $x_1 = -2$, $x_2 = 1$. Therefore,

$$-2\mathbf{v}_1 + \mathbf{v}_2 + \mathbf{v}_3 = \boldsymbol{\theta}.$$

Note that from this equation we can express $\mathbf{v}_3$ as a linear combination of $\mathbf{v}_1$ and $\mathbf{v}_2$:

$$\mathbf{v}_3 = 2\mathbf{v}_1 - \mathbf{v}_2.$$

Similarly, of course, $\mathbf{v}_1$ can be expressed as a linear combination of $\mathbf{v}_2$ and $\mathbf{v}_3$, and $\mathbf{v}_2$ can be expressed as a linear combination of $\mathbf{v}_1$ and $\mathbf{v}_3$. ■

EXAMPLE 3 Determine whether or not the set $\{\mathbf{v}_1, \mathbf{v}_2, \mathbf{v}_3\}$ is linearly dependent, where

$$\mathbf{v}_1 = \begin{bmatrix} 1 \\ 2 \\ -3 \end{bmatrix}, \quad \mathbf{v}_2 = \begin{bmatrix} -2 \\ 1 \\ 1 \end{bmatrix}, \quad \text{and} \quad \mathbf{v}_3 = \begin{bmatrix} 1 \\ -1 \\ -2 \end{bmatrix}.$$

Solution If $V = [\mathbf{v}_1, \mathbf{v}_2, \mathbf{v}_3]$, then the augmented matrix $[V \mid \boldsymbol{\theta}]$ is row equivalent to

$$\begin{bmatrix} 1 & 0 & 0 & 0 \\ 0 & 1 & 0 & 0 \\ 0 & 0 & 1 & 0 \end{bmatrix}.$$

Thus the only solution of $x_1\mathbf{v}_1 + x_2\mathbf{v}_2 + x_3\mathbf{v}_3 = \boldsymbol{\theta}$ is the trivial solution $x_1 = x_2 = x_3 = 0$; so the set $\{\mathbf{v}_1, \mathbf{v}_2, \mathbf{v}_3\}$ is linearly independent.

In contrast to the preceding example, note that $\mathbf{v}_3$ cannot be expressed as a linear combination of $\mathbf{v}_1$ and $\mathbf{v}_2$. If there were scalars a_1 and a_2 such that

$$\mathbf{v}_3 = a_1\mathbf{v}_1 + a_2\mathbf{v}_2,$$

then there would be a nontrivial solution to $x_1\mathbf{v}_1 + x_2\mathbf{v}_2 + x_3\mathbf{v}_3 = \boldsymbol{\theta}$; namely, $x_1 = -a_1$, $x_2 = -a_2$, $x_3 = 1$. ■

We note that a set of vectors is linearly dependent if and only if one of the vectors is a linear combination of the remaining ones (see the exercises). It is also worth noting

THE VECTOR SPACE R^n, $n > 3$ The extension of vectors and their corresponding algebra into more than three dimensions was an extremely important step in the development of mathematics. This advancement is attributed largely to Hermann Grassmann (1809–1877) in his *Ausdehnungslehre*. In this work Grassmann discussed linear independence and dependence and many concepts dealing with the algebraic structure of R^n (such as dimension and subspaces), which we will study in Chapter 3. Unfortunately, Grassmann's work was so difficult to read that it went almost unnoticed for a long period of time, and he did not receive as much credit as he deserved.

that any set of vectors that contains the zero vector is linearly dependent (again, see the exercises).

The ***unit vectors*** $\mathbf{e}_1, \mathbf{e}_2, \ldots, \mathbf{e}_n$ in R^n are defined by

$$\mathbf{e}_1 = \begin{bmatrix} 1 \\ 0 \\ 0 \\ \vdots \\ 0 \end{bmatrix}, \quad \mathbf{e}_2 = \begin{bmatrix} 0 \\ 1 \\ 0 \\ \vdots \\ 0 \end{bmatrix}, \quad \mathbf{e}_3 = \begin{bmatrix} 0 \\ 0 \\ 1 \\ \vdots \\ 0 \end{bmatrix}, \quad \ldots, \quad \mathbf{e}_n = \begin{bmatrix} 0 \\ 0 \\ 0 \\ \vdots \\ 1 \end{bmatrix}. \tag{8}$$

It is easy to see that $\{\mathbf{e}_1, \mathbf{e}_2, \ldots, \mathbf{e}_n\}$ is linearly independent. To illustrate, consider the unit vectors

$$\mathbf{e}_1 = \begin{bmatrix} 1 \\ 0 \\ 0 \end{bmatrix}, \quad \mathbf{e}_2 = \begin{bmatrix} 0 \\ 1 \\ 0 \end{bmatrix}, \quad \text{and} \quad \mathbf{e}_3 = \begin{bmatrix} 0 \\ 0 \\ 1 \end{bmatrix}$$

in R^3. If $V = [\mathbf{e}_1, \mathbf{e}_2, \mathbf{e}_3]$, then

$$[V \mid \boldsymbol{\theta}] = \begin{bmatrix} 1 & 0 & 0 & 0 \\ 0 & 1 & 0 & 0 \\ 0 & 0 & 1 & 0 \end{bmatrix},$$

so clearly the only solution of $V\mathbf{x} = \boldsymbol{\theta}$ (or equivalently, of $x_1\mathbf{e}_1 + x_2\mathbf{e}_2 + x_3\mathbf{e}_3 = \boldsymbol{\theta}$) is the trivial solution $x_1 = 0, x_2 = 0, x_3 = 0$.

The next example illustrates that, in some cases, the linear dependence of a set of vectors can be determined by inspection. The example is a special case of Theorem 11, which follows.

EXAMPLE 4 Let $\{\mathbf{v}_1, \mathbf{v}_2, \mathbf{v}_3\}$ be the set of vectors in R^2 given by

$$\mathbf{v}_1 = \begin{bmatrix} 1 \\ 2 \end{bmatrix}, \quad \mathbf{v}_2 = \begin{bmatrix} 3 \\ 1 \end{bmatrix}, \quad \text{and} \quad \mathbf{v}_3 = \begin{bmatrix} 2 \\ 3 \end{bmatrix}.$$

Without solving the corresponding homogeneous system of equations, show that the set is linearly dependent.

Solution The vector equation $x_1\mathbf{v}_1 + x_2\mathbf{v}_2 + x_3\mathbf{v}_3 = \boldsymbol{\theta}$ is equivalent to the homogeneous system of equations $V\mathbf{x} = \boldsymbol{\theta}$, where $V = [\mathbf{v}_1, \mathbf{v}_2, \mathbf{v}_3]$. But this is the homogeneous system

$$\begin{aligned} x_1 + 3x_2 + 2x_3 &= 0 \\ 2x_1 + x_2 + 3x_3 &= 0, \end{aligned}$$

consisting of two equations in three unknowns. By Theorem 4 of Section 1.3, the system has nontrivial solutions; hence the set $\{\mathbf{v}_1, \mathbf{v}_2, \mathbf{v}_3\}$ is linearly dependent. ■

Example 4 is a particular case of the following general result.

THEOREM 11 Let $\{\mathbf{v}_1, \mathbf{v}_2, \ldots, \mathbf{v}_p\}$ be a set of vectors in R^m. If $p > m$, then this set is linearly dependent.

Proof The set $\{\mathbf{v}_1, \mathbf{v}_2, \ldots, \mathbf{v}_p\}$ is linearly dependent if the equation $V\mathbf{x} = \boldsymbol{\theta}$ has a nontrivial solution, where $V = [\mathbf{v}_1, \mathbf{v}_2, \ldots, \mathbf{v}_p]$. But $V\mathbf{x} = \boldsymbol{\theta}$ represents a homogeneous $(m \times p)$ system of linear equations with $m < p$. By Theorem 4 of Section 1.3, $V\mathbf{x} = \boldsymbol{\theta}$ has nontrivial solutions. ■

Note that Theorem 11 does not say that if $p \le m$, then the set $\{\mathbf{v}_1, \mathbf{v}_2, \ldots, \mathbf{v}_p\}$ is linearly independent. Indeed Examples 2 and 3 illustrate that if $p \le m$, then the set may be either linearly independent or linearly dependent.

Nonsingular Matrices

The concept of linear independence allows us to state precisely which $(n \times n)$ systems of linear equations always have a unique solution. We begin with the following definition.

DEFINITION 12 An $(n \times n)$ matrix A is ***nonsingular*** if the only solution to $A\mathbf{x} = \boldsymbol{\theta}$ is $\mathbf{x} = \boldsymbol{\theta}$. Furthermore, A is said to be ***singular*** if A is not nonsingular.

If $A = [\mathbf{A}_1, \mathbf{A}_2, \ldots, \mathbf{A}_n]$, then $A\mathbf{x} = \boldsymbol{\theta}$ can be written as

$$x_1\mathbf{A}_1 + x_2\mathbf{A}_2 + \cdots + x_n\mathbf{A}_n = \boldsymbol{\theta},$$

so it is an immediate consequence of Definition 12 that A is nonsingular if and only if the column vectors of A form a linearly independent set. This observation is important enough to be stated as a theorem.

THEOREM 12 The $(n \times n)$ matrix $A = [\mathbf{A}_1, \mathbf{A}_2, \ldots, \mathbf{A}_n]$ is nonsingular if and only if $\{\mathbf{A}_1, \mathbf{A}_2, \ldots, \mathbf{A}_n\}$ is a linearly independent set. ■

EXAMPLE 5 Determine whether each of the matrices

$$A = \begin{bmatrix} 1 & 3 \\ 2 & 2 \end{bmatrix} \quad \text{and} \quad B = \begin{bmatrix} 1 & 2 \\ 2 & 4 \end{bmatrix}$$

is singular or nonsingular.

Solution The augmented matrix $[A \mid \boldsymbol{\theta}]$ for the system $A\mathbf{x} = \boldsymbol{\theta}$ is row equivalent to

$$\begin{bmatrix} 1 & 0 & 0 \\ 0 & 1 & 0 \end{bmatrix},$$

so the trivial solution $x_1 = 0, x_2 = 0$ (or $\mathbf{x} = \boldsymbol{\theta}$) is the unique solution. Thus A is nonsingular.

The augmented matrix $[B \mid \boldsymbol{\theta}]$ for the system $B\mathbf{x} = \boldsymbol{\theta}$ is row equivalent to

$$\begin{bmatrix} 1 & 2 & 0 \\ 0 & 0 & 0 \end{bmatrix}.$$

Thus, B is singular because the vector

$$\mathbf{x} = \begin{bmatrix} -2 \\ 1 \end{bmatrix}$$

is a nontrivial solution of $B\mathbf{x} = \boldsymbol{\theta}$. Equivalently, the columns of B are linearly dependent because

$$-2\mathbf{B}_1 + \mathbf{B}_2 = \boldsymbol{\theta}.$$ ■

The next theorem demonstrates the importance of nonsingular matrices with respect to linear systems.

THEOREM 13 Let A be an $(n \times n)$ matrix. The equation $A\mathbf{x} = \mathbf{b}$ has a unique solution for every $(n \times 1)$ column vector $\mathbf{b}$ if and only if A is nonsingular.

Proof Suppose first that $A\mathbf{x} = \mathbf{b}$ has a unique solution no matter what choice we make for $\mathbf{b}$. Choosing $\mathbf{b} = \boldsymbol{\theta}$ implies, by Definition 12, that A is nonsingular.

Conversely, suppose that $A = [\mathbf{A}_1, \mathbf{A}_2, \dots, \mathbf{A}_n]$ is nonsingular, and let $\mathbf{b}$ be any $(n \times 1)$ column vector. We first show that $A\mathbf{x} = \mathbf{b}$ has a solution. To see this, observe first that

$$\{\mathbf{A}_1, \mathbf{A}_2, \dots, \mathbf{A}_n, \mathbf{b}\}$$

is a set of $(n \times 1)$ vectors in R^n; so by Theorem 11 this set is linearly dependent. Thus there are scalars $a_1, a_2, \dots, a_n, a_{n+1}$ such that

$$a_1\mathbf{A}_1 + a_2\mathbf{A}_2 + \cdots + a_n\mathbf{A}_n + a_{n+1}\mathbf{b} = \boldsymbol{\theta}; \tag{9}$$

and moreover not all these scalars are zero. In fact, if $a_{n+1} = 0$ in Eq. (9), then

$$a_1\mathbf{A}_1 + a_2\mathbf{A}_2 + \cdots + a_n\mathbf{A}_n = \boldsymbol{\theta},$$

and it follows that $\{\mathbf{A}_1, \mathbf{A}_2, \dots, \mathbf{A}_n\}$ is a linearly dependent set. Since this contradicts the assumption that A is nonsingular, we know that a_{n+1} is nonzero. It follows from Eq. (9) that

$$s_1\mathbf{A}_1 + s_2\mathbf{A}_2 + \cdots + s_n\mathbf{A}_n = \mathbf{b},$$

where

$$s_1 = \frac{-a_1}{a_{n+1}}, \quad s_2 = \frac{-a_2}{a_{n+1}}, \dots, \quad s_n = \frac{-a_n}{a_{n+1}}.$$

Thus $A\mathbf{x} = \mathbf{b}$ has a solution $\mathbf{s}$ given by

$$\mathbf{s} = \begin{bmatrix} s_1 \\ s_2 \\ \vdots \\ s_n \end{bmatrix}.$$

This shows that $A\mathbf{x} = \mathbf{b}$ is always consistent when A is nonsingular.

To show that the solution is unique, suppose that the $(n \times 1)$ vector $\mathbf{u}$ is any solution whatsoever to $A\mathbf{x} = \mathbf{b}$; that is, $A\mathbf{u} = \mathbf{b}$. Then $A\mathbf{s} - A\mathbf{u} = \mathbf{b} - \mathbf{b}$, or

$$A(\mathbf{s} - \mathbf{u}) = \boldsymbol{\theta};$$

therefore, $\mathbf{y} = \mathbf{s} - \mathbf{u}$ is a solution to $A\mathbf{x} = \boldsymbol{\theta}$. But A is nonsingular, so $\mathbf{y} = \boldsymbol{\theta}$; that is $\mathbf{s} = \mathbf{u}$. Thus $A\mathbf{x} = \mathbf{b}$ has one, and only one, solution. ■

In closing we note that for a specific system $A\mathbf{x} = \mathbf{b}$, it is usually easier to demonstrate the existence and/or uniqueness of a solution by using Gaussian elimination and actually solving the system. There are many instances, however, in which theoretical information about existence and uniqueness is extremely valuable to practical computations. A specific instance of this is provided in the next section.

1.7 EXERCISES

The vectors listed in Eq. (10) are used in several of the exercises that follow.

$$\mathbf{v}_1 = \begin{bmatrix} 1 \\ 2 \end{bmatrix}, \quad \mathbf{v}_2 = \begin{bmatrix} 2 \\ 3 \end{bmatrix}, \quad \mathbf{v}_3 = \begin{bmatrix} 2 \\ 4 \end{bmatrix},$$

$$\mathbf{v}_4 = \begin{bmatrix} 1 \\ 1 \end{bmatrix}, \quad \mathbf{v}_5 = \begin{bmatrix} 3 \\ 6 \end{bmatrix},$$

$$\mathbf{u}_0 = \begin{bmatrix} 1 \\ 0 \\ 0 \end{bmatrix}, \quad \mathbf{u}_1 = \begin{bmatrix} 1 \\ 2 \\ -1 \end{bmatrix}, \quad \mathbf{u}_2 = \begin{bmatrix} 2 \\ 1 \\ -3 \end{bmatrix},$$

$$\mathbf{u}_3 = \begin{bmatrix} -1 \\ 4 \\ 3 \end{bmatrix}, \quad \mathbf{u}_4 = \begin{bmatrix} 4 \\ 4 \\ 0 \end{bmatrix}, \quad \mathbf{u}_5 = \begin{bmatrix} 1 \\ 1 \\ 0 \end{bmatrix} \qquad (10)$$

In Exercises 1–14, use Eq. (6) to determine whether the given set of vectors is linearly independent or linearly dependent. If the set is linearly dependent, express one vector in the set as a linear combination of the others.

1. $\{\mathbf{v}_1, \mathbf{v}_2\}$ **2.** $\{\mathbf{v}_1, \mathbf{v}_3\}$

3. $\{\mathbf{v}_1, \mathbf{v}_5\}$ **4.** $\{\mathbf{v}_2, \mathbf{v}_3\}$

5. $\{\mathbf{v}_1, \mathbf{v}_2, \mathbf{v}_3\}$ **6.** $\{\mathbf{v}_2, \mathbf{v}_3, \mathbf{v}_4\}$

7. $\{\mathbf{u}_4, \mathbf{u}_5\}$ **8.** $\{\mathbf{u}_3, \mathbf{u}_4\}$

9. $\{\mathbf{u}_1, \mathbf{u}_2, \mathbf{u}_5\}$ **10.** $\{\mathbf{u}_1, \mathbf{u}_4, \mathbf{u}_5\}$

11. $\{\mathbf{u}_2, \mathbf{u}_4, \mathbf{u}_5\}$ **12.** $\{\mathbf{u}_1, \mathbf{u}_2, \mathbf{u}_4\}$

13. $\{\mathbf{u}_0, \mathbf{u}_1, \mathbf{u}_2, \mathbf{u}_4\}$ **14.** $\{\mathbf{u}_0, \mathbf{u}_2, \mathbf{u}_3, \mathbf{u}_4\}$

15. Consider the sets of vectors in Exercises 1–14. Using Theorem 11, determine by inspection which of these sets are known to be linearly dependent.

The matrices listed in Eq. (11) are used in some of the exercises that follow.

$$A = \begin{bmatrix} 1 & 2 \\ 3 & 4 \end{bmatrix}, \quad B = \begin{bmatrix} 1 & 2 \\ 2 & 4 \end{bmatrix}, \quad C = \begin{bmatrix} 1 & 3 \\ 2 & 4 \end{bmatrix},$$

$$D = \begin{bmatrix} 1 & 0 & 0 \\ 0 & 1 & 0 \\ 0 & 1 & 0 \end{bmatrix}, \quad E = \begin{bmatrix} 0 & 1 & 0 \\ 0 & 0 & 2 \\ 0 & 1 & 3 \end{bmatrix},$$

$$F = \begin{bmatrix} 1 & 2 & 1 \\ 0 & 3 & 2 \\ 0 & 0 & 1 \end{bmatrix} \qquad (11)$$

In Exercises 16–27, use Definition 12 to determine whether the given matrix is singular or nonsingular. If a matrix M is singular, give all solutions of $M\mathbf{x} = \boldsymbol{\theta}$.

16. A **17.** B **18.** C
19. AB **20.** BA **21.** D
22. F **23.** $D + F$ **24.** E
25. EF **26.** DE **27.** F^T

In Exercises 28–33, determine conditions on the scalars so that the set of vectors is linearly dependent.

28. $\mathbf{v}_1 = \begin{bmatrix} 1 \\ a \end{bmatrix}$, $\mathbf{v}_2 = \begin{bmatrix} 2 \\ 3 \end{bmatrix}$

29. $\mathbf{v}_1 = \begin{bmatrix} 1 \\ 2 \end{bmatrix}$, $\mathbf{v}_2 = \begin{bmatrix} 3 \\ a \end{bmatrix}$

30. $\mathbf{v}_1 = \begin{bmatrix} 1 \\ 2 \\ 1 \end{bmatrix}$, $\mathbf{v}_2 = \begin{bmatrix} 1 \\ 3 \\ 2 \end{bmatrix}$, $\mathbf{v}_3 = \begin{bmatrix} 0 \\ 1 \\ a \end{bmatrix}$

31. $\mathbf{v}_1 = \begin{bmatrix} 1 \\ 2 \\ 1 \end{bmatrix}$, $\mathbf{v}_2 = \begin{bmatrix} 1 \\ a \\ 3 \end{bmatrix}$, $\mathbf{v}_3 = \begin{bmatrix} 0 \\ 2 \\ b \end{bmatrix}$

32. $\mathbf{v}_1 = \begin{bmatrix} a \\ 1 \end{bmatrix}$, $\mathbf{v}_2 = \begin{bmatrix} b \\ 3 \end{bmatrix}$

33. $\mathbf{v}_1 = \begin{bmatrix} 1 \\ a \end{bmatrix}$, $\mathbf{v}_2 = \begin{bmatrix} b \\ c \end{bmatrix}$

In Exercises 34–39, the vectors and matrices are from Eq. (10) and Eq. (11). The equations listed in Exercises 34–39 all have the form $M\mathbf{x} = \mathbf{b}$, and all the equations are consistent. In each exercise, solve the equation and express $\mathbf{b}$ as a linear combination of the columns of M.

34. $A\mathbf{x} = \mathbf{v}_1$ **35.** $A\mathbf{x} = \mathbf{v}_3$
36. $C\mathbf{x} = \mathbf{v}_4$ **37.** $C\mathbf{x} = \mathbf{v}_2$
38. $F\mathbf{x} = \mathbf{u}_1$ **39.** $F\mathbf{x} = \mathbf{u}_3$

In Exercises 40–45, express the given vector $\mathbf{b}$ as a linear combination of $\mathbf{v}_1$ and $\mathbf{v}_2$, where $\mathbf{v}_1$ and $\mathbf{v}_2$ are in Eq. (10).

40. $\mathbf{b} = \begin{bmatrix} 2 \\ 7 \end{bmatrix}$ **41.** $\mathbf{b} = \begin{bmatrix} 3 \\ -1 \end{bmatrix}$

42. $\mathbf{b} = \begin{bmatrix} 0 \\ 4 \end{bmatrix}$ **43.** $\mathbf{b} = \begin{bmatrix} 0 \\ 0 \end{bmatrix}$

44. $\mathbf{b} = \begin{bmatrix} 1 \\ 2 \end{bmatrix}$ **45.** $\mathbf{b} = \begin{bmatrix} 1 \\ 0 \end{bmatrix}$

In Exercises 46–47, let $S = \{\mathbf{v}_1, \mathbf{v}_2, \mathbf{v}_3\}$.

a) For what value(s) a is the set S linearly dependent?

b) For what value(s) a can $\mathbf{v}_3$ be expressed as a linear combination of $\mathbf{v}_1$ and $\mathbf{v}_2$?

46. $\mathbf{v}_1 = \begin{bmatrix} 1 \\ -1 \end{bmatrix}$, $\mathbf{v}_2 = \begin{bmatrix} -2 \\ 2 \end{bmatrix}$, $\mathbf{v}_3 = \begin{bmatrix} 3 \\ a \end{bmatrix}$

47. $\mathbf{v}_1 = \begin{bmatrix} 1 \\ 0 \end{bmatrix}$, $\mathbf{v}_2 = \begin{bmatrix} 1 \\ 1 \end{bmatrix}$, $\mathbf{v}_3 = \begin{bmatrix} 3 \\ a \end{bmatrix}$

48. Let $S = \{\mathbf{v}_1, \mathbf{v}_2, \mathbf{v}_3\}$ be a set of vectors in R^3, where $\mathbf{v}_1 = \boldsymbol{\theta}$. Show that S is a linearly dependent set of vectors. [*Hint:* Exhibit a nontrivial solution for either Eq. (5) or Eq. (6).)]

49. Let $\{\mathbf{v}_1, \mathbf{v}_2, \mathbf{v}_3\}$ be a set of nonzero vectors in R^m such that $\mathbf{v}_i^T\mathbf{v}_j = 0$ when $i \neq j$. Show that the set is linearly independent. [*Hint:* Set $a_1\mathbf{v}_1 + a_2\mathbf{v}_2 + a_3\mathbf{v}_3 = \boldsymbol{\theta}$ and consider $\boldsymbol{\theta}^T\boldsymbol{\theta}$.]

50. If the set $\{\mathbf{v}_1, \mathbf{v}_2, \mathbf{v}_3\}$ of vectors in R^m is linearly dependent, then argue that the set $\{\mathbf{v}_1, \mathbf{v}_2, \mathbf{v}_3, \mathbf{v}_4\}$ is also linearly dependent for every choice of $\mathbf{v}_4$ in R^m.

51. Suppose that $\{\mathbf{v}_1, \mathbf{v}_2, \mathbf{v}_3\}$ is a linearly independent subset of R^m. Show that the set $\{\mathbf{v}_1, \mathbf{v}_1 + \mathbf{v}_2, \mathbf{v}_1 + \mathbf{v}_2 + \mathbf{v}_3\}$ is also linearly independent.

52. If A and B are $(n \times n)$ matrices such that A is nonsingular and $AB = \mathcal{O}$, then prove that $B = \mathcal{O}$. [*Hint:* Write $B = [\mathbf{B}_1, \ldots, \mathbf{B}_n]$ and consider $AB = [A\mathbf{B}_1, \ldots, A\mathbf{B}_n]$.]

53. If A, B, and C are $(n \times n)$ matrices such that A is nonsingular and $AB = AC$, then prove that $B = C$. [*Hint:* Consider $A(B - C)$ and use the preceding exercise.]

54. Let $A = [\mathbf{A}_1, \ldots, \mathbf{A}_{n-1}]$ be an $(n \times (n-1))$ matrix. Show that $B = [\mathbf{A}_1, \ldots, \mathbf{A}_{n-1}, A\mathbf{b}]$ is singular for every choice of $\mathbf{b}$ in R^{n-1}.

55. Suppose that C and B are (2×2) matrices and that B is singular. Show that CB is singular. [*Hint:* By Definition 12, there is a vector $\mathbf{x}_1$ in R^2, $\mathbf{x}_1 \neq \boldsymbol{\theta}$, such that $B\mathbf{x}_1 = \boldsymbol{\theta}$.]

56. Let $\{\mathbf{w}_1, \mathbf{w}_2\}$ be a linearly independent set of vectors in R^2. Show that if $\mathbf{b}$ is any vector in R^2, then $\mathbf{b}$ is a linear combination of $\mathbf{w}_1$ and $\mathbf{w}_2$. [*Hint:* Consider the (2×2) matrix $A = [\mathbf{w}_1, \mathbf{w}_2]$.]

57. Let A be an $(n \times n)$ nonsingular matrix. Show that A^T is nonsingular as follows:

a) Suppose that $\mathbf{v}$ is a vector in R^n such that $A^T\mathbf{v} = \boldsymbol{\theta}$. Cite a theorem from this section that guarantees there is a vector $\mathbf{w}$ in R^n such that $A\mathbf{w} = \mathbf{v}$.

b) By part (a), $A^TA\mathbf{w} = \boldsymbol{\theta}$, and therefore $\mathbf{w}^TA^TA\mathbf{w} = \mathbf{w}^T\boldsymbol{\theta} = 0$. Cite results from Section 1.6 that allow you to conclude that $\|A\mathbf{w}\| = 0$. [*Hint:* What is $(A\mathbf{w})^T$?]

c) Use parts (a) and (b) to conclude that if $A^T\mathbf{v} = \boldsymbol{\theta}$, then $\mathbf{v} = \boldsymbol{\theta}$; this shows that A^T is nonsingular.

58. Let T be an $(n \times n)$ upper-triangular matrix

$$T = \begin{bmatrix} t_{11} & t_{12} & t_{13} & \cdots & t_{1n} \\ 0 & t_{22} & t_{23} & \cdots & t_{2n} \\ 0 & 0 & t_{33} & \cdots & t_{3n} \\ \vdots & & & & \vdots \\ 0 & 0 & 0 & \cdots & t_{nn} \end{bmatrix}.$$

Prove that if $t_{ii} = 0$ for some i, $1 \le i \le n$, then T is singular. [*Hint:* If $t_{11} = 0$, find a nonzero vector $\mathbf{v}$ such that $T\mathbf{v} = \boldsymbol{\theta}$. If $t_{rr} = 0$, but $t_{ii} \ne 0$ for $1, 2, \ldots, r-1$, use Theorem 4 of Section 1.3 to show that columns $\mathbf{T}_1, \mathbf{T}_2, \ldots, \mathbf{T}_r$ of T are linearly dependent. Then select a nonzero vector $\mathbf{v}$ such that $T\mathbf{v} = \boldsymbol{\theta}$.]

59. Let T be an $(n \times n)$ upper-triangular matrix as in Exercise 58. Prove that if $t_{ii} \ne 0$ for $i = 1, 2, \ldots, n$, then T is nonsingular. [*Hint:* Let $T = [\mathbf{T}_1, \mathbf{T}_2, \ldots, \mathbf{T}_n]$, and suppose that $a_1\mathbf{T}_1 + a_2\mathbf{T}_2 + \cdots + a_n\mathbf{T}_n = \boldsymbol{\theta}$ for some scalars $a_1, a_2, \ldots, a_n$. First deduce that $a_n = 0$. Next show $a_{n-1} = 0$, and so on.] Note that Exercises 58 and 59 establish that an upper-triangular matrix is singular if and only if one of the entries $t_{11}, t_{22}, \ldots, t_{nn}$ is zero. By Exercise 57 the same result is true for lower-triangular matrices.

60. Suppose that the $(n \times n)$ matrices A and B are row equivalent. Prove that A is nonsingular if and only if B is nonsingular. [*Hint:* The homogeneous systems $A\mathbf{x} = \boldsymbol{\theta}$ and $B\mathbf{x} = \boldsymbol{\theta}$ are equivalent by Theorem 1 of Section 1.1.]

1.8 DATA FITTING, NUMERICAL INTEGRATION, AND NUMERICAL DIFFERENTIATION (OPTIONAL)

In this section we present four applications of matrix theory toward the solution of a practical problem. Three of the applications involve numerical approximation techniques, and the fourth relates to solving certain types of differential equations. In each case, solving the general problem depends on being able to solve a system of linear equations, and the theory of nonsingular matrices will guarantee that a solution exists and is unique.

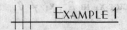

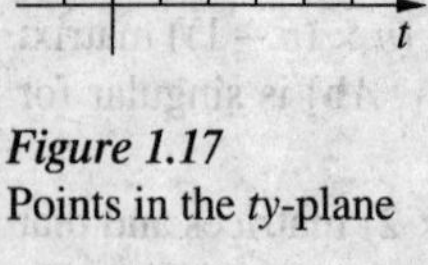

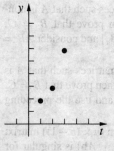

Figure 1.17
Points in the *ty*-plane

Polynomial Interpolation

We begin by applying matrix theory to the problem of interpolating data with polynomials. In particular, Theorem 13 of Section 1.7 is used to establish a general existence and uniqueness result for polynomial interpolation. The following example is a simple illustration of polynomial interpolation.

EXAMPLE 1 Find a quadratic polynomial, $q(t)$, such that the graph of $q(t)$ goes through the points $(1, 2)$, $(2, 3)$, and $(3, 6)$ in the ty-plane (see Fig. 1.17).

Solution A quadratic polynomial $q(t)$ has the form

$$q(t) = a + bt + ct^2, \tag{1a}$$

so our problem reduces to determining constants a, b, and c such that

$$\begin{aligned} q(1) &= 2 \\ q(2) &= 3 \\ q(3) &= 6. \end{aligned} \tag{1b}$$

The constraints in (1b) are, by (1a), equivalent to

$$\begin{aligned} a + b + c &= 2 \\ a + 2b + 4c &= 3 \\ a + 3b + 9c &= 6. \end{aligned} \tag{1c}$$

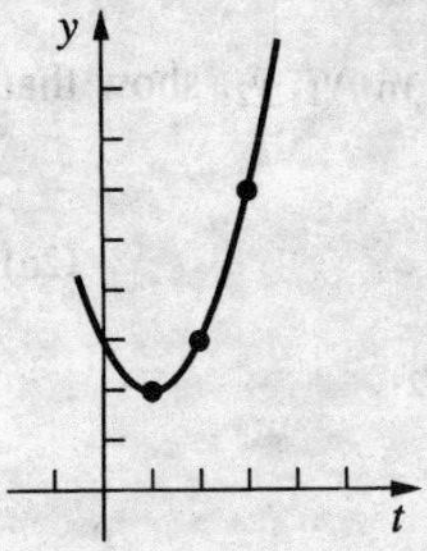

Figure 1.18
Graph of $q(t)$

Clearly (1c) is a system of three linear equations in the three unknowns a, b, and c; so solving (1c) will determine the polynomial $q(t)$. Solving (1c), we find the unique solution $a = 3$, $b = -2$, $c = 1$; therefore, $q(t) = 3 - 2t + t^2$ is the unique quadratic polynomial satisfying the conditions (1b). A portion of the graph of $q(t)$ is shown in Fig. 1.18. ∎

Table 1.1

t	$f(t)$
t_0	y_0
t_1	y_1
t_2	y_2
$\vdots$	$\vdots$
t_n	y_n

Frequently polynomial interpolation is used when values of a function $f(t)$ are given in tabular form. For example, given a table of $n + 1$ values of $f(t)$ (see Table 1.1), an ***interpolating polynomial*** for $f(t)$ is a polynomial, $p(t)$, of the form

$$p(t) = a_0 + a_1 t + a_2 t^2 + \cdots + a_n t^n$$

such that $p(t_i) = y_i = f(t_i)$ for $0 \le i \le n$. Problems of interpolating data in tables are quite common in scientific and engineering work; for example, $y = f(t)$ might describe a temperature distribution as a function of time with $y_i = f(t_i)$ being observed (measured) temperatures. For a time $\hat{t}$ not listed in the table, $p(\hat{t})$ provides an approximation for $f(\hat{t})$.

EXAMPLE 2 Find an interpolating polynomial for the four observations given in Table 1.2. Give an approximation for $f(1.5)$.

Solution In this case, the interpolating polynomial is a polynomial of degree 3 or less,

$$p(t) = a_0 + a_1 t + a_2 t^2 + a_3 t^3,$$

Table 1.2

t	$f(t)$
0	3
1	0
2	−1
3	6

where $p(t)$ satisfies the four constraints $p(0) = 3$, $p(1) = 0$, $p(2) = -1$, and $p(3) = 6$. As in the previous example, these constraints are equivalent to the (4×4) system of equations

$$\begin{aligned} a_0 \qquad\qquad\qquad &= 3 \\ a_0 + a_1 + a_2 + a_3 &= 0 \\ a_0 + 2a_1 + 4a_2 + 8a_3 &= -1 \\ a_0 + 3a_1 + 9a_2 + 27a_3 &= 6. \end{aligned}$$

Solving this system, we find that $a_0 = 3$, $a_1 = -2$, $a_2 = -2$, $a_3 = 1$ is the unique solution. Hence the unique polynomial that interpolates the tabular data for $f(t)$ is

$$p(t) = 3 - 2t - 2t^2 + t^3.$$

The desired approximation for $f(1.5)$ is $p(1.5) = -1.125$. ∎

Note that in each of the two preceding examples, the interpolating polynomial was unique. Theorem 14, on page 83, states that this is always the case. The next example considers the general problem of fitting a quadratic polynomial to three data points and illustrates the proof of Theorem 14.

EXAMPLE 3 Given three distinct numbers t_0, t_1, t_2 and any set of three values y_0, y_1, y_2, show that there exists a unique polynomial,

$$p(t) = a_0 + a_1 t + a_2 t^2, \tag{2a}$$

of degree 2 or less such that $p(t_0) = y_0$, $p(t_1) = y_1$, and $p(t_2) = y_2$.

Solution The given constraints and (2a) define a (3×3) linear system,

$$\begin{aligned} a_0 + a_1 t_0 + a_2 t_0^2 &= y_0 \\ a_0 + a_1 t_1 + a_2 t_1^2 &= y_1 \\ a_0 + a_1 t_2 + a_2 t_2^2 &= y_2, \end{aligned} \tag{2b}$$

where a_0, a_1, and a_2 are the unknowns. The problem is to show that system (2b) has a unique solution. We can write system (2b) in matrix form as $T\mathbf{a} = \mathbf{y}$, where

$$T = \begin{bmatrix} 1 & t_0 & t_0^2 \\ 1 & t_1 & t_1^2 \\ 1 & t_2 & t_2^2 \end{bmatrix}, \quad \mathbf{a} = \begin{bmatrix} a_0 \\ a_1 \\ a_2 \end{bmatrix}, \quad \text{and} \quad \mathbf{y} = \begin{bmatrix} y_0 \\ y_1 \\ y_2 \end{bmatrix}. \tag{2c}$$

By Theorem 13, the system is guaranteed to have a unique solution if T is nonsingular. To establish that T is nonsingular, it suffices to show that if

$$\mathbf{c} = \begin{bmatrix} c_0 \\ c_1 \\ c_2 \end{bmatrix}$$

is a solution to the homogeneous system $T\mathbf{x} = \boldsymbol{\theta}$, then $\mathbf{c} = \boldsymbol{\theta}$. But $T\mathbf{c} = \boldsymbol{\theta}$ is equivalent to

$$\begin{aligned} c_0 + c_1 t_0 + c_2 t_0^2 &= 0 \\ c_0 + c_1 t_1 + c_2 t_1^2 &= 0 \\ c_0 + c_1 t_2 + c_2 t_2^2 &= 0. \end{aligned} \tag{2d}$$

Let $q(t) = c_0 + c_1 t + c_2 t^2$. Then $q(t)$ has degree at most 2 and, by system (2d), $q(t_0) = q(t_1) = q(t_2) = 0$. Thus $q(t)$ has three distinct real zeros. By Exercise 25, if a quadratic polynomial has three distinct real zeros, then it must be identically zero. That is, $c_0 = c_1 = c_2 = 0$, or $\mathbf{c} = \boldsymbol{\theta}$. Hence T is nonsingular, and so system (2b) has a unique solution. ■

The matrix T given in (2c) is the (3×3) Vandermonde matrix. More generally, for real numbers $t_0, t_1, \ldots, t_n$, the $[(n+1) \times (n+1)]$ ***Vandermonde matrix*** T

is defined by

$$T = \begin{bmatrix} 1 & t_0 & t_0^2 & \cdots & t_0^n \\ 1 & t_1 & t_1^2 & \cdots & t_1^n \\ \vdots & & & & \vdots \\ 1 & t_n & t_n^2 & \cdots & t_n^n \end{bmatrix}. \quad (3)$$

Following the argument given in Example 3 and making use of Exercise 26, we can show that if $t_0, t_1, \ldots, t_n$ are distinct, then T is nonsingular. Thus, by Theorem 13, the linear system $T\mathbf{x} = \mathbf{y}$ has a unique solution for each choice of $\mathbf{y}$ in R^{n+1}. As a consequence, we have the following theorem.

THEOREM 14 Given $n+1$ distinct numbers $t_0, t_1, \ldots, t_n$ and any set of $n+1$ values $y_0, y_1, \ldots, y_n$, there is one and only one polynomial $p(t)$ of degree n or less, $p(t) = a_0 + a_1 t + \cdots + a_n t^n$, such that $p(t_i) = y_i$, $i = 0, 1, \ldots, n$. ■

Solutions to Initial Value Problems

The following example provides yet another application of the fact that the Vandermonde matrix T given in (3) is nonsingular when $t_0, t_1, \ldots, t_n$ are distinct. Problems of this sort arise in solving initial value problems in differential equations.

EXAMPLE 4 Given $n + 1$ distinct numbers $t_0, t_1, \ldots, t_n$ and any set of $n + 1$ values $y_0, y_1, \ldots, y_n$, show that there is one, and only one, function that has the form

$$y = a_0 e^{t_0 x} + a_1 e^{t_1 x} + \cdots + a_n e^{t_n x} \quad (4a)$$

and that satisfies the constraints $y(0) = y_0$, $y'(0) = y_1, \ldots, y^{(n)}(0) = y_n$.

Solution Calculating the first n derivatives of y gives

$$\begin{aligned} y &= a_0 e^{t_0 x} + a_1 e^{t_1 x} + \cdots + a_n e^{t_n x} \\ y' &= a_0 t_0 e^{t_0 x} + a_1 t_1 e^{t_1 x} + \cdots + a_n t_n e^{t_n x} \\ y'' &= a_0 t_0^2 e^{t_0 x} + a_1 t_1^2 e^{t_1 x} + \cdots + a_n t_n^2 e^{t_n x} \\ &\vdots \\ y^{(n)} &= a_0 t_0^n e^{t_0 x} + a_1 t_1^n e^{t_1 x} + \cdots + a_n t_n^n e^{t_n x}. \end{aligned} \quad (4b)$$

Substituting $x = 0$ in each equation of system (4b) and setting $y^{(k)}(0) = y_k$ yields the system

$$\begin{aligned} y_0 &= a_0 + a_1 + \cdots + a_n \\ y_1 &= a_0 t_0 + a_1 t_1 + \cdots + a_n t_n \\ y_2 &= a_0 t_0^2 + a_1 t_1^2 + \cdots + a_n t_n^2 \\ &\vdots \\ y_n &= a_0 t_0^n + a_1 t_1^n + \cdots + a_n t_n^n \end{aligned} \quad (4c)$$

with unknowns $a_0, a_1, \ldots, a_n$. Note that the coefficient matrix for the linear system (4c) is

$$T^T = \begin{bmatrix} 1 & 1 & \cdots & 1 \\ t_0 & t_1 & \cdots & t_n \\ t_0^2 & t_1^2 & \cdots & t_n^2 \\ \vdots & & & \vdots \\ t_0^n & t_1^n & \cdots & t_n^n \end{bmatrix}, \tag{4d}$$

where T is the $[(n+1) \times (n+1)]$ Vandermonde matrix given in Eq. (3). It is left as an exercise (see Exercise 57 of Section 1.7) to show that because T is nonsingular, the transpose T^T is also nonsingular. Thus by Theorem 13, the linear system (4c) has a unique solution. ■

The next example is a specific case of Example 4.

EXAMPLE 5 Find the unique function $y = c_1e^x + c_2e^{2x} + c_3e^{3x}$ that satisfies the constraints $y(0) = 1$, $y'(0) = 2$, and $y''(0) = 0$.

Solution The given function and its first two derivatives are

$$\begin{aligned} y &= c_1e^x + c_2e^{2x} + c_3e^{3x} \\ y' &= c_1e^x + 2c_2e^{2x} + 3c_3e^{3x} \\ y'' &= c_1e^x + 4c_2e^{2x} + 9c_3e^{3x}. \end{aligned} \tag{5a}$$

From (5a) the given constraints are equivalent to

$$\begin{aligned} 1 &= c_1 + c_2 + c_3 \\ 2 &= c_1 + 2c_2 + 3c_3 \\ 0 &= c_1 + 4c_2 + 9c_3. \end{aligned} \tag{5b}$$

The augmented matrix for system (5b) is

$$\begin{bmatrix} 1 & 1 & 1 & 1 \\ 1 & 2 & 3 & 2 \\ 1 & 4 & 9 & 0 \end{bmatrix},$$

and solving in the usual manner yields the unique solution $c_1 = -2$, $c_2 = 5$, $c_3 = -2$. Therefore, the function $y = -2e^x + 5e^{2x} - 2e^{3x}$ is the unique function that satisfies the given constraints. ■

Numerical Integration

The Vandermonde matrix also arises in problems where it is necessary to estimate numerically an integral or a derivative. For example, let $I(f)$ denote the definite integral

$$I(f) = \int_a^b f(t)\,dt.$$

If the integrand is fairly complicated or if the integrand is not a standard form that can be found in a table of integrals, then it will be necessary to approximate the value $I(f)$ numerically.

One effective way to approximate $I(f)$ is first to find a polynomial p that approximates f on $[a, b]$,

$$p(t) \approx f(t), \qquad a \le t \le b.$$

Next, given that p is a good approximation to f, we would expect that the approximation that follows is also a good one:

$$\int_a^b p(t)\,dt \approx \int_a^b f(t)\,dt. \tag{6}$$

Of course, since p is a polynomial, the integral on the left-hand side of Eq. (6) can be easily evaluated and provides a computable estimate to the unknown integral, $I(f)$.

One way to generate a polynomial approximation to f is through interpolation. If we select $n + 1$ points $t_0, t_1, \ldots, t_n$ in $[a, b]$, then the nth-degree polynomial p that satisfies $p(t_i) = f(t_i), 0 \le i \le n$, is an approximation to f that can be used in Eq. (6) to estimate $I(f)$.

In summary, the numerical integration process proceeds as follows:

1. Given f, construct the interpolating polynomial, p.
2. Given p, calculate the integral, $\int_a^b p(t)\,dt$.
3. Use $\int_a^b p(t)\,dt$ as the approximation to $\int_a^b f(t)\,dt$.

It turns out that this approximation scheme can be simplified considerably, and step 1 can be skipped entirely. That is, it is not necessary to construct the actual interpolating polynomial p in order to know the integral of p, $\int_a^b p(t)\,dt$.

We will illustrate the idea with a quadratic interpolating polynomial. Suppose p is the quadratic polynomial that interpolates f at t_0, t_1, and t_2. Next, suppose we can find scalars A_0, A_1, A_2 such that

$$\begin{aligned} A_0 + A_1 + A_2 &= \int_a^b 1\,dt \\ A_0t_0 + A_1t_1 + A_2t_2 &= \int_a^b t\,dt \\ A_0t_0^2 + A_1t_1^2 + A_2t_2^2 &= \int_a^b t^2\,dt. \end{aligned} \tag{7}$$

Now, if the interpolating polynomial p is given by $p(t) = a_0 + a_1t + a_2t^2$, then the equations in (7) give

$$\begin{aligned}\int_a^b p(t)\,dt &= \int_a^b [a_0 + a_1 t + a_2 t^2]\,dt \\ &= a_0 \int_a^b 1\,dt + a_1 \int_a^b t\,dt + a_2 \int_a^b t^2\,dt \\ &= a_0 \sum_{i=0}^{2} A_i + a_1 \sum_{i=0}^{2} A_i t_i + a_2 \sum_{i=0}^{2} A_i t_i^2 \\ &= \sum_{i=0}^{2} A_i [a_0 + a_1 t_i + a_2 t_i^2] \\ &= \sum_{i=0}^{2} A_i p(t_i).\end{aligned}$$

The previous calculations demonstrate the following: If we know the values of a quadratic polynomial p at three points t_0, t_1, t_2 and if we can find scalars A_0, A_1, A_2 that satisfy system (7), then we can evaluate the integral of p with the formula

$$\int_a^b p(t)\,dt = \sum_{i=0}^{2} A_i p(t_i). \tag{8}$$

Next, since p is the quadratic interpolating polynomial for f, we see that the values of $p(t_i)$ are known to us; that is, $p(t_0) = f(t_0)$, $p(t_1) = f(t_1)$, and $p(t_2) = f(t_2)$. Thus, combining Eq. (8) and Eq. (6), we obtain

$$\int_a^b p(t)\,dt = \sum_{i=0}^{2} A_i p(t_i) = \sum_{i=0}^{2} A_i f(t_i) \approx \int_a^b f(t)\,dt,$$

or equivalently,

$$\int_a^b f(t)\,dt \approx \sum_{i=0}^{2} A_i f(t_i). \tag{9}$$

The approximation $\sum_{i=0}^{2} A_i f(t_i)$ in (9) is known as a numerical integration formula. Observe that once the evaluation points t_0, t_1, t_2 are selected, the scalars A_0, A_1, A_2 are determined by system (7). The coefficient matrix for system (7) has the form

$$A = \begin{bmatrix} 1 & 1 & 1 \\ t_0 & t_1 & t_2 \\ t_0^2 & t_1^2 & t_2^2 \end{bmatrix},$$

and so we see that A is nonsingular since A is the transpose of a Vandermonde matrix (recall matrix (4d)).

In general, if $t_0, t_1, \ldots, t_n$ are $n+1$ points in $[a, b]$, we can proceed exactly as in the derivation of formula (9) and produce a numerical integration formula of the form

$$\int_a^b f(t)\,dt \approx \sum_{i=0}^{n} A_i f(t_i). \tag{10}$$

The weights A_i in formula (10) would be determined by solving the Vandermonde system:

$$\begin{aligned}
A_0 \quad + A_1 \quad + \cdots + A_n \quad &= \int_a^b 1\,dt \\
A_0t_0 + A_1t_1 + \cdots + A_nt_n &= \int_a^b t\,dt \\
\vdots \qquad \vdots \qquad\quad \vdots \quad & \quad \vdots \\
A_0t_0^n + A_1t_1^n + \cdots + A_nt_n^n &= \int_a^b t^n\,dt.
\end{aligned} \tag{11}$$

The approximation $\sum_{i=0}^{n} A_i f(t_i)$ is the same number that would be produced by calculating the polynomial p of degree n that interpolates f at $t_0, t_1, \ldots, t_n$ and then evaluating $\int_a^b p(t)\,dt$.

EXAMPLE 6 For an interval $[a, b]$ let $t_0 = a$, $t_1 = (a+b)/2$, and $t_2 = b$. Construct the corresponding numerical integration formula.

Solution For $t_0 = a$, $t_1 = (a + b)/2$, and $t_2 = b$, the system to be solved is given by (11) with $n = 2$. We write system (11) as $C\mathbf{x} = \mathbf{d}$, where

$$C = \begin{bmatrix} 1 & 1 & 1 \\ a & t_1 & b \\ a^2 & t_1^2 & b^2 \end{bmatrix} \quad \text{and} \quad \mathbf{d} = \begin{bmatrix} b-a \\ (b^2-a^2)/2 \\ (b^3-a^3)/3 \end{bmatrix}.$$

It can be shown (see Exercise 23) that the solution of $C\mathbf{x} = \mathbf{d}$ is $A_0 = (b - a)/6$, $A_1 = 4(b-a)/6$, $A_2 = (b-a)/6$. The corresponding numerical integration formula is

$$\int_a^b f(t)\,dt \approx [(b-a)/6]\{f(a) + 4f[(a+b)/2] + f(b)\}. \tag{12}$$

The reader may be familiar with the preceding approximation, which is known as Simpson's rule. ■

EXAMPLE 7 Use the integration formula (12) to approximate the integral

$$I(f) = \int_0^{1/2} \cos(\pi t^2/2)\,dt.$$

Solution With $a = 0$ and $b = 1/2$, formula (12) becomes

$$\begin{aligned}
I(f) &\approx 1/12[\cos(0) + 4\cos(\pi/32) + \cos(\pi/8)] \\
&= (1/12)[1.0 + 4(0.995184\ldots) + 0.923879\ldots] \\
&= 0.492051\ldots.
\end{aligned}$$ ■

Note that in Example 7, the number $I(f)$ is equal to $C(0.5)$, where $C(x)$ denotes the Fresnel integral

$$C(x) = \int_0^x \cos(\pi t^2/2)\,dt.$$

The function $C(x)$ is important in applied mathematics, and extensive tables of the function $C(x)$ are available. The integrand is not a standard form, and $C(x)$ must be evaluated numerically. From a table, $C(0.5) = 0.49223442\ldots$.

Numerical Differentiation

Numerical differentiation formulas can also be derived in the same fashion as numerical integration formulas. In particular, suppose that f is a differentiable function and we wish to estimate the value $f'(a)$, where f is differentiable at $t = a$.

Let p be the polynomial of degree n that interpolates f at $t_0, t_1, \ldots, t_n$, where the interpolation nodes t_i are clustered near $t = a$. Then p provides us with an approximation for f, and we can estimate the value $f'(a)$ by evaluating the derivative of p at $t = a$:

$$f'(a) \approx p'(a).$$

As with a numerical integration formula, it can be shown that the value $p'(a)$ can be expressed as

$$p'(a) = A_0 p(t_0) + A_1 p(t_1) + \cdots + A_n p(t_n). \tag{13}$$

In formula (13), the weights A_i are determined by the system of equations

$$\begin{aligned} q_0'(a) &= A_0 q_0(t_0) + A_1 q_0(t_1) + \cdots + A_n q_0(t_n) \\ q_1'(a) &= A_0 q_1(t_0) + A_1 q_1(t_1) + \cdots + A_n q_1(t_n) \\ &\vdots \\ q_n'(a) &= A_0 q_n(t_0) + A_1 q_n(t_1) + \cdots + A_n q_n(t_n), \end{aligned}$$

where $q_0(t) = 1, q_1(t) = t, \ldots, q_n(t) = t^n$. So if formula (13) holds for the $n + 1$ special polynomials $1, t, \ldots, t^n$, then it holds for every polynomial p of degree n or less.

If p interpolates f at $t_0, t_1, \ldots, t_n$ so that $p(t_i) = f(t_i), 0 \le i \le n$, then (by formula 13) the approximation $f'(a) \approx p'(a)$ leads to

$$f'(a) \approx A_0 f(t_0) + A_1 f(t_1) + \cdots + A_n f(t_n). \tag{14}$$

An approximation of the form (14) is called a numerical differentiation formula.

EXAMPLE 8 Derive a numerical differentiation formula of the form

$$f'(a) \approx A_0 f(a - h) + A_1 f(a) + A_2 f(a + h).$$

Solution The weights A_0, A_1, and A_2 are determined by forcing Eq. (13) to hold for $p(t) = 1$, $p(t) = t$, and $p(t) = t^2$. Thus the weights are found by solving the system

$$\begin{aligned} &[p(t) = 1] & 0 &= A_0 + A_1 + A_2 \\ &[p(t) = t] & 1 &= A_0(a - h) + A_1(a) + A_2(a + h) \\ &[p(t) = t^2] & 2a &= A_0(a - h)^2 + A_1(a)^2 + A_2(a + h)^2. \end{aligned}$$

In matrix form, the system above can be expressed as $C\mathbf{x} = \mathbf{d}$, where

$$C = \begin{bmatrix} 1 & 1 & 1 \\ a-h & a & a+h \\ (a-h)^2 & a^2 & (a+h)^2 \end{bmatrix} \quad \text{and} \quad \mathbf{d} = \begin{bmatrix} 0 \\ 1 \\ 2a \end{bmatrix}.$$

By (4d), the matrix C is nonsingular and (see Exercise 24) the solution is $A_0 = -1/2h$, $A_1 = 0$, $A_2 = 1/2h$. The numerical differentiation formula has the form

$$f'(a) \approx [f(a+h) - f(a-h)]/2h. \tag{15}$$

(***Note:*** Formula (15) in this example is known as the centered-difference approximation to $f'(a)$.) ■

The same techniques can be used to derive formulas for estimating higher derivatives.

EXAMPLE 9 Construct a numerical differentiation formula of the form

$$f''(a) \approx A_0 f(a) + A_1 f(a+h) + A_2 f(a+2h) + A_3 f(a+3h).$$

Solution The weights A_0, A_1, A_2, and A_3 are determined by forcing the preceding approximation to be an equality for $p(t) = 1$, $p(t) = t$, $p(t) = t^2$, and $p(t) = t^3$. These constraints lead to the equations

$$\begin{array}{lll} [p(t)=1] & 0 &= A_0 + A_1 + A_2 + A_3 \\ [p(t)=t] & 0 &= A_0(a) + A_1(a+h) + A_2(a+2h) + A_3(a+3h) \\ [p(t)=t^2] & 2 &= A_0(a)^2 + A_1(a+h)^2 + A_2(a+2h)^2 + A_3(a+3h)^2 \\ [p(t)=t^3] & 6a &= A_0(a)^3 + A_1(a+h)^3 + A_2(a+2h)^3 + A_3(a+3h)^3. \end{array}$$

Since this system is a bit cumbersome to solve by hand, we decided to use the computer algebra system Derive. (Because the coefficient matrix has symbolic rather than numerical entries, we had to use a computer algebra system rather than numerical software such as MATLAB. In particular, Derive is a popular computer algebra system that is menu-driven and very easy to use.)

Figure 1.19 shows the results from Derive. Line 2 gives the command to row reduce the augmented matrix for the system. Line 3 gives the results. Therefore, the numerical differentiation formula is

$$f''(a) \approx \frac{1}{h^2}[2f(a) - 5f(a+h) + 4f(a+2h) - f(a+3h)].$$ ■

$$\text{2: ROW\_REDUCE}\begin{bmatrix} 1 & 1 & 1 & 1 & 0 \\ a & a+h & a+2h & a+3h & 0 \\ a^2 & (a+h)^2 & (a+2h)^2 & (a+3h)^2 & 2 \\ a^3 & (a+h)^3 & (a+2h)^3 & (a+3h)^3 & 6a \end{bmatrix}$$

$$\text{3:}\begin{bmatrix} 1 & 0 & 0 & 0 & \dfrac{2}{h^2} \\ 0 & 1 & 0 & 0 & -\dfrac{5}{h^2} \\ 0 & 0 & 1 & 0 & \dfrac{4}{h^2} \\ 0 & 0 & 0 & 1 & -\dfrac{1}{h^2} \end{bmatrix}$$

Figure 1.19 Using Derive to solve the system of equations in Example 9

1.8 EXERCISES

In Exercises 1–6, find the interpolating polynomial for the given table of data. [*Hint:* If the data table has k entries, the interpolating polynomial will be of degree $k-1$ or less.]

1.

t	0	1	2
y	−1	3	6

2.

t	−1	0	2
y	6	1	−3

3.

t	−1	1	2
y	1	5	7

4.

t	1	3	4
y	5	11	14

5.

t	−1	0	1	2
y	−6	1	4	15

6.

t	−2	−1	1	2
y	−3	1	3	13

In Exercises 7–10, find the constants so that the given function satisfies the given conditions.

7. $y = c_1e^{2x} + c_2e^{3x}$; $y(0) = 3$, $y'(0) = 7$

8. $y = c_1e^{(x-1)} + c_2e^{3(x-1)}$; $y(1) = 1$, $y'(1) = 5$

9. $y = c_1e^{-x} + c_2e^{x} + c_3e^{2x}$; $y(0) = 8$, $y'(0) = 3$, $y''(0) = 11$

10. $y = c_1e^{x} + c_2e^{2x} + c_3e^{3x}$; $y(0) = -1$, $y'(0) = -3$, $y''(0) = -5$

As in Example 6, find the weights A_i for the numerical integration formulas listed in Exercises 11–16. [*Note:* It can be shown that the special formulas developed in Exercises 11–16 can be translated to any interval of the general form $[a, b]$. Similarly, the numerical differentiation formulas in Exercises 17–22 can also be translated.]

11. $\int_0^{3h} f(t)\,dt \approx A_0 f(h) + A_1 f(2h)$

12. $\int_0^{h} f(t)\,dt \approx A_0 f(0) + A_1 f(h)$

13. $\int_0^{3h} f(t)\,dt \approx A_0 f(0) + A_1 f(h) + A_2 f(2h) + A_3 f(3h)$

14. $\int_0^{4h} f(t)\,dt \approx A_0 f(h) + A_1 f(2h) + A_2 f(3h)$

15. $\int_0^{h} f(t)\,dt \approx A_0 f(-h) + A_1 f(0)$

16. $\int_0^{h} f(t)\,dt \approx A_0 f(-h) + A_1 f(0) + A_2 f(h)$

As in Example 8, find the weights for the numerical differentiation formulas in Exercises 17–22. For Exercises 21 and 22, replace $p'(a)$ in formula (13) by $p''(a)$.

17. $f'(0) \approx A_0 f(0) + A_1 f(h)$

18. $f'(0) \approx A_0 f(-h) + A_1 f(0)$

19. $f'(0) \approx A_0 f(0) + A_1 f(h) + A_2 f(2h)$

20. $f'(0) \approx A_0 f(0) + A_1 f(h) + A_2 f(2h) + A_3 f(3h)$

21. $f''(0) \approx A_0 f(-h) + A_1 f(0) + A_2 f(h)$

22. $f''(0) \approx A_0 f(0) + A_1 f(h) + A_2 f(2h)$

23. Complete the calculations in Example 6 by transforming the augmented matrix $[C \mid \mathbf{d}]$ to reduced echelon form.

24. Complete the calculations in Example 8 by transforming the augmented matrix $[C \mid \mathbf{d}]$ to reduced echelon form.

25. Let p denote the quadratic polynomial defined by $p(t) = at^2 + bt + c$, where a, b, and c are real numbers. Use Rolle's theorem to prove the following: If t_0, t_1, and t_2 are real numbers such that $t_0 < t_1 < t_2$ and if $p(t_0) = 0$, $p(t_1) = 0$, and $p(t_2) = 0$, then $a = b = c = 0$. (Recall that Rolle's theorem states there are values u_1 and u_2 such that u_1 is in (t_0, t_1), u_2 is in (t_1, t_2), $p'(u_1) = 0$, and $p'(u_2) = 0$.)

26. Use mathematical induction to prove that a polynomial of the form $p(t) = a_n t^n + \cdots + a_1 t + a_0$ can have $n+1$ distinct real zeros only if $a_n = a_{n-1} = \cdots = a_1 = a_0 = 0$. [*Hint:* Use Rolle's theorem, as in Exercise 25.]

Exercises 27–33 concern ***Hermite interpolation***, where Hermite interpolation means the process of constructing polynomials that match both function values and derivative values.

In Exercises 27–30, find a polynomial p of the form $p(t) = at^3 + bt^2 + ct + d$ that satisfies the given conditions.

27. $p(0) = 2,\ p'(0) = 3,\ p(1) = 8,\ p'(1) = 10$

28. $p(0) = 1,\ p'(0) = 2,\ p(1) = 4,\ p'(1) = 4$

29. $p(-1) = -1,\ p'(-1) = 5,\ p(1) = 9,\ p'(1) = 9$

30. $p(1) = 3,\ p'(1) = 4,\ p(2) = 15,\ p'(2) = 22$

31. Suppose that t_0 and t_1 are distinct real numbers, where $t_0 < t_1$. Prove: If p is any polynomial of the form $p(t) = at^3 + bt^2 + ct + d$, where $p(t_0) = p(t_1) = 0$ and $p'(t_0) = p'(t_1) = 0$, then $a = b = c = d = 0$. [*Hint:* Apply Rolle's theorem.]

32. Suppose t_0 and t_1 are distinct real numbers, where $t_0 < t_1$. Suppose y_0, y_1, s_0, and s_1 are given real numbers. Prove that there is one, and only one, polynomial p of the form $p(t) = at^3 + bt^2 + ct + d$ such that $p(t_0) = y_0$, $p'(t_0) = s_0$, $p(t_1) = y_1$, and $p'(t_1) = s_1$. [*Hint:* Set up a system of four equations corresponding to the four interpolation constraints. Use Exercise 31 to show that the coefficient matrix is nonsingular.]

33. Let $t_0 < t_1 < \cdots < t_n$ be $n+1$ distinct real numbers. Let $y_0, y_1, \ldots, y_n$ and $s_0, s_1, \ldots, s_n$ be given real numbers. Show that there is one, and only one, polynomial p of degree $2n+1$ or less such that $p(t_i) = y_i, 0 \le i \le n$, and $p'(t_i) = s_i, 0 \le i \le n$. [*Hint:* As in Exercise 31, show that all the coefficients of p are zero if $y_i = s_i = 0, 0 \le i \le n$. Next, as in Exercise 32, write the system of equations corresponding to the interpolation constraints and verify that the coefficient matrix is nonsingular.]

In Exercises 34 and 35, use linear algebra software, such as Derive, to construct the formula.

34. $\int_0^{5h} f(x)dx \approx \sum_{j=0}^{5} A_j f(jh)$

35. $f'(a) \approx A_0 f(a-2h) + A_1 f(a-h) + A_2 f(a) + A_3 f(a+h) + A_4 f(a+2h)$

1.9 MATRIX INVERSES AND THEIR PROPERTIES

In the preceding sections the matrix equation

$$A\mathbf{x} = \mathbf{b} \tag{1}$$

has been used extensively to represent a system of linear equations. Equation (1) looks, symbolically, like the single linear equation

$$ax = b, \tag{2}$$

where a and b are real numbers. Since Eq. (2) has the unique solution

$$x = a^{-1}b$$

when $a \neq 0$, it is natural to ask whether Eq. (1) can also be solved as

$$\mathbf{x} = A^{-1}\mathbf{b}.$$

In this section we investigate this question. We begin by defining the inverse of a matrix, showing how to calculate it, and then showing how the inverse can be used to solve systems of the form $A\mathbf{x} = \mathbf{b}$.

The Matrix Inverse

For a nonzero real number a, the inverse of a is the unique real number a^{-1} having the property that

$$a^{-1}a = aa^{-1} = 1. \tag{3}$$

In Eq. (3), the number 1 is the multiplicative identity for real number multiplication. In an analogous fashion, let A be an $(n \times n)$ matrix. We now ask if we can find a matrix A^{-1} with the property that

$$A^{-1}A = AA^{-1} = I. \tag{4}$$

(In Eq. (4) I denotes the $(n \times n)$ identity matrix; see Section 1.6.)

We formalize the idea suggested by Eq. (4) in the next definition. Note that the commutativity condition $A^{-1}A = AA^{-1}$ means that A and A^{-1} must be square and of the same size; see Exercise 75.

DEFINITION 13 Let A be an $(n \times n)$ matrix. We say that A is ***invertible*** if we can find an $(n \times n)$ matrix A^{-1} such that

$$A^{-1}A = AA^{-1} = I.$$

The matrix A^{-1} is called an ***inverse*** for A.

(***Note:*** It is shown in Exercise 77 that if A is invertible, then A^{-1} is unique.

As an example of an invertible matrix, consider

$$A = \begin{bmatrix} 1 & 2 \\ 3 & 4 \end{bmatrix}.$$

It is simple to show that A is invertible and that A^{-1} is given by

$$A^{-1} = \begin{bmatrix} -2 & 1 \\ 3/2 & -1/2 \end{bmatrix}.$$

(To show that the preceding matrix is indeed the inverse of A, we need only form the products $A^{-1}A$ and AA^{-1} and then verify that both products are equal to I.)

Not every square matrix is invertible, as the next example shows.

EXAMPLE 1 Let A be the (2×2) matrix

$$A = \begin{bmatrix} 1 & 2 \\ 3 & 6 \end{bmatrix}.$$

Show that A has no inverse.

Solution An inverse for A must be a (2×2) matrix

$$B = \begin{bmatrix} a & b \\ c & d \end{bmatrix}$$

such that $AB = BA = I$. If such a matrix B exists, it must satisfy the following equation:

$$\begin{bmatrix} 1 & 0 \\ 0 & 1 \end{bmatrix} = \begin{bmatrix} 1 & 2 \\ 3 & 6 \end{bmatrix}\begin{bmatrix} a & b \\ c & d \end{bmatrix} = \begin{bmatrix} a+2c & b+2d \\ 3a+6c & 3b+6d \end{bmatrix}.$$

The preceding equation requires that $a + 2c = 1$ and $3a + 6c = 0$. This is clearly impossible, so A has no inverse.

Using Inverses to Solve Systems of Linear Equations

One major use of inverses is to solve systems of linear equations. In particular, consider the equation

$$A\mathbf{x} = \mathbf{b}, \tag{5}$$

where A is an $(n \times n)$ matrix and where A^{-1} exists. Then, to solve $A\mathbf{x} = \mathbf{b}$, we might think of multiplying both sides of the equation by A^{-1}:

$$A^{-1}A\mathbf{x} = A^{-1}\mathbf{b}$$

or

$$\mathbf{x} = A^{-1}\mathbf{b}.$$

The preceding calculations suggest the following: To solve $A\mathbf{x} = \mathbf{b}$ we need only compute the vector $\mathbf{x}$ given by

$$\mathbf{x} = A^{-1}\mathbf{b}. \tag{6}$$

To verify that the vector $\mathbf{x} = A^{-1}\mathbf{b}$ is indeed a solution, we need only insert it into the equation:

Existence of Inverses

As we saw earlier in Example 1, some matrices do not have an inverse. We now turn our attention to determining exactly which matrices *are* invertible. In the process, we will also develop a simple algorithm for calculating A^{-1}.

Let A be an $(n \times n)$ matrix. If A does have an inverse, then that inverse is an $(n \times n)$ matrix B such that

$$AB = I. \tag{7a}$$

(Of course, to be an inverse, the matrix B must also satisfy the condition $BA = I$. We will put this additional requirement aside for the moment and concentrate solely on the condition $AB = I$.)

Expressing B and I in column form, the equation $AB = I$ can be rewritten as

$$A[\mathbf{b}_1, \mathbf{b}_2, \ldots, \mathbf{b}_n] = [\mathbf{e}_1, \mathbf{e}_2, \ldots, \mathbf{e}_n]$$

or

$$[A\mathbf{b}_1, A\mathbf{b}_2, \ldots, A\mathbf{b}_n] = [\mathbf{e}_1, \mathbf{e}_2, \ldots, \mathbf{e}_n]. \tag{7b}$$

If A has an inverse, therefore, it follows that we must be able to solve each of the following n equations:

$$\begin{aligned} A\mathbf{x} &= \mathbf{e}_1 \\ A\mathbf{x} &= \mathbf{e}_2 \\ &\vdots \\ A\mathbf{x} &= \mathbf{e}_n. \end{aligned} \tag{7c}$$

In particular, if A is invertible, then the kth column of A^{-1} can be found by solving $A\mathbf{x} = \mathbf{e}_k$, $k = 1, 2, \ldots, n$.

We know (recall Theorem 13) that all the equations listed in (7c) can be solved if A is nonsingular. We suspect, therefore, that a nonsingular matrix always has an inverse. In fact, as is shown in Theorem 15, A has an inverse if and only if A is nonsingular.

Before stating Theorem 15, we give a lemma. (Although we do not need it here, the converse of the lemma is also valid; see Exercise 70.)

LEMMA Let P, Q, and R be $(n \times n)$ matrices such that $PQ = R$. If either P or Q is singular, then so is R.

Proof Suppose first that Q is singular. Then there is a nonzero vector $\mathbf{x}_1$ such that $Q\mathbf{x}_1 = \boldsymbol{\theta}$. Therefore, using associativity of matrix multiplication,

$$\begin{aligned} R\mathbf{x}_1 &= (PQ)\mathbf{x}_1 \\ &= P(Q\mathbf{x}_1) \\ &= P\boldsymbol{\theta} \\ &= \boldsymbol{\theta}. \end{aligned}$$

So, Q singular implies R is singular.

Now, suppose Q is nonsingular but the other factor, P, is singular. Then there is a nonzero vector $\mathbf{x}_1$ such that $P\mathbf{x}_1 = \boldsymbol{\theta}$. Also, Q nonsingular means we can find a vector

$\mathbf{x}_2$ such that $Q\mathbf{x}_2 = \mathbf{x}_1$. (In addition, note that $\mathbf{x}_2$ must be nonzero because $\mathbf{x}_1$ is nonzero.) Therefore,

$$\begin{aligned} R\mathbf{x}_2 &= (PQ)\mathbf{x}_2 \\ &= P(Q\mathbf{x}_2) \\ &= P\mathbf{x}_1 \\ &= \boldsymbol{\theta}. \end{aligned}$$

Thus, if either P or Q is singular, then the product PQ is also singular. ∎

We are now ready to characterize invertible matrices.

THEOREM 15 Let A be an $(n \times n)$ matrix. Then A has an inverse if and only if A is nonsingular.

Proof Suppose first that A has an inverse. That is, as in equation (7a), there is a matrix B such that $AB = I$. Now, as Exercise 74 proves, I is nonsingular. Therefore, by the lemma, neither A nor B can be singular. This argument shows that invertibility implies nonsingularity.

For the converse, suppose A is nonsingular. Since A is nonsingular, we see from equations (7a)–(7c) that there is a unique matrix B such that $AB = I$. This matrix B will be the inverse of A if we can show that A and B commute; that is, if we can also show that $BA = I$.

We will use a common algebraic trick to prove $BA = I$. First of all, note that the matrix B must also be nonsingular since $AB = I$. Therefore, just as with equations (7a)–(7c), there is a matrix C such that $BC = I$. Then, combining the expressions $AB = I$ and $BC = I$, we obtain

$$A = AI = A(BC) = (AB)C = IC = C.$$

Since $A = C$, we also have $BA = BC = I$. Therefore, $BA = I$, and this shows that B is the inverse of A. Hence, A nonsingular implies that A is invertible. ∎

Calculating the Inverse

In this subsection we give a simple algorithm for finding the inverse of a matrix A, provided that A has an inverse. The algorithm is based on the system of equations (7c):

$$A\mathbf{x} = \mathbf{e}_1,\ A\mathbf{x} = \mathbf{e}_2,\ \ldots,\ A\mathbf{x} = \mathbf{e}_n.$$

We first observe that there is a very efficient way to organize the solution of these n systems; we simply row reduce the associated augmented matrix $[A \,|\, \mathbf{e}_1, \mathbf{e}_2, \ldots, \mathbf{e}_n]$. The procedure is illustrated in the next example.

EXAMPLE 2 Find the inverse of the (3×3) matrix

$$A = \begin{bmatrix} 1 & 2 & 3 \\ 2 & 5 & 4 \\ 1 & -1 & 10 \end{bmatrix}.$$

Solution The augmented matrix $[A \mid \mathbf{e}_1, \mathbf{e}_2, \mathbf{e}_3]$ is given by

$$\begin{bmatrix} 1 & 2 & 3 & 1 & 0 & 0 \\ 2 & 5 & 4 & 0 & 1 & 0 \\ 1 & -1 & 10 & 0 & 0 & 1 \end{bmatrix}.$$

(Note that the augmented matrix has the form $[A \mid I]$.)

We now perform appropriate row operations to transform $[A \mid I]$ to reduced echelon form.

$R_2 - 2R_1, R_3 - R_1$:

$$\begin{bmatrix} 1 & 2 & 3 & 1 & 0 & 0 \\ 0 & 1 & -2 & -2 & 1 & 0 \\ 0 & -3 & 7 & -1 & 0 & 1 \end{bmatrix}$$

$R_1 - 2R_2, R_3 + 3R_2$:

$$\begin{bmatrix} 1 & 0 & 7 & 5 & -2 & 0 \\ 0 & 1 & -2 & -2 & 1 & 0 \\ 0 & 0 & 1 & -7 & 3 & 1 \end{bmatrix}$$

$R_1 - 7R_3, R_2 + 2R_3$:

$$\begin{bmatrix} 1 & 0 & 0 & 54 & -23 & -7 \\ 0 & 1 & 0 & -16 & 7 & 2 \\ 0 & 0 & 1 & -7 & 3 & 1 \end{bmatrix}.$$

Having the reduced echelon form above, we easily find the solutions of the three systems $A\mathbf{x} = \mathbf{e}_1$, $A\mathbf{x} = \mathbf{e}_2$, $A\mathbf{x} = \mathbf{e}_3$. In particular,

$A\mathbf{x} = \mathbf{e}_1$ ***has solution:*** $A\mathbf{x} = \mathbf{e}_2$ ***has solution:*** $A\mathbf{x} = \mathbf{e}_3$ ***has solution:***

$$\mathbf{x}_1 = \begin{bmatrix} 54 \\ -16 \\ -7 \end{bmatrix} \qquad \mathbf{x}_2 = \begin{bmatrix} -23 \\ 7 \\ 3 \end{bmatrix} \qquad \mathbf{x}_3 = \begin{bmatrix} -7 \\ 2 \\ 1 \end{bmatrix}.$$

Therefore, $A^{-1} = [\mathbf{x}_1, \mathbf{x}_2, \mathbf{x}_3]$ or

$$A^{-1} = \begin{bmatrix} 54 & -23 & -7 \\ -16 & 7 & 2 \\ -7 & 3 & 1 \end{bmatrix}.$$ ■

This procedure illustrated in Example 2 can be summarized by the following algorithm for calculating A^{-1}.

Computation of A^{-1}

To calculate the inverse of a nonsingular $(n \times n)$ matrix, we can proceed as follows:

Step 1. Form the $(n \times 2n)$ matrix $[A \mid I]$.

Step 2. Use elementary row operations to transform $[A \mid I]$ to the form $[I \mid B]$.

Step 3. Reading from this final form, $A^{-1} = B$.

(***Note:*** Step 2 of the algorithm above assumes that $[A \mid I]$ can always be row reduced to the form $[I \mid B]$ when A is nonsingular. This is indeed the case, and we ask you to prove it in Exercise 76 by showing that the reduced echelon form for any nonsingular matrix A is I. In fact, Exercise 76 actually establishes the stronger result listed next in Theorem 16.)

THEOREM 16 Let A be an $(n \times n)$ matrix. Then A is nonsingular if and only if A is row equivalent to I. ■

The next example illustrates the algorithm for calculating A^{-1} and also illustrates how to compute the solution to $A\mathbf{x} = \mathbf{b}$ by forming $\mathbf{x} = A^{-1}\mathbf{b}$.

EXAMPLE 3 Consider the system of equations

$$\begin{aligned} x_1 + 2x_2 &= -1 \\ 2x_1 + 5x_2 &= -10. \end{aligned}$$

(a) Use the algorithm to find the inverse of the coefficient matrix A.

(b) Use the inverse to calculate the solution of the system.

Solution

(a) We begin by forming the (2×4) matrix $[A \mid I]$,

$$[A \mid I] = \begin{bmatrix} 1 & 2 & 1 & 0 \\ 2 & 5 & 0 & 1 \end{bmatrix}.$$

We next row reduce $[A \mid I]$ to $[I \mid B]$ as follows:

$\boldsymbol{R_2 - 2R_1}$:

$$\begin{bmatrix} 1 & 2 & 1 & 0 \\ 0 & 1 & -2 & 1 \end{bmatrix}$$

$\boldsymbol{R_1 - 2R_2}$:

$$\begin{bmatrix} 1 & 0 & 5 & -2 \\ 0 & 1 & -2 & 1 \end{bmatrix}.$$

Thus, A^{-1} is the matrix

$$\begin{bmatrix} 5 & -2 \\ -2 & 1 \end{bmatrix}.$$

(b) The solution to the system is $\mathbf{x} = A^{-1}\mathbf{b}$ where

$$\mathbf{b} = \begin{bmatrix} -1 \\ -10 \end{bmatrix}.$$

Now, $A^{-1}\mathbf{b} = [15, -8]^T$, so the solution is $x_1 = 15$, $x_2 = -8$.

Inverses for (2 x 2) Matrices

There is a simple formula for the inverse of a (2×2) matrix, which we give in the remark that follows.

Remark Let A be a (2×2) matrix,

$$A = \begin{bmatrix} a & b \\ c & d \end{bmatrix},$$

and set $\Delta = ad - bc$.

(a) If $\Delta = 0$, then A does not have an inverse.
(b) If $\Delta \neq 0$, then A has an inverse given by

$$A^{-1} = \frac{1}{\Delta}\begin{bmatrix} d & -b \\ -c & a \end{bmatrix}. \quad (8)$$

Part (a) of the remark is Exercise 69. To verify the formula given in (b), suppose that $\Delta \neq 0$, and define B to be the matrix

$$B = \frac{1}{\Delta}\begin{bmatrix} d & -b \\ -c & a \end{bmatrix}.$$

Then

$$BA = \frac{1}{\Delta}\begin{bmatrix} d & -b \\ -c & a \end{bmatrix}\begin{bmatrix} a & b \\ c & d \end{bmatrix} = \frac{1}{\Delta}\begin{bmatrix} ad - bc & 0 \\ 0 & ad - bc \end{bmatrix} = \begin{bmatrix} 1 & 0 \\ 0 & 1 \end{bmatrix}.$$

Similarly, $AB = I$, so $B = A^{-1}$.

The reader familiar with determinants will recognize the number Δ in the remark as the determinant of the matrix A. We make use of the remark in the following example.

EXAMPLE 4 Let A and B be given by

$$A = \begin{bmatrix} 6 & 8 \\ 3 & 4 \end{bmatrix} \quad \text{and} \quad B = \begin{bmatrix} 1 & 7 \\ 3 & 5 \end{bmatrix}.$$

For each matrix, determine whether an inverse exists and calculate the inverse if it does exist.

Solution For the matrix A, the number Δ is

$$\Delta = 6(4) - 8(3) = 0,$$

so, by the remark, A cannot have an inverse. For the matrix B, the number Δ is

$$\Delta = 1(5) - 7(3) = -16.$$

According to formula (8)

$$B^{-1} = -\frac{1}{16}\begin{bmatrix} 5 & -7 \\ -3 & 1 \end{bmatrix}.$$

EXAMPLE 5 Consider the matrix A

$$A = \begin{bmatrix} \lambda & 2 \\ 2 & \lambda - 3 \end{bmatrix}.$$

For what values of λ is the matrix A nonsingular? Find A^{-1} if A is nonsingular.

Solution The number Δ is given by

$$\Delta = \lambda(\lambda - 3) - 4 = \lambda^2 - 3\lambda - 4 = (\lambda - 4)(\lambda + 1).$$

Thus, A is singular if and only if $\lambda = 4$ or $\lambda = -1$. For values other than these two, A^{-1} is given by

$$A^{-1} = \frac{1}{\lambda^2 - 3\lambda - 4}\begin{bmatrix} \lambda - 3 & -2 \\ -2 & \lambda \end{bmatrix}.$$

Properties of Matrix Inverses

The following theorem lists some of the properties of matrix inverses.

THEOREM 17 Let A and B be $(n \times n)$ matrices, each of which has an inverse. Then:

1. A^{-1} has an inverse, and $(A^{-1})^{-1} = A$.
2. AB has an inverse, and $(AB)^{-1} = B^{-1}A^{-1}$.
3. If k is a nonzero scalar, then kA has an inverse, and $(kA)^{-1} = (1/k)A^{-1}$.
4. A^T has an inverse, and $(A^T)^{-1} = (A^{-1})^T$.

Proof

1. Since $AA^{-1} = A^{-1}A = I$, the inverse of A^{-1} is A; that is, $(A^{-1})^{-1} = A$.
2. Note that $(AB)(B^{-1}A^{-1}) = A(BB^{-1})A^{-1} = A(IA^{-1}) = AA^{-1} = I$. Similarly, $(B^{-1}A^{-1})(AB) = I$, so, by Definition 13, $B^{-1}A^{-1}$ is the inverse for AB. Thus $(AB)^{-1} = B^{-1}A^{-1}$.
3. The proof of property 3 is similar to the proofs given for properties 1 and 2 and is left as an exercise.

4. It follows from Theorem 10, property 2, of Section 1.6 that $A^T(A^{-1})^T = (A^{-1}A)^T = I^T = I$. Similarly, $(A^{-1})^T A^T = I$. Therefore, A^T has inverse $(A^{-1})^T$. ∎

Note that the familiar formula $(ab)^{-1} = a^{-1}b^{-1}$ for real numbers is valid only because multiplication of real numbers is commutative. We have already noted that matrix multiplication is not commutative, so, as the following example demonstrates, $(AB)^{-1} \neq A^{-1}B^{-1}$.

EXAMPLE 6 Let A and B be the (2×2) matrices

$$A = \begin{bmatrix} 1 & 3 \\ 2 & 4 \end{bmatrix} \quad \text{and} \quad B = \begin{bmatrix} 3 & -2 \\ 1 & -1 \end{bmatrix}.$$

1. Use formula (8) to calculate A^{-1}, B^{-1}, and $(AB)^{-1}$.
2. Use Theorem 17, property 2, to calculate $(AB)^{-1}$.
3. Show that $(AB)^{-1} \neq A^{-1}B^{-1}$.

Solution For A the number Δ is $\Delta = 1(4) - 3(2) = -2$, so by formula (8)

$$A^{-1} = \begin{bmatrix} -2 & 3/2 \\ 1 & -1/2 \end{bmatrix}.$$

For B the number Δ is $3(-1) - 1(-2) = -1$, so

$$B^{-1} = \begin{bmatrix} 1 & -2 \\ 1 & -3 \end{bmatrix}.$$

The product AB is given by

$$AB = \begin{bmatrix} 6 & -5 \\ 10 & -8 \end{bmatrix},$$

so by formula (8)

$$(AB)^{-1} = \begin{bmatrix} -4 & 5/2 \\ -5 & 3 \end{bmatrix}.$$

By Theorem 17, property 2,

$$(AB)^{-1} = B^{-1}A^{-1} = \begin{bmatrix} 1 & -2 \\ 1 & -3 \end{bmatrix}\begin{bmatrix} -2 & 3/2 \\ 1 & -1/2 \end{bmatrix} = \begin{bmatrix} -4 & 5/2 \\ -5 & 3 \end{bmatrix}.$$

Finally,

$$A^{-1}B^{-1} = \begin{bmatrix} -2 & 3/2 \\ 1 & -1/2 \end{bmatrix}\begin{bmatrix} 1 & -2 \\ 1 & -3 \end{bmatrix} = \begin{bmatrix} -1/2 & -1/2 \\ 1/2 & -1/2 \end{bmatrix} \neq (AB)^{-1}.$$ ∎

The following theorem summarizes some of the important properties of nonsingular matrices.

THEOREM 18 Let A be an $(n \times n)$ matrix. The following are equivalent:

(a) A is nonsingular; that is, the only solution of $A\mathbf{x} = \boldsymbol{\theta}$ is $\mathbf{x} = \boldsymbol{\theta}$.

(b) The column vectors of A are linearly independent.

(c) $A\mathbf{x} = \mathbf{b}$ always has a unique solution.

(d) A has an inverse.

(e) A is row equivalent to I.

Ill-Conditioned Matrices

In applications the equation $A\mathbf{x} = \mathbf{b}$ often serves as a mathematical model for a physical problem. In these cases it is important to know whether solutions to $A\mathbf{x} = \mathbf{b}$ are sensitive to small changes in the right-hand side $\mathbf{b}$. If small changes in $\mathbf{b}$ can lead to relatively large changes in the solution $\mathbf{x}$, then the matrix A is called ***ill-conditioned***.

The concept of an ill-conditioned matrix is related to the size of A^{-1}. This connection is explained after the next example.

EXAMPLE 7 The $(n \times n)$ Hilbert matrix is the matrix whose ijth entry is $1/(i + j - 1)$. For example, the (3×3) Hilbert matrix is

$$\begin{bmatrix} 1 & 1/2 & 1/3 \\ 1/2 & 1/3 & 1/4 \\ 1/3 & 1/4 & 1/5 \end{bmatrix}.$$

Let A denote the (6×6) Hilbert matrix, and consider the vectors $\mathbf{b}$ and $\mathbf{b} + \Delta\mathbf{b}$:

$$\mathbf{b} = \begin{bmatrix} 1 \\ 2 \\ 1 \\ 1.414 \\ 1 \\ 2 \end{bmatrix}, \quad \mathbf{b} + \Delta\mathbf{b} = \begin{bmatrix} 1 \\ 2 \\ 1 \\ 1.4142 \\ 1 \\ 2 \end{bmatrix}.$$

Note that $\mathbf{b}$ and $\mathbf{b} + \Delta\mathbf{b}$ differ slightly in their fourth components. Compare the solutions of $A\mathbf{x} = \mathbf{b}$ and $A\mathbf{x} = \mathbf{b} + \Delta\mathbf{b}$.

Solution We used MATLAB to solve these two equations. If $\mathbf{x}_1$ denotes the solution of $A\mathbf{x} = \mathbf{b}$, and $\mathbf{x}_2$ denotes the solution of $A\mathbf{x} = \mathbf{b} + \Delta\mathbf{b}$, the results are (rounded to the nearest integer):

$$x_1 = \begin{bmatrix} -6538 \\ 185706 \\ -1256237 \\ 3271363 \\ -3616326 \\ 1427163 \end{bmatrix} \quad \text{and} \quad x_2 = \begin{bmatrix} -6539 \\ 185747 \\ -1256519 \\ 3272089 \\ -3617120 \\ 1427447 \end{bmatrix}.$$

(*Note:* Despite the fact that $\mathbf{b}$ and $\mathbf{b}+\Delta\mathbf{b}$ are nearly equal, $\mathbf{x}_1$ and $\mathbf{x}_2$ differ by almost 800 in their fifth components.)

Example 7 illustrates that the solutions of $A\mathbf{x}=\mathbf{b}$ and $A\mathbf{x}=\mathbf{b}+\Delta\mathbf{b}$ may be quite different even though $\Delta\mathbf{b}$ is a small vector. In order to explain these differences, let $\mathbf{x}_1$ denote the solution of $A\mathbf{x}=\mathbf{b}$ and $\mathbf{x}_2$ the solution of $A\mathbf{x}=\mathbf{b}+\Delta\mathbf{b}$. Therefore, $A\mathbf{x}_1=\mathbf{b}$ and $A\mathbf{x}_2=\mathbf{b}+\Delta\mathbf{b}$. To assess the difference, $\mathbf{x}_2-\mathbf{x}_1$, we proceed as follows:

$$A\mathbf{x}_2 - A\mathbf{x}_1 = (\mathbf{b}+\Delta\mathbf{b}) - \mathbf{b} = \Delta\mathbf{b}.$$

Therefore, $A(\mathbf{x}_2-\mathbf{x}_1)=\Delta\mathbf{b}$, or

$$\mathbf{x}_2 - \mathbf{x}_1 = A^{-1}\Delta\mathbf{b}.$$

If A^{-1} contains large entries, then we see from the equation above that $\mathbf{x}_2-\mathbf{x}_1$ can be large even though $\Delta\mathbf{b}$ is small.

The Hilbert matrices described in Example 7 are well-known examples of ill-conditioned matrices and have large inverses. For example, the inverse of the (6×6) Hilbert matrix is

$$A^{-1} = \begin{bmatrix} 36 & -630 & 3360 & -7560 & 7560 & -2772 \\ -630 & 14700 & -88200 & 211680 & -220500 & 83160 \\ 3360 & -88200 & 564480 & -1411200 & 1512000 & -582120 \\ -7560 & 211680 & -1411200 & 3628800 & -3969000 & 1552320 \\ 7560 & -220500 & 1512000 & -3969000 & 4410000 & -1746360 \\ -2772 & 83160 & -582120 & 1552320 & -1746360 & 698544 \end{bmatrix}.$$

Because of the large entries in A^{-1}, we should not be surprised at the large difference between $\mathbf{x}_1$ and $\mathbf{x}_2$, the two solutions in Example 7.

1.9 EXERCISES

In Exercises 1–4, verify that B is the inverse of A by showing that $AB=BA=I$.

1. $A=\begin{bmatrix} 7 & 4 \\ 5 & 3 \end{bmatrix}$, $B=\begin{bmatrix} 3 & -4 \\ -5 & 7 \end{bmatrix}$

2. $A=\begin{bmatrix} 3 & 10 \\ 2 & 10 \end{bmatrix}$, $B=\begin{bmatrix} 1 & -1 \\ -.2 & .3 \end{bmatrix}$

3. $A=\begin{bmatrix} -1 & -2 & 11 \\ 1 & 3 & -15 \\ 0 & -1 & 5 \end{bmatrix}$, $B=\begin{bmatrix} 0 & 1 & 3 \\ 5 & 5 & 4 \\ 1 & 1 & 1 \end{bmatrix}$

4. $A=\begin{bmatrix} 1 & 0 & 0 \\ 2 & 1 & 0 \\ 3 & 4 & 1 \end{bmatrix}$, $B=\begin{bmatrix} 1 & 0 & 0 \\ -2 & 1 & 0 \\ 5 & -4 & 1 \end{bmatrix}$

In Exercises 5–8, use the appropriate inverse matrix from Exercises 1–4 to solve the given system of linear equations.

5. $\begin{aligned} 3x_1 + 10x_2 &= 6 \\ 2x_1 + 10x_2 &= 9 \end{aligned}$

6. $\begin{aligned} 7x_1 + 4x_2 &= 5 \\ 5x_1 + 3x_2 &= 2 \end{aligned}$

7. $\begin{aligned} x_2 + 3x_3 &= 4 \\ 5x_1 + 5x_2 + 4x_3 &= 2 \\ x_1 + x_2 + x_3 &= 2 \end{aligned}$

8. $\begin{aligned} x_1 \qquad\qquad &= 2 \\ -2x_1 + x_2 \qquad &= 3 \\ 5x_1 - 4x_2 + x_3 &= 2 \end{aligned}$

In Exercises 9–12, verify that the given matrix A does not have an inverse. [*Hint:* One of $AB=I$ or $BA=I$ leads to an easy contradiction.]

9. $A=\begin{bmatrix} 0 & 0 & 0 \\ 1 & 2 & 1 \\ 3 & 2 & 1 \end{bmatrix}$

10. $A=\begin{bmatrix} 0 & 4 & 2 \\ 0 & 1 & 7 \\ 0 & 3 & 9 \end{bmatrix}$

11. $A = \begin{bmatrix} 2 & 2 & 4 \\ 1 & 1 & 7 \\ 3 & 3 & 9 \end{bmatrix}$ 12. $A = \begin{bmatrix} 1 & 1 & 1 \\ 1 & 1 & 1 \\ 2 & 3 & 2 \end{bmatrix}$

In Exercises 13–21, reduce $[A \mid I]$ to find A^{-1}. In each case, check your calculations by multiplying the given matrix by the derived inverse.

13. $\begin{bmatrix} 1 & 1 \\ 2 & 3 \end{bmatrix}$ 14. $\begin{bmatrix} 2 & 3 \\ 6 & 7 \end{bmatrix}$

15. $\begin{bmatrix} 1 & 2 \\ 2 & 1 \end{bmatrix}$ 16. $\begin{bmatrix} -1 & -2 & 11 \\ 1 & 3 & -15 \\ 0 & -1 & 5 \end{bmatrix}$

17. $\begin{bmatrix} 1 & 0 & 0 \\ 2 & 1 & 0 \\ 3 & 4 & 1 \end{bmatrix}$ 18. $\begin{bmatrix} 1 & 3 & 5 \\ 0 & 1 & 4 \\ 0 & 2 & 7 \end{bmatrix}$

19. $\begin{bmatrix} 1 & 4 & 2 \\ 0 & 2 & 1 \\ 3 & 5 & 3 \end{bmatrix}$ 20. $\begin{bmatrix} 1 & -2 & 2 & 1 \\ 1 & -1 & 5 & 0 \\ 2 & -2 & 11 & 2 \\ 0 & 2 & 8 & 1 \end{bmatrix}$

21. $\begin{bmatrix} 1 & 2 & 3 & 1 \\ -1 & 0 & 2 & 1 \\ 2 & 1 & -3 & 0 \\ 1 & 1 & 2 & 1 \end{bmatrix}$

As in Example 5, determine whether the (2×2) matrices in Exercises 22–26 have an inverse. If A has an inverse, find A^{-1} and verify that $A^{-1}A = I$.

22. $A = \begin{bmatrix} -3 & 2 \\ 1 & 1 \end{bmatrix}$ 23. $A = \begin{bmatrix} 2 & -2 \\ 2 & 3 \end{bmatrix}$

24. $A = \begin{bmatrix} -1 & 3 \\ 2 & 1 \end{bmatrix}$ 25. $A = \begin{bmatrix} 2 & 1 \\ 4 & 2 \end{bmatrix}$

26. $A = \begin{bmatrix} 6 & -2 \\ 9 & -3 \end{bmatrix}$

In Exercises 27–28 determine the value(s) of λ for which A has an inverse.

27. $A = \begin{bmatrix} \lambda & 4 \\ 1 & \lambda \end{bmatrix}$ 28. $A = \begin{bmatrix} 1 & -2 & 3 \\ 4 & -1 & 4 \\ 2 & -3 & \lambda \end{bmatrix}$

In Exercises 29–34, solve the given system by forming $\mathbf{x} = A^{-1}\mathbf{b}$, where A is the coefficient matrix for the system.

29. $2x_1 + x_2 = 4$
$3x_1 + 2x_2 = 2$

30. $x_1 + x_2 = 0$
$2x_1 + 3x_2 = 4$

31. $x_1 - x_2 = 5$
$3x_1 - 4x_2 = 2$

32. $2x_1 + 3x_2 = 1$
$3x_1 + 4x_2 = 7$

33. $3x_1 + x_2 = 10$
$-x_1 + 3x_2 = 5$

34. $x_1 - x_2 = 10$
$2x_1 + 3x_2 = 4$

The following matrices are used in Exercises 35–45.

$$A^{-1} = \begin{bmatrix} 3 & 1 \\ 0 & 2 \end{bmatrix}, B = \begin{bmatrix} 1 & 2 \\ 2 & 1 \end{bmatrix}, C^{-1} = \begin{bmatrix} -1 & 1 \\ 1 & 2 \end{bmatrix}. \quad (9)$$

In Exercises 35–45, use Theorem 17 and the matrices in (9) to form Q^{-1}, where Q is the given matrix.

35. $Q = AC$ 36. $Q = CA$

37. $Q = A^T$ 38. $Q = A^TC$

39. $Q = C^TA^T$ 40. $Q = B^{-1}A$

41. $Q = CB^{-1}$ 42. $Q = B^{-1}$

43. $Q = 2A$ 44. $Q = 10C$

45. $Q = (AC)B^{-1}$

46. Let A be the matrix given in Exercise 13. Use the inverse found in Exercise 13 to obtain matrices B and C such that $AB = D$ and $CA = E$, where

$$D = \begin{bmatrix} -1 & 2 & 3 \\ 1 & 0 & 2 \end{bmatrix} \text{ and } E = \begin{bmatrix} 2 & -1 \\ 1 & 1 \\ 0 & 3 \end{bmatrix}.$$

47. Repeat Exercise 46 with A being the matrix given in Exercise 16 and where

$$D = \begin{bmatrix} 2 & -1 \\ 1 & 1 \\ 0 & 3 \end{bmatrix} \text{ and } E = \begin{bmatrix} -1 & 2 & 3 \\ 1 & 0 & 2 \end{bmatrix}.$$

48. For what values of a is

$$A = \begin{bmatrix} 1 & 1 & -1 \\ 0 & 1 & 2 \\ 1 & 1 & a \end{bmatrix}$$

nonsingular?

49. Find $(AB)^{-1}$, $(3A)^{-1}$, and $(A^T)^{-1}$ given that

$$A^{-1} = \begin{bmatrix} 1 & 2 & 5 \\ 3 & 1 & 6 \\ 2 & 8 & 1 \end{bmatrix} \text{ and } B^{-1} = \begin{bmatrix} 3 & -3 & 4 \\ 5 & 1 & 3 \\ 7 & 6 & -1 \end{bmatrix}.$$

50. Find the (3×3) nonsingular matrix A if $A^2 = AB + 2A$, where

$$B = \begin{bmatrix} 2 & 1 & -1 \\ 0 & 3 & 2 \\ -1 & 4 & 1 \end{bmatrix}.$$

51. Simplify $(A^{-1}B)^{-1}(C^{-1}A)^{-1}(B^{-1}C)^{-1}$ for $(n \times n)$ invertible matrices A, B, and C.

52. The equation $x^2 = 1$ can be solved by setting $x^2 - 1 = 0$ and factoring the expression to obtain $(x-1)(x+1) = 0$. This yields solutions $x = 1$ and $x = -1$.

a) Using the factorization technique given above, what (2×2) matrix solutions do you obtain for the matrix equation $X^2 = I$?

b) Show that

$$A = \begin{bmatrix} a & 1-a^2 \\ 1 & -a \end{bmatrix}$$

is a solution to $X^2 = I$ for every real number a.

c) Let $b = \pm 1$. Show that

$$B = \begin{bmatrix} b & 0 \\ c & -b \end{bmatrix}$$

is a solution to $X^2 = I$ for every real number c.

d) Explain why the factorization technique used in part (a) did not yield all the solutions to the matrix equation $X^2 = I$.

53. Suppose that A is a (2×2) matrix with columns $\mathbf{u}$ and $\mathbf{v}$, so that $A = [\mathbf{u}, \mathbf{v}]$, $\mathbf{u}$ and $\mathbf{v}$ in R^2. Suppose also that $\mathbf{u}^T\mathbf{u} = 1$, $\mathbf{u}^T\mathbf{v} = 0$, and $\mathbf{v}^T\mathbf{v} = 1$. Prove that $A^TA = I$. [*Hint:* Express the matrix A as

$$A = \begin{bmatrix} u_1 & v_1 \\ u_2 & v_2 \end{bmatrix}, \quad \mathbf{u} = \begin{bmatrix} u_1 \\ u_2 \end{bmatrix}, \quad \mathbf{v} \begin{bmatrix} v_1 \\ v_2 \end{bmatrix}$$

and form the product A^TA.]

54. Let $\mathbf{u}$ be a vector in R^n such that $\mathbf{u}^T\mathbf{u} = 1$. Let $A = I - \mathbf{u}\mathbf{u}^T$, where I is the $(n \times n)$ identity. Verify that $AA = A$. [*Hint:* Write the product $\mathbf{u}\mathbf{u}^T\mathbf{u}\mathbf{u}^T$ as $\mathbf{u}\mathbf{u}^T\mathbf{u}\mathbf{u}^T = \mathbf{u}(\mathbf{u}^T\mathbf{u})\mathbf{u}^T$, and note that $\mathbf{u}^T\mathbf{u}$ is a scalar.]

55. Suppose that A is an $(n \times n)$ matrix such that $AA = A$, as in Exercise 54. Show that if A has an inverse, then $A = I$.

56. Let $A = I - a\mathbf{v}\mathbf{v}^T$, where $\mathbf{v}$ is a nonzero vector in R^n, I is the $(n \times n)$ identity, and a is the scalar given by $a = 2/(\mathbf{v}^T\mathbf{v})$. Show that A is symmetric and that $AA = I$; that is, $A^{-1} = A$.

57. Consider the $(n \times n)$ matrix A defined in Exercise 56. For $\mathbf{x}$ in R^n, show that the product $A\mathbf{x}$ has the form $A\mathbf{x} = \mathbf{x} - \lambda\mathbf{v}$, where λ is a scalar. What is the value of λ for a given $\mathbf{x}$?

58. Suppose that A is an $(n \times n)$ matrix such that $A^TA = I$ (the matrix defined in Exercise 56 is such a matrix). Let $\mathbf{x}$ be any vector in R^n. Show that $\|A\mathbf{x}\| = \|\mathbf{x}\|$; that is, multiplication of $\mathbf{x}$ by A produces a vector $A\mathbf{x}$ having the same length as $\mathbf{x}$.

59. Let $\mathbf{u}$ and $\mathbf{v}$ be vectors in R^n, and let I denote the $(n \times n)$ identity. Let $A = I + \mathbf{u}\mathbf{v}^T$, and suppose $\mathbf{v}^T\mathbf{u} \neq -1$. Establish the ***Sherman–Woodberry*** formula:

$$A^{-1} = I - a\mathbf{u}\mathbf{v}^T, \quad a = 1/(1 + \mathbf{v}^T\mathbf{u}). \qquad (10)$$

[*Hint:* Form AA^{-1}, where A^{-1} is given by formula (10).]

60. If A is a square matrix, we define the powers A^2, A^3, and so on, as follows: $A^2 = AA$, $A^3 = A(A^2)$, and so on. Suppose A is an $(n \times n)$ matrix such that

$$A^3 - 2A^2 + 3A - I = \mathcal{O}.$$

Show that $AB = I$, where $B = A^2 - 2A + 3I$.

61. Suppose that A is $(n \times n)$ and

$$A^2 + b_1A + b_0I = \mathcal{O}, \qquad (11)$$

where $b_0 \neq 0$. Show that $AB = I$, where $B = (-1/b_0)[A + b_1I]$.

It can be shown that when A is a (2×2) matrix such that A^{-1} exists, then there are constants b_1 and b_0 such that Eq. (11) holds. Moreover, $b_0 \neq 0$ in Eq. (11) unless A is a multiple of I. In Exercises 62–65, find the constants b_1 and b_0 in Eq. (11) for the given (2×2) matrix. Also, verify that $A^{-1} = (-1/b_0)[A + b_1I]$.

62. A in Exercise 13.

63. A in Exercise 15.

64. A in Exercise 14.

65. A in Exercise 22.

66. a) If linear algebra software is available, solve the systems $A\mathbf{x} = \mathbf{b}_1$ and $A\mathbf{x} = \mathbf{b}_2$, where

$$A = \begin{bmatrix} 0.932 & 0.443 & 0.417 \\ 0.712 & 0.915 & 0.887 \\ 0.632 & 0.514 & 0.493 \end{bmatrix},$$

$$\mathbf{b}_1 = \begin{bmatrix} 1 \\ 1 \\ -1 \end{bmatrix}, \quad \mathbf{b}_2 = \begin{bmatrix} 1.01 \\ 1.01 \\ -1.01 \end{bmatrix}.$$

Note the large difference between the two solutions.

b) Calculate A^{-1} and use it to explain the results of part (a).

67. a) Give examples of nonsingular (2×2) matrices A and B such that $A + B$ is singular.

b) Give examples of singular (2×2) matrices A and B such that $A + B$ is nonsingular.

68. Let A be an $(n \times n)$ nonsingular symmetric matrix. Show that A^{-1} is also symmetric.

69. a) Suppose that $AB = \mathcal{O}$, where A is nonsingular. Prove that $B = \mathcal{O}$.

b) Find a (2×2) matrix B such that $AB = \mathcal{O}$, where B has nonzero entries and where A is the matrix

$$A = \begin{bmatrix} 1 & 1 \\ 1 & 1 \end{bmatrix}.$$

Why does this example not contradict part (a)?

70. Let A, B, and C be matrices such that A is nonsingular and $AB = AC$. Prove that $B = C$.

71. Let A be the (2×2) matrix

$$A = \begin{bmatrix} a & b \\ c & d \end{bmatrix},$$

and set $\Delta = ad - bc$. Prove that if $\Delta = 0$, then A is singular. Conclude that A has no inverse. [*Hint:* Consider the vector

$$\mathbf{v} = \begin{bmatrix} d \\ -c \end{bmatrix};$$

also treat the special case when $d = c = 0$.]

72. Let A and B be $(n \times n)$ nonsingular matrices. Show that AB is also nonsingular.

73. What is wrong with the following argument that if AB is nonsingular, then each of A and B is also nonsingular?

Since AB is nonsingular, $(AB)^{-1}$ exists. But by Theorem 17, property 2, $(AB)^{-1} = B^{-1}A^{-1}$. Therefore, A^{-1} and B^{-1} exist, so A and B are nonsingular.

74. Let A and B be $(n \times n)$ matrices such that AB is nonsingular.

a) Prove that B is nonsingular. [*Hint:* Suppose $\mathbf{v}$ is any vector such that $B\mathbf{v} = \boldsymbol{\theta}$, and write $(AB)\mathbf{v}$ as $A(B\mathbf{v})$.]

b) Prove that A is nonsingular. [*Hint:* By part (a), B^{-1} exists. Apply Exercise 72 to the matrices AB and B^{-1}.]

75. Let A be a singular $(n \times n)$ matrix. Argue that at least one of the systems $A\mathbf{x} = \mathbf{e}_k$, $k = 1, 2, \ldots, n$, must be inconsistent, where $\mathbf{e}_1, \mathbf{e}_2, \ldots, \mathbf{e}_n$ are the n-dimensional unit vectors.

76. Show that the $(n \times n)$ identity matrix, I, is nonsingular.

77. Let A and B be matrices such that $AB = BA$. Show that A and B must be square and of the same order. [*Hint:* Let A be $(p \times q)$ and let B be $(r \times s)$. Now show that $p = r$ and $q = s$.]

78. Use Theorem 3 to prove Theorem 16.

79. Let A be $(n \times n)$ and invertible. Show that A^{-1} is unique.

SUPPLEMENTARY EXERCISES

1. Consider the system of equations

$$\begin{aligned} x_1 \qquad\qquad\qquad &= 1 \\ 2x_1 + (a^2 + a - 2)x_2 &= a^2 - a - 4. \end{aligned}$$

For what values of a does the system have infinitely many solutions? No solutions? A unique solution in which $x_2 = 0$?

2. Let

$$A = \begin{bmatrix} 1 & -1 & -1 \\ 2 & -1 & 1 \\ -3 & 1 & -3 \end{bmatrix}, \quad \mathbf{x} = \begin{bmatrix} x_1 \\ x_2 \\ x_3 \end{bmatrix}, \text{ and}$$

$$\mathbf{b} = \begin{bmatrix} b_1 \\ b_2 \\ b_3 \end{bmatrix}.$$

a) Determine conditions on b_1, b_2, and b_3 that are necessary and sufficient for the system of equations $A\mathbf{x} = \mathbf{b}$ to be consistent. [*Hint:* Reduce the augmented matrix $[A \mid \mathbf{b}]$.]

b) For each of the following choices of $\mathbf{b}$, either show that the system $A\mathbf{x} = \mathbf{b}$ is inconsistent or exhibit the solution.

i) $\mathbf{b} = \begin{bmatrix} 1 \\ 1 \\ 1 \end{bmatrix}$ ii) $\mathbf{b} = \begin{bmatrix} 5 \\ 2 \\ 1 \end{bmatrix}$

iii) $\mathbf{b} = \begin{bmatrix} 7 \\ 3 \\ 1 \end{bmatrix}$ iv) $\mathbf{b} = \begin{bmatrix} 0 \\ 1 \\ 2 \end{bmatrix}$

3. Let

$$A = \begin{bmatrix} 1 & -1 & 3 \\ 2 & -1 & 5 \\ -3 & 5 & -10 \\ 1 & 0 & 4 \end{bmatrix} \quad \text{and} \quad \mathbf{x} = \begin{bmatrix} x_1 \\ x_2 \\ x_3 \end{bmatrix}.$$

a) Simultaneously solve each of the systems $A\mathbf{x} = \mathbf{b}_i$, $i = 1, 2, 3$, where

$$\mathbf{b}_1 = \begin{bmatrix} -5 \\ -17 \\ 19 \\ 24 \end{bmatrix}, \quad \mathbf{b}_2 = \begin{bmatrix} 5 \\ 11 \\ -12 \\ 8 \end{bmatrix}, \text{ and}$$

$$\mathbf{b}_3 = \begin{bmatrix} 1 \\ 2 \\ -1 \\ 5 \end{bmatrix}.$$

b) Let $B = [\mathbf{b}_1, \mathbf{b}_2, \mathbf{b}_3]$. Use the results of part (a) to exhibit a (3×3) matrix C such that $AC = B$.

4. Let

$$A = \begin{bmatrix} 1 & -1 & 3 \\ 2 & -1 & 4 \end{bmatrix} \quad \text{and} \quad C = \begin{bmatrix} 1 & 2 \\ 3 & 1 \end{bmatrix}.$$

Find a (3×2) matrix B such that $AB = C$.

5. Let A be the nonsingular (5×5) matrix

$$A = [\mathbf{A}_1, \mathbf{A}_2, \mathbf{A}_3, \mathbf{A}_4, \mathbf{A}_5],$$

and let $B = [\mathbf{A}_5, \mathbf{A}_1, \mathbf{A}_4, \mathbf{A}_2, \mathbf{A}_3]$. For a given vector $\mathbf{b}$, suppose that $[1, 3, 5, 7, 9]^T$ is the solution to $B\mathbf{x} = \mathbf{b}$. What is the solution of $A\mathbf{x} = \mathbf{b}$?

6. Let

$$\mathbf{v}_1 = \begin{bmatrix} 1 \\ 1 \\ 3 \end{bmatrix}, \quad \mathbf{v}_2 = \begin{bmatrix} 2 \\ 1 \\ 4 \end{bmatrix}, \quad \text{and} \quad \mathbf{v}_3 = \begin{bmatrix} 5 \\ 2 \\ 9 \end{bmatrix}.$$

a) Solve the vector equation $x_1\mathbf{v}_1 + x_2\mathbf{v}_2 + x_3\mathbf{v}_3 = \mathbf{b}$, where

$$\mathbf{b} = \begin{bmatrix} 8 \\ 5 \\ 18 \end{bmatrix}.$$

b) Show that the set of vectors $\{\mathbf{v}_1, \mathbf{v}_2, \mathbf{v}_3\}$ is linearly dependent by exhibiting a nontrivial solution to the vector equation $x_1\mathbf{v}_1 + x_2\mathbf{v}_2 + x_3\mathbf{v}_3 = \boldsymbol{\theta}$.

7. Let

$$A = \begin{bmatrix} 1 & -1 & 3 \\ 2 & -1 & 5 \\ -1 & 4 & -5 \end{bmatrix}$$

and define a function $T: R^3 \to R^3$ by $T(\mathbf{x}) = A\mathbf{x}$ for each

$$\mathbf{x} = \begin{bmatrix} x_1 \\ x_2 \\ x_3 \end{bmatrix}$$

in R^3.

a) Find a vector $\mathbf{x}$ in R^3 such that $T(\mathbf{x}) = \mathbf{b}$, where

$$\mathbf{b} = \begin{bmatrix} 1 \\ 3 \\ 2 \end{bmatrix}.$$

b) If $\boldsymbol{\theta}$ is the zero vector of R^3, then clearly $T(\boldsymbol{\theta}) = \boldsymbol{\theta}$. Describe all vectors $\mathbf{x}$ in R^3 such that $T(\mathbf{x}) = \boldsymbol{\theta}$.

8. Let

$$\mathbf{v}_1 = \begin{bmatrix} 1 \\ -1 \\ 3 \end{bmatrix}, \quad \mathbf{v}_2 = \begin{bmatrix} 2 \\ -1 \\ 5 \end{bmatrix}, \quad \text{and} \quad \mathbf{v}_3 = \begin{bmatrix} -1 \\ 4 \\ -5 \end{bmatrix}.$$

Find

$$\mathbf{x} = \begin{bmatrix} x_1 \\ x_2 \\ x_3 \end{bmatrix}$$

so that $\mathbf{x}^T\mathbf{v}_1 = 2$, $\mathbf{x}^T\mathbf{v}_2 = 3$, and $\mathbf{x}^T\mathbf{v}_3 = -4$.

9. Find A^{-1} for each of the following matrices A

a) $A = \begin{bmatrix} 1 & 2 & 1 \\ 2 & 5 & 4 \\ 1 & 1 & 0 \end{bmatrix}$

b) $A = \begin{bmatrix} \cos\theta & -\sin\theta \\ \sin\theta & \cos\theta \end{bmatrix}$

10. For what values of λ is the matrix

$$A = \begin{bmatrix} \lambda - 4 & -1 \\ 2 & \lambda - 1 \end{bmatrix}$$

singular? Find A^{-1} if A is nonsingular.

11. Find A if A is (2×2) and $(4A)^{-1} = \begin{bmatrix} 3 & 1 \\ 5 & 2 \end{bmatrix}$.

12. Find A and B if they are (2×2) and

$$A + B = \begin{bmatrix} 4 & 6 \\ 8 & 10 \end{bmatrix} \quad \text{and} \quad A - B = \begin{bmatrix} 2 & 2 \\ 4 & 6 \end{bmatrix}.$$

13. Let

$$A = \begin{bmatrix} 1 & 0 & 0 \\ 0 & -1 & 0 \\ 0 & 0 & -1 \end{bmatrix}.$$

Calculate A^{99} and A^{100}.

In Exercises 14–18, A and B are (3×3) matrices such that

$$A^{-1} = \begin{bmatrix} 2 & 3 & 5 \\ 7 & 2 & 1 \\ 4 & -4 & 3 \end{bmatrix} \quad \text{and} \quad B^{-1} = \begin{bmatrix} -6 & 4 & 3 \\ 7 & -1 & 5 \\ 2 & 3 & 1 \end{bmatrix}.$$

14. Without calculating A, solve the system of equations $A\mathbf{x} = \mathbf{b}$, where

$$\mathbf{x} = \begin{bmatrix} x_1 \\ x_2 \\ x_3 \end{bmatrix} \quad \text{and} \quad \mathbf{b} = \begin{bmatrix} -1 \\ 0 \\ 1 \end{bmatrix}.$$

15. Without calculating A or B, find $(AB)^{-1}$.

16. Without calculating A, find $(3A)^{-1}$.

17. Without calculating A or B, find $(A^TB)^{-1}$.

18. Without calculating A or B, find $[(A^{-1}B^{-1})^{-1}A^{-1}B]^{-1}$.

CONCEPTUAL EXERCISES

In Exercises 1–8, answer true or false. Justify your answer by providing a counterexample if the statement is false or an outline of a proof if the statement is true.

1. If A and B are symmetric $(n \times n)$ matrices, then AB is also symmetric.
2. If A is an $(n \times n)$ matrix, then $A + A^T$ is symmetric.
3. If A and B are nonsingular $(n \times n)$ matrices such that $A^2 = I$ and $B^2 = I$, then $(AB)^{-1} = BA$.
4. If A and B are nonsingular $(n \times n)$ matrices, then $A + B$ is also nonsingular.
5. A consistent (3×2) linear system of equations can never have a unique solution.
6. If A is an $(m \times n)$ matrix such that $A\mathbf{x} = \boldsymbol{\theta}$ for every $\mathbf{x}$ in R^n, then A is the $(m \times n)$ zero matrix.
7. If A is a (2×2) nonsingular matrix and $\mathbf{u}_1$ and $\mathbf{u}_2$ are nonzero vectors in R^2, then $\{A\mathbf{u}_1, A\mathbf{u}_2\}$ is linearly independent.
8. Let A be $(m \times n)$ and B be $(p \times q)$. If AB is defined and square, then BA is also defined and square.

In Exercises 9–16, give a brief answer.

9. Let P, Q, and R be nonsingular $(n \times n)$ matrices such that $PQR = I$. Express Q^{-1} in terms of P and R.

10. Suppose that each of A, B, and AB are symmetric $(n \times n)$ matrices. Show that $AB = BA$.

11. Let $\mathbf{u}_1$, $\mathbf{u}_2$, and $\mathbf{u}_3$ be nonzero vectors in R^n such that $\mathbf{u}_1^T\mathbf{u}_2 = 0$, $\mathbf{u}_1^T\mathbf{u}_3 = 0$, and $\mathbf{u}_2^T\mathbf{u}_3 = 0$. Show that $\{\mathbf{u}_1, \mathbf{u}_2, \mathbf{u}_3\}$ is a linearly independent set.

12. Let $\mathbf{u}_1$ and $\mathbf{u}_2$ be linearly dependent vectors in R^2, and let A be a (2×2) matrix. Show that the vectors $A\mathbf{u}_1$ and $A\mathbf{u}_2$ are linearly dependent.

13. An $(n \times n)$ matrix A is ***orthogonal*** provided that $A^T = A^{-1}$, that is, if $AA^T = A^TA = I$. If A is an $(n \times n)$ orthogonal matrix, then prove that $\|\mathbf{x}\| = \|A\mathbf{x}\|$ for every vector $\mathbf{x}$ in R^n.

14. An $(n \times n)$ matrix A is ***idempotent*** if $A^2 = A$. What can you say about A if it is both idempotent and nonsingular?

15. Let A and B be $(n \times n)$ idempotent matrices such that $AB = BA$. Show that AB is also idempotent.

16. An $(n \times n)$ matrix A is ***nilpotent of index*** k if $A^k = \mathcal{O}$ but $A^i \neq \mathcal{O}$ for $1 \leq i \leq k - 1$.
    a) Show: If A is nilpotent of index 2 or 3, then A is singular.
    b) (Optional) Show: If A is nilpotent of index k, $k \geq 2$, then A is singular. [*Hint:* Consider a proof by contradiction.]

MATLAB EXERCISES

Exercise 1 illustrates some ideas associated with population dynamics. We will look at this topic again in Chapter 4, after we have developed the necessary analytical tools—eigenvalues and eigenvectors.

1. **Population dynamics** An island is divided into three regions, A, B, and C. The yearly migration of a certain animal among these regions is described by the following table.

	From A	*From* B	*From* C
To A	70%	15%	10%
To B	15%	80%	30%
To C	15%	5%	60%

For example, the first column in the table tells us, in any given year, that 70% of the population in A remains in region A, 15% migrates to B, and 15% migrates to C.

The total population of animals on the island is expected to remain stable for the foreseeable future and a census finds the current population consists of 300 in region A, 350 in region B, and 200 in region C. Corresponding to the migration table and the census, we define a matrix A and a vector $\mathbf{x}_0$:

$$A = \begin{bmatrix} .70 & .15 & .10 \\ .15 & .80 & .30 \\ .15 & .05 & .60 \end{bmatrix} \qquad \mathbf{x}_0 = \begin{bmatrix} 300 \\ 350 \\ 200 \end{bmatrix}.$$

The matrix A is called the ***transition matrix*** and the vector $\mathbf{x}_0$ is the initial ***state vector***. In general, let $\mathbf{x}_k = [x_1, x_2, x_3]^T$ denote the state vector for year k. (The state vector tells us that in year k there are x_1 animals in region A, x_2 in region B, and x_3 in region C.) Then, using the transition matrix, we find in year $k + 1$ that the population distribution is given by

$$\mathbf{x}_{k+1} = A\mathbf{x}_k. \tag{1}$$

a) Use Eq. (1) to find the population distribution one year after the census.

b) Give a formula for $\mathbf{x}_n$ in terms of powers of A and $\mathbf{x}_0$.

c) Calculate the state vectors $\mathbf{x}_1, \mathbf{x}_2, \ldots, \mathbf{x}_{10}$. Observe that the population distribution seems to be reaching a ***steady state***. Estimate the steady-state population for each region.

d) Calculate $\mathbf{x}_{20}$ and compare it with your estimate from part c).

e) Let $\mathbf{x}_{-1}$ denote the state vector one year prior to the census. Calculate $\mathbf{x}_{-1}$.

f) Demonstrate that Eq. (1) has not always been an accurate model for population distribution by calculating the state vector four years prior to the census.

g) How should we rearrange the population just after the census so that the distribution three years later is $\mathbf{x}_3 = [250, 400, 200]^T$? That is, what should $\mathbf{x}_0$ be in order to hit the target $\mathbf{x}_3$?

We have already seen one example of a ***partitioned matrix*** (also called a ***block matrix***) when we wrote A in column form as $A = [\mathbf{A}_1, \mathbf{A}_2, \ldots, \mathbf{A}_n]$; recall Section 1.6. Exercise 2 expands on this idea and illustrates how partitioned matrices can be multiplied in a natural way.

2. Partitioned matrices A matrix A is a (2×2) ***block matrix*** if it is represented in the form

$$A = \begin{bmatrix} A_1 & A_2 \\ A_3 & A_4 \end{bmatrix},$$

where each of the A_i are matrices. Note that the matrix A need not be a square matrix; for instance, A might be (7×12) with A_1 being (3×5), A_2 being (3×7), A_3 being (4×5), and A_4 being (4×7). We can imagine creating a (2×2) block matrix by dividing the array into four pieces using a horizontal line and a vertical line.

Now suppose B is also a (2×2) block matrix given by

$$B = \begin{bmatrix} B_1 & B_2 \\ B_3 & B_4 \end{bmatrix}.$$

Finally, let us suppose that the product AB can be formed and that B has been partitioned in a way such that the following matrix is defined:

$$\begin{bmatrix} A_1B_1 + A_2B_3 & A_1B_2 + A_2B_4 \\ A_3B_1 + A_4B_3 & A_3B_2 + A_4B_4 \end{bmatrix}.$$

It turns out that the product AB is given by this block matrix. That is, if all the submatrix products are defined, then we can treat the blocks in a partitioned matrix as though they were scalars when forming products. It is tedious to prove this result in general, so we ask you to illustrate its validity with some randomly chosen matrices.

a) Using the MATLAB command `round(10*rand(6, 6))` generate two randomly selected (6×6) matrices A and B. Compute the product AB. Then write each of A and B as a block matrix of the form

$$A = \begin{bmatrix} A_1 & A_2 \\ A_3 & A_4 \end{bmatrix} \quad B = \begin{bmatrix} B_1 & B_2 \\ B_3 & B_4 \end{bmatrix}.$$

Above, each A_i and B_i should be a (3×3) block. Using matrix surgery (see Section 4 of Appendix A) extract the A_i and B_i matrices and form the new block matrix:

$$\begin{bmatrix} A_1B_1 + A_2B_3 & A_1B_2 + A_2B_4 \\ A_3B_1 + A_4B_3 & A_3B_2 + A_4B_4 \end{bmatrix}.$$

Compare the preceding block matrix with AB and confirm that they are equal.

b) Repeat this calculation on three other matrices (not necessarily (6×6) matrices). Break some of these matrices into blocks of unequal sizes. You need to make sure that corresponding blocks are the correct size so that matrix multiplication is defined.

c) Repeat the calculation in (a) with the product of a (2×3) block matrix times a (3×3) block matrix.

In Exercise 3, determine how many places were lost to round-off error when $A\mathbf{x} = \mathbf{b}$ was solved on the computer?

3. This exercise expands on the topic of ill-conditioned matrices, introduced at the end of Section 1.9. In general, a mathematician speaks of a problem as being ***ill conditioned*** if *small* changes in the parameters of the problem lead to *large* changes in the solution to the problem.

Part d) of this exercise also discusses a very practical question:

> *How much reliance can I place in the solution to* $A\mathbf{x} = \mathbf{b}$ *that my computer gives me?*

A reasonably precise assessment of this question can be made using the concept of a **condition number** for A.

An easily understood example of an ill-conditioned problem is the equation $A\mathbf{x} = \mathbf{b}$ where A is the $(n \times n)$ Hilbert matrix (see Example 7, Section 1.9 for the definition of the Hilbert matrix). When A is the Hilbert matrix, then a small change in any entry of A or a small change in any entry of $\mathbf{b}$ will lead to a large change in the solution of $A\mathbf{x} = \mathbf{b}$.

Let A denote the $(n \times n)$ Hilbert matrix; in MATLAB, A can be created by the command $A = \text{hilb}(n, n)$.

a) Let B denote the inverse of A, as calculated by MATLAB. For $n = 8, 9, 10, 11$, and 12, form the product AB and note how the product looks less and less like the identity. In order to have the results clearly displayed, you might want to use the MATLAB Bank format for your output. For each value n, list the difference of the (1, 1) entries, $(AB)_{11} - I_{11}$. [Note that it is not MATLAB's fault that the inverse cannot be calculated with any accuracy. MATLAB's calculations are all done with 17-place arithmetic, but the Hilbert matrix is so sensitive that seventeen places are not enough.]

b) This exercise illustrates how small changes in $\mathbf{b}$ can sometimes dramatically shift the solution of $A\mathbf{x} = \mathbf{b}$ when A is an ill-conditioned matrix. Let A denote the (9×9) Hilbert matrix and let $\mathbf{b}$ denote the (9×1) column vector consisting entirely of 1's. Use MATLAB to calculate the solution $\mathbf{u} = \text{inv}(A)*\mathbf{b}$. Next change the fourth component of $\mathbf{b}$ to 1.001 and let $\mathbf{v} = \text{inv}(A)*\mathbf{b}$. Compare the difference between the two solution vectors $\mathbf{u}$ and $\mathbf{v}$; what is the largest component (in absolute value) of the difference vector $\mathbf{u} - \mathbf{v}$? For ease of comparison, you might form the matrix $[\mathbf{u}, \mathbf{v}]$ and display it using Bank format.

c) This exercise illustrates that different methods of solving $A\mathbf{x} = \mathbf{b}$ may lead to wildly different numerical answers in the computer when A is ill-conditioned. For A and $\mathbf{b}$

as in part b), compare the solution vector **u** found using the MATLAB command `u = inv(A)*b` with the solution **w** found using the MATLAB command `ww = rref([A, b])`. For comparison, display the matrix [**u**, **w**] using Bank format. What is the largest component (in absolute value) of the difference vector $\mathbf{u} - \mathbf{w}$?

d) To give a numerical measure for how ill conditioned a matrix is, mathematicians use the concept of a ***condition number***. You can find the definition of the condition number in a numerical analysis text. The condition number has many uses, one of which is to estimate the error between a machine-calculated solution to $A\mathbf{x} = \mathbf{b}$ and the true solution. To explain, let $\mathbf{x}_c$ denote the machine-calculated solution and let $\mathbf{x}_t$ denote the true solution. For a machine that uses d-place arithmetic, we can bound the relative error between the true solution and the machine solution as follows:

$$\frac{\|\mathbf{x}_c - \mathbf{x}_t\|}{\|\mathbf{x}_t\|} \le 10^{-d}\,\mathrm{Cond}(A). \tag{2}$$

In inequality (2), Cond(A) denotes the condition number. The left-hand side of the inequality is the ***relative error*** (sometimes also called the ***percentage error***). The relative error has the following interpretation: If the relative error is about 10^{-k}, then the two vectors $\mathbf{x}_c$ and $\mathbf{x}_t$ agree to about k places. Thus, using inequality (2), suppose Cond(A) is about 10^c and suppose we are using MATLAB so that $d = 17$. Then the right-hand side of inequality (2) is roughly $(10^{-17})(10^c) = 10^{-(17-c)}$. In other words, we might have as few as $17 - c$ correct places in the computer-calculated solution (we might have more than $17 - c$ correct places, but inequality (2) is sharp and so there will be problems for which the inequality is nearly an equality). If $c = 14$, for instance, then we might have as few as 3 correct places in our answer.

Test inequality (2) using the $(n \times n)$ Hilbert matrix for $n = 3, 4, \ldots, 9$. As the vector **b**, use the n-dimensional vector consisting entirely of 1's. For a calculated solution, use MATLAB to calculate $\mathbf{x}_c = \mathrm{inv}(A)^*\mathbf{b}$ where A is the $(n \times n)$ Hilbert matrix. For this illustration we also need to determine the true solution $\mathbf{x}_t$. Now, it is known that the Hilbert matrix has an inverse with only integer entries, see Example 6 in Section 1.9 for a listing of the inverse of the (6×6) Hilbert matrix. (In fact, there is a known formula giving the entries of Hilbert matrix inverses.) Therefore, the true solution to our problem is a vector $\mathbf{x}_t$ that has only integer entries. The calculated solution found by MATLAB can be rounded in order to generate the true solution. Do so, using the MATLAB rounding command: `xt = round(xc)`. Finally, the MATLAB command `cond(A)` will calculate the condition number for A. Prepare a table listing n, the left-hand side of inequality (2), and the right-hand side of inequality (2) with $d = 17$. Next, using the long format, display several of the pairs $\mathbf{x}_c$ and $\mathbf{x}_t$ and comment on how well the order of magnitude of the relative error compares with the number of correct places in $\mathbf{x}_c$.

2 VECTORS IN 2-SPACE AND 3-SPACE

Readers already familiar with the material in this chapter can go directly to Chapter 3 with no loss of continuity.

OVERVIEW

In this chapter we review the related concepts of physical vectors, geometric vectors, and algebraic vectors. To provide maximum geometric insight, we concentrate on vectors in two-space and three-space.

Later, in Chapter 3, we will generalize many of the ideas developed in this chapter and apply them to a study of vectors in n-space, that is, to vectors in R^n. A major emphasis in Chapter 3 is on certain fundamental ideas such as subspaces of R^n and the dimension of a subspace. As we will see in Chapter 3, concepts such as subspace and dimension are directly related to the geometrically familiar notions of lines and planes in three-space.

CORE SECTIONS

2.1 *Vectors in the Plane*

2.2 *Vectors in Space*

2.3 *The Dot Product and the Cross Product*

2.4 *Lines and Planes in Space*

2.1 VECTORS IN THE PLANE

The word ***vector*** has its origins in physics where it is used to denote a quantity having both magnitude and direction—quantities such as force and velocity. In this chapter we see how matrix algebra can help us solve the problems involving vectors that arise in science and engineering.

Three Types of Vectors

To minimize confusion, we will be careful to distinguish among three different types of vectors:

(a) Physical vectors
(b) Geometric vectors
(c) Algebraic vectors

We will use the term ***physical vector*** when we refer to a physical quantity such as a force or a velocity.

If we want to visualize a physical vector, we can draw a directed line segment in the xy-plane. We will refer to such a directed line segment as a ***geometric vector.***

Finally, as we will see, any geometric vector in the plane can be represented as an ordered pair. We will call such a representation an ***algebraic vector.*** We will use algebraic vectors when we need to make a calculation.

Physical Vectors

Some physical quantities, such as air pressure in a tire or the weight of a metal bar, can be described by a single real number. Such quantities are called ***scalar quantities.*** Frequently, however, a single real number is not sufficient to describe a physical situation. For example, consider a wind blowing from the southwest toward the northeast at 10 miles per hour. This wind has both magnitude and direction and so we need two numbers to describe it.

In general, a physical quantity having both magnitude and direction is called a ***vector quantity*** or simply, a ***vector.*** Typical physical vectors are forces, displacements, velocities, and so forth.

Geometric Vectors

We use geometric vectors to visualize a problem that involves physical vectors. For instance, consider Fig. 2.1, which shows two wires pulling on a pin. If the pin tears loose from the block, which direction will it fly?

We can visualize the problem described in Fig. 2.1 by sketching it in the xy-plane; see Fig. 2.2. Note in Fig. 2.2 that the directed line segment OP representing the horizontal force has a length of 50. Similarly, OQ, which represents the other force, has a length of 90. The directed line segments (or arrows) in Fig. 2.2 are examples of geometric vectors.

In general, let $A = (a_1, a_2)$ and $B = (b_1, b_2)$ be two points in the xy-plane. The directed line segment from A to B is called a ***geometric vector*** and is denoted by

$$\mathbf{v} = \overrightarrow{AB}.$$

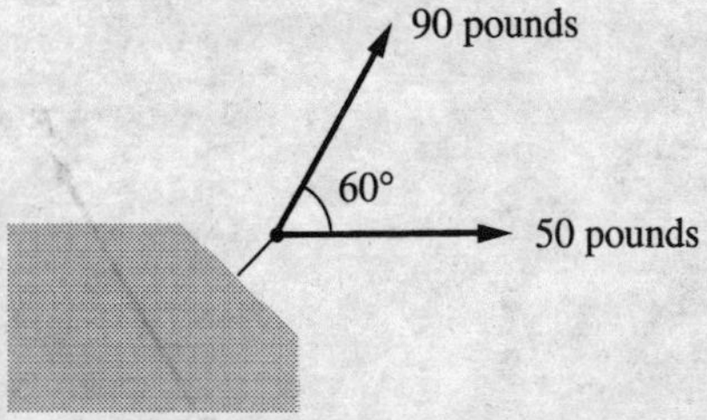

Figure 2.1 The tension in the horizontal wire is 50 pounds, and the tension in the other wire is 90 pounds. If the pin tears loose from the block, which direction will it fly?

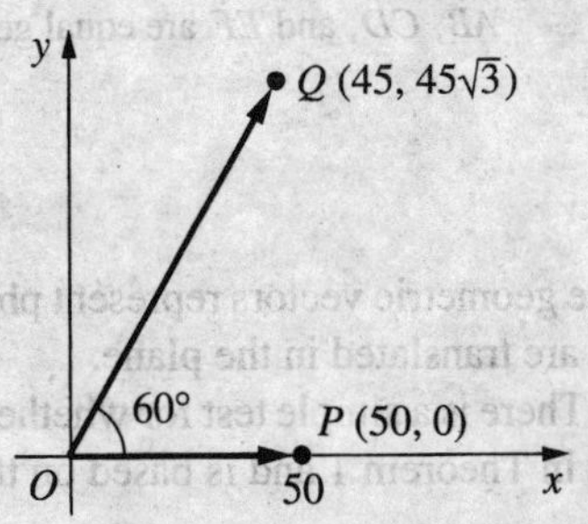

Figure 2.2 Geometric vectors representing the physical vectors in Fig. 2.1

For a given geometric vector $\overrightarrow{AB}$, the endpoint A is called the ***initial point*** and B is the ***terminal point***. A geometric vector has both magnitude (its length) and direction—therefore, it is natural to represent physical vectors as geometric vectors.

Equality of Geometric Vectors

Because we are going to use geometric vectors to represent physical vectors, we adopt the following rule:

> *All geometric vectors having the same direction and magnitude will be regarded as* ***equal****, regardless of whether or not they have the same endpoints.*

For example, in Fig. 2.3, the geometric vectors $\overrightarrow{AB}$, $\overrightarrow{CD}$, and $\overrightarrow{EF}$ are all equal.

We use this definition of equality for geometric vectors because it agrees with the definition of equality for physical vectors. For instance, suppose we place a brick weighing five pounds on a desk. The brick exerts the same five-pound force (directed downward) no matter where we place it on the desk. Similarly, if we move the brick from the desk and place it on the floor, it still exerts a five-pound force directed downward. In other words, the force vector does not change even if its point of application is changed.

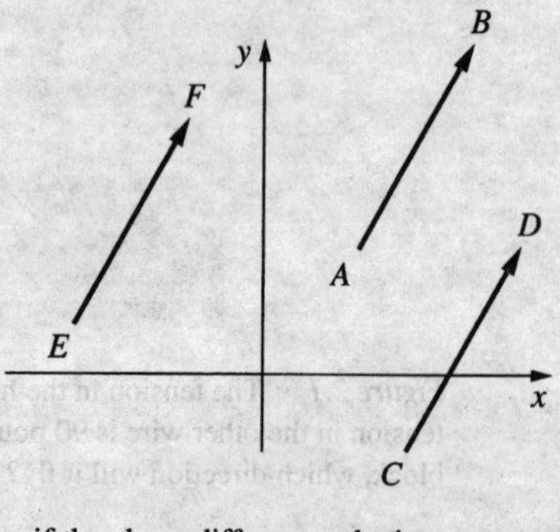

Figure 2.3 Even if they have different endpoints, geometric vectors are equal whenever they have the same magnitude and direction. Thus, $\overrightarrow{AB}$, $\overrightarrow{CD}$, and $\overrightarrow{EF}$ are equal geometric vectors.

Since geometric vectors represent physical vectors, we do not want them to change when they are translated in the plane.

There is a simple test for whether two geometric vectors are equal. This test is given later in Theorem 1 and is based on the idea of a *position vector.*

Position Vectors

Let $\mathbf{v} = \overrightarrow{AB}$ be a geometric vector having initial point $A = (a_1, a_2)$ and having terminal point $B = (b_1, b_2)$; see Fig. 2.4. Among all geometric vectors $\overrightarrow{CD}$ that are equal to $\overrightarrow{AB}$, there is exactly one of the form $\mathbf{v} = \overrightarrow{OP}$ where the initial point $O = (0, 0)$ is at the origin; see Fig. 2.4. This vector $\overrightarrow{OP}$ is called the ***position vector*** for $\mathbf{v}$. From geometry, it follows that the terminal point P has coordinates equal to $(b_1 - a_1, b_2 - a_2)$.

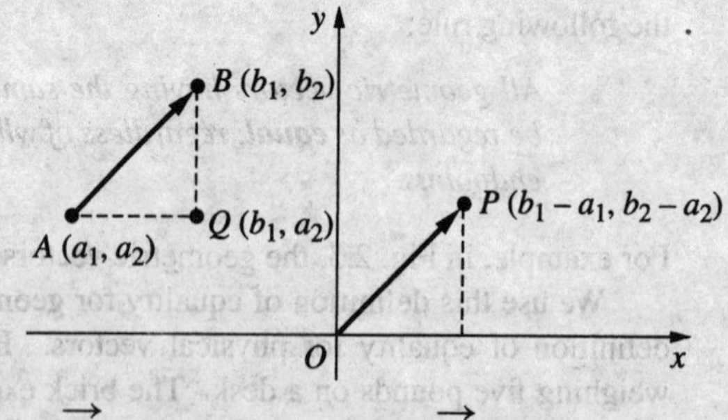

Figure 2.4 $\overrightarrow{OP}$ is the position vector for $\overrightarrow{AB}$. From geometry, P has coordinates $(b_1 - a_1, b_2 - a_2)$.

Components of a Vector

Let $\mathbf{v} = \overrightarrow{OP}$ be the position vector for $\mathbf{v} = \overrightarrow{AB}$. The coordinates of P are called the ***components*** of $\mathbf{v}$. If $A = (a_1, a_2)$ and $B = (b_1, b_2)$, then we see from Fig. 2.4:

$$\text{The } x\text{-component of } \overrightarrow{AB} \text{ is } b_1 - a_1 \tag{1a}$$

$$\text{The } y\text{-component of } \overrightarrow{AB} \text{ is } b_2 - a_2 \tag{1b}$$

EXAMPLE 1 Let $A = (7, 3)$ and $B = (2, 5)$. Find the components of $\mathbf{v} = \overrightarrow{AB}$.

Solution By (1), the x-component of $\overrightarrow{AB}$ is $2 - 7 = -5$. Similarly, the y-component of $\overrightarrow{AB}$ is $5 - 3 = 2$. (In terms of Fig. 2.4, the position vector $\overrightarrow{OP}$ has its terminal point given by $P = (-5, 2)$.) ■

An Equality Test for Geometric Vectors

As we see from the following theorem, two geometric vectors are equal if and only if they have the same components.

THEOREM 1 Let $\overrightarrow{AB}$ and $\overrightarrow{CD}$ be geometric vectors. Then $\overrightarrow{AB} = \overrightarrow{CD}$ if and only if their components are equal.

Proof If two geometric vectors are equal, then they have the same position vector; hence, they have the same components. On the other hand, if two geometric vectors have the same components, then they have the same position vector; hence, they are equal. ■

The following example illustrates Theorem 1.

EXAMPLE 2 Let $A = (2, 2)$, $B = (4, 5)$, $C = (3, -2)$, and $D = (5, 1)$. Use Theorem 1 to show that $\overrightarrow{AB} = \overrightarrow{CD}$.

Solution Calculating x-components, we have

For $\overrightarrow{\mathbf{AB}}$**:** $b_1 - a_1 = 4 - 2 = 2$

For $\overrightarrow{\mathbf{CD}}$**:** $d_1 - c_1 = 5 - 3 = 2.$

Similarly, calculating y-components, we find

For $\overrightarrow{\mathbf{AB}}$**:** $b_2 - a_2 = 5 - \quad 2 = 3$

For $\overrightarrow{\mathbf{CD}}$**:** $d_2 - c_2 = 1 - (-2) = 3.$

Since both vectors have the same components, Theorem 1 tells us they are equal. ■

If we know the components of a geometric vector $\mathbf{v}$, then it is easy to draw $\mathbf{v}$ using any desired initial point or terminal point. For example, suppose we know that $\mathbf{v}$ has an x-component v_1 and a y-component v_2. Suppose we want to represent $\mathbf{v}$ as the directed line segment $\overrightarrow{AB}$, where $A = (a_1, a_2)$. The terminal point B is found by moving v_1 units in the x direction and then v_2 units in the y direction. In other words

$$B = (a_1 + v_1, a_2 + v_2). \tag{2}$$

If we want to specify the terminal point B, a similar calculation is used to find the initial point A; see part (**b**) of the next example.

EXAMPLE 3 A geometric vector **v** has x-component 3 and y-component -5.

(a) If we want to represent **v** in the form $\mathbf{v} = \overrightarrow{AB}$ where $A = (1, 2)$, what are the coordinates of the terminal point B?

(b) If we want to represent **v** in the form $\mathbf{v} = \overrightarrow{CD}$ where $D = (5, 7)$, what are the coordinates of the initial point C?

Solution

(a) By (2), the coordinates of B are $(1 + 3, 2 + (-5)) = (4, -3)$; see Fig. 2.5.

(b) Given the coordinates of the terminal point D, we find the initial point C by moving "backward"; that is, see Fig. 2.5,

$$C = (5 - v_1, 7 - v_2) = (5 - 3, 7 - (-5)) = (2, 12).$$

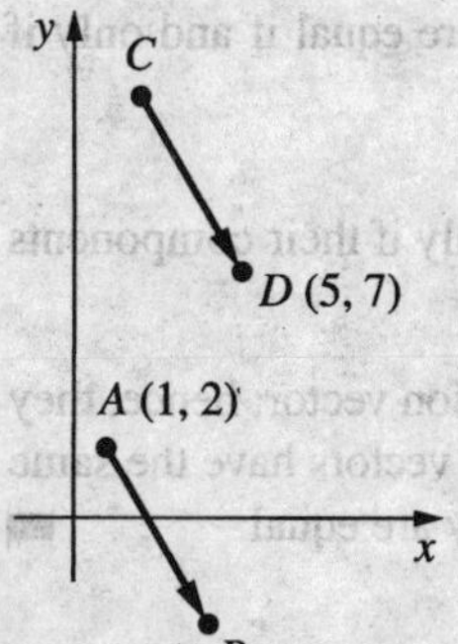

Figure 2.5
A geometric vector **v** has x-component 3 and y-component -5. In Example 3 we saw how to draw **v** with initial point A and how to draw **v** with terminal point D.

Algebraic Vectors

Let **v** be a geometric vector with x-component v_1 and y-component v_2. Figure 2.6 shows $\overrightarrow{OP}$, the position vector for **v**, where

$$P = (v_1, v_2).$$

Since **v** is completely characterized by its components, it is natural to associate **v** with the algebraic vector

$$\mathbf{v} = \begin{bmatrix} v_1 \\ v_2 \end{bmatrix}.$$

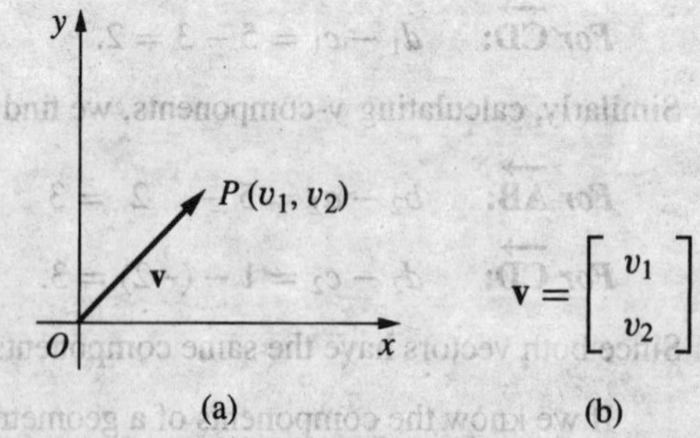

Figure 2.6 (a) $\overrightarrow{OP}$ is the position vector for **v**; the *coordinates* of P are equal to the components of **v**. (b) In the algebraic representation for **v**, the *entries* of the column vector are the components of **v**.

The connection between a geometric vector $\mathbf{v} = \overrightarrow{AB}$ and its algebraic representation

$$\mathbf{v} = \begin{bmatrix} v_1 \\ v_2 \end{bmatrix}$$

is so close that we will not distinguish between the two. We simply use the term ***vector*** to refer to either representation. Each representation for **v** has its own advantages. The geometric representation allows us to draw diagrams as an aid for our intuition. On the other hand, the algebraic representation is very efficient when we need to make mathematical calculations.

Table 2.1 summarizes the relationship between geometric vectors and algebraic vectors.

Table 2.1

(a) Let $\mathbf{v} = \overrightarrow{AB}$ be a geometric vector, with $A = (a_1, a_2)$ and $B = (b_1, b_2)$. Then **v** can be represented by the algebraic vector

$$\mathbf{v} = \begin{bmatrix} b_1 - a_1 \\ b_2 - a_2 \end{bmatrix}.$$

(b) Let $\mathbf{v} = \begin{bmatrix} v_1 \\ v_2 \end{bmatrix}$. Given $A = (a_1, a_2)$, **v** can be represented as the geometric vector $\overrightarrow{AB}$ where the terminal point B is given by

$$B = (a_1 + v_1, a_2 + v_2).$$

EXAMPLE 4

(a) Let $\mathbf{v} = \overrightarrow{AB}$ where $A = (1, 5)$ and $B = (3, 2)$. Represent **v** as an algebraic vector.

(b) Let $\mathbf{u} = \begin{bmatrix} 4 \\ 7 \end{bmatrix}$. Represent **u** as a geometric vector with initial point $C = (5, -2)$.

Solution

(a) Using part **(a)** of Table 2.1,

$$\mathbf{v} = \begin{bmatrix} 2 \\ -3 \end{bmatrix}.$$

(b) Using part **(b)** of Table 2.1, $\mathbf{u} = \overrightarrow{CD}$ where $D = (5 + 4, -2 + 7) = (9, 5)$. ∎

Adding Physical Vectors

As you might recall from your physics or statics courses, physical vectors (forces, displacements, velocities, and so forth) can be summed.

For instance, consider Fig. 2.7 which shows two forces, $\mathbf{F}_1$ and $\mathbf{F}_2$, applied at the same point A. We know from physics that the net effect of applying these two forces is exactly the same as applying a single force $\mathbf{F}$. This single force $\mathbf{F}$ is called the ***resultant force*** and can be calculated by adding $\mathbf{F}_1$ and $\mathbf{F}_2$ according to the rules for adding geometric vectors.

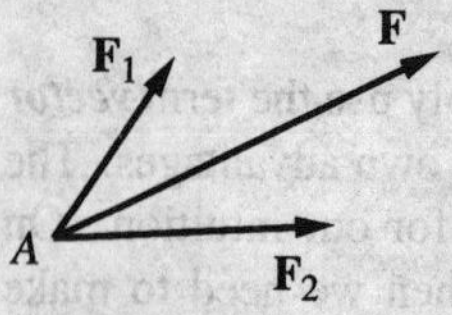

Figure 2.7
The net effect of the two forces $\mathbf{F}_1$ and $\mathbf{F}_2$ is the same as the effect of the single resultant force $\mathbf{F}$. The resultant force $\mathbf{F}$ can be calculated using the rules for adding geometric vectors.

Adding Geometric Vectors

You are familiar with the rules for adding geometric vectors from your physics courses. We review those rules now.

As in Fig. 2.8(a), let $\mathbf{u}$ and $\mathbf{v}$ be geometric vectors. The ***sum***, denoted by $\mathbf{u} + \mathbf{v}$, is the geometric vector found as follows [see Fig. 2.8(b)]:

(a) Translate $\mathbf{v}$ so that its initial point coincides with the terminal point of $\mathbf{u}$.

(b) Then, $\mathbf{u} + \mathbf{v}$ is the geometric vector having the same initial point as $\mathbf{u}$ and the same terminal point as the translated vector $\mathbf{v}$.

As will be shown shortly, it does not matter which vector is translated—we can move $\mathbf{v}$ to the tip of $\mathbf{u}$ as in Fig. 2.8(b), or we can move $\mathbf{u}$ to the tip of $\mathbf{v}$. We will always get the same sum, $\mathbf{u} + \mathbf{v}$, in either case.

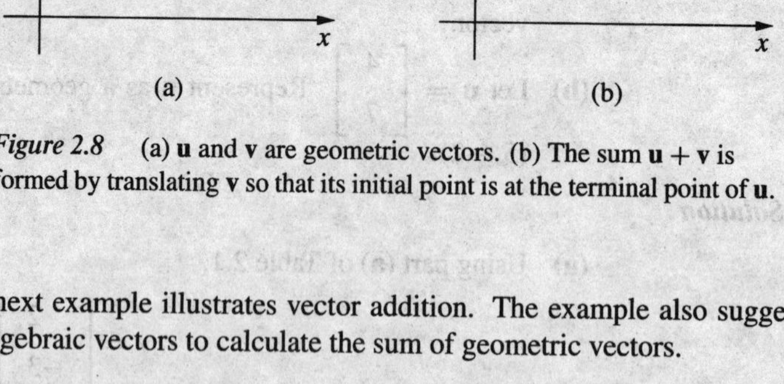

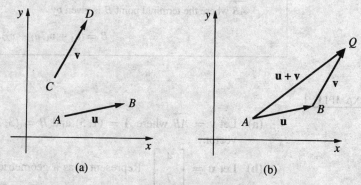

Figure 2.8 (a) $\mathbf{u}$ and $\mathbf{v}$ are geometric vectors. (b) The sum $\mathbf{u} + \mathbf{v}$ is formed by translating $\mathbf{v}$ so that its initial point is at the terminal point of $\mathbf{u}$.

The next example illustrates vector addition. The example also suggests that we can use algebraic vectors to calculate the sum of geometric vectors.

EXAMPLE 5 Let $\mathbf{u} = \overrightarrow{AB}$ where $A = (1, 2)$ and $B = (4, 6)$; see Fig. 2.9. Let $\mathbf{v} = \overrightarrow{CD}$ where $C = (-4, 3)$ and $D = (-2, 1)$. Find the sum $\mathbf{u} + \mathbf{v}$.

Solution In Fig. 2.9(b) we translate **v** so that its initial point is at $B = (4, 6)$. As can be seen, the terminal point of **v** is now at $Q = (6, 4)$. Thus, we see that the sum $\mathbf{u} + \mathbf{v}$ is given by $\mathbf{u} + \mathbf{v} = \overrightarrow{AQ}$. ■

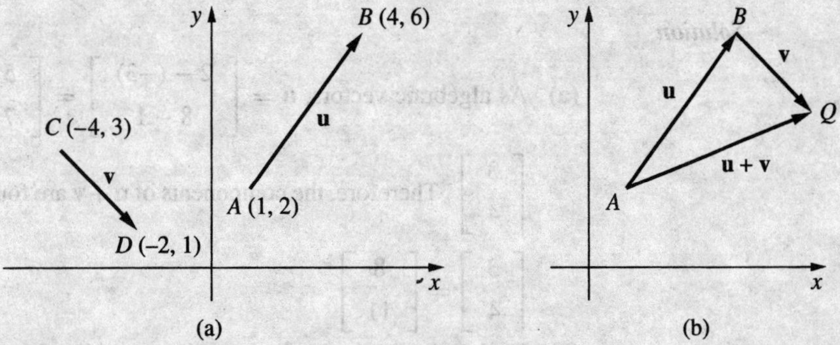

Figure 2.9 Forming the sum $\mathbf{u} + \mathbf{v}$, see Example 5

If we examine the geometric construction used in Fig. 2.9, we see that the coordinates of Q are found by adding the *components* of **v** to the *coordinates* of B. Therefore, Fig. 2.9 suggests that we can use algebraic vectors to calculate vector sums; this idea is stated formally below, in Theorem 2.

Using Algebraic Vectors to Calculate the Sum of Geometric Vectors

The following theorem shows that we can find the components of $\mathbf{u} + \mathbf{v}$ by adding their corresponding algebraic vector representations. In words: the components of the sum are the sums of the components.

THEOREM 2 Let **u** and **v** be geometric vectors with algebraic representations given by $\mathbf{u} = \begin{bmatrix} u_1 \\ u_2 \end{bmatrix}$ and $\mathbf{v} = \begin{bmatrix} v_1 \\ v_2 \end{bmatrix}$. Then the sum $\mathbf{u} + \mathbf{v}$ has the following algebraic representation:

$$\mathbf{u} + \mathbf{v} = \begin{bmatrix} u_1 + v_1 \\ u_2 + v_2 \end{bmatrix}.$$

Proof The proof is based on Fig. 2.8 where $\mathbf{u} = \overrightarrow{AB}$. Let $A = (a_1, a_2)$ and let $B = (b_1, b_2)$. Note that, $\mathbf{u} + \mathbf{v} = \overrightarrow{AQ}$ where $Q = (b_1 + v_1, b_2 + v_2)$. Therefore, the components of $\mathbf{u} + \mathbf{v} = \overrightarrow{AQ}$ are:

The x-component: $(b_1 + v_1) - a_1 = (b_1 - a_1) + v_1 = u_1 + v_1$

The y-component: $(b_2 + v_2) - a_2 = (b_2 - a_2) + v_2 = u_2 + v_2.$ ■

EXAMPLE 6 Let $\mathbf{u} = \overrightarrow{AB}$ where $A = (-3, 1)$ and $B = (2, 8)$. Let $\mathbf{v} = \overrightarrow{CD}$ where $C = (1, 3)$ and $D = (4, 7)$.

(a) Use Theorem 2 to find the components of $\mathbf{u} + \mathbf{v}$.

(b) Find S so that $\mathbf{u} + \mathbf{v} = \overrightarrow{RS}$ when the initial point is $R = (-1, 1)$.

Solution

(a) As algebraic vectors, $\mathbf{u} = \begin{bmatrix} 2-(-3) \\ 8-1 \end{bmatrix} = \begin{bmatrix} 5 \\ 7 \end{bmatrix}$ and $\mathbf{v} = \begin{bmatrix} 4-1 \\ 7-3 \end{bmatrix} = \begin{bmatrix} 3 \\ 4 \end{bmatrix}$. Therefore, the components of $\mathbf{u}+\mathbf{v}$ are found from $\mathbf{u}+\mathbf{v} = \begin{bmatrix} 5 \\ 7 \end{bmatrix} + \begin{bmatrix} 3 \\ 4 \end{bmatrix} = \begin{bmatrix} 8 \\ 11 \end{bmatrix}$.

(b) Having the components of $\mathbf{u} + \mathbf{v}$ we see that the terminal point S is given by $S = (-1 + 8, 1 + 11) = (7, 12)$. ■

Scalar Multiplication

Suppose you initially push on an object with a certain force, but later decide you need to push twice as hard in the same direction. Let $\mathbf{u} = \overrightarrow{OP}$ be the position vector representing the first force, where $P = (u_1, u_2)$. Let $\mathbf{v} = \overrightarrow{OQ}$ represent the second force (see Fig. 2.10). Since $\mathbf{u}$ and $\mathbf{v}$ are in the same direction, Q must be on the line through O and P. But, since the second force $\mathbf{v}$ is twice as strong, the line segment OQ is twice as long as the segment OP (again, see Fig. 2.10). Thus, the coordinates of Q are twice that of the coordinates of P; that is, $Q = (v_1, v_2) = (2u_1, 2u_2)$.

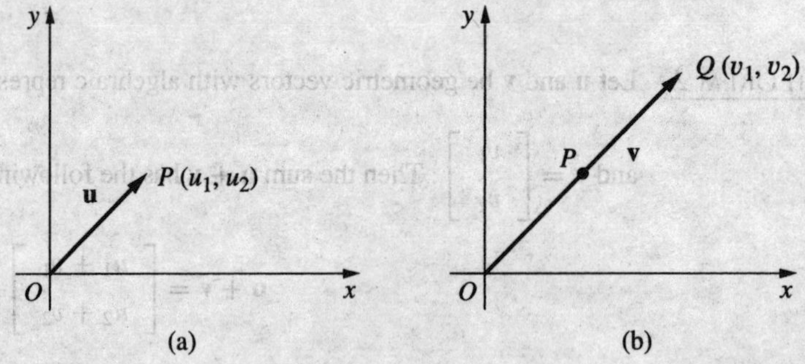

Figure 2.10 The vector $\mathbf{v} = \overrightarrow{OQ}$ is twice as long as the vector $u = \overrightarrow{OP}$. We will write $\mathbf{v} = 2\mathbf{u}$.

Interpreting Fig. 2.10 in terms of algebraic vectors, we have

$$\mathbf{v} = \begin{bmatrix} v_1 \\ v_2 \end{bmatrix} = \begin{bmatrix} 2u_1 \\ 2u_2 \end{bmatrix} = 2\mathbf{u}.$$

The rules for forming the scalar multiple of a geometric vector are suggested by Fig. 2.10. In particular, let $\mathbf{u} = \overrightarrow{AB}$ be a geometric vector and let c denote a scalar. The ***scalar multiple***, denoted $c\mathbf{u}$, is defined as follows:

(a) If $c > 0$, then $c\mathbf{u}$ is the geometric vector having the same direction as $\mathbf{u}$, but with a magnitude that is c times as large.

(b) If $c < 0$, then $c\mathbf{u}$ is the geometric vector having the opposite direction as $\mathbf{u}$, but with a magnitude that is c times as large.

The definition of scalar multiplication is illustrated in Fig. 2.11.

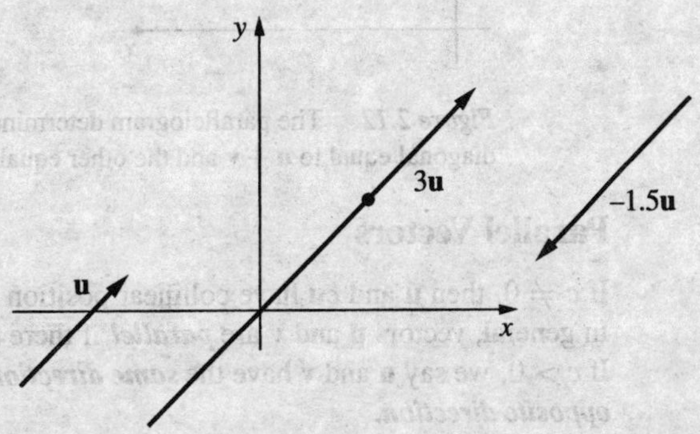

Figure 2.11 The vector $3\mathbf{u}$ is three times as long as $\mathbf{u}$, in the same direction. The vector $-1.5\mathbf{u}$ is 1.5 times as long as $\mathbf{u}$, but is in the opposite direction.

Theorem 2 shows how to use algebraic vectors to calculate the components of the sum, $\mathbf{u} + \mathbf{v}$. As might be expected from Fig. 2.11, a similar result holds for scalar multiplication.

THEOREM 3 Let $\mathbf{u}$ be a geometric vector with algebraic representation

$$\mathbf{u} = \begin{bmatrix} u_1 \\ u_2 \end{bmatrix}.$$

Then the scalar multiple $c\mathbf{u}$ has the following algebraic representation:

$$c\mathbf{u} = \begin{bmatrix} cu_1 \\ cu_2 \end{bmatrix}.$$

Subtracting Geometric Vectors

Having defined the scalar multiple of a geometric vector, we are ready to define the difference, $\mathbf{u} - \mathbf{v}$, of two vectors. We define vector subtraction as follows:

$$\mathbf{u} - \mathbf{v} = \mathbf{u} + (-1)\mathbf{v}.$$

Vector addition and vector subtraction are often visualized in terms of the diagonals of a parallelogram; see Fig. 2.12.

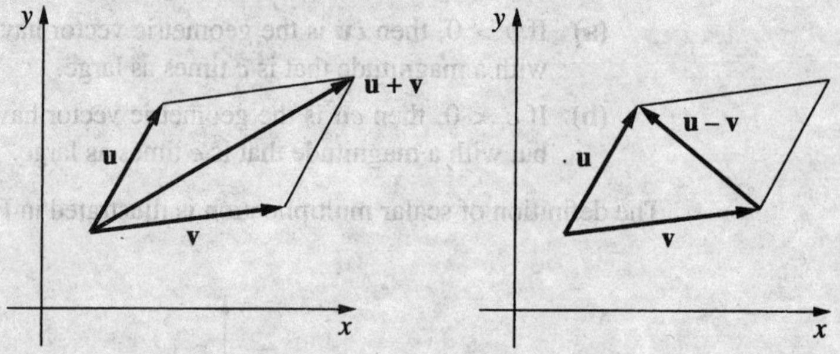

Figure 2.12 The parallelogram determined by **u** and **v** has one diagonal equal to **u** + **v** and the other equal to **u** − **v**.

Parallel Vectors

If $c \neq 0$, then **u** and c**u** have collinear position vectors and we say they are "parallel." In general, vectors **u** and **v** are ***parallel*** if there is a nonzero scalar c such that $\mathbf{v} = c\mathbf{u}$. If $c > 0$, we say **u** and **v** have the ***same direction*** but if $c < 0$, we say **u** and **v** have the ***opposite direction.***

To determine whether vectors are parallel, it is easier to use the algebraic representation than the geometric representation. The next example illustrates this fact.

EXAMPLE 7 Let $\mathbf{u} = \overrightarrow{AB}$ and $\mathbf{v} = \overrightarrow{CD}$ where $A = (1, 2)$, $B = (3, 5)$, $C = (1, 7)$, and $D = (-3, 1)$. Show that **u** and **v** are parallel vectors. Does **v** have the same direction or the opposite direction as **u**?

Solution The algebraic representations for **u** and **v** are (respectively)

$$\mathbf{u} = \begin{bmatrix} 3-1 \\ 5-2 \end{bmatrix} = \begin{bmatrix} 2 \\ 3 \end{bmatrix} \quad \text{and} \quad \mathbf{v} = \begin{bmatrix} -3-1 \\ 1-7 \end{bmatrix} = \begin{bmatrix} -4 \\ -6 \end{bmatrix}.$$

We see that $\mathbf{v} = -2\mathbf{u}$. Hence **v** is parallel to **u**, and has the opposite direction. ■

Lengths of Vectors and Unit Vectors

The length or magnitude of a geometric vector $\mathbf{u} = \overrightarrow{AB}$ is the length of the line segment joining A and B. Therefore, from analytic geometry, the length of $\mathbf{u} = \overrightarrow{AB}$ is equal to

$$\sqrt{(u_1)^2 + (u_2)^2} = \sqrt{(b_1 - a_1)^2 + (b_2 - a_2)^2}.$$

As in Section 1.7, we use the symbol $\|\mathbf{u}\|$, read as the ***norm of u***, to denote the length of **u**:

$$\text{If } \mathbf{u} = \begin{bmatrix} u_1 \\ u_2 \end{bmatrix}, \quad \text{then} \quad \|\mathbf{u}\| = \sqrt{(u_1)^2 + (u_2)^2}.$$

If a vector $\mathbf{w}$ has length equal to 1, we say that $\mathbf{w}$ is a ***unit vector***. That is, $\mathbf{w}$ is a ***unit vector*** if and only if

$$\|\mathbf{w}\| = 1.$$

For example, the following vector $\mathbf{w}$ is a unit vector

$$\mathbf{w} = \begin{bmatrix} 0.6 \\ 0.8 \end{bmatrix}.$$

We often use a unit vector to specify *direction.* In particular, if $\mathbf{u}$ is any nonzero vector, then Eq. (3) gives a formula for a unit vector $\mathbf{w}$ in the same direction as $\mathbf{u}$,

$$\mathbf{w} = \frac{1}{\|\mathbf{u}\|}\mathbf{u}. \quad (3)$$

In Exercise 40 we ask you to verify that the vector $\mathbf{w}$ defined in Eq. (3) is indeed a unit vector. Then, because $\mathbf{w}$ is a positive scalar multiple of $\mathbf{u}$, it will follow that $\mathbf{w}$ is a unit vector in the direction of $\mathbf{u}$. (Similarly, the vector $-\mathbf{w}$ is a unit vector in the direction opposite to $\mathbf{u}$.)

EXAMPLE 8 Find a vector $\mathbf{v}$ having the opposite direction as $\mathbf{u} = \begin{bmatrix} 1 \\ 7 \end{bmatrix}$ and where $\|\mathbf{v}\| = 10$.

Solution We first choose a unit vector $\mathbf{w}$ in the direction we want (opposite the direction of $\mathbf{u}$) and then multiply $\mathbf{w}$ by 10 to produce the desired vector $\mathbf{v}$. Now, $\|\mathbf{u}\| = \sqrt{50}$. Therefore, using (3), a unit vector $\mathbf{w}$ having the same direction as $\mathbf{u}$ is given by

$$\mathbf{w} = \frac{1}{\|\mathbf{u}\|}\mathbf{u} = \frac{1}{\sqrt{50}}\begin{bmatrix} 1 \\ 7 \end{bmatrix}.$$

Since $\mathbf{w}$ has the same direction as $\mathbf{u}$, we know $-\mathbf{w}$ is a unit vector in the direction opposite $\mathbf{u}$. Multiplying $-\mathbf{w}$ by 10 will produce the vector $\mathbf{v}$ asked for in this example:

$$\mathbf{v} = -10\mathbf{w} = -\frac{10}{\sqrt{50}}\begin{bmatrix} 1 \\ 7 \end{bmatrix} = -\frac{10}{5\sqrt{2}}\begin{bmatrix} 1 \\ 7 \end{bmatrix} = -\sqrt{2}\begin{bmatrix} 1 \\ 7 \end{bmatrix}.$$ ■

The Basic Vectors i and j

Let $\mathbf{u} = \begin{bmatrix} u_1 \\ u_2 \end{bmatrix}$ be a vector. Then:

$$\mathbf{u} = \begin{bmatrix} u_1 \\ u_2 \end{bmatrix} = \begin{bmatrix} u_1 \\ 0 \end{bmatrix} + \begin{bmatrix} 0 \\ u_2 \end{bmatrix} = u_1\begin{bmatrix} 1 \\ 0 \end{bmatrix} + u_2\begin{bmatrix} 0 \\ 1 \end{bmatrix} = u_1\mathbf{i} + u_2\mathbf{j} \quad (4)$$

where the special vectors $\mathbf{i}$ and $\mathbf{j}$ are defined by

$$\mathbf{i} = \begin{bmatrix} 1 \\ 0 \end{bmatrix} \quad \text{and} \quad \mathbf{j} = \begin{bmatrix} 0 \\ 1 \end{bmatrix}.$$

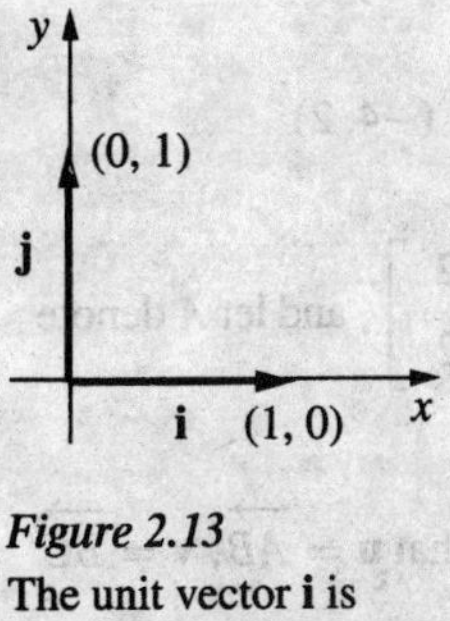

Figure 2.13
The unit vector **i** is parallel to the x-axis; **j** is parallel to the y-axis.

As you can see, the vectors $\mathbf{i}$ and $\mathbf{j}$ are unit vectors; they are shown in Fig. 2.13. From Eq. (4) we see that $\mathbf{i}$ and $\mathbf{j}$ are *basic* in the sense that any vector $\mathbf{u}$ can be formed by adding a scalar multiple of $\mathbf{i}$ to a scalar multiple of $\mathbf{j}$.

EXAMPLE 9 Let $\mathbf{u} = 2\mathbf{i} - 4\mathbf{j}$ and $\mathbf{v} = \mathbf{i} + 6\mathbf{j}$. Find the components of $\mathbf{w} = 2\mathbf{u} + \mathbf{v}$.

Solution We find

$$\mathbf{w} = 2(2\mathbf{i} - 4\mathbf{j}) + (\mathbf{i} + 6\mathbf{j}) = 5\mathbf{i} - 2\mathbf{j} = 5\begin{bmatrix} 1 \\ 0 \end{bmatrix} - 2\begin{bmatrix} 0 \\ 1 \end{bmatrix} = \begin{bmatrix} 5 \\ -2 \end{bmatrix}.$$

2.1 EXERCISES

In Exercises 1–4, graph the geometric vectors $\mathbf{u} = \overrightarrow{AB}$ and $\mathbf{v} = \overrightarrow{CD}$. Determine by inspection whether the two vectors are equal; then use Theorem 1 to verify your answers.

1. $A = (0, -2)$, $B = (-4, 3)$, $C = (1, 2)$, $D = (-3, 7)$
2. $A = (-1, 3)$, $B = (3, -2)$, $C = (5, -1)$, $D = (1, 4)$
3. $A = (-4, -2)$, $B = (0, 1)$, $C = (0, -2)$, $D = (3, 2)$
4. $A = (3, 1)$, $B = (-1, 1)$, $C = (0, 3)$, $D = (-6, 0)$
5. Let $\mathbf{u} = \overrightarrow{AB}$ and $\mathbf{v} = \overrightarrow{CD}$ where $A = (-3, 5)$, $B = (2, 2)$, $C = (3, 4)$, $D = (-2, 7)$.
   - **a)** Verify that $\mathbf{u}$ and $\mathbf{v}$ have the same length.
   - **b)** Verify that the line segments AB and CD have the same slope.
   - **c)** Use Theorem 1 to show that $\mathbf{u} \neq \mathbf{v}$.
   - **d)** Graph $\mathbf{u}$ and $\mathbf{v}$ and use the graph to explain why $\mathbf{u} \neq \mathbf{v}$.

In Exercises 6–9, find the unspecified coordinates so that $\overrightarrow{AB} = \overrightarrow{CD}$.

6. $A = (-1, -3)$, $B = (3, 2)$, $C = (0, 2)$, $D = (d_1, d_2)$
7. $A = (3, -2)$, $B = (0, 3)$, $C = (1, 0)$, $D = (d_1, d_2)$
8. $A = (-2, 3)$, $B = (2, -1)$, $C = (c_1, c_2)$, $D = (3, 2)$
9. $A = (3, -2)$, $B = (3, 4)$, $C = (c_1, c_2)$, $D = (-1, 7)$
10. A force of 10 pounds is directed from left to right along a line at an angle of 30° (measured clockwise) from the horizontal. Represent this force as a geometric vector $\overrightarrow{OP}$ where $O = (0, 0)$. Sketch a graph of $\overrightarrow{OP}$.

In Exercises 11–14, express the geometric vector $\mathbf{v} = \overrightarrow{AB}$ as an algebraic vector $\mathbf{v} = \begin{bmatrix} v_1 \\ v_2 \end{bmatrix}$.

11. $A = (-1, -2)$, $B = (4, 1)$
12. $A = (1, 3)$, $B = (6, -1)$
13. $A = (2, -1)$, $B = (-4, 4)$
14. $A = (3, 2)$, $B = (0, -2)$

In Exercises 15–16, find $B = (b_1, b_2)$ such that $\mathbf{v} = \overrightarrow{AB}$.

15. $\mathbf{v} = \begin{bmatrix} 2 \\ 5 \end{bmatrix}$ and $A = (1, -2)$
16. $\mathbf{v} = \begin{bmatrix} -3 \\ 4 \end{bmatrix}$ and $A = (2, -2)$

In Exercises 17–18, find $A = (a_1, a_2)$ such that $\mathbf{v} = \overrightarrow{AB}$.

17. $\mathbf{v} = \begin{bmatrix} 3 \\ -3 \end{bmatrix}$ and $B = (5, 1)$
18. $\mathbf{v} = \begin{bmatrix} -4 \\ -1 \end{bmatrix}$ and $B = (-4, 2)$
19. Let $\mathbf{u} = \begin{bmatrix} 1 \\ 3 \end{bmatrix}$ and $\mathbf{v} = \begin{bmatrix} 2 \\ -2 \end{bmatrix}$, and let A denote the point $(2, -1)$.
    - **a)** Find points B and C such that $\mathbf{u} = \overrightarrow{AB}$, $\mathbf{v} = \overrightarrow{BC}$ and $\mathbf{u} + \mathbf{v} = \overrightarrow{AC}$.
    - **b)** Graph $\mathbf{u} = \overrightarrow{AB}$, $\mathbf{v} = \overrightarrow{BC}$ and $\mathbf{u} + \mathbf{v} = \overrightarrow{AC}$.

20. Repeat Exercise 19 for $\mathbf{u} = \begin{bmatrix} -2 \\ 4 \end{bmatrix}$ and $\mathbf{v} = \begin{bmatrix} 3 \\ 1 \end{bmatrix}$ and $A = (0, -1)$.

21. Let $\mathbf{u} = \overrightarrow{AB}$ and $\mathbf{v} = \overrightarrow{CD}$, where $A = (-1, 2)$, $B = (3, 5)$, $C = (0, 3)$, $D = (4, -1)$.

a) Find a point Q such that $\mathbf{v} = \overrightarrow{BQ}$ and $\mathbf{u} + \mathbf{v} = \overrightarrow{AQ}$.

b) Graph $\mathbf{u} = \overrightarrow{AB}$, $\mathbf{v} = \overrightarrow{CD}$, $\mathbf{v} = \overrightarrow{BQ}$, and $\mathbf{u} + \mathbf{v} = \overrightarrow{AQ}$.

22. Repeat Exercise 21 with $A = (-2, 4)$, $B = (1, -3)$, $C = (0, 1)$, $D = (3, 5)$.

23. Let $\mathbf{u} = \begin{bmatrix} 1 \\ 3 \end{bmatrix}$ and $\mathbf{v} = \begin{bmatrix} 2 \\ -2 \end{bmatrix}$, and let A denote the point $(-2, 1)$.

a) Find points B and C such that $\mathbf{u} = \overrightarrow{AB}$, $\mathbf{v} = \overrightarrow{AC}$, and $\mathbf{u} - \mathbf{v} = \overrightarrow{CB}$.

b) Graph $\mathbf{u} = \overrightarrow{AB}$, $\mathbf{v} = \overrightarrow{AC}$, and $\mathbf{u} - \mathbf{v} = \overrightarrow{CB}$.

24. Let $\mathbf{u} = \overrightarrow{AB}$ and $\mathbf{v} = \overrightarrow{CD}$ where $A = (-1, 2)$, $B = (3, 5)$, $C = (0, 3)$, $D = (4, -1)$.

a) Find a point Q such that $\mathbf{v} = \overrightarrow{AQ}$ and $\mathbf{u} - \mathbf{v} = \overrightarrow{QB}$.

b) Graph $\mathbf{u} = \overrightarrow{AB}$, $\mathbf{v} = \overrightarrow{CD}$, $\mathbf{v} = \overrightarrow{AQ}$, and $\mathbf{u} - \mathbf{v} = \overrightarrow{QB}$.

25. Let $\mathbf{v} = \begin{bmatrix} 3 \\ -2 \end{bmatrix}$ and $A = (0, 5)$.

a) Find points B and C such that $\mathbf{v} = AB$ and $2\mathbf{v} = \overrightarrow{AC}$.

b) Graph $\mathbf{v} = \overrightarrow{AB}$ and $2\mathbf{v} = \overrightarrow{AC}$.

26. Let $\mathbf{v} = 2\mathbf{i} + 6\mathbf{j}$ and $A = (-2, 1)$.

a) Find points B and C such that $\mathbf{v} = \overrightarrow{AB}$ and $\left(\frac{-1}{2}\right)\mathbf{v} = \overrightarrow{AC}$.

b) Graph $\mathbf{v} = \overrightarrow{AB}$ and $\left(\frac{-1}{2}\right)\mathbf{v} = \overrightarrow{AC}$.

27. Let $\mathbf{v} = \overrightarrow{AB}$ where $A = (1, 4)$ and $B = (5, -1)$.

a) If $C = (-2, 7)$, find D such that $2\mathbf{v} = \overrightarrow{CD}$.

b) Graph $\mathbf{v} = \overrightarrow{AB}$ and $2\mathbf{v} = \overrightarrow{CD}$.

In Exercises 28–31, find a unit vector $\mathbf{u}$ that has the same direction as the given vector $\mathbf{v}$.

28. $\mathbf{v} = \begin{bmatrix} -1 \\ 2 \end{bmatrix}$ **29.** $\mathbf{v} = \begin{bmatrix} 3 \\ 4 \end{bmatrix}$

30. $\mathbf{v} = \mathbf{i} + \mathbf{j}$ **31.** $\mathbf{v} = 3\mathbf{i} - 2\mathbf{j}$

In Exercises 32–35, determine the terminal point B such that $\mathbf{v} = \overrightarrow{AB}$.

32. $\mathbf{v}$ has the same direction as $\begin{bmatrix} 2 \\ 1 \end{bmatrix}$, $\|\mathbf{v}\| = 4\sqrt{5}$, $A = (-4, -2)$.

33. $\mathbf{v}$ has opposite direction to $\begin{bmatrix} 1 \\ 3 \end{bmatrix}$, $\|\mathbf{v}\| = 3\sqrt{10}$, $A = (4, 7)$.

34. $\mathbf{v}$ is parallel to $\mathbf{i} + 2\mathbf{j}$, $A = (3, 1)$, B is on the y-axis.

35. $\mathbf{v}$ is parallel to $\mathbf{i} + 3\mathbf{j}$, $A = (3, 1)$, B is on the line $y = -7$.

In Exercises 36–39, find the components of $\mathbf{u} + \mathbf{v}$ and $\mathbf{u} - 3\mathbf{v}$.

36. $\mathbf{u} = \begin{bmatrix} 1 \\ 1 \end{bmatrix}$, $\mathbf{v} = \begin{bmatrix} 1 \\ 2 \end{bmatrix}$

37. $\mathbf{u} = \begin{bmatrix} 0 \\ 5 \end{bmatrix}$, $\mathbf{v} = \begin{bmatrix} 2 \\ -1 \end{bmatrix}$

38. $\mathbf{u} = \mathbf{i} + 2\mathbf{j}$, $\mathbf{v} = \mathbf{i} - \mathbf{j}$

39. $\mathbf{u} = 2\mathbf{i} - \mathbf{j}$, $\mathbf{v} = 2\mathbf{i} + 2\mathbf{j}$

40. Let $\mathbf{u} = \begin{bmatrix} a \\ b \end{bmatrix}$ where at least one of a or b is nonzero and set $\mathbf{w} = \frac{1}{\|\mathbf{u}\|}\|\mathbf{u}\|$. Verify that $\|\mathbf{w}\| = 1$.

2.2 VECTORS IN SPACE

So far, our study has focused on vectors in the plane, that is, on two-dimensional problems. But, since we live and work in a three-dimensional world, we need to extend vector concepts to three dimensions. As we know, a vector is a quantity that has both direction and magnitude. In order to discuss direction and magnitude in three dimensions, it is convenient to have a coordinate system for three-dimensional space.

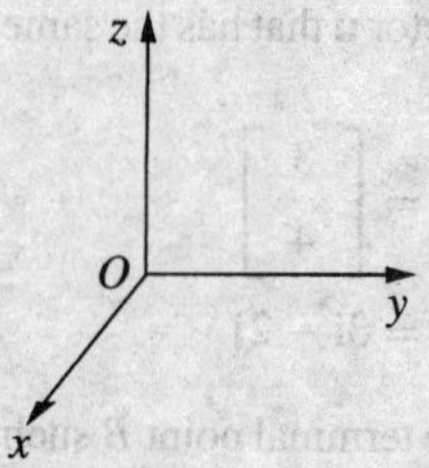

Figure 2.14
The rectangular axis system consists of three mutually perpendicular axes that meet at the origin, O.

Coordinate Axes in Three Space

There are a number of different coordinate systems we can use in three-dimensional space—for airline navigation we might use a system of geographical coordinates (latitude, longitude, and altitude). The system we introduce here is called the ***rectangular coordinate system*** or the ***Cartesian coordinate system.*** It is a direct generalization of the familiar xy-coordinate system for the plane.

We begin with three mutually perpendicular axes, called the x-axis, the y-axis, and the z-axis. We require that these axes intersect at a point designated as the ***origin,*** O; see Fig. 2.14.

The Right-Hand Rule

When the coordinate axes are oriented as in Fig. 2.14, the coordinate system is called a ***right-handed*** system. If the x-axis and y-axis are interchanged, the system is a ***left-handed*** system. The orientation of the right-handed system can be remembered with the ***right-hand rule***:

> *If the fingers of the right-hand are pointed in the direction of the positive x-axis and curled in the direction of the positive y-axis, then the thumb points in the direction of the positive z-axis.*

We will see the right-hand rule again when we study the cross product of two vectors.

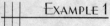

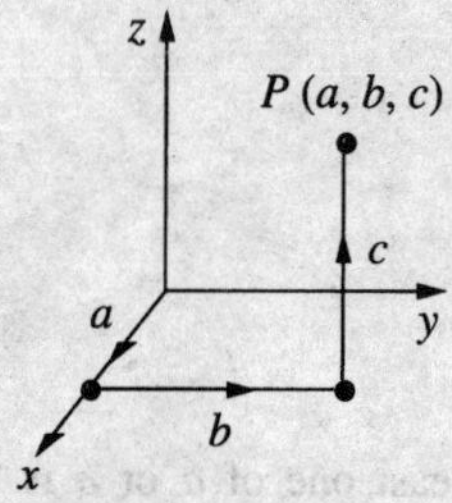

Figure 2.15
The point P has rectangular coordinates (a, b, c).

Rectangular Coordinates for Points in Three Space

Let P denote a point in space. We can locate P by moving a directed distance of a units along the x-axis, then b units along the y-axis, and then c units along the z-axis; see Fig. 2.15. When the point P is located in this fashion, we say that P has coordinates (a, b, c).

The plane containing the x and y axes is called the ***xy-plane.*** Similarly, the ***yz-plane*** contains the y and z axes and the ***xz-plane*** contains the x and z axes. Collectively, these planes are known as the ***coordinate planes***. The coordinate planes divide three space into eight subregions called ***octants***. The ***first octant*** consists of all points $P = (a, b, c)$ where $a > 0$, $b > 0$, and $c > 0$. The other seven octants are usually not given numbers.

EXAMPLE 1 Graph the points $P = (2, 3, 2)$ and $Q = (1, -2, 1)$.

Solution The points P and Q are shown in Fig. 2.16. ■

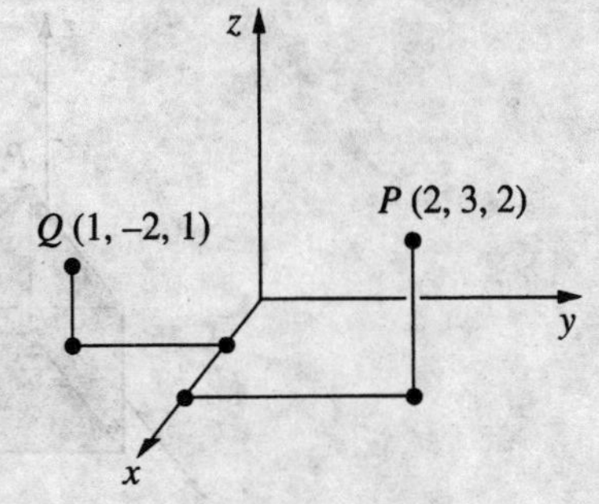

Figure 2.16 The points $P = (2, 3, 2)$ and $Q = (1, -2, 1)$; see Example 1.

EXAMPLE 2 Describe the graph of the equation $z = 2$ in three space.

Solution In three space, the graph of $z = 2$ consists of all points that have coordinates of the form $(x, y, 2)$, where x and y are arbitrary. Thus, the graph of $z = 2$ can be viewed as the xy-plane translated up 2 units; see Fig. 2.17.

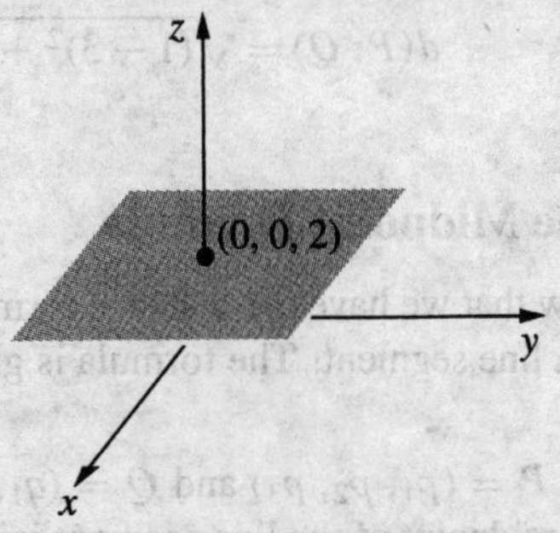

Figure 2.17 The graph of the equation $z = 2$; see Example 2

The Distance Formula

Consider a geometric vector $\mathbf{u} = \overrightarrow{AB}$ in the plane. The magnitude of $\mathbf{u}$ is found by measuring the distance between the endpoints, A and B. Similarly, to define the magnitude of a vector in three space, we will need a formula for the distance between two points in space. A formula for the distance between two points in space is given by Theorem 4.

THEOREM 4 Let $P = (p_1, p_2, p_3)$ and $Q = (q_1, q_2, q_3)$ be two points in three space. The distance between P and Q, denoted by $d(P, Q)$, is given by

$$d(P, Q) = \sqrt{(q_1 - p_1)^2 + (q_2 - p_2)^2 + (q_3 - p_3)^2}.$$

Proof The proof follows from Fig. 2.18, after two applications of the Pythagorean formula. We ask you to supply the details in Exercise 17.

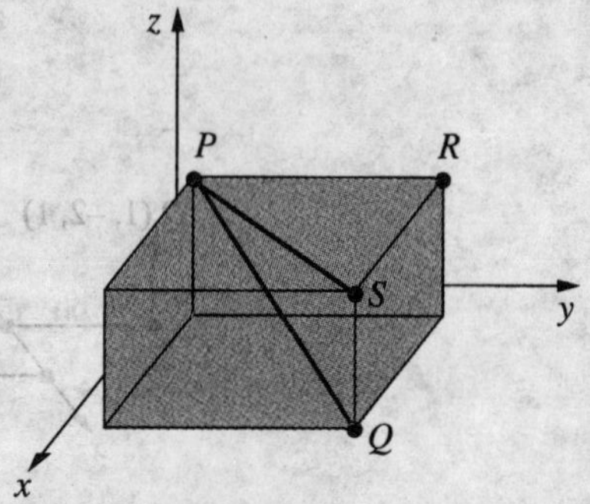

Figure 2.18   The triangle *PRS* is in a plane. The Pythagorean theorem gives the length of *PS*. Similarly, the triangle *PSQ* is in a plane and we can use the Pythagorean theorem to find the length of *PQ*.

EXAMPLE 3   Find $d(P, Q)$ where $P = (3, 2, -4)$ and $Q = (1, -1, 2)$.

Solution   By Theorem 4,

$$d(P, Q) = \sqrt{(1 - 3)^2 + ((-1) - 2)^2 + (2 - (-4))^2} = \sqrt{49} = 7. \qquad \blacksquare$$

The Midpoint Formula

Now that we have the distance formula, it is easy to develop a formula for the midpoint of a line segment. The formula is given in Theorem 5.

THEOREM 5   Let $P = (p_1, p_2, p_3)$ and $Q = (q_1, q_2, q_3)$ be two points in three space. Let M denote the midpoint of the line segment joining P and Q. Then, M is given by

$$M = \left(\frac{p_1 + q_1}{2}, \frac{p_2 + q_2}{2}, \frac{p_3 + q_3}{2} \right).$$

Proof   We leave the proof to the reader—it requires you to establish that $d(P, M) = d(Q, M)$. $\blacksquare$

EXAMPLE 4   Find the midpoint, M, of the line segment joining the points $P = (3, 2, -4)$ and $Q = (1, -6, 2)$.

Solution   By the midpoint formula, we find

$$M = \left(\frac{3 + 1}{2}, \frac{2 - 6}{2}, \frac{-4 + 2}{2} \right) = (2, -2, -1). \qquad \blacksquare$$

Geometric Vectors and Their Components

The vector concepts from two dimensions can be extended directly to three dimensions. The next few subsections briefly describe the extension. As we did in the plane, we can represent physical vectors in three dimensions by a directed line segment $\mathbf{v} = \overrightarrow{AB}$. This directed line segment is called a ***geometric vector***. The length of the line segment represents the magnitude of the physical vector and the orientation of the line segment represents the direction of the physical vector.

Let $\mathbf{v} = \overrightarrow{AB}$ be a geometric vector with ***initial point*** $A = (a_1, a_2, a_3)$ and ***terminal point*** $B = (b_1, b_2, b_3)$. The ***components*** of $\mathbf{v} = \overrightarrow{AB}$ are defined for three-dimensional vectors just as they are for two-dimensional vectors. In particular:

The x-component of $\overrightarrow{AB}$ is $b_1 - a_1$.

The y-component of $\overrightarrow{AB}$ is $b_2 - a_2$.

The z-component of $\overrightarrow{AB}$ is $b_3 - a_3$.

As before, two geometric vectors are ***equal*** if they have the same components. Among all geometric vectors $\mathbf{v} = \overrightarrow{CD}$ that are equal to $\mathbf{v} = \overrightarrow{AB}$, there is exactly one of the form $\mathbf{v} = \overrightarrow{OP}$ whose initial point is at the origin. The vector $\mathbf{v} = \overrightarrow{OP}$ is the ***position vector*** for $\mathbf{v}$. Because $\overrightarrow{OP}$ and $\overrightarrow{AB}$ are equal, we know that $P = (b_1 - a_1, b_2 - a_2, b_3 - a_3)$.

Algebraic Vectors

Since all geometric vectors equal to $\mathbf{v} = \overrightarrow{AB}$ have the same position vector, we use the following ***algebraic vector*** to represent $\overrightarrow{AB}$ (as in two dimensions, the *components* of $\mathbf{v}$ are the *coordinates* of P):

$$\mathbf{v} = \begin{bmatrix} b_1 - a_1 \\ b_2 - a_2 \\ b_3 - a_3 \end{bmatrix}. \tag{1}$$

EXAMPLE 5 Let $A = (1, -1, 2)$ and $B = (2, 1, 3)$.

(a) Represent $\mathbf{v} = \overrightarrow{AB}$ as an algebraic vector.

(b) For $C = (2, 2, 1)$, find the point D such that $\mathbf{v} = \overrightarrow{CD}$.

Solution

(a) Using formula (1), we have

$$\mathbf{v} = \begin{bmatrix} 2-1 \\ 1-(-1) \\ 3-2 \end{bmatrix} = \begin{bmatrix} 1 \\ 2 \\ 1 \end{bmatrix}.$$

(b) To find the terminal point D, we add the components of $\mathbf{v}$ to the coordinates of the initial point C. Thus, $D = (2+1, 2+2, 1+1) = (3, 4, 2)$. ■

Addition and Scalar Multiplication for Vectors

There is an ***addition*** and a ***scalar multiplication*** defined for geometric vectors in three space. These operations are defined exactly as they are for geometric vectors in the plane.

For instance, we find the geometric vector $\mathbf{u}+\mathbf{v}$ by translating $\mathbf{v}$ so that its initial point is at the terminal point of $\mathbf{u}$—the initial point of $\mathbf{u}+\mathbf{v}$ is the initial point of $\mathbf{u}$ while the terminal point of $\mathbf{u}+\mathbf{v}$ is the terminal point of the translated vector $\mathbf{v}$.

As with geometric vectors in the plane, these geometric operations are easily performed using algebraic representations; see Theorem 6.

THEOREM 6

(a) Let $\mathbf{u} = \overrightarrow{AB}$ and $\mathbf{v} = \overrightarrow{CD}$. The algebraic representation for the geometric vector $\mathbf{u}+\mathbf{v}$ is:

$$\mathbf{u}+\mathbf{v} = \begin{bmatrix} u_1 \\ u_2 \\ u_3 \end{bmatrix} + \begin{bmatrix} v_1 \\ v_2 \\ v_3 \end{bmatrix} = \begin{bmatrix} u_1+v_1 \\ u_2+v_2 \\ u_3+v_3 \end{bmatrix}.$$

(b) Let $\mathbf{u} = \overrightarrow{AB}$ and let c be a scalar. The algebraic representation for the geometric vector $c\mathbf{u}$ is:

$$c\mathbf{u} = c\begin{bmatrix} u_1 \\ u_2 \\ u_3 \end{bmatrix} = \begin{bmatrix} cu_1 \\ cu_2 \\ cu_3 \end{bmatrix}.$$ ■

Parallel Vectors, Lengths of Vectors, and Unit Vectors

As before, if $\mathbf{u} = c\mathbf{v}$ for some nonzero scalar c, we say $\mathbf{u}$ is ***parallel*** to $\mathbf{v}$. If c is positive, then $\mathbf{u}$ has the ***same direction*** as $\mathbf{v}$. If c is negative, then $\mathbf{u}$ has the ***opposite direction*** as $\mathbf{v}$.

Let $\mathbf{u}$ be given by

$$\mathbf{u} = \begin{bmatrix} u_1 \\ u_2 \\ u_3 \end{bmatrix}.$$

The ***length*** of $\mathbf{u}$ (or the ***norm*** of $\mathbf{u}$) is defined to be:

$$\|\mathbf{u}\| = \sqrt{(u_1)^2 + (u_2)^2 + (u_3)^2}.$$

If a vector $\mathbf{w}$ has length equal to 1, we say $\mathbf{w}$ is a ***unit vector.***

In applications we often need to calculate a unit vector in the direction of a given vector. This is an easy task. In particular, given a vector $\mathbf{u}$, the following vector $\mathbf{w}$ is a unit vector in the same direction as **u**:

$$\mathbf{w} = \frac{1}{\|\mathbf{u}\|}\mathbf{u}. \tag{2}$$

If we need a vector **v** having a given length, m, and in the same direction as a given vector **u**, we can find **v** with the following formula derived from Eq. (2).

$$\mathbf{v} = m\left(\frac{1}{\|\mathbf{u}\|}\mathbf{u}\right). \tag{3}$$

EXAMPLE 6 Find a vector of length 7 in the direction opposite $\mathbf{u} = \begin{bmatrix} 1 \\ 2 \\ 2 \end{bmatrix}$.

Solution A calculation shows $\|\mathbf{u}\| = 3$. Therefore, a unit vector in the direction of **u** is given by

$$\mathbf{w} = \frac{1}{3}\begin{bmatrix} 1 \\ 2 \\ 2 \end{bmatrix} = \begin{bmatrix} 1/3 \\ 2/3 \\ 2/3 \end{bmatrix}.$$

The vector $-\mathbf{w}$ is a unit vector in the direction we are interested in (since $-\mathbf{w}$ is opposite **u**). Thus, the vector **v** we seek is given by $\mathbf{v} = -7\mathbf{w}$:

$$\mathbf{v} = -7\mathbf{w} = \begin{bmatrix} -7/3 \\ -14/3 \\ -14/3 \end{bmatrix}.$$

The Basic Unit Vectors in Three Space

In three space, the basic unit vectors are denoted **i**, **j**, and **k**. In particular, **i** is along the x-axis, **j** is along the y-axis, and **k** is along the z-axis. These vectors are

$$\mathbf{i} = \begin{bmatrix} 1 \\ 0 \\ 0 \end{bmatrix}, \quad \mathbf{j} = \begin{bmatrix} 0 \\ 1 \\ 0 \end{bmatrix}, \quad \mathbf{k} = \begin{bmatrix} 0 \\ 0 \\ 1 \end{bmatrix}.$$

A given vector $\mathbf{u} = \begin{bmatrix} u_1 \\ u_2 \\ u_3 \end{bmatrix}$ can be expressed in terms of these basic unit vectors:

$$\mathbf{u} = u_1\mathbf{i} + u_2\mathbf{j} + u_3\mathbf{k}.$$

EXAMPLE 7 Let $\mathbf{u} = 2\mathbf{i} - \mathbf{j} + 3\mathbf{k}$ and $\mathbf{v} = 6\mathbf{i} + 4\mathbf{j} + \mathbf{k}$. Find a unit vector in the direction of $\mathbf{u} - \mathbf{v}$.

Solution The vector $\mathbf{u}-\mathbf{v}$ is given by $\mathbf{u}-\mathbf{v} = -4\mathbf{i}-5\mathbf{j}+2\mathbf{k} = \begin{bmatrix} -4 \\ -5 \\ 2 \end{bmatrix}$. The length of $\mathbf{u}-\mathbf{v}$ is $\sqrt{45} = 3\sqrt{5}$. Thus a unit vector in the direction of $\mathbf{u}-\mathbf{v}$ is

$$\mathbf{w} = \frac{1}{\|\mathbf{u}-\mathbf{v}\|}(\mathbf{u}-\mathbf{v}) = \frac{1}{3\sqrt{5}} \begin{bmatrix} -4 \\ -5 \\ 2 \end{bmatrix}.$$

2.2 EXERCISES

In Exercises 1–4, plot the points P and Q and determine $d(P, Q)$.

1. $P = (1, 2, 1)$, $Q = (0, 2, 2)$

2. $P = (1, 1, 0)$, $Q = (0, 0, 1)$

3. $P = (1, 0, 0)$, $Q = (0, 0, 1)$

4. $P = (1, 1, 1)$, $Q = (0, 0, 0)$

In Exercises 5–6, find the coordinates of the segment PQ. Calculate the distance from the midpoint to the origin.

5. $P = (2, 3, 1)$, $Q = (0, 5, 7)$

6. $P = (1, 0, 3)$, $Q = (3, 2, 5)$

7. Let $A = (-1, 0, -3)$ and $E = (3, 6, 3)$. Find points B, C, and D on the line segment AE such that $d(A, B) = d(B, C) = d(C, D) = d(D, E) = \frac{1}{4}d(A, E)$.

In Exercises 8–12, identify the given set of points in space as being a plane or a line.

8. $\{(x, y, z) : z = 4\}$

9. $\{(x, y, z) : x = 4, y = 2\}$

10. $\{(x, y, z) : x = y = z\}$

11. $\{(x, y, z) : y = 2\}$

12. The set of all points equidistant from (5, 0, 0) and (0, 5, 0).

In Exercises 13–16, graph the given region R.

13. $R = \{(x, y, z) : |x| \le 1, |y| \le 2, |z| \le 3\}$

14. $R = \{(x, y, z) : 0 \le x \le 1, 0 \le y \le 2, z = 2\}$

15. $R = \{(x, y, z) : 0 \le x \le 1, 0 \le y \le 2x, 0 \le z \le 1\}$

16. $R = \{(x, y, z) : 0 \le x, 0 \le y, x + y \le 1, 0 \le z \le 1\}$

17. Let $P = (p_1, p_2, p_3)$ and $Q = (q_1, q_2, q_3)$ be two points in space. As in Fig. 2.18, let $R = (p_1, q_2, p_3)$ and $S = (q_1, q_2, p_3)$.

a) Apply the Pythagorean theorem to the triangle PRS to show that
$$d(P, S) = \sqrt{(q_1 - p_1)^2 + (q_2 - p_2)^2}.$$

b) Apply the Pythagorean theorem to the triangle PSQ to establish the distance formula,
$$d(P, Q) = \sqrt{(q_1 - p_1)^2 + (q_2 - p_2)^2 + (q_3 - p_3)^2}.$$

In Exercises 18–21, (a) give the algebraic representation for $\mathbf{v} = \overrightarrow{AB}$; (b) for $C = (-1, 2, 1)$, find D such that $\mathbf{v} = \overrightarrow{CD}$.

18. $A = (2, 0, 7)$, $B = (0, 3, 4)$

19. $A = (-1, 2, 3)$, $B = (2, 4, 0)$

20. $A = (2, 4, 0)$, $B = (-1, 2, 3)$

21. $A = (1, -2, 4)$, $B = (1, 3, -3)$

In Exercises 22–25, determine a point A such that $\mathbf{v} = \overrightarrow{AB}$ where $B = (4, 3, 2)$.

22. $\mathbf{v} = \begin{bmatrix} 0 \\ 3 \\ 2 \end{bmatrix}$ **23.** $\mathbf{v} = \begin{bmatrix} 1 \\ 1 \\ 1 \end{bmatrix}$

24. $\mathbf{v} = 2\mathbf{j}$ **25.** $\mathbf{v} = 6\mathbf{i} + 3\mathbf{k}$

In Exercises 26–29, find: (a) $\mathbf{u} + 2\mathbf{v}$; (b) $\|\mathbf{u} - \mathbf{v}\|$; (c) a vector $\mathbf{w}$ such that $\mathbf{u} + 2\mathbf{w} = \mathbf{v}$.

26. $\mathbf{u} = \begin{bmatrix} 1 \\ 3 \\ 2 \end{bmatrix}$, $\mathbf{v} = \begin{bmatrix} 4 \\ 3 \\ 6 \end{bmatrix}$

27. $\mathbf{u} = \begin{bmatrix} 1 \\ 3 \\ 2 \end{bmatrix}$, $\mathbf{v} = \begin{bmatrix} 3 \\ 2 \\ 4 \end{bmatrix}$

28. $\mathbf{u} = 9\mathbf{i} - 3\mathbf{j} + 2\mathbf{k}$, $\mathbf{v} = \mathbf{i} + \mathbf{k}$

29. $\mathbf{u} = -5\mathbf{i} + 7\mathbf{j}$, $\mathbf{v} = 2\mathbf{i} - 3\mathbf{j} + \mathbf{k}$

In Exercises 30–35, determine a vector $\mathbf{u}$ that satisfies the given conditions.

30. $\mathbf{u}$ has the same direction as $\mathbf{v} = \mathbf{i} + \mathbf{j}$ and $\|\mathbf{u}\| = \sqrt{8}$.

31. $\mathbf{u}$ has the same direction as $\mathbf{v} = \mathbf{k}$ and $\|\mathbf{u}\| = 2$.

32. $\mathbf{u}$ has opposite direction to $\mathbf{v} = \begin{bmatrix} 1 \\ 0 \\ 1 \end{bmatrix}$ and $\|\mathbf{u}\| = \sqrt{32}$.

33. $\mathbf{u}$ has opposite direction to $\mathbf{v} = \begin{bmatrix} -1 \\ 2 \\ 2 \end{bmatrix}$ and $\|\mathbf{u}\| = 5$.

34. $\mathbf{u}$ is parallel to $\mathbf{v} = \begin{bmatrix} 1 \\ 2 \\ 0 \end{bmatrix}$ and $\mathbf{u} = \overrightarrow{AB}$ where $A = (1, 1, 1)$ and B is in the xz-plane.

35. $\mathbf{u}$ is parallel to $\mathbf{v} = \begin{bmatrix} 4 \\ 8 \\ 2 \end{bmatrix}$ and $\mathbf{u} = \overrightarrow{AB}$ where $A = (1, 1, 1)$ and B is in the xy-plane.

2.3 THE DOT PRODUCT AND THE CROSS PRODUCT

Applications such as calculating the work done by a force often require us to determine the angle between two geometric vectors. Figure 2.19 shows the angle $\boldsymbol{\theta}$ between two vectors $\mathbf{u}$ and $\mathbf{v}$. As we will see, $\boldsymbol{\theta}$ can be found using the *dot product,* one of the topics of this section.

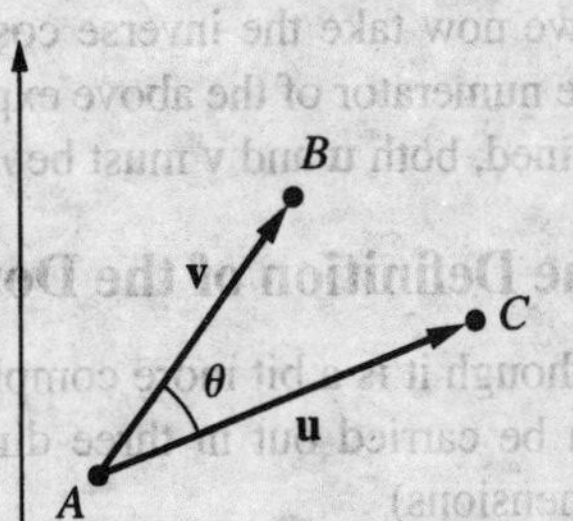

Figure 2.19 When geometric vectors $\mathbf{u}$ and $\mathbf{v}$ are translated to have the same initial point, we can measure the angle $\boldsymbol{\theta}$ between them.

The Dot Product of Two Vectors

To find the angle $\boldsymbol{\theta}$ in Fig. 2.19, we consider the triangle ABC and interpret the vectors $\mathbf{v} = \overrightarrow{AB}$, $\mathbf{u} = \overrightarrow{AC}$, and $\mathbf{u} - \mathbf{v} = \overrightarrow{BC}$ as the sides of ABC (see Fig. 2.20).

Applying the ***Law of Cosines*** to the triangle in Fig. 2.20, we obtain

$$\|\mathbf{u} - \mathbf{v}\|^2 = \|\mathbf{u}\|^2 + \|\mathbf{v}\|^2 - 2\|\mathbf{u}\|\|\mathbf{v}\| \cos\boldsymbol{\theta}. \tag{1}$$

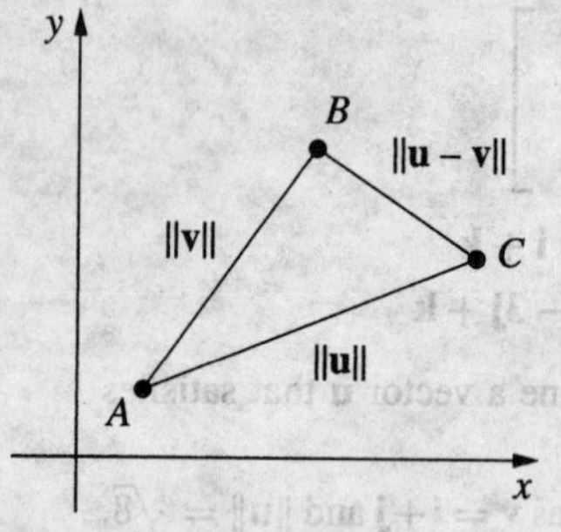

Figure 2.20 The sides of the triangle ABC can be interpreted in terms of the lengths of **u**, **v**, and **u** − **v**.

To solve (1) for cos θ, let **u** and **v** be given by

$$\mathbf{u} = \begin{bmatrix} u_1 \\ u_2 \end{bmatrix}, \quad \mathbf{v} = \begin{bmatrix} v_1 \\ v_2 \end{bmatrix}.$$

If we insert **u** and **v** into Eq. (1) and simplify, we obtain

$$u_1v_1 + u_2v_2 = \|\mathbf{u}\|\|\mathbf{v}\| \cos\theta. \tag{2a}$$

Solving Eq. (2a) for cos θ, we arrive at

$$\cos\theta = \frac{u_1v_1 + u_2v_2}{\|\mathbf{u}\|\|\mathbf{v}\|}.$$

If we now take the inverse cosine of the above expression, we will have the angle θ. The numerator of the above expression is called the ***dot product*** of **u** and **v**. (For θ to be defined, both **u** and **v** must be *nonzero* vectors.)

The Definition of the Dot Product

Although it is a bit more complicated, the calculations leading from Eq. (1) to Eq. (2a) can be carried out in three dimensions as well. In fact, Eq. (2a) becomes (in three dimensions)

$$u_1v_1 + u_2v_2 + u_3v_3 = \|\mathbf{u}\|\|\mathbf{v}\| \cos\theta. \tag{2b}$$

The left-hand side of (2b) defines the dot product in three space. In general,

DEFINITION 1

(a) If **u** and **v** are two-dimensional vectors, then the ***dot product*** of **u** and **v**, denoted **u** · **v**, is defined by

$$\mathbf{u}\cdot\mathbf{v} = u_1v_1 + u_2v_2.$$

(b) If **u** and **v** are three-dimensional vectors, then

$$\mathbf{u}\cdot\mathbf{v} = u_1v_1 + u_2v_2 + u_3v_3.$$

(*Note:* We actually introduced the dot product (or scalar product) for n-dimensional vectors in Section 1.6. In that section we defined the dot product as

$$\mathbf{u}^T\mathbf{v}.$$

Of course, these two definitions are exactly the same in two dimensions or three dimensions. In this chapter, however, we will use the "dot" notation, $\mathbf{u} \cdot \mathbf{v}$, that is customary in the study of geometric vectors rather than $\mathbf{u}^T\mathbf{v}$.)

The Angle Between Two Vectors

We use the dot product notation to summarize Eq. (2a) and (2b).

THEOREM 7 Let $\mathbf{u}$ and $\mathbf{v}$ be two nonzero vectors in the plane or in three space. If $\boldsymbol{\theta}$ denotes the angle between $\mathbf{u}$ and $\mathbf{v}$, then

$$\mathbf{u} \cdot \mathbf{v} = \|\mathbf{u}\|\|\mathbf{v}\| \cos \boldsymbol{\theta}.$$

The next example illustrates the use of Theorem 7.

EXAMPLE 1 Let $\mathbf{u} = \begin{bmatrix} 1 \\ 3 \\ -2 \end{bmatrix}$ and $\mathbf{v} = \begin{bmatrix} 4 \\ -1 \\ -3 \end{bmatrix}$.

(a) Calculate $\mathbf{u} \cdot \mathbf{v}$.

(b) Using Theorem 7, find the angle between $\mathbf{u}$ and $\mathbf{v}$.

Solution

(a) The number $\mathbf{u} \cdot \mathbf{v}$ is given by

$$\mathbf{u} \cdot \mathbf{v} = (1)(4) + (3)(-1) + (-2)(-3) = 4 - 3 + 6 = 7.$$

(b) Solving for $\cos \boldsymbol{\theta}$ in Theorem 7, we have

$$\cos \boldsymbol{\theta} = \frac{\mathbf{u} \cdot \mathbf{v}}{\|\mathbf{u}\|\|\mathbf{v}\|} = \frac{7}{\sqrt{14}\sqrt{26}} = \frac{7}{\sqrt{364}} = 0.366899\ldots.$$

Taking the inverse cosine, we find $\boldsymbol{\theta} = 1.1951\ldots$ radians $(68.4755\ldots$ degrees).

Algebraic Properties of the Dot Product

The following theorem lists some of the algebraic properties of the dot product.

THEOREM 8 Let $\mathbf{u}$, $\mathbf{v}$, and $\mathbf{w}$ denote vectors in space or in the plane, and let c denote a scalar. Then:

(a) $\mathbf{u} \cdot \mathbf{u} \geq 0$

(b) $\mathbf{u} \cdot \mathbf{v} = \mathbf{v} \cdot \mathbf{u}$

(c) $\mathbf{u} \cdot (c\mathbf{v}) = c(\mathbf{u} \cdot \mathbf{v})$

(d) $\mathbf{u} \cdot (\mathbf{v} + \mathbf{w}) = \mathbf{u} \cdot \mathbf{v} + \mathbf{u} \cdot \mathbf{w}$

We leave the verification of Theorem 8 to the exercises.

Orthogonal Vectors

Let **u** and **v** be nonzero vectors and let θ denote the angle between them. When $\theta = \pi/2$, we say that **u** and **v** are ***perpendicular*** or ***orthogonal***. By Theorem 7, we see that **u** and **v** are orthogonal if and only if

$$\mathbf{u} \cdot \mathbf{v} = 0.$$

In the plane, the basic unit vectors **i** and **j** are orthogonal. In three space, the basic unit vectors **i**, **j**, and **k** are mutually orthogonal. The next example also illustrates the concept of orthogonality.

EXAMPLE 2 Consider the vectors

$$\mathbf{u} = \begin{bmatrix} 2 \\ -3 \\ 7 \end{bmatrix}, \quad \mathbf{v} = \begin{bmatrix} 1 \\ 3 \\ 1 \end{bmatrix} \quad \text{and} \quad \mathbf{w} = \begin{bmatrix} 3 \\ 2 \\ 0 \end{bmatrix}.$$

Show that **u** is orthogonal to both **v** and **w**, but that **v** and **w** are not orthogonal.

Solution Forming dot products, we find

$$\mathbf{u} \cdot \mathbf{v} = (2)(1) + (-3)(3) + (7)(1) = 2 - 9 + 7 = 0$$
$$\mathbf{u} \cdot \mathbf{w} = (2)(3) + (-3)(2) + (7)(0) = 6 - 6 + 0 = 0$$
$$\mathbf{v} \cdot \mathbf{w} = (1)(3) + (3)(2) + (1)(0) = 3 + 6 + 0 = 9.$$

Thus, **u** and **v** are orthogonal; **u** and **w** are orthogonal; but **v** and **w** are not orthogonal.

Projections

In applications it is often necessary to express a given vector **u** in the form

$$\mathbf{u} = \mathbf{v} + \mathbf{w}$$

where

(a) The vector **v** is parallel to a given nonzero vector **q**.

(b) The vector **w** is orthogonal to **q**.

As an example, consider Fig. 2.21, illustrating a block on an inclined plane. In Fig. 2.21, the downward directed force **u** is the weight of the block. As you can see, the force **u** has been expressed as the sum of two forces:

$$\mathbf{u} = \mathbf{v} + \mathbf{w}.$$

The force **v** is normal (perpendicular) to the inclined plane and because of friction it tends to hold the block stationary on the plane. The force **w** is tangential to the inclined

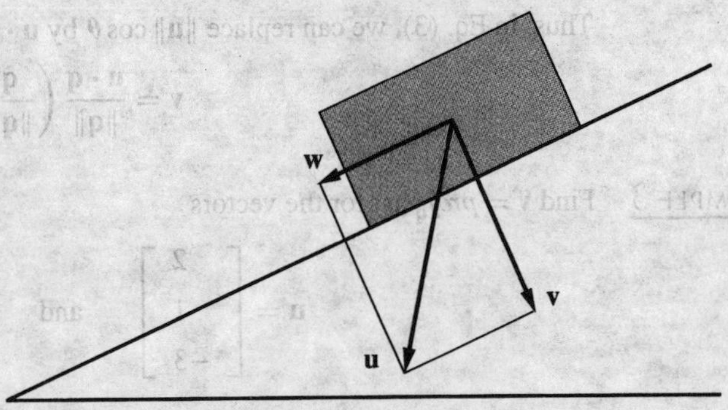

Figure 2.21 The vector **u** represents the weight of the block. We want to express **u** in the form $\mathbf{u} = \mathbf{v} + \mathbf{w}$ where **v** is normal to the plane and **w** is parallel to the plane.

plane and because of gravitational forces it tends to make the block slide downward. The relative magnitudes of **v** and **w** (along with the frictional characteristics of the block and the plane) determine whether the block remains stationary or slides.

The situation shown in Fig. 2.21 is a special case of the general problem we discuss next. The general problem is illustrated in Fig. 2.22. As you can see, Fig. 2.22 shows a given vector **u** and a given direction defined by the vector **q**. The vector **v** shown in Fig. 2.22 is parallel to **q** and is called the ***projection of* u *onto* q**. For notation, we write

$$\mathbf{v} = proj_{\mathbf{q}}(\mathbf{u}) \qquad \text{(read as "}\mathbf{v}\text{ is the projection of }\mathbf{u}\text{ onto }\mathbf{q}\text{")}.$$

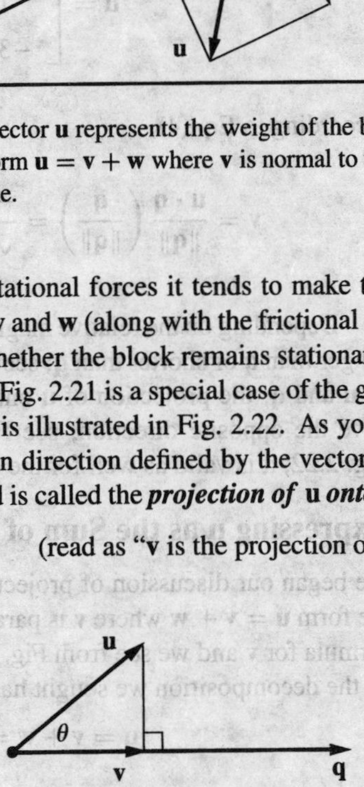

Figure 2.22 The vector **v** is called the projection of **u** onto **q**.

Calculating the Projection

To calculate the projection **v** shown in Fig. 2.22, we first write **v** as

$$\mathbf{v} = \|\mathbf{v}\|\left(\frac{\mathbf{q}}{\|\mathbf{q}\|}\right).$$

Next, from Fig. 2.22, we see that $\|\mathbf{v}\| = \|\mathbf{u}\|\cos\theta$, and thus we have

$$\mathbf{v} = \|\mathbf{u}\|\cos\theta\left(\frac{\mathbf{q}}{\|\mathbf{q}\|}\right). \tag{3}$$

If we know the angle θ, then Eq. (3) gives us the projection. In certain applications, especially in three dimensions, we might need to use the dot product to find the term $\cos\theta$ that appears in Eq. (3). In such an event, recall from Theorem 7 that $\mathbf{u}\cdot\mathbf{q} = \|\mathbf{u}\|\|\mathbf{q}\|\cos\theta$.

Thus, in Eq. (3), we can replace $\|\mathbf{u}\| \cos\theta$ by $\mathbf{u}\cdot\mathbf{q}/\|\mathbf{q}\|$, finding

$$\mathbf{v} = \frac{\mathbf{u}\cdot\mathbf{q}}{\|\mathbf{q}\|}\left(\frac{\mathbf{q}}{\|\mathbf{q}\|}\right). \tag{4}$$

EXAMPLE 3 Find $\mathbf{v} = proj_{\mathbf{q}}(\mathbf{u})$ for the vectors

$$\mathbf{u} = \begin{bmatrix} 2 \\ 1 \\ -3 \end{bmatrix} \quad \text{and} \quad \mathbf{q} = \begin{bmatrix} 1 \\ 0 \\ 2 \end{bmatrix}.$$

Solution According to Eq. (4),

$$\mathbf{v} = \frac{\mathbf{u}\cdot\mathbf{q}}{\|\mathbf{q}\|}\left(\frac{\mathbf{q}}{\|\mathbf{q}\|}\right) = \frac{-4}{\sqrt{5}}\left(\frac{\mathbf{q}}{\sqrt{5}}\right) = \frac{-4}{5}\begin{bmatrix} 1 \\ 0 \\ 2 \end{bmatrix} = \begin{bmatrix} -0.8 \\ 0 \\ -1.6 \end{bmatrix}.$$

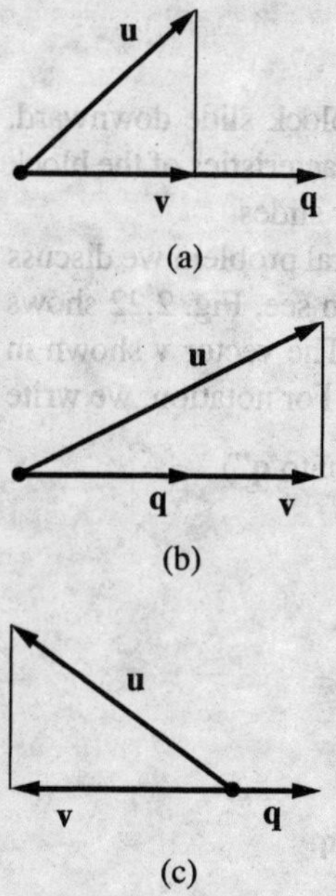

Figure 2.23 The projection of **u** onto **q** might be shorter or longer than **q** and might have the same or opposite direction as **q**.

Depending on the relative magnitudes of **q** and **u**, the projection of **u** onto **q** might be longer than **q** or shorter than **q**; see Fig. 2.23. Also, depending on the relative directions of **u** and **q**, the projection of **u** onto **q** might be in the same direction as **q** or it might have the opposite direction; see Fig. 2.23. Although formula (4) was derived from Fig. 2.22, it is valid as well for the configurations shown in Fig. 2.23(b)–(c).

Expressing u as the Sum of Two Orthogonal Vectors

We began our discussion of projections with the important problem of expressing **u** in the form $\mathbf{u} = \mathbf{v} + \mathbf{w}$ where **v** is parallel to **q** and **w** is orthogonal to **q**. Eq. (4) gives us a formula for **v** and we see from Fig. 2.24 that $\mathbf{w} = \mathbf{u} - \mathbf{v}$ is indeed orthogonal to **q**. That is, the decomposition we sought has the form

$$\mathbf{u} = \mathbf{v} + \mathbf{w} = proj_{\mathbf{q}}(\mathbf{u}) + (\mathbf{u} - proj_{\mathbf{q}}(\mathbf{u})). \tag{5}$$

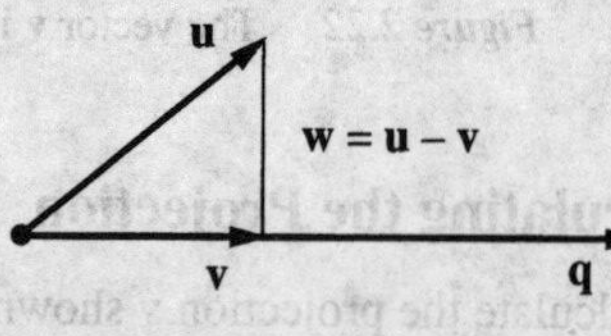

Figure 2.24 Here, $\mathbf{u} = \mathbf{v} + \mathbf{w}$. The vector **v** is the projection of **u** along **q**. The vector $\mathbf{w} = \mathbf{u} - \mathbf{v}$ is orthogonal to **q**, by construction.

EXAMPLE 4 Let $\mathbf{u} = \begin{bmatrix} 4 \\ -2 \\ 3 \end{bmatrix}$ and $\mathbf{q} = \begin{bmatrix} 3 \\ 0 \\ 1 \end{bmatrix}$. Express **u** in the form $\mathbf{u} = \mathbf{v} + \mathbf{w}$ where **u** is parallel to **q** and **w** is orthogonal to **q**; see Eq. (5).

Solution We first calculate the projection **v** as in Example 3:

$$\mathbf{v} = \frac{\mathbf{u}\cdot\mathbf{q}}{\|\mathbf{q}\|}\left(\frac{\mathbf{q}}{\|\mathbf{q}\|}\right) = \frac{15}{\sqrt{10}}\left(\frac{\mathbf{q}}{\sqrt{10}}\right) = \frac{15}{10}\begin{bmatrix}3\\0\\1\end{bmatrix} = \begin{bmatrix}4.5\\0\\1.5\end{bmatrix}.$$

Then, $\mathbf{w} = \mathbf{u} - \mathbf{v} = \begin{bmatrix}4\\-2\\3\end{bmatrix} - \begin{bmatrix}4.5\\0\\1.5\end{bmatrix} = \begin{bmatrix}-0.5\\-2\\1.5\end{bmatrix}$. As we see, **v** is parallel to **q** since $\mathbf{v} = 1.5\mathbf{q}$, **w** is orthogonal to **q**, and $\mathbf{u} = \mathbf{v} + \mathbf{w}$. ■

The Cross Product

To introduce the cross product, let us consider the problem stated below and illustrated in Fig. 2.25.

> ***Problem:*** *Given nonzero vectors* **u** *and* **v** *in three space, find a vector* **w** *that is orthogonal to both* **u** *and* **v**.

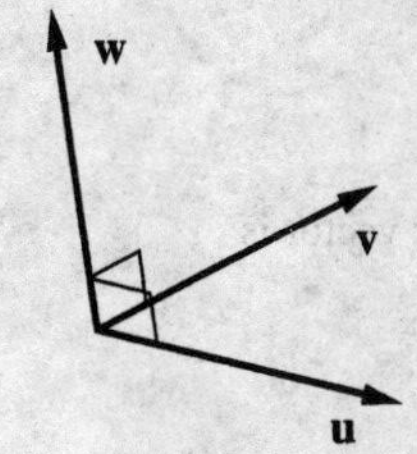

Figure 2.25
Given vectors **u** and **v** in three space, how do we find a vector **w** that is orthogonal to **u** and to **v**?

A solution to this problem is the *cross product vector*, the topic of the remainder of this section.

Derivation of the Cross Product

To solve the problem posed in Fig. 2.25, let $\mathbf{u} = \begin{bmatrix}u_1\\u_2\\u_3\end{bmatrix}$ and $\mathbf{v} = \begin{bmatrix}v_1\\v_2\\v_3\end{bmatrix}$. We want a nonzero vector $\mathbf{w} = \begin{bmatrix}x\\y\\z\end{bmatrix}$ such that $\mathbf{w}\cdot\mathbf{u} = 0$ and $\mathbf{w}\cdot\mathbf{v} = 0$. In terms of the components of **u**, **v**, and **w**, the orthogonality conditions lead to a system of two equations in three unknowns:

$$\begin{aligned} u_1x + u_2y + u_3z &= 0 \\ v_1x + v_2y + v_3z &= 0. \end{aligned}$$

The system above is homogeneous and has more unknowns than equations. Thus, we know the system always has nonzero solutions (see Theorem 4 in Section 1.3). In the exercises, we ask you to show that one nonzero solution is

$$x = u_2v_3 - u_3v_2, \qquad y = u_3v_1 - u_1v_3, \qquad z = u_1v_2 - u_2v_1. \tag{6}$$

The vector **w** having components (6) is called the ***cross product*** of **u** and **v**.

The Definition of the Cross Product

Drawing on the derivation above, we are led to the following definition.

DEFINITION 2 Let $\mathbf{u} = \begin{bmatrix} u_1 \\ u_2 \\ u_3 \end{bmatrix}$ and $\mathbf{v} = \begin{bmatrix} v_1 \\ v_2 \\ v_3 \end{bmatrix}$ be vectors in three space. The ***cross product*** of **u** and **v**, denoted by **u** × **v**, is the vector given by

$$\mathbf{u} \times \mathbf{v} = \begin{bmatrix} u_2v_3 - u_3v_2 \\ u_3v_1 - u_1v_3 \\ u_1v_2 - u_2v_1 \end{bmatrix}.$$

The next example illustrates a typical cross product calculation.

EXAMPLE 5 Find **u** × **v** for $\mathbf{u} = \begin{bmatrix} 2 \\ 1 \\ 3 \end{bmatrix}$ and $\mathbf{v} = \begin{bmatrix} 1 \\ -3 \\ 4 \end{bmatrix}$. Verify that the cross product vector is orthogonal to both **u** and **v**.

Solution Using Definition 2, we find the cross product vector

$$\mathbf{u} \times \mathbf{v} = \begin{bmatrix} (1)(4) - (3)(-3) \\ (3)(1) - (2)(4) \\ (2)(-3) - (1)(1) \end{bmatrix} = \begin{bmatrix} 13 \\ -5 \\ -7 \end{bmatrix}.$$

Calculating shows that $(\mathbf{u} \times \mathbf{v}) \cdot \mathbf{u} = 0$ and $(\mathbf{u} \times \mathbf{v}) \cdot \mathbf{v} = 0$. ■

Using Determinants to Remember the Form of the Cross Product

We can use a "symbolic determinant" to help us remember the cross product. (A detailed discussion of determinants can be found in Chapters 4 and 6. Many people, however, will recall seeing (2 × 2) and (3 × 3) determinants in their high school algebra courses.) The cross product can be remembered as

$$\mathbf{u} \times \mathbf{v} = \begin{vmatrix} \mathbf{i} & \mathbf{j} & \mathbf{k} \\ u_1 & u_2 & u_3 \\ v_1 & v_2 & v_3 \end{vmatrix} = (u_2v_3 - u_3v_2)\mathbf{i} - (u_1v_3 - u_3v_1)\mathbf{j} + (u_1v_2 - u_2v_1)\mathbf{k}. \quad (7)$$

EXAMPLE 6 Use the symbolic determinant (7) to calculate **u** × **v** and **v** × **u**, where

$$\mathbf{u} = \begin{bmatrix} 1 \\ 1 \\ -1 \end{bmatrix} \text{ and } \mathbf{v} = \begin{bmatrix} 2 \\ -1 \\ 3 \end{bmatrix}.$$

Solution Using (7), we obtain

$$\mathbf{u} \times \mathbf{v} = \begin{vmatrix} \mathbf{i} & \mathbf{j} & \mathbf{k} \\ 1 & 1 & -1 \\ 2 & -1 & 3 \end{vmatrix} = (3-1)\mathbf{i} - (3+2)\mathbf{j} + (-1-2)\mathbf{k} = 2\mathbf{i} - 5\mathbf{j} - 3\mathbf{k} = \begin{bmatrix} 2 \\ -5 \\ -3 \end{bmatrix}.$$

To calculate $\mathbf{v} \times \mathbf{u}$, we switch the rows in the symbolic determinant for $\mathbf{u} \times \mathbf{v}$

$$\mathbf{v} \times \mathbf{u} = \begin{vmatrix} \mathbf{i} & \mathbf{j} & \mathbf{k} \\ 2 & -1 & 3 \\ 1 & 1 & -1 \end{vmatrix}.$$

From the properties of determinants, we know that the determinant changes sign when two rows are interchanged. Thus, even without expanding the determinant for $\mathbf{v} \times \mathbf{u}$,

$$\text{we know that } \mathbf{v} \times \mathbf{u} = -\mathbf{u} \times \mathbf{v} = \begin{bmatrix} -2 \\ 5 \\ 3 \end{bmatrix}.$$

Algebraic Properties of the Cross Product

We have to be careful with cross product calculations since properties that we intuitively expect to hold might not be true. For instance, we saw in Example 6 that the expected equality, $\mathbf{u} \times \mathbf{v} = \mathbf{v} \times \mathbf{u}$, might not be true. A summary of several important algebraic properties of the cross product is given in Theorem 9.

THEOREM 9 Let $\mathbf{u}$, $\mathbf{v}$, and $\mathbf{w}$ be three-dimensional vectors and let c be a scalar. Then

(a) $\mathbf{u} \times \mathbf{v} = -\mathbf{v} \times \mathbf{u}$

(b) $\mathbf{u} \times \mathbf{u} = \mathbf{0}$

(c) $(c\mathbf{u}) \times \mathbf{v} = \mathbf{u} \times (c\mathbf{v}) = c(\mathbf{u} \times \mathbf{v})$

(d) $\mathbf{u} \times (\mathbf{v} + \mathbf{w}) = \mathbf{u} \times \mathbf{v} + \mathbf{u} \times \mathbf{w}$

(e) $\mathbf{u} \cdot (\mathbf{v} \times \mathbf{w}) = (\mathbf{u} \times \mathbf{v}) \cdot \mathbf{w}$

Proof The proof of Theorem 9 follows from the definition of the cross product.

It is worth noting that the cross product operation is not associative. That is, in general, $(\mathbf{u} \times \mathbf{v}) \times \mathbf{w}$ is not equal to $\mathbf{u} \times (\mathbf{v} \times \mathbf{w})$. See the exercises for an example of this fact.

The Right-Hand Rule

By Theorem 9, $\mathbf{u} \times \mathbf{v} = -\mathbf{v} \times \mathbf{u}$. Therefore, both of the vectors $\mathbf{u} \times \mathbf{v}$ and $\mathbf{v} \times \mathbf{u}$ are perpendicular to $\mathbf{u}$ and to $\mathbf{v}$. The orientation of $\mathbf{u} \times \mathbf{v}$ can be found by using the ***right-hand rule:***

> *Let* $\mathbf{u}$, $\mathbf{v}$, *and* $\mathbf{u} \times \mathbf{v}$ *have a common initial point A. Imagine placing your right hand near A with your fingers pointing along* $\mathbf{u}$. *Let your fingers curl from* $\mathbf{u}$ *toward* $\mathbf{v}$. *Your thumb points in the direction of* $\mathbf{u} \times \mathbf{v}$.

Cross products of the basic unit vectors illustrate the right-hand rule. The first line of cross products can be found using Definition 2 or the determinant (7). The other two lines follow from Theorem 9.

$$\begin{array}{lll} \mathbf{i} \times \mathbf{j} = \mathbf{k} & \mathbf{j} \times \mathbf{k} = \mathbf{i} & \mathbf{k} \times \mathbf{i} = \mathbf{j} \\ \mathbf{j} \times \mathbf{i} = -\mathbf{k} & \mathbf{k} \times \mathbf{j} = -\mathbf{i} & \mathbf{i} \times \mathbf{k} = -\mathbf{j} \\ \mathbf{i} \times \mathbf{i} = \mathbf{0} & \mathbf{j} \times \mathbf{j} = \mathbf{0} & \mathbf{k} \times \mathbf{k} = \mathbf{0}. \end{array} \tag{8}$$

When $\mathbf{u}$ and $\mathbf{v}$ are given in terms of the basic unit vectors, we can use Theorem 9 and Eq. (8) to calculate $\mathbf{u} \times \mathbf{v}$. The next example illustrates this idea.

EXAMPLE 7 Let $\mathbf{u} = 3\mathbf{i} + 2\mathbf{k}$ and let $\mathbf{v} = 4\mathbf{i} + \mathbf{j} + 5\mathbf{k}$. Calculate $\mathbf{u} \times \mathbf{v}$.

Solution We have

$$\begin{aligned} \mathbf{u} \times \mathbf{v} &= (3\mathbf{i} + 2\mathbf{k}) \times (4\mathbf{i} + \mathbf{j} + 5\mathbf{k}) \\ &= 12\mathbf{i} \times \mathbf{i} + 3\mathbf{i} \times \mathbf{j} + 15\mathbf{i} \times \mathbf{k} + 8\mathbf{k} \times \mathbf{i} + 2\mathbf{k} \times \mathbf{j} + 10\mathbf{k} \times \mathbf{k} \\ &= (12)\mathbf{0} + (10)\mathbf{0} \\ &= -2\mathbf{i} - 7\mathbf{j} + 3\mathbf{k}. \end{aligned}$$

Geometric Properties of the Cross Product

The right-hand rule gives us the direction of $\mathbf{u} \times \mathbf{v}$. Theorem 10 tells us the magnitude of $\mathbf{u} \times \mathbf{v}$.

THEOREM 10 Let $\mathbf{u}$ and $\mathbf{v}$ be nonzero three-dimensional vectors and let θ be the angle between $\mathbf{u}$ and $\mathbf{v}$. The length of $\mathbf{u} \times \mathbf{v}$ is given by

$$\|\mathbf{u} \times \mathbf{v}\| = \|\mathbf{u}\|\|\mathbf{v}\| \sin\theta.$$

We leave the proof of Theorem 10 as an exercise. Note that Theorem 10 can be used as a test of whether or not nonzero vectors $\mathbf{u}$ and $\mathbf{v}$ are parallel; see Theorem 12 at the end of this section.

An interesting application of Theorem 10 involves using $\mathbf{u} \times \mathbf{v}$ to find the area of a parallelogram. Let $ABCD$ denote a parallelogram determined by four points A, B, C, and D; see Fig. 2.26.

The following result can be established with the help of Fig. 2.26.

THEOREM 11 Let $ABCD$ be the parallelogram where A and D are opposite vertices. The area of $ABCD$ is equal to the length of the cross product vector, $\overrightarrow{AB} \times \overrightarrow{AC}$.

Proof We can verify Theorem 11 by appealing to Fig. 2.26:

$$\begin{aligned} \text{Area} &= \|\overrightarrow{AB}\|h && \text{(area = base} \times \text{height)} \\ &= \|\overrightarrow{AB}\|\|\overrightarrow{AC}\| \sin\theta && (\text{since } h = \|\overrightarrow{AC}\| \sin\theta) \\ &= \|\overrightarrow{AB} \times \overrightarrow{AC}\| && \text{(by Theorem 2)} \end{aligned}$$

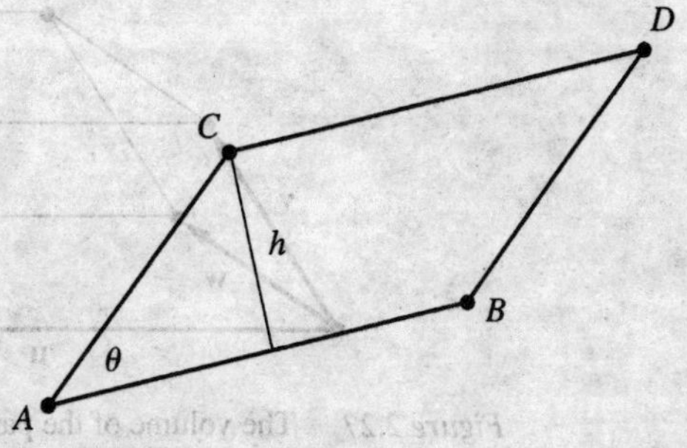

Figure 2.26 The parallelogram *ABCD*. The area of *ABCD* is equal to the magnitude of $\overrightarrow{AB} \times \overrightarrow{AC}$.

EXAMPLE 8 Use Theorem 11 to find the area of the triangle *ABC* where the vertices are $A = (1, 2, 2)$, $B = (3, 1, 4)$, and $C = (5, 2, 1)$.

Solution From geometry, we know that the triangle *ABC* has half the area of the parallelogram *ABCD*; see Fig. 2.26. So, as in Fig. 2.26, let $\mathbf{v} = \overrightarrow{AB}$ and let $\mathbf{u} = \overrightarrow{AC}$. Forming $\mathbf{u} \times \mathbf{v}$ we find

$$\mathbf{u} \times \mathbf{v} = \begin{vmatrix} \mathbf{i} & \mathbf{j} & \mathbf{k} \\ 4 & 0 & -1 \\ 2 & -1 & 2 \end{vmatrix} = -\mathbf{i} - 10\mathbf{j} - 4\mathbf{k}.$$

Calculating the magnitude of $\mathbf{u} \times \mathbf{v}$, we obtain $\sqrt{117}$. Thus, the area of the triangle *ABC* is equal to $\sqrt{117}/2$. ■

Triple Products

The products $\mathbf{u} \cdot (\mathbf{v} \times \mathbf{w})$ and $\mathbf{u} \times (\mathbf{v} \times \mathbf{w})$ are called ***triple products***. The triple product $\mathbf{u} \cdot (\mathbf{v} \times \mathbf{w})$ is known as the ***scalar triple product***, and $\mathbf{u} \times (\mathbf{v} \times \mathbf{w})$ is called the ***vector triple product***.

The magnitude of the scalar triple product has an interesting geometric interpretation. Suppose *PQ*, *PR*, and *PS* are adjacent edges of a parallelepiped, as in Fig. 2.27. Let $\mathbf{u} = \overrightarrow{PQ}$, $\mathbf{v} = \overrightarrow{PR}$, and $\mathbf{w} = \overrightarrow{PS}$. In the exercises we ask you to verify that the volume, V, of the parallelepiped is given by

$$V = |\mathbf{u} \cdot (\mathbf{v} \times \mathbf{w})|. \tag{9}$$

Tests for Collinearity and Coplanarity

Let *AP* be the area of a parallelogram with adjacent edges $\mathbf{u} = \overrightarrow{AB}$ and $\mathbf{v} = \overrightarrow{AC}$. Then, $AP = 0$ if and only if $\mathbf{u}$ and $\mathbf{v}$ are collinear (see Fig. 2.26). Similarly, let V be the volume of the parallelepiped in Fig. 2.27. We see that $V = 0$ if and only if the vectors $\mathbf{u}$, $\mathbf{v}$, and $\mathbf{w}$ are coplanar.

Combining $AP = 0$ with Theorem 11 and $V = 0$ with Eq. (9), we obtain the following useful test.

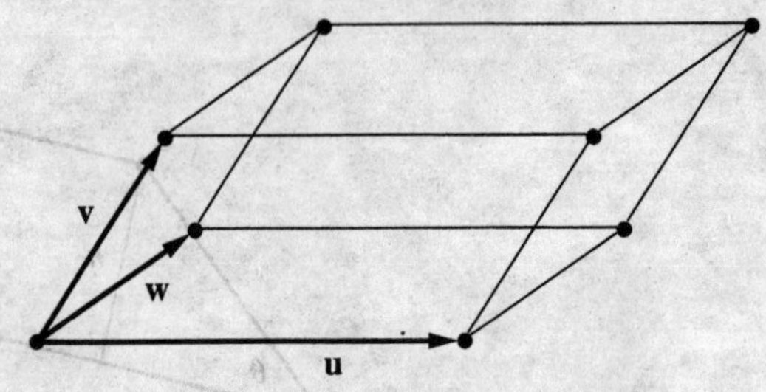

Figure 2.27 The volume of the parallelepiped is $|\mathbf{u} \cdot (\mathbf{v} \times \mathbf{w})|$.

THEOREM 12 Let **u**, **v**, and **w** be nonzero three dimensional vectors.

(a) **u** and **v** are collinear if and only if $\mathbf{u} \times \mathbf{v} = \mathbf{0}$.

(b) **u**, **v**, and **w** are coplanar if and only if $\mathbf{u} \cdot (\mathbf{v} \times \mathbf{w}) = 0$.

2.3 EXERCISES

In Exercises 1–4, calculate the dot product $\mathbf{u} \cdot \mathbf{v}$.

1. $\mathbf{u} = \begin{bmatrix} 1 \\ 3 \end{bmatrix}, \quad \mathbf{v} = \begin{bmatrix} 4 \\ -2 \end{bmatrix}$

2. $\mathbf{u} = \begin{bmatrix} 2 \\ 3 \end{bmatrix}, \quad \mathbf{v} = \begin{bmatrix} -3 \\ 2 \end{bmatrix}$

3. $\mathbf{u} = \begin{bmatrix} 1 \\ -2 \\ 1 \end{bmatrix}, \quad \mathbf{v} = \begin{bmatrix} 3 \\ -1 \\ 2 \end{bmatrix}$

4. $\mathbf{u} = 4\mathbf{i} + 2\mathbf{j} - 3\mathbf{k}, \quad \mathbf{v} = -2\mathbf{i} + \mathbf{j} - 2\mathbf{k}$

In Exercises 5–8, determine $\cos\theta$ where θ is the angle between **u** and **v**.

5. $\mathbf{u} = \begin{bmatrix} 3 \\ 1 \end{bmatrix}, \quad \mathbf{v} = \begin{bmatrix} 2 \\ 5 \end{bmatrix}$

6. $\mathbf{u} = \begin{bmatrix} 2 \\ 3 \end{bmatrix}, \quad \mathbf{v} = \begin{bmatrix} -3 \\ 1 \end{bmatrix}$

7. $\mathbf{u} = \begin{bmatrix} 1 \\ 2 \\ 1 \end{bmatrix}, \quad \mathbf{v} = \begin{bmatrix} 2 \\ -1 \\ 1 \end{bmatrix}$

8. $\mathbf{u} = 2\mathbf{i} - 3\mathbf{j} + \mathbf{k}, \quad \mathbf{v} = \mathbf{i} - 2\mathbf{j} + 3\mathbf{k}$

In Exercises 9–12, find θ (in radians) where θ is the angle between **u** and **v**.

9. $\mathbf{u} = \begin{bmatrix} 3 \\ \sqrt{3} \end{bmatrix}, \quad \mathbf{v} = \begin{bmatrix} 2 \\ 2\sqrt{3} \end{bmatrix}$

10. $\mathbf{u} = \begin{bmatrix} \sqrt{3} \\ 1 \end{bmatrix}, \quad \mathbf{v} = \begin{bmatrix} -3 \\ \sqrt{3} \end{bmatrix}$

11. $\mathbf{u} = \begin{bmatrix} 1 \\ 3 \\ -1 \end{bmatrix}, \quad \mathbf{v} = \begin{bmatrix} 2 \\ -2 \\ -4 \end{bmatrix}$

12. $\mathbf{u} = \mathbf{i} + 2\mathbf{j} + \mathbf{k}, \quad \mathbf{v} = 3\mathbf{i} + 6\mathbf{j} + 3\mathbf{k}$

In Exercises 13–18, there are at most two three-dimensional vectors **u** that satisfy the given conditions. Determine these vector(s) **u**.

13. $\mathbf{u} \cdot \mathbf{i} = 1, \quad \mathbf{u} \cdot \mathbf{j} = 3, \quad \mathbf{u} \cdot \mathbf{k} = 4$

14. $\mathbf{u} \cdot \mathbf{i} = 0, \quad \mathbf{u} \cdot \mathbf{j} = 0, \quad \mathbf{u} \cdot \mathbf{k} = 4$

15. $\mathbf{u} \cdot \mathbf{i} = 3, \quad \mathbf{u} \cdot \mathbf{k} = 4, \quad \|\mathbf{u}\| = 5$

16. $\mathbf{u} \cdot \mathbf{i} = 12, \quad \mathbf{u} \cdot \mathbf{k} = 3, \quad \|\mathbf{u}\| = 13$

17. $\mathbf{u} \cdot (\mathbf{i} + \mathbf{j}) = 2, \quad \mathbf{u} \cdot (\mathbf{j} + \mathbf{k}) = 4, \quad \mathbf{u} \cdot \mathbf{k} = 1$

18. $\mathbf{u} \cdot (\mathbf{i} + \mathbf{j}) = 2, \quad \mathbf{u} \cdot (\mathbf{j} + \mathbf{k}) = 3, \quad \mathbf{u} \cdot \mathbf{k} = 2$

In Exercises 19–22, $\mathbf{u} = \overrightarrow{OP}$, $\mathbf{v} = \overrightarrow{OQ}$ and $\mathbf{w} = proj_{\mathbf{q}}\mathbf{u}$. Find the point R such that $\mathbf{w} = \overrightarrow{OR}$. Graph **u**, **v**, and **w**.

19. $P = (2, 5)$, $Q = (6, 2)$

20. $P = (7, 6)$, $Q = (4, 1)$

21. $P = (-4, 2)$, $Q = (6, 2)$

22. $P = (-2, 4)$, $Q = (4, 2)$

In Exercises 23–26, find $\mathbf{u}_1$ and $\mathbf{u}_2$ such that $\mathbf{u}_1 = proj_{\mathbf{q}}\mathbf{u}$, $\mathbf{u}_1$ and $\mathbf{u}_2$ are orthogonal, and $\mathbf{u} = \mathbf{u}_1 + \mathbf{u}_2$.

23. $\mathbf{u} = \begin{bmatrix} 7 \\ 3 \end{bmatrix}$, $\mathbf{q} = \begin{bmatrix} 1 \\ 1 \end{bmatrix}$

24. $\mathbf{u} = \begin{bmatrix} 6 \\ 2 \end{bmatrix}$, $\mathbf{q} = \begin{bmatrix} 1 \\ -1 \end{bmatrix}$

25. $\mathbf{u} = \begin{bmatrix} 6 \\ 4 \\ -2 \end{bmatrix}$, $\mathbf{q} = \begin{bmatrix} 1 \\ 2 \\ 1 \end{bmatrix}$

26. $\mathbf{u} = 2\mathbf{i} + \mathbf{j} + 6\mathbf{k}$, $\mathbf{q} = \mathbf{i} + \mathbf{j} + \mathbf{k}$

In Exercises 27–30,

let $\mathbf{u} = \begin{bmatrix} u_1 \\ u_2 \\ u_3 \end{bmatrix}$, $\mathbf{v} = \begin{bmatrix} v_1 \\ v_2 \\ v_3 \end{bmatrix}$, $\mathbf{w} = \begin{bmatrix} w_1 \\ w_2 \\ w_3 \end{bmatrix}$.

27. Prove part **(a)** of Theorem 8.

28. Prove part **(b)** of Theorem 8.

29. Prove part **(c)** of Theorem 8.

30. Prove part **(d)** of Theorem 8.

31. Let $\mathbf{u} = \begin{bmatrix} u_1 \\ u_2 \end{bmatrix}$ and $\mathbf{v} = \begin{bmatrix} v_1 \\ v_2 \end{bmatrix}$. Show that Eq. (1) simplifies to Eq. (2a).

In Exercises 32–35, calculate the cross product $\mathbf{u} \times \mathbf{v}$.

32. $\mathbf{u} = \begin{bmatrix} 1 \\ 3 \\ 0 \end{bmatrix}$, $\mathbf{v} = \begin{bmatrix} 4 \\ 1 \\ 0 \end{bmatrix}$

33. $\mathbf{u} = \begin{bmatrix} 4 \\ 0 \\ 1 \end{bmatrix}$, $\mathbf{v} = \begin{bmatrix} 2 \\ 2 \\ 0 \end{bmatrix}$

34. $\mathbf{u} = \mathbf{i} + \mathbf{j} + 3\mathbf{k}$, $\mathbf{v} = 2\mathbf{i} + 2\mathbf{j} + 6\mathbf{k}$

35. $\mathbf{u} = \mathbf{i} + 3\mathbf{j}$, $\mathbf{v} = 2\mathbf{i} + \mathbf{j} + \mathbf{k}$

In Exercises 36–39, find a vector $\mathbf{w}$ such that $\mathbf{u} \cdot \mathbf{w} = 0$ and $\mathbf{v} \cdot \mathbf{w} = 0$.

36. $\mathbf{u} = \begin{bmatrix} 3 \\ 1 \\ 2 \end{bmatrix}$, $\mathbf{v} = \begin{bmatrix} 1 \\ 1 \\ 1 \end{bmatrix}$

37. $\mathbf{u} = \begin{bmatrix} 2 \\ 0 \\ 1 \end{bmatrix}$, $\mathbf{v} = \begin{bmatrix} 1 \\ 2 \\ 3 \end{bmatrix}$

38. $\mathbf{u} = \mathbf{i} + \mathbf{j}$, $\mathbf{v} = \mathbf{i} + \mathbf{k}$

39. $\mathbf{u} = \mathbf{i} - 2\mathbf{k}$, $\mathbf{v} = \mathbf{j} + 3\mathbf{k}$

In Exercises 40–41, find a vector $\mathbf{w}$ that is perpendicular to the plane containing the given points A, B, and C.

40. $A = (-1, 1, 2)$, $B = (2, 1, -1)$, $C = (0, -2, 4)$

41. $A = (1, 0, 0)$, $B = (0, 1, 0)$, $C = (2, 3, 1)$

In Exercises 42–43, two sides of a parallelogram coincide with the position vectors for $\mathbf{u}$ and $\mathbf{v}$. Find the area of the parallelogram.

42. $\mathbf{u} = \begin{bmatrix} 1 \\ 2 \\ 4 \end{bmatrix}$, $\mathbf{v} = \begin{bmatrix} 0 \\ 2 \\ 1 \end{bmatrix}$

43. $\mathbf{u} = \begin{bmatrix} 4 \\ -1 \\ 2 \end{bmatrix}$, $\mathbf{v} = \begin{bmatrix} 0 \\ 1 \\ 2 \end{bmatrix}$

In Exercises 44–45, find the area of the triangle having the given points as vertices.

44. $A = (0, 0, 0)$, $B = (2, 3, 4)$, $C = (1, -1, 2)$

45. $A = (5, -1, 1)$, $B = (4, 3, 0)$, $C = (0, 1, 2)$

In Exercises 46–47, three edges of a parallelepiped coincide with the position vectors for $\mathbf{u}$, $\mathbf{v}$, and $\mathbf{w}$. Find the volume of the parallelepiped.

46. $\mathbf{u} = \begin{bmatrix} 0 \\ 1 \\ 3 \end{bmatrix}$, $\mathbf{v} = \begin{bmatrix} -2 \\ 1 \\ 0 \end{bmatrix}$, $\mathbf{w} = \begin{bmatrix} 0 \\ 4 \\ 1 \end{bmatrix}$

47. $\mathbf{u} = \begin{bmatrix} 2 \\ 2 \\ 0 \end{bmatrix}$, $\mathbf{v} = \begin{bmatrix} 1 \\ 4 \\ 0 \end{bmatrix}$, $\mathbf{w} = \begin{bmatrix} 1 \\ 2 \\ 4 \end{bmatrix}$

In Exercises 48–49, determine if the three vectors are coplanar.

48. $\mathbf{u} = \begin{bmatrix} 1 \\ -1 \\ 0 \end{bmatrix}, \quad \mathbf{v} = \begin{bmatrix} 2 \\ 0 \\ 1 \end{bmatrix}, \quad \mathbf{w} = \begin{bmatrix} 0 \\ 2 \\ 1 \end{bmatrix}$

49. $\mathbf{u} = \begin{bmatrix} 2 \\ -2 \\ 1 \end{bmatrix}, \quad \mathbf{v} = \begin{bmatrix} 0 \\ 1 \\ -1 \end{bmatrix}, \quad \mathbf{w} = \begin{bmatrix} -1 \\ 0 \\ 3 \end{bmatrix}$

50. Verify that $x = u_2v_3 - u_3v_2$, $y = u_3v_1 - u_1v_3$, $z = u_1v_2 - u_2v_1$ is a solution of the system of equations

$$u_1x + u_2y + u_3z = 0$$
$$v_1x + v_2y + v_3z = 0$$

51. Show that $(\mathbf{i} \times \mathbf{i}) \times \mathbf{j} \neq \mathbf{i} \times (\mathbf{i} \times \mathbf{j})$.

52. Let $\mathbf{u} = \begin{bmatrix} u_1 \\ u_2 \\ u_3 \end{bmatrix}$ and $\mathbf{v} = \begin{bmatrix} v_1 \\ v_2 \\ v_3 \end{bmatrix}$.

a) Verify that $\|\mathbf{u} \times \mathbf{v}\|^2 = \|\mathbf{u}\|^2\|\mathbf{v}\|^2 - (\mathbf{u} \cdot \mathbf{v})^2$

b) Use the equation in part (a) to show $\|\mathbf{u} \times \mathbf{v}\| = \|\mathbf{u}\|\|\mathbf{v}\| \sin\theta$ where θ is the angle between $\mathbf{u}$ and $\mathbf{v}$.

53. Suppose PQ, PR, and PS are adjacent edges of a rectangular parallelepiped, as in Fig. 2.27. Let $\mathbf{u} = \overrightarrow{PQ}$, $\mathbf{v} = \overrightarrow{PR}$, $\mathbf{w} = \overrightarrow{PS}$. Show that the volume, V, of the parallelepiped is given by $V = |\mathbf{u} \cdot (\mathbf{v} \times \mathbf{w})|$.

2.4 LINES AND PLANES IN SPACE

Many physical problems involve motion along a curve in three space. Examples include satellite trajectories, the arc of a slicing golf ball, the flight path of an airliner, and so forth. The simplest curve in three space is a line and we now discuss how lines are defined in three space.

The Equation of a Line in the *xy*-Plane

As we know, a line in the xy-plane is determined by a point on the line and the slope of the line (see Fig. 2.28). If a line l passes through the point $P_0 = (x_0, y_0)$ and if l has slope m, then the equation of the line is

$$y = m(x - x_0) + y_0.$$

That is, the line l is completely determined once we specify two pieces of information:

(a) A direction for the line, given by the slope m.
(b) A point $P_0 = (x_0, y_0)$ on the line.

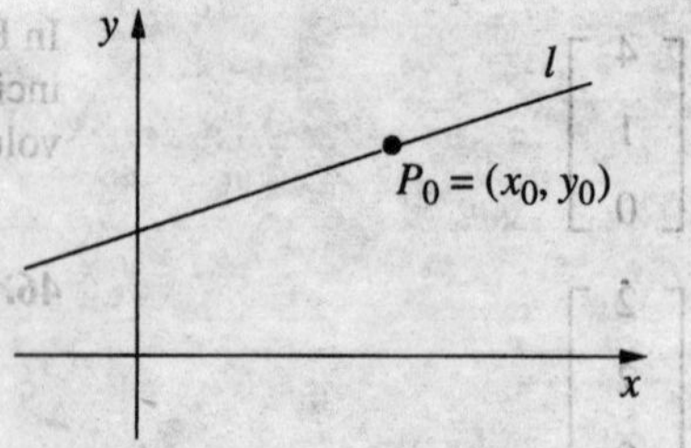

Figure 2.28 The line l has slope m and passes through the point $P_0 = (x_0, y_0)$. In general, a line in the xy-plane is determined by its direction (the slope of the line) and a point P_0 on the line.

The Vector Form for the Equation of a Line in Three Space

As with lines in the xy-plane, a line L in three space is completely determined once we specify the *direction* of the line and a *point* on the line. In three space, vectors are used to specify direction. Therefore, a line L is determined once we specify a direction vector $\mathbf{u}$ for the line and a point $P_0 = (x_0, y_0, z_0)$ on the line (see Fig. 2.29). As you can see from Fig. 2.29, a point $P = (x, y, z)$ is on the line L if and only if the vector $\overrightarrow{P_0P}$ is parallel to $\mathbf{u}$; that is, if and only if $\overrightarrow{P_0P} = t\mathbf{u}$ for some scalar t.

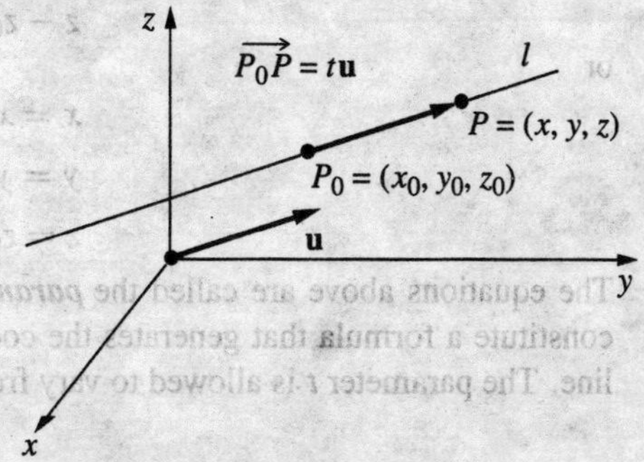

Figure 2.29 A line L in space is determined by a direction vector, $\mathbf{u}$, and a point P_0 on L. As we see, a point $P = (x, y, z)$ is on L if and only if $\overrightarrow{P_0P} = t\mathbf{u}$ for some value t.

The geometric view given in Fig. 2.29 leads us to the ***vector form for the equation of a line:***

> **Vector Form for the Equation of a Line**
>
> Let L be the line through $P_0 = (x_0, y_0, z_0)$ having direction vector $\mathbf{u}$. A point $P = (x, y, z)$ is on the line L if and only if
>
> $$\overrightarrow{P_0P} = t\mathbf{u} \text{ for some scalar } t,\ -\infty < t < \infty.$$

Parametric Equations for a Line in Three Space

We can use the vector form for the equation of a line to derive a formula for the coordinates of every point P on the line. Let L be a line through $P_0 = (x_0, y_0, z_0)$ and let L have direction vector $\mathbf{u}$ where

$$\mathbf{u} = \begin{bmatrix} u_1 \\ u_2 \\ u_3 \end{bmatrix}.$$

Let $P = (x, y, z)$ be any point on the line L. The vector $\overrightarrow{P_0P}$ is given by

$$\overrightarrow{P_0P} = \begin{bmatrix} x - x_0 \\ y - y_0 \\ z - z_0 \end{bmatrix}.$$

Since P is on the line L, we know there is some scalar t such that $\overrightarrow{P_0P} = t\mathbf{u}$. Therefore,

$$x - x_0 = tu_1$$
$$y - y_0 = tu_2$$
$$z - z_0 = tu_3$$

or

$$x = x_0 + tu_1$$
$$y = y_0 + tu_2$$
$$z = z_0 + tu_3.$$

The equations above are called the ***parametric equations of the line***. As such, they constitute a formula that generates the coordinates, (x, y, z), of every point P on the line. The parameter t is allowed to vary from $-\infty$ to ∞.

Parametric Equations for a Line

Let L be a line with direction vector $\mathbf{u} = \begin{bmatrix} u_1 \\ u_2 \\ u_3 \end{bmatrix}$ where $P_0 = (x_0, y_0, z_0)$ is on the line. A point $P = (x, y, z)$ is on the line if and only if

$$x = x_0 + tu_1, \qquad y = y_0 + tu_2, \qquad z = z_0 + tu_3$$

for some real number t.

EXAMPLE 1 Let L be the line through $P_0 = (2, 1, 6)$, having direction vector $\mathbf{u}$ given by

$$\mathbf{u} = \begin{bmatrix} 4 \\ -1 \\ 3 \end{bmatrix}.$$

(a) Find parametric equations for the line L.

(b) Does the line L intersect the xy-plane? If so, what are the coordinates of the point of intersection?

Solution

(a) One set of parametric equations for L is

$$x = 2 + 4t, \qquad y = 1 - t, \qquad z = 6 + 3t.$$

(b) If L intersects the xy-plane, it must do so at a point P_1 having z-coordinate equal to zero—a point of the form $P_1 = (x_1, y_1, 0)$. Since the z-coordinate of points on L is given by $z = 6 + 3t$, it follows that $t = -2$. When $t = -2$, we see that $x = -6$ and $y = 3$. Thus, the line L intersects the xy-plane at the point $P_1 = (-6, 3, 0)$.

As we know from geometry, two points determine a line. The next example illustrates how we can find the equation of a line L given two points on L.

EXAMPLE 2 Find parametric equations for the line L passing through $P_0 = (2, 5, 7)$ and $P_1 = (4, 9, 8)$.

Solution As a direction vector for L, we use $\mathbf{u} = \overrightarrow{P_0P_1}$:

$$\overrightarrow{P_0P_1} = \begin{bmatrix} 2 \\ 4 \\ 1 \end{bmatrix}.$$

Therefore, one set of parametric equations for L is

$$x = 2 + 2t, \qquad y = 5 + 4t, \qquad z = 7 + t.$$

(***Note:*** In Examples 1 and 2, we were careful to say that we had found *one* set of parametric equations for the line L. In particular, there are many other ways to describe the line L. For example, we could replace the parameter t by a new parameter t^3 and the parametric equations in Examples 1 and 2 would still trace out the same line L.)

Line Segments

We can use the ideas described above to specify line segments instead of entire lines. To specify the line segment joining P_0 and P_1, we first find parametric equations for the line passing through P_0 and P_1, as in Example 2. We then restrict the parameter t to the interval $[0, 1]$; when $t = 0$, we are at P_0 and when $t = 1$, we are at P_1.

EXAMPLE 3 Find parametric equations for the line segment joining $P_0 = (2, 5, 7)$ and the point $P_1 = (4, 9, 8)$; recall Example 2.

Solution Drawing on the results of Example 2, one set of parametric equations for the line segment is

$$x = 2 + 2t, \qquad y = 5 + 4t, \qquad z = 7 + t, \qquad 0 \le t \le 1.$$

As you can see, $t = 0$ gives P_0 and $t = 1$ gives P_1.

Planes in Space and Their Normal Vectors

A line L is determined by a point P_0 on the line and a direction vector $\mathbf{u}$ for the line. Similarly, a plane Π is determined by a point P_0 on the plane and a vector $\mathbf{n}$ that gives us the "orientation" of the plane. In particular, a vector **n** is said to be ***normal*** to the plane Π if **n** is perpendicular (orthogonal) to every vector **u** in the plane (see Fig. 2.30).

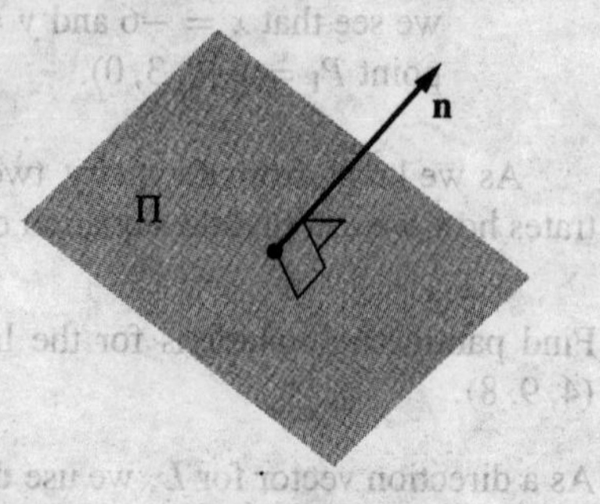

Figure 2.30 The vector **n** is normal (that is, perpendicular) to the plane Π. The vector **n** tells us the orientation of the plane.

One way to think of a normal is to imagine that the plane Π is an infinite sheet of plywood. Then a normal is like a nail hammered perpendicularly into the plywood. When we turn the plywood, we can deduce the orientation of the sheet simply by looking at the direction the nail is pointing.

From our work in Section 2.3, we know that two nonzero vectors **r** and **s** are perpendicular if and only if $\mathbf{r} \cdot \mathbf{s} = 0$. Therefore, a vector **n** is normal to a plane Π if and only if

$$\mathbf{n} \cdot \mathbf{u} = 0 \quad \text{for every vector } \mathbf{u} \text{ in } \Pi.$$

The following example illustrates the concept of a normal to a plane.

EXAMPLE 4 Let Π denote the *xy*-plane. Which of the following vectors are normal to Π?

(a) $\mathbf{n}_1 = \begin{bmatrix} 2 \\ 1 \\ 3 \end{bmatrix}$

(b) $\mathbf{n}_2 = \begin{bmatrix} 3 \\ 2 \\ 0 \end{bmatrix}$

(c) $\mathbf{n}_3 = \begin{bmatrix} 0 \\ 0 \\ 5 \end{bmatrix}$

Solution A vector **u** is in the *xy*-plane if and only if **u** has the form

$$\mathbf{u} = \begin{bmatrix} u_1 \\ u_2 \\ 0 \end{bmatrix}.$$

Forming the dot products $\mathbf{n}_1 \cdot \mathbf{u}$, $\mathbf{n}_2 \cdot \mathbf{u}$, and $\mathbf{n}_3 \cdot \mathbf{u}$, we find

$$\mathbf{n}_1 \cdot \mathbf{u} = 2u_1 + u_2$$
$$\mathbf{n}_2 \cdot \mathbf{u} = 3u_1 + 2u_2$$
$$\mathbf{n}_3 \cdot \mathbf{u} = 0.$$

Thus, $\mathbf{n}_3$ is normal to the plane Π. Observe that $\mathbf{n}_1$ and $\mathbf{n}_2$ are not normal to Π because they are not perpendicular to *every* vector $\mathbf{u}$ in Π.

(***Note:*** Parallel planes have the same orientation and hence have the same normals. For example, the plane $z = 3$ is parallel to the xy-plane. In particular, the plane $z = 3$ consists of all vectors $\mathbf{u}$ having the form

$$\mathbf{u} = \begin{bmatrix} u_1 \\ u_2 \\ 3 \end{bmatrix}.$$

Recalling Example 4, the vector $\mathbf{n}_3$ is normal to the xy-plane. Clearly, this vector $\mathbf{n}_3$ is also normal to the plane $z = 3$. Thus, we have an illustration of the fact that parallel planes have the same normals.)

The Vector Form for the Equation of a Plane in Three Space

Let Π be a plane in three space and let $\mathbf{n}$ be a normal for Π. As noted above, the normal vector $\mathbf{n}$ tells us the orientation of Π. But, since parallel planes all have the same orientation (that is, the same normals) we also need to give a point P_0 on Π in order to specify completely.

So, let Π be a plane with normal $\mathbf{n}$ where P_0 is a point on Π. If P is any other point on Π, then the vector $\mathbf{u} = \overrightarrow{PP_0}$ lies in Π (see Fig. 2.31). Since $\mathbf{n}$ is normal to Π, it follows that

$$\mathbf{n} \cdot \overrightarrow{PP_0} = 0.$$

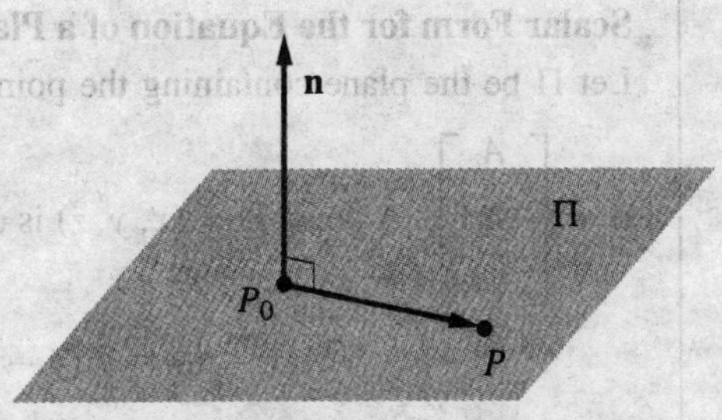

Figure 2.31 The vector $\mathbf{n}$ is normal to the plane Π. The point $P = (x, y, z)$ is in Π if and only if the vector $\overrightarrow{PP_0}$ lies in Π and hence, if and only if $\mathbf{n} \cdot \overrightarrow{PP_0} = 0$.

The geometric view given in Fig. 2.31 leads us to the ***vector form for the equation of a plane***:

> **Vector Form for the Equation of a Plane**
> Let Π be the plane containing the point $P_0 = (x_0, y_0, z_0)$ and having normal $\mathbf{n}$. A point $P = (x, y, z)$ is in the plane Π if and only if
> $$\mathbf{n} \cdot \overrightarrow{PP_0} = 0.$$

The Scalar Form for the Equation of a Plane

Let Π be a plane and let $P_0 = (x_0, y_0, z_0)$ be a point in Π. Let $\mathbf{n}$ be a normal vector for Π where

$$\mathbf{n} = \begin{bmatrix} A \\ B \\ C \end{bmatrix}.$$

As we saw above, a point $P = (x, y, z)$ is in Π if and only if $\mathbf{n} \cdot \overrightarrow{PP_0} = 0$. Expanding this dot product condition, we obtain:

$$\begin{bmatrix} A \\ B \\ C \end{bmatrix} \cdot \begin{bmatrix} x - x_0 \\ y - y_0 \\ z - z_0 \end{bmatrix} = 0$$

or,

$$A(x - x_0) + B(y - y_0) + C(z - z_0) = 0.$$

The equation above is the scalar form for the equation of a plane.

> **Scalar Form for the Equation of a Plane**
> Let Π be the plane containing the point $P_0 = (x_0, y_0, z_0)$ and having a normal $\mathbf{n} = \begin{bmatrix} A \\ B \\ C \end{bmatrix}$. A point $P = (x, y, z)$ is on the plane Π if and only if
> $$A(x - x_0) + B(y - y_0) + C(z - z_0) = 0. \qquad (1)$$

EXAMPLE 5 Find the equation of the plane containing the point $P_0 = (1, 3, -2)$ and having normal

$$\mathbf{n} = \begin{bmatrix} 5 \\ -2 \\ 2 \end{bmatrix}.$$

Solution The equation of the plane is $\mathbf{n} \cdot \overrightarrow{PP_0} = 0$,

$$5(x-1) - 2(y-3) + 2(z+2) = 0$$

or

$$5x - 2y + 2z = -5.$$

When simplified, the scalar form (1) for the equation of a plane Π has the form

$$Ax + By + Cz = D.$$

We can read the components of a normal vector for Π from this equation; the components are A, B, and C.

EXAMPLE 6 The equation of a plane Π is given by

$$2x + y - 2z = 8.$$

Find a unit normal for Π (by a unit normal, we mean a normal vector that has length 1).

Solution From the equation for Π, we see that a normal vector $\mathbf{n}$ is given by

$$\mathbf{n} = \begin{bmatrix} 2 \\ 1 \\ -2 \end{bmatrix}.$$

We get a *unit* normal, $\mathbf{v}$, by dividing $\mathbf{n}$ by its length:

$$\mathbf{v} = \frac{\mathbf{n}}{\|\mathbf{n}\|} = \frac{1}{3}\mathbf{n} = \begin{bmatrix} 2/3 \\ 1/3 \\ -2/3 \end{bmatrix}.$$

Using the Cross Product to Find a Normal

We have often heard that "two points determine a line." Similarly, three points determine a plane. To explain how, suppose P_0, P_1, and P_2 are three points on a plane Π (see Fig. 2.32). Clearly, the vectors $\mathbf{u} = \overrightarrow{P_0P_1}$ and $\mathbf{v} = \overrightarrow{P_0P_2}$ lie in the plane Π. To find a normal for Π (a vector $\mathbf{n}$ that is perpendicular to both $\mathbf{u}$ and $\mathbf{v}$), we need only form the cross product of $\mathbf{u}$ and $\mathbf{v}$. Thus, a normal for Π is given by:

$$\mathbf{n} = \mathbf{u} \times \mathbf{v}.$$

EXAMPLE 7 Find the equation of the plane passing through the points $P_0 = (1, 3, 2)$, $P_1 = (2, 0, -1)$, and $P_2 = (4, 5, 1)$.

Solution The vectors $\mathbf{u} = \overrightarrow{P_0P_1}$ and $\mathbf{v} = \overrightarrow{P_0P_2}$ are given by

$$\mathbf{u} = \begin{bmatrix} 1 \\ -3 \\ -3 \end{bmatrix} \quad \text{and} \quad \mathbf{v} = \begin{bmatrix} 3 \\ 2 \\ -1 \end{bmatrix}.$$

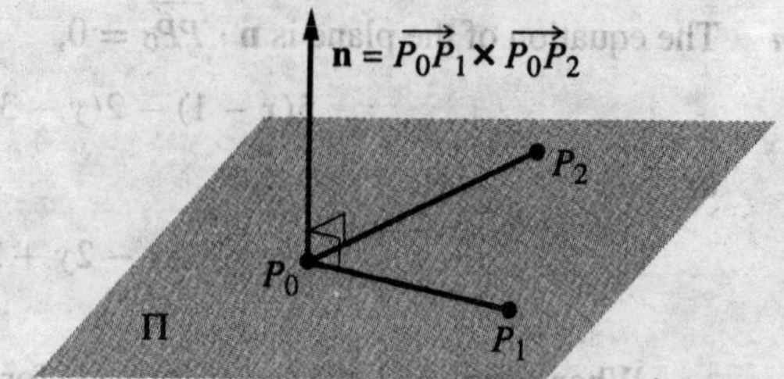

Figure 2.32 Since P_0, P_1, and P_2 are in the plane Π, the vectors $\mathbf{u} = \overrightarrow{P_0P_1}$ and $\mathbf{v} = \overrightarrow{P_0P_2}$ also lie in Π. Therefore, $\mathbf{n} = \mathbf{u} \times \mathbf{v}$ is a normal for Π.

We use a symbolic determinant to find the cross product of **u** and **v**:

$$\mathbf{n} = \mathbf{u} \times \mathbf{v} = \begin{vmatrix} \mathbf{i} & \mathbf{j} & \mathbf{k} \\ 1 & -3 & -3 \\ 3 & 2 & -1 \end{vmatrix} = 9\mathbf{i} - 8\mathbf{j} + 11\mathbf{k} = \begin{bmatrix} 9 \\ -8 \\ 11 \end{bmatrix}.$$

Having **n**, we use Eq. (1) to calculate the equation of the plane:

$$9(x-1) - 8(y-3) + 11(z-2) = 0$$

or,

$$9x - 8y + 11z = 7.$$

(*Note:* The method for finding a normal used in Example 7 will only work if the three points P_0, P_1, and P_2 do not lie on a line.)

Parallel Planes

As we indicated earlier, parallel planes have the same normals. This observation leads to a formal definition. Let Π_1 and Π_2 be planes in space with normals $\mathbf{n}_1$ and $\mathbf{n}_2$, respectively. We say that Π_1 and Π_2 are ***parallel*** if the normal $\mathbf{n}_1$ is parallel to the normal $\mathbf{n}_2$.

EXAMPLE 8 Let Π_1, Π_2, and Π_3 be planes having the following equations:

Equation of Π_1: $6x + 4y + 8z = 2$

Equation of Π_2: $x + 5y + 3z = 4$

Equation of Π_3: $3x + 2y + 4z = 9$

(a) Determine if any two of these three planes are parallel.

(b) Find the equation of the plane parallel to Π_1 passing through $P_0 = (1, 2, 1)$.

Solution

(a) Let $\mathbf{n}_1$, $\mathbf{n}_2$, and $\mathbf{n}_3$ denote the normals for Π_1, Π_2, and Π_3, respectively. Then

$$\mathbf{n}_1 = \begin{bmatrix} 6 \\ 4 \\ 8 \end{bmatrix}, \quad \mathbf{n}_2 = \begin{bmatrix} 1 \\ 5 \\ 3 \end{bmatrix}, \quad \mathbf{n}_3 = \begin{bmatrix} 3 \\ 2 \\ 4 \end{bmatrix}.$$

Clearly, $\mathbf{n}_1 = 2\mathbf{n}_3$, and so $\mathbf{n}_1$ and $\mathbf{n}_3$ are parallel vectors. Therefore, Π_1 and Π_3 are parallel planes.

(b) Any plane parallel to Π_1 has a normal equal to $\mathbf{n}_1$. Thus, using Eq. (1), we find the equation of the plane parallel to Π_1 and containing $P_0 = (1, 2, 1)$ has equation

$$6x + 4y + 8z = 22$$

or, after canceling a common factor of 2,

$$3x + 2y + 4z = 11. \quad \blacksquare$$

2.4 EXERCISES

In Exercises 1–2, give parametric equations for the line L through P_0 in the direction $\mathbf{u}$.

1. $P_0 = (2, 4, -3), \quad \mathbf{u} = \begin{bmatrix} 3 \\ 2 \\ 4 \end{bmatrix}$

2. $P_0 = (1, 1, -1), \quad \mathbf{u} = \begin{bmatrix} 2 \\ 0 \\ 3 \end{bmatrix}$

In Exercises 3–4, give parametric equations for the line L through the two points.

3. $P_0 = (0, 4, 1), \quad P_1 = (1, 2, 4)$

4. $P_0 = (5, 1, -3), \quad P_1 = (6, 6, 4)$

In Exercises 5–8, determine whether the given lines are parallel.

5. $\begin{aligned} x &= 3 + 2t \\ y &= 2 - t \\ z &= 1 + 3t \end{aligned} \qquad \begin{aligned} x &= 5 - 4t \\ y &= 6 + 2t \\ z &= 2 - 6t \end{aligned}$

6. $\begin{aligned} x &= 2 + 6t \\ y &= 2 + 4t \\ z &= -1 + 3t \end{aligned} \qquad \begin{aligned} x &= 4 + 3t \\ y &= 7 + 2t \\ z &= 2 + 3t \end{aligned}$

7. $\begin{aligned} x &= 1 - 2t \\ y &= 5 + 3t \\ z &= 4 - 2t \end{aligned} \qquad \begin{aligned} x &= 7 + 2t \\ y &= 2 - 3t \\ z &= 3 + 4t \end{aligned}$

8. $\begin{aligned} x &= 5 - t \\ y &= 3 + 2t \\ z &= 2 - 3t \end{aligned} \qquad \begin{aligned} x &= 4 + 3t \\ y &= 6 - 6t \\ z &= 8 + 9t \end{aligned}$

In Exercises 9–10, find parametric equations for the line L through the point P_0 and normal to the given plane.

9. $P_0 = (1, 2, 1), \quad 3x + 4y - z = 9$

10. $P_0 = (2, 0, -3), \quad x - y + 2z = 8$

In Exercises 11–14, find a point P where the line intersects the given plane or decide that the line does not intersect the plane.

11. $\begin{aligned} x &= 1 + 2t \\ y &= 3 - t, \\ z &= 5 + 4t \end{aligned} \qquad x + y - z = 2$

12. $\begin{aligned} x &= 4 + 2t \\ y &= 7 + 2t, \\ z &= 5 + 4t \end{aligned} \qquad x + y - z = 2$

13. $\begin{aligned} x &= 8 + 4t \\ y &= 3 + 4t, \\ z &= 4 - 8t \end{aligned} \qquad x + 2y + z = 2$

14. $x = 1 + 2t$
$y = 3 - t, \quad x + 2y + z = 4$
$z = 5 + 4t$

In Exercises 15–16, find the equation of the plane through P_0 with the given normal $\mathbf{n}$.

15. $P_0 = (3, 1, 3), \quad \mathbf{n} = \begin{bmatrix} 6 \\ 1 \\ -1 \end{bmatrix}$

16. $P_0 = (4, -2, 3), \quad \mathbf{n} = \begin{bmatrix} 1 \\ -2 \\ 3 \end{bmatrix}$

In Exercises 17–20, find the equation of the plane through the given (noncollinear) points P, Q, and R.

17. $P = (1, 0, 3)$
$Q = (2, 1, 5)$
$R = (1, 4, 4)$

18. $P = (5, 1, 7)$
$Q = (6, 9, 2)$
$R = (7, 2, 9)$

19. $P = (3, 2, 3)$
$Q = (1, 1, 4)$
$R = (6, 2, 5)$

20. $P = (4, 1, 0)$
$Q = (3, 2, 1)$
$R = (5, 1, 1)$

In Exercises 21–22, find a unit normal for the given plane.

21. $2x + y - 2z = 6$

22. $4x - 4y + 2z = 10$

In Exercises 23–24, find the equation of the plane through the point P_0 and parallel to the given plane.

23. $P_0 = (3, 8, 1), \quad x + 2y - 2z = 4$

24. $P_0 = (1, 1, 3), \quad 2x - 3y + 2z = 6$

In Exercises 25–26, the given planes intersect in a line. Find parametric equations for the line of intersection. [*Hint:* The line of intersection consists of all points (x, y, z) that satisfy both equations. Solve the system and designate the unconstrained variable as t.]

25. $x + z = 4, \quad 2x - y + 3z = 3$

26. $x + 2y + z = 1, \quad 2x + 5y + 3z = 4$

SUPPLEMENTARY EXERCISES

1. Let $\mathbf{u} = \begin{bmatrix} 5 \\ 2 \end{bmatrix}$, $\mathbf{v} = \begin{bmatrix} 7 \\ 1 \end{bmatrix}$, $\mathbf{x} = \begin{bmatrix} 1 \\ 4 \end{bmatrix}$.

Write $\mathbf{x}$ in the form $\mathbf{x} = \mathbf{x}_1 + \mathbf{x}_2$ where $\mathbf{x}_1$ is parallel to $\mathbf{u}$ and $\mathbf{x}_2$ is parallel to $\mathbf{v}$.

2. A boat leaves its mainland dock and sails 10 miles in the direction 60° north of east, to an island dock. The boat then leaves the island, sailing 10 miles due northwest, to a buoy. Place an xy-coordinate system so that its origin is at the mainland dock and so that the y-axis points north. Give the coordinates of the island dock and the buoy. How far is the buoy from the mainland dock?

3. Let $P = (16, 20)$ and $Q = (12, -8)$. Find the coordinates of the point R that is halfway between the midpoint of the segment PQ and the point Q.

4. Let $\mathbf{u}$ and $\mathbf{v}$ be orthogonal unit vectors and let $\mathbf{a} = 2\mathbf{u} + 3\mathbf{v}$. Find $\|\mathbf{a}\|$.

5. Let $\mathbf{u}$, $\mathbf{v}$, and $\mathbf{w}$ be mutually orthogonal vectors such that $\|\mathbf{u}\| = 2$, $\|\mathbf{v}\| = 1$, and $\|\mathbf{w}\| = 2$. Let $\mathbf{a} = \mathbf{u} + \mathbf{v} + \mathbf{w}$. What is $\|\mathbf{a}\|$?

6. Let $\mathbf{u}$ and $\mathbf{v}$ be orthogonal vectors such that $\|\mathbf{u}\| = 2$ and $\|\mathbf{v}\| = 3$. Calculate the dot product $(\mathbf{u} - \mathbf{v}) \cdot (\mathbf{u} + \mathbf{v})$.

7. Let $\mathbf{u}$ and $\mathbf{v}$ be as in Exercise 6. Calculate $\|\mathbf{u} \times \mathbf{v}\|$.

8. Let $\mathbf{u}$ and $\mathbf{v}$ be as in Exercise 6. Calculate $\|(\mathbf{u} - \mathbf{v}) \times (\mathbf{u} + \mathbf{v})\|$.

9. Find all unit vectors in R^3 parallel to the xz-plane and orthogonal to $\begin{bmatrix} 3 \\ -2 \\ 4 \end{bmatrix}$.

10. A plane intersects the x-axis at the point $(a, 0, 0)$, the y-axis at $(0, b, 0)$ and the z-axis at $(0, 0, c)$, where a, b, and c are nonzero. Find the equation of the plane and express it in the form $\alpha x + \beta y + \gamma z = 1$.

11. Do the four points (1, 1, 2), (2, 3, 9), (−2, 1, −1), and (1, 2, 5) all lie on the same plane?

12. Let A, B, and C be distinct points on a circle of radius r in the plane where A and B are endpoints of a diameter of the circle. Show that the triangle ABC is a right triangle. [*Hint:* Set up a coordinate system in the plane with the origin at the center of the circle and such that $A = (-r, 0)$, $B = (r, 0)$.]

13. Let A, B, C, and D be verticles, not endpoints of a quadrilateral in the plane. Show that the line segments joining the midpoints of opposite sides of $ABCD$ bisect each other. [*Hint:* Set up a coordinate system in the plane with $A = (a_1, a_2)$, $B = (b_1, b_2)$, $C = (c_1, c_2)$, $D = (d_1, d_2)$.]

CONCEPTUAL EXERCISES

1. True or False: If $\mathbf{u} \cdot \mathbf{v} = 0$, then either $\mathbf{u} = \mathbf{0}$ or $\mathbf{v} = \mathbf{0}$.

2. True or False: If $\mathbf{u} \times \mathbf{v} = \mathbf{0}$, then either $\mathbf{u} = \mathbf{0}$ or $\mathbf{v} = \mathbf{0}$.

3. Prove the Parallelogram Law: $\|\mathbf{u}+\mathbf{v}\|^2 + \|\mathbf{u}-\mathbf{v}\|^2 = 2\|\mathbf{u}\|^2 + 2\|\mathbf{v}\|^2$.

4. Let $\mathbf{u}$ and $\mathbf{v}$ be nonzero vectors in the plane. Assume that $\mathbf{u}$ and $\mathbf{v}$ are not parallel vectors and that they have the same initial point. Draw the vectors $\mathbf{u} - \mathbf{v}$ and $\mathbf{u} + \mathbf{v}$. Use your sketch to explain why the result of Exercise 3 is called the Parallelogram Law.

5. Give an example of three distinct vectors $\mathbf{u}$, $\mathbf{v}$, and $\mathbf{w}$ such that $\mathbf{u} \times (\mathbf{v} \times \mathbf{w}) \neq (\mathbf{u} \times \mathbf{v}) \times \mathbf{w}$.

6. Let A be a (3×3) matrix, given in column form as $A = [\mathbf{A}_1, \mathbf{A}_2, \mathbf{A}_3]$. Suppose each column vector is nonzero and that $\mathbf{A}_1 \cdot \mathbf{A}_2 = 0$, $\mathbf{A}_1 \cdot \mathbf{A}_3 = 0$, and $\mathbf{A}_2 \cdot \mathbf{A}_3 = 0$. Recall, for $\mathbf{b}$ a (3×1) vector, that the equation $A\mathbf{x} = \mathbf{b}$ can be written in the form
$$x_1\mathbf{A}_1 + x_2\mathbf{A}_2 + x_3\mathbf{A}_3 = \mathbf{b}. \tag{1}$$
Use the orthogonality of the columns of A to give a formula for x_1, x_2, x_3. [*Hint:* Form the dot product of $\mathbf{A}_i$ with both sides of (1).]

7. Let A be as in Exercise 6. Show that A is nonsingular.

8. Let A be as in Exercise 6, along with the additional conditions that the columns of A are unit vectors. That is, $\mathbf{A}_1 \cdot \mathbf{A}_1 = 1$, $\mathbf{A}_2 \cdot \mathbf{A}_2 = 1$, and $\mathbf{A}_3 \cdot \mathbf{A}_3 = 1$. Use the formula developed in Exercise 6 to show that $A^{-1} = A^T$. [*Hint:* Recall Eq. (7c) in Section 1.9.]

9. Let A be as in Exercise 8; that is, $A^TA = I$. Show that the function $\mathbf{y} = A\mathbf{x}$ preserves lengths; that is, show that if $\mathbf{x}$ is (3×1), then $\|A\mathbf{x}\| = \|\mathbf{x}\|$.

10. Let A be as in Exercise 8; that is, $A^TA = I$. Show that the function $\mathbf{y} = A\mathbf{x}$ preserves dot products; that is, show that if $\mathbf{u}$ and $\mathbf{v}$ are (3×1), then $(A\mathbf{u}) \cdot (A\mathbf{v}) = \mathbf{u} \cdot \mathbf{v}$.

11. Let A be as in Exercise 8; that is, $A^TA = I$. Use the results of Exercises 9 and 10 to show that the function $\mathbf{y} = A\mathbf{x}$ preserves angles between vectors; that is, show that if the angle between $\mathbf{u}$ and $\mathbf{v}$ is $\boldsymbol{\theta}$, then the angle between $A\mathbf{u}$ and $A\mathbf{v}$ is also $\boldsymbol{\theta}$.

12. Let $\mathbf{u}$ and $\mathbf{v}$ be nonzero vectors such that $\|\mathbf{u}\| = \|\mathbf{v}\|$. Show that $\mathbf{u} - \mathbf{v}$ and $\mathbf{u} + \mathbf{v}$ are orthogonal.

MATLAB EXERCISES

Exercises 1–4 are introductory exercises in programming. Each exercise asks you to write a MATLAB function (that is, a function M-file) that calculates the given quantity. If you are not familiar with MATLAB scripts and functions, you can read Section A-11 in the Appendix.

1. Recall that we can use Theorem 11 to find the area of a triangle whose vertices are $A = (a_1, a_2, a_3)$, $B = (b_1, b_2, b_3)$, and $C = (c_1, c_2, c_3)$ (see Example 8 in Section 2.3). Write a function M-file that calculates the area of a triangle having three given vertices. The function M-file should have the form

```
area = triangle(a,b,c)
```

where a, b, and c are MATLAB row vectors representing the vertices of the triangle; that is, $a = [a_1, a_2, a_3]$, $b = [b_1, b_2, b_3]$, and $c = [c_1, c_2, c_3]$. As an option, you might want your function to issue a warning if the three vertices a, b, and c are collinear. (See Exercise 4 where we discuss such a feature.)

2. Write a function M-file that calculates the volume of a parallelepiped whose sides are determined by given vectors

$$\mathbf{u} = \begin{bmatrix} u_1 \\ u_2 \\ u_3 \end{bmatrix}, \quad \mathbf{v} = \begin{bmatrix} v_1 \\ v_2 \\ v_3 \end{bmatrix}, \quad \mathbf{w} = \begin{bmatrix} w_1 \\ w_2 \\ w_3 \end{bmatrix}.$$

The function M-file should have the form

```
volume = parallelepiped(u,v,w).
```

3. Write a function M-file that calculates the area of a parallelogram having given vertices $a = [a_1, a_2, a_3]$, $b = [b_1, b_2, b_3]$, $c = [c_1, c_2, c_3]$, and $d = [d_1, d_2, d_3]$. The function M-file should have the form

```
area = parallelogram(a,b,c,d).
```

4. Write a function M-file that calculates the equation of the plane that passes through three given points $a = [a_1, a_2, a_3]$, $b = [b_1, b_2, b_3]$, and $c = [c_1, c_2, c_3]$. The equation of the plane should be given in the form

$$Ax + By + Cz = D.$$

Your function program should check to see if the given points a, b, and c are collinear. To determine collinearity, you can calculate the cross product of $\mathbf{u}$ and $\mathbf{v}$ where

$$\mathbf{u} = \overrightarrow{ab} \text{ and } \mathbf{v} = \overrightarrow{ac}$$

(recall Theorem 12 in Section 2.3). If a, b, and c are collinear, there is not a unique plane containing the three points and your program should communicate this fact to the user. The normal method of communicating whether or not a function encounters an abnormal situation is by "setting a flag." That is, a variable (a flag) is given one of several values in the function, depending on the circumstances encountered when the function is invoked. The flag is returned by the function and the user can tell what happened in the function by evaluating the flag.

To illustrate the ideas, we list the first few lines of one possible program for this exercise.

```
function [coefficients,ier]=plane(a,b,c)
%
%  This function calculates the equation of the plane
%     that passes through the points a, b and c.  The
%     flag ier is set to -1 if a, b and c are collinear
%     and is set to 1 otherwise.  When ier = 1, the
%     equation of the plane is Ax+By+Cz=D and this is
%     returned in the vector coefficients, where
%
%             coefficients = [A, B, C, D].
%
%
ier = 1;
coefficients = [0,0,0,0];
u=b-a;
v=c-a;
w = cross(u,v);
normw = norm(w);
if normw == 0
   ier = -1;
   return
end
```

⋮

[The rest of the program goes here, lines that calculate the coefficients A, B, C, and D.]

⋮

The return statement in the lines above returns control to the calling program (the program that invoked the function "plane"). If $\mathbf{w} = \mathbf{u} \times \mathbf{v}$ is not the zero vector, then the return is not executed because a, b, and c are not collinear. We leave it for you to complete this program. Test your function using the three points in Example 7 of Section 2.4. Also, test your function using the three collinear points

$$a = (2, 1, 5), \quad b = (6, 3, 15), \quad c = (-4, -2, -10).$$

3

THE VECTOR SPACE R^n

OVERVIEW

In Chapter 2 we discussed geometric vector concepts in the familiar setting of two-space and three-space. In this chapter, we extend these concepts to n-dimensional space. For instance, we will see that lines and planes in three-space give rise to the idea of a subspace of R^n.

Many of the results in this chapter are grounded in the basic idea of linear independence that was introduced in Chapter 1. Linear independence is key, for example, to defining the concept of the dimension of a subspace or a basis for a subspace.

In turn, ideas such as subspace and basis are fundamental to modern mathematics and applications. We will see how these ideas are used to solve applied problems involving least-squares fits to data, Fourier series approximations of functions, systems of differential equations, and so forth.

In this chapter, for example, Sections 3.8 and 3.9 deal with least-squares fits to data. As we see in these two sections, methods for determining a least-squares fit (and a framework for interpreting the results of a least-squares fit) cannot be understood without a thorough appreciation of the basic topics in this chapter—subspace, basis, and dimension.

CORE SECTIONS

3.2 Vector Space Properties of R^n

3.3 Examples of Subspaces

3.4 Bases for Subspaces

3.5 Dimension

3.6 Orthogonal Bases for Subspaces

3.1 INTRODUCTION

In mathematics and the physical sciences, the term *vector* is applied to a wide variety of objects. Perhaps the most familiar application of the term is to quantities, such as force and velocity, that have both magnitude and direction. Such vectors can be represented in two-space or in three-space as directed line segments or arrows. (A review of geometric vectors is given in Chapter 2.) As we will see in Chapter 5, the term *vector* may also be used to describe objects such as matrices, polynomials, and continuous real-valued functions. In this section we demonstrate that R^n, the set of n-dimensional vectors, provides a natural bridge between the intuitive and natural concept of a geometric vector and that of an abstract vector in a general vector space. The remainder of the chapter is concerned with the algebraic and geometric structure of R^n and subsets of R^n. Some of the concepts fundamental to describing this structure are subspace, basis, and dimension. These concepts are introduced and discussed in the first few sections. Although these ideas are relatively abstract, they are easy to understand in R^n, and they also have application to concrete problems. Thus R^n will serve as an example and as a model for the study in Chapter 5 of general vector spaces.

To make the transition from geometric vectors in two-space and three-space to two-dimensional and three-dimensional vectors in R^2 and R^3, recall that the geometric vector, $\mathbf{v}$, can be uniquely represented as a directed line segment OP, with initial point at the origin, O, and with terminal point P. If $\mathbf{v}$ is in two-space and point P has coordinates (a, b), then it is natural to represent $\mathbf{v}$ in R^2 as the vector

$$\mathbf{x} = \begin{bmatrix} a \\ b \end{bmatrix}.$$

Similarly, if $\mathbf{v}$ is in three-space and point P has coordinates (a, b, c), then $\mathbf{v}$ can be represented by the vector

$$\mathbf{x} = \begin{bmatrix} a \\ b \\ c \end{bmatrix}$$

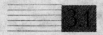

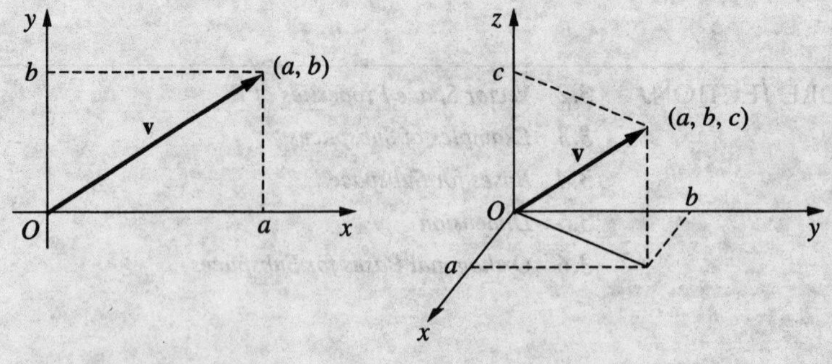

Figure 3.1 Geometric vectors

in R^3 (see Fig. 3.1). Under the correspondence $\mathbf{v} \to \mathbf{x}$ described above, the usual geometric addition of vectors translates to the standard algebraic addition in R^2 and R^3. Similarly, geometric multiplication by a scalar corresponds precisely to the standard algebraic scalar multiplication (see Fig. 3.2). Thus the study of R^2 and R^3 allows us to translate the geometric properties of vectors to algebraic properties. As we consider vectors from the algebraic viewpoint, it becomes natural to extend the concept of a vector to other objects that satisfy the same algebraic properties but for which there is no geometric representation. The elements of R^n, $n \geq 4$, are an immediate example.

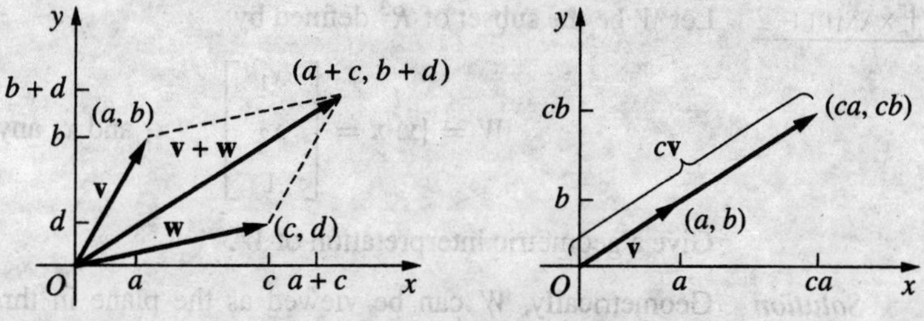

Figure 3.2 Addition and scalar multiplication of vectors

We conclude this section by noting a useful geometric interpretation for vectors in R^2 and R^3. A vector

$$\mathbf{x} = \begin{bmatrix} a \\ b \end{bmatrix}$$

in R^2 can be represented geometrically as the point in the plane that has coordinates (a, b). Similarly, the vector

$$\mathbf{x} = \begin{bmatrix} a \\ b \\ c \end{bmatrix}$$

in R^3 corresponds to the point in three-space that has coordinates (a, b, c). As the next two examples illustrate, this correspondence allows us to interpret subsets of R^2 and R^3 geometrically.

EXAMPLE 1 Give a geometric interpretation of the subset W of R^2 defined by

$$W = \{\mathbf{x}: \mathbf{x} = \begin{bmatrix} x_1 \\ x_2 \end{bmatrix}, \quad x_1 + x_2 = 2\}.$$

Solution Geometrically, W is the line in the plane with equation $x + y = 2$ (see Fig. 3.3). ■

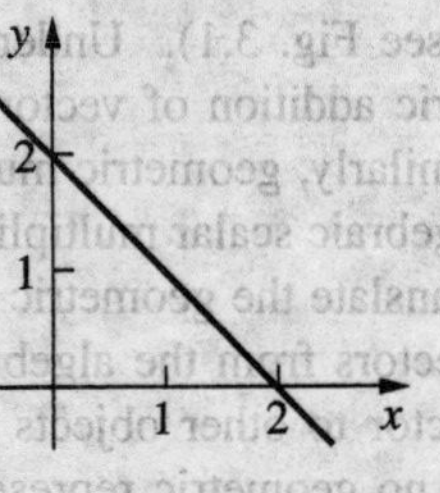

Figure 3.3 The line $x + y = 2$

EXAMPLE 2 Let W be the subset of R^3 defined by

$$W = \{\mathbf{x}\colon \mathbf{x} = \begin{bmatrix} x_1 \\ x_2 \\ 1 \end{bmatrix}, \quad x_1 \text{ and } x_2 \text{ any real numbers}\}.$$

Give a geometric interpretation of W.

Solution Geometrically, W can be viewed as the plane in three-space with equation $z = 1$ (see Fig. 3.4).

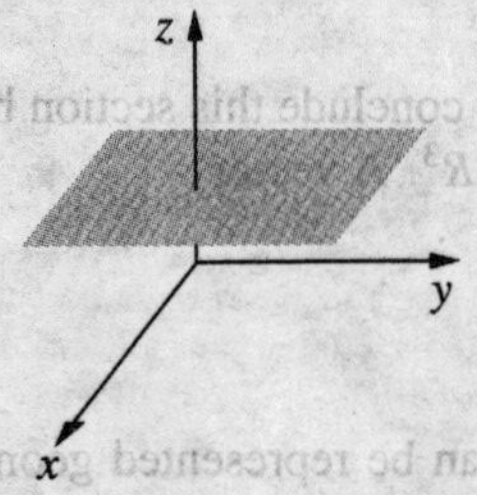

Figure 3.4 The plane $z = 1$

3.1 EXERCISES

Exercises 1–11 refer to the vectors given in (1).

$$\mathbf{u} = \begin{bmatrix} 3 \\ 1 \end{bmatrix}, \quad \mathbf{v} = \begin{bmatrix} 1 \\ 2 \end{bmatrix},$$
$$\mathbf{x} = \begin{bmatrix} 0 \\ 1 \\ 3 \end{bmatrix}, \quad \mathbf{y} = \begin{bmatrix} 2 \\ 1 \\ 0 \end{bmatrix}, \qquad (1)$$

In Exercises 1–11, sketch the geometric vector (with initial point at the origin) corresponding to each of the vectors given.

1. **u** and −**u**

2. **v** and 2**v**

3. **u** and −3**u**

4. **v** and −2**v**

5. **u**, **v**, and **u** + **v**

6. **u**, 2**v**, and **u** + 2**v**

7. **u**, **v**, and **u** − **v**

8. **u**, **v**, and **v** − **u**

9. **x** and 2**x**

10. **y** and −**y**

11. **x**, **y**, and **x** + **y**

In Exercises 12–17, interpret the subset W of R^2 geometrically by sketching a graph for W.

12. $W = \{\mathbf{x}\colon \mathbf{x} = \begin{bmatrix} a \\ b \end{bmatrix}, \quad a + b = 1\}$

13. $W = \{\mathbf{x}\colon \mathbf{x} = \begin{bmatrix} x_1 \\ x_2 \end{bmatrix},\ x_1 = -3x_2,$ x_2 any real number$\}$

14. $W = \{\mathbf{w}\colon \mathbf{w} = \begin{bmatrix} 0 \\ b \end{bmatrix},\ b$ any real number$\}$

15. $W = \{\mathbf{u}\colon \mathbf{u} = \begin{bmatrix} c \\ d \end{bmatrix},\ c + d \geq 0\}$

16. $W = \{\mathbf{x}\colon \mathbf{x} = t\begin{bmatrix} 1 \\ 3 \end{bmatrix},\ t$ any real number$\}$

17. $W = \{\mathbf{x}\colon \mathbf{x} = \begin{bmatrix} a \\ b \end{bmatrix},\ a^2 + b^2 = 4\}$

In Exercises 18–21, interpret the subset W of R^3 geometrically by sketching a graph for W.

18. $W = \{\mathbf{x}\colon \mathbf{x} = \begin{bmatrix} a \\ 0 \\ 0 \end{bmatrix},\ a > 0\}$

19. $W = \{\mathbf{x}\colon \mathbf{x} = \begin{bmatrix} x_1 \\ x_2 \\ x_3 \end{bmatrix},\ x_1 = -x_2 - 2x_3\}$

20. $W = \{\mathbf{w}\colon \mathbf{w} = r\begin{bmatrix} 2 \\ 0 \\ 1 \end{bmatrix},\ r$ any real number$\}$

21. $W = \{\mathbf{u}\colon \mathbf{u} = \begin{bmatrix} a \\ b \\ c \end{bmatrix},\ a^2 + b^2 + c^2 = 1$ and $c \geq 0\}$

In Exercises 22–26, give a set-theoretic description of the given points as a subset W of R^2.

22. The points on the line $x - 2y = 1$

23. The points on the x-axis

24. The points in the upper half-plane

25. The points on the line $y = 2$

26. The points on the parabola $y = x^2$

In Exercises 27–30, give a set-theoretic description of the given points as a subset W of R^3.

27. The points on the plane $x + y - 2z = 0$

28. The points on the line with parametric equations $x = 2t$, $y = -3t$, and $z = t$

29. The points in the yz-plane

30. The points in the plane $y = 2$

3.2 VECTOR SPACE PROPERTIES OF R^n

Recall that R^n is the set of all n-dimensional vectors with real components:

$$R^n = \{\mathbf{x}\colon \mathbf{x} = \begin{bmatrix} x_1 \\ x_2 \\ \vdots \\ x_n \end{bmatrix},\ x_1, x_2, \ldots, x_n \text{ real numbers}\}.$$

If $\mathbf{x}$ and $\mathbf{y}$ are elements of R^n with

$$\mathbf{x} = \begin{bmatrix} x_1 \\ x_2 \\ \vdots \\ x_n \end{bmatrix} \quad \text{and} \quad \mathbf{y} = \begin{bmatrix} y_1 \\ y_2 \\ \vdots \\ y_n \end{bmatrix},$$

then (see Section 1.5) the vector $\mathbf{x}+\mathbf{y}$ is defined by

$$\mathbf{x}+\mathbf{y}=\begin{bmatrix} x_1+y_1 \\ x_2+y_2 \\ \vdots \\ x_n+y_n \end{bmatrix},$$

and if a is a real number, then the vector $a\mathbf{x}$ is defined to be

$$a\mathbf{x}=\begin{bmatrix} ax_1 \\ ax_2 \\ \vdots \\ ax_n \end{bmatrix}.$$

In the context of R^n, scalars are always real numbers. In particular, throughout this chapter, the term *scalar* always means a real number.

The following theorem gives the arithmetic properties of vector addition and scalar multiplication. Note that the statements in this theorem are already familiar from Section 1.6, which discusses the arithmetic properties of matrix operations (a vector in R^n is an $(n \times 1)$ matrix, and hence the properties of matrix addition and scalar multiplication listed in Section 1.6 are inherited by vectors in R^n).

As we will see in Chapter 5, any set that satisfies the properties of Theorem 1 is called a ***vector space***; thus for each positive integer n, R^n is an example of a vector space.

THEOREM 1 If $\mathbf{x}$, $\mathbf{y}$, and $\mathbf{z}$ are vectors in R^n and a and b are scalars, then the following properties hold:

Closure properties:

(c1) $\mathbf{x}+\mathbf{y}$ is in R^n.
(c2) $a\mathbf{x}$ is in R^n.

Properties of addition:

(a1) $\mathbf{x}+\mathbf{y}=\mathbf{y}+\mathbf{x}$.
(a2) $\mathbf{x}+(\mathbf{y}+\mathbf{z})=(\mathbf{x}+\mathbf{y})+\mathbf{z}$.
(a3) R^n contains the zero vector, $\boldsymbol{\theta}$, and $\mathbf{x}+\boldsymbol{\theta}=\mathbf{x}$ for all $\mathbf{x}$ in R^n.
(a4) For each vector $\mathbf{x}$ in R^n, there is a vector $-\mathbf{x}$ in R^n such that $\mathbf{x}+(-\mathbf{x})=\boldsymbol{\theta}$.

Properties of scalar multiplication:

(m1) $a(b\mathbf{x})=(ab)\mathbf{x}$.
(m2) $a(\mathbf{x}+\mathbf{y})=a\mathbf{x}+a\mathbf{y}$.
(m3) $(a+b)\mathbf{x}=a\mathbf{x}+b\mathbf{x}$.
(m4) $1\mathbf{x}=\mathbf{x}$ for all $\mathbf{x}$ in R^n.

Subspaces of R^n

In this chapter we are interested in subsets, W, of R^n that satisfy all the properties of Theorem 1 (with R^n replaced by W throughout). Such a subset W is called a ***subspace***

ORIGINS OF HIGHER-DIMENSIONAL SPACES In addition to Grassmann (see Section 1.7), Sir William Hamilton (1805–1865) also envisioned algebras of n-tuples (which he called *polyplets*). In 1833, Hamilton gave rules for the addition and multiplication of ordered pairs, (a, b), which became the algebra of complex numbers, $z = a + bi$. He searched for years for an extension to 3-tuples. He finally discovered, in a flash of inspiration while crossing a bridge, that the extension was possible if he used 4-tuples $(a, b, c, d) = a + bi + cj + dk$. In this algebra of quaternions, however, multiplication is not commutative; for example, $ij = k$, but $ji = -k$. Hamilton stopped and carved the basic formula, $i^2 = j^2 = k^2 = ijk$, on the bridge. He considered the quaternions his greatest achievement, even though his so-called Hamiltonian principle is considered fundamental to modern physics.

of R^n. For example, consider the subset W of R^3 defined by

$$W = \{\mathbf{x}: \mathbf{x} = \begin{bmatrix} x_1 \\ x_2 \\ 0 \end{bmatrix}, \quad x_1 \text{ and } x_2 \text{ real numbers}\}.$$

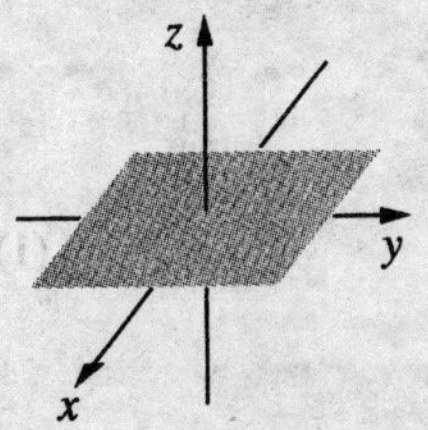

Figure 3.5
W as a subset of R^3

Viewed geometrically, W is the xy-plane (see Fig. 3.5), so it can be represented by R^2. Therefore, as can be easily shown, W is a subspace of R^3.

The following theorem provides a convenient way of determining when a subset W of R^n is a subspace of R^n.

THEOREM 2 A subset W of R^n is a subspace of R^n if and only if the following conditions are met:

(s1)* The zero vector, $\boldsymbol{\theta}$, is in W.

(s2) $\mathbf{x} + \mathbf{y}$ is in W whenever $\mathbf{x}$ and $\mathbf{y}$ are in W.

(s3) $a\mathbf{x}$ is in W whenever $\mathbf{x}$ is in W and a is any scalar.

Proof Suppose that W is a subset of R^n that satisfies conditions (s1)–(s3). To show that W is a subspace of R^n, we must show that the 10 properties of Theorem 1 (with R^n replaced by W throughout) are satisfied. But properties (a1), (a2), (m1), (m2), (m3), and (m4) are satisfied by every subset of R^n and so hold in W. Condition (a3) is satisfied by W because the hypothesis (s1) guarantees that $\boldsymbol{\theta}$ is in W. Similarly, (c1) and (c2) are given by the hypotheses (s2) and (s3), respectively. The only remaining condition is (a4), and we can easily see that $-\mathbf{x} = (-1)\mathbf{x}$. Thus if $\mathbf{x}$ is in W, then, by (s3), $-\mathbf{x}$ is also in W. Therefore, all the conditions of Theorem 1 are satisfied by W, and W is a subspace of R^n.

For the converse, suppose W is a subspace of R^n. The conditions (a3), (c1), and (c2) of Theorem 1 imply that properties (s1), (s2), and (s3) hold in W. ∎

The next example illustrates the use of Theorem 2 to verify that a subset W of R^n is a subspace of R^n.

*The usual statement of Theorem 2 lists only conditions (s2) and (s3) but assumes that the subset W is nonempty. Thus (s1) replaces the assumption that W is nonempty. The two versions are equivalent (see Exercise 34).

EXAMPLE 1 Let W be the subset of R^3 defined by

$$W = \{\mathbf{x}\colon \mathbf{x} = \begin{bmatrix} x_1 \\ x_2 \\ x_3 \end{bmatrix},\quad x_1 = x_2 - x_3,\quad x_2 \text{ and } x_3 \text{ any real numbers}\}.$$

Verify that W is a subspace of R^3 and give a geometric interpretation of W.

Solution To show that W is a subspace of R^3, we must check that properties (s1)–(s3) of Theorem 2 are satisfied by W. Clearly the zero vector, $\boldsymbol{\theta}$, satisfies the condition $x_1 = x_2 - x_3$. Therefore, $\boldsymbol{\theta}$ is in W, showing that (s1) holds. Now let $\mathbf{u}$ and $\mathbf{v}$ be in W, where

$$\mathbf{u} = \begin{bmatrix} u_1 \\ u_2 \\ u_3 \end{bmatrix} \quad \text{and} \quad \mathbf{v} = \begin{bmatrix} v_1 \\ v_2 \\ v_3 \end{bmatrix},$$

and let a be an arbitrary scalar. Since $\mathbf{u}$ and $\mathbf{v}$ are in W,

$$u_1 = u_2 - u_3 \quad \text{and} \quad v_1 = v_2 - v_3. \tag{1}$$

The sum $\mathbf{u} + \mathbf{v}$ and the scalar product $a\mathbf{u}$ are given by

$$\mathbf{u} + \mathbf{v} = \begin{bmatrix} u_1 + v_1 \\ u_2 + v_2 \\ u_3 + v_3 \end{bmatrix} \quad \text{and} \quad a\mathbf{u} = \begin{bmatrix} au_1 \\ au_2 \\ au_3 \end{bmatrix}.$$

To see that $\mathbf{u} + \mathbf{v}$ is in W, note that (1) gives

$$u_1 + v_1 = (u_2 - u_3) + (v_2 - v_3) = (u_2 + v_2) - (u_3 + v_3). \tag{2}$$

Thus if the components of $\mathbf{u}$ and $\mathbf{v}$ satisfy the condition $x_1 = x_2 - x_3$, then so do the components of the sum $\mathbf{u} + \mathbf{v}$. This argument shows that condition (s2) is met by W. Similarly, from (1),

$$au_1 = a(u_2 - u_3) = au_2 - au_3, \tag{3}$$

so $a\mathbf{u}$ is in W. Therefore, W is a subspace of R^3.

Geometrically, W is the plane whose equation is $x - y + z = 0$ (see Fig. 3.6). ■

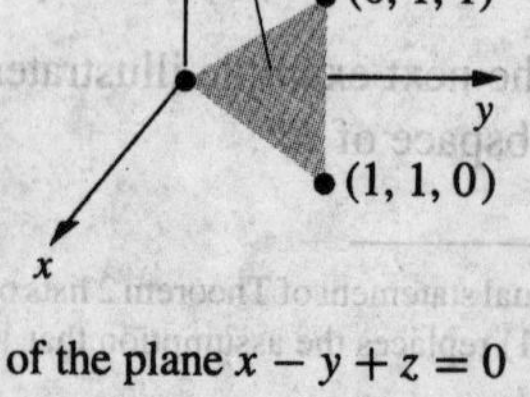

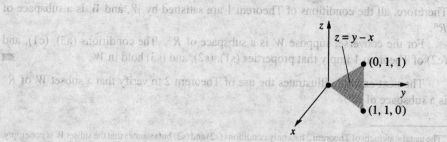

Figure 3.6 A portion of the plane $x - y + z = 0$

Verifying that Subsets are Subspaces

Example 1 illustrates the typical procedure for verifying that a subset W of R^n is a subspace of R^n. In general such a verification proceeds along the following lines:

Verifying that W Is a Subspace of R^n

Step 1. An algebraic specification for the subset W is given, and this specification serves as a test for determining whether a vector in R^n is or is not in W.

Step 2. Test the zero vector, $\boldsymbol{\theta}$, of R^n to see whether it satisfies the algebraic specification required to be in W. (This shows that W is nonempty.)

Step 3. Choose two arbitrary vectors $\mathbf{x}$ and $\mathbf{y}$ from W. Thus $\mathbf{x}$ and $\mathbf{y}$ are in R^n, and both vectors satisfy the algebraic specification of W.

Step 4. Test the sum $\mathbf{x}+\mathbf{y}$ to see whether it meets the specification of W.

Step 5. For an arbitrary scalar, a, test the scalar multiple $a\mathbf{x}$ to see whether it meets the specification of W.

The next example illustrates again the use of the procedure described above to verify that a subset W of R^n is a subspace.

EXAMPLE 2 Let W be the subset of R^3 defined by

$$W = \{\mathbf{x}\colon \mathbf{x} = \begin{bmatrix} x_1 \\ x_2 \\ x_3 \end{bmatrix}, \quad x_2 = 2x_1, \quad x_3 = 3x_1, \quad x_1 \text{ any real number}\}.$$

Verify that W is a subspace of R^3 and give a geometric interpretation of W.

Solution For clarity in this initial example, we explicitly number the five steps used to verify that W is a subspace.

1. The algebraic condition for $\mathbf{x}$ to be in W is

$$x_2 = 2x_1 \quad \text{and} \quad x_3 = 3x_1. \tag{4}$$

In words, $\mathbf{x}$ is in W if and only if the second component of $\mathbf{x}$ is twice the first component and the third component of $\mathbf{x}$ is three times the first.

2. Note that the zero vector, $\boldsymbol{\theta}$, clearly satisfies (4). Therefore, $\boldsymbol{\theta}$ is in W.

3. Next, let $\mathbf{u}$ and $\mathbf{v}$ be two arbitrary vectors in W:

$$\mathbf{u} = \begin{bmatrix} u_1 \\ u_2 \\ u_3 \end{bmatrix} \quad \text{and} \quad \mathbf{v} = \begin{bmatrix} v_1 \\ v_2 \\ v_3 \end{bmatrix}.$$

Because **u** and **v** are in W, each must satisfy the algebraic specification of W. That is,

$$u_2 = 2u_1 \quad \text{and} \quad u_3 = 3u_1 \tag{5a}$$

$$v_2 = 2v_1 \quad \text{and} \quad v_3 = 3v_1. \tag{5b}$$

4. Next, check whether the sum, $\mathbf{u}+\mathbf{v}$, is in W. (That is, does the vector $\mathbf{u}+\mathbf{v}$ satisfy Eq. (4)?) Now, the sum $\mathbf{u}+\mathbf{v}$ is given by

$$\mathbf{u}+\mathbf{v} = \begin{bmatrix} u_1+v_1 \\ u_2+v_2 \\ u_3+v_3 \end{bmatrix}.$$

By (5a) and (5b), we have

$$u_2+v_2 = 2(u_1+v_1) \quad \text{and} \quad (u_3+v_3) = 3(u_1+v_1).$$

Thus $\mathbf{u}+\mathbf{v}$ is in W whenever **u** and **v** are both in W (see Eq. (4)).

5. Similarly, for any scalar a, the scalar multiple $a\mathbf{u}$ is given by

$$a\mathbf{u} = \begin{bmatrix} au_1 \\ au_2 \\ au_3 \end{bmatrix}.$$

Using (5a) gives $au_2 = a(2u_1) = 2(au_1)$ and $au_3 = a(3u_1) = 3(au_1)$. Therefore, $a\mathbf{u}$ is in W whenever **u** is in W (see Eq. (4)).

Thus, by Theorem 2, W is a subspace of R^3. Geometrically, W is a line through the origin with parametric equations

$$\begin{aligned} x &= x_1 \\ y &= 2x_1 \\ z &= 3x_1. \end{aligned}$$

The graph of the line is given in Fig. 3.7. ■

Exercise 29 shows that any line in three-space through the origin is a subspace of R^3, and Example 3 of Section 3.3 shows that in three-space any plane through the origin is a subspace. Also note that for each positive integer n, R^n is a subspace of itself and $\{\boldsymbol{\theta}\}$ is a subspace of R^n. We conclude this section with examples of subsets that are not subspaces.

EXAMPLE 3 Let W be the subset of R^3 defined by

$$W = \left\{\mathbf{x}\colon \mathbf{x} = \begin{bmatrix} x_1 \\ x_2 \\ 1 \end{bmatrix}, \quad x_1 \text{ and } x_2 \text{ any real numbers}\right\}.$$

Show that W is not a subspace of R^3.

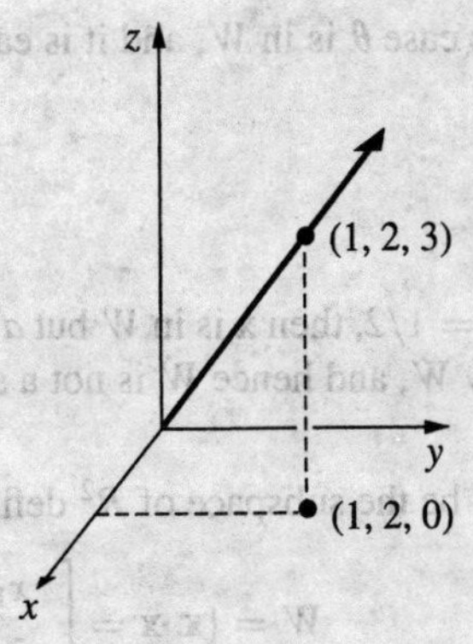

Figure 3.7 A geometric representation of the subspace W (see Example 2)

Solution To show that W is not a subspace of R^3, we need only verify that at least one of the properties (s1)–(s3) of Theorem 2 fails. Note that geometrically W can be interpreted as the plane $z = 1$, which does not contain the origin. In other words, the zero vector, $\boldsymbol{\theta}$, is not in W. Because condition (s1) of Theorem 2 is not met, W is not a subspace of R^3. Although it is not necessary to do so, in this example we can also show that both conditions (s2) and (s3) of Theorem 2 fail. To see this, let $\mathbf{x}$ and $\mathbf{y}$ be in W, where

$$\mathbf{x} = \begin{bmatrix} x_1 \\ x_2 \\ 1 \end{bmatrix} \quad \text{and} \quad \mathbf{y} = \begin{bmatrix} y_1 \\ y_2 \\ 1 \end{bmatrix}.$$

Then $\mathbf{x} + \mathbf{y}$ is given by

$$\mathbf{x} + \mathbf{y} = \begin{bmatrix} x_1 + y_1 \\ x_2 + y_2 \\ 2 \end{bmatrix}.$$

In particular, $\mathbf{x} + \mathbf{y}$ is not in W, because the third component of $\mathbf{x} + \mathbf{y}$ does not have the value 1. Similarly,

$$a\mathbf{x} = \begin{bmatrix} ax_1 \\ ax_2 \\ a \end{bmatrix}.$$

So if $a \neq 1$, then $a\mathbf{x}$ is not in W.

EXAMPLE 4 Let W be the subset of R^2 defined by

$$W = \{\mathbf{x}: \mathbf{x} = \begin{bmatrix} x_1 \\ x_2 \end{bmatrix}, \quad x_1 \text{ and } x_2 \text{ any integers}\}.$$

Demonstrate that W is not a subspace of R^2.

Solution In this case $\boldsymbol{\theta}$ is in W, and it is easy to see that if $\mathbf{x}$ and $\mathbf{y}$ are in W, then so is $\mathbf{x}+\mathbf{y}$. If we set

$$\mathbf{x}=\begin{bmatrix}1\\1\end{bmatrix}$$

and $a=1/2$, then $\mathbf{x}$ is in W but $a\mathbf{x}$ is not. Therefore, condition (s3) of Theorem 2 is not met by W, and hence W is not a subspace of R^2. ■

EXAMPLE 5 Let W be the subspace of R^2 defined by

$$W=\{\mathbf{x}\colon \mathbf{x}=\begin{bmatrix}x_1\\x_2\end{bmatrix},\quad \text{where either } x_1=0 \text{ or } x_2=0\}.$$

Show that W is not a subspace of R^2.

Solution Let $\mathbf{x}$ and $\mathbf{y}$ be defined by

$$\mathbf{x}=\begin{bmatrix}1\\0\end{bmatrix} \quad\text{and}\quad \mathbf{y}=\begin{bmatrix}0\\1\end{bmatrix}.$$

Then $\mathbf{x}$ and $\mathbf{y}$ are in W. But

$$\mathbf{x}+\mathbf{y}=\begin{bmatrix}1\\1\end{bmatrix}$$

is not in W, so W is not a subspace of R^2. Note that $\boldsymbol{\theta}$ is in W, and for any vector $\mathbf{x}$ in W and any scalar a, $a\mathbf{x}$ is again in W. Geometrically, W is the set of points in the plane that lie either on the x-axis or on the y-axis. Either of these axes alone is a subspace of R^2, but, as this example demonstrates, their union is not a subspace. ■

3.2 EXERCISES

In Exercises 1–8, W is a subset of R^2 consisting of vectors of the form

$$\mathbf{x}=\begin{bmatrix}x_1\\x_2\end{bmatrix}.$$

In each case determine whether W is a subspace of R^2. If W is a subspace, then give a geometric description of W.

1. $W=\{\mathbf{x}\colon x_1=2x_2\}$

2. $W=\{\mathbf{x}\colon x_1-x_2=2\}$

3. $W=\{\mathbf{x}\colon x_1=x_2 \text{ or } x_1=-x_2\}$

4. $W=\{\mathbf{x}\colon x_1 \text{ and } x_2 \text{ are rational numbers}\}$

5. $W=\{\mathbf{x}\colon x_1=0\}$

6. $W=\{\mathbf{x}\colon |x_1|+|x_2|=0\}$

7. $W=\{\mathbf{x}\colon x_1^2+x_2=1\}$

8. $W=\{\mathbf{x}\colon x_1x_2=0\}$

In Exercises 9–17, W is a subset of R^3 consisting of vectors of the form

$$\mathbf{x}=\begin{bmatrix}x_1\\x_2\\x_3\end{bmatrix}.$$

In each case, determine whether W is a subspace of R^3. If W is a subspace, then give a geometric description of W.

9. $W=\{\mathbf{x}\colon x_3=2x_1-x_2\}$

10. $W=\{\mathbf{x}\colon x_2=x_3+x_1\}$

11. $W=\{\mathbf{x}\colon x_1x_2=x_3\}$

12. $W = \{\mathbf{x}: x_1 = 2x_3\}$
13. $W = \{\mathbf{x}: x_1^2 = x_1 + x_2\}$
14. $W = \{\mathbf{x}: x_2 = 0\}$
15. $W = \{\mathbf{x}: x_1 = 2x_3, \quad x_2 = -x_3\}$
16. $W = \{\mathbf{x}: x_3 = x_2 = 2x_1\}$
17. $W = \{\mathbf{x}: x_2 = x_3 = 0\}$
18. Let **a** be a fixed vector in R^3, and define W to be the subset of R^3 given by

$$W = \{\mathbf{x}: \mathbf{a}^T\mathbf{x} = 0\}.$$

Prove that W is a subspace of R^3.

19. Let W be the subspace defined in Exercise 18, where

$$\mathbf{a} = \begin{bmatrix} 1 \\ 2 \\ 3 \end{bmatrix}.$$

Give a geometric description for W.

20. Let W be the subspace defined in Exercise 18, where

$$\mathbf{a} = \begin{bmatrix} 1 \\ 0 \\ 0 \end{bmatrix}.$$

Give a geometric description of W.

21. Let **a** and **b** be fixed vectors in R^3, and let W be the subset of R^3 defined by

$$W = \{\mathbf{x}: \mathbf{a}^T\mathbf{x} = 0 \text{ and } \mathbf{b}^T\mathbf{x} = 0\}.$$

Prove that W is a subspace of R^3.

In Exercises 22–25, W is the subspace of R^3 defined in Exercise 21. For each choice of **a** and **b**, give a geometric description of W.

22. $\mathbf{a} = \begin{bmatrix} 1 \\ -1 \\ 2 \end{bmatrix}, \quad \mathbf{b} = \begin{bmatrix} 2 \\ -1 \\ 3 \end{bmatrix}$

23. $\mathbf{a} = \begin{bmatrix} 1 \\ 2 \\ 2 \end{bmatrix}, \quad \mathbf{b} = \begin{bmatrix} 1 \\ 3 \\ 0 \end{bmatrix}$

24. $\mathbf{a} = \begin{bmatrix} 1 \\ 1 \\ 1 \end{bmatrix}, \quad \mathbf{b} = \begin{bmatrix} 2 \\ 2 \\ 2 \end{bmatrix}$

25. $\mathbf{a} = \begin{bmatrix} 1 \\ 0 \\ -1 \end{bmatrix}, \quad \mathbf{b} = \begin{bmatrix} -2 \\ 0 \\ 2 \end{bmatrix}$

26. In R^4, let $\mathbf{x} = [1, -3, 2, 1]^T$, $\mathbf{y} = [2, 1, 3, 2]^T$, and $\mathbf{z} = [-3, 2, -1, 4]^T$. Set $a = 2$ and $b = -3$. Illustrate that the ten properties of Theorem 1 are satisfied by **x**, **y**, **z**, a, and b.

27. In R^2, suppose that scalar multiplication were defined by

$$a\mathbf{x} = a\begin{bmatrix} x_1 \\ x_2 \end{bmatrix} = \begin{bmatrix} 2ax_1 \\ 2ax_2 \end{bmatrix}$$

for every scalar a. Illustrate with specific examples those properties of Theorem 1 that are not satisfied.

28. Let

$$W = \left\{\mathbf{x}: \mathbf{x} = \begin{bmatrix} x_1 \\ x_2 \end{bmatrix}, \quad x_2 \geq 0\right\}.$$

In the statement of Theorem 1, replace each occurrence of R^n with W. Illustrate with specific examples each of the ten properties of Theorem 1 that are not satisfied.

29. In R^3, a line through the origin is the set of all points in R^3 whose coordinates satisfy $x_1 = at$, $x_2 = bt$, and $x_3 = ct$, where t is a variable and a, b, and c are not all zero. Show that a line through the origin is a subspace of R^3.

30. If U and V are subsets of R^n, then the set $U + V$ is defined by

$$U + V = \{\mathbf{x}: \mathbf{x} = \mathbf{u} + \mathbf{v}, \quad \mathbf{u} \text{ in } U \text{ and } \mathbf{v} \text{ in } V\}.$$

Prove that if U and V are subspaces of R^n, then $U + V$ is a subspace of R^n.

31. Let U and V be subspaces of R^n. Prove that the intersection, $U \cap V$, is also a subspace of R^n.

32. Let U and V be the subspaces of R^3 defined by

$$U = \{\mathbf{x}: \mathbf{a}^T\mathbf{x} = 0\} \text{ and } V = \{\mathbf{x}: \mathbf{b}^T\mathbf{x} = 0\},$$

where

$$\mathbf{a} = \begin{bmatrix} 1 \\ 1 \\ 0 \end{bmatrix} \text{ and } \mathbf{b} = \begin{bmatrix} 0 \\ 1 \\ -1 \end{bmatrix}.$$

Demonstrate that the union, $U \cup V$, is not a subspace of R^3 (see Exercise 18).

33. Let U and V be subspaces of R^n.

a) Show that the union, $U \cup V$, satisfies properties (s1) and (s3) of Theorem 2.

b) If neither U nor V is a subset of the other, show that $U \cup V$ does not satisfy condition (s2) of

Theorem 2. [*Hint*: Choose vectors $\mathbf{u}$ and $\mathbf{v}$ such that $\mathbf{u}$ is in U but not in V and $\mathbf{v}$ is in V but not in U. Assume that $\mathbf{u}+\mathbf{v}$ is in either U or V and reach a contradiction.]

34. Let W be a nonempty subset of R^n that satisfies conditions (s2) and (s3) of Theorem 2. Prove that $\boldsymbol{\theta}$ is in W and conclude that W is a subspace of R^n. (Thus property (s1) of Theorem 2 can be replaced with the assumption that W is nonempty.)

3.3 EXAMPLES OF SUBSPACES

In this section we introduce several important and particularly useful examples of subspaces of R^n.

The Span of a Subset

To begin, recall that if $\mathbf{v}_1, \ldots, \mathbf{v}_r$ are vectors in R^n, then a vector $\mathbf{y}$ in R^n is a linear combination of $\mathbf{v}_1, \ldots, \mathbf{v}_r$, provided that there exist scalars $a_1, \ldots, a_r$ such that

$$\mathbf{y} = a_1\mathbf{v}_1 + \cdots + a_r\mathbf{v}_r.$$

The next theorem shows that the set of all linear combinations of $\mathbf{v}_1, \ldots, \mathbf{v}_r$ is a subspace of R^n.

THEOREM 3 If $\mathbf{v}_1, \ldots, \mathbf{v}_r$ are vectors in R^n, then the set W consisting of all linear combinations of $\mathbf{v}_1, \ldots, \mathbf{v}_r$ is a subspace of R^n.

Proof To show that W is a subspace of R^n, we must verify that the three conditions of Theorem 2 are satisfied. Now $\boldsymbol{\theta}$ is in W because

$$\boldsymbol{\theta} = 0\mathbf{v}_1 + \cdots + 0\mathbf{v}_r.$$

Next, suppose that $\mathbf{y}$ and $\mathbf{z}$ are in W. Then there exist scalars $a_1, \ldots, a_r, b_1, \ldots, b_r$ such that

$$\mathbf{y} = a_1\mathbf{v}_1 + \cdots + a_r\mathbf{v}_r$$

and

$$\mathbf{z} = b_1\mathbf{v}_1 + \cdots + b_r\mathbf{v}_r.$$

Thus,

$$\mathbf{y}+\mathbf{z} = (a_1+b_1)\mathbf{v}_1 + \cdots + (a_r+b_r)\mathbf{v}_r,$$

so $\mathbf{y}+\mathbf{z}$ is a linear combination of $\mathbf{v}_1, \ldots, \mathbf{v}_r$; that is, $\mathbf{y}+\mathbf{z}$ is in W. Also, for any scalar c,

$$c\mathbf{y} = (ca_1)\mathbf{v}_1 + \cdots + (ca_r)\mathbf{v}_r.$$

In particular, $c\mathbf{y}$ is in W. It follows from Theorem 2 that W is a subspace of R^n. ∎

If $S = \{\mathbf{v}_1, \ldots, \mathbf{v}_r\}$ is a subset of R^n, then the subspace W consisting of all linear combinations of $\mathbf{v}_1, \ldots, \mathbf{v}_r$ is called the ***subspace spanned by S*** and will be denoted by

$$\mathrm{Sp}(S) \quad \text{or} \quad \mathrm{Sp}\{\mathbf{v}_1, \ldots, \mathbf{v}_r\}.$$

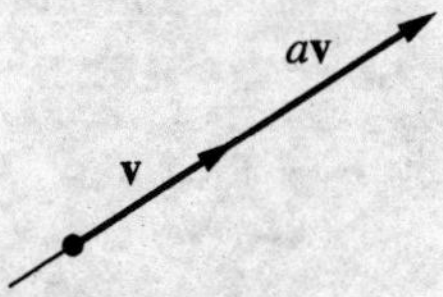

Figure 3.8
Sp{**v**}

For a single vector **v** in R^n, Sp{**v**} is the subspace

$$\mathrm{Sp}\{\mathbf{v}\} = \{a\mathbf{v}\text{: } a \text{ is any real number}\}.$$

If **v** is a nonzero vector in R^2 or R^3, then Sp{**v**} can be interpreted as the line determined by **v** (see Fig. 3.8). As a specific example, consider

$$\mathbf{v} = \begin{bmatrix} 1 \\ 2 \\ 3 \end{bmatrix}.$$

Then

$$\mathrm{Sp}\{\mathbf{v}\} = \{t \begin{bmatrix} 1 \\ 2 \\ 3 \end{bmatrix} : t \text{ is any real number}\}.$$

Thus Sp{**v**} is the line with parametric equations

$$\begin{aligned} x &= t \\ y &= 2t \\ z &= 3t. \end{aligned}$$

Equivalently, Sp{**v**} is the line that passes through the origin and through the point with coordinates 1, 2, and 3 (see Fig. 3.9).

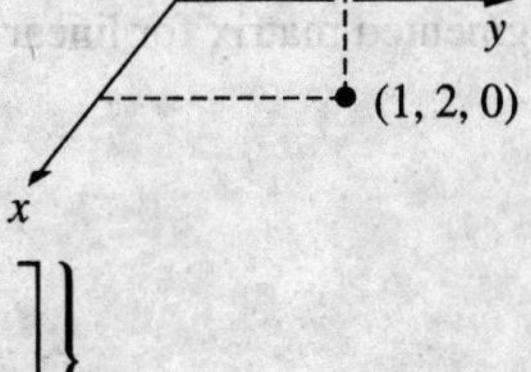

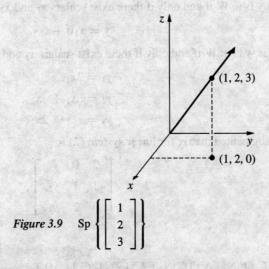

Figure 3.9 $\mathrm{Sp}\left\{\begin{bmatrix} 1 \\ 2 \\ 3 \end{bmatrix}\right\}$

If **u** and **v** are noncollinear geometric vectors, then

$$\mathrm{Sp}\{\mathbf{u}, \mathbf{v}\} = \{a\mathbf{u} + b\mathbf{v}\text{: } a, b \text{ any real numbers}\}$$

is the plane containing **u** and **v** (see Fig. 3.10). The following example illustrates this case with a subspace of R^3.

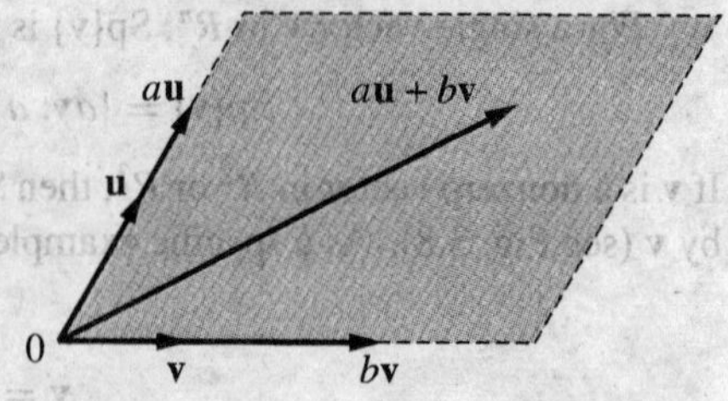

Figure 3.10 Sp{**u**, **v**}

EXAMPLE 1 Let **u** and **v** be the three-dimensional vectors

$$\mathbf{u} = \begin{bmatrix} 2 \\ 1 \\ 0 \end{bmatrix} \quad \text{and} \quad \mathbf{v} = \begin{bmatrix} 0 \\ 1 \\ 2 \end{bmatrix}.$$

Determine $W = \text{Sp}\{\mathbf{u}, \mathbf{v}\}$ and give a geometric interpretation of W.

Solution Let **y** be an arbitrary vector in R^3, where

$$\mathbf{y} = \begin{bmatrix} y_1 \\ y_2 \\ y_3 \end{bmatrix}.$$

Then **y** is in W if and only if there exist scalars x_1 and x_2 such that

$$\mathbf{y} = x_1\mathbf{u} + x_2\mathbf{v}. \tag{1}$$

That is, **y** is in W if and only if there exist scalars x_1 and x_2 such that

$$\begin{aligned} y_1 &= 2x_1 \\ y_2 &= x_1 + x_2 \\ y_3 &= 2x_2. \end{aligned} \tag{2}$$

The augmented matrix for linear system (2) is

$$\begin{bmatrix} 2 & 0 & y_1 \\ 1 & 1 & y_2 \\ 0 & 2 & y_3 \end{bmatrix},$$

PHYSICAL REPRESENTATIONS OF VECTORS The vector space work of Grassmann and Hamilton was distilled and popularized for the case of R^3 by a Yale University physicist, Josiah Willard Gibbs (1839–1903). Gibbs produced a pamphlet, "Elements of Vector Analysis," mainly for the use of his students. In it, and subsequent articles, Gibbs simplified and improved Hamilton's work in multiple algebras with regard to three-dimensional space. This led to the familiar geometrical representation of vector algebra in terms of operations on directed line segments.

and this matrix is row equivalent to the matrix

$$\begin{bmatrix} 1 & 0 & (1/2)y_1 \\ 0 & 1 & y_2 - (1/2)y_1 \\ 0 & 0 & (1/2)y_3 + (1/2)y_1 - y_2 \end{bmatrix} \quad (3)$$

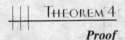

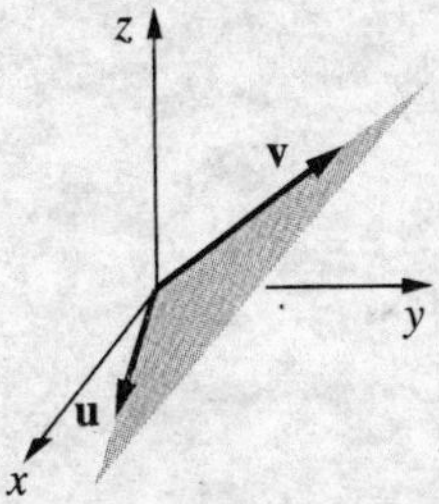

Figure 3.11
A portion of the plane $x - 2y + z = 0$

in echelon form. Therefore, linear system (2) is consistent if and only if $(1/2)y_1 - y_2 + (1/2)y_3 = 0$, or equivalently, if and only if

$$y_1 - 2y_2 + y_3 = 0. \quad (4)$$

Thus W is the subspace given by

$$W = \{\mathbf{y} = \begin{bmatrix} y_1 \\ y_2 \\ y_3 \end{bmatrix} : y_1 - 2y_2 + y_3 = 0\}. \quad (5)$$

It also follows from Eq. (5) that geometrically W is the plane in three-space with equation $x - 2y + z = 0$ (see Fig. 3.11). ■

The Null Space of a Matrix

We now introduce two subspaces that have particular relevance to the linear system of equations $A\mathbf{x} = \mathbf{b}$, where A is an $(m \times n)$ matrix. The first of these subspaces is called the ***null space*** of A (or the ***kernel*** of A) and consists of all solutions of $A\mathbf{x} = \boldsymbol{\theta}$.

DEFINITION 1 Let A be an $(m \times n)$ matrix. The ***null space*** of A [denoted $\mathcal{N}(A)$] is the set of vectors in R^n defined by

$$\mathcal{N}(A) = \{\mathbf{x}: A\mathbf{x} = \boldsymbol{\theta}, \quad \mathbf{x} \text{ in } R^n\}.$$

In words, the null space consists of all those vectors $\mathbf{x}$ such that $A\mathbf{x}$ is the zero vector. The next theorem shows that the null space of an $(m \times n)$ matrix A is a subspace of R^n.

THEOREM 4 If A is an $(m \times n)$ matrix, then $\mathcal{N}(A)$ is a subspace of R^n.

Proof To show that $\mathcal{N}(A)$ is a subspace of R^n, we must verify that the three conditions of Theorem 2 hold. Let $\boldsymbol{\theta}$ be the zero vector in R^n. Then

$$A\boldsymbol{\theta} = \boldsymbol{\theta}, \quad (6)$$

and so $\boldsymbol{\theta}$ is in $\mathcal{N}(A)$. (*Note*: In Eq. (6), the left $\boldsymbol{\theta}$ is in R^n but the right $\boldsymbol{\theta}$ is in R^m.) Now let $\mathbf{u}$ and $\mathbf{v}$ be vectors in $\mathcal{N}(A)$. Then $\mathbf{u}$ and $\mathbf{v}$ are in R^n and

$$A\mathbf{u} = \boldsymbol{\theta} \quad \text{and} \quad A\mathbf{v} = \boldsymbol{\theta}. \quad (7)$$

To see that $\mathbf{u} + \mathbf{v}$ is in $\mathcal{N}(A)$, we must test $\mathbf{u} + \mathbf{v}$ against the algebraic specification of $\mathcal{N}(A)$; that is, we must show that $A(\mathbf{u} + \mathbf{v}) = \boldsymbol{\theta}$. But it follows from Eq. (7) that

$$A(\mathbf{u} + \mathbf{v}) = A\mathbf{u} + A\mathbf{v} = \boldsymbol{\theta} + \boldsymbol{\theta} = \boldsymbol{\theta},$$

and therefore $\mathbf{u}+\mathbf{v}$ is in $\mathcal{N}(A)$. Similarly, for any scalar a, it follows from Eq. (7) that

$$A(a\mathbf{u}) = aA\mathbf{u} = a\boldsymbol{\theta} = \boldsymbol{\theta}.$$

Therefore, $a\mathbf{u}$ is in $\mathcal{N}(A)$. By Theorem 2, $\mathcal{N}(A)$ is a subspace of R^n. ■

EXAMPLE 2 Describe $\mathcal{N}(A)$, where A is the (3×4) matrix

$$A = \begin{bmatrix} 1 & 1 & 3 & 1 \\ 2 & 1 & 5 & 4 \\ 1 & 2 & 4 & -1 \end{bmatrix}.$$

Solution $\mathcal{N}(A)$ is determined by solving the homogeneous system

$$A\mathbf{x} = \boldsymbol{\theta}. \tag{8}$$

This is accomplished by reducing the augmented matrix $[A \,|\, \boldsymbol{\theta}]$ to echelon form. It is easy to verify that $[A \,|\, \boldsymbol{\theta}]$ is row equivalent to

$$\begin{bmatrix} 1 & 0 & 2 & 3 & 0 \\ 0 & 1 & 1 & -2 & 0 \\ 0 & 0 & 0 & 0 & 0 \end{bmatrix}.$$

Solving the corresponding reduced system yields

$$\begin{aligned} x_1 &= -2x_3 - 3x_4 \\ x_2 &= -\ \ x_3 + 2x_4 \end{aligned}$$

as the solution to Eq. (8). Thus a vector $\mathbf{x}$ in R^4,

$$\mathbf{x} = \begin{bmatrix} x_1 \\ x_2 \\ x_3 \\ x_4 \end{bmatrix},$$

is in $\mathcal{N}(A)$ if and only if $\mathbf{x}$ can be written in the form

$$\mathbf{x} = \begin{bmatrix} -2x_3 - 3x_4 \\ -x_3 + 2x_4 \\ x_3 \\ x_4 \end{bmatrix} = x_3 \begin{bmatrix} -2 \\ -1 \\ 1 \\ 0 \end{bmatrix} + x_4 \begin{bmatrix} -3 \\ 2 \\ 0 \\ 1 \end{bmatrix},$$

where x_3 and x_4 are arbitrary; that is,

$$\mathcal{N}(A) = \left\{\mathbf{x}\colon \mathbf{x} = x_3 \begin{bmatrix} -2 \\ -1 \\ 1 \\ 0 \end{bmatrix} + x_4 \begin{bmatrix} -3 \\ 2 \\ 0 \\ 1 \end{bmatrix},\quad x_3 \text{ and } x_4 \text{ any real numbers}\right\}.$$ ■

As the next example demonstrates, the fact that $\mathcal{N}(A)$ is a subspace can be used to show that in three-space every plane through the origin is a subspace.

EXAMPLE 3 Verify that any plane through the origin in R^3 is a subspace of R^3.

Solution The equation of a plane in three-space through the origin is

$$ax + by + cz = 0, \tag{9}$$

where a, b, and c are specified constants not all of which are zero. Now, Eq. (9) can be written as

$$A\mathbf{x} = \boldsymbol{\theta},$$

where A is a (1×3) matrix and $\mathbf{x}$ is in R^3:

$$A = [a \quad b \quad c] \quad \text{and} \quad \mathbf{x} = \begin{bmatrix} x \\ y \\ z \end{bmatrix}.$$

Thus $\mathbf{x}$ is on the plane defined by Eq. (9) if and only if $\mathbf{x}$ is in $\mathcal{N}(A)$. Since $\mathcal{N}(A)$ is a subspace of R^3 by Theorem 4, any plane through the origin is a subspace of R^3. ■

The Range of a Matrix

Another important subspace associated with an $(m \times n)$ matrix A is the ***range*** of A, defined as follows.

DEFINITION 2

Let A be an $(m \times n)$ matrix. The ***range*** of A [denoted $\mathcal{R}(A)$] is the set of vectors in R^m defined by

$$\mathcal{R}(A) = \{\mathbf{y}: \mathbf{y} = A\mathbf{x} \text{ for some } \mathbf{x} \text{ in } R^n\}.$$

In words, the range of A consists of the set of all vectors $\mathbf{y}$ in R^m such that the linear system

$$A\mathbf{x} = \mathbf{y}$$

is consistent. As another way to view $\mathcal{R}(A)$, suppose that A is an $(m \times n)$ matrix. We can regard multiplication by A as defining a function from R^n to R^m. In this sense, as $\mathbf{x}$ varies through R^n, the set of all vectors

$$\mathbf{y} = A\mathbf{x}$$

produced in R^m constitutes the "range" of the function.

We saw in Section 1.5 (see Theorem 5) that if the $(m \times n)$ matrix A has columns $\mathbf{A}_1, \mathbf{A}_2, \ldots, \mathbf{A}_n$ and if

$$\mathbf{x} = \begin{bmatrix} x_1 \\ x_2 \\ \vdots \\ x_n \end{bmatrix},$$

then the matrix equation

$$A\mathbf{x} = \mathbf{y}$$

is equivalent to the vector equation

$$x_1\mathbf{A}_1 + x_2\mathbf{A}_2 + \cdots + x_n\mathbf{A}_n = \mathbf{y}.$$

Therefore, it follows that

$$\mathcal{R}(A) = \text{Sp}\{\mathbf{A}_1, \mathbf{A}_2, \ldots, \mathbf{A}_n\}.$$

By Theorem 3, $\text{Sp}\{\mathbf{A}_1, \mathbf{A}_2, \ldots, \mathbf{A}_n\}$ is a subspace of R^m. (This subspace is also called the ***column space*** of matrix A.) Consequently, $\mathcal{R}(A)$ is a subspace of R^m, and we have proved the following theorem.

THEOREM 5 If A is an $(m \times n)$ matrix and if $\mathcal{R}(A)$ is the range of A, then $\mathcal{R}(A)$ is a subspace of R^m. ■

The next example illustrates a way to give an algebraic specification for $\mathcal{R}(A)$.

EXAMPLE 4 Describe the range of A, where A is the (3×4) matrix

$$A = \begin{bmatrix} 1 & 1 & 3 & 1 \\ 2 & 1 & 5 & 4 \\ 1 & 2 & 4 & -1 \end{bmatrix}.$$

Solution Let $\mathbf{b}$ be an arbitrary vector in R^3,

$$\mathbf{b} = \begin{bmatrix} b_1 \\ b_2 \\ b_3 \end{bmatrix}.$$

Then $\mathbf{b}$ is in $\mathcal{R}(A)$ if and only if the system of equations

$$A\mathbf{x} = \mathbf{b}$$

is consistent. The augmented matrix for the system is

$$[A \mid \mathbf{b}] = \begin{bmatrix} 1 & 1 & 3 & 1 & b_1 \\ 2 & 1 & 5 & 4 & b_2 \\ 1 & 2 & 4 & -1 & b_3 \end{bmatrix},$$

which is equivalent to

$$\begin{bmatrix} 1 & 0 & 2 & 3 & b_2 - b_1 \\ 0 & 1 & 1 & -2 & 2b_1 - b_2 \\ 0 & 0 & 0 & 0 & -3b_1 + b_2 + b_3 \end{bmatrix}.$$

It follows that $A\mathbf{x} = \mathbf{b}$ has a solution [or equivalently, $\mathbf{b}$ is in $\mathcal{R}(A)$] if and only if $-3b_1 + b_2 + b_3 = 0$, or $b_3 = 3b_1 - b_2$, where b_1 and b_2 are arbitrary. Thus

$$\mathcal{R}(A) = \{\mathbf{b}\colon \mathbf{b} = \begin{bmatrix} b_1 \\ b_2 \\ 3b_1 - b_2 \end{bmatrix}$$

$$= b_1 \begin{bmatrix} 1 \\ 0 \\ 3 \end{bmatrix} + b_2 \begin{bmatrix} 0 \\ 1 \\ -1 \end{bmatrix}, \quad b_1 \text{ and } b_2 \text{ any real numbers}\}.$$ ■

The Row Space of a Matrix

If A is an $(m \times n)$ matrix with columns $\mathbf{A}_1, \mathbf{A}_2, \ldots, \mathbf{A}_n$, then we have already defined the ***column space*** of A to be

$$\mathrm{Sp}\{\mathbf{A}_1, \mathbf{A}_2, \ldots, \mathbf{A}_n\}.$$

In a similar fashion, the rows of A can be regarded as vectors $\mathbf{a}_1, \mathbf{a}_2, \ldots, \mathbf{a}_m$ in R^n, and the ***row space*** of A is defined to be

$$\mathrm{Sp}\{\mathbf{a}_1, \mathbf{a}_2, \ldots, \mathbf{a}_m\}.$$

For example, if

$$A = \begin{bmatrix} 1 & 2 & 3 \\ 1 & 0 & 1 \end{bmatrix},$$

then the row space of A is $\mathrm{Sp}\{\mathbf{a}_1, \mathbf{a}_2\}$, where

$$\mathbf{a}_1 = [1 \ \ 2 \ \ 3] \quad \text{and} \quad \mathbf{a}_2 = [1 \ \ 0 \ \ 1].$$

The following theorem shows that row-equivalent matrices have the same row space.

THEOREM 6 Let A be an $(m \times n)$ matrix, and suppose that A is row equivalent to the $(m \times n)$ matrix B. Then A and B have the same row space. ■

The proof of Theorem 6 is given at the end of this section. To illustrate Theorem 6, let A be the (3×3) matrix

$$A = \begin{bmatrix} 1 & -1 & 1 \\ 2 & -1 & 4 \\ 1 & 1 & 5 \end{bmatrix}.$$

By performing the elementary row operations R_2-2R_1, R_3-R_1, R_1+R_2, and R_3-2R_2, we obtain the matrix

$$B = \begin{bmatrix} 1 & 0 & 3 \\ 0 & 1 & 2 \\ 0 & 0 & 0 \end{bmatrix}.$$

By Theorem 6, matrices A and B have the same row space. Clearly the zero row of B contributes nothing as an element of the spanning set, so the row space of B is $\mathrm{Sp}\{\mathbf{b}_1, \mathbf{b}_2\}$, where

$$\mathbf{b}_1 = [1 \quad 0 \quad 3] \quad \text{and} \quad \mathbf{b}_2 = [0 \quad 1 \quad 2].$$

If the rows of A are denoted by $\mathbf{a}_1$, $\mathbf{a}_2$, and $\mathbf{a}_3$, then

$$\mathrm{Sp}\{\mathbf{a}_1, \mathbf{a}_2, \mathbf{a}_3\} = \mathrm{Sp}\{\mathbf{b}_1, \mathbf{b}_2\}.$$

More generally, given a subset $S = \{\mathbf{v}_1, \ldots, \mathbf{v}_m\}$ of R^n, Theorem 6 allows us to obtain a "nicer" subset $T = \{\mathbf{w}_1, \ldots, \mathbf{w}_k\}$ of R^n such that $\mathrm{Sp}(S) = \mathrm{Sp}(T)$. The next example illustrates this.

EXAMPLE 5 Let $S = \{\mathbf{v}_1, \mathbf{v}_2, \mathbf{v}_3, \mathbf{v}_4\}$ be a subset of R^3, where

$$\mathbf{v}_1 = \begin{bmatrix} 1 \\ 2 \\ 1 \end{bmatrix}, \quad \mathbf{v}_2 = \begin{bmatrix} 2 \\ 3 \\ 5 \end{bmatrix}, \quad \mathbf{v}_3 = \begin{bmatrix} 1 \\ 4 \\ -5 \end{bmatrix}, \quad \text{and} \quad \mathbf{v}_4 = \begin{bmatrix} 2 \\ 5 \\ -1 \end{bmatrix}.$$

Show that there exists a set $T = \{\mathbf{w}_1, \mathbf{w}_2\}$ consisting of two vectors in R^3 such that $\mathrm{Sp}(S) = \mathrm{Sp}(T)$.

Solution Let A be the (3×4) matrix

$$A = [\mathbf{v}_1, \mathbf{v}_2, \mathbf{v}_3, \mathbf{v}_4];$$

that is,

$$A = \begin{bmatrix} 1 & 2 & 1 & 2 \\ 2 & 3 & 4 & 5 \\ 1 & 5 & -5 & -1 \end{bmatrix}.$$

The matrix A^T is the (4×3) matrix

$$A^T = \begin{bmatrix} 1 & 2 & 1 \\ 2 & 3 & 5 \\ 1 & 4 & -5 \\ 2 & 5 & -1 \end{bmatrix},$$

and the row vectors of A^T are precisely the vectors $\mathbf{v}_1^T$, $\mathbf{v}_2^T$, $\mathbf{v}_3^T$, and $\mathbf{v}_4^T$. It is straightforward to see that A^T reduces to the matrix

$$B^T = \begin{bmatrix} 1 & 0 & 7 \\ 0 & 1 & -3 \\ 0 & 0 & 0 \\ 0 & 0 & 0 \end{bmatrix}.$$

So, by Theorem 6, A^T and B^T have the same row space. Thus A and B have the same column space, where

$$B = \begin{bmatrix} 1 & 0 & 0 & 0 \\ 0 & 1 & 0 & 0 \\ 7 & -3 & 0 & 0 \end{bmatrix}.$$

In particular, $\mathrm{Sp}(S) = \mathrm{Sp}(T)$, where $T = \{\mathbf{w}_1, \mathbf{w}_2\}$,

$$\mathbf{w}_1 = \begin{bmatrix} 1 \\ 0 \\ 7 \end{bmatrix} \quad \text{and} \quad \mathbf{w}_2 = \begin{bmatrix} 0 \\ -1 \\ 3 \end{bmatrix}.$$ ■

Proof of Theorem 6 (Optional)

Assume that A and B are row-equivalent $(m \times n)$ matrices. Then there is a sequence of matrices

$$A = A_1, A_2, \ldots, A_{k-1}, A_k = B$$

such that for $2 \le j \le k$, A_j is obtained by performing a single elementary row operation on A_{j-1}. It suffices, then, to show that A_{j-1} and A_j have the same row space for each j, $2 \le j \le k$. This means that it is sufficient to consider only the case in which B is obtained from A by a single elementary row operation.

Let A have rows $\mathbf{a}_1, \ldots, \mathbf{a}_m$; that is, A is the $(m \times n)$ matrix

$$A = \begin{bmatrix} \mathbf{a}_1 \\ \vdots \\ \mathbf{a}_j \\ \vdots \\ \mathbf{a}_k \\ \vdots \\ \mathbf{a}_m \end{bmatrix},$$

where each $\mathbf{a}_i$ is a $(1 \times n)$ row vector;

$$\mathbf{a}_i = [a_{i1} \quad a_{i2} \quad \cdots \quad a_{in}].$$

Clearly the order of the rows is immaterial; that is, if B is obtained by interchanging the jth and kth rows of A,

$$B = \begin{bmatrix} \mathbf{a}_1 \\ \vdots \\ \mathbf{a}_k \\ \vdots \\ \mathbf{a}_j \\ \vdots \\ \mathbf{a}_m \end{bmatrix},$$

then A and B have the same row space because

$$\mathrm{Sp}\{\mathbf{a}_1, \ldots, \mathbf{a}_j, \ldots, \mathbf{a}_k, \ldots, \mathbf{a}_m\} = \mathrm{Sp}\{\mathbf{a}_1, \ldots, \mathbf{a}_k, \ldots, \mathbf{a}_j, \ldots, \mathbf{a}_m\}.$$

Next, suppose that B is obtained by performing the row operation $R_k + cR_j$ on A; thus,

$$B = \begin{bmatrix} \mathbf{a}_1 \\ \vdots \\ \mathbf{a}_j \\ \vdots \\ \mathbf{a}_k + c\mathbf{a}_j \\ \vdots \\ \mathbf{a}_m \end{bmatrix}.$$

If the vector $\mathbf{x}$ is in the row space of A, then there exist scalars $b_1, \ldots, b_m$ such that

$$\mathbf{x} = b_1\mathbf{a}_1 + \cdots + b_j\mathbf{a}_j + \cdots + b_k\mathbf{a}_k + \cdots + b_m\mathbf{a}_m. \tag{10}$$

The vector equation (10) can be rewritten as

$$\mathbf{x} = b_1\mathbf{a}_1 + \cdots + (b_j - cb_k)\mathbf{a}_j + \cdots + b_k(\mathbf{a}_k + c\mathbf{a}_j) + \cdots + b_m\mathbf{a}_m, \tag{11}$$

and hence $\mathbf{x}$ is in the row space of B. Conversely, if the vector $\mathbf{y}$ is in the row space of B, then there exist scalars $d_1, \ldots, d_m$ such that

$$\mathbf{y} = d_1\mathbf{a}_1 + \cdots + d_j\mathbf{a}_j + \cdots + d_k(\mathbf{a}_k + c\mathbf{a}_j) + \cdots + d_m\mathbf{a}_m. \tag{12}$$

But Eq. (12) can be rearranged as

$$\mathbf{y} = d_1\mathbf{a}_1 + \cdots + (d_j + cd_k)\mathbf{a}_j + \cdots + d_k\mathbf{a}_k + \cdots + d_m\mathbf{a}_m, \tag{13}$$

so $\mathbf{y}$ is in the row space of A. Therefore, A and B have the same row space.

The remaining case is the one in which B is obtained from A by multiplying the jth row by the nonzero scalar c. This case is left as Exercise 54 at the end of this section.

3.3 EXERCISES

Exercises 1–11 refer to the vectors in Eq. (14).

$$\mathbf{a} = \begin{bmatrix} 1 \\ -1 \end{bmatrix}, \quad \mathbf{b} = \begin{bmatrix} 2 \\ -3 \end{bmatrix}, \quad \mathbf{c} = \begin{bmatrix} -2 \\ 2 \end{bmatrix},$$

$$\mathbf{d} = \begin{bmatrix} 1 \\ 0 \end{bmatrix}, \quad \mathbf{e} = \begin{bmatrix} 0 \\ 0 \end{bmatrix}. \tag{14}$$

In Exercises 1–11, either show that $\mathrm{Sp}(S) = R^2$ or give an algebraic specification for $\mathrm{Sp}(S)$. If $\mathrm{Sp}(S) \neq R^2$, then give a geometric description of $\mathrm{Sp}(S)$.

1. $S = \{\mathbf{a}\}$ **2.** $S = \{\mathbf{b}\}$ **3.** $S = \{\mathbf{e}\}$

4. $S = \{\mathbf{a}, \mathbf{b}\}$ **5.** $S = \{\mathbf{a}, \mathbf{d}\}$ **6.** $S = \{\mathbf{a}, \mathbf{c}\}$

7. $S = \{\mathbf{b}, \mathbf{e}\}$ **8.** $S = \{\mathbf{a}, \mathbf{b}, \mathbf{d}\}$

9. $S = \{\mathbf{b}, \mathbf{c}, \mathbf{d}\}$ **10.** $S = \{\mathbf{a}, \mathbf{b}, \mathbf{e}\}$

11. $S = \{\mathbf{a}, \mathbf{c}, \mathbf{e}\}$

Exercises 12–19 refer to the vectors in Eq. (15).

$$\mathbf{v} = \begin{bmatrix} 1 \\ 2 \\ 0 \end{bmatrix}, \quad \mathbf{w} = \begin{bmatrix} 0 \\ -1 \\ 1 \end{bmatrix}, \quad \mathbf{x} = \begin{bmatrix} 1 \\ 1 \\ -1 \end{bmatrix},$$

$$\mathbf{y} = \begin{bmatrix} -2 \\ -2 \\ 2 \end{bmatrix}, \quad \mathbf{z} = \begin{bmatrix} 1 \\ 0 \\ 2 \end{bmatrix} \tag{15}$$

In Exercises 12–19, either show that $\mathrm{Sp}(S) = R^3$ or give an algebraic specification for $\mathrm{Sp}(S)$. If $\mathrm{Sp}(S) \neq R^3$, then give a geometric description of $\mathrm{Sp}(S)$.

12. $S = \{\mathbf{v}\}$ **13.** $S = \{\mathbf{w}\}$

14. $S = \{\mathbf{v}, \mathbf{w}\}$ **15.** $S = \{\mathbf{v}, \mathbf{x}\}$

16. $S = \{\mathbf{v}, \mathbf{w}, \mathbf{x}\}$ **17.** $S = \{\mathbf{w}, \mathbf{x}, \mathbf{z}\}$

18. $S = \{\mathbf{v}, \mathbf{w}, \mathbf{z}\}$ **19.** $S = \{\mathbf{w}, \mathbf{x}, \mathbf{y}\}$

20. Let S be the set given in Exercise 14. For each vector given below, determine whether the vector is in $\mathrm{Sp}(S)$. Express those vectors that are in $\mathrm{Sp}(S)$ as a linear combination of $\mathbf{v}$ and $\mathbf{w}$.

a) $\begin{bmatrix} 1 \\ 1 \\ 1 \end{bmatrix}$ **b)** $\begin{bmatrix} 1 \\ 1 \\ -1 \end{bmatrix}$ **c)** $\begin{bmatrix} 1 \\ 2 \\ 0 \end{bmatrix}$

d) $\begin{bmatrix} 2 \\ 3 \\ 1 \end{bmatrix}$ **e)** $\begin{bmatrix} -1 \\ 2 \\ 4 \end{bmatrix}$ **f)** $\begin{bmatrix} 1 \\ 1 \\ 3 \end{bmatrix}$

21. Repeat Exercise 20 for the set S given in Exercise 15.

22. Determine which of the vectors listed in Eq. (14) is in the null space of the matrix

$$A = \begin{bmatrix} 2 & 2 \\ 3 & 3 \end{bmatrix}.$$

23. Determine which of the vectors listed in Eq. (14) is in the null space of the matrix

$$A = \begin{bmatrix} 0 & 1 \\ 0 & 2 \\ 0 & 3 \end{bmatrix}.$$

24. Determine which of the vectors listed in Eq. (15) is in the null space of the matrix

$$A = [-2 \ \ 1 \ \ 1].$$

25. Determine which of the vectors listed in Eq. (15) is in the null space of the matrix

$$A = \begin{bmatrix} 1 & -1 & 0 \\ 2 & -1 & 1 \\ 3 & -5 & -2 \end{bmatrix}.$$

In Exercises 26–37, give an algebraic specification for the null space and the range of the given matrix A.

26. $A = \begin{bmatrix} 1 & -2 \\ -3 & 6 \end{bmatrix}$ **27.** $A = \begin{bmatrix} -1 & 3 \\ 2 & -6 \end{bmatrix}$

28. $A = \begin{bmatrix} 1 & 1 \\ 1 & 2 \end{bmatrix}$ **29.** $A = \begin{bmatrix} 1 & 1 \\ 2 & 5 \end{bmatrix}$

30. $A = \begin{bmatrix} 1 & -1 & 2 \\ 2 & -1 & 5 \end{bmatrix}$ **31.** $A = \begin{bmatrix} 1 & 2 & 1 \\ 3 & 6 & 4 \end{bmatrix}$

32. $A = \begin{bmatrix} 1 & 3 \\ 2 & 7 \\ 1 & 5 \end{bmatrix}$ **33.** $A = \begin{bmatrix} 0 & 1 \\ 0 & 2 \\ 0 & 3 \end{bmatrix}$

34. $A = \begin{bmatrix} 1 & -2 & 1 \\ 2 & -3 & 5 \\ 1 & 0 & 7 \end{bmatrix}$ **35.** $A = \begin{bmatrix} 1 & 2 & 3 \\ 1 & 3 & 1 \\ 2 & 2 & 10 \end{bmatrix}$

36. $A = \begin{bmatrix} 1 & 0 & -1 \\ -1 & 1 & 2 \\ 1 & 2 & 2 \end{bmatrix}$

37. $A = \begin{bmatrix} 1 & 2 & 1 \\ 2 & 5 & 4 \\ 1 & 3 & 4 \end{bmatrix}$

38. Let A be the matrix given in Exercise 26.

a) For each vector $\mathbf{b}$ that follows, determine whether $\mathbf{b}$ is in $\mathcal{R}(A)$.

b) If $\mathbf{b}$ is in $\mathcal{R}(A)$, then exhibit a vector $\mathbf{x}$ in R^2 such that $A\mathbf{x} = \mathbf{b}$.

c) If $\mathbf{b}$ is in $\mathcal{R}(A)$, then write $\mathbf{b}$ as a linear combination of the columns of A.

i) $\mathbf{b} = \begin{bmatrix} 1 \\ -3 \end{bmatrix}$ **ii)** $\mathbf{b} = \begin{bmatrix} -1 \\ 2 \end{bmatrix}$

iii) $\mathbf{b} = \begin{bmatrix} 1 \\ 1 \end{bmatrix}$ **iv)** $\mathbf{b} = \begin{bmatrix} -2 \\ 6 \end{bmatrix}$

v) $\mathbf{b} = \begin{bmatrix} 3 \\ -6 \end{bmatrix}$ **vi)** $\mathbf{b} = \begin{bmatrix} 0 \\ 0 \end{bmatrix}$

39. Repeat Exercise 38 for the matrix A given in Exercise 27.

40. Let A be the matrix given in Exercise 34.

a) For each vector $\mathbf{b}$ that follows, determine whether $\mathbf{b}$ is in $\mathcal{R}(A)$.

b) If $\mathbf{b}$ is in $\mathcal{R}(A)$, then exhibit a vector $\mathbf{x}$ in R^3 such that $A\mathbf{x} = \mathbf{b}$.

c) If $\mathbf{b}$ is in $\mathcal{R}(A)$, then write $\mathbf{b}$ as a linear combination of the columns of A.

i) $\mathbf{b} = \begin{bmatrix} 1 \\ 2 \\ 0 \end{bmatrix}$ **ii)** $\mathbf{b} = \begin{bmatrix} 1 \\ 1 \\ -1 \end{bmatrix}$

iii) $\mathbf{b} = \begin{bmatrix} 4 \\ 7 \\ 2 \end{bmatrix}$ **iv)** $\mathbf{b} = \begin{bmatrix} 0 \\ 1 \\ 2 \end{bmatrix}$

v) $\mathbf{b} = \begin{bmatrix} 0 \\ 1 \\ -2 \end{bmatrix}$ **vi)** $\mathbf{b} = \begin{bmatrix} 0 \\ 0 \\ 0 \end{bmatrix}$

41. Repeat Exercise 40 for the matrix A given in Exercise 35.

42. Let

$$W = \{\mathbf{y} = \begin{bmatrix} 2x_1 - 3x_2 + x_3 \\ -x_1 + 4x_2 - 2x_3 \\ 2x_1 + x_2 + 4x_3 \end{bmatrix} : x_1, x_2, x_3 \text{ real}\}.$$

Exhibit a (3×3) matrix A such that $W = \mathcal{R}(A)$. Conclude that W is a subspace of R^3.

43. Let

$$W = \{\mathbf{x} = \begin{bmatrix} x_1 \\ x_2 \\ x_3 \end{bmatrix} : 3x_1 - 4x_2 + 2x_3 = 0\}.$$

Exhibit a (1×3) matrix A such that $W = \mathcal{N}(A)$. Conclude that W is a subspace of R^3.

44. Let S be the set of vectors given in Exercise 16. Exhibit a matrix A such that $\text{Sp}(S) = \mathcal{R}(A)$.

45. Let S be the set of vectors given in Exercise 17. Exhibit a matrix A such that $\text{Sp}(S) = \mathcal{R}(A)$.

In Exercises 46–49, use the technique illustrated in Example 5 to find a set $T = \{\mathbf{w}_1, \mathbf{w}_2\}$ consisting of two vectors such that $\text{Sp}(S) = \text{Sp}(T)$.

46. $S = \left\{ \begin{bmatrix} 1 \\ 0 \\ -1 \end{bmatrix}, \begin{bmatrix} 2 \\ 2 \\ 1 \end{bmatrix}, \begin{bmatrix} 1 \\ 2 \\ 2 \end{bmatrix} \right\}$

47. $S = \left\{ \begin{bmatrix} -2 \\ 1 \\ 3 \end{bmatrix}, \begin{bmatrix} 2 \\ 2 \\ -1 \end{bmatrix}, \begin{bmatrix} -2 \\ 7 \\ 7 \end{bmatrix} \right\}$

48. $S = \left\{ \begin{bmatrix} 1 \\ 0 \\ 1 \end{bmatrix}, \begin{bmatrix} -2 \\ 0 \\ -2 \end{bmatrix}, \begin{bmatrix} 1 \\ 1 \\ 2 \end{bmatrix}, \begin{bmatrix} -2 \\ 3 \\ 1 \end{bmatrix} \right\}$

49. $S = \left\{ \begin{bmatrix} 1 \\ 2 \\ 2 \end{bmatrix}, \begin{bmatrix} 1 \\ 5 \\ 3 \end{bmatrix}, \begin{bmatrix} 0 \\ 6 \\ 2 \end{bmatrix}, \begin{bmatrix} 1 \\ -1 \\ 1 \end{bmatrix} \right\}$

50. Identify the range and the null space for each of the following.

a) The $(n \times n)$ identity matrix

b) The $(n \times n)$ zero matrix

c) Any $(n \times n)$ nonsingular matrix A

51. Let A and B be $(n \times n)$ matrices. Verify that $\mathcal{N}(A) \cap \mathcal{N}(B) \subseteq \mathcal{N}(A + B)$.

52. Let A be an $(m \times r)$ matrix and B an $(r \times n)$ matrix.

a) Show that $\mathcal{N}(B) \subseteq \mathcal{N}(AB)$.

b) Show that $\mathcal{R}(AB) \subseteq \mathcal{R}(A)$.

53. Let W be a subspace of R^n, and let A be an $(m \times n)$ matrix. Let V be the subset of R^m defined by

$$V = \{\mathbf{y}\text{: } \mathbf{y} = A\mathbf{x} \text{ for some } \mathbf{x} \text{ in } W\}.$$

Prove that V is a subspace of R^m.

54. Let A be an $(m \times n)$ matrix, and let B be obtained by multiplying the kth row of A by the nonzero scalar c. Prove that A and B have the same row space.

3.4 BASES FOR SUBSPACES

Two of the most fundamental concepts of geometry are those of dimension and the use of coordinates to locate a point in space. In this section and the next, we extend these notions to an arbitrary subspace of R^n by introducing the idea of a basis for a subspace. The first part of this section is devoted to developing the definition of a basis, and in the latter part of the section, we present techniques for obtaining bases for the subspaces introduced in Section 3.3. We will consider the concept of dimension in Section 3.5.

An example from R^2 will serve to illustrate the transition from geometry to algebra. We have already seen that each vector $\mathbf{v}$ in R^2,

$$\mathbf{v} = \begin{bmatrix} a \\ b \end{bmatrix}, \tag{1}$$

can be interpreted geometrically as the point with coordinates a and b. Recall that in R^2 the vectors $\mathbf{e}_1$ and $\mathbf{e}_2$ are defined by

$$\mathbf{e}_1 = \begin{bmatrix} 1 \\ 0 \end{bmatrix} \quad \text{and} \quad \mathbf{e}_2 = \begin{bmatrix} 0 \\ 1 \end{bmatrix}.$$

Clearly the vector $\mathbf{v}$ in (1) can be expressed uniquely as a linear combination of $\mathbf{e}_1$ and $\mathbf{e}_2$:

$$\mathbf{v} = a\mathbf{e}_1 + b\mathbf{e}_2. \tag{2}$$

As we will see later, the set $\{\mathbf{e}_1, \mathbf{e}_2\}$ is an example of a ***basis*** for R^2 (indeed, it is called the ***natural basis*** for R^2). In Eq. (2), the vector $\mathbf{v}$ is determined by the coefficients a and b (see Fig. 3.12). Thus the geometric concept of characterizing a point by its coordinates can be interpreted algebraically as determining a vector by its coefficients when the vector is expressed as a linear combination of "basis" vectors. (In fact, the coefficients obtained are often referred to as the coordinates of the vector. This idea will be developed further in Chapter 5.) We turn now to the task of making these ideas precise in the context of an arbitrary subspace W of R^n.

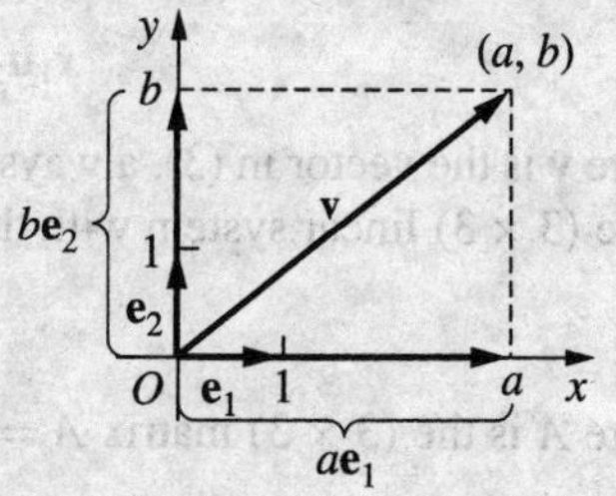

Figure 3.12 $\mathbf{v} = a\mathbf{e}_1 + b\mathbf{e}_2$

Spanning Sets

Let W be a subspace of R^n, and let S be a subset of W. The discussion above suggests that the first requirement for S to be a basis for W is that each vector in W be expressible as a linear combination of the vectors in S. This leads to the following definition.

DEFINITION 3 Let W be a subspace of R^n, and let $S = \{\mathbf{w}_1, \ldots, \mathbf{w}_m\}$ be a subset of W. We say that S is a ***spanning set*** for W, or simply that S ***spans*** W, if every vector $\mathbf{w}$ in W can be expressed as a linear combination of vectors in S;

$$\mathbf{w} = a_1\mathbf{w}_1 + \cdots + a_m\mathbf{w}_m.$$

A restatement of Definition 3 in the notation of the previous section is that S is a spanning set of W provided that $\mathrm{Sp}(S) = W$. It is evident that the set $S = \{\mathbf{e}_1, \mathbf{e}_2, \mathbf{e}_3\}$, consisting of the unit vectors in R^3, is a spanning set for R^3. Specifically, if $\mathbf{v}$ is in R^3,

$$\mathbf{v} = \begin{bmatrix} a \\ b \\ c \end{bmatrix}, \tag{3}$$

then $\mathbf{v} = a\mathbf{e}_1 + b\mathbf{e}_2 + c\mathbf{e}_3$. The next two examples consider other subsets of R^3.

EXAMPLE 1 In R^3, let $S = \{\mathbf{u}_1, \mathbf{u}_2, \mathbf{u}_3\}$, where

$$\mathbf{u}_1 = \begin{bmatrix} 1 \\ -1 \\ 0 \end{bmatrix}, \quad \mathbf{u}_2 = \begin{bmatrix} -2 \\ 3 \\ 1 \end{bmatrix}, \quad \text{and} \quad \mathbf{u}_3 = \begin{bmatrix} 1 \\ 2 \\ 4 \end{bmatrix}.$$

Determine whether S is a spanning set for R^3.

Solution We must determine whether an arbitrary vector $\mathbf{v}$ in R^3 can be expressed as a linear combination of $\mathbf{u}_1$, $\mathbf{u}_2$, and $\mathbf{u}_3$. In other words, we must decide whether the vector equation

$$x_1\mathbf{u}_1 + x_2\mathbf{u}_2 + x_3\mathbf{u}_3 = \mathbf{v}, \tag{4}$$

where $\mathbf{v}$ is the vector in (3), always has a solution. The vector equation (4) is equivalent to the (3×3) linear system with the matrix equation

$$A\mathbf{x} = \mathbf{v}, \tag{5}$$

where A is the (3×3) matrix $A = [\mathbf{u}_1, \mathbf{u}_2, \mathbf{u}_3]$. The augmented matrix for Eq. (5) is

$$[A \mid \mathbf{v}] = \begin{bmatrix} 1 & -2 & 1 & a \\ -1 & 3 & 2 & b \\ 0 & 1 & 4 & c \end{bmatrix},$$

and this matrix is row equivalent to

$$\begin{bmatrix} 1 & 0 & 0 & 10a + 9b - 7c \\ 0 & 1 & 0 & 4a + 4b - 3c \\ 0 & 0 & 1 & -a - b + c \end{bmatrix}.$$

Therefore,

$$\begin{aligned} x_1 &= 10a + 9b - 7c \\ x_2 &= 4a + 4b - 3c \\ x_3 &= -a - b + c \end{aligned}$$

is the solution of Eq. (4). In particular, Eq. (4) always has a solution, so S is a spanning set for R^3. ■

EXAMPLE 2 Let $S = \{\mathbf{v}_1, \mathbf{v}_2, \mathbf{v}_3\}$ be the subset of R^3 defined by

$$\mathbf{v}_1 = \begin{bmatrix} 1 \\ 2 \\ 3 \end{bmatrix}, \quad \mathbf{v}_2 = \begin{bmatrix} -1 \\ 0 \\ -7 \end{bmatrix}, \quad \text{and} \quad \mathbf{v}_3 = \begin{bmatrix} 2 \\ 7 \\ 0 \end{bmatrix}.$$

Does S span R^3?

Solution Let $\mathbf{v}$ be the vector given in Eq. (3). As before, the vector equation

$$x_1\mathbf{v}_1 + x_2\mathbf{v}_2 + x_3\mathbf{v}_3 = \mathbf{v} \tag{6}$$

is equivalent to the (3×3) system of equations

$$A\mathbf{x} = \mathbf{v}, \tag{7}$$

where $A = [\mathbf{v}_1, \mathbf{v}_2, \mathbf{v}_3]$. The augmented matrix for Eq. (7) is

$$[A \mid \mathbf{v}] = \begin{bmatrix} 1 & -1 & 2 & a \\ 2 & 0 & 7 & b \\ 3 & -7 & 0 & c \end{bmatrix},$$

and the matrix $[A \mid \mathbf{v}]$ is row equivalent to

$$\begin{bmatrix} 1 & 0 & 7/2 & b/2 \\ 0 & 1 & 3/2 & -a + (1/2)b \\ 0 & 0 & 0 & -7a + 2b + c \end{bmatrix}.$$

It follows that Eq. (6) has a solution if and only if $-7a + 2b + c = 0$. In particular, S does not span R^3. Indeed,

$$\text{Sp}(S) = \{\mathbf{v}\colon \mathbf{v} = \begin{bmatrix} a \\ b \\ c \end{bmatrix}, \quad \text{where} -7a + 2b + c = 0\}.$$

For example, the vector

$$\mathbf{w} = \begin{bmatrix} 1 \\ 1 \\ 1 \end{bmatrix}$$

is in R^3 but is not in Sp(S); that is, $\mathbf{w}$ cannot be expressed as a linear combination of $\mathbf{v}_1$, $\mathbf{v}_2$, and $\mathbf{v}_3$. ■

The next example illustrates a procedure for constructing a spanning set for the null space, $\mathcal{N}(A)$, of a matrix A.

EXAMPLE 3 Let A be the (3×4) matrix

$$A = \begin{bmatrix} 1 & 1 & 3 & 1 \\ 2 & 1 & 5 & 4 \\ 1 & 2 & 4 & -1 \end{bmatrix}.$$

Exhibit a spanning set for $\mathcal{N}(A)$, the null space of A.

Solution The first step toward obtaining a spanning set for $\mathcal{N}(A)$ is to obtain an algebraic specification for $\mathcal{N}(A)$ by solving the homogeneous system $A\mathbf{x} = \boldsymbol{\theta}$. For the given matrix A, this was done in Example 2 of Section 3.3. Specifically,

$$\mathcal{N}(A) = \{\mathbf{x}\text{: } \mathbf{x} = \begin{bmatrix} -2x_3 - 3x_4 \\ -x_3 + 2x_4 \\ x_3 \\ x_4 \end{bmatrix}, \quad x_3 \text{ and } x_4 \text{ any real numbers}\}.$$

Thus a vector $\mathbf{x}$ in $\mathcal{N}(A)$ is totally determined by the unconstrained parameters x_3 and x_4. Separating those parameters gives a decomposition of $\mathbf{x}$:

$$\mathbf{x} = \begin{bmatrix} -2x_3 - 3x_4 \\ -x_3 + 2x_4 \\ x_3 \\ x_4 \end{bmatrix} = \begin{bmatrix} -2x_3 \\ -\ x_3 \\ x_3 \\ 0 \end{bmatrix} + \begin{bmatrix} -3x_4 \\ 2x_4 \\ 0 \\ x_4 \end{bmatrix} = x_3 \begin{bmatrix} -2 \\ -1 \\ 1 \\ 0 \end{bmatrix} + x_4 \begin{bmatrix} -3 \\ 2 \\ 0 \\ 1 \end{bmatrix}. \quad (8)$$

Let $\mathbf{u}_1$ and $\mathbf{u}_2$ be the vectors

$$\mathbf{u}_1 = \begin{bmatrix} -2 \\ -1 \\ 1 \\ 0 \end{bmatrix} \quad \text{and} \quad \mathbf{u}_2 = \begin{bmatrix} -3 \\ 2 \\ 0 \\ 1 \end{bmatrix}.$$

By setting $x_3 = 1$ and $x_4 = 0$ in Eq. (8), we obtain $\mathbf{u}_1$, so $\mathbf{u}_1$ is in $\mathcal{N}(A)$. Similarly, $\mathbf{u}_2$ can be obtained by setting $x_3 = 0$ and $x_4 = 1$, so $\mathbf{u}_2$ is in $\mathcal{N}(A)$. Moreover, it is an immediate consequence of Eq. (8) that each vector $\mathbf{x}$ in $\mathcal{N}(A)$ is a linear combination of $\mathbf{u}_1$ and $\mathbf{u}_2$. Therefore, $\mathcal{N}(A) = \text{Sp}\{\mathbf{u}_1, \mathbf{u}_2\}$; that is, $\{\mathbf{u}_1, \mathbf{u}_2\}$ is a spanning set for $\mathcal{N}(A)$. ■

The remaining subspaces introduced in Section 3.3 were either defined or characterized by a spanning set. If $S = \{\mathbf{v}_1, \ldots, \mathbf{v}_r\}$ is a subset of R^n, for instance, then obviously S is a spanning set for $\text{Sp}(S)$. If A is an $(m \times n)$ matrix,

$$A = [\mathbf{A}_1, \ldots, \mathbf{A}_n],$$

then, as we saw in Section 3.3, $\{\mathbf{A}_1, \ldots, \mathbf{A}_n\}$ is a spanning set for $\mathcal{R}(A)$, the range of A. Finally, if

$$A = \begin{bmatrix} \mathbf{a}_1 \\ \mathbf{a}_2 \\ \vdots \\ \mathbf{a}_m \end{bmatrix},$$

where $\mathbf{a}_i$ is the ith-row vector of A, then, by definition, $\{\mathbf{a}_1, \ldots, \mathbf{a}_m\}$ is a spanning set for the row space of A.

Minimal Spanning Sets

If W is a subspace of R^n, $W \neq \{\boldsymbol{\theta}\}$, then spanning sets for W abound. For example, a vector $\mathbf{v}$ in a spanning set can always be replaced by $a\mathbf{v}$, where a is any nonzero scalar. It is easy to demonstrate, however, that not all spanning sets are equally desirable. For example, define $\mathbf{u}$ in R^2 by

$$\mathbf{u} = \begin{bmatrix} 1 \\ 1 \end{bmatrix}.$$

The set $S = \{\mathbf{e}_1, \mathbf{e}_2, \mathbf{u}\}$ is a spanning set for R^2. Indeed, for an arbitrary vector $\mathbf{v}$ in R^2,

$$\mathbf{v} = \begin{bmatrix} a \\ b \end{bmatrix},$$

$\mathbf{v} = (a - c)\mathbf{e}_1 + (b - c)\mathbf{e}_2 + c\mathbf{u}$, where c is any real number whatsoever. But the subset $\{\mathbf{e}_1, \mathbf{e}_2\}$ already spans R^2, so the vector $\mathbf{u}$ is unnecessary.

Recall that a set $\{\mathbf{v}_1, \ldots, \mathbf{v}_m\}$ of vectors in R^n is linearly independent if the vector equation

$$x_1\mathbf{v}_1 + \cdots + x_m\mathbf{v}_m = \boldsymbol{\theta} \tag{9}$$

has only the trivial solution $x_1 = \cdots = x_m = 0$; if Eq. (9) has a nontrivial solution, then the set is linearly dependent. The set $S = \{\mathbf{e}_1, \mathbf{e}_2, \mathbf{u}\}$ is linearly dependent because

$$\mathbf{e}_1 + \mathbf{e}_2 - \mathbf{u} = \boldsymbol{\theta}.$$

Our next example illustrates that a linearly dependent set is not an efficient spanning set; that is, fewer vectors will span the same space.

EXAMPLE 4 Let $S = \{\mathbf{v}_1, \mathbf{v}_2, \mathbf{v}_3\}$ be the subset of R^3, where

$$\mathbf{v}_1 = \begin{bmatrix} 1 \\ 1 \\ 1 \end{bmatrix}, \quad \mathbf{v}_2 = \begin{bmatrix} 2 \\ 3 \\ 1 \end{bmatrix}, \quad \text{and} \quad \mathbf{v}_3 = \begin{bmatrix} 3 \\ 5 \\ 1 \end{bmatrix}.$$

Show that S is a linearly dependent set, and exhibit a subset T of S such that T contains only two vectors but $\mathrm{Sp}(T) = \mathrm{Sp}(S)$.

Solution The vector equation

$$x_1\mathbf{v}_1 + x_2\mathbf{v}_2 + x_3\mathbf{v}_3 = \boldsymbol{\theta} \tag{10}$$

is equivalent to the (3×3) homogeneous system of equations with augmented matrix

$$A = \begin{bmatrix} 1 & 2 & 3 & 0 \\ 1 & 3 & 5 & 0 \\ 1 & 1 & 1 & 0 \end{bmatrix}.$$

Matrix A is row equivalent to

$$B = \begin{bmatrix} 1 & 0 & -1 & 0 \\ 0 & 1 & 2 & 0 \\ 0 & 0 & 0 & 0 \end{bmatrix}$$

in echelon form. Solving the system with augmented matrix B gives

$$\begin{aligned} x_1 &= x_3 \\ x_2 &= -2x_3. \end{aligned}$$

Because Eq. (10) has nontrivial solutions, the set S is linearly dependent. Taking $x_3 = 1$, for example, gives $x_1 = 1$, $x_2 = -2$. Therefore,

$$\mathbf{v}_1 - 2\mathbf{v}_2 + \mathbf{v}_3 = \boldsymbol{\theta}. \tag{11}$$

Equation (11) allows us to express $\mathbf{v}_3$ as a linear combination of $\mathbf{v}_1$ and $\mathbf{v}_2$:

$$\mathbf{v}_3 = -\mathbf{v}_1 + 2\mathbf{v}_2.$$

(Note that we could just as easily have solved Eq. (11) for either $\mathbf{v}_1$ or $\mathbf{v}_2$.) It now follows that

$$\mathrm{Sp}\{\mathbf{v}_1, \mathbf{v}_2\} = \mathrm{Sp}\{\mathbf{v}_1, \mathbf{v}_2, \mathbf{v}_3\}.$$

To illustrate, let $\mathbf{v}$ be in the subspace $\mathrm{Sp}\{\mathbf{v}_1, \mathbf{v}_2, \mathbf{v}_3\}$:

$$\mathbf{v} = a_1\mathbf{v}_1 + a_2\mathbf{v}_2 + a_3\mathbf{v}_3.$$

Making the substitution $\mathbf{v}_3 = -\mathbf{v}_1 + 2\mathbf{v}_2$, yields

$$\mathbf{v} = a_1\mathbf{v}_1 + a_2\mathbf{v}_2 + a_3(-\mathbf{v}_1 + 2\mathbf{v}_2).$$

This expression simplifies to

$$\mathbf{v} = (a_1 - a_3)\mathbf{v}_1 + (a_2 + 2a_3)\mathbf{v}_2;$$

in particular, $\mathbf{v}$ is in $\mathrm{Sp}\{\mathbf{v}_1, \mathbf{v}_2\}$. Clearly any linear combination of $\mathbf{v}_1$ and $\mathbf{v}_2$ is in $\mathrm{Sp}(S)$ because

$$b_1\mathbf{v}_1 + b_2\mathbf{v}_2 = b_1\mathbf{v}_1 + b_2\mathbf{v}_2 + 0\mathbf{v}_3.$$

Thus if $T = \{\mathbf{v}_1, \mathbf{v}_2\}$, then $\mathrm{Sp}(T) = \mathrm{Sp}(S)$. ■

The lesson to be drawn from Example 4 is that a linearly dependent spanning set contains redundant information. That is, if $S = \{\mathbf{w}_1, \ldots, \mathbf{w}_r\}$ is a linearly dependent spanning set for a subspace W, then at least one vector from S is a linear combination of the other $r - 1$ vectors and can be discarded from S to produce a smaller spanning set. On the other hand, if $B = \{\mathbf{v}_1, \ldots, \mathbf{v}_m\}$ is a linearly independent spanning set for W, then no vector in B is a linear combination of the other $m - 1$ vectors in B. Hence if a vector is removed from B, this smaller set cannot be a spanning set for W (in particular, the vector removed from B is in W but cannot be expressed as a linear combination of the vectors retained). In this sense a linearly independent spanning set is a minimal spanning set and hence represents the most efficient way of characterizing the subspace. This idea leads to the following definition.

DEFINITION 4 **Let W be a nonzero subspace of R^n. A *basis* for W is a linearly independent spanning set for W.**

Note that the zero subspace of R^n, $W = \{\theta\}$, contains only the vector θ. Although it is the case that $\{\theta\}$ is a spanning set for W, the set $\{\theta\}$ is linearly dependent. Thus the concept of a basis is not meaningful for $W = \{\theta\}$.

Uniqueness of Representation

Let $B = \{\mathbf{v}_1, \mathbf{v}_2, \ldots, \mathbf{v}_p\}$ be a basis for a subspace W of R^n, and let $\mathbf{x}$ be a vector in W. Because B is a spanning set, we know that there are scalars $a_1, a_2, \ldots, a_p$ such that

$$\mathbf{x} = a_1\mathbf{v}_1 + a_2\mathbf{v}_2 + \cdots + a_p\mathbf{v}_p. \tag{12}$$

Because B is also a linearly independent set, we can show that the representation of $\mathbf{x}$ in Eq. (12) is unique. That is, if we have any representation of the form $\mathbf{x} = b_1\mathbf{v}_1 + b_2\mathbf{v}_2 + \cdots + b_p\mathbf{v}_p$, then $a_1 = b_1, a_2 = b_2, \ldots, a_p = b_p$. To establish this uniqueness, suppose that $b_1, b_2, \ldots, b_p$ are any scalars such that

$$\mathbf{x} = b_1\mathbf{v}_1 + b_2\mathbf{v}_2 + \cdots + b_p\mathbf{v}_p.$$

Subtracting the preceding equation from Eq. (12), we obtain

$$\theta = (a_1 - b_1)\mathbf{v}_1 + (a_2 - b_2)\mathbf{v}_2 + \cdots + (a_p - b_p)\mathbf{v}_p.$$

Then, using the fact that $\{\mathbf{v}_1, \mathbf{v}_2, \ldots, \mathbf{v}_p\}$ is linearly independent, we see that $a_1 - b_1 = 0$, $a_2 - b_2 = 0, \ldots, a_p - b_p = 0$. This discussion of uniqueness leads to the following remark.

Remark Let $B = \{\mathbf{v}_1, \mathbf{v}_2, \ldots, \mathbf{v}_p\}$ be a basis for W, where W is a subspace of R^n. If $\mathbf{x}$ is in W, then $\mathbf{x}$ can be represented uniquely in terms of the basis B. That is, there are unique scalars $a_1, a_2, \ldots, a_p$ such that

$$\mathbf{x} = a_1\mathbf{v}_1 + a_2\mathbf{v}_2 + \cdots + a_p\mathbf{v}_p.$$

As we see later, these scalars are called the **coordinates** of x with respect to the basis.

Examples of Bases

It is easy to show that the unit vectors

$$\mathbf{e}_1 = \begin{bmatrix} 1 \\ 0 \\ 0 \end{bmatrix}, \quad \mathbf{e}_2 = \begin{bmatrix} 0 \\ 1 \\ 0 \end{bmatrix}, \quad \text{and} \quad \mathbf{e}_3 = \begin{bmatrix} 0 \\ 0 \\ 1 \end{bmatrix}$$

constitute a basis for R^3. In general, the n-dimensional vectors $\mathbf{e}_1, \mathbf{e}_2, \ldots, \mathbf{e}_n$ form a basis for R^n, frequently called the natural basis.

In Exercise 30, the reader is asked to use Theorem 13 of Section 1.7 to prove that any linearly independent subset $B = \{\mathbf{v}_1, \mathbf{v}_2, \mathbf{v}_3\}$ of R^3 is actually a basis for R^3. Thus, for example, the vectors

$$\mathbf{v}_1 = \begin{bmatrix} 1 \\ 0 \\ 0 \end{bmatrix}, \quad \mathbf{v}_2 = \begin{bmatrix} 1 \\ 1 \\ 0 \end{bmatrix}, \quad \text{and} \quad \mathbf{v}_3 = \begin{bmatrix} 1 \\ 1 \\ 1 \end{bmatrix}$$

provide another basis for R^3.

In Example 3, a procedure for determining a spanning set for $\mathcal{N}(A)$, the null space of a matrix A, was illustrated. Note in Example 3 that the spanning set $\{\mathbf{u}_1, \mathbf{u}_2\}$ obtained is linearly independent, so it is a basis for $\mathcal{N}(A)$. Oftentimes, if a subspace W of R^n has an algebraic specification in terms of unconstrained variables, the procedure illustrated in Example 3 yields a basis for W. The next example provides another illustration.

EXAMPLE 5 Let A be the (3×4) matrix given in Example 4 of Section 3.3. Use the algebraic specification of $\mathcal{R}(A)$ derived in that example to obtain a basis for $\mathcal{R}(A)$.

Solution In Example 4 of Section 3.3, the range of A was determined to be

$$\mathcal{R}(A) = \{\mathbf{b}\colon \mathbf{b} = \begin{bmatrix} b_1 \\ b_2 \\ 3b_1 - b_2 \end{bmatrix}, \quad b_1 \text{ and } b_2 \text{ any real numbers}\}.$$

Thus b_1 and b_2 are unconstrained variables, and a vector $\mathbf{b}$ in $\mathcal{R}(A)$ can be decomposed as

$$\mathbf{b} = \begin{bmatrix} b_1 \\ b_2 \\ 3b_1 - b_2 \end{bmatrix} = \begin{bmatrix} b_1 \\ 0 \\ 3b_1 \end{bmatrix} + \begin{bmatrix} 0 \\ b_2 \\ -b_2 \end{bmatrix} = b_1 \begin{bmatrix} 1 \\ 0 \\ 3 \end{bmatrix} + b_2 \begin{bmatrix} 0 \\ 1 \\ -1 \end{bmatrix}. \tag{13}$$

If $\mathbf{u}_1$ and $\mathbf{u}_2$ are defined by

$$\mathbf{u}_1 = \begin{bmatrix} 1 \\ 0 \\ 3 \end{bmatrix} \quad \text{and} \quad \mathbf{u} = \begin{bmatrix} 0 \\ 1 \\ -1 \end{bmatrix},$$

then $\mathbf{u}_1$ and $\mathbf{u}_2$ are in $\mathcal{R}(A)$. One can easily check that $\{\mathbf{u}_1, \mathbf{u}_2\}$ is a linearly independent set, and it is evident from Eq. (13) that $\mathcal{R}(A)$ is spanned by $\mathbf{u}_1$ and $\mathbf{u}_2$. Therefore, $\{\mathbf{u}_1, \mathbf{u}_2\}$ is a basis for $\mathcal{R}(A)$. ■

The previous example illustrates how to obtain a basis for a subspace W, given an algebraic specification for W. The last two examples of this section illustrate two different techniques for constructing a basis for W from a spanning set.

EXAMPLE 6 Let W be the subspace of R^4 spanned by the set $S = \{\mathbf{v}_1, \mathbf{v}_2, \mathbf{v}_3, \mathbf{v}_4, \mathbf{v}_5\}$, where

$$\mathbf{v}_1 = \begin{bmatrix} 1 \\ 1 \\ 2 \\ -1 \end{bmatrix}, \quad \mathbf{v}_2 = \begin{bmatrix} 1 \\ 2 \\ 1 \\ 1 \end{bmatrix}, \quad \mathbf{v}_3 = \begin{bmatrix} 1 \\ 4 \\ -1 \\ 5 \end{bmatrix},$$

$$\mathbf{v}_4 = \begin{bmatrix} 1 \\ 0 \\ 4 \\ -1 \end{bmatrix}, \text{ and } \mathbf{v}_5 = \begin{bmatrix} 2 \\ 5 \\ 0 \\ 2 \end{bmatrix}.$$

Find a subset of S that is a basis for W.

Solution The procedure is suggested by Example 4. The idea is to solve the dependence relation

$$x_1\mathbf{v}_1 + x_2\mathbf{v}_2 + x_3\mathbf{v}_3 + x_4\mathbf{v}_4 + x_5\mathbf{v}_5 = \boldsymbol{\theta} \tag{14}$$

and then determine which of the $\mathbf{v}_j$'s can be eliminated. If V is the (4×5) matrix

$$V = [\mathbf{v}_1, \mathbf{v}_2, \mathbf{v}_3, \mathbf{v}_4, \mathbf{v}_5],$$

then the augmented matrix $[V \mid \boldsymbol{\theta}]$ reduces to

$$\begin{bmatrix} 1 & 0 & -2 & 0 & 1 & 0 \\ 0 & 1 & 3 & 0 & 2 & 0 \\ 0 & 0 & 0 & 1 & -1 & 0 \\ 0 & 0 & 0 & 0 & 0 & 0 \end{bmatrix}. \tag{15}$$

The system of equations with augmented matrix (15) has solution

$$\begin{aligned} x_1 &= 2x_3 - x_5 \\ x_2 &= -3x_3 - 2x_5 \\ x_4 &= x_5, \end{aligned} \tag{16}$$

where x_3 and x_5 are unconstrained variables. In particular, the set S is linearly dependent. Moreover, taking $x_3 = 1$ and $x_5 = 0$ yields $x_1 = 2$, $x_2 = -3$, and $x_4 = 0$. Thus Eq. (14) becomes

$$2\mathbf{v}_1 - 3\mathbf{v}_2 + \mathbf{v}_3 = \boldsymbol{\theta}. \tag{17}$$

Since Eq. (17) can be solved for $\mathbf{v}_3$,

$$\mathbf{v}_3 = -2\mathbf{v}_1 + 3\mathbf{v}_2,$$

it follows that $\mathbf{v}_3$ is redundant and can be removed from the spanning set. Similarly, setting $x_3 = 0$ and $x_5 = 1$ gives $x_1 = -1$, $x_2 = -2$, and $x_4 = 1$. In this case, Eq. (14) becomes

$$-\mathbf{v}_1 - 2\mathbf{v}_2 + \mathbf{v}_4 + \mathbf{v}_5 = \boldsymbol{\theta},$$

and hence

$$\mathbf{v}_5 = \mathbf{v}_1 + 2\mathbf{v}_2 - \mathbf{v}_4.$$

Since both $\mathbf{v}_3$ and $\mathbf{v}_5$ are in $\text{Sp}\{\mathbf{v}_1, \mathbf{v}_2, \mathbf{v}_4\}$, it follows (as in Example 4) that $\mathbf{v}_1$, $\mathbf{v}_2$, and $\mathbf{v}_4$ span W.

To see that the set $\{\mathbf{v}_1, \mathbf{v}_2, \mathbf{v}_4\}$ is linearly independent, note that the dependence relation

$$x_1\mathbf{v}_1 + x_2\mathbf{v}_2 + x_4\mathbf{v}_4 = \boldsymbol{\theta} \tag{18}$$

is just Eq. (14) with $\mathbf{v}_3$ and $\mathbf{v}_5$ removed. Thus the augmented matrix $[\mathbf{v}_1, \mathbf{v}_2, \mathbf{v}_4 \,|\, \boldsymbol{\theta}]$, for Eq. (18) reduces to

$$\begin{bmatrix} 1 & 0 & 0 & 0 \\ 0 & 1 & 0 & 0 \\ 0 & 0 & 1 & 0 \\ 0 & 0 & 0 & 0 \end{bmatrix}, \tag{19}$$

which is matrix (15) with the third and fifth columns removed. From matrix (19), it is clear that Eq. (18) has only the trivial solution; so $\{\mathbf{v}_1, \mathbf{v}_2, \mathbf{v}_4\}$ is a linearly independent set and therefore a basis for W.

The procedure demonstrated in the preceding example can be outlined as follows:

1. A spanning set $S\{\mathbf{v}_1, \ldots, \mathbf{v}_m\}$ for a subspace W is given.
2. Solve the vector equation
$$x_1\mathbf{v}_1 + \cdots + x_m\mathbf{v}_m = \boldsymbol{\theta}. \tag{20}$$
3. If Eq. (20) has only the trivial solution $x_1 = \cdots = x_m = 0$, then S is a linearly independent set and hence is a basis for W.
4. If Eq. (20) has nontrivial solutions, then there are unconstrained variables. For each x_j that is designated as an unconstrained variable, delete the vector $\mathbf{v}_j$ from the set S. The remaining vectors constitute a basis for W.

Our final technique for constructing a basis uses Theorem 7.

THEOREM 7 If the nonzero matrix A is row equivalent to the matrix B in echelon form, then the nonzero rows of B form a basis for the row space of A.

Proof By Theorem 6, A and B have the same row space. It follows that the nonzero rows of B span the row space of A. Since the nonzero rows of an echelon matrix are linearly independent vectors, it follows that the nonzero rows of B form a basis for the row space of A.

EXAMPLE 7 Let W be the subspace of R^4 given in Example 6. Use Theorem 7 to construct a basis for W.

Solution As in Example 6, let V be the (4×5) matrix

$$V = [\mathbf{v}_1, \mathbf{v}_2, \mathbf{v}_3, \mathbf{v}_4, \mathbf{v}_5].$$

Thus W can be viewed as the row space of the matrix V^T, where

$$V^T = \begin{bmatrix} 1 & 1 & 2 & -1 \\ 1 & 2 & 1 & 1 \\ 1 & 4 & -1 & 5 \\ 1 & 0 & 4 & -1 \\ 2 & 5 & 0 & 2 \end{bmatrix}.$$

Since V^T is row equivalent to the matrix

$$B^T = \begin{bmatrix} 1 & 0 & 0 & -9 \\ 0 & 1 & 0 & 4 \\ 0 & 0 & 1 & 2 \\ 0 & 0 & 0 & 0 \\ 0 & 0 & 0 & 0 \end{bmatrix}$$

in echelon form, it follows from Theorem 7 that the nonzero rows of B^T form a basis for the row space of V^T. Consequently the nonzero columns of

$$B = \begin{bmatrix} 1 & 0 & 0 & 0 & 0 \\ 0 & 1 & 0 & 0 & 0 \\ 0 & 0 & 1 & 0 & 0 \\ -9 & 4 & 2 & 0 & 0 \end{bmatrix}$$

are a basis for W. Specifically, the set $\{\mathbf{u}_1, \mathbf{u}_2, \mathbf{u}_3\}$ is a basis of W, where

$$\mathbf{u}_1 = \begin{bmatrix} 1 \\ 0 \\ 0 \\ -9 \end{bmatrix}, \quad \mathbf{u}_2 = \begin{bmatrix} 0 \\ 1 \\ 0 \\ 4 \end{bmatrix}, \quad \text{and} \quad \mathbf{u}_3 = \begin{bmatrix} 0 \\ 0 \\ 1 \\ 2 \end{bmatrix}.$$ ■

The procedure used in the preceding example can be summarized as follows:

1. A spanning set $S = \{\mathbf{v}_1, \ldots, \mathbf{v}_m\}$ for a subspace W of R^n is given.
2. Let V be the $(n \times m)$ matrix $V = [\mathbf{v}_1, \ldots \mathbf{v}_m]$. Use elementary row operations to transform V^T to a matrix B^T in echelon form.
3. The nonzero columns of B are a basis for W.

3.4 EXERCISES

In Exercises 1–8, let W be the subspace of R^4 consisting of vectors of the form

$$\mathbf{x} = \begin{bmatrix} x_1 \\ x_2 \\ x_3 \\ x_4 \end{bmatrix}.$$

Find a basis for W when the components of $\mathbf{x}$ satisfy the given conditions.

1. $\begin{aligned} x_1 + x_2 - x_3 \quad &= 0 \\ x_2 \quad - x_4 &= 0 \end{aligned}$

2. $\begin{aligned} x_1 + x_2 - x_3 + x_4 &= 0 \\ x_2 - 2x_3 - x_4 &= 0 \end{aligned}$

3. $x_1 - x_2 + x_3 - 3x_4 = 0$

4. $x_1 - x_2 + x_3 = 0$

5. $x_1 + x_2 = 0$

6. $\begin{aligned} x_1 - x_2 \quad &= 0 \\ x_2 - 2x_3 \quad &= 0 \\ x_3 - x_4 &= 0 \end{aligned}$

7. $\begin{aligned} -x_1 + 2x_2 \quad - x_4 &= 0 \\ x_2 + x_3 \quad &= 0 \end{aligned}$

8. $\begin{aligned} x_1 - x_2 - x_3 + x_4 &= 0 \\ x_2 + x_3 \quad &= 0 \end{aligned}$

9. Let W be the subspace described in Exercise 1. For each vector $\mathbf{x}$ that follows, determine if $\mathbf{x}$ is in W. If $\mathbf{x}$ is in W, then express $\mathbf{x}$ as a linear combination of the basis vectors found in Exercise 1.

a) $\mathbf{x} = \begin{bmatrix} 1 \\ 1 \\ 2 \\ 1 \end{bmatrix}$ **b)** $\mathbf{x} = \begin{bmatrix} -1 \\ 2 \\ 3 \\ 2 \end{bmatrix}$

c) $\mathbf{x} = \begin{bmatrix} 3 \\ -3 \\ 0 \\ -3 \end{bmatrix}$ **d)** $\mathbf{x} = \begin{bmatrix} 2 \\ 0 \\ 2 \\ 0 \end{bmatrix}$

10. Let W be the subspace described in Exercise 2. For each vector $\mathbf{x}$ that follows, determine if $\mathbf{x}$ is in W. If $\mathbf{x}$ is in W, then express $\mathbf{x}$ as a linear combination of the basis vectors found in Exercise 2.

a) $\mathbf{x} = \begin{bmatrix} -3 \\ 3 \\ 1 \\ 1 \end{bmatrix}$ **b)** $\mathbf{x} = \begin{bmatrix} 0 \\ 3 \\ 2 \\ -1 \end{bmatrix}$

c) $\mathbf{x} = \begin{bmatrix} 7 \\ 8 \\ 3 \\ 2 \end{bmatrix}$ **d)** $\mathbf{x} = \begin{bmatrix} 4 \\ -2 \\ 0 \\ -2 \end{bmatrix}$

In Exercises 11–16:

a) Find a matrix B in reduced echelon form such that B is row equivalent to the given matrix A.

b) Find a basis for the null space of A.

c) As in Example 6, find a basis for the range of A that consists of columns of A. For each column, $\mathbf{A}_j$, of A that does not appear in the basis, express $\mathbf{A}_j$ as a linear combination of the basis vectors.

d) Exhibit a basis for the row space of A.

11. $A = \begin{bmatrix} 1 & 2 & 3 & -1 \\ 3 & 5 & 8 & -2 \\ 1 & 1 & 2 & 0 \end{bmatrix}$

12. $A = \begin{bmatrix} 1 & 1 & 2 \\ 1 & 1 & 2 \\ 2 & 3 & 5 \end{bmatrix}$

13. $A = \begin{bmatrix} 1 & 2 & 1 & 0 \\ 2 & 5 & 3 & -1 \\ 2 & 2 & 0 & 2 \\ 0 & 1 & 1 & -1 \end{bmatrix}$

14. $A = \begin{bmatrix} 2 & 2 & 0 \\ 2 & 1 & 1 \\ 2 & 3 & 0 \end{bmatrix}$

15. $A = \begin{bmatrix} 1 & 2 & 1 \\ 2 & 4 & 1 \\ 3 & 6 & 2 \end{bmatrix}$

16. $A = \begin{bmatrix} 2 & 1 & 2 \\ 2 & 2 & 1 \\ 2 & 3 & 0 \end{bmatrix}$

17. Use the technique illustrated in Example 7 to obtain a basis for the range of A, where A is the matrix given in Exercise 11.

18. Repeat Exercise 17 for the matrix given in Exercise 12.

19. Repeat Exercise 17 for the matrix given in Exercise 13.

20. Repeat Exercise 17 for the matrix given in Exercise 14.

In Exercises 21–24 for the given set S:

a) Find a subset of S that is a basis for Sp(S) using the technique illustrated in Example 6.

b) Find a basis for Sp(S) using the technique illustrated in Example 7.

21. $S = \left\{ \begin{bmatrix} 1 \\ 2 \end{bmatrix}, \begin{bmatrix} 2 \\ 4 \end{bmatrix} \right\}$

22. $S = \left\{ \begin{bmatrix} 1 \\ 2 \end{bmatrix}, \begin{bmatrix} 2 \\ 1 \end{bmatrix}, \begin{bmatrix} 3 \\ 2 \end{bmatrix} \right\}$

23. $S = \left\{ \begin{bmatrix} 1 \\ 2 \\ 1 \end{bmatrix}, \begin{bmatrix} 2 \\ 5 \\ 0 \end{bmatrix}, \begin{bmatrix} 3 \\ 7 \\ 1 \end{bmatrix}, \begin{bmatrix} 1 \\ 1 \\ 3 \end{bmatrix} \right\}$

24. $S = \left\{ \begin{bmatrix} 1 \\ 2 \\ -1 \\ 3 \end{bmatrix}, \begin{bmatrix} -2 \\ 1 \\ 2 \\ -1 \end{bmatrix}, \begin{bmatrix} -1 \\ -1 \\ 1 \\ -3 \end{bmatrix}, \begin{bmatrix} -2 \\ 2 \\ 2 \\ 0 \end{bmatrix} \right\}$

25. Find a basis for the null space of each of the following matrices.

a) $\begin{bmatrix} 1 & 0 & 0 \\ 1 & 0 & 1 \end{bmatrix}$ b) $\begin{bmatrix} 1 & 1 & 0 \\ 1 & 1 & 0 \end{bmatrix}$

c) $\begin{bmatrix} 1 & 1 & 0 \\ 1 & 1 & 1 \end{bmatrix}$

26. Find a basis for the range of each matrix in Exercise 25.

27. Let $S = \{\mathbf{v}_1, \mathbf{v}_2, \mathbf{v}_3\}$, where

$$\mathbf{v}_1 = \begin{bmatrix} 1 \\ 2 \\ 1 \end{bmatrix}, \quad \mathbf{v}_2 = \begin{bmatrix} -1 \\ -1 \\ 1 \end{bmatrix}, \quad \text{and}$$

$$\mathbf{v}_3 = \begin{bmatrix} -1 \\ 1 \\ 5 \end{bmatrix}.$$

Show that S is a linearly dependent set, and verify that $\text{Sp}\{\mathbf{v}_1, \mathbf{v}_2, \mathbf{v}_3\} = \text{Sp}\{\mathbf{v}_1, \mathbf{v}_2\}$.

28. Let $S = \{\mathbf{v}_1, \mathbf{v}_2, \mathbf{v}_3\}$, where

$$\mathbf{v}_1 = \begin{bmatrix} 1 \\ 0 \end{bmatrix}, \quad \mathbf{v}_2 = \begin{bmatrix} 0 \\ 1 \end{bmatrix}, \quad \text{and}$$

$$\mathbf{v}_3 = \begin{bmatrix} -1 \\ 1 \end{bmatrix}.$$

Find every subset of S that is a basis for R^2.

29. Let $S = \{\mathbf{v}_1, \mathbf{v}_2, \mathbf{v}_3, \mathbf{v}_4\}$, where

$$\mathbf{v}_1 = \begin{bmatrix} 1 \\ 2 \\ 1 \end{bmatrix}, \quad \mathbf{v}_2 = \begin{bmatrix} -1 \\ -1 \\ 1 \end{bmatrix},$$

$$\mathbf{v}_3 = \begin{bmatrix} -1 \\ 1 \\ 7 \end{bmatrix}, \quad \text{and} \quad \mathbf{v}_4 = \begin{bmatrix} -2 \\ -4 \\ -4 \end{bmatrix}.$$

Find every subset of S that is a basis for R^3.

30. Let $B = \{\mathbf{v}_1, \mathbf{v}_2, \mathbf{v}_3\}$ be a set of linearly independent vectors in R^3. Prove that B is a basis for R^3. [*Hint:* Use Theorem 13 of Section 1.7 to show that B is a spanning set for R^3.]

31. Let $B = \{\mathbf{v}_1, \mathbf{v}_2, \mathbf{v}_3\}$ be a subset of R^3 such that $\text{Sp}(B) = R^3$. Prove that B is a basis for R^3. [*Hint:* Use Theorem 13 of Section 1.7 to show that B is a linearly independent set.]

In Exercises 32–35, determine whether the given set S is a basis for R^3.

32. $S = \left\{ \begin{bmatrix} 1 \\ -1 \\ -2 \end{bmatrix}, \begin{bmatrix} 1 \\ 1 \\ 2 \end{bmatrix}, \begin{bmatrix} 2 \\ -3 \\ -3 \end{bmatrix} \right\}$

33. $S = \left\{ \begin{bmatrix} 1 \\ 1 \\ -2 \end{bmatrix}, \begin{bmatrix} 2 \\ 5 \\ 2 \end{bmatrix}, \begin{bmatrix} 1 \\ 3 \\ 2 \end{bmatrix} \right\}$

34. $S = \left\{ \begin{bmatrix} 1 \\ -1 \\ -2 \end{bmatrix}, \begin{bmatrix} 1 \\ 1 \\ 2 \end{bmatrix}, \begin{bmatrix} 2 \\ -3 \\ -3 \end{bmatrix}, \begin{bmatrix} 1 \\ 4 \\ 5 \end{bmatrix} \right\}$

35. $S = \left\{ \begin{bmatrix} 1 \\ 1 \\ -2 \end{bmatrix}, \begin{bmatrix} 2 \\ 5 \\ 2 \end{bmatrix} \right\}$

36. Find a vector $\mathbf{w}$ in R^3 such that $\mathbf{w}$ is not a linear combination of $\mathbf{v}_1$ and $\mathbf{v}_2$:

$$\mathbf{v}_1 = \begin{bmatrix} 1 \\ 2 \\ -1 \end{bmatrix}, \quad \text{and} \quad \mathbf{v}_2 = \begin{bmatrix} 2 \\ -1 \\ -2 \end{bmatrix}.$$

37. Prove that every basis for R^2 contains exactly two vectors. Proceed by showing the following:

a) A basis for R^2 cannot have more than two vectors.

b) A basis for R^2 cannot have one vector. [*Hint:* Suppose that a basis for R^2 could contain one vector. Represent $\mathbf{e}_1$ and $\mathbf{e}_2$ in terms of the basis and obtain a contradiction.]

38. Show that any spanning set for R^n must contain at least n vectors. Proceed by showing that if $\mathbf{u}_1, \mathbf{u}_2, \ldots, \mathbf{u}_p$ are vectors in R^n, and if $p < n$, then there is a nonzero vector $\mathbf{v}$ in R^n such that $\mathbf{v}^T\mathbf{u}_i = 0$, $1 \le i \le p$. [*Hint:* Write the constraints as a $(p \times n)$ system and use Theorem 4 of Section 1.3.] Given $\mathbf{v}$ as above, can $\mathbf{v}$ be a linear combination of $\mathbf{u}_1, \mathbf{u}_2, \ldots, \mathbf{u}_p$?

39. Recalling Exercise 38, prove that every basis for R^n contains exactly n vectors.

3.5 DIMENSION

In this section we translate the geometric concept of dimension into algebraic terms. Clearly R^2 and R^3 have dimension 2 and 3, respectively, since these vector spaces are simply algebraic interpretations of two-space and three-space. It would be natural to extrapolate from these two cases and declare that R^n has dimension n for each positive integer n; indeed, we have earlier referred to elements of R^n as n-dimensional vectors. But if W is a subspace of R^n, how is the dimension of W to be determined? An examination of the subspace, W, of R^3 defined by

$$W = \{\mathbf{x}\colon \mathbf{x} = \begin{bmatrix} x_2 - 2x_3 \\ x_2 \\ x_3 \end{bmatrix}, \quad x_2 \text{ and } x_3 \text{ any real numbers}\}$$

suggests a possibility. Geometrically, W is the plane with equation $x = y - 2z$, so naturally the dimension of W is 2. The techniques of the previous section show that W has a basis $\{\mathbf{v}_1, \mathbf{v}_2\}$ consisting of the two vectors

$$\mathbf{v}_1 = \begin{bmatrix} 1 \\ 1 \\ 0 \end{bmatrix} \quad \text{and} \quad \mathbf{v}_2 = \begin{bmatrix} -2 \\ 0 \\ 1 \end{bmatrix}.$$

Thus in this case the dimension of W is equal to the number of vectors in a basis for W.

The Definition of Dimension

More generally, for any subspace W of R^n, we wish to define the dimension of W to be the number of vectors in a basis for W. We have seen, however, that a subspace W

may have many different bases. In fact, Exercise 30 of Section 3.4 shows that any set of three linearly independent vectors in R^3 is a basis for R^3. Therefore, for the concept of dimension to make sense, we must show that all bases for a given subspace W contain the same number of vectors. This fact will be an easy consequence of the following theorem.

THEOREM 8 Let W be a subspace of R^n, and let $B = \{\mathbf{w}_1, \mathbf{w}_2, \ldots, \mathbf{w}_p\}$ be a spanning set for W containing p vectors. Then any set of $p+1$ or more vectors in W is linearly dependent.

Proof Let $\{\mathbf{s}_1, \mathbf{s}_2, \ldots, \mathbf{s}_m\}$ be any set of m vectors in W, where $m > p$. To show that this set is linearly dependent, we first express each $\mathbf{s}_i$ in terms of the spanning set B:

$$\begin{aligned} \mathbf{s}_1 &= a_{11}\mathbf{w}_1 + a_{21}\mathbf{w}_2 + \cdots + a_{p1}\mathbf{w}_p \\ \mathbf{s}_2 &= a_{12}\mathbf{w}_1 + a_{22}\mathbf{w}_2 + \cdots + a_{p2}\mathbf{w}_p \\ &\vdots \\ \mathbf{s}_m &= a_{1m}\mathbf{w}_1 + a_{2m}\mathbf{w}_2 + \cdots + a_{pm}\mathbf{w}_p. \end{aligned} \tag{1}$$

To show that $\{\mathbf{s}_1, \mathbf{s}_2, \ldots, \mathbf{s}_m\}$ is linearly dependent, we must show that there is a nontrivial solution of

$$c_1\mathbf{s}_1 + c_2\mathbf{s}_2 + \cdots + c_m\mathbf{s}_m = \boldsymbol{\theta}. \tag{2}$$

Now using system (1), we can rewrite Eq. (2) in terms of the vectors in B as

$$\begin{aligned} &c_1(a_{11}\mathbf{w}_1 + a_{21}\mathbf{w}_2 + \cdots + a_{p1}\mathbf{w}_p) + \\ &c_2(a_{12}\mathbf{w}_1 + a_{22}\mathbf{w}_2 + \cdots + a_{p2}\mathbf{w}_p) + \\ &\cdots + c_m(a_{1m}\mathbf{w}_1 + a_{2m}\mathbf{w}_2 + \cdots + a_{pm}\mathbf{w}_p) = \boldsymbol{\theta}. \end{aligned} \tag{3a}$$

Equation (3a) can be regrouped as

$$\begin{aligned} &(c_1a_{11} + c_2a_{12} + \cdots + c_ma_{1m})\mathbf{w}_1 + \\ &(c_1a_{21} + c_2a_{22} + \cdots + c_ma_{2m})\mathbf{w}_2 + \\ &\cdots + (c_1a_{p1} + c_2a_{p2} + \cdots + c_ma_{pm})\mathbf{w}_p = \boldsymbol{\theta}. \end{aligned} \tag{3b}$$

Now finding $c_1, c_2, \ldots, c_m$ to satisfy Eq. (2) is the same as finding $c_1, c_2, \ldots, c_m$ to satisfy Eq. (3b). Furthermore, we can clearly satisfy Eq. (3b) if we can choose zero for each coefficient of each $\mathbf{w}_i$. Therefore, to obtain one solution of Eq. (3b), it suffices to solve the system

$$\begin{aligned} a_{11}c_1 + a_{12}c_2 + \cdots + a_{1m}c_m &= 0 \\ a_{21}c_1 + a_{22}c_2 + \cdots + a_{2m}c_m &= 0 \\ \vdots \\ a_{p1}c_1 + a_{p2}c_2 + \cdots + a_{pm}c_m &= 0. \end{aligned} \tag{4}$$

[Recall that each a_{ij} is a specified constant determined by system (1), whereas each c_i is an unknown parameter of Eq. (2).] The homogeneous system in (4) has more unknowns than equations, so by Theorem 4 of Section 1.3 there is a nontrivial solution to system (4). But a solution to system (4) is also a solution to Eq. (2), so Eq. (2) has a nontrivial solution, and the theorem is established. ∎

As an immediate corollary of Theorem 8, we can show that all bases for a subspace contain the same number of vectors.

COROLLARY Let W be a subspace of R^n, and let $B = \{\mathbf{w}_1, \mathbf{w}_2, \ldots, \mathbf{w}_p\}$ be a basis for W containing p vectors. Then every basis for W contains p vectors.

Proof Let $Q = \{\mathbf{u}_1, \mathbf{u}_2, \ldots, \mathbf{u}_r\}$ be any basis for W. Since Q is a spanning set for W, by Theorem 8 any set of $r + 1$ or more vectors in W is linearly dependent. Since B is a linearly independent set of p vectors in W, we know that $p \le r$. Similarly, since B is a spanning set of p vectors for W, any set of $p + 1$ or more vectors in W is linearly dependent. By assumption, Q is a set of r linearly independent vectors in W; so $r \le p$. Now, since we have $p \le r$ and $r \le p$, it must be that $r = p$. ∎

Given that every basis for a subspace contains the same number of vectors, we can make the following definition without any possibility of ambiguity.

DEFINITION 5 Let W be a subspace of R^n. If W has a basis $B = \{\mathbf{w}_1, \mathbf{w}_2, \ldots, \mathbf{w}_p\}$ of p vectors, then we say that W is a subspace of ***dimension p***, and we write $\dim(W) = p$.

In Exercise 30, the reader is asked to show that every nonzero subspace of R^n does have a basis. Thus a value for dimension can be assigned to any subspace of R^n, where for completeness we define $\dim(W) = 0$ if W is the zero subspace.

Since R^3 has a basis $\{\mathbf{e}_1, \mathbf{e}_2, \mathbf{e}_3\}$ containing three vectors, we see that $\dim(R^3) = 3$. In general, R^n has a basis $\{\mathbf{e}_1, \mathbf{e}_2, \ldots, \mathbf{e}_n\}$ that contains n vectors; so $\dim(R^n) = n$. Thus the definition of dimension—the number of vectors in a basis—agrees with the usual terminology; R^3 is three-dimensional, and in general, R^n is n-dimensional.

EXAMPLE 1 Let W be the subspace of R^3 defined by

$$W = \{\mathbf{x}\colon \mathbf{x} = \begin{bmatrix} x_1 \\ x_2 \\ x_3 \end{bmatrix}, \quad x_1 = -2x_3, x_2 = x_3, x_3 \text{ arbitrary}\}.$$

Exhibit a basis for W and determine $\dim(W)$.

Solution A vector $\mathbf{x}$ in W can be written in the form

$$\mathbf{x} = \begin{bmatrix} -2x_3 \\ x_3 \\ x_3 \end{bmatrix} = x_3 \begin{bmatrix} -2 \\ 1 \\ 1 \end{bmatrix}.$$

Therefore, the set $\{\mathbf{u}\}$ is a basis for W, where

$$\mathbf{u} = \begin{bmatrix} -2 \\ 1 \\ 1 \end{bmatrix}.$$

It follows that $\dim(W) = 1$. Geometrically, W is the line through the origin and through the point with coordinates $(-2, 1, 1)$, so again the definition of dimension coincides with our geometric intuition.

The next example illustrates the importance of the corollary to Theorem 8.

EXAMPLE 2 Let W be the subspace of R^3, $W = \text{span}\{\mathbf{u}_1, \mathbf{u}_2, \mathbf{u}_3, \mathbf{u}_4\}$, where

$$\mathbf{u}_1 = \begin{bmatrix} 1 \\ 1 \\ 2 \end{bmatrix}, \quad \mathbf{u}_2 = \begin{bmatrix} 2 \\ 4 \\ 0 \end{bmatrix}, \quad \mathbf{u}_3 = \begin{bmatrix} 3 \\ 5 \\ 2 \end{bmatrix}, \quad \text{and} \quad \mathbf{u}_4 = \begin{bmatrix} 2 \\ 5 \\ -2 \end{bmatrix}.$$

Use the techniques illustrated in Examples 5, 6, and 7 of Section 3.4 to find three different bases for W. Give the dimension of W.

Solution

(a) The technique used in Example 5 consisted of finding a basis for W by using the algebraic specification for W. In particular, let $\mathbf{b}$ be a vector in R^3:

$$\mathbf{b} = \begin{bmatrix} a \\ b \\ c \end{bmatrix}.$$

Then $\mathbf{b}$ is in W if and only if the vector equation

$$x_1\mathbf{u}_1 + x_2\mathbf{u}_2 + x_3\mathbf{u}_3 + x_4\mathbf{u}_4 = \mathbf{b} \tag{5a}$$

is consistent. The matrix equation for (5a) is $U\mathbf{x} = \mathbf{b}$, where U is the (3×4) matrix $U = [\mathbf{u}_1, \mathbf{u}_2, \mathbf{u}_3, \mathbf{u}_4]$. Now, the augmented matrix $[U \mid \mathbf{b}]$ is row equivalent to the matrix

$$\begin{bmatrix} 1 & 0 & 1 & -1 & 2a - b \\ 0 & 1 & 1 & 3/2 & -a/2 + b/2 \\ 0 & 0 & 0 & 0 & -4a + 2b + c \end{bmatrix}. \tag{5b}$$

Thus $\mathbf{b}$ is in W if and only if $-4a + 2b + c = 0$ or, equivalently, $c = 4a - 2b$. The subspace W can then be described by

$$W = \left\{\mathbf{b}\colon \mathbf{b} = \begin{bmatrix} a \\ b \\ 4a - 2b \end{bmatrix},\ a \text{ and } b \text{ any real numbers}\right\}.$$

From this description it follows that W has a basis $\{\mathbf{v}_1, \mathbf{v}_2\}$, where

$$\mathbf{v}_1 = \begin{bmatrix} 1 \\ 0 \\ 4 \end{bmatrix} \quad \text{and} \quad \mathbf{v}_2 = \begin{bmatrix} 0 \\ 1 \\ -2 \end{bmatrix}.$$

(b) The technique used in Example 6 consisted of discarding redundant vectors from a spanning set for W. In particular since $\{\mathbf{u}_1, \mathbf{u}_2, \mathbf{u}_3, \mathbf{u}_4\}$ spans W, this technique gives a basis for W that is a subset of $\{\mathbf{u}_1, \mathbf{u}_2, \mathbf{u}_3, \mathbf{u}_4\}$. To obtain such a subset, solve the dependence relation

$$x_1\mathbf{u}_1 + x_2\mathbf{u}_2 + x_3\mathbf{u}_3 + x_4\mathbf{u}_4 = \boldsymbol{\theta}. \tag{5c}$$

Note that Eq. (5c) is just Eq. (5a) with $\mathbf{b} = \boldsymbol{\theta}$. It is easily seen from matrix (5b) that Eq. (5c) is equivalent to the reduced system

$$\begin{aligned} x_1 \quad + x_3 \quad - \quad\quad x_4 &= 0 \\ x_2 + x_3 + (3/2)x_4 &= 0. \end{aligned} \tag{5d}$$

Backsolving (5d) yields

$$\begin{aligned} x_1 &= -x_3 + x_4 \\ x_2 &= -x_3 - (3/2)x_4, \end{aligned}$$

where x_3 and x_4 are arbitrary. Therefore, the vectors $\mathbf{u}_3$ and $\mathbf{u}_4$ can be deleted from the spanning set for W, leaving $\{\mathbf{u}_1, \mathbf{u}_2\}$ as a basis for W.

(c) Let U be the (3×4) matrix whose columns span W, $U = [\mathbf{u}_1, \mathbf{u}_2, \mathbf{u}_3, \mathbf{u}_4]$. Following the technique of Example 7, reduce U^T to the matrix

$$C^T = \begin{bmatrix} 1 & 0 & 4 \\ 0 & 1 & -2 \\ 0 & 0 & 0 \\ 0 & 0 & 0 \end{bmatrix}$$

in echelon form. In this case the nonzero columns of

$$C = \begin{bmatrix} 1 & 0 & 0 & 0 \\ 0 & 1 & 0 & 0 \\ 4 & -2 & 0 & 0 \end{bmatrix}$$

form a basis for W; that is, $\{\mathbf{w}_1, \mathbf{w}_2\}$ is a basis for W, where

$$\mathbf{w}_1 = \begin{bmatrix} 1 \\ 0 \\ 4 \end{bmatrix} \quad \text{and} \quad \mathbf{w}_2 = \begin{bmatrix} 0 \\ 1 \\ -2 \end{bmatrix}.$$

In each case the basis obtained for W contains two vectors, so $\dim(W) = 2$. Indeed, viewed geometrically, W is the plane with equation $-4x + 2y + z = 0$. ■

Properties of a p-Dimensional Subspace

An important feature of dimension is that a p-dimensional subspace W has many of the same properties as R^p. For example, Theorem 11 of Section 1.7 shows that any set of $p + 1$ or more vectors in R^p is linearly dependent. The following theorem shows that this same property and others hold in W when $\dim(W) = p$.

THEOREM 9 Let W be a subspace of R^n with $\dim(W) = p$.

1. Any set of $p + 1$ or more vectors in W is linearly dependent.
2. Any set of fewer than p vectors in W does not span W.
3. Any set of p linearly independent vectors in W is a basis for W.
4. Any set of p vectors that spans W is a basis for W.

Proof Property 1 follows immediately from Theorem 8, because $\dim(W) = p$ means that W has a basis (and hence a spanning set) of p vectors.

Property 2 is equivalent to the statement that a spanning set for W must contain at least p vectors. Again, this is an immediate consequence of Theorem 8.

To establish property 3, let $\{\mathbf{u}_1, \mathbf{u}_2, \ldots, \mathbf{u}_p\}$ be a set of p linearly independent vectors in W. To see that the given set spans W, let $\mathbf{v}$ be any vector in W. By property 1, the set $\{\mathbf{v}, \mathbf{u}_1, \mathbf{u}_2, \ldots, \mathbf{u}_p\}$ is a linearly dependent set of vectors because the set contains $p + 1$ vectors. Thus there are scalars $a_0, a_1, \ldots, a_p$ (not all of which are zero) such that

$$a_0\mathbf{v} + a_1\mathbf{u}_1 + a_2\mathbf{u}_2 + \cdots + a_p\mathbf{u}_p = \boldsymbol{\theta}. \tag{6}$$

In addition, in Eq. (6), a_0 cannot be zero because $\{\mathbf{u}_1, \mathbf{u}_2, \ldots, \mathbf{u}_p\}$ is a linearly independent set. Therefore, Eq. (6) can be rewritten as

$$\mathbf{v} = (-1/a_0)[a_1\mathbf{u}_1 + a_2\mathbf{u}_2 + \cdots + a_p\mathbf{u}_p]. \tag{7}$$

It is clear from Eq. (7) that any vector in W can be expressed as a linear combination of $\mathbf{u}_1, \mathbf{u}_2, \ldots, \mathbf{u}_p$, so the given linearly independent set also spans W. Therefore, the set is a basis.

The proof of property 4 is left as an exercise. ■

EXAMPLE 3 Let W be the subspace of R^3 given in Example 2, and let $\{\mathbf{v}_1, \mathbf{v}_2, \mathbf{v}_3\}$ be the subset of W defined by

$$\mathbf{v}_1 = \begin{bmatrix} 1 \\ -1 \\ 6 \end{bmatrix}, \quad \mathbf{v}_2 = \begin{bmatrix} 1 \\ 2 \\ 0 \end{bmatrix}, \quad \text{and} \quad \mathbf{v}_3 = \begin{bmatrix} 2 \\ 1 \\ 6 \end{bmatrix}.$$

Determine which of the subsets $\{\mathbf{v}_1\}$, $\{\mathbf{v}_2\}$, $\{\mathbf{v}_1, \mathbf{v}_2\}$, $\{\mathbf{v}_1, \mathbf{v}_3\}$, $\{\mathbf{v}_2, \mathbf{v}_3\}$, and $\{\mathbf{v}_1, \mathbf{v}_2, \mathbf{v}_3\}$ is a basis for W.

Solution In Example 2, the subspace W was described as

$$W = \{\mathbf{b}\colon \mathbf{b} = \begin{bmatrix} a \\ b \\ 4a - 2b \end{bmatrix}, \quad a \text{ and } b \text{ any real numbers}\}. \tag{8}$$

Using Eq. (8), we can easily check that $\mathbf{v}_1$, $\mathbf{v}_2$, and $\mathbf{v}_3$ are in W. We saw further in Example 2 that $\dim(W) = 2$. By Theorem 9, property 2, neither of the sets $\{\mathbf{v}_1\}$ or $\{\mathbf{v}_2\}$ spans W. By Theorem 9, property 1, the set $\{\mathbf{v}_1, \mathbf{v}_2, \mathbf{v}_3\}$ is linearly dependent. We can easily check that each of the sets $\{\mathbf{v}_1, \mathbf{v}_2\}$, $\{\mathbf{v}_1, \mathbf{v}_3\}$, and $\{\mathbf{v}_2, \mathbf{v}_3\}$, is linearly independent, so by Theorem 9, property 3, each is a basis for W. ■

The Rank of a Matrix

In this subsection we use the concept of dimension to characterize nonsingular matrices and to determine precisely when a system of linear equations $A\mathbf{x} = \mathbf{b}$ is consistent. For an $(m \times n)$ matrix A, the dimension of the null space is called the ***nullity of** A*, and the dimension of the range of A is called the ***rank of** A*. The following example will illustrate the relationship between the rank of A and the nullity of A, as well as the relationship between the rank of A and the dimension of the row space of A.

EXAMPLE 4 Find the rank, nullity, and dimension of the row space for the matrix A, where

$$A = \begin{bmatrix} 1 & 1 & 1 & 2 \\ -1 & 0 & 2 & -3 \\ 2 & 4 & 8 & 5 \end{bmatrix}.$$

Solution To find the dimension of the row space of A, observe that A is row equivalent to the matrix

$$B = \begin{bmatrix} 1 & 0 & -2 & 0 \\ 0 & 1 & 3 & 0 \\ 0 & 0 & 0 & 1 \end{bmatrix},$$

and B is in echelon form. Since the nonzero rows of B form a basis for the row space of A, the row space of A has dimension 3.

To find the nullity of A, we must determine the dimension of the null space. Since the homogeneous system $A\mathbf{x} = \boldsymbol{\theta}$ is equivalent to $B\mathbf{x} = \boldsymbol{\theta}$, the null space of A can be determined by solving $B\mathbf{x} = \boldsymbol{\theta}$. This gives

$$\begin{aligned} x_1 &= 2x_3 \\ x_2 &= -3x_3 \\ x_4 &= 0. \end{aligned}$$

Thus $\mathcal{N}(A)$ can be described by

$$\mathcal{N}(A) = \{\mathbf{x}\colon \mathbf{x} = \begin{bmatrix} 2x_3 \\ -3x_3 \\ x_3 \\ 0 \end{bmatrix}, \quad x_3 \text{ any real number}\}.$$

It now follows that the nullity of A is 1 because the vector

$$\mathbf{v} = \begin{bmatrix} 2 \\ -3 \\ 1 \\ 0 \end{bmatrix}$$

forms a basis for $\mathcal{N}(A)$.

To find the rank of A, we must determine the dimension of the range of A. Recall that $\mathcal{R}(A)$, the range of A, equals the column space of A, so a basis for $\mathcal{R}(A)$ can be found by reducing A^T to echelon form. It is straightforward to show that A^T is row equivalent to the matrix C^T, where

$$C^T = \begin{bmatrix} 1 & 0 & 0 \\ 0 & 1 & 0 \\ 0 & 0 & 1 \\ 0 & 0 & 0 \end{bmatrix}.$$

The nonzero columns of the matrix C,

$$C = \begin{bmatrix} 1 & 0 & 0 & 0 \\ 0 & 1 & 0 & 0 \\ 0 & 0 & 1 & 0 \end{bmatrix},$$

form a basis for $\mathcal{R}(A)$. Thus the rank of A is 3.

Note in the previous example that the row space of A is a subspace of R^4, whereas the column space (or range) of A is a subspace of R^3. Thus they are entirely different subspaces; even so, the dimensions are the same, and the next theorem states that this is always the case.

THEOREM 10 If A is an $(m \times n)$ matrix, then the rank of A is equal to the rank of A^T.

The proof of Theorem 10 will be given at the end of this section. Note that the range of A^T is equal to the column space of A^T. But the column space of A^T is precisely the row space of A, so the following corollary is actually a restatement of Theorem 10.

COROLLARY If A is an $(m \times n)$ matrix, then the row space and the column space of A have the same dimension.

This corollary provides a useful way to determine the rank of a matrix A. Specifically, if A is row equivalent to a matrix B in echelon form, then the number, r, of nonzero rows in B equals the rank of A.

The null space of an $(m \times n)$ matrix A is determined by solving the homogeneous system of equations $A\mathbf{x} = \boldsymbol{\theta}$. Suppose the augmented matrix $[A \mid \boldsymbol{\theta}]$ for the system is row equivalent to the matrix $[B \mid \boldsymbol{\theta}]$, which is in echelon form. Then clearly A is row equivalent to B, and the number, r, of nonzero rows of B equals the rank of A. But r is also the number of nonzero rows of $[B \mid \boldsymbol{\theta}]$. It follows from Theorem 3 of Section 1.3 that there are $n - r$ free variables in a solution for $A\mathbf{x} = \boldsymbol{\theta}$. But the number of vectors in a basis for $\mathcal{N}(A)$ equals the number of free variables in the solution for $A\mathbf{x} = \boldsymbol{\theta}$ (see Example 3 of Section 3.4); that is, the nullity of A is $n - r$. Thus we have shown, informally, that the following formula holds.

Remark If A is an $(m \times n)$ matrix, then

$$n = \text{rank}(A) + \text{nullity}(A).$$

This remark will be proved formally in a more general context in Chapter 5.

Example 4 illustrates the argument preceding the remark. If A is the matrix given in Example 4,

$$A = \begin{bmatrix} 1 & 1 & 1 & 2 \\ -1 & 0 & 2 & -3 \\ 2 & 4 & 8 & 5 \end{bmatrix},$$

then the augmented matrix $[A \mid \boldsymbol{\theta}]$ is row equivalent to

$$[B \mid \boldsymbol{\theta}] = \begin{bmatrix} 1 & 0 & -2 & 0 & 0 \\ 0 & 1 & 3 & 0 & 0 \\ 0 & 0 & 0 & 1 & 0 \end{bmatrix}.$$

Since A is row equivalent to B, the corollary to Theorem 10 implies that A has rank 3. Further, in the notation of Theorem 3 of Section 1.3, the system $A\mathbf{x} = \boldsymbol{\theta}$ has $n = 4$ unknowns, and the reduced matrix $[B \mid \boldsymbol{\theta}]$ has $r = 3$ nonzero rows. Therefore, the solution for $A\mathbf{x} = \boldsymbol{\theta}$ has $n - r = 4 - 3 = 1$ independent variables, and it follows that the nullity of A is 1. In particular,

$$\text{rank}(A) + \text{nullity}(A) = 3 + 1 = 4,$$

as is guaranteed by the remark.

The following theorem uses the concept of the rank of a matrix to establish necessary and sufficient conditions for a system of equations, $A\mathbf{x} = \mathbf{b}$, to be consistent.

THEOREM 11 An $(m \times n)$ system of linear equations, $A\mathbf{x} = \mathbf{b}$, is consistent if and only if

$$\text{rank}(A) = \text{rank}([A \mid \mathbf{b}]).$$

Proof Suppose that $A = [\mathbf{A}_1, \mathbf{A}_2, \ldots, \mathbf{A}_n]$. Then the rank of A is the dimension of the column space of A, that is, the subspace

$$\text{Sp}\{\mathbf{A}_1, \mathbf{A}_2, \ldots, \mathbf{A}_n\}. \tag{9}$$

Similarly, the rank of $[A \mid \mathbf{b}]$ is the dimension of the subspace

$$\text{Sp}\{\mathbf{A}_1, \mathbf{A}_2, \ldots, \mathbf{A}_n, \mathbf{b}\}. \tag{10}$$

But we already know that $A\mathbf{x} = \mathbf{b}$ is consistent if and only if $\mathbf{b}$ is in the column space of A. It follows that $A\mathbf{x} = \mathbf{b}$ is consistent if and only if the subspaces given in Eq. (9) and Eq. (10) are equal and consequently have the same dimension. ■

Our final theorem in this section shows that rank can be used to determine nonsingular matrices.

THEOREM 12 An $(n \times n)$ matrix A is nonsingular if and only if the rank of A is n.

Proof Suppose that $A = [\mathbf{A}_1, \mathbf{A}_2, \ldots, \mathbf{A}_n]$. The proof of Theorem 12 rests on the observation that the range of A is given by

$$\mathcal{R}(A) = \text{Sp}\{\mathbf{A}_1, \mathbf{A}_2, \ldots, \mathbf{A}_n\}. \tag{11}$$

If A is nonsingular then, by Theorem 12 of Section 1.7, the columns of A are linearly independent. Thus $\{\mathbf{A}_1, \mathbf{A}_2, \ldots, \mathbf{A}_n\}$ is a basis for $\mathcal{R}(A)$, and the rank of A is n.

Conversely, suppose that A has rank n; that is, $\mathcal{R}(A)$ has dimension n. It is an immediate consequence of Eq. (11) and Theorem 9, property 4, that $\{\mathbf{A}_1, \mathbf{A}_2, \ldots, \mathbf{A}_n\}$ is a basis for $\mathcal{R}(A)$. In particular, the columns of A are linearly independent, so, by Theorem 12 of Section 1.7, A is nonsingular. ■

Proof of Theorem 10 (Optional)

To prove Theorem 10, let $A = (a_{ij})$ be an $(m \times n)$ matrix. Denote the rows of A by $\mathbf{a}_1, \mathbf{a}_2, \ldots, \mathbf{a}_m$. Thus,

$$\mathbf{a}_i = [a_{i1}, a_{i2}, \ldots, a_{in}].$$

Similarly, let $\mathbf{A}_1, \mathbf{A}_2, \ldots, \mathbf{A}_n$ be the columns of A, where

$$\mathbf{A}_j = \begin{bmatrix} a_{1j} \\ a_{2j} \\ \vdots \\ a_{mj} \end{bmatrix}.$$

Suppose that A^T has rank k. Since the columns of A^T are $\mathbf{a}_1^T, \mathbf{a}_2^T, \ldots, \mathbf{a}_m^T$, it follows that if

$$W = \mathrm{Sp}\{\mathbf{a}_1, \mathbf{a}_2, \ldots, \mathbf{a}_m\},$$

then $\dim(W) = k$. Therefore, W has a basis $\{\mathbf{w}_1, \mathbf{w}_2, \ldots, \mathbf{w}_k\}$, and, by Theorem 9, property 2, $m \geq k$. For $1 \leq j \leq k$, suppose that $\mathbf{w}_j$ is the $(1 \times n)$ vector

$$\mathbf{w}_j = [w_{j1}, w_{j2}, \ldots, w_{jn}].$$

Writing each $\mathbf{a}_i$ in terms of the basis yields

$$\begin{aligned}
[a_{11}, a_{12}, \ldots, a_{1n}] &= \mathbf{a}_1 = c_{11}\mathbf{w}_1 + c_{12}\mathbf{w}_2 + \cdots + c_{1k}\mathbf{w}_k \\
[a_{21}, a_{22}, \ldots, a_{2n}] &= \mathbf{a}_2 = c_{21}\mathbf{w}_1 + c_{22}\mathbf{w}_2 + \cdots + c_{2k}\mathbf{w}_k \\
&\;\;\vdots \\
[a_{m1}, a_{m2}, \ldots, a_{mn}] &= \mathbf{a}_m = c_{m1}\mathbf{w}_1 + c_{m2}\mathbf{w}_2 + \cdots + c_{mk}\mathbf{w}_k.
\end{aligned} \tag{12}$$

Equating the jth component of the left side of system (12) with the jth component of the right side yields

$$\begin{bmatrix} a_{1j} \\ a_{2j} \\ \vdots \\ a_{mj} \end{bmatrix} = w_{1j}\begin{bmatrix} c_{11} \\ c_{21} \\ \vdots \\ c_{m1} \end{bmatrix} + w_{2j}\begin{bmatrix} c_{12} \\ c_{22} \\ \vdots \\ c_{m2} \end{bmatrix} + \cdots + w_{kj}\begin{bmatrix} c_{1k} \\ c_{2k} \\ \vdots \\ c_{mk} \end{bmatrix} \tag{13}$$

for $1 \leq j \leq n$. For $1 \leq i \leq k$, define $\mathbf{c}_i$ to be the $(m \times 1)$ column vector

$$\mathbf{c}_i = \begin{bmatrix} c_{1i} \\ c_{2i} \\ \vdots \\ c_{mi} \end{bmatrix}.$$

Then system (13) becomes

$$\mathbf{A}_j = w_{1j}\mathbf{c}_1 + w_{2j}\mathbf{c}_2 + \cdots + w_{kj}\mathbf{c}_k, \quad 1 \le j \le n. \tag{14}$$

It follows from the equations in (14) that

$$\mathcal{R}(A) = \mathrm{Sp}\{\mathbf{A}_1, \mathbf{A}_2, \ldots \mathbf{A}_n\} \subseteq \mathrm{Sp}\{\mathbf{c}_1, \mathbf{c}_2, \ldots, \mathbf{c}_k\}.$$

It follows from Theorem 8 that the subspace

$$V = \mathrm{Sp}\{\mathbf{c}_1, \mathbf{c}_2, \ldots, \mathbf{c}_k\}$$

has dimension k, at most. By Exercise 32, $\dim[\mathcal{R}(A)] \le \dim(V) \le k$; that is, $\mathrm{rank}(A) \le \mathrm{rank}(A^T)$.

Since $(A^T)^T = A$, the same argument implies that $\mathrm{rank}(A^T) \le \mathrm{rank}(A)$. Thus $\mathrm{rank}(A) = \mathrm{rank}(A^T)$. ∎

3.5 EXERCISES

Exercises 1–14 refer to the vectors in (15).

$$\mathbf{u}_1 = \begin{bmatrix} 1 \\ 1 \end{bmatrix}, \quad \mathbf{u}_2 = \begin{bmatrix} 1 \\ 2 \end{bmatrix}, \quad \mathbf{u}_3 = \begin{bmatrix} -1 \\ 1 \end{bmatrix},$$

$$\mathbf{u}_4 = \begin{bmatrix} 0 \\ 0 \end{bmatrix}, \quad \mathbf{u}_5 = \begin{bmatrix} 3 \\ 3 \end{bmatrix}, \quad \mathbf{v}_1 = \begin{bmatrix} 1 \\ -1 \\ 1 \end{bmatrix}$$

$$\mathbf{v}_2 = \begin{bmatrix} 0 \\ 1 \\ 2 \end{bmatrix}, \quad \mathbf{v}_3 = \begin{bmatrix} 1 \\ -1 \\ 0 \end{bmatrix}, \quad \mathbf{v}_4 = \begin{bmatrix} -1 \\ 3 \\ 3 \end{bmatrix} \tag{15}$$

In Exercises 1–6, determine by inspection why the given set S is not a basis for R^2. (That is, either S is linearly dependent or S does not span R^2.)

1. $S = \{\mathbf{u}_1\}$

2. $S = \{\mathbf{u}_2\}$

3. $S = \{\mathbf{u}_1, \mathbf{u}_2, \mathbf{u}_3\}$

4. $S = \{\mathbf{u}_2, \mathbf{u}_3, \mathbf{u}_5\}$

5. $S = \{\mathbf{u}_1, \mathbf{u}_4\}$

6. $S = \{\mathbf{u}_1, \mathbf{u}_5\}$

In Exercises 7–9, determine by inspection why the given set S is not a basis for R^3. (That is, either S is linearly dependent or S does not span R^3.)

7. $S = \{\mathbf{v}_1, \mathbf{v}_2\}$

8. $S = \{\mathbf{v}_1, \mathbf{v}_3\}$

9. $S = \{\mathbf{v}_1, \mathbf{v}_2, \mathbf{v}_3, \mathbf{v}_4\}$

In Exercises 10–14, use Theorem 9, property 3, to determine whether the given set is a basis for the indicated vector space.

10. $S = \{\mathbf{u}_1, \mathbf{u}_2\}$ for R^2

11. $S = \{\mathbf{u}_2, \mathbf{u}_3\}$ for R^2

12. $S = \{\mathbf{v}_1, \mathbf{v}_2, \mathbf{v}_3\}$ for R^3

13. $S = \{\mathbf{v}_1, \mathbf{v}_2, \mathbf{v}_4\}$ for R^3

14. $S = \{\mathbf{v}_2, \mathbf{v}_3, \mathbf{v}_4\}$ for R^3

In Exercises 15–20, W is a subspace of R^4 consisting of vectors of the form

$$\mathbf{x} = \begin{bmatrix} x_1 \\ x_2 \\ x_3 \\ x_4 \end{bmatrix}.$$

Determine $\dim(W)$ when the components of $\mathbf{x}$ satisfy the given conditions.

15. $x_1 - 2x_2 + x_3 - x_4 = 0$

16. $x_1 - 2x_3 = 0$

17. $\begin{aligned} x_1 &= -x_2 + 2x_4 \\ x_3 &= -x_4 \end{aligned}$

18. $\begin{aligned} x_1 + x_3 - 2x_4 &= 0 \\ x_2 + 2x_3 - 3x_4 &= 0 \end{aligned}$

19. $\begin{aligned} x_1 &= -x_4 \\ x_2 &= 3x_4 \\ x_3 &= 2x_4 \end{aligned}$

20. $\begin{aligned} x_1 - x_2 &= 0 \\ x_2 - 2x_3 &= 0 \\ x_3 - x_4 &= 0 \end{aligned}$

In Exercises 21–24, find a basis for $\mathcal{N}(A)$ and give the nullity and the rank of A.

21. $A = \begin{bmatrix} 1 & 2 \\ -2 & -4 \end{bmatrix}$

22. $A = \begin{bmatrix} -1 & 2 & 0 \\ 2 & -5 & 1 \end{bmatrix}$

23. $A = \begin{bmatrix} 1 & -1 & 3 \\ 2 & -1 & 8 \\ -1 & 4 & 3 \end{bmatrix}$

24. $A = \begin{bmatrix} 1 & 2 & 0 & 5 \\ 1 & 3 & 1 & 7 \\ 2 & 3 & -1 & 9 \end{bmatrix}$

In Exercises 25 and 26, find a basis for $\mathcal{R}(A)$ and give the nullity and the rank of A.

25. $A = \begin{bmatrix} 1 & 2 & 1 \\ -1 & 0 & 3 \\ 1 & 5 & 7 \end{bmatrix}$

26. $A = \begin{bmatrix} 1 & 1 & 2 & 0 \\ 2 & 4 & 2 & 4 \\ 2 & 1 & 5 & -2 \end{bmatrix}$

27. Let W be a subspace, and let S be a spanning set for W. Find a basis for W, and calculate $\dim(W)$ for each set S.

a) $S = \left\{ \begin{bmatrix} 1 \\ 1 \\ -2 \end{bmatrix}, \begin{bmatrix} -1 \\ -2 \\ 3 \end{bmatrix}, \begin{bmatrix} 1 \\ 0 \\ -1 \end{bmatrix}, \begin{bmatrix} 2 \\ -1 \\ 0 \end{bmatrix} \right\}$

b) $S = \left\{ \begin{bmatrix} 1 \\ 2 \\ -1 \\ 1 \end{bmatrix}, \begin{bmatrix} 3 \\ 1 \\ 1 \\ 2 \end{bmatrix}, \begin{bmatrix} -1 \\ 1 \\ -2 \\ 2 \end{bmatrix}, \begin{bmatrix} 0 \\ -2 \\ 1 \\ 2 \end{bmatrix} \right\}$

28. Let W be the subspace of R^4 defined by $W = \{\mathbf{x}: \mathbf{v}^T\mathbf{x} = 0\}$. Calculate $\dim(W)$, where

$$\mathbf{v} = \begin{bmatrix} 1 \\ 2 \\ -3 \\ -1 \end{bmatrix}.$$

29. Let W be the subspace of R^4 defined by $W = \{\mathbf{x}: \mathbf{a}^T\mathbf{x} = 0 \text{ and } \mathbf{b}^T\mathbf{x} = 0 \text{ and } \mathbf{c}^T\mathbf{x} = 0\}$. Calculate $\dim(W)$ for

$$\mathbf{a} = \begin{bmatrix} 1 \\ -1 \\ 0 \\ 0 \end{bmatrix}, \quad \mathbf{b} = \begin{bmatrix} 1 \\ 0 \\ -1 \\ 0 \end{bmatrix}, \text{ and}$$

$$\mathbf{c} = \begin{bmatrix} 0 \\ 1 \\ -1 \\ 0 \end{bmatrix}.$$

30. Let W be a nonzero subspace of R^n. Show that W has a basis. [*Hint:* Let $\mathbf{w}_1$ be any nonzero vector in W. If $\{\mathbf{w}_1\}$ is a spanning set for W, then we are done. If not, there is a vector $\mathbf{w}_2$ in W such that $\{\mathbf{w}_1, \mathbf{w}_2\}$ is linearly independent. Why? Continue by asking whether this is a spanning set for W. Why must this process eventually stop?]

31. Suppose that $\{\mathbf{u}_1, \mathbf{u}_2, \ldots, \mathbf{u}_p\}$ is a basis for a subspace W, and suppose that $\mathbf{x}$ is in W with $\mathbf{x} = a_1\mathbf{u}_1 + a_2\mathbf{u}_2 + \cdots + a_p\mathbf{u}_p$. Show that this representation for $\mathbf{x}$ in terms of the basis is unique—that is, if $\mathbf{x} = b_1\mathbf{u}_1 + b_2\mathbf{u}_2 + \cdots + b_p\mathbf{u}_p$, then $b_1 = a_1, b_2 = a_2, \ldots, b_p = a_p$.

32. Let U and V be subspaces of R^n, and suppose that U is a subset of V. Prove that $\dim(U) \le \dim(V)$. If $\dim(U) = \dim(V)$, prove that V is contained in U, and thus conclude that $U = V$.

33. For each of the following, determine the largest possible value for the rank of A and the smallest possible value for the nullity of A.

a) A is (3×3)

b) A is (3×4)

c) A is (5×4)

34. If A is a (3×4) matrix, prove that the columns of A are linearly dependent.

35. If A is a (4×3) matrix, prove that the rows of A are linearly dependent.

36. Let A be an $(m \times n)$ matrix. Prove that $\text{rank}(A) \le m$ and $\text{rank}(A) \le n$.

37. Let A be a (2×3) matrix with rank 2. Show that the (2×3) system of equations $A\mathbf{x} = \mathbf{b}$ is consistent for every choice of $\mathbf{b}$ in R^2.

38. Let A be a (3×4) matrix with nullity 1. Prove that the (3×4) system of equations $A\mathbf{x} = \mathbf{b}$ is consistent for every choice of $\mathbf{b}$ in R^3.

39. Prove that an $(n \times n)$ matrix A is nonsingular if and only if the nullity of A is zero.

40. Let A be an $(m \times m)$ nonsingular matrix, and let B be an $(m \times n)$ matrix. Prove that $\mathcal{N}(AB) = \mathcal{N}(B)$ and conclude that rank $(AB) =$ rank (B).

41. Prove property 4 of Theorem 9 as follows: Assume that $\dim(W) = p$ and let $S = \{\mathbf{w}_1, \ldots, \mathbf{w}_p\}$ be a set of p vectors that spans W. To see that S is linearly independent, suppose that $c_1\mathbf{w}_1 + \cdots + c_p\mathbf{w}_p = \boldsymbol{\theta}$. If $c_i \neq 0$, show that $W = \text{Sp}\{\mathbf{w}_1, \ldots, \mathbf{w}_{i-1}, \mathbf{w}_{i+1}, \ldots, \mathbf{w}_p\}$. Finally, use Theorem 8 to reach a contradiction.

42. Suppose that $S = \{\mathbf{u}_1, \mathbf{u}_2, \ldots, \mathbf{u}_p\}$ is a set of linearly independent vectors in a subspace W, where $\dim(W) = m$ and $m > p$. Prove that there is a vector $\mathbf{u}_{p+1}$ in W such that $\{\mathbf{u}_1, \mathbf{u}_2, \ldots, \mathbf{u}_p, \mathbf{u}_{p+1}\}$ is linearly independent. Use this proof to show that a basis including all the vectors in S can be constructed for W.

3.6 ORTHOGONAL BASES FOR SUBSPACES

We have seen that a basis provides a very efficient way to characterize a subspace. Also, given a subspace W, we know that there are many different ways to construct a basis for W. In this section we focus on a particular type of basis called an *orthogonal basis*.

Orthogonal Bases

The idea of orthogonality is a generalization of the vector geometry concept of perpendicularity. If $\mathbf{u}$ and $\mathbf{v}$ are two vectors in R^2 or R^3, then we know that $\mathbf{u}$ and $\mathbf{v}$ are perpendicular if $\mathbf{u}^T\mathbf{v} = 0$ (see Theorem 7 in Section 2.3). For example, consider the vectors $\mathbf{u}$ and $\mathbf{v}$ given by

$$\mathbf{u} = \begin{bmatrix} 1 \\ -2 \end{bmatrix} \quad \text{and} \quad \mathbf{v} = \begin{bmatrix} 6 \\ 3 \end{bmatrix}.$$

Clearly $\mathbf{u}^T\mathbf{v} = 0$, and these two vectors are perpendicular when viewed as directed line segments in the plane (see Fig. 3.13).

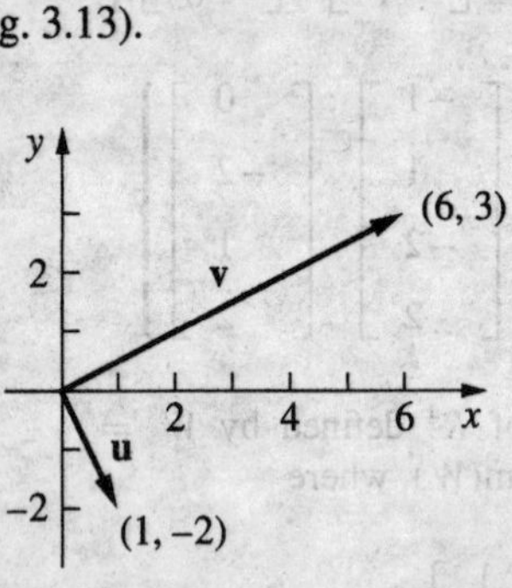

Figure 3.13 In R^2, nonzero vectors $\mathbf{u}$ and $\mathbf{v}$ are perpendicular if and only if $\mathbf{u}^T\mathbf{v} = 0$.

In general, for vectors in R^n, we use the term *orthogonal* rather than the term *perpendicular.* Specifically, if $\mathbf{u}$ and $\mathbf{v}$ are vectors in R^n, we say that $\mathbf{u}$ and $\mathbf{v}$ are ***orthogonal*** if

$$\mathbf{u}^T\mathbf{v} = 0.$$

We will also find the concept of an orthogonal set of vectors to be useful.

DEFINITION 6 Let $S = \{\mathbf{u}_1, \mathbf{u}_2, \ldots, \mathbf{u}_p\}$ be a set of vectors in R^n. The set S is said to be an ***orthogonal set*** if each pair of distinct vectors from S is orthogonal; that is, $\mathbf{u}_i^T\mathbf{u}_j = 0$ when $i \neq j$.

EXAMPLE 1 Verify that S is an orthogonal set of vectors, where

$$S = \left\{ \begin{bmatrix} 1 \\ 0 \\ 1 \\ 2 \end{bmatrix}, \begin{bmatrix} 1 \\ 1 \\ -1 \\ 0 \end{bmatrix}, \begin{bmatrix} 1 \\ -2 \\ -1 \\ 0 \end{bmatrix} \right\},$$

Solution If we use the notation $S = \{\mathbf{u}_1, \mathbf{u}_2, \mathbf{u}_3\}$, then

$$\mathbf{u}_1^T\mathbf{u}_2 = [1 \quad 0 \quad 1 \quad 2] \begin{bmatrix} 1 \\ 1 \\ -1 \\ 0 \end{bmatrix} = 1 + 0 - 1 + 0 = 0$$

$$\mathbf{u}_1^T\mathbf{u}_3 = [1 \quad 0 \quad 1 \quad 2] \begin{bmatrix} 1 \\ -2 \\ -1 \\ 0 \end{bmatrix} = 1 + 0 - 1 + 0 = 0$$

$$\mathbf{u}_2^T\mathbf{u}_3 = [1 \quad 1 \quad -1 \quad 0] \begin{bmatrix} 1 \\ -2 \\ -1 \\ 0 \end{bmatrix} = 1 - 2 + 1 + 0 = 0.$$

Therefore, $S = \{\mathbf{u}_1, \mathbf{u}_2, \mathbf{u}_3\}$ is an orthogonal set of vectors in R^4. ■

An important property of an orthogonal set S is that S is necessarily linearly independent (so long as S does not contain the zero vector).

THEOREM 13 Let $S = \{\mathbf{u}_1, \mathbf{u}_2, \ldots, \mathbf{u}_p\}$ be a set of nonzero vectors in R^n. If S is an orthogonal set of vectors, then S is a linearly independent set of vectors.

Proof Let $c_1, c_2, \ldots, c_p$ be any scalars that satisfy

$$c_1\mathbf{u}_1 + c_2\mathbf{u}_2 + \cdots + c_p\mathbf{u}_p = \boldsymbol{\theta}. \tag{1}$$

Form the scalar product

$$\mathbf{u}_1^T(c_1\mathbf{u}_1 + c_2\mathbf{u}_2 + \cdots + c_p\mathbf{u}_p) = \mathbf{u}_1^T\boldsymbol{\theta}$$

or

$$c_1(\mathbf{u}_1^T\mathbf{u}_1) + c_2(\mathbf{u}_1^T\mathbf{u}_2) + \cdots + c_p(\mathbf{u}_1^T\mathbf{u}_p) = 0.$$

Since $\mathbf{u}_1^T\mathbf{u}_j = 0$ for $2 \le j \le p$, the expression above reduces to

$$c_1(\mathbf{u}_1^T\mathbf{u}_1) = 0. \qquad (2)$$

Next, because $\mathbf{u}_1^T\mathbf{u}_1 > 0$ when $\mathbf{u}_1$ is nonzero, we see from Eq. (2) that $c_1 = 0$.

Similarly, forming the scalar product of both sides of Eq. (1) with $\mathbf{u}_i$, we see that $c_i(\mathbf{u}_i^T\mathbf{u}_i) = 0$ or $c_i = 0$ for $1 \le i \le p$. Thus S is a linearly independent set of vectors. ∎

By Theorem 13, any orthogonal set S containing p nonzero vectors from a p-dimensional subspace W will be a basis for W (since S is a linearly independent subset of p vectors from W, where $\dim(W) = p$). Such a basis is called an orthogonal basis. In the following definition, recall that the symbol $\|\mathbf{v}\|$ denotes the length of $\mathbf{v}$, $\|\mathbf{v}\| = \sqrt{\mathbf{v}^T\mathbf{v}}$.

DEFINITION 7 Let W be a subspace of R^n, and let $B = \{\mathbf{u}_1, \mathbf{u}_2, \ldots, \mathbf{u}_p\}$ be a basis for W. If B is an orthogonal set of vectors, then B is called an ***orthogonal basis*** for W.

Furthermore, if $\|\mathbf{u}_i\| = 1$ for $1 \le i \le p$, then B is said to be an ***orthonormal basis*** for W.

The word *orthonormal* suggests both *ortho*gonal and *normal*ized. Thus an orthonormal basis is an orthogonal basis consisting of vectors having length 1, where a vector of length 1 is a unit vector or a normalized vector. Observe that the unit vectors $\mathbf{e}_1, \mathbf{e}_2, \ldots, \mathbf{e}_n$ form an orthonormal basis for R^n.

EXAMPLE 2 Verify that the set $B = \{\mathbf{v}_1, \mathbf{v}_2, \mathbf{v}_3\}$ is an orthogonal basis for R^3, where

$$\mathbf{v}_1 = \begin{bmatrix} 1 \\ 2 \\ 1 \end{bmatrix}, \quad \mathbf{v}_2 = \begin{bmatrix} 3 \\ -1 \\ -1 \end{bmatrix}, \quad \text{and} \quad \mathbf{v}_3 = \begin{bmatrix} 1 \\ -4 \\ 7 \end{bmatrix}.$$

Solution We first verify that B is an orthogonal set by calculating

$$\mathbf{v}_1^T\mathbf{v}_2 = 3 - 2 - 1 = 0$$
$$\mathbf{v}_1^T\mathbf{v}_3 = 1 - 8 + 7 = 0$$
$$\mathbf{v}_2^T\mathbf{v}_3 = 3 + 4 - 7 = 0.$$

Now, R^3 has dimension 3. Thus, since B is a set of three vectors and is also a linearly independent set (see Theorem 13), it follows that B is an orthogonal basis for R^3. ∎

These observations are stated formally in the following corollary of Theorem 13.

COROLLARY Let W be a subspace of R^n, where $\dim(W) = p$. If S is an orthogonal set of p nonzero vectors and is also a subset of W, then S is an orthogonal basis for W.

Orthonormal Bases

If $B = \{\mathbf{u}_1, \mathbf{u}_2, \ldots, \mathbf{u}_p\}$ is an orthogonal set, then $C = \{a_1\mathbf{u}_1, a_2\mathbf{u}_2, \ldots, a_p\mathbf{u}_p\}$ is also an orthogonal set for any scalars $a_1, a_2, \ldots, a_p$. If B contains only nonzero vectors and if we define the scalars a_i by

$$a_i = \frac{1}{\sqrt{\mathbf{u}_i^T \mathbf{u}_i}},$$

then C is an ***orthonormal*** set. That is, we can convert an orthogonal set of nonzero vectors into an orthonormal set by dividing each vector by its length.

EXAMPLE 3 Recall that the set B in Example 2 is an orthogonal basis for R^3. Modify B so that it is an orthonormal basis.

Solution Given that $B = \{\mathbf{v}_1, \mathbf{v}_2, \mathbf{v}_3\}$ is an orthogonal basis for R^3, we can modify B to be an orthonormal basis by dividing each vector by its length. In particular (see Example 2), the lengths of $\mathbf{v}_1$, $\mathbf{v}_2$, and $\mathbf{v}_3$ are

$$\|\mathbf{v}_1\| = \sqrt{6}, \quad \|\mathbf{v}_2\| = \sqrt{11}, \quad \text{and} \quad \|\mathbf{v}_3\| = \sqrt{66}.$$

Therefore, the set $C = \{\mathbf{w}_1, \mathbf{w}_2, \mathbf{w}_3\}$ is an orthonormal basis for R^3, where

$$\mathbf{w}_1 = \frac{1}{\sqrt{6}}\mathbf{v}_1 = \begin{bmatrix} 1/\sqrt{6} \\ 2/\sqrt{6} \\ 1/\sqrt{6} \end{bmatrix}, \quad \mathbf{w}_2 = \frac{1}{\sqrt{11}}\mathbf{v}_2 = \begin{bmatrix} 3/\sqrt{11} \\ -1/\sqrt{11} \\ -1/\sqrt{11} \end{bmatrix}, \quad \text{and}$$

$$\mathbf{w}_3 = \frac{1}{\sqrt{66}}\mathbf{v}_3 = \begin{bmatrix} 1/\sqrt{66} \\ -4/\sqrt{66} \\ 7/\sqrt{66} \end{bmatrix}.$$

Determining Coordinates

Suppose that W is a p-dimensional subspace of R^n, and $B = \{\mathbf{w}_1, \mathbf{w}_2, \ldots, \mathbf{w}_p\}$ is a basis for W. If $\mathbf{v}$ is any vector in W, then $\mathbf{v}$ can be written uniquely in the form

$$\mathbf{v} = a_1\mathbf{w}_1 + a_2\mathbf{w}_2 + \cdots + a_p\mathbf{w}_p. \tag{3}$$

(In Eq. (3), the fact that the scalars $a_1, a_2, \ldots, a_p$ are unique is proved in Exercise 31 of Section 3.5.) The scalars $a_1, a_2, \ldots, a_p$ in Eq. (3) are called the ***coordinates of*** $\mathbf{v}$ with respect to the basis B.

As we will see, it is fairly easy to determine the coordinates of a vector with respect to an orthogonal basis. To appreciate the savings in computation, consider how coordinates are found when the basis is not orthogonal. For instance, the set $B_1 = \{\mathbf{v}_1, \mathbf{v}_2, \mathbf{v}_3\}$ is a basis for R^3, where

$$\mathbf{v}_1 = \begin{bmatrix} 1 \\ 1 \\ -1 \end{bmatrix}, \quad \mathbf{v}_2 = \begin{bmatrix} -1 \\ 2 \\ 1 \end{bmatrix}, \quad \text{and} \quad \mathbf{v}_3 = \begin{bmatrix} 2 \\ -2 \\ 1 \end{bmatrix}.$$

As can be seen, $\mathbf{v}_1^T\mathbf{v}_3 \neq 0$, and so B_1 is not an orthogonal basis. Next, suppose we wish to express some vector $\mathbf{v}$ in R^3, say $\mathbf{v} = [5, -5, -2]^T$, in terms of B_1. We must solve the (3×3) system: $a_1\mathbf{v}_1 + a_2\mathbf{v}_2 + a_3\mathbf{v}_3 = \mathbf{v}$. In matrix terms the coordinates a_1, a_2, and a_3 are found by solving the equation

$$\begin{bmatrix} 1 & -1 & 2 \\ 1 & 2 & -2 \\ -1 & 1 & 1 \end{bmatrix} \begin{bmatrix} a_1 \\ a_2 \\ a_3 \end{bmatrix} = \begin{bmatrix} 5 \\ -5 \\ -2 \end{bmatrix}.$$

(By Gaussian elimination, the solution is $a_1 = 1$, $a_2 = -2$, $a_3 = 1$.)

By contrast, if $B_2 = \{\mathbf{w}_1, \mathbf{w}_2, \mathbf{w}_3\}$ is an orthogonal basis for R^3, it is easy to determine a_1, a_2, and a_3 so that

$$\mathbf{v} = a_1\mathbf{w}_1 + a_2\mathbf{w}_2 + a_3\mathbf{w}_3. \tag{4}$$

To find the coordinate a_1 in Eq. (4), we form the scalar product

$$\begin{aligned} \mathbf{w}_1^T\mathbf{v} &= \mathbf{w}_1^T(a_1\mathbf{w}_1 + a_2\mathbf{w}_2 + a_3\mathbf{w}_3) \\ &= a_1(\mathbf{w}_1^T\mathbf{w}_1) + a_2(\mathbf{w}_1^T\mathbf{w}_2) + a_3(\mathbf{w}_1^T\mathbf{w}_3) \\ &= a_1(\mathbf{w}_1^T\mathbf{w}_1). \end{aligned}$$

The last equality follows because $\mathbf{w}_1^T\mathbf{w}_2 = 0$ and $\mathbf{w}_1^T\mathbf{w}_3 = 0$. Therefore, from above

$$a_1 = \frac{\mathbf{w}_1^T\mathbf{v}}{\mathbf{w}_1^T\mathbf{w}_1}.$$

Similarly,

$$a_2 = \frac{\mathbf{w}_2^T\mathbf{v}}{\mathbf{w}_2^T\mathbf{w}_2} \quad \text{and} \quad a_3 = \frac{\mathbf{w}_3^T\mathbf{v}}{\mathbf{w}_3^T\mathbf{w}_3}.$$

(*Note:* Since B_2 is a basis, $\mathbf{w}_i^T\mathbf{w}_i > 0$, $1 \leq i \leq 3$.)

EXAMPLE 4 Express the vector $\mathbf{v}$ in terms of the orthogonal basis $B = \{\mathbf{w}_1, \mathbf{w}_2, \mathbf{w}_3\}$, where

$$\mathbf{v} = \begin{bmatrix} 12 \\ -3 \\ 6 \end{bmatrix}, \quad \mathbf{w}_1 = \begin{bmatrix} 1 \\ 2 \\ 1 \end{bmatrix}, \quad \mathbf{w}_2 = \begin{bmatrix} 3 \\ -1 \\ -1 \end{bmatrix}, \quad \text{and} \quad \mathbf{w}_3 = \begin{bmatrix} 1 \\ -4 \\ 7 \end{bmatrix}.$$

Solution Beginning with the equation

$$\mathbf{v} = a_1\mathbf{w}_1 + a_2\mathbf{w}_2 + a_3\mathbf{w}_3,$$

we form scalar products to obtain

$$\mathbf{w}_1^T\mathbf{v} = a_1(\mathbf{w}_1^T\mathbf{w}_1), \quad \text{or} \quad 12 = 6a_1$$
$$\mathbf{w}_2^T\mathbf{v} = a_2(\mathbf{w}_2^T\mathbf{w}_2), \quad \text{or} \quad 33 = 11a_2$$
$$\mathbf{w}_3^T\mathbf{v} = a_3(\mathbf{w}_3^T\mathbf{w}_3), \quad \text{or} \quad 66 = 66a_3.$$

Thus $a_1 = 2$, $a_2 = 3$, and $a_3 = 1$. Therefore, as can be verified directly, $\mathbf{v} = 2\mathbf{w}_1 + 3\mathbf{w}_2 + \mathbf{w}_3$. ■

In general, let W be a subspace of R^n, and let $B = \{\mathbf{w}_1, \mathbf{w}_2, \ldots, \mathbf{w}_p\}$ be an orthogonal basis for W. If $\mathbf{v}$ is any vector in W, then $\mathbf{v}$ can be expressed uniquely in the form

$$\mathbf{v} = a_1\mathbf{w}_1 + a_2\mathbf{w}_2 + \cdots + a_p\mathbf{w}_p, \tag{5a}$$

where

$$a_i = \frac{\mathbf{w}_i^T\mathbf{v}}{\mathbf{w}_i^T\mathbf{w}_i}, \quad 1 \le i \le p. \tag{5b}$$

Constructing an Orthogonal Basis

The next theorem gives a procedure that can be used to generate an orthogonal basis from any given basis. This procedure, called the Gram–Schmidt process, is quite practical from a computational standpoint (although some care must be exercised when programming the procedure for the computer). Generating an orthogonal basis is often the first step in solving problems in least-squares approximation; so Gram–Schmidt orthogonalization is of more than theoretical interest.

THEOREM 14 **Gram–Schmidt** Let W be a p-dimensional subspace of R^n, and let $\{\mathbf{w}_1, \mathbf{w}_2, \ldots, \mathbf{w}_p\}$ be any basis for W. Then the set of vectors $\{\mathbf{u}_1, \mathbf{u}_2, \ldots, \mathbf{u}_p\}$ is an orthogonal basis for W, where

$$\mathbf{u}_1 = \mathbf{w}_1$$
$$\mathbf{u}_2 = \mathbf{w}_2 - \frac{\mathbf{u}_1^T\mathbf{w}_2}{\mathbf{u}_1^T\mathbf{u}_1}\mathbf{u}_1$$
$$\mathbf{u}_3 = \mathbf{w}_3 - \frac{\mathbf{u}_1^T\mathbf{w}_3}{\mathbf{u}_1^T\mathbf{u}_1}\mathbf{u}_1 - \frac{\mathbf{u}_2^T\mathbf{w}_3}{\mathbf{u}_2^T\mathbf{u}_2}\mathbf{u}_2,$$

and where, in general,

$$\mathbf{u}_i = \mathbf{w}_i - \sum_{k=1}^{i-1}\frac{\mathbf{u}_k^T\mathbf{w}_i}{\mathbf{u}_k^T\mathbf{u}_k}\mathbf{u}_k, \quad 2 \le i \le p. \tag{6}$$

■

The proof of Theorem 14 is somewhat technical, and we defer it to the end of this section.

In Eq. (6) we have explicit expressions that can be used to generate an orthogonal set of vectors $\{\mathbf{u}_1, \mathbf{u}_2, \ldots, \mathbf{u}_p\}$ from a given set of linearly independent vectors. These explicit expressions are especially useful if we have reason to implement the Gram–Schmidt process on a computer.

However, for hand calculations, it is not necessary to memorize formula (6). All we need to remember is the form or the general pattern of the Gram–Schmidt process. In particular, the Gram–Schmidt process starts with a basis $\{\mathbf{w}_1, \mathbf{w}_2, \ldots, \mathbf{w}_p\}$ and generates new vectors $\mathbf{u}_1, \mathbf{u}_2, \mathbf{u}_3, \ldots$ according to the following pattern:

$$\begin{aligned}
\mathbf{u}_1 &= \mathbf{w}_1\\
\mathbf{u}_2 &= \mathbf{w}_2 + a\mathbf{u}_1\\
\mathbf{u}_3 &= \mathbf{w}_3 + b\mathbf{u}_1 + c\mathbf{u}_2\\
\mathbf{u}_4 &= \mathbf{w}_4 + d\mathbf{u}_1 + e\mathbf{u}_2 + f\mathbf{u}_3\\
&\ \vdots\\
\mathbf{u}_i &= \mathbf{w}_i + \alpha_1\mathbf{u}_1 + \alpha_2\mathbf{u}_2 + \cdots + \alpha_{i-1}\mathbf{u}_{i-1}\\
&\ \vdots
\end{aligned}$$

In this sequence, the scalars can be determined in a step-by-step fashion from the orthogonality conditions.

For instance, to determine the scalar a in the definition of $\mathbf{u}_2$, we use the condition $\mathbf{u}_1^T\mathbf{u}_2 = 0$:

$$\begin{aligned}
&0 = \mathbf{u}_1^T\mathbf{u}_2 = \mathbf{u}_1^T\mathbf{w}_2 + a\mathbf{u}_1^T\mathbf{u}_1;\\
&\textit{Therefore:}\quad a = -(\mathbf{u}_1^T\mathbf{w}_2)/(\mathbf{u}_1^T\mathbf{u}_1).
\end{aligned} \tag{7}$$

To determine the two scalars b and c in the definition of $\mathbf{u}_3$, we use the two conditions $\mathbf{u}_1^T\mathbf{u}_3 = 0$ and $\mathbf{u}_2^T\mathbf{u}_3 = 0$. In particular,

$$\begin{aligned}
0 = \mathbf{u}_1^T\mathbf{u}_3 &= \mathbf{u}_1^T\mathbf{w}_3 + b\mathbf{u}_1^T\mathbf{u}_1 + c\mathbf{u}_1^T\mathbf{u}_2\\
&= \mathbf{u}_1^T\mathbf{w}_3 + b\mathbf{u}_1^T\mathbf{u}_1 \quad (\text{since } \mathbf{u}_1^T\mathbf{u}_2 = 0 \ \text{ by Eq. (7)})\\
\textit{Therefore:}\quad b &= -(\mathbf{u}_1^T\mathbf{w}_3)/(\mathbf{u}_1^T\mathbf{u}_1).
\end{aligned}$$

Similarly,

$$\begin{aligned}
0 = \mathbf{u}_2^T\mathbf{u}_3 &= \mathbf{u}_2^T\mathbf{w}_3 + b\mathbf{u}_2^T\mathbf{u}_1 + c\mathbf{u}_2^T\mathbf{u}_2\\
&= \mathbf{u}_2^T\mathbf{w}_3 + c\mathbf{u}_2^T\mathbf{u}_2 \quad (\text{since } \mathbf{u}_2^T\mathbf{u}_1 = 0 \ \text{ by Eq. (7)})\\
\textit{Therefore:}\quad c &= -(\mathbf{u}_2^T\mathbf{w}_3)/(\mathbf{u}_2^T\mathbf{u}_2).
\end{aligned}$$

The examples that follow illustrate the previous calculations.

Finally, to use the Gram–Schmidt orthogonalization process to find an orthogonal basis for W, we need some basis for W as a starting point. In many of the applications that require an orthogonal basis for a subspace W, it is relatively easy to produce this initial basis—we will give some examples in a later section. Given a basis for W, the Gram–Schmidt process proceeds in a mechanical fashion using Eq. (6). (*Note:* It was shown in Exercise 30 of Section 3.5 that every nonzero subspace of R^n has a basis. Therefore, by Theorem 14, every nonzero subspace of R^n has an orthogonal basis.)

Example 5 Let W be the subspace of R^3 defined by $W = \text{Sp}\{\mathbf{w}_1, \mathbf{w}_2\}$, where

$$\mathbf{w}_1 = \begin{bmatrix} 1 \\ 1 \\ 2 \end{bmatrix} \quad \text{and} \quad \mathbf{w}_2 = \begin{bmatrix} 0 \\ 2 \\ -4 \end{bmatrix}.$$

Use the Gram–Schmidt process to construct an orthogonal basis for W.

Solution We define vectors $\mathbf{u}_1$ and $\mathbf{u}_2$ of the form

$$\mathbf{u}_1 = \mathbf{w}_1$$
$$\mathbf{u}_2 = \mathbf{w}_2 + a\mathbf{u}_1,$$

where the scalar a is found from the condition $\mathbf{u}_1^T\mathbf{u}_2 = 0$. Now, $\mathbf{u}_1 = [1, 1, 2]^T$ and thus $\mathbf{u}_1^T\mathbf{u}_2$ is given by

$$\mathbf{u}_1^T\mathbf{u}_2 = \mathbf{u}_1^T(\mathbf{w}_2 + a\mathbf{u}_1) = \mathbf{u}_1^T\mathbf{w}_2 + a\mathbf{u}_1^T\mathbf{u}_1 = -6 + 6a.$$

Therefore, to have $\mathbf{u}_1^T\mathbf{u}_2 = 0$, we need $a = 1$. With $a = 1$, $\mathbf{u}_2$ is given by $\mathbf{u}_2 = \mathbf{w}_2 + \mathbf{u}_1 = [1, 3, -2]^T$.

In detail, an orthogonal basis for W is $B = \{\mathbf{u}_1, \mathbf{u}_2\}$, where

$$\mathbf{u}_1 = \begin{bmatrix} 1 \\ 1 \\ 2 \end{bmatrix} \quad \text{and} \quad \mathbf{u}_2 = \begin{bmatrix} 1 \\ 3 \\ -2 \end{bmatrix}.$$

For convenience in hand calculations, we can always eliminate fractional components in a set of orthogonal vectors. Specifically, if $\mathbf{x}$ and $\mathbf{y}$ are orthogonal, then so are $a\mathbf{x}$ and $\mathbf{y}$ for any scalar a:

$$\text{If} \quad \mathbf{x}^T\mathbf{y} = 0, \quad \text{then} \quad (a\mathbf{x})^T\mathbf{y} = a(\mathbf{x}^T\mathbf{y}) = 0.$$

We will make use of this observation in the following example.

Example 6 Use the Gram–Schmidt orthogonalization process to generate an orthogonal basis for $W = \text{Sp}\{\mathbf{w}_1, \mathbf{w}_2, \mathbf{w}_3\}$, where

$$\mathbf{w}_1 = \begin{bmatrix} 0 \\ 1 \\ 2 \\ 1 \end{bmatrix}, \quad \mathbf{w}_2 = \begin{bmatrix} 0 \\ 1 \\ 3 \\ 1 \end{bmatrix}, \quad \text{and} \quad \mathbf{w}_3 = \begin{bmatrix} 1 \\ 1 \\ 1 \\ 0 \end{bmatrix}.$$

Solution First we should check to be sure that $\{\mathbf{w}_1, \mathbf{w}_2, \mathbf{w}_3\}$ is a linearly independent set. A calculation shows that the vectors are linearly independent. (Exercise 27 illustrates what happens when the Gram–Schmidt algorithm is applied to a linearly dependent set.)

To generate an orthogonal basis $\{\mathbf{u}_1, \mathbf{u}_2, \mathbf{u}_3\}$ from $\{\mathbf{w}_1, \mathbf{w}_2, \mathbf{w}_3\}$, we first set

$$\mathbf{u}_1 = \mathbf{w}_1$$
$$\mathbf{u}_2 = \mathbf{w}_2 + a\mathbf{u}_1$$
$$\mathbf{u}_3 = \mathbf{w}_3 + b\mathbf{u}_1 + c\mathbf{u}_2.$$

With $\mathbf{u}_1 = [0, 1, 2, 1]^T$, the orthogonality condition $\mathbf{u}_1^T \mathbf{u}_2 = 0$ leads to $\mathbf{u}_1^T \mathbf{w}_2 + a\mathbf{u}_1^T \mathbf{u}_1 = 0$, or $8 + 6a = 0$. Therefore, $a = -4/3$ and hence

$$\mathbf{u}_2 = \mathbf{w}_2 - (4/3)\mathbf{u}_1 = [0, -1/3, 1/3, -1/3]^T.$$

Next, the conditions $\mathbf{u}_1^T \mathbf{u}_3 = 0$ and $\mathbf{u}_2^T \mathbf{u}_3 = 0$ lead to

$$0 = \mathbf{u}_1^T(\mathbf{w}_3 + b\mathbf{u}_1 + c\mathbf{u}_2) = 3 + 6b$$
$$0 = \mathbf{u}_2^T(\mathbf{w}_3 + b\mathbf{u}_1 + c\mathbf{u}_2) = 0 + (1/3)c.$$

Therefore, $b = -1/2$ and $c = 0$. Having the scalars b and c,

$$\mathbf{u}_3 = \mathbf{w}_3 - (1/2)\mathbf{u}_1 - (0)\mathbf{u}_2 = [1, 1/2, 0, -1/2]^T.$$

For convenience, we can eliminate the fractional components in $\mathbf{u}_2$ and $\mathbf{u}_3$ and obtain an orthogonal basis $\{\mathbf{v}_1, \mathbf{v}_2, \mathbf{v}_3\}$, where

$$\mathbf{v}_1 = \begin{bmatrix} 0 \\ 1 \\ 2 \\ 1 \end{bmatrix}, \quad \mathbf{v}_2 = \begin{bmatrix} 0 \\ -1 \\ 1 \\ -1 \end{bmatrix}, \quad \text{and} \quad \mathbf{v}_3 = \begin{bmatrix} 2 \\ 1 \\ 0 \\ -1 \end{bmatrix}. \quad \blacksquare$$

(*Note:* In Example 6, we could have also eliminated fractional components in the middle of the Gram–Schmidt process. That is, we could have redefined $\mathbf{u}_2$ to be the vector $\mathbf{u}_2 = [0, -1, 1, -1]^T$ and then calculated $\mathbf{u}_3$ with this new, redefined multiple of $\mathbf{u}_2$.)

As a final example, we use MATLAB to construct orthogonal bases.

EXAMPLE 7   Let A be the (3×5) matrix

$$A = \begin{bmatrix} 1 & 2 & 1 & 3 & 2 \\ 4 & 1 & 0 & 6 & 1 \\ 1 & 1 & 2 & 4 & 5 \end{bmatrix}.$$

Find an orthogonal basis for $\mathcal{R}(A)$ and an orthogonal basis for $\mathcal{N}(A)$.

Solution   The MATLAB command orth(A) gives an orthonormal basis for the range of A. The command null(A) gives an orthonormal basis for the null space of A. The results are shown in Fig. 3.14. Observe that the basis for $\mathcal{R}(A)$ has three vectors; that is, the dimension of $\mathcal{R}(A)$ is three or, equivalently, A has rank three. The basis for $\mathcal{N}(A)$ has two vectors; that is, the dimension of $\mathcal{N}(A)$ is two, or equivalently, A has nullity two. $\blacksquare$

Proof of Theorem 14 (Optional)

We first show that the expression given in Eq. (6) is always defined and that the vectors $\mathbf{u}_1, \mathbf{u}_2, \ldots, \mathbf{u}_p$ are all nonzero. To begin, $\mathbf{u}_1$ is a nonzero vector since $\mathbf{u}_1 = \mathbf{w}_1$. Thus $\mathbf{u}_1^T \mathbf{u}_1 > 0$, and so we can define $\mathbf{u}_2$. Furthermore, we observe that $\mathbf{u}_2$ has the form $\mathbf{u}_2 = \mathbf{w}_2 - b\mathbf{u}_1 = \mathbf{w}_2 - b_1 \mathbf{w}_1$; so $\mathbf{u}_2$ is nonzero since it is a nontrivial linear combination

```
A=
     1    2    1    3    2
     4    1    0    6    1
     1    1    2    4    5

>>orth(A)

ans=
     0.3841        -0.1173        -0.9158
     0.7682         0.5908         0.2466
     0.5121        -0.7983         0.3170

>>null(A)

ans=
     -0.7528        -0.0690
     -0.2063         0.1800
     -0.1069        -0.9047
      0.5736        -0.0469
     -0.2243         0.3772
```

Figure 3.14 The MATLAB command `orth(A)` produces an orthonormal basis for the range of A. The command `null(A)` gives an orthonormal basis for the null space of A.

of $\mathbf{w}_1$ and $\mathbf{w}_2$. Proceeding inductively, suppose that $\mathbf{u}_1, \mathbf{u}_2, \ldots, \mathbf{u}_{i-1}$ have been generated by Eq. (6); and suppose that each $\mathbf{u}_k$ has the form

$$\mathbf{u}_k = \mathbf{w}_k - c_1\mathbf{w}_1 - c_2\mathbf{w}_2 - \cdots - c_{k-1}\mathbf{w}_{k-1}.$$

From this equation, each $\mathbf{u}_k$ is nonzero; and it follows that Eq. (6) is a well-defined expression [since $\mathbf{u}_k^T\mathbf{u}_k > 0$ for $1 \le k \le (i-1)$]. Finally, since each $\mathbf{u}_k$ in Eq. (6) is a linear combination of $\mathbf{w}_1, \mathbf{w}_2, \ldots, \mathbf{w}_k$, we see that $\mathbf{u}_i$ is a nontrivial linear combination of $\mathbf{w}_1, \mathbf{w}_2, \ldots, \mathbf{w}_i$; and therefore $\mathbf{u}_i$ is nonzero.

All that remains to be proved is that the vectors generated by Eq. (6) are orthogonal. Clearly $\mathbf{u}_1^T\mathbf{u}_2 = 0$. Proceeding inductively again, suppose that $\mathbf{u}_j^T\mathbf{u}_k = 0$ for any j and k, where $j \neq k$ and $1 \le j, k \le i-1$. From (6) we have

$$\begin{aligned}\mathbf{u}_j^T\mathbf{u}_i = \mathbf{u}_j^T\left(\mathbf{w}_i - \sum_{k=1}^{i-1}\frac{\mathbf{u}_k^T\mathbf{w}_i}{\mathbf{u}_k^T\mathbf{u}_k}\mathbf{u}_k\right) &= \mathbf{u}_j^T\mathbf{w}_i - \sum_{k=1}^{i-1}\left(\frac{\mathbf{u}_k^T\mathbf{w}_i}{\mathbf{u}_k^T\mathbf{u}_k}\right)(\mathbf{u}_j^T\mathbf{u}_k)\\ &= \mathbf{u}_j^T\mathbf{w}_i - \left(\frac{\mathbf{u}_j^T\mathbf{w}_i}{\mathbf{u}_j^T\mathbf{u}_j}\right)(\mathbf{u}_j^T\mathbf{u}_j) = 0.\end{aligned}$$

Thus $\mathbf{u}_i$ is orthogonal to $\mathbf{u}_j$ for $1 \le j \le i-1$. Having this result, we have shown that $\{\mathbf{u}_1, \mathbf{u}_2, \ldots, \mathbf{u}_p\}$ is an orthogonal set of p nonzero vectors. So, by the corollary of Theorem 13, the vectors $\mathbf{u}_1, \mathbf{u}_2, \ldots, \mathbf{u}_p$ are an orthogonal basis for W.

3.6 EXERCISES

In Exercises 1–4, verify that $\{\mathbf{u}_1, \mathbf{u}_2, \mathbf{u}_3\}$ is an orthogonal set for the given vectors.

1. $\mathbf{u}_1 = \begin{bmatrix} 1 \\ 1 \\ 1 \end{bmatrix}$, $\mathbf{u}_2 = \begin{bmatrix} -1 \\ 0 \\ 1 \end{bmatrix}$, $\mathbf{u}_3 = \begin{bmatrix} -1 \\ 2 \\ -1 \end{bmatrix}$

2. $\mathbf{u}_1 = \begin{bmatrix} 1 \\ 0 \\ 1 \end{bmatrix}$, $\mathbf{u}_2 = \begin{bmatrix} -1 \\ 0 \\ 1 \end{bmatrix}$, $\mathbf{u}_3 = \begin{bmatrix} 0 \\ 1 \\ 0 \end{bmatrix}$

3. $\mathbf{u}_1 = \begin{bmatrix} 1 \\ 1 \\ 2 \end{bmatrix}$, $\mathbf{u}_2 = \begin{bmatrix} 2 \\ 0 \\ -1 \end{bmatrix}$, $\mathbf{u}_3 = \begin{bmatrix} 1 \\ -5 \\ 2 \end{bmatrix}$

4. $\mathbf{u}_1 = \begin{bmatrix} 2 \\ 1 \\ 2 \end{bmatrix}$, $\mathbf{u}_2 = \begin{bmatrix} 1 \\ 2 \\ -2 \end{bmatrix}$, $\mathbf{u}_3 = \begin{bmatrix} -2 \\ 2 \\ 1 \end{bmatrix}$

In Exercises 5–8, find values a, b, and c such that $\{\mathbf{u}_1, \mathbf{u}_2, \mathbf{u}_3\}$ is an orthogonal set.

5. $\mathbf{u}_1 = \begin{bmatrix} 1 \\ 1 \\ 1 \end{bmatrix}$, $\mathbf{u}_2 = \begin{bmatrix} 2 \\ 2 \\ -4 \end{bmatrix}$, $\mathbf{u}_3 = \begin{bmatrix} a \\ b \\ c \end{bmatrix}$

6. $\mathbf{u}_1 = \begin{bmatrix} 2 \\ 0 \\ 1 \end{bmatrix}$, $\mathbf{u}_2 = \begin{bmatrix} 1 \\ 1 \\ -2 \end{bmatrix}$, $\mathbf{u}_3 = \begin{bmatrix} a \\ b \\ c \end{bmatrix}$

7. $\mathbf{u}_1 = \begin{bmatrix} 1 \\ 1 \\ 1 \end{bmatrix}$, $\mathbf{u}_2 = \begin{bmatrix} -2 \\ -1 \\ a \end{bmatrix}$, $\mathbf{u}_3 = \begin{bmatrix} 4 \\ b \\ c \end{bmatrix}$

8. $\mathbf{u}_1 = \begin{bmatrix} 2 \\ 1 \\ -1 \end{bmatrix}$, $\mathbf{u}_2 = \begin{bmatrix} a \\ 1 \\ -1 \end{bmatrix}$, $\mathbf{u}_3 = \begin{bmatrix} b \\ 3 \\ c \end{bmatrix}$

In Exercises 9–12, express the given vector $\mathbf{v}$ in terms of the orthogonal basis $B = \{\mathbf{u}_1, \mathbf{u}_2, \mathbf{u}_3\}$, where $\mathbf{u}_1$, $\mathbf{u}_2$, and $\mathbf{u}_3$ are as in Exercise 1.

9. $\mathbf{v} = \begin{bmatrix} 1 \\ 1 \\ 0 \end{bmatrix}$ **10.** $\mathbf{v} = \begin{bmatrix} 0 \\ 1 \\ 2 \end{bmatrix}$

11. $\mathbf{v} = \begin{bmatrix} 3 \\ 3 \\ 3 \end{bmatrix}$ **12.** $\mathbf{v} = \begin{bmatrix} 1 \\ 2 \\ 1 \end{bmatrix}$

In Exercises 13–18, use the Gram–Schmidt process to generate an orthogonal set from the given linearly independent vectors.

13. $\begin{bmatrix} 0 \\ 0 \\ 1 \\ 0 \end{bmatrix}, \begin{bmatrix} 1 \\ 1 \\ 2 \\ 1 \end{bmatrix}, \begin{bmatrix} 1 \\ 0 \\ 1 \\ 1 \end{bmatrix}$

14. $\begin{bmatrix} 1 \\ 0 \\ 1 \\ 2 \end{bmatrix}, \begin{bmatrix} 2 \\ 1 \\ 0 \\ 2 \end{bmatrix}, \begin{bmatrix} 1 \\ -1 \\ 0 \\ 1 \end{bmatrix}$

15. $\begin{bmatrix} 1 \\ 1 \\ 0 \end{bmatrix}, \begin{bmatrix} 0 \\ 2 \\ 1 \end{bmatrix}, \begin{bmatrix} 1 \\ 1 \\ 6 \end{bmatrix}$

16. $\begin{bmatrix} 0 \\ 1 \\ 2 \end{bmatrix}, \begin{bmatrix} 3 \\ 6 \\ 2 \end{bmatrix}, \begin{bmatrix} 10 \\ -5 \\ 5 \end{bmatrix}$

17. $\begin{bmatrix} 0 \\ 1 \\ 0 \\ 1 \end{bmatrix}, \begin{bmatrix} 1 \\ 2 \\ 0 \\ 0 \end{bmatrix}, \begin{bmatrix} 0 \\ 2 \\ 1 \\ 0 \end{bmatrix}$

18. $\begin{bmatrix} 1 \\ 1 \\ 0 \\ 2 \end{bmatrix}, \begin{bmatrix} 0 \\ 2 \\ 1 \\ 2 \end{bmatrix}, \begin{bmatrix} 0 \\ 1 \\ 0 \\ 2 \end{bmatrix}$

In Exercises 19 and 20, find a basis for the null space and the range of the given matrix. Then use Gram–Schmidt to obtain orthogonal bases.

19. $\begin{bmatrix} 1 & -2 & 1 & -5 \\ 2 & 1 & 7 & 5 \\ 1 & -1 & 2 & -2 \end{bmatrix}$

20. $\begin{bmatrix} 1 & 3 & 10 & 11 & 9 \\ -1 & 2 & 5 & 4 & 1 \\ 2 & -1 & -1 & 1 & 4 \end{bmatrix}$

21. Argue that any set of four or more nonzero vectors in R^3 cannot be an orthogonal set.

22. Let $S = \{\mathbf{u}_1, \mathbf{u}_2, \mathbf{u}_3\}$ be an orthogonal set of nonzero vectors in R^3. Define the (3×3) matrix A by $A = [\mathbf{u}_1, \mathbf{u}_2, \mathbf{u}_3]$. Show that A is nonsingular and $A^T A = D$, where D is a diagonal matrix. Calculate the diagonal matrix D when A is created from the orthogonal vectors in Exercise 1.

23. Let W be a p-dimensional subspace of R^n. If $\mathbf{v}$ is a vector in W such that $\mathbf{v}^T\mathbf{w} = 0$ for every $\mathbf{w}$ in W, show that $\mathbf{v} = \boldsymbol{\theta}$. [*Hint:* Consider $\mathbf{w} = \mathbf{v}$.]

24. *The Cauchy–Schwarz inequality.* Let $\mathbf{x}$ and $\mathbf{y}$ be vectors in R^n. Prove that $|\mathbf{x}^T\mathbf{y}| \le \|\mathbf{x}\|\|\mathbf{y}\|$. [*Hint:* Observe that $\|\mathbf{x} - c\mathbf{y}\|^2 \ge 0$ for any scalar c. If $\mathbf{y} \ne \boldsymbol{\theta}$, let $c = \mathbf{x}^T\mathbf{y}/\mathbf{y}^T\mathbf{y}$ and expand $(\mathbf{x} - c\mathbf{y})^T(\mathbf{x} - c\mathbf{y}) \ge 0$. Also treat the case $\mathbf{y} = \boldsymbol{\theta}$.]

25. *The triangle inequality.* Let $\mathbf{x}$ and $\mathbf{y}$ be vectors in R^n. Prove that $\|\mathbf{x}+\mathbf{y}\| \le \|\mathbf{x}\| + \|\mathbf{y}\|$. [*Hint:* Expand $\|\mathbf{x} + \mathbf{y}\|^2$ and use Exercise 24.]

26. Let $\mathbf{x}$ and $\mathbf{y}$ be vectors in R^n. Prove that $|\|\mathbf{x}\| - \|\mathbf{y}\|| \le \|\mathbf{x} - \mathbf{y}\|$. [*Hint:* For one part consider $\|\mathbf{x} + (\mathbf{y} - \mathbf{x})\|$ and Exercise 25.]

27. If the hypotheses for Theorem 14 were altered so that $\{\mathbf{w}_i\}_{i=1}^{p-1}$ is linearly independent and $\{\mathbf{w}_i\}_{i=1}^{p}$ is linearly dependent, use Exercise 23 to show that Eq. (6) yields $\mathbf{u}_p = \boldsymbol{\theta}$.

28. Let $B = \{\mathbf{u}_1, \mathbf{u}_2, \ldots, \mathbf{u}_p\}$ be an *orthonormal* basis for a subspace W. Let $\mathbf{v}$ be any vector in W, where $\mathbf{v} = a_1\mathbf{u}_1 + a_2\mathbf{u}_2 + \cdots + a_p\mathbf{u}_p$. Show that

$$\|\mathbf{v}\|^2 = a_1^2 + a_2^2 + \cdots + a_p^2.$$

3.7 LINEAR TRANSFORMATIONS FROM R^n TO R^m

In this section we consider a special class of functions, called *linear transformations*, that map vectors to vectors. As we will presently observe, linear transformations arise naturally as a generalization of matrices. Moreover, linear transformations have important applications in engineering science, the social sciences, and various branches of mathematics.

The notation for linear transformations follows the usual notation for functions. If V is a subspace of R^n and W is a subspace of R^m, then the notation

$$F\colon V \to W$$

will denote a function, F, whose domain is the subspace V and whose range is contained in W. Furthermore, for $\mathbf{v}$ in V we write

$$\mathbf{w} = F(\mathbf{v})$$

to indicate that F maps $\mathbf{v}$ to $\mathbf{w}$. To illustrate, let $F\colon R^3 \to R^2$ be defined by

$$F(\mathbf{x}) = \begin{bmatrix} x_1 - x_2 \\ x_2 + x_3 \end{bmatrix},$$

where

$$\mathbf{x} = \begin{bmatrix} x_1 \\ x_2 \\ x_3 \end{bmatrix}.$$

In this case if, for example, **v** is the vector

$$\mathbf{v} = \begin{bmatrix} 1 \\ 2 \\ 3 \end{bmatrix},$$

then $F(\mathbf{v}) = \mathbf{w}$, where

$$\mathbf{w} = \begin{bmatrix} -1 \\ 5 \end{bmatrix}.$$

In earlier sections we have seen that an $(m \times n)$ matrix A determines a function from R^n to R^m. Specifically for **x** in R^n, the formula

$$T(\mathbf{x}) = A\mathbf{x} \tag{1}$$

defines a function $T: R^n \to R^m$. To illustrate, let A be the (3×2) matrix

$$A = \begin{bmatrix} 1 & -1 \\ 0 & 2 \\ 3 & 1 \end{bmatrix}.$$

In this case Eq. (1) defines a function $T: R^2 \to R^3$, and the formula for T is

$$T(\mathbf{x}) = T\left(\begin{bmatrix} x_1 \\ x_2 \end{bmatrix}\right) = \begin{bmatrix} 1 & -1 \\ 0 & 2 \\ 3 & 1 \end{bmatrix}\begin{bmatrix} x_1 \\ x_2 \end{bmatrix} = \begin{bmatrix} x_1 - x_2 \\ 2x_2 \\ 3x_1 + x_2 \end{bmatrix};$$

for instance,

$$T\left(\begin{bmatrix} 1 \\ 1 \end{bmatrix}\right) = \begin{bmatrix} 0 \\ 2 \\ 4 \end{bmatrix}.$$

Returning to the general case in which A is an $(m \times n)$ matrix, note that the function T defined by Eq. (1) satisfies the following linearity properties:

$$\begin{aligned} T(\mathbf{v} + \mathbf{w}) &= A(\mathbf{v} + \mathbf{w}) = A\mathbf{v} + A\mathbf{w} = T(\mathbf{v}) + T(\mathbf{w}) \\ T(c\mathbf{v}) &= A(c\mathbf{v}) = cA\mathbf{v} = cT(\mathbf{v}), \end{aligned} \tag{2}$$

where **v** and **w** are any vectors in R^n and c is an arbitrary scalar. We next define a linear transformation to be a function that satisfies the two linearity properties given in Eq. (2).

DEFINITION 8

Let V and W be subspaces of R^n and R^m, respectively, and let T be a function from V to W, $T: V \to W$. We say that T is a ***linear transformation*** if for all **u** and **v** in V and for all scalars a

$$T(\mathbf{u} + \mathbf{v}) = T(\mathbf{u}) + T\mathbf{v})$$

and

$$T(a\mathbf{u}) = aT(\mathbf{u}). \tag{3}$$

It is apparent from Eq. (2) that the function T defined in Eq. (1) by matrix multiplication is a linear transformation. Conversely, if $T: R^n \to R^m$ is a linear transformation, then (see Theorem 15 on page 232) there is an $(m \times n)$ matrix A such that T is defined by Eq. (1). Thus linear transformations from R^n to R^m are precisely those functions that can be defined by matrix multiplication as in Eq. (1). The situation is not so simple for linear transformations on arbitrary vector spaces or even for linear transformations on subspaces of R^n. Thus the concept of a linear transformation is a convenient and useful generalization to arbitrary subspaces of matrix functions defined as in Eq. (1).

Examples of Linear Transformations

Most of the familiar functions from the reals to the reals are not linear transformations. For example, none of the functions

$$f(x) = x + 1, \qquad g(x) = x^2, \qquad h(x) = \sin x, \qquad k(x) = e^x$$

is a linear transformation. Indeed, it will follow from the exercises that a function $f: R \to R$ is a linear transformation if and only if f is defined by $f(x) = ax$ for some scalar a.

We now give several examples to illustrate the use of Definition 8 in verifying whether a function is or is not a linear transformation.

EXAMPLE 1 Let $F: R^3 \to R^2$ be the function defined by

$$F(\mathbf{x}) = \begin{bmatrix} x_1 - x_2 \\ x_2 + x_3 \end{bmatrix}, \quad \text{where } \mathbf{x} = \begin{bmatrix} x_1 \\ x_2 \\ x_3 \end{bmatrix}.$$

Determine whether F is a linear transformation.

Solution We must determine whether the two linearity properties in Eq. (3) are satisfied by F. Thus let $\mathbf{u}$ and $\mathbf{v}$ be in R^3,

$$\mathbf{u} = \begin{bmatrix} u_1 \\ u_2 \\ u_3 \end{bmatrix} \quad \text{and} \quad \mathbf{v} = \begin{bmatrix} v_1 \\ v_2 \\ v_3 \end{bmatrix},$$

and let c be a scalar. Then

$$\mathbf{u} + \mathbf{v} = \begin{bmatrix} u_1 + v_1 \\ u_2 + v_2 \\ u_3 + v_3 \end{bmatrix}.$$

Therefore, from the rule defining F,

$$\begin{aligned} F(\mathbf{u} + \mathbf{v}) &= \begin{bmatrix} (u_1 + v_1) - (u_2 + v_2) \\ (u_2 + v_2) + (u_3 + v_3) \end{bmatrix} \\ &= \begin{bmatrix} u_1 - u_2 \\ u_2 + u_3 \end{bmatrix} + \begin{bmatrix} v_1 - v_2 \\ v_2 + v_3 \end{bmatrix} \\ &= F(\mathbf{u}) + F(\mathbf{v}). \end{aligned}$$

Similarly,

$$F(c\mathbf{u}) = \begin{bmatrix} cu_1 - cu_2 \\ cu_2 + cu_3 \end{bmatrix} = c\begin{bmatrix} u_1 - u_2 \\ u_2 + u_3 \end{bmatrix} = cF(\mathbf{u}),$$

so F is a linear transformation.

Note that F can also be defined as $F(\mathbf{x}) = A\mathbf{x}$, where A is the (2×3) matrix

$$A = \begin{bmatrix} 1 & -1 & 0 \\ 0 & 1 & 1 \end{bmatrix}.$$

EXAMPLE 2 Define $H: R^2 \to R^2$ by

$$H(\mathbf{x}) = \begin{bmatrix} x_1 - x_2 + 1 \\ 3x_2 \end{bmatrix}, \quad \text{where } \mathbf{x} = \begin{bmatrix} x_1 \\ x_2 \end{bmatrix}.$$

Determine whether H is a linear transformation.

Solution Let $\mathbf{u}$ and $\mathbf{v}$ be in R^2:

$$\mathbf{u} = \begin{bmatrix} u_1 \\ u_2 \end{bmatrix} \quad \text{and} \quad \mathbf{v} = \begin{bmatrix} v_1 \\ v_2 \end{bmatrix}.$$

Then

$$H(\mathbf{u}+\mathbf{v}) = \begin{bmatrix} (u_1 + v_1) - (u_2 + v_2) + 1 \\ 3(u_2 + v_2) \end{bmatrix},$$

while

$$H(\mathbf{u}) + H(\mathbf{v}) = \begin{bmatrix} u_1 - u_2 + 1 \\ 3u_2 \end{bmatrix} + \begin{bmatrix} v_1 - v_2 + 1 \\ 3v_2 \end{bmatrix}$$

$$= \begin{bmatrix} (u_1 + v_1) - (u_2 + v_2) + 2 \\ 3(u_2 + v_2) \end{bmatrix}.$$

Thus we see that $H(\mathbf{u}+\mathbf{v}) \neq H(\mathbf{u}) + H(\mathbf{v})$. Therefore, H is not a linear transformation. Although it is not necessary, it can also be verified easily that if $c \neq 1$, then $H(c\mathbf{u}) \neq cH(\mathbf{u})$.

EXAMPLE 3 Let W be a subspace of R^n such that $\dim(W) = p$, and let $S = \{\mathbf{w}_1, \mathbf{w}_2, \ldots, \mathbf{w}_p\}$ be an orthonormal basis for W. Define $T: R^n \to W$ by

$$T(\mathbf{v}) = (\mathbf{v}^T\mathbf{w}_1)\mathbf{w}_1 + (\mathbf{v}^T\mathbf{w}_2)\mathbf{w}_2 + \cdots + (\mathbf{v}^T\mathbf{w}_p)\mathbf{w}_p. \tag{4}$$

Prove that T is a linear transformation.

Solution If $\mathbf{u}$ and $\mathbf{v}$ are in R^n, then

$$\begin{aligned} T(\mathbf{u}+\mathbf{v}) &= [(\mathbf{u}+\mathbf{v})^T\mathbf{w}_1]\mathbf{w}_1 + [(\mathbf{u}+\mathbf{v})^T\mathbf{w}_2]\mathbf{w}_2 + \cdots + [(\mathbf{u}+\mathbf{v})^T\mathbf{w}_p]\mathbf{w}_p \\ &= [(\mathbf{u}^T+\mathbf{v}^T)\mathbf{w}_1]\mathbf{w}_1 + [(\mathbf{u}^T+\mathbf{v}^T)\mathbf{w}_2]\mathbf{w}_2 + \cdots + [(\mathbf{u}^T+\mathbf{v}^T)\mathbf{w}_p]\mathbf{w}_p \\ &= (\mathbf{u}^T\mathbf{w}_1)\mathbf{w}_1 + (\mathbf{u}^T\mathbf{w}_2)\mathbf{w}_2 + \cdots + (\mathbf{u}^T\mathbf{w}_p)\mathbf{w}_p \\ &\quad + (\mathbf{v}^T\mathbf{w}_1)\mathbf{w}_1 + (\mathbf{v}^T\mathbf{w}_2)\mathbf{w}_2 + \cdots + (\mathbf{v}^T\mathbf{w}_p)\mathbf{w}_p \\ &= T(\mathbf{u}) + T(\mathbf{v}). \end{aligned}$$

It can be shown similarly that $T(c\mathbf{u}) = cT(\mathbf{u})$ for each scalar c, so T is a linear transformation. ■

The vector $T(\mathbf{v})$ defined by Eq. (4) is called the orthogonal projection of $\mathbf{v}$ onto W and will be considered further in Sections 3.8 and 3.9. As a specific illustration of Example 3, let W be the subspace of R^3 consisting of all vectors of the form

$$\mathbf{x} = \begin{bmatrix} x_1 \\ x_2 \\ 0 \end{bmatrix}.$$

Thus W is the *xy*-plane, and the set $\{\mathbf{e}_1, \mathbf{e}_2\}$ is an orthonormal basis for W. For $\mathbf{x}$ in R^3,

$$\mathbf{x} = \begin{bmatrix} x_1 \\ x_2 \\ x_3 \end{bmatrix},$$

the formula in Eq. (4) yields

$$T(\mathbf{x}) = (\mathbf{x}^T\mathbf{e}_1)\mathbf{e}_1 + (\mathbf{x}^T\mathbf{e}_2)\mathbf{e}_2 = x_1\mathbf{e}_1 + x_2\mathbf{e}_2.$$

Thus,

$$T(\mathbf{x}) = \begin{bmatrix} x_1 \\ x_2 \\ 0 \end{bmatrix}.$$

This transformation is illustrated geometrically by Fig. 3.15.

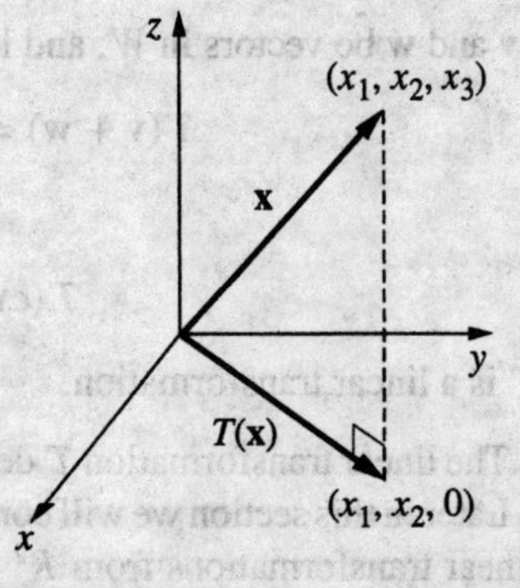

Figure 3.15 Orthogonal projection onto the *xy*-plane

EXAMPLE 4 Let W be a subspace of R^n, and let a be a scalar. Define $T: W \to W$ by $T(\mathbf{w}) = a\mathbf{w}$. Demonstrate that T is a linear transformation.

Solution If $\mathbf{v}$ and $\mathbf{w}$ are in W, then

$$T(\mathbf{v} + \mathbf{w}) = a(\mathbf{v} + \mathbf{w}) = a\mathbf{v} + a\mathbf{w} = T(\mathbf{v}) + T(\mathbf{w}).$$

Likewise, if c is a scalar, then

$$T(c\mathbf{w}) = a(c\mathbf{w}) = c(a\mathbf{w}) = cT(\mathbf{w}).$$

It follows that T is a linear transformation. ∎

The linear transformation defined in Example 4 is called a ***dilation*** when $a > 1$ and a ***contraction*** when $0 < a < 1$. These cases are illustrated geometrically in Fig. 3.16.

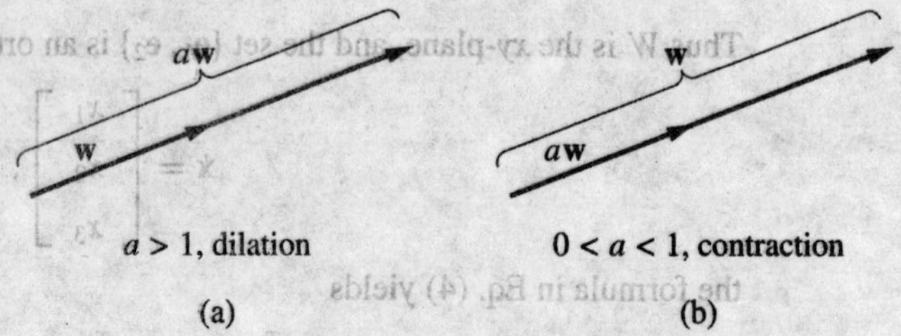

Figure 3.16 Dilations and contractions

The mapping I: $W \rightarrow W$ defined by $I(\mathbf{w}) = \mathbf{w}$ is the special case of Example 4 in which $a = 1$. The linear transformation I is called the ***identity transformation***.

EXAMPLE 5 Let W be a subspace of R^n, and let $\boldsymbol{\theta}$ be the zero vector in R^m. Define T: $W \rightarrow R^m$ by $T(\mathbf{w}) = \boldsymbol{\theta}$ for each $\mathbf{w}$ in W. Show that T is a linear transformation.

Solution Let $\mathbf{v}$ and $\mathbf{w}$ be vectors in W, and let c be a scalar. Then

$$T(\mathbf{v} + \mathbf{w}) = \boldsymbol{\theta} = \boldsymbol{\theta} + \boldsymbol{\theta} = T(\mathbf{v}) + T(\mathbf{w})$$

and

$$T(c\mathbf{v}) = \boldsymbol{\theta} = c\boldsymbol{\theta} = cT(\mathbf{v}),$$

so T is a linear transformation. ∎

The linear transformation T defined in Example 5 is called the ***zero transformation***. Later in this section we will consider other examples when we study a particular class of linear transformations from R^2 to R^2. For the present, we turn to further properties of linear transformations.

The Matrix of a Transformation

Let V and W be subspaces, and let T: $V \rightarrow W$ be a linear transformation. If $\mathbf{u}$ and $\mathbf{v}$ are vectors in V and if a and b are scalars, then the linearity properties (3) yield

$$T(a\mathbf{u} + b\mathbf{v}) = T(a\mathbf{u}) + T(b\mathbf{v}) = aT(\mathbf{u}) + bT(\mathbf{v}). \tag{5}$$

Inductively we can extend Eq. (5) to any finite subset of V. That is, if $\mathbf{v}_1, \mathbf{v}_2, \ldots, \mathbf{v}_r$ are vectors in V and if $c_1, c_2, \ldots, c_r$ are scalars, then

$$T(c_1\mathbf{v}_1 + c_2\mathbf{v}_2 + \cdots + c_r\mathbf{v}_r) = c_1T(\mathbf{v}_1) + c_2T(\mathbf{v}_2) + \cdots + c_rT(\mathbf{v}_r). \qquad (6)$$

The following example illustrates an application of Eq. (6).

EXAMPLE 6 Let W be the subspace of R^3 defined by

$$W = \{\mathbf{x}: \mathbf{x} = \begin{bmatrix} x_2 + 2x_3 \\ x_2 \\ x_3 \end{bmatrix}, \quad x_2 \text{ and } x_3 \text{ any real numbers}\}.$$

Then $\{\mathbf{w}_1, \mathbf{w}_2\}$ is a basis for W, where

$$\mathbf{w}_1 = \begin{bmatrix} 1 \\ 1 \\ 0 \end{bmatrix} \quad \text{and} \quad \mathbf{w}_2 = \begin{bmatrix} 2 \\ 0 \\ 1 \end{bmatrix}.$$

Suppose that $T: W \to R^2$ is a linear transformation such that $T(\mathbf{w}_1) = \mathbf{u}_1$ and $T(\mathbf{w}_2) = \mathbf{u}_2$, where

$$\mathbf{u}_1 = \begin{bmatrix} 1 \\ 1 \end{bmatrix} \quad \text{and} \quad \mathbf{u}_2 = \begin{bmatrix} 1 \\ -1 \end{bmatrix}.$$

Let the vector $\mathbf{w}$ be given by

$$\mathbf{w} = \begin{bmatrix} -1 \\ 3 \\ -2 \end{bmatrix}.$$

Show that $\mathbf{w}$ is in W, express $\mathbf{w}$ as a linear combination of $\mathbf{w}_1$ and $\mathbf{w}_2$, and use Eq. (6) to determine $T(\mathbf{w})$.

Solution It follows from the description of W that $\mathbf{w}$ is in W. Furthermore, it is easy to see that

$$\mathbf{w} = 3\mathbf{w}_1 - 2\mathbf{w}_2.$$

By Eq. (6),

$$T(\mathbf{w}) = 3T(\mathbf{w}_1) - 2T(\mathbf{w}_2) = 3\mathbf{u}_1 - 2\mathbf{u}_2 = 3\begin{bmatrix} 1 \\ 1 \end{bmatrix} - 2\begin{bmatrix} 1 \\ -1 \end{bmatrix}.$$

Thus,

$$T(\mathbf{w}) = \begin{bmatrix} 1 \\ 5 \end{bmatrix}.$$

Example 6 illustrates that the action of a linear transformation T on a subspace W is completely determined once the action of T on a basis for W is known. Our next example provides yet another illustration of this fact.

EXAMPLE 7 Let $T: R^3 \to R^2$ be a linear transformation such that

$$T(\mathbf{e}_1) = \begin{bmatrix} 1 \\ 2 \end{bmatrix}, \quad T(\mathbf{e}_2) = \begin{bmatrix} -1 \\ 1 \end{bmatrix}, \quad \text{and} \quad T(\mathbf{e}_3) = \begin{bmatrix} 2 \\ 3 \end{bmatrix}.$$

For an arbitrary vector $\mathbf{x}$ in R^3,

$$\mathbf{x} = \begin{bmatrix} x_1 \\ x_2 \\ x_3 \end{bmatrix},$$

give a formula for $T(\mathbf{x})$.

Solution The vector $\mathbf{x}$ can be written in the form

$$\mathbf{x} = x_1\mathbf{e}_1 + x_2\mathbf{e}_2 + x_3\mathbf{e}_3,$$

so by Eq. (6),

$$T(\mathbf{x}) = x_1T(\mathbf{e}_1) + x_2T(\mathbf{e}_2) + x_3T(\mathbf{e}_3). \tag{7}$$

Thus,

$$T(\mathbf{x}) = x_1\begin{bmatrix} 1 \\ 2 \end{bmatrix} + x_2\begin{bmatrix} -1 \\ 1 \end{bmatrix} + x_3\begin{bmatrix} 2 \\ 3 \end{bmatrix} = \begin{bmatrix} x_1 - x_2 + 2x_3 \\ 2x_1 + x_2 + 3x_3 \end{bmatrix}.$$ ■

Continuing with the notation of the preceding example, let A be the (2×3) matrix with columns $T(\mathbf{e}_1)$, $T(\mathbf{e}_2)$, $T(\mathbf{e}_3)$; thus,

$$A = [T(\mathbf{e}_1), T(\mathbf{e}_2), T(\mathbf{e}_3)] = \begin{bmatrix} 1 & -1 & 2 \\ 2 & 1 & 3 \end{bmatrix}.$$

It is an immediate consequence of Eq. (7) and Theorem 5 of Section 1.5 that $T(\mathbf{x}) = A\mathbf{x}$. Thus Example 7 illustrates the following theorem.

THEOREM 15 Let $T: R^n \to R^m$ be a linear transformation, and let $\mathbf{e}_1, \mathbf{e}_2, \ldots, \mathbf{e}_n$ be the unit vectors in R^n. If A is the $(m \times n)$ matrix defined by

$$A = [T(\mathbf{e}_1), T(\mathbf{e}_2), \ldots, T(\mathbf{e}_n)],$$

then $T(\mathbf{x}) = A\mathbf{x}$ for all $\mathbf{x}$ in R^n.

Proof If $\mathbf{x}$ is a vector in R^n,

$$\mathbf{x} = \begin{bmatrix} x_1 \\ x_2 \\ \vdots \\ x_n \end{bmatrix},$$

then $\mathbf{x}$ can be expressed in the form

$$\mathbf{x} = x_1\mathbf{e}_1 + x_2\mathbf{e}_2 + \cdots + x_n\mathbf{e}_n.$$

It now follows from Eq. (6) that

$$T(\mathbf{x}) = x_1T(\mathbf{e}_1) + x_2T(\mathbf{e}_2) + \cdots + x_nT(\mathbf{e}_n). \tag{8}$$

If $A = [T(\mathbf{e}_1), T(\mathbf{e}_2), \ldots, T(\mathbf{e}_n)]$, then by Theorem 5 of Section 1.5, the right-hand side of Eq. (8) is simply $A\mathbf{x}$. Thus Eq. (8) is equivalent to $T(\mathbf{x}) = A\mathbf{x}$. ■

EXAMPLE 8 Let $T: R^2 \to R^3$ be the linear transformation defined by the formula

$$T\left(\begin{bmatrix} x_1 \\ x_2 \end{bmatrix}\right) = \begin{bmatrix} x_1 + 2x_2 \\ -x_1 + x_2 \\ 2x_1 - x_2 \end{bmatrix}.$$

Find a matrix A such that $T(\mathbf{x}) = A\mathbf{x}$ for each $\mathbf{x}$ in R^2.

Solution By Theorem 15, A is the (3×2) matrix

$$A = [T(\mathbf{e}_1), T(\mathbf{e}_2)].$$

It is an easy calculation that

$$T(\mathbf{e}_1) = \begin{bmatrix} 1 \\ -1 \\ 2 \end{bmatrix} \quad \text{and} \quad T(\mathbf{e}_2) = \begin{bmatrix} 2 \\ 1 \\ -1 \end{bmatrix}.$$

Therefore,

$$A = \begin{bmatrix} 1 & 2 \\ -1 & 1 \\ 2 & -1 \end{bmatrix}.$$

One can easily verify that $T(\mathbf{x}) = A\mathbf{x}$ for each $\mathbf{x}$ in R^2. ■

Null Space and Range

Associated with a linear transformation, T, are two important and useful subspaces called the null space and the range of T. These are defined as follows.

DEFINITION 9 Let V and W be subspaces, and let $T: V \to W$ be a linear transformation. The ***null space*** of T, denoted by $\mathcal{N}(T)$, is the subset of V given by

$$\mathcal{N}(T) = \{\mathbf{v}: \mathbf{v} \text{ is in } V \text{ and } T(\mathbf{v}) = \boldsymbol{\theta}\}.$$

The ***range*** of T, denoted by $\mathcal{R}(T)$, is the subset of W defined by

$$\mathcal{R}(T) = \{\mathbf{w}: \mathbf{w} \text{ is in } W \text{ and } \mathbf{w} = T(\mathbf{v}) \text{ for some } \mathbf{v} \text{ in } V\}.$$

That $\mathcal{N}(T)$ and $\mathcal{R}(T)$ are subspaces will be proved in the more general context of Chapter 5. If T maps R^n into R^m, then by Theorem 15 there exists an $(m \times n)$ matrix

A such that $T(\mathbf{x}) = A\mathbf{x}$. In this case it is clear that the null space of T is the null space of A and the range of T coincides with the range of A.

As with matrices, the dimension of the null space of a linear transformation T is called the ***nullity*** of T, and the dimension of the range of T is called the ***rank*** of T. If T is defined by matrix multiplication, $T(\mathbf{x}) = A\mathbf{x}$, then the transformation T and the matrix A have the same nullity and the same rank. Moreover, if T: $R^n \to R^m$, then A is an $(m \times n)$ matrix, so it follows from the remark in Section 3.5 that

$$\text{rank}(T) + \text{nullity}(T) = n. \tag{9}$$

Formula (9) will be proved in a more general setting in Chapter 5.

The next two examples illustrate the use of the matrix of T to determine the null space and the range of T.

EXAMPLE 9 Let F be the linear transformation given in Example 1, F: $R^3 \to R^2$. Describe the null space and the range of F, and determine the nullity and the rank of F.

Solution It follows from Theorem 15 that $F(\mathbf{x}) = A\mathbf{x}$, where A is the (2×3) matrix

$$A = [F(\mathbf{e}_1), F(\mathbf{e}_2), F(\mathbf{e}_3)] = \begin{bmatrix} 1 & -1 & 0 \\ 0 & 1 & 1 \end{bmatrix}.$$

Thus the null space and the range of F coincide, respectively, with the null space and the range of A. The null space of A is determined by backsolving the homogeneous system $A\mathbf{x} = \boldsymbol{\theta}$, where $\mathbf{x}$ is in R^3:

$$\mathbf{x} = \begin{bmatrix} x_1 \\ x_2 \\ x_3 \end{bmatrix}.$$

This gives

$$\mathcal{N}(F) = \mathcal{N}(A) = \{\mathbf{x} : x_1 = -x_3 \text{ and } x_2 = -x_3\}.$$

Using the techniques of Section 3.4, we can easily see that the vector

$$\mathbf{u} = \begin{bmatrix} -1 \\ -1 \\ 1 \end{bmatrix}$$

is a basis for $\mathcal{N}(F)$, so F has nullity 1. By Eq. (9),

$$\text{rank}(F) = n - \text{nullity}(F) = 3 - 1 = 2.$$

Thus $\mathcal{R}(F)$ is a two-dimensional subspace of R^2, and hence $\mathcal{R}(F) = R^2$.

Alternatively, note that the system of equations $A\mathbf{x} = \mathbf{b}$ has a solution for each $\mathbf{b}$ in R^2, so $\mathcal{R}(F) = \mathcal{R}(A) = R^2$. ■

EXAMPLE 10 Let T: $R^2 \to R^3$ be the linear transformation given in Example 8. Describe the null space and the range of T, and determine the nullity and the rank of T.

Solution In Example 8 it was shown that $T(\mathbf{x}) = A\mathbf{x}$, where A is the (3×2) matrix

$$A = \begin{bmatrix} 1 & 2 \\ -1 & 1 \\ 2 & -1 \end{bmatrix}.$$

If $\mathbf{b}$ is the (3×1) vector,

$$\mathbf{b} = \begin{bmatrix} b_1 \\ b_2 \\ b_3 \end{bmatrix},$$

then the augmented matrix $[A \mid \mathbf{b}]$ for the linear system $A\mathbf{x} = \mathbf{b}$ is row equivalent to

$$\begin{bmatrix} 1 & 0 & (1/3)b_1 - (2/3)b_2 \\ 0 & 1 & (1/3)b_1 + (1/3)b_2 \\ 0 & 0 & (-1/3)b_1 + (5/3)b_2 + b_3 \end{bmatrix}. \tag{10}$$

Therefore, $T(\mathbf{x}) = A\mathbf{x} = \mathbf{b}$ can be solved if and only if $0 = (-1/3)b_1 + (5/3)b_2 + b_3$. The range of T can thus be described as

$$\begin{aligned} \mathcal{R}(T) &= \mathcal{R}(A) \\ &= \left\{\mathbf{b}\colon \mathbf{b} = \begin{bmatrix} b_1 \\ b_2 \\ (1/3)b_1 - (5/3)b_2 \end{bmatrix},\quad b_1 \text{ and } b_2 \text{ any real numbers}\right\}. \end{aligned}$$

A basis for $\mathcal{R}(T)$ is $\{\mathbf{u}_1, \mathbf{u}_2\}$ where

$$\mathbf{u}_1 = \begin{bmatrix} 1 \\ 0 \\ 1/3 \end{bmatrix} \quad \text{and} \quad \mathbf{u}_2 = \begin{bmatrix} 0 \\ 1 \\ -5/3 \end{bmatrix}.$$

Thus T has rank 2, and by Eq. (9),

$$\text{nullity}(T) = n - \text{rank}(T) = 2 - 2 = 0.$$

It follows that T has null space $\{\boldsymbol{\theta}\}$. Alternatively, it is clear from matrix (10), with $\mathbf{b} = \boldsymbol{\theta}$, that the homogeneous system of equations $A\mathbf{x} = \boldsymbol{\theta}$ has only the trivial solution. Therefore, $\mathcal{N}(T) = \mathcal{N}(A) = \{\boldsymbol{\theta}\}$. ■

Orthogonal Transformations on R^2 (Optional)

It is often informative and useful to view linear transformations on either R^2 or R^3 from a geometric point of view. To illustrate this general notion, the remainder of this section is devoted to determining those linear transformations $T\colon R^2 \to R^2$ that preserve the length of a vector; that is, we are interested in linear transformations T such that

$$\|T(\mathbf{v})\| = \|\mathbf{v}\| \tag{11}$$

for all $\mathbf{v}$ in R^2. Transformations that satisfy Eq. (11) are called ***orthogonal transformations***. We begin by giving some examples of orthogonal transformations.

EXAMPLE 11 Let θ be a fixed angle, and let $T: R^2 \rightarrow R^2$ be the linear transformation defined by $T(\mathbf{v}) = A\mathbf{v}$, where A is the (2×2) matrix

$$A = \begin{bmatrix} \cos\theta & -\sin\theta \\ \sin\theta & \cos\theta \end{bmatrix}.$$

Give a geometric interpretation of T, and show that T is an orthogonal transformation.

Solution Suppose that $\mathbf{v}$ and $T(\mathbf{v})$ are given by

$$\mathbf{v} = \begin{bmatrix} a \\ b \end{bmatrix} \quad \text{and} \quad T(\mathbf{v}) = \begin{bmatrix} c \\ d \end{bmatrix}.$$

Then $T(\mathbf{v}) = A\mathbf{v}$, so

$$\begin{bmatrix} c \\ d \end{bmatrix} = \begin{bmatrix} \cos\theta & -\sin\theta \\ \sin\theta & \cos\theta \end{bmatrix} \begin{bmatrix} a \\ b \end{bmatrix} = \begin{bmatrix} a\cos\theta - b\sin\theta \\ a\sin\theta + b\cos\theta \end{bmatrix}. \tag{12}$$

We proceed now to show that $T(\mathbf{v})$ is obtained geometrically by rotating the vector $\mathbf{v}$ through the angle θ. To see this, let ϕ be the angle between $\mathbf{v}$ and the positive x-axis (see Fig. 3.17), and set $r = \|\mathbf{v}\|$. Then the coordinates a and b can be written as

$$a = r\cos\phi, \quad b = r\sin\phi. \tag{13}$$

Making the substitution (13) for a and b in (12) yields

$$c = r\cos\phi\cos\theta - r\sin\phi\sin\theta = r\cos(\phi + \theta)$$

and

$$d = r\cos\phi\sin\theta + r\sin\phi\cos\theta = r\sin(\phi + \theta).$$

Therefore, c and d are the coordinates of the point obtained by rotating the point (a, b) through the angle θ. Clearly then, $\|T(\mathbf{v})\| = \|\mathbf{v}\|$, and T is an orthogonal linear transformation. ■

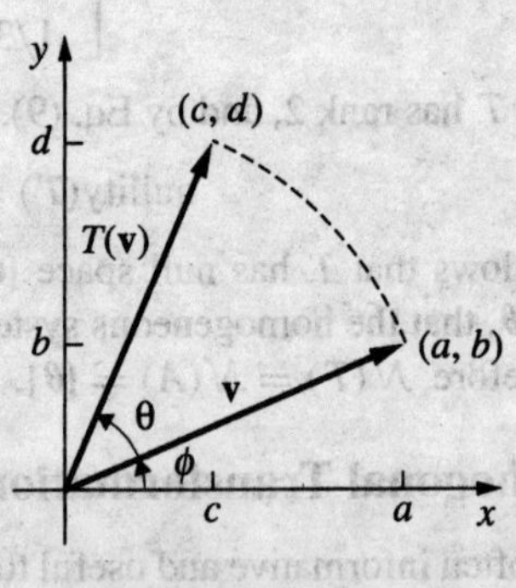

Figure 3.17 Rotation through the angle θ

The linear transformation T defined in Example 11 is called a ***rotation***. Thus if A is a (2×2) matrix,

$$A = \begin{bmatrix} a & -b \\ b & a \end{bmatrix},$$

where $a^2 + b^2 = 1$, then the linear transformation $T(\mathbf{v}) = A\mathbf{v}$ is the rotation through the angle θ, $0 \le \theta < 2\pi$, where $\cos\theta = a$ and $\sin\theta = b$.

EXAMPLE 12 Define $T\colon R^2 \to R^2$ by $T(\mathbf{v}) = A\mathbf{v}$, where

$$A = \begin{bmatrix} -1/2 & \sqrt{3}/2 \\ -\sqrt{3}/2 & -1/2 \end{bmatrix}.$$

Give a geometric interpretation of T.

Solution Since $\cos(4\pi/3) = -1/2$ and $\sin(4\pi/3) = -\sqrt{3}/2$, T is the rotation through the angle $4\pi/3$. ■

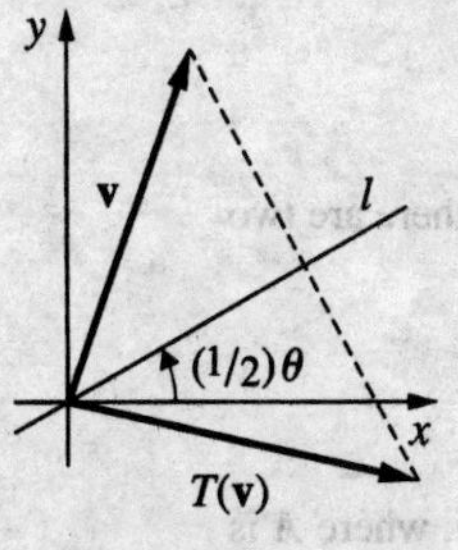

Figure 3.18
Reflection about a line

Now let l be a line in the plane that passes through the origin, and let $\mathbf{v}$ be a vector in the plane. If we define $T(\mathbf{v})$ to be the symmetric image of $\mathbf{v}$ relative to l (see Fig. 3.18), then clearly T preserves the length of $\mathbf{v}$. It can be shown that T is multiplication by the matrix

$$A = \begin{bmatrix} \cos\theta & \sin\theta \\ \sin\theta & -\cos\theta \end{bmatrix},$$

where $(1/2)\theta$ is the angle between l and the positive x-axis. Any such transformation is called a ***reflection***. Note that a reflection T is also an orthogonal linear transformation.

EXAMPLE 13 Let $T\colon R^2 \to R^2$ be defined by $T(\mathbf{v}) = A\mathbf{v}$, where A is the (2×2) matrix

$$A = \begin{bmatrix} 1/2 & \sqrt{3}/2 \\ \sqrt{3}/2 & -1/2 \end{bmatrix}.$$

Give a geometric interpretation of T.

Solution Since $\cos(\pi/3) = 1/2$ and $\sin(\pi/3) = \sqrt{3}/2$, T is the reflection about the line l, where l is the line that passes through the origin at an angle of 30 degrees. ■

The next theorem gives a characterization of orthogonal transformations on R^2. A consequence of this theorem will be that every orthogonal transformation is either a rotation or a reflection.

THEOREM 16 Let $T\colon R^2 \to R^2$ be a linear transformation. Then T is an orthogonal transformation if and only if $\|T(\mathbf{e}_1)\| = \|T(\mathbf{e}_2)\| = 1$ and $T(\mathbf{e}_1)$ is perpendicular to $T(\mathbf{e}_2)$.

Proof If T is an orthogonal transformation, then $\|T(\mathbf{v})\| = \|\mathbf{v}\|$ for every vector $\mathbf{v}$ in R^2. In particular, $\|T(\mathbf{e}_1)\| = \|\mathbf{e}_1\| = 1$, and similarly $\|T(\mathbf{e}_2)\| = 1$. Set $\mathbf{u}_1 = T(\mathbf{e}_1)$, $\mathbf{u}_2 = T(\mathbf{e}_2)$, and $\mathbf{v} = [1, 1]^T = \mathbf{e}_1 + \mathbf{e}_2$. Then

$$2 = \|\mathbf{v}\|^2 = \|T(\mathbf{v})\|^2 = \|T(\mathbf{e}_1 + \mathbf{e}_2)\|^2 = \|T(\mathbf{e}_1) + T(\mathbf{e}_2)\|^2.$$

Thus,

$$\begin{aligned}2 &= \|\mathbf{u}_1 + \mathbf{u}_2\|^2 \\ &= (\mathbf{u}_1 + \mathbf{u}_2)^T(\mathbf{u}_1 + \mathbf{u}_2) \\ &= (\mathbf{u}_1^T + \mathbf{u}_2^T)(\mathbf{u}_1 + \mathbf{u}_2) \\ &= \mathbf{u}_1^T\mathbf{u}_1 + \mathbf{u}_1^T\mathbf{u}_2 + \mathbf{u}_2^T\mathbf{u}_1 + \mathbf{u}_2^T\mathbf{u}_2 \\ &= \|\mathbf{u}_1\|^2 + 2\mathbf{u}_1^T\mathbf{u}_2 + \|\mathbf{u}_2\|^2 \\ &= 2 + 2\mathbf{u}_1^T\mathbf{u}_2.\end{aligned}$$

It follows that $\mathbf{u}_1^T\mathbf{u}_2 = 0$, so $\mathbf{u}_1$ is perpendicular to $\mathbf{u}_2$.

The proof of the converse is Exercise 47. ■

We can now use Theorem 16 to give a geometric description for any orthogonal linear transformation, T, on R^2. First, suppose that $T(\mathbf{e}_1) = \mathbf{u}_1$ and $T(\mathbf{e}_2) = \mathbf{u}_2$. If

$$\mathbf{u}_1 = \begin{bmatrix} a \\ b \end{bmatrix},$$

then $1 = \|\mathbf{u}_1\|^2 = a^2 + b^2$. Since $\|\mathbf{u}_2\| = 1$ and $\mathbf{u}_2$ is perpendicular to $\mathbf{u}_1$, there are two choices for $\mathbf{u}_2$ (see Fig. 3.19): either

$$\mathbf{u}_2 = \begin{bmatrix} -b \\ a \end{bmatrix} \quad \text{or} \quad \mathbf{u}_2 = \begin{bmatrix} b \\ -a \end{bmatrix}.$$

In either case, it follows from Theorem 15 that T is defined by $T(\mathbf{v}) = A\mathbf{v}$, where A is the (2×2) matrix $A = [\mathbf{u}_1, \mathbf{u}_2]$. Thus if

$$\mathbf{u}_2 = \begin{bmatrix} -b \\ a \end{bmatrix},$$

then

$$A = \begin{bmatrix} a & -b \\ b & a \end{bmatrix},$$

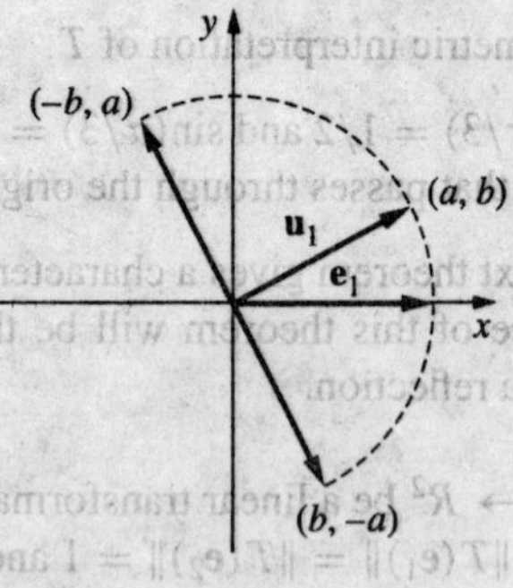

Figure 3.19 Choices for $\mathbf{u}_2$

so T is a rotation. If

$$\mathbf{u}_2 = \begin{bmatrix} b \\ -a \end{bmatrix},$$

then

$$A = \begin{bmatrix} a & b \\ b & -a \end{bmatrix},$$

and T is a reflection. In either case note that $A^TA = I$, so $A^T = A^{-1}$ (see Exercise 48). An $(n \times n)$ real matrix with the property that $A^TA = I$ is called an ***orthogonal matrix***. Thus we have shown that an orthogonal transformation on R^2 is defined by

$$T(\mathbf{x}) = A\mathbf{x},$$

where A is an orthogonal matrix.

3.7 EXERCISES

1. Define T: $R^2 \to R^2$ by

$$T\left(\begin{bmatrix} x_1 \\ x_2 \end{bmatrix}\right) = \begin{bmatrix} 2x_1 - 3x_2 \\ -x_1 + x_2 \end{bmatrix}.$$

Find each of the following.

a) $T\left(\begin{bmatrix} 0 \\ 0 \end{bmatrix}\right)$ **b)** $T\left(\begin{bmatrix} 1 \\ 1 \end{bmatrix}\right)$

c) $T\left(\begin{bmatrix} 2 \\ 1 \end{bmatrix}\right)$ **d)** $T\left(\begin{bmatrix} -1 \\ 0 \end{bmatrix}\right)$

2. Define T: $R^2 \to R^2$ by $T(\mathbf{x}) = A\mathbf{x}$, where

$$A = \begin{bmatrix} 1 & -1 \\ -3 & 3 \end{bmatrix}.$$

Find each of the following.

a) $T\left(\begin{bmatrix} 2 \\ 2 \end{bmatrix}\right)$ **b)** $T\left(\begin{bmatrix} 3 \\ 1 \end{bmatrix}\right)$

c) $T\left(\begin{bmatrix} 2 \\ 0 \end{bmatrix}\right)$ **d)** $T\left(\begin{bmatrix} 0 \\ 0 \end{bmatrix}\right)$

3. Let T: $R^3 \to R^2$ be the linear transformation defined by

$$T\left(\begin{bmatrix} x_1 \\ x_2 \\ x_3 \end{bmatrix}\right) = \begin{bmatrix} x_1 + 2x_2 + 4x_3 \\ 2x_1 + 3x_2 + 5x_3 \end{bmatrix}.$$

Which of the following vectors are in the null space of T?

a) $\begin{bmatrix} 0 \\ 0 \\ 0 \end{bmatrix}$ **b)** $\begin{bmatrix} 2 \\ -3 \\ 1 \end{bmatrix}$

c) $\begin{bmatrix} 1 \\ 2 \\ 1 \end{bmatrix}$ **d)** $\begin{bmatrix} -1 \\ 3/2 \\ -1/2 \end{bmatrix}$

4. Let T: $R^2 \to R^2$ be the function defined in Exercise 1. Find $\mathbf{x}$ in R^2 such that $T(\mathbf{x}) = \mathbf{b}$, where

$$\mathbf{b} = \begin{bmatrix} 2 \\ -2 \end{bmatrix}.$$

5. Let T: $R^2 \to R^2$ be the function given in Exercise 1. Show that for each $\mathbf{b}$ in R^2, there is an $\mathbf{x}$ in R^2 such that $T(\mathbf{x}) = \mathbf{b}$.

6. Let T be the linear transformation given in Exercise 2. Find $\mathbf{x}$ in R^2 such that $T(\mathbf{x}) = \mathbf{b}$, where

$$\mathbf{b} = \begin{bmatrix} -2 \\ 6 \end{bmatrix}.$$

7. Let T be the linear transformation given in Exercise 2. Show that there is no $\mathbf{x}$ in R^2 such that

$T(\mathbf{x}) = \mathbf{b}$ for

$$\mathbf{b} = \begin{bmatrix} 1 \\ 1 \end{bmatrix}.$$

In Exercises 8–17, determine whether the function F is a linear transformation.

8. F: $R^2 \to R^2$ defined by

$$F\left(\begin{bmatrix} x_1 \\ x_2 \end{bmatrix}\right) = \begin{bmatrix} 2x_1 - x_2 \\ x_1 + 3x_2 \end{bmatrix}$$

9. F: $R^2 \to R^2$ defined by

$$F\left(\begin{bmatrix} x_1 \\ x_2 \end{bmatrix}\right) = \begin{bmatrix} x_2 \\ x_1 \end{bmatrix}$$

10. F: $R^2 \to R^2$ defined by

$$F\left(\begin{bmatrix} x_1 \\ x_2 \end{bmatrix}\right) = \begin{bmatrix} x_1 + x_2 \\ 1 \end{bmatrix}$$

11. F: $R^2 \to R^2$ defined by

$$F\left(\begin{bmatrix} x_1 \\ x_2 \end{bmatrix}\right) = \begin{bmatrix} x_1^2 \\ x_1x_2 \end{bmatrix}$$

12. F: $R^3 \to R^2$ defined by

$$F\left(\begin{bmatrix} x_1 \\ x_2 \\ x_3 \end{bmatrix}\right) = \begin{bmatrix} x_1 - x_2 + x_3 \\ -x_1 + 3x_2 - 2x_3 \end{bmatrix}$$

13. F: $R^3 \to R^2$ defined by

$$F\left(\begin{bmatrix} x_1 \\ x_2 \\ x_3 \end{bmatrix}\right) = \begin{bmatrix} x_1 \\ x_2 \end{bmatrix}$$

14. F: $R^2 \to R^3$ defined by

$$F\left(\begin{bmatrix} x_1 \\ x_2 \end{bmatrix}\right) = \begin{bmatrix} x_1 - x_2 \\ -x_1 + x_2 \\ x_2 \end{bmatrix}$$

15. F: $R^2 \to R^3$ defined by

$$F\left(\begin{bmatrix} x_1 \\ x_2 \end{bmatrix}\right) = \begin{bmatrix} x_1 \\ x_2 \\ 0 \end{bmatrix}$$

16. F: $R^2 \to R$ defined by

$$F\left(\begin{bmatrix} x_1 \\ x_2 \end{bmatrix}\right) = 2x_1 + 3x_2$$

17. F: $R^2 \to R$ defined by

$$F\left(\begin{bmatrix} x_1 \\ x_2 \end{bmatrix}\right) = |x_1| + |x_2|$$

18. Let W be the subspace of R^3 defined by

$$W = \{\mathbf{x}\colon \mathbf{x} = \begin{bmatrix} x_1 \\ x_2 \\ x_3 \end{bmatrix}, \quad x_2 = x_3 = 0\}.$$

Find an orthonormal basis for W, and use Eq. (4) of Example 3 to give a formula for the orthogonal projection T: $R^3 \to W$; that is, determine $T(\mathbf{v})$ for arbitrary $\mathbf{v}$ in R^3:

$$\mathbf{v} = \begin{bmatrix} a \\ b \\ c \end{bmatrix}.$$

Give a geometric interpretation of W, $\mathbf{v}$, and $T(\mathbf{v})$.

19. Let T: $R^2 \to R^3$ be a linear transformation such that $T(\mathbf{e}_1) = \mathbf{u}_1$ and $T(\mathbf{e}_2) = \mathbf{u}_2$, where

$$\mathbf{u}_1 = \begin{bmatrix} 1 \\ 0 \\ -1 \end{bmatrix} \quad \text{and} \quad \mathbf{u}_2 = \begin{bmatrix} 2 \\ 1 \\ 0 \end{bmatrix}.$$

Find each of the following.

a) $T\left(\begin{bmatrix} 1 \\ 1 \end{bmatrix}\right)$

b) $T\left(\begin{bmatrix} 2 \\ -1 \end{bmatrix}\right)$

c) $T\left(\begin{bmatrix} 3 \\ 2 \end{bmatrix}\right)$

20. Let T: $R^2 \to R^2$ be a linear transformation such that $T(\mathbf{v}_1) = \mathbf{u}_1$ and $T(\mathbf{v}_2) = \mathbf{u}_2$, where

$$\mathbf{v}_1 = \begin{bmatrix} 0 \\ 1 \end{bmatrix}, \quad \mathbf{v}_2 = \begin{bmatrix} -1 \\ 1 \end{bmatrix},$$

$$\mathbf{u}_1 = \begin{bmatrix} 0 \\ 2 \end{bmatrix}, \quad \text{and} \quad \mathbf{u}_2 = \begin{bmatrix} 3 \\ 1 \end{bmatrix}.$$

Find each of the following.

a) $T\left(\begin{bmatrix} 1 \\ 1 \end{bmatrix}\right)$

b) $T\left(\begin{bmatrix} 2 \\ -1 \end{bmatrix}\right)$

c) $T\left(\begin{bmatrix} 3 \\ 2 \end{bmatrix}\right)$

In Exercises 21–24, the action of a linear transformation T on a basis for either R^2 or R^3 is given. In each case use Eq. (6) to derive a formula for T.

21. $T\left(\begin{bmatrix} 1 \\ 1 \end{bmatrix}\right) = \begin{bmatrix} 2 \\ -1 \end{bmatrix}$ and

$T\left(\begin{bmatrix} 1 \\ -1 \end{bmatrix}\right) = \begin{bmatrix} 0 \\ 3 \end{bmatrix}$

22. $T\left(\begin{bmatrix} 1 \\ 1 \end{bmatrix}\right) = \begin{bmatrix} 1 \\ 2 \\ 1 \end{bmatrix}$ and

$T\left(\begin{bmatrix} 1 \\ -1 \end{bmatrix}\right) = \begin{bmatrix} 0 \\ 2 \\ 2 \end{bmatrix}$

23. $T\left(\begin{bmatrix} 1 \\ 0 \\ 1 \end{bmatrix}\right) = \begin{bmatrix} 0 \\ 1 \end{bmatrix}$,

$T\left(\begin{bmatrix} 0 \\ -1 \\ 1 \end{bmatrix}\right) = \begin{bmatrix} 1 \\ 0 \end{bmatrix}$,

$T\left(\begin{bmatrix} 1 \\ -1 \\ 0 \end{bmatrix}\right) = \begin{bmatrix} 0 \\ 0 \end{bmatrix}$

24. $T\left(\begin{bmatrix} 1 \\ 0 \\ 1 \end{bmatrix}\right) = \begin{bmatrix} 0 \\ -1 \\ 1 \end{bmatrix}$,

$T\left(\begin{bmatrix} 0 \\ -1 \\ 1 \end{bmatrix}\right) = \begin{bmatrix} 2 \\ 1 \\ 0 \end{bmatrix}$,

$T\left(\begin{bmatrix} 1 \\ -1 \\ 0 \end{bmatrix}\right) = \begin{bmatrix} 0 \\ 0 \\ 1 \end{bmatrix}$

In Exercises 25–30, a linear transformation T is given. In each case find a matrix A such that $T(\mathbf{x}) = A\mathbf{x}$. Also describe the null space and the range of T and give the rank and the nullity of T.

25. $T\colon R^2 \to R^2$ defined by

$$T\left(\begin{bmatrix} x_1 \\ x_2 \end{bmatrix}\right) = \begin{bmatrix} x_1 + 3x_2 \\ 2x_1 + x_2 \end{bmatrix}$$

26. $T\colon R^2 \to R^3$ defined by

$$T\left(\begin{bmatrix} x_1 \\ x_2 \end{bmatrix}\right) = \begin{bmatrix} x_1 - x_2 \\ x_1 + x_2 \\ x_2 \end{bmatrix}$$

27. $T\colon R^2 \to R$ defined by

$$T\left(\begin{bmatrix} x_1 \\ x_2 \end{bmatrix}\right) = 3x_1 + 2x_2$$

28. $T\colon R^3 \to R^3$ defined by

$$T\left(\begin{bmatrix} x_1 \\ x_2 \\ x_3 \end{bmatrix}\right) = \begin{bmatrix} x_1 + x_2 \\ x_3 \\ x_2 \end{bmatrix}$$

29. $T\colon R^3 \to R^2$ defined by

$$T\left(\begin{bmatrix} x_1 \\ x_2 \\ x_3 \end{bmatrix}\right) = \begin{bmatrix} x_1 - x_2 \\ x_2 - x_3 \end{bmatrix}$$

30. $T\colon R^3 \to R$ defined by

$$T\left(\begin{bmatrix} x_1 \\ x_2 \\ x_3 \end{bmatrix}\right) = 2x_1 - x_2 + 4x_3$$

31. Let a be a real number, and define $f\colon R \to R$ by $f(x) = ax$ for each x in R. Show that f is a linear transformation.

32. Let T: $R \to R$ be a linear transformation, and suppose that $T(1) = a$. Show that $T(x) = ax$ for each x in R.

33. Let T: $R^2 \to R^2$ be the function that maps each point in R^2 to its reflection with respect to the x-axis. Give a formula for T and show that T is a linear transformation.

34. Let T: $R^2 \to R^2$ be the function that maps each point in R^2 to its reflection with respect to the line $y = x$. Give a formula for T and show that T is a linear transformation.

35. Let V and W be subspaces, and let F: $V \to W$ and G: $V \to W$ be linear transformations. Define $F + G$: $V \to W$ by $[F + G](\mathbf{v}) = F(\mathbf{v}) + G(\mathbf{v})$ for each $\mathbf{v}$ in V. Prove that $F + G$ is a linear transformation.

36. Let F: $R^3 \to R^2$ and G: $R^3 \to R^2$ be defined by

$$F\left(\begin{bmatrix} x_1 \\ x_2 \\ x_3 \end{bmatrix}\right) = \begin{bmatrix} 2x_1 - 3x_2 + x_3 \\ 4x_1 + 2x_2 - 5x_3 \end{bmatrix}$$

and

$$G\left(\begin{bmatrix} x_1 \\ x_2 \\ x_3 \end{bmatrix}\right) = \begin{bmatrix} -x_1 + 4x_2 + 2x_3 \\ -2x_1 + 3x_2 + 3x_3 \end{bmatrix}.$$

a) Give a formula for the linear transformation $F + G$ (see Exercise 35).

b) Find matrices A, B, and C such that $F(\mathbf{x}) = A\mathbf{x}$, $G(\mathbf{x}) = B\mathbf{x}$, and $(F + G)(\mathbf{x}) = C\mathbf{x}$.

c) Verify that $C = A + B$.

37. Let V and W be subspaces, and let T: $V \to W$ be a linear transformation. If a is a scalar, define aT: $V \to W$ by $[aT](\mathbf{v}) = a[T(\mathbf{v})]$ for each $\mathbf{v}$ in V. Show that aT is a linear transformation.

38. Let T: $R^3 \to R^2$ be the linear transformation defined in Exercise 29. The linear transformation $[3T]$: $R^3 \to R^2$ is defined in Exercise 37.

a) Give a formula for the transformation $3T$.

b) Find matrices A and B such that $T(\mathbf{x}) = A\mathbf{x}$ and $[3T](\mathbf{x}) = B\mathbf{x}$.

c) Verify that $B = 3A$.

39. Let U, V, and W be subspaces, and let F: $U \to V$ and G: $V \to W$ be linear transformations. Prove that the composition $G \circ F$: $U \to W$ of F and G, defining by $[G \circ F](\mathbf{u}) = G(F(\mathbf{u}))$ for each $\mathbf{u}$ in U, is a linear transformation.

40. Let F: $R^3 \to R^2$ and G: $R^2 \to R^3$ be linear transformations defined by

$$F\left(\begin{bmatrix} x_1 \\ x_2 \\ x_3 \end{bmatrix}\right) = \begin{bmatrix} -x_1 + 2x_2 - 4x_3 \\ 2x_1 + 5x_2 + x_3 \end{bmatrix}$$

and

$$G\left(\begin{bmatrix} x_1 \\ x_2 \end{bmatrix}\right) = \begin{bmatrix} x_1 - 2x_2 \\ 3x_1 + 2x_2 \\ -x_1 + x_2 \end{bmatrix}.$$

a) By Exercise 39, $G \circ F$: $R^3 \to R^3$ is a linear transformation. Give a formula for $G \circ F$.

b) Find matrices A, B, and C such that $F(\mathbf{x}) = A\mathbf{x}$, $G(\mathbf{x}) = B\mathbf{x}$, and $[G \circ F](\mathbf{x}) = C\mathbf{x}$.

c) Verify that $C = BA$.

41. Let B be an $(m \times n)$ matrix, and let T: $R^n \to R^m$ be defined by $T(\mathbf{x}) = B\mathbf{x}$ for each $\mathbf{x}$ in R^n. If A is the matrix for T given by Theorem 15, show that $A = B$.

42. Let F: $R^n \to R^p$ and G: $R^p \to R^m$ be linear transformations, and assume that Theorem 15 yields matrices A and B, respectively, for F and G. Show that the matrix for the composition $G \circ F$ (see Exercise 39) is BA. [*Hint:* Show that $(G \circ F)(\mathbf{x}) = BA\mathbf{x}$ for $\mathbf{x}$ in R^n and then apply Exercise 41.]

43. Let I: $R^n \to R^n$ be the identity transformation. Determine the matrix A such that $I(\mathbf{x}) = A\mathbf{x}$ for each $\mathbf{x}$ in R^n.

44. Let a be a real number and define T: $R^n \to R^n$ by $T(\mathbf{x}) = a\mathbf{x}$ (see Example 4). Determine the matrix A such that $T(\mathbf{x}) = A\mathbf{x}$ for each $\mathbf{x}$ in R^n.

Exercises 45–49 are based on the optional material.

45. Let T: $R^2 \to R^2$ be a rotation through the angle θ. In each of the following cases, exhibit the matrix for T. Also represent $\mathbf{v}$ and $T(\mathbf{v})$ geometrically, where

$$\mathbf{v} = \begin{bmatrix} 1 \\ 1 \end{bmatrix}.$$

a) $\theta = \pi/2$ **b)** $\theta = \pi/3$ **c)** $\theta = 2\pi/3$

46. Let T: $R^2 \to R^2$ be the reflection with respect to the line l. In each of the following cases, exhibit

the matrix for T. Also represent $\mathbf{e}_1$, $\mathbf{e}_2$, $T(\mathbf{e}_1)$, and $T(\mathbf{e}_2)$ geometrically.
a) l is the x-axis. **b)** l is the y-axis.
c) l is the line with equation $y = x$.
d) l is the line with equation $y = \sqrt{3}x$.

47. Let $T: R^2 \to R^2$ be a linear transformation that satisfies the conditions of Theorem 16. Show that T is orthogonal. [*Hint:* If $\mathbf{v} = [a, b]^T$, then $\mathbf{v} = a\mathbf{e}_1 + b\mathbf{e}_2$. Now use Eq. (6).]

48. Let $T: R^2 \to R^2$ be an orthogonal linear transformation, and let A be the corresponding (2×2) matrix. Show that $A^TA = I$. [*Hint:* Use Theorem 16.]

49. Let $A = [\mathbf{A}_1, \mathbf{A}_2]$ be a (2×2) matrix such that $A^TA = I$, and define $T: R^2 \to R^2$ by $T(\mathbf{x}) = A\mathbf{x}$.
a) Show that $\{\mathbf{A}_1, \mathbf{A}_2\}$ is an orthonormal set.
b) Use Theorem 16 to show that T is an orthogonal transformation.

3.8 LEAST-SQUARES SOLUTIONS TO INCONSISTENT SYSTEMS, WITH APPLICATIONS TO DATA FITTING

When faced with solving a linear system of the form $A\mathbf{x} = \mathbf{b}$, our procedure has been to describe all solutions if the system is consistent but merely to say "there are no solutions" if the system is inconsistent. We now want to go a step further with regard to inconsistent systems. If a given linear system $A\mathbf{x} = \mathbf{b}$ has no solution, then we would like to do the next best thing—find a vector $\mathbf{x}^*$ such that the residual vector, $\mathbf{r} = A\mathbf{x}^* - \mathbf{b}$, is as small as possible. In terms of practical applications, we shall see that any technique for minimizing the residual vector can also be used to find best least-squares fits to data.

A common source of inconsistent systems are ***overdetermined systems*** (that is, systems with more equations than unknowns). The system that follows is an example of an overdetermined system:

$$\begin{aligned} x_1 + 4x_2 &= -2 \\ x_1 + 2x_2 &= 6 \\ 2x_1 + 3x_2 &= 1. \end{aligned}$$

Overdetermined systems are often inconsistent, and the preceding example is no exception. Given that the above system has no solution, a reasonable goal is to find values for x_1 and x_2 that come as close as possible to satisfying all three equations. Methods for achieving that goal are the subject of this section.

Least-Squares Solutions to $A\mathbf{x} = \mathbf{b}$

Consider the linear system $A\mathbf{x} = \mathbf{b}$ where A is $(m \times n)$. If $\mathbf{x}$ is a vector in R^n, then the vector $\mathbf{r} = A\mathbf{x} - \mathbf{b}$ is called a ***residual vector***. A vector $\mathbf{x}^*$ in R^n that yields the smallest possible residual vector is called a least-squares solution to $A\mathbf{x} = \mathbf{b}$. More precisely, $\mathbf{x}^*$ is a ***least-squares solution*** to $A\mathbf{x} = \mathbf{b}$ if

$$\|A\mathbf{x}^* - \mathbf{b}\| \le \|A\mathbf{x} - \mathbf{b}\|, \quad \text{for all } \mathbf{x} \text{ in } R^n.$$

(If $A\mathbf{x} = \mathbf{b}$ happens to be consistent, then a least-squares solution $\mathbf{x}^*$ is also a solution in the usual sense since $\|A\mathbf{x}^* - \mathbf{b}\| = 0$.)

The special case of an inconsistent (3×2) system $A\mathbf{x} = \mathbf{b}$ suggests how we can calculate least-squares solutions. In particular, consider Fig. 3.20 which illustrates a vector $\mathbf{b}$ that is not in $\mathcal{R}(A)$; that is, $A\mathbf{x} = \mathbf{b}$ is inconsistent.

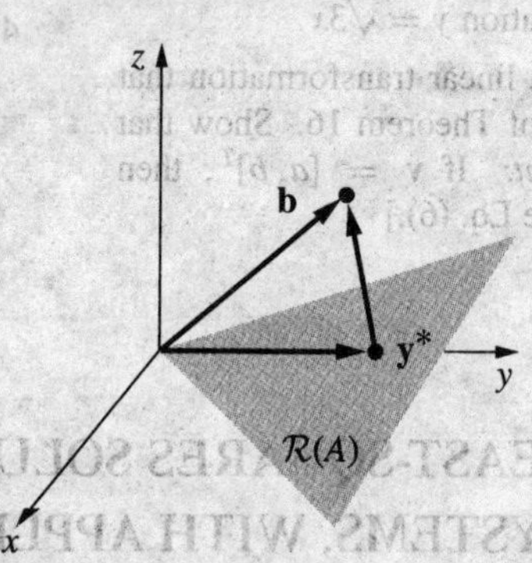

Figure 3.20 **$\mathbf{y}^*$ is the closest vector in $\mathcal{R}(A)$ to $\mathbf{b}$**

Let the vector $\mathbf{y}^*$ in $\mathcal{R}(A)$ be the closest vector in $\mathcal{R}(A)$ to $\mathbf{b}$; that is

$$\|\mathbf{y}^* - \mathbf{b}\| \leq \|\mathbf{y} - \mathbf{b}\|, \quad \text{for all } \mathbf{y} \text{ in } \mathcal{R}(A).$$

Geometry suggests (see Fig. 3.20) that the vector $\mathbf{y}^* - \mathbf{b}$ is orthogonal to every vector in $\mathcal{R}(A)$. Since the columns of A form a spanning set for $\mathcal{R}(A)$, this orthogonality condition leads to

$$\mathbf{A}_1^T(\mathbf{y}^* - \mathbf{b}) = 0$$
$$\mathbf{A}_2^T(\mathbf{y}^* - \mathbf{b}) = 0$$

or, in matrix-vector terms,

$$A^T(\mathbf{y}^* - \mathbf{b}) = \boldsymbol{\theta}.$$

Since $\mathbf{y}^* = A\mathbf{x}^*$ for some $\mathbf{x}^*$ in R^2, the preceding equation becomes $A^T(A\mathbf{x}^* - \mathbf{b}) = \boldsymbol{\theta}$, or

$$A^TA\mathbf{x}^* = A^T\mathbf{b}.$$

Thus, the geometry of the (3×2) system, as illustrated in Fig. 3.20, suggests that we can find least-squares solutions by solving the associated system (1):

$$A^TA\mathbf{x} = A^T\mathbf{b}. \tag{1}$$

As the following theorem asserts, this solution procedure is indeed valid.

THEOREM 17 Consider the $(m \times n)$ system $A\mathbf{x} = \mathbf{b}$.

(a) The associated system $A^TA\mathbf{x} = A^T\mathbf{b}$ is always consistent.

(b) The least-squares solutions of $A\mathbf{x} = \mathbf{b}$ are precisely the solutions of $A^TA\mathbf{x} = A^T\mathbf{b}$.

(c) The least-squares solution is unique if and only if A has rank n. ■

We will give the proof of Theorem 17 in the next section. For now, we will illustrate the use of Theorem 17 and also give some examples showing the connections between data-fitting problems and least-squares solutions of inconsistent systems. (In parts (a) and (b) of Theorem 17, the associated equations $A^TA\mathbf{x} = A^T\mathbf{b}$ are called the ***normal equations***.)

EXAMPLE 1 Find the least-squares solutions to the inconsistent system

$$\begin{aligned} x_1 + 4x_2 &= -2 \\ x_1 + 2x_2 &= 6 \\ 2x_1 + 3x_2 &= 1. \end{aligned}$$

Solution By Theorem 17, we can find the least-squares solutions by solving the normal equations, $A^TA\mathbf{x} = A^T\mathbf{b}$, where

$$A = \begin{bmatrix} 1 & 4 \\ 1 & 2 \\ 2 & 3 \end{bmatrix} \quad \text{and} \quad \mathbf{b} = \begin{bmatrix} -2 \\ 6 \\ 1 \end{bmatrix}.$$

Forming A^TA and $A^T\mathbf{b}$, we obtain

$$A^TA = \begin{bmatrix} 6 & 12 \\ 12 & 29 \end{bmatrix} \quad \text{and} \quad A^T\mathbf{b} = \begin{bmatrix} 6 \\ 7 \end{bmatrix}.$$

Solving the system $A^TA\mathbf{x} = A^T\mathbf{b}$, we find the least-squares solution

$$\mathbf{x}^* = \begin{bmatrix} 3 \\ -1 \end{bmatrix}.$$

Least-Squares Fits to Data

One of the major applications for least-squares solutions is to the problem of determining best least-squares fits to data. To introduce this important topic, consider a table of data such as the one displayed next.

Table 3.1

t	t_0	t_1	t_2	$\cdots$	t_n
y	y_0	y_1	y_2	$\cdots$	y_n

Suppose, when we plot the data in Table 3.1, that it has a distribution such as the one shown in Fig. 3.21. When we examine Fig. 3.21, it appears that the data points nearly fall along a line of the form $y = mt + c$. A logical question is: "What is the best line that we can draw through the data, one that comes closest to representing the data?"

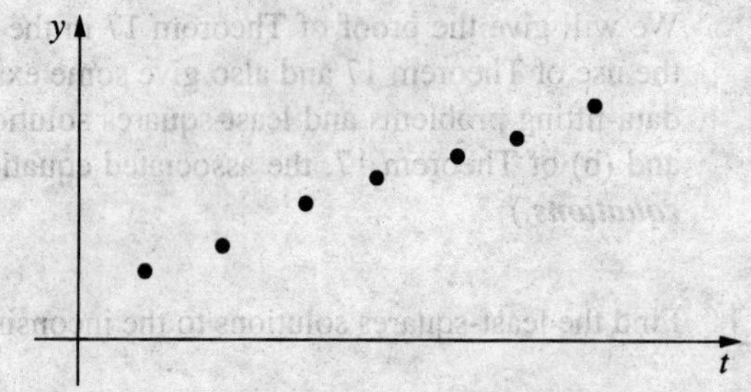

Figure 3.21 A nearly linear distribution of data points

In order to answer this question, we need a way to quantify the terms *best* and *closest*. There are many different methods we might use to measure best, but one of the most useful is the ***least-squares criterion***:

$$\text{Find } m \text{ and } c \text{ to minimize } \sum_{i=0}^{n} [(mt_i + c) - y_i]^2 \tag{2}$$

The particular linear polynomial $y = mt + c$ that minimizes the sum of squares in Eq. (2) is called the ***best least-squares linear fit*** to the data in Table 3.1. (We see in the next section that best least-squares linear fits always exist and are unique.)

Similarly, suppose the set of data points from Table 1 has a distribution such as the one displayed in Fig. 3.22. In this case, it appears that the data might nearly fall along the graph of a quadratic polynomial $y = at^2 + bt + c$. As in Eq. (2), we can use a least-squares criterion to choose the *best least-squares quadratic fit*:

$$\text{Find } a, b, \text{ and } c \text{ to minimize } \sum_{i=0}^{n} [(at_i^2 + bt_i + c) - y_i]^2.$$

In a like manner, we can consider fitting data in a least-squares sense with polynomials of any appropriate degree.

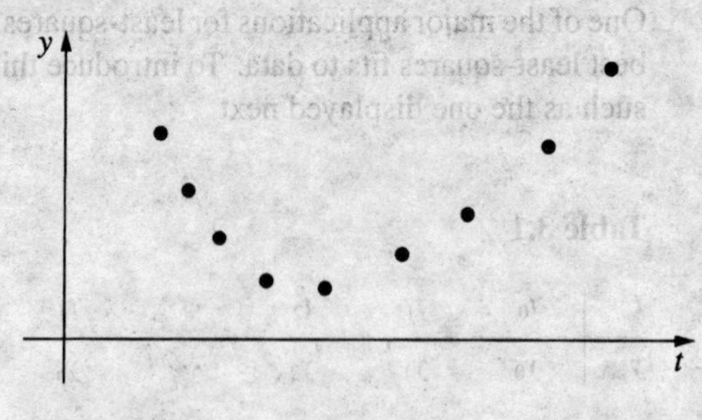

Figure 3.22 A nearly parabolic distribution of data points

In the next several subsections, we examine the connection between least-squares fits to data and least-squares solutions to $A\mathbf{x} = \mathbf{b}$.

Least-Squares Linear Fits to Data

Suppose the laws of physics tell us that two measurable quantities, t and y, are related in a linear fashion:

$$y = mt + c. \tag{3}$$

Suppose also that we wish to determine experimentally the values of m and c. If we know that Eq. (3) models the phenomena exactly and that we have made no experimental error, then we can determine m and c with only two experimental observations. For instance, if $y = y_0$ when $t = t_0$ and if $y = y_1$ when $t = t_1$, we can solve for m and c from

$$\begin{aligned} mt_0 + c &= y_0 \\ mt_1 + c &= y_1 \end{aligned} \quad \text{or} \quad \begin{bmatrix} t_0 & 1 \\ t_1 & 1 \end{bmatrix} \begin{bmatrix} m \\ c \end{bmatrix} = \begin{bmatrix} y_0 \\ y_1 \end{bmatrix}.$$

Usually we must be resigned to experimental errors or to imperfections in the model given by Eq. (3). In this case, we would probably make a number of experimental observations, (t_i, y_i) for $i = 0, 1, \ldots, k$. Using these observed values in Eq. (3) leads to an overdetermined system of the form

$$\begin{aligned} mt_0 + c &= y_0 \\ mt_1 + c &= y_1 \\ &\vdots \\ mt_k + c &= y_k. \end{aligned}$$

In matrix terms, this overdetermined system can be expressed as $A\mathbf{x} = \mathbf{b}$, where

$$A = \begin{bmatrix} t_0 & 1 \\ t_1 & 1 \\ \vdots & \vdots \\ t_k & 1 \end{bmatrix}, \quad \mathbf{x} = \begin{bmatrix} m \\ c \end{bmatrix}, \quad \text{and} \quad \mathbf{b} = \begin{bmatrix} y_0 \\ y_1 \\ \vdots \\ y_k \end{bmatrix}.$$

In this context, a least-squares solution to $A\mathbf{x} = \mathbf{b}$ is a vector $\mathbf{x}^* = [m^*, c^*]^T$ that minimizes $\|A\mathbf{x} - \mathbf{b}\|$, where

$$\|A\mathbf{x} - \mathbf{b}\|^2 = \sum_{i=0}^{k} [(mt_i + c) - y_i]^2.$$

Comparing the equation above with the least-squares criterion (2), we see that the best least-squares linear fit, $y = m^*t + c^*$, can be determined by finding the least-squares solution of $A\mathbf{x} = \mathbf{b}$.

EXAMPLE 2 Consider the experimental observations given in the following table:

t	1	4	8	11
y	1	2	4	5

Find the least-squares linear fit to the data.

Solution For the function defined by $y = mt + c$, the data lead to the overdetermined system

$$\begin{aligned} m + c &= 1 \\ 4m + c &= 2 \\ 8m + c &= 4 \\ 11m + c &= 5. \end{aligned}$$

In matrix terms, the system is $A\mathbf{x} = \mathbf{b}$, where

$$A = \begin{bmatrix} 1 & 1 \\ 4 & 1 \\ 8 & 1 \\ 11 & 1 \end{bmatrix}, \quad \mathbf{x} = \begin{bmatrix} m \\ c \end{bmatrix}, \quad \text{and} \quad \mathbf{b} = \begin{bmatrix} 1 \\ 2 \\ 4 \\ 5 \end{bmatrix}.$$

The least-squares solution, $\mathbf{x}^*$, is found by solving $A^T A\mathbf{x} = A^T\mathbf{b}$, where

$$A^T A = \begin{bmatrix} 202 & 24 \\ 24 & 4 \end{bmatrix} \quad \text{and} \quad A^T\mathbf{b} = \begin{bmatrix} 96 \\ 12 \end{bmatrix}.$$

There is a unique solution to $A^T A\mathbf{x} = A^T\mathbf{b}$ because A has rank 2. The solution is

$$\mathbf{x}^* = \begin{bmatrix} 12/29 \\ 15/29 \end{bmatrix}.$$

Thus the least-squares linear fit is defined by

$$y = \frac{12}{29}t + \frac{15}{29}.$$

The data points and the linear fit are sketched in Fig. 3.23. ∎

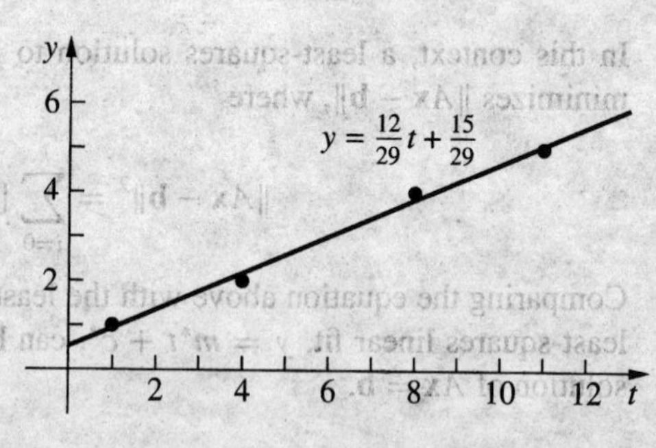

Figure 3.23 The least-squares linear fit to the data in Example 2

Using MATLAB to Find Least-Squares Solutions

Up to now we have been finding least-squares solutions to inconsistent systems by solving the normal equations $A^T A\mathbf{x} = A^T\mathbf{b}$. This method is fine in theory but (because of roundoff error) it is not reliable for machine calculations—especially for large systems

$A\mathbf{x} = \mathbf{b}$. MATLAB has several reliable alternatives for finding least-squares solutions to inconsistent systems; these methods do not depend on solving the normal equations.

If A is not square, the simple MATLAB command `x = A\b` produces a least-squares solution to $A\mathbf{x} = \mathbf{b}$ using a QR-factorization of A. (In Chapter 7, we give a thorough discussion of how to find least-squares solutions using QR-factorizations and Householder transformations.) If A is square but inconsistent, then the command `x = A\b` results in a warning but does not return a least-squares solution. If A is not square, a warning is also issued when A does not have full rank. In the next section we will give more details about these matters and about using MATLAB to find least-squares solutions.

EXAMPLE 3 Lubricating characteristics of oils deteriorate at elevated temperatures, and the amount of bearing wear, y, is normally a linear function of the operating temperature, t. That is, $y = mt + b$. By weighing bearings before and after operation at various temperatures, the following table was constructed:

Operating temperature, °C	120	148	175	204	232	260	288	316	343	371
Amount of wear, gm/10,000 hr	3	4	5	5.5	6	7.5	8.8	10	11.1	12

Determine the least-squares linear fit from these readings and use it to determine an operating temperature that should limit bearing wear to 7 gm/10,000 hr of operation.

Solution For the system $A\mathbf{x} = \mathbf{b}$, we see that A and $\mathbf{b}$ are given by

$$A = \begin{bmatrix} 120 & 148 & 175 & 204 & 232 & 260 & 288 & 316 & 343 & 371 \\ 1 & 1 & 1 & 1 & 1 & 1 & 1 & 1 & 1 & 1 \end{bmatrix}^T$$

$$\mathbf{b} = [3,\ 4,\ 5,\ 5.5,\ 6,\ 7.5,\ 8.8,\ 10,\ 11.1,\ 12]^T.$$

The least-squares solution to $A\mathbf{x} = \mathbf{b}$ is found from the MATLAB commands in Fig. 3.24.

```
>>A=[120 148 175 204 232 260 288 316 343 371;
       1   1   1   1   1   1   1   1   1   1]';
>>b=[3 4 5 5.5 6 7.5 8.8 10 11.1 12]';
>>x=A\b

x=

   0.0362
  -1.6151
```

Figure 3.24 The MATLAB commands for Example 3

From Fig. 3.24 we see that the least-squares linear fit is

$$y = (0.0362)t - 1.6151.$$

Setting $y = 7$ yields $t = 237.986$. Hence an operating temperature of about 238°C should limit bearing wear to 7 gm/10,000 hr. ■

General Least-Squares Fits

Consider the following table of data:

t	t_0	t_1	t_2	$\cdots$	t_m
y	y_0	y_1	y_2	$\cdots$	y_m

When the data points (t_i, y_i) are plotted in the ty-plane, the plot may reveal a trend that is nonlinear (see Fig. 3.25). For a set of data such as that sketched in Fig. 3.25, a linear fit would not be appropriate. However, we might choose a polynomial function, $y = p(t)$, where

$$p(t_i) \simeq y_i, \quad 0 \le i \le m.$$

In particular, suppose we decide to fit the data with an nth-degree polynomial:

$$p(t) = a_n t^n + a_{n-1} t^{n-1} + \cdots + a_1 t + a_0, \quad m \ge n.$$

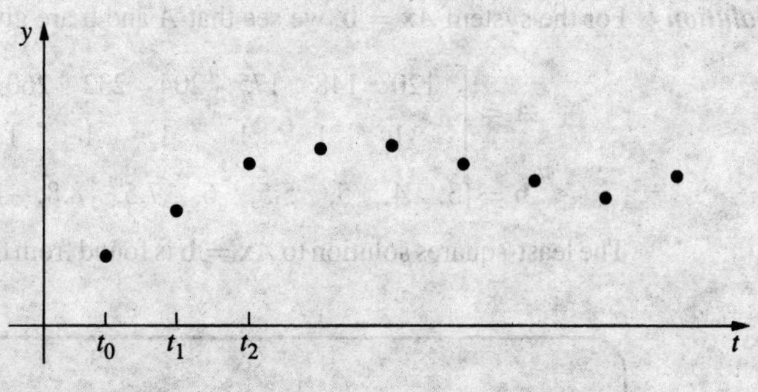

Figure 3.25 Nonlinear data

As a measure for goodness of fit, we can ask for coefficients $a_0, a_1, \ldots, a_n$ that minimize the quantity $Q(a_0, a_1, \ldots, a_n)$, where

$$\begin{aligned} Q(a_0, a_1, \ldots, a_n) &= \sum_{i=0}^{m} [p(t_i) - y_i]^2 \\ &= \sum_{i=0}^{m} [(a_0 + a_1 t_i + \cdots + a_n t_i^n) - y_i]^2. \end{aligned} \tag{4}$$

As can be seen by inspection, minimizing $Q(a_0, a_1, \ldots, a_n)$ is the same as minimizing $\|A\mathbf{x} - \mathbf{b}\|^2$, where

$$A = \begin{bmatrix} 1 & t_0 & t_0^2 & \cdots & t_0^n \\ 1 & t_1 & t_1^2 & \cdots & t_1^n \\ \vdots & & & & \vdots \\ 1 & t_m & t_m^2 & \cdots & t_m^n \end{bmatrix}, \quad \mathbf{x} = \begin{bmatrix} a_0 \\ a_1 \\ \vdots \\ a_n \end{bmatrix}, \quad \text{and} \quad \mathbf{b} = \begin{bmatrix} y_0 \\ y_1 \\ \vdots \\ y_m \end{bmatrix}. \tag{5}$$

As before, we can minimize $\|A\mathbf{x} - \mathbf{b}\|^2 = Q(a_0, a_1, \ldots, a_n)$ by solving $A^TA\mathbf{x} = A^T\mathbf{b}$. The nth-degree polynomial p^* that minimizes Eq. (4) is called the least-squares nth-degree fit.

EXAMPLE 4 Consider the data from the following table:

t	−2	−1	0	1	2
y	12	5	3	2	4

Find the least-squares quadratic fit to the data.

Solution Since we want a quadratic fit, we are trying to match the form $y = a_0 + a_1t + a_2t^2$ to the data. The equations are

$$\begin{aligned} a_0 - 2a_1 + 4a_2 &= 12 \\ a_0 - a_1 + a_2 &= 5 \\ a_0 &= 3 \\ a_0 + a_1 + a_2 &= 2 \\ a_0 + 2a_1 + 4a_2 &= 4. \end{aligned}$$

This overdetermined system can be shown to be inconsistent. Therefore, we look for a least-squares solution to $A\mathbf{x} = \mathbf{b}$, where A and $\mathbf{b}$ are as in system (5), with $n = 2$ and $m = 4$.

The matrix A and the vectors $\mathbf{x}$ and $\mathbf{b}$ are

$$A = \begin{bmatrix} 1 & -2 & 4 \\ 1 & -1 & 1 \\ 1 & 0 & 0 \\ 1 & 1 & 1 \\ 1 & 2 & 4 \end{bmatrix}, \quad \mathbf{x} = \begin{bmatrix} a_0 \\ a_1 \\ a_2 \end{bmatrix}, \quad \text{and} \quad \mathbf{b} = \begin{bmatrix} 12 \\ 5 \\ 3 \\ 2 \\ 4 \end{bmatrix}.$$

The least-squares solution of $A\mathbf{x} = \mathbf{b}$ is found by solving $A^TA\mathbf{x} = A^T\mathbf{b}$, where

$$A^TA = \begin{bmatrix} 5 & 0 & 10 \\ 0 & 10 & 0 \\ 10 & 0 & 34 \end{bmatrix} \quad \text{and} \quad A^T\mathbf{b} = \begin{bmatrix} 26 \\ -19 \\ 71 \end{bmatrix}.$$

The solution is $\mathbf{x}^* = [87/35, -19/10, 19/14]$, and hence the least-squares quadratic fit is

$$p(t) = \frac{19}{14}t^2 - \frac{19}{10}t + \frac{87}{35}.$$

A graph of $y = p(t)$ and the data points are sketched in Fig. 3.26. ∎

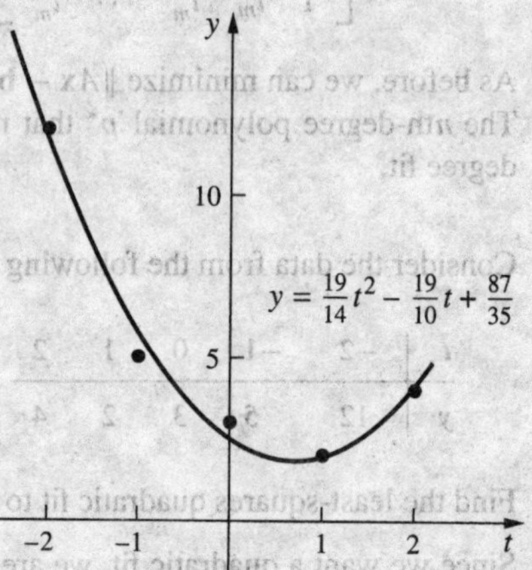

Figure 3.26 Least-squares quadratic fit for the data in Example 4

The same principles apply when we decide to fit data with any linear combination of functions. For example, suppose $y = f(t)$ is defined by

$$f(t) = a_1g_1(t) + a_2g_2(t) + \cdots + a_ng_n(t),$$

where $g_1, g_2, \ldots, g_n$ are given functions. We can use the method of least squares to determine scalars $a_1, a_2, \ldots, a_n$ that will minimize

$$Q(a_1, a_2, \ldots, a_n) = \sum_{i=1}^{m} [f(t_i) - y_i]^2 = \sum_{i=1}^{m} \{[a_1g_1(t_i) + a_2g_2(t_i) + \cdots + a_ng_n(t_i)] - y_i\}^2. \quad (6)$$

The ideas associated with minimizing $Q(a_1, a_2, \ldots, a_n)$ are explored in the exercises.

Rank Deficient Matrices

In each of Examples 1–4, the least-squares solution to $A\mathbf{x} = \mathbf{b}$ was unique. Indeed, if A is $(m \times n)$, then part (c) of Theorem 17 states that least-squares solutions are unique if and only if the rank of A is equal to n. If the rank of A is less than n, then we say that A is ***rank deficient***, or A does not have ***full rank***.

Therefore, when A is rank deficient, there is an infinite family of least-squares solutions to $A\mathbf{x} = \mathbf{b}$. Such an example is given next. This example is worked using MATLAB, and we note that MATLAB produces only a single least-squares solution but does give a warning that A is rank deficient. In Section 3.9 we will discuss this topic in more detail.

EXAMPLE 5 For A and $\mathbf{b}$ as given, the system $A\mathbf{x} = \mathbf{b}$ has no solution. Find all the least-squares solutions

$$A = \begin{bmatrix} 1 & 0 & 2 \\ 0 & 2 & 2 \\ -1 & 1 & -1 \\ -1 & 2 & 0 \end{bmatrix}, \quad \mathbf{b} = \begin{bmatrix} 3 \\ -3 \\ 0 \\ -3 \end{bmatrix}.$$

Solution The MATLAB calculation is displayed in Fig. 3.27(a). Notice that MATLAB warns us that A is rank deficient, having rank two. In Exercise 18 we ask you to verify that A does indeed have rank two. ∎

```
>>A=[1 0 2;0 2 2;-1 1 -1;-1 2 0];
>>b=[3 -3 0 -3]';
>>x=A\b

Warning: Rank deficient, rank = 2  tol =   2.6645e-15

x=

        0
  -1.5000
   0.5000
```

Figure 3.27(a) The MATLAB commands for Example 5

Since A is rank deficient, there are infinitely many least-squares solutions to the inconsistent system $A\mathbf{x} = \mathbf{b}$. MATLAB returned just one of these solutions, namely $\mathbf{x} = [0, -1.5, 0.5]^T$. We can find all the solutions by solving the normal equations $A^TA\mathbf{x} = A^T\mathbf{b}$.

Fig. 3.27(b) shows the result of using MATLAB to solve the normal equations for the original system (since A and $\mathbf{b}$ have already been defined, in Fig. 3.27(a), MATLAB

```
>>NormEqn=[A'*A,A'*b]

NormEqn =

     3    -3     3     6
    -3     9     3   -12
     3     3     9     0

>>rref(NormEqn)

ans =

     1     0     2     1
     0     1     1    -1
     0     0     0     0
```

Figure 3.27(b) Setting up and solving the normal equations for Example 5

makes it very easy to define the augmented matrix for $A^TA\mathbf{x} = A^T\mathbf{b}$). The complete solution is $x_1 = 1 - 2x_3$, $x_2 = -1 - x_3$, or in vector form:

$$\mathbf{x}^* = \begin{bmatrix} 1-2x_3 \\ -1-x_3 \\ x_3 \end{bmatrix} = \begin{bmatrix} 1 \\ -1 \\ 0 \end{bmatrix} + x_3 \begin{bmatrix} -2 \\ -1 \\ 1 \end{bmatrix}.$$

As can be seen from the complete solution just displayed, the particular MATLAB least-squares solution can be recovered by setting $x_3 = 0.5$.

3.8 EXERCISES

In Exercises 1–6, find all vectors $\mathbf{x}^*$ that minimize $\|A\mathbf{x}-\mathbf{b}\|$, where A and $\mathbf{b}$ are as given. Use the procedure suggested by Theorem 17, as illustrated in Examples 1 and 5.

1. $A = \begin{bmatrix} 1 & 2 \\ -1 & 1 \\ 1 & 3 \end{bmatrix}$, $\mathbf{b} = \begin{bmatrix} 1 \\ 1 \\ 1 \end{bmatrix}$

2. $A = \begin{bmatrix} 1 & 2 & 4 \\ -2 & -3 & -7 \\ 1 & 3 & 5 \end{bmatrix}$, $\mathbf{b} = \begin{bmatrix} 1 \\ 1 \\ 2 \end{bmatrix}$

3. $A = \begin{bmatrix} 1 & 2 & 1 \\ 3 & 5 & 4 \\ -1 & 1 & -4 \end{bmatrix}$, $\mathbf{b} = \begin{bmatrix} 1 \\ 3 \\ 0 \end{bmatrix}$

4. $A = \begin{bmatrix} 1 & 2 & -1 \\ 2 & 3 & 1 \\ -1 & -1 & -2 \\ 3 & 5 & 0 \end{bmatrix}$, $\mathbf{b} = \begin{bmatrix} 1 \\ 0 \\ 1 \\ 0 \end{bmatrix}$

5. $A = \begin{bmatrix} 1 & 2 \\ 2 & 4 \\ 3 & 6 \end{bmatrix}$, $\mathbf{b} = \begin{bmatrix} 0 \\ 2 \\ 16 \end{bmatrix}$

6. $A = \begin{bmatrix} 1 & 0 & 0 \\ 3 & 0 & 0 \\ 1 & 1 & 1 \end{bmatrix}$, $\mathbf{b} = \begin{bmatrix} 11 \\ 3 \\ 1 \end{bmatrix}$

In Exercises 7–10, find the least-squares linear fit to the given data. In each exercise, plot the data points and the linear approximation.

7.

t	−1	0	1	2
y	0	1	2	4

8.

t	−2	0	1	2
y	2	1	0	0

9.

t	−1	0	1	2
y	−1	1	2	3

10.

t	0	1	2	3
y	−2	3	7	10

In Exercises 11–14, find the least-squares quadratic fit to the given data. In each exercise, plot the data points and the quadratic approximation.

11.

t	−2	−1	1	2
y	2	0	1	2

12.

t	0	1	2	3
y	0	0	1	2

13.

t	−2	−1	0	1
y	−3	−1	0	3

14.

t	−2	0	1	2
y	5	1	1	5

15. Consider the following table of data:

t	t_1	t_2	$\cdots$	t_m
y	y_1	y_2	$\cdots$	y_m

For given functions g_1 and g_2, consider a function f defined by $f(t) = a_1 g_1(t) + a_2 g_2(t)$. Show that

$$\sum_{i=1}^{m} [f(t_i) - y_i]^2 = \|A\mathbf{x} - \mathbf{b}\|^2,$$

where

$$A = \begin{bmatrix} g_1(t_1) & g_2(t_1) \\ g_1(t_2) & g_2(t_2) \\ \vdots & \vdots \\ g_1(t_m) & g_2(t_m) \end{bmatrix}, \quad \mathbf{x} = \begin{bmatrix} a_1 \\ a_2 \end{bmatrix}, \quad \text{and}$$

$$\mathbf{b} = \begin{bmatrix} y_1 \\ y_2 \\ \vdots \\ y_m \end{bmatrix}.$$

16. Let $g_1(t) = \sqrt{t}$ and $g_2(t) = \cos \pi t$, and consider the data points (t_i, y_i), $1 \le i \le 4$, defined by

t	1	4	9	16
y	0	2	4	5

As in Eq. (6), let $Q(a_1, a_2) = \sum_{i=1}^{4} [a_1 g_1(t_i) + a_2 g_2(t_i) - y_i]^2$, where $g_1(t_i) = \sqrt{t_i}$ and $g_2(t_i) = \cos \pi t_i$.

a) Use the result of Exercise 15 to determine A, $\mathbf{x}$, and $\mathbf{b}$ so that $Q(a_1, a_2) = \|A\mathbf{x} - \mathbf{b}\|^2$.

b) Find the coefficients for $f(t) = a_1\sqrt{t} + a_2 \cos \pi t$ that minimize $Q(a_1, a_2)$.

17. Consider the $[(m+1) \times (n+1)]$ matrix A in Eq. (5), where $m \ge n$. Show that A has rank $n + 1$. [*Hint:* Suppose that $A\mathbf{x} = \boldsymbol{\theta}$, where $\mathbf{x} = [a_0, a_1, \ldots, a_n]^T$. What can you say about the polynomial $p(t) = a_0 + a_1 t + \cdots + a_n t^n$?]

18. Find the rank of the matrix A in Example 5.

3.9 THEORY AND PRACTICE OF LEAST SQUARES

In the previous section, we discussed least-squares solutions to $A\mathbf{x} = \mathbf{b}$ and the closely related idea of best least-squares fits to data. In this section, we have two major objectives:

(a) Develop the theory for the least-squares problem in R^n

(b) Use the theory to explain some of the technical language associated with least squares so that we can become comfortable using computational packages such as MATLAB for least-squares problems.

The Least-Squares Problem in R^n

The theory necessary for a complete understanding of least squares is fairly concise and geometric. To ensure our development is completely unambiguous, we begin by reviewing some familiar terminology and notation. In particular, let $\mathbf{x}$ be a vector in R^n,

$$\mathbf{x} = \begin{bmatrix} x_1 \\ x_2 \\ \vdots \\ x_n \end{bmatrix}.$$

We define the ***distance*** between two vectors $\mathbf{x}$ and $\mathbf{y}$ to be the length of the vector $\mathbf{x} - \mathbf{y}$; recall that the length of $\mathbf{x} - \mathbf{y}$ is the number $\|\mathbf{x} - \mathbf{y}\|$ where

$$\begin{aligned}\|\mathbf{x} - \mathbf{y}\| &= \sqrt{(\mathbf{x} - \mathbf{y})^T(\mathbf{x} - \mathbf{y})} \\ &= \sqrt{(x_1 - y_1)^2 + (x_2 - y_2)^2 + \cdots + (x_n - y_n)^2}.\end{aligned}$$

The problem we wish to consider is stated next.

> **The Least-Squares Problem in R^n**
>
> Let W be a p-dimensional subspace of R^n. Given a vector $\mathbf{v}$ in R^n, find a vector $\mathbf{w}^*$ in W such that
>
> $$\|\mathbf{v} - \mathbf{w}^*\| \le \|\mathbf{v} - \mathbf{w}\|, \quad \text{for all } \mathbf{w} \text{ in } W.$$
>
> The vector $\mathbf{w}^*$ is called the ***best least-squares approximation to v***.

That is, among all vectors $\mathbf{w}$ in W, we want to find the special vector $\mathbf{w}^*$ in W that is closest to $\mathbf{v}$. Although this problem can be extended to some very complicated and abstract settings, examination of the geometry of a simple special case will exhibit a fundamental principle that extends to all such problems.

Consider the special case where W is a two-dimensional subspace of R^3. Geometrically, we can visualize W as a plane through the origin (see Fig. 3.28). Given a point $\mathbf{v}$ not on W, we wish to find the point in the plane, $\mathbf{w}^*$, that is closest to $\mathbf{v}$. The geometry of this problem seems to insist (see Fig. 3.28) that $\mathbf{w}^*$ is characterized by the fact that the vector $\mathbf{v} - \mathbf{w}^*$ is perpendicular to the plane W.

The next theorem shows that Fig. 3.28 is not misleading. That is, if $\mathbf{v} - \mathbf{w}^*$ is orthogonal to every vector in W, then $\mathbf{w}^*$ is the best least-squares approximation to $\mathbf{v}$.

THEOREM 18 Let W be a p-dimensional subspace of R^n, and let $\mathbf{v}$ be a vector in R^n. Suppose there is a vector $\mathbf{w}^*$ in W such that $(\mathbf{v} - \mathbf{w}^*)^T\mathbf{w} = 0$ for every vector $\mathbf{w}$ in W. Then $\mathbf{w}^*$ is the best least-squares approximation to $\mathbf{v}$.

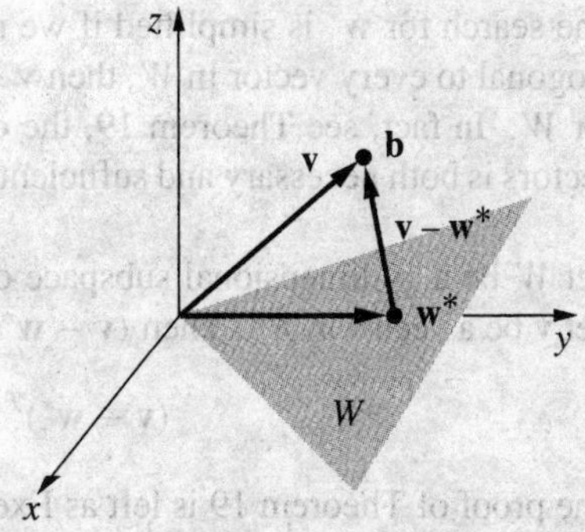

Figure 3.28 $\mathbf{w}^*$ is the closest point in the plane W to $\mathbf{v}$

Proof Let $\mathbf{w}$ be any vector in W and consider the following calculation for the distance from $\mathbf{v}$ to $\mathbf{w}$:

$$\begin{aligned}\|\mathbf{v}-\mathbf{w}\|^2 &= \|(\mathbf{v}-\mathbf{w}^*)+(\mathbf{w}^*-\mathbf{w})\|^2\\ &= (\mathbf{v}-\mathbf{w}^*)^T(\mathbf{v}-\mathbf{w}^*)+2(\mathbf{v}-\mathbf{w}^*)^T(\mathbf{w}^*-\mathbf{w})\\ &\quad+(\mathbf{w}^*-\mathbf{w})^T(\mathbf{w}^*-\mathbf{w})\\ &= \|\mathbf{v}-\mathbf{w}^*\|^2+\|\mathbf{w}^*-\mathbf{w}\|^2.\end{aligned} \tag{1}$$

(The last equality follows because $\mathbf{w}^*-\mathbf{w}$ is a vector in W, and therefore $(\mathbf{v}-\mathbf{w}^*)^T(\mathbf{w}^*-\mathbf{w})=0$.) Since $\|\mathbf{w}^*-\mathbf{w}\|^2 \geq 0$, it follows from Eq. (1) that $\|\mathbf{v}-\mathbf{w}\|^2 \geq \|\mathbf{v}-\mathbf{w}^*\|^2$. Therefore, $\mathbf{w}^*$ is the best approximation to $\mathbf{v}$. ∎

The equality in calculation (1), $\|\mathbf{v}-\mathbf{w}\|^2=\|\mathbf{v}-\mathbf{w}^*\|^2+\|\mathbf{w}^*-\mathbf{w}\|^2$, is reminiscent of the Pythagorean theorem. A schematic view of this connection is sketched in Fig. 3.29.

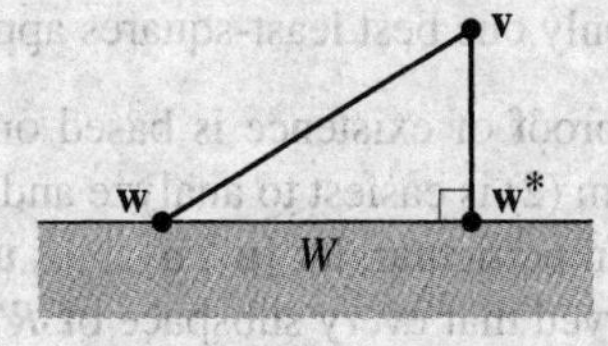

Figure 3.29 A geometric interpretation of the vector $\mathbf{w}^*$ in W closest to $\mathbf{v}$

In a later theorem, we will show that there is always one, and only one, vector $\mathbf{w}^*$ in W such that $\mathbf{v}-\mathbf{w}^*$ is orthogonal to every vector in W. Thus it will be established that the best approximation always exists and is always unique. The proof of this fact will be constructive, so we now concentrate on methods for finding $\mathbf{w}^*$.

Finding Best Approximations

Theorem 18 suggests a procedure for finding the best approximation $\mathbf{w}^*$. In particular, we should search for a vector $\mathbf{w}^*$ in W that satisfies the following condition:

$$\text{If } \mathbf{w} \text{ is any vector in } W, \quad \text{then } (\mathbf{v}-\mathbf{w}^*)^T\mathbf{w}=0.$$

The search for $\mathbf{w}^*$ is simplified if we make the following observation: If $\mathbf{v} - \mathbf{w}^*$ is orthogonal to every vector in W, then $\mathbf{v} - \mathbf{w}^*$ is also orthogonal to every vector in a basis for W. In fact, see Theorem 19, the condition that $\mathbf{v} - \mathbf{w}^*$ be orthogonal to the basis vectors is both necessary and sufficient for $\mathbf{v} - \mathbf{w}^*$ to be orthogonal to every vector in W.

THEOREM 19 Let W be a p-dimensional subspace of R^n, and let $\{\mathbf{u}_1, \mathbf{u}_2, \ldots, \mathbf{u}_p\}$ be a basis for W. Let $\mathbf{v}$ be a vector in R^n. Then $(\mathbf{v} - \mathbf{w}^*)^T\mathbf{w} = 0$ for all $\mathbf{w}$ in W if and only if

$$(\mathbf{v} - \mathbf{w}^*)^T\mathbf{u}_i = 0, \quad 1 \le i \le p.$$

The proof of Theorem 19 is left as Exercise 17.

As Theorem 19 states, the best approximation $\mathbf{w}^*$ can be found by solving the p equations:

$$\begin{aligned}(\mathbf{v} - \mathbf{w}^*)^T\mathbf{u}_1 &= 0\\ (\mathbf{v} - \mathbf{w}^*)^T\mathbf{u}_2 &= 0\\ &\vdots\\ (\mathbf{v} - \mathbf{w}^*)^T\mathbf{u}_p &= 0\end{aligned} \tag{2}$$

Suppose we can show that these p equations always have a unique solution. Then, by Theorem 18, it will follow that the best approximation exists and is unique.

Existence and Uniqueness of Best Approximations

We saw above that $\mathbf{w}^*$ is a best least-squares approximation to $\mathbf{v}$ if the vector $\mathbf{v} - \mathbf{w}^*$ satisfies system (2). We now use this result to prove that best approximations always exist and are always unique. In addition, we will give a formula for the best approximation.

THEOREM 20 Let W be a p-dimensional subspace of R^n and let $\mathbf{v}$ be a vector in R^n. Then there is one and only one best least-squares approximation in W to $\mathbf{v}$.

Proof The proof of existence is based on finding a solution to the system of Eq. (2). Now, system (2) is easiest to analyze and solve if we assume the basis vectors are orthogonal.

In particular, let $\{\mathbf{u}_1, \mathbf{u}_2, \ldots, \mathbf{u}_p\}$ be an orthogonal basis for W (in Section 3.6 we observed that every subspace of R^n has an orthogonal basis). Let $\mathbf{w}^*$ be a vector in W where

$$\mathbf{w}^* = a_1\mathbf{u}_1 + a_2\mathbf{u}_2 + \cdots + a_p\mathbf{u}_p. \tag{3}$$

Using Eq. (3), the equations in system (2) become

$$(\mathbf{v} - (a_1\mathbf{u}_1 + a_2\mathbf{u}_2 + \cdots + a_p\mathbf{u}_p))^T\mathbf{u}_i = 0, \quad \text{for } i = 1, 2, \ldots, p.$$

Then, because the basis vectors are orthogonal, the preceding equations simplify considerably:

$$\mathbf{v}^T\mathbf{u}_i - a_i\mathbf{u}_i^T\mathbf{u}_i = 0, \quad \text{for } i = 1, 2, \ldots, p.$$

Solving for the coefficients a_i, we obtain

$$a_i = \frac{\mathbf{v}^T\mathbf{u}_i}{\mathbf{u}_i^T\mathbf{u}_i}.$$

Note that the preceding expression for a_i is well defined since $\mathbf{u}_i$ is a basis vector, and hence the denominator $\mathbf{u}_i^T\mathbf{u}_i$ cannot be zero.

Having solved the system (2), we can write down an expression for a vector $\mathbf{w}^*$ such that $(\mathbf{v}-\mathbf{w}^*)^T\mathbf{w}=0$ for all $\mathbf{w}$ in W. By Theorem 18, this vector $\mathbf{w}^*$ is a best approximation to $\mathbf{v}$:

$$\mathbf{w}^* = \sum_{i=1}^{p} \frac{\mathbf{v}^T\mathbf{u}_i}{\mathbf{u}_i^T\mathbf{u}_i}\mathbf{u}_i. \tag{4}$$

Having established the existence of best approximations with formula (4), we turn now to the question of uniqueness. To begin, suppose $\mathbf{w}$ is any best approximation to $\mathbf{v}$, and $\mathbf{w}^*$ is the best approximation defined by Eq. (4). Since the vector $\mathbf{v}-\mathbf{w}^*$ was constructed so as to be orthogonal to every vector in W, we can make a calculation similar to the one in Eq. (1) and conclude the following:

$$\|\mathbf{v}-\mathbf{w}\|^2 = \|\mathbf{v}-\mathbf{w}^*\|^2 + \|\mathbf{w}^*-\mathbf{w}\|^2.$$

But, if $\mathbf{w}$ and $\mathbf{w}^*$ are both best approximations to $\mathbf{v}$, then it follows from the equation above that $\|\mathbf{w}^*-\mathbf{w}\|^2=0$. This equality implies that $\mathbf{w}^*-\mathbf{w}=\boldsymbol{\theta}$ or $\mathbf{w}^*=\mathbf{w}$. Therefore, uniqueness of best approximations is established. ∎

The following example illustrates how a best approximation can be found from Eq. (4).

EXAMPLE 1 Let W be the subspace of R^3 defined by

$$W = \{\mathbf{x}\colon \mathbf{x} = \begin{bmatrix} x_1 \\ x_2 \\ x_3 \end{bmatrix},\quad x_1+x_2-3x_3=0\}.$$

Let $\mathbf{v}$ be the vector $\mathbf{v}=[1,-2,-4]^T$. Use Eq. (4) to find the best least-squares approximation to $\mathbf{v}$.

Solution Our first task is to find an orthogonal basis for W. We will use the Gram–Schmidt process to find such a basis.

To begin, $\mathbf{x}$ is in W if and only if $x_1=-x_2+3x_3$. That is, if and only if $\mathbf{x}$ has the form

$$\mathbf{x} = \begin{bmatrix} -x_2+3x_3 \\ x_2 \\ x_3 \end{bmatrix} = x_2\begin{bmatrix} -1 \\ 1 \\ 0 \end{bmatrix} + x_3\begin{bmatrix} 3 \\ 0 \\ 1 \end{bmatrix}.$$

Therefore, a natural basis for W consists of the two vectors $\mathbf{w}_1=[-1,1,0]^T$ and $\mathbf{w}_2=[3,0,1]^T$.

We now use the Gram–Schmidt process to derive an orthogonal basis $\{\mathbf{u}_1,\mathbf{u}_2\}$ from the natural basis $\{\mathbf{w}_1,\mathbf{w}_2\}$. In particular,

(a) Let $\mathbf{u}_1=\mathbf{w}_1$.
(b) Choose a scalar a so that $\mathbf{u}_2=\mathbf{w}_2+a\mathbf{u}_1$ is orthogonal to $\mathbf{u}_1$.

To find the scalar a in (b), consider

$$\begin{aligned}\mathbf{u}_1^T\mathbf{u}_2 &= \mathbf{u}_1^T(\mathbf{w}_2 + a\mathbf{u}_1)\\ &= \mathbf{u}_1^T\mathbf{w}_2 + a\mathbf{u}_1^T\mathbf{u}_1.\end{aligned}$$

Thus, to have $\mathbf{u}_1^T\mathbf{u}_2 = 0$, we need $\mathbf{u}_1^T\mathbf{w}_2 + a\mathbf{u}_1^T\mathbf{u}_1 = 0$, or

$$\begin{aligned}a &= -\frac{\mathbf{u}_1^T\mathbf{w}_2}{\mathbf{u}_1^T\mathbf{u}_1}\\ &= -\frac{-3}{2}\\ &= 1.5.\end{aligned}$$

Having found a, we calculate the second vector in the orthogonal basis for W, finding $\mathbf{u}_2 = \mathbf{w}_2 + 1.5\mathbf{u}_1 = [3, 0, 1]^T + 1.5[-1, 1, 0]^T = [1.5, 1.5, 1]^T$.

Next, let $\mathbf{w}^* = a_1\mathbf{u}_1 + a_2\mathbf{u}_2$ denote the best approximation, and determine the coefficients of $\mathbf{w}^*$ using Eq. (4):

$$a_1 = \frac{\mathbf{v}^T\mathbf{u}_1}{\mathbf{u}_1^T\mathbf{u}_1} = \frac{-3}{2} = -1.5$$

$$a_2 = \frac{\mathbf{v}^T\mathbf{u}_2}{\mathbf{u}_2^T\mathbf{u}_2} = \frac{-5.5}{5.5} = -1.$$

Therefore, the best approximation is given by

$$\mathbf{w}^* = -1.5\mathbf{u}_1 - \mathbf{u}_2 = -1.5[-1, 1, 0]^T - [1.5, 1.5, 1]^T = [0, -3, -1]^T.$$

(As a check for the calculations, we can form $\mathbf{v} - \mathbf{w}^* = [1, 1, -3]^T$ and verify that $\mathbf{v} - \mathbf{w}^*$ is orthogonal to each of the original basis vectors, $\mathbf{w}_1 = [-1, 1, 0]^T$ and $\mathbf{w}_2 = [3, 0, 1]^T$.) ■

Least-Squares Solutions to Inconsistent Systems $A\mathbf{x} = \mathbf{b}$

In Section 3.8 we were interested in a special case of least-squares approximations—finding least-squares solutions to inconsistent systems $A\mathbf{x} = \mathbf{b}$. Recall that our method for finding least-squares solutions consisted of solving the normal equations $A^TA\mathbf{x} = A^T\mathbf{b}$. In turn, the validity of the normal equations approach was based on Theorem 17, which said:

(a) The normal equations are always consistent.

(b) The solutions of the normal equations are precisely the least-squares solutions of $A\mathbf{x} = \mathbf{b}$.

(c) If A is $(m \times n)$, then least-squares solutions of $A\mathbf{x} = \mathbf{b}$ are unique if and only if A has rank n.

We are now in a position to sketch a proof of Theorem 17. The basic ideas supporting Theorem 17 are very important to a complete understanding of least-squares solutions of inconsistent systems. These ideas are easy to explain and are illustrated in Fig. 3.30.

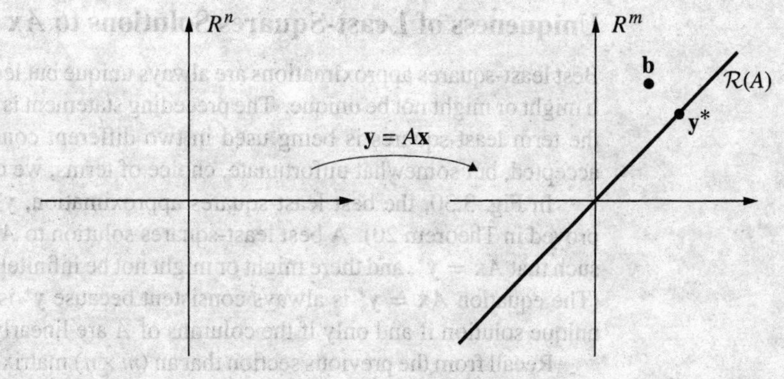

Figure 3.30 A geometric visualization of Theorem 17

In Fig. 3.30, we think of the $(m \times n)$ matrix A as defining a function of the form $\mathbf{y} = A\mathbf{x}$ from R^n to R^m. The subspace $\mathcal{R}(A)$ represents the range of A; it is a p-dimensional subspace of R^m. We have drawn the vector $\mathbf{b}$ so that it is not in $\mathcal{R}(A)$, illustrating the case where the system $A\mathbf{x} = \mathbf{b}$ is inconsistent. The vector $\mathbf{y}^*$ represents the (unique) best approximation in $\mathcal{R}(A)$ to $\mathbf{b}$.

Proof of Theorem 17 Because $\mathbf{y}^*$ is in $\mathcal{R}(A)$, there must be vectors $\mathbf{x}$ in R^n such that $A\mathbf{x} = \mathbf{y}^*$. In addition, because $\mathbf{y}^*$ is the closest point in $\mathcal{R}(A)$ to $\mathbf{b}$, we can say:

A vector $\mathbf{x}$ in $\mathcal{R}^n$ is a best least-squares solution to $A\mathbf{x} = \mathbf{b}$ if and only if $A\mathbf{x} = \mathbf{y}^*$. (5)

In order to locate $\mathbf{y}^*$ in W, we note that $\mathbf{y}^*$ is characterized by $\mathbf{w}^T(\mathbf{y}^* - \mathbf{b}) = 0$ for any vector $\mathbf{w}$ in $\mathcal{R}(A)$. Then, since the columns of A form a spanning set for $\mathcal{R}(A)$, $\mathbf{y}^*$ can be characterized by the conditions:

$$\mathbf{A}_i^T(\mathbf{y}^* - \mathbf{b}) = 0, \quad \text{for } i = 1, 2, \ldots, n. \tag{6}$$

The orthogonality conditions above can be rewritten in matrix/vector terms as

$$A^T(\mathbf{y}^* - \mathbf{b}) = \boldsymbol{\theta}. \tag{7}$$

Finally, since $\mathbf{y}^*$ is in $\mathcal{R}(A)$, finding $\mathbf{y}^*$ to solve Eq. (7) is the same as finding vectors $\mathbf{x}$ in R^n that satisfy the normal equations:

$$A^T(A\mathbf{x} - \mathbf{b}) = \boldsymbol{\theta}. \tag{8}$$

We can now complete the proof of Theorem 17 by making the observation that Eq. (6) and Eq. (8) are equivalent in the following sense: A vector $\mathbf{x}$ in R^n satisfies Eq. (8) if and only if the vector $\mathbf{y}^*$ satisfies Eq. (6), where $\mathbf{y}^* = A\mathbf{x}$.

To establish part (a) of Theorem 17, we note that Eq. (6) is consistent, and hence the normal equations given in Eq. (8) are consistent as well. Part (b) of Theorem 17 follows from rule (5) and the equivalence of equations (6) and (8). Part (c) of Theorem 17 follows because $A\mathbf{x} = \mathbf{y}^*$ has a unique solution if and only if the columns of A are linearly independent. ∎

Uniqueness of Least-Squares Solutions to $A\mathbf{x} = \mathbf{b}$

Best least-squares approximations are always unique but least-squares solutions to $A\mathbf{x} = \mathbf{b}$ might or might not be unique. The preceding statement is somewhat confusing because the term least-squares is being used in two different contexts. To clarify this widely accepted, but somewhat unfortunate, choice of terms, we can refer to Fig. 3.30.

In Fig. 3.30, the best least-squares approximation, $\mathbf{y}^*$, is unique (uniqueness was proved in Theorem 20). A best least-squares solution to $A\mathbf{x} = \mathbf{b}$, however, is a vector $\mathbf{x}$ such that $A\mathbf{x} = \mathbf{y}^*$, and there might or might not be infinitely many solutions to $A\mathbf{x} = \mathbf{y}^*$. (The equation $A\mathbf{x} = \mathbf{y}^*$ is always consistent because $\mathbf{y}^*$ is in $\mathcal{R}(A)$; the equation has a unique solution if and only if the columns of A are linearly independent.)

Recall from the previous section that an $(m \times n)$ matrix A is called ***rank deficient*** if it has rank less than n (that is, if the columns of A are linearly dependent). When A is rank deficient, there are infinitely many least-squares solutions to $A\mathbf{x} = \mathbf{b}$. In this instance, we might want to select the minimum norm solution as the least-squares solution we use in our application. To explain, we say $\mathbf{x}^*$ is the **minimum norm** least-squares solution to $A\mathbf{x} = \mathbf{b}$ if $\|\mathbf{x}^*\|$ minimizes $\|\mathbf{x}\|$ among all least-squares solutions. That is,

$$\|\mathbf{x}^*\| = \min\{\|\mathbf{x}\| : A\mathbf{x} = \mathbf{y}^*\}.$$

It can be shown that the minimum norm solution always exists and is always unique.

The minimum norm solution is associated with another least-squares concept, that of the pseudoinverse of A. The pseudoinverse of A is, in a sense, the closest thing to an inverse that a rectangular matrix can have. To explain the idea, we first introduce the **Frobenius norm** for an $(m \times n)$ matrix A. The Frobenius norm, denoted $\|A\|_F$, is defined by the following:

$$\|A\|_F = \sqrt{\sum_{i=1}^{m}\sum_{j=1}^{n} a_{ij}^2}.$$

Just as $\|\mathbf{x}\|$ measures the size of a vector $\mathbf{x}$, $\|A\|_F$ measures the size of a matrix A.

Now, let A be an $(m \times n)$ matrix. The ***pseudoinverse*** of A, denoted A^+, is the $(n \times m)$ matrix that minimizes $\|AX - I\|_F$ where I denotes the $(m \times m)$ identity matrix. It can be shown that such a minimizing matrix always exists and is always unique. As can be seen from the definition of the pseudoinverse, it is the closest thing (in a least-squares sense) to an inverse for a rectangular matrix. In the event that A is square and invertible, then the pseudoinverse coincides with the usual inverse, A^{-1}. It can be shown that the minimum norm least-squares solution of $A\mathbf{x} = \mathbf{b}$ can be found from

$$\mathbf{x}^* = A^+\mathbf{b}.$$

An actual calculation of the pseudoinverse is usually made with the aid of another type of decomposition, the singular-value decomposition. A discussion of the singular-value decomposition would lead us too far afield, and so we ask the interested reader to consult a reference, such as Golub and Van Loan, *Matrix Computations*.

MATLAB and Least-Squares Solutions

As we noted in the previous section, there are several ways to solve least-squares problems using MATLAB.

(a) If A is $(m \times n)$ with $m \neq n$, then the MATLAB command `A\b` returns a least-squares solution to $A\mathbf{x} = \mathbf{b}$. If A happens to be rank deficient, then MATLAB selects a least-squares solution with no more than p nonzero entries (where p denotes the rank of A). The least-squares solution is calculated using a QR-factorization for A (see Chapter 7).

(b) If A is square and inconsistent, then the MATLAB command `A\b` will produce a warning that A is singular or nearly singular, but will not give a least-squares solution. One way to use MATLAB to find a least-squares solution for a square but inconsistent system is to set up and solve the normal equations.

(c) Whether A is square or rectangular, the MATLAB command `x = pinv(A)*b` will give the minimum norm least-squares solution; the command `pinv(A)` generates the pseudoinverse A^+.

EXAMPLE 2 The following sample values from the function $z = f(x, y)$ were obtained from experimental observations:

$$f(1,1) = -1.1 \qquad f(1,2) = 0.9$$
$$f(2,1) = 0.2 \qquad f(2,2) = 2.0$$
$$f(3,1) = 0.9 \qquad f(3,2) = 3.1$$

We would like to approximate the surface $z = f(x, y)$ by a plane of the form $z = ax + by + c$. Use a least-squares criterion to choose the parameters a, b, and c.

Solution The conditions implied by the experimental observations are

$$\begin{aligned} a + b + c &= -1.1 \\ 2a + b + c &= 0.2 \\ 3a + b + c &= 0.9 \\ a + 2b + c &= 0.9 \\ 2a + 2b + c &= 2.0 \\ 3a + 2b + c &= 3.1. \end{aligned}$$

A least-squares solution,

$$a = 1.05, b = 2.00, c = -4.10,$$

to this overdetermined system $A\mathbf{x} = \mathbf{b}$ was found using MATLAB, see Fig. 3.31. Since MATLAB did not issue a rank deficient warning, we can assume that A has full rank (rank equal to 3) and therefore that the least-squares solution is unique. ■

EXAMPLE 3 Find a least-squares solution to the equation $A\mathbf{x} = \mathbf{b}$ where

$$A = \begin{bmatrix} 1 & 1 & 2 \\ 1 & 2 & 3 \\ 1 & 3 & 4 \\ 1 & 4 & 5 \end{bmatrix}, \qquad \mathbf{b} = \begin{bmatrix} 1 \\ 2 \\ 1 \\ 2 \end{bmatrix}.$$

```
>>A=[1,1,1;2,1,1;3,1,1;1,2,1;2,2,1;3,2,1];
>>b=[-1.1,.2,.9,.9,2.,3.1]';
>>x=A\b

x =

   1.0500
   2.0000
  -4.1000
```

Figure 3.31 The results of Example 2

Solution The results are shown in Fig. 3.32(a). Note that MATLAB has issued a rank deficient warning and concluded that A has rank 2. Because A is not full rank, least-squares solutions to $A\mathbf{x} = \mathbf{b}$ are not unique. Since A has rank 2, the MATLAB command `A\b` selects a solution with no more than 2 nonzero components, namely $\mathbf{x}_1 = [0.0, -0.8, 1.1]^T$.

As an alternative, we can use the pseudoinverse to calculate the minimum-norm least-squares solution (see Fig. 3.32(b)). As can be seen from Fig. 3.32(b), the MATLAB command `pinv(A)*b` has produced the least-squares solution $\mathbf{x}_2 = [0.6, -0.2, 0.4]^T$. A calculation shows that $\|\mathbf{x}_1\| = 1.2806$, while the minimum norm solution in Fig. 3.32(b) has $\|\mathbf{x}_2\| = 0.7483$.

Finally, to complete this example, we can find all possible least-squares solutions by solving the normal equations. We find, using the MATLAB command `rref(B)`,

```
>>x=A\b

Warning: Rank deficient, rank = 2

x =

        0
  -0.8000
   1.1000
```

(a)

```
x=pinv(A)*b

x =

   0.6000
  -0.2000
   0.4000
```

(b)

Figure 3.32 (a) Using the command `A\b` to find a least-squares solution for Example 3. (b) Using the pseudoinverse to find a least-squares solution for Example 3.

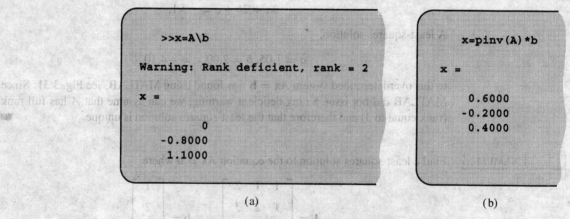

that the augmented matrix $B = [A^T A \mid A^T\mathbf{b}]$ is row equivalent to

$$\begin{bmatrix} 1 & 0 & 1 & 1 \\ 0 & 1 & 1 & .2 \\ 0 & 0 & 0 & 0 \end{bmatrix}.$$

Thus, the set of all least-squares solutions are found from $\mathbf{x} = [1 - x_3, 0.2 - x_3, x_3]^T = [1, 0.2, 0]^T + x_3[-1, -1, 1]^T$. ■

EXAMPLE 4 As a final example to illustrate how MATLAB treats inconsistent square systems, find a least-squares solution to $A\mathbf{x} = \mathbf{b}$ where

$$A = \begin{bmatrix} 2 & 3 & 5 \\ 1 & 0 & 3 \\ 3 & 3 & 8 \end{bmatrix}, \quad \mathbf{b} = \begin{bmatrix} 1 \\ 1 \\ 1 \end{bmatrix}.$$

Solution The results are given in Fig. 3.33 where, for clarity, we used the rational format to display the calculations. As can be seen, the MATLAB command A\b results in a warning that A may be ill conditioned and may have a solution vector with very large components.

Then, a least-squares solution is calculated using the pseudoinverse. The least-squares solution found is $\mathbf{x} = [2/39, -2/13, 8/39]^T$. ■

```
   >>A=[2,3,5;1,0,3;3,3,8];
   >>b=[1,1,1]';
   >>x=A\b

Warning: Matrix is close to singular or badly scaled.
         Results may be inaccurate. RCOND = 6.405133e-18

x =

-6755399441055744
750599937895082
2251799813685248

   >>x=pinv(A)*b

x =

     2/39
    -2/13
     8/39
```

Figure 3.33 The results from Example 4

3.9 EXERCISES

Exercises 1–16 refer to the following subspaces:

a) $W =$

$$\left\{\mathbf{x}: \mathbf{x} = \begin{bmatrix} x_1 \\ x_2 \\ x_3 \end{bmatrix}, \quad x_1 - 2x_2 + x_3 = 0\right\}$$

b) $W = \mathcal{R}(B), \quad B = \begin{bmatrix} 1 & 2 \\ 1 & 1 \\ 0 & 1 \end{bmatrix}$

c) $W = \mathcal{R}(B), \quad B = \begin{bmatrix} 1 & 2 & 4 \\ -1 & 0 & -2 \\ 1 & 1 & 3 \end{bmatrix}$

d) $W =$

$$\left\{\mathbf{x}: \mathbf{x} = \begin{bmatrix} x_1 \\ x_2 \\ x_3 \end{bmatrix}, \quad \begin{matrix} x_1 + x_2 + x_3 = 0 \\ x_1 - x_2 - x_3 = 0 \end{matrix}\right\}$$

In Exercises 1–10, find a basis for the indicated subspace W. For the given vector $\mathbf{v}$, solve the normal equations (2) and determine the best approximation $\mathbf{w}^*$. Verify that $\mathbf{v} - \mathbf{w}^*$ is orthogonal to the basis vectors.

1. W given by (a), $\mathbf{v} = [1, 2, 6]^T$

2. W given by (a), $\mathbf{v} = [3, 0, 3]^T$

3. W given by (a), $\mathbf{v} = [1, 1, 1]^T$

4. W given by (b), $\mathbf{v} = [1, 1, 6]^T$

5. W given by (b), $\mathbf{v} = [3, 3, 3]^T$

6. W given by (b), $\mathbf{v} = [3, 0, 3]^T$

7. W given by (c), $\mathbf{v} = [2, 0, 4]^T$

8. W given by (c), $\mathbf{v} = [4, 0, -1]^T$

9. W given by (d), $\mathbf{v} = [1, 3, 1]^T$

10. W given by (d), $\mathbf{v} = [3, 4, 0]^T$

In Exercises 11–16, find an orthogonal basis for the indicated subspace W. Use Eq. (4) to determine the best approximation $\mathbf{w}^*$ for the given vector $\mathbf{v}$.

11. W and $\mathbf{v}$ as in Exercise 1

12. W and $\mathbf{v}$ as in Exercise 2

13. W and $\mathbf{v}$ as in Exercise 4

14. W and $\mathbf{v}$ as in Exercise 5

15. W and $\mathbf{v}$ as in Exercise 7

16. W and $\mathbf{v}$ as in Exercise 8

17. Prove Theorem 19.

SUPPLEMENTARY EXERCISES

1. Let

$$W = \{\mathbf{x}: \mathbf{x} = \begin{bmatrix} x_1 \\ x_2 \end{bmatrix}, \quad x_1 x_2 = 0\}.$$

Verify that W satisfies properties (s1) and (s3) of Theorem 2. Illustrate by example that W does not satisfy (s2).

2. Let

$$W = \{\mathbf{x}: \mathbf{x} = \begin{bmatrix} x_1 \\ x_2 \end{bmatrix}, \quad x_1 \ge 0, \quad x_2 \ge 0\}.$$

Verify that W satisfies properties (s1) and (s2) of Theorem 2. Illustrate by example that W does not satisfy (s3).

3. Let

$$A = \begin{bmatrix} 2 & -1 & 1 \\ 1 & 4 & -1 \\ 2 & 2 & 1 \end{bmatrix}$$

and

$$W = \{\mathbf{x}: \mathbf{x} = \begin{bmatrix} x_1 \\ x_2 \\ x_3 \end{bmatrix}, \quad A\mathbf{x} = 3\mathbf{x}\}.$$

a) Show that W is a subspace of R^3.

b) Find a basis for W and determine $\dim(W)$.

4. If

$$S = \left\{ \begin{bmatrix} 1 \\ 1 \\ -2 \end{bmatrix}, \begin{bmatrix} 2 \\ 1 \\ 3 \end{bmatrix} \right\}$$

and

$$T = \left\{ \begin{bmatrix} 1 \\ 0 \\ 5 \end{bmatrix}, \begin{bmatrix} 0 \\ 1 \\ -7 \end{bmatrix}, \begin{bmatrix} 3 \\ 2 \\ 1 \end{bmatrix} \right\},$$

then show that $\mathrm{Sp}(S) = \mathrm{Sp}(T)$. [*Hint:* Obtain an algebraic specification for each of $\mathrm{Sp}(S)$ and $\mathrm{Sp}(T)$.]

5. Let

$$A = \begin{bmatrix} 1 & -1 & 2 & 3 \\ 2 & -2 & 5 & 4 \\ 1 & -1 & 0 & 7 \end{bmatrix}.$$

a) Reduce the matrix A to echelon form, and determine the rank and the nullity of A.

b) Exhibit a basis for the row space of A.

c) Find a basis for the column space of A (that is, for $\mathcal{R}(A)$) consisting of columns of A.

d) Use the answers obtained in parts b) and c) to exhibit bases for the row space and the column space of A^T.

e) Find a basis for $\mathcal{N}(A)$.

6. Let $S = \{\mathbf{v}_1, \mathbf{v}_2, \mathbf{v}_3\}$, where

$$\mathbf{v}_1 = \begin{bmatrix} 1 \\ -1 \\ 1 \end{bmatrix}, \quad \mathbf{v}_2 = \begin{bmatrix} 1 \\ 2 \\ -1 \end{bmatrix}, \quad \text{and}$$

$$\mathbf{v}_3 = \begin{bmatrix} 3 \\ 3 \\ -1 \end{bmatrix}.$$

a) Find a subset of S that is a basis for $\mathrm{Sp}(S)$.

b) Find a basis for $\mathrm{Sp}(S)$ by setting $A = [\mathbf{v}_1, \mathbf{v}_2, \mathbf{v}_3]$ and reducing A^T to echelon form.

c) Give an algebraic specification for $\mathrm{Sp}(S)$, and use that specification to obtain a basis for $\mathrm{Sp}(S)$.

7. Let A be the $(m \times n)$ matrix defined by

$$A = \begin{bmatrix} n+1 & n+2 & \cdots & 2n-1 & 2n \\ 2n+1 & 2n+2 & \cdots & 3n-1 & 3n \\ \vdots & \vdots & & & \\ mn+1 & mn+2 & \cdots & (m+1)n-1 & (m+1)n \end{bmatrix}.$$

Find a basis for the row space of A, and determine the rank and the nullity of A.

8. In a)–c), use the given information to determine the nullity of T.

a) $T\colon R^3 \to R^2$ and the rank of T is 2.

b) $T\colon R^3 \to R^3$ and the rank of T is 2.

c) $T\colon R^3 \to R^3$ and the rank of T is 3.

9. In a)–c), use the given information to determine the rank of T.

a) $T\colon R^3 \to R^2$ and the nullity of T is 2.

b) $T\colon R^3 \to R^3$ and the nullity of T is 1.

c) $T\colon R^2 \to R^3$ and the nullity of T is 0.

10. Let $B = \{\mathbf{x}_1, \mathbf{x}_2\}$ be a basis for R^2, and let $T\colon R^2 \to R^2$ be a linear transformation such that

$$T(\mathbf{x}_1) = \begin{bmatrix} 1 \\ 1 \end{bmatrix} \quad \text{and} \quad T(\mathbf{x}_2) = \begin{bmatrix} 2 \\ -1 \end{bmatrix}.$$

If $\mathbf{e}_1 = \mathbf{x}_1 - 2\mathbf{x}_2$ and $\mathbf{e}_2 = 2\mathbf{x}_1 + \mathbf{x}_2$, where $\mathbf{e}_1$ and $\mathbf{e}_2$ are the unit vectors in R^2, then find the matrix of T.

11. Let

$$\mathbf{b} = \begin{bmatrix} a \\ b \end{bmatrix},$$

and suppose that $T\colon R^3 \to R^2$ is a linear transformation defined by $T(\mathbf{x}) = A\mathbf{x}$, where A is a (2×3) matrix such that the augmented matrix $[A \,|\, \mathbf{b}]$ reduces to

$$\begin{bmatrix} 1 & 0 & 8 & -5a+3b \\ 0 & 1 & -3 & 2a-b \end{bmatrix}.$$

a) Find vectors $\mathbf{x}_1$ and $\mathbf{x}_2$ in R^3 such that $T(\mathbf{x}_1) = \mathbf{e}_1$ and $T(\mathbf{x}_2) = \mathbf{e}_2$, where $\mathbf{e}_1$ and $\mathbf{e}_2$ are the unit vectors in R^2.

b) Exhibit a nonzero vector $\mathbf{x}_3$ in R^3 such that $\mathbf{x}_3$ is in $\mathcal{N}(T)$.

c) Show that $B = \{\mathbf{x}_1, \mathbf{x}_2, \mathbf{x}_3\}$ is a basis for R^3.

d) Express each of the unit vectors $\mathbf{e}_1, \mathbf{e}_2, \mathbf{e}_3$ of R^3 as a linear combination of the vectors in B. Now calculate $T(\mathbf{e}_i)$, $i = 1, 2, 3$, and determine the matrix A.

In Exercises 12–18, $\mathbf{b} = [a, b, c, d]^T$, $T: R^6 \to R^4$ is a linear transformation defined by $T(\mathbf{x}) = A\mathbf{x}$, and A is a (4×6) matrix such that the augmented matrix $[A \mid \mathbf{b}]$ reduces to

$$\left[\begin{array}{rrrrrr|c} 1 & 0 & 2 & 0 & -3 & 1 & 4a + b - 2c \\ 0 & 1 & -1 & 0 & 2 & 2 & 12a + 5b - 7c \\ 0 & 0 & 0 & 1 & -1 & -2 & -5a - 2b + 3c \\ 0 & 0 & 0 & 0 & 0 & 0 & -16a - 7b + 9c + d \end{array}\right].$$

12. Exhibit a basis for the row space of A, and determine the rank and the nullity of A.

13. Determine which of the following vectors are in $\mathcal{R}(T)$. Explain how you can tell.

$$\mathbf{w}_1 = \begin{bmatrix} 1 \\ -1 \\ 1 \\ 0 \end{bmatrix}, \quad \mathbf{w}_2 = \begin{bmatrix} 1 \\ 1 \\ 3 \\ 2 \end{bmatrix},$$

$$\mathbf{w}_3 = \begin{bmatrix} 2 \\ -2 \\ 1 \\ 9 \end{bmatrix}, \quad \mathbf{w}_4 = \begin{bmatrix} 2 \\ 1 \\ 4 \\ 3 \end{bmatrix}$$

14. For each vector $\mathbf{w}_i$, $i = 1, 2, 3, 4$ listed in Exercise 13, if the system of equations $A\mathbf{x} = \mathbf{w}_i$ is consistent, then exhibit a solution.

15. For each vector $\mathbf{w}_i$, $i = 1, 2, 3, 4$ listed in Exercise 13, if $\mathbf{w}_i$ is in $\mathcal{R}(T)$, then find a vector $\mathbf{x}$ in R^6 such that $T(\mathbf{x}) = \mathbf{w}_i$.

16. Suppose that $A = [\mathbf{A}_1, \mathbf{A}_2, \mathbf{A}_3, \mathbf{A}_4, \mathbf{A}_5, \mathbf{A}_6]$.

a) For each vector $\mathbf{w}_i$, $i = 1, 2, 3, 4$, listed in Exercise 13, if $\mathbf{w}_i$ is in the column space of A, then express $\mathbf{w}_i$ as a linear combination of the columns of A.

b) Find a subset of $\{\mathbf{A}_1, \mathbf{A}_2, \mathbf{A}_3, \mathbf{A}_4, \mathbf{A}_5, \mathbf{A}_6\}$ that is a basis for the column space of A.

c) For each column, $\mathbf{A}_j$, of A that does not appear in the basis obtained in part b), express $\mathbf{A}_j$ as a linear combination of the basis vectors.

d) Let $\mathbf{b} = [1, -2, 1, -7]^T$. Show that $\mathbf{b}$ is in the column space of A, and express $\mathbf{b}$ as a linear combination of the basis vectors found in part b).

e) If $\mathbf{x} = [2, 3, 1, -1, 1, 1]^T$, then express $A\mathbf{x}$ as a linear combination of the basis vectors found in part b).

17. a) Give an algebraic specification for $\mathcal{R}(T)$, and use that specification to determine a basis for $\mathcal{R}(T)$.

b) Show that $\mathbf{b} = [1, 2, 3, 3]^T$ is in $\mathcal{R}(T)$, and express $\mathbf{b}$ as a linear combination of the basis vectors found in part a).

18. a) Exhibit a basis for $\mathcal{N}(T)$.

b) Show that $\mathbf{x} = [6, 1, 1, -2, 2, -2]^T$ is in $\mathcal{N}(T)$, and express $\mathbf{x}$ as a linear combination of the basis vectors found in part a).

CONCEPTUAL EXERCISES

In Exercises 1–12, answer true or false. Justify your answer by providing a counterexample if the statement is false or an outline of a proof if the statement is true.

1. If W is a subspace of R^n and $\mathbf{x}$ and $\mathbf{y}$ are vectors in R^n such that $\mathbf{x} + \mathbf{y}$ is in W, then $\mathbf{x}$ is in W and $\mathbf{y}$ is in W.

2. If W is a subspace of R^n and $a\mathbf{x}$ is in W, where a is a nonzero scalar and $\mathbf{x}$ is in R^n, then $\mathbf{x}$ is in W.

3. If $S = \{\mathbf{x}_1, \ldots, \mathbf{x}_k\}$ is a subset of R^n and $k \le n$, then S is a linearly independent set.

4. If $S = \{\mathbf{x}_1, \ldots, \mathbf{x}_k\}$ is a subset of R^n and $k > n$, then S is a linearly dependent set.

5. If $S = \{\mathbf{x}_1, \ldots, \mathbf{x}_k\}$ is a subset of R^n and $k < n$, then S is not a spanning set for R^n.

6. If $S = \{\mathbf{x}_1, \ldots, \mathbf{x}_k\}$ is a subset of R^n and $k \ge n$, then S is a spanning set for R^n.

7. If S_1 and S_2 are linearly independent subsets of R^n, then the set $S_1 \cup S_2$ is also linearly independent.

8. If W is a subspace of R^n, then W has exactly one basis.

9. If W is a subspace of R^n, and $\dim(W) = k$, then W contains exactly k vectors.

10. If B is a basis for R^n and W is a subspace of R^n, then some subset of B is a basis for W.

11. If W is a subspace of R^n, and $\dim(W) = n$, then $W = R^n$.

12. Let W_1 and W_2 be subspaces of R^n with bases B_1 and B_2, respectively. Then $B_1 \cap B_2$ is a basis for $W_1 \cap W_2$.

In Exercises 13–23, give a brief answer.

13. Let W be a subspace of R^n, and set $V = \{\mathbf{x}: \mathbf{x}$ is in R^n but $\mathbf{x}$ is not in $W\}$. Determine if V is a subspace of R^n.

14. Explain what is wrong with the following argument: Let W be a subspace of R^n, and let $B = \{\mathbf{e}_1, \ldots, \mathbf{e}_n\}$ be the basis of R^n consisting of the unit vectors. Since B is linearly independent and since every vector $\mathbf{w}$ in W can be written as a linear combination of the vectors in B, it follows that B is a basis for W.

15. If $B = \{\mathbf{x}_1, \mathbf{x}_2, \mathbf{x}_3\}$ is a basis for R^3, show that $B' = \{\mathbf{x}_1, \mathbf{x}_1 + \mathbf{x}_2, \mathbf{x}_1 + \mathbf{x}_2 + \mathbf{x}_3\}$ is also a basis for R^3.

16. Let W be a subspace of R^n, and let $S = \{\mathbf{w}_1, \ldots, \mathbf{w}_k\}$ be a linearly independent subset of W such that $\{\mathbf{w}_1, \ldots, \mathbf{w}_k, \mathbf{w}\}$ is linearly dependent for every $\mathbf{w}$ in W. Prove that S is a basis for W.

17. Let $\{\mathbf{u}_1, \ldots, \mathbf{u}_n\}$ be a linearly independent subset of R^n, and let $\mathbf{x}$ in R^n be such that $\mathbf{u}_1^T\mathbf{x} = \cdots = \mathbf{u}_n^T\mathbf{x} = 0$. Show that $\mathbf{x} = \boldsymbol{\theta}$.

18. Let $\mathbf{u}$ be a nonzero vector in R^n, and let W be the subset of R^n defined by $W = \{\mathbf{x}: \mathbf{u}^T\mathbf{x} = 0\}$.
    a) Prove that W is a subspace of R^n.
    b) Show that $\dim(W) = n - 1$.
    c) If $\boldsymbol{\theta} = \mathbf{w} + c\mathbf{u}$, where $\mathbf{w}$ is in W and c is a scalar, show that $\mathbf{w} = \boldsymbol{\theta}$ and $c = 0$. [*Hint:* Consider $\mathbf{u}^T(\mathbf{w} + c\mathbf{u})$.]
    d) If $\{\mathbf{w}_1, \ldots, \mathbf{w}_{n-1}\}$ is a basis for W, show that $\{\mathbf{w}_1, \ldots, \mathbf{w}_{n-1}, \mathbf{u}\}$ is a basis for R^n. [*Hint:* Suppose that $c_1\mathbf{w}_1 + \cdots + c_{n-1}\mathbf{w}_{n-1} + c\mathbf{u} = \boldsymbol{\theta}$. Now set $\mathbf{w} = c_1\mathbf{w}_1 + \cdots + c_{n-1}\mathbf{w}_{n-1}$ and use part c).]

19. Let V and W be subspaces of R^n such that $V \cap W = \{\boldsymbol{\theta}\}$ and $\dim(V) + \dim(W) = n$.
    a) If $\mathbf{v} + \mathbf{w} = \boldsymbol{\theta}$, where $\mathbf{v}$ is in V and $\mathbf{w}$ is in W, show that $\mathbf{v} = \boldsymbol{\theta}$ and $\mathbf{w} = \boldsymbol{\theta}$.
    b) If B_1 is a basis for V and B_2 is a basis for W, show that $B_1 \cup B_2$ is a basis for R^n. [*Hint:* Use part a) to show that $B_1 \cup B_2$ is linearly independent.]
    c) If $\mathbf{x}$ is in R^n, show that $\mathbf{x}$ can be written in the form $\mathbf{x} = \mathbf{v} + \mathbf{w}$, where $\mathbf{v}$ is in V and $\mathbf{w}$ is in W. [*Hint:* First note that $\mathbf{x}$ can be written as a linear combination of the vectors in $B_1 \cup B_2$.]
    d) Show that the representation obtained in part c) is unique; that is, if $\mathbf{x} = \mathbf{v}_1 + \mathbf{w}_1$, where $\mathbf{v}_1$ is in V and $\mathbf{w}_1$ is in W, then $\mathbf{v} = \mathbf{v}_1$ and $\mathbf{w} = \mathbf{w}_1$.

20. A linear transformation $T: R^n \to R^n$ is ***onto*** provided that $\mathcal{R}(T) = R^n$. Prove each of the following.
    a) If the rank of T is n, then T is onto.
    b) If the nullity of T is zero, then T is onto.
    c) If T is onto, then the rank of T is n and the nullity of T is zero.

21. If $T: R^n \to R^m$ is a linear transformation, then show that $T(\boldsymbol{\theta}_n) = \boldsymbol{\theta}_m$, where $\boldsymbol{\theta}_n$ and $\boldsymbol{\theta}_m$ are the zero vectors in R^n and R^m, respectively.

22. Let $T: R^n \to R^m$ be a linear transformation, and suppose that $S = \{\mathbf{x}_1, \ldots, \mathbf{x}_k\}$ is a subset of R^n such that $\{T(\mathbf{x}_1), \ldots, T(\mathbf{x}_k)\}$ is a linearly independent subset of R^m. Show that the set S is linearly independent.

23. Let $T: R^n \to R^m$ be a linear transformation with nullity zero. If $S = \{\mathbf{x}_1, \ldots, \mathbf{x}_k\}$ is a linearly independent subset of R^n, then show that $\{T(\mathbf{x}_1), \ldots, T(\mathbf{x}_k)\}$ is a linearly independent subset of R^m.

MATLAB EXERCISES

A continuing problem for university administrations is managing admissions so that the freshman class entering in the fall is neither too large nor too small. As you know, most high school seniors apply simultaneously for admission to several different universities. Therefore, a university must accept more applicants than it can handle in order to compensate for the expected number who decline an offer of admission.

Least-squares fits to historical data is often used for forecasting, whether it be forecasting university enrollments, or for business applications such as inventory control, or for technical applications such as modeling drag based on wind-tunnel data. In this exercise, we use a linear least-squares fit to model enrollment data.

1. **Forecasting enrollments** The following enrollment data is from Virginia Tech. It lists the total number of students, both undergraduate and graduate.

Total enrollment at Virginia Tech, 1979–1996

Year	Number	Year	Number	Year	Number
1979	20414	1985	22044	1991	23912
1980	21071	1986	22345	1992	23637
1981	21586	1987	22702	1993	23865
1982	21510	1988	22361	1994	23873
1983	21356	1989	22922	1995	23674
1984	22454	1990	23365	1996	24812

a) To get a feeling for the data, enter the numbers of students in a vector called TOTAL. Then, issue the MATLAB command `plot(TOTAL,'o')`. This command will give a scatterplot of the sixteen data points. If you want the years listed on the horizontal axis, you can define the vector YEAR with the command `YEAR = 1979:1996` and then use the plot command `plot(YEAR, TOTAL,'o')`. Note that the scatterplot indicates a general trend of increasing enrollments, but with enrollments that decrease from time to time.

b) Because it is such a common but important problem, MATLAB has commands that can be used to generate best least-squares polynomial approximations. In particular, given data vectors X and Y, the command `A = polyfit(X, Y, n)` gives the vector of coefficients for the best least-squares polynomial of degree n to the data. Given a vector of evaluation points T, the command `POFT = polyval(A, T)` will evaluate (at each point of T) the polynomial having a vector of coefficients given by A. Use the polyfit command `A = polyfit(YEAR,TOTAL,1)` to generate the coefficients for a linear fit of the data graphed in part a). Issue the hold command to hold the graph from part a). Generate the vector Y from `Y=polyval(A,YEAR)` and note that Y is the vector of values of the linear fit. Issue the command `plot(YEAR,Y)` to superimpose the graph of the linear fit on the scatterplot from part a).

c) In order to gain a feeling for how well the linear fit works as a forecasting tool, imagine that you do not know the enrollments for 1996 and 1995. Calculate the linear fit for the smaller set of data, the years 1979–1994, a set of 16 points. How well does the linear fit over these sixteen points predict the actual enrollment numbers for 1995 and 1996?

d) Use the linear fit calculated in part b) to estimate the year when enrollment can be expected to reach 30,000 and the year when enrollment should reach 35,000.

How does a computer evaluate functions such as $y = \cos x$ or $y = e^x$? Exercises 2–5 illustrate how mathematical functions such as $y = \tan x$ are evaluated on a computer or calculator. By way of introduction, note that the only operations a computer can actually perform are addition, subtraction, multiplication, and division. A computer cannot actually evaluate functions such as $y = \sqrt{x}$ or $y = \sin x$; instead, whenever a number such as $y = \sqrt{2.7}$ or $y = \sin 2.7$ is requested, the computer executes an algorithm that yields an *approximation* of the requested number. We now consider some computer algorithms for approximating mathematical functions.

2. We begin by formulating a method for estimating the function $y = \cos x$. Recall that $y = \cos x$ is periodic with period 2π. Therefore, if we can find a polynomial $y = g(x)$ that is a good approximation when x is $[-\pi, \pi]$, then we can also use it to approximate $y = \cos a$ for any real number a. To illustrate this point, consider the value $a = 17.3$ and note that $5\pi < 17.3 < 7\pi$. Now, let $x = 17.3 - 6\pi$ and note:

$$x = 17.3 - 6\pi \text{ is in the interval } [-\pi, \pi]. \tag{1}$$

$$\cos 17.3 = \cos(17.3 - 6\pi) = \cos x \approx g(x). \tag{2}$$

In general, if a is any real number, then we can always locate a between two successive odd multiples of π, $(2k-1)\pi \le a \le (2k+1)\pi$. Having located a, we see that $x = a - 2k\pi$ is in the interval $[-\pi, \pi]$ and therefore we have a good approximation for the value $\cos(a - 2k\pi)$, namely $g(a - 2k\pi)$. But, because of periodicity, $\cos(a - 2k\pi) = \cos a$, and so $g(a - 2k\pi)$ is also a good approximation for $\cos a$.

In light of the preceding observations, we turn our attention to the problem of approximating $y = \cos x$, for x in the interval $[-\pi, \pi]$. First, note that the approximation interval can be further reduced from $[-\pi, \pi]$ to $[0, \pi/2]$. In particular, if we have an approximation to $y = \cos x$ that is good in $[0, \pi/2]$, then we can use it to give a good approximation in $[-\pi, \pi]$. We ask you to establish this fact in part a).

a) Suppose $y = g(x)$ is a good approximation to $y = \cos x$ whenever x is in the interval $[0, \pi/2]$. Now, let a be in the interval $[\pi/2, \pi]$. Use inequalities to show that $\pi - a$ is in the interval $[0, \pi/2]$. Next, use trigonometric identities to show that $\cos a = -\cos(\pi - a)$. Thus, for a in $[\pi/2, \pi]$, we can use the approximation:

$$\cos a = -\cos(\pi - a) \approx -g(\pi - a).$$

Finally, since $\cos -x = \cos x$, the approximation $\cos x \approx g(x)$ can be extended to the interval $[-\pi, \pi]$.

b) In part a) we saw that if we had an approximation for $y = \cos x$ that is a good one in $[0, \pi/2]$, then we could use it to approximate $y = \cos a$ for any real value a. In this part, we see how a least-squares approximation $y = g(x)$ will serve as a good way to estimate $y = \cos x$ in $[0, \pi/2]$.

If we want to generate a least-squares approximation to $y = \cos x$, we need a collection of data points $(x_i, \cos x_i)$, $i = 1, 2, \ldots, m$. Given these m data points, we can choose $y = g(x)$ to be the best least-squares polynomial approximation of degree n for the data. In order to carry out this project, however, we need to select appropriate values for both m and n. There is a rule of thumb that is well known among people who need to analyze data:

The degree of the least-squares fit should be about half the number of data points.

So, when we have $m = 10$ data points, we might guess that a polynomial of degree $n = 5$ will provide a reasonable least-squares fit. (By increasing the degree of the fitting polynomial, we can drive the error at the data points to zero; in fact, when $n = m - 1$, the fitting polynomial becomes an ***interpolating polynomial***, matching the data points exactly. However, the graph of a high-degree interpolating polynomial often oscillates wildly and leads to a poor approximation between the data points. This deficiency of interpolating polynomials is one of the main reasons for using least-squares fits—we are looking for an approximation that behaves smoothly over the entire interval and the choice $n \approx m/2$ seems to work well in practice. In a later MATLAB exercise (see Chapter 4) we will explore some of the problems associated with polynomial interpolation.)

So, for $m = 10, 12, 14, 16, 18$, and 20, let us choose $y = g(x)$ to be the least-squares polynomial approximation of degree $n = 5, 6, 7, 8, 9$, and 10 respectively. As data values x_i, let us choose m points equally spaced in $[0, \pi/2]$. We also need a measure of goodness for the approximation $\cos x \approx g(x)$. Let $t_1, t_2, \ldots, t_{100}$ denote 100 points, equally spaced in $[0, \pi/2]$ and let D denote the maximum value of $|\cos t_i - g(t_i)|$, $i = 1, 2, \ldots, 100$. The size of D will serve as a measure of how well $g(x)$ approximates $\cos x$.

For each value of m, find the least-squares polynomial approximation of degree n and list the coefficients of the polynomial, using long format. Next, calculate the number D defined in the previous paragraph. Finally, list in column form and in long format, the 100 values $(\cos t_i, g(t_i))$. Write a brief report summarizing your conclusions.

Note: MATLAB provides a number of computational tools (see Appendix A) that make it very easy to carry out the investigations in Exercise 1. In particular, the command `linspace` generates vectors with equally-spaced components (the data values x_i and t_i). If X denotes the vector of data values x_i, then the command `Y = cos(X)` generates a vector of data values x_i, $y_i = \cos x_i$. In MATLAB, the number π can be entered by typing `pi`. Recall from part b) of Exercise 1 that the MATLAB function ***polyfit*** will calculate the coefficients for a best least-squares approximation and the function ***polyval*** will evaluate the approximation at a given set of points. Finally, to calculate the largest entry in absolute value of a vector **v**, use the command `maximum(abs(v))`.

Note: Exercise 1 illustrates the basic ideas underlying computer evaluation of mathematical functions. For obvious competitive reasons, computer and calculator manufacturers generally will not reveal the details of how their particular machine evaluates mathematical functions. If you are interested in knowing more about this topic, you might consult the *Computer Evaluation of Mathematical Functions* by C. T. Fike. In addition, the now outdated line of IBM 360 and 370 mainframe computers provided a manual giving the exact description of how each FORTRAN command was implemented by their compiler (for instance, the FORTRAN command `y = sqrt(α)` was executed by carrying out two steps of Newton's method for the equation $x^2 = \alpha$, starting with an initial guess generated from the value α).

3. If you enjoy programming, write a MATLAB function that calculates $y = \cos x$ for any real input value x. You could draw on the ideas in Exercise 1.

4. Repeat Exercise 1 for the function $y = e^x$. Consider choosing a least-squares polynomial approximation $y = g(x)$ that is good on the interval $[0, 1]$ and then using the fact that $e^{a+b} = e^a e^b$. For example, suppose $x = 4.19$. You could approximate $e^{4.19}$ as follows:

$$e^{4.19} = e^4 e^{0.19} \approx e^4 g(0.19).$$

For the preceding approximation, we would have the constant e precalculated and stored. Then, the evaluation of e^4 just requires multiplication.

5. Repeat Exercise 1 for the function $y = \tan x$. This time, a polynomial approximation will not be effective since the tangent has vertical asymptotes at $x = -\pi/2$ and $x = \pi/2$ and polynomial functions cannot imitate such behavior. For functions having either vertical or horizontal asymptotes, you can try approximating by a ***rational function*** (that is, by a quotient of polynomials).

In particular, let $y = f(x)$ denote the function that we wish to approximate. A rational function approximation for f will typically take the following form:

$$f(x) \approx \frac{a_0 + a_1 x + \cdots + a_m x^m}{b_0 + b_1 x + \cdots + b_n x^n}.$$

The preceding approximation actually has $m + n + 1$ parameters because we can divide numerator and denominator by a constant. For example, we can assume that $b_0 = 1$ if we want an approximation that is valid for $x = 0$.

An example should clarify the ideas. Suppose for $0 \le x < \pi/2$, we want to approximate $y = \tan x$ by a rational function of the form

$$g(x) = \frac{a_0 + a_1 x + a_2 x^2}{1 + b_1 x + b_2 x^2}.$$

Since g is a five parameter function, we will use a least-squares criterion involving ten data values to determine a_0, a_1, a_2, b_1, and b_2. Since we want $g(x)$ to approximate $\tan x$, the ten data values will be $y_i = \tan x_i$ for $i = 1, 2, \ldots, 10$. In particular, the ten conditions $y_i = g(x_i)$ lead to the system:

$$\begin{aligned}
y_1(1 + b_1 x_1 + b_2 x_1^2) &= a_0 + a_1 x_1 + a_2 x_1^2 \\
y_2(1 + b_1 x_2 + b_2 x_2^2) &= a_0 + a_1 x_2 + a_2 x_2^2 \\
&\vdots \\
y_{10}(1 + b_1 x_{10} + b_2 x_{10}^2) &= a_0 + a_1 x_{10} + a_2 x_{10}^2
\end{aligned}$$

In matrix terms, this system is

$$\begin{bmatrix} 1 & x_1 & x_1^2 & -x_1 y_1 & -x_1^2 y_1 \\ 1 & x_2 & x_2^2 & -x_2 y_2 & -x_2^2 y_2 \\ \vdots & & & & \vdots \\ 1 & x_{10} & x_{10}^2 & -x_{10} y_{10} & -x_{10}^2 y_{10} \end{bmatrix} \begin{bmatrix} a_0 \\ a_1 \\ a_2 \\ b_1 \\ b_2 \end{bmatrix} = \begin{bmatrix} y_1 \\ y_2 \\ \vdots \\ y_{10} \end{bmatrix}.$$

As in Exercise 1, try various choices for m and n until you obtain a good approximation $g(x)$ for $\tan x$. Since the tangent function is odd, you might want to select m to be an odd integer and n to be an even integer.

There are other ways you might think of to approximate $y = \tan x$. For instance, if you have separate polynomial approximations for $y = \sin x$ and $y = \cos x$, then it also makes sense to use the quotient of these two approximations; you will find, however, that the choice of a rational function determined as above will be better.

THE EIGENVALUE PROBLEM

4

An understanding of the eigenvalue problem requires several results about determinants. We review the necessary results in Section 4.2.

Readers familiar with determinants may omit Sections 4.2 and 4.3 with no loss of continuity.

A thorough treatment of determinants is given in Chapter 6. Chapter 6 is designed so that it can be covered now (before eigenvalues) or later (after eigenvalues).

OVERVIEW

As we shall see, the eigenvalue problem is of great practical importance in mathematics and applications. In Section 4.1 we introduce the eigenvalue problem for the special case of (2×2) matrices; this special case can be handled using ideas developed in Chapter 1. In Section 4.4 we move on to the general case, the eigenvalue problem for $(n \times n)$ matrices. The general case requires several results from determinant theory, and these are summarized in Section 4.2. If you are familiar with these results, you can proceed directly to the general $(n \times n)$ case in Section 4.4.

If you have time and if you want a thorough discussion of determinants, you might want to cover Chapter 6 (Determinants) before Chapter 4 (The Eigenvalue Problem). Chapters 4 and 6 are independent, and they are designed to be read in any order.

CORE SECTIONS

4.1 *The Eigenvalue Problem for (2×2) Matrices*
4.2 *Determinants and the Eigenvalue Problem (or Sections 6.1–6.3)*
4.4 *Eigenvalues and the Characteristic Polynomial*
4.5 *Eigenvectors and Eigenspaces*
4.6 *Complex Eigenvalues and Eigenvectors*
4.7 *Similarity Transformations and Diagonalization*

4.1 THE EIGENVALUE PROBLEM FOR (2 × 2) MATRICES

The ***eigenvalue problem***, the topic of this chapter, is a problem of considerable theoretical interest and wide-ranging application. For instance, applications found in Sections 4.8 and 5.10 and Chapter 7 include procedures for:

(a) solving systems of differential equations;
(b) analyzing population growth models;
(c) calculating powers of matrices;
(d) diagonalizing linear transformations; and
(e) simplifying and describing the graphs of quadratic forms in two and three variables.

The eigenvalue problem is formulated as follows.

The Eigenvalue Problem

For an $(n \times n)$ matrix A, find all scalars λ such that the equation

$$A\mathbf{x} = \lambda\mathbf{x} \tag{1}$$

has a nonzero solution, $\mathbf{x}$. Such a scalar λ is called an ***eigenvalue*** of A, and any nonzero $(n \times 1)$ vector $\mathbf{x}$ satisfying Eq. (1) is called an ***eigenvector*** corresponding to λ.

Let $\mathbf{x}$ be an eigenvector of A corresponding to an eigenvalue λ. Then the vector $A\mathbf{x}$ is a scalar multiple of $\mathbf{x}$ (see Eq. (1)). Represented as geometric vectors, $\mathbf{x}$ and $A\mathbf{x}$ have the same direction if λ is positive and the opposite direction if λ is negative (see Fig. 4.1).

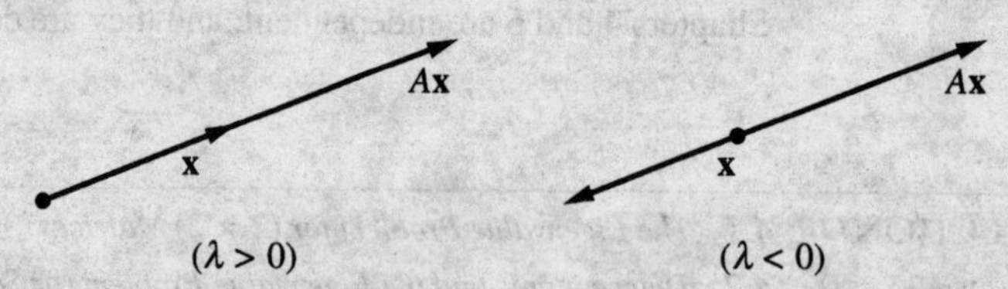

Figure 4.1 Let $A\mathbf{x} = \lambda\mathbf{x}$, where $\mathbf{x}$ is a nonzero vector. Then $\mathbf{x}$ and $A\mathbf{x}$ are parallel vectors.

Now, we can rewrite Eq. (1) as

$$A\mathbf{x} - \lambda\mathbf{x} = \boldsymbol{\theta},$$

or

$$(A - \lambda I)\mathbf{x} = \boldsymbol{\theta}, \quad \mathbf{x} \neq \boldsymbol{\theta}, \tag{2}$$

where I is the $(n \times n)$ identity matrix. If Eq. (2) is to have nonzero solutions, then λ must be chosen so that the $(n \times n)$ matrix $A - \lambda I$ is singular. Therefore, the eigenvalue problem consists of two parts:

1. Find all scalars λ such that $A - \lambda I$ is singular.
2. Given a scalar λ such that $A - \lambda I$ is singular, find all nonzero vectors $\mathbf{x}$ such that $(A - \lambda I)\mathbf{x} = \boldsymbol{\theta}$.

If we know an eigenvalue of A, then the variable-elimination techniques described in Chapter 1 provide an efficient way to find the eigenvectors. The new feature of the eigenvalue problem is in part 1, determining all scalars λ such that the matrix $A - \lambda I$ is singular. In the next subsection, we discuss how such values λ are found.

Eigenvalues for (2 × 2) Matrices

Before discussing how the eigenvalue problem is solved for a general $(n \times n)$ matrix A, we first consider the special case where A is a (2×2) matrix. In particular, suppose we want to solve the eigenvalue problem for a matrix A of the form

$$A = \begin{bmatrix} a & b \\ c & d \end{bmatrix}.$$

As we noted above, the first step is to find all scalars λ such that $A - \lambda I$ is singular. The matrix $A - \lambda I$ is given by

$$A - \lambda I = \begin{bmatrix} a & b \\ c & d \end{bmatrix} - \begin{bmatrix} \lambda & 0 \\ 0 & \lambda \end{bmatrix},$$

or

$$A - \lambda I = \begin{bmatrix} a - \lambda & b \\ c & d - \lambda \end{bmatrix}.$$

Next we recall (see Exercise 68 in Section 1.9) that a (2×2) matrix is singular if and only if the product of the diagonal entries is equal to the product of the off-diagonal entries. That is, if B is the (2×2) matrix

$$B = \begin{bmatrix} r & s \\ t & u \end{bmatrix}, \tag{3a}$$

then

$$B \text{ is singular} \Leftrightarrow ru - st = 0. \tag{3b}$$

If we apply the result in (3b) to the matrix $A - \lambda I$, it follows that $A - \lambda I$ is singular if and only if λ is a value such that

$$(a - \lambda)(d - \lambda) - bc = 0. \tag{4}$$

Expanding the equation for λ given above, we obtain the following condition on λ:

$$\lambda^2 - (a + d)\lambda + (ad - bc) = 0.$$

Equivalently, $A - \lambda I$ is singular if and only if λ is a root of the polynomial equation

$$t^2 - (a+d)t + (ad - bc) = 0. \tag{5}$$

An example will serve to illustrate this idea.

EXAMPLE 1 Find all scalars λ such that $A - \lambda I$ is singular, where

$$A = \begin{bmatrix} 5 & -2 \\ 6 & -2 \end{bmatrix}.$$

Solution The matrix $A - \lambda I$ has the form

$$A - \lambda I = \begin{bmatrix} 5-\lambda & -2 \\ 6 & -2-\lambda \end{bmatrix}.$$

As in Eq. (4), $A - \lambda I$ is singular if and only if

$$-(5-\lambda)(2+\lambda) + 12 = 0,$$

or $\lambda^2 - 3\lambda + 2 = 0$. Since $\lambda^2 - 3\lambda + 2 = (\lambda - 2)(\lambda - 1)$, it follows that $A - \lambda I$ is singular if and only if $\lambda = 2$ or $\lambda = 1$. ■

As a check for the calculations in Example 1, we list the matrices $A - \lambda I$ for $\lambda = 2$ and $\lambda = 1$:

$$A - 2I = \begin{bmatrix} 3 & -2 \\ 6 & -4 \end{bmatrix}, \quad A - I = \begin{bmatrix} 4 & -2 \\ 6 & -3 \end{bmatrix}. \tag{6}$$

Note that these matrices, $A - 2I$ and $A - I$, are singular.

Eigenvectors for (2 x 2) Matrices

As we observed earlier, the eigenvalue problem consists of two steps: First find the eigenvalues (the scalars λ such that $A - \lambda I$ is singular). Next find the eigenvectors (the nonzero vectors $\mathbf{x}$ such that $(A - \lambda I)\mathbf{x} = \boldsymbol{\theta}$).

In the following example, we find the eigenvectors for matrix A in Example 1.

EXAMPLE 2 For matrix A in Example 1, determine the eigenvectors corresponding to $\lambda = 2$ and to $\lambda = 1$.

Solution According to Eq. (2), the eigenvectors corresponding to $\lambda = 2$ are the nonzero solutions of $(A - 2I)\mathbf{x} = \boldsymbol{\theta}$. Thus, for the singular matrix $A - 2I$ listed in (6), we need to solve the homogeneous system

$$\begin{aligned} 3x_1 - 2x_2 &= 0 \\ 6x_1 - 4x_2 &= 0. \end{aligned}$$

The solution of this system is given by $3x_1 = 2x_2$, or $x_1 = (2/3)x_2$. Thus all the nonzero solutions of $(A - 2I)\mathbf{x} = \boldsymbol{\theta}$ are of the form

$$\mathbf{x} = \begin{bmatrix} (2/3)x_2 \\ x_2 \end{bmatrix} = x_2 \begin{bmatrix} 2/3 \\ 1 \end{bmatrix}, \quad x_2 \neq 0.$$

For $\lambda = 1$, the solutions of $(A - I)\mathbf{x} = \boldsymbol{\theta}$ are found by solving

$$4x_1 - 2x_2 = 0$$
$$6x_1 - 3x_2 = 0.$$

The nonzero solutions of this system are all of the form

$$\mathbf{x} = \begin{bmatrix} (1/2)x_2 \\ x_2 \end{bmatrix} = x_2 \begin{bmatrix} 1/2 \\ 1 \end{bmatrix}, \quad x_2 \neq 0.$$

The results of Examples 1 and 2 provide the solution to the eigenvalue problem for the matrix A, where A is given by

$$A = \begin{bmatrix} 5 & -2 \\ 6 & -2 \end{bmatrix}.$$

In a summary form, the eigenvalues and corresponding eigenvectors are as listed below:

Eigenvalue: $\lambda = 2$; *Eigenvectors:* $\mathbf{x} = a\begin{bmatrix} 2/3 \\ 1 \end{bmatrix}, \quad a \neq 0.$

Eigenvalue: $\lambda = 1$; *Eigenvectors:* $\mathbf{x} = a\begin{bmatrix} 1/2 \\ 1 \end{bmatrix}, \quad a \neq 0.$

Note that for a given eigenvalue λ, there are infinitely many eigenvectors corresponding to λ. Since Eq. (2) is a homogeneous system, it follows that if $\mathbf{x}$ is an eigenvector corresponding to λ, then so is $a\mathbf{x}$ for any nonzero scalar a.

Finally, we make the following observation: If A is a (2×2) matrix, then we have a simple test for determining those values λ such that $A - \lambda I$ is singular. But if A is an $(n \times n)$ matrix with $n > 2$, we do not (as yet) have a test for determining whether $A - \lambda I$ is singular. In the next section a singularity test based on the theory of determinants will be developed.

4.1 EXERCISES

In Exercises 1–12, find the eigenvalues and the eigenvectors for the given matrix.

1. $A = \begin{bmatrix} 1 & 0 \\ 2 & 3 \end{bmatrix}$
2. $A = \begin{bmatrix} 2 & 1 \\ 0 & -1 \end{bmatrix}$
3. $A = \begin{bmatrix} 2 & -1 \\ -1 & 2 \end{bmatrix}$
4. $A = \begin{bmatrix} 1 & -2 \\ 1 & 4 \end{bmatrix}$
5. $A = \begin{bmatrix} 2 & 1 \\ 1 & 2 \end{bmatrix}$
6. $A = \begin{bmatrix} 3 & -1 \\ 5 & -3 \end{bmatrix}$
7. $A = \begin{bmatrix} 1 & 0 \\ 2 & 1 \end{bmatrix}$
8. $A = \begin{bmatrix} 2 & 3 \\ 0 & 2 \end{bmatrix}$
9. $A = \begin{bmatrix} 2 & 2 \\ 3 & 3 \end{bmatrix}$
10. $A = \begin{bmatrix} 1 & 2 \\ 4 & 8 \end{bmatrix}$
11. $A = \begin{bmatrix} 1 & -1 \\ 1 & 3 \end{bmatrix}$
12. $A = \begin{bmatrix} 2 & -1 \\ 1 & 4 \end{bmatrix}$

Using Eq. (4), apply the singularity test to the matrices in Exercises 13–16. Show that there is no *real* scalar λ such that $A-\lambda I$ is singular. [*Note:* Complex eigenvalues are discussed in Section 4.6.]

13. $A = \begin{bmatrix} -2 & -1 \\ 5 & 2 \end{bmatrix}$ **14.** $A = \begin{bmatrix} 3 & -2 \\ 5 & -3 \end{bmatrix}$

15. $A = \begin{bmatrix} 2 & -1 \\ 1 & 2 \end{bmatrix}$ **16.** $A = \begin{bmatrix} 1 & -1 \\ 1 & 1 \end{bmatrix}$

17. Consider the (2×2) *symmetric* matrix

$$A = \begin{bmatrix} a & b \\ b & d \end{bmatrix}.$$

Show that there are always real scalars λ such that $A-\lambda I$ is singular. [*Hint:* Use the quadratic formula for the roots of Eq. (5).]

18. Consider the (2×2) matrix A given by

$$A = \begin{bmatrix} a & b \\ -b & a \end{bmatrix}, \quad b \neq 0.$$

Show that there are no real scalars λ such that $A-\lambda I$ is singular.

19. Let A be a (2×2) matrix. Show that A and A^T have the same set of eigenvalues by considering the polynomial equation (5).

4.2 DETERMINANTS AND THE EIGENVALUE PROBLEM

Now we turn our attention to the eigenvalue problem for a general $(n \times n)$ matrix A. As we observed in the last section, the first task is to determine all scalars λ such that the matrix $A - \lambda I$ given by

$$A - \lambda I = \begin{bmatrix} a-\lambda & b \\ c & d-\lambda \end{bmatrix},$$

we have a simple test for singularity:

$$A - \lambda I \text{ is singular} \Leftrightarrow (a-\lambda)(d-\lambda) - bc = 0.$$

For a general $(n \times n)$ matrix A, the theory of determinants can be used to discover those values λ such that $A - \lambda I$ is singular.

Determinant theory has long intrigued mathematicians. The reader has probably learned how to calculate determinants, at least for (2×2) and (3×3) matrices. The purpose of this section is to briefly review those aspects of determinant theory that can be used in the eigenvalue problem. A formal development of determinants, including proofs, definitions, and the important properties of determinants, can be found in Chapter 6. In this section we present three basic results: an algorithm for evaluating determinants, a characterization of singular matrices in terms of determinants, and a result concerning determinants of matrix products.

Determinants of (2 × 2) Matrices

We begin with the definition for the determinant of a (2×2) matrix.

DEFINITION 1 Let A be the (2×2) matrix

$$A = \begin{bmatrix} a_{11} & a_{12} \\ a_{21} & a_{22} \end{bmatrix}.$$

The ***determinant*** of A, denoted by $\det(A)$, is the number

$$\det(A) = \begin{vmatrix} a_{11} & a_{12} \\ a_{21} & a_{22} \end{vmatrix} = a_{11}a_{22} - a_{21}a_{12}.$$

(*Note:* As Definition 1 indicates, the determinant of a (2×2) matrix is simply the difference of the products of the diagonal entries and the off-diagonal entries. Thus, in the context of the singularity test displayed in Eqs. (3a) and (3b) in the previous section, a (2×2) matrix A is singular if and only if $\det(A) = 0$. Also note that we designate the determinant of A by vertical bars when we wish to exhibit the entries of A.)

EXAMPLE 1 Find $\det(A)$, where

$$A = \begin{bmatrix} 2 & 4 \\ 1 & 3 \end{bmatrix}.$$

Solution By Definition 1,

$$\det(A) = \begin{vmatrix} 2 & 4 \\ 1 & 3 \end{vmatrix} = 2 \cdot 3 - 1 \cdot 4 = 2.$$

EXAMPLE 2 Find $\det(A)$, where

$$A = \begin{bmatrix} 2 & 4 \\ 3 & 6 \end{bmatrix}.$$

DETERMINANTS Determinants were studied and extensively used long before matrix algebra was developed. In 1693, the co-founder of calculus, Gottfried Wilhelm Leibniz (1646–1716), essentially used determinants to determine if a (3×3) linear system was consistent. (Similar work was done ten years earlier in Japan by Seki-Kowa.) Cramer's Rule (see Section 6.4), which uses determinants to solve linear systems, was developed in 1729 by Colin Maclaurin (1698–1746). Joseph Louis Lagrange (1736–1813) used determinants to express the area of a triangle and the volume of a tetrahedron.

It was Augustin-Louis Cauchy (1789–1857) who first coined the term "determinant" and in 1812 published a unification of the theory of determinants. In subsequent publications Cauchy used determinants in a variety of ways such as the development of the functional determinant commonly called the *Jacobian*.

Solution By Definition 1,

$$\det(A) = \begin{vmatrix} 2 & 4 \\ 3 & 6 \end{vmatrix} = 2 \cdot 6 - 3 \cdot 4 = 0.$$

Again, Examples 1 and 2 are special instances that reaffirm our earlier observation about the singularity of a (2×2) matrix A. That is, A is singular if and only if $\det(A) = 0$.

Determinants of (3 x 3) Matrices

In Definition 1, we associated a number, $\det(A)$, with a (2×2) matrix A. This number assignment had the property that $\det(A) = 0$ if and only if A is singular. We now develop a similar association of a number, $\det(A)$, with an $(n \times n)$ matrix A.

We first consider the case in which $n = 3$.

DEFINITION 2 Let A be the (3×3) matrix

$$A = \begin{bmatrix} a_{11} & a_{12} & a_{13} \\ a_{21} & a_{22} & a_{23} \\ a_{31} & a_{32} & a_{33} \end{bmatrix}.$$

The ***determinant of*** A is the number $\det(A)$, where

$$\det(A) = a_{11} \begin{vmatrix} a_{22} & a_{23} \\ a_{32} & a_{33} \end{vmatrix} - a_{12} \begin{vmatrix} a_{21} & a_{23} \\ a_{31} & a_{33} \end{vmatrix} + a_{13} \begin{vmatrix} a_{21} & a_{22} \\ a_{31} & a_{32} \end{vmatrix}. \quad (1)$$

(*Note:* The determinant of a (3×3) matrix is defined to be the *weighted sum* of three (2×2) determinants. Similarly, the determinant of an $(n \times n)$ matrix will be defined as the weighted sum of n determinants each of order $[(n-1) \times (n-1)]$.)

EXAMPLE 3 Find $\det(A)$, where

$$A = \begin{bmatrix} 1 & 2 & -1 \\ 5 & 3 & 4 \\ -2 & 0 & 1 \end{bmatrix}.$$

Solution From Definition 2,

$$\begin{aligned} \det(A) &= (1) \begin{vmatrix} 3 & 4 \\ 0 & 1 \end{vmatrix} - (2) \begin{vmatrix} 5 & 4 \\ -2 & 1 \end{vmatrix} + (-1) \begin{vmatrix} 5 & 3 \\ -2 & 0 \end{vmatrix} \\ &= 1(3 \cdot 1 - 4 \cdot 0) - 2[5 \cdot 1 - 4(-2)] - 1[5 \cdot 0 - 3(-2)] \\ &= 3 - 26 - 6 = -29. \end{aligned}$$

Minors and Cofactors

If we examine the three (2×2) determinants that appear in Eq. (1), we can see a pattern. In particular, the entries in the first (2×2) determinant can be obtained from the matrix A by striking out the first row and column of A. Similarly, the entries in the second (2×2) determinant can be obtained by striking out the first row and second column of A. Finally, striking out the first row and third column yields the third (2×2) determinant.

The process of generating submatrices by striking out rows and columns is fundamental to the definition of a general $(n \times n)$ determinant. For a general $(n \times n)$ matrix A, we will use the notation M_{rs} to designate the $[(n-1) \times (n-1)]$ matrix generated by removing row r and column s from A (see Definition 3).

DEFINITION 3 Let $A = (a_{ij})$ be an $(n \times n)$ matrix. The $[(n-1) \times (n-1)]$ matrix that results from removing the rth row and sth column from A is called a ***minor matrix of A*** and is designated by M_{rs}.

Example 4 illustrates the idea in Definition 3.

EXAMPLE 4 List the minor matrices M_{21}, M_{23}, M_{42}, and M_{11} for the (4×4) matrix A given by

$$A = \begin{bmatrix} 1 & 2 & 1 & 3 \\ 0 & 1 & 2 & 0 \\ 4 & 2 & 0 & -1 \\ -2 & 3 & 1 & 1 \end{bmatrix}.$$

Solution The minor matrix M_{21} is obtained from A by removing the second row and the first column from A:

$$M_{21} = \begin{bmatrix} 2 & 1 & 3 \\ 2 & 0 & -1 \\ 3 & 1 & 1 \end{bmatrix}.$$

Similarly, we have

$$M_{23} = \begin{bmatrix} 1 & 2 & 3 \\ 4 & 2 & -1 \\ -2 & 3 & 1 \end{bmatrix}, \quad M_{42} = \begin{bmatrix} 1 & 1 & 3 \\ 0 & 2 & 0 \\ 4 & 0 & -1 \end{bmatrix}, \text{ and}$$

$$M_{11} = \begin{bmatrix} 1 & 2 & 0 \\ 2 & 0 & -1 \\ 3 & 1 & 1 \end{bmatrix}.$$ ■

Using the notation for a minor matrix, we can reinterpret the definition of a (3×3) determinant as follows: If $A = (a_{ij})$ is a (3×3) matrix, then from Eq. (1) and Definition 3,

$$\det(A) = a_{11}\det(M_{11}) - a_{12}\det(M_{12}) + a_{13}\det(M_{13}). \tag{2}$$

In determinant theory, the number $\det(M_{ij})$ is called a minor. Precisely, if $A = (a_{ij})$ is an $(n \times n)$ matrix, then the number $\det(M_{ij})$ is the ***minor of the (i, j)th entry, a_{ij}***. In addition, the numbers A_{ij} defined by

$$A_{ij} = (-1)^{i+j}\det(M_{ij})$$

are known as ***cofactors*** (or ***signed minors***). Thus the expression for $\det(A)$ in Eq. (2) is known as a ***cofactor expansion*** corresponding to the first row.

It is natural, then, to wonder about other cofactor expansions of A that parallel the one given in Eq. (2). For instance, what is the cofactor expansion of A corresponding to the second row or even, perhaps, corresponding to the third column?

By analogy, a cofactor expansion along the second row would have the form

$$-a_{21}\det(M_{21}) + a_{22}\det(M_{22}) - a_{23}\det(M_{23}). \tag{3}$$

An expansion along the third column would take the form

$$a_{13}\det(M_{13}) - a_{23}\det(M_{23}) + a_{33}\det(M_{33}). \tag{4}$$

EXAMPLE 5 Let A denote the (3×3) matrix from Example 3,

$$A = \begin{bmatrix} 1 & 2 & -1 \\ 5 & 3 & 4 \\ -2 & 0 & 1 \end{bmatrix}.$$

Calculate the second-row and third-column cofactor expansions defined by Eqs. (3) and (4), respectively.

Solution According to the pattern in Eq. (3), a second-row expansion has the value

$$-5\begin{vmatrix} 2 & -1 \\ 0 & 1 \end{vmatrix} + 3\begin{vmatrix} 1 & -1 \\ -2 & 1 \end{vmatrix} - 4\begin{vmatrix} 1 & 2 \\ -2 & 0 \end{vmatrix} = -10 - 3 - 16 = -29.$$

Using Eq. (4), we obtain a third-column expansion given by

$$-\begin{vmatrix} 5 & 3 \\ -2 & 0 \end{vmatrix} - 4\begin{vmatrix} 1 & 2 \\ -2 & 0 \end{vmatrix} + \begin{vmatrix} 1 & 2 \\ 5 & 3 \end{vmatrix} = -6 - 16 - 7 = -29.$$ ■

(*Note:* For the (3×3) matrix A in Example 5, there are three possible row expansions and three possible column expansions. It can be shown that each of these six expansions yields exactly the same value, namely, -29. In general, as we observe in the next subsection, all row expansions and all column expansions produce the same value for any $(n \times n)$ matrix.)

The Determinant of an $(n \times n)$ Matrix

We now give an inductive definition for $\det(A)$, the determinant of an $(n \times n)$ matrix. That is, $\det(A)$ is defined in terms of determinants of $[(n-1) \times (n-1)]$ matrices. The natural extension of Definition 2 is the following.

DEFINITION 4 Let $A = (a_{ij})$ be an $(n \times n)$ matrix. The ***determinant of*** A is the number $\det(A)$, where

$$\begin{aligned}\det(A) &= a_{11}\det(M_{11}) - a_{12}\det(M_{12}) + \cdots + (-1)^{n+1}a_{1n}\det(M_{1n}) \\ &= \sum_{j=1}^{n}(-1)^{j+1}a_{1j}\det(M_{1j}).\end{aligned} \tag{5}$$

The definition for $\det(A)$ can be stated in a briefer form if we recall the notation A_{ij} for a cofactor. That is, $A_{ij} = (-1)^{i+j}\det(M_{ij})$. Using the cofactor notation, we can rephrase Definition 4 as

$$\det(A) = \sum_{j=1}^{n} a_{1j}A_{1j}. \tag{6}$$

In the following example we see how Eq. (5) gives the determinant of a (4×4) matrix as the sum of four (3×3) determinants, where each (3×3) determinant is the sum of three (2×2) determinants.

EXAMPLE 6 Use Definition 4 to calculate the $\det(A)$, where

$$A = \begin{bmatrix} 1 & 2 & -1 & 1 \\ -1 & 0 & 2 & -2 \\ 3 & -1 & 1 & 1 \\ 2 & 0 & -1 & 2 \end{bmatrix}.$$

Solution The determinants of the minor matrices M_{11}, M_{12}, M_{13}, and M_{14} are (3×3) determinants and are calculated as before with Definition 2:

$$\det(M_{11}) = \begin{vmatrix} 0 & 2 & -2 \\ -1 & 1 & 1 \\ 0 & -1 & 2 \end{vmatrix} = 0\begin{vmatrix} 1 & 1 \\ -1 & 2 \end{vmatrix} - 2\begin{vmatrix} -1 & 1 \\ 0 & 2 \end{vmatrix} + (-2)\begin{vmatrix} -1 & 1 \\ 0 & -1 \end{vmatrix} = 2$$

$$\det(M_{12}) = \begin{vmatrix} -1 & 2 & -2 \\ 3 & 1 & 1 \\ 2 & -1 & 2 \end{vmatrix} = (-1)\begin{vmatrix} 1 & 1 \\ -1 & 2 \end{vmatrix} - 2\begin{vmatrix} 3 & 1 \\ 2 & 2 \end{vmatrix} + (-2)\begin{vmatrix} 3 & 1 \\ 2 & -1 \end{vmatrix} = -1$$

$$\det(M_{13}) = \begin{vmatrix} -1 & 0 & -2 \\ 3 & -1 & 1 \\ 2 & 0 & 2 \end{vmatrix} = (-1)\begin{vmatrix} -1 & 1 \\ 0 & 2 \end{vmatrix} - 0\begin{vmatrix} 3 & 1 \\ 2 & 2 \end{vmatrix} + (-2)\begin{vmatrix} 3 & -1 \\ 2 & 0 \end{vmatrix} = -2$$

$$\det(M_{14}) = \begin{vmatrix} -1 & 0 & 2 \\ 3 & -1 & 1 \\ 2 & 0 & -1 \end{vmatrix} = (-1)\begin{vmatrix} -1 & 1 \\ 0 & -1 \end{vmatrix} - 0\begin{vmatrix} 3 & 1 \\ 2 & -1 \end{vmatrix} + 2\begin{vmatrix} 3 & -1 \\ 2 & 0 \end{vmatrix} = 3.$$

Hence, from Eq. (5) with $n = 4$,

$$\det(A) = 1(2) - 2(-1) + (-1)(-2) - 1(3) = 3.$$

EXAMPLE 7 For the (4×4) matrix A in Example 6, calculate the second-column cofactor expansion given by

$$-a_{12}\det(M_{12}) + a_{22}\det(M_{22}) - a_{32}\det(M_{32}) + a_{42}\det(M_{42}).$$

Solution From Example 6, $\det(M_{12}) = -1$. Since $a_{22} = 0$ and $a_{42} = 0$, we need not calculate $\det(M_{22})$ and $\det(M_{42})$. The only other value needed is $\det(M_{32})$, where

$$\det(M_{32}) = \begin{vmatrix} 1 & -1 & 1 \\ -1 & 2 & -2 \\ 2 & -1 & 2 \end{vmatrix} = 1\begin{vmatrix} 2 & -2 \\ -1 & 2 \end{vmatrix} - (-1)\begin{vmatrix} -1 & -2 \\ 2 & 2 \end{vmatrix} + 1\begin{vmatrix} -1 & 2 \\ 2 & -1 \end{vmatrix} = 1.$$

Thus the second-column expansion gives the value

$$-2(-1) + 0\det(M_{22}) - (-1)(1) + 0\det(M_{42}) = 3.$$

From Example 6, $\det(A) = 3$. From Example 7, a second-column expansion also produces the same value, 3. The next theorem states that a cofactor expansion along any row or any column always produces the same number, $\det(A)$. The expansions in the theorem are phrased in the same brief notation as in Eq. (6). The proof of Theorem 1 is given in Chapter 6.

THEOREM 1 Let $A = (a_{ij})$ be an $(n \times n)$ matrix with minor matrices M_{ij} and cofactors $A_{ij} = (-1)^{i+j}\det(M_{ij})$. Then

$$\det(A) = \sum_{j=1}^{n} a_{ij} A_{ij} \quad (i\text{th-row expansion})$$

$$= \sum_{i=1}^{n} a_{ij} A_{ij} \quad (j\text{th-column expansion}) \quad \blacksquare$$

Because of Theorem 1, we can always find $\det(A)$ by choosing the row or column of A with the most zeros for the cofactor expansion. (If $a_{ij} = 0$, then $a_{ij} A_{ij} = 0$, and we need not compute A_{ij}.) In the next section we consider how to use elementary row or column operations to create zeros and hence simplify determinant calculations.

Determinants and Singular Matrices

Theorems 2 and 3, which follow, are fundamental to our study of eigenvalues. These theorems are stated here and their proofs are given in Chapter 6.

THEOREM 2 Let A and B be $(n \times n)$ matrices. Then

$$\det(AB) = \det(A) \det(B).$$
$\blacksquare$

The following example illustrates Theorem 2.

EXAMPLE 8 Calculate $\det(A)$, $\det(B)$, and $\det(AB)$ for the matrices

$$A = \begin{bmatrix} 1 & 2 \\ -1 & 1 \end{bmatrix} \quad \text{and} \quad B = \begin{bmatrix} 2 & 3 \\ 1 & -1 \end{bmatrix}.$$

Solution The product, AB, is given by

$$AB = \begin{bmatrix} 4 & 1 \\ -1 & -4 \end{bmatrix}.$$

Clearly $\det(AB) = -15$. We also see that $\det(A) = 3$ and $\det(B) = -5$. Observe, for this special case, that $\det(A) \det(B) = \det(AB)$. $\blacksquare$

To study the eigenvalue problem for an $(n \times n)$ matrix, we need a test for singularity. The following theorem shows that determinant theory provides a simple and elegant test.

THEOREM 3 Let A be an $(n \times n)$ matrix. Then

$$A \text{ is singular if and only if } \det(A) = 0. \quad \blacksquare$$

Theorem 3 is already familiar for the case in which A is a (2×2) matrix (recall Definition 1 and Examples 1 and 2). An outline for the proof of Theorem 3 is given in the next section. Finally, in Section 4.4 we will be able to use Theorem 3 to devise a procedure for solving the eigenvalue problem.

We conclude this brief introduction to determinants by observing that it is easy to calculate the determinant of a triangular matrix.

THEOREM 4 Let $T = (t_{ij})$ be an $(n \times n)$ triangular matrix. Then

$$\det(T) = t_{11}t_{22}\ldots t_{nn}.$$

The proof of Theorem 4 is left to the exercises. The next example illustrates how a proof for Theorem 4 might be constructed.

EXAMPLE 9 Use a cofactor expansion (as in Definition 4 or Theorem 1) to calculate $\det(T)$:

$$T = \begin{bmatrix} 2 & 1 & 3 & 7 \\ 0 & 4 & 8 & 1 \\ 0 & 0 & 1 & 5 \\ 0 & 0 & 0 & 3 \end{bmatrix}.$$

Solution By Theorem 1, we can use a cofactor expansion along any row or column to calculate $\det(T)$. Because of the structure of T, an expansion along the first column or the fourth row will be easiest.

Expanding along the first column, we find

$$\det(T) = \begin{vmatrix} 2 & 1 & 3 & 7 \\ 0 & 4 & 8 & 1 \\ 0 & 0 & 1 & 5 \\ 0 & 0 & 0 & 3 \end{vmatrix} = 2\begin{vmatrix} 4 & 8 & 1 \\ 0 & 1 & 5 \\ 0 & 0 & 3 \end{vmatrix}$$

$$= (2)(4)\begin{vmatrix} 1 & 5 \\ 0 & 3 \end{vmatrix} = 24.$$

This example provides a special case of Theorem 4.

(*Note:* An easy corollary to Theorem 4 is the following: If I is the $(n \times n)$ identity matrix, then $\det(I) = 1$. In the exercises that follow, some additional results are derived from the theorems in this section and from the fact that $\det(I) = 1$.)

4.2 EXERCISES

In Exercises 1–6, list the minor matrix M_{ij}, and calculate the cofactor $A_{ij} = (-1)^{i+j}\det(M_{ij})$ for the matrix A given by

$$A = \begin{bmatrix} 2 & -1 & 3 & 1 \\ 4 & 1 & 3 & -1 \\ 6 & 2 & 4 & 1 \\ 2 & 2 & 0 & -2 \end{bmatrix} \qquad (7)$$

1. M_{11} **2.** M_{21} **3.** M_{31}
4. M_{41} **5.** M_{34} **6.** M_{43}

7. Use the results of Exercises 1–4 to calculate $\det(A)$ for the matrix A given in (7).

In Exercises 8–19, calculate the determinant of the given matrix. Use Theorem 3 to state whether the matrix is singular or nonsingular.

8. $A = \begin{bmatrix} 2 & 1 \\ -1 & 2 \end{bmatrix}$ **9.** $A = \begin{bmatrix} 1 & -1 \\ -2 & 2 \end{bmatrix}$

10. $A = \begin{bmatrix} 2 & 3 \\ 4 & 6 \end{bmatrix}$ **11.** $A = \begin{bmatrix} 1 & 1 \\ 2 & 1 \end{bmatrix}$

12. $A = \begin{bmatrix} 1 & 2 & 4 \\ 2 & 3 & 7 \\ 4 & 2 & 10 \end{bmatrix}$ **13.** $A = \begin{bmatrix} 2 & -3 & 2 \\ -1 & -2 & 1 \\ 3 & 1 & -1 \end{bmatrix}$

14. $A = \begin{bmatrix} 1 & 2 & 1 \\ 0 & 3 & 2 \\ -1 & 1 & 1 \end{bmatrix}$ **15.** $A = \begin{bmatrix} 2 & 0 & 0 \\ 1 & 3 & 2 \\ 2 & 1 & 4 \end{bmatrix}$

16. $A = \begin{bmatrix} 2 & 0 & 0 \\ 3 & 1 & 0 \\ 2 & 4 & 2 \end{bmatrix}$ **17.** $A = \begin{bmatrix} 1 & 2 & 1 & 5 \\ 0 & 3 & 0 & 0 \\ 0 & 4 & 1 & 2 \\ 0 & 3 & 1 & 4 \end{bmatrix}$

18. $A = \begin{bmatrix} 0 & 1 & 0 & 0 \\ 0 & 0 & 1 & 0 \\ 1 & 0 & 0 & 0 \\ 0 & 0 & 0 & 1 \end{bmatrix}$

19. $A = \begin{bmatrix} 0 & 0 & 0 & 2 \\ 0 & 0 & 3 & 1 \\ 0 & 2 & 1 & 2 \\ 3 & 4 & 1 & 4 \end{bmatrix}$

20. Let $A = (a_{ij})$ be a given (3×3) matrix. Form the associated (3×5) matrix B shown next:

$$B = \begin{bmatrix} a_{11} & a_{12} & a_{13} & a_{11} & a_{12} \\ a_{21} & a_{22} & a_{23} & a_{21} & a_{22} \\ a_{31} & a_{32} & a_{33} & a_{31} & a_{32} \end{bmatrix}$$

a) Subtract the sum of the three upward diagonal products from the sum of the three downward diagonal products and argue that your result is equal to $\det(A)$.

b) Show, by example, that a similar basketweave algorithm cannot be used to calculate the determinant of a (4×4) matrix.

In Exercises 21 and 22, find all ordered pairs (x, y) such that A is singular.

21. $A = \begin{bmatrix} x & y & 1 \\ 2 & 3 & 1 \\ 0 & -1 & 1 \end{bmatrix}$ **22.** $A = \begin{bmatrix} x & 1 & 1 \\ 2 & 1 & 1 \\ 0 & -1 & y \end{bmatrix}$

23. Let $A = (a_{ij})$ be the $(n \times n)$ matrix specified thus: $a_{ij} = d$ for $i = j$ and $a_{ij} = 1$ for $i \neq j$. For $n = 2$, 3, and 4, show that

$$\det(A) = (d-1)^{n-1}(d-1+n).$$

24. Let A and B be $(n \times n)$ matrices. Use Theorems 2 and 3 to give a quick proof of each of the following.

a) If either A or B is singular, then AB is singular.

b) If AB is singular, then either A or B is singular.

25. Suppose that A is an $(n \times n)$ nonsingular matrix, and recall that $\det(I) = 1$, where I is the $(n \times n)$ identity matrix. Show that $\det(A^{-1}) = 1/\det(A)$.

26. If A and B are $(n \times n)$ matrices, then usually $AB \neq BA$. Nonetheless, argue that always $\det(AB) = \det(BA)$.

In Exercises 27–30, use Theorem 2 and Exercise 25 to evaluate the given determinant, where A and B are $(n \times n)$ matrices with $\det(A) = 3$ and $\det(B) = 5$.

27. $\det(ABA^{-1})$ **28.** $\det(A^2B)$

29. $\det(A^{-1}B^{-1}A^2)$ **30.** $\det(AB^{-1}A^{-1}B)$

31. a) Let A be an $(n \times n)$ matrix. If $n = 3$, $\det(A)$ can be found by evaluating three (2×2) determinants. If $n = 4$, $\det(A)$ can be found by evaluating twelve (2×2) determinants. Give a formula, $H(n)$, for the number of (2×2) determinants necessary to find $\det(A)$ for an arbitrary n.

b) Suppose you can perform additions, subtractions, multiplications, and divisions each at a rate of one per second. How long does it take to evaluate $H(n)$ (2×2) determinants when $n = 2$, $n = 5$, and $n = 10$?

32. Let U and V be $(n \times n)$ upper-triangular matrices. Prove a special case of Theorem 2: $\det(UV) = \det(U)\det(V)$. [*Hint:* Use the definition for matrix multiplication to calculate the diagonal entries of the product UV, and then apply Theorem 4. You will also need to recall from Exercise 67 in Section 1.5 that UV is an upper-triangular matrix.]

33. Let V be an $(n \times n)$ triangular matrix. Use Theorem 4 to prove that $\det(V^T) = \det(V)$.

34. Let $T = (t_{ij})$ be an $(n \times n)$ upper-triangular matrix. Prove that $\det(T) = t_{11}t_{22}\ldots t_{nn}$. [*Hint:* Use mathematical induction, beginning with a (2×2) upper-triangular determinant.]

ELEMENTARY OPERATIONS AND DETERMINANTS (OPTIONAL)*

We saw in Section 4.2 that having many zero entries in a matrix simplifies the calculation of its determinant. The ultimate case is given in Theorem 4. If $T = (t_{ij})$ is an $(n \times n)$ triangular matrix, then it is very easy to calculate $\det(T)$:

$$\det(T) = t_{11}t_{22}\ldots t_{nn}.$$

In Chapter 1, we used elementary row operations to create zero entries. We now consider these row operations (along with similar column operations) and describe their effect on the value of the determinant. For instance, consider the (2×2) matrices

$$A = \begin{bmatrix} 1 & 2 \\ 3 & 4 \end{bmatrix} \quad \text{and} \quad B = \begin{bmatrix} 3 & 4 \\ 1 & 2 \end{bmatrix}.$$

Clearly B is the result of interchanging the first and second rows of A (an elementary row operation). Also, we see that $\det(A) = -2$, whereas $\det(B) = 2$. This computation demonstrates that performing an elementary operation may change the value of the determinant. As we will see, however, it is possible to predict in advance the nature of any changes that might be produced by an elementary operation. For example, we will see that a row interchange always reverses the sign of the determinant.

Before studying the effects of elementary row operations on determinants, we consider the following theorem, which is an immediate consequence of Theorem 1.

THEOREM 5 If A is an $(n \times n)$ matrix, then

$$\det(A) = \det(A^T).$$

Proof The proof is by induction, and we begin with the case $n = 2$. Let $A = (a_{ij})$ be a (2×2) matrix:

$$A = \begin{bmatrix} a_{11} & a_{12} \\ a_{21} & a_{22} \end{bmatrix}, \quad A^T = \begin{bmatrix} a_{11} & a_{21} \\ a_{12} & a_{22} \end{bmatrix}.$$

Hence it is clear that $\det(A) = \det(A^T)$ when A is a (2×2) matrix.

The inductive step hinges on the following observation about minor matrices: Suppose that B is a square matrix, and let $C = B^T$. Next, let M_{rs} and N_{rs} denote minor matrices of B and C, respectively. Then these minor matrices are related by

$$N_{ij} = (M_{ji})^T. \tag{1}$$

(In words, the ijth minor matrix of B^T is equal to the transpose of the jith minor matrix of B.)

To proceed with the induction, suppose that Theorem 5 is valid for all $(k \times k)$ matrices, $2 \le k \le n - 1$. Let A be an $(n \times n)$ matrix, where $n > 2$. Let M_{rs} denote the

*The results in this section are not required for a study of the eigenvalue problem. They are included here for the convenience of the reader and because they follow naturally from definitions and theorems in the previous section. See Chapter 6 for proofs.

minor matrices of A, and let N_{rs} denote the minor matrices of A^T. Consider an expansion of $\det(A)$ along the first row and an expansion of $\det(A^T)$ along the first column:

$$\begin{aligned}\det(A) &= a_{11}\det(M_{11}) - a_{12}\det(M_{12}) + \cdots + (-1)^{n+1}a_{1n}\det(M_{1n})\\ \det(A^T) &= a_{11}\det(N_{11}) - a_{12}\det(N_{21}) + \cdots + (-1)^{n+1}a_{1n}\det(N_{n1}).\end{aligned} \quad (2)$$

(The expansion for $\det(A^T)$ in Eq. (2) incorporates the fact that the first-column entries for A^T are the same as the first-row entries of A.)

By Eq. (1), the minor matrices N_{j1} in Eq. (2) satisfy $N_{j1} = (M_{1j})^T$, $1 \le j \le n$. By the inductive hypotheses, $\det(M_{1j}^T) = \det(M_{1j})$, since M_{1j} is a matrix of order $n-1$. Therefore, both expansions in Eq. (2) have the same value, showing that $\det(A^T) = \det(A)$. ■

One valuable aspect of Theorem 5 is that it tells us an elementary column operation applied to a square matrix A will affect $\det(A)$ in precisely the same way as the corresponding elementary row operation.

Effects of Elementary Operations

We first consider how the determinant changes when rows of a matrix are interchanged.

THEOREM 6 Let A be an $(n \times n)$ matrix, and let B be formed by interchanging any two rows (or columns) of A. Then

$$\det(B) = -\det(A).$$

Proof First we consider the case where the two rows to be interchanged are adjacent, say, the ith and $(i+1)$st rows. Let M_{ij}, $1 \le j \le n$, be the minor matrices of A from the ith row, and let $N_{i+1,j}$, $1 \le j \le n$, be the minor matrices of B from the $(i+1)$st row. A bit of reflection will reveal that $N_{i+1,j} = M_{ij}$. Since $a_{i1}, a_{i2}, \ldots, a_{in}$ are the elements of the $(i+1)$st row of B, we have

$$\begin{aligned}\det(B) &= \sum_{j=1}^{n}(-1)^{i+1+j}a_{ij}\det(N_{i+1,j})\\ &= -\sum_{j=1}^{n}(-1)^{i+j}a_{ij}\det(N_{i+1,j})\\ &= -\sum_{j=1}^{n}(-1)^{i+j}a_{ij}\det(M_{ij}), \quad \text{since } N_{i+1,j} = M_{ij}\\ &= -\det(A).\end{aligned}$$

Thus far we know that interchanging any two *adjacent* rows changes the sign of the determinant. Now suppose that B is formed by interchanging the ith and kth rows of A, where $k \ge i+1$. The ith row can be moved to the kth row by $(k-i)$ successive interchanges of adjacent rows. The original kth row at this point is now the $(k-1)$st row. This row can be moved to the ith row by $(k-1-i)$ successive interchanges of adjacent rows. At this point all other rows are in their original positions. Hence, we have formed B with $2k-1-2i$ successive interchanges of adjacent rows. Thus,

$$\det(B) = (-1)^{(2k-1-2i)}\det(A) = -\det(A).$$ ■

COROLLARY If A is an $(n \times n)$ matrix with two identical rows (columns), then $\det(A) = 0$.

We leave the proof of the corollary as an exercise.

EXAMPLE 1 Find $\det(A)$, where

$$A = \begin{bmatrix} 0 & 0 & 0 & 4 \\ 0 & 0 & 3 & 2 \\ 0 & 1 & 2 & 5 \\ 2 & 3 & 1 & 3 \end{bmatrix}.$$

Solution We could calculate $\det(A)$ by using a cofactor expansion, but we also see that we can rearrange the rows of A to produce a triangular matrix.

Adopting the latter course of action, we have

$$\det(A) = \begin{vmatrix} 0 & 0 & 0 & 4 \\ 0 & 0 & 3 & 2 \\ 0 & 1 & 2 & 5 \\ 2 & 3 & 1 & 3 \end{vmatrix} = - \begin{vmatrix} 2 & 3 & 1 & 3 \\ 0 & 0 & 3 & 2 \\ 0 & 1 & 2 & 5 \\ 0 & 0 & 0 & 4 \end{vmatrix} = \begin{vmatrix} 2 & 3 & 1 & 3 \\ 0 & 1 & 2 & 5 \\ 0 & 0 & 3 & 2 \\ 0 & 0 & 0 & 4 \end{vmatrix} = 24.$$

Next we consider the effect of another elementary operation.

THEOREM 7 Suppose that B is obtained from the $(n \times n)$ matrix A by multiplying one row (or column) of A by a nonzero scalar c and leaving the other rows (or columns) unchanged. Then

$$\det(B) = c\det(A).$$

Proof Suppose that $[ca_{i1}, ca_{i2}, \ldots, ca_{in}]$ is the ith row of B. Since the other rows of B are unchanged from A, the minor matrices of B from the ith row are the same as M_{ij}, the minor matrices of A from the ith row. Using a cofactor expansion from the ith row of B to calculate $\det(B)$ gives

$$\begin{aligned} \det(B) &= \sum_{j=1}^{n} (ca_{ij})(-1)^{i+j}\det(M_{ij}) \\ &= c\sum_{j=1}^{n} a_{ij}(-1)^{i+j}\det(M_{ij}) \\ &= c\det(A). \end{aligned}$$

As we see in the next theorem, the third elementary operation leaves the determinant unchanged. (*Note:* Theorem 8 is also valid when the word *column* is substituted for the word *row*.)

THEOREM 8 Let A be an $(n \times n)$ matrix. Suppose that B is the matrix obtained from A by replacing the ith row of A by the ith row of A plus a constant multiple of the kth row of A, $k \neq i$. Then

$$\det(B) = \det(A).$$

Proof Note that the ith row of B has the form

$$[a_{i1} + ca_{k1}, a_{i2} + ca_{k2}, \ldots, a_{in} + ca_{kn}].$$

Since the other rows of B are unchanged from A, the minor matrices taken with respect to the ith row of B are the same as the minor matrices M_{ij} of A.

Using a cofactor expansion of $\det(B)$ from the ith row, we have

$$\begin{aligned}
\det(B) &= \sum_{j=1}^{n}(a_{ij} + ca_{kj})(-1)^{i+j}\det(M_{ij}) \\
&= \sum_{j=1}^{n} a_{ij}(-1)^{i+j}\det(M_{ij}) + c\sum_{j=1}^{n} a_{kj}(-1)^{i+j}\det(M_{ij}) \qquad (3) \\
&= \det(A) + c\sum_{j=1}^{n} a_{kj}(-1)^{i+j}\det(M_{ij}).
\end{aligned}$$

Theorem 8 will be proved if we can show that the last summation on the right-hand side of Eq. (3) has the value zero. In order to prove that the summation has the value zero, construct a matrix Q by replacing the ith row of A by the kth row of A. The matrix Q so constructed has two identical rows (the kth row of A appears both as the kth row and the ith row of Q). Therefore, by the corollary to Theorem 6, $\det(Q) = 0$. Next, expanding $\det(Q)$ along the ith row of Q, we obtain (since the ith-row minors of Q are the same as those of A and since the ijth entry of Q is a_{kj})

$$0 = \det(Q) = \sum_{j=1}^{n} a_{kj}(-1)^{i+j}\det(M_{ij}). \qquad (4)$$

Substituting Eq. (4) into Eq. (3) establishes the theorem. ■

EXAMPLE 2 Evaluate $\det(A)$, where

$$A = \begin{bmatrix} 1 & 2 & 1 \\ 0 & 3 & 2 \\ -2 & 1 & 1 \end{bmatrix}.$$

Solution The value of $\det(A)$ is unchanged if we add a multiple of 2 times row 1 to row 3. The effect of this row operation will be to introduce another zero entry in the first column. Specifically,

$$\det(A) = \begin{vmatrix} 1 & 2 & 1 \\ 0 & 3 & 2 \\ -2 & 1 & 1 \end{vmatrix} \xrightarrow[=]{(R_3 + 2R_1)} \begin{vmatrix} 1 & 2 & 1 \\ 0 & 3 & 2 \\ 0 & 5 & 3 \end{vmatrix} = -1. \qquad ■$$

Using Elementary Operations to Simplify Determinants

Clearly it is usually easier to calculate the determinant of a matrix with several zero entries than to calculate one with no zero entries. Therefore, a common strategy in determinant evaluation is to mimic the steps of Gaussian elimination—that is, to use elementary row or column operations to reduce the matrix to triangular form.

EXAMPLE 3 Evaluate det(A), where

$$A = \begin{bmatrix} 1 & 2 & -1 \\ 5 & 3 & 4 \\ -2 & 0 & 1 \end{bmatrix}.$$

Solution With Gaussian elimination, we would first form the matrix B by the following operations: Replace R_2 by $R_2 - 5R_1$ and replace R_3 by $R_3 + 2R_1$. From Theorem 8, the matrix B produced by these two row operations has the same determinant as the original matrix A. In detail:

$$\det(A) = \begin{vmatrix} 1 & 2 & -1 \\ 5 & 3 & 4 \\ -2 & 0 & 1 \end{vmatrix} = \begin{vmatrix} 1 & 2 & -1 \\ 0 & -7 & 9 \\ 0 & 4 & -1 \end{vmatrix} = 1\begin{vmatrix} -7 & 9 \\ 4 & -1 \end{vmatrix} = 7 - 36 = -29. \blacksquare$$

We could have created a zero in the (2, 1) position of the last (2 × 2) determinant. The formula for (2 × 2) determinants is so simple, however, that it is customary to evaluate a (2 × 2) determinant directly. The next example illustrates that we need not always attempt to go to a triangular form in order to simplify a determinant.

EXAMPLE 4 Evaluate det(A), where

$$A = \begin{bmatrix} 1 & 2 & -1 & 1 \\ -1 & 0 & 2 & -2 \\ 3 & -1 & 1 & 1 \\ 2 & 0 & -1 & 2 \end{bmatrix}.$$

Solution We can introduce a third zero in the second column if we replace R_1 by $R_1 + 2R_3$:

$$\det(A) = \begin{vmatrix} 1 & 2 & -1 & 1 \\ -1 & 0 & 2 & -2 \\ 3 & -1 & 1 & 1 \\ 2 & 0 & -1 & 2 \end{vmatrix} = \begin{vmatrix} 7 & 0 & 1 & 3 \\ -1 & 0 & 2 & -2 \\ 3 & -1 & 1 & 1 \\ 2 & 0 & -1 & 2 \end{vmatrix}$$

$$= -(-1)\begin{vmatrix} 7 & 1 & 3 \\ -1 & 2 & -2 \\ 2 & -1 & 2 \end{vmatrix}.$$

(The second equality is from Theorem 8. The third equality is from an expansion along the second column.) Next we replace R_2 by $R_2 - 2R_1$ and R_3 by $R_1 + R_3$.

The details are

$$\det(A) = \begin{vmatrix} 7 & 1 & 3 \\ -1 & 2 & -2 \\ 2 & -1 & 2 \end{vmatrix} = \begin{vmatrix} 7 & 1 & 3 \\ -15 & 0 & -8 \\ 9 & 0 & 5 \end{vmatrix}$$

$$= -1 \begin{vmatrix} -15 & -8 \\ 9 & 5 \end{vmatrix} = (75 - 72) = 3.$$

The next example illustrates that if the entries in a determinant are integers, then we can avoid working with fractions until the last step. The technique involves multiplying various rows by constants to make each entry in a column divisible by the pivot entry in the column.

Example 5 Find $\det(A)$, where

$$A = \begin{bmatrix} 2 & 3 & -2 & 4 \\ 3 & -3 & 5 & 2 \\ 5 & 2 & 4 & 3 \\ -3 & 4 & -3 & 2 \end{bmatrix}.$$

Solution We first multiply rows 2, 3, and 4 by 2 to make them divisible by 2. The row reduction operations to create zeros in the first column can then proceed without using fractions. The row operations are $R_2 - 3R_1$, $R_3 - 5R_1$, and $R_4 + 3R_1$:

$$\det(A) = \begin{vmatrix} 2 & 3 & -2 & 4 \\ 3 & -3 & 5 & 2 \\ 5 & 2 & 4 & 3 \\ -3 & 4 & -3 & 2 \end{vmatrix} = \frac{1}{8} \begin{vmatrix} 2 & 3 & -2 & 4 \\ 6 & -6 & 10 & 4 \\ 10 & 4 & 8 & 6 \\ -6 & 8 & -6 & 4 \end{vmatrix}$$

$$= \frac{1}{8} \begin{vmatrix} 2 & 3 & -2 & 4 \\ 0 & -15 & 16 & -8 \\ 0 & -11 & 18 & -14 \\ 0 & 17 & -12 & 16 \end{vmatrix} = \frac{2}{8} \begin{vmatrix} -15 & 16 & -8 \\ -11 & 18 & -14 \\ 17 & -12 & 16 \end{vmatrix}$$

$$= \frac{1}{4} \begin{vmatrix} -15 & 2(8) & 2(-4) \\ -11 & 2(9) & 2(-7) \\ 17 & 2(-6) & 2(8) \end{vmatrix} = \frac{2(2)}{4} \begin{vmatrix} -15 & 8 & -4 \\ -11 & 9 & -7 \\ 17 & -6 & 8 \end{vmatrix}.$$

We now multiply the second row by 4 and use $R_2 - 7R_1$ and $R_3 + 2R_1$:

$$\det(A) = \frac{1}{4} \begin{vmatrix} -15 & 8 & -4 \\ -44 & 36 & -28 \\ 17 & -6 & 8 \end{vmatrix} = \frac{1}{4} \begin{vmatrix} -15 & 8 & -4 \\ 61 & -20 & 0 \\ -13 & 10 & 0 \end{vmatrix}$$

$$= \frac{-4}{4}(610 - 260) = -350. \qquad \blacksquare$$

The preceding examples illustrate that there are many strategies that will lead to a simpler determinant calculation. Exactly which choices are made are determined by experience and personal preference.

Proof of Theorem 3

In the last section we stated Theorem 3: An $(n \times n)$ matrix A is singular if and only if $\det(A) = 0$. The results of this section enable us to sketch a proof for Theorem 3.

If A is an $(n \times n)$ matrix, then we know from Chapter 1 that we can use Gaussian elimination to produce a row-equivalent upper-triangular matrix T. This matrix T can be formed by using row interchanges and adding multiples of one row to other rows. Thus, by Theorems 6 and 8,

$$\det(A) = \pm \det(T). \qquad (5)$$

An outline for the proof of Theorem 3 is given below. We use t_{ij} to denote the entries of the upper-triangular matrix T:

1. $\det(A) = 0 \Leftrightarrow \det(T) = 0$, by Eq. (5);
2. $\det(T) = 0 \Leftrightarrow t_{ii} = 0$ for some i, by Theorem 4;
3. $t_{ii} = 0$ for some $i \Leftrightarrow T$ singular (see Exercise 56 of Section 1.7);
4. T singular $\Leftrightarrow A$ singular, since T and A are row equivalent. $\blacksquare$

4.3   EXERCISES

In Exercises 1–6, evaluate $\det(A)$ by using row operations to introduce zeros into the second and third entries of the first column.

1. $A = \begin{bmatrix} 1 & 2 & 1 \\ 3 & 0 & 2 \\ -1 & 1 & 3 \end{bmatrix}$ 2. $A = \begin{bmatrix} 2 & 4 & 6 \\ 3 & 1 & 2 \\ 1 & 2 & 1 \end{bmatrix}$

3. $A = \begin{bmatrix} 3 & 6 & 9 \\ 2 & 0 & 2 \\ 1 & 2 & 0 \end{bmatrix}$ 4. $A = \begin{bmatrix} 1 & 1 & 2 \\ -2 & 1 & 3 \\ 1 & 4 & 1 \end{bmatrix}$

5. $A = \begin{bmatrix} 2 & 4 & -3 \\ 3 & 2 & 5 \\ 2 & 3 & 4 \end{bmatrix}$ 6. $A = \begin{bmatrix} 3 & 4 & -2 \\ 2 & 3 & 5 \\ 2 & 4 & 3 \end{bmatrix}$

In Exercises 7–12, use only column interchanges or row interchanges to produce a triangular determinant and then find the value of the original determinant.

7. $\begin{vmatrix} 1 & 0 & 0 & 0 \\ 2 & 0 & 0 & 3 \\ 1 & 1 & 0 & 1 \\ 1 & 4 & 2 & 2 \end{vmatrix}$ 8. $\begin{vmatrix} 0 & 0 & 3 & 1 \\ 2 & 1 & 0 & 1 \\ 0 & 0 & 0 & 2 \\ 0 & 2 & 2 & 1 \end{vmatrix}$

9. $\begin{vmatrix} 0 & 0 & 2 & 0 \\ 0 & 0 & 1 & 3 \\ 0 & 4 & 1 & 3 \\ 2 & 1 & 5 & 6 \end{vmatrix}$

10. $\begin{vmatrix} 0 & 0 & 1 & 0 \\ 1 & 2 & 1 & 3 \\ 0 & 0 & 0 & 5 \\ 0 & 3 & 1 & 2 \end{vmatrix}$

11. $\begin{vmatrix} 0 & 0 & 1 & 0 \\ 0 & 2 & 6 & 3 \\ 2 & 4 & 1 & 5 \\ 0 & 0 & 0 & 4 \end{vmatrix}$

12. $\begin{vmatrix} 0 & 1 & 0 & 0 \\ 0 & 2 & 0 & 3 \\ 2 & 1 & 0 & 6 \\ 3 & 2 & 2 & 4 \end{vmatrix}$

In Exercises 13–18, assume that the (3×3) matrix A satisfies $\det(A) = 2$, where A is given by

$$A = \begin{bmatrix} a & b & c \\ d & e & f \\ g & h & i \end{bmatrix}.$$

Calculate $\det(B)$ in each case.

13. $B = \begin{bmatrix} a & b & 3c \\ d & e & 3f \\ g & h & 3i \end{bmatrix}$

14. $B = \begin{bmatrix} d & e & f \\ g & h & i \\ a & b & c \end{bmatrix}$

15. $B = \begin{bmatrix} b & a & c \\ e & d & f \\ h & g & i \end{bmatrix}$

16. $B = \begin{bmatrix} a & b & c \\ a+d & b+e & c+f \\ g & h & i \end{bmatrix}$

17. $B = \begin{bmatrix} d & e & f \\ 2a & 2b & 2c \\ g & h & i \end{bmatrix}$

18. $B = \begin{bmatrix} d & f & e \\ a & c & b \\ g & i & h \end{bmatrix}$

In Exercises 19–22, evaluate the (4×4) determinants. Theorems 6–8 can be used to simplify the calculations.

19. $\begin{vmatrix} 2 & 4 & 2 & 6 \\ 1 & 3 & 2 & 1 \\ 2 & 1 & 2 & 3 \\ 1 & 2 & 1 & 1 \end{vmatrix}$

20. $\begin{vmatrix} 0 & 2 & 1 & 3 \\ 1 & 2 & 1 & 0 \\ 0 & 1 & 1 & 3 \\ 2 & 2 & 1 & 2 \end{vmatrix}$

21. $\begin{vmatrix} 0 & 4 & 1 & 3 \\ 0 & 2 & 2 & 1 \\ 1 & 3 & 1 & 2 \\ 2 & 2 & 1 & 4 \end{vmatrix}$

22. $\begin{vmatrix} 2 & 2 & 4 & 4 \\ 1 & 1 & 3 & 3 \\ 1 & 0 & 2 & 1 \\ 4 & 1 & 3 & 2 \end{vmatrix}$

In Exercises 23 and 24, use row operations to obtain a triangular determinant and find the value of the original Vandermonde determinant.

23. $\begin{vmatrix} 1 & a & a^2 \\ 1 & b & b^2 \\ 1 & c & c^2 \end{vmatrix}$

24. $\begin{vmatrix} 1 & a & a^2 & a^3 \\ 1 & b & b^2 & b^3 \\ 1 & c & c^2 & c^3 \\ 1 & d & d^2 & d^3 \end{vmatrix}$

25. Let A be an $(n \times n)$ matrix. Use Theorem 7 to argue that $\det(cA) = c^n \det(A)$.

26. Prove the corollary to Theorem 6. [*Hint:* Suppose that the ith and jth rows of A are identical. Interchange these two rows and let B denote the matrix that results. How are $\det(A)$ and $\det(B)$ related?]

27. Find examples of (2×2) matrices A and B such that $\det(A + B) \neq \det(A) + \det(B)$.

28. An $(n \times n)$ matrix A is called ***skew symmetric*** if $A^T = -A$. Show that if A is skew symmetric, then $\det(A) = (-1)^n \det(A)$. [*Hint:* Use Theorem 5 and Exercise 25.] Now, argue that an $(n \times n)$ skew-symmetric matrix is singular when n is an odd integer.

4.4 EIGENVALUES AND THE CHARACTERISTIC POLYNOMIAL

Having given the brief introduction to determinant theory presented in Section 4.2, we return to the central topic of this chapter, the eigenvalue problem. For reference, recall that the eigenvalue problem for an $(n \times n)$ matrix A has two parts:

1. Find all scalars λ such that $A - \lambda I$ is singular. (Such scalars are the ***eigenvalues*** of A.)
2. Given an eigenvalue λ, find all nonzero vectors $\mathbf{x}$ such that $(A - \lambda I)\mathbf{x} = \boldsymbol{\theta}$. (Such vectors are the ***eigenvectors*** corresponding to the eigenvalue λ.)

In this section we focus on part 1, finding the eigenvalues. In the next section we discuss eigenvectors.

In Section 4.1, we were able to determine the eigenvalues of a (2×2) matrix by using a test for singularity given by Eq. (4) in Section 4.1. Knowing Theorem 3 from Section 4.2, we now have a test for singularity that is applicable to any $(n \times n)$ matrix. As applied to the eigenvalue problem, Theorem 3 can be used as follows:

$$A - \lambda I \text{ is singular} \Leftrightarrow \det(A - \lambda I) = 0. \tag{1}$$

An example will illustrate how the singularity test given in Eq. (1) is used in practice.

EXAMPLE 1 Use the singularity test given in Eq. (1) to determine the eigenvalues of the (3×3) matrix A, where

$$A = \begin{bmatrix} 1 & 1 & 1 \\ 0 & 3 & 3 \\ -2 & 1 & 1 \end{bmatrix}.$$

Solution A scalar λ is an eigenvalue of A if and only if $A - \lambda I$ is singular. According to the singularity test in Eq. (1), λ is an eigenvalue of A if and only if λ is a scalar such that

$$\det(A - \lambda I) = 0.$$

Thus we focus on $\det(A - \lambda I)$, where $A - \lambda I$ is the matrix given by

$$A - \lambda I = \begin{bmatrix} 1 & 1 & 1 \\ 0 & 3 & 3 \\ -2 & 1 & 1 \end{bmatrix} - \begin{bmatrix} \lambda & 0 & 0 \\ 0 & \lambda & 0 \\ 0 & 0 & \lambda \end{bmatrix}$$

$$= \begin{bmatrix} 1-\lambda & 1 & 1 \\ 0 & 3-\lambda & 3 \\ -2 & 1 & 1-\lambda \end{bmatrix}.$$

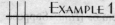

Expanding $\det(A - \lambda I)$ along the first column, we have

$$\det(A - \lambda I) = \begin{vmatrix} 1-\lambda & 1 & 1 \\ 0 & 3-\lambda & 3 \\ -2 & 1 & 1-\lambda \end{vmatrix}$$

$$= (1-\lambda)\begin{vmatrix} 3-\lambda & 3 \\ 1 & 1-\lambda \end{vmatrix} - (0)\begin{vmatrix} 1 & 1 \\ 1 & 1-\lambda \end{vmatrix}$$

$$+ (-2)\begin{vmatrix} 1 & 1 \\ 3-\lambda & 3 \end{vmatrix}$$

$$\begin{aligned} &= (1-\lambda)[(3-\lambda)(1-\lambda) - 3] - 2[3 - (3-\lambda)] \\ &= (1-\lambda)[\lambda^2 - 4\lambda] - 2[\lambda] \\ &= [-\lambda^3 + 5\lambda^2 - 4\lambda] - [2\lambda] \\ &= -\lambda^3 + 5\lambda^2 - 6\lambda \\ &= -\lambda(\lambda^2 - 5\lambda + 6) \\ &= -\lambda(\lambda - 3)(\lambda - 2). \end{aligned}$$

From the singularity test in Eq. (1), we see that $A - \lambda I$ is singular if and only if $\lambda = 0$, $\lambda = 3$, or $\lambda = 2$.

The ideas developed in Example 1 will be formalized in the next subsection.

The Characteristic Polynomial

From the singularity condition given in Eq. (1), we know that $A - \lambda I$ is singular if and only if $\det(A - \lambda I) = 0$. In Example 1, for a (3×3) matrix A, we saw that the expression $\det(A - \lambda I)$ was a polynomial of degree 3 in λ. In general, it can be shown that $\det(A - \lambda I)$ is a polynomial of degree n in λ when A is $(n \times n)$. Then, since $A - \lambda I$ is singular if and only if $\det(A - \lambda I) = 0$, it follows that the eigenvalues of A are precisely the zeros of the polynomial $\det(A - \lambda I)$.

To avoid any possible confusion between the eigenvalues λ of A and the problem of finding the zeros of this associated polynomial (called the characteristic polynomial of A), we will use the variable t instead of λ in the characteristic polynomial and write $p(t) = \det(A - tI)$. To summarize this discussion, we give Theorems 9 and 10.

THEOREM 9 Let A be an $(n \times n)$ matrix. Then $\det(A - tI)$ is a polynomial of degree n in t.

The proof of Theorem 9 is somewhat tedious, and we omit it. The fact that $\det(A - tI)$ is a polynomial leads us to the next definition.

DEFINITION 5 Let A be an $(n \times n)$ matrix. The nth-degree polynomial, $p(t)$, given by

$$p(t) = \det(A - tI)$$

is called the ***characteristic polynomial*** for A.

Again, in the context of the singularity test in Eq. (1), the roots of $p(t) = 0$ are the eigenvalues of A. This observation is stated formally in the next theorem.

THEOREM 10 Let A be an $(n \times n)$ matrix, and let p be the characteristic polynomial for A. Then the eigenvalues of A are precisely the roots of $p(t) = 0$. ■

Theorem 10 has the effect of replacing the original problem—determining values λ for which $A - \lambda I$ is singular—by an equivalent problem, finding the roots of a polynomial equation $p(t) = 0$. Since polynomials are familiar and an immense amount of theoretical and computational machinery has been developed for solving polynomial equations, we should feel more comfortable with the eigenvalue problem.

The equation $p(t) = 0$ that must be solved to find the eigenvalues of A is called the ***characteristic equation***. Suppose that $p(t)$ has degree n, where $n \geq 1$. Then the equation $p(t) = 0$ can have no more than n distinct roots. From this fact, it follows that:

(a) An $(n \times n)$ matrix can have no more than n distinct eigenvalues.

Also, by the fundamental theorem of algebra, the equation $p(t) = 0$ always has at least one root (possibly complex). Therefore:

(b) An $(n \times n)$ matrix always has at least one eigenvalue (possibly complex).

Finally, we recall that any nth-degree polynomial $p(t)$ can be written in the factored form

$$p(t) = a(t - r_1)(t - r_2) \cdots (t - r_n).$$

The zeros of $p, r_1, r_2, \ldots, r_n$, however, need not be distinct or real. The number of times the factor $(t - r)$ appears in the factorization of $p(t)$ given above is called the ***algebraic multiplicity*** of r.

EXAMPLE 2 Find the characteristic polynomial and the eigenvalues for the (2×2) matrix

$$A = \begin{bmatrix} 1 & 5 \\ 3 & 3 \end{bmatrix}.$$

Solution By Definition 5, the characteristic polynomial is found by calculating $p(t) = \det(A - tI)$, or

$$p(t) = \begin{vmatrix} 1 - t & 5 \\ 3 & 3 - t \end{vmatrix} = (1 - t)(3 - t) - 15$$

$$= t^2 - 4t - 12 = (t - 6)(t + 2).$$

THE FUNDAMENTAL THEOREM OF ALGEBRA The eigenvalues of an $(n \times n)$ matrix A are the zeros of $p(t) = \det(A - tI)$, a polynomial of degree n. The fundamental theorem of algebra states that the equation $p(t) = 0$ has a solution, r_1, in the field of complex numbers. Since $q(t) = p(t)/(t - r_1)$ is a polynomial of degree $n - 1$, repeated use of this result allows us to write

$$p(t) = a(t - r_1)(t - r_2)\cdots(t - r_n).$$

A number of famous mathematicians (including Newton, Euler, d'Alembert, and Lagrange) attempted proofs of the fundamental theorem. In 1799, Gauss critiqued these attempts and presented a proof of his own. He admitted that his proof contained an unestablished assertion, but he stated that its validity could not be doubted. Gauss gave three more proofs in his lifetime, but all suffered from an imperfect understanding of the concept of continuity and the structure of the complex number system. These properties were established in 1874 by Weierstrass and not only made the proofs by Gauss rigorous, but a 1746 proof due to d'Alembert as well.

By Theorem 10, the eigenvalues of A are the roots of $p(t) = 0$; thus the eigenvalues are $\lambda = 6$ and $\lambda = -2$. ■

EXAMPLE 3 Find the characteristic polynomial and the eigenvalues for the (2×2) matrix

$$A = \begin{bmatrix} 2 & -1 \\ 1 & 2 \end{bmatrix}$$

Solution The characteristic polynomial is

$$p(t) = \begin{vmatrix} 2-t & -1 \\ 1 & 2-t \end{vmatrix} = t^2 - 4t + 5.$$

By the quadratic formula, the eigenvalues are $\lambda = 2 + i$ and $\lambda = 2 - i$. Therefore, this example illustrates that a matrix with real entries can have eigenvalues that are complex. In Section 4.6, we discuss complex eigenvalues and eigenvectors at length. ■

EXAMPLE 4 Find the characteristic polynomial and the eigenvalues for the (3×3) matrix

$$A = \begin{bmatrix} 3 & -1 & -1 \\ -12 & 0 & 5 \\ 4 & -2 & -1 \end{bmatrix}.$$

Solution By Definition 5, the characteristic polynomial is given by $p(t) = \det(A - tI)$, or

$$p(t) = \begin{vmatrix} 3-t & -1 & -1 \\ -12 & -t & 5 \\ 4 & -2 & -1-t \end{vmatrix}.$$

Expanding along the first column, we have

$$\begin{aligned}
p(t) &= (3-t)\begin{vmatrix} -t & 5 \\ -2 & -1-t \end{vmatrix} + 12\begin{vmatrix} -1 & -1 \\ -2 & -1-t \end{vmatrix} + 4\begin{vmatrix} -1 & -1 \\ -t & 5 \end{vmatrix} \\
&= (3-t)[t(1+t)+10] + 12[(1+t)-2] + 4[-5-t] \\
&= (3-t)[t^2+t+10] + 12[t-1] + 4[-t-5] \\
&= [-t^3+2t^2-7t+30] + [12t-12] + [-4t-20] \\
&= -t^3+2t^2+t-2.
\end{aligned}$$

By Theorem 10, the eigenvalues of A are the roots of $p(t) = 0$. We can write $p(t)$ as

$$p(t) = -(t-2)(t-1)(t+1),$$

and thus the eigenvalues of A are $\lambda = 2$, $\lambda = 1$, and $\lambda = -1$. ■

(*Note:* Finding or approximating the root of a polynomial equation is a task that is generally best left to the computer. Therefore, so that the theory associated with the eigenvalue problem is not hidden by a mass of computational details, the examples and exercises in this chapter will usually be constructed so that the characteristic equation has integer roots.)

Special Results

If we know the eigenvalues of a matrix A, then we also know the eigenvalues of certain matrices associated with A. A list of such results is found in Theorems 11 and 12.

THEOREM 11 Let A be an $(n \times n)$ matrix, and let λ be an eigenvalue of A. Then:

(a) λ^k is an eigenvalue of A^k, $k = 2, 3, \ldots$.

(b) If A is nonsingular, then $1/\lambda$ is an eigenvalue of A^{-1}.

(c) If α is any scalar, then $\lambda + \alpha$ is an eigenvalue of $A + \alpha I$.

Proof Property (a) is proved by induction, and we begin with the case $k = 2$. Suppose that λ is an eigenvalue of A with an associated eigenvector, $\mathbf{x}$. That is,

$$A\mathbf{x} = \lambda\mathbf{x}, \quad \mathbf{x} \neq \boldsymbol{\theta}. \tag{2}$$

Multiplying both sides of Eq. (2) by the matrix A gives

$$\begin{aligned}
A(A\mathbf{x}) &= A(\lambda\mathbf{x}) \\
A^2\mathbf{x} &= \lambda(A\mathbf{x}) \\
A^2\mathbf{x} &= \lambda(\lambda\mathbf{x}) \\
A^2\mathbf{x} &= \lambda^2\mathbf{x}, \quad \mathbf{x} \neq \boldsymbol{\theta}.
\end{aligned}$$

Thus λ^2 is an eigenvalue of A^2 with a corresponding eigenvector, $\mathbf{x}$.

In the exercises the reader is asked to finish the proof of property (a) and prove properties (b) and (c) of Theorem 11. (*Note:* As the proof of Theorem 11 will demonstrate, if $\mathbf{x}$ is any eigenvector of A, then $\mathbf{x}$ is also an eigenvector of A^k, A^{-1}, and $A + \alpha I$.) ■

EXAMPLE 5 Let A be the (3×3) matrix in Example 4. Determine the eigenvalues of A^5, A^{-1}, and $A + 2I$.

Solution From Example 4, the eigenvalues of A are $\lambda = 2$, $\lambda = 1$, and $\lambda = -1$. By Theorem 11, A^5 has eigenvalues $\lambda = 2^5 = 32$, $\lambda = 1^5 = 1$, and $\lambda = (-1)^5 = -1$. Since A^5 is a (3×3) matrix and can have no more than three eigenvalues, those eigenvalues must be 32, 1, and -1.

Similarly, the eigenvalues of A^{-1} are $\lambda = 1/2$, $\lambda = 1$, and $\lambda = -1$. The eigenvalues of $A + 2I$ are $\lambda = 4$, $\lambda = 3$, and $\lambda = 1$. ■

The proof of the next theorem rests on the following fact (see Section 1.7): If B is a square matrix, then both B and B^T are nonsingular or both B and B^T are singular. (See also Exercise 30.)

THEOREM 12 Let A be an $(n \times n)$ matrix. Then A and A^T have the same eigenvalues.

Proof Observe that $(A - \lambda I)^T = A^T - \lambda I$. By our earlier remark, $A - \lambda I$ and $(A - \lambda I)^T$ are either both singular or both nonsingular. Thus λ is an eigenvalue of A if and only if λ is an eigenvalue of A^T. ■

The next result follows immediately from the definition of an eigenvalue. We write the result as a theorem because it provides another important characterization of singularity.

THEOREM 13 Let A be an $(n \times n)$ matrix. Then A is singular if and only if $\lambda = 0$ is an eigenvalue of A. ■

(*Note:* If A is singular, then the eigenvectors corresponding to $\lambda = 0$ are in the null space of A.)

Our final theorem treats a class of matrices for which eigenvalues can be determined by inspection.

THEOREM 14 Let $T = (t_{ij})$ be an $(n \times n)$ triangular matrix. Then the eigenvalues of T are the diagonal entries, $t_{11}, t_{22}, \ldots, t_{nn}$.

Proof Since T is triangular, the matrix $T - tI$ is also triangular. The diagonal entries of $T - tI$ are $t_{11} - t, t_{22} - t, \ldots, t_{nn} - t$. Thus, by Theorem 4, the characteristic polynomial is given by

$$p(t) = \det(T - tI) = (t_{11} - t)(t_{22} - t)\cdots(t_{nn} - t).$$

By Theorem 10, the eigenvalues are $\lambda = t_{11}, \lambda = t_{22}, \ldots, \lambda = t_{nn}$. ■

EXAMPLE 6 Find the characteristic polynomial and the eigenvalues for the matrix A given by

$$A = \begin{bmatrix} 1 & 2 & 1 & 0 \\ 0 & 3 & -1 & 1 \\ 0 & 0 & 2 & 1 \\ 0 & 0 & 0 & 3 \end{bmatrix}.$$

Solution By Theorem 4, $p(t) = \det(A - tI)$ has the form

$$p(t) = (1 - t)(3 - t)^2(2 - t).$$

The eigenvalues are $\lambda = 1$, $\lambda = 2$, and $\lambda = 3$. The eigenvalues $\lambda = 1$ and $\lambda = 2$ have algebraic multiplicity 1, whereas the eigenvalue $\lambda = 3$ has algebraic multiplicity 2. ∎

Computational Considerations

In all the examples we have considered so far, it was possible to factor the characteristic polynomial and thus determine the eigenvalues by inspection. In reality we can rarely expect to be able to factor the characteristic polynomial; so we must solve the characteristic equation by using numerical root-finding methods. To be more specific about root finding, we recall that there are formulas for the roots of some polynomial equations. For instance, the solution of the linear equation

$$at + b = 0, \quad a \neq 0,$$

is given by

$$t = -\frac{b}{a};$$

and the roots of the quadratic equation

$$at^2 + bt + c = 0, \quad a \neq 0,$$

are given by the familiar quadratic formula

$$t = \frac{-b \pm \sqrt{b^2 - 4ac}}{2a}.$$

There are similar (although more complicated) formulas for the roots of third-degree and fourth-degree polynomial equations. Unfortunately there are no such formulas for polynomials of degree 5 or higher [that is, formulas that express the zeros of $p(t)$ as a simple function of the coefficients of $p(t)$]. Moreover, in the mid-nineteenth century Abel *proved* that such formulas cannot exist for polynomials of degree 5 or higher.* This means that in general we cannot expect to find the eigenvalues of a large matrix exactly—the best we can do is to find good approximations to the eigenvalues. The eigenvalue problem differs qualitatively from the problem of solving $A\mathbf{x} = \mathbf{b}$. For a system $A\mathbf{x} = \mathbf{b}$, if we are willing to invest the effort required to solve the system by hand, we can obtain the exact solution in a finite number of steps. On the other hand, we cannot in general expect to find roots of a polynomial equation in a finite number of steps.

Finding roots of the characteristic equation is not the only computational aspect of the eigenvalue problem that must be considered. In fact, it is not hard to see that special techniques must be developed even to find the characteristic polynomial. To see the dimensions of this problem, consider the characteristic polynomial of an $(n \times n)$ matrix A: $p(t) = \det(A - tI)$. The evaluation of $p(t)$ from a cofactor expansion of $\det(A - tI)$

*For a historical discussion, see J. E. Maxfield and M. W. Maxfield, *Abstract Algebra and Solution by Radicals* (Dover, 1992).

ultimately requires the evaluation of $n!/2$ determinants of order (2×2). Even for modest values of n, the number $n!/2$ is alarmingly large. For instance,

$$10!/2 = 1{,}814{,}400,$$

whereas

$$20!/2 > 1.2\times 10^{18}.$$

The enormous number of calculations required to compute $\det(A-tI)$ means that we cannot find $p(t)$ in any practical sense by expanding $\det(A-tI)$. In Chapter 6, we note that there are relatively efficient ways of finding $\det(A)$, but these techniques (which amount to using elementary row operations to triangularize A) are not useful in our problem of computing $\det(A-tI)$ because of the variable t. In Section 7.3, we resolve this difficulty by using similarity transformations to transform A to a matrix H, where A and H have the same characteristic polynomial, and where it is a trivial matter to calculate the characteristic polynomial for H. Moreover, these transformation methods will give us some other important results as a by-product, results such as the Cayley–Hamilton theorem, which have some practical computational significance.

4.4 EXERCISES

In Exercises 1–14, find the characteristic polynomial and the eigenvalues for the given matrix. Also, give the algebraic multiplicity of each eigenvalue. [*Note:* In each case the eigenvalues are integers.]

1. $\begin{bmatrix} 1 & 0\\ 2 & 3\end{bmatrix}$ **2.** $\begin{bmatrix} 2 & 1\\ 0 & -1\end{bmatrix}$

3. $\begin{bmatrix} 2 & -1\\ -1 & 2\end{bmatrix}$ **4.** $\begin{bmatrix} 13 & -16\\ 9 & -11\end{bmatrix}$

5. $\begin{bmatrix} 1 & -1\\ 1 & 3\end{bmatrix}$ **6.** $\begin{bmatrix} 2 & 2\\ 3 & 3\end{bmatrix}$

7. $\begin{bmatrix} -6 & -1 & 2\\ 3 & 2 & 0\\ -14 & -2 & 5\end{bmatrix}$ **8.** $\begin{bmatrix} -2 & -1 & 0\\ 0 & 1 & 1\\ -2 & -2 & -1\end{bmatrix}$

9. $\begin{bmatrix} 3 & -1 & -1\\ -12 & 0 & 5\\ 4 & -2 & -1\end{bmatrix}$ **10.** $\begin{bmatrix} -7 & 4 & -3\\ 8 & -3 & 3\\ 32 & -16 & 13\end{bmatrix}$

11. $\begin{bmatrix} 2 & 4 & 4\\ 0 & 1 & -1\\ 0 & 1 & 3\end{bmatrix}$ **12.** $\begin{bmatrix} 6 & 4 & 4 & 1\\ 4 & 6 & 1 & 4\\ 4 & 1 & 6 & 4\\ 1 & 4 & 4 & 6\end{bmatrix}$

13. $\begin{bmatrix} 5 & 4 & 1 & 1\\ 4 & 5 & 1 & 1\\ 1 & 1 & 4 & 2\\ 1 & 1 & 2 & 4\end{bmatrix}$ **14.** $\begin{bmatrix} 1 & -1 & -1 & -1\\ -1 & 1 & -1 & -1\\ -1 & -1 & 1 & -1\\ -1 & -1 & -1 & 1\end{bmatrix}$

15. Prove property (b) of Theorem 11. [*Hint:* Begin with $A\mathbf{x} = \lambda\mathbf{x}$, $\mathbf{x}\neq\boldsymbol{\theta}$.]

16. Prove property (c) of Theorem 11.

17. Complete the proof of property (a) of Theorem 11.

18. Let $q(t) = t^3 - 2t^2 - t + 2$; and for any $(n\times n)$ matrix H, define the matrix polynomial $q(H)$ by

$$q(H) = H^3 - 2H^2 - H + 2I,$$

where I is the $(n\times n)$ identity matrix.

a) Prove that if λ is an eigenvalue of H, then the number $q(\lambda)$ is an eigenvalue of the matrix $q(H)$. [*Hint:* Suppose that $H\mathbf{x} = \lambda\mathbf{x}$, where $\mathbf{x}\neq\boldsymbol{\theta}$, and use Theorem 11 to evaluate $q(H)\mathbf{x}$.]

b) Use part a) to calculate the eigenvalues of $q(A)$ and $q(B)$, where A and B are from Exercises 7 and 8, respectively.

19. With $q(t)$ as in Exercise 18, verify that $q(C)$ is the zero matrix, where C is from Exercise 9. (Note that $q(t)$ is the characteristic polynomial for C. See Exercises 20–23.)

Exercises 20–23 illustrate the ***Cayley–Hamilton theorem***, which states that if $p(t)$ is the characteristic polynomial for A, then $p(A)$ is the zero matrix. (As in Exercise 18, $p(A)$ is the $(n \times n)$ matrix that comes from substituting A for t in $p(t)$.) In Exercises 20–23, verify that $p(A) = \mathcal{O}$ for the given matrix A.

20. A in Exercise 3

21. A in Exercise 4

22. A in Exercise 9

23. A in Exercise 13

24. This problem establishes a special case of the Cayley–Hamilton theorem.

a) Prove that if B is a (3×3) matrix, and if $B\mathbf{x} = \boldsymbol{\theta}$ for every $\mathbf{x}$ in R^3, then B is the zero matrix. [*Hint:* Consider $B\mathbf{e}_1$, $B\mathbf{e}_2$, and $B\mathbf{e}_3$.]

b) Suppose that λ_1, λ_2, and λ_3 are the eigenvalues of a (3×3) matrix A, and suppose that $\mathbf{u}_1$, $\mathbf{u}_2$, and $\mathbf{u}_3$ are corresponding eigenvectors. Prove that if $\{\mathbf{u}_1, \mathbf{u}_2, \mathbf{u}_3\}$ is a linearly independent set, and if $p(t)$ is the characteristic polynomial for A, then $p(A)$ is the zero matrix. [*Hint:* Any vector $\mathbf{x}$ in R^3 can be expressed as a linear combination of $\mathbf{u}_1$, $\mathbf{u}_2$, and $\mathbf{u}_3$.]

25. Consider the (2×2) matrix A given by

$$A = \begin{bmatrix} a & b \\ c & d \end{bmatrix}.$$

The characteristic polynomial for A is $p(t) = t^2 - (a+d)t + (ad - bc)$. Verify the Cayley–Hamilton theorem for (2×2) matrices by forming A^2 and showing that $p(A)$ is the zero matrix.

26. Let A be the (3×3) upper-triangular matrix given by

$$A = \begin{bmatrix} a & d & f \\ 0 & b & e \\ 0 & 0 & c \end{bmatrix}.$$

The characteristic polynomial for A is $p(t) = -(t-a)(t-b)(t-c)$. Verify that $p(A)$ has the form $p(A) = -(A - aI)(A - bI)(A - cI)$. [*Hint:* Expand $p(t)$ and $p(A)$; for instance, $(A - bI)(A - cI) = A^2 - (b+c)A + bcI$]. Next, show that $p(A)$ is the zero matrix by forming the product of the matrices $A - aI$, $A - bI$, and $A - cI$. [*Hint:* Form the product $(A - bI)(A - cI)$ first.]

27. Let $q(t) = t^n + a_{n-1}t^{n-1} + \cdots + a_1 t + a_0$, and define the $(n \times n)$ "companion" matrix by

$$A = \begin{bmatrix} -a_{n-1} & -a_{n-2} & \cdots & -a_1 & -a_0 \\ 1 & 0 & \cdots & 0 & 0 \\ 0 & 1 & \cdots & 0 & 0 \\ \vdots & & & & \vdots \\ 0 & 0 & \cdots & 1 & 0 \end{bmatrix}.$$

a) For $n = 2$ and for $n = 3$, show that $\det(A - tI) = (-1)^n q(t)$.

b) Give the companion matrix A for the polynomial $q(t) = t^4 + 3t^3 - t^2 + 2t - 2$. Verify that $q(t)$ is the characteristic polynomial for A.

c) Prove for all n that $\det(A - tI) = (-1)^n q(t)$.

28. The power method is a numerical method used to estimate the dominant eigenvalue of a matrix A. (By the dominant eigenvalue, we mean the one that is largest in absolute value.) The algorithm proceeds as follows:

a) Choose any starting vector $\mathbf{x}_0$, $\mathbf{x}_0 \neq \boldsymbol{\theta}$.

b) Let $\mathbf{x}_{k+1} = A\mathbf{x}_k$, $k = 0, 1, 2, \ldots$.

c) Let $\beta_k = \mathbf{x}_k^T \mathbf{x}_{k+1} / \mathbf{x}_k^T \mathbf{x}_k$, $k = 0, 1, 2, \ldots$.

Under suitable conditions, it can be shown that $\{\beta_k\} \to \lambda_1$, where λ_1 is the dominant eigenvalue of A. Use the power method to estimate the dominant eigenvalue of the matrix in Exercise 9. Use the starting vector

$$\mathbf{x} = \begin{bmatrix} 1 \\ 1 \\ 1 \end{bmatrix}$$

and calculate β_0, β_1, β_2, β_3, and β_4.

29. This exercise gives a condition under which the power method (see Exercise 28) converges. Suppose that A is an $(n \times n)$ matrix and has real eigenvalues $\lambda_1, \lambda_2, \ldots, \lambda_n$ with corresponding eigenvectors $\mathbf{u}_1, \mathbf{u}_2, \ldots, \mathbf{u}_n$. Furthermore, suppose that $|\lambda_1| > |\lambda_2| \geq \cdots \geq |\lambda_n|$, and the starting vector $\mathbf{x}_0$ satisfies $\mathbf{x}_0 = c_1\mathbf{u}_1 + c_2\mathbf{u}_2 + \cdots + c_n\mathbf{u}_n$, where $c_1 \neq 0$. Prove that

$$\lim_{k \to \infty} \beta_k = \lambda_1.$$

[*Hint:* Observe that $\mathbf{x}_j = A^j \mathbf{x}_0$, $j = 1, 2, \ldots$, and use Theorem 11 to calculate $\mathbf{x}_{k+1}$ and $\mathbf{x}_k$. Next, factor all powers of λ_1 from the numerator and denominator of $\beta_k = \mathbf{x}_k^T \mathbf{x}_{k+1} / \mathbf{x}_k^T \mathbf{x}_k$.]

30. Theorem 12 shows that A and A^T have the same eigenvalues. In Theorem 5 of Section 4.3, it was shown that $\det(A) = \det(A^T)$. Use this result to show that A and A^T have the same characteristic polynomial. [*Note:* Theorem 12 proves that $A - \lambda I$ and $A^T - \lambda I$ are singular or nonsingular together. This exercise shows that the eigenvalues of A and A^T have the same algebraic multiplicity.]

The characteristic polynomial $p(t) = \det(A - tI)$ has the form $p(t) = (-1)^n t^n + a_{n-1}t^{n-1} + \cdots + a_1 t + a_0$. The coefficients of $p(t)$ can be found by evaluating $\det(A - tI)$ at n distinct values of t and solving the resulting Vandermonde system for $a_{n-1}, \ldots, a_1, a_0$. Employ this technique in Exercises 31–34 to find the characteristic polynomial for the indicated matrix A.

31. A in Exercise 5

32. A in Exercise 6

33. A in Exercise 7

34. A in Exercise 8

4.5 EIGENVECTORS AND EIGENSPACES

As we saw in the previous section, we can find the eigenvalues of a matrix A by solving the characteristic equation $\det(A - tI) = 0$. Once we know the eigenvalues, the familiar technique of Gaussian elimination can be employed to find the eigenvectors that correspond to the various eigenvalues.

In particular, the eigenvectors corresponding to an eigenvalue λ of A are the nonzero solutions of

$$(A - \lambda I)\mathbf{x} = \boldsymbol{\theta}. \tag{1}$$

Given a value for λ, the equations in (1) can be solved for $\mathbf{x}$ by using Gaussian elimination.

EXAMPLE 1 Find the eigenvectors that correspond to the eigenvalues of matrix A in Example 1 of Section 4.4.

Solution For matrix A in Example 1, $A - \lambda I$ is the matrix

$$A - \lambda I = \begin{bmatrix} 1-\lambda & 1 & 1 \\ 0 & 3-\lambda & 3 \\ -2 & 1 & 1-\lambda \end{bmatrix}.$$

Also, from Example 1 we know that the eigenvalues of A are given by $\lambda = 0$, $\lambda = 2$, and $\lambda = 3$.

For each eigenvalue λ, we find the eigenvectors that correspond to λ by solving the system $(A - \lambda I)\mathbf{x} = \boldsymbol{\theta}$. For the eigenvalue $\lambda = 0$, we have $(A - 0I)\mathbf{x} = \boldsymbol{\theta}$, or $A\mathbf{x} = \boldsymbol{\theta}$, to solve:

$$\begin{aligned} x_1 + x_2 + x_3 &= 0 \\ 3x_2 + 3x_3 &= 0 \\ -2x_1 + x_2 + x_3 &= 0. \end{aligned}$$

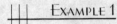

The solution of this system is $x_1 = 0$, $x_2 = -x_3$, with x_3 arbitrary. Thus the eigenvectors of A corresponding to $\lambda = 0$ are given by

$$\mathbf{x} = \begin{bmatrix} 0 \\ -a \\ a \end{bmatrix} = a \begin{bmatrix} 0 \\ -1 \\ 1 \end{bmatrix}, \quad a \neq 0,$$

and any such vector $\mathbf{x}$ satisfies $A\mathbf{x} = 0 \cdot \mathbf{x}$. This equation illustrates that the definition of eigenvalues does allow the possibility that $\lambda = 0$ is an eigenvalue. We stress, however, that the zero vector is never considered an eigenvector (after all, $A\mathbf{x} = \lambda\mathbf{x}$ is always satisfied for $\mathbf{x} = \boldsymbol{\theta}$, no matter what value λ has).

The eigenvectors corresponding to the eigenvalue $\lambda = 3$ are found by solving $(A - 3I)\mathbf{x} = \boldsymbol{\theta}$:

$$\begin{aligned} -2x_1 + x_2 + x_3 &= 0 \\ 3x_3 &= 0 \\ -2x_1 + x_2 - 2x_3 &= 0. \end{aligned}$$

The solution of this system is $x_3 = 0$, $x_2 = 2x_1$, with x_1 arbitrary. Thus the nontrivial solutions of $(A - 3I)\mathbf{x} = \boldsymbol{\theta}$ (the eigenvectors of A corresponding to $\lambda = 3$) all have the form

$$\mathbf{x} = \begin{bmatrix} a \\ 2a \\ 0 \end{bmatrix} = a \begin{bmatrix} 1 \\ 2 \\ 0 \end{bmatrix}, \quad a \neq 0.$$

Finally, the eigenvectors corresponding to $\lambda = 2$ are found from $(A - 2I)\mathbf{x} = \boldsymbol{\theta}$, and the solution is $x_1 = -2x_3$, $x_2 = -3x_3$, with x_3 arbitrary. So the eigenvectors corresponding to $\lambda = 2$ are of the form

$$\mathbf{x} = \begin{bmatrix} -2a \\ -3a \\ a \end{bmatrix} = a \begin{bmatrix} -2 \\ -3 \\ 1 \end{bmatrix}, \quad a \neq 0.$$ ■

We pause here to make several comments. As Example 1 shows, there are infinitely many eigenvectors that correspond to a given eigenvalue. This comment should be obvious, for if $A - \lambda I$ is a singular matrix, there are infinitely many nontrivial solutions of $(A - \lambda I)\mathbf{x} = \boldsymbol{\theta}$. In particular, if $A\mathbf{x} = \lambda\mathbf{x}$ for some nonzero vector $\mathbf{x}$, then we also have $A\mathbf{y} = \lambda\mathbf{y}$ when $\mathbf{y} = a\mathbf{x}$, with a being any scalar. Thus any nonzero multiple of an eigenvector is again an eigenvector.

Next, we again note that the scalar $\lambda = 0$ may be an eigenvalue of a matrix, as Example 1 showed. In fact, from Theorem 13 of Section 4.4 we know that $\lambda = 0$ is an eigenvalue of A whenever A is singular.

Last, we observe from Example 1 that finding all the eigenvectors corresponding to $\lambda = 0$ is precisely the same as finding the null space of A and then deleting the zero vector, $\boldsymbol{\theta}$. Likewise, the eigenvectors of A corresponding to $\lambda = 2$ and $\lambda = 3$ are the nonzero vectors in the null space of $A - 2I$ and $A - 3I$, respectively.

Eigenspaces and Geometric Multiplicity

In the preceding discussion, we made the following observation: If λ is an eigenvalue of A, then the eigenvectors corresponding to λ are precisely the nonzero vectors in the null space of $A - \lambda I$. It is convenient to formalize this observation.

DEFINITION 6 Let A be an $(n \times n)$ matrix. If λ is an eigenvalue of A, then:

(a) The null space of $A - \lambda I$ is denoted by E_λ and is called the ***eigenspace*** of λ.

(b) The dimension of E_λ is called the ***geometric multiplicity*** of λ.

(*Note:* Since $A - \lambda I$ is singular, the dimension of E_λ, the geometric multiplicity of λ, is always at least 1 and may be larger. It can be shown that the geometric multiplicity of λ is never larger than the algebraic multiplicity of λ. The next three examples illustrate some of the possibilities.)

EXAMPLE 2 Determine the algebraic and geometric multiplicities for the eigenvalues of A

$$A = \begin{bmatrix} 1 & 1 & 0 \\ 0 & 1 & 1 \\ 0 & 0 & 1 \end{bmatrix}.$$

Solution The characteristic polynomial is $p(t) = (1 - t)^3$, and thus the only eigenvalue of A is $\lambda = 1$. The eigenvalue $\lambda = 1$ has algebraic multiplicity 3.

The eigenspace is found by solving $(A - I)\mathbf{x} = \boldsymbol{\theta}$. The system $(A - I)\mathbf{x} = \boldsymbol{\theta}$ is

$$x_2 = 0$$
$$x_3 = 0.$$

Thus $\mathbf{x}$ is in the eigenspace E_λ corresponding to $\lambda = 1$ if and only if $\mathbf{x}$ has the form

$$\mathbf{x} = \begin{bmatrix} x_1 \\ 0 \\ 0 \end{bmatrix} = x_1 \begin{bmatrix} 1 \\ 0 \\ 0 \end{bmatrix}. \qquad (2)$$

The geometric multiplicity of the eigenvalue $\lambda = 1$ is 1, and $\mathbf{x}$ is an eigenvector if $\mathbf{x}$ has the form (2) with $x_1 \neq 0$. ∎

EXAMPLE 3 Determine the algebraic and geometric multiplicities for the eigenvalues of B,

$$B = \begin{bmatrix} 1 & 1 & 0 \\ 0 & 1 & 0 \\ 0 & 0 & 1 \end{bmatrix}.$$

Solution The characteristic polynomial is $p(t) = (1-t)^3$, so $\lambda = 1$ is the only eigenvalue, and it has algebraic multiplicity 3.

The corresponding eigenspace is found by solving $(B-I)\mathbf{x} = \boldsymbol{\theta}$. Now $(B-I)\mathbf{x} = \boldsymbol{\theta}$ if and only if $\mathbf{x}$ has the form

$$\mathbf{x} = \begin{bmatrix} x_1 \\ 0 \\ x_3 \end{bmatrix} = x_1 \begin{bmatrix} 1 \\ 0 \\ 0 \end{bmatrix} + x_3 \begin{bmatrix} 0 \\ 0 \\ 1 \end{bmatrix}. \tag{3}$$

By (3), the eigenspace has dimension 2, and so the eigenvalue $\lambda = 1$ has geometric multiplicity 2. The eigenvectors of B are the nonzero vectors of the form (3). ■

EXAMPLE 4 Determine the algebraic and geometric multiplicities for the eigenvalues of C,

$$C = \begin{bmatrix} 1 & 0 & 0 \\ 0 & 1 & 0 \\ 0 & 0 & 1 \end{bmatrix}.$$

Solution The characteristic polynomial is $p(t) = (1-t)^3$, so $\lambda = 1$ has algebraic multiplicity 3.

The eigenspace is found by solving $(C - I)\mathbf{x} = \boldsymbol{\theta}$, and since $C - I$ is the zero matrix, every vector in R^3 is in the null space of $C - I$. The geometric multiplicity of the eigenvalue $\lambda = 1$ is equal to 3. ■

(*Note:* The matrices in Examples 2, 3, and 4 all have the same characteristic polynomial, $p(t) = (1-t)^3$. However, the respective eigenspaces are different.)

Defective Matrices

For applications (such as diagonalization) it will be important to know whether an $(n \times n)$ matrix A has a set of n linearly independent eigenvectors. As we will see later, if A is an $(n \times n)$ matrix and if some eigenvalue of A has a geometric multiplicity that is less than its algebraic multiplicity, then A will not have a set of n linearly independent eigenvectors. Such a matrix is called defective.

DEFINITION 7 Let A be an $(n \times n)$ matrix. If there is an eigenvalue λ of A such that the geometric multiplicity of λ is less than the algebraic multiplicity of λ, then A is called a ***defective*** matrix.

Note that the matrices in Examples 1 and 4 are not defective. The matrices in Examples 2 and 3 are defective. Example 5 provides another instance of a defective matrix.

EXAMPLE 5 Find all the eigenvalues and eigenvectors of the matrix A:

$$A = \begin{bmatrix} -4 & 1 & 1 & 1 \\ -16 & 3 & 4 & 4 \\ -7 & 2 & 2 & 1 \\ -11 & 1 & 3 & 4 \end{bmatrix}.$$

Also, determine the algebraic and geometric multiplicities of the eigenvalues.

Solution Omitting the details, a cofactor expansion yields

$$\begin{aligned}\det(A - tI) &= t^4 - 5t^3 + 9t^2 - 7t + 2 \\ &= (t-1)^3(t-2).\end{aligned}$$

Hence the eigenvalues are $\lambda = 1$ (algebraic multiplicity 3) and $\lambda = 2$ (algebraic multiplicity 1).

In solving $(A - 2I)\mathbf{x} = \boldsymbol{\theta}$, we reduce the augmented matrix $[A - 2I \mid \boldsymbol{\theta}]$ as follows, multiplying rows 2, 3, and 4 by constants to avoid working with fractions:

$$[A - 2I \mid \boldsymbol{\theta}] = \begin{bmatrix} -6 & 1 & 1 & 1 & 0 \\ -16 & 1 & 4 & 4 & 0 \\ -7 & 2 & 0 & 1 & 0 \\ -11 & 1 & 3 & 2 & 0 \end{bmatrix} \sim \begin{bmatrix} -6 & 1 & 1 & 1 & 0 \\ -48 & 3 & 12 & 12 & 0 \\ -42 & 12 & 0 & 6 & 0 \\ -66 & 6 & 18 & 12 & 0 \end{bmatrix}$$

$$\sim \begin{bmatrix} -6 & 1 & 1 & 1 & 0 \\ 0 & -5 & 4 & 4 & 0 \\ 0 & 5 & -7 & -1 & 0 \\ 0 & -5 & 7 & 1 & 0 \end{bmatrix} \sim \begin{bmatrix} -6 & 1 & 1 & 1 & 0 \\ 0 & -5 & 4 & 4 & 0 \\ 0 & 0 & -3 & 3 & 0 \\ 0 & 0 & 0 & 0 & 0 \end{bmatrix}.$$

Backsolving yields $x_1 = 3x_4/5$, $x_2 = 8x_4/5$, $x_3 = x_4$. Hence $\mathbf{x}$ is an eigenvector corresponding to $\lambda = 2$ only if

$$\mathbf{x} = \begin{bmatrix} x_1 \\ x_2 \\ x_3 \\ x_4 \end{bmatrix} = \begin{bmatrix} 3x_4/5 \\ 8x_4/5 \\ x_4 \\ x_4 \end{bmatrix} = \frac{x_4}{5}\begin{bmatrix} 3 \\ 8 \\ 5 \\ 5 \end{bmatrix}, \quad x_4 \neq 0.$$

Thus the algebraic and geometric multiplicities of the eigenvalue $\lambda = 2$ are equal to 1.

In solving $(A - I)\mathbf{x} = \boldsymbol{\theta}$, we reduce the augmented matrix $[A - I \mid \boldsymbol{\theta}]$:

$$[A - I \mid \boldsymbol{\theta}] = \begin{bmatrix} -5 & 1 & 1 & 1 & 0 \\ -16 & 2 & 4 & 4 & 0 \\ -7 & 2 & 1 & 1 & 0 \\ -11 & 1 & 3 & 3 & 0 \end{bmatrix} \sim \begin{bmatrix} -5 & 1 & 1 & 1 & 0 \\ -80 & 10 & 20 & 20 & 0 \\ -35 & 10 & 5 & 5 & 0 \\ -55 & 5 & 15 & 15 & 0 \end{bmatrix}$$

$$\sim \begin{bmatrix} -5 & 1 & 1 & 1 & 0 \\ 0 & -6 & 4 & 4 & 0 \\ 0 & 3 & -2 & -2 & 0 \\ 0 & -6 & 4 & 4 & 0 \end{bmatrix}$$

$$\sim \begin{bmatrix} -5 & 1 & 1 & 1 & 0 \\ 0 & 3 & -2 & -2 & 0 \\ 0 & 0 & 0 & 0 & 0 \\ 0 & 0 & 0 & 0 & 0 \end{bmatrix}.$$

Backsolving yields $x_1 = (x_3 + x_4)/3$ and $x_2 = 2(x_3 + x_4)/3$. Thus $\mathbf{x}$ is an eigenvector corresponding to $\lambda = 1$ only if $\mathbf{x}$ is a nonzero vector of the form

$$\mathbf{x} = \begin{bmatrix} x_1 \\ x_2 \\ x_3 \\ x_4 \end{bmatrix} = \begin{bmatrix} (x_3 + x_4)/3 \\ 2(x_3 + x_4)/3 \\ x_3 \\ x_4 \end{bmatrix} = \frac{x_3}{3}\begin{bmatrix} 1 \\ 2 \\ 3 \\ 0 \end{bmatrix} + \frac{x_4}{3}\begin{bmatrix} 1 \\ 2 \\ 0 \\ 3 \end{bmatrix}. \tag{4}$$

By (4), the eigenspace E_λ corresponding to $\lambda = 1$ has a basis consisting of the vectors

$$\begin{bmatrix} 1 \\ 2 \\ 3 \\ 0 \end{bmatrix} \text{ and } \begin{bmatrix} 1 \\ 2 \\ 0 \\ 3 \end{bmatrix}.$$

Since E_λ has dimension 2, the eigenvalue $\lambda = 1$ has geometric multiplicity 2 and algebraic multiplicity 3. (Matrix A is defective.) ■

The next theorem shows that a matrix can be defective only if it has repeated eigenvalues. (As shown in Example 4, however, repeated eigenvalues do not necessarily mean that a matrix is defective.)

THEOREM 15 Let $\mathbf{u}_1, \mathbf{u}_2, \ldots, \mathbf{u}_k$ be eigenvectors of an $(n \times n)$ matrix A corresponding to distinct eigenvalues $\lambda_1, \lambda_2, \ldots, \lambda_k$. That is,

$$A\mathbf{u}_j = \lambda_j \mathbf{u}_j \quad \text{for } j = 1, 2, \ldots, k; \quad k \le n \tag{5}$$

$$\lambda_i \ne \lambda_j \quad \text{for } i \ne j; \quad 1 \le i, j \le k. \tag{6}$$

Then $\{\mathbf{u}_1, \mathbf{u}_2, \ldots, \mathbf{u}_k\}$ is a linearly independent set.

Proof Since $\mathbf{u}_1 \neq \boldsymbol{\theta}$, the set $\{\mathbf{u}_1\}$ is trivially linearly independent. If the set $\{\mathbf{u}_1, \mathbf{u}_2, \ldots, \mathbf{u}_k\}$ were linearly dependent, then there would exist an integer m, $2 \leq m \leq k$, such that:

(a) $S_1 = \{\mathbf{u}_1, \mathbf{u}_2, \ldots, \mathbf{u}_{m-1}\}$ is linearly independent.

(b) $S_2 = \{\mathbf{u}_1, \mathbf{u}_2, \ldots, \mathbf{u}_{m-1}, \mathbf{u}_m\}$ is linearly dependent.

Now since S_2 is linearly dependent, there exist scalars $c_1, c_2, \ldots, c_m$ (not all zero) such that

$$c_1\mathbf{u}_1 + c_2\mathbf{u}_2 + \cdots + c_{m-1}\mathbf{u}_{m-1} + c_m\mathbf{u}_m = \boldsymbol{\theta}. \tag{7}$$

Furthermore, c_m in Eq. (7) cannot be zero. (If $c_m = 0$, then Eq. (7) would imply that S_1 is linearly dependent, contradicting (a).)

Multiplying both sides of Eq. (7) by A and using $A\mathbf{u}_j = \lambda_j\mathbf{u}_j$, we obtain

$$c_1\lambda_1\mathbf{u}_1 + c_2\lambda_2\mathbf{u}_2 + \cdots + c_{m-1}\lambda_{m-1}\mathbf{u}_{m-1} + c_m\lambda_m\mathbf{u}_m = \boldsymbol{\theta}. \tag{8}$$

Multiplying both sides of Eq. (7) by λ_m yields

$$c_1\lambda_m\mathbf{u}_1 + c_2\lambda_m\mathbf{u}_2 + \cdots + c_{m-1}\lambda_m\mathbf{u}_{m-1} + c_m\lambda_m\mathbf{u}_m = \boldsymbol{\theta}. \tag{9}$$

Subtracting Eq. (8) from Eq. (9), we find that

$$c_1(\lambda_m - \lambda_1)\mathbf{u}_1 + c_2(\lambda_m - \lambda_2)\mathbf{u}_2 + \cdots + c_{m-1}(\lambda_m - \lambda_{m-1})\mathbf{u}_{m-1} = \boldsymbol{\theta}. \tag{10}$$

If we set $\beta_j = c_j(\lambda_m - \lambda_j)$, $1 \leq j \leq m-1$, Eq. (10) becomes

$$\beta_1\mathbf{u}_1 + \beta_2\mathbf{u}_2 + \cdots + \beta_{m-1}\mathbf{u}_{m-1} = \boldsymbol{\theta}.$$

Since S_1 is linearly independent, it then follows that

$$\beta_1 = \beta_2 = \cdots = \beta_{m-1} = 0,$$

or

$$c_j(\lambda_m - \lambda_j) = 0, \quad \text{for } j = 1, 2, \ldots, m-1.$$

Because $\lambda_m \neq \lambda_j$ for $j \neq m$, we must have $c_j = 0$ for $1 \leq j \leq m-1$.

Finally (see Eq. 7), if $c_j = 0$ for $1 \leq j \leq m-1$, then $c_m\mathbf{u}_m = \boldsymbol{\theta}$. Since $c_m \neq 0$, it follows that $\mathbf{u}_m = \boldsymbol{\theta}$. But $\mathbf{u}_m$ is an eigenvector, and so $\mathbf{u}_m \neq \boldsymbol{\theta}$. Hence we have contradicted the assumption that there is an m, $m \leq k$, such that S_2 is linearly dependent. Thus $\{\mathbf{u}_1, \mathbf{u}_2, \ldots, \mathbf{u}_k\}$ is linearly independent. ■

An important and useful corollary to Theorem 15 is given next.

COROLLARY Let A be an $(n \times n)$ matrix. If A has n distinct eigenvalues, then A has a set of n linearly independent eigenvectors. ■

4.5 EXERCISES

The following list of matrices and their respective characteristic polynomials is referred to in Exercises 1–11.

$$A = \begin{bmatrix} 2 & -1 \\ -1 & 2 \end{bmatrix},\quad B = \begin{bmatrix} 1 & -1 \\ 1 & 3 \end{bmatrix},$$
$$p(t) = (t-3)(t-1),\qquad p(t) = (t-2)^2,$$

$$C = \begin{bmatrix} -6 & -1 & 2 \\ 3 & 2 & 0 \\ -14 & -2 & 5 \end{bmatrix},\quad D = \begin{bmatrix} -7 & 4 & -3 \\ 8 & -3 & 3 \\ 32 & -16 & 13 \end{bmatrix},$$
$$p(t) = -(t-1)^2(t+1),\qquad p(t) = -(t-1)^3,$$

$$E = \begin{bmatrix} 6 & 4 & 4 & 1 \\ 4 & 6 & 1 & 4 \\ 4 & 1 & 6 & 4 \\ 1 & 4 & 4 & 6 \end{bmatrix},\quad F = \begin{bmatrix} 1 & -1 & -1 & -1 \\ -1 & 1 & -1 & -1 \\ -1 & -1 & 1 & -1 \\ -1 & -1 & -1 & 1 \end{bmatrix},$$
$$p(t) = (t+1)(t+5)^2(t-15),\qquad p(t) = (t+2)(t-2)^3$$

In Exercises 1–11, find a basis for the eigenspace E_λ for the given matrix and the value of λ. Determine the algebraic and geometric multiplicities of λ.

1. $A, \lambda = 3$ **2.** $A, \lambda = 1$ **3.** $B, \lambda = 2$

4. $C, \lambda = 1$ **5.** $C, \lambda = -1$ **6.** $D, \lambda = 1$

7. $E, \lambda = -1$ **8.** $E, \lambda = 5$ **9.** $E, \lambda = 15$

10. $F, \lambda = -2$ **11.** $F, \lambda = 2$

In Exercises 12–17, find the eigenvalues and the eigenvectors for the given matrix. Is the matrix defective?

12. $\begin{bmatrix} 1 & 1 & -1 \\ 0 & 2 & -1 \\ 0 & 0 & 1 \end{bmatrix}$ **13.** $\begin{bmatrix} 2 & 1 & 2 \\ 0 & 3 & 2 \\ 0 & 0 & 2 \end{bmatrix}$

14. $\begin{bmatrix} 1 & 2 & 1 \\ 0 & 1 & 2 \\ 0 & 0 & 1 \end{bmatrix}$ **15.** $\begin{bmatrix} 2 & 0 & 3 \\ 0 & 2 & 1 \\ 0 & 0 & 1 \end{bmatrix}$

16. $\begin{bmatrix} -1 & 6 & 2 \\ 0 & 5 & -6 \\ 1 & 0 & -2 \end{bmatrix}$ **17.** $\begin{bmatrix} 3 & -1 & -1 \\ -12 & 0 & 5 \\ 4 & -2 & -1 \end{bmatrix}$

18. If a vector $\mathbf{x}$ is a linear combination of eigenvectors of a matrix A, then it is easy to calculate the product $\mathbf{y} = A^k\mathbf{x}$ for any positive integer k. For instance, suppose that $A\mathbf{u}_1 = \lambda_1\mathbf{u}_1$ and $A\mathbf{u}_2 = \lambda_2\mathbf{u}_2$, where $\mathbf{u}_1$ and $\mathbf{u}_2$ are nonzero vectors. If $\mathbf{x} = a_1\mathbf{u}_1 + a_2\mathbf{u}_2$, then (see Theorem 11 of Section 4.4) $\mathbf{y} = A^k\mathbf{x} = A^k(a_1\mathbf{u}_1 + a_2\mathbf{u}_2) = a_1A^k\mathbf{u}_1 + a_2A^k\mathbf{u}_2 = a_1(\lambda_1)^k\mathbf{u}_1 + a_2(\lambda_2)^k\mathbf{u}_2$. Find $A^{10}\mathbf{x}$, where

$$A = \begin{bmatrix} 4 & -2 \\ 5 & -3 \end{bmatrix} \quad\text{and}\quad \mathbf{x} = \begin{bmatrix} 0 \\ 9 \end{bmatrix}.$$

19. As in Exercise 18, calculate $A^{10}\mathbf{x}$ for

$$A = \begin{bmatrix} 1 & 2 & -1 \\ 0 & 5 & -2 \\ 0 & 6 & -2 \end{bmatrix} \quad\text{and}\quad \mathbf{x} = \begin{bmatrix} 2 \\ 4 \\ 7 \end{bmatrix}.$$

20. Consider a (4×4) matrix H of the form

$$H = \begin{bmatrix} \times & \times & \times & \times \\ a & \times & \times & \times \\ 0 & b & \times & \times \\ 0 & 0 & c & \times \end{bmatrix} \qquad (11)$$

In matrix (11) the entries designated $\times$ may be zero or nonzero. Suppose, in matrix (11), that a, b, and c are nonzero. Let λ be any eigenvalue of H. Show that the geometric multiplicity of λ is equal to 1. [*Hint:* Verify that the rank of $H - \lambda I$ is exactly equal to 3.]

21. An $(n \times n)$ matrix P is called ***idempotent*** if $P^2 = P$. Show that if P is an invertible idempotent matrix, then $P = I$.

22. Let P be an idempotent matrix. Show that the only eigenvalues of P are $\lambda = 0$ and $\lambda = 1$. [*Hint:* Suppose that $P\mathbf{x} = \lambda\mathbf{x}, \mathbf{x} \neq \boldsymbol{\theta}$.]

23. Let $\mathbf{u}$ be a vector in R^n such that $\mathbf{u}^T\mathbf{u} = 1$. Show that the $(n \times n)$ matrix $P = \mathbf{u}\mathbf{u}^T$ is an idempotent matrix. [*Hint:* Use the associative properties of matrix multiplication.]

24. Verify that if Q is idempotent, then so is $I - Q$. Also verify that $(I - 2Q)^{-1} = I - 2Q$.

25. Suppose that $\mathbf{u}$ and $\mathbf{v}$ are vectors in R^n such that $\mathbf{u}^T\mathbf{u} = 1$, $\mathbf{v}^T\mathbf{v} = 1$, and $\mathbf{u}^T\mathbf{v} = 0$. Show that $P = \mathbf{u}\mathbf{u}^T + \mathbf{v}\mathbf{v}^T$ is idempotent.

26. Show that any nonzero vector of the form $a\mathbf{u} + b\mathbf{v}$ is an eigenvector corresponding to $\lambda = 1$ for the matrix P in Exercise 25.

27. Let A be an $(n \times n)$ symmetric matrix, with (real) distinct eigenvalues $\lambda_1, \lambda_2, \ldots, \lambda_n$. Let the corresponding eigenvectors $\mathbf{u}_1, \mathbf{u}_2, \ldots, \mathbf{u}_n$ be chosen so that $\|\mathbf{u}_i\| = 1$ (that is, $\mathbf{u}_i^T\mathbf{u}_i = 1$). Exercise 29 shows that A can be decomposed as

$$A = \lambda_1\mathbf{u}_1\mathbf{u}_1^T + \lambda_2\mathbf{u}_2\mathbf{u}_2^T + \cdots + \lambda_n\mathbf{u}_n\mathbf{u}_n^T. \quad (12)$$

Verify decomposition (12) for each of the following matrices.

a) $B = \begin{bmatrix} 2 & -1 \\ -1 & 2 \end{bmatrix}$ b) $C = \begin{bmatrix} 1 & 2 \\ 2 & 1 \end{bmatrix}$

c) $D = \begin{bmatrix} 3 & 2 \\ 2 & 0 \end{bmatrix}$

28. Let A be a symmetric matrix and suppose that $A\mathbf{u} = \lambda\mathbf{u}$, $\mathbf{u} \neq \boldsymbol{\theta}$ and $A\mathbf{v} = \beta\mathbf{v}$, $\mathbf{v} \neq \boldsymbol{\theta}$. Also suppose that $\lambda \neq \beta$. Show that $\mathbf{u}^T\mathbf{v} = 0$. [*Hint:* Since $A\mathbf{v}$ and $\mathbf{u}$ are vectors, $(A\mathbf{v})^T\mathbf{u} = \mathbf{u}^T(A\mathbf{v})$. Rewrite the term $(A\mathbf{v})^T\mathbf{u}$ by using Theorem 10, property 2, of Section 1.6.]

29. Having A as in Exercise 27, we see from Exercise 28 that $\mathbf{u}_i^T\mathbf{u}_j = 0$, $i \neq j$. By the corollary to Theorem 15, $\{\mathbf{u}_1, \mathbf{u}_2, \ldots, \mathbf{u}_n\}$ is an orthonormal basis for R^n. To show that decomposition (12) is valid, let C denote the right-hand side of (12). Then show that $(A - C)\mathbf{u}_i = \boldsymbol{\theta}$ for $1 \leq i \leq n$. Finally, show that $A - C$ is the zero matrix. [*Hint:* Look at Exercise 24 in Section 4.4.]

(*Note:* We will see in the next section that a real symmetric matrix has only real eigenvalues. It can also be shown that the eigenvectors can be chosen to be orthonormal, even when the eigenvalues are not distinct. Thus decomposition (12) is valid for any real symmetric matrix A.)

4.6 COMPLEX EIGENVALUES AND EIGENVECTORS

Up to now we have not examined in detail the case in which the characteristic equation has complex roots—that is, the case in which a matrix has complex eigenvalues. We will see that the possibility of complex eigenvalues does not pose any additional problems except that the eigenvectors corresponding to complex eigenvalues will have complex components, and complex arithmetic will be required to find these eigenvectors.

EXAMPLE 1 Find the eigenvalues and the eigenvectors for

$$A = \begin{bmatrix} 3 & 1 \\ -2 & 1 \end{bmatrix}.$$

Solution The characteristic polynomial for A is $p(t) = t^2 - 4t + 5$. The eigenvalues of A are the roots of $p(t) = 0$, which we can find from the quadratic formula,

$$\lambda = \frac{4 \pm \sqrt{-4}}{2} = 2 \pm i,$$

where $i = \sqrt{-1}$. Thus despite the fact that A is a real matrix, the eigenvalues of A are complex, $\lambda = 2 + i$ and $\lambda = 2 - i$. To find the eigenvectors of A corresponding to $\lambda = 2 + i$, we must solve $[A - (2+i)I]\mathbf{x} = \boldsymbol{\theta}$, which leads to the (2×2) homogeneous system

$$\begin{aligned} (1-i)x_1 + \quad\quad x_2 &= 0 \\ -2x_1 - (1+i)x_2 &= 0. \end{aligned} \quad (1)$$

COMPLEX NUMBERS Ancient peoples knew that certain quadratic equations, such as $x^2+1=0$, had no real solutions. This posed no difficulty, however, because their particular problems (such as finding the intersections of a line and a circle) did not require complex solutions. Hence people paid complex numbers little attention and referred to them as *imaginary numbers*. In 1545, however, Cardano published a formula for finding the roots of a cubic equation that often required algebraic manipulation of $\sqrt{-1}$ in order to find certain real solutions. Guided by Cardano's formula, Bombelli, in 1572, is credited with working out the algebra of complex numbers. However, the important link to geometry, the association of $a+bi$ with the point (a, b), was not developed for another hundred years.

Probably the two people most influential in developing complex numbers into their essential role in describing scientific phenomena were Leonhard Euler (1707–1783) and Augustin-Louis Cauchy (1789–1857). Besides introducing much of the mathematical notation used today, Euler used complex numbers to unify the study of exponential, logarithmic, and trigonometric functions. Cauchy is regarded as the founder of the field of functions of a complex variable. Many terms and results in the extension of calculus to complex variables are due to Cauchy and are named after him.

At the end of this section, we will discuss the details of how such a system is solved. For the moment, we merely note that if the first equation is multiplied by $1+i$, then Eq. (1) is equivalent to

$$\begin{aligned} 2x_1 + (1+i)x_2 &= 0 \\ -2x_1 - (1+i)x_2 &= 0. \end{aligned}$$

Thus the solutions of Eq. (1) are determined by $x_1 = -(1+i)x_2/2$. The nonzero solutions of Eq. (1), the eigenvectors corresponding to $\lambda = 2+i$, are of the form

$$\mathbf{x} = a\begin{bmatrix} 1+i \\ -2 \end{bmatrix}, \quad a \neq 0.$$

Similar calculations show that the eigenvectors of A corresponding to $\lambda = 2-i$ are all of the form

$$\mathbf{x} = b\begin{bmatrix} 1-i \\ -2 \end{bmatrix}, \quad b \neq 0.$$

Complex Arithmetic and Complex Vectors

Before giving the major theoretical results of this section, we briefly review several of the details of complex arithmetic. We will usually represent a complex number z in the form $z = a + ib$, where a and b are real numbers and $i^2 = -1$. In the representation $z = a + ib$, a is called the ***real part*** of z, and b is called the ***imaginary part*** of z. If $z = a + ib$ and $w = c + id$, then $z + w = (a + c) + i(b + d)$, whereas $zw = (ac - bd) + i(ad + bc)$. Thus, for example, if $z_1 = 2 + 3i$ and $z_2 = 1 - i$, then

$$z_1 + z_2 = 3 + 2i \quad \text{and} \quad z_1z_2 = 5 + i.$$

If z is the complex number $z = a + ib$, then the ***conjugate*** of z (denoted by $\bar{z}$) is defined to be $\bar{z} = a - ib$. We list several properties of the conjugate operation:

$$\begin{aligned}(\overline{z+w}) &= \bar{z} + \bar{w}\\ (\overline{zw}) &= \bar{z}\bar{w}\\ z + \bar{z} &= 2a\\ z - \bar{z} &= 2ib\\ z\bar{z} &= a^2 + b^2.\end{aligned} \tag{2}$$

From the last equality, we note that $z\bar{z}$ is a positive real quantity when $z \neq 0$. In fact, if we visualize z as the point (a, b) in the coordinate plane (called the ***complex plane***), then $\sqrt{a^2 + b^2}$ is the distance from (a, b) to the origin (see Fig. 4.2). Hence we define the ***magnitude*** of z to be $|z|$, where

$$|z| = \sqrt{\bar{z}z} = \sqrt{a^2 + b^2}.$$

We also note from (2) that if $z = \bar{z}$, then $b = 0$ and so z is a real number.

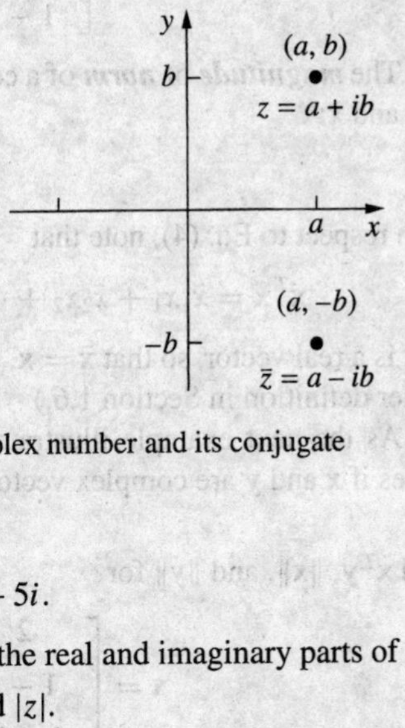

Figure 4.2 A complex number and its conjugate

EXAMPLE 2 Let $z = 4 - 2i$ and $w = 3 + 5i$.

(a) Find the values of the real and imaginary parts of w.

(b) Calculate $\bar{z}$, $\bar{w}$, and $|z|$.

(c) Find $u = 2z + 3\bar{w}$ and $v = \bar{z}w$.

Solution

(a) Since $w = 3 + 5i$, the real part of w is 3, and the imaginary part is 5.

(b) For $z = 4 - 2i$, $\bar{z} = 4 + 2i$. Similarly, since $w = 3 + 5i$, we have $\bar{w} = 3 - 5i$. Finally, $|z| = \sqrt{(4)^2 + (-2)^2} = \sqrt{20}$.

(c) Here, $2z = 2(4-2i) = 8-4i$, whereas $3\bar{w} = 3(3-5i) = 9-15i$. Therefore,

$$u = 2z + 3\bar{w} = (8 - 4i) + (9 - 15i) = 17 - 19i.$$

The product $v = \bar{z}w$ is calculated as follows:

$$\begin{aligned} v = \bar{z}w &= (4+2i)(3+5i) \\ &= 12 + 6i + 20i + 10i^2 \\ &= 2 + 26i. \end{aligned}$$

The conjugate operation is useful when dealing with matrices and vectors that have complex components. We define the conjugate of a vector as follows: If $\mathbf{x} = [x_1, x_2, \ldots, x_n]^T$, then the ***conjugate vector*** (denoted by $\bar{\mathbf{x}}$) is given by

$$\bar{\mathbf{x}} = \begin{bmatrix} \bar{x}_1 \\ \bar{x}_2 \\ \vdots \\ \bar{x}_n \end{bmatrix}.$$

In (3), an example of a vector $\mathbf{x}$ and its conjugate, $\bar{\mathbf{x}}$, is given:

$$\mathbf{x} = \begin{bmatrix} 2+3i \\ 4 \\ 1-7i \end{bmatrix}, \quad \bar{\mathbf{x}} = \begin{bmatrix} 2-3i \\ 4 \\ 1+7i \end{bmatrix}. \tag{3}$$

The ***magnitude*** or ***norm*** of a complex vector $\mathbf{x}$ (denoted by $\|\mathbf{x}\|$) is defined in terms of $\mathbf{x}$ and $\bar{\mathbf{x}}$:

$$\|\mathbf{x}\| = \sqrt{\bar{\mathbf{x}}^T\mathbf{x}}. \tag{4}$$

With respect to Eq. (4), note that

$$\bar{\mathbf{x}}^T\mathbf{x} = \bar{x}_1x_1 + \bar{x}_2x_2 + \cdots + \bar{x}_nx_n = |x_1|^2 + |x_2|^2 + \cdots + |x_n|^2.$$

(If $\mathbf{x}$ is a real vector, so that $\bar{\mathbf{x}} = \mathbf{x}$, then the definition for $\|\mathbf{x}\|$ in Eq. (4) agrees with our earlier definition in Section 1.6.)

As the next example illustrates, the scalar product $\mathbf{x}^T\mathbf{y}$ will usually be complex values if $\mathbf{x}$ and $\mathbf{y}$ are complex vectors.

EXAMPLE 3 Find $\mathbf{x}^T\mathbf{y}$, $\|\mathbf{x}\|$, and $\|\mathbf{y}\|$ for

$$\mathbf{x} = \begin{bmatrix} 2 \\ 1-i \\ 3+2i \end{bmatrix} \quad \text{and} \quad \mathbf{y} = \begin{bmatrix} i \\ 1+i \\ 2-i \end{bmatrix}.$$

Solution For $\mathbf{x}^T\mathbf{y}$, we find

$$\begin{aligned} \mathbf{x}^T\mathbf{y} &= (2)(i) + (1-i)(1+i) + (3+2i)(2-i) \\ &= (2i) + (2) + (8+i) \\ &= 10 + 3i. \end{aligned}$$

Similarly, $\|\mathbf{x}\| = \sqrt{\bar{\mathbf{x}}^T\mathbf{x}} = \sqrt{4+2+13} = \sqrt{19}$, whereas $\|\mathbf{y}\| = \sqrt{\bar{\mathbf{y}}^T\mathbf{y}} = \sqrt{1+2+5} = \sqrt{8}$.

Eigenvalues of Real Matrices

In a situation where complex numbers might arise, it is conventional to refer to a vector $\mathbf{x}$ as a real vector if all the components of $\mathbf{x}$ are known to be real numbers. Similarly, we use the term *real matrix* to denote a matrix A, all of whose entries are real.

With these preliminaries, we can present two important results. The first result was illustrated in Example 1. We found $\lambda = 2 + i$ to be an eigenvalue with a corresponding eigenvector $\mathbf{x} = [1 + i, -2]^T$. We also found that the conjugates, $\bar{\lambda} = 2 - i$ and $\bar{\mathbf{x}} = [1 - i, -2]^T$, were the other eigenvalue/eigenvector pair. That is, the eigenvalues and eigenvectors occurred in conjugate pairs. The next theorem tells us that Example 1 is typical.

THEOREM 16 Let A be a real $(n \times n)$ matrix with an eigenvalue λ and corresponding eigenvector $\mathbf{x}$. Then $\bar{\lambda}$ is also an eigenvalue of A, and $\bar{\mathbf{x}}$ is an eigenvector corresponding to $\bar{\lambda}$.

Proof It can be shown (see Exercise 36) that $\overline{\lambda \mathbf{x}} = \bar{\lambda}\bar{\mathbf{x}}$. Furthermore, since A is real, it can be shown (see Exercise 36) that

$$\overline{A\mathbf{x}} = \bar{A}\bar{\mathbf{x}} = A\bar{\mathbf{x}}.$$

Using these two results and the assumption $A\mathbf{x} = \lambda\mathbf{x}$, we obtain

$$A\bar{\mathbf{x}} = \overline{A\mathbf{x}} = \overline{\lambda\mathbf{x}} = \bar{\lambda}\bar{\mathbf{x}}, \quad \bar{\mathbf{x}} \neq \boldsymbol{\theta}.$$

Thus $\bar{\lambda}$ is an eigenvalue corresponding to the eigenvector $\bar{\mathbf{x}}$. ∎

Finally, as the next theorem shows, there is an important class of matrices for which the possibility of complex eigenvalues is precluded.

THEOREM 17 If A is an $(n \times n)$ real symmetric matrix, then all the eigenvalues of A are real.

Proof Let A by any $(n \times n)$ real symmetric matrix, and suppose that $A\mathbf{x} = \lambda\mathbf{x}$, where $\mathbf{x} \neq \boldsymbol{\theta}$ and where we allow the possibility that $\mathbf{x}$ is a complex vector. To isolate λ, we first note that

$$\bar{\mathbf{x}}^T(A\mathbf{x}) = \bar{\mathbf{x}}^T(\lambda\mathbf{x}) = \lambda(\bar{\mathbf{x}}^T\mathbf{x}). \tag{5}$$

Regarding $A\mathbf{x}$ as a vector, we see that $\bar{\mathbf{x}}^T(A\mathbf{x}) = (A\mathbf{x})^T\bar{\mathbf{x}}$ (since, in general, $\mathbf{u}^T\mathbf{v} = \mathbf{v}^T\mathbf{u}$ for complex vectors $\mathbf{u}$ and $\mathbf{v}$). Using this observation in Eq. (5), we obtain

$$\lambda\bar{\mathbf{x}}^T\mathbf{x} = \bar{\mathbf{x}}^T(A\mathbf{x}) = (A\mathbf{x})^T\bar{\mathbf{x}} = \mathbf{x}^TA^T\bar{\mathbf{x}} = \mathbf{x}^TA\bar{\mathbf{x}}, \tag{6}$$

with the last equality holding because $A = A^T$. Since A is real, we also know that $A\bar{\mathbf{x}} = \overline{\lambda\mathbf{x}}$; hence we deduce from Eq. (6) that

$$\lambda\bar{\mathbf{x}}^T\mathbf{x} = \mathbf{x}^TA\bar{\mathbf{x}} = \mathbf{x}^T(\bar{\lambda}\bar{\mathbf{x}}) = \bar{\lambda}\mathbf{x}^T\bar{\mathbf{x}},$$

or

$$\lambda\bar{\mathbf{x}}^T\mathbf{x} = \bar{\lambda}\mathbf{x}^T\bar{\mathbf{x}}. \tag{7}$$

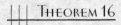

Because $\mathbf{x} \neq \boldsymbol{\theta}$, $\bar{\mathbf{x}}^T\mathbf{x}$ is nonzero, and so from Eq. (7) we see that $\bar{\lambda} = \lambda$, which means that λ is real. ∎

Gaussian Elimination for Systems with Complex Coefficients (Optional)

The remainder of this section is concerned with the computational details of solving $(A - \lambda I)\mathbf{x} = \boldsymbol{\theta}$ when λ is complex. We will see that although the arithmetic is tiresome, we can use Gaussian elimination to solve a system of linear equations that has some complex coefficients in exactly the same way that we solve systems of linear equations having real coefficients. For example, consider the (2×2) system

$$\begin{aligned} a_{11}x_1 + a_{12}x_2 &= b_1 \\ a_{21}x_1 + a_{22}x_2 &= b_2, \end{aligned}$$

where the coefficients a_{ij} may be complex. Just as before, we can multiply the first equation by $-a_{21}/a_{11}$, add the result to the second equation to eliminate x_1 from the second equation, and then backsolve to find x_2 and x_1. For larger systems with complex coefficients, the principles of Gaussian elimination are exactly the same as they are for real systems; only the computational details are different.

One computational detail that might be unfamiliar is dividing one complex number by another (the first step of Gaussian elimination for the (2×2) system above is to form a_{21}/a_{11}). To see how a complex division is carried out, let $z = a + ib$ and $w = c + id$, where $w \neq 0$. To form the quotient z/w, we multiply numerator and denominator by $\bar{w}$:

$$\frac{z}{w} = \frac{z\bar{w}}{w\bar{w}}.$$

In detail, we have

$$\frac{z}{w} = \frac{z\bar{w}}{w\bar{w}} = \frac{(a+ib)(c-id)}{c^2+d^2} = \frac{(ac+bd)+i(bc-ad)}{c^2+d^2}. \tag{8}$$

Our objective is to express the quotient z/w in the standard form $z/w = r + is$, where r and s are real numbers; from Eq. (8), r and s are given by

$$r = \frac{ac+bd}{c^2+d^2} \quad \text{and} \quad s = \frac{bc-ad}{c^2+d^2}.$$

For instance,

$$\frac{2+3i}{1+2i} = \frac{(2+3i)(1-2i)}{(1+2i)(1-2i)} = \frac{8-i}{5} = \frac{8}{5} - \frac{1}{5}i.$$

EXAMPLE 4 Use Gaussian elimination to solve the system in (1):

$$\begin{aligned} (1-i)x_1 + x_2 &= 0 \\ -2x_1 - (1+i)x_2 &= 0. \end{aligned}$$

Solution The initial step in solving this system is to multiply the first equation by $2/(1-i)$ and then add the result to the second equation. Following the discussion above, we write $2/(1-i)$ as

$$\frac{2}{1-i} = \frac{2(1+i)}{(1-i)(1+i)} = \frac{2+2i}{2} = 1+i.$$

Multiplying the first equation by $1+i$ and adding the result to the second equation produces the equivalent system

$$\begin{aligned}(1-i)x_1 + x_2 &= 0\\ 0 &= 0,\end{aligned}$$

which leads to $x_1 = -x_2/(1-i)$. Simplifying, we obtain

$$x_1 = \frac{-x_2}{1-i} = \frac{-x_2(1+i)}{(1-i)(1+i)} = \frac{-(1+i)}{2}x_2.$$

With $x_2 = -2a$, the solutions are all of the form

$$\mathbf{x} = a\begin{bmatrix} 1+i \\ -2 \end{bmatrix}.$$

(*Note:* Since we are allowing the possibility of vectors with complex components, we will also allow the parameter a in Example 4 to be complex. For example, with $a = i$ we see that

$$\mathbf{x} = \begin{bmatrix} -1+i \\ -2i \end{bmatrix}$$

is also a solution.)

EXAMPLE 5 Find the eigenvalues and the eigenvectors of A, where

$$A = \begin{bmatrix} -2 & -2 & -9 \\ -1 & 1 & -3 \\ 1 & 1 & 4 \end{bmatrix}.$$

Solution The characteristic polynomial of A is

$$p(t) = -(t-1)(t^2 - 2t + 2).$$

Thus the eigenvalues of A are $\lambda = 1$, $\lambda = 1+i$, $\lambda = 1-i$.

As we noted earlier, the complex eigenvalues occur in conjugate pairs; and if we find an eigenvector $\mathbf{x}$ for $\lambda = 1+i$, then we immediately see that $\bar{\mathbf{x}}$ is an eigenvector for $\bar{\lambda} = 1-i$. In this example we find the eigenvectors for $\lambda = 1+i$ by reducing the augmented matrix $[A - \lambda I \mid \boldsymbol{\theta}]$ to echelon form. Now for $\lambda = 1+i$,

$$[A - \lambda I \mid \boldsymbol{\theta}] = \begin{bmatrix} -3-i & -2 & -9 & 0 \\ -1 & -i & -3 & 0 \\ 1 & 1 & 3-i & 0 \end{bmatrix}.$$

To introduce a zero into the (2, 1) position, we use the multiple m, where

$$m = \frac{1}{-3-i} = \frac{-1}{3+i} = \frac{-(3-i)}{(3+i)(3-i)} = \frac{-3+i}{10}.$$

Multiplying the first row by m and adding the result to the second row, and then multiplying the first row by $-m$ and adding the result to the third row, we find that $[A - \lambda I \mid \boldsymbol{\theta}]$ is row equivalent to

$$\begin{bmatrix} -3-i & -2 & -9 & 0 \\ 0 & \dfrac{6-12i}{10} & \dfrac{-3-9i}{10} & 0 \\ 0 & \dfrac{4+2i}{10} & \dfrac{3-i}{10} & 0 \end{bmatrix}.$$

Multiplying the second and third rows by 10 in the preceding matrix, we obtain a row-equivalent matrix:

$$\begin{bmatrix} -3-i & -2 & -9 & 0 \\ 0 & 6-12i & -3-9i & 0 \\ 0 & 4+2i & 3-i & 0 \end{bmatrix}.$$

Completing the reduction, we multiply the second row by r and add the result to the third row, where r is the multiple

$$r = \frac{-(4+2i)}{6-12i} = \frac{-(4+2i)(6+12i)}{(6-12i)(6+12i)} = \frac{-60i}{180} = \frac{-i}{3}.$$

We obtain the row-equivalent matrix

$$\begin{bmatrix} -3-i & -2 & -9 & 0 \\ 0 & 6-12i & -3-9i & 0 \\ 0 & 0 & 0 & 0 \end{bmatrix};$$

and the eigenvectors of A corresponding to $\lambda = 1 + i$ are found by solving

$$\begin{aligned} -(3+i)x_1 - \quad 2x_2 &= \quad 9x_3 \\ (6-12i)x_2 &= (3+9i)x_3, \end{aligned} \tag{9}$$

with x_3 arbitrary, $x_3 \neq 0$. We first find x_2 from

$$x_2 = \frac{3+9i}{6-12i}x_3 = \frac{(3+9i)(6+12i)}{180}x_3 = \frac{-90+90i}{180}x_3,$$

or

$$x_2 = \frac{-1+i}{2}x_3.$$

From the first equation in (9), we obtain

$$-(3+i)x_1 = 2x_2 + 9x_3 = (8+i)x_3,$$

or

$$x_1 = \frac{-(8+i)}{3+i}x_3 = \frac{-(8+i)(3-i)}{10}x_3 = \frac{-25+5i}{10}x_3 = \frac{-5+i}{2}x_3.$$

Setting $x_3 = 2a$, we have $x_2 = (-1+i)a$ and $x_1 = (-5+i)a$; so the eigenvectors of A corresponding to $\lambda = 1+i$ are all of the form

$$\mathbf{x} = \begin{bmatrix} (-5+i)a \\ (-1+i)a \\ 2a \end{bmatrix} = a\begin{bmatrix} -5+i \\ -1+i \\ 2 \end{bmatrix}, \quad a \neq 0.$$

Furthermore, we know that eigenvectors of A corresponding to $\bar{\lambda} = 1-i$ have the form

$$\bar{\mathbf{x}} = b\begin{bmatrix} -5-i \\ -1-i \\ 2 \end{bmatrix}, \quad b \neq 0.$$

If linear algebra software is available, then finding eigenvalues and eigenvectors is a simple matter.

EXAMPLE 6 Find the eigenvalues and the eigenvectors for the (4×4) matrix

$$A = \begin{bmatrix} 3 & 3 & 6 & 9 \\ 1 & 4 & 3 & 7 \\ 2 & -5 & 8 & 3 \\ 2 & -9 & 7 & 4 \end{bmatrix}.$$

Solution We used MATLAB to solve this problem. The command `[V, D] = eig(A)` produces a diagonal matrix D and a matrix of eigenvectors V. That is, $AV = DV$ or (if A is not defective) $V^{-1}AV = D$. The results from MATLAB are shown in Fig. 4.3. As can be seen from the matrix D in Fig. 4.3, A has two complex eigenvalues, which are (to the places shown) $\lambda = 6.9014 + 5.3028i$ and $\lambda = 6.9014 - 5.3028i$. In addition, A has two real eigenvalues $\lambda = 4.0945$ and $\lambda = 1.1027$. Eigenvectors are found in the corresponding columns of V.

As the preceding examples indicate, finding eigenvectors that correspond to a complex eigenvalue proceeds exactly as for a real eigenvalue except for the additional details required by complex arithmetic.

Although complex eigenvalues and eigenvectors may seem an undue complication, they are in fact fairly important to applications. For instance, we note (without trying to be precise) that oscillatory and periodic solutions to first-order systems of differential equations correspond to complex eigenvalues; and since many physical systems exhibit such behavior, we need some way to model them.

```
A=
     3      3      6      9
     1      4      3      7
     2     -5      8      3
     2     -9      7      4

>>[V,D]=eig(A)

V =
   0.6897 + 0.2800i   0.6897 - 0.2800i   0.8216    0.9609
   0.4761 + 0.2051i   0.4761 - 0.2051i   0.4196   -0.0067
   0.1338 + 0.2255i   0.1338 - 0.2255i   0.3014   -0.2765
  -0.1139 + 0.3090i  -0.1139 - 0.3090i  -0.2409   -0.0160

D =
   6.9014 + 5.3028i        0                 0         0
        0             6.9014 - 5.3028i       0         0
        0                  0             4.0945        0
        0                  0                 0    1.1027
```

Figure 4.3 MATLAB was used to find the eigenvalues and eigenvectors of matrix A in Example 6—that is, $AV = VD$ or $V^{-1}AV = D$, where D is diagonal.

4.6 EXERCISES

In Exercises 1–18, $s = 1 + 2i$, $u = 3 - 2i$, $v = 4 + i$, $w = 2 - i$, and $z = 1 + i$. In each exercise, perform the indicated calculation and express the result in the form $a + ib$.

1. $\bar{u}$ **2.** $\bar{z}$ **3.** $u + \bar{v}$

4. $\bar{z} + w$ **5.** $u + \bar{u}$ **6.** $s - \bar{s}$

7. $v\bar{v}$ **8.** $u\bar{v}$ **9.** $s^2 - w$

10. $z^2 w$ **11.** $\bar{u}w^2$ **12.** $s(u^2 + v)$

13. u/v **14.** v/u^2 **15.** s/z

16. $(w + \bar{v})/u$ **17.** $w + iz$ **18.** $s - iw$

Find the eigenvalues and the eigenvectors for the matrices in Exercises 19–24. (For the matrix in Exercise 24, one eigenvalue is $\lambda = 1 + 5i$.)

19. $\begin{bmatrix} 6 & 8 \\ -1 & 2 \end{bmatrix}$ **20.** $\begin{bmatrix} 2 & 4 \\ -2 & -2 \end{bmatrix}$

21. $\begin{bmatrix} -2 & -1 \\ 5 & 2 \end{bmatrix}$ **22.** $\begin{bmatrix} 5 & -5 & -5 \\ -1 & 4 & 2 \\ 3 & -5 & -3 \end{bmatrix}$

23. $\begin{bmatrix} 1 & -4 & -1 \\ 3 & 2 & 3 \\ 1 & 1 & 3 \end{bmatrix}$ **24.** $\begin{bmatrix} 1 & -5 & 0 & 0 \\ 5 & 1 & 0 & 0 \\ 0 & 0 & 1 & -2 \\ 0 & 0 & 2 & 1 \end{bmatrix}$

In Exercises 25 and 26, solve the linear system.

25. $(1 + i)x + iy = 5 + 4i$
$(1 - i)x - 4y = -11 + 5i$

26. $(1 - i)x - (3 + i)y = -5 - i$
$(2 + i)x + (1 + 2i)y = 1 + 6i$

In Exercises 27–30, calculate $\|\mathbf{x}\|$.

27. $\mathbf{x} = \begin{bmatrix} 1+i \\ 2 \end{bmatrix}$ **28.** $\mathbf{x} = \begin{bmatrix} 3+i \\ 2-i \end{bmatrix}$

29. $\mathbf{x} = \begin{bmatrix} 1-2i \\ i \\ 3+i \end{bmatrix}$ **30.** $\mathbf{x} = \begin{bmatrix} 2i \\ 1-i \\ 3 \end{bmatrix}$

In Exercises 31–34, use linear algebra software to find the eigenvalues and the eigenvectors.

31. $\begin{bmatrix} 2 & 2 & 5 \\ 5 & 3 & 7 \\ 1 & 5 & 3 \end{bmatrix}$ **32.** $\begin{bmatrix} 1 & 2 & 8 \\ 8 & 4 & 9 \\ 2 & 6 & 1 \end{bmatrix}$

33. $\begin{bmatrix} 5 & -1 & 0 & 8 \\ 3 & 6 & 8 & -3 \\ 1 & 1 & 4 & 2 \\ 9 & 7 & 6 & 9 \end{bmatrix}$ **34.** $\begin{bmatrix} 5 & 5 & 4 & 6 \\ 0 & 8 & 6 & 7 \\ 1 & 2 & 3 & 1 \\ 6 & 3 & 8 & 5 \end{bmatrix}$

35. Establish the five properties of the conjugate operation listed in (2).

36. Let A be an $(m \times n)$ matrix, and let B be an $(n \times p)$ matrix, where the entries of A and B may be complex. Use Exercise 35 and the definition of AB to show that $\overline{AB} = \bar{A}\bar{B}$. (By $\bar{A}$, we mean the matrix whose ijth entry is the conjugate of the ijth entry of A.) If A is a real matrix and $\mathbf{x}$ is an $(n \times 1)$ vector, show that $\overline{A\mathbf{x}} = A\bar{\mathbf{x}}$.

37. Let A be an $(m \times n)$ matrix, where the entries of A may be complex. It is customary to use the symbol A^* to denote the matrix

$$A^* = (\bar{A})^T.$$

Suppose that A is an $(m \times n)$ matrix and B is an $(n \times p)$ matrix. Use Exercise 36 and the properties of the transpose operation to give a quick proof that $(AB)^* = B^*A^*$.

38. An $(n \times n)$ matrix A is called ***Hermitian*** if $A^* = A$.

a) Prove that a Hermitian matrix A has only real eigenvalues. [*Hint:* Observing that $\bar{\mathbf{x}}^T\mathbf{x} = \mathbf{x}^*\mathbf{x}$, modify the proof of Theorem 17.]

b) Let $A = (a_{ij})$ be an $(n \times n)$ Hermitian matrix. Show that a_{ii} is real for $1 \le i \le n$.

39. Let $p(t) = a_0 + a_1 t + \cdots + a_n t^n$, where the coefficients $a_0, a_1, \ldots, a_n$ are all real.

a) Prove that if r is a complex root of $p(t) = 0$, then $\bar{r}$ is also a root of $p(t) = 0$.

b) If $p(t)$ has degree 3, argue that $p(t)$ must have at least one real root.

c) If A is a (3×3) real matrix, argue that A must have at least one real eigenvalue.

40. An $(n \times n)$ real matrix A is called ***orthogonal*** if $A^TA = I$. Let λ be an eigenvalue of an orthogonal matrix A, where $\lambda = r + is$. Prove that $\lambda\bar{\lambda} = r^2 + s^2 = 1$. [*Hint:* First show that $\|A\mathbf{x}\| = \|\mathbf{x}\|$ for any vector $\mathbf{x}$.]

41. A real symmetric $(n \times n)$ matrix A is called ***positive definite*** if $\mathbf{x}^TA\mathbf{x} > 0$ for all $\mathbf{x}$ in R^n, $\mathbf{x} \ne \boldsymbol{\theta}$. Prove that the eigenvalues of a real symmetric positive-definite matrix A are all positive.

42. An $(n \times n)$ matrix A is called ***unitary*** if $A^*A = I$. (If A is a real unitary matrix, then A is orthogonal; see Exercise 40.) Show that if A is unitary and λ is an eigenvalue for A, then $|\lambda| = 1$.

4.7 SIMILARITY TRANSFORMATIONS AND DIAGONALIZATION

In Chapter 1, we saw that two linear systems of equations have the same solution if their augmented matrices are row equivalent. In this chapter, we are interested in identifying classes of matrices that have the same eigenvalues.

As we know, the eigenvalues of an $(n \times n)$ matrix A are the zeros of its characteristic polynomial,

$$p(t) = \det(A - tI).$$

Thus if an $(n \times n)$ matrix B has the same characteristic polynomial as A, then A and B have the same eigenvalues. As we will see, it is fairly simple to find such matrices B.

Similarity

In particular, let A be an $(n \times n)$ matrix, and let S be a nonsingular $(n \times n)$ matrix. Then, as the following calculation shows, the matrices A and $B = S^{-1}AS$ have the same characteristic polynomial. To establish this fact, observe that the characteristic polynomial for $S^{-1}AS$ is given by

$$\begin{aligned} p(t) &= \det(S^{-1}AS - tI) \\ &= \det(S^{-1}AS - tS^{-1}S) \\ &= \det[S^{-1}(A - tI)S] \\ &= \det(S^{-1})\det(A - tI)\det(S), \quad \text{by Theorem 2} \\ &= [\det(S^{-1})\det(S)]\det(A - tI) \\ &= \det(A - tI). \end{aligned} \tag{1}$$

(The last equality given follows because $\det(S^{-1})\det(S) = \det(S^{-1}S) = \det(I) = 1$.)

Thus, by (1), the matrices $S^{-1}AS$ and A have the same characteristic polynomial and hence the same set of eigenvalues. The discussion above leads to the next definition.

DEFINITION 8 The $(n \times n)$ matrices A and B are said to be ***similar*** if there is a nonsingular $(n \times n)$ matrix S such that $B = S^{-1}AS$.

The calculations carried out in (1) show that similar matrices have the same characteristic polynomial. Consequently the following theorem is immediate.

THEOREM 18 If A and B are similar $(n \times n)$ matrices, then A and B have the same eigenvalues. Moreover, these eigenvalues have the same algebraic multiplicity. ∎

Although similar matrices always have the same characteristic polynomial, it is not true that two matrices with the same characteristic polynomial are necessarily similar. As a simple example, consider the two matrices

$$A = \begin{bmatrix} 1 & 0 \\ 1 & 1 \end{bmatrix} \quad \text{and} \quad I = \begin{bmatrix} 1 & 0 \\ 0 & 1 \end{bmatrix}.$$

Now $p(t) = (1-t)^2$ is the characteristic polynomial for both A and I; so A and I have the same set of eigenvalues. If A and I were similar, however, there would be a (2×2) matrix S such that

$$I = S^{-1}AS.$$

But the equation $I = S^{-1}AS$ is equivalent to $S = AS$, which is in turn equivalent to $SS^{-1} = A$ or $I = A$. Thus I and A cannot be similar. (A repetition of this argument shows that the only matrix similar to the identity matrix is I itself.) In this respect, similarity is a more fundamental concept for the eigenvalue problem than is the characteristic polynomial; two matrices can have exactly the same characteristic polynomial without being similar; so similarity leads to a more finely detailed way of distinguishing matrices.

Although similar matrices have the same eigenvalues, they do not generally have the same eigenvectors. For example, if $B = S^{-1}AS$ and if $B\mathbf{x} = \lambda\mathbf{x}$, then

$$S^{-1}AS\mathbf{x} = \lambda\mathbf{x} \quad \text{or} \quad A(S\mathbf{x}) = \lambda(S\mathbf{x}).$$

Thus if $\mathbf{x}$ is an eigenvector for B corresponding to λ, then $S\mathbf{x}$ is an eigenvector for A corresponding to λ.

Diagonalization

Computations involving an $(n \times n)$ matrix A can often be simplified if we know that A is similar to a diagonal matrix. To illustrate, suppose $S^{-1}AS = D$, where D is a diagonal matrix. Next, suppose we need to calculate the power A^k, here k is a positive integer. Knowing that $D = S^{-1}AS$, we can proceed as follows:

$$\begin{aligned} D^k &= (S^{-1}AS)^k \\ &= S^{-1}A^kS. \end{aligned} \tag{2}$$

(The fact that $(S^{-1}AS)^k = S^{-1}A^kS$ is established in Exercise 25.) Note that because D is a diagonal matrix, it is easy to form the power D^k.

Once the matrix D^k is computed, the matrix A^k can be recovered from Eq. (2) by forming SD^kS^{-1}:

$$SD^kS^{-1} = S(S^{-1}A^kS)S^{-1} = A^k.$$

Whenever an $(n \times n)$ matrix A is similar to a diagonal matrix, we say that A is ***diagonalizable***. The next theorem gives a characterization of diagonalizable matrices.

THEOREM 19 An $(n \times n)$ matrix A is diagonalizable if and only if A possesses a set of n linearly independent eigenvectors.

Proof Suppose that $\{\mathbf{u}_1, \mathbf{u}_2, \ldots, \mathbf{u}_n\}$ is a set of n linearly independent eigenvectors for A:

$$A\mathbf{u}_k = \lambda_k\mathbf{u}_k, \quad k = 1, 2, \ldots, n.$$

Let S be the $(n \times n)$ matrix whose column vectors are the eigenvectors of A:

$$S = [\mathbf{u}_1, \mathbf{u}_2, \ldots, \mathbf{u}_n].$$

Now S is a nonsingular matrix; so S^{-1} exists where

$$S^{-1}S = [S^{-1}\mathbf{u}_1, S^{-1}\mathbf{u}_2, \ldots, S^{-1}\mathbf{u}_n] = [\mathbf{e}_1, \mathbf{e}_2, \ldots, \mathbf{e}_n] = I. \tag{3}$$

Furthermore, since $A\mathbf{u}_k = \lambda_k\mathbf{u}_k$, we obtain

$$AS = [A\mathbf{u}_1, A\mathbf{u}_2, \ldots, A\mathbf{u}_n] = [\lambda_1\mathbf{u}_1, \lambda_2\mathbf{u}_2, \ldots, \lambda_n\mathbf{u}_n];$$

and so from Eq. (3),

$$S^{-1}AS = [\lambda_1S^{-1}\mathbf{u}_1, \lambda_2S^{-1}\mathbf{u}_2, \ldots, \lambda_nS^{-1}\mathbf{u}_n] = [\lambda_1\mathbf{e}_1, \lambda_2\mathbf{e}_2, \ldots, \lambda_n\mathbf{e}_n].$$

Therefore, $S^{-1}AS$ has the form

$$S^{-1}AS = \begin{bmatrix} \lambda_1 & 0 & 0 & \cdots & 0 \\ 0 & \lambda_2 & 0 & \cdots & 0 \\ 0 & 0 & \lambda_3 & \cdots & 0 \\ \vdots & & & & \vdots \\ 0 & 0 & 0 & \cdots & \lambda_n \end{bmatrix} = D;$$

and we have shown that if A has n linearly independent eigenvectors, then A is similar to a diagonal matrix.

Now suppose that $C^{-1}AC = D$, where C is nonsingular and D is a diagonal matrix. Let us write C and D in column form as

$$C = [\mathbf{C}_1, \mathbf{C}_2, \ldots, \mathbf{C}_n] \quad \text{and} \quad D = [d_1\mathbf{e}_1, d_2\mathbf{e}_2, \ldots, d_n\mathbf{e}_n].$$

From $C^{-1}AC = D$, we obtain $AC = CD$, and we write both of these in column form as

$$AC = [A\mathbf{C}_1, A\mathbf{C}_2, \ldots, A\mathbf{C}_n]$$
$$CD = [d_1C\mathbf{e}_1, d_2C\mathbf{e}_2, \ldots, d_nC\mathbf{e}_n].$$

But since $C\mathbf{e}_k = \mathbf{C}_k$ for $k = 1, 2, \ldots, n$, we see that $AC = CD$ implies

$$A\mathbf{C}_k = d_k\mathbf{C}_k, \quad k = 1, 2, \ldots, n.$$

Since C is nonsingular, the vectors $\mathbf{C}_1, \mathbf{C}_2, \ldots, \mathbf{C}_n$ are linearly independent (and in particular, no $\mathbf{C}_k$ is the zero vector). Thus the diagonal entries of D are the eigenvalues of A, and the column vectors of C are a set of n linearly independent eigenvectors. ∎

Note that the proof of Theorem 19 gives a procedure for diagonalizing an $(n \times n)$ matrix A. That is, if A has n linearly independent eigenvectors $\mathbf{u}_1, \mathbf{u}_2, \ldots, \mathbf{u}_n$, then the matrix $S = [\mathbf{u}_1, \mathbf{u}_2, \ldots, \mathbf{u}_n]$ will diagonalize A.

EXAMPLE 1 Show that A is diagonalizable by finding a matrix S such that $S^{-1}AS = D$:

$$A = \begin{bmatrix} 5 & -6 \\ 3 & -4 \end{bmatrix}.$$

Solution It is easy to verify that A has eigenvalues $\lambda_1 = 2$ and $\lambda_2 = -1$ with corresponding eigenvectors

$$\mathbf{u}_1 = \begin{bmatrix} 2 \\ 1 \end{bmatrix} \quad \text{and} \quad \mathbf{u}_2 = \begin{bmatrix} 1 \\ 1 \end{bmatrix}.$$

Forming $S = [\mathbf{u}_1, \mathbf{u}_2]$, we obtain

$$S = \begin{bmatrix} 2 & 1 \\ 1 & 1 \end{bmatrix}, \quad S^{-1} = \begin{bmatrix} 1 & -1 \\ -1 & 2 \end{bmatrix}.$$

As a check on the calculations, we form $S^{-1}AS$. The matrix AS is given by

$$AS = \begin{bmatrix} 5 & -6 \\ 3 & -4 \end{bmatrix} \begin{bmatrix} 2 & 1 \\ 1 & 1 \end{bmatrix} = \begin{bmatrix} 4 & -1 \\ 2 & -1 \end{bmatrix}.$$

Next, forming $S^{-1}(AS)$, we obtain

$$S^{-1}(AS) = \begin{bmatrix} 1 & -1 \\ -1 & 2 \end{bmatrix} \begin{bmatrix} 4 & -1 \\ 2 & -1 \end{bmatrix} = \begin{bmatrix} 2 & 0 \\ 0 & -1 \end{bmatrix} = D.$$

EXAMPLE 2 Use the result of Example 1 to calculate A^{10}, where

$$A = \begin{bmatrix} 5 & -6 \\ 3 & -4 \end{bmatrix}.$$

Solution As was noted in Eq. (2), $D^{10} = S^{-1}A^{10}S$. Therefore, $A^{10} = SD^{10}S^{-1}$. Now by Example 1,

$$D^{10} = \begin{bmatrix} 2^{10} & 0 \\ 0 & (-1)^{10} \end{bmatrix} = \begin{bmatrix} 1024 & 0 \\ 0 & 1 \end{bmatrix}.$$

Hence $A^{10} = SD^{10}S^{-1}$ is given by

$$A^{10} = \begin{bmatrix} 2047 & -2046 \\ 1023 & -1022 \end{bmatrix}.$$

Sometimes complex arithmetic is necessary to diagonalize a real matrix.

EXAMPLE 3 Show that A is diagonalizable by finding a matrix S such that $S^{-1}AS = D$:

$$A = \begin{bmatrix} 1 & 1 \\ -1 & 1 \end{bmatrix}.$$

Solution A has eigenvalues $\lambda_1 = 1 + i$ and $\lambda_2 = 1 - i$, with corresponding eigenvectors

$$\mathbf{u}_1 = \begin{bmatrix} 1 \\ i \end{bmatrix} \quad \text{and} \quad \mathbf{u}_2 = \begin{bmatrix} 1 \\ -i \end{bmatrix}.$$

Forming the matrix $S = [\mathbf{u}_1, \mathbf{u}_2]$, we obtain

$$S = \begin{bmatrix} 1 & 1 \\ i & -i \end{bmatrix}, \qquad S^{-1} = \begin{bmatrix} \frac{1}{2} & -\frac{i}{2} \\ \frac{1}{2} & \frac{i}{2} \end{bmatrix}.$$

As a check, note that AS is given by

$$AS = \begin{bmatrix} 1 & 1 \\ -1 & 1 \end{bmatrix} \begin{bmatrix} 1 & 1 \\ i & -i \end{bmatrix} = \begin{bmatrix} 1+i & 1-i \\ -1+i & -1-i \end{bmatrix}.$$

Next, $S^{-1}(AS)$ is the matrix

$$S^{-1}(AS) = \frac{1}{2} \begin{bmatrix} 1 & -i \\ 1 & i \end{bmatrix} \begin{bmatrix} 1+i & 1-i \\ -1+i & -1-i \end{bmatrix} = \begin{bmatrix} 1+i & 0 \\ 0 & 1-i \end{bmatrix} = D.$$

Some types of matrices are known to be diagonalizable. The next theorem lists one such condition. Then, in the last subsection, we prove the important theorem: If A is a real symmetric matrix, then A is diagonalizable.

THEOREM 20 Let A be an $(n \times n)$ matrix with n distinct eigenvalues. Then A is diagonalizable.

Proof By Theorem 15, if A has n distinct eigenvalues, then A has a set of n linearly independent eigenvectors. Thus by Theorem 19, A is diagonalizable. ■

As the next example shows, a matrix A may be diagonalizable even though it has repeated eigenvalues.

EXAMPLE 4 Show that A is diagonalizable, where

$$A = \begin{bmatrix} 25 & -8 & 30 \\ 24 & -7 & 30 \\ -12 & 4 & -14 \end{bmatrix}.$$

Solution The eigenvalues of A are $\lambda_1 = \lambda_2 = 1$ and $\lambda_3 = 2$. The eigenspace corresponding to $\lambda_1 = \lambda_2 = 1$ has dimension 2, with a basis $\{\mathbf{u}_1, \mathbf{u}_2\}$, where

$$\mathbf{u}_1 = \begin{bmatrix} 1 \\ 3 \\ 0 \end{bmatrix} \text{ and } \mathbf{u}_2 = \begin{bmatrix} -4 \\ 3 \\ 4 \end{bmatrix}.$$

An eigenvector corresponding to $\lambda_3 = 2$ is

$$\mathbf{u}_3 = \begin{bmatrix} 4 \\ 4 \\ -2 \end{bmatrix}.$$

Defining S by $S = [\mathbf{u}_1, \mathbf{u}_2, \mathbf{u}_3]$, we can verify that

$$S^{-1}AS = D = \begin{bmatrix} 1 & 0 & 0 \\ 0 & 1 & 0 \\ 0 & 0 & 2 \end{bmatrix}.$$ ■

Orthogonal Matrices

A remarkable and useful fact about symmetric matrices is that they are always diagonalizable. Moreover, the diagonalization of a symmetric matrix A can be accomplished with a special type of matrix known as an orthogonal matrix.

DEFINITION 9 A real $(n \times n)$ matrix Q is called an ***orthogonal*** matrix if Q is invertible and $Q^{-1} = Q^T$.

Definition 9 can be rephrased as follows: A real square matrix Q is orthogonal if and only if

$$Q^TQ = I. \tag{4}$$

Another useful description of orthogonal matrices can be obtained from Eq. (4). In particular, suppose that $Q = [\mathbf{q}_1, \mathbf{q}_2, \ldots, \mathbf{q}_n]$ is an $(n \times n)$ matrix. Since the ith row of Q^T is equal to $\mathbf{q}_i^T$, the definition of matrix multiplication tells us:

The ijth entry of Q^TQ is equal to $\mathbf{q}_i^T\mathbf{q}_j$.

Therefore, by Eq. (4), an $(n \times n)$ matrix $Q = [\mathbf{q}_1, \mathbf{q}_2, \ldots, \mathbf{q}_n]$ is orthogonal if and only if:

The columns of Q, $\{\mathbf{q}_1, \mathbf{q}_2, \ldots, \mathbf{q}_n\}$, form an orthonormal set of vectors. (5)

EXAMPLE 5 Verify that the matrices, Q_1 and Q_2 are orthogonal:

$$Q_1 = \frac{1}{\sqrt{2}}\begin{bmatrix} 1 & 0 & 1 \\ 0 & \sqrt{2} & 0 \\ -1 & 0 & 1 \end{bmatrix} \quad \text{and} \quad Q_2 = \begin{bmatrix} 0 & 0 & 1 \\ 1 & 0 & 0 \\ 0 & 1 & 0 \end{bmatrix}.$$

Solution We use Eq. (4) to show that Q_1 is orthogonal. Specifically,

$$Q_1^TQ_1 = \frac{1}{2}\begin{bmatrix} 1 & 0 & -1 \\ 0 & \sqrt{2} & 0 \\ 1 & 0 & 1 \end{bmatrix}\begin{bmatrix} 1 & 0 & 1 \\ 0 & \sqrt{2} & 0 \\ -1 & 0 & 1 \end{bmatrix} = \frac{1}{2}\begin{bmatrix} 2 & 0 & 0 \\ 0 & 2 & 0 \\ 0 & 0 & 2 \end{bmatrix} = I.$$

We use condition Eq. (5) to show that Q_2 is orthogonal. The column vectors of Q_2 are, in the order they appear, $\{\mathbf{e}_2, \mathbf{e}_3, \mathbf{e}_1\}$. Since these vectors are orthonormal, it follows from Eq. (5) that Q_2 is orthogonal. ■

From the characterization of orthogonal matrices given in condition Eq. (5), the following observation can be made: If $Q = [\mathbf{q}_1, \mathbf{q}_2, \ldots, \mathbf{q}_n]$ is an $(n \times n)$ orthogonal matrix and if $P = [\mathbf{p}_1, \mathbf{p}_2, \ldots, \mathbf{p}_n]$ is formed by rearranging the columns of Q, then P is also an orthogonal matrix.

As a special case of this observation, suppose that P is a matrix formed by rearranging the columns of the identity matrix, I. Then, since I is an orthogonal matrix, it follows that P is orthogonal as well. Such a matrix P, formed by rearranging the columns of I, is called a ***permutation*** matrix. The matrix Q_2 in Example 5 is a specific instance of a (3×3) permutation matrix.

Orthogonal matrices have some special properties that make them valuable tools for applications. These properties were mentioned in Section 3.7 with regard to (2×2) orthogonal matrices. Suppose we think of an $(n \times n)$ matrix Q as defining a function (or linear transformation) from R^n to R^n. That is, for $\mathbf{x}$ in R^n, consider the function defined by

$$\mathbf{y} = Q\mathbf{x}.$$

As the next theorem shows, if Q is orthogonal, then the function $\mathbf{y} = Q\mathbf{x}$ preserves the lengths of vectors and the angles between pairs of vectors.

THEOREM 21 Let Q be an $(n \times n)$ orthogonal matrix.

(a) If $\mathbf{x}$ is in R^n, then $\|Q\mathbf{x}\| = \|\mathbf{x}\|$.

(b) If $\mathbf{x}$ and $\mathbf{y}$ are in R^n, then $(Q\mathbf{x})^T(Q\mathbf{y}) = \mathbf{x}^T\mathbf{y}$.

(c) $\text{Det}(Q) = \pm 1$.

Proof We will prove property (a) and leave properties (b) and (c) to the exercises. Let $\mathbf{x}$ be a vector in R^n. Then

$$\|Q\mathbf{x}\| = \sqrt{(Q\mathbf{x})^T(Q\mathbf{x})} = \sqrt{\mathbf{x}^T Q^T Q\mathbf{x}} = \sqrt{\mathbf{x}^T I\mathbf{x}} = \sqrt{\mathbf{x}^T\mathbf{x}} = \|\mathbf{x}\|.$$

The fact that $\mathbf{x}^T(Q^TQ)\mathbf{x} = \mathbf{x}^T I\mathbf{x}$ comes from Eq. (4). ∎

Theorem 21 can be illustrated geometrically (see Figs. 4.4 and 4.5). In Fig. 4.4(a), a vector $\mathbf{x}$ in R^2 is shown, where $\|\mathbf{x}\| = 1$. The vector $Q\mathbf{x}$ is shown in Fig. 4.4(b), where, by Theorem 21, $Q\mathbf{x}$ also has length 1. In Fig. 4.5(a), vectors $\mathbf{x}$ and $\mathbf{y}$ are shown, where $\|\mathbf{x}\| = 1$ and $\|\mathbf{y}\| = 2$. From vector geometry, we know that the angle θ between $\mathbf{x}$ and $\mathbf{y}$ satisfies the condition

$$\mathbf{x}^T\mathbf{y} = \|\mathbf{x}\|\|\mathbf{y}\|\cos\theta, \quad 0 \le \theta \le \pi. \tag{6}$$

In Fig. 4.5(b), the vectors $Q\mathbf{x}$ and $Q\mathbf{y}$ are shown, where the angle between $Q\mathbf{x}$ and $Q\mathbf{y}$ is also equal to θ. To establish that the angle between $\mathbf{x}$ and $\mathbf{y}$ is equal to the angle between $Q\mathbf{x}$ and $Q\mathbf{y}$, we can argue as follows: Let γ denote the angle between $Q\mathbf{x}$ and $Q\mathbf{y}$, where $0 \le \gamma \le \pi$. As in Eq. (6), the angle γ satisfies the condition

$$(Q\mathbf{x})^T(Q\mathbf{y}) = \|Q\mathbf{x}\|\|Q\mathbf{y}\|\cos\gamma, \quad 0 \le \gamma \le \pi. \tag{7}$$

By Theorem 21, $(Q\mathbf{x})^T(Q\mathbf{y}) = \mathbf{x}^T\mathbf{y}$ and $\|Q\mathbf{x}\|\|Q\mathbf{y}\| = \|\mathbf{x}\|\|\mathbf{y}\|$. Thus, from Eq. (6) and Eq. (7), $\cos\theta = \cos\gamma$. Since the cosine function is one-to-one on $[0, \pi]$, the condition $\cos\theta = \cos\gamma$ implies that $\theta = \gamma$.

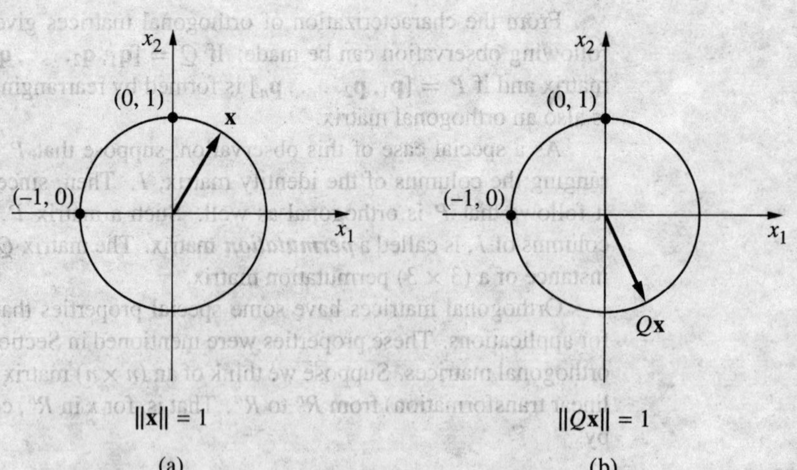

Figure 4.4 The length of $\mathbf{x}$ is equal to the length of $Q\mathbf{x}$

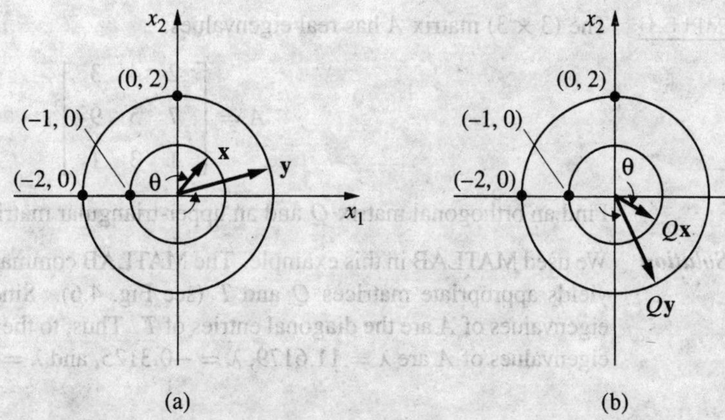

Figure 4.5 The angle between **x** and **y** is equal to the angle between $Q\mathbf{x}$ and $Q\mathbf{y}$.

Diagonalization of Symmetric Matrices

We conclude this section by showing that every symmetric matrix can be diagonalized by an orthogonal matrix. Several approaches can be used to establish this diagonalization result. We choose to demonstrate it by first stating a special case of a theorem known as Schur's theorem.

THEOREM 22 Let A be an $(n \times n)$ matrix, where A has only real eigenvalues. Then there is an $(n \times n)$ orthogonal matrix Q such that

$$Q^T A Q = T,$$

where T is an $(n \times n)$ upper-triangular matrix.

We leave the proof of Theorem 22 as a series of somewhat challenging exercises. It is important to observe that the triangular matrix T in Theorem 22 is similar to A. That is, since $Q^{-1} = Q^T$, it follows that $Q^T A Q$ is a similarity transformation.

Schur's theorem (of which Theorem 22 is a special case) states that any $(n \times n)$ matrix A is unitarily similar to a triangular matrix T. The definition of a unitary matrix is given in the exercises of the previous section.

Linear algebra software can be used to find matrices Q and T that satisfy the conclusions of Schur's theorem: $Q^T A Q = T$. Note that we can rewrite $Q^T A Q = T$ as

$$A = Q T Q^T.$$

The decomposition $A = QTQ^T$ is called a ***Schur decomposition*** or a ***Schur factorization*** of A.

EXAMPLE 6 The (3×3) matrix A has real eigenvalues:

$$A = \begin{bmatrix} 2 & 4 & 3 \\ 7 & 5 & 9 \\ 1 & 3 & 1 \end{bmatrix}.$$

Find an orthogonal matrix Q and an upper-triangular matrix T such that $Q^T A Q = T$.

Solution We used MATLAB in this example. The MATLAB command `[Q, T] = schur(A)` yields appropriate matrices Q and T (see Fig. 4.6). Since A and T are similar, the eigenvalues of A are the diagonal entries of T. Thus, to the places shown in Fig. 4.6, the eigenvalues of A are $\lambda = 11.6179$, $\lambda = -0.3125$, and $\lambda = -3.3055$. ■

```
A=

     2     4     3
     7     5     9
     1     3     1

>>[Q,T]=schur(A)

Q=
   -0.4421    0.7193   -0.5359
   -0.8514   -0.1486    0.5030
   -0.2822   -0.6786   -0.6781

T=
   11.6179    2.1869    6.6488
         0   -0.3125    0.1033
         0         0   -3.3055
```

Figure 4.6 MATLAB was used in Example 6 to find matrices Q and T such that $Q^T A Q = T$.

With Theorem 22, it is a simple matter to show that any real symmetric matrix can be diagonalized by an orthogonal matrix. In fact, as the next theorem states, a matrix is orthogonally diagonalizable if and only if the matrix is symmetric. We will use this result in Section 7.1 when we discuss diagonalizing quadratic forms.

THEOREM 23 Let A be a real $(n \times n)$ matrix.

(a) If A is symmetric, then there is an orthogonal matrix Q such that $Q^T A Q = D$, where D is diagonal.

(b) If $Q^T A Q = D$, where Q is orthogonal and D is diagonal, then A is a symmetric matrix.

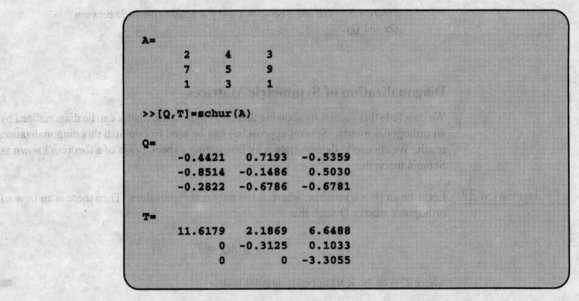

Proof To prove property (a), suppose A is symmetric. Recall, by Theorem 17, that A has only real eigenvalues. Thus, by Theorem 22, there is an orthogonal matrix Q such that $Q^TAQ = M$, where M is an upper-triangular matrix. Using the transpose operation on the equality $M = Q^TAQ$ and also using the fact that $A^T = A$, we obtain

$$M^T = (Q^TAQ)^T = Q^TA^TQ = Q^TAQ = M.$$

Thus, since M is upper triangular and $M^T = M$, it follows that M is a diagonal matrix.

To prove property (b), suppose that $Q^TAQ = D$, where Q is orthogonal and D is diagonal. Since D is diagonal, we know that $D^T = D$. Thus, using the transpose operation on the equality $Q^TAQ = D$, we obtain

$$Q^TAQ = D = D^T = (Q^TAQ)^T = Q^TA^TQ.$$

From this result, we see that $Q^TAQ = Q^TA^TQ$. Multiplying by Q and Q^T, we obtain

$$\begin{aligned} Q(Q^TAQ)Q^T &= Q(Q^TA^TQ)Q^T \\ (QQ^T)A(QQ^T) &= (QQ^T)A^T(QQ^T) \\ A &= A^T. \end{aligned}$$

Thus, since $A = A^T$, matrix A is symmetric. ∎

Theorem 23 states that every real symmetric matrix A is orthogonally diagonalizable; that is, $Q^TAQ = D$, where Q is orthogonal and D is diagonal. From the proof of Theorem 19 (also, see Examples 1, 3, and 4), the eigenvalues of A are the diagonal entries of D, and eigenvectors of A can be chosen as the columns of Q. Since the columns of Q form an orthonormal set, the following result is a corollary of Theorem 23.

COROLLARY Let A be a real $(n \times n)$ symmetric matrix. It is possible to choose eigenvectors $\mathbf{u}_1, \mathbf{u}_2, \ldots, \mathbf{u}_n$ for A such that $\{\mathbf{u}_1, \mathbf{u}_2, \ldots, \mathbf{u}_n\}$ is an orthonormal basis for R^n. ∎

The corollary is illustrated in the next example. Before presenting the example, we note the following fact, which is established in Exercise 43:

If $\mathbf{u}$ and $\mathbf{v}$ are eigenvectors of a symmetric matrix and if $\mathbf{u}$ and $\mathbf{v}$ belong to different eigenspaces, then $\mathbf{u}^T\mathbf{v} = 0$. (8)

Note that if A is not symmetric, then eigenvectors corresponding to different eigenvalues are not generally orthogonal.

EXAMPLE 7 Find an orthonormal basis for R^4 consisting of eigenvectors of the matrix

$$A = \begin{bmatrix} 1 & -1 & -1 & -1 \\ -1 & 1 & -1 & -1 \\ -1 & -1 & 1 & -1 \\ -1 & -1 & -1 & 1 \end{bmatrix}.$$

Solution Matrix A is a special case of the Rodman matrix (see Exercise 42). The characteristic polynomial for A is given by

$$p(t) = \det(A - tI) = (t-2)^3(t+2).$$

Thus the eigenvalues of A are $\lambda_1 = \lambda_2 = \lambda_3 = 2$ and $\lambda_4 = -2$.

It is easy to verify that corresponding eigenvectors are given by

$$\mathbf{w}_1 = \begin{bmatrix} 1 \\ -1 \\ 0 \\ 0 \end{bmatrix}, \quad \mathbf{w}_2 = \begin{bmatrix} 1 \\ 0 \\ -1 \\ 0 \end{bmatrix}, \quad \mathbf{w}_3 = \begin{bmatrix} 1 \\ 0 \\ 0 \\ -1 \end{bmatrix}, \quad \text{and} \quad \mathbf{w}_4 = \begin{bmatrix} 1 \\ 1 \\ 1 \\ 1 \end{bmatrix}.$$

Note that $\mathbf{w}_1$, $\mathbf{w}_2$, and $\mathbf{w}_3$ belong to the eigenspace associated with $\lambda = 2$, whereas $\mathbf{w}_4$ is in the eigenspace associated with $\lambda = -2$. As is promised by condition (8), $\mathbf{w}_1^T\mathbf{w}_4 = \mathbf{w}_2^T\mathbf{w}_4 = \mathbf{w}_3^T\mathbf{w}_4 = 0$. Also note that the matrix S defined by $S = [\mathbf{w}_1, \mathbf{w}_2, \mathbf{w}_3, \mathbf{w}_4]$ will diagonalize A. However, S is not an orthogonal matrix.

To obtain an orthonormal basis for R^4 (and hence an orthogonal matrix Q that diagonalizes A), we first find an orthogonal basis for the eigenspace associated with $\lambda = 2$. Applying the Gram–Schmidt process to the set $\{\mathbf{w}_1, \mathbf{w}_2, \mathbf{w}_3\}$, we produce orthogonal vectors

$$\mathbf{x}_1 = \begin{bmatrix} 1 \\ -1 \\ 0 \\ 0 \end{bmatrix}, \quad \mathbf{x}_2 = \begin{bmatrix} 1/2 \\ 1/2 \\ -1 \\ 0 \end{bmatrix}, \quad \text{and} \quad \mathbf{x}_3 = \begin{bmatrix} 1/3 \\ 1/3 \\ 1/3 \\ -1 \end{bmatrix}.$$

Thus the set $\{\mathbf{x}_1, \mathbf{x}_2, \mathbf{x}_3, \mathbf{w}_4\}$ is an orthogonal basis for R^4 consisting of eigenvectors of A. This set can then be normalized to determine an orthonormal basis for R^4 and an orthogonal matrix Q that diagonalizes A. ■

We conclude by mentioning a result that is useful in applications. Let A be an $(n \times n)$ symmetric matrix with eigenvalues $\lambda_1, \lambda_2, \ldots, \lambda_n$. Let $\mathbf{u}_1, \mathbf{u}_2, \ldots, \mathbf{u}_n$ be a corresponding set of orthonormal eigenvectors, where $A\mathbf{u}_i = \lambda_i\mathbf{u}_i$, $1 \le i \le n$. Matrix A can be expressed in the form

$$A = \lambda_1\mathbf{u}_1\mathbf{u}_1^T + \lambda_2\mathbf{u}_2\mathbf{u}_2^T + \cdots + \lambda_n\mathbf{u}_n\mathbf{u}_n^T. \tag{9}$$

In Eq. (9), each $(n \times n)$ matrix $\mathbf{u}_i\mathbf{u}_i^T$ is a rank-one matrix. Expression (9) is called a ***spectral decomposition for A***. A proof for Eq. (9) can be constructed along the lines of Exercise 29 of Section 4.5.

4.7 EXERCISES

In Exercises 1–12, determine whether the given matrix A is diagonalizable. If A is diagonalizable, calculate A^5 using the method of Example 2.

1. $A = \begin{bmatrix} 2 & -1 \\ -1 & 2 \end{bmatrix}$

2. $A = \begin{bmatrix} 1 & -1 \\ -1 & 1 \end{bmatrix}$

3. $A = \begin{bmatrix} -3 & 2 \\ -2 & 1 \end{bmatrix}$ 4. $A = \begin{bmatrix} 1 & 3 \\ 0 & 1 \end{bmatrix}$

5. $A = \begin{bmatrix} 1 & 0 \\ 10 & 2 \end{bmatrix}$ 6. $A = \begin{bmatrix} -1 & 7 \\ 0 & 1 \end{bmatrix}$

7. $A = \begin{bmatrix} 3 & -2 & -4 \\ 8 & -7 & -16 \\ -3 & 3 & 7 \end{bmatrix}$

8. $A = \begin{bmatrix} -1 & -1 & -4 \\ -8 & -3 & -16 \\ 1 & 2 & 7 \end{bmatrix}$

9. $A = \begin{bmatrix} 3 & -1 & -1 \\ -12 & 0 & 5 \\ 4 & -2 & -1 \end{bmatrix}$

10. $A = \begin{bmatrix} 1 & 1 & -1 \\ 0 & 2 & -1 \\ 0 & 0 & 1 \end{bmatrix}$ 11. $A = \begin{bmatrix} 1 & 1 & -2 \\ 0 & 2 & -1 \\ 0 & 0 & 1 \end{bmatrix}$

12. $A = \begin{bmatrix} 1 & 3 & 3 \\ 0 & 5 & 4 \\ 0 & 0 & 1 \end{bmatrix}$

In Exercises 13–18, use condition (5) to determine whether the given matrix Q is orthogonal.

13. $Q = \begin{bmatrix} 0 & 1 \\ 1 & 0 \end{bmatrix}$ 14. $Q = \frac{1}{\sqrt{5}}\begin{bmatrix} 1 & -2 \\ 2 & 1 \end{bmatrix}$

15. $Q = \begin{bmatrix} 2 & -1 \\ 1 & 2 \end{bmatrix}$ 16. $Q = \begin{bmatrix} 3 & 2 \\ -2 & 3 \end{bmatrix}$

17. $Q = \frac{1}{\sqrt{6}}\begin{bmatrix} \sqrt{3} & 1 & \sqrt{2} \\ 0 & -2 & \sqrt{2} \\ -\sqrt{3} & 1 & \sqrt{2} \end{bmatrix}$

18. $Q = \begin{bmatrix} 1 & 1 & -4 \\ 2 & -2 & 1 \\ 1 & 3 & 2 \end{bmatrix}$

In Exercises 19 and 20, find values α, β, a, b, and c such that matrix Q is orthogonal. Choose positive values for α and β. [*Hint:* Use condition (5) to determine the values.]

19. $Q = \begin{bmatrix} \alpha & \beta & a \\ 0 & 2\beta & b \\ \alpha & -\beta & c \end{bmatrix}$ 20. $Q = \begin{bmatrix} \alpha & -\beta & a \\ \alpha & 3\beta & b \\ \alpha & -2\beta & c \end{bmatrix}$

In Exercises 21–24, use linear algebra software to find an orthogonal matrix Q and an upper-triangular matrix T such that $Q^TAQ = T$. [*Note:* In each exercise, the matrix A has only real eigenvalues.]

21. $\begin{bmatrix} 1 & 0 & 1 \\ 3 & 3 & 5 \\ 2 & 6 & 2 \end{bmatrix}$ 22. $\begin{bmatrix} 3 & 0 & 7 \\ 9 & -6 & 4 \\ 1 & 1 & 4 \end{bmatrix}$

23. $\begin{bmatrix} 4 & 5 & 2 & 8 \\ 0 & 6 & 7 & 5 \\ 2 & 4 & 5 & 3 \\ 9 & 7 & 3 & 6 \end{bmatrix}$ 24. $\begin{bmatrix} 4 & 7 & 3 & 5 \\ 8 & 5 & 7 & 8 \\ 2 & 4 & 3 & 5 \\ 0 & 5 & 7 & 4 \end{bmatrix}$

25. Let A be an $(n \times n)$ matrix, and let S be a nonsingular $(n \times n)$ matrix.
   a) Verify that $(S^{-1}AS)^2 = S^{-1}A^2S$ and that $(S^{-1}AS)^3 = S^{-1}A^3S$.
   b) Prove by induction that $(S^{-1}AS)^k = S^{-1}A^kS$ for any positive integer k.

26. Show that if A is diagonalizable and if B is similar to A, then B is diagonalizable. [*Hint:* Suppose that $S^{-1}AS = D$ and $W^{-1}AW = B$.]

27. Suppose that B is similar to A. Show each of the following.
   a) $B + \alpha I$ is similar to $A + \alpha I$.
   b) B^T is similar to A^T.
   c) If A is nonsingular, then B is nonsingular and, moreover, B^{-1} is similar to A^{-1}.

28. Prove properties (b) and (c) of Theorem 21. [*Hint:* For property (c), use the fact that $Q^TQ = I$.]

29. Let $\mathbf{u}$ be a vector in R^n such that $\mathbf{u}^T\mathbf{u} = 1$. Let $Q = I - 2\mathbf{u}\mathbf{u}^T$. Show that Q is an orthogonal matrix. Also, calculate the vector $Q\mathbf{u}$. Is $\mathbf{u}$ an eigenvector for Q?

30. Suppose that A and B are orthogonal $(n \times n)$ matrices. Show that AB is an orthogonal matrix.

31. Let $\mathbf{x}$ be a nonzero vector in R^2, $\mathbf{x} = [a, b]^T$. Find a vector $\mathbf{y}$ in R^2 such that $\mathbf{x}^T\mathbf{y} = 0$ and $\mathbf{y}^T\mathbf{y} = 1$.

32. Let A be a real (2×2) matrix with only real eigenvalues. Suppose that $A\mathbf{u} = \lambda\mathbf{u}$, where $\mathbf{u}^T\mathbf{u} = 1$. By Exercise 31, there is a vector $\mathbf{v}$ in R^2 such that

$\mathbf{u}^T\mathbf{v} = 0$ and $\mathbf{v}^T\mathbf{v} = 1$. Let Q be the (2×2) matrix given by $Q = [\mathbf{u}, \mathbf{v}]$, and note that Q is an orthogonal matrix. Verify that

$$Q^TAQ = \begin{bmatrix} \lambda & \mathbf{u}^TA\mathbf{v} \\ 0 & \mathbf{v}^TA\mathbf{v} \end{bmatrix}.$$

(Thus Theorem 22 is proved for a (2×2) matrix A.)

In Exercises 33–36, use the procedure outlined in Exercise 32 to find an orthogonal matrix Q such that $Q^TAQ = T$, T upper triangular.

33. $A = \begin{bmatrix} 1 & -1 \\ 1 & 3 \end{bmatrix}$ **34.** $A = \begin{bmatrix} 5 & -2 \\ 6 & -2 \end{bmatrix}$

35. $A = \begin{bmatrix} 2 & -1 \\ -1 & 2 \end{bmatrix}$ **36.** $A = \begin{bmatrix} 2 & 2 \\ 3 & 3 \end{bmatrix}$

37. Let A and R be $(n \times n)$ matrices. Show that the ijth entry of R^TAR is given by $\mathbf{R}_i^T A\mathbf{R}_j$, where $R = [\mathbf{R}_1, \mathbf{R}_2, \ldots, \mathbf{R}_n]$.

38. Let A be a real (3×3) matrix with only real eigenvalues. Suppose that $A\mathbf{u} = \lambda\mathbf{u}$, where $\mathbf{u}^T\mathbf{u} = 1$. By the Gram–Schmidt process, there are vectors $\mathbf{v}$ and $\mathbf{w}$ in R^3 such that $\{\mathbf{u}, \mathbf{v}, \mathbf{w}\}$ is an orthonormal set. Consider the orthogonal matrix Q given by $Q = [\mathbf{u}, \mathbf{v}, \mathbf{w}]$. Verify that

$$Q^TAQ = \begin{bmatrix} \lambda & \mathbf{u}^TA\mathbf{v} & \mathbf{u}^TA\mathbf{w} \\ 0 & \mathbf{v}^TA\mathbf{v} & \mathbf{v}^TA\mathbf{w} \\ 0 & \mathbf{w}^TA\mathbf{v} & \mathbf{w}^TA\mathbf{w} \end{bmatrix}$$

$$= \left[\begin{array}{c|cc} \lambda & \mathbf{u}^TA\mathbf{v} & \mathbf{u}^TA\mathbf{w} \\ \hline 0 & \multicolumn{2}{c}{\multirow{2}{*}{A_1}} \\ 0 & & \end{array}\right].$$

39. Let $B = Q^TAQ$, where Q and A are as in Exercise 38. Consider the (2×2) submatrix of B given by A_1 in Exercise 38. Show that the eigenvalues of A_1 are real. [*Hint:* Calculate $\det(B - tI)$, and show that every eigenvalue of A_1 is an eigenvalue of B. Then make a statement showing that all the eigenvalues of B are real.]

40. Let $B = Q^TAQ$, where Q and A are as in Exercise 38. By Exercises 32 and 39, there is a (2×2) matrix S such that $S^TS = I$, $S^TA_1S = T_1$, where T_1 is upper triangular. Form the (3×3) matrix R:

$$R = \left[\begin{array}{c|cc} 1 & 0 & 0 \\ \hline 0 & \multicolumn{2}{c}{\multirow{2}{*}{S}} \\ 0 & & \end{array}\right].$$

Verify each of the following.

a) $R^TR = I$.

b) R^TQ^TAQR is an upper-triangular matrix.

(Note that this exercise verifies Theorem 22 for a (3×3) matrix A.)

41. Following the outline of Exercises 38–40, use induction to prove Theorem 22.

42. Consider the $(n \times n)$ symmetric matrix $A = (a_{ij})$ defined as follows:

a) $a_{ii} = 1, 1 \le i \le n$;

b) $a_{ij} = -1, i \ne j, 1 \le i, j \le n$.

(A (4×4) version of this matrix is given in Example 7.) Verify that the eigenvalues of A are $\lambda = 2$ (geometric multiplicity $n - 1$) and $\lambda = 2 - n$ (geometric multiplicity 1). [*Hint:* Show that the following are eigenvectors: $\mathbf{u}_i = \mathbf{e}_1 - \mathbf{e}_i$, $2 \le i \le n$ and $\mathbf{u}_1 = [1, 1, \ldots, 1]^T$.]

43. Suppose that A is a real symmetric matrix and that $A\mathbf{u} = \lambda\mathbf{u}$, $A\mathbf{v} = \beta\mathbf{v}$, where $\lambda \ne \beta$, $\mathbf{u} \ne \boldsymbol{\theta}$, and $\mathbf{v} \ne \boldsymbol{\theta}$. Show that $\mathbf{u}^T\mathbf{v} = 0$. [*Hint:* Consider $\mathbf{u}^TA\mathbf{v}$.]

4.8 DIFFERENCE EQUATIONS; MARKOV CHAINS; SYSTEMS OF DIFFERENTIAL EQUATIONS (OPTIONAL)

In this section we examine how eigenvalues can be used to solve difference equations and systems of differential equations. In Chapter 7, we treat other applications of eigenvalues and also return to a deeper study of systems of differential equations.

Let A be an $(n \times n)$ matrix, and let $\mathbf{x}_0$ be a vector in R^n. Consider the sequence of vectors $\{\mathbf{x}_k\}$ defined by

$$\begin{aligned}\mathbf{x}_1 &= A\mathbf{x}_0\\ \mathbf{x}_2 &= A\mathbf{x}_1\\ \mathbf{x}_3 &= A\mathbf{x}_2\\ &\vdots\end{aligned}$$

In general, this sequence is given by

$$\mathbf{x}_k = A\mathbf{x}_{k-1}, \quad k = 1, 2, \ldots. \tag{1}$$

Vector sequences that are generated as in Eq. (1) occur in a variety of applications and serve as mathematical models to describe population growth, ecological systems, radar tracking of airborne objects, digital control of chemical processes, and the like. One of the objectives in such models is to describe the behavior of the sequence $\{\mathbf{x}_k\}$ in qualitative or quantitative terms. In this section we see that the behavior of the sequence $\{\mathbf{x}_k\}$ can be analyzed from the eigenvalues of A.

The following simple example illustrates a typical sequence of the form (1).

EXAMPLE 1 Let $\mathbf{x}_k = A\mathbf{x}_{k-1}$, $k = 1, 2, \ldots$. Calculate $\mathbf{x}_1$, $\mathbf{x}_2$, $\mathbf{x}_3$, $\mathbf{x}_4$, and $\mathbf{x}_5$, where

$$A = \begin{bmatrix} .8 & .2\\ .2 & .8 \end{bmatrix} \quad \text{and} \quad \mathbf{x}_0 = \begin{bmatrix} 1\\ 2 \end{bmatrix}.$$

Solution Some routine but tedious calculations show that

$$\mathbf{x}_1 = A\mathbf{x}_0 = \begin{bmatrix} 1.2\\ 1.8 \end{bmatrix}, \quad \mathbf{x}_2 = A\mathbf{x}_1 = \begin{bmatrix} 1.32\\ 1.68 \end{bmatrix}, \quad \mathbf{x}_3 = A\mathbf{x}_2 = \begin{bmatrix} 1.392\\ 1.608 \end{bmatrix}$$

$$\mathbf{x}_4 = A\mathbf{x}_3 = \begin{bmatrix} 1.4352\\ 1.5648 \end{bmatrix}, \quad \text{and} \quad \mathbf{x}_5 = A\mathbf{x}_4 = \begin{bmatrix} 1.46112\\ 1.53888 \end{bmatrix}.$$

In Example 1, the first six terms of a vector sequence $\{\mathbf{x}_k\}$ are listed. An inspection of these first few terms suggests that the sequence might have some regular pattern of behavior. For instance, the first components of these vectors are steadily increasing, whereas the second components are steadily decreasing. In fact, as shown in Example 3, this monotonic behavior persists for all terms of the sequence $\{\mathbf{x}_k\}$. Moreover, it can be shown that

$$\lim_{k\to\infty} \mathbf{x}_k = \mathbf{x}^*,$$

where the limit vector $\mathbf{x}^*$ is given by

$$\mathbf{x}^* = \begin{bmatrix} 1.5\\ 1.5 \end{bmatrix}.$$

Difference Equations

Let A be an $(n \times n)$ matrix. The equation

$$\mathbf{x}_k = A\mathbf{x}_{k-1} \tag{2}$$

is called a ***difference equation***. A ***solution*** to the difference equation is any sequence of vectors $\{\mathbf{x}_k\}$ that satisfies Eq. (2). That is, a solution is a sequence $\{\mathbf{x}_k\}$ whose successive terms are related by $\mathbf{x}_1 = A\mathbf{x}_0$, $\mathbf{x}_2 = A\mathbf{x}_1, \ldots, \mathbf{x}_k = A\mathbf{x}_{k-1}, \ldots$. (Equation 2 is not the most general form of a difference equation.)

The basic challenge posed by a difference equation is to describe the behavior of the sequence $\{\mathbf{x}_k\}$. Some specific questions are:

1. For a given starting vector $\mathbf{x}_0$, is there a vector $\mathbf{x}^*$ such that

$$\lim_{k \to \infty} \mathbf{x}_k = \mathbf{x}^*?$$

2. If the sequence $\{\mathbf{x}_k\}$ does have a limit, $\mathbf{x}^*$, what is the limit vector?

3. Find a "formula" that can be used to calculate $\mathbf{x}_k$ in terms of the starting vector $\mathbf{x}_0$.

4. Given a vector $\mathbf{b}$ and an integer k, determine $\mathbf{x}_0$ so that $\mathbf{x}_k = \mathbf{b}$.

5. Given a vector $\mathbf{b}$, characterize the set of starting vectors $\mathbf{x}_0$ for which $\{\mathbf{x}_k\} \to \mathbf{b}$.

Unlike many equations, the Difference Eq. in (2) does not raise any interesting questions concerning the existence or uniqueness of solutions. For a given starting vector $\mathbf{x}_0$, we see that a solution to Eq. (2) always exists because it can be constructed. For instance, in Example 1 we found the first six terms of the solution to the given difference equation. In terms of uniqueness, suppose $\mathbf{x}_0$ is a given starting vector. It can be shown (see Exercise 21) that if $\{\mathbf{w}_k\}$ is any sequence satisfying Eq. (2) and if $\mathbf{w}_0 = \mathbf{x}_0$, then $\mathbf{w}_k = \mathbf{x}_k$, $k = 1, 2, \ldots$.

The next example shows how a difference equation might serve as a mathematical model for a physical process. The model is kept very simple so that the details do not obscure the ideas. Thus the example should be considered illustrative rather than realistic.

EXAMPLE 2 Suppose that animals are being raised for market, and the grower wishes to determine how the annual rate of harvesting animals will affect the yearly size of the herd.

Solution To begin, let $x_1(k)$ and $x_2(k)$ be the state variables that measure the size of the herd in the kth year of operation, where

$$x_1(k) = \text{number of animals less than one year old at year } k$$
$$x_2(k) = \text{number of animals more than one year old at year } k.$$

We assume that animals less than one year old do not reproduce, and that animals more than one year old have a reproduction rate of b per year. Thus if the herd has $x_2(k)$ mature animals at year k, we expect to have $x_1(k+1)$ young animals at year $k+1$, where

$$x_1(k+1) = bx_2(k).$$

Next we assume that the young animals have a death rate of d_1 per year, and the mature animals have a death rate of d_2 per year. Furthermore, we assume that the mature animals are harvested at a rate of h per year and that young animals are not harvested. Thus we expect to have $x_2(k+1)$ mature animals at year $k+1$, where

$$x_2(k+1) = x_1(k) + x_2(k) - d_1x_1(k) - d_2x_2(k) - hx_2(k).$$

This equation reflects the following facts: An animal that is young at year k will mature by year $k+1$; an animal that is mature at year k is still mature at year $k+1$; a certain percentage of young and mature animals will die during the year; and a certain percentage of mature animals will be harvested during the year. Collecting like terms in the second equation and combining the two equations, we obtain the state equations for the herd:

$$\begin{aligned} x_1(k+1) &= bx_2(k) \\ x_2(k+1) &= (1-d_1)x_1(k) + (1-d_2-h)x_2(k). \end{aligned} \tag{3}$$

The state equations give the size and composition of the herd at year $k+1$ in terms of the size and composition of the herd at year k. For example, if we know the initial composition of the herd at year zero, $x_1(0)$ and $x_2(0)$, we can use (3) to calculate the composition of the herd after one year, $x_1(1)$ and $x_2(1)$.

In matrix form, (3) becomes

$$\mathbf{x}(k) = A\mathbf{x}(k-1), \quad k = 1, 2, 3, \ldots,$$

where

$$\mathbf{x}(k) = \begin{bmatrix} x_1(k) \\ x_2(k) \end{bmatrix} \quad \text{and} \quad A = \begin{bmatrix} 0 & b \\ (1-d_1) & (1-d_2-h) \end{bmatrix}.$$

In the context of this example, the growth and composition of the herd are governed by the eigenvalues of A, and these can be controlled by varying the parameter h. ■

Solving Difference Equations

Consider the difference equation

$$\mathbf{x}_k = A\mathbf{x}_{k-1}, \tag{4}$$

where A is an $(n \times n)$ matrix. The key to finding a useful form for solutions of Eq. (4) is to observe that the sequence $\{\mathbf{x}_k\}$ can be calculated by multiplying powers of A by the starting vector $\mathbf{x}_0$. That is,

$$\begin{aligned} \mathbf{x}_1 &= A\mathbf{x}_0 \\ \mathbf{x}_2 &= A\mathbf{x}_1 = A(A\mathbf{x}_0) = A^2\mathbf{x}_0 \\ \mathbf{x}_3 &= A\mathbf{x}_2 = A(A^2\mathbf{x}_0) = A^3\mathbf{x}_0 \\ \mathbf{x}_4 &= A\mathbf{x}_3 = A(A^3\mathbf{x}_0) = A^4\mathbf{x}_0, \end{aligned}$$

and, in general,

$$\mathbf{x}_k = A^k\mathbf{x}_0, \quad k = 1, 2, \ldots. \tag{5}$$

Next, let A have eigenvalues $\lambda_1, \lambda_2, \ldots, \lambda_n$ and corresponding eigenvectors $\mathbf{u}_1$, $\mathbf{u}_2$, $\ldots$, $\mathbf{u}_n$. We now make a critical assumption: Let us suppose that matrix A is not defective. That is, let us suppose that the set of eigenvectors $\{\mathbf{u}_1, \mathbf{u}_2, \ldots, \mathbf{u}_n\}$ is linearly independent.

With the assumption that A is not defective, we can use the set of eigenvectors as a basis for R^n. In particular, any starting vector $\mathbf{x}_0$ can be expressed as a linear combination of the eigenvectors:

$$\mathbf{x}_0 = a_1\mathbf{u}_1 + a_2\mathbf{u}_2 + \cdots + a_n\mathbf{u}_n.$$

Then, using Eq. (5), we can obtain the following expression for $\mathbf{x}_k$:

$$\begin{aligned}\mathbf{x}_k &= A^k\mathbf{x}_0 \\ &= A^k(a_1\mathbf{u}_1 + a_2\mathbf{u}_2 + \cdots + a_n\mathbf{u}_n) \\ &= a_1A^k\mathbf{u}_1 + a_2A^k\mathbf{u}_2 + \cdots + a_nA^k\mathbf{u}_n \\ &= a_1(\lambda_1)^k\mathbf{u}_1 + a_2(\lambda_2)^k\mathbf{u}_2 + \cdots + a_n(\lambda_n)^k\mathbf{u}_n.\end{aligned} \tag{6}$$

(This last equality comes from Theorem 11 of Section 4.4: If $A\mathbf{u} = \lambda\mathbf{u}$, then $A^k\mathbf{u} = \lambda^k\mathbf{u}$.)

Note that if A does not have a set of n linearly independent eigenvectors, then the expression for $\mathbf{x}_k$ in Eq. (6) must be modified. The modification depends on the idea of a generalized eigenvector. It can be shown (see Section 7.8) that we can always choose a basis for R^n consisting of eigenvectors and generalized eigenvectors of A.

EXAMPLE 3 Use Eq. (6) to find an expression for $\mathbf{x}_k$, where $\mathbf{x}_k$ is the kth term of the sequence in Example 1. Use your expression to calculate $\mathbf{x}_k$ for $k = 10$ and $k = 20$. Determine whether the sequence $\{\mathbf{x}_k\}$ converges.

Solution The sequence $\{\mathbf{x}_k\}$ in Example 1 is generated by $\mathbf{x}_k = A\mathbf{x}_{k-1}$, $k = 1, 2, \ldots$, where

$$A = \begin{bmatrix} .8 & .2 \\ .2 & .8 \end{bmatrix} \quad\text{and}\quad \mathbf{x}_0 = \begin{bmatrix} 1 \\ 2 \end{bmatrix}.$$

Now the characteristic polynomial for A is

$$p(t) = t^2 - 1.6t + 0.6 = (t - 1)(t - 0.6).$$

Therefore, the eigenvalues of A are $\lambda_1 = 1$ and $\lambda_2 = 0.6$. Corresponding eigenvectors are

$$\mathbf{u}_1 = \begin{bmatrix} 1 \\ 1 \end{bmatrix} \quad\text{and}\quad \mathbf{u}_2 = \begin{bmatrix} 1 \\ -1 \end{bmatrix}.$$

The starting vector $\mathbf{x}_0$ can be expressed in terms of the eigenvectors as $\mathbf{x}_0 = 1.5\mathbf{u}_1 - 0.5\mathbf{u}_2$:

$$\mathbf{x}_0 = \begin{bmatrix} 1 \\ 2 \end{bmatrix} = 1.5\begin{bmatrix} 1 \\ 1 \end{bmatrix} - 0.5\begin{bmatrix} 1 \\ -1 \end{bmatrix}.$$

Therefore, the terms of the sequence $\{\mathbf{x}_k\}$ are given by

$$\begin{aligned}\mathbf{x}_k = A^k\mathbf{x}_0 &= A^k(1.5\mathbf{u}_1 - 0.5\mathbf{u}_2) \\ &= 1.5A^k\mathbf{u}_1 - 0.5A^k\mathbf{u}_2 \\ &= 1.5(1)^k\mathbf{u}_1 - 0.5(0.6)^k\mathbf{u}_2 \\ &= 1.5\mathbf{u}_1 - 0.5(0.6)^k\mathbf{u}_2.\end{aligned}$$

In detail, the components of $\mathbf{x}_k$ are

$$\mathbf{x}_k = \begin{bmatrix} 1.5 - 0.5(0.6)^k \\ 1.5 + 0.5(0.6)^k \end{bmatrix}, \quad k = 0, 1, 2, \ldots. \tag{7}$$

For $k = 10$ and $k = 20$, we calculate $\mathbf{x}_k$ from Eq. (7), finding

$$\mathbf{x}_{10} = \begin{bmatrix} 1.496976\ldots \\ 1.503023\ldots \end{bmatrix} \text{ and } \mathbf{x}_{20} = \begin{bmatrix} 1.499981\ldots \\ 1.500018\ldots \end{bmatrix}.$$

Finally, since $\lim_{k\to\infty}(0.6)^k = 0$, we see from Eq. (7) that

$$\lim_{k\to\infty} \mathbf{x}_k = \mathbf{x}^* = \begin{bmatrix} 1.5 \\ 1.5 \end{bmatrix}$$

Types of Solutions to Difference Equations

If we reflect about the results of Example 3, the following observations emerge: Suppose a sequence $\{\mathbf{x}_k\}$ is generated by $\mathbf{x}_k = A\mathbf{x}_{k-1}$, $k = 1, 2, \ldots$, where A is the (2×2) matrix

$$A = \begin{bmatrix} .8 & .2 \\ .2 & .8 \end{bmatrix}.$$

Then, no matter what starting vector $\mathbf{x}_0$ is selected, the sequence $\{\mathbf{x}_k\}$ will either converge to the zero vector, or the sequence will converge to a multiple of $\mathbf{u}_1 = [1, 1]^T$.

To verify this observation, let $\mathbf{x}_0$ be any given initial vector. We can express $\mathbf{x}_0$ in terms of the eigenvectors:

$$\mathbf{x}_0 = a_1\mathbf{u}_1 + a_2\mathbf{u}_2.$$

Since the eigenvalues of A are $\lambda_1 = 1$ and $\lambda_2 = 0.6$, the vector $\mathbf{x}_k$ is given by

$$\mathbf{x}_k = A^k\mathbf{x}_0 = a_1(1)^k\mathbf{u}_1 + a_2(0.6)^k\mathbf{u}_2 = a_1\mathbf{u}_1 + a_2(0.6)^k\mathbf{u}_2.$$

Given this expression for $\mathbf{x}_k$, there are only two possibilities:

1. If $a_1 \neq 0$, then $\lim_{k\to\infty} \mathbf{x}_k = a_1\mathbf{u}_1$.
2. If $a_1 = 0$, then $\lim_{k\to\infty} \mathbf{x}_k = \boldsymbol{\theta}$.

In general, an analogous description can be given for the possible solutions of any difference equation. Specifically, let A be a nondefective $(n \times n)$ matrix with eigenvalues $\lambda_1, \lambda_2, \ldots, \lambda_n$. For convenience, let us assume the eigenvalues are indexed according to their magnitude, where

$$|\lambda_1| \geq |\lambda_2| \geq \cdots \geq |\lambda_n|.$$

Let $\mathbf{x}_0$ be any initial vector, and consider the sequence $\{\mathbf{x}_k\}$, where $\mathbf{x}_k = A\mathbf{x}_{k-1}$, $k = 1, 2, \ldots$. Finally, suppose $\mathbf{x}_0$ is expressed as

$$\mathbf{x}_0 = a_1\mathbf{u}_1 + a_2\mathbf{u}_2 + \cdots + a_n\mathbf{u}_n,$$

where $a_1 \neq 0$.

From Eq. (6), we have the following possibilities for the sequence $\{\mathbf{x}_k\}$:

1. If $|\lambda_1| < 1$, then $\lim_{k\to\infty} \mathbf{x}_k = \boldsymbol{\theta}$.
2. If $|\lambda_1| = 1$, then there is a constant $M > 0$ such that $\|\mathbf{x}_k\| \le M$, for all k.
3. If $\lambda_1 = 1$ and $|\lambda_2| < 1$, then $\lim_{k\to\infty} \mathbf{x}_k = a_1\mathbf{u}_1$.
4. If $|\lambda_1| > 1$, then $\lim_{k\to\infty} \|\mathbf{x}_k\| = \infty$.

Other possibilities exist that are not listed. For example, if $\lambda_1 = 1$, $\lambda_2 = 1$, and $|\lambda_3| < 1$, then $\{\mathbf{x}_k\} \to a_1\mathbf{u}_1 + a_2\mathbf{u}_2$.

Also, in listing the possibilities we assumed that A was not defective and that $a_1 \neq 0$. If $a_1 = 0$ but $a_2 \neq 0$, it should be clear that a similar list can be made by using λ_2 in place of λ_1. If matrix A is defective, it can be shown (see Section 7.8) that the list above is still valid, with the following exception (see Exercise 19 for an example): If $|\lambda_1| = 1$ and if the geometric multiplicity of λ_1 is less than the algebraic multiplicity, then it will usually be the case that $\|\mathbf{x}_k\| \to \infty$ as $k \to \infty$.

EXAMPLE 4 For the herd model described in Example 2, let the parameters be given by $b = 0.9$, $d_1 = 0.1$, and $d_2 = 0.2$. Thus $\mathbf{x}_k = A\mathbf{x}_{k-1}$, where

$$A = \begin{bmatrix} 0 & .9 \\ .9 & .8 - h \end{bmatrix}.$$

Determine a harvest rate h so that the herd neither dies out nor grows without bound.

Solution For any given harvest rate h, the matrix A will have eigenvalues λ_1 and λ_2, where $|\lambda_1| \ge |\lambda_2|$. If $|\lambda_1| < 1$, then $\{\mathbf{x}_k\} \to \boldsymbol{\theta}$, and the herd is dying out. If $|\lambda_1| > 1$, then $\{\|\mathbf{x}_k\|\} \to \infty$, which indicates that the herd is increasing without bound.

Therefore, we want to select h so that $\lambda_1 = 1$. For any given h, λ_1 and λ_2 are roots of the characteristic equation $p(t) = 0$, where

$$p(t) = \det(A - tI) = t^2 - (.8 - h)t - .81.$$

To have $\lambda_1 = 1$, we need $p(1) = 0$, or

$$(1)^2 - (.8 - h)(1) - .81 = 0,$$

or

$$h - .61 = 0.$$

Thus a harvest rate of $h = 0.61$ will lead to $\lambda_1 = 1$ and $\lambda_2 = -0.81$. ■

Note that to the extent the herd model in Examples 2 and 4 is valid, a harvest rate of less than 0.61 will cause the herd to grow, whereas a rate greater than 0.61 will cause the herd to decrease. A harvest rate of 0.61 will cause the herd to approach a steady-state distribution of 9 young animals for every 10 mature animals. That is, for any initial vector $\mathbf{x}_0 = a_1\mathbf{u}_1 + a_2\mathbf{u}_2$, we have (with $h = 0.61$)

$$\mathbf{x}_k = a_1\mathbf{u}_1 + a_2(-0.81)^k\mathbf{u}_2,$$

where the eigenvectors $\mathbf{u}_1$ and $\mathbf{u}_2$ are given by

$$\mathbf{u}_1 = \begin{bmatrix} 9 \\ 10 \end{bmatrix} \quad \text{and} \quad \mathbf{u}_2 = \begin{bmatrix} 10 \\ -9 \end{bmatrix}.$$

Markov Chains

A special type of difference equation arises in the study of Markov chains or Markov processes. We cannot go into the interesting theory of Markov chains, but we will give an example that illustrates some of the ideas.

EXAMPLE 5 An automobile rental company has three locations, which we designate as P, Q, and R. When an automobile is rented at one of the locations, it may be returned to any of the three locations.

Suppose, at some specific time, that there are p cars at location P, q cars at Q, and r cars at R. Experience has shown, in any given week, that the p cars at location P are distributed as follows: 10% are rented and returned to Q, 30% are rented and returned to R, and 60% remain at P (these either are not rented or are rented and returned to P). Similar rental histories are known for locations Q and R, as summarized below.

Weekly Distribution History

Location P: 60% stay at P, 10% go to Q, 30% go to R.

Location Q: 10% go to P, 80% stay at Q, 10% go to R.

Location R: 10% go to P, 20% go to Q, 70% stay at R.

Solution Let $\mathbf{x}_k$ represent the state of the rental fleet at the beginning of week k:

$$\mathbf{x}_k = \begin{bmatrix} p(k) \\ q(k) \\ r(k) \end{bmatrix}.$$

For the state vector $\mathbf{x}_k$, $p(k)$ denotes the number of cars at location P, $q(k)$ the number at Q, and $r(k)$ the number at R.

From the weekly distribution history, we see that

$$\begin{aligned} p(k+1) &= .6p(k) + .1q(k) + .1r(k) \\ q(k+1) &= .1p(k) + .8q(k) + .2r(k) \\ r(k+1) &= .3p(k) + .1q(k) + .7r(k). \end{aligned}$$

(For instance, the number of cars at P when week $k+1$ begins is determined by the 60% that remain at P, the 10% that arrive from Q, and the 10% that arrive from R.)

To the extent that the weekly distribution percentages do not change, the rental fleet is rearranged among locations P, Q, and R according to the rule $\mathbf{x}_{k+1} = A\mathbf{x}_k$, $k = 0, 1, \ldots$, where A is the (3×3) matrix

$$A = \begin{bmatrix} .6 & .1 & .1 \\ .1 & .8 & .2 \\ .3 & .1 & .7 \end{bmatrix}.$$ ■

Example 5 represents a situation in which a fixed population (the rental fleet) is rearranged in stages (week by week) among a fixed number of categories (the locations P, Q, and R). Moreover, in Example 5 the rules governing the rearrangement remain fixed from stage to stage (the weekly distribution percentages stay constant). In general, such problems can be modeled by a difference equation of the form

$$\mathbf{x}_{k+1} = A\mathbf{x}_k, \quad k = 0, 1, \ldots.$$

For such problems the matrix A is often called a ***transition*** matrix. Such a matrix has two special properties:

The entries of A are all nonnegative. **(8a)**

In each column of A, the sum of the entries has the value 1. **(8b)**

It turns out that a matrix having properties (8a) and (8b) always has an eigenvalue of $\lambda = 1$. This fact is established in Exercise 26 and illustrated in the next example.

EXAMPLE 6 Suppose the automobile rental company described in Example 5 has a fleet of 600 cars. Initially an equal number of cars is based at each location, so that $p(0) = 200$, $q(0) = 200$, and $r(0) = 200$. As in Example 5, let the week-by-week distribution of cars be governed by $\mathbf{x}_{k+1} = A\mathbf{x}_k$, $k = 0, 1, \ldots$, where

$$\mathbf{x}_k = \begin{bmatrix} p(k) \\ q(k) \\ r(k) \end{bmatrix}, \quad A = \begin{bmatrix} .6 & .1 & .1 \\ .1 & .8 & .2 \\ .3 & .1 & .7 \end{bmatrix}, \quad \text{and} \quad \mathbf{x}_0 = \begin{bmatrix} 200 \\ 200 \\ 200 \end{bmatrix}.$$

Find $\lim_{k\to\infty} \mathbf{x}_k$. Determine the number of cars at each location in the kth week, for $k = 1, 5$, and 10.

Solution If A is not defective, we can use Eq. (6) to express $\mathbf{x}_k$ as

$$\mathbf{x}_k = a_1(\lambda_1)^k\mathbf{u}_1 + a_2(\lambda_2)^k\mathbf{u}_2 + a_3(\lambda_3)^k\mathbf{u}_3,$$

where $\{\mathbf{u}_1, \mathbf{u}_2, \mathbf{u}_3\}$ is a basis for R^3, consisting of eigenvectors of A.

It can be shown that A has eigenvalues $\lambda_1 = 1$, $\lambda_2 = .6$, and $\lambda_3 = .5$. Thus A has three linearly independent eigenvectors:

$$\lambda_1 = 1, \quad \mathbf{u}_1 = \begin{bmatrix} 4 \\ 9 \\ 7 \end{bmatrix}; \quad \lambda_2 = .6 \quad \mathbf{u}_2 = \begin{bmatrix} 0 \\ 1 \\ -1 \end{bmatrix};$$

$$\lambda_3 = .5, \quad \mathbf{u}_3 = \begin{bmatrix} -1 \\ -1 \\ 2 \end{bmatrix}.$$

The initial vector, $\mathbf{x}_0 = [200, 200, 200]^T$, can be written as

$$\mathbf{x}_0 = 30\mathbf{u}_1 - 150\mathbf{u}_2 - 80\mathbf{u}_3.$$

Thus the vector $\mathbf{x}_k = [p(k), q(k), r(k)]^T$ is given by

$$\begin{aligned} \mathbf{x}_k &= A^k\mathbf{x}_0 \\ &= A^k(30\mathbf{u}_1 - 150\mathbf{u}_2 - 80\mathbf{u}_3) \\ &= 30(\lambda_1)^k\mathbf{u}_1 - 150(\lambda_2)^k\mathbf{u}_2 - 80(\lambda_3)^k\mathbf{u}_3 \\ &= 30\mathbf{u}_1 - 150(.6)^k\mathbf{u}_2 - 80(.5)^k\mathbf{u}_3. \end{aligned} \qquad (9)$$

From the expression above, we see that

$$\lim_{k\to\infty} \mathbf{x}_k = 30\mathbf{u}_1 = \begin{bmatrix} 120 \\ 270 \\ 210 \end{bmatrix}.$$

Therefore, as the weeks proceed, the rental fleet will tend to an equilibrium state with 120 cars at P, 270 cars at Q, and 210 cars at R. To the extent that the model is valid, location Q will require the largest facility for maintenance, parking, and the like.

Finally, using Eq. (9), we can calculate the state of the fleet for the kth week:

$$\mathbf{x}_1 = \begin{bmatrix} 160 \\ 220 \\ 220 \end{bmatrix}, \quad \mathbf{x}_5 = \begin{bmatrix} 122.500 \\ 260.836 \\ 216.664 \end{bmatrix}, \quad \text{and} \quad \mathbf{x}_{10} = \begin{bmatrix} 120.078 \\ 269.171 \\ 210.751 \end{bmatrix}. \quad \blacksquare$$

Note that the components of $\mathbf{x}_{10}$ are rounded to three places. Of course, for an actual fleet the state vectors $\mathbf{x}_k$ must have only integer components. The fact that the sequence defined in Eq. (9) need not have integer components represents a limitation of the assumed distribution model.

Systems of Differential Equations

Difference equations are useful for describing the state of a physical system at discrete values of time. Mathematical models that describe the evolution of a physical system for all values of time are frequently expressed in terms of a differential equation or a system of differential equations. A simple example of a system of differential equations is

$$\begin{aligned} v'(t) &= av(t) + bw(t) \\ w'(t) &= cv(t) + dw(t). \end{aligned} \tag{10}$$

In Eq. (10), the problem is to find functions $v(t)$ and $w(t)$ that simultaneously satisfy these equations and in which initial conditions $v(0)$ and $w(0)$ may also be specified. We can express Eq. (10) in matrix terms if we let

$$\mathbf{x}(t) = \begin{bmatrix} v(t) \\ w(t) \end{bmatrix}.$$

Then Eq. (10) can be written as $\mathbf{x}'(t) = A\mathbf{x}(t)$, where

$$\mathbf{x}'(t) = \begin{bmatrix} v'(t) \\ w'(t) \end{bmatrix} \quad \text{and} \quad A = \begin{bmatrix} a & b \\ c & d \end{bmatrix}.$$

The equation $\mathbf{x}'(t) = A\mathbf{x}(t)$ is reminiscent of the simple scalar differential equation, $y'(t) = \alpha y(t)$, which is frequently used in calculus to model problems such as radioactive decay or bacterial growth. To find a function $y(t)$ that satisfies the identity $y'(t) = \alpha y(t)$, we rewrite the equation as $y'(t)/y(t) = \alpha$. Integrating both sides with respect to t yields $\ln|y(t)| = \alpha t + \beta$, or equivalently $y(t) = y_0 e^{\alpha t}$, where $y_0 = y(0)$.

Using the scalar equation as a guide, we assume the vector equation $\mathbf{x}'(t) = A\mathbf{x}(t)$ has a solution of the form

$$\mathbf{x}(t) = e^{\lambda t}\mathbf{u}, \tag{11}$$

where $\mathbf{u}$ is a constant vector. To see if the function $\mathbf{x}(t)$ in Eq. (11) can be a solution, we differentiate and get $\mathbf{x}'(t) = \lambda e^{\lambda t}\mathbf{u}$. On the other hand, $A\mathbf{x}(t) = e^{\lambda t}A\mathbf{u}$; so Eq. (11) will be a solution of $\mathbf{x}'(t) = A\mathbf{x}(t)$ if and only if

$$e^{\lambda t}(A - \lambda I)\mathbf{u} = \boldsymbol{\theta}. \tag{12}$$

Now $e^{\lambda t} \neq 0$ for all values of t; so Eq. (12) will be satisfied only if $(A - \lambda I)\mathbf{u} = \boldsymbol{\theta}$. Therefore, if λ is an eigenvalue of A and $\mathbf{u}$ is a corresponding eigenvector, then $\mathbf{x}(t)$ given in Eq. (11) is a solution to $\mathbf{x}'(t) = A\mathbf{x}(t)$. (*Note:* The choice $\mathbf{u} = \boldsymbol{\theta}$ will also give a solution, but it is a trivial solution.)

If the (2×2) matrix A has eigenvalues λ_1 and λ_2 with corresponding eigenvectors $\mathbf{u}_1$ and $\mathbf{u}_2$, then two solutions of $\mathbf{x}'(t) = A\mathbf{x}(t)$ are $\mathbf{x}_1(t) = e^{\lambda_1 t}\mathbf{u}_1$ and $\mathbf{x}_2(t) = e^{\lambda_2 t}\mathbf{u}_2$. It is easy to verify that any linear combination of $\mathbf{x}_1(t)$ and $\mathbf{x}_2(t)$ is also a solution; so

$$\mathbf{x}(t) = a_1\mathbf{x}_1(t) + a_2\mathbf{x}_2(t) \tag{13}$$

will solve $\mathbf{x}'(t) = A\mathbf{x}(t)$ for any choice of scalars a_1 and a_2. Finally, the initial-value problem consists of finding a solution to $\mathbf{x}'(t) = A\mathbf{x}(t)$ that satisfies an initial condition, $\mathbf{x}(0) = \mathbf{x}_0$, where $\mathbf{x}_0$ is some specified vector. Given the form of $\mathbf{x}_1(t)$ and $\mathbf{x}_2(t)$, it is clear from Eq. (13) that $\mathbf{x}(0) = a_1\mathbf{u}_1 + a_2\mathbf{u}_2$. If the eigenvectors $\mathbf{u}_1$ and $\mathbf{u}_2$ are linearly independent, we can always choose scalars b_1 and b_2 so that $\mathbf{x}_0 = b_1\mathbf{u}_1 + b_2\mathbf{u}_2$; and therefore $\mathbf{x}(t) = b_1\mathbf{x}_1(t) + b_2\mathbf{x}_2(t)$ is the solution of $\mathbf{x}'(t) = A\mathbf{x}(t)$, $\mathbf{x}(0) = \mathbf{x}_0$.

EXAMPLE 7 Solve the initial-value problem

$$\begin{aligned} v'(t) &= v(t) - 2w(t), \quad v(0) = 4 \\ w'(t) &= v(t) + 4w(t), \quad w(0) = -3. \end{aligned}$$

Solution In vector form, the given equation can be expressed as $\mathbf{x}'(t) = A\mathbf{x}(t)$, $\mathbf{x}(0) = \mathbf{x}_0$, where

$$\mathbf{x}(t) = \begin{bmatrix} v(t) \\ w(t) \end{bmatrix}, \quad A = \begin{bmatrix} 1 & -2 \\ 1 & 4 \end{bmatrix}, \quad \text{and} \quad \mathbf{x}_0 = \begin{bmatrix} 4 \\ -3 \end{bmatrix}.$$

The eigenvalues of A are $\lambda_1 = 2$ and $\lambda_2 = 3$, with corresponding eigenvectors

$$\mathbf{u}_1 = \begin{bmatrix} 2 \\ -1 \end{bmatrix} \quad \text{and} \quad \mathbf{u}_2 = \begin{bmatrix} 1 \\ -1 \end{bmatrix}.$$

As before, $\mathbf{x}_1(t) = e^{2t}\mathbf{u}_1$ and $\mathbf{x}_2(t) = e^{3t}\mathbf{u}_2$ are solutions of $\mathbf{x}'(t) = A\mathbf{x}(t)$, as is any linear combination, $\mathbf{x}(t) = b_1\mathbf{x}_1(t) + b_2\mathbf{x}_2(t)$. We now need only choose appropriate constants b_1 and b_2 so that $\mathbf{x}(0) = \mathbf{x}_0$, where we know $\mathbf{x}(0) = b_1\mathbf{u}_1 + b_2\mathbf{u}_2$. For $\mathbf{x}_0$ as given, it is routine to find $\mathbf{x}_0 = \mathbf{u}_1 + 2\mathbf{u}_2$. Thus the solution of $\mathbf{x}'(t) = A\mathbf{x}(t)$, $\mathbf{x}(0) = \mathbf{x}_0$ is $\mathbf{x}(t) = \mathbf{x}_1(t) + 2\mathbf{x}_2(t)$, or

$$\mathbf{x}(t) = e^{2t}\mathbf{u}_1 + 2e^{3t}\mathbf{u}_2.$$

In terms of the functions v and w, we have

$$\mathbf{x}(t) = \begin{bmatrix} v(t) \\ w(t) \end{bmatrix} = e^{2t}\begin{bmatrix} 2 \\ -1 \end{bmatrix} + 2e^{3t}\begin{bmatrix} 1 \\ -1 \end{bmatrix} = \begin{bmatrix} 2e^{2t} + 2e^{3t} \\ -e^{2t} - 2e^{3t} \end{bmatrix}.$$

In general, given the problem of solving

$$\mathbf{x}'(t) = A\mathbf{x}(t), \quad \mathbf{x}(0) = \mathbf{x}_0, \tag{14}$$

where A is an $(n \times n)$ matrix, we can proceed just as above. We first find the eigenvalues $\lambda_1, \lambda_2, \ldots, \lambda_n$ of A and corresponding eigenvectors $\mathbf{u}_1, \mathbf{u}_2, \ldots, \mathbf{u}_n$. For each i, $\mathbf{x}_i(t) = e^{\lambda_i t}\mathbf{u}_i$ is a solution of $\mathbf{x}'(t) = A\mathbf{x}(t)$, as is the general expression

$$\mathbf{x}(t) = b_1\mathbf{x}_1(t) + b_2\mathbf{x}_2(t) + \cdots + b_n\mathbf{x}_n(t). \tag{15}$$

As before, $\mathbf{x}(0) = b_1\mathbf{u}_1 + b_2\mathbf{u}_2 + \cdots + b_n\mathbf{u}_n$; so if $\mathbf{x}_0$ can be expressed as a linear combination of $\mathbf{u}_1, \mathbf{u}_2, \ldots, \mathbf{u}_n$, then we can construct a solution to Eq. (14) in the form of Eq. (15). If the eigenvectors of A do not form a basis for R^n, we can still get a solution of the form Eq. (15); but a more detailed analysis is required. See Example 4, Section 7.8.

4.8 EXERCISES

In Exercises 1–6, consider the vector sequence $\{\mathbf{x}_k\}$, where $\mathbf{x}_k = A\mathbf{x}_{k-1}$, $k = 1, 2, \ldots$. For the given starting vector $\mathbf{x}_0$, calculate $\mathbf{x}_1$, $\mathbf{x}_2$, $\mathbf{x}_3$, and $\mathbf{x}_4$ by using direct multiplication, as in Example 1.

1. $A = \begin{bmatrix} 0 & 1 \\ 1 & 0 \end{bmatrix}, \quad \mathbf{x}_0 = \begin{bmatrix} 2 \\ 4 \end{bmatrix}$

2. $A = \begin{bmatrix} .5 & .5 \\ .5 & .5 \end{bmatrix}, \quad \mathbf{x}_0 = \begin{bmatrix} 16 \\ 8 \end{bmatrix}$

3. $A = \begin{bmatrix} .5 & .25 \\ .5 & .75 \end{bmatrix}, \quad \mathbf{x}_0 = \begin{bmatrix} 128 \\ 64 \end{bmatrix}$

4. $A = \begin{bmatrix} 2 & -1 \\ -1 & 2 \end{bmatrix}, \quad \mathbf{x}_0 = \begin{bmatrix} 3 \\ 1 \end{bmatrix}$

5. $A = \begin{bmatrix} 1 & 4 \\ 1 & 1 \end{bmatrix}, \quad \mathbf{x}_0 = \begin{bmatrix} -1 \\ 2 \end{bmatrix}$

6. $A = \begin{bmatrix} 3 & 1 \\ 4 & 3 \end{bmatrix}, \quad \mathbf{x}_0 = \begin{bmatrix} 2 \\ 0 \end{bmatrix}$

In Exercises 7–14, let $\mathbf{x}_k = A\mathbf{x}_{k-1}$, $k = 1, 2, \ldots$, for the given A and $\mathbf{x}_0$. Find an expression for $\mathbf{x}_k$ by using Eq. (6), as in Example 3. With a calculator, compute $\mathbf{x}_4$ and $\mathbf{x}_{10}$ from the expression. Comment on $\lim_{k\to\infty} \mathbf{x}_k$.

7. A and $\mathbf{x}_0$ in Exercise 1
8. A and $\mathbf{x}_0$ in Exercise 2
9. A and $\mathbf{x}_0$ in Exercise 3
10. A and $\mathbf{x}_0$ in Exercise 4
11. A and $\mathbf{x}_0$ in Exercise 5
12. A and $\mathbf{x}_0$ in Exercise 6
13. $A = \begin{bmatrix} 3 & -1 & -1 \\ -12 & 0 & 5 \\ 4 & -2 & -1 \end{bmatrix}, \quad \mathbf{x}_0 = \begin{bmatrix} 3 \\ -14 \\ 8 \end{bmatrix}$
14. $A = \begin{bmatrix} -6 & 1 & 3 \\ -3 & 0 & 2 \\ -20 & 2 & 10 \end{bmatrix}, \quad \mathbf{x}_0 = \begin{bmatrix} 1 \\ 1 \\ -1 \end{bmatrix}$

In Exercises 15–18, solve the initial-value problem.

15. $u'(t) = 5u(t) - 6v(t), \quad u(0) = 4$
$v'(t) = 3u(t) - 4v(t), \quad v(0) = 1$
16. $u'(t) = u(t) + 2v(t), \quad u(0) = 1$
$v'(t) = 2u(t) + v(t), \quad v(0) = 5$
17. $u'(t) = u(t) + v(t) + w(t), \quad u(0) = 3$
$v'(t) = 3v(t) + 3w(t), \quad v(0) = 3$
$w'(t) = -2u(t) + v(t) + w(t), \quad w(0) = 1$
18. $u'(t) = -2u(t) + 2v(t) - 3w(t), \quad u(0) = 3$
$v'(t) = 2u(t) + v(t) - 6w(t), \quad v(0) = -1$
$w'(t) = -u(t) - 2v(t), \quad w(0) = 3$
19. Consider the matrix A given by

$$A = \begin{bmatrix} 1 & 2 \\ 0 & 1 \end{bmatrix}.$$

Note that $\lambda = 1$ is the only eigenvalue of A.

a) Verify that A is defective.

b) Consider the sequence $\{\mathbf{x}_k\}$ determined by $\mathbf{x}_k = A\mathbf{x}_{k-1}$, $k = 1, 2, \ldots$, where $\mathbf{x}_0 = [1, 1]^T$. Use induction to show that

$\mathbf{x}_k = [2k+1, 1]^T$. (This exercise gives an example of a sequence $\mathbf{x}_k = A\mathbf{x}_{k-1}$, where $\lim_{k\to\infty} \|\mathbf{x}_k\| = \infty$, even though A has no eigenvalue larger than 1 in magnitude.)

In Exercises 20 and 21, choose a value α so that the matrix A has an eignevalue of $\lambda = 1$. Then, for $\mathbf{x}_0 = [1, 1]^T$, calculate $\lim_{k\to\infty} \mathbf{x}_k$, where $\mathbf{x}_k = A\mathbf{x}_{k-1}$, $k = 1, 2, \ldots$.

20. $A = \begin{bmatrix} .5 & .5 \\ .5 & 1+\alpha \end{bmatrix}$

21. $A = \begin{bmatrix} 0 & .3 \\ .6 & 1+\alpha \end{bmatrix}$

22. Suppose that $\{\mathbf{u}_k\}$ and $\{\mathbf{v}_k\}$ are sequences satisfying $\mathbf{u}_k = A\mathbf{u}_{k-1}$, $k = 1, 2, \ldots$, and $\mathbf{v}_k = A\mathbf{v}_{k-1}$, $k = 1, 2, \ldots$. Show that if $\mathbf{u}_0 = \mathbf{v}_0$, then $\mathbf{u}_i = \mathbf{v}_i$ for all i.

23. Let $B = (b_{ij})$ be an $(n \times n)$ matrix. Matrix B is called a stochastic matrix if B contains only nonnegative entries and if $b_{i1} + b_{i2} + \cdots + b_{in} = 1$, $1 \le i \le n$. (That is, B is a stochastic matrix if B^T satisfies conditions 8a and 8b.) Show that $\lambda = 1$ is an eigenvalue of B. [*Hint:* Consider the vector $\mathbf{w} = [1, 1, \ldots, 1]^T$.]

24. Suppose that B is a stochastic matrix whose entries are all positive. By Exercise 23, $\lambda = 1$ is an eigenvalue of B. Show that if $B\mathbf{u} = \mathbf{u}$, $\mathbf{u} \ne \boldsymbol{\theta}$, then $\mathbf{u}$ is a multiple of the vector $\mathbf{w}$ defined in Exercise 23. [*Hint:* Define $\mathbf{v} = \alpha\mathbf{u}$ so that $v_i = 1$ and $|v_j| \le 1$, $1 \le j \le n$. Consider the ith equations in $B\mathbf{w} = \mathbf{w}$ and $B\mathbf{v} = \mathbf{v}$.]

25. Let B be a stochastic matrix, and let λ by any eigenvalue of B. Show that $|\lambda| \le 1$. For simplicity, assume that λ is real. [*Hint:* Suppose that $B\mathbf{u} = \lambda\mathbf{u}$, $\mathbf{u} \ne \boldsymbol{\theta}$. Define a vector $\mathbf{v}$ as in Exercise 24.]

26. Let A be an $(n \times n)$ matrix satisfying conditions (8a) and (8b). Show that $\lambda = 1$ is an eigenvalue of A and that if $A\mathbf{u} = \beta\mathbf{u}$, $\mathbf{u} \ne \boldsymbol{\theta}$, then $|\beta| \le 1$. [*Hint:* Matrix A^T is stochastic.]

27. Suppose that $(A - \lambda I)\mathbf{u} = \boldsymbol{\theta}$, $\mathbf{u} \ne \boldsymbol{\theta}$, and there is a vector $\mathbf{v}$ such that $(A - \lambda I)\mathbf{v} = \mathbf{u}$. Then $\mathbf{v}$ is called a ***generalized eigenvector***. Show that $\{\mathbf{u}, \mathbf{v}\}$ is a linearly independent set. [*Hint:* Note that $A\mathbf{v} = \lambda\mathbf{v} + \mathbf{u}$. Suppose that $a\mathbf{u} + b\mathbf{v} = \boldsymbol{\theta}$, and multiply this equation by A.]

28. Let A, $\mathbf{u}$, and $\mathbf{v}$ be as in Exercise 27. Show that $A^k\mathbf{v} = \lambda^k\mathbf{v} + k\lambda^{k-1}\mathbf{u}$, $k = 1, 2, \ldots$.

29. Consider matrix A in Exercise 19.

a) Find an eigenvector $\mathbf{u}$ and a generalized eigenvector $\mathbf{v}$ for A.

b) Express $\mathbf{x}_0 = [1, 1]^T$ as $\mathbf{x}_0 = a\mathbf{u} + b\mathbf{v}$.

c) Using the result of Exercise 28, find an expression for $A^k\mathbf{x}_0 = A^k(a\mathbf{u} + b\mathbf{v})$.

d) Verify that $A^k\mathbf{x}_0 = [2k+1, 1]^T$ as was shown by other means in Exercise 19.

SUPPLEMENTARY EXERCISES

1. Find all values x such that A is singular, where

$$A = \begin{bmatrix} x & 1 & 2 \\ 3 & x & 0 \\ 0 & -1 & 1 \end{bmatrix}.$$

2. For what values x does A have only real eigenvalues, where

$$A = \begin{bmatrix} 2 & 1 \\ x & 3 \end{bmatrix}?$$

3. Let

$$A = \begin{bmatrix} a & b \\ c & d \end{bmatrix},$$

where $a + b = 2$ and $c + d = 2$. Show that $\lambda = 2$ is an eigenvalue for A. [*Hint:* Guess an eigenvector.]

4. Let A and B be (3×3) matrices such that $\det(A) = 2$ and $\det(B) = 9$. Find the values of each of the following.

a) $\det(A^{-1}B^2)$

b) $\det(3A)$

c) $\det(AB^2A^{-1})$

5. For what values x is A defective, where

$$A = \begin{bmatrix} 2 & x \\ 0 & 2 \end{bmatrix}.$$

In Exercises 6–9, A is a (2×2) matrix such that $A^2 + 3A - I = \mathcal{O}$.

6. Suppose we know that

$$A\mathbf{u} = \begin{bmatrix} 2 \\ 1 \end{bmatrix}, \quad \text{where } \mathbf{u} = \begin{bmatrix} 1 \\ 3 \end{bmatrix}.$$

Find $A^2\mathbf{u}$ and $A^3\mathbf{u}$.

7. Show that A is nonsingular. [*Hint:* Is there a nonzero vector $\mathbf{x}$ such that $A\mathbf{x} = \boldsymbol{\theta}$?]

8. Find $A^{-1}\mathbf{u}$, where $\mathbf{u}$ is as in Exercise 6.

9. Using the fact that $A^2 = I - 3A$, we can find scalars a_k and b_k such that $A^k = a_k A + b_k I$. Find these scalars for $k = 2, 3, 4$, and 5.

In Exercises 10 and 11, find the eigenvalues λ_i given the corresponding eigenvector $\mathbf{u}_i$. Do not calculate the characteristic polynomial for A.

10. $A = \begin{bmatrix} 2 & -12 \\ 1 & -5 \end{bmatrix}, \quad \mathbf{u}_1 = \begin{bmatrix} 4 \\ 1 \end{bmatrix},$

$\mathbf{u}_2 = \begin{bmatrix} 3 \\ 1 \end{bmatrix}$

11. $A = \begin{bmatrix} 1 & 2 \\ -1 & 4 \end{bmatrix}, \quad \mathbf{u}_1 = \begin{bmatrix} 2 \\ 1 \end{bmatrix},$

$\mathbf{u}_2 = \begin{bmatrix} 1 \\ 1 \end{bmatrix}$

12. Find x so that $\mathbf{u}$ is an eigenvector. What is the corresponding eigenvalue λ?

$$A = \begin{bmatrix} 2 & x \\ 1 & -5 \end{bmatrix}, \quad \mathbf{u} = \begin{bmatrix} 1 \\ -1 \end{bmatrix}$$

13. Find x and y so that $\mathbf{u}$ is an eigenvector corresponding to the eigenvalue $\lambda = 1$:

$$A = \begin{bmatrix} x & y \\ 2x & -y \end{bmatrix}, \quad \mathbf{u} = \begin{bmatrix} -1 \\ 1 \end{bmatrix}$$

14. Find x and y so that $\mathbf{u}$ is an eigenvector corresponding to the eigenvalue $\lambda = 4$:

$$A = \begin{bmatrix} x+y & y \\ x-3 & 1 \end{bmatrix}, \quad \mathbf{u} = \begin{bmatrix} -3 \\ 1 \end{bmatrix}$$

CONCEPTUAL EXERCISES

In Exercises 1–8, answer true or false. Justify your answer by providing a counterexample if the statement is false or an outline of a proof if the statement is true. In each exercise, A is a real $(n \times n)$ matrix.

1. If A is nonsingular with $A^{-1} = A^T$, then $\det(A) = 1$.
2. If $\mathbf{x}$ is an eigenvector for A, where A is nonsingular, then $\mathbf{x}$ is also an eigenvector for A^{-1}.
3. If A is nonsingular, then $\det(A^4)$ is positive.
4. If A is defective, then A is singular.
5. If A is an orthogonal matrix and if $\mathbf{x}$ is in R^n, then $\|A\mathbf{x}\| = \|\mathbf{x}\|$.
6. If S is $(n \times n)$ and nonsingular, then A and $S^{-1}AS$ have the same eigenvalues.
7. If A and B are diagonal $(n \times n)$ matrices, then $\det(A + B) = \det(A) + \det(B)$.
8. If A is singular, then A is defective.

In Exercises 9–14, give a brief answer.

9. Suppose that A and Q are $(n \times n)$ matrices where Q is orthogonal. Then we know that A and $B = Q^TAQ$ have the same eigenvalues.

   a) If $\mathbf{x}$ is an eigenvector of B corresponding to λ, give an eigenvector of A corresponding to λ.

b) If $\mathbf{u}$ is an eigenvector of A corresponding to λ, give an eigenvector of B corresponding to λ.

10. Suppose that A is $(n \times n)$ and $A^3 = \mathcal{O}$. Show that 0 is the only eigenvalue of A.

11. Show that if A is $(n \times n)$ and is similar to the $(n \times n)$ identity I, then $A = I$.

12. Let A and B be $(n \times n)$ with A nonsingular. Show that AB and BA are similar. [*Hint:* Consider $S^{-1}ABS = BA$.]

13. Suppose that A and B are $(n \times n)$ and A is similar to B. Show that A^k is similar to B^k for $k = 2, 3$, and 4.

14. Let $\mathbf{u}$ be a vector in R^n such that $\mathbf{u}^T\mathbf{u} = 1$, and let A denote the $(n \times n)$ matrix $A = I - 2\mathbf{u}\mathbf{u}^T$.

a) Is A symmetric?

b) Is A orthogonal?

c) Calculate $A\mathbf{u}$.

d) Suppose that $\mathbf{w}$ is in R^n and $\mathbf{u}^T\mathbf{w} = 0$. What is $A\mathbf{w}$?

e) Give the eigenvalues of A and give the geometric multiplicity for each eignevalue.

MATLAB EXERCISES

1. Recognizing eigenvectors geometrically Let $x = [x_1, x_2]^T$ and let $\mathbf{y} = [y_1, y_2]^T$ be vectors in R^2. The following MATLAB command gives us a geometric representation of $\mathbf{x}$ and $\mathbf{y}$:

```
plot([0, x(1)], [0, x(2)], [0, y(1)], [0, y(2)]).     (1)
```

(In particular, the single command `plot([0, x(1)], [0, x(2)])` draws a line from the origin (0, 0) to the point $(x(1), x(2))$; this line is a geometric representation of the vector $\mathbf{x}$. The longer command (1) draws two lines, one representing $\mathbf{x}$ and the other $\mathbf{y}$.)

a) Let A be the (2×2) matrix

$$A = \begin{bmatrix} 3 & 7 \\ 1 & 3 \end{bmatrix}.$$

For each of the following vectors $\mathbf{x}$, use the command (1) to plot $\mathbf{x}$ and $\mathbf{y} = A\mathbf{x}$. Which of the vectors $\mathbf{x}$ is an eigenvector for A? How can you tell from the geometric representation drawn by MATLAB?

i) $\mathbf{x} = \begin{bmatrix} 0.3536 \\ 0.9354 \end{bmatrix}$ **ii)** $\mathbf{x} = \begin{bmatrix} 0.9354 \\ 0.3536 \end{bmatrix}$

iii) $\mathbf{x} = \begin{bmatrix} -0.3536 \\ 0.9354 \end{bmatrix}$ **iv)** $\mathbf{x} = \begin{bmatrix} -0.9354 \\ 0.3536 \end{bmatrix}$.

b) Let λ be an eigenvalue for A with corresponding eigenvector $\mathbf{x}$. Then:

$$\frac{(A\mathbf{x})^T\mathbf{x}}{\mathbf{x}^T\mathbf{x}} = \frac{(\lambda\mathbf{x})^T\mathbf{x}}{\mathbf{x}^T\mathbf{x}} = \frac{\lambda\mathbf{x}^T\mathbf{x}}{\mathbf{x}^T\mathbf{x}} = \lambda.$$

The expression $(A\mathbf{u})^T\mathbf{u}/\mathbf{u}^T\mathbf{u}$ is called a ***Rayleigh quotient***. Therefore, the preceding formula says that if $\mathbf{u}$ is an eigenvector for A, then the value of the Rayleigh quotient is equal to an eigenvalue corresponding to $\mathbf{u}$.

For each of the eigenvectors found in part a), use MATLAB to compute the Rayleigh quotient and hence determine the corresponding eigenvalue λ. Check your calculations by comparing $A\mathbf{x}$ and $\lambda\mathbf{x}$.

c) Repeat parts a) and b) for the following matrix A and vectors given in i)–iv):

$$A = \begin{bmatrix} 1 & 3 \\ 1 & 1 \end{bmatrix}$$

and

$$\textbf{i)}\ \mathbf{x} = \begin{bmatrix} -0,8660 \\ 0.5000 \end{bmatrix} \qquad \textbf{ii)}\ \mathbf{x} = \begin{bmatrix} 0.5000 \\ 0.8660 \end{bmatrix}$$

$$\textbf{iii)}\ \mathbf{x} = \begin{bmatrix} -0.5000 \\ 0.8660 \end{bmatrix} \qquad \textbf{iv)}\ \mathbf{x} = \begin{bmatrix} -0.8660 \\ 0.5000 \end{bmatrix}.$$

2. Determinants of block matrices In the MATLAB exercises for Chapter 1, we discussed how block matrices could be multiplied by thinking of the blocks as numbers. In this exercise, we extend the ideas to include determinants of block matrices.

Consider a (2×2) block matrix A of the form

$$A = \begin{bmatrix} A_1 & A_2 \\ A_3 & A_4 \end{bmatrix}. \tag{2}$$

We would like to be able to say that $\det(A) = \det(A_1)\det(A_4) - \det(A_3)\det(A_2)$ and, in fact, sometimes we can; but, sometimes we cannot.

a) Generate a random (6×6) matrix A and partition it into four (3×3) blocks in order to create a (2×2) block matrix of the form displayed in Eq. (2). Use the MATLAB determinant command to calculate $\det(A)$—as you might expect, the command is `det(A)`. Use MATLAB to calculate the determinant of each block and compare your result with the value: $\det(A_1)\det(A_4) - \det(A_3)\det(A_2)$. Is the formula $\det(A) = \det(A_1)\det(A_4) - \det(A_3)\det(A_2)$ valid in general?

b) Now, let us do part a) again. This time, however, we will choose A_3 to be the (3×3) zero matrix. That is, A is a ***block upper-triangular*** matrix. Verify for your randomly chosen matrix that the expected result holds:

If A is block upper triangular, then $\det(A) = \det(A_1)\det(A_4)$.

c) The result in part b) suggests the following theorem:

The determinant of a block triangular matrix is equal to the product of the determinants of its diagonal blocks.

This theorem is indeed true and it is valid for a matrix with any number of blocks, so long as the matrix is partitioned in such a way that the diagonal blocks are square. Illustrate this result by generating a random (12×12) matrix A and partitioning it as follows:

$$A = \begin{bmatrix} A_{11} & A_{12} & A_{13} \\ 0 & A_{22} & A_{23} \\ 0 & 0 & A_{33} \end{bmatrix}.$$

Your (3×3) block upper-triangular matrix A must have its diagonal blocks square, but there is no other requirement. For example, A_{11} could be (2×2), A_{22} could be (7×7), and A_{33} could be (3×3). The proof of the theorem stated above can be established using techniques discussed in Chapter 6.

3. **Dominant eigenvalues** An eigenvalue λ for a matrix A is called a ***dominant eigenvalue*** if $|\lambda| > |\beta|$ for any other eigenvalue β of A. This exercise will illustrate how powers of A multiplying a starting vector $\mathbf{x}_0$ will line up along a ***dominant eigenvector***. That is, given a starting vector $\mathbf{x}_0$, the following sequence of vectors will tend to become a multiple of an eigenvector associated with the dominant eigenvalue λ.

$$\mathbf{x}_1 = A\mathbf{x}_0, \mathbf{x}_2 = A\mathbf{x}_1, \ldots, \mathbf{x}_k = A\mathbf{x}_{k-1}, \ldots. \tag{3}$$

The sequence of vectors defined above was discussed in Section 4.8 under the topics of ***difference equations*** and ***Markov chains***. In that section we saw how the dominant eigenvalue/eigenvector pair determined the steady-state solution of the difference equation. The sequence of vectors was also introduced in Exercise 28 in Section 4.4. In that exercise, we saw the converse; that estimates of the steady-state solution can be used to estimate a dominant eigenvalue and eigenvector (this procedure is the ***power method***).

The point of this exercise is to illustrate numerically and graphically how the sequence (3) lines up in the direction of a dominant eigenvector. First, however, we want to recall why this sequence behaves in such a fashion.

As an example, suppose A is a (3×3) matrix with eigenvalues λ_1, λ_2, λ_3 and eigenvectors $\mathbf{u}_1$, $\mathbf{u}_2$, $\mathbf{u}_3$. Further, suppose λ_1 is a dominant eigenvalue. Now we know that the kth term in sequence (3) can be expressed as $\mathbf{x}_k = A^k\mathbf{x}_0$ (see Eqs. (4) and (5) in Section 4.8). Finally, let us suppose that $\mathbf{x}_0$ can be expessed as a linear combination of the eigenvectors:

$$\mathbf{x}_0 = c_1\mathbf{u}_1 + c_2\mathbf{u}_2 + c_3\mathbf{u}_3.$$

Using the fact that $\mathbf{x}_k = A^k\mathbf{x}_0$, we see from the preceding representation for $\mathbf{x}_0$ that we have

$$\mathbf{x}_k = c_1(\lambda_1)^k\mathbf{u}_1 + c_2(\lambda_2)^k\mathbf{u}_2 + c_3(\lambda_3)^k\mathbf{u}_3$$

or

$$\mathbf{x}_k = c_1\lambda_1^k\left(\mathbf{u}_1 + \frac{c_2}{c_1}\left(\frac{\lambda_2}{\lambda_1}\right)^k\mathbf{u}_2 + \frac{c_3}{c_1}\left(\frac{\lambda_3}{\lambda_1}\right)^k\mathbf{u}_3\right). \tag{4}$$

Since λ_1 is a dominant eigenvalue, the reason that $\mathbf{x}_k$ lines up in the direction of the dominant eigenvector $\mathbf{u}_1$ is clear from formula (4) for $\mathbf{x}_k$.

We note that formula (4) can be used in two different ways. For a given starting vector $\mathbf{x}_0$, we can use (4) to estimate the steady-state vector $\mathbf{x}_k$ at some future time t_k (this use is discussed in Section 4.8). Conversely, given a matrix A, we can calculate the sequence (3) and use formula (4) to estimate the dominant eigenvalue (this use is the power method).

a) Let the matrix A and the starting vector $\mathbf{x}_0$ be as follows:

$$A = \begin{bmatrix} 3 & -1 & -1 \\ -12 & 0 & 5 \\ 4 & -2 & -1 \end{bmatrix}, \quad \mathbf{x}_0 = \begin{bmatrix} 1 \\ 1 \\ 1 \end{bmatrix}.$$

Use MATLAB to generate $\mathbf{x}_1, \mathbf{x}_2, \ldots, \mathbf{x}_{10}$. (You need not use subscripted vectors, you can simply repeat the following command ten times: `x = A*x`. This assignment statement replaces $\mathbf{x}$ by $A\mathbf{x}$ each time it is executed.) As you can see, the vectors $\mathbf{x}_k$ are lining up in a certain direction. To conveniently identify that direction, divide each component of $\mathbf{x}_{10}$ by the first component of $\mathbf{x}_{10}$. Calculate the next three vectors in the sequence (the vectors $\mathbf{x}_{11}$, $\mathbf{x}_{12}$, and $\mathbf{x}_{13}$) normalizing each one as you did for $\mathbf{x}_{10}$. What is your guess as to a dominant eigenvector for A?

b) From formula (4) we see that $\mathbf{x}_{k+1} \approx \lambda_1 \mathbf{x}_k$. Use this approximation and the results of part a) to estimate the dominant eigenvalue of A.

c) As you can see from part a), when we generate the sequence (3) we obtain vectors with larger and larger components when the dominant eigenvalue is larger than 1 in absolute value. To avoid vectors with large components, it is customary to normalize each vector in the sequence. Thus, rather than generating sequence (3), we instead generate the following sequence (5) of unit vectors:

$$\mathbf{x}_1 = \frac{A\mathbf{x}_0}{\|A\mathbf{x}_0\|}, \mathbf{x}_2 = \frac{A\mathbf{x}_1}{\|A\mathbf{x}_1\|}, \ldots, \mathbf{x}_k = \frac{A\mathbf{x}_{k-1}}{A\mathbf{x}_{k-1}\|}, \ldots \tag{5}$$

A slight modification of formula (4) shows that the normalized sequence (5) also lines up along the dominant eigenvector. Repeat part a) using the normalized sequence (5) and observe that you find the same dominant eigenvector. Try several different starting vectors, such as $\mathbf{x}_0 = [1, 2, 3]^T$.

d) This exercise illustrates graphically the ideas in parts a)–c). Consider the matrix A and starting vector $\mathbf{x}_0$ given by

$$A = \begin{bmatrix} 2.8 & -1.6 \\ -1.6 & 5.2 \end{bmatrix}, \quad \mathbf{x}_0 = \begin{bmatrix} 1/\sqrt{2} \\ 1/\sqrt{2} \end{bmatrix}.$$

Use MATLAB to calculate the sequence of vectors defined by (5). In order to give a geometric representation of each term in the sequence, we can use the following MATLAB commands:

```
x=[1,1]'
x=x/norm(x)
plot([0, x(1)], [0, x(2)])
hold
x = A*x/norm(A*x)
plot([0, x(1)], [0, x(2)])
x = A*x/norm(A*x)
plot([0, x(1)], [0, x(2)])
  etc.
```

Continue until the sequences appear to be stabilizing.

e) Exercise 28 in Section 4.4 describes the power method, which is based on the ideas discussed so far in this exercise. Exercise 28 gives an easy way (based on Rayleigh quotients) to estimate the dominant eigenvalue that corresponds to the dominant eigenvectors generated by the sequence (5); see the definition of β_k in part c) of Exercise 28. Use this idea to estimate the dominant eigenvalue for the matrix A in part d) of this MATLAB exercise.

VECTOR SPACES AND LINEAR TRANSFORMATIONS

5

OVERVIEW

In Chapter 3 we saw, by using an algebraic perspective, that we could extend geometric vector concepts to R^n. In this chapter, using R^n as a model, we further extend the idea of a vector to include objects such as matrices, polynomials, functions, infinite sequences, and so forth.

As we will see in this chapter, concepts introduced in Chapter 3 (such as subspace, basis, and dimension) have natural extensions to the general vector space setting. In addition, applications treated in Chapter 3 (such as least squares fits to data) also have extensions to the general vector space setting.

CORE SECTIONS

5.2 *Vector Spaces*

5.3 *Subspaces*

5.4 *Linear Independence, Bases, and Coordinates*

5.5 *Dimension*

5.7 *Linear Transformations*

5.8 *Operations with Linear Transformations*

5.9 *Matrix Representations for Linear Transformations*

5.10 *Change of Basis and Diagonalization*

5.1 INTRODUCTION

Chapter 3 illustrated that by passing from a purely geometric view of vectors to an algebraic perspective we could, in a natural way, extend the concept of a vector to include elements of R^n. Using R^n as a model, this chapter extends the notion of a vector even further to include objects such as matrices, polynomials, functions continuous on a given interval, and solutions to certain differential equations. Most of the elementary concepts (such as subspace, basis, and dimension) that are important to understanding vector spaces are immediate generalizations of the same concepts in R^n.

Linear transformations were also introduced in Chapter 3, and we showed in Section 3.7 that a linear transformation, T, from R^n to R^m is always defined by matrix multiplication; that is,

$$T(\mathbf{x}) = A\mathbf{x} \tag{1}$$

for some $(m \times n)$ matrix A. In Sections 5.7–5.10, we will consider linear transformations on arbitrary vector spaces, thus extending the theory of mappings defined as in Eq. (1) to a more general setting. For example, differentiation and integration can be viewed as linear transformations.

Although the theory of vector spaces is relatively abstract, the vector-space structure provides a unifying framework of great flexibility, and many important practical problems fit naturally into a vector-space framework. As examples, the set of all solutions to a differential equation such as

$$a(x)y'' + b(x)y' + c(x)y = 0$$

can be shown to be a two-dimensional vector space. Thus if two *linearly independent* solutions are known, then all the solutions are determined. The previously defined notion of dot product can be extended to more general vector spaces and used to define the distance between two vectors. This notion is essential when one wishes to approximate one object with another (for example, to approximate a function with a polynomial). Linear transformations permit a natural extension of the important concepts of eigenvalues and eigenvectors to arbitrary vector spaces.

A basic feature of vector spaces is that they possess both an algebraic character and a geometric character. In this regard the geometric character frequently gives a pictorial insight into how a particular problem can be solved, whereas the algebraic character is used actually to calculate a solution.

As an example of how we can use this dual geometric/algebraic character of vector spaces, consider the following. In 1811 and 1822, Fourier, in his *Mathematical Theory of Heat*, made extremely important discoveries by using trigonometric series of the form

$$s(x) = \sum_{k=0}^{\infty}(a_k \cos kx + b_k \sin kx)$$

to represent functions, $f(x)$, $-\pi \le x \le \pi$. Today these representations can be visualized and utilized in a simple way using vector-space concepts.

For any positive integer n, let $\mathcal{S}_n$ represent the set of all trigonometric polynomials of degree at most n:

$$\mathcal{S}_n = \left\{ s_n(x)\colon s_n(x) = \sum_{k=0}^{n}(a_k \cos kx + b_k \sin kx), \quad a_k \text{ and } b_k \text{ real numbers} \right\}.$$

Now, if $s_n^*(x)$ is the best approximation in $\mathcal{S}_n$ to $f(x)$, then we might hope that $s(x) = \lim_{n\to\infty} s_n^*(x)$. A heuristic picture of this setting is shown in Fig. 5.1, where $\mathcal{F}[-\pi, \pi]$ denotes all functions defined on $[-\pi, \pi]$.

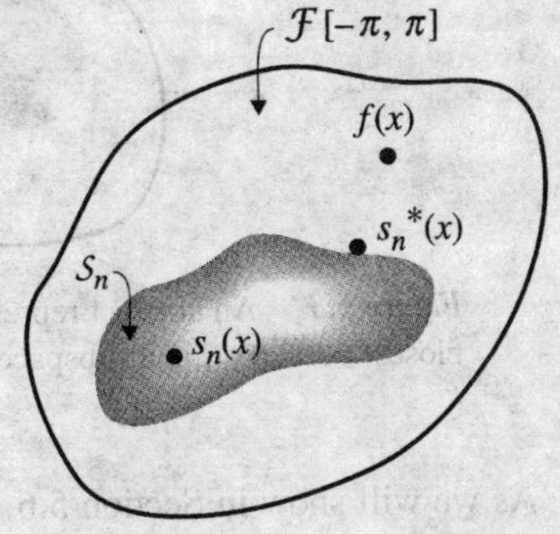

Figure 5.1 Among all $s_n(x)$ in $\mathcal{S}_n$, we are searching for $s^*(x)$, which best approximates $f(x)$, $-\pi \le x \le \pi$.

In Fig. 5.2, we have a vector approximation problem that we already know how to work from calculus. Here Π is a plane through the origin, and we are searching for a point y^* in Π that is closer to the given point b than any other point y in Π. Using $\mathbf{b}$, $\mathbf{y}$, and $\mathbf{y}^*$ as the position vectors for the points b, y, and y^*, respectively, we know that $\mathbf{y}^*$ is characterized by the fact that the remainder vector, $\mathbf{b} - \mathbf{y}^*$, is perpendicular to every position vector $\mathbf{y}$ in Π. That is, we can find $\mathbf{y}^*$ by setting $(\mathbf{b} - \mathbf{y}^*)^T\mathbf{u}_1 = 0$ and $(\mathbf{b} - \mathbf{y}^*)^T\mathbf{u}_2 = 0$, where $\{\mathbf{u}_1, \mathbf{u}_2\}$ is any basis for Π.

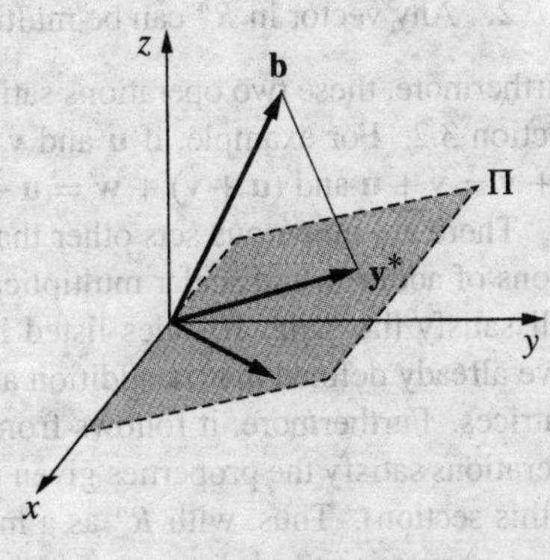

Figure 5.2 The vector $\mathbf{y}^*$ in Π is closer to $\mathbf{b}$ than is any other vector $\mathbf{y}$ in Π if and only if $\mathbf{b} - \mathbf{y}^*$ is perpendicular to all $\mathbf{y}$ in Π.

Figure 5.3 gives another way of visualizing this problem. We see a striking similarity between Figs. 5.1 and 5.3. It gives us the inspiration to ask if we can find $s_n^*(x)$ in Fig. 5.1 by choosing its coefficients, a_k and b_k, so that the remainder function, $f(x) - s_n^*(x)$, is in some way "perpendicular" to every $s_n(x)$ in $\mathcal{S}_n$.

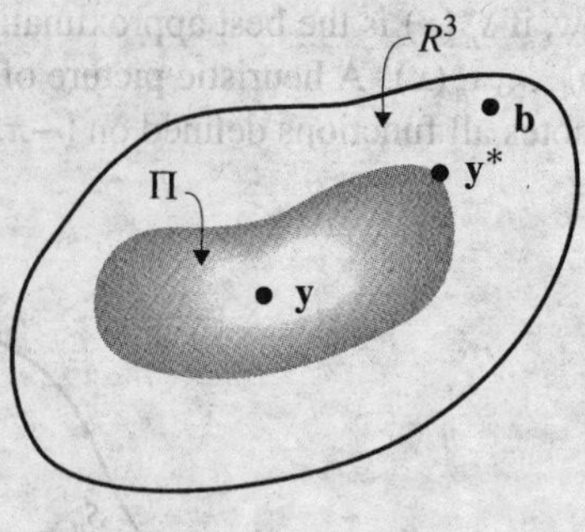

Figure 5.3 An abstract representation of the problem of finding the closest vector, $\mathbf{y}^*$, in a subspace Π to a vector $\mathbf{b}$.

As we will show in Section 5.6, this is precisely the approach we use to compute $s_n^*(x)$. Thus the geometric character of the vector-space setting provides our intuition with a possible procedure for solution. We must then use the algebraic character to:

(a) argue that our intuition is valid, and

(b) perform the actual calculation of the coefficients a_k and b_k for $s_n^*(x)$.

5.2 VECTOR SPACES

We begin our study of vector spaces by recalling the basic properties of R^n. First recall that there are two algebraic operations in R^n:

1. Vectors in R^n can be added.
2. Any vector in R^n can be multiplied by a scalar.

Furthermore, these two operations satisfy the 10 basic properties given in Theorem 1 of Section 3.2. For example, if $\mathbf{u}$ and $\mathbf{v}$ are in R^n, then $\mathbf{u} + \mathbf{v}$ is also in R^n. Moreover, $\mathbf{u} + \mathbf{v} = \mathbf{v} + \mathbf{u}$ and $(\mathbf{u} + \mathbf{v}) + \mathbf{w} = \mathbf{u} + (\mathbf{v} + \mathbf{w})$ for all $\mathbf{u}$, $\mathbf{v}$, and $\mathbf{w}$ in R^n.

There are numerous sets other than R^n on which there are defined algebraic operations of addition and scalar multiplication. Moreover, in many cases these operations will satisfy the same 10 rules listed in Theorem 1 of Section 3.2. For example, we have already defined matrix addition and scalar multiplication on the set of all $(m \times n)$ matrices. Furthermore, it follows from Theorems 7, 8, and 9 of Section 1.6 that these operations satisfy the properties given in Theorem 1 of Section 3.2 (see Example 2 later in this section). Thus, with R^n as a model, we could just as easily study the set of all $(m \times n)$ matrices and derive most of the properties and concepts given in Chapter 3, but in the context of matrices. Rather than study each such set individually, however, it is more efficient to define a *vector space* in the abstract as any set of objects that has algebraic operations that satisfy a given list of basic properties. Using only these assumed properties, we can prove other properties and develop further concepts. The results obtained in this manner then apply to any specific vector space. For example, later in this chapter the term *linearly independent* will be applied to a set of matrices, a set of polynomials, or a set of continuous functions.

Drawing on this discussion, we see that a general vector space should consist of a set of elements (or vectors), V, and a set of scalars, S, together with two algebraic operations:

1. An addition, which is defined between any two elements of V and which produces a sum that is in V;
2. A scalar multiplication, which defines how to multiply any element of V by a scalar from S.

In practice the set V can consist of any collection of objects for which meaningful operations of addition and scalar multiplication can be defined. For example, V might be the set of all (2×3) matrices, the set R^4 of all four-dimensional vectors, a set of functions, a set of polynomials, or the set of all solutions to a linear homogeneous differential equation. We will take the set S of scalars to be the set of real numbers, although for added flexibility other sets of scalars may be used (for example, S could be the set of complex numbers). Throughout this chapter the term *scalar* will always denote a real number.

Using R^n as a model and the properties of R^n listed in Theorem 1 of Section 3.2 as a guide, we now define a general vector space. Note that the definition says nothing about the set V but rather specifies rules that the algebraic operations must satisfy.

DEFINITION 1 A set of elements V is said to be a ***vector space*** over a scalar field S if an addition operation is defined between any two elements of V and a scalar multiplication operation is defined between any element of S and any vector in V. Moreover, if $\mathbf{u}$, $\mathbf{v}$, and $\mathbf{w}$ are vectors in V, and if a and b are any two scalars, then these 10 properties must hold.

Closure properties:

(c1) $\mathbf{u} + \mathbf{v}$ is a vector in V.
(c2) $a\mathbf{v}$ is a vector in V.

Properties of addition:

(a1) $\mathbf{u} + \mathbf{v} = \mathbf{v} + \mathbf{u}$.
(a2) $\mathbf{u} + (\mathbf{v} + \mathbf{w}) = (\mathbf{u} + \mathbf{v}) + \mathbf{w}$.
(a3) There is a vector $\boldsymbol{\theta}$ in V such that $\mathbf{v} + \boldsymbol{\theta} = \mathbf{v}$ for all $\mathbf{v}$ in V.
(a4) Given a vector $\mathbf{v}$ in V, there is a vector $-\mathbf{v}$ in V such that $\mathbf{v} + (-\mathbf{v}) = \boldsymbol{\theta}$.

Properties of scalar multiplication:

(m1) $a(b\mathbf{v}) = (ab)\mathbf{v}$.
(m2) $a(\mathbf{u} + \mathbf{v}) = a\mathbf{u} + a\mathbf{v}$.
(m3) $(a + b)\mathbf{v} = a\mathbf{v} + b\mathbf{v}$.
(m4) $1\mathbf{v} = \mathbf{v}$ for all $\mathbf{v}$ in V.

The first two conditions, (c1) and (c2), in Definition 1, called ***closure properties***, ensure that the sum of any two vectors in V remains in V and that any scalar multiple of a vector in V remains in V. In condition (a3), $\boldsymbol{\theta}$ is naturally called the ***zero vector*** (or the ***additive identity***). In (a4), the vector $-\mathbf{v}$ is called the ***additive inverse*** of $\mathbf{v}$, and (a4) asserts that the equation $\mathbf{v} + \mathbf{x} = \boldsymbol{\theta}$ has a solution in V. When the set of scalars S is the set of real numbers, V is called a ***real vector space***; and as we have said, we will consider only real vector spaces.

Example of Vector Spaces

We already have two familiar examples of vector spaces, namely, R^n and the set of all $(m \times n)$ matrices. It is easy to verify that these are vector spaces, and the verification is sketched in the next two examples.

EXAMPLE 1 For any positive integer n, verify that R^n is a real vector space.

Solution Theorem 1 of Section 3.2 shows that R^n satisfies the properties listed in Definition 1, so R^n is a real vector space.

Example 2 may strike the reader as being a little unusual since we are considering matrices as elements in a vector space. The example, however, illustrates the flexibility of the vector-space concept; any set of entities that has addition and scalar multiplication operations can be a vector space, provided that addition and scalar multiplication satisfy the requirements of Definition 1.

EXAMPLE 2 Verify that the set of all (2×3) matrices with real entries is a real vector space.

Solution Let A and B be any (2×3) matrices, and let addition and scalar multiplication be defined as in Definitions 6 and 7 of Section 1.5. Therefore, $A + B$ and aA are defined by

$$A + B = \begin{bmatrix} a_{11} & a_{12} & a_{13} \\ a_{21} & a_{22} & a_{23} \end{bmatrix} + \begin{bmatrix} b_{11} & b_{12} & b_{13} \\ b_{21} & b_{22} & b_{23} \end{bmatrix}$$

$$= \begin{bmatrix} a_{11} + b_{11} & a_{12} + b_{12} & a_{13} + b_{13} \\ a_{21} + b_{21} & a_{22} + b_{22} & a_{23} + b_{23} \end{bmatrix}$$

$$aA = a\begin{bmatrix} a_{11} & a_{12} & a_{13} \\ a_{21} & a_{22} & a_{23} \end{bmatrix} = \begin{bmatrix} aa_{11} & aa_{12} & aa_{13} \\ aa_{21} & aa_{22} & aa_{23} \end{bmatrix}.$$

From these definitions it is obvious that both the sum $A + B$ and the scalar multiple aA are again (2×3) matrices; so (c1) and (c2) of Definition 1 hold. Properties (a1), (a2), (a3), and (a4) follow from Theorem 7 of Section 1.6; and (m1), (m2), and (m3) are proved in Theorems 8 and 9 of Section 1.6. Property (m4) is immediate from the definition of scalar multiplication [clearly $1A = A$ for any (2×3) matrix A]. For emphasis we recall that the zero element in this vector space is the matrix

$$\mathcal{O} = \begin{bmatrix} 0 & 0 & 0 \\ 0 & 0 & 0 \end{bmatrix},$$

and clearly $A + \mathcal{O} = A$ for any (2×3) matrix A. We further observe that $(-1)A$ is the additive inverse for A because

$$A + (-1)A = \mathcal{O}.$$

[That is, $(-1)A$ is a matrix we can add to A to produce the zero element $\mathcal{O}$.] A duplication of these arguments shows that for any m and n the set of all $(m \times n)$ matrices with real entries is a real vector space.

The next three examples show that certain sets of functions have a natural vector-space structure.

EXAMPLE 3 Let $\mathcal{P}_2$ denote the set of all real polynomials of degree 2 or less. Verify that $\mathcal{P}_2$ is a real vector space.

Solution Note that a natural addition is associated with polynomials. For example, let $p(x)$ and $q(x)$ be the polynomials

$$p(x) = 2x^2 - x + 3 \text{ and } q(x) = x^2 + 2x - 1.$$

Then the sum $r(x) = p(x) + q(x)$ is the polynomial $r(x) = 3x^2 + x + 2$. Scalar multiplication is defined similarly; so if $s(x) = 2q(x)$, then

$$s(x) = 2x^2 + 4x - 2.$$

Given this natural addition and scalar multiplication associated with the set $\mathcal{P}_2$, it seems reasonable to expect that $\mathcal{P}_2$ is a real vector space.

To establish this conclusion rigorously, we must be a bit more careful. To begin, we define $\mathcal{P}_2$ to be the set of all expressions (or functions) of the form

$$p(x) = a_2x^2 + a_1x + a_0, \tag{1}$$

where a_2, a_1, and a_0 are any real constants. Thus the following polynomials are vectors in $\mathcal{P}_2$:

$$p_1(x) = x^2 - x + 3, \quad p_2(x) = x^2 + 1, \quad p_3(x) = x - 2,$$
$$p_4(x) = 2x, \quad p_5(x) = 7, \quad p_6(x) = 0.$$

For instance, we see that $p_2(x)$ has the form of Eq. (1), with $a_2 = 1, a_1 = 0$, and $a_0 = 1$. Similarly, $p_4(x)$ is in $\mathcal{P}_2$ because $p_4(x)$ is a function of the form (1), where $a_2 = 0, a_1 = 2$, and $a_0 = 0$. Finally, $p_6(x)$ has the form (1) with $a_2 = 0, a_1 = 0$, and $a_0 = 0$. To define addition precisely, let

$$p(x) = a_2x^2 + a_1x + a_0 \text{ and } q(x) = b_2x^2 + b_1x + b_0$$

be two vectors in $\mathcal{P}_2$. We define the sum $r(x) = p(x) + q(x)$ to be the polynomial

$$r(x) = (a_2 + b_2)x^2 + (a_1 + b_1)x + (a_0 + b_0);$$

and we define the scalar multiple $s(x) = cp(x)$ to be the polynomial

$$s(x) = (ca_2)x^2 + (ca_1)x + (ca_0).$$

We leave it to the reader to verify that these algebraic operations meet the requirements of Definition 1; we note only that we choose the zero vector to be the polynomial that is identically zero. That is, the zero element in $\mathcal{P}_2$ is the polynomial $\theta(x)$, where $\theta(x) = 0$; or in terms of Eq. (1), $\theta(x)$ is defined by

$$\theta(x) = 0x^2 + 0x + 0.$$

EXAMPLE 4 In this example we take $\mathcal{P}_n$ to be the set of all real polynomials of degree n or less. That is, $\mathcal{P}_n$ consists of all functions $p(x)$ of the form

$$p(x) = a_n x^n + a_{n-1}x^{n-1} + \cdots + a_2 x^2 + a_1 x + a_0,$$

where $a_n, a_{n-1}, \ldots, a_2, a_1, a_0$ are any real constants. With addition and scalar multiplication defined as in Example 3, it is easy to show that $\mathcal{P}_n$ is a real vector space. ■

The next example presents one of the more important vector spaces in applications.

EXAMPLE 5 Let $C[a, b]$ be the set of functions defined by

$$C[a, b] = \{f(x)\colon f(x) \text{ is a real-valued continuous function, } \ a \le x \le b\}.$$

Verify that $C[a, b]$ is a real vector space.

Solution $C[a, b]$ has a natural addition, just as $\mathcal{P}_n$. If f and g are vectors in $C[a, b]$, then we define the sum $h = f + g$ to be the function h given by

$$h(x) = f(x) + g(x), \quad a \le x \le b.$$

Similarly, if c is a scalar, then the scalar multiple $q = cf$ is the function

$$q(x) = cf(x), \quad a \le x \le b.$$

As a concrete example, if $f(x) = e^x$ and $g(x) = \sin x$, then $3f + g$ is the function r, where the action of r is defined by $r(x) = 3e^x + \sin x$. Note that the closure properties, (c1) and (c2), follow from elementary results of calculus—sums and scalar multiples of continuous functions are again continuous functions. The remaining eight properties of Definition 1 are easily seen to hold in $C[a, b]$; the verification proceeds exactly as in $\mathcal{P}_n$. ■

Note that any polynomial can be regarded as a continuous function on any interval $[a, b]$. Thus for any given positive integer n, $\mathcal{P}_n$ is not only a subset of $C[a, b]$ but also a vector space contained in the vector space $C[a, b]$. This concept of a vector space that contains a smaller vector space (or a vector subspace) is quite important and is one topic of the next section.

FUNCTION SPACES The giant step of expanding vector spaces from R^n to spaces of functions was a combined effort of many mathematicians. Probably foremost among them, however, was David Hilbert (1862–1943), for whom Hilbert spaces are named. Hilbert had great success in solving several important contemporary problems by emphasizing abstraction and an axiomatic approach. His ideas on abstract spaces came largely from his work on important integral equations in physics. Hilbert related integral equations to problems of infinitely-many equations in infinitely-many unknowns, a natural extension of a fundamental problem in the setting of R^n. Great credit for expansion of vector-space ideas is also given to the work of Riesz, Fischer, Fréchet, and Weyl. In particular, Hermann Weyl (1885–1955) was known for his stress on the rigorous application of axiomatic logic rather than visual plausibility, which was all too often accepted as proof.

Further Vector-Space Properties

The algebraic operations in a vector space have additional properties that can be derived from the 10 fundamental properties listed in Definition 1. The first of these, the cancellation laws for vector addition, are straightforward to prove and will be left as exercises.

> **Cancellation Laws for Vector Addition**
>
> Let V be a vector space, and let $\mathbf{u}$, $\mathbf{v}$, and $\mathbf{w}$ be vectors in V.
>
> **1.** If $\mathbf{u} + \mathbf{v} = \mathbf{u} + \mathbf{w}$, then $\mathbf{v} = \mathbf{w}$.
>
> **2.** If $\mathbf{v} + \mathbf{u} = \mathbf{w} + \mathbf{u}$, then $\mathbf{v} = \mathbf{w}$.

Some additional properties of vector spaces are summarized in Theorem 1.

THEOREM 1 If V is a vector space, then:

1. The zero vector, $\boldsymbol{\theta}$, is unique.

2. For each $\mathbf{v}$, the additive inverse $-\mathbf{v}$ is unique.

3. $0\mathbf{v} = \boldsymbol{\theta}$ for every $\mathbf{v}$ in V, where 0 is the zero scalar.

4. $a\boldsymbol{\theta} = \boldsymbol{\theta}$ for every scalar a.

5. If $a\mathbf{v} = \boldsymbol{\theta}$, then $a = 0$ or $\mathbf{v} = \boldsymbol{\theta}$.

6. $(-1)\mathbf{v} = -\mathbf{v}$.

Proof [We prove properties 1, 4, and 6 and leave the remaining properties as exercises.] We first prove property 1. Suppose that ζ is a vector in V such that $\mathbf{v} + \zeta = \mathbf{v}$ for all $\mathbf{v}$ in V. Then setting $\mathbf{v} = \boldsymbol{\theta}$, we have

$$\boldsymbol{\theta} + \zeta = \boldsymbol{\theta}. \tag{2}$$

By property (a3) of Definition 1, we know also that

$$\zeta + \boldsymbol{\theta} = \zeta. \tag{3}$$

But from property (a1) of Definition 1, we know that $\zeta + \boldsymbol{\theta} = \boldsymbol{\theta} + \zeta$; so using Eq. (2), property (a1), and Eq. (3), we conclude that

$$\boldsymbol{\theta} = \boldsymbol{\theta} + \zeta = \zeta + \boldsymbol{\theta} = \zeta,$$

or $\boldsymbol{\theta} = \zeta$.

We next prove property 4 of Theorem 1. We do so by observing that $\boldsymbol{\theta} + \boldsymbol{\theta} = \boldsymbol{\theta}$, from property (a3) of Definition 1. Therefore if a is any scalar, we see from property (m2) of Definition 1 that

$$a\boldsymbol{\theta} = a(\boldsymbol{\theta} + \boldsymbol{\theta}) = a\boldsymbol{\theta} + a\boldsymbol{\theta}. \tag{4}$$

Since $a\boldsymbol{\theta} = a\boldsymbol{\theta} + \boldsymbol{\theta}$ by property (a3) of Definition 1, Eq. (4) becomes

$$a\boldsymbol{\theta} + \boldsymbol{\theta} = a\boldsymbol{\theta} + a\boldsymbol{\theta}.$$

The cancellation laws now yield $\boldsymbol{\theta} = a\boldsymbol{\theta}$.

Finally, we outline a proof for property 6 of Theorem 1 by displaying a sequence of equalities (the last equality is based on property 3, which is an exercise):

$$\mathbf{v} + (-1)\mathbf{v} = (1)\mathbf{v} + (-1)\mathbf{v} = [1 + (-1)]\mathbf{v} = 0\mathbf{v} = \boldsymbol{\theta}.$$

Thus $(-1)\mathbf{v}$ is a solution to the equation $\mathbf{v} + \mathbf{x} = \boldsymbol{\theta}$. But from property 2 of Theorem 1, the additive inverse $-\mathbf{v}$ is the only solution of $\mathbf{v} + \mathbf{x} = \boldsymbol{\theta}$; so we must have $(-1)\mathbf{v} = -\mathbf{v}$. Thus property 6 constitutes a formula for the additive inverse. This formula is not totally unexpected, but neither is it so obvious as it might seem, since a number of vector-space properties were required to prove it. ■

EXAMPLE 6 We conclude this section by introducing the ***zero vector space***. The zero vector space contains only one vector, $\boldsymbol{\theta}$; the arithmetic operations are defined by

$$\boldsymbol{\theta} + \boldsymbol{\theta} = \boldsymbol{\theta}$$
$$k\boldsymbol{\theta} = \boldsymbol{\theta}.$$

It is easy to verify that the set $\{\boldsymbol{\theta}\}$ with the operations just defined is a vector space. ■

5.2 EXERCISES

For $\mathbf{u}$, $\mathbf{v}$, and $\mathbf{w}$ given in Exercises 1–3, calculate $\mathbf{u} - 2\mathbf{v}$, $\mathbf{u} - (2\mathbf{v} - 3\mathbf{w})$, and $-2\mathbf{u} - \mathbf{v} + 3\mathbf{w}$.

1. In the vector space of (2×3) matrices

$$\mathbf{u} = \begin{bmatrix} 2 & 1 & 3 \\ -1 & 1 & 2 \end{bmatrix}, \quad \mathbf{v} = \begin{bmatrix} 1 & 4 & -1 \\ 5 & 2 & 7 \end{bmatrix},$$
$$\mathbf{w} = \begin{bmatrix} 4 & -5 & 11 \\ -13 & -1 & -1 \end{bmatrix}.$$

2. In the vector space $\mathcal{P}_2$

$$\mathbf{u} = x^2 - 2, \quad \mathbf{v} = x^2 + 2x - 1, \quad \mathbf{w} = 2x + 1.$$

3. In the vector space $C[0, 1]$

$$\mathbf{u} = e^x, \quad \mathbf{v} = \sin x, \quad \mathbf{w} = \sqrt{x^2 + 1}.$$

4. For $\mathbf{u}$, $\mathbf{v}$, and $\mathbf{w}$ in Exercise 2, find nonzero scalars c_1, c_2, c_3 such that $c_1\mathbf{u} + c_2\mathbf{v} + c_3\mathbf{w} = \boldsymbol{\theta}$. Are there nonzero scalars c_1, c_2, c_3 such that $c_1\mathbf{u} + c_2\mathbf{v} + c_3\mathbf{w} = \boldsymbol{\theta}$ for $\mathbf{u}$, $\mathbf{v}$, and $\mathbf{w}$ in Exercise 1?

5. For $\mathbf{u}$, $\mathbf{v}$, and $\mathbf{w}$ in Exercise 2, find scalars c_1, c_2, c_3 such that $c_1\mathbf{u} + c_2\mathbf{v} + c_3\mathbf{w} = x^2 + 6x + 1$. Show that there are no scalars c_1, c_2, c_3 such that $c_1\mathbf{u} + c_2\mathbf{v} + c_3\mathbf{w} = x^2$.

In Exercises 6–11, the given set is a subset of a vector space. Which of these subsets are also vector spaces in their own right? To answer this question, determine whether the subset satisfies the 10 properties of Definition 1. (*Note:* Because these sets are subsets of a vector space, properties (a1), (a2), (m1), (m2), (m3), and (m4) are automatically satisfied.)

6. $S = \{\mathbf{v} \text{ in } R^4\colon v_1 + v_4 = 0\}$

7. $S = \{\mathbf{v} \text{ in } R^4\colon v_1 + v_4 = 1\}$

8. $P = \{p(x) \text{ in } \mathcal{P}_2\colon p(0) = 0\}$

9. $P = \{p(x) \text{ in } \mathcal{P}_2\colon p''(0) \neq 0\}$

10. $P = \{p(x) \text{ in } \mathcal{P}_2\colon p(x) = p(-x) \text{ for all } x\}$

11. $P = \{p(x) \text{ in } \mathcal{P}_2\colon p(x) \text{ has degree } 2\}$

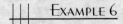

In Exercises 12–16, V is the vector space of all real (3×4) matrices. Which of the given subsets of V are also vector spaces?

12. $S = \{A \text{ in } V: a_{11} = 0\}$

13. $S = \{A \text{ in } V: a_{11} + a_{23} = 0\}$

14. $S = \{A \text{ in } V: |a_{11}| + |a_{21}| = 1\}$

15. $S = \{A \text{ in } V: a_{32} \neq 0\}$

16. $S = \{A \text{ in } V: \text{ each } a_{ij} \text{ is an integer}\}$

17. Let Q denote the set of all (2×2) nonsingular matrices with the usual matrix addition and scalar multiplication. Show that Q is not a vector space by exhibiting specific matrices in Q that violate property (c1) of Definition 1. Also show that properties (c2) and (a3) are not met.

18. Let Q denote the set of all (2×2) singular matrices with the usual matrix addition and scalar multiplication. Determine whether Q is a vector space.

19. Let Q denote the set of all (2×2) symmetric matrices with the usual matrix addition and scalar multiplication. Verify that Q is a vector space.

20. Prove the cancellation laws for vector addition.

21. Prove property 2 of Theorem 1. [*Hint:* See the proof of Theorem 15 in Section 1.9.]

22. Prove property 3 of Theorem 1. [*Hint:* Note that $0\mathbf{v} = (0 + 0)\mathbf{v}$. Now mimic the proof given for property 4.]

23. Prove property 5 of Theorem 1. (If $a \neq 0$ then multiply both sides of $a\mathbf{v} = \boldsymbol{\theta}$ by a^{-1}. Use properties (m1) and (m4) of Definition 1 and use property 4 of Theorem 1.)

24. Prove that the zero vector space, defined in Example 6, is indeed a vector space.

In Exercises 25–29, the given set is a subset of $C[-1, 1]$. Which of these are also vector spaces?

25. $F = \{f(x) \text{ in } C[-1, 1]: f(-1) = f(1)\}$

26. $F = \{f(x) \text{ in } C[-1, 1]: f(x) = 0 \text{ for } -1/2 \leq x \leq 1/2\}$

27. $F = \{f(x) \text{ in } C[-1, 1]: f(1) = 1\}$

28. $F = \{f(x) \text{ in } C[-1, 1]: f(1) = 0\}$

29. $F = \left\{f(x) \text{ in } C[-1, 1]: \int_{-1}^{1} f(x)\,dx = 0\right\}$

30. The set $C^2[a, b]$ is defined to be the set of all real-valued functions $f(x)$ defined on $[a, b]$, where $f(x)$, $f'(x)$, and $f''(x)$ are continuous on $[a, b]$. Verify that $C^2[a, b]$ is a vector space by citing the appropriate theorems on continuity and differentiability from calculus.

31. The following are subsets of the vector space $C^2[-1, 1]$. Which of these are vector spaces?

a) $F = \{f(x) \text{ in } C^2[-1, 1]: f''(x) + f(x) = 0, -1 \leq x \leq 1\}$

b) $F = \{f(x) \text{ in } C^2[-1, 1]: f''(x) + f(x) = x^2, -1 \leq x \leq 1\}$

32. Show that the set $\mathcal{P}$ of all real polynomials is a vector space.

33. Let $\mathcal{F}(R)$ denote the set of all real-valued functions defined on the reals. Thus

$$\mathcal{F}(R) = \{f: f \text{ is a function}, f: R \to R\}.$$

With addition of functions and scalar multiplication defined as in Example 5, show that $\mathcal{F}(R)$ is a vector space.

34. Let

$$V = \left\{\mathbf{x}: \mathbf{x} = \begin{bmatrix} x_1 \\ x_2 \end{bmatrix}, \text{ where } x_1 \text{ and } x_2 \text{ are in } R\right\}.$$

For $\mathbf{u}$ and $\mathbf{v}$ in V and c in R, define the operations of addition and scalar multiplication on V by

$$\mathbf{u} + \mathbf{v} = \begin{bmatrix} u_1 \\ u_2 \end{bmatrix} + \begin{bmatrix} v_1 \\ v_2 \end{bmatrix} = \begin{bmatrix} u_1 + v_1 + 1 \\ u_2 + v_2 - 1 \end{bmatrix} \text{ and}$$

$$c\mathbf{u} = \begin{bmatrix} cu_1 \\ cu_2 \end{bmatrix}. \qquad (5)$$

a) Show that the operations defined in (5) satisfy properties (c1), (c2), (a1)–(a4), (m1), and (m4) of Definition 1.

b) Give examples to illustrate that properties (m2) and (m3) are not satisfied by the operations defined in (5).

35. Let

$$V = \left\{\mathbf{x}: \mathbf{x} = \begin{bmatrix} x_1 \\ x_2 \end{bmatrix}, \text{ where } x_1 \text{ and } x_2 \text{ are in } R\right\}.$$

For $\mathbf{u}$ and $\mathbf{v}$ in V and c in R, define the operations of addition and scalar multiplication on V by

$$\mathbf{u}+\mathbf{v}=\begin{bmatrix} u_1 \\ u_2 \end{bmatrix}+\begin{bmatrix} v_1 \\ v_2 \end{bmatrix}=\begin{bmatrix} u_1+v_1 \\ u_2+v_2 \end{bmatrix} \text{ and}$$

$$c\mathbf{u}=\begin{bmatrix} 0 \\ 0 \end{bmatrix}. \qquad (6)$$

Show that the operations defined in (6) satisfy all the properties of Definition 1 except (m4). (Note that the addition given in (6) is the usual addition of R^2. Since R^2 is a vector space, all the additive properties of Definition 1 are satisfied.)

36. Let

$$V = \{\mathbf{x}\colon \mathbf{x} = \begin{bmatrix} x_1 \\ x_2 \end{bmatrix}, \text{ where } x_2 > 0\}.$$

For $\mathbf{u}$ and $\mathbf{v}$ in V and c in R, define addition and scalar multiplication by

$$\mathbf{u}+\mathbf{v}=\begin{bmatrix} u_1 \\ u_2 \end{bmatrix}+\begin{bmatrix} v_1 \\ v_2 \end{bmatrix}=\begin{bmatrix} u_1+v_1 \\ u_2v_2 \end{bmatrix} \text{ and}$$

$$c\mathbf{u}=\begin{bmatrix} cu_1 \\ u_2^c \end{bmatrix}. \qquad (7)$$

With the operations defined in (7), show that V is a vector space.

5.3 SUBSPACES

Chapter 3 demonstrated that whenever W is a p-dimensional subspace of R^n, then W behaves essentially like R^p (for instance, any set of $p+1$ vectors in W is linearly dependent). The situation is much the same in a general vector space V. In this setting, certain subsets of V inherit the vector-space structure of V and are vector spaces in their own right.

DEFINITION 2 If V and W are real vector spaces, and if W is a nonempty subset of V, then W is called a ***subspace*** of V.

Subspaces have considerable practical importance and are useful in problems involving approximation, optimization, differential equations, and so on. The vector-space/subspace framework allows us to pose and rigorously answer questions such as, *How can we find good polynomial approximations to complicated functions?* and *How can we generate good approximate solutions to differential equations?* Questions such as these are at the heart of many technical problems; and vector-space techniques, together with the computational power of the computer, are useful in helping to answer them.

As was the case in R^n, it is fairly easy to recognize when a subset of a vector space V is actually a subspace. Specifically, the following restatement of Theorem 2 of Section 3.2 holds in any vector space.

THEOREM 2 Let W be a subset of a vector space V. Then W is a subspace of V if and only if the following conditions are met:

(s1) The zero vector, $\boldsymbol{\theta}$, of V is in W.

(s2) $\mathbf{u}+\mathbf{v}$ is in W whenever $\mathbf{u}$ and $\mathbf{v}$ are in W.

(s3) $a\mathbf{u}$ is in W whenever $\mathbf{u}$ is in W and a is any scalar.

The proof of Theorem 2 coincides with the proof given in Section 3.2 with one minor exception. In R^n it is easily seen that $-\mathbf{v} = (-1)\mathbf{v}$ for any vector $\mathbf{v}$. In a general vector space V, this is a consequence of Theorem 1 of Section 5.2.

Examples of Subspaces

If we are given that W is a subset of a known vector space V, Theorem 2 simplifies the task of determining whether or not W is itself a vector space. Instead of testing all 10 properties of Definition 1, Theorem 2 states that we need only verify that properties (s1)–(s3) hold. Furthermore, just as in Chapter 3, a subset W of V will be specified by certain defining relationships that tell whether a vector $\mathbf{u}$ is in W. Thus to verify that (s1) holds, it must be shown that the zero vector, $\boldsymbol{\theta}$, of V satisfies the specification given for W. To check (s2) and (s3), we select two arbitrary vectors, say $\mathbf{u}$ and $\mathbf{v}$, that satisfy the defining relationships of W (that is, $\mathbf{u}$ and $\mathbf{v}$ are in W). We then test $\mathbf{u}+\mathbf{v}$ and $a\mathbf{u}$ to see whether they also satisfy the defining relationships of W. (That is, do $\mathbf{u}+\mathbf{v}$ and $a\mathbf{u}$ belong to W?) The next three examples illustrate the use of Theorem 2.

EXAMPLE 1 Let V be the vector space of all real (2×2) matrices, and let W be the subset of V specified by

$$W = \{A\colon A = \begin{bmatrix} 0 & a_{12} \\ a_{21} & 0 \end{bmatrix},\ a_{12} \text{ and } a_{21} \text{ any real scalars}\}.$$

Verify that W is a subspace of V.

Solution The zero vector for V is the (2×2) zero matrix $\mathcal{O}$, and $\mathcal{O}$ is in W since it satisfies the defining relationships of W. If A and B are any two vectors in W, then A and B have the form

$$A = \begin{bmatrix} 0 & a_{12} \\ a_{21} & 0 \end{bmatrix}, \quad B = \begin{bmatrix} 0 & b_{12} \\ b_{21} & 0 \end{bmatrix}.$$

Thus $A+B$ and aA have the form

$$A+B = \begin{bmatrix} 0 & a_{12}+b_{12} \\ a_{21}+b_{21} & 0 \end{bmatrix}, \quad aA = \begin{bmatrix} 0 & aa_{12} \\ aa_{21} & 0 \end{bmatrix}.$$

Therefore, $A+B$ and aA are in W, and we conclude that W is a subspace of the set of all real (2×2) matrices. ■

EXAMPLE 2 Let W be the subset of $C[a, b]$ (see Example 5 of Section 5.2) defined by

$$W = \{f(x) \text{ in } C[a, b]\colon f(a) = f(b)\}.$$

Verify that W is a subspace of $C[a, b]$.

Solution The zero vector in $C[a, b]$ is the zero function, $\theta(x)$, defined by $\theta(x) = 0$ for all x in the interval $[a, b]$. In particular, $\theta(a) = \theta(b)$ since $\theta(a) = 0$ and $\theta(b) = 0$. Therefore, $\theta(x)$ is in W. Now let $g(x)$ and $h(x)$ be any two functions that are in W, that is,

$$g(a) = g(b) \text{ and } h(a) = h(b). \tag{1}$$

The sum of $g(x)$ and $h(x)$ is the function $s(x)$ defined by $s(x) = g(x) + h(x)$. To see that $s(x)$ is in W, note that property (1) gives

$$s(a) = g(a) + h(a) = g(b) + h(b) = s(b).$$

Similarly, if c is a scalar, then it is immediate from property (1) that $cg(a) = cg(b)$. It follows that $cg(x)$ is in W. Theorem 2 now implies that W is a subspace of $C[a, b]$. ∎

The next example illustrates how to use Theorem 2 to show that a subset of a vector space is not a vector space. Recall from Chapter 3 that if a subset fails to satisfy any one of the properties (s1), (s2), or (s3), then it is not a subspace.

EXAMPLE 3 Let V be the vector space of all (2×2) matrices, and let W be the subspace of V specified by

$$W = \{A \colon A = \begin{bmatrix} a & b \\ c & d \end{bmatrix}, \quad ad = 0 \text{ and } bc = 0\}.$$

Show that W is not a subspace of V.

Solution It is straightforward to show that W satisfies properties (s1) and (s3) of Theorem 2. Thus to demonstrate that W is not a subspace of V, we must show that (s2) fails. It suffices to give a specific example that illustrates the failure of (s2). For example, define A and B by

$$A = \begin{bmatrix} 1 & 0 \\ 0 & 0 \end{bmatrix} \quad \text{and} \quad B = \begin{bmatrix} 0 & 0 \\ 0 & 1 \end{bmatrix}.$$

Then A and B are in W, but $A + B$ is not, since

$$A + B = \begin{bmatrix} 1 & 0 \\ 0 & 1 \end{bmatrix}.$$

In particular, $ad = (1)(1) = 1$, so $ad \neq 0$. ∎

If $n \leq m$, then $\mathcal{P}_n$ is a subspace of $\mathcal{P}_m$. We can verify this assertion directly from Definition 2 since we have already shown that $\mathcal{P}_n$ and $\mathcal{P}_m$ are each real vector spaces, and $\mathcal{P}_n$ is a subset of $\mathcal{P}_m$. Similarly, for any n, $\mathcal{P}_n$ is a subspace of $C[a, b]$. Again this assertion follows directly from Definition 2 since any polynomial is continuous on any interval $[a, b]$. Therefore, $\mathcal{P}_n$ can be considered a subspace of $C[a, b]$, as well as a vector space in its own right.

Spanning Sets

The vector-space structure as given in Definition 1 guarantees that the notion of a linear combination makes sense in a general vector space. Specifically, the vector **v** is a ***linear***

combination of the vectors $\mathbf{v}_1, \mathbf{v}_2, \ldots, \mathbf{v}_m$ provided that there exist scalars $a_1, a_2, \ldots, a_m$ such that

$$\mathbf{v} = a_1\mathbf{v}_1 + a_2\mathbf{v}_2 + \cdots + a_m\mathbf{v}_m.$$

The next example illustrates this concept in the vector space $\mathcal{P}_2$.

EXAMPLE 4 In $\mathcal{P}_2$ let $p(x)$, $p_1(x)$, $p_2(x)$, and $p_3(x)$ be defined by $p(x) = -1 + 2x^2$, $p_1(x) = 1 + 2x - 2x^2$, $p_2(x) = -1 - x$, and $p_3(x) = -3 - 4x + 4x^2$. Express $p(x)$ as a linear combination of $p_1(x)$, $p_2(x)$, and $p_3(x)$.

Solution Setting $p(x) = a_1p_1(x) + a_2p_2(x) + a_3p_3(x)$ yields

$$-1 + 2x^2 = a_1(1 + 2x - 2x^2) + a_2(-1 - x) + a_3(-3 - 4x + 4x^2).$$

Equating coefficients yields the system of equations

$$\begin{aligned} a_1 - a_2 - 3a_3 &= -1 \\ 2a_1 - a_2 - 4a_3 &= 0 \\ -2a_1 + 4a_3 &= 2. \end{aligned}$$

This system has the unique solution $a_1 = 3$, $a_2 = -2$, and $a_3 = 2$. We can easily check that

$$p(x) = 3p_1(x) - 2p_2(x) + 2p_3(x).$$

The very useful concept of a spanning set is suggested by the preceding discussion.

DEFINITION 3 Let V be a vector space, and let $Q = \{\mathbf{v}_1, \mathbf{v}_2, \ldots, \mathbf{v}_m\}$ be a set of vectors in V. If every vector $\mathbf{v}$ in V is a linear combination of vectors in Q,

$$\mathbf{v} = a_1\mathbf{v}_1 + a_2\mathbf{v}_2 + \cdots + a_m\mathbf{v}_m,$$

then we say that Q is a ***spanning set*** for V.

For many vector spaces V, it is relatively easy to find a natural spanning set. For example, it is easily seen that $\{1, x, x^2\}$ is a spanning set for $\mathcal{P}_2$ and, in general, $\{1, x, \ldots, x^n\}$ is a spanning set for $\mathcal{P}_n$. The vector space of all (2×2) matrices is spanned by the set $\{E_{11}, E_{12}, E_{21}, E_{22}\}$, where

$$E_{11} = \begin{bmatrix} 1 & 0 \\ 0 & 0 \end{bmatrix}, \quad E_{12} = \begin{bmatrix} 0 & 1 \\ 0 & 0 \end{bmatrix}, \quad E_{21} = \begin{bmatrix} 0 & 0 \\ 1 & 0 \end{bmatrix}, \quad \text{and} \quad E_{22} = \begin{bmatrix} 0 & 0 \\ 0 & 1 \end{bmatrix}.$$

More generally, if the $(m \times n)$ matrix E_{ij} is the matrix with 1 as the ijth entry and zeros elsewhere, then $\{E_{ij}: 1 \le i \le m, 1 \le j \le n\}$ is a spanning set for the vector space of $(m \times n)$ real matrices.

If $Q = \{\mathbf{v}_1, \mathbf{v}_2, \ldots, \mathbf{v}_k\}$ is a set of vectors in a vector space V, then, as in Section 3.3, the ***span*** of Q, denoted $\mathrm{Sp}(Q)$, is the set of all linear combinations of $\mathbf{v}_1, \mathbf{v}_2, \ldots, \mathbf{v}_k$:

$$\mathrm{Sp}(Q) = \{\mathbf{v}: \mathbf{v} = a_1\mathbf{v}_1 + a_2\mathbf{v}_2 + \cdots + a_k\mathbf{v}_k\}.$$

From closure properties (c1) and (c2) of Definition 1, it is obvious that Sp(Q) is a subset of V. In fact, the proof of Theorem 3 in Section 3.3 is valid in a general vector space, so we have the following theorem.

THEOREM 3 If V is a vector space and $Q = \{\mathbf{v}_1, \mathbf{v}_2, \ldots, \mathbf{v}_k\}$ is a set of vectors in V, then Sp(Q) is a subspace of V. ■

The connection between spanning sets and the span of a set is fairly obvious. If W is a subspace of V and $Q \subseteq W$, then Q is a spanning set for W if and only if $W = \text{Sp}(Q)$. As the next three examples illustrate, it is often easy to obtain a spanning set for a subspace W when an algebraic specification for W is given.

EXAMPLE 5 Let V be the vector space of all real (2×2) matrices, and let W be the subspace given in Example 1:

$$W = \{A\colon A = \begin{bmatrix} 0 & a_{12} \\ a_{21} & 0 \end{bmatrix}, \quad a_{12} \text{ and } a_{21} \text{ any real scalars}\}.$$

Find a spanning set for W.

Solution One obvious spanning set for W is seen to be the set of vectors $Q = \{A_1, A_2\}$, where

$$A_1 = \begin{bmatrix} 0 & 1 \\ 0 & 0 \end{bmatrix} \quad \text{and} \quad A_2 = \begin{bmatrix} 0 & 0 \\ 1 & 0 \end{bmatrix}.$$

To verify this assertion, suppose A is in W, where

$$A = \begin{bmatrix} 0 & a_{12} \\ a_{21} & 0 \end{bmatrix}.$$

Then clearly $A = a_{12}A_1 + a_{21}A_2$, and therefore Q is a spanning set for W. ■

EXAMPLE 6 Let W be the subspace of $\mathcal{P}_2$ defined by

$$W = \{p(x)\colon p(x) = a_0 + a_1x + a_2x^2, \quad \text{where } a_2 = -a_1 + 2a_0\}.$$

Exhibit a spanning set for W.

Solution Let $p(x) = a_0 + a_1x + a_2x^2$ be a vector in W. From the specifications of W, we know that $a_2 = -a_1 + 2a_0$. That is,

$$\begin{aligned} p(x) &= a_0 + a_1x + a_2x^2 \\ &= a_0 + a_1x + (-a_1 + 2a_0)x^2 \\ &= a_0(1 + 2x^2) + a_1(x - x^2). \end{aligned}$$

Since every vector p in W is a linear combination of $p_1(x) = 1 + 2x^2$ and $p_2(x) = x - x^2$, we see that $\{p_1(x), p_2(x)\}$ is a spanning set for W. ■

A square matrix, $A = (a_{ij})$, is called ***skew symmetric*** if $A^T = -A$. Recall that the ijth entry of A^T is a_{ji}, the jith entry of A. Thus the entries of A must satisfy $a_{ji} = -a_{ij}$ in order for A to be skew symmetric. In particular, each entry, a_{ii}, on the main diagonal must be zero since $a_{ii} = -a_{ii}$.

EXAMPLE 7 Let W be the set of all (3×3) skew-symmetric matrices. Show that W is a subspace of the vector space V of all (3×3) matrices, and exhibit a spanning set for W.

Solution Let $\mathcal{O}$ denote the (3×3) zero matrix. Clearly $\mathcal{O}^T = \mathcal{O} = -\mathcal{O}$, so $\mathcal{O}$ is in W. If A and B are in W, then $A^T = -A$ and $B^T = -B$. Therefore,

$$(A + B)^T = A^T + B^T = -A - B = -(A + B).$$

It follows that $A + B$ is skew symmetric; that is, $A + B$ is in W. Likewise, if c is a scalar, then

$$(cA)^T = cA^T = c(-A) = -(cA),$$

so cA is in W. By Theorem 2, W is a subspace of V. Moreover, the remarks preceding the example imply that W can be described by

$$W = \{A\colon A = \begin{bmatrix} 0 & a & b \\ -a & 0 & c \\ -b & -c & 0 \end{bmatrix}, \quad a, b, c \text{ any real numbers}\}.$$

From this description it is easily seen that a natural spanning set for W is the set $Q = \{A_1, A_2, A_3\}$, where

$$A_1 = \begin{bmatrix} 0 & 1 & 0 \\ -1 & 0 & 0 \\ 0 & 0 & 0 \end{bmatrix}, \quad A_2 = \begin{bmatrix} 0 & 0 & 1 \\ 0 & 0 & 0 \\ -1 & 0 & 0 \end{bmatrix}, \quad \text{and} \quad A_3 = \begin{bmatrix} 0 & 0 & 0 \\ 0 & 0 & 1 \\ 0 & -1 & 0 \end{bmatrix}.$$

Finally, note that in Definition 3 we have implicitly assumed that spanning sets are finite. This is not a required assumption, and frequently $\mathrm{Sp}(Q)$ is defined as the set of all finite linear combinations of vectors from Q, where Q may be either an infinite set or a finite set. We do not need this full generality, and we will explore this idea no further other than to note later that one contrast between the vector space R^n and a general vector space V is that V might not possess a finite spanning set. An example of a vector space where the most natural spanning set is infinite is the vector space $\mathcal{P}$, consisting of all polynomials (we place no upper limit on the degree). Then, for instance, $\mathcal{P}_n$ is a subspace of $\mathcal{P}$ for each n, $n = 1, 2, 3, \ldots$. A natural spanning set for $\mathcal{P}$ (in the generalized sense described earlier) is the infinite set

$$Q = \{1, x, x^2, \ldots, x^k, \ldots\}.$$

5.3 EXERCISES

Let V be the vector space of all (2×3) matrices. Which of the subsets in Exercises 1–4 are subspaces of V?

1. $W = \{A \text{ in } V\colon a_{11} + a_{13} = 1\}$

2. $W = \{A \text{ in } V\colon a_{11} - a_{12} + 2a_{13} = 0\}$

3. $W = \{A \text{ in } V\colon a_{11} - a_{12} = 0, a_{12} + a_{13} = 0, \text{ and } a_{23} = 0\}$

4. $W = \{A \text{ in } V\colon a_{11}a_{12}a_{13} = 0\}$

In Exercises 5–8, which of the given subsets of $\mathcal{P}_2$ are subspaces of $\mathcal{P}_2$?

5. $W = \{p(x) \text{ in } \mathcal{P}_2\colon p(0) + p(2) = 0\}$

6. $W = \{p(x) \text{ in } \mathcal{P}_2\colon p(1) = p(3)\}$

7. $W = \{p(x) \text{ in } \mathcal{P}_2\colon p(1)p(3) = 0\}$

8. $W = \{p(x) \text{ in } \mathcal{P}_2\colon p(1) = -p(-1)\}$

In Exercises 9–12, which of the given subsets of $C[1, -1]$ are subspaces of $C[-1, 1]$?

9. $F = \{f(x) \text{ in } C[-1, 1]: f(-1) = -f(1)\}$
10. $F = \{f(x) \text{ in } C[-1, 1]: f(x) \geq 0 \text{ for all } x \text{ in } [-1, 1]\}$
11. $F = \{f(x) \text{ in } C[-1, 1]: f(-1) = -2 \text{ and } f(1) = 2\}$
12. $F = \{f(x) \text{ in } C[-1, 1]: f(1/2) = 0\}$

In Exercises 13–16, which of the given subsets of $C^2[-1, 1]$ (see Exercise 30 of Section 5.2) are subspaces of $C^2[-1, 1]$?

13. $F = \{f(x) \text{ in } C^2[-1, 1]: f''(0) = 0\}$
14. $F = \{f(x) \text{ in } C^2[-1, 1]: f''(x) - e^x f'(x) + xf(x) = 0, -1 \leq x \leq 1\}$
15. $F = \{f(x) \text{ in } C^2[-1, 1]: f''(x) + f(x) = \sin x, -1 \leq x \leq 1\}$
16. $F = \{f(x) \text{ in } C^2[-1, 1]: f''(x) = 0, -1 \leq x \leq 1\}$

In Exercises 17–21, express the given vector as a linear combination of the vectors in the given set Q.

17. $p(x) = -1 - 3x + 3x^2$ and $Q = \{p_1(x), p_2(x), p_3(x)\}$, where $p_1(x) = 1 + 2x + x^2$, $p_2(x) = 2 + 5x$, and $p_3(x) = 3 + 8x - 2x^2$
18. $p(x) = -2 - 4x + x^2$ and
$$Q = \{p_1(x), p_2(x), p_3(x), p_4(x)\},$$
and where $p_1(x) = 1 + 2x^2 + x^3$, $p_2(x) = 1 + x + 2x^3$, $p_3(x) = -1 - 3x + 4x^2 - 4x^3$, and $p_4(x) = 1 + 2x - x^2 + x^3$.
19. $A = \begin{bmatrix} -2 & -4 \\ 1 & 0 \end{bmatrix}$ and $Q = \{B_1, B_2, B_3, B_4\}$,

where $B_1 = \begin{bmatrix} 1 & 0 \\ 2 & 1 \end{bmatrix}$, $B_2 = \begin{bmatrix} 1 & 1 \\ 0 & 2 \end{bmatrix}$,

$B_3 = \begin{bmatrix} -1 & -3 \\ 4 & -4 \end{bmatrix}$, and $B_4 = \begin{bmatrix} 1 & 2 \\ -1 & 1 \end{bmatrix}$.
20. $f(x) = e^x$ and $Q = \{\sinh x, \cosh x\}$
21. $f(x) = \cos 2x$ and $Q = \{\sin^2 x, \cos^2 x\}$
22. Let V be the vector space of all (2×2) matrices. The subset W of V defined by
$$W = \{A \text{ in } V: a_{11} - a_{12} = 0, a_{12} + a_{22} = 0\}$$
is a subspace of V. Find a spanning set for W. [*Hint:* Observe that A is in W if and only if A has the form
$$A = \begin{bmatrix} a_{11} & a_{11} \\ a_{21} & -a_{11} \end{bmatrix},$$
where a_{11} and a_{21} are arbitrary.]
23. Let W be the subset of $\mathcal{P}_3$ defined by
$$W = \{p(x) \text{ in } \mathcal{P}_3: p(1) = p(-1) \text{ and } p(2) = p(-2)\}.$$
Show that W is a subspace of $\mathcal{P}_3$, and find a spanning set for W.
24. Let W be the subset of $\mathcal{P}_3$ defined by
$$W = \{p(x) \text{ in } \mathcal{P}_3: p(1) = 0 \text{ and } p'(-1) = 0\}.$$
Show that W is a subspace of $\mathcal{P}_3$, and find a spanning set for W.
25. Find a spanning set for each of the subsets that is a subspace in Exercises 1–8.
26. Show that the set W of all symmetric (3×3) matrices is a subspace of the vector space of all (3×3) matrices. Find a spanning set for W.
27. The trace of an $(n \times n)$ matrix $A = (a_{ij})$, denoted $\text{tr}(A)$, is defined to be the sum of the diagonal elements of A; that is, $\text{tr}(A) = a_{11} + a_{22} + \cdots + a_{nn}$. Let V be the vector space of all (3×3) matrices, and let W be defined by
$$W = \{A \text{ in } V: \text{tr}(A) = 0\}.$$
Show that W is a subspace of V, and exhibit a spanning set for W.
28. Let A be an $(n \times n)$ matrix. Show that $B = (A + A^T)/2$ is symmetric and that $C = (A - A^T)/2$ is skew symmetric.
29. Use Exercise 28 to show that every $(n \times n)$ matrix can be expressed as the sum of a symmetric matrix and a skew-symmetric matrix.
30. Use Exercises 26 and 29 and Example 7 to construct a spanning set for the vector space of all (3×3) matrices where the spanning set consists entirely of symmetric and skew-symmetric matrices. Specify how a (3×3) matrix $A = (a_{ij})$ can be expressed by using this spanning set.
31. Let V be the set of all (3×3) upper-triangular matrices, and note that V is a vector space. Each of the subsets W is a subspace of V. Find a spanning set for W.
   a) $W = \{A \text{ in } V: a_{11} = 0, a_{22} = 0, a_{33} = 0\}$
   b) $W = \{A \text{ in } V: a_{11} + a_{22} + a_{33} = 0, a_{12} + a_{23} = 0\}$

c) $W = \{A \text{ in } V: a_{11} = a_{12}, a_{13} = a_{23}, a_{22} = a_{33}\}$

d) $W = \{A \text{ in } V: a_{11} = a_{22}, a_{22} - a_{33} = 0, a_{12} + a_{23} = 0\}$

32. Let $p(x) = a_0 + a_1x + a_2x^2$ be a vector in $\mathcal{P}_2$. Find b_0, b_1, and b_2 in terms of a_0, a_1, and a_2 so that $p(x) = b_0 + b_1(x+1) + b_2(x+1)^2$. [*Hint:* Equate the coefficients of like powers of x.] Represent $q(x) = 1 - x + 2x^2$ and $r(x) = 2 - 3x + x^2$ in terms of the spanning set $\{1, x+1, (x+1)^2\}$.

33. Let A be an arbitrary matrix in the vector space of all (2×2) matrices:

$$A = \begin{bmatrix} a & b \\ c & d \end{bmatrix}.$$

Find scalars x_1, x_2, x_3, x_4 in terms of a, b, c, and d such that $A = x_1B_1 + x_2B_2 + x_3B_3 + x_4B_4$, where

$$B_1 = \begin{bmatrix} 1 & 0 \\ 1 & -2 \end{bmatrix}, \quad B_2 = \begin{bmatrix} 2 & 1 \\ 1 & -2 \end{bmatrix},$$

$$B_3 = \begin{bmatrix} -1 & 3 \\ -3 & 6 \end{bmatrix}, \quad \text{and} \quad B_4 = \begin{bmatrix} 1 & 1 \\ -2 & 5 \end{bmatrix}.$$

Represent the matrices

$$C = \begin{bmatrix} 0 & 2 \\ -1 & 1 \end{bmatrix} \quad \text{and} \quad D = \begin{bmatrix} 2 & 1 \\ 0 & 1 \end{bmatrix}$$

in terms of the spanning set $\{B_1, B_2, B_3, B_4\}$.

5.4 LINEAR INDEPENDENCE, BASES, AND COORDINATES

One of the central ideas of Chapters 1 and 3 is linear independence. As we will see, this concept generalizes directly to vector spaces. With the concepts of linear independence and spanning sets, it is easy to extend the idea of a basis to our vector-space setting. The notion of a basis is one of the most fundamental concepts in the study of vector spaces. For example, in certain vector spaces a basis can be used to produce a coordinate system for the space. As a consequence, a real vector space with a basis of n vectors behaves essentially like R^n. Moreover, this coordinate system sometimes permits a geometric perspective in an otherwise nongeometric setting.

Linear Independence

We begin by restating Definition 11 of Section 1.7 in a general vector-space setting.

DEFINITION 4 Let V be a vector space, and let $\{\mathbf{v}_1, \mathbf{v}_2, \ldots, \mathbf{v}_p\}$ be a set of vectors in V. This set is ***linearly dependent*** if there are scalars $a_1, a_2, \ldots, a_p$, not all of which are zero, such that

$$a_1\mathbf{v}_1 + a_2\mathbf{v}_2 + \cdots + a_p\mathbf{v}_p = \boldsymbol{\theta}. \tag{1}$$

The set $\{\mathbf{v}_1, \mathbf{v}_2, \ldots, \mathbf{v}_p\}$ is ***linearly independent*** if it is not linearly dependent; that is, the only scalars for which Eq. (1) holds are the scalars $a_1 = a_2 = \cdots = a_p = 0$.

Note that as a consequence of property 3 of Theorem 1 in Section 5.2, the vector equation (1) in Definition 4 always has the trivial solution $a_1 = a_2 = \cdots = a_p = 0$. Thus the set $\{\mathbf{v}_1, \mathbf{v}_2, \ldots, \mathbf{v}_p\}$ is linearly independent if the trivial solution is the only solution to Eq. (1). If another solution exists, then the set is linearly dependent.

As before, it is easy to prove that a set $\{\mathbf{v}_1, \mathbf{v}_2, \ldots, \mathbf{v}_p\}$ is linearly dependent if and only if some $\mathbf{v}_i$ is a linear combination of the other $p-1$ vectors in the set. The only real distinction between linear independence/dependence in R^n and in a general vector space is that we cannot always test for dependence by solving a homogeneous system of equations. That is, in a general vector space we may have to go directly to the defining equation

$$a_1\mathbf{v}_1 + a_2\mathbf{v}_2 + \cdots + a_p\mathbf{v}_p = \boldsymbol{\theta}$$

and attempt to determine whether there are nontrivial solutions. Examples 2 and 3 illustrate the point.

EXAMPLE 1 Let V be the vector space of (2×2) matrices, and let W be the subspace

$$W = \{A\colon A = \begin{bmatrix} 0 & a_{12} \\ a_{21} & 0 \end{bmatrix}, \quad a_{12} \text{ and } a_{21} \text{ any real scalars}\}.$$

Define matrices B_1, B_2, and B_3 in W by

$$B_1 = \begin{bmatrix} 0 & 2 \\ 1 & 0 \end{bmatrix}, \quad B_2 = \begin{bmatrix} 0 & 1 \\ 0 & 0 \end{bmatrix}, \quad \text{and} \quad B_3 = \begin{bmatrix} 0 & 2 \\ 3 & 0 \end{bmatrix}.$$

Show that the set $\{B_1, B_2, B_3\}$ is linearly dependent, and express B_3 as a linear combination of B_1 and B_2. Show that $\{B_1, B_2\}$ is a linearly independent set.

Solution According to Definition 4, the set $\{B_1, B_2, B_3\}$ is linearly dependent provided that there exist nontrivial solutions to the equation

$$a_1B_1 + a_2B_2 + a_3B_3 = \mathcal{O}, \tag{2}$$

where $\mathcal{O}$ is the zero element in V [that is, $\mathcal{O}$ is the (2×2) zero matrix]. Writing Eq. (2) in detail, we see that a_1, a_2, a_3 are solutions of Eq. (2) if

$$\begin{bmatrix} 0 & 2a_1 \\ a_1 & 0 \end{bmatrix} + \begin{bmatrix} 0 & a_2 \\ 0 & 0 \end{bmatrix} + \begin{bmatrix} 0 & 2a_3 \\ 3a_3 & 0 \end{bmatrix} = \begin{bmatrix} 0 & 0 \\ 0 & 0 \end{bmatrix}.$$

With corresponding entries equated, a_1, a_2, a_3 must satisfy

$$2a_1 + a_2 + 2a_3 = 0 \quad \text{and} \quad a_1 + 3a_3 = 0.$$

This (2×3) homogeneous system has nontrivial solutions by Theorem 4 of Section 1.3, and one such solution is $a_1 = -3$, $a_2 = 4$, $a_3 = 1$. In particular,

$$-3B_1 + 4B_2 + B_3 = \mathcal{O}; \tag{3}$$

so the set $\{B_1, B_2, B_3\}$ is a linearly dependent set of vectors in W. It is an immediate consequence of Eq. (3) that

$$B_3 = 3B_1 - 4B_2.$$

To see that the set $\{B_1, B_2\}$ is linearly independent, let a_1 and a_2 be scalars such that $a_1B_1 + a_2B_2 = \mathcal{O}$. Then we must have

$$2a_1 + a_2 = 0 \quad \text{and} \quad a_1 = 0.$$

Hence $a_1 = 0$ and $a_2 = 0$; so if $a_1B_1 + a_2B_2 = \mathcal{O}$, then $a_1 = a_2 = 0$. Thus $\{B_1, B_2\}$ is a linearly independent set of vectors in W. ■

Establishing linear independence/dependence in a vector space of functions such as $\mathcal{P}_n$ or $C[a, b]$ may sometimes require techniques from calculus. We illustrate one such technique in the following example.

EXAMPLE 2 Show that $\{1, x, x^2\}$ is a linearly independent set in $\mathcal{P}_2$.

Solution Suppose that a_0, a_1, a_2 are any scalars that satisfy the defining equation

$$a_0 + a_1x + a_2x^2 = \theta(x), \tag{4}$$

where $\theta(x)$ is the zero polynomial. If Eq. (4) is to be an identity holding for all values of x, then [since $\theta'(x) = \theta(x)$] we can differentiate both sides of Eq. (4) to obtain

$$a_1 + 2a_2x = \theta(x). \tag{5}$$

Similarly, differentiating both sides of Eq. (5), we obtain

$$2a_2 = \theta(x). \tag{6}$$

From Eq. (6) we must have $a_2 = 0$. If $a_2 = 0$, then Eq. (5) requires $a_1 = 0$; hence in Eq. (4), $a_0 = 0$ as well. Therefore, the only scalars that satisfy Eq. (4) are $a_0 = a_1 = a_2 = 0$, and thus $\{1, x, x^2\}$ is linearly independent in $\mathcal{P}_2$. (Also see the material on Wronskians in Section 6.5.) ■

The following example illustrates another procedure for showing that a set of functions is linearly independent.

EXAMPLE 3 Show that $\{\sqrt{x}, 1/x, x^2\}$ is a linearly independent subset of $C[1, 10]$.

Solution If the equation

$$a_1\sqrt{x} + a_2(1/x) + a_3x^2 = 0 \tag{7}$$

holds for all x, $1 \le x \le 10$, then it must hold for any three values of x in the interval. Successively letting $x = 1$, $x = 4$, and $x = 9$ in Eq. (7) yields the system of equations

$$\begin{aligned} a_1 + a_2 + a_3 &= 0 \\ 2a_1 + (1/4)a_2 + 16a_3 &= 0 \\ 3a_1 + (1/9)a_2 + 81a_3 &= 0. \end{aligned} \tag{8}$$

It is easily shown that the trivial solution $a_1 = a_2 = a_3 = 0$ is the unique solution for system (8). It follows that the set $\{\sqrt{x}, 1/x, x^2\}$ is linearly independent.

Note that a nontrivial solution for system (8) would have yielded no information regarding the linear independence/dependence of the given set of functions. We could have concluded only that Eq. (7) holds when $x = 1$, $x = 4$, or $x = 9$. ■

Vector-Space Bases

It is now straightforward to combine the concepts of linear independence and spanning sets to define a basis for a vector space.

DEFINITION 5 Let V be a vector space, and let $B = \{\mathbf{v}_1, \mathbf{v}_2, \ldots, \mathbf{v}_p\}$ be a spanning set for V. If B is linearly independent, then B is a ***basis*** for V.

Thus as before, a basis for V is a linearly independent spanning set for V. (Again we note the implicit assumption that a basis contains only a finite number of vectors.)

There is often a "natural" basis for a vector space. We have seen in Chapter 3 that the set of unit vectors $\{\mathbf{e}_1, \mathbf{e}_2, \ldots, \mathbf{e}_n\}$ in R^n is a basis for R^n. In the preceding section we noted that the set $\{1, x, x^2\}$ is a spanning set for $\mathcal{P}_2$. Example 2 showed further that $\{1, x, x^2\}$ is linearly independent and hence is a basis for $\mathcal{P}_2$. More generally, the set $\{1, x, \ldots, x^n\}$ is a natural basis for $\mathcal{P}_n$. Similarly, the matrices

$$E_{11} = \begin{bmatrix} 1 & 0 \\ 0 & 0 \end{bmatrix}, \quad E_{12} = \begin{bmatrix} 0 & 1 \\ 0 & 0 \end{bmatrix}, \quad E_{21} = \begin{bmatrix} 0 & 0 \\ 1 & 0 \end{bmatrix}, \quad \text{and} \quad E_{22} = \begin{bmatrix} 0 & 0 \\ 0 & 1 \end{bmatrix}$$

constitute a basis for the vector space of all (2×2) real matrices (see Exercise 11). In general, the set of $(m \times n)$ matrices $\{E_{ij}: 1 \le i \le m, 1 \le j \le n\}$ defined in Section 5.3 is a natural basis for the vector space of all $(m \times n)$ real matrices.

Examples 5, 6, and 7 in Section 5.3 demonstrated a procedure for obtaining a natural spanning set for a subspace W when an algebraic specification for W is given. The spanning set obtained in this manner is often a basis for W. The following example provides another illustration.

EXAMPLE 4 Let V be the vector space of all (2×2) real matrices, and let W be the subspace defined by

$$W = \left\{A\colon A = \begin{bmatrix} a & a+b \\ a-b & b \end{bmatrix}, \quad a \text{ and } b \text{ any real numbers}\right\}.$$

Exhibit a basis for W.

Solution In the specification for W, a and b are unconstrained variables. Assigning values $a = 1, b = 0$ and then $a = 0, b = 1$ yields the matrices

$$B_1 = \begin{bmatrix} 1 & 1 \\ 1 & 0 \end{bmatrix} \quad \text{and} \quad B_2 = \begin{bmatrix} 0 & 1 \\ -1 & 1 \end{bmatrix}$$

in W. Since

$$\begin{bmatrix} a & a+b \\ a-b & b \end{bmatrix} = a \begin{bmatrix} 1 & 1 \\ 1 & 0 \end{bmatrix} + b \begin{bmatrix} 0 & 1 \\ -1 & 1 \end{bmatrix},$$

the set $\{B_1, B_2\}$ is clearly a spanning set for W. The equation

$$c_1 B_1 + c_2 B_2 = \mathcal{O}$$

(where $\mathcal{O}$ is the (2×2) zero matrix) is equivalent to

$$\begin{bmatrix} c_1 & c_1 + c_2 \\ c_1 - c_2 & c_2 \end{bmatrix} = \begin{bmatrix} 0 & 0 \\ 0 & 0 \end{bmatrix}.$$

Equating entries immediately yields $c_1 = c_2 = 0$; so the set $\{B_1, B_2\}$ is linearly independent and hence is a basis for W. ■

Coordinate Vectors

As we noted in Chapter 3 a basis is a minimal spanning set; as such, a basis contains no redundant information. This lack of redundance is an important feature of a basis in the general vector-space setting and allows every vector to be represented uniquely in terms of the basis (see Theorem 4). We cannot make such an assertion of unique representation about a spanning set that is linearly dependent; in fact, in this case, the representation is never unique.

THEOREM 4 Let V be a vector space, and let $B = \{\mathbf{v}_1, \mathbf{v}_2, \ldots, \mathbf{v}_p\}$ be a basis for V. For each vector $\mathbf{w}$ in V, there exists a unique set of scalars $w_1, w_2, \ldots, w_p$ such that

$$\mathbf{w} = w_1\mathbf{v}_1 + w_2\mathbf{v}_2 + \cdots + w_p\mathbf{v}_p.$$

Proof Let $\mathbf{w}$ be a vector in V and suppose that $\mathbf{w}$ is represented in two ways as

$$\mathbf{w} = w_1\mathbf{v}_1 + w_2\mathbf{v}_2 + \cdots + w_p\mathbf{v}_p$$
$$\mathbf{w} = u_1\mathbf{v}_1 + u_2\mathbf{v}_2 + \cdots + u_p\mathbf{v}_p.$$

Subtracting, we obtain

$$\boldsymbol{\theta} = (w_1 - u_1)\mathbf{v}_1 + (w_2 - u_2)\mathbf{v}_2 + \cdots + (w_p - u_p)\mathbf{v}_p.$$

Therefore, since $\{\mathbf{v}_1, \mathbf{v}_2, \ldots, \mathbf{v}_p\}$ is a linearly independent set, it follows that $w_1 - u_1 = 0, w_2 - u_2 = 0, \ldots, w_p - u_p = 0$. That is, a vector $\mathbf{w}$ cannot be represented in two different ways in terms of a basis B. ■

Now, let V be a vector space with a basis $B = \{\mathbf{v}_1, \mathbf{v}_2, \ldots, \mathbf{v}_p\}$. Given that each vector $\mathbf{w}$ in V has a unique representation in terms of B as

$$\mathbf{w} = w_1\mathbf{v}_1 + w_2\mathbf{v}_2 + \cdots + w_p\mathbf{v}_p, \tag{9}$$

it follows that the scalars $w_1, w_2, \ldots, w_p$ serve to characterize $\mathbf{w}$ completely in terms of the basis B. In particular, we can identify $\mathbf{w}$ unambiguously with the vector $[\mathbf{w}]_B$ in R^p, where

$$[\mathbf{w}]_B = \begin{bmatrix} w_1 \\ w_2 \\ \vdots \\ w_p \end{bmatrix}.$$

We will call the unique scalars $w_1, w_2, \ldots, w_p$ in Eq. (9) the ***coordinates of* w** with respect to the basis B, and we will call the vector $[\mathbf{w}]_B$ in R_p the ***coordinate vector of*** w with respect to B. This idea is a useful one; for example, we will show that a set of vectors $\{\mathbf{u}_1, \mathbf{u}_2, \ldots, \mathbf{u}_r\}$ in V is linearly independent if and only if the coordinate vectors $[\mathbf{u}_1]_B, [\mathbf{u}_2]_B, \ldots, [\mathbf{u}_r]_B$ are linearly independent in R^n. Since we know how to determine whether vectors in R^p are linearly independent or not, we can use the idea of coordinates to reduce a problem of linear independence/dependence in a general vector space to an equivalent problem in R^p, which we can work. Finally, we note that the subscript B is necessary when we write $[\mathbf{w}]_B$, since the coordinate vector for $\mathbf{w}$ changes when we change the basis.

EXAMPLE 5 Let V be the vector space of all real (2×2) matrices. Let $B = \{E_{11}, E_{12}, E_{21}, E_{22}\}$ and $Q = \{E_{11}, E_{21}, E_{12}, E_{22}\}$, where

$$E_{11} = \begin{bmatrix} 1 & 0 \\ 0 & 0 \end{bmatrix}, E_{12} = \begin{bmatrix} 0 & 1 \\ 0 & 0 \end{bmatrix}, E_{21} = \begin{bmatrix} 0 & 0 \\ 1 & 0 \end{bmatrix}, \text{ and } E_{22} = \begin{bmatrix} 0 & 0 \\ 0 & 1 \end{bmatrix}.$$

Let the matrix A be defined by

$$A = \begin{bmatrix} 2 & -1 \\ -3 & 4 \end{bmatrix}.$$

Find $[A]_B$ and $[A]_Q$.

Solution We have already noted that B is the natural basis for V. Since Q contains the same vectors as B, but in a different order, Q is also a basis for V. It is easy to see that

$$A = 2E_{11} - E_{12} - 3E_{21} + 4E_{22},$$

so

$$[A]_B = \begin{bmatrix} 2 \\ -1 \\ -3 \\ 4 \end{bmatrix}.$$

Similarly,

$$A = 2E_{11} - 3E_{21} - E_{12} + 4E_{22},$$

so

$$[A]_Q = \begin{bmatrix} 2 \\ -3 \\ -1 \\ 4 \end{bmatrix}.$$ ■

It is apparent in the preceding example that the ordering of the basis vectors determined the ordering of the components of the coordinate vectors. A basis with such an implicitly fixed ordering is usually called an ***ordered basis.*** Although we do not intend to dwell on this point, we do have to be careful to work with a fixed ordering in a basis.

If V is a vector space with (ordered) basis $B = \{\mathbf{v}_1, \mathbf{v}_2, \ldots, \mathbf{v}_p\}$, then the correspondence

$$\mathbf{v} \to [\mathbf{v}]_B$$

provides an identification between vectors in V and elements of R^p. For instance, the preceding example identified a (2×2) matrix with a vector in R^4. The following lemma lists some of the properties of this correspondence. (The lemma hints at the idea of an isomorphism that will be developed in detail later.)

LEMMA Let V be a vector space that has a basis $B = \{\mathbf{v}_1, \mathbf{v}_2, \ldots, \mathbf{v}_p\}$. If $\mathbf{u}$ and $\mathbf{v}$ are vectors in V and if c is a scalar, then the following hold:

$$[\mathbf{u}+\mathbf{v}]_B = [\mathbf{u}]_B + [\mathbf{v}]_B$$

and

$$[c\mathbf{u}]_B = c[\mathbf{u}]_B.$$

Proof Suppose that $\mathbf{u}$ and $\mathbf{v}$ are expressed in terms of the basis vectors in B as

$$\mathbf{u} = a_1\mathbf{v}_1 + a_2\mathbf{v}_2 + \cdots + a_p\mathbf{v}_p$$

and

$$\mathbf{v} = b_1\mathbf{v}_1 + b_2\mathbf{v}_2 + \cdots + b_p\mathbf{v}_p.$$

Then clearly

$$\mathbf{u}+\mathbf{v} = (a_1+b_1)\mathbf{v}_1 + (a_2+b_2)\mathbf{v}_2 + \cdots + (a_p+b_p)\mathbf{v}_p$$

and

$$c\mathbf{u} = (ca_1)\mathbf{v}_1 + (ca_2)\mathbf{v}_2 + \cdots + (ca_p)\mathbf{v}_p.$$

Therefore,

$$[\mathbf{u}]_B = \begin{bmatrix} a_1 \\ a_2 \\ \vdots \\ a_p \end{bmatrix}, \quad [\mathbf{v}]_B = \begin{bmatrix} b_1 \\ b_2 \\ \vdots \\ b_p \end{bmatrix},$$

$$[\mathbf{u}+\mathbf{v}]_B = \begin{bmatrix} a_1+b_1 \\ a_2+b_2 \\ \vdots \\ a_p+b_p \end{bmatrix}, \quad \text{and} \quad [c\mathbf{u}] = \begin{bmatrix} ca_1 \\ ca_2 \\ \vdots \\ ca_p \end{bmatrix}.$$

We can now easily see that $[\mathbf{u}+\mathbf{v}]_B = [\mathbf{u}]_B + [\mathbf{v}]_B$ and $[c\mathbf{u}]_B = c[\mathbf{u}]_B$. ■

The following example illustrates the preceding lemma.

EXAMPLE 6 In $\mathcal{P}_2$, let $p(x) = 3 - 2x + x^2$ and $q(x) = -2 + 3x - 4x^2$. Show that

$$[p(x)+q(x)]_B = [p(x)]_B + [q(x)]_B \quad \text{and} \quad [2p(x)]_B = 2[p(x)]_B,$$

where B is the natural basis for $\mathcal{P}_2$: $B = \{1, x, x^2\}$.

Solution The coordinate vectors for $p(x)$ and $q(x)$ are

$$[p(x)]_B = \begin{bmatrix} 3 \\ -2 \\ 1 \end{bmatrix} \quad \text{and} \quad [q(x)]_B = \begin{bmatrix} -2 \\ 3 \\ -4 \end{bmatrix}.$$

Furthermore, $p(x) + q(x) = 1 + x - 3x^2$ and $2p(x) = 6 - 4x + 2x^2$. Thus

$$[p(x) + q(x)]_B = \begin{bmatrix} 1 \\ 1 \\ -3 \end{bmatrix} \text{ and } [2p(x)]_B = \begin{bmatrix} 6 \\ -4 \\ 2 \end{bmatrix}.$$

Therefore, $[p(x) + q(x)]_B = [p(x)]_B + [q(x)]_B$ and $[2p(x)]_B = 2[p(x)]_B$.

Suppose that the vector space V has basis $B = \{\mathbf{v}_1, \mathbf{v}_2, \ldots, \mathbf{v}_p\}$, and let $\{\mathbf{u}_1, \mathbf{u}_2, \ldots, \mathbf{u}_m\}$ be a subset of V. The two properties in the preceding lemma can easily be combined and extended to give

$$[c_1\mathbf{u}_1 + c_2\mathbf{u}_2 + \cdots + c_m\mathbf{u}_m]_B = c_1[\mathbf{u}_1]_B + c_2[\mathbf{u}_2]_B + \cdots + c_m[\mathbf{u}_m]_B. \tag{10}$$

This observation will be useful in proving the next theorem.

THEOREM 5 Suppose that V is a vector space with a basis $B = \{\mathbf{v}_1, \mathbf{v}_2, \ldots, \mathbf{v}_p\}$. Let $S = \{\mathbf{u}_1, \mathbf{u}_2, \ldots, \mathbf{u}_m\}$ be a subset of V, let $T = \{[\mathbf{u}_1]_B, [\mathbf{u}_2]_B, \ldots, [\mathbf{u}_m]_B\}$.

1. A vector $\mathbf{u}$ in V is in Sp(S) if and only if $[\mathbf{u}]_B$ is in Sp(T).
2. The set S is linearly independent in V if and only if the set T is linearly independent in R^p.

Proof The vector equation

$$\mathbf{u} = x_1\mathbf{u}_1 + x_2\mathbf{u}_2 + \cdots + x_m\mathbf{u}_m \tag{11}$$

in V is equivalent to the equation

$$[\mathbf{u}]_B = [x_1\mathbf{u}_1 + x_2\mathbf{u}_2 + \cdots + x_m\mathbf{u}_m]_B \tag{12}$$

in R^p. It follows from Eq. (10) that Eq. (12) is equivalent to

$$[\mathbf{u}]_B = x_1[\mathbf{u}_1]_B + x_2[\mathbf{u}_2]_B + \cdots + x_m[\mathbf{u}_m]_B. \tag{13}$$

Therefore, the vector equation (11) in V is equivalent to the vector equation (13) in R^p. In particular, Eq. (11) has a solution $x_1 = c_1, x_2 = c_2, \ldots, x_m = c_m$ if and only if Eq. (13) has the same solution. Thus $\mathbf{u}$ is in Sp(S) if and only if $[\mathbf{u}]_B$ is in Sp(T).

To avoid confusion in the proof of property 2, let $\boldsymbol{\theta}_V$ denote the zero vector for V and let $\boldsymbol{\theta}_p$ denote the p-dimensional zero vector in R^p. Then $[\boldsymbol{\theta}_V]_B = \boldsymbol{\theta}_p$. Thus setting $\mathbf{u} = \boldsymbol{\theta}_V$ in Eq. (11) and Eq. (13) implies that the vector equations

$$\boldsymbol{\theta}_V = x_1\mathbf{u}_1 + x_2\mathbf{u}_2 + \cdots + x_m\mathbf{u}_m \tag{14}$$

and

$$\boldsymbol{\theta}_p = x_1[\mathbf{u}_1]_B + x_2[\mathbf{u}_2]_B + \cdots + x_m[\mathbf{u}_m]_B \tag{15}$$

have the same solutions. In particular, Eq. (14) has *only* the trivial solution if and only if Eq. (15) has *only* the trivial solution; that is, S is a linearly independent set in V if and only if T is linearly independent in R^p.

An immediate corollary to Theorem 5 is as follows.

COROLLARY Let V be a vector space with a basis $B = \{\mathbf{v}_1, \mathbf{v}_2, \ldots, \mathbf{v}_p\}$. Let $S = \{\mathbf{u}_1, \mathbf{u}_2, \ldots, \mathbf{u}_m\}$ be a subset of V, and let $T = \{[\mathbf{u}_1]_B, [\mathbf{u}_2]_B, \ldots, [\mathbf{u}_m]_B\}$. Then S is a basis for V if and only if T is a basis for R^p.

Proof By Theorem 5, S is both linearly independent and a spanning set for V if and only if T is both linearly independent and a spanning set for R^p. ■

Theorem 5 and its corollary allow us to use the techniques developed in Chapter 3 to solve analogous problems in vector spaces other than R^p. The next two examples provide illustrations.

EXAMPLE 7 Use the corollary to Theorem 5 to show that the set $\{1, 1+x, 1+2x+x^2\}$ is a basis for $\mathcal{P}_2$.

Solution Let B be the standard basis for $\mathcal{P}_2$: $B = \{1, x, x^2\}$. The coordinate vectors of $1, 1+x$, and $1+2x+x^2$ are

$$[1]_B = \begin{bmatrix} 1 \\ 0 \\ 0 \end{bmatrix}, \quad [1+x]_B = \begin{bmatrix} 1 \\ 1 \\ 0 \end{bmatrix}, \quad \text{and} \quad [1+2x+x^2]_B = \begin{bmatrix} 1 \\ 2 \\ 1 \end{bmatrix}.$$

Clearly the coordinate vectors $[1]_B$, $[1+x]_B$, and $[1+2x+x^2]_B$ are linearly independent in R^3. Since R^3 has dimension 3, the coordinate vectors constitute a basis for R^3. It now follows that $\{1, 1+x, 1+2x+x^2\}$ is a basis for $\mathcal{P}_2$. ■

EXAMPLE 8 Let V be the vector space of all (2×2) matrices, and let the subset S of V be defined by $S = \{A_1, A_2, A_3, A_4\}$, where

$$A_1 = \begin{bmatrix} 1 & 2 \\ -1 & 3 \end{bmatrix}, \quad A_2 = \begin{bmatrix} 0 & -1 \\ 1 & 4 \end{bmatrix},$$

$$A_3 = \begin{bmatrix} -1 & 0 \\ 1 & -10 \end{bmatrix}, \quad \text{and} \quad A_4 = \begin{bmatrix} 3 & 7 \\ -2 & 6 \end{bmatrix}.$$

Use the corollary to Theorem 5 and the techniques of Section 3.4 to obtain a basis for Sp(S).

Solution If B is the natural basis for V, $B = \{E_{11}, E_{12}, E_{21}, E_{22}\}$, then

$$[A_1]_B = \begin{bmatrix} 1 \\ 2 \\ -1 \\ 3 \end{bmatrix}, \quad [A_2]_B = \begin{bmatrix} 0 \\ -1 \\ 1 \\ 4 \end{bmatrix},$$

$$[A_3]_B = \begin{bmatrix} -1 \\ 0 \\ 1 \\ -10 \end{bmatrix}, \quad \text{and} \quad [A_4]_B = \begin{bmatrix} 3 \\ 7 \\ -2 \\ 6 \end{bmatrix}.$$

Let $T = \{[A_1]_B, [A_2]_B, [A_3]_B, [A_4]_B\}$. Several techniques for obtaining a basis for Sp(T) were illustrated in Section 3.4. For example, using the method demonstrated in Example 7 of Section 3.4, we form the matrix

$$C = \begin{bmatrix} 1 & 0 & -1 & 3 \\ 2 & -1 & 0 & 7 \\ -1 & 1 & 1 & -2 \\ 3 & 4 & -10 & 6 \end{bmatrix}.$$

The matrix C^T can be reduced to the matrix

$$D^T = \begin{bmatrix} 1 & 2 & -1 & 3 \\ 0 & -1 & 1 & 4 \\ 0 & 0 & 2 & 1 \\ 0 & 0 & 0 & 0 \end{bmatrix}.$$

Thus

$$D = \begin{bmatrix} 1 & 0 & 0 & 0 \\ 2 & -1 & 0 & 0 \\ -1 & 1 & 2 & 0 \\ 3 & 4 & 1 & 0 \end{bmatrix},$$

and the nonzero columns of D constitute a basis for Sp(T). Denote the nonzero columns of D by $\mathbf{w}_1$, $\mathbf{w}_2$, and $\mathbf{w}_3$, respectively. Thus

$$\mathbf{w}_1 = \begin{bmatrix} 1 \\ 2 \\ -1 \\ 3 \end{bmatrix}, \quad \mathbf{w}_2 = \begin{bmatrix} 0 \\ -1 \\ 1 \\ 4 \end{bmatrix}, \quad \text{and} \quad \mathbf{w}_3 = \begin{bmatrix} 0 \\ 0 \\ 2 \\ 1 \end{bmatrix},$$

and $\{\mathbf{w}_1, \mathbf{w}_2, \mathbf{w}_3\}$ is a basis for Sp(T). If B_1, B_2, and B_3 are (2×2) matrices such that $[B_1]_B = \mathbf{w}_1$, $[B_2]_B = \mathbf{w}_2$, and $[B_3]_B = \mathbf{w}_3$, then it follows from Theorem 5 that $\{B_1, B_2, B_3\}$ is a basis for Sp(S). If

$$B_1 = E_{11} + 2E_{12} - E_{21} + 3E_{22},$$

then clearly $[B_1]_B = \mathbf{w}_1$. B_2 and B_3 are obtained in the same fashion, and

$$B_1 = \begin{bmatrix} 1 & 2 \\ -1 & 3 \end{bmatrix}, \quad B_2 = \begin{bmatrix} 0 & -1 \\ 1 & 4 \end{bmatrix}, \quad \text{and} \quad B_3 = \begin{bmatrix} 0 & 0 \\ 2 & 1 \end{bmatrix}.$$ ■

Examples 7 and 8 illustrate an important point. Although Theorem 5 shows that questions regarding the span or the linear dependence/independence of a subset of V can be translated to an equivalent problem in R^p, we do need one basis for V as a point of reference. For example, in $\mathcal{P}_2$, once we know that $B = \{1, x, x^2\}$ is a basis, we can use Theorem 5 to pass from a problem in $\mathcal{P}_2$ to an analogous problem in R^3. In order to obtain the first basis B, however, we cannot use Theorem 5.

EXAMPLE 9 In $\mathcal{P}_4$, consider the set of vectors $S = \{p_1, p_2, p_3, p_4, p_5\}$, where $p_1(x) = x^4 + 3x^3 + 2x + 4$, $p_2(x) = x^3 - x^2 + 5x + 1$, $p_3(x) = x^4 + x + 3$, $p_4(x) = x^4 + x^3 - x + 2$, and $p_5(x) = x^4 + x^2$. Is S a basis for $\mathcal{P}_4$?

Solution Let B denote the standard basis for $\mathcal{P}_4$, $B = \{1, x, x^2, x^3, x^4\}$. By the corollary to Theorem 5, S is a basis for $\mathcal{P}_4$ if and only if T is a basis for R^5, where $T = \{[p_1]_B, [p_2]_B, [p_3]_B, [p_4]_B, [p_5]_B\}$. In particular, the coordinate vectors in T are

$$[p_1]_B = \begin{bmatrix} 4 \\ 2 \\ 0 \\ 3 \\ 1 \end{bmatrix}, \quad [p_2]_B = \begin{bmatrix} 1 \\ 5 \\ -1 \\ 1 \\ 0 \end{bmatrix}, \quad [p_3]_B = \begin{bmatrix} 3 \\ 1 \\ 0 \\ 0 \\ 1 \end{bmatrix},$$

$$[p_4]_B = \begin{bmatrix} 2 \\ -1 \\ 0 \\ 1 \\ 1 \end{bmatrix}, \quad \text{and} \quad [p_5]_B = \begin{bmatrix} 0 \\ 0 \\ 1 \\ 0 \\ 1 \end{bmatrix}.$$

Since R^5 has dimension 5 and T contains 5 vectors, T will be a basis for R^5 if T is a linearly independent set. To check whether T is linearly independent, we form the matrix A whose columns are the vectors in T and use MATLAB to reduce A to echelon form. As can be seen from the results in Fig. 5.4, the columns of A are linearly independent. Hence, T is a basis for R^5. Therefore, S is a basis for $\mathcal{P}_4$. ■

```
A=
     4     1     3     2     0
     2     5     1    -1     0
     0    -1     0     0     1
     3     1     0     1     0
     1     0     1     1     1

>>rref(A)

ans=
     1     0     0     0     0
     0     1     0     0     0
     0     0     1     0     0
     0     0     0     1     0
     0     0     0     0     1
```

Figure 5.4 MATLAB was used for Example 9 to determine whether the columns of A are linearly independent. Since A is row equivalent to the identity, its columns are linearly independent.

5.4 EXERCISES

In Exercises 1–4, W is a subspace of the vector space V of all (2×2) matrices. A matrix A in W is written as

$$A = \begin{bmatrix} a & b \\ c & d \end{bmatrix}.$$

In each case exhibit a basis for W.

1. $W = \{A: a + b + c + d = 0\}$
2. $W = \{A: a = -d,\ \ b = 2d,\ \ c = -3d\}$
3. $W = \{A: a = 0\}$
4. $W = \{A: b = a - c,\ \ d = 2a + c\}$

In Exercises 5–8, W is a subspace of $\mathcal{P}_2$. In each case exhibit a basis for W.

5. $W = \{p(x) = a_0 + a_1x + a_2x^2: a_2 = a_0 - 2a_1\}$
6. $W = \{p(x) = a_0 + a_1x + a_2x^2: a_0 = 3a_2,\ a_1 = -a_2\}$
7. $W = \{p(x) = a_0 + a_1x + a_2x^2: p(0) = 0\}$
8. $W = \{p(x) = a_0 + a_1x + a_2x^2: p(1) = p'(1) = 0\}$
9. Find a basis for the subspace V of $\mathcal{P}_4$, where $V = \{p(x) \text{ in } \mathcal{P}_4\text{: } p(0) = 0, p'(1) = 0, p''(-1) = 0\}$.
10. Prove that the set of all real (2×2) symmetric matrices is a subspace of the vector space of all real (2×2) matrices. Find a basis for this subspace (see Exercise 26 of Section 5.3).
11. Let V be the vector space of all (2×2) real matrices. Show that $B = \{E_{11}, E_{12}, E_{21}, E_{22}\}$ (see Example 5) is a basis for V.
12. With respect to the basis $B = \{1, x, x^2\}$ for $\mathcal{P}_2$, find the coordinate vector for each of the following.
    a) $p(x) = x^2 - x + 1$
    b) $p(x) = x^2 + 4x - 1$
    c) $p(x) = 2x + 5$
13. With respect to the basis $B = \{E_{11}, E_{12}, E_{21}, E_{22}\}$ for the vector space V of all (2×2) matrices, find the coordinate vector for each of the following.
    a) $A_1 = \begin{bmatrix} 2 & -1 \\ 3 & 2 \end{bmatrix}$ b) $A_2 = \begin{bmatrix} 1 & 0 \\ -1 & 1 \end{bmatrix}$
    c) $A_3 = \begin{bmatrix} 2 & 3 \\ 0 & 0 \end{bmatrix}$
14. Prove that $\{1, x, x^2, \ldots, x^n\}$ is a linearly independent set in $\mathcal{P}_n$ by supposing that $p(x) = \theta(x)$, where $p(x) = a_0 + a_1x + \cdots + a_nx^n$. Next, take successive derivatives as in Example 2.

In Exercises 15–17, use the basis B of Exercise 11 and property 2 of Theorem 5 to test for linear independence in the vector space of (2×2) matrices.

15. $A_1 = \begin{bmatrix} 2 & 1 \\ 2 & 1 \end{bmatrix}$, $A_2 = \begin{bmatrix} 3 & 0 \\ 0 & 2 \end{bmatrix}$, $A_3 = \begin{bmatrix} 1 & 1 \\ 2 & 1 \end{bmatrix}$
16. $A_1 = \begin{bmatrix} 1 & 3 \\ 2 & 1 \end{bmatrix}$, $A_2 = \begin{bmatrix} 4 & -2 \\ 0 & 6 \end{bmatrix}$, $A_3 = \begin{bmatrix} 6 & 4 \\ 4 & 8 \end{bmatrix}$
17. $A_1 = \begin{bmatrix} 2 & 2 \\ 1 & 3 \end{bmatrix}$, $A_2 = \begin{bmatrix} 1 & 4 \\ 0 & 5 \end{bmatrix}$, $A_3 = \begin{bmatrix} 4 & 10 \\ 1 & 13 \end{bmatrix}$

In Exercises 18–21, use Exercise 14 and property 2 of Theorem 5 to test for linear independence in $\mathcal{P}_3$.

18. $\{x^3 - x, x^2 - 1, x + 4\}$
19. $\{x^2 + 2x - 1, x^2 - 5x + 2, 3x^2 - x\}$
20. $\{x^3 - x^2, x^2 - x, x - 1, x^3 - 1\}$
21. $\{x^3 + 1, x^2 + 1, x + 1, 1\}$
22. In $\mathcal{P}_2$, let $S = \{p_1(x), p_2(x), p_3(x), p_4(x)\}$, where $p_1(x) = 1 + 2x + x^2$, $p_2(x) = 2 + 5x$, $p_3(x) = 3 + 7x + x^2$, and $p_4(x) = 1 + x + 3x^2$. Use the method illustrated in Example 8 to obtain a basis for Sp(S). [*Hint:* Use the basis $B = \{1, x, x^2\}$ to obtain coordinate vectors for $p_1(x)$, $p_2(x)$, $p_3(x)$, and $p_4(x)$. Now use the method illustrated in Example 7 of Section 3.4.]
23. Let S be the subset of $\mathcal{P}_2$ given in Exercise 22. Find a subset of S that is a basis for Sp(S). [*Hint:* Proceed as in Exercise 22, but use the technique illustrated in Example 6 of Section 3.4.]
24. Let V be the vector space of all (2×2) matrices and let $S = \{A_1, A_2, A_3, A_4\}$, where

$$A_1 = \begin{bmatrix} 1 & 2 \\ -1 & 3 \end{bmatrix}, \quad A_2 = \begin{bmatrix} -2 & 1 \\ 2 & -1 \end{bmatrix},$$

$$A_3 = \begin{bmatrix} -1 & -1 \\ 1 & -3 \end{bmatrix}, \text{ and } A_4 = \begin{bmatrix} -2 & 2 \\ 2 & 0 \end{bmatrix}.$$

As in Example 8, find a basis for Sp(S).

25. Let V and S be as in Exercise 24. Find a subset of S that is a basis for Sp(S). [*Hint:* Use Theorem 5 and the technique illustrated in Example 6 of Section 3.4.]

26. In $\mathcal{P}_2$, let $Q = \{p_1(x), p_2(x), p_3(x)\}$, where $p_1(x) = -1 + x + 2x^2$, $p_2(x) = x + 3x^2$, and $p_3(x) = 1+2x+8x^2$. Use the basis $B = \{1, x, x^2\}$ to show that Q is a basis for $\mathcal{P}_2$.

27. Let Q be the basis for $\mathcal{P}_2$ given in Exercise 26. Find $[p(x)]_Q$ for $p(x) = 1 + x + x^2$.

28. Let Q be the basis for $\mathcal{P}_2$ given in Exercise 26. Find $[p(x)]_Q$ for $p(x) = a_0 + a_1x + a_2x^2$.

29. In the vector space V of (2×2) matrices, let $Q = \{A_1, A_2, A_3, A_4\}$ where

$$A_1 = \begin{bmatrix} 1 & 0 \\ 0 & 0 \end{bmatrix}, \quad A_2 = \begin{bmatrix} 1 & -1 \\ 0 & 0 \end{bmatrix},$$

$$A_3 = \begin{bmatrix} 0 & 2 \\ 0 & 0 \end{bmatrix}, \text{ and } A_4 = \begin{bmatrix} -3 & 0 \\ 2 & 1 \end{bmatrix}.$$

Use the corollary to Theorem 5 and the natural basis for V to show that Q is a basis for V.

30. With V and Q as in Exercise 29, find $[A]_Q$ for

$$A = \begin{bmatrix} 7 & 3 \\ -3 & -1 \end{bmatrix}.$$

31. With V and Q as in Exercise 29, find $[A]_Q$ for

$$A = \begin{bmatrix} a & b \\ c & d \end{bmatrix}.$$

32. Give an alternative proof that $\{1, x, x^2\}$ is a linearly independent set in $\mathcal{P}_2$ as follows: Let $p(x) = a_0 + a_1x + a_2x^2$, and suppose that $p(x) = \theta(x)$. Then $p(-1) = 0$, $p(0) = 0$, and $p(1) = 0$. These three equations can be used to show that $a_0 = a_1 = a_2 = 0$.

33. The set $\{\sin x, \cos x\}$ is a subset of the vector space $C[-\pi, \pi]$. Prove that the set is linearly independent. [*Hint:* Set $f(x) = c_1 \sin x + c_2 \cos x$, and assume that $f(x) = \theta(x)$. Then $f(0) = 0$ and $f(\pi/2) = 0$.]

In Exercises 34 and 35, V is the set of functions

$$V = \{f(x)\colon f(x) = ae^x + be^{2x} + ce^{3x} + de^{4x} \text{ for real numbers } a, b, c, d\}.$$

It can be shown that V is a vector space.

34. Show that $B = \{e^x, e^{2x}, e^{3x}, e^{4x}\}$ is a basis for V. [*Hint:* To see that B is a linearly independent set, let $h(x) = c_1e^x + c_2e^{2x} + c_3e^{3x} + c_4e^{4x}$ and assume that $h(x) = \theta(x)$. Then $h'(x) = \theta(x)$, $h''(x) = \theta(x)$, and $h'''(x) = \theta(x)$. Therefore, $h(0) = 0$, $h'(0) = 0$, $h''(0) = 0$, and $h'''(0) = 0$.]

35. Let $S = \{g_1(x), g_2(x), g_3(x)\}$ be the subset of V, where $g_1(x) = e^x - e^{4x}$, $g_2(x) = e^{2x} + e^{3x}$, and $g_3(x) = -e^x + e^{3x} + e^{4x}$. Use Theorem 5 and basis B of Exercise 34 to show that S is a linearly independent set.

36. Prove that if $Q = \{\mathbf{v}_1, \mathbf{v}_2, \ldots, \mathbf{v}_m\}$ is a linearly independent subset of a vector space V, and if $\mathbf{w}$ is a vector in V such that $\mathbf{w}$ is not in Sp(Q), then $\{\mathbf{v}_1, \mathbf{v}_2, \ldots, \mathbf{v}_m, \mathbf{w}\}$ is also a linearly independent set in V. [*Note:* $\boldsymbol{\theta}$ is always in Sp(Q).]

37. Let $S = \{\mathbf{v}_1, \mathbf{v}_2, \ldots, \mathbf{v}_n\}$ be a subset of a vector space V, where $n \geq 2$. Prove that set S is linearly dependent if and only if at least one of the vectors, $\mathbf{v}_j$, can be expressed as a linear combination of the remaining vectors.

38. Use Exercise 37 to obtain necessary and sufficient conditions for a set $\{\mathbf{u}, \mathbf{v}\}$ of two vectors to be linearly dependent. Determine by inspection whether each of the following sets is linearly dependent or linearly independent.

a) $\{1 + x, x^2\}$

b) $\{x, e^x\}$

c) $\{x, 3x\}$

d) $\left\{\begin{bmatrix} -1 & 2 \\ 1 & 3 \end{bmatrix}, \begin{bmatrix} 2 & -4 \\ -2 & -6 \end{bmatrix}\right\}$

e) $\left\{\begin{bmatrix} 0 & 0 \\ 0 & 0 \end{bmatrix}, \begin{bmatrix} 1 & 0 \\ 0 & 1 \end{bmatrix}\right\}$

5.5 DIMENSION

We now use Theorem 5 to generalize the idea of dimension to the general vector-space setting. We begin with two theorems that will be needed to show that dimension is a well-defined concept. These theorems are direct applications of the corollary to Theorem 5, and the proofs are left to the exercises because they are essentially the same as the proofs of the analogous theorems from Section 3.5.

THEOREM 6 If V is a vector space and if $B = \{\mathbf{v}_1, \mathbf{v}_2, \ldots, \mathbf{v}_p\}$ is a basis of V, then any set of $p+1$ vectors in V is linearly dependent. ■

THEOREM 7 Let V be a vector space, and let $B = \{\mathbf{v}_1, \mathbf{v}_2, \ldots, \mathbf{v}_p\}$ be a basis for V. If $Q = \{\mathbf{u}_1, \mathbf{u}_2, \ldots, \mathbf{u}_m\}$ is also a basis for V, then $m = p$. ■

If V is a vector space that has a basis of p vectors, then no ambiguity can arise if we define the dimension of V to be p (since the number of vectors in a basis for V is an invariant property of V by Theorem 7). There is, however, one extreme case, which is also included in Definition 6. That is, there may not be a finite set of vectors that spans V; in this case we call V an infinite-dimensional vector space.

DEFINITION 6 Let V be a vector space.

1. If V has a basis $B = \{\mathbf{v}_1, \mathbf{v}_2, \ldots, \mathbf{v}_n\}$ of n vectors, then V has ***dimension n***, and we write $\dim(V) = n$. [If $V = \{\boldsymbol{\theta}\}$, then $\dim(V) = 0$.]
2. If V is nontrivial and does not have a basis containing a finite number of vectors, then V is an ***infinite-dimensional*** vector space.

We already know from Chapter 3 that R^n has dimension n. In the preceding section it was shown that $\{1, x, x^2\}$ is a basis for $\mathcal{P}_2$, so $\dim(\mathcal{P}_2) = 3$. Similarly, the set $\{1, x, \ldots, x^n\}$ is a basis for $\mathcal{P}_n$, so $\dim(\mathcal{P}_n) = n + 1$. The vector space V consisting of all (2×2) real matrices has a basis with four vectors, namely, $B = \{E_{11}, E_{12}, E_{21}, E_{22}\}$. Therefore, $\dim(V) = 4$. More generally, the space of all $(m \times n)$ real matrices has dimension mn because the $(m \times n)$ matrices E_{ij}, $1 \le i \le m$, $1 \le j \le n$, constitute a basis for the space.

EXAMPLE 1 Let W be the subspace of the set of all (2×2) matrices defined by

$$W = \{A = \begin{bmatrix} a & b \\ c & d \end{bmatrix} : 2a - b + 3c + d = 0\}.$$

Determine the dimension of W.

Solution The algebraic specification for W can be rewritten as $d = -2a + b - 3c$. Thus an element of W is completely determined by the three independent variables a, b, and c.

In succession, let $a = 1, b = 0, c = 0$; $a = 0, b = 1, c = 0$; and $a = 0, b = 0, c = 1$. This yields three matrices

$$A_1 = \begin{bmatrix} 1 & 0 \\ 0 & -2 \end{bmatrix}, \quad A_2 = \begin{bmatrix} 0 & 1 \\ 0 & 1 \end{bmatrix}, \quad \text{and} \quad A_3 = \begin{bmatrix} 0 & 0 \\ 1 & -3 \end{bmatrix}$$

in W. The matrix A is in W if and only if $A = aA_1 + bA_2 + cA_3$, so $\{A_1, A_2, A_3\}$ is a spanning set for W. It is easy to show that the set $\{A_1, A_2, A_3\}$ is linearly independent, so it is a basis for W. It follows that $\dim(W) = 3$. ■

An example of an infinite-dimensional vector space is given next, in Example 2. As Example 2 illustrates, we can show that a vector space V is infinite dimensional if we can show that V contains subspaces of dimension k for $k = 1, 2, 3, \ldots$.

If W is a subspace of a vector space V, and if $\dim(W) = k$, then it is almost obvious that $\dim(V) \geq \dim(W) = k$ (we leave the proof of this as an exercise). This observation can be used to show that $C[a, b]$ is an infinite-dimensional vector space.

EXAMPLE 2 Show that $C[a, b]$ is an infinite-dimensional vector space.

Solution To show that $C[a, b]$ is not a finite-dimensional vector space, we merely note that $\mathcal{P}_n$ is a subspace of $C[a, b]$ for every n. But $\dim(\mathcal{P}_n) = n + 1$; and so $C[a, b]$ contains subspaces of arbitrarily large dimension. Thus $C[a, b]$ must be an infinite-dimensional vector space. ■

Properties of a p-Dimensional Vector Space

The next two theorems summarize some of the properties of a p-dimensional vector space V and show how properties of R^p carry over into V.

THEOREM 8 Let V be a finite-dimensional vector space with $\dim(V) = p$.

1. Any set of $p + 1$ or more vectors in V is linearly dependent.
2. Any set of p linearly independent vectors in V is a basis for V. ■

This theorem is a direct generalization from R^p (Exercise 20). To complete our discussion of finite-dimensional vector spaces, we state the following lemma.

LEMMA Let V be a vector space, and let $Q = \{\mathbf{u}_1, \mathbf{u}_2, \ldots, \mathbf{u}_p\}$ be a spanning set for V. Then there is a subset Q' of Q that is a basis for V.

Proof (We only sketch the proof of this lemma because the proof follows familiar lines.) If Q is linearly independent, then Q itself is a basis for V. If Q is linearly dependent, we can express some vector from Q in terms of the other $p - 1$ vectors in Q. Without loss of generality, let us suppose we can express $\mathbf{u}_1$ in terms of $\mathbf{u}_2, \mathbf{u}_3, \ldots, \mathbf{u}_p$. In that event we have

$$\text{Sp}\{\mathbf{u}_2, \mathbf{u}_3, \ldots, \mathbf{u}_p\} = \text{Sp}\{\mathbf{u}_1, \mathbf{u}_2, \mathbf{u}_3, \ldots, \mathbf{u}_p\} = V;$$

if $\{\mathbf{u}_2, \mathbf{u}_3, \ldots, \mathbf{u}_p\}$ is linearly independent, it is a basis for V. If $\{\mathbf{u}_2, \mathbf{u}_3, \ldots, \mathbf{u}_p\}$ is linearly dependent, we continue discarding redundant vectors until we obtain a linearly independent spanning set, Q'. ■

The following theorem is a companion to Theorem 8.

THEOREM 9 Let V be a finite-dimensional vector space with $\dim(V) = p$.

1. Any spanning set for V must contain at least p vectors.
2. Any set of p vectors that spans V is a basis for V.

Proof Property 1 follows immediately from the preceding lemma, for if there were a spanning set Q for V that contained fewer than p vectors, then we could find a subset Q' of Q that is a basis for V containing fewer than p vectors. This finding would contradict Theorem 7, so property 1 must be valid.

Property 2 also follows from the lemma, because we know there is a subset Q' of Q such that Q' is a basis for V. Since $\dim(V) = p$, Q' must have p vectors, and since $Q' \subseteq Q$, where Q has p vectors, we must have $Q' = Q$. ∎

EXAMPLE 3 Let V be the vector space of all (2×2) real matrices. In V, set

$$A_1 = \begin{bmatrix} 1 & 0 \\ -1 & 0 \end{bmatrix}, \quad A_2 = \begin{bmatrix} 0 & 1 \\ 2 & 0 \end{bmatrix}, \quad A_3 = \begin{bmatrix} 0 & 0 \\ -1 & 3 \end{bmatrix},$$

$$A_4 = \begin{bmatrix} 1 & 0 \\ -1 & 1 \end{bmatrix}, \quad \text{and} \quad A_5 = \begin{bmatrix} 2 & 1 \\ 3 & 1 \end{bmatrix}.$$

For each of the sets $\{A_1, A_2, A_3\}$, $\{A_1, A_2, A_3, A_4\}$, and $\{A_1, A_2, A_3, A_4, A_5\}$, determine whether the set is a basis for V.

Solution We have already noted that $\dim(V) = 4$ and that $B = \{E_{11}, E_{12}, E_{21}, E_{22}\}$ is a basis for V. It follows from property 1 of Theorem 9 that the set $\{A_1, A_2, A_3\}$ does not span V. Likewise, property 1 of Theorem 8 implies that $\{A_1, A_2, A_3, A_4, A_5\}$ is a linearly dependent set. By property 2 of Theorem 8, the set $\{A_1, A_2, A_3, A_4\}$ is a basis for V if and only if it is a linearly independent set. It is straightforward to see that the set of coordinate vectors $\{[A_1]_B, [A_2]_B, [A_3]_B, [A_4]_B\}$ is a linearly independent set. By Theorem 5 of Section 5.4, the set $\{A_1, A_2, A_3, A_4\}$ is also linearly independent; thus the set is a basis for V. ∎

5.5 EXERCISES

1. Let V be the set of all real (3×3) matrices, and let V_1 and V_2 be subsets of V, where V_1 consists of all the (3×3) lower-triangular matrices and V_2 consists of all the (3×3) upper-triangular matrices.

a) Show that V_1 and V_2 are subspaces of V.

b) Find bases for V_1 and V_2.

c) Calculate $\dim(V)$, $\dim(V_1)$, and $\dim(V_2)$.

2. Suppose that V_1 and V_2 are subspaces of a vector space V. Show that $V_1 \cap V_2$ is also a subspace of V. It is not necessarily true that $V_1 \cup V_2$ is a subspace of V. Let $V = R^2$ and find two subspaces of R^2 whose union is not a subspace of R^2.

3. Let V, V_1, and V_2 be as in Exercise 1. By Exercise 2, $V_1 \cap V_2$ is a subspace of V. Describe $V_1 \cap V_2$ and calculate its dimension.

4. Let V be as in Exercise 1, and let W be the subset of all the (3×3) symmetric matrices in V. Clearly W is a subspace of V. What is $\dim(W)$?

5. Recall that a square matrix A is called skew symmetric if $A^T = -A$. Let V be as in Exercise 1 and let W be the subset of all the (3×3) skew-symmetric matrices in V. Calculate $\dim(W)$.

6. Let W be the subspace of $\mathcal{P}_2$ consisting of polynomials $p(x) = a_0 + a_1x + a_2x^2$ such that $2a_0 - a_1 + 3a_2 = 0$. Determine $\dim(W)$.

7. Let W be the subspace of $\mathcal{P}_4$ defined thus: $p(x)$ is in W if and only if $p(1) + p(-1) = 0$ and $p(2) + p(-2) = 0$. What is $\dim(W)$?

In Exercises 8–13, a subset S of a vector space V is given. In each case choose one of the statements i), ii), or iii) that holds for S and verify that this is the case.

i) S is a basis for V.

ii) S does not span V.

iii) S is linearly dependent.

8. $S = \{1 + x - x^2, x + x^3, -x^2 + x^3\}$; $V = \mathcal{P}_3$

9. $S = \{1 + x^2, x - x^2, 1 + x, 2 - x + x^2\}$; $V = \mathcal{P}_2$

10. $S = \{1 + x + x^2, x + x^2, x^2\}$; $V = \mathcal{P}_2$

11. $S = \left\{\begin{bmatrix} 0 & 1 \\ 1 & 0 \end{bmatrix}, \begin{bmatrix} 1 & 0 \\ 0 & 1 \end{bmatrix}\right\}$;

V is the set of all (2×2) real matrices.

12. $S = \left\{\begin{bmatrix} 0 & 0 \\ 0 & 1 \end{bmatrix}, \begin{bmatrix} 0 & 1 \\ 0 & 1 \end{bmatrix}, \begin{bmatrix} 1 & 1 \\ 1 & 1 \end{bmatrix}, \begin{bmatrix} 0 & 1 \\ 1 & 1 \end{bmatrix}\right\}$;

V is the set of all (2×2) real matrices.

13. $S = \left\{\begin{bmatrix} 1 & 0 \\ -1 & 0 \end{bmatrix}, \begin{bmatrix} 1 & 2 \\ 1 & -2 \end{bmatrix}, \begin{bmatrix} 1 & -1 \\ 1 & 4 \end{bmatrix}, \begin{bmatrix} 3 & 4 \\ 0 & 4 \end{bmatrix}, \begin{bmatrix} 0 & 1 \\ -1 & 3 \end{bmatrix}\right\}$;

V is the set of all (2×2) real matrices.

14. Let W be the subspace of $C[-\pi, \pi]$ consisting of functions of the form $f(x) = a \sin x + b \cos x$. Determine the dimension of W.

15. Let V denote the set of all infinite sequences of real numbers:

$$V = \{\mathbf{x}: \mathbf{x} = \{x_i\}_{i=1}^{\infty}, \quad x_i \text{ in } R\}.$$

If $\mathbf{x} = \{x_i\}_{i=1}^{\infty}$ and $\mathbf{y} = \{y_i\}_{i=1}^{\infty}$ are in V, then $\mathbf{x} + \mathbf{y}$ is the sequence $\{x_i + y_i\}_{i=1}^{\infty}$. If c is a real number, then $c\mathbf{x}$ is the sequence $\{cx_i\}_{i=1}^{\infty}$.

a) Prove that V is a vector space.

b) Show that V has infinite dimension. [*Hint:* For each positive integer, k, let $\mathbf{s}_k$ denote the sequence $\mathbf{s}_k = \{e_{ki}\}_{i=1}^{\infty}$, where $e_{kk} = 1$, but $e_{ki} = 0$ for $i \neq k$. For each positive integer n, show that $\{\mathbf{s}_1, \mathbf{s}_2, \ldots, \mathbf{s}_n\}$ is a linearly independent subset of V.]

16. Let V be a vector space, and let W be a subspace of V, where $\dim(W) = k$. Prove that if V is finite dimensional, then $\dim(V) \geq k$. [*Hint:* W must contain a set of k linearly independent vectors.]

17. Let W be a subspace of a finite-dimensional vector space V, where W contains at least one nonzero vector. Prove that W has a basis and that $\dim(W) \leq \dim(V)$. [*Hint:* Use Exercise 36 of Section 5.4 to show that W has a basis.]

18. Prove Theorem 6. [*Hint:* Let $\{\mathbf{u}_1, \mathbf{u}_2, \ldots, \mathbf{u}_k\}$ be a subset of V, where $k \geq p + 1$. Consider the vectors $[\mathbf{u}_1]_B, [\mathbf{u}_2]_B, \ldots, [\mathbf{u}_k]_B$ in R^p and apply Theorem 5 of Section 5.4.]

19. Prove Theorem 7.

20. Prove Theorem 8.

21. (*Change of basis;* see also Section 5.10). Let V be a vector space, where $\dim(V) = n$, and let $B = \{\mathbf{v}_1, \mathbf{v}_2, \ldots, \mathbf{v}_n\}$ and $C = \{\mathbf{u}_1, \mathbf{u}_2, \ldots, \mathbf{u}_n\}$ be two bases for V. Let $\mathbf{w}$ be any vector in V, and suppose that $\mathbf{w}$ has these representations in terms of the bases B and C:

$$\mathbf{w} = d_1\mathbf{v}_1 + d_2\mathbf{v}_2 + \cdots + d_n\mathbf{v}_n$$
$$\mathbf{w} = c_1\mathbf{u}_1 + c_2\mathbf{u}_2 + \cdots + c_n\mathbf{u}_n.$$

By considering Eq. (10) of Section 5.4, convince yourself that the coordinate vectors for $\mathbf{w}$ satisfy

$$[\mathbf{w}]_B = A[\mathbf{w}]_C,$$

where A is the $(n \times n)$ matrix whose ith column is equal to $[\mathbf{u}_i]_B$, $1 \leq i \leq n$. As an application, consider the two bases for $\mathcal{P}_2$: $C = \{1, x, x^2\}$ and $B = \{1, x + 1, (x + 1)^2\}$.

a) Calculate the (3×3) matrix A just described.

b) Using the identity $[p]_B = A[p]_c$, calculate the coordinate vector of $p(x) = x^2 + 4x + 8$ with respect to B.

22. The matrix A in Exercise 21 is called a transition matrix and shows how to transform a representation with respect to one basis into a representation with respect to another. Use the matrix in part a) of Exercise 21 to convert $p(x) = c_0 + c_1x + c_2x^2$ to the form $p(x) = a_0 + a_1(x + 1) + a_2(x + 1)^2$, where:

a) $p(x) = x^2 + 3x - 2$;
b) $p(x) = 2x^2 - 5x + 8$;
c) $p(x) = -x^2 - 2x + 3$;
d) $p(x) = x - 9$.

23. By Theorem 5 of Section 5.4, an $(n \times n)$ transition matrix (see Exercises 21 and 22) is always nonsingular. Thus if $[\mathbf{w}]_B = A[\mathbf{w}]_c$, then $[\mathbf{w}]_C = A^{-1}[\mathbf{w}]_B$. Calculate A^{-1} for the matrix in part a) of Exercise 21 and use the result to transform each of the following polynomials to the form $a_0 + a_1x + a_2x^2$.

a) $p(x) = 2 - 3(x+1) + 7(x+1)^2$
b) $p(x) = 1 + 4(x+1) - (x+1)^2$
c) $p(x) = 4 + (x+1)$
d) $p(x) = 9 - (x+1)^2$

24. Find a matrix A such that $[p]_B = A[p]_c$ for all $p(x)$ in $\mathcal{P}_3$, where $C = \{1, x, x^2, x^3\}$ and $B = \{1, x, x(x-1), x(x-1)(x-2)\}$. Use A to convert each of the following to the form $p(x) = a_0 + a_1x + a_2x(x-1) + a_3x(x-1)(x-2)$.

a) $p(x) = x^3 - 2x^2 + 5x - 9$
b) $p(x) = x^2 + 7x - 2$
c) $p(x) = x^3 + 1$
d) $p(x) = x^3 + 2x^2 + 2x + 3$

5.6 INNER-PRODUCT SPACES, ORTHOGONAL BASES, AND PROJECTIONS (OPTIONAL)

Up to now we have considered a vector space solely as an entity with an algebraic structure. We know, however, that R^n possesses more than just an algebraic structure; in particular, we know that we can measure the size or length of a vector $\mathbf{x}$ in R^n by the quantity $\|\mathbf{x}\| = \sqrt{\mathbf{x}^T\mathbf{x}}$. Similarly, we can define the distance from $\mathbf{x}$ to $\mathbf{y}$ as $\|\mathbf{x} - \mathbf{y}\|$. The ability to measure distances means that R^n has a geometric structure, which supplements the algebraic structure. The geometric structure can be employed to study problems of convergence, continuity, and the like. In this section we briefly describe how a suitable measure of distance might be imposed on a general vector space. Our development will be brief, and we will leave most of the details to the reader; but the ideas parallel those in Sections 3.6 and 3.8–3.9.

Inner-Product Spaces

To begin, we observe that the geometric structure for R^n is based on the scalar product $\mathbf{x}^T\mathbf{y}$. Essentially the scalar product is a real-valued function of two vector variables: Given $\mathbf{x}$ and $\mathbf{y}$ in R^n, the scalar product produces a number $\mathbf{x}^T\mathbf{y}$. Thus to derive a geometric structure for a vector space V, we should look for a generalization of the scalar-product function. A consideration of the properties of the scalar-product function leads to the definition of an inner-product function for a vector space. (With reference to Definition 7, which follows, we note that the expression $\mathbf{u}^T\mathbf{v}$ does not make sense in a general vector space V. Thus not only does the nomenclature change—scalar product becomes inner product—but also the notation changes as well, with $\langle \mathbf{u}, \mathbf{v} \rangle$ denoting the inner product of $\mathbf{u}$ and $\mathbf{v}$.)

DEFINITION 7 An ***inner product*** on a real vector space V is a function that assigns a real number, $\langle \mathbf{u}, \mathbf{v} \rangle$, to each pair of vectors $\mathbf{u}$ and $\mathbf{v}$ in V, and that satisfies these properties:

1. $\langle \mathbf{u}, \mathbf{u} \rangle \geq 0$ and $\langle \mathbf{u}, \mathbf{u} \rangle = 0$ if and only if $\mathbf{u} = \boldsymbol{\theta}$.
2. $\langle \mathbf{u}, \mathbf{v} \rangle = \langle \mathbf{v}, \mathbf{u} \rangle$.
3. $\langle a\mathbf{u}, \mathbf{v} \rangle = a\langle \mathbf{u}, \mathbf{v} \rangle$.
4. $\langle \mathbf{u}, \mathbf{v} + \mathbf{w} \rangle = \langle \mathbf{u}, \mathbf{v} \rangle + \langle \mathbf{u}, \mathbf{w} \rangle$.

The usual scalar product in R^n is an inner product in the sense of Definition 7, where $\langle \mathbf{x}, \mathbf{y} \rangle = \mathbf{x}^T\mathbf{y}$. To illustrate the flexibility of Definition 7, we also note that there are other sorts of inner products for R^n. The following example gives another inner product for R^2.

EXAMPLE 1 Let V be the vector space R^2, and let A be the (2×2) matrix

$$A = \begin{bmatrix} 3 & 2 \\ 2 & 4 \end{bmatrix}.$$

Verify that the function $\langle \mathbf{u}, \mathbf{v} \rangle = \mathbf{u}^T A\mathbf{v}$ is an inner product for R^2.

Solution Let $\mathbf{u}$ be a vector in R^2:

$$\mathbf{u} = \begin{bmatrix} u_1 \\ u_2 \end{bmatrix}.$$

Then

$$\langle \mathbf{u}, \mathbf{u} \rangle = \mathbf{u}^T A\mathbf{u} = [u_1, u_2] \begin{bmatrix} 3 & 2 \\ 2 & 4 \end{bmatrix} \begin{bmatrix} u_1 \\ u_2 \end{bmatrix},$$

so $\langle \mathbf{u}, \mathbf{u} \rangle = 3u_1^2 + 4u_1u_2 + 4u_2^2 = 2u_1^2 + (u_1 + 2u_2)^2$. Thus $\langle \mathbf{u}, \mathbf{u} \rangle \geq 0$ and $\langle \mathbf{u}, \mathbf{u} \rangle = 0$ if and only if $u_1 = u_2 = 0$. This shows that property 1 of Definition 7 is satisfied.

To see that property 2 of Definition 7 holds, note that A is symmetric; that is, $A^T = A$. Also observe that if $\mathbf{u}$ and $\mathbf{v}$ are in R^2, then $\mathbf{u}^T A\mathbf{v}$ is a (1×1) matrix, so $(\mathbf{u}^T A\mathbf{v})^T = \mathbf{u}^T A\mathbf{v}$. It now follows that $\langle \mathbf{u}, \mathbf{v} \rangle = \mathbf{u}^T A\mathbf{v} = (\mathbf{u}^T A\mathbf{v})^T = \mathbf{v}^T A^T (\mathbf{u}^T)^T = \mathbf{v}^T A^T \mathbf{u} = \langle \mathbf{v}, \mathbf{u} \rangle$.

Properties 3 and 4 of Definition 7 follow easily from the properties of matrix multiplication, so $\langle \mathbf{u}, \mathbf{v} \rangle$ is an inner product for R^2. ■

In Example 1, an inner product for R^2 was defined in terms of a matrix A:

$$\langle \mathbf{u}, \mathbf{v} \rangle = \mathbf{u}^T A\mathbf{v}.$$

In general, we might ask the following question:

"For what $(n \times n)$ matrices, A, does the operation $\mathbf{u}^T A\mathbf{v}$ define an inner product on R^n?"

The answer to this question is suggested by the solution to Example 1. In particular (see Exercises 3 and 32), the operation $\langle \mathbf{u}, \mathbf{v} \rangle = \mathbf{u}^T A \mathbf{v}$ is an inner product for R^n if and only if A is a symmetric positive-definite matrix.

There are a number of ways in which inner products can be defined on spaces of functions. For example, Exercise 6 will show that

$$\langle p, q \rangle = p(0)q(0) + p(1)q(1) + p(2)q(2)$$

defines one inner product for $\mathcal{P}_2$. The following example gives yet another inner product for $\mathcal{P}_2$.

EXAMPLE 2 For $p(t)$ and $q(t)$ in $\mathcal{P}_2$, verify that

$$\langle p, q \rangle = \int_0^1 p(t)q(t)\,dt$$

is an inner product.

Solution To check property 1 of Definition 7, note that

$$\langle p, p \rangle = \int_0^1 p(t)^2\,dt,$$

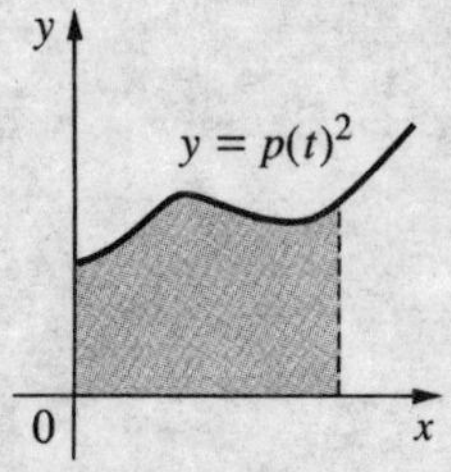

Figure 5.5
The value $\langle p, p \rangle$ is equal to the area under the graph of $y = p(t)^2$.

and $p(t)^2 \geq 0$ for $0 \leq t \leq 1$. Thus $\langle p, p \rangle$ is the area under the curve $p(t)^2, 0 \leq t \leq 1$. Hence $\langle p, p \rangle \geq 0$, and equality holds if and only if $p(t) = 0, 0 \leq t \leq 1$ (see Fig. 5.5).

Properties 2, 3, and 4 of Definition 7 are straightforward to verify, and we include here only the verification of property 4. If $p(t)$, $q(t)$, and $r(t)$ are in $\mathcal{P}_2$, then

$$\begin{aligned}\langle p, q + r \rangle &= \int_0^1 p(t)[q(t) + r(t)]\,dt = \int_0^1 [p(t)q(t) + p(t)r(t)]\,dt \\ &= \int_0^1 p(t)q(t)dt + \int_0^1 p(t)r(t)dt = \langle p, q \rangle + \langle p, r \rangle,\end{aligned}$$

as required by property 4. ■

After the key step of defining a vector-space analog of the scalar product, the rest is routine. For purposes of reference we call a vector space with an inner product an ***inner-product space***. As in R^n, we can use the inner product as a measure of size: If V is an inner-product space, then for each $\mathbf{v}$ in V we define $\|\mathbf{v}\|$ (the ***norm*** of $\mathbf{v}$) as

$$\|\mathbf{v}\| = \sqrt{\langle \mathbf{v}, \mathbf{v} \rangle}.$$

Note that $\langle \mathbf{v}, \mathbf{v} \rangle \geq 0$ for all $\mathbf{v}$ in V, so the norm function is always defined.

EXAMPLE 3 Use the inner product for $\mathcal{P}_2$ defined in Example 2 to determine $\|t^2\|$.

Solution By definition, $\|t^2\| = \sqrt{\langle t^2, t^2 \rangle}$. But $\langle t^2, t^2 \rangle = \int_0^1 t^2 t^2\,dt = \int_0^1 t^4\,dt = 1/5$, so $\|t^2\| = 1/\sqrt{5}$. ■

Before continuing, we pause to illustrate one way in which the inner-product space framework is used in practice. One of the many inner products for the vector space $C[0, 1]$ is

$$\langle f, g \rangle = \int_0^1 f(x)g(x)\,dx.$$

If f is a relatively complicated function in $C[0, 1]$, we might wish to approximate f by a simpler function, say a polynomial. For definiteness suppose we want to find a polynomial p in $\mathcal{P}_2$ that is a good approximation to f. The phrase "good approximation" is too vague to be used in any calculation, but the inner-product space framework allows us to measure size and thus to pose some meaningful problems. In particular, we can ask for a polynomial p^* in $\mathcal{P}_2$ such that

$$\|f - p^*\| \leq \|f - p\|$$

for all p in $\mathcal{P}_2$. Finding such a polynomial p^* in this setting is equivalent to minimizing

$$\int_0^1 [f(x) - p(x)]^2\, dx$$

among all p in $\mathcal{P}_2$. We will present a procedure for doing this shortly.

Orthogonal Bases

If $\mathbf{u}$ and $\mathbf{v}$ are vectors in an inner-product space V, we say that $\mathbf{u}$ and $\mathbf{v}$ are ***orthogonal*** if $\langle \mathbf{u}, \mathbf{v} \rangle = 0$. Similarly, $B = \{\mathbf{v}_1, \mathbf{v}_2, \ldots, \mathbf{v}_p\}$ is an ***orthogonal set*** in V if $\langle \mathbf{v}_i, \mathbf{v}_j \rangle = 0$ when $i \neq j$. In addition, if an orthogonal set of vectors B is a basis for V, we call B an ***orthogonal basis***. The next two theorems correspond to their analogs in R^n, and we leave the proofs to the exercises. [See Eq. (5a), Eq. (5b), and Theorem 14 of Section 3.6.]

THEOREM 10 Let $B = \{\mathbf{v}_1, \mathbf{v}_2, \ldots, \mathbf{v}_n\}$ be an orthogonal basis for an inner-product space V. If $\mathbf{u}$ is any vector in V, then

$$\mathbf{u} = \frac{\langle \mathbf{v}_1, \mathbf{u} \rangle}{\langle \mathbf{v}_1, \mathbf{v}_1 \rangle}\mathbf{v}_1 + \frac{\langle \mathbf{v}_2, \mathbf{u} \rangle}{\langle \mathbf{v}_2, \mathbf{v}_2 \rangle}\mathbf{v}_2 + \cdots + \frac{\langle \mathbf{v}_n, \mathbf{u} \rangle}{\langle \mathbf{v}_n, \mathbf{v}_n \rangle}\mathbf{v}_n.$$

THEOREM 11 **Gram–Schmidt Orthogonalization** Let V be an inner-product space, and let $\{\mathbf{u}_1, \mathbf{u}_2, \ldots, \mathbf{u}_n\}$ be a basis for V. Let $\mathbf{v}_1 = \mathbf{u}_1$, and for $2 \leq k \leq n$ define $\mathbf{v}_k$ by

$$\mathbf{v}_k = \mathbf{u}_k - \sum_{j=1}^{k-1} \frac{\langle \mathbf{u}_k, \mathbf{v}_j \rangle}{\langle \mathbf{v}_j, \mathbf{v}_j \rangle}\mathbf{v}_j.$$

Then $\{\mathbf{v}_1, \mathbf{v}_2, \ldots, \mathbf{v}_n\}$ is an orthogonal basis for V.

EXAMPLE 4 Let the inner product on $\mathcal{P}_2$ be the one given in Example 2. Starting with the natural basis $\{1, x, x^2\}$, use Gram–Schmidt orthogonalization to obtain an orthogonal basis for $\mathcal{P}_2$.

Solution If we let $\{p_0, p_1, p_2\}$ denote the orthogonal basis, we have $p_0(x) = 1$ and find $p_1(x)$ from

$$p_1(x) = x - \frac{\langle p_0, x \rangle}{\langle p_0, p_0 \rangle} p_0(x).$$

We calculate

$$\langle p_0, x \rangle = \int_0^1 x\, dx = 1/2 \text{ and } \langle p_0, p_0 \rangle = \int_0^1 dx = 1;$$

so $p_1(x) = x - 1/2$. The next step of the Gram–Schmidt orthogonalization process is to form

$$p_2(x) = x^2 - \frac{\langle p_1, x^2\rangle}{\langle p_1, p_1\rangle} p_1(x) - \frac{\langle p_0, x^2\rangle}{\langle p_0, p_0\rangle} p_0(x).$$

The required constants are

$$\langle p_1, x^2\rangle = \int_0^1 (x^3 - x^2/2)\, dx = 1/12$$

$$\langle p_1, p_1\rangle = \int_0^1 (x^2 - x + 1/4)\, dx = 1/12$$

$$\langle p_0, x^2\rangle = \int_0^1 x^2\, dx = 1/3$$

$$\langle p_0, p_0\rangle = \int_0^1 dx = 1.$$

Therefore, $p_2(x) = x^2 - p_1(x) - p_0(x)/3 = x^2 - x + 1/6$, and $\{p_0, p_1, p_2\}$ is an orthogonal basis for $\mathcal{P}_2$ with respect to the inner product. ■

EXAMPLE 5 Let $B = \{p_0, p_1, p_2\}$ be the orthogonal basis for $\mathcal{P}_2$ obtained in Example 4. Find the coordinates of x^2 relative to B.

Solution By Theorem 10, $x^2 = a_0 p_0(x) + a_1 p_1(x) + a_2 p_2(x)$, where

$$a_0 = \langle p_0, x^2\rangle / \langle p_0, p_0\rangle$$
$$a_1 = \langle p_1, x^2\rangle / \langle p_1, p_1\rangle$$
$$a_2 = \langle p_2, x^2\rangle / \langle p_2, p_2\rangle.$$

The necessary calculations are

$$\langle p_0, x^2\rangle = \int_0^1 x^2\, dx = 1/3$$

$$\langle p_1, x^2\rangle = \int_0^1 [x^3 - (1/2)x^2]\, dx = 1/12$$

$$\langle p_2, x^2\rangle = \int_0^1 [x^4 - x^3 + (1/6)x^2]\, dx = 1/180$$

$$\langle p_0, p_0\rangle = \int_0^1 dx = 1$$

$$\langle p_1, p_1\rangle = \int_0^1 [x^2 - x + 1/4]\, dx = 1/12$$

$$\langle p_2, p_2\rangle = \int_0^1 [x^2 - x + 1/6]^2\, dx = 1/180.$$

Thus $a_0 = 1/3$, $a_1 = 1$, and $a_2 = 1$. We can easily check that $x^2 = (1/3)p_0(x) + p_1(x) + p_2(x)$. ■

Orthogonal Projections

We return now to the previously discussed problem of finding a polynomial p^* in $\mathcal{P}_2$ that is the best approximation of a function f in $C[0, 1]$. Note that the problem amounts to determining a vector p^* in a subspace of an inner-product space, where p^* is closer to f than any other vector in the subspace. The essential aspects of this problem can be stated formally as the following general problem:

Let V be an inner-product space and let W be a subspace of V. Given a vector $\mathbf{v}$ in V, find a vector $\mathbf{w}^*$ in W such that

$$\|\mathbf{v} - \mathbf{w}^*\| \leq \|\mathbf{v} - \mathbf{w}\| \quad \text{for all } \mathbf{w} \text{ in } W. \tag{1}$$

A vector $\mathbf{w}^*$ in W satisfying inequality (1) is called the ***projection of v*** onto W, or (frequently) the ***best least-squares approximation*** to $\mathbf{v}$. Intuitively $\mathbf{w}^*$ is the nearest vector in W to $\mathbf{v}$.

The solution process for this problem is almost exactly the same as that for the least-squares problem in R^n. One distinction in our general setting is that the subspace W might not be finite dimensional. If W is an infinite-dimensional subspace of V, then there may or may not be a projection of $\mathbf{v}$ onto W. If W is finite dimensional, then a projection always exists, is unique, and can be found explicitly. The next two theorems outline this concept, and again we leave the proofs to the reader since they parallel the proof of Theorem 18 of Section 3.9.

THEOREM 12 Let V be an inner-product space, and let W be a subspace of V. Let $\mathbf{v}$ be a vector in V, and suppose $\mathbf{w}^*$ is a vector in W such that

$$\langle \mathbf{v} - \mathbf{w}^*, \mathbf{w} \rangle = 0 \quad \text{for all } \mathbf{w} \text{ in } W.$$

Then $\|\mathbf{v} - \mathbf{w}^*\| \leq \|\mathbf{v} - \mathbf{w}\|$ for all $\mathbf{w}$ in W with equality holding only for $\mathbf{w} = \mathbf{w}^*$. ■

THEOREM 13 Let V be an inner-product space, and let $\mathbf{v}$ be a vector in V. Let W be an n-dimensional subspace of V, and let $\{\mathbf{u}_1, \mathbf{u}_2, \ldots, \mathbf{u}_n\}$ be an orthogonal basis for W. Then

$$\|\mathbf{v} - \mathbf{w}^*\| \leq \|\mathbf{v} - \mathbf{w}\| \text{ for all } \mathbf{w} \text{ in } W$$

if and only if

$$\mathbf{w}^* = \frac{\langle \mathbf{v}, \mathbf{u}_1 \rangle}{\langle \mathbf{u}_1, \mathbf{u}_1 \rangle}\mathbf{u}_1 + \frac{\langle \mathbf{v}, \mathbf{u}_2 \rangle}{\langle \mathbf{u}_2, \mathbf{u}_2 \rangle}\mathbf{u}_2 + \cdots + \frac{\langle \mathbf{v}, \mathbf{u}_n \rangle}{\langle \mathbf{u}_n, \mathbf{u}_n \rangle}\mathbf{u}_n. \tag{2}$$

■

In view of Theorem 13, it follows that when W is a finite-dimensional subspace of an inner-product space V, we can always find projections by first finding an orthogonal basis for W (by using Theorem 11) and then calculating the projection $\mathbf{w}^*$ from Eq. (2).

To illustrate the process of finding a projection, we return to the inner-product space $C[0, 1]$ with the subspace $\mathcal{P}_2$. As a specific but rather unrealistic function, f, we choose $f(x) = \cos x$, x in radians. The inner product is

$$\langle f, g \rangle = \int_0^1 f(x)g(x)\, dx.$$

EXAMPLE 6 In the vector space $C[0, 1]$, let $f(x) = \cos x$. Find the projection of f onto the subspace $\mathcal{P}_2$.

Solution Let $\{p_0, p_1, p_2\}$ be the orthogonal basis for $\mathcal{P}_2$ found in Example 4. (Note that the inner product used in Example 4 coincides with the present inner product on $C[0, 1]$. By Theorem 13, the projection of f onto $\mathcal{P}_2$ is the polynomial p^* defined by

$$p^*(x) = \frac{\langle f, p_0 \rangle}{\langle p_0, p_0 \rangle} p_0(x) + \frac{\langle f, p_1 \rangle}{\langle p_1, p_1 \rangle} p_1(x) + \frac{\langle f, p_2 \rangle}{\langle p_2, p_2 \rangle} p_2(x),$$

where

$$\langle f, p_0 \rangle = \int_0^1 \cos(x)\, dx \simeq .841471$$

$$\langle f, p_1 \rangle = \int_0^1 (x - 1/2) \cos(x)\, dx \simeq .038962$$

$$\langle f, p_2 \rangle = \int_0^1 (x^2 - x + 1/6) \cos(x)\, dx \simeq -.002394.$$

From Example 5, we have $\langle p_0, p_0 \rangle = 1$, $\langle p_1, p_1 \rangle = 1/12$, and $\langle p_2, p_2 \rangle = 1/180$. Therefore, $p^*(x)$ is given by

$$\begin{aligned} p^*(x) &= \langle f, p_0 \rangle p_0(x) + 12\langle f, p_1 \rangle p_1(x) + 180\langle f, p_2 \rangle p_2(x) \\ &\simeq .841471 p_0(x) + .467544 p_1(x) - .430920 p_2(x). \end{aligned}$$

In order to assess how well $p^*(x)$ approximates $\cos x$ in the interval $[0, 1]$, we can tabulate $p^*(x)$ and $\cos x$ at various values of x (see Table 5.1). ∎

EXAMPLE 7 The function $\text{Si}(x)$ (important in applications such as optics) is defined as follows:

$$\text{Si}(x) = \int_0^x \frac{\sin u}{u}\, du, \quad \text{for } x \neq 0. \tag{3}$$

The integral in (3) is not an elementary one and so, for a given value of x, $\text{Si}(x)$ must be evaluated using a numerical integration procedure. In this example, we approximate

Table 5.1

x	$p^*(x)$	$\cos x$	$p^*(x) - \cos x$
0.0	1.0034	1.000	.0034
0.2	.9789	.9801	−.0012
0.4	.9198	.9211	−.0013
0.6	.8263	.8253	.0010
0.8	.6983	.6967	.0016
1.0	.5359	.5403	−.0044

Si(x) by a cubic polynomial for $0 \le x \le 1$. In particular, it can be shown that if we define Si(0) $= 0$, then Si(x) is continuous for all x. Thus we can ask:

"What is the projection of Si(x) onto the subspace $\mathcal{P}_3$ of $C[0, 1]$?"

This projection will serve as an approximation to Si(x) for $0 \le x \le 1$.

Solution We used the computer algebra system Derive to carry out the calculations. Some of the steps are shown in Fig. 5.6. To begin, let $\{p_0, p_1, p_2, p_3\}$ be the orthogonal basis for $\mathcal{P}_3$ found by the Gram–Schmidt process. From Example 4, we already know that

$$6:\quad \int_0^1 x^3 \,\mathrm{P1}(x)\, dx$$

$$7:\quad \frac{3}{40}$$

$$8:\quad \int_0^1 x^3 \,\mathrm{P2}(x)\, dx$$

$$9:\quad \frac{1}{120}$$

$$15:\quad \mathrm{P3}(x) := x^3 - \frac{1}{4}\mathrm{P0}(x) - \frac{9}{10}\mathrm{P1}(x) - \frac{3}{2}\mathrm{P2}(x)$$

$$16:\quad \mathrm{P3}(x) := x^3 - \frac{3x^2}{2} + \frac{3x}{5} - \frac{1}{20}$$

$$17:\quad \int_0^1 \mathrm{P3}(x)\,\mathrm{P3}(x)\, dx$$

$$18:\quad \frac{1}{2800}$$

$$49:\quad \int_0^1 180\,\mathrm{P2}(x) \int_0^x \frac{\mathrm{SIN}(u)}{u}\, du\, dx$$

$$50:\quad -0.0804033$$

$$51:\quad \int_0^1 2800\,\mathrm{P3}(x) \int_0^x \frac{\mathrm{SIN}(u)}{u}\, du\, dx$$

$$52:\quad -0.0510442$$

Figure 5.6 Some of the steps used by Derive to generate the projection of Si(x) onto $\mathcal{P}_3$ in Example 7

$p_0(x) = 1$, $p_1(x) = x - 1/2$, and $p_2(x) = x^2 - x + 1/6$. To find p_3, we first calculate the inner products

$$\langle p_0, x^3 \rangle, \langle p_1, x^3 \rangle, \langle p_2, x^3 \rangle$$

(see steps 6–9 in Fig. 5.6 for $\langle p_1, x^3 \rangle$ and $\langle p_2, x^3 \rangle$).

Using Theorem 11, we find p_3 and, for later use, $\langle p_3, p_3 \rangle$:

$$p_3(x) = x^3 - (3/2)x^2 + (3/5)x - 1/20$$
$$\langle p_3, p_3 \rangle = 1/2800$$

(see steps 15–18 in Fig. 5.6). Finally, by Theorem 13, the projection of $\mathrm{Si}(x)$ onto $\mathcal{P}_3$ is the polynomial p^* defined by

$$\begin{aligned} p^*(x) &= \frac{\langle \mathrm{Si}, p_0 \rangle}{\langle p_0, p_0 \rangle} p_0(x) + \frac{\langle \mathrm{Si}, p_1 \rangle}{\langle p_1, p_1 \rangle} p_1(x) + \frac{\langle \mathrm{Si}, p_2 \rangle}{\langle p_2, p_2 \rangle} p_2(x) + \frac{\langle \mathrm{Si}, p_3 \rangle}{\langle p_3, p_3 \rangle} p_3(x) \\ &= \langle \mathrm{Si}, p_0 \rangle p_0(x) + 12\langle \mathrm{Si}, p_1 \rangle p_1(x) + 180\langle \mathrm{Si}, p_2 \rangle p_2(x) + 2800\langle \mathrm{Si}, p_3 \rangle p_3(x). \end{aligned}$$

In the expression above for p^*, the inner products $\langle \mathrm{Si}, p_k \rangle$ for $k = 0, 1, 2$, and 3 are given by

$$\langle \mathrm{Si}, p_k \rangle = \int_0^1 p_k(x)\mathrm{Si}(x)\,dx = \int_0^1 p_k(x) \left\{ \int_0^x \frac{\sin u}{u} du \right\} dx$$

(see steps 49–52 in Fig. 5.6 for $180\langle \mathrm{Si}, p_2 \rangle$ and $2800\langle \mathrm{Si}, p_3 \rangle$).

Now, since $\mathrm{Si}(x)$ must be estimated numerically, it follows that the inner products $\langle \mathrm{Si}, p_k \rangle$ must be estimated as well. Using Derive to approximate the inner products, we obtain the projection (or best least-squares approximation)

$$p^*(x) = .486385 p_0(x) + .951172 p_1(x) - .0804033 p_2(x) - .0510442 p_3(x).$$

To assess how well $p^*(x)$ approximates $\mathrm{Si}(x)$ in $[0, 1]$, we tabulate each function at a few selected points (see Table 5.2). As can be seen from Table 5.2, it appears that $p^*(x)$ is a very good approximation to $\mathrm{Si}(x)$. ■

Table 5.2

x	$p^*(x)$	$\mathrm{Si}(x)$	$p^*(x) - \mathrm{Si}(x)$
0.0	.000049	.000000	.000049
0.2	.199578	.199556	.000028
0.4	.396449	.396461	−.000012
0.6	.588113	.588128	−.000015
0.8	.772119	.772095	.000024
1.0	.946018	.946083	−.000065

5.6 EXERCISES

1. Prove that $\langle \mathbf{x}, \mathbf{y} \rangle = 4x_1y_1 + x_2y_2$ is an inner product on R^2, where

$$\mathbf{x} = \begin{bmatrix} x_1 \\ x_2 \end{bmatrix} \text{ and } \mathbf{y} = \begin{bmatrix} y_1 \\ y_2 \end{bmatrix}.$$

2. Prove that $\langle \mathbf{x}, \mathbf{y} \rangle = a_1x_1y_1 + a_2x_2y_2 + \cdots + a_nx_ny_n$ is an inner product on R^n, where $a_1, a_2, \ldots, a_n$ are positive real numbers and where

$$\mathbf{x} = [x_1, x_2, \ldots, x_n]^T \text{ and}$$
$$\mathbf{y} = [y_1, y_2, \ldots, y_n]^T.$$

3. A real $(n \times n)$ symmetric matrix A is called ***positive definite*** if $\mathbf{x}^TA\mathbf{x} > 0$ for all $\mathbf{x}$ in R^n, $\mathbf{x} \neq \boldsymbol{\theta}$. Let A be a symmetric positive-definite matrix, and verify that

$$\langle \mathbf{x}, \mathbf{y} \rangle = \mathbf{x}^TA\mathbf{y}$$

defines an inner product on R^n; that is, verify that the four properties of Definition 7 are satisfied.

4. Prove that the following symmetric matrix A is positive definite. Prove this by choosing an arbitrary vector $\mathbf{x}$ in R^2, $\mathbf{x} \neq \boldsymbol{\theta}$, and calculating $\mathbf{x}^TA\mathbf{x}$.

$$A = \begin{bmatrix} 1 & 1 \\ 1 & 2 \end{bmatrix}$$

5. In $\mathcal{P}_2$ let $p(x) = a_0 + a_1x + a_2x^2$ and $q(x) = b_0 + b_1x + b_2x^2$. Prove that $\langle p, q \rangle = a_0b_0 + a_1b_1 + a_2b_2$ is an inner product on $\mathcal{P}_2$.

6. Prove that $\langle p, q \rangle = p(0)q(0) + p(1)q(1) + p(2)q(2)$ is an inner product on $\mathcal{P}_2$.

7. Let $A = (a_{ij})$ and $B = (b_{ij})$ be (2×2) matrices. Show that $\langle A, B \rangle = a_{11}b_{11} + a_{12}b_{12} + a_{21}b_{21} + a_{22}b_{22}$ is an inner product for the vector space of all (2×2) matrices.

8. For $\mathbf{x} = [1, -2]^T$ and $\mathbf{y} = [0, 1]^T$ in R^2, find $\langle \mathbf{x}, \mathbf{y} \rangle$, $\|\mathbf{x}\|$, $\|\mathbf{y}\|$, and $\|\mathbf{x} - \mathbf{y}\|$ using the inner product given in Exercise 1.

9. Repeat Exercise 8 with the inner product defined in Exercise 3 and the matrix A given in Exercise 4.

10. In $\mathcal{P}_2$ let $p(x) = -1 + 2x + x^2$ and $q(x) = 1 - x + 2x^2$. Using the inner product given in Exercise 5, find $\langle p, q \rangle$, $\|p\|$, $\|q\|$, and $\|p - q\|$.

11. Repeat Exercise 10 using the inner product defined in Exercise 6.

12. Show that $\{1, x, x^2\}$ is an orthogonal basis for $\mathcal{P}_2$ with the inner product defined in Exercise 5 but not with the inner product in Exercise 6.

13. In R^2 let $S = \{\mathbf{x}\colon \|\mathbf{x}\| = 1\}$. Sketch a graph of S if $\langle \mathbf{x}, \mathbf{y} \rangle = \mathbf{x}^T\mathbf{y}$. Now graph S using the inner product given in Exercise 1.

14. Let A be the matrix given in Exercise 4, and for $\mathbf{x}, \mathbf{y}$ in R^2 define $\langle \mathbf{x}, \mathbf{y} \rangle = \mathbf{x}^TA\mathbf{y}$ (see Exercise 3). Starting with the natural basis $\{\mathbf{e}_1, \mathbf{e}_2\}$, use Theorem 11 to obtain an orthogonal basis $\{\mathbf{u}_1, \mathbf{u}_2\}$ for R^2.

15. Let $\{\mathbf{u}_1, \mathbf{u}_2\}$ be the orthogonal basis for R^2 obtained in Exercise 14 and let $\mathbf{v} = [3, 4]^T$. Use Theorem 10 to find scalars a_1, a_2 such that $\mathbf{v} = a_1\mathbf{u}_1 + a_2\mathbf{u}_2$.

16. Use Theorem 11 to calculate an orthogonal basis $\{p_0, p_1, p_2\}$ for $\mathcal{P}_2$ with respect to the inner product in Exercise 6. Start with the natural basis $\{1, x, x^2\}$ for $\mathcal{P}_2$.

17. Use Theorem 10 to write $q(x) = 2 + 3x - 4x^2$ in terms of the orthogonal basis $\{p_0, p_1, p_2\}$ obtained in Exercise 16.

18. Show that the function defined in Exercise 6 is not an inner product for $\mathcal{P}_3$. [*Hint:* Find $p(x)$ in $\mathcal{P}_3$ such that $\langle p, p \rangle = 0$, but $p \neq \boldsymbol{\theta}$.]

19. Starting with the natural basis $\{1, x, x^2, x^3, x^4\}$, generate an orthogonal basis for $\mathcal{P}_4$ with respect to the inner product

$$\langle p, q \rangle = \sum_{i=-2}^{2} p(i)q(i).$$

20. If V is an inner-product space, show that $\langle \mathbf{v}, \boldsymbol{\theta} \rangle = 0$ for each vector $\mathbf{v}$ in V.

21. Let V be an inner-product space, and let $\mathbf{u}$ be a vector in V such that $\langle \mathbf{u}, \mathbf{v} \rangle = 0$ for every vector $\mathbf{v}$ in V. Show that $\mathbf{u} = \boldsymbol{\theta}$.

22. Let a be a scalar and $\mathbf{v}$ a vector in an inner-product space V. Prove that $\|a\mathbf{v}\| = |a|\|\mathbf{v}\|$.

23. Prove that if $\{\mathbf{v}_1, \mathbf{v}_2, \ldots, \mathbf{v}_k\}$ is an orthogonal set of nonzero vectors in an inner-product space, then this set is linearly independent.

24. Prove Theorem 10.

25. Approximate x^3 with a polynomial in $\mathcal{P}_2$. [*Hint:* Use the inner product

$$\langle p, q\rangle = \int_0^1 p(t)q(t)\,dt,$$

and let $\{p_0, p_1, p_2\}$ be the orthogonal basis for $\mathcal{P}_2$ obtained in Example 4. Now apply Theorem 13.]

26. In Examples 4 and 7 we found $p_0(x), \ldots, p_3(x)$, which are orthogonal with respect to

$$\langle f, g\rangle = \int_0^1 f(x)g(x)\,dx.$$

Continue the process, and find $p_4(x)$ so that $\{p_0, p_1, \ldots, p_4\}$ is an orthogonal basis for $\mathcal{P}_4$. (Clearly there is an infinite sequence of polynomials $p_0, p_1, \ldots, p_n, \ldots$ that satisfy

$$\int_0^1 p_i(x)p_j(x)\,dx = 0, \quad i \neq j.$$

These are called the ***Legendre polynomials***.)

27. With the orthogonal basis for $\mathcal{P}_3$ obtained in Example 7, use Theorem 13 to find the projection of $f(x) = \cos x$ in $\mathcal{P}_3$. Construct a table similar to Table 5.1 and note the improvement.

28. An inner product on $C[-1, 1]$ is

$$\langle f, g\rangle = \frac{2}{\pi}\int_{-1}^{1} \frac{f(x)g(x)}{\sqrt{1-x^2}}\,dx.$$

Starting with the set $\{1, x, x^2, x^3, \ldots\}$, use the Gram–Schmidt process to find polynomials $T_0(x)$, $T_1(x)$, $T_2(x)$, and $T_3(x)$ such that $\langle T_i, T_j\rangle = 0$ when $i \neq j$. These polynomials are called the ***Chebyshev polynomials of the first kind***. [*Hint:* Make a change of variables $x = \cos\theta$.]

29. A sequence of orthogonal polynomials usually satisfies a three-term recurrence relation. For example, the Chebyshev polynomials are related by

$$T_{n+1}(x) = 2xT_n(x) - T_{n-1}(x), \quad n = 1, 2, \ldots, \tag{R}$$

where $T_0(x) = 1$ and $T_1(x) = x$. Verify that the polynomials defined by the relation (R) above are indeed orthogonal in $C[-1, 1]$ with respect to the inner product in Exercise 28. Verify this as follows:

a) Make the change of variables $x = \cos\theta$, and use induction to show that $T_k(\cos\theta) = \cos k\theta$, $k = 0, 1, \ldots$, where $T_k(x)$ is defined by (R).

b) Using part a), show that $\langle T_i, T_j\rangle = 0$ when $i \neq j$.

c) Use induction to show that $T_k(x)$ is a polynomial of degree k, $k = 0, 1, \ldots$.

d) Use (R) to calculate T_2, T_3, T_4, and T_5.

30. Let $C[-1, 1]$ have the inner product of Exercise 28, and let f be in $C[-1, 1]$. Use Theorem 13 to prove that $\|f - p^*\| \leq \|f - p\|$ for all p in $\mathcal{P}_n$ if

$$p^*(x) = \frac{a_0}{2} + \sum_{j=1}^{n} a_j T_j(x),$$

where $a_j = \langle f, T_j\rangle$, $j = 0, 1, \ldots, n$.

31. The iterated trapezoid rule provides a good estimate of $\int_a^b f(x)\,dx$ when $f(x)$ is periodic in $[a, b]$. In particular, let N be a positive integer, and let $h = (b-a)/N$. Next, define x_i by $x_i = a + ih$, $i = 0, 1, \ldots, N$, and suppose $f(x)$ is in $C[a, b]$. If we define $A(f)$ by

$$A(f) = \frac{h}{2}f(x_0) + h\sum_{j=1}^{N-1} f(x_j) + \frac{h}{2}f(x_N),$$

then $A(f)$ is the iterated trapezoid rule applied to $f(x)$. Using the result in Exercise 30, write a computer program that generates a good approximation to $f(x)$ in $C[-1, 1]$. That is, for an input function $f(x)$ and a specified value of n, calculate estimates of $a_0, a_1, \ldots, a_n$, where

$$a_k = \langle f, T_k\rangle \simeq A(fT_k).$$

To do this calculation, make the usual change of variables $x = \cos\theta$ so that

$$a_k = \frac{2}{\pi}\int_0^{\pi} f(\cos\theta)\cos(k\theta)d\theta, \quad k = 0, 1, \ldots, n.$$

Use the iterated trapezoid rule to estimate each a_k. Test your program on $f(x) = e^{2x}$ and note that (R) can be used to evaluate $p^*(x)$ at any point x in $[-1, 1]$.

32. Show that if A is a real $(n \times n)$ matrix and if the expression $\langle \mathbf{u}, \mathbf{v}\rangle = \mathbf{u}^T A\mathbf{v}$ defines an inner product on R^n, then A must be symmetric and positive definite (see Exercise 3 for the definition of positive definite). [*Hint:* Consider $\langle \mathbf{e}_i, \mathbf{e}_j\rangle$.]

5.7 LINEAR TRANSFORMATIONS

Linear transformations on subspaces of R^n were introduced in Section 3.7. The definition given there extends naturally to the general vector-space setting. In this section and the next, we develop the basic properties of linear transformations, and in Section 5.8 we will use linear transformations and the concept of coordinate vectors to show that an n-dimensional vector space is essentially just R^n.

If $T: R^n \to R^m$ is a linear transformation, there exists an $(m \times n)$ matrix A such that $T(\mathbf{x}) = A\mathbf{x}$. Although this is not the case in the general vector-space setting, we will show in Section 5.9 that there is still a close relationship between linear transformations and matrices, provided that the domain space is finite dimensional.

We begin with the definition of a linear transformation.

DEFINITION 8 Let U and V be vector spaces, and let T be a function from U to V, $T: U \to V$. We say that T is a ***linear transformation*** if for all $\mathbf{u}$ and $\mathbf{w}$ in U and all scalars a

$$T(\mathbf{u} + \mathbf{w}) = T(\mathbf{u}) + T(\mathbf{w})$$

and

$$T(a\mathbf{u}) = aT(\mathbf{u}).$$

Examples of Linear Transformations

To illustrate Definition 8, we now provide several examples of linear transformations.

EXAMPLE 1 Let $T: \mathcal{P}_2 \to R^1$ be defined by $T(p) = p(2)$. Verify that T is a linear transformation.

Solution First note that R^1 is just the set R of real numbers, but in this context R is regarded as a vector space. To illustrate the definition of T, if $p(x) = x^2 - 3x + 1$, then $T(p) = p(2) = -1$.

To verify that T is a linear transformation, let $p(x)$ and $q(x)$ be in $\mathcal{P}_2$ and let a be a scalar. Then $T(p + q) = (p + q)(2) = p(2) + q(2) = T(p) + T(q)$. Likewise, $T(ap) = (ap)(2) = ap(2) = aT(p)$. Thus T is a linear transformation. ■

In general, if W is any subspace of $C[a, b]$ and if x_0 is any number in $[a, b]$, then the function $T: W \to R^1$ defined by $T(f) = f(x_0)$ is a linear transformation.

EXAMPLE 2 Let V be a p-dimensional vector space with basis $B = \{\mathbf{v}_1, \mathbf{v}_2, \ldots, \mathbf{v}_p\}$. Show that $T: V \to R^p$ defined by $T(\mathbf{v}) = [\mathbf{v}]_B$ is a linear transformation.

Solution That T is a linear transformation is a direct consequence of the lemma in Section 5.4. Specifically, if $\mathbf{u}$ and $\mathbf{v}$ are vectors in V, then $T(\mathbf{u} + \mathbf{v}) = [\mathbf{u} + \mathbf{v}]_B = [\mathbf{u}]_B + [\mathbf{v}]_B = T(\mathbf{u}) + T(\mathbf{v})$. Also, if a is a scalar, then $T(a\mathbf{u}) = [a\mathbf{u}]_B = a[\mathbf{u}]_B = aT(\mathbf{u})$. ■

EXAMPLE 3 Let $T: C[0, 1] \rightarrow R^1$ be defined by

$$T(f) = \int_0^1 f(t)\,dt.$$

Prove that T is a linear transformation.

Solution If $f(x)$ and $g(x)$ are functions in $C[0, 1]$, then

$$\begin{aligned} T(f+g) &= \int_0^1 [f(t) + g(t)]\,dt \\ &= \int_0^1 f(t)\,dt + \int_0^1 g(t)\,dt \\ &= T(f) + T(g). \end{aligned}$$

Likewise, if a is a scalar, the properties of integration give

$$\begin{aligned} T(af) &= \int_0^1 af(t)\,dt \\ &= a\int_0^1 f(t)\,dt \\ &= aT(f). \end{aligned}$$

Therefore, T is a linear transformation. ■

EXAMPLE 4 Let $C^1[0, 1]$ denote the set of all functions that have a continuous first derivative in the interval $[0, 1]$. (Note that $C^1[0, 1]$ is a subspace of $C[0, 1]$.) Let $k(x)$ be a fixed function in $C[0, 1]$ and define $T: C^1[0, 1] \rightarrow C[0, 1]$ by

$$T(f) = f' + kf.$$

Verify that T is a linear transformation.

Solution To illustrate the definition of T, suppose, for example, that $k(x) = x^2$. If $f(x) = \sin x$, then $T(f)$ is the function defined by $T(f)(x) = f'(x) + k(x)f(x) = \cos x + x^2 \sin x$.

To see that T is a linear transformation, let g and h be functions in $C^1[0, 1]$. Then

$$\begin{aligned} T(g+h) &= (g+h)' + k(g+h) \\ &= g' + h' + kg + kh \\ &= (g' + kg) + (h' + kh) \\ &= T(g) + T(h). \end{aligned}$$

Also, for a scalar c, $T(cg) = (cg)' + k(cg) = c(g' + kg) = cT(g)$. Hence T is a linear transformation. ■

The linear transformation in Example 4 is an example of a differential operator. We will return to differential operators later and only mention here that the term *operator* is traditional in the study of differential equations. Operator is another term for function or transformation, and we could equally well speak of T as a differential transformation.

For any vector space V, the mapping $I\colon V \to V$ defined by $I(\mathbf{v}) = \mathbf{v}$ is a linear transformation called the ***identity transformation***. Between any two vector spaces U and V, there is always at least one linear transformation, called the ***zero transformation***. If $\boldsymbol{\theta}_V$ is the zero vector in V, then the zero transformation $T\colon U \to V$ is defined by $T(\mathbf{u}) = \boldsymbol{\theta}_V$ for all $\mathbf{u}$ in U.

Properties of Linear Transformations

One of the important features of the two linearity properties in Definition 8 is that if $T\colon U \to V$ is a linear transformation and if U is a finite-dimensional vector space, then the action of T on U is completely determined by the action of T on a basis for U. To see why this statement is true, suppose U has a basis $B = \{\mathbf{u}_1, \mathbf{u}_2, \ldots, \mathbf{u}_p\}$. Then given any $\mathbf{u}$ in U, we know that $\mathbf{u}$ can be expressed uniquely as

$$\mathbf{u} = a_1\mathbf{u}_1 + a_2\mathbf{u}_2 + \cdots + a_p\mathbf{u}_p.$$

From this expression it follows that $T(\mathbf{u})$ is given by

$$\begin{aligned} T(\mathbf{u}) &= T(a_1\mathbf{u}_1 + a_2\mathbf{u}_2 + \cdots + a_p\mathbf{u}_p) \\ &= a_1T(\mathbf{u}_1) + a_2T(\mathbf{u}_2) + \cdots + a_pT(\mathbf{u}_p). \end{aligned} \tag{1}$$

Clearly Eq. (1) shows that if we know the vectors $T(\mathbf{u}_1), T(\mathbf{u}_2), \ldots, T(\mathbf{u}_p)$, then we know $T(\mathbf{u})$ for any $\mathbf{u}$ in U; T is completely determined once T is defined on the basis. The next example illustrates this concept.

EXAMPLE 5 Let $T\colon \mathcal{P}_3 \to \mathcal{P}_2$ be a linear transformation such that $T(1) = 1 - x$, $T(x) = x + x^2$, $T(x^2) = 1 + 2x$, and $T(x^3) = 2 - x^2$. Find $T(2 - 3x + x^2 - 2x^3)$.

Solution Applying Eq. (1) yields

$$\begin{aligned} T(2 - 3x + x^2 - 2x^3) &= 2T(1) - 3T(x) + T(x^2) - 2T(x^3) \\ &= 2(1-x) - 3(x + x^2) + (1 + 2x) - 2(2 - x^2) \\ &= -1 - 3x - x^2. \end{aligned}$$

Similarly,

$$\begin{aligned} &T(a_0 + a_1x + a_2x^2 + a_3x^3) \\ &= a_0T(1) + a_1T(x) + a_2T(x^2) + a_3T(x^3) \\ &= a_0(1-x) + a_1(x + x^2) + a_2(1 + 2x) + a_3(2 - x^2) \\ &= (a_0 + a_2 + 2a_3) + (-a_0 + a_1 + 2a_2)x + (a_1 - a_3)x^2. \end{aligned}$$

Before giving further properties of linear transformations, we require several definitions. Let $T\colon U \to V$ be a linear transformation, and for clarity let us denote the zero vectors in U and V as $\boldsymbol{\theta}_U$ and $\boldsymbol{\theta}_V$, respectively. The ***null space*** (or ***kernel***) of T, denoted by $\mathcal{N}(T)$, is the subset of U defined by

$$\mathcal{N}(T) = \{\mathbf{u} \text{ in } U\colon T(\mathbf{u}) = \boldsymbol{\theta}_V\}.$$

The ***range*** of T, denoted by $\mathcal{R}(T)$, is the subset of V defined by

$$\mathcal{R}(T) = \{\mathbf{v} \text{ in } V\colon \mathbf{v} = T(\mathbf{u}) \text{ for some } \mathbf{u} \text{ in } U\}.$$

As before, the dimension of $\mathcal{N}(T)$ is called the ***nullity*** of T and is denoted by nullity(T). Likewise, the dimension of $\mathcal{R}(T)$ is called the ***rank*** of T and is denoted by rank(T). Finally, we say a linear transformation is ***one to one*** if $T(\mathbf{u}) = T(\mathbf{w})$ implies $\mathbf{u} = \mathbf{w}$ for all $\mathbf{u}$ and $\mathbf{w}$ in U. Some of the elementary properties of linear transformations are given in the next theorem.

THEOREM 14 Let $T\colon U \to V$ be a linear transformation. Then:

1. $T(\boldsymbol{\theta}_U) = \boldsymbol{\theta}_V$.
2. $\mathcal{N}(T)$ is a subspace of U.
3. $\mathcal{R}(T)$ is a subspace of V.
4. T is one to one if and only if $\mathcal{N}(T) = \{\boldsymbol{\theta}_U\}$; that is, T is one to one if and only if nullity$(T) = 0$.

Proof To prove property 1, note that $0\boldsymbol{\theta}_U = \boldsymbol{\theta}_U$, so

$$T(\boldsymbol{\theta}_U) = T(0\boldsymbol{\theta}_U) = 0T(\boldsymbol{\theta}_U) = \boldsymbol{\theta}_V.$$

To prove property 2, we must verify that $\mathcal{N}(T)$ satisfies the three properties of Theorem 2 in Section 5.3. It follows from property 1 that $\boldsymbol{\theta}_U$ is in $\mathcal{N}(T)$. Next, let $\mathbf{u}_1$ and $\mathbf{u}_2$ be in $\mathcal{N}(T)$ and let a be a scalar. Then $T(\mathbf{u}_1+\mathbf{u}_2) = T(\mathbf{u}_1)+T(\mathbf{u}_2) = \boldsymbol{\theta}_V+\boldsymbol{\theta}_V = \boldsymbol{\theta}_V$, so $\mathbf{u}_1 + \mathbf{u}_2$ is in $\mathcal{N}(T)$. Similarly, $T(a\mathbf{u}_1) = aT(\mathbf{u}_1) = a\boldsymbol{\theta}_V = \boldsymbol{\theta}_V$, so $a\mathbf{u}_1$ is in $\mathcal{N}(T)$. Therefore, $\mathcal{N}(T)$ is a subspace of U.

The proof of property 3 is left as an exercise. To prove property 4, suppose that $\mathcal{N}(T) = \{\boldsymbol{\theta}_U\}$. In order to show that T is one to one, let $\mathbf{u}$ and $\mathbf{w}$ be vectors in U such that $T(\mathbf{u}) = T(\mathbf{w})$. Then $\boldsymbol{\theta}_V = T(\mathbf{u}) - T(\mathbf{w}) = T(\mathbf{u}) + (-1)T(\mathbf{w}) = T[\mathbf{u} + (-1)\mathbf{w}] = T(\mathbf{u} - \mathbf{w})$. It follows that $\mathbf{u} - \mathbf{w}$ is in $\mathcal{N}(T)$. But $\mathcal{N}(T) = \{\boldsymbol{\theta}_U\}$, so $\mathbf{u} - \mathbf{w} = \boldsymbol{\theta}_U$. Therefore, $\mathbf{u} = \mathbf{w}$ and T is one to one. The converse is Exercise 24. ■

When $T\colon R^n \to R^m$ is given by $T(\mathbf{x}) = A\mathbf{x}$, with A an $(m \times n)$ matrix, then $\mathcal{N}(T)$ is the null space of A and $\mathcal{R}(T)$ is the range of A. In this setting, property 4 of Theorem 14 states that a consistent system of equations $A\mathbf{x} = \mathbf{b}$ has a unique solution if and only if the trivial solution is the unique solution for the homogeneous system $A\mathbf{x} = \boldsymbol{\theta}$.

The following theorem gives additional properties of a linear transformation $T\colon U \to V$, where U is a finite-dimensional vector space.

THEOREM 15 Let $T\colon U \to V$ be a linear transformation and let U be p-dimensional, where $B = \{\mathbf{u}_1, \mathbf{u}_2, \ldots, \mathbf{u}_p\}$ is a basis for U.

1. $\mathcal{R}(T) = \mathrm{Sp}\{T(\mathbf{u}_1), T(\mathbf{u}_2), \ldots, T(\mathbf{u}_p)\}$.
2. T is one to one if and only if $\{T(\mathbf{u}_1), T(\mathbf{u}_2), \ldots, T(\mathbf{u}_p)\}$ is linearly independent in V.
3. rank(T) + nullity$(T) = p$.

Proof Property 1 is immediate from Eq. (1). That is, if $\mathbf{v}$ is in $\mathcal{R}(T)$, then $\mathbf{v} = T(\mathbf{u})$ for some $\mathbf{u}$ in U. But B is a basis for U; so $\mathbf{u}$ is of the form $\mathbf{u} = a_1\mathbf{u}_1 + a_2\mathbf{u}_2 + \cdots + a_p\mathbf{u}_p$; and hence $T(\mathbf{u}) = \mathbf{v} = a_1T(\mathbf{u}_1) + a_2T(\mathbf{u}_2) + \cdots + a_pT(\mathbf{u}_p)$. Therefore, $\mathbf{v}$ is in $\mathrm{Sp}\{T(\mathbf{u}_1), T(\mathbf{u}_2), \ldots, T(\mathbf{u}_p)\}$.

To prove property 2, we can use property 4 of Theorem 14; T is one to one if and only if $\boldsymbol{\theta}_U$ is the only vector in $\mathcal{N}(T)$. In particular, let us suppose that $\mathbf{u}$ is some vector in $\mathcal{N}(T)$, where $\mathbf{u} = b_1\mathbf{u}_1 + b_2\mathbf{u}_2 + \cdots + b_p\mathbf{u}_p$. Then $T(\mathbf{u}) = \boldsymbol{\theta}_V$, or

$$b_1T(\mathbf{u}_1) + b_2T(\mathbf{u}_2) + \cdots + b_pT(\mathbf{u}_p) = \boldsymbol{\theta}_V. \tag{2}$$

If $\{T(\mathbf{u}_1), T(\mathbf{u}_2), \ldots, T(\mathbf{u}_p)\}$ is a linearly independent set in V, then the only scalars satisfying Eq. (2) are $b_1 = b_2 = \cdots = b_p = 0$. Therefore, $\mathbf{u}$ must be $\boldsymbol{\theta}_U$; so T is one to one. On the other hand, if T is one to one, then there cannot be a nontrivial solution to Eq. (2); for if there were, $\mathcal{N}(T)$ would contain the nonzero vector $\mathbf{u}$.

To prove property 3, we first note that $0 \le \text{rank}(T) \le p$ by property 1. We leave the two extreme cases, $\text{rank}(T) = p$ and $\text{rank}(T) = 0$, to the exercises and consider only $0 < \text{rank}(T) < p$. [Note that $\text{rank}(T) < p$ implies that $\text{nullity}(T) \ge 1$, so T is not one to one. We mention this point because we will need to choose a basis for $\mathcal{N}(T)$ below.]

It is conventional to let r denote $\text{rank}(T)$, so let us suppose $\mathcal{R}(T)$ has a basis of r vectors, $\{\mathbf{v}_1, \mathbf{v}_2, \ldots, \mathbf{v}_r\}$. From the definition of $\mathcal{R}(T)$, we know there are vectors $\mathbf{w}_1, \mathbf{w}_2, \ldots, \mathbf{w}_r$, in U such that

$$T(\mathbf{w}_i) = \mathbf{v}_i, \quad 1 \le i \le r. \tag{3}$$

Now suppose that $\text{nullity}(T) = k$ and let $\{\mathbf{x}_1, \mathbf{x}_2, \ldots, \mathbf{x}_k\}$ be a basis for $\mathcal{N}(T)$. We now show that the set

$$Q = \{\mathbf{x}_1, \mathbf{x}_2, \ldots, \mathbf{x}_k, \mathbf{w}_1, \mathbf{w}_2, \ldots, \mathbf{w}_r\}$$

is a basis for U (therefore, $k + r = p$, which proves property 3).

We first establish that Q is a linearly independent set in U by considering

$$c_1\mathbf{x}_1 + c_2\mathbf{x}_2 + \cdots + c_k\mathbf{x}_k + a_1\mathbf{w}_1 + a_2\mathbf{w}_2 + \cdots + a_r\mathbf{w}_r = \boldsymbol{\theta}_U. \tag{4}$$

Applying T to both sides of Eq. (4) yields

$$T(c_1\mathbf{x}_1 + \cdots + c_k\mathbf{x}_k + a_1\mathbf{w}_1 + \cdots + a_r\mathbf{w}_r) = T(\boldsymbol{\theta}_U). \tag{5a}$$

Using Eq. (1) and property 1 of Theorem 14, Eq. (5a) becomes

$$c_1T(\mathbf{x}_1) + \cdots + c_kT(\mathbf{x}_k) + a_1T(\mathbf{w}_1) + \cdots + a_rT(\mathbf{w}_r) = \boldsymbol{\theta}_V. \tag{5b}$$

Since each $\mathbf{x}_i$ is in $\mathcal{N}(T)$ and $T(\mathbf{w}_i) = \mathbf{v}_i$, Eq. (5b) becomes

$$a_1\mathbf{v}_1 + a_2\mathbf{v}_2 + \cdots + a_r\mathbf{v}_r = \boldsymbol{\theta}_V. \tag{5c}$$

Since the set $\{\mathbf{v}_1, \mathbf{v}_2, \ldots, \mathbf{v}_r\}$ is linearly independent, $a_1 = a_2 = \cdots = a_r = 0$. The vector equation (4) now becomes

$$c_1\mathbf{x}_1 + c_2\mathbf{x}_2 + \cdots + c_k\mathbf{x}_k = \boldsymbol{\theta}_U. \tag{6}$$

But $\{\mathbf{x}_1, \mathbf{x}_2, \ldots, \mathbf{x}_k\}$ is a linearly independent set in U, so we must have $c_1 = c_2 = \cdots = c_k = 0$. Therefore, Q is a linearly independent set.

To complete the argument, we need to show that Q is a spanning set for U. So let $\mathbf{u}$ be any vector in U. Then $\mathbf{v} = T(\mathbf{u})$ is a vector in $\mathcal{R}(T)$; so

$$T(\mathbf{u}) = b_1\mathbf{v}_1 + b_2\mathbf{v}_2 + \cdots + b_r\mathbf{v}_r.$$

Consider an associated vector $\mathbf{x}$ in U, where $\mathbf{x}$ is defined by

$$\mathbf{x} = b_1\mathbf{w}_1 + b_2\mathbf{w}_2 + \cdots + b_r\mathbf{w}_r. \tag{7}$$

We observe that $T(\mathbf{u} - \mathbf{x}) = \boldsymbol{\theta}_V$; so obviously $\mathbf{u} - \mathbf{x}$ is in $\mathcal{N}(T)$ and can be written as

$$\mathbf{u} - \mathbf{x} = d_1\mathbf{x}_1 + d_2\mathbf{x}_2 + \cdots + d_k\mathbf{x}_k. \tag{8}$$

Placing $\mathbf{x}$ on the right-hand side of Eq. (8) and using Eq. (7), we have shown that $\mathbf{u}$ is a linear combination of vectors in Q. Thus Q is a basis for U, and property 3 is proved since $k + r$ must equal p. ■

As the following example illustrates, property 1 of Theorem 15 and the techniques of Section 5.4 give a method for obtaining a basis for $\mathcal{R}(T)$.

EXAMPLE 6 Let V be the vector space of all (2×2) matrices, and let $T\colon \mathcal{P}_3 \to V$ be the linear transformation defined by

$$T(a_0 + a_1x + a_2x^2 + a_3x^3) = \begin{bmatrix} a_0 + a_2 & a_0 + a_3 \\ a_1 + a_2 & a_1 + a_3 \end{bmatrix}.$$

Find a basis for $\mathcal{R}(T)$ and determine $\operatorname{rank}(T)$ and $\operatorname{nullity}(T)$. Finally, show that T is not one to one.

Solution By property 1 of Theorem 15, $\mathcal{R}(T) = \operatorname{Sp}\{T(1), T(x), T(x^2), T(x^3)\}$. Thus $\mathcal{R}(T) = \operatorname{Sp}(S)$, where $S = \{A_1, A_2, A_3, A_4\}$ and

$$A_1 = \begin{bmatrix} 1 & 1 \\ 0 & 0 \end{bmatrix},\quad A_2 = \begin{bmatrix} 0 & 0 \\ 1 & 1 \end{bmatrix},\quad A_3 = \begin{bmatrix} 1 & 0 \\ 1 & 0 \end{bmatrix},\quad \text{and}\quad A_4 = \begin{bmatrix} 0 & 1 \\ 0 & 1 \end{bmatrix}.$$

Let B be the natural basis for V: $B = \{E_{11}, E_{12}, E_{21}, E_{22}\}$. Form the (4×4) matrix C with column vectors $[A_1]_B, [A_2]_B, [A_3]_B, [A_4]_B$; thus

$$C = \begin{bmatrix} 1 & 0 & 1 & 0 \\ 1 & 0 & 0 & 1 \\ 0 & 1 & 1 & 0 \\ 0 & 1 & 0 & 1 \end{bmatrix}.$$

EMMY NOETHER Emmy Noether (1882–1935) is the most heralded female mathematician of the early twentieth century. Overcoming great obstacles for women in mathematics at the time, she received her doctorate from Göttingen and went on to work with David Hilbert and Felix Klein on the general theory of relativity. Among her most highly regarded results are the representation of noncommutative algebras as linear transformations and Noether's Theorem, which is used to explain the correspondences between certain invariants and physical conservation laws. She fled from Germany in 1933 and spent the last two years of her life on the faculty at Bryn Mawr College in Philadelphia.

The matrix C^T reduces to the matrix

$$D^T = \begin{bmatrix} 1 & 1 & 0 & 0 \\ 0 & 1 & 0 & 1 \\ 0 & 0 & 1 & 1 \\ 0 & 0 & 0 & 0 \end{bmatrix}$$

in echelon form. Therefore,

$$D = \begin{bmatrix} 1 & 0 & 0 & 0 \\ 1 & 1 & 0 & 0 \\ 0 & 0 & 1 & 0 \\ 0 & 1 & 1 & 0 \end{bmatrix},$$

and the nonzero columns of D constitute a basis for the subspace $\text{Sp}\{[A_1]_B, [A_2]_B, [A_3]_B, [A_4]_B\}$ of R^4. If the matrices B_1, B_2, and B_3 are defined by

$$B_1 = \begin{bmatrix} 1 & 1 \\ 0 & 0 \end{bmatrix}, \quad B_2 = \begin{bmatrix} 0 & 1 \\ 0 & 1 \end{bmatrix}, \quad \text{and} \quad B_3 = \begin{bmatrix} 0 & 0 \\ 1 & 1 \end{bmatrix},$$

then $[B_1]_B, [B_2]_B$, and $[B_3]_B$ are the nonzero columns of D. It now follows from Theorem 5 of Section 5.4 that $\{B_1, B_2, B_3\}$ is a basis for $\mathcal{R}(T)$.

By property 3 of Theorem 15,

$$\dim(\mathcal{P}_3) = \text{rank}(T) + \text{nullity}(T).$$

We have just shown that $\text{rank}(T) = 3$. Since $\dim(\mathcal{P}_3) = 4$, it follows that $\text{nullity}(T) = 1$. In particular, T is not one to one by property 4 of Theorem 14. ■

EXAMPLE 7 Let $T: \mathcal{P}_2 \to R^1$ be defined by $T(p(x)) = p(2)$. Exhibit a basis for $\mathcal{N}(T)$ and determine the rank and nullity of T.

Solution By definition, $T(a_0 + a_1x + a_2x^2) = a_0 + 2a_1 + 4a_2$. Thus

$$\mathcal{N}(T) = \{p(x) \colon p(x) \text{ is in } \mathcal{P}_2 \text{ and } a_0 + 2a_1 + 4a_2 = 0\}.$$

In the algebraic specification for $\mathcal{N}(T)$, a_1 and a_2 can be designated as unconstrained variables, and $a_0 = -2a_1 - 4a_2$. Thus $p(x)$ in $\mathcal{N}(T)$ can be decomposed as

$$p(x) = (-2a_1 - 4a_2) + a_1x + a_2x^2 = a_1(-2 + x) + a_2(-4 + x^2).$$

It follows that $\{-2 + x, -4 + x^2\}$ is a basis for $\mathcal{N}(T)$. In particular, $\text{nullity}(T) = 2$. Then $\text{rank}(T) = \dim(\mathcal{P}_2) - \text{nullity}(T) = 3 - 2 = 1$. ■

We have already noted that if A is an $(m \times n)$ matrix and $T: R^n \to R^m$ is defined by $T(\mathbf{x}) = A\mathbf{x}$, then $\mathcal{R}(T) = \mathcal{R}(A)$ and $\mathcal{N}(T) = \mathcal{N}(A)$. The following corollary, given as a remark in Section 3.5, is now an immediate consequence of these observations and property 3 of Theorem 15.

COROLLARY If A is an $(m \times n)$ matrix, then

$$n = \text{rank}(A) + \text{nullity}(A).$$ ■

5.7 EXERCISES

In Exercises 1–4, V is the vector space of all (2×2) matrices and A has the form

$$A = \begin{bmatrix} a & b \\ c & d \end{bmatrix}.$$

Determine whether the function $T: V \to R^1$ is a linear transformation.

1. $T(A) = \det(A)$
2. $T(A) = a + 2b - c + d$
3. $T(A) = \operatorname{tr}(A)$, where $\operatorname{tr}(A)$ denotes the trace of A and is defined by $\operatorname{tr}(A) = a + d$.
4. $T(A) = (a - d)(b - c)$

In Exercises 5–8, determine whether T is a linear transformation.

5. $T: C^1[-1, 1] \to R^1$ defined by $T(f) = f'(0)$
6. $T: C[0, 1] \to C[0, 1]$ defined by $T(f) = g$, where $g(x) = e^x f(x)$
7. $T: \mathcal{P}_2 \to \mathcal{P}_2$ defined by $T(a_0 + a_1x + a_2x^2) = (a_0 + 1) + (a_1 + 1)x + (a_2 + 1)x^2$
8. $T: \mathcal{P}_2 \to \mathcal{P}_2$ defined by $T(p(x)) = p(0) + xp'(x)$
9. Suppose that $T: \mathcal{P}_2 \to \mathcal{P}_3$ is a linear transformation, where $T(1) = 1 + x^2$, $T(x) = x^2 - x^3$, and $T(x^2) = 2 + x^3$.
   a) Find $T(p)$, where $p(x) = 3 - 2x + 4x^2$.
   b) Give a formula for T; that is, find
   $$T(a_0 + a_1x + a_2x^2).$$
10. Suppose that $T: \mathcal{P}_2 \to \mathcal{P}_4$ is a linear transformation, where $T(1) = x^4$, $T(x + 1) = x^3 - 2x$, and $T(x^2 + 2x + 1) = x$. Find $T(p)$ and $T(q)$, where $p(x) = x^2 + 5x - 1$ and $q(x) = x^2 + 9x + 5$.
11. Let V be the set of all (2×2) matrices and suppose that $T: V \to \mathcal{P}_2$ is a linear transformation such that $T(E_{11}) = 1 - x$, $T(E_{12}) = 1 + x + x^2$, $T(E_{21}) = 2x - x^2$, and $T(E_{22}) = 2 + x - 2x^2$.
    a) Find $T(A)$, where
    $$A = \begin{bmatrix} -2 & 2 \\ 3 & 4 \end{bmatrix}.$$
    b) Give a formula for T; that is, find
    $$T\left(\begin{bmatrix} a & b \\ c & d \end{bmatrix}\right).$$
12. With V as in Exercise 11, define $T: V \to R^2$ by
    $$T\left(\begin{bmatrix} a & b \\ c & d \end{bmatrix}\right) = \begin{bmatrix} a + 2d \\ b - c \end{bmatrix}.$$
    a) Prove that T is a linear transformation.
    b) Give an algebraic specification for $\mathcal{N}(T)$.
    c) Exhibit a basis for $\mathcal{N}(T)$.
    d) Determine the nullity and the rank of T.
    e) Without doing any calculations, argue that $\mathcal{R}(T) = R^2$.
    f) Prove $\mathcal{R}(T) = R^2$ as follows: Let $\mathbf{v}$ be in R^2,
    $$\mathbf{v} = \begin{bmatrix} x \\ y \end{bmatrix}.$$
    Exhibit a (2×2) matrix A in V such that $T(A) = \mathbf{v}$.
13. Let $T: \mathcal{P}_4 \to \mathcal{P}_2$ be the linear transformation defined by $T(p) = p''(x)$.
    a) Exhibit a basis for $\mathcal{R}(T)$ and conclude that $\mathcal{R}(T) = \mathcal{P}_2$.
    b) Determine the nullity of T and conclude that T is not one to one.
    c) Give a direct proof that $\mathcal{R}(T) = \mathcal{P}_2$; that is, for $p(x) = a_0 + a_1x + a_2x^2$ in $\mathcal{P}_2$, exhibit a polynomial $q(x)$ in $\mathcal{P}_4$ such that $T(q) = p$.
14. Define $T: \mathcal{P}_4 \to \mathcal{P}_3$ by
    $$\begin{aligned} T(a_0 + a_1x + a_2x^2 + a_3x^3 + a_4x^4) &= (a_0 - a_1 + 2a_2 - a_3 + a_4) \\ &+ (-a_0 + 3a_1 - 2a_2 + 3a_3 - a_4)x \\ &+ (2a_0 - 3a_1 + 5a_2 - a_3 + a_4)x^2 \\ &+ (3a_0 - a_1 + 7a_2 + 2a_3 + 2a_4)x^3. \end{aligned}$$
    Find a basis for $\mathcal{R}(T)$ (see Example 6) and show that T is not one to one.
15. Identify $\mathcal{N}(T)$ and $\mathcal{R}(T)$ for the linear transformation T given in Example 1.
16. Identify $\mathcal{N}(T)$ and $\mathcal{R}(T)$ for the linear transformation T given in Example 3.
17. Let $I: V \to V$ be defined by $I(\mathbf{v}) = \mathbf{v}$ for each $\mathbf{v}$ in V.
    a) Prove that I is a linear transformation.
    b) Determine $\mathcal{N}(I)$ and $\mathcal{R}(I)$.

18. Let U and V be vector spaces and define $T: U \to V$ by $T(\mathbf{u}) = \boldsymbol{\theta}_V$ for each $\mathbf{u}$ in U.

   a) Prove that T is a linear transformation.

   b) Determine $\mathcal{N}(T)$ and $\mathcal{R}(T)$.

19. Suppose that $T: \mathcal{P}_4 \to \mathcal{P}_2$ is a linear transformation. Enumerate the various possibilities for rank(T) and nullity(T). Can T possibly be one to one?

20. Let $T: U \to V$ be a linear transformation and let U be finite dimensional. Prove that if $\dim(U) > \dim(V)$, then T cannot be one to one.

21. Suppose that $T: \mathcal{R}_3 \to \mathcal{P}_3$ is a linear transformation. Enumerate the various possibilities for rank(T) and nullity(T). Is $\mathcal{R}(T) = \mathcal{P}_3$ a possibility?

22. Let $T: U \to V$ be a linear transformation and let U be finite dimensional. Prove that if $\dim(U) < \dim(V)$, then $\mathcal{R}(T) = V$ is not possible.

23. Prove property 3 of Theorem 14.

24. Complete the proof of property 4 of Theorem 14 by showing that if T is one to one, then $\mathcal{N}(T) = \{\boldsymbol{\theta}_U\}$.

25. Complete the proof of property 3 of Theorem 15 as follows:

   a) If rank$(T) = p$, prove that nullity$(T) = 0$.

   b) If rank$(T) = 0$, show that nullity$(T) = p$.

26. Let $T: R^n \to R^n$ be defined by $T(\mathbf{x}) = A\mathbf{x}$, where A is an $(n \times n)$ matrix. Use property 4 of Theorem 14 to show that T is one to one if and only if A is nonsingular.

27. Let V be the vector space of all (2×2) matrices and define $T: V \to V$ by $T(A) = A^T$.

   a) Show that T is a linear transformation.

   b) Determine the nullity and rank of T. Conclude that T is one to one and $\mathcal{R}(T) = V$.

   c) Show directly that $\mathcal{R}(T) = V$; that is, for B in V exhibit a matrix C in V such that $T(C) = B$.

5.8 OPERATIONS WITH LINEAR TRANSFORMATIONS

We know that a useful arithmetic structure is associated with matrices: Matrices can be added and multiplied, nonsingular matrices have inverses, and so on. Much of this structure is available also for linear transformations. For our explanation we will need some definitions. Let U and V be vector spaces and let T_1 and T_2 be linear transformations, where $T_1: U \to V$ and $T_2: U \to V$. By the ***sum*** $T_3 = T_1 + T_2$, we mean the function $T_3: U \to V$, where $T_3(\mathbf{u}) = T_1(\mathbf{u}) + T_2(\mathbf{u})$ for all $\mathbf{u}$ in U. The following example illustrates this concept.

EXAMPLE 1 Let $T_1: \mathcal{P}_4 \to \mathcal{P}_2$ be given by $T_1(p) = p''(x)$, and suppose that $T_2: \mathcal{P}_4 \to \mathcal{P}_2$ is defined by $T_2(p) = xp(1)$. If $S = T_1 + T_2$, give the formula for S.

Solution By definition, the sum $T_1 + T_2$ is the linear transformation $S: \mathcal{P}_4 \to \mathcal{P}_2$ defined by $S(p) = T_1(p) + T_2(p) = p''(x) + xp(1)$.

If $T: U \to V$ is a linear transformation and a is a scalar, then aT denotes the function $aT: U \to V$ defined by $aT(\mathbf{u}) = a(T(\mathbf{u}))$ for all $\mathbf{u}$ in U. Again, we illustrate with an example.

EXAMPLE 2 Let V be the vector space of all (2×2) matrices and define $T: V \to R^1$ by $T(A) = 2a - b + 3c + 4d$, where

$$A = \begin{bmatrix} a & b \\ c & d \end{bmatrix}.$$

Give the formula for $3T$.

Solution By definition, $3T(A) = 3(T(A)) = 3(2a - b + 3c + 4d) = 6a - 3b + 9c + 12d$. ∎

It is straightforward to show that the functions $T_1 + T_2$ and aT, previously defined, are linear transformations (see Exercises 13 and 14).

Now let U, V, and W be vector spaces and let S and T be linear transformations, where $S\colon U \to V$ and $T\colon V \to W$. The ***composition***, $L = T \circ S$, of S and T is defined to be function $L\colon U \to W$ given by $L(\mathbf{u}) = T(S(\mathbf{u}))$ for all $\mathbf{u}$ in U (see Fig. 5.7).

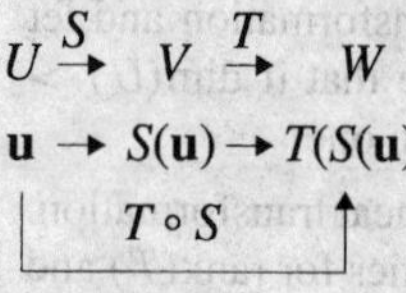

Figure 5.7 The composition of linear transformations is a linear transformation (see Example 3).

EXAMPLE 3 Let $S\colon U \to V$ and $T\colon V \to W$ be linear transformations. Verify that the composition $L = T \circ S$ is also a linear transformation.

Solution Let $\mathbf{u}_1, \mathbf{u}_2$ be vectors in U. Then $L(\mathbf{u}_1 + \mathbf{u}_2) = T(S(\mathbf{u}_1 + \mathbf{u}_2))$. Since S is a linear transformation, $S(\mathbf{u}_1 + \mathbf{u}_2) = S(\mathbf{u}_1) + S(\mathbf{u}_2)$. But T is also a linear transformation, so $L(\mathbf{u}_1 + \mathbf{u}_2) = T(S(\mathbf{u}_1) + S(\mathbf{u}_2)) = T(S(\mathbf{u}_1)) + T(S(\mathbf{u}_2)) = L(\mathbf{u}_1) + L(\mathbf{u}_2)$. Similarly, if $\mathbf{u}$ is in U and a is a scalar, $L(a\mathbf{u}) = T(S(a\mathbf{u})) = T(aS(\mathbf{u})) = aT(S(\mathbf{u})) = aL(\mathbf{u})$. This shows that $L = T \circ S$ is a linear transformation. ∎

The next two examples provide specific illustrations of the composition of two linear transformations.

EXAMPLE 4 Let U be the vector space of all (2×2) matrices. Define $S\colon U \to \mathcal{P}_2$ by $S(A) = (a - c) + (b + 2c)x + (3c - d)x^2$, where

$$A = \begin{bmatrix} a & b \\ c & d \end{bmatrix}.$$

Define $T\colon \mathcal{P}_2 \to R^2$ by

$$T(a_0 + a_1x + a_2x^2) = \begin{bmatrix} a_0 - a_1 \\ 2a_1 + a_2 \end{bmatrix}.$$

Give the formula for $T \circ S$ and show that $S \circ T$ is not defined.

Solution The composition $T \circ S\colon U \to R^2$ is defined by $(T \circ S)(A) = T(S(A)) = T[(a - c) + (b + 2c)x + (3c - d)x^2]$. Thus

$$(T \circ S)\left(\begin{bmatrix} a & b \\ c & d \end{bmatrix}\right) = \begin{bmatrix} a - b - 3c \\ 2b + 7c - d \end{bmatrix}.$$

If $p(x)$ is in $\mathcal{P}_2$, then $T(p(x)) = \mathbf{v}$, where $\mathbf{v}$ is in R^2. Thus $(S \circ T)(p(x)) = S(T(p(x))) = S(\mathbf{v})$. But $\mathbf{v}$ is not in the domain of S, so $S(\mathbf{v})$ is not defined. Therefore, $S \circ T$ is undefined. ∎

Example 4 illustrates that, as with matrix multiplication, $T \circ S$ may be defined, whereas $S \circ T$ is not defined. The next example illustrates that even when both are defined, they may be different transformations.

EXAMPLE 5 Let $S: \mathcal{P}_4 \to \mathcal{P}_4$ be given by $S(p) = p''(x)$ and define $T: \mathcal{P}_4 \to \mathcal{P}_4$ by $T(q) = xq(1)$. Give the formulas for $T \circ S$ and $S \circ T$.

Solution The linear transformation $T \circ S: \mathcal{P}_4 \to \mathcal{P}_4$ is defined by

$$(T \circ S)(p) = T(S(p)) = T(p''(x)) = xp''(1),$$

and $S \circ T: \mathcal{P}_4 \to \mathcal{P}_4$ is given by

$$(S \circ T)(p) = S(T(p)) = S(xp(1)) = [xp(1)]'' = \boldsymbol{\theta}(x).$$

In particular, $S \circ T \neq T \circ S$. ∎

Invertible Transformations

As we have previously noted, linear transformations can be viewed as an extension of the notion of a matrix to general vector spaces. In this subsection we introduce those linear transformations that correspond to nonsingular (or invertible) matrices. First, suppose X and Y are any sets and $f: X \to Y$ is a function; and suppose $\mathcal{R}(f)$ denotes the range of f where $\mathcal{R}(f) \subseteq Y$. Recall that f is ***onto*** provided that $\mathcal{R}(f) = Y$; that is, f is onto if for each element y in Y there exists an element x in X such that $f(x) = y$.

In order to show that a linear transformation $T: U \to V$ is onto, it is frequently convenient to use the results of Section 5.7 and a dimension argument to determine whether $\mathcal{R}(T) = V$. To be more specific, suppose V has finite dimension. If $\mathcal{R}(T)$ has the same dimension, then, since $\mathcal{R}(T)$ is a subspace of V, it must be the case that $\mathcal{R}(T) = V$. Thus in order to show that T is onto when the dimension of V is finite, it suffices to demonstrate that $\text{rank}(T) = \dim(V)$. Alternatively, an elementwise argument can be used to show that T is onto. The next two examples illustrate both procedures.

EXAMPLE 6 Let U be the subspace of (2×2) matrices defined by

$$U = \{A: A = \begin{bmatrix} a & -b \\ b & a \end{bmatrix}, \text{ where } a \text{ and } b \text{ are in } R\},$$

and let $V = \{f(x) \text{ in } C[0, 1]: f(x) = ce^x + de^{-x}$, where c and d are in $R\}$. Define $T: U \to V$ by

$$T\left(\begin{bmatrix} a & -b \\ b & a \end{bmatrix}\right) = (a + b)e^x + (a - b)e^{-x}.$$

Show that $\mathcal{R}(T) = V$.

Solution Note that U has basis $\{A_1, A_2\}$, where

$$A_1 = \begin{bmatrix} 1 & 0 \\ 0 & 1 \end{bmatrix} \text{ and } A_2 = \begin{bmatrix} 0 & -1 \\ 1 & 0 \end{bmatrix}.$$

It follows from Theorem 15, property 1, of Section 5.7 that $\mathcal{R}(T) = \mathrm{Sp}\{T(A_1), T(A_2)\} = \mathrm{Sp}\{e^x + e^{-x}, e^x - e^{-x}\}$. It is easily shown that the set $\{e^x + e^{-x}, e^x - e^{-x}\}$ is linearly independent. It follows that $\mathrm{rank}(T) = 2$. Since $\{e^x, e^{-x}\}$ is a linearly independent set and $V = \mathrm{Sp}\{e^x, e^{-x}\}$, the set is a basis for V. In particular, $\dim(V) = 2$. Since $\mathcal{R}(T) \subseteq V$ and $\mathrm{rank}(T) = \dim(V)$, it follows that $\mathcal{R}(T) = V$. ■

EXAMPLE 7 Let $T: \mathcal{P} \to \mathcal{P}$ be defined by $T(p) = p''(x)$. Show that $\mathcal{R}(T) = \mathcal{P}$.

Solution Recall that $\mathcal{P}$ is the vector space of all polynomials, with no bound on the degree. We have previously seen that $\mathcal{P}$ does not have a finite basis, so the techniques of Example 6 do not apply. To show that $\mathcal{R}(T) = \mathcal{P}$, let $q(x) = a_0 + a_1 x + \cdots + a_n x^n$ be an arbitrary polynomial in $\mathcal{P}$. We must exhibit a polynomial $p(x)$ in $\mathcal{P}$ such that $T(p) = p''(x) = q(x)$. It is easy to see that $p(x) = (1/2)a_0 x^2 + (1/6)a_1 x^3 + \cdots + [1/(n+1)(n+2)]a_n x^{n+2}$ is one choice for $p(x)$. Thus T is onto. ■

Let $f: X \to Y$ be a function. If f is both one to one and onto, then the ***inverse*** of f, $f^{-1}: Y \to X$, is the function defined by

$$f^{-1}(y) = x \text{ if and only if } f(x) = y. \tag{1}$$

Therefore, if $T: U \to V$ is a linear transformation that is both one to one and onto, then the inverse function $T^{-1}: V \to U$ is defined. The next two examples illustrate this concept.

EXAMPLE 8 Let $T: \mathcal{P}_4 \to \mathcal{P}_3$ be defined by $T(p) = p''(x)$. Show that T^{-1} is not defined.

Solution It is easy to see that $\mathcal{N}(T) = \mathcal{P}_1$. In particular, by property 4 of Theorem 14 (Section 5.7), T is not one to one. Thus T^{-1} is not defined. To illustrate specifically, note that $T(x) = T(x+1) = \boldsymbol{\theta}(x)$. Thus by formula (1) above, we have both $T^{-1}(\boldsymbol{\theta}(x)) = x$ and $T^{-1}(\boldsymbol{\theta}(x)) = x + 1$. Since $T^{-1}(\boldsymbol{\theta}(x))$ is not uniquely determined, T^{-1} does not exist.

Since $\mathcal{N}(T) = \mathcal{P}_1$, it follows that $\mathrm{nullity}(T) = 2$. By property 3 of Theorem 15 (Section 5.7), $\mathrm{rank}(T) = \dim(\mathcal{P}_4) - \mathrm{nullity}(T) = 5 - 2 = 3$. But $\dim(\mathcal{P}_3) = 4$, so T is not onto. In particular, x^3 is in $\mathcal{P}_3$, and it is easy to see that there is no polynomial $p(x)$ in $\mathcal{P}_4$ such that $T(p(x)) = p''(x) = x^3$. Thus $T^{-1}(x^3)$ remains undefined by formula (1). ■

Example 8 illustrates the following: If $T: U \to V$ is not one to one, then there exists $\mathbf{v}$ in V such that $T^{-1}(\mathbf{v})$ is not uniquely determined by formula (1), since there exists $\mathbf{u}_1$ and $\mathbf{u}_2$ in U such that $\mathbf{u}_1 \neq \mathbf{u}_2$ but $T(\mathbf{u}_1) = \mathbf{v} = T(\mathbf{u}_2)$. On the other hand, if T is not onto, there exists $\mathbf{v}$ in V such that $T^{-1}(\mathbf{v})$ is not defined by formula (1), since there exists no vector $\mathbf{u}$ in U such that $T(\mathbf{u}) = \mathbf{v}$.

EXAMPLE 9 Let $T: U \to V$ be the linear transformation defined in Example 6. Show that T is both one to one and onto, and give the formula for T^{-1}.

Solution We showed in Example 6 that T is onto. In order to show that T is one to one, it suffices, by Theorem 14, property 4 of Section 5.7, to show that if $A \in \mathcal{N}(T)$, then $A = \mathcal{O}$

[where $\mathcal{O}$ is the (2×2) zero matrix]. Thus suppose that

$$A = \begin{bmatrix} a & -b \\ b & a \end{bmatrix}$$

and $T(A) = \boldsymbol{\theta}(x)$; that is, $(a+b)e^x + (a-b)e^{-x} = \boldsymbol{\theta}(x)$. Since the set $\{e^x, e^{-x}\}$ is linearly independent, it follows that $a + b = 0$ and $a - b = 0$. Therefore, $a = b = 0$ and $A = \mathcal{O}$.

To determine the formula for T^{-1}, let $f(x) = ce^x + de^{-x}$ be in V. By formula (1), $T^{-1}(f) = A$, where A is a matrix such that $T(A) = f(x)$; that is,

$$T(A) = (a+b)e^x + (a-b)e^{-x} = ce^x + de^{-x}. \tag{2}$$

Since $\{e^x, e^{-x}\}$ is a linearly independent set, Eq. (2) requires that $a+b = c$ and $a-b = d$. This yields $a = (1/2)c + (1/2)d$ and $b = (1/2)c - (1/2)d$. Therefore, the formula for T^{-1} is given by

$$T^{-1}(ce^x + de^{-x}) = (1/2)\begin{bmatrix} c+d & -c+d \\ c-d & c+d \end{bmatrix}.$$ ■

A linear transformation $T: U \to V$ that is both one to one and onto is called an ***invertible*** linear transformation. Thus if T is invertible, then the mapping $T^{-1}: V \to U$ exists and is defined by formula (1). The next theorem lists some of the properties of T^{-1}.

THEOREM 16 Let U and V be vector spaces, and let $T: U \to V$ be an invertible linear transformation. Then:

1. $T^{-1}: V \to U$ is a linear transformation.
2. T^{-1} is invertible and $(T^{-1})^{-1} = T$.
3. $T^{-1} \circ T = I_U$ and $T \circ T^{-1} = I_V$, where I_U and I_V are the identity transformations on U and V, respectively.

Proof For property 1, we need to show that $T^{-1}: V \to U$ satisfies Definition 8. Suppose that $\mathbf{v}_1$ and $\mathbf{v}_2$ are vectors in V. Since T is onto, there are vectors $\mathbf{u}_1$ and $\mathbf{u}_2$ in U such that $T(\mathbf{u}_1) = \mathbf{v}_1$ and $T(\mathbf{u}_1) = \mathbf{v}_2$. By formula (1),

$$T^{-1}(\mathbf{v}_1) = \mathbf{u}_1 \text{ and } T^{-1}(\mathbf{v}_2) = \mathbf{u}_2. \tag{3}$$

Furthermore, $\mathbf{v}_1 + \mathbf{v}_2 = T(\mathbf{u}_1) + T(\mathbf{u}_2) = T(\mathbf{u}_1 + \mathbf{u}_2)$, so by formula (1),

$$T^{-1}(\mathbf{v}_1 + \mathbf{v}_2) = \mathbf{u}_1 + \mathbf{u}_2 = T^{-1}(\mathbf{v}_1) + T^{-1}\mathbf{v}_2.$$

It is equally easy to see that $T^{-1}(c\mathbf{v}) = cT^{-1}(\mathbf{v})$ for all $\mathbf{v}$ in V and for any scalar c (see Exercise 15).

The proof of property 2 requires showing that T^{-1} is both one to one and onto. To see that T^{-1} is one to one, let $\mathbf{v}$ be in $\mathcal{N}(T^{-1})$. Then $T^{-1}(\mathbf{v}) = \boldsymbol{\theta}_U$, so by formula (1), $T(\boldsymbol{\theta}_U) = \mathbf{v}$. By Theorem 14, property 1, of Section 5.7, $\mathbf{v} = \boldsymbol{\theta}_V$ so Theorem 14, property 4, implies that T is one to one. To see that T^{-1} is onto, let $\mathbf{u}$ be an arbitrary vector in U. If $\mathbf{v} = T(\mathbf{u})$, then $\mathbf{v}$ is in V and, by formula (1), $T^{-1}(\mathbf{v}) = \mathbf{u}$. Therefore, T^{-1} is onto, and it follows that T is invertible.

That $(T^{-1})^{-1} = T$ is an easy consequence of formula (1), as are the equalities given in property 3, and the proofs are left as exercises. ■

As might be guessed from the corresponding theorems for nonsingular matrices, other properties of invertible transformations can be established. For example, if $T: U \to V$ is an invertible transformation, then for each vector $\mathbf{b}$ in V, $\mathbf{x} = T^{-1}(\mathbf{b})$ is the unique solution of $T(\mathbf{x}) = \mathbf{b}$. Also, if S and T are invertible and $S \circ T$ is defined, then $S \circ T$ is invertible and $(S \circ T)^{-1} = T^{-1} \circ S^{-1}$.

Isomorphic Vector Spaces

Suppose that a linear transformation $T: U \to V$ is invertible. Since T is both one to one and onto, T establishes an exact pairing between elements of U and V. Moreover, because T is a linear transformation, this pairing preserves algebraic properties. Therefore, although U and V may be different sets, they may be regarded as indistinguishable (or equivalent) algebraically. Stated another way, U and V both represent just one underlying vector space but perhaps with different "labels" for the elements. The invertible linear transformation T acts as a translation from one set of labels to another.

If U and V are vector spaces and if $T: U \to V$ is an invertible linear transformation, then U and V are said to be ***isomorphic*** vector spaces. Also, an invertible transformation T is called an ***isomorphism***. For instance, the vector spaces U and V given in Example 6 are isomorphic, as shown in Example 9. The next example provides another illustration.

EXAMPLE 10 Let U be the subspace of $\mathcal{P}_3$ defined by

$$U = \{p(x) = a_0 + a_1x + a_2x^2 + a_3x^3 \colon a_3 = -2a_0 + 3a_1 + a_2\}.$$

Show that U is isomorphic to R^3.

Solution Note that $\dim(U) = 3$ and the set $\{1 - 2x^3, x + 3x^3, x^2 + x^3\}$ is a basis for U. Moreover, each polynomial $p(x)$ in U can be decomposed as

$$\begin{aligned} p(x) &= a_0 + a_1x + a_2x^2 + a_3x^3 \\ &= a_0(1 - 2x^3) + a_1(x + 3x^3) + a_2(x^2 + x^3). \end{aligned} \tag{4}$$

It is reasonable to expect that an isomorphism $T: U \to R^3$ will map a basis of U to a basis of R^3. Since $\{\mathbf{e}_1, \mathbf{e}_2, \mathbf{e}_3\}$ is a basis for R^3, we seek a linear transformation T such that

$$T(1 - 2x^3) = \mathbf{e}_1, \quad T(x + 3x^3) = \mathbf{e}_2, \quad \text{and} \quad T(x^2 + x^3) = \mathbf{e}_3. \tag{5}$$

It follows from Eq. (4) in this example and from Eq. (1) of Section 5.7 that if such a linear transformation exists, then it is defined by

$$\begin{aligned} T(a_0 + a_1x + a_2x^2 + a_3x^3) &= a_0T(1 - 2x^3) + a_1T(x + 3x^3) + a_2T(x^2 + x^3) \\ &= a_0\mathbf{e}_1 + a_1\mathbf{e}_2 + a_2\mathbf{e}_3. \end{aligned}$$

That is,

$$T(a_0 + a_1x + a_2x^2 + a_3x^3) = \begin{bmatrix} a_0 \\ a_1 \\ a_2 \end{bmatrix}. \tag{6}$$

It is straightforward to show that the function T defined by Eq. (6) is a linear transformation. Moreover, the constraints placed on T by (5) imply, by Theorem 15, property 1, of Section 5.7, that $\mathcal{R}(T) = R^3$. Likewise, by Theorem 15, property 2, T is one to one. Therefore, T is an isomorphism and U and R^3 are isomorphic vector spaces. ∎

The previous example is actually just a special case of the following theorem, which states that every real n-dimensional vector space is isomorphic to R^n.

THEOREM 17 If U is a real n-dimensional vector space, then U and R^n are isomorphic.

Proof To prove this theorem, we need only exhibit the isomorphism, and a coordinate system on U will provide the means. Let $B = \{\mathbf{u}_1, \mathbf{u}_2, \ldots, \mathbf{u}_n\}$ be a basis for U, and let $T: U \to R^n$ be the linear transformation defined by

$$T(\mathbf{u}) = [\mathbf{u}]_B.$$

Since B is a basis, $\boldsymbol{\theta}_U$ is the only vector in $\mathcal{N}(T)$; and therefore T is one to one. Furthermore, $T(\mathbf{u}_i)$ is the vector $\mathbf{e}_i$ in R^n; so

$$\mathcal{R}(T) = \mathrm{Sp}\{T(\mathbf{u}_1), T(\mathbf{u}_2), \ldots, T(\mathbf{u}_n)\} = \mathrm{Sp}\{\mathbf{e}_1, \mathbf{e}_2, \ldots, \mathbf{e}_n\} = R^n.$$

Hence T is one to one and onto. ∎

As an illustration of Theorem 17, note that $\dim(\mathcal{P}_2) = 3$, so $\mathcal{P}_2$ and R^3 are isomorphic. Moreover, if $B = \{1, x, x^2\}$ is the natural basis for $\mathcal{P}_2$, then the linear transformation $T: \mathcal{P}_2 \to R^3$ defined by $T(p) = [p]_B$ is an isomorphism; thus

$$T(a_0 + a_1x + a_2x^2) = \begin{bmatrix} a_0 \\ a_1 \\ a_2 \end{bmatrix}.$$

The isomorphism T "pairs" the elements of $\mathcal{P}_2$ with elements of R^3, $p(x) \leftrightarrow [p(x)]_B$. Furthermore, under this correspondence the sum of two polynomials, $p(x) + q(x)$, is paired with the sum of the corresponding coordinate vectors:

$$p(x) + q(x) \leftrightarrow [p(x)]_B + [q(x)]_B.$$

Similarly, a scalar multiple, $ap(x)$, of a polynomial $p(x)$ is paired with the corresponding scalar multiple of $[p(x)]_B$:

$$ap(x) \leftrightarrow a[p(x)]_B.$$

In this sense, $\mathcal{P}_2$ and R^3 have the same algebraic character.

It is easy to show that if U is isomorphic to V and V is isomorphic to W, then U and W are also isomorphic (see Exercise 19). Using this fact, we obtain the following corollary of Theorem 17.

COROLLARY If U and V are real n-dimensional vector spaces, then U and V are isomorphic. ∎

5.8 EXERCISES

In Exercises 1–6, the linear transformations S, T, and H are defined as follows:

$S:\mathcal{P}_3 \to \mathcal{P}_4$ is defined by $S(p) = p'(0)$.

$T:\mathcal{P}_3 \to \mathcal{P}_4$ is defined by $T(p) = (x+2)p(x)$.

$H:\mathcal{P}_4 \to \mathcal{P}_3$ is defined by $H(p) = p'(x) + p(0)$.

1. Give the formula for $S+T$. Calculate $(S+T)(x)$ and $(S+T)(x^2)$.

2. Give the formula for $2T$. Calculate $(2T)(x)$.

3. Give the formula for $H \circ T$. What is the domain for $H \circ T$? Calculate $(H \circ T)(x)$.

4. Give the formula for $T \circ H$. What is the domain for $T \circ H$? Calculate $(T \circ H)(x)$.

5. **a)** Prove that T is one to one but not onto.

b) Attempt to define $T^{-1}: \mathcal{P}_4 \to \mathcal{P}_3$ as in formula (1) by setting $T^{-1}(q) = p$ if and only if $T(p) = q$. What is $T^{-1}(x)$?

6. **a)** Prove that H is onto but not one to one.

b) Attempt to define $H^{-1}: \mathcal{P}_3 \to \mathcal{P}_4$ as in formula (1) by setting $H^{-1}(q) = p$ if and only if $H(p) = q$. Show that $H^{-1}(x)$ is not uniquely determined.

7. The functions e^x, e^{2x}, and e^{3x} are linearly independent in $C[0,1]$. Let V be the subspace of $C[0,1]$ defined by $V = \mathrm{Sp}\{e^x, e^{2x}, e^{3x}\}$, and let $T: V \to V$ be given by $T(p) = p'(x)$. Show that T is invertible and calculate $T^{-1}(e^x)$, $T^{-1}(e^{2x})$, and $T^{-1}(e^{3x})$. What is $T^{-1}(ae^x + be^{2x} + ce^{3x})$?

8. Let V be the subspace of $C[0,1]$ defined by $V = \mathrm{Sp}\{\sin x, \cos x, e^{-x}\}$, and let $T: V \to V$ be given by $T(f) = f'(x)$. Given that the set $\{\sin x, \cos x, e^{-x}\}$ is linearly independent, show that T is invertible. Calculate $T^{-1}(\sin x)$, $T^{-1}(\cos x)$, and $T^{-1}(e^{-x})$ and give the formula for T^{-1}; that is, determine $T^{-1}(a\sin x + b\cos x + ce^{-x})$.

9. Let V be the vector space of all (2×2) matrices and define $T: V \to V$ by $T(A) = A^T$. Show that T is invertible and give the formula for T^{-1}.

10. Let V be the vector space of all (2×2) matrices, and let Q be a given nonsingular (2×2) matrix. If $T: V \to V$ is defined by $T(A) = Q^{-1}AQ$, prove that T is invertible and give the formula for T^{-1}.

11. Let V be the vector space of all (2×2) matrices.

a) Use Theorem 17 to show that V is isomorphic to R^4.

b) Use the corollary to Theorem 17 to show that V is isomorphic to $\mathcal{P}_3$.

c) Exhibit an isomorphism $T: V \to \mathcal{P}_3$. [*Hint:* See Example 10.]

12. Let U be the vector space of all (2×2) symmetric matrices.

a) Use Theorem 17 to show that U is isomorphic to R^3.

b) Use the corollary to Theorem 17 to show that U is isomorphic to $\mathcal{P}_2$.

c) Exhibit an isomorphism $T: U \to \mathcal{P}_2$.

13. Let $T_1: U \to V$ and $T_2: U \to V$ be linear transformations. Prove that $S: U \to V$, where $S = T_1 + T_2$, is a linear transformation.

14. If $T: U \to V$ is a linear transformation and a is a scalar, show that $aT: U \to V$ is a linear transformation.

15. Complete the proof of property 1 of Theorem 16 by showing that $T^{-1}(c\mathbf{v}) = cT^{-1}(\mathbf{v})$ for all $\mathbf{v}$ in V and for an arbitrary scalar c.

16. Complete the proof of property 2 of Theorem 16 by showing that $(T^{-1})^{-1} = T$. [*Hint:* Use formula 1.]

17. Prove property 3 of Theorem 16.

18. Let $S: U \to V$ and $T: V \to W$ be linear transformations.

a) Prove that if S and T are both one to one, then $T \circ S$ is one to one.

b) Prove that if S and T are both onto, then $T \circ S$ is onto.

c) Prove that if S and T are both invertible, then $T \circ S$ is invertible and $(T \circ S)^{-1} = S^{-1} \circ T^{-1}$.

19. Let U, V, and W be vector spaces such that U and V are isomorphic and V and W are isomorphic. Use Exercise 18 to show that U and W are isomorphic.

20. Let U and V both be n-dimensional vector spaces, and suppose that $T: U \to V$ is a linear transformation.

a) If T is one to one, prove that T is invertible. [*Hint:* Use property 3 of Theorem 15 to prove that $\mathcal{R}(T) = V$.]

b) If T is onto, prove that T is invertible. [*Hint:* Use property 3 of Theorem 15 and property 4 of Theorem 14 to prove that T is one to one.]

21. Define $T: \mathcal{P} \to \mathcal{P}$ by $T(a_0 + a_1x + \cdots + a_nx^n) = a_0x + (1/2)a_1x^2 + \cdots + (1/(n+1))a_nx^{n+1}$. Prove that T is one to one but not onto. Why is this example not a contradiction of part a) of Exercise 20?

22. Define $S: \mathcal{P} \to \mathcal{P}$ by $S(p) = p'(x)$. Prove that S is onto but not one to one. Why is this example not a contradiction of part b) of Exercise 20?

In Exercises 23–25, $S: U \to V$ and $T: V \to W$ are linear transformations.

23. Show that $\mathcal{N}(S) \subseteq \mathcal{N}(T \circ S)$. Conclude that if $T \circ S$ is one to one, then S is one to one.

24. Show that $\mathcal{R}(T \circ S) \subseteq \mathcal{R}(T)$. Conclude that if $T \circ S$ is onto, then T is onto.

25. Assume that U, V, and W all have dimension n. Prove that if $T \circ S$ is invertible, then both T and S are invertible. [*Hint:* Use Exercises 20, 23, and 24.]

26. Let A be an $(m \times p)$ matrix and B a $(p \times n)$ matrix. Use Exercises 23 and 24 to show that nullity$(B) \le$ nullity(AB) and rank$(AB) \le$ rank(A).

27. Let A be an $(n \times n)$ matrix, and suppose that $T: R^n \to R^n$ is defined by $T(\mathbf{x}) = A\mathbf{x}$. Show that T is invertible if and only if A is nonsingular. If T is invertible, give a formula for T^{-1}.

28. Let A and B be $(n \times n)$ matrices such that AB is nonsingular. Use Exercises 25 and 27 to show that each of the matrices A and B is nonsingular.

29. Let U and V be vector spaces, and let $L(U, V) = \{T: T \text{ is a linear transformation from } U \text{ to } V\}$. With the operations of addition and scalar multiplication defined in this section, show that $L(U, V)$ is a vector space.

5.9 MATRIX REPRESENTATIONS FOR LINEAR TRANSFORMATIONS

In Section 3.7 we showed that a linear transformation $T: R^n \to R^m$ can be represented as multiplication by an $(m \times n)$ matrix A; that is, $T(\mathbf{x}) = A\mathbf{x}$ for all $\mathbf{x}$ in R^n. In the general vector-space setting, we have viewed a linear transformation $T: U \to V$ as an extension of this notion. Now suppose that U and V both have finite dimension, say $\dim(U) = n$ and $\dim(V) = m$. By Theorem 17 of Section 5.8, U is isomorphic to R^n and V is isomorphic to R^m. To be specific, let B be a basis for U and let C be a basis for V. Then each vector $\mathbf{u}$ in U can be represented by the vector $[\mathbf{u}]_B$ in R^n, and similarly each vector $\mathbf{v}$ in V can be represented by the vector $[\mathbf{v}]_C$ in R^m. In this section we show that T can be represented by an $(m \times n)$ matrix Q in the sense that if $T(\mathbf{u}) = \mathbf{v}$, then $Q[\mathbf{u}]_B = [\mathbf{v}]_C$.

The Matrix of a Transformation

We begin by defining the matrix of a linear transformation. Thus let $T: U \to V$ be a linear transformation, where $\dim(U) = n$ and $\dim(V) = m$. Let $B = \{\mathbf{u}_1, \mathbf{u}_2, \ldots, \mathbf{u}_n\}$ be a basis for U, and let $C = \{\mathbf{v}_1, \mathbf{v}_2, \ldots, \mathbf{v}_m\}$ be a basis for V. The ***matrix representation*** for T with respect to the bases B and C is the $(m \times n)$ matrix Q defined by

$$Q = [\mathbf{Q}_1, \mathbf{Q}_2, \ldots, \mathbf{Q}_n],$$

where

$$\mathbf{Q}_j = [T(\mathbf{u}_j)]_C.$$

Thus to determine Q, we first represent each of the vectors $T(\mathbf{u}_1), T(\mathbf{u}_2), \ldots, T(\mathbf{u}_n)$ in terms of the basis C for V:

$$\begin{aligned} T(\mathbf{u}_1) &= q_{11}\mathbf{v}_1 + q_{21}\mathbf{v}_2 + \cdots + q_{m1}\mathbf{v}_m \\ T(\mathbf{u}_2) &= q_{12}\mathbf{v}_1 + q_{22}\mathbf{v}_2 + \cdots + q_{m2}\mathbf{v}_m \\ &\vdots \\ T(\mathbf{u}_n) &= q_{1n}\mathbf{v}_1 + q_{2n}\mathbf{v}_2 + \cdots + q_{mn}\mathbf{v}_m. \end{aligned} \tag{1}$$

It follows from system (1) that

$$\mathbf{Q}_1 = [T(\mathbf{u}_1)]_C = \begin{bmatrix} q_{11} \\ q_{21} \\ \vdots \\ q_{m1} \end{bmatrix}, \ldots, \mathbf{Q}_n = [T(\mathbf{u}_n)]_C = \begin{bmatrix} q_{1n} \\ q_{2n} \\ \vdots \\ q_{mn} \end{bmatrix}. \tag{2}$$

The following example provides a specific illustration.

EXAMPLE 1 Let U be the vector space of all (2×2) matrices and define $T: U \to \mathcal{P}_2$ by

$$T\left(\begin{bmatrix} a & b \\ c & d \end{bmatrix}\right) = (a - d) + (a + 2b)x + (b - 3c)x^2.$$

Find the matrix of T relative to the natural bases for U and $\mathcal{P}_2$.

Solution Let $B = \{E_{11}, E_{12}, E_{21}, E_{22}\}$ be the natural basis for U, and let $C = \{1, x, x^2\}$ be the natural basis for $\mathcal{P}_2$. Then $T(E_{11}) = 1 + x$, $T(E_{12}) = 2x + x^2$, $T(E_{21}) = -3x^2$, and $T(E_{22}) = -1$. In this example system (1) becomes

$$\begin{aligned} T(E_{11}) &= 1 + 1x + 0x^2 \\ T(E_{12}) &= 0 + 2x + 1x^2 \\ T(E_{21}) &= 0 + 0x - 3x^2 \\ T(E_{22}) &= -1 + 0x + 0x^2. \end{aligned}$$

Therefore, the matrix of T is the (3×4) matrix Q given by

$$Q = \begin{bmatrix} 1 & 0 & 0 & -1 \\ 1 & 2 & 0 & 0 \\ 0 & 1 & -3 & 0 \end{bmatrix}.$$

The Representation Theorem

The next theorem shows that if we translate from general vector spaces to coordinate vectors, the action of a linear transformation T translates to multiplication by its matrix representative.

THEOREM 18 Let $T: U \to V$ be a linear transformation, where $\dim(U) = n$ and $\dim(V) = m$. Let B and C be bases for U and V, respectively, and let Q be the matrix of T relative to B and C. If $\mathbf{u}$ is a vector in U and if $T(\mathbf{u}) = \mathbf{v}$, then

$$Q[\mathbf{u}]_B = [\mathbf{v}]_C. \tag{3}$$

Moreover, Q is the unique matrix that satisfies (3). ■

The representation of T by Q is illustrated in Fig. 5.8. Before giving the proof of Theorem 18, we illustrate the result with an example.

$$\begin{array}{ccc} \mathbf{u} & \longrightarrow & T(\mathbf{u}) = \mathbf{v} \\ \downarrow & & \downarrow \\ [\mathbf{u}]_B & \rightarrow & Q[\mathbf{u}]_B = [\mathbf{v}]_C \end{array}$$

Figure 5.8 The matrix of T

EXAMPLE 2 Let $T: U \to \mathcal{P}_2$ be the linear transformation defined in Example 1, and let Q be the matrix representation determined in that example. Show by direct calculation that if $T(A) = p(x)$, then

$$Q[A]_B = [p(x)]_C. \tag{4}$$

Solution Recall that $B = \{E_{11}, E_{12}, E_{21}, E_{22}\}$ and $C = \{1, x, x^2\}$. Equation (4) is, of course, an immediate consequence of Eq. (3). To verify Eq. (4) directly, note that if

$$A = \begin{bmatrix} a & b \\ c & d \end{bmatrix},$$

then

$$[A]_B = \begin{bmatrix} a \\ b \\ c \\ d \end{bmatrix}.$$

Further, if $p(x) = T(A)$, then $p(x) = (a - d) + (a + 2b)x + (b - 3c)x^2$, so

$$[p(x)]_C = \begin{bmatrix} a - d \\ a + 2b \\ b - 3c \end{bmatrix}.$$

Therefore,

$$Q[A]_B = \begin{bmatrix} 1 & 0 & 0 & -1 \\ 1 & 2 & 0 & 0 \\ 0 & 1 & -3 & 0 \end{bmatrix} \begin{bmatrix} a \\ b \\ c \\ d \end{bmatrix} = \begin{bmatrix} a - d \\ a + 2b \\ b - 3c \end{bmatrix} = [p(x)]_C.$$ ■

Proof of Theorem 18 Let $B = \{\mathbf{u}_1, \mathbf{u}_2, \ldots, \mathbf{u}_n\}$ be the given basis for U, let $\mathbf{u}$ be in U, and set $T(\mathbf{u}) = \mathbf{v}$. First write $\mathbf{u}$ in terms of the basis vectors:

$$\mathbf{u} = a_1\mathbf{u}_1 + a_2\mathbf{u}_2 + \cdots + a_n\mathbf{u}_n. \tag{5}$$

It follows from Eq. (5) that the coordinate vector for $\mathbf{u}$ is

$$[\mathbf{u}]_B = \begin{bmatrix} a_1 \\ a_2 \\ \vdots \\ a_n \end{bmatrix}.$$

Furthermore, the action of T is completely determined by its action on a basis for U (see Eq. (1) of Section 5.7), so Eq. (5) implies that

$$T(\mathbf{u}) = a_1T(\mathbf{u}_1) + a_2T(\mathbf{u}_2) + \cdots + a_nT(\mathbf{u}_n) = \mathbf{v}. \tag{6}$$

The vectors in Eq. (6) are in V, and passing to coordinate vectors relative to the basis C yields, by Eq. (10) of Section 5.4,

$$a_1[T(\mathbf{u}_1)]_C + a_2[T(\mathbf{u}_2)]_C + \cdots + a_n[T(\mathbf{u}_n)]_C = [\mathbf{v}]_C. \tag{7}$$

Recall that the matrix Q of T is the $(m \times n)$ matrix $Q = [\mathbf{Q}_1, \mathbf{Q}_2, \ldots, \mathbf{Q}_n]$, where

$$\mathbf{Q}_j = [T(\mathbf{u}_j)]_C.$$

Thus Eq. (7) can be rewritten as

$$a_1\mathbf{Q}_1 + a_2\mathbf{Q}_2 + \cdots + a_n\mathbf{Q}_n = [\mathbf{v}]_C. \tag{8}$$

Since Eq. (8) is equivalent to the matrix equation

$$Q[\mathbf{u}]_B = [\mathbf{v}]_C,$$

this shows that Eq. (3) of Theorem 18 holds. The uniqueness of Q is left as an exercise. ∎

EXAMPLE 3 Let $S: \mathcal{P}_2 \to \mathcal{P}_3$ be the differential operator defined by $S(f) = x^2f'' - 2f' + xf$. Find the (4×3) matrix P that represents S with respect to the natural bases $C = \{1, x, x^2\}$ and $D = \{1, x, x^2, x^3\}$ for $\mathcal{P}_2$ and $\mathcal{P}_3$, respectively. Also, illustrate that P satisfies Eq. (3) of Theorem 18.

Solution To construct the (4×3) matrix P that represents S, we need to find the coordinate vectors of $S(1)$, $S(x)$, and $S(x^2)$ with respect to D. We calculate that $S(1) = x$, $S(x) = x^2 - 2$, and $S(x^2) = x^3 + 2x^2 - 4x$; so the coordinate vectors of $S(1)$, $S(x)$, and $S(x^2)$ are

$$[S(1)]_D = \begin{bmatrix} 0 \\ 1 \\ 0 \\ 0 \end{bmatrix}, \quad [S(x)]_D = \begin{bmatrix} -2 \\ 0 \\ 1 \\ 0 \end{bmatrix}, \quad \text{and} \quad [S(x^2)]_D = \begin{bmatrix} 0 \\ -4 \\ 2 \\ 1 \end{bmatrix}.$$

Thus the matrix representation for S is the (4×3) matrix

$$P = \begin{bmatrix} 0 & -2 & 0 \\ 1 & 0 & -4 \\ 0 & 1 & 2 \\ 0 & 0 & 1 \end{bmatrix}.$$

To see that Eq. (3) of Theorem 18 holds, let $p(x) = a_0 + a_1x + a_2x^2$ be in $\mathcal{P}_2$. Then $S(p) = -2a_1 + (a_0 - 4a_2)x + (a_1 + 2a_2)x^2 + a_2x^3$. In this case

$$[p(x)]_C = \begin{bmatrix} a_0 \\ a_1 \\ a_2 \end{bmatrix},$$

and if $S(p) = q(x)$, then

$$[q(x)]_D = \begin{bmatrix} -2a_1 \\ a_0 - 4a_2 \\ a_1 + 2a_2 \\ a_2 \end{bmatrix}.$$

A straightforward calculation shows that $P[p(x)]_C = [q(x)]_D$. ■

EXAMPLE 4 Let A be an $(m \times n)$ matrix and consider the linear transformation $T: R^n \to R^m$ defined by $T(\mathbf{x}) = A\mathbf{x}$. Show that relative to the natural bases for R^n and R^m, the matrix for T is A.

Solution Let $B = \{\mathbf{e}_1, \mathbf{e}_2, \ldots, \mathbf{e}_n\}$ be the natural basis for R^n, and let C denote the natural basis for R^m. First note that for each vector $\mathbf{y}$ in R^m, $\mathbf{y} = [\mathbf{y}]_C$. Now let Q denote the matrix of T relative to B and C, $Q = [\mathbf{Q}_1, \mathbf{Q}_2, \ldots, \mathbf{Q}_n]$, and write $A = [\mathbf{A}_1, \mathbf{A}_2, \ldots, \mathbf{A}_n]$. The definition of Q gives

$$\mathbf{Q}_j = [T(\mathbf{e}_j)]_C = T(\mathbf{e}_j) = A\mathbf{e}_j = \mathbf{A}_j.$$

It now follows that $Q = A$. ■

If V is a vector space, then linear transformations of the form $T: V \to V$ are of considerable interest and importance. In this case, the same basis B is normally chosen for both the domain and the range of T, and we refer to the representation as the matrix of T with respect to B. In this case, if Q is the matrix of T and if $\mathbf{v}$ is in V, then Eq. (3) of Theorem 18 becomes

$$Q[\mathbf{v}]_B = [T(\mathbf{v})]_B.$$

The next example illustrates this special case.

EXAMPLE 5 Let $T: \mathcal{P}_2 \to \mathcal{P}_2$ be the linear transformation defined by $T(p) = xp'(x)$. Find the matrix, Q, of T relative to the natural basis for $\mathcal{P}_2$.

Solution Let $B = \{1, x, x^2\}$. Then $T(1) = 0, T(x) = x$, and $T(x^2) = 2x^2$. The coordinate vectors for $T(1), T(x), T(x^2)$ relative to B are

$$[T(1)]_B = \begin{bmatrix} 0 \\ 0 \\ 0 \end{bmatrix}, \quad [T(x)]_B = \begin{bmatrix} 0 \\ 1 \\ 0 \end{bmatrix}, \quad \text{and} \quad [T(x^2)]_B = \begin{bmatrix} 0 \\ 0 \\ 2 \end{bmatrix}.$$

It follows that the matrix of T with respect to B is the (3×3) matrix

$$Q = \begin{bmatrix} 0 & 0 & 0 \\ 0 & 1 & 0 \\ 0 & 0 & 2 \end{bmatrix}.$$

If $p(x) = a_0 + a_1x + a_2x^2$, then $T[p(x)] = x(a_1 + 2a_2x) = a_1x + 2a_2x^2$. Thus

$$[p(x)]_B = \begin{bmatrix} a_0 \\ a_1 \\ a_2 \end{bmatrix} \quad \text{and} \quad [T(p(x))]_B = \begin{bmatrix} 0 \\ a_1 \\ 2a_2 \end{bmatrix}.$$

A direct calculation verifies that $Q[p(x)]_B = [T(p(x))]_B$. ■

Algebraic Properties

In Section 5.8, we defined the algebraic operations of addition, scalar multiplication, and composition for linear transformations. We now examine the matrix representations of the resulting transformations. We begin with the following theorem.

THEOREM 19 Let U and V be vector spaces, with $\dim(U) = n$ and $\dim(V) = m$, and suppose that B and C are bases for U and V, respectively. Let T_1, T_2, and T be transformations from U to V and let Q_1, Q_2, and Q be the matrix representations with respect to B and C for T_1, T_2, and T, respectively. Then:

1. $Q_1 + Q_2$ is the matrix representation for $T_1 + T_2$ with respect to B and C.
2. For a scalar a, aQ is the matrix representation for aT with respect to B and C.

Proof We include here only the proof of property 1. The proof of property 2 is left for Exercises 26 and 27.

To prove property 1, set $T_3 = T_1 + T_2$ and let Q_3 be the matrix of T_3. By Eq. (3) of Theorem 18, Q_3 satisfies the equation

$$Q_3[\mathbf{u}]_B = [T_3(\mathbf{u})]_C \tag{9}$$

for every vector $\mathbf{u}$ in U; moreover, any other matrix that satisfies Eq. (9) is equal to Q_3. We also know from Theorem 18 that

$$Q_1[\mathbf{u}]_B = [T_1(\mathbf{u})]_C \quad \text{and} \quad Q_2[\mathbf{u}]_B = [T_2(\mathbf{u})]_C \tag{10}$$

for every vector $\mathbf{u}$ in U. Using Eq. (10) in Section 5.4 gives

$$[T_1(\mathbf{u}) + T_2(\mathbf{u})]_C = [T_1(\mathbf{u})]_C + [T_2(\mathbf{u})]_C. \tag{11}$$

It follows from Eqs. (10) and (11) that

$$(Q_1 + Q_2)[\mathbf{u}]_B = [T_1(\mathbf{u}) + T_2(\mathbf{u})]_C = [T_3(\mathbf{u})]_C;$$

therefore, $Q_3 = Q_1 + Q_2$. ∎

The following example illustrates the preceding theorem.

EXAMPLE 6 Let T_1 and T_2 be the linear transformations from $\mathcal{P}_2$ to R^2 defined by

$$T_1(p) = \begin{bmatrix} p(0) \\ p(1) \end{bmatrix} \quad \text{and} \quad T_2(p) = \begin{bmatrix} p'(0) \\ p(-1) \end{bmatrix}.$$

Set $T_3 = T_1 + T_2$ and $T_4 = 3T_1$ and let $B = \{1, x, x^2\}$ and $C = \{\mathbf{e}_1, \mathbf{e}_2\}$. Use the definition to calculate the matrices Q_1, Q_2, Q_3, and Q_4 for T_1, T_2, T_3, and T_4, respectively, relative to the bases B and C. Note that $Q_3 = Q_1 + Q_2$ and $Q_4 = 3Q_1$.

Solution Since

$$T_1(1) = \begin{bmatrix} 1 \\ 1 \end{bmatrix}, \quad T_1(x) = \begin{bmatrix} 0 \\ 1 \end{bmatrix}, \quad \text{and} \quad T_1(x^2) = \begin{bmatrix} 0 \\ 1 \end{bmatrix},$$

it follows that Q_1 is the (2×3) matrix given by

$$Q_1 = \begin{bmatrix} 1 & 0 & 0 \\ 1 & 1 & 1 \end{bmatrix}.$$

Similarly,

$$T_2(1) = \begin{bmatrix} 0 \\ 1 \end{bmatrix}, \quad T_2(x) = \begin{bmatrix} 1 \\ -1 \end{bmatrix}, \quad \text{and} \quad T_2(x^2) = \begin{bmatrix} 0 \\ 1 \end{bmatrix},$$

so Q_2 is given by

$$Q_2 = \begin{bmatrix} 0 & 1 & 0 \\ 1 & -1 & 1 \end{bmatrix}.$$

Now $T_3(p) = T_1(p) + T_2(p)$, so

$$T_3(p) = \begin{bmatrix} p(0) + p'(0) \\ p(1) + p(-1) \end{bmatrix}.$$

Proceeding as before, we obtain

$$T_3(1) = \begin{bmatrix} 1 \\ 2 \end{bmatrix}, \quad T_3(x) = \begin{bmatrix} 1 \\ 0 \end{bmatrix}, \quad \text{and} \quad T_3(x^2) = \begin{bmatrix} 0 \\ 2 \end{bmatrix}.$$

Thus

$$Q_3 = \begin{bmatrix} 1 & 1 & 0 \\ 2 & 0 & 2 \end{bmatrix},$$

and clearly $Q_3 = Q_1 + Q_2$.

The formula for T_4 is

$$T_4(p) = 3T_1(p) = 3\begin{bmatrix} p(0) \\ p(1) \end{bmatrix} = \begin{bmatrix} 3p(0) \\ 3p(1) \end{bmatrix}.$$

The matrix, Q_4, for T_4 is easily obtained and is given by

$$Q_4 = \begin{bmatrix} 3 & 0 & 0 \\ 3 & 3 & 3 \end{bmatrix}.$$

In particular, $Q_4 = 3Q_1$. ■

The following theorem shows that the composition of two linear transformations corresponds to the product of the matrix representations.

THEOREM 20 Let $T: U \to V$ and $S: V \to W$ be linear transformations, and suppose $\dim(U) = n$, $\dim(V) = m$, and $\dim(W) = k$. Let B, C, and D be bases for U, V, and W, respectively. If the matrix for T relative to B and C is $Q[Q$ is $(m \times n)]$ and the matrix for S relative to C and D is $P[P$ is $(k \times m)]$, then the matrix representation for $S \circ T$ is PQ.

Proof The composition of T and S is illustrated in Fig. 5.9(a), and the matrix representation is illustrated in 5.9(b).

$$U \xrightarrow{T} V \xrightarrow{S} W \qquad\qquad R^n \xrightarrow{Q} R^m \xrightarrow{P} R^k$$

$$\mathbf{u} \longrightarrow T(\mathbf{u}) \longrightarrow S[T(\mathbf{u})] \qquad [\mathbf{u}]_B \longrightarrow Q[\mathbf{u}]_B \longrightarrow PQ[\mathbf{u}]_B$$

(a) (b)

Figure 5.9 The matrix for $S \circ T$

To prove Theorem 20, let N be the matrix of $S \circ T$ with respect to the bases B and D. Then N is the unique matrix with the property that

$$N[\mathbf{u}]_B = [(S \circ T)(\mathbf{u})]_D \tag{12}$$

for every vector $\mathbf{u}$ in U. Similarly, Q and P are characterized by

$$Q[\mathbf{u}]_B = [T(\mathbf{u})]_C \quad \text{and} \quad P[\mathbf{v}]_C = [S(\mathbf{v})]_D \tag{13}$$

for all $\mathbf{u}$ in U and $\mathbf{v}$ in V. It follows from Eq. (13) that

$$PQ[\mathbf{u}]_B = P[T(\mathbf{u})]_C = [S(T(\mathbf{u}))]_D = [(S \circ T)(\mathbf{u})]_D.$$

The uniqueness of N in Eq. (12) now implies that $PQ = N$. ■

EXAMPLE 7 Let U be the vector space of (2×2) matrices. If $T: U \to \mathcal{P}_2$ is the transformation given in Example 1 and $S: \mathcal{P}_2 \to \mathcal{P}_3$ is the transformation described in Example 3, give the formula for $S \circ T$. By direct calculation, find the matrix of $S \circ T$ with respect to the bases $B = \{E_{11}, E_{12}, E_{21}, E_{22}\}$ and $D = \{1, x, x^2, x^3\}$ for U and $\mathcal{P}_3$, respectively.

Finally, use Theorem 20 and the matrices found in Examples 1 and 3 to calculate the matrix for $S \circ T$.

Solution Recall that $T: U \to \mathcal{P}_2$ is given by

$$T\left(\begin{bmatrix} a & b \\ c & d \end{bmatrix}\right) = (a-d) + (a+2b)x + (b-3c)x^2,$$

and $S: \mathcal{P}_2 \to \mathcal{P}_3$ is defined by

$$S(p) = x^2 p'' - 2p' + xp.$$

Therefore, $S \circ T: U \to \mathcal{P}_3$ is defined by

$$\begin{aligned}(S \circ T)(A) = S(T(A)) &= S((a-d) + (a+2b)x + (b-3c)x^2) \\ &= (-2a-4b) + (a-4b+12c-d)x + (a+4b-6c)x^2 \\ &\quad + (b-3c)x^3.\end{aligned}$$

The matrix, N, of $S \circ T$ relative to the given bases B and D is easily determined to be the (4×4) matrix

$$N = \begin{bmatrix} -2 & -4 & 0 & 0 \\ 1 & -4 & 12 & -1 \\ 1 & 4 & -6 & 0 \\ 0 & 1 & -3 & 0 \end{bmatrix}.$$

Moreover, $N = PQ$, where Q is the matrix for T found in Example 1 and P is the matrix for S determined in Example 3. ■

A particularly useful case of Theorem 20 is the one in which S and T both map V to V, $\dim(V) = n$, and the same basis B is used for both the domain and the range. In this case, the composition $S \circ T$ is always defined, and the matrices P and Q for S and T, respectively, are both $(n \times n)$ matrices. Using Theorem 20, we can easily show that if T is invertible, then Q is nonsingular, and furthermore the matrix representation for T^{-1} is Q^{-1}. The matrix representation for the identity transformation on V, I_V, is the $(n \times n)$ identity matrix I. The matrix representation for the zero transformation on V is the $(n \times n)$ zero matrix. (Observe that the identity and the zero transformations always have the same matrix representations, regardless of what basis we choose for V. Thus changing the basis for V may change the matrix representation for T or may leave the representation unchanged.)

The Vector Space $L(U, V)$ (Optional)

If U and V are vector spaces, then $L(U, V)$ denotes the set of all linear transformations from U to V:

$$L(U, V) = \{T: T \text{ is a linear transformation; } T: U \to V\}.$$

If T, T_1, and T_2 are in $L(U, V)$ and a is a scalar, we have seen in Section 5.8 that $T_1 + T_2$ and aT are again in $L(U, V)$. In fact, with these operations of addition and scalar multiplication, we have the following.

Remark The set $L(U, V)$ is a vector space.

The proof of this remark is Exercise 29 of Section 5.8. We note here only that the zero of $L(U, V)$ is the zero transformation $T_0: U \to V$ defined by $T_0(\mathbf{u}) = \boldsymbol{\theta}_V$ for all $\mathbf{u}$ in U. To see this, let T be in $L(U, V)$. Then $(T+T_0)(\mathbf{u}) = T(\mathbf{u})+T_0(\mathbf{u}) = T(\mathbf{u})+\boldsymbol{\theta}_V = T(\mathbf{u})$. This shows that $T + T_0 = T$, so T_0 is the zero vector in $L(U, V)$.

Now let R_{mn} denote the vector space of $(m \times n)$ real matrices. If $\dim(U) = n$ and $\dim(V) = m$, then we can define a function $\psi: L(U, V) \to R_{mn}$ as follows: Let B and C be bases for U and V, respectively. For a transformation T in $L(U, V)$, set $\psi(T) = Q$, where Q is the matrix of T with respect to B and C. We will now show that ψ is an isomorphism. In particular, the following theorem holds.

THEOREM 21 If U and V are vector spaces such that $\dim(U) = n$ and $\dim(V) = m$, then $L(U, V)$ is isomorphic to R_{mn}.

Proof It is an immediate consequence of Theorem 19 that the function ψ defined previously is a linear transformation; that is, if S and T are in $L(U, V)$ and a is a scalar, then $\psi(S+T) = \psi(S) + \psi(T)$ and $\psi(aT) = a\psi(T)$.

To show that ψ maps $L(U, V)$ onto R_{mn}, let $Q = [q_{ij}]$ be an $(m \times n)$ matrix. Assume that $B = \{\mathbf{u}_1, \mathbf{u}_2, \dots, \mathbf{u}_n\}$ and $C = \{\mathbf{v}_1, \mathbf{v}_2, \dots, \mathbf{v}_m\}$ are the given bases for U and V, respectively. Define a subset $\{\mathbf{w}_1, \mathbf{w}_2, \dots, \mathbf{w}_n\}$ of V as follows:

$$\begin{aligned} \mathbf{w}_1 &= q_{11}\mathbf{v}_1 + q_{21}\mathbf{v}_2 + \cdots + q_{m1}\mathbf{v}_m \\ \mathbf{w}_2 &= q_{12}\mathbf{v}_1 + q_{22}\mathbf{v}_2 + \cdots + q_{m2}\mathbf{v}_m \\ &\;\;\vdots \\ \mathbf{w}_n &= q_{1n}\mathbf{v}_1 + q_{2n}\mathbf{v}_2 + \cdots + q_{mn}\mathbf{v}_m. \end{aligned} \tag{14}$$

Each vector $\mathbf{u}$ in U can be expressed uniquely in the form

$$\mathbf{u} = a_1\mathbf{u}_1 + a_2\mathbf{u}_2 + \cdots + a_n\mathbf{u}_n.$$

If $T: U \to V$ is a function defined by

$$T(\mathbf{u}) = a_1\mathbf{w}_1 + a_2\mathbf{w}_2 + \cdots + a_n\mathbf{w}_n,$$

then T is a linear transformation and $T(\mathbf{u}_j) = \mathbf{w}_j$ for each j, $1 \le j \le n$. By comparing systems (14) and (1), it becomes clear that the matrix of T with respect to B and C is Q; that is, $\psi(T) = Q$.

The proof that ψ is one to one is Exercise 33. ∎

The following example illustrates the method, described in the proof of Theorem 21, for obtaining the transformation when its matrix representation is given.

EXAMPLE 8 Let Q be the (3×4) matrix

$$Q = \begin{bmatrix} 1 & 0 & -1 & 0 \\ 0 & 1 & 1 & 0 \\ 2 & 0 & 3 & 1 \end{bmatrix}.$$

Give the formula for a linear transformation $T: \mathcal{P}_3 \to \mathcal{P}_2$ such that the matrix of T relative to the natural bases for $\mathcal{P}_3$ and $\mathcal{P}_2$ is Q.

Solution Let $B = \{1, x, x^2, x^3\}$ and let $C = \{1, x, x^2\}$. Following the proof of Theorem 21, we form a subset $\{q_0(x), q_1(x), q_2(x), q_3(x)\}$ of $\mathcal{P}_2$ by using the columns of Q. Thus

$$\begin{aligned} q_0(x) &= (1)1 + 0x + 2x^2 = 1 + 2x^2 \\ q_1(x) &= (0)1 + 1x + 0x^2 = x \\ q_2(x) &= (-1)1 + 1x + 3x^2 = -1 + x + 3x^2 \\ q_3(x) &= (0)1 + 0x + 1x^2 = x^2. \end{aligned}$$

If $p(x) = a_0 + a_1x + a_2x^2 + a_3x^3$ is an arbitrary polynomial in $\mathcal{P}_3$, then define $T: \mathcal{P}_3 \to \mathcal{P}_2$ by $T(p(x)) = a_0q_0(x) + a_1q_1(x) + a_2q_2(x) + a_3q_3(x)$. Thus

$$T(p(x)) = (a_0 - a_2) + (a_1 + a_2)x + (2a_0 + 3a_2 + a_3)x^2.$$

It is straightforward to show that T is a linear transformation. Moreover, $T(1) = q_0(x), T(x) = q_1(x), T(x^2) = q_2(x)$, and $T(x^3) = q_3(x)$. It follows that Q is the matrix of T with respect to B and C. ■

Let U and V be vector spaces such that $\dim(U) = n$ and $\dim(V) = m$. Theorem 21 implies that $L(U, V)$ and R_{mn} are essentially the same vector space. Thus, for example, we can now conclude that $L(U, V)$ has dimension mn. Furthermore, if T is a linear transformation in $L(U, V)$ and Q is the corresponding matrix in R_{mn}, then properties of T can be ascertained by studying Q. For example, a vector $\mathbf{u}$ in U is in $\mathcal{N}(T)$ if and only if $[\mathbf{u}]_B$ is in $\mathcal{N}(Q)$ and a vector $\mathbf{v}$ in V is in $\mathcal{R}(T)$ if and only if $[\mathbf{v}]_C$ is in $\mathcal{R}(Q)$. It follows that nullity(T) = nullity(Q) and rank(T) = rank(Q). In summary, the correspondence between $L(U, V)$ and R_{mn} allows both the computational and the theoretical aspects of linear transformations to be studied in the more familiar context of matrices.

5.9 EXERCISES

In Exercises 1–10, the linear transformations S, T, H are defined as follows:

$S: \mathcal{P}_3 \to \mathcal{P}_4$ is defined by $S(p) = p'(0)$.

$T: \mathcal{P}_3 \to \mathcal{P}_4$ is defined by $T(p) = (x + 2)p(x)$.

$H: \mathcal{P}_4 \to \mathcal{P}_3$ is defined by $H(p) = p'(x) + p(0)$.

Also, $B = \{1, x, x^2, x^3\}$ is the natural basis for $\mathcal{P}_3$, and $C = \{1, x, x^2, x^3, x^4\}$ is the natural basis for $\mathcal{P}_4$.

1. Find the matrix for S with respect to B and C.

2. Find the matrix for T with respect to B and C.

3. a) Use the formula for $S + T$ (see Exercise 1 of Section 5.8) to calculate the matrix of $S + T$ relative to B and C.

b) Use Theorem 19 and the matrices found in Exercises 1 and 2 to obtain the matrix representation of $S + T$.

4. a) Use the formula for $2T$ (see Exercise 2 of Section 5.8) to calculate the matrix of $2T$ with respect to B and C.

b) Use Theorem 19 and the matrix found in Exercise 2 to find the matrix for $2T$.

5. Find the matrix for H with respect to C and B.

6. a) Use the formula for $H \circ T$ (see Exercise 3 of Section 5.8) to determine the matrix of $H \circ T$ with respect to B.

---

*Exercises that are based on optional material.

b) Use Theorem 20 and the matrices obtained in Exercises 2 and 5 to obtain the matrix representation for $H \circ T$.

7. a) Use the formula for $T \circ H$ (see Exercise 4 of Section 5.8) to determine the matrix of $T \circ H$ with respect to C.

b) Use Theorem 20 and the matrices obtained in Exercises 2 and 5 to obtain the matrix representation for $T \circ H$.

8. Let $p(x) = a_0 + a_1x + a_2x^2 + a_3x^3$ be an arbitrary polynomial in $\mathcal{P}_3$.

a) Exhibit the coordinate vectors $[p]_B$ and $[S(p)]_C$.

b) If P is the matrix for S obtained in Exercise 1, demonstrate that $P[p]_B = [S(p)]_C$.

9. Let $p(x) = a_0 + a_1x + a_2x^2 + a_3x^3$ be an arbitrary polynomial in $\mathcal{P}_3$.

a) Exhibit the coordinate vectors $[p]_B$ and $[T(p)]_C$.

b) If Q is the matrix for T obtained in Exercise 2, demonstrate that $Q[p]_B = [T(p)]_C$.

10. Let N be the matrix representation obtained for H in Exercise 5. Demonstrate that $N[q]_C = [H(q)]_B$ for $q(x) = a_0 + a_1x + a_2x^2 + a_3x^3 + a_4x^4$ in $\mathcal{P}_4$.

11. Let $T: V \to V$ be the linear transformation defined in Exercise 7 of Section 5.8, and let $B = \{e^x, e^{2x}, e^{3x}\}$.

a) Find the matrix, Q, of T with respect to B.

b) Find the matrix, P, of T^{-1} with respect to B.

c) Show that $P = Q^{-1}$.

12. Let $T: V \to V$ be the linear transformation defined in Exercise 8 of Section 5.8, and let $B = \{\sin x, \cos x, e^{-x}\}$. Repeat Exercise 11.

13. Let V be the vector space of (2×2) matrices and define $T: V \to V$ by $T(A) = A^T$ (see Exercise 9 of Section 5.8). Let $B = \{E_{11}, E_{12}, E_{21}, E_{22}\}$ be the natural basis for V.

a) Find the matrix, Q, of T with respect to B.

b) For arbitrary A in V, show that $Q[A]_B = [A^T]_B$.

14. Let $S: \mathcal{P}_2 \to \mathcal{P}_3$ be given by $S(p) = x^3p'' - x^2p' + 3p$. Find the matrix representation of S with respect to the natural bases $B = \{1, x, x^2\}$ for $\mathcal{P}_2$ and $C = \{1, x, x^2, x^3\}$ for $\mathcal{P}_3$.

15. Let S be the transformation in Exercise 14, let the basis for $\mathcal{P}_2$ be $B = \{x + 1, x + 2, x^2\}$, and let the basis for $\mathcal{P}_3$ be $C = \{1, x, x^2, x^3\}$. Find the matrix representation for S.

16. Let S be the transformation in Exercise 14, let the basis for $\mathcal{P}_2$ be $B = \{1, x, x^2\}$, and let the basis for $\mathcal{P}_3$ be $D = \{3, 3x - x^2, 3x^2, x^3\}$. Find the matrix for S.

17. Let $T: \mathcal{P}_2 \to R^3$ be given by

$$T(p) = \begin{bmatrix} p(0) \\ 3p'(1) \\ p'(1) + p''(0) \end{bmatrix}.$$

Find the representation of T with respect to the natural bases for $\mathcal{P}_2$ and R^3.

18. Find the representation for the transformation in Exercise 17 with respect to the natural basis for $\mathcal{P}_2$ and the basis $\{\mathbf{u}_1, \mathbf{u}_2, \mathbf{u}_3\}$ for R^3, where

$$\mathbf{u}_1 = \begin{bmatrix} 1 \\ 0 \\ 1 \end{bmatrix}, \quad \mathbf{u}_2 = \begin{bmatrix} 0 \\ 1 \\ 1 \end{bmatrix}, \quad \text{and}$$

$$\mathbf{u}_3 = \begin{bmatrix} 1 \\ 1 \\ 1 \end{bmatrix}.$$

19. Let $T: V \to V$ be a linear transformation, where $B = \{\mathbf{v}_1, \mathbf{v}_2, \mathbf{v}_3, \mathbf{v}_4\}$ is a basis for V. Find the matrix representation of T with respect to B if $T(\mathbf{v}_1) = \mathbf{v}_2$, $T(\mathbf{v}_2) = \mathbf{v}_3$, $T(\mathbf{v}_3) = \mathbf{v}_1 + \mathbf{v}_2$, and $T(\mathbf{v}_4) = \mathbf{v}_1 + 3\mathbf{v}_4$.

20. Let $T: R^3 \to R^2$ be given by $T(\mathbf{x}) = A\mathbf{x}$, where

$$A = \begin{bmatrix} 1 & 2 & 1 \\ 3 & 0 & 4 \end{bmatrix}.$$

Find the representation of T with respect to the natural bases for R^2 and R^3.

21. Let $T: \mathcal{P}_2 \to \mathcal{P}_2$ be defined by $T(a_0 + a_1x + a_2x^2) = (-4a_0 - 2a_1) + (3a_0 + 3a_1)x + (-a_0 + 2a_1 + 3a_2)x^2$. Determine the matrix of T relative to the natural basis B for $\mathcal{P}_2$.

22. Let T be the linear transformation defined in Exercise 21. If Q is the matrix representation found in Exercise 21, show that $Q[p]_B = [T(p)]_B$ for $p(x) = a_0 + a_1x + a_2x^2$.

23. Let T be the linear transformation defined in Exercise 21. Find the matrix of T with respect to the basis $C = \{1 - 3x + 7x^2, 6 - 3x + 2x^2, x^2\}$.

24. Complete the proof of Theorem 18 by showing that Q is the unique matrix that satisfies Equation 3. [*Hint:* Suppose $P = [\mathbf{P}_1, \mathbf{P}_2, \dots, \mathbf{P}_n]$ is an $(m \times n)$ matrix such that $P[\mathbf{u}]_B = [T(\mathbf{u})]_C$ for each $\mathbf{u}$ in U. By taking $\mathbf{u}$ in B, show that $\mathbf{P}_j = \mathbf{Q}_j$ for $1 \le j \le n$.]

25. Give another proof of property 1 of Theorem 19 by constructing matrix representations for T_1, T_2, and $T_1 + T_2$.

26. Give a proof of property 2 of Theorem 19 by constructing matrix representations for T and aT.

27. Give a proof of property 2 of Theorem 19 that uses the uniqueness assertion in Theorem 18.

28. Let V be an n-dimensional vector space, and let $I_V: V \to V$ be the identity transformation on V. [Recall that $I_V(\mathbf{v}) = \mathbf{v}$ for all $\mathbf{v}$ in V.] Show that the matrix representation for I_V with respect to any basis for V is the $(n \times n)$ identity matrix I.

29. Let V be an n-dimensional vector space, and let $T_0: V \to V$ be the zero transformation in V; that is, $T_0(\mathbf{v}) = \boldsymbol{\theta}_V$ for all $\mathbf{v}$ in V. Show that the matrix representation for T_0 with respect to any basis for V is the $(n \times n)$ zero matrix.

30. Let V be an n-dimensional vector space with basis B, and let $T: V \to V$ be an invertible linear transformation. Let Q be the matrix of T with respect to B, and let P be the matrix of T^{-1} with respect to B. Prove that $P = Q^{-1}$. [*Hint:* Note that $T^{-1} \circ T = I_V$. Now apply Theorem 20 and Exercise 28.]

In Exercises 31 and 32, Q is the (3×4) matrix given by

$$Q = \begin{bmatrix} 1 & 0 & 2 & 0 \\ 0 & 1 & 0 & 1 \\ -1 & 1 & 0 & -1 \end{bmatrix}.$$

*31. Give the formula for a linear transformation $T: \mathcal{P}_3 \to \mathcal{P}_2$ such that Q is the matrix of T with respect to the natural bases for $\mathcal{P}_3$ and $\mathcal{P}_2$.

*32. Let V be the vector space of all (2×2) matrices. Give the formula for a linear transformation $S: \mathcal{P}_2 \to V$ such that Q^T is the matrix of S with respect to the natural bases for $\mathcal{P}_2$ and V.

*33. Complete the proof of Theorem 21 by showing that the mapping described in the proof of the theorem is one to one.

5.10 CHANGE OF BASIS AND DIAGONALIZATION

In Section 5.9, we saw that a linear transformation from U to V could be represented as an $(m \times n)$ matrix when $\dim(U) = n$ and $\dim(V) = m$. A consequence of this representation is that properties of transformations can be studied by examining their corresponding matrix representations. Moreover, we have a great deal of machinery in place for matrix theory; so matrices will provide a suitable analytical and computational framework for studying a linear transformation. To simplify matters somewhat, we consider only transformations from V to V, where $\dim(V) = n$. So let $T: V \to V$ be a linear transformation and suppose that Q is the matrix representation for T with respect to a basis B; that is,

$$\text{if } \mathbf{w} = T(\mathbf{u}), \quad \text{then} \quad [\mathbf{w}]_B = Q[\mathbf{u}]_B. \qquad (1)$$

As we know, when we change the basis B for V, we may change the matrix representation for T. If we are interested in the properties of T, then it is reasonable to search for a basis for V that makes the matrix representation for T as simple as possible. Finding such a basis is the subject of this section.

Diagonalizable Transformations

A particularly nice matrix to deal with computationally is a diagonal matrix. If $T: V \to V$ is a linear transformation whose matrix representation with respect to B is a diagonal matrix,

$$D = \begin{bmatrix} d_1 & 0 & 0 & \cdots & 0 \\ 0 & d_2 & 0 & \cdots & 0 \\ \vdots & & & & \vdots \\ 0 & 0 & 0 & \cdots & d_n \end{bmatrix}, \tag{2}$$

then it is easy to analyze the action of T on V, as the following example illustrates.

EXAMPLE 1 Let V be a three-dimensional vector space with basis $B = \{\mathbf{v}_1, \mathbf{v}_2, \mathbf{v}_3\}$, and suppose that $T: V \to V$ is a linear transformation with matrix

$$D = \begin{bmatrix} 2 & 0 & 0 \\ 0 & 3 & 0 \\ 0 & 0 & 0 \end{bmatrix}$$

with respect to B. Describe the action of T in terms of the basis vectors and determine bases for $\mathcal{N}(T)$ and $\mathcal{R}(T)$.

Solution It follows from the definition of D that $T(\mathbf{v}_1) = 2\mathbf{v}_1$, $T(\mathbf{v}_2) = 3\mathbf{v}_2$, and $T(\mathbf{v}_3) = \boldsymbol{\theta}$. If $\mathbf{u}$ is any vector in V and

$$\mathbf{u} = a\mathbf{v}_1 + b\mathbf{v}_2 + c\mathbf{v}_3,$$

then

$$T(\mathbf{u}) = aT(\mathbf{v}_1) + bT(\mathbf{v}_2) + cT(\mathbf{v}_3).$$

Therefore, the action of T on $\mathbf{u}$ is given by

$$T(\mathbf{u}) = 2a\mathbf{v}_1 + 3b\mathbf{v}_2.$$

It follows that $\mathbf{u}$ is in $\mathcal{N}(T)$ if and only if $a = b = 0$; that is,

$$\mathcal{N}(T) = \mathrm{Sp}\{\mathbf{v}_3\}. \tag{3}$$

Further, $\mathcal{R}(T) = \mathrm{Sp}\{T(\mathbf{v}_1), T(\mathbf{v}_2), T(\mathbf{v}_3)\}$, and since $T(\mathbf{v}_3) = \boldsymbol{\theta}$, it follows that

$$\mathcal{R}(T) = \mathrm{Sp}\{T(\mathbf{v}_1), T(\mathbf{v}_2)\} = \mathrm{Sp}\{2\mathbf{v}_1, 3\mathbf{v}_2\}. \tag{4}$$

One can easily see that the spanning sets given in Eqs. (3) and (4) are linearly independent, so they are bases for $\mathcal{N}(T)$ and $\mathcal{R}(T)$, respectively. ■

If T is a linear transformation with a matrix representation that is diagonal, then T is called ***diagonalizable***. Before characterizing diagonalizable linear transformations, we need to extend the concepts of eigenvalues and eigenvectors to the general vector-space setting. Specifically, a scalar λ is called an ***eigenvalue*** for a linear transformation $T: V \to V$ provided that there is a nonzero vector $\mathbf{v}$ in V such that $T(\mathbf{v}) = \lambda\mathbf{v}$. The vector $\mathbf{v}$ is called an ***eigenvector*** for T corresponding to λ. The following example illustrates these concepts.

EXAMPLE 2 Let $T: \mathcal{P}_2 \to \mathcal{P}_2$ be defined by

$$T(a_0 + a_1x + a_2x^2) = (2a_1 - 2a_2) + (2a_0 + 3a_2)x + 3a_2x^2.$$

Show that $C = \{1 + x, 1 - x, x + x^2\}$ is a basis of V consisting of eigenvectors for T, and exhibit the matrix of T with respect to C.

Solution It is straightforward to show that C is a basis for $\mathcal{P}_2$. Also,

$$\begin{aligned} T(1+x) &= \;\; 2+2x \;\; = \;\; 2(1+x) \\ T(1-x) &= -2+2x = -2(1-x) \\ T(x+x^2) &= \;\; 3x+3x^2 = \;\; 3(x+x^2). \end{aligned} \tag{5}$$

Thus T has eigenvalues 2, −2, and 3 with corresponding eigenvectors $1 + x$, $1 - x$, and $x + x^2$, respectively. Moreover, it follows from (5) that the matrix of T with respect to C is the (3×3) diagonal matrix

$$Q = \begin{bmatrix} 2 & 0 & 0 \\ 0 & -2 & 0 \\ 0 & 0 & 3 \end{bmatrix}.$$

In particular, T is a diagonalizable linear transformation. ∎

The linear transformation in Example 2 provides an illustration of the following general result.

THEOREM 22 Let V be an n-dimensional vector space. A linear transformation $T: V \to V$ is diagonalizable if and only if there exists a basis for V consisting of eigenvectors for T.

Proof First, suppose that $B = \{\mathbf{v}_1, \mathbf{v}_2, \ldots, \mathbf{v}_n\}$ is a basis for V consisting entirely of eigenvectors—say, $T(\mathbf{v}_1) = d_1\mathbf{v}_1$, $T(\mathbf{v}_2) = d_2\mathbf{v}_2, \ldots, T(\mathbf{v}_n) = d_n\mathbf{v}_n$. It follows that the coordinate vectors for $T(\mathbf{v}_1), T(\mathbf{v}_2), \ldots, T(\mathbf{v}_n)$ are the n-dimensional vectors

$$[T(\mathbf{v}_1)]_B = \begin{bmatrix} d_1 \\ 0 \\ \vdots \\ 0 \end{bmatrix}, \quad [T(\mathbf{v}_2)]_B = \begin{bmatrix} 0 \\ d_2 \\ \vdots \\ 0 \end{bmatrix}, \ldots, \quad [T(\mathbf{v}_n)]_B = \begin{bmatrix} 0 \\ 0 \\ \vdots \\ d_n \end{bmatrix}. \tag{6}$$

Therefore, the matrix representation for T with respect to B is the $(n \times n)$ diagonal matrix D given in (2). In particular, T is diagonalizable.

Conversely, assume that T is diagonalizable and that the matrix for T with respect to the basis $B = \{\mathbf{v}_1, \mathbf{v}_2, \ldots, \mathbf{v}_n\}$ is the diagonal matrix D given in (2). Then the coordinate vectors for $T(\mathbf{v}_1), T(\mathbf{v}_2), \ldots, T(\mathbf{v}_n)$ are given by (6), so it follows that

$$\begin{aligned} T(\mathbf{v}_1) &= d_1\mathbf{v}_1 + 0\mathbf{v}_2 + \cdots + 0\mathbf{v}_n = d_1\mathbf{v}_1 \\ T(\mathbf{v}_2) &= 0\mathbf{v}_1 + d_2\mathbf{v}_2 + \cdots + 0\mathbf{v}_n = d_2\mathbf{v}_2 \\ &\vdots \\ T(\mathbf{v}_n) &= 0\mathbf{v}_1 + 0\mathbf{v}_2 + \cdots + d_n\mathbf{v}_n = d_n\mathbf{v}_n. \end{aligned}$$

Thus B consists of eigenvectors for T. ∎

As with matrices, not every linear transformation is diagonalizable. Equivalently, if $T: V \to V$ is a linear transformation, it may be that no matter what basis we choose for V, we never obtain a matrix representation for T that is diagonal. Moreover, even if T is diagonalizable, Theorem 22 provides no procedure for calculating a basis for V consisting of eigenvectors for T. Before providing such a procedure, we will examine the relationship between matrix representations of a single transformation with respect to different bases. First we need to facilitate the process of changing bases.

The Transition Matrix

Let B and C be bases for an n-dimensional vector space V. Theorem 23, which follows, relates the coordinate vectors $[\mathbf{v}]_B$ and $[\mathbf{v}]_C$ for an arbitrary vector $\mathbf{v}$ in V. Using this theorem, we will be able to show later that if Q is the matrix of a linear transformation T with respect to B, and if P is the matrix of T relative to C, then Q and P are similar. Since we know how to determine whether a matrix is similar to a diagonal matrix, we will be able to determine when T is diagonalizable.

THEOREM 23 **Change of Basis** Let B and C be bases for the vector space V, with $B = \{\mathbf{u}_1, \mathbf{u}_2, \ldots, \mathbf{u}_n\}$, and let P be the $(n \times n)$ matrix given by $P = [\mathbf{P}_1, \mathbf{P}_2, \ldots, \mathbf{P}_n]$, where the ith column of P is

$$\mathbf{P}_i = [\mathbf{u}_i]_C. \tag{7}$$

Then P is a nonsingular matrix and

$$[\mathbf{v}]_C = P[\mathbf{v}]_B \tag{8}$$

for each vector $\mathbf{v}$ in V.

Proof Let I_V denote the identity transformation on V; that is, $I_V(\mathbf{v}) = \mathbf{v}$ for all $\mathbf{v}$ in V. Recall that the ith column of the matrix of I_V with respect to B and C is the coordinate vector $[I_V(\mathbf{u}_i)]_C$. But $I_V(\mathbf{u}_i) = \mathbf{u}_i$, so it follows that the matrix P described above is just the matrix representation of I_V with respect to B and C. It now follows from Eq. (3) of Theorem 18 that

$$P[\mathbf{v}]_B = [I_V(\mathbf{v})]_C = [\mathbf{v}]_C$$

for each $\mathbf{v}$ in V; in particular, Eq. (8) is proved. The proof that P is nonsingular is left as Exercise 17. ∎

The matrix P given in Theorem 23 is called the ***transition matrix***. Since P is nonsingular, we have, in addition to Eq. (8), the relationship

$$[\mathbf{v}]_B = P^{-1}[\mathbf{v}]_C \tag{9}$$

for each vector $\mathbf{v}$ in V. The following example illustrates the use of the transition matrix.

EXAMPLE 3 Let B and C be the bases for $\mathcal{P}_2$ given by $B = \{1, x, x^2\}$ and $C = \{1, x+1, (x+1)^2\}$. Find the transition matrix P such that

$$P[q]_B = [q]_C$$

for each polynomial $q(x)$ in $\mathcal{P}_2$.

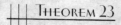

Solution Following Theorem 23, we determine the coordinates of 1, x, and x^2 in terms of 1, $x+1$, and $(x+1)^2$. This determination is easy, and we find

$$1 = 1$$
$$x = (x+1) - 1$$
$$x^2 = (x+1)^2 - 2(x+1) + 1.$$

Thus with respect to C the coordinate vectors of B are

$$[1]_C = \begin{bmatrix} 1 \\ 0 \\ 0 \end{bmatrix}, \quad [x]_C = \begin{bmatrix} -1 \\ 1 \\ 0 \end{bmatrix}, \quad \text{and} \quad [x^2]_C = \begin{bmatrix} 1 \\ -2 \\ 1 \end{bmatrix}.$$

The transition matrix P is therefore

$$P = \begin{bmatrix} 1 & -1 & 1 \\ 0 & 1 & -2 \\ 0 & 0 & 1 \end{bmatrix}.$$

In particular, any polynomial $q(x) = a_0 + a_1x + a_2x^2$ can be expressed in terms of $1, x+1$, and $(x+1)^2$ by forming $[q]_C = P[q]_B$. Forming this, we find

$$[q]_C = \begin{bmatrix} a_0 - a_1 + a_2 \\ a_1 - 2a_2 \\ a_2 \end{bmatrix}.$$

So with respect to C, we can write $q(x)$ as $q(x) = (a_0 - a_1 + a_2) + (a_1 - 2a_2)(x+1) + a_2(x+1)^2$ [a result that we can verify directly by multiplying out the new expression for $q(x)$]. ■

Matrix Representation and Change of Basis

In terms of the transition matrix, we can now state precisely the relationship between the matrix representations of a linear transformation with respect to two different bases B and C. Moreover, given a basis B, the relationship suggests how to determine a basis C such that the matrix relative to C is a simpler matrix.

THEOREM 24 Let B and C be bases for the n-dimensional vector space V, and let $T: V \to V$ be a linear transformation. If Q_1 is the matrix of T with respect to B and if Q_2 is the matrix of T with respect to C, then

$$Q_2 = P^{-1}Q_1P, \tag{10}$$

where P is the transition matrix from C to B.

Proof First note that the notation is reversed from Theorem 23; P is the transition matrix from C to B, so

$$[\mathbf{v}]_B = P[\mathbf{v}]_C \tag{11}$$

for all $\mathbf{v}$ in V. Also,

$$P^{-1}[\mathbf{w}]_B = [\mathbf{w}]_C \tag{12}$$

for each $\mathbf{w}$ in V. If $\mathbf{v}$ is in V and if $T(\mathbf{v}) = \mathbf{w}$, then (1) implies that

$$Q_1[\mathbf{v}]_B = [\mathbf{w}]_B \text{ and } Q_2[\mathbf{v}]_C = [\mathbf{w}]_C. \tag{13}$$

From the equations given in (11), (12), and (13), we obtain

$$P^{-1}Q_1P[\mathbf{v}]_C = P^{-1}Q_1[\mathbf{v}]_B = P^{-1}[\mathbf{w}]_B = [\mathbf{w}]_C;$$

that is, the matrix $P^{-1}Q_1P$ satisfies the same property as Q_2 in (13). By the uniqueness of Q_2, we conclude that $Q_2 = P^{-1}Q_1P$. ■

The following example provides an illustration of Theorem 24.

EXAMPLE 4 Let $T: \mathcal{P}_2 \to \mathcal{P}_2$ be the linear transformation given in Example 2, and let B and C be the bases for $\mathcal{P}_2$ given by $B = \{1, x, x^2\}$ and $C = \{1 + x, 1 - x, x + x^2\}$. Calculate the matrix of T with respect to B and use Theorem 24 to find the matrix of T with respect to C.

Solution Recall that T is defined by

$$T(a_0 + a_1x + a_2x^2) = (2a_1 - 2a_2) + (2a_0 + 3a_2)x + 3a_2x^2.$$

In particular, $T(1) = 2x$, $T(x) = 2$, and $T(x^2) = -2 + 3x + 3x^2$. Thus

$$[T(1)]_B = \begin{bmatrix} 0 \\ 2 \\ 0 \end{bmatrix}, \quad [T(x)]_B = \begin{bmatrix} 2 \\ 0 \\ 0 \end{bmatrix}, \quad \text{and} \quad [T(x^2)]_B = \begin{bmatrix} -2 \\ 3 \\ 3 \end{bmatrix}.$$

It follows that the matrix of T with respect to B is the matrix Q_1 given by

$$Q_1 = \begin{bmatrix} 0 & 2 & -2 \\ 2 & 0 & 3 \\ 0 & 0 & 3 \end{bmatrix}.$$

Now let P be the transition matrix from C to B; that is, $P[\mathbf{v}]_C = [\mathbf{v}]_B$ for each vector $\mathbf{v}$ in V (note that the roles of B and C are reversed from Theorem 23). By Theorem 23, P is the (3×3) matrix $P = [\mathbf{P}_1, \mathbf{P}_2, \mathbf{P}_3]$, where

$$\mathbf{P}_1 = [1 + x]_B, \quad \mathbf{P}_2 = [1 - x]_B, \quad \text{and} \quad \mathbf{P}_3 = [x + x^2]_B.$$

Thus P is given by

$$P = \begin{bmatrix} 1 & 1 & 0 \\ 1 & -1 & 1 \\ 0 & 0 & 1 \end{bmatrix}.$$

The inverse of P can be easily be calculated and is given by

$$P^{-1} = (1/2)\begin{bmatrix} 1 & 1 & -1 \\ 1 & -1 & 1 \\ 0 & 0 & 2 \end{bmatrix}.$$

By Theorem 24, the matrix of T with respect to C is the matrix Q_2 determined by $Q_2 = P^{-1}Q_1P$. This yields

$$Q_2 = \begin{bmatrix} 2 & 0 & 0 \\ 0 & -2 & 0 \\ 0 & 0 & 3 \end{bmatrix}.$$

Although the preceding example serves to illustrate the statement of Theorem 2, a comparison of Examples 2 and 4 makes it clear that when the basis C is given, it may be easier to calculate the matrix of T with respect to C directly from the definition. Theorem 24, however, suggests the following idea: If we are given a linear transformation $T: V \to V$ and the matrix representation, Q, for T with respect to a given basis B, then we should look for a simple matrix R (diagonal if possible) that is similar to Q, $R = S^{-1}QS$. In this case we can use S^{-1} as a transition matrix to obtain a new basis C for V, where $[\mathbf{u}]_C = S^{-1}[\mathbf{u}]_B$. With respect to the basis C, T will have the matrix representation R, where $R = S^{-1}QS$.

Given the transition matrix S^{-1}, it is an easy matter to find the actual basis vectors of C. In particular, suppose that $B = \{\mathbf{u}_1, \mathbf{u}_2, \ldots, \mathbf{u}_n\}$ is the given basis for V, and we wish to find vectors in $C = \{\mathbf{v}_1, \mathbf{v}_2, \ldots, \mathbf{v}_n\}$. Since $[\mathbf{u}]_C = S^{-1}[\mathbf{u}]_B$ for all $\mathbf{u}$ in V, we know that $S[\mathbf{u}]_C = [\mathbf{u}]_B$. Moreover, with respect to C, $[\mathbf{v}_i]_C = \mathbf{e}_i$. So from $S[\mathbf{v}_i]_C = [\mathbf{v}_i]_B$ we obtain

$$S\mathbf{e}_i = [\mathbf{v}_i]_B, \quad 1 \le i \le n. \tag{14}$$

But if $S = [\mathbf{S}_1, \mathbf{S}_2, \ldots, \mathbf{S}_n]$, then $S\mathbf{e}_i = \mathbf{S}_i$, and Eq. (14) tells us that the coordinate vector of $\mathbf{v}_i$ with respect to the known basis B is the ith column of S. The procedure just described can be summarized as follows:

Summary

Let $T: V \to V$ be a linear transformation and let $B = \{\mathbf{u}_1, \mathbf{u}_2, \ldots, \mathbf{u}_n\}$ be a given basis for V.

Step 1. Calculate the matrix, Q, for T with respect to the basis B.

Step 2. Use matrix techniques to find a "simple" matrix R and a nonsingular matrix S such that $R = S^{-1}QS$.

Step 3. Determine vectors $\mathbf{v}_1, \mathbf{v}_2, \ldots, \mathbf{v}_n$ in V so that $[\mathbf{v}_i]_B = \mathbf{S}_i$, $1 \le i \le n$, where $\mathbf{S}_i$ is the ith column of S.

Then $C = \{\mathbf{v}_1, \mathbf{v}_2, \ldots, \mathbf{v}_n\}$ is a basis for V and R is the matrix of T with respect to C.

The case of particular interest is the one in which Q is similar to a diagonal matrix R. In this case, if we choose $\{\mathbf{S}_1, \mathbf{S}_2, \ldots, \mathbf{S}_n\}$ to be a basis of R^n consisting of eigenvectors for Q, then

$$R = S^{-1}QS = \begin{bmatrix} d_1 & 0 & \cdots & 0 \\ 0 & d_2 & \cdots & 0 \\ \vdots & & & \vdots \\ 0 & 0 & \cdots & d_n \end{bmatrix},$$

where $d_1, d_2, \ldots, d_n$ are the (not necessarily distinct) eigenvalues for Q and where $Q\mathbf{S}_i = d_i\mathbf{S}_i$. Since R is the matrix of T with respect to C, $C = \{\mathbf{v}_1, \mathbf{v}_2, \ldots, \mathbf{v}_n\}$ is a basis of V consisting of eigenvectors for T; specifically, $T(\mathbf{v}_i) = d_i\mathbf{v}_i$ for $1 \le i \le n$. The following example provides an illustration.

EXAMPLE 5 Show that the differential operator $T: \mathcal{P}_2 \to \mathcal{P}_2$ defined by $T(p) = x^2p'' + (2x-1)p' + 3p$ is diagonalizable.

Solution With respect to the basis $B = \{1, x, x^2\}$, T has the matrix representation

$$Q = \begin{bmatrix} 3 & -1 & 0 \\ 0 & 5 & -2 \\ 0 & 0 & 9 \end{bmatrix}.$$

Since Q is triangular, we see that the eigenvalues are 3, 5, and 9; and since Q has distinct eigenvalues, Q can be diagonalized where the matrix S of eigenvectors will diagonalize Q.

We calculate the eigenvectors $\mathbf{u}_1, \mathbf{u}_2, \mathbf{u}_3$ for Q and form $S = [\mathbf{u}_1, \mathbf{u}_2, \mathbf{u}_3]$, which yields

$$S = \begin{bmatrix} 1 & 1 & 1 \\ 0 & -2 & -6 \\ 0 & 0 & 12 \end{bmatrix}.$$

In this case it follows that

$$S^{-1}QS = \begin{bmatrix} 3 & 0 & 0 \\ 0 & 5 & 0 \\ 0 & 0 & 9 \end{bmatrix} = R.$$

In view of our remarks above, R is the matrix representation for T with respect to the basis $C = \{\mathbf{v}_1, \mathbf{v}_2, \mathbf{v}_3\}$, where $[\mathbf{v}_i]_B = \mathbf{S}_i$, or

$$[\mathbf{v}_1]_B = \begin{bmatrix} 1 \\ 0 \\ 0 \end{bmatrix}, \quad [\mathbf{v}_2]_B = \begin{bmatrix} 1 \\ -2 \\ 0 \end{bmatrix}, \quad \text{and} \quad [\mathbf{v}_3]_B = \begin{bmatrix} 1 \\ -6 \\ 12 \end{bmatrix}.$$

Therefore, the basis C is given precisely as $C = \{1, 1-2x, 1-6x+12x^2\}$. Moreover, it is easy to see that $T(\mathbf{v}_1) = 3\mathbf{v}_1$, $T(\mathbf{v}_2) = 5\mathbf{v}_2$, and $T(\mathbf{v}_3) = 9\mathbf{v}_3$, where $\mathbf{v}_1 = 1$, $\mathbf{v}_2 = 1-2x$, and $\mathbf{v}_3 = 1 - 6x + 12x^2$. ■

5.10 EXERCISES

1. Let $T: R^2 \to R^2$ be defined by

$$T\left(\begin{bmatrix} x_1 \\ x_2 \end{bmatrix}\right) = \begin{bmatrix} 2x_1 + x_2 \\ x_1 + 2x_2 \end{bmatrix}.$$

Define $\mathbf{u}_1, \mathbf{u}_2$ in R^2 by

$$\mathbf{u}_1 = \begin{bmatrix} -1 \\ 1 \end{bmatrix} \quad \text{and} \quad \mathbf{u}_2 = \begin{bmatrix} 1 \\ 1 \end{bmatrix}.$$

Show that $C = \{\mathbf{u}_1, \mathbf{u}_2\}$ is a basis of R^2 consisting of eigenvectors for T. Calculate the matrix of T with respect to C.

2. Let $T: \mathcal{P}_2 \to \mathcal{P}_2$ be defined by

$$T(a_0 + a_1x + a_2x^2) = (2a_0 - a_1 - a_2) + (a_0 - a_2)x + (-a_0 + a_1 + 2a_2)x^2.$$

Show that $C = \{1+x-x^2, 1+x^2, 1+x\}$ is a basis of $\mathcal{P}_2$ consisting of eigenvectors for T, and find the matrix of T with respect to C.

3. Let V be the vector space of (2×2) matrices, and let $T: V \to V$ be defined by

$$T\left(\begin{bmatrix} a & b \\ c & d \end{bmatrix}\right) = \begin{bmatrix} -3a+5d & 3b-5c \\ -2c & 2d \end{bmatrix}.$$

If $C = \{A_1, A_2, A_3, A_4\}$, where

$$A_1 = \begin{bmatrix} 1 & 0 \\ 0 & 1 \end{bmatrix}, \quad A_2 = \begin{bmatrix} 0 & 1 \\ 1 & 0 \end{bmatrix},$$

$$A_3 = \begin{bmatrix} 0 & 1 \\ 0 & 0 \end{bmatrix}, \quad \text{and} \quad A_4 = \begin{bmatrix} 1 & 0 \\ 0 & 0 \end{bmatrix},$$

then show that C is a basis of V consisting of eigenvectors for T. Find the matrix of T with respect to C.

4. Let C be the basis for R^2 given in Exercise 1, and let B be the natural basis for R^2. Find the transition matrix and represent the following vectors in terms of C:

$$\mathbf{a} = \begin{bmatrix} 4 \\ 2 \end{bmatrix}, \quad \mathbf{b} = \begin{bmatrix} -2 \\ 0 \end{bmatrix},$$

$$\mathbf{c} = \begin{bmatrix} 9 \\ 5 \end{bmatrix}, \quad \text{and} \quad \mathbf{d} = \begin{bmatrix} a \\ b \end{bmatrix}.$$

5. Let C be the basis for $\mathcal{P}_2$ given in Exercise 2 and let $B = \{1, x, x^2\}$. Find the transition matrix and represent the following polynomials in terms of C:

$$p(x) = 2 + x, \quad q(x) = -1 + 2x + 2x^2,$$

$$s(x) = -1 + x^2, \quad \text{and} \quad r(x) = a_0 + a_1x + a_2x^2.$$

6. Let V be the vector space of (2×2) matrices, and let C be the basis given in Exercise 3. If B is the natural basis for V, $B = \{E_{11}, E_{12}, E_{21}, E_{22}\}$, then find the transition matrix and express the following matrices in terms of the vectors in C:

$$A = \begin{bmatrix} 1 & 2 \\ 3 & 4 \end{bmatrix}, \quad B = \begin{bmatrix} -1 & 1 \\ 0 & 3 \end{bmatrix}, \quad \text{and}$$

$$C = \begin{bmatrix} a & b \\ c & d \end{bmatrix}.$$

7. Find the transition matrix for R^2 when $B = \{\mathbf{u}_1, \mathbf{u}_2\}$ and $C = \{\mathbf{w}_1, \mathbf{w}_2\}$:

$$\mathbf{w}_1 = \begin{bmatrix} 2 \\ 1 \end{bmatrix}, \quad \mathbf{w}_2 = \begin{bmatrix} 1 \\ 2 \end{bmatrix},$$

$$\mathbf{u}_1 = \begin{bmatrix} 1 \\ 1 \end{bmatrix}, \quad \text{and} \quad \mathbf{u}_2 = \begin{bmatrix} 3 \\ 1 \end{bmatrix}.$$

8. Repeat Exercise 7 for the basis vectors

$$\mathbf{w}_1 = \begin{bmatrix} 4 \\ 3 \end{bmatrix}, \quad \mathbf{w}_2 = \begin{bmatrix} 2 \\ 3 \end{bmatrix},$$

$$\mathbf{u}_1 = \begin{bmatrix} 4 \\ 1 \end{bmatrix}, \quad \text{and} \quad \mathbf{u}_2 = \begin{bmatrix} 2 \\ 1 \end{bmatrix}.$$

9. Let $B = \{1, x, x^2, x^3\}$ and $C = \{x, x+1, x^2 - 2x, x^3 + 3\}$ be bases for $\mathcal{P}_3$. Find the transition matrix and use it to represent the following in terms of C:

$$p(x) = x^2 - 7x + 2, \quad q(x) = x^3 + 9x - 1,$$

$$\text{and} \quad r(x) = x^3 - 2x^2 + 6.$$

10. Represent the following quadratic polynomials in the form $a_0 + a_1x + a_2x(x-1)$ by constructing the appropriate transition matrix:

$$p(x) = x^2 + 5x - 3, \quad q(x) = 2x^2 - 6x + 8,$$

$$\text{and} \quad r(x) = x^2 - 5$$

11. Let $T: R^2 \to R^2$ be the linear transformation defined in Exercise 1. Find the matrix of T with respect to the natural basis $B = \{\mathbf{e}_1, \mathbf{e}_2\}$. If C is the basis for R^2 given in Exercise 1, use Theorem 24 to calculate the matrix of T with respect to C.

12. Let $T: \mathcal{P}_2 \to \mathcal{P}_2$ be the linear transformation given in Exercise 2. Find the matrix representation of T with respect to the natural basis $B = \{1, x, x^2\}$ and then use Theorem 24 to calculate the matrix of T relative to the basis C given in Exercise 2.

13. Let V and T be as in Exercise 3. Find the matrix representation of T with respect to the natural basis $B = \{E_{11}, E_{12}, E_{21}, E_{22}\}$. If C is the basis for V given in Exercise 3, use Theorem 24 to determine the matrix of T with respect to C.

In Exercises 14–16, proceed through the following steps:

a) Find the matrix, Q, of T with respect to the natural basis B for V.

b) Show that Q is similar to a diagonal matrix; that is, find a nonsingular matrix S and a diagonal matrix R such that $R = S^{-1}QS$.

c) Exhibit a basis C of V such that R is the matrix representation of T with respect to C.

d) Calculate the transition matrix, P, from B to C.

e) Use the transition matrix P and the formula $R[\mathbf{v}]_C = [T(\mathbf{v})]_C$ to calculate $T(\mathbf{w}_1)$, $T(\mathbf{w}_2)$, and $T(\mathbf{w}_3)$.

14. $V = \mathcal{P}_1$ and $T: V \to V$ is defined by $T(a_0+a_1x) = (4a_0 + 3a_1) + (-2a_0 - 3a_1)x$. Also,

$$\mathbf{w}_1 = 2 + 3x, \quad \mathbf{w}_2 = -1 + x, \quad \text{and}$$

$$\mathbf{w}_3 = x.$$

15. $V = \mathcal{P}_2$ and $T: V \to V$ is defined by $T(p) = xp'' + (x + 1)p' + p$. Also,

$$\mathbf{w}_1 = -8 + 7x + x^2, \quad \mathbf{w}_2 = 5 + x^2, \quad \text{and}$$

$$\mathbf{w}_3 = 4 - 3x + 2x^2.$$

16. V is the vector space of (2×2) matrices and $T: V \to V$ is given by

$$T\left(\begin{bmatrix} a & b \\ c & d \end{bmatrix}\right) = \begin{bmatrix} a - b & 2b - 2c \\ 5c - 3d & 10d \end{bmatrix}.$$

Also,

$$\mathbf{w}_1 = \begin{bmatrix} 0 & 3 \\ 0 & 1 \end{bmatrix}, \quad \mathbf{w}_2 = \begin{bmatrix} 2 & -3 \\ 1 & 0 \end{bmatrix}, \quad \text{and}$$

$$\mathbf{w}_3 = \begin{bmatrix} 8 & -7 \\ 0 & 2 \end{bmatrix}.$$

17. Complete the proof of Theorem 23 by showing that the transition matrix P is nonsingular. [*Hint:* We have already noted in the proof of Theorem 23 that P is the matrix representation of I_V with respect to the bases B and C. Let Q be the matrix representation of I_V with respect to C and B. Now apply Theorem 20 with $T = S = I_V$.]

18. Let V be an n-dimensional vector space with basis B, and assume that $T: V \to V$ is a linear transformation with matrix representation Q relative to B.

a) If $\mathbf{v}$ is an eigenvector for T associated with the eigenvalue λ, then prove that $[\mathbf{v}]_B$ is an eigenvector for Q associated with λ.

b) If the vector $\mathbf{x}$ in R^n is an eigenvector for Q corresponding to the eigenvalue λ and if $\mathbf{v}$ in V is a vector such that $[\mathbf{v}]_B = \mathbf{x}$, prove that $\mathbf{v}$ is an eigenvector for T corresponding to the eigenvalue λ. [*Hint:* Make use of Eq. (1).]

19. Let $T: V \to V$ be a linear transformation, and let λ be an eigenvalue for T. Show that λ^2 is an eigenvalue for $T^2 = T \circ T$.

20. Prove that a linear transformation $T: V \to V$ is one to one if and only if zero is not an eigenvalue for T. [*Hint:* Use Theorem 14, property 4, of Section 5.7.]

21. Let $T: V \to V$ be an invertible linear transformation. If λ is an eigenvalue for T, prove that λ^{-1} is an eigenvalue for T^{-1}. (Note that $\lambda \neq 0$ by Exercise 20.)

SUPPLEMENTARY EXERCISES

1. Let V be the set of all (2×2) matrices with real entries and with the usual operation of addition. Suppose, however, that scalar multiplication in V is defined by

$$k\begin{bmatrix} a & b \\ c & d \end{bmatrix} = \begin{bmatrix} ka & 0 \\ 0 & kd \end{bmatrix}.$$

Determine whether V is a real vector space.

2. Recall that $\mathcal{F}(R)$ denotes the set of all functions from R to R; that is, $\mathcal{F}(R) = \{f: R \to R\}$. A function g in $\mathcal{F}(R)$ is called an even function if $g(-x) = g(x)$ for every x in R. Prove that the set of all even functions in $\mathcal{F}(R)$ is a subspace of $\mathcal{F}(R)$.

3. In each of parts a)–c), show that the set S is linearly dependent, and write one of the vectors in S as a linear combination of the remaining vectors.

a) $S = \{A_1, A_2, A_3, A_4\}$, where

$$A_1 = \begin{bmatrix} 1 & 0 \\ -1 & 1 \end{bmatrix}, \quad A_2 = \begin{bmatrix} -1 & 1 \\ 0 & 1 \end{bmatrix},$$

$$A_3 = \begin{bmatrix} -1 & 3 \\ -2 & 5 \end{bmatrix}, \text{ and } A_4 = \begin{bmatrix} -3 & 2 \\ 2 & 0 \end{bmatrix}.$$

b) $S = \{p_1(x), p_2(x), p_3(x), p_4(x)\}$, where $p_1(x) = 1 - x^2 + x^3$, $p_2(x) = -1 + x + x^3$, $p_3(x) = -1 + 3x - 2x^2 + 5x^3$, and $p_4(x) = -3 + 2x + 2x^2$.

c) $S = \{\mathbf{v}_1, \mathbf{v}_2, \mathbf{v}_3, \mathbf{v}_4\}$, where

$$\mathbf{v}_1 = \begin{bmatrix} 1 \\ 0 \\ -1 \\ 1 \end{bmatrix}, \quad \mathbf{v}_2 = \begin{bmatrix} -1 \\ 1 \\ 0 \\ 1 \end{bmatrix},$$

$$\mathbf{v}_3 = \begin{bmatrix} -1 \\ 3 \\ -2 \\ 5 \end{bmatrix}, \text{ and } \mathbf{v}_4 = \begin{bmatrix} -3 \\ 2 \\ 2 \\ 0 \end{bmatrix}.$$

4. Let W be the subspace of the set of (2×2) real matrices defined by

$$W = \{A = \begin{bmatrix} a & b \\ c & d \end{bmatrix}: a - 2b + 3c + d = 0\}.$$

a) Exhibit a basis B for W.

b) Find a matrix A in W such that $[A]_B = [2, 1, -2]^T$.

5. In $\mathcal{P}_2$, let $S = \{p_1(x), p_2(x), p_3(x)\}$, where $p_1(x) = 1 - x + 2x^2$, $p_2(x) = 2 + 3x + x^2$, and $p_3(x) = 1 - 6x + 5x^2$.

a) Obtain an algebraic specification for Sp(S).

b) Determine which of the following polynomials are in Sp(S):

$$q_1(x) = 5 + 5x + 4x^2, \quad q_2(x) = 5 - 5x + 8x^2,$$
$$q_3(x) = -5x + 3x^2, \quad \text{and} \quad q_4(x) = 5 + 7x^2.$$

c) Use the algebraic specification obtained in part a) to determine a basis, B, of Sp(S).

d) For each polynomial $q_i(x)$, $i = 1, 2, 3, 4$, given in part b), if $q_i(x)$ is in Sp(S), then find $[q_i(x)]_B$.

6. In parts a)–c), find a subset of S that is a basis for Sp(S). Express each element of S that does not appear in the basis as a linear combination of the basis vectors.

a) $S = \{A_1, A_2, A_3, A_4, A_5\}$, where

$$A_1 = \begin{bmatrix} 1 & -2 \\ 1 & -1 \end{bmatrix}, \quad A_2 = \begin{bmatrix} 2 & -3 \\ 4 & -3 \end{bmatrix},$$

$$A_3 = \begin{bmatrix} -1 & 1 \\ -3 & 2 \end{bmatrix}, \quad A_4 = \begin{bmatrix} 1 & -1 \\ 4 & 0 \end{bmatrix}, \text{ and}$$

$$A_5 = \begin{bmatrix} 12 & -17 \\ 30 & -11 \end{bmatrix}.$$

b) $S = \{p_1(x), p_2(x), p_3(x), p_4(x), p_5(x)\}$, where

$$p_1(x) = 1 - 2x + x^2 - x^3,$$
$$p_2(x) = 2 - 3x + 4x^2 - 3x^3,$$
$$p_3(x) = -1 + x - 3x^2 + 2x^3,$$
$$p_4(x) = 1 - x + 4x^2, \quad \text{and}$$
$$p_5(x) = 12 - 17x + 30x^2 - 11x^3$$

c) $S = \{f_1(x), f_2(x), f_3(x), f_4(x), f_5(x)\}$, where

$$f_1(x) = e^x - 2e^{2x} + e^{3x} - e^{4x},$$
$$f_2(x) = 2e^x - 3e^{2x} + 4e^{3x} - 3e^{4x},$$
$$f_3(x) = -e^x + e^{2x} - 3e^{3x} + 2e^{4x},$$
$$f_4(x) = e^x - e^{2x} + 4e^{3x}, \quad \text{and}$$
$$f_5(x) = 12e^x - 17e^{2x} + 30e^{3x} - 11e^{4x}$$

In Exercises 7–11, use the fact that the matrix

$$[A \mid \mathbf{b}] = \left[\begin{array}{rrrrrr|c} 1 & -1 & 3 & 1 & 3 & 2 & a \\ 1 & 0 & 2 & 3 & 2 & 3 & b \\ 0 & -2 & 2 & -4 & 3 & 0 & c \\ 2 & -1 & 5 & 4 & 6 & 7 & d \end{array}\right]$$

is row equivalent to

$$\left[\begin{array}{cccccc|c} 1 & 0 & 2 & 3 & 0 & -1 & 4a-3b-2c \\ 0 & 1 & -1 & 2 & 0 & 3 & -3a+3b+c \\ 0 & 0 & 0 & 0 & 1 & 2 & -2a+2b+c \\ 0 & 0 & 0 & 0 & 0 & 0 & a-3b-c+d \end{array}\right].$$

7. Find a basis for Sp$\{A_1, A_2, A_3, A_4\}$, where

$$A_1 = \begin{bmatrix} 1 & -1 & 3 \\ 1 & 3 & 2 \end{bmatrix}, \quad A_2 = \begin{bmatrix} 1 & 0 & 2 \\ 3 & 2 & 3 \end{bmatrix},$$

$$A_3 = \begin{bmatrix} 0 & -2 & 2 \\ -4 & 3 & 0 \end{bmatrix}, \quad \text{and} \quad A_4 = \begin{bmatrix} 2 & -1 & 5 \\ 4 & 6 & 7 \end{bmatrix}.$$

8. Let $S = \{p_1(x), p_2(x), p_3(x), p_4(x), p_5(x), p_6(x)\}$, where

$$p_1(x) = 1 + x + 2x^3,$$
$$p_2(x) = -1 - 2x^2 - x^3,$$
$$p_3(x) = 3 + 2x + 2x^2 + 5x^3,$$
$$p_4(x) = 1 + 3x - 4x^2 + 4x^3,$$
$$p_5(x) = 3 + 2x + 3x^2 + 6x^3, \quad \text{and}$$
$$p_6(x) = 2 + 3x + 7x^3.$$

Find a subset of S that is a basis for Sp(S).

9. Let S be the set of polynomials given in Exercise 8. Show that $q(x) = 1 + 2x - x^2 + 4x^3$ is in Sp(S), and express $q(x)$ as a linear combination of the basis vector found in Exercise 8.

10. If

$$S = \left\{ \begin{bmatrix} 1 & 1 \\ 0 & 2 \end{bmatrix}, \begin{bmatrix} -1 & 0 \\ -2 & -1 \end{bmatrix}, \begin{bmatrix} 3 & 2 \\ 2 & 5 \end{bmatrix}, \begin{bmatrix} 1 & 3 \\ -4 & 4 \end{bmatrix}, \begin{bmatrix} 3 & 2 \\ 3 & 6 \end{bmatrix}, \begin{bmatrix} 2 & 3 \\ 0 & 7 \end{bmatrix} \right\},$$

then give an algebraic specification for Sp(S) and use the specification to determine a basis for Sp(S).

11. Let V be the vector space for all (2×3) matrices, and suppose that $T: V \to \mathcal{P}_3$ is the linear transformation defined by

$$T\left(\begin{bmatrix} a_{11} & a_{12} & a_{13} \\ a_{21} & a_{22} & a_{23} \end{bmatrix}\right)$$
$$= (a_{11} - a_{12} + 3a_{13} + a_{21} + 3a_{22} + 2a_{23})$$
$$+ (a_{11} + 2a_{13} + 3a_{21} + 2a_{22} + 3a_{23})x$$
$$+ (-2a_{12} + 2a_{13} - 4a_{21} + 3a_{22})x^2$$
$$+ (2a_{11} - a_{12} + 5a_{13} + 4a_{21} + 6a_{22} + 7a_{23})x^3.$$

a) Calculate the matrix of T relative to the natural bases B and C for V and $\mathcal{P}_3$, respectively.
b) Determine the rank and the nullity of T.
c) Give an algebraic specification for $\mathcal{R}(T)$ and use the specification to determine a basis for $\mathcal{R}(T)$.
d) Show that $q(x) = 1 + 2x - x^2 + 4x^3$ is in $\mathcal{R}(T)$ and find a matrix A in V such that $T(A) = q(x)$.
e) Find a basis for $\mathcal{N}(T)$.

12. Show that there is a linear transformation $T: R^2 \to \mathcal{P}_2$ such that

$$T\left(\begin{bmatrix} 0 \\ 1 \end{bmatrix}\right) = 1 + 2x + x^2 \quad \text{and}$$

$$T\left(\begin{bmatrix} -1 \\ 1 \end{bmatrix}\right) = 2 - x.$$

Give a formula for

$$T\left(\begin{bmatrix} a \\ b \end{bmatrix}\right).$$

13. Show that there are infinitely many linear transformations $T: \mathcal{P}_2 \to R^2$ such that

$$T(x) = \begin{bmatrix} 1 \\ 0 \end{bmatrix} \quad \text{and} \quad T(x^2) = \begin{bmatrix} 0 \\ 1 \end{bmatrix}.$$

Give a formula for $T(a + bx + cx^2)$ for one such linear transformation.

14. Let V be the vector space of (2×2) matrices, and let $T: V \to \mathcal{P}_2$ be the linear transformation defined by

$$T\left(\begin{bmatrix} a & b \\ c & d \end{bmatrix}\right) = (a - b + c - 4d) + (b + c + 3d)x + (a + 2c - d)x^2.$$

a) Find the matrix of T relative to the natural bases, B and C, for V and $\mathcal{P}_2$, respectively.

b) Give an algebraic specification for $\mathcal{R}(T)$ and use the specification to obtain a basis S for $\mathcal{R}(T)$.

c) For each polynomial $q(x)$ in S, find a matrix A in V such that $T(A) = q(x)$. Let B_1 denote the set of matrices found.

d) Find a basis, B_2, for $\mathcal{N}(T)$.

e) Show that $B_1 \cup B_2$ is a basis for V.

(*Note:* This exercise illustrates the proof that $\text{rank}(T) + \text{nullity}(T) = \dim(V)$.)

CONCEPTUAL EXERCISES

In Exercises 1–10, answer true or false. Justify your answer by providing a counterexample if the statement is false or an outline of a proof if the statement is true.

1. If a is a nonzero scalar and $\mathbf{u}$ and $\mathbf{v}$ are vectors in a vector space V such that $a\mathbf{u} = a\mathbf{v}$, then $\mathbf{u} = \mathbf{v}$.

2. If $\mathbf{v}$ is a nonzero vector in a vector space V and a and b are scalars such that $a\mathbf{v} = b\mathbf{v}$, then $a = b$.

3. Every vector space V contains a unique vector called the additive inverse of V.

4. If V consists of all real polynomials of degree exactly n together with the zero polynomial, then V is a vector space.

5. If W is a subspace of the vector space V and $\dim(W) = \dim(V) = n$, then $W = V$.

6. If $\dim(V) = n$ and W is a subspace of V, then $\dim(W) \le n$.

7. The subset $\{\boldsymbol{\theta}\}$ of a vector space is linearly dependent.

8. Let S_1 and S_2 be subsets of a vector space V such that $S_1 \subseteq S_2$. If S_1 is linearly dependent, then so is S_2.

9. Let S_1 and S_2 be subsets of a vector space V such that $S_1 \subseteq S_2$. If S_1 is linearly independent, then so is S_2.

10. Suppose that $S_1 = \{\mathbf{v}_1, \ldots, \mathbf{v}_k\}$ and $S_2 = \{\mathbf{w}_1, \ldots, \mathbf{w}_l\}$ are subsets of a vector space V. If $V = \text{Sp}(S_1)$ and S_2 is linearly independent, then $l \le k$.

In Exercises 11–19, give a brief answer.

11. Let W be a subspace of the vector space V. If $\mathbf{u}$ and $\mathbf{v}$ are elements of V such that $\mathbf{u} + \mathbf{v}$ and $\mathbf{u} - \mathbf{v}$ are in W, show that $\mathbf{u}$ and $\mathbf{v}$ are in W.

12. Let W be a subset of a vector space V that satisfies the following properties:

i) $\boldsymbol{\theta}$ is in W.

ii) If $\mathbf{x}$ and $\mathbf{y}$ are in W and a is a scalar, then $a\mathbf{x} + \mathbf{y}$ is in W. Prove that W is a subspace of V.

13. If W is a subspace of a vector space V, show that $\text{Sp}(W) = W$.

14. Give examples of subsets of S_1 and S_2 of a vector space V such that $\text{Sp}(S_1) \cap \text{Sp}(S_2) \ne \text{Sp}(S_1 \cap S_2)$.

15. If U and W are subspaces of a vector space V, then $U + W = \{\mathbf{u} + \mathbf{w}\colon \mathbf{u} \text{ is in } U \text{ and } \mathbf{w} \text{ is in } W\}$.

a) Prove that $U + W$ is a subspace of V.

b) Let $S_1 = \{\mathbf{x}_1, \ldots, \mathbf{x}_m\}$ and $S_2 = \{\mathbf{y}_1, \ldots, \mathbf{y}_n\}$ be subsets of V. Show that $\text{Sp}(S_1 \cup S_2) = \text{Sp}(S_1) + \text{Sp}(S_2)$.

16. Let $B = \{\mathbf{v}_1, \ldots, \mathbf{v}_n\}$ be a basis for a vector space V, and let $\mathbf{v}$ be a nonzero vector in V. Prove that there exists a vector $\mathbf{v}_j$ in B, $1 \le j \le n$, such that $\mathbf{v}_j$ can be replaced by $\mathbf{v}$ and the resulting set, B', is still a basis for V.

17. Let $B = \{\mathbf{v}_1, \ldots, \mathbf{v}_n\}$ be a basis for a vector space V, and let $S: V \to W$ and $T: V \to W$ be linear transformations such that $S(\mathbf{v}_i) = T(\mathbf{v}_i)$ for $i = 1, 2, \ldots, n$. Show that $S = T$.

18. Let $T: V \to W$ be a linear transformation.

a) If T is one to one, then show that T carries linearly independent subsets of V to linearly independent subsets of W.

b) If T carries linearly independent subsets of V to linearly independent subsets of W, then prove that T is one to one.

19. Give an example of a linear transformation $T: R^2 \to R^2$ such that $\mathcal{N}(T) = \mathcal{R}(T)$.

MATLAB EXERCISES

In these exercises we expand on least-squares approximation of functions, an important topic introduced in Section 5.6. As an inner-product space, we use $C[a, b]$ with an inner product given by

$$\langle f, g \rangle = \int_a^b w(x) f(x) g(x)\, dx.$$

For the inner product just defined, $y = w(x)$ denotes a function that is positive and continuous on (a, b); the function w is called a ***weight function***.

Let $y = f(x)$ denote a function we wish to approximate. Let $y = p^*(x)$ denote the best approximation to f in $\mathcal{P}_n$. In particular, if $y = q(x)$ is any polynomial in $\mathcal{P}_n$, then we have

$$\int_a^b w(x)[f(x) - p^*(x)]^2\, dx \leq \int_a^b w(x)[f(x) - q(x)]^2\, dx. \tag{1}$$

By Theorem 12, the best approximation p^* is characterized by the condition:

$$\langle f - p^*, q \rangle = 0, \quad \text{for all } q \text{ in } \mathcal{P}_n.$$

Let $\{q_j\}_{j=0}^n$ be any basis for $\mathcal{P}_n$. The preceding condition can be replaced by the set of $n + 1$ equations $\langle f - p^*, q_j \rangle = 0$, $j = 0, 1, \ldots, n$. Equivalently, p^* is characterized by

$$\langle p^*, q_j \rangle = \langle f, q_j \rangle,\ j = 0, 1, \ldots, n. \tag{2}$$

Now, suppose that p^* has the following representation in terms of the basis:

$$p^*(x) = a_0 q_0(x) + a_1 q_1(x) + \cdots + a_n q_n(x).$$

Inserting this representation into Eq. (2), we obtain a system of $n + 1$ equations in the $n + 1$ unknowns $a_0, a_1, \ldots, a_n$:

$$\begin{aligned}
a_0\langle q_0, q_0\rangle + a_1\langle q_1, q_0\rangle + \cdots + a_n\langle q_n, q_0\rangle &= \langle f, q_0\rangle \\
a_0\langle q_0, q_1\rangle + a_1\langle q_1, q_1\rangle + \cdots + a_n\langle q_n, q_1\rangle &= \langle f, q_1\rangle \\
&\ \ \vdots \\
a_0\langle q_0, q_n\rangle + a_1\langle q_1, q_n\rangle + \cdots + a_n\langle q_n, q_n\rangle &= \langle f, q_n\rangle
\end{aligned} \tag{3}$$

The equations above are called the ***normal equations,*** and the coefficient matrix for the system is known as the ***Gram matrix***. For notation, let us denote the system (3) by

$$G\mathbf{a} = \mathbf{f} \tag{4}$$

where

$$G = \begin{bmatrix} \langle q_0, q_0 \rangle & \langle q_1, q_0 \rangle & \cdots & \langle q_n, q_0 \rangle \\ \langle q_0, q_1 \rangle & \langle q_1, q_1 \rangle & \cdots & \langle q_n, q_1 \rangle \\ \vdots & & & \vdots \\ \langle q_0, q_n \rangle & \langle q_1, q_n \rangle & \cdots & \langle q_n, q_n \rangle \end{bmatrix}, \quad \mathbf{a} = \begin{bmatrix} a_0 \\ a_1 \\ \vdots \\ a_n \end{bmatrix}, \quad \mathbf{f} = \begin{bmatrix} \langle f, q_0 \rangle \\ \langle f, q_1 \rangle \\ \vdots \\ \langle f, q_n \rangle \end{bmatrix}.$$

Thus, to find the best least-squares polynomial approximation to a function f, we can use the following algorithm:

1. choose a basis for $\mathcal{P}_n$
2. set up the Gram matrix G and the vector $\mathbf{f}$ and then solve Eq. (4).

Note: The preceding process is not restricted to polynomial approximations of f. In particular, without loss of generality, we can replace the subspace $\mathcal{P}_n$ by any finite-dimensional subspace of $C[a, b]$.

1. Let $f(x) = \cos x$, $[a, b] = [0, 1]$, and $w(x) = 1$. Also, let $n = 2$ and $q_j(x) = x^j$ for $j = 0, 1, 2$. Find the best least-squares approximation to f by solving Eq. (4). In setting up the matrix G and the vector $\mathbf{f}$, you can evaluate the inner products using an integral table or by using the MATLAB numerical integration routine `quad8` to estimate the inner products. If you use `quad8`, you might want to test the effects of using different tolerances.

2. In Example 6, Section 5.6, the least-squares approximation problem in Exercise 1 was worked using a different basis for $\mathcal{P}_2$. Verify that you got the same polynomial p^* in Exercise 1 even though the basis was different. On the same MATLAB plot, compare the graph of $y = \cos x$ and $y = p^*(x)$. Next, plot the difference function $y = \cos x - p^*(x)$ and use your graph to estimate the maximum error.

3. Repeat Exercise 1, only this time use the basis from Example 6: $q_0(x) = 1, q_1(x) = x - 1/2$, and $q_2(x) = x^2 - x + 1/6$. What differences are there between the Gram matrix G in this exercise and the matrix G in Exercise 1?

4. If you did not already do so in Exercise 1, calculate by hand the *ij*-th entry of the Gram matrix for the basis of Exercise 1. Is the Gram matrix you find equal to the (3×3) Hilbert matrix? Suppose we were looking for an n-th degree polynomial approximation. Would the Gram matrix be the $((n+1) \times (n+1))$ Hilbert matrix? If we used an orthogonal basis in Eqs. (3) and (4), would the Gram matrix be a diagonal matrix? (Note that Eq. (4) is ill conditioned when G is the Hilbert matrix, but we would hope that it might be better conditioned when G is a diagonal matrix.)

5. Many applications of mathematics require the use of functions defined by integrals of the form

$$f(x) = \int_0^x g(t)\,dt. \tag{5}$$

Quite often the integral defining f is not an elementary one and can only be evaluated numerically. Some examples are

$$\textbf{a) } g(x) = \int_0^x e^{t^2}\,dt \qquad \textbf{b) } f(x) = \int_0^x \frac{\sin t}{t}\,dt \qquad \textbf{c) } f(x) = \int_0^x \cos t^2\,dt.$$

These functions are, respectively, the ***error function***, the ***sine integral***, and the ***Fresnel integral***. In each case, the integral defining $f(x)$ must be evaluated numerically.

Rather than calling a numerical integration routine whenever we need the value $f(x)$, we might consider approximating f by a polynomial. That idea is the theme of this exercise.

Now, if we are to approximate f by its best least-squares polynomial approximation p^*, we first have to choose a basis for $\mathcal{P}_n$ and then solve the normal equations (represented in Eq. (4) by $G\mathbf{a} = \mathbf{f}$). As we can see from Eqs. (3) and (4), the vector $\mathbf{f}$ has components $\langle f, q_0\rangle, \langle f, q_1\rangle, \ldots, \langle f, q_n\rangle$. Since f itself must be evaluated numerically, we will have to do the same for each of the components $\langle f, q_k\rangle$. However, using a numerical integration routine to estimate $\langle f, q_k\rangle$ requires us to supply a formula of some sort for $f(x)$. In order to avoid this requirement by a numerical integration routine, we use integration by parts to replace evaluations of f by evaluations of f'.

In particular, suppose we want to approximate $y = f(x)$ for x in $[0, 1]$. Let us choose $y = \rho(x)$ to be an antiderivative for $q_k(x)$ with the property that $\rho(1)$ is 0. Then, using integration by parts, we have:

$$\begin{aligned} \langle f, q_k\rangle &= \int_0^1 f(x)q_k(x)\,dx \\ &= \rho(x)f(x)\big|_0^1 - \int_0^1 \rho(x)f'(x)\,dx \qquad (6) \\ &= -\int_0^1 \rho(x)g(x)\,dx. \end{aligned}$$

To explain the preceding calculations, we used integration by parts with $u = f(x)$, $dv = q_k(x)dx$, $v = \rho(x)$, and $du = f'(x)\,dx$. To obtain the final result, we used the fact that $\rho(1) = 0$ and $f(0) = 0$, and also the fact that $f'(x) = g(x)$ by the fundamental theorem of calculus.

Let $g(x) = \cos x^2$ and use the preceding ideas to find the best least-squares approximation to the Fresnel integral $f(x)$. Use $n = 2, 4$, and 6. For ease of calculation, use the standard basis for $\mathcal{P}_n$, $q_k(x) = x^k$, $k = 0, 1, \ldots, n$. (Note that this choice of basis will mean that the Gram matrix will be a Hilbert matrix. However, for the small values of n we are using, the Hilbert matrix is not that badly behaved. You can use the MATLAB command `hilb(n)` to create the matrix G in Eq. (4).) In order to find the components of the vector $\mathbf{f}$ on the right-hand side of Eq. (4), use a numerical integration routine such as `quad8`. Because of Eq. (6), the components of $\mathbf{f}$ can be found by evaluating the following integral numerically:

$$\langle f, q_k\rangle = -\int_0^1 \frac{x^{k+1} - 1}{k+1}\cos(x^2)\,dx.$$

6

DETERMINANTS

This chapter may be covered at any time after Chapter 1

OVERVIEW

In this chapter we introduce the idea of the determinant of a square matrix. We also investigate some of the properties of the determinant. For example, a square matrix is singular if and only if its determinant is zero.

We also consider applications of determinants in matrix theory. For instance, we describe Cramer's Rule for solving $A\mathbf{x} = \mathbf{b}$, see how to express A^{-1} in terms of the adjoint matrix, and show how the Wronskian can be used as a device for determining linear independence of a set of functions.

CORE SECTIONS

6.2 *Cofactor Expansions of Determinants*
6.3 *Elementary Operations and Determinants*
6.4 *Cramer's Rule*
6.5 *Applications of Determinants: Inverses and Wronskians*

6.1 INTRODUCTION

Determinants have played a major role in the historical development of matrix theory, and they possess a number of properties that are theoretically pleasing. For example, in terms of linear algebra, determinants can be used to characterize nonsingular matrices, to express solutions of nonsingular systems $A\mathbf{x} = \mathbf{b}$, and to calculate the dimension of subspaces. In analysis, determinants are used to express vector cross products, to express the conversion factor (the Jacobian) when a change of variables is needed to evaluate a multiple integral, to serve as a convenient test (the Wronskian) for linear independence of sets of functions, and so on. We explore the theory and some of the applications of determinants in this chapter.

The material in Sections 6.2 and 6.3 duplicates the material in Sections 4.2 and 4.3 in order to present a contiguous coverage of determinants. The treatment is slightly different because the material in Chapter 6 is self-contained, whereas Chapter 4 uses a result (Theorem 6.13) that is stated in Chapter 4 but actually proved in Chapter 6. Hence, the reader who has seen the results of Sections 4.2 and 4.3 might want to proceed directly to Section 6.4.

6.2 COFACTOR EXPANSIONS OF DETERMINANTS

If A is an $(n \times n)$ matrix, the determinant of A, denoted $\det(A)$, is a number that we associate with A. Determinants are usually defined either in terms of *cofactors* or in terms of *permutations*, and we elect to use the cofactor definition here. We begin with the definition of $\det(A)$ when A is a (2×2) matrix.

DEFINITION 1 Let $A = (a_{ij})$ be a (2×2) matrix. The ***determinant*** of A is given by

$$\det(A) = a_{11}a_{22} - a_{12}a_{21}.$$

For notational purposes the determinant is often expressed by using vertical bars:

$$\det(A) = \begin{vmatrix} a_{11} & a_{12} \\ a_{21} & a_{22} \end{vmatrix}.$$

EXAMPLE 1 Find the determinants of the following matrices:

$$A = \begin{bmatrix} 1 & 2 \\ -1 & 3 \end{bmatrix}, \quad B = \begin{bmatrix} 4 & 1 \\ 2 & 1 \end{bmatrix}, \quad \text{and} \quad C = \begin{bmatrix} 3 & 4 \\ 6 & 8 \end{bmatrix}.$$

Solution

$$\det(A) = \begin{vmatrix} 1 & 2 \\ -1 & 3 \end{vmatrix} = 1 \cdot 3 - 2(-1) = 5;$$

$$\det(B) = \begin{vmatrix} 4 & 1 \\ 2 & 1 \end{vmatrix} = 4 \cdot 1 - 1 \cdot 2 = 2;$$

$$\det(C) = \begin{vmatrix} 3 & 4 \\ 6 & 8 \end{vmatrix} = 3 \cdot 8 - 4 \cdot 6 = 0$$

We now define the determinant of an $(n \times n)$ matrix as a *weighted sum* of $[(n-1) \times (n-1)]$ determinants. It is convenient to make a preliminary definition.

DEFINITION 2 Let $A = (a_{ij})$ be an $(n \times n)$ matrix, and let M_{rs} denote the $[(n-1) \times (n-1)]$ matrix obtained by deleting the rth row and sth column from A. Then M_{rs} is called a ***minor matrix*** of A, and the number $\det(M_{rs})$ is the ***minor of the (r,s)th entry***, a_{rs}. In addition, the numbers

$$A_{ij} = (-1)^{i+j} \det(M_{ij})$$

are called ***cofactors*** (or ***signed minors***).

EXAMPLE 2 Determine the minor matrices M_{11}, M_{23}, and M_{32} for the matrix A given by

$$A = \begin{bmatrix} 1 & -1 & 2 \\ 2 & 3 & -3 \\ 4 & 5 & 1 \end{bmatrix}.$$

Also, calculate the cofactors A_{11}, A_{23}, and A_{32}.

Solution Deleting row 1 and column 1 from A, we obtain M_{11}:

$$M_{11} = \begin{bmatrix} 3 & -3 \\ 5 & 1 \end{bmatrix}.$$

Similarly, the minor matrices M_{23} and M_{32} are

$$M_{23} = \begin{bmatrix} 1 & -1 \\ 4 & 5 \end{bmatrix} \quad \text{and} \quad M_{32} = \begin{bmatrix} 1 & 2 \\ 2 & -3 \end{bmatrix}.$$

The associated cofactors, $A_{ij} = (-1)^{i+j}\det(M_{ij})$ are given by

$$A_{11} = (-1)^{1+1}\begin{vmatrix} 3 & -3 \\ 5 & 1 \end{vmatrix} = 3 + 15 = 18;$$

$$A_{23} = (-1)^{2+3}\begin{vmatrix} 1 & -1 \\ 4 & 5 \end{vmatrix} = -(5 + 4) = -9;$$

$$A_{32} = (-1)^{3+2}\begin{vmatrix} 1 & 2 \\ 2 & -3 \end{vmatrix} = -(-3 - 4) = 7.$$

We use cofactors in our definition of the determinant.

DEFINITION 3 Let $A = (a_{ij})$ be an $(n \times n)$ matrix. Then the ***determinant*** of A is

$$\det(A) = a_{11}A_{11} + a_{12}A_{12} + \cdots + a_{1n}A_{1n},$$

where A_{ij} is the cofactor of a_{1j}, $1 \le j \le n$.

Determinants are defined only for square matrices. Note also the inductive nature of the definition. For example, if A is (3×3), then $\det(A) = a_{11}A_{11} + a_{12}A_{12} + a_{13}A_{13}$, and the cofactors A_{11}, A_{12}, and A_{13} can be evaluated from Definition 1. Similarly, the determinant of a (4×4) matrix is the sum of four (3×3) determinants, where each (3×3) determinant is in turn the sum of three (2×2) determinants.

EXAMPLE 3 Compute $\det(A)$, where

$$A = \begin{bmatrix} 3 & 2 & 1 \\ 2 & 1 & -3 \\ 4 & 0 & 1 \end{bmatrix}.$$

Solution The matrix A is (3×3). Using $n = 3$ in Definition 3, we have

$$\begin{aligned}\det(A) &= a_{11}A_{11} + a_{12}A_{12} + a_{13}A_{13} \\ &= 3\begin{vmatrix} 1 & -3 \\ 0 & 1 \end{vmatrix} - 2\begin{vmatrix} 2 & -3 \\ 4 & 1 \end{vmatrix} + 1\begin{vmatrix} 2 & 1 \\ 4 & 0 \end{vmatrix} \\ &= 3(1) - 2(14) + 1(-4) = -29.\end{aligned}$$

DETERMINANTS BY PERMUTATIONS The determinant of an $(n \times n)$ matrix A can be defined in terms of permutations rather than cofactors. Specifically, let $S = \{1, 2, \ldots, n\}$ denote the set consisting of the first n positive integers. A ***permutation*** $(j_1, j_2, \ldots, j_n)$ of the set $S = \{1, 2, \ldots, n\}$ is just a rearrangement of the numbers in S. An ***inversion*** of this permutation occurs whenever a number j_r is followed by a smaller number j_s. For example, the permutation (1, 3, 2) has one inversion, but (2, 3, 1) has two inversions. A permutation of S is called *odd* or *even* if it has an odd or even number of inversions.

It can be shown that $\det(A)$ is the sum of all possible terms of the form $\pm a_{1j_1}a_{2j_2}\ldots a_{nj_n}$, where $(j_1, j_2, \ldots, j_n)$ is a permutation of S and the sign is taken as $+$ or $-$, depending on whether the permutation is even or odd. For instance,

$$\begin{vmatrix} a_{11} & a_{12} \\ a_{21} & a_{22} \end{vmatrix} = +a_{11}a_{22} - a_{12}a_{21};$$

$$\begin{vmatrix} a_{11} & a_{12} & a_{13} \\ a_{21} & a_{22} & a_{23} \\ a_{31} & a_{32} & a_{33} \end{vmatrix} = +a_{11}a_{22}a_{33} - a_{11}a_{23}a_{32} - a_{12}a_{21}a_{33} + a_{12}a_{23}a_{31} + a_{13}a_{21}a_{32} - a_{13}a_{22}a_{31}.$$

Since there are $n!$ different permutations when $S = \{1, 2, \ldots, n\}$, you can see why this definition is not suitable for calculation. For example, calculating the determinant of a (10×10) matrix requires us to evaluate $10! = 3{,}628{,}800$ different terms of the form $\pm a_{1j_1}a_{2j_2}\ldots a_{10j_{10}}$. The permutation definition is useful for theoretical purposes, however. For instance, the permutation definition gives immediately that $\det(A) = 0$ when A has a row of zeros.

EXAMPLE 4 Compute $\det(A)$, where

$$A = \begin{bmatrix} 1 & 2 & 0 & 2 \\ -1 & 2 & 3 & 1 \\ -3 & 2 & -1 & 0 \\ 2 & -3 & -2 & 1 \end{bmatrix}.$$

Solution The matrix A is (4×4). Using $n = 4$ in Definition 3, we have

$$\det(A) = a_{11}A_{11} + a_{12}A_{12} + a_{13}A_{13} + a_{14}A_{14} = A_{11} + 2A_{12} + 2A_{14}.$$

The required cofactors, A_{11}, A_{12}, and A_{14}, are calculated as in Example 3 (note that the cofactor A_{13} is not needed, since $a_{13} = 0$).

In detail,

$$A_{11} = \begin{vmatrix} 2 & 3 & 1 \\ 2 & -1 & 0 \\ -3 & -2 & 1 \end{vmatrix}$$

$$= 2\begin{vmatrix} -1 & 0 \\ -2 & 1 \end{vmatrix} - 3\begin{vmatrix} 2 & 0 \\ -3 & 1 \end{vmatrix} + 1\begin{vmatrix} 2 & -1 \\ -3 & -2 \end{vmatrix} = -15;$$

$$A_{12} = -\begin{vmatrix} -1 & 3 & 1 \\ -3 & -1 & 0 \\ 2 & -2 & 1 \end{vmatrix}$$

$$= -\left(-1\begin{vmatrix} -1 & 0 \\ -2 & 1 \end{vmatrix} - 3\begin{vmatrix} -3 & 0 \\ 2 & 1 \end{vmatrix} + 1\begin{vmatrix} -3 & -1 \\ 2 & -2 \end{vmatrix}\right) = -18;$$

$$A_{14} = -\begin{vmatrix} -1 & 2 & 3 \\ -3 & 2 & -1 \\ 2 & -3 & -2 \end{vmatrix}$$

$$= -\left(-1\begin{vmatrix} 2 & -1 \\ -3 & -2 \end{vmatrix} - 2\begin{vmatrix} -3 & -1 \\ 2 & -2 \end{vmatrix} + 3\begin{vmatrix} -3 & 2 \\ 2 & -3 \end{vmatrix}\right) = -6.$$

Thus it follows that

$$\det(A) = A_{11} + 2A_{12} + 2A_{14} = -15 - 36 - 12 = -63.$$

The definition of $\det(A)$ given in Definition 3 and used in Examples 3 and 4 is based on a cofactor expansion along the first row of A. In Section 6.5 (see Theorem 13), we prove that the value $\det(A)$ can be calculated from a cofactor expansion along any row or any column.

Also, note in Example 4 that the calculation of the (4×4) determinant was simplified because of the zero entry in the $(1, 3)$ position. Clearly, if we had some procedure for creating zero entries, we could simplify the computation of determinants since the cofactor of a zero entry need not be calculated. We will develop such simplifications in the next section.

EXAMPLE 5 Compute the determinant of the lower-triangular matrix T, where

$$T = \begin{bmatrix} 3 & 0 & 0 & 0 \\ 1 & 2 & 0 & 0 \\ 2 & 3 & 2 & 0 \\ 1 & 4 & 5 & 1 \end{bmatrix}.$$

Solution We have $\det(T) = t_{11}T_{11} + t_{12}T_{12} + t_{13}T_{13} + t_{14}T_{14}$. Since $t_{12} = 0$, $t_{13} = 0$, and $t_{14} = 0$, the calculation simplifies to

$$\det(T) = t_{11}T_{11} = 3\begin{vmatrix} 2 & 0 & 0 \\ 3 & 2 & 0 \\ 4 & 5 & 1 \end{vmatrix}$$

$$= 3 \cdot 2 \begin{vmatrix} 2 & 0 \\ 5 & 1 \end{vmatrix}$$

$$= 3 \cdot 2 \cdot 2 \cdot 1 = 12.$$

In Example 5, we saw that the determinant of the lower-triangular matrix T was the product of the diagonal entries, $\det(T) = t_{11}t_{22}t_{33}t_{44}$. This simple relationship is valid for any lower-triangular matrix.

THEOREM 1 Let $T = (t_{ij})$ be an $(n \times n)$ lower-triangular matrix. Then

$$\det(T) = t_{11} \cdot t_{22} \cdot \cdots \cdot t_{nn}.$$

Proof If T is a (2×2) lower-triangular matrix, then

$$\det(T) = \begin{vmatrix} t_{11} & 0 \\ t_{21} & t_{22} \end{vmatrix} = t_{11}t_{22}.$$

Proceeding inductively, suppose that the theorem is true for any $(k \times k)$ lower-triangular matrix, where $2 \le k \le n-1$. If T is an $(n \times n)$ lower-triangular matrix, then

$$\det(T) = \begin{vmatrix} t_{11} & 0 & 0 & \cdots & 0 \\ t_{21} & t_{22} & 0 & \cdots & 0 \\ \vdots & & & & \vdots \\ t_{n1} & t_{n2} & t_{n3} & \cdots & t_{nn} \end{vmatrix} = t_{11}, T_{11}, \quad \text{where } T_{11} = \begin{vmatrix} t_{22} & 0 & \cdots & 0 \\ t_{32} & t_{33} & \cdots & 0 \\ \vdots & & & \vdots \\ t_{n2} & t_{n3} & \cdots & t_{nn} \end{vmatrix}.$$

Clearly, T_{11} is the determinant of an $[(n-1) \times (n-1)]$ lower-triangular matrix, so $T_{11} = t_{22}t_{33} \cdots t_{nn}$. Thus $\det(T) = t_{11}t_{22} \cdots t_{nn}$, and the theorem is proved.

EXAMPLE 6 Let I denote the $(n \times n)$ identity matrix. Calculate $\det(I)$.

Solution Since I is a lower-triangular matrix with diagonal entries equal to 1, we see from Theorem 1 that

$$\det(T) = \underbrace{1 \cdot 1 \cdot \cdots \cdot 1}_{n \text{ factors}} = 1.$$

6.2 EXERCISES

In Exercises 1–8, evaluate the determinant of the given matrix. If the determinant is zero, find a nonzero vector $\mathbf{x}$ such that $A\mathbf{x} = \boldsymbol{\theta}$. (We will see later that $\det(A) = 0$ if and only if A is singular.)

1. $\begin{bmatrix} 1 & 3 \\ 2 & 1 \end{bmatrix}$

2. $\begin{bmatrix} 6 & 7 \\ 7 & 3 \end{bmatrix}$

3. $\begin{bmatrix} 2 & 4 \\ 4 & 8 \end{bmatrix}$ 4. $\begin{bmatrix} 1 & 3 \\ 0 & 2 \end{bmatrix}$

5. $\begin{bmatrix} 4 & 3 \\ 1 & 7 \end{bmatrix}$ 6. $\begin{bmatrix} 2 & -1 \\ 1 & 1 \end{bmatrix}$

7. $\begin{bmatrix} 4 & 1 \\ -2 & 1 \end{bmatrix}$ 8. $\begin{bmatrix} 1 & 3 \\ 2 & 6 \end{bmatrix}$

In Exercises 9–14, calculate the cofactors A_{11}, A_{12}, A_{13}, and A_{33} for the given matrix A.

9. $A = \begin{bmatrix} 1 & 2 & 1 \\ 0 & 1 & 3 \\ 2 & 1 & 1 \end{bmatrix}$ 10. $A = \begin{bmatrix} 1 & 4 & 0 \\ 1 & 0 & 2 \\ 3 & 1 & 2 \end{bmatrix}$

11. $A = \begin{bmatrix} 2 & -1 & 3 \\ -1 & 2 & 2 \\ 3 & 2 & 1 \end{bmatrix}$

12. $A = \begin{bmatrix} 1 & 1 & 1 \\ 1 & 1 & 2 \\ 2 & 1 & 1 \end{bmatrix}$ 13. $A = \begin{bmatrix} -1 & 1 & -1 \\ 2 & 1 & 0 \\ 0 & 1 & 3 \end{bmatrix}$

14. $A = \begin{bmatrix} 4 & 2 & 1 \\ 4 & 3 & 1 \\ 0 & 0 & 2 \end{bmatrix}$

In Exercises 15–20, use the results of Exercises 9–14 to find $\det(A)$, where:

15. A is in Exercise 9. 16. A is in Exercise 10.

17. A is in Exercise 11. 18. A is in Exercise 12.

19. A is in Exercise 13. 20. A is in Exercise 14.

In Exercises 21–24, calculate $\det(A)$.

21. $A = \begin{bmatrix} 2 & 1 & -1 & 2 \\ 3 & 0 & 0 & 1 \\ 2 & 1 & 2 & 0 \\ 3 & 1 & 1 & 2 \end{bmatrix}$

22. $A = \begin{bmatrix} 1 & -1 & 1 & 2 \\ 1 & 0 & 1 & 3 \\ 0 & 0 & 2 & 4 \\ 1 & 1 & -1 & 1 \end{bmatrix}$

23. $A = \begin{bmatrix} 2 & 0 & 2 & 0 \\ 1 & 3 & 1 & 2 \\ 0 & 1 & 2 & 1 \\ 0 & 3 & 1 & 4 \end{bmatrix}$

24. $A = \begin{bmatrix} 1 & 2 & 1 & 1 \\ 0 & 2 & 0 & 3 \\ 1 & 4 & 1 & 2 \\ 0 & 2 & 1 & 3 \end{bmatrix}$

In Exercises 25 and 26, show that the quantities $\det(A)$, $a_{21}A_{21} + a_{22}A_{22} + a_{23}A_{23}$, and $a_{31}A_{31} + a_{32}A_{32} + a_{33}A_{33}$ are all equal. (This is a special case of a general result given later in Theorem 13.)

25. $A = \begin{bmatrix} 1 & 3 & 2 \\ -1 & 4 & 1 \\ 2 & 2 & 3 \end{bmatrix}$ 26. $A = \begin{bmatrix} 2 & 4 & 1 \\ 3 & 1 & 3 \\ 2 & 3 & 2 \end{bmatrix}$

In Exercises 27 and 28, show that $a_{11}A_{21} + a_{12}A_{22} + a_{13}A_{23} = 0$, and $a_{11}A_{31} + a_{12}A_{32} + a_{13}A_{33} = 0$. (This is a special case of a general result given later in the lemma to Theorem 14.)

27. A as in Exercise 25 28. A as in Exercise 26

In Exercises 29 and 30, form the (3×3) matrix of cofactors C where $c_{ij} = A_{ij}$ and then calculate BA where $B = C^T$. How can you use this result to find A^{-1}?

29. A as in Exercise 25 30. A as in Exercise 26

31. Verify that $\det(A) = 0$ when

$$A = \begin{bmatrix} 0 & a_{12} & a_{13} \\ 0 & a_{22} & a_{23} \\ 0 & a_{32} & a_{33} \end{bmatrix}.$$

32. Use the result of Exercise 31 to prove that if $U = (u_{ij})$ is a (4×4) upper-triangular matrix, then $\det(U) = u_{11}u_{22}u_{33}u_{44}$.

33. Let $A = (a_{ij})$ be a (2×2) matrix. Show that $\det(A^T) = \det(A)$.

34. An $(n \times n)$ symmetric matrix A is called positive definite if $\mathbf{x}^T A\mathbf{x} > 0$ for all $\mathbf{x}$ in R^n, $\mathbf{x} \neq \boldsymbol{\theta}$. Let A be a (2×2) symmetric matrix. Prove the following:

a) If A is positive definite, then $a_{11} > 0$ and $\det(A) > 0$.

b) If $a_{11} > 0$ and $\det(A) > 0$, then A is positive definite. [*Hint:* For part a), consider $\mathbf{x} = \mathbf{e}_1$.

Then consider $\mathbf{x} = [u, v]^T$ and use the fact that A is symmetric.]

35. a) Let A be an $(n \times n)$ matrix. If $n = 3$, $\det(A)$ can be found by evaluating three (2×2) determinants. If $n = 4$, $\det(A)$ can be found by evaluating twelve (2×2) determinants. Give a formula, $H(n)$, for the number of (2×2) determinants necessary to find $\det(A)$ for an arbitrary n.

b) Suppose you can perform additions, subtractions, multiplications, and divisions each at a rate of one per second. How long does it take to evaluate $H(n)$ determinants of order (2×2) when $n = 2$, $n = 5$, and $n = 10$?

6.3 ELEMENTARY OPERATIONS AND DETERMINANTS

In this section we show how certain column operations simplify the calculation of determinants. In addition, the properties we develop will be used later to demonstrate some of the connections between determinant theory and linear algebra. We use three elementary column operations, which are analogous to the elementary row operations defined in Chapter 1. For a matrix A, the elementary column operations are as follows:

1. Interchange two columns of A.
2. Multiply a column of A by a scalar c, $c \neq 0$.
3. Add a scalar multiple of one column of A to another column of A.

From Chapter 1, we know that row operations can be used to reduce a square matrix A to an upper-triangular matrix (that is, we know A can be reduced to echelon form, and a square matrix in echelon form is upper triangular). Similarly, it is easy to show that column operations can be used to reduce a square matrix to lower-triangular form. One reason for reducing an $(n \times n)$ matrix A to a lower-triangular matrix T is that $\det(T)$ is trivial to evaluate (see Theorem 1). Thus if we can calculate the effect that column operations have on the determinant, we can relate $\det(A)$ to $\det(T)$.

Before proceeding, we wish to make the following statement about elementary row and column operations. We will prove a succession of results dealing only with column operations. These results lead to a proof in Section 6.5 of the following theorem (see Theorem 12):

THEOREM If A is an $(n \times n)$ matrix, then

$$\det(A^T) = \det(A). \tag{1}$$

Once Eq. (1) is formally established, we will immediately know that the theorems for column operations are also valid for row operations. (Row operations on A are precisely mirrored by column operations on A^T.) Therefore the following theorems are stated in terms of elementary row operations, as well as elementary column operations, although the row results will not be truly established until Theorem 12 is proved.

Elementary Operations

Our purpose is to describe how the determinant of a matrix A changes when an elementary column operation is applied to A. The description will take the form of a series of theorems. Because of the technical nature of the first three theorems, we defer their proofs to the end of the section.

Our first result relating to elementary operations is given in Theorem 2. This theorem asserts that a column interchange (or a row interchange) will change the sign of the determinant.

THEOREM 2 Let $A = [\mathbf{A}_1, \mathbf{A}_2, \ldots, \mathbf{A}_n]$ be an $(n \times n)$ matrix. If B is obtained from A by interchanging two columns (or rows) of A, then $\det(B) = -\det(A)$.

The proof of Theorem 2 is at the end of this section.

EXAMPLE 1 Verify Theorem 2 for the (2×2) matrix

$$A = \begin{bmatrix} a_{11} & a_{12} \\ a_{21} & a_{22} \end{bmatrix}.$$

Solution Let B denote the matrix obtained by interchanging the first and second columns of A. Thus B is given by

$$B = \begin{bmatrix} a_{12} & a_{11} \\ a_{22} & a_{21} \end{bmatrix}.$$

Now $\det(B) = a_{12}a_{21} - a_{11}a_{22}$, and $\det(A) = a_{11}a_{22} - a_{12}a_{21}$. Thus $\det(B) = -\det(A)$.

EXAMPLE 2 Let A be the (3×3) matrix

$$A = \begin{bmatrix} 1 & 3 & 1 \\ 2 & 0 & 4 \\ 1 & 2 & 3 \end{bmatrix}.$$

The determinant of A is -10. Use the fact that $\det(A) = -10$ to find the determinants of B, C, and F, where

$$B = \begin{bmatrix} 3 & 1 & 1 \\ 0 & 2 & 4 \\ 2 & 1 & 3 \end{bmatrix}, \quad C = \begin{bmatrix} 1 & 1 & 3 \\ 2 & 4 & 0 \\ 1 & 3 & 2 \end{bmatrix}, \quad \text{and} \quad F = \begin{bmatrix} 1 & 1 & 3 \\ 4 & 2 & 0 \\ 3 & 1 & 2 \end{bmatrix}.$$

Solution If A is given in column form as $A = [\mathbf{A}_1, \mathbf{A}_2, \mathbf{A}_3]$, then $B = [\mathbf{A}_2, \mathbf{A}_1, \mathbf{A}_3]$, $C = [\mathbf{A}_1, \mathbf{A}_3, \mathbf{A}_2]$, and $F = [\mathbf{A}_3, \mathbf{A}_1, \mathbf{A}_2]$. Since both B and C are obtained from A by a single column interchange, it follows from Theorem 2 that

$$\det(B) = \det(C) = -\det(A) = 10.$$

We can obtain F from A by two column interchanges as follows:

$$A \rightarrow G = [\mathbf{A}_2, \mathbf{A}_1, \mathbf{A}_3] \rightarrow F = [\mathbf{A}_3, \mathbf{A}_1, \mathbf{A}_2].$$

From Theorem 2, $\det(G) = -\det(A)$ and $\det(F) = -\det(G)$. Therefore $\det(F) = -\det(G) = -[-\det(A)] = \det(A) = -10$.

By performing a sequence of column interchanges, we can produce any rearrangement of columns that we wish; and Theorem 2 can be used to find the determinant of the end result. For example, if $A = [\mathbf{A}_1, \mathbf{A}_2, \mathbf{A}_3, \mathbf{A}_4]$ is a (4×4) matrix and $B = [\mathbf{A}_4, \mathbf{A}_3, \mathbf{A}_1, \mathbf{A}_2]$ then we can relate $\det(B)$ to $\det(A)$ as follows: Form $B_1 = [\mathbf{A}_4, \mathbf{A}_2, \mathbf{A}_3, \mathbf{A}_1]$; then form $B_2 = [\mathbf{A}_4, \mathbf{A}_3, \mathbf{A}_2, \mathbf{A}_1]$; and then form B by interchanging the last two columns of B_2. In this sequence, $\det(B) = -\det(A)$ and $\det(B_2) = -\det(B_1)$, so $\det(B) = -\det(B_2) = \det(B_1) = -\det(A)$.

Our next theorem shows that multiplying all entries in a column of A by a scalar c has the effect of multiplying the determinant by c.

THEOREM 3   If A is an $(n \times n)$ matrix, and if B is the $(n \times n)$ matrix resulting from multiplying the kth column (or row) of A by a scalar c, then $\det(B) = c \det(A)$. ■

Again, the proof of Theorem 3 is rather technical, so we defer it to the end of this section. The next example, however, verifies Theorem 3 for a (2×2) matrix A.

EXAMPLE 3   Verify Theorem 3 for the (2×2) matrix

$$A = \begin{bmatrix} a_{11} & a_{12} \\ a_{21} & a_{22} \end{bmatrix}.$$

Solution   Consider the matrices A' and A'' given by

$$A' = \begin{bmatrix} ca_{11} & a_{12} \\ ca_{21} & a_{22} \end{bmatrix} \quad \text{and} \quad A'' = \begin{bmatrix} a_{11} & ca_{12} \\ a_{21} & ca_{22} \end{bmatrix}.$$

Clearly, $\det(A') = ca_{11}a_{22} - ca_{21}a_{12} = c(a_{11}a_{22} - a_{21}a_{12}) = c \det(A)$. Similarly,

$$\det(A'') = ca_{11}a_{22} - ca_{21}a_{12} = c(a_{11}a_{22} - a_{21}a_{12}) = c \det(A).$$

These calculations prove Theorem 3 for a (2×2) matrix A. ■

We emphasize that Theorem 3 is valid when $c = 0$. That is, if A has a column of zeros, then $\det(A) = 0$.

EXAMPLE 4   Let A be the (3×3) matrix

$$A = \begin{bmatrix} 1 & 3 & 1 \\ 2 & 0 & 4 \\ 1 & 2 & 3 \end{bmatrix}.$$

The determinant of A is -10. Use the fact that $\det(A) = -10$ to find the determinants of G, H, and J, where

$$G = \begin{bmatrix} 2 & 3 & 1 \\ 4 & 0 & 4 \\ 2 & 2 & 3 \end{bmatrix}, \quad H = \begin{bmatrix} 2 & -3 & 1 \\ 4 & 0 & 4 \\ 2 & -2 & 3 \end{bmatrix}, \quad \text{and} \quad J = \begin{bmatrix} 2 & -3 & 2 \\ 4 & 0 & 8 \\ 2 & -2 & 6 \end{bmatrix}.$$

Solution Let $A = [\mathbf{A}_1, \mathbf{A}_2, \mathbf{A}_3]$. Then

$$G = [2\mathbf{A}_1, \mathbf{A}_2, \mathbf{A}_3],\quad H = [2\mathbf{A}_1, -\mathbf{A}_2, \mathbf{A}_3],\quad \text{and}\quad J = [2\mathbf{A}_1, -\mathbf{A}_2, 2\mathbf{A}_3].$$

By Theorem 3, $\det(G) = 2\det(A) = -20$.

Next, H is obtained from G by multiplying the second column of G by -1. Therefore, $\det(H) = -\det(G) = 20$. Finally, J is obtained from H by multiplying the third column of H by 2. Thus, $\det(J) = 2\det(H) = 40$. ■

The following result is a corollary of Theorem 3:

COROLLARY Let A be an $(n \times n)$ matrix and let c be a scalar. Then

$$\det(cA) = c^n \det(A).$$ ■

We leave the proof of the corollary as Exercise 32.

EXAMPLE 5 Find $\det(3A)$, where

$$A = \begin{bmatrix} 1 & 2 \\ 4 & 1 \end{bmatrix}.$$

Solution Clearly, $\det(A) = -7$. Therefore, by the corollary, $\det(3A) = 3^2\det(A) = -63$. As a check, note that the matrix $3A$ is given by

$$3A = \begin{bmatrix} 3 & 6 \\ 12 & 3 \end{bmatrix}.$$

Thus, $\det(3A) = 9 - 72 = -63$, confirming the calculation above. ■

So far we have considered the effect of two elementary column operations: column interchanges and multiplication of a column by a scalar. We now wish to show that the addition of a constant multiple of one column to another column does not change the determinant. We need several preliminary results to prove this.

THEOREM 4 If A, B, and C are $(n\times n)$ matrices that are equal except that the sth column (or row) of A is equal to the sum of the sth columns (or rows) of B and C, then $\det(A) = \det(B) + \det(C)$. ■

As before, the proof of Theorem 4 is somewhat technical and is deferred to the end of this section.

EXAMPLE 6 Verify Theorem 4 where A, B, and C are (2×2) matrices.

Solution Suppose that A, B, and C are (2×2) matrices such that the first column of A is equal to the sum of the first columns of B and C. Thus,

$$B = \begin{bmatrix} b_1 & \alpha \\ b_2 & \beta \end{bmatrix},\quad C = \begin{bmatrix} c_1 & \alpha \\ c_2 & \beta \end{bmatrix},\quad \text{and}\quad A = \begin{bmatrix} b_1 + c_1 & \alpha \\ b_2 + c_2 & \beta \end{bmatrix}.$$

Calculating $\det(A)$, we have

$$\begin{aligned}\det(A) &= (b_1 + c_1)\beta - \alpha(b_2 + c_2)\\ &= (b_1\beta - \alpha b_2) + (c_1\beta - \alpha c_2)\\ &= \det(B) + \det(C).\end{aligned}$$

The case in which A, B, and C have the same first column is left as an exercise.

EXAMPLE 7 Given that $\det(B) = 22$ and $\det(C) = 29$, find $\det(A)$, where

$$A = \begin{bmatrix} 1 & 3 & 2 \\ 0 & 4 & 7 \\ 2 & 1 & 8 \end{bmatrix}, \quad B = \begin{bmatrix} 1 & 1 & 2 \\ 0 & 2 & 7 \\ 2 & 0 & 8 \end{bmatrix}, \quad \text{and} \quad C = \begin{bmatrix} 1 & 2 & 2 \\ 0 & 2 & 7 \\ 2 & 1 & 8 \end{bmatrix}.$$

Solution In terms of column vectors, $\mathbf{A}_1 = \mathbf{B}_1 = \mathbf{C}_1$, $\mathbf{A}_3 = \mathbf{B}_3 = \mathbf{C}_3$, and $\mathbf{A}_2 = \mathbf{B}_2 + \mathbf{C}_2$. Thus,

$$\det(A) = \det(B) + \det(C) = 22 + 29 = 51.$$

THEOREM 5 Let A be an $(n \times n)$ matrix. If the jth column (or row) of A is a multiple of the kth column (or row) of A, then $\det(A) = 0$.

Proof Let $A = [\mathbf{A}_1, \mathbf{A}_2, \ldots, \mathbf{A}_j, \ldots, \mathbf{A}_k, \ldots, \mathbf{A}_n]$ and suppose that $\mathbf{A}_j = c\mathbf{A}_k$. Define B to be the matrix $B = [\mathbf{A}_1, \mathbf{A}_2, \ldots, \mathbf{A}_k, \ldots, \mathbf{A}_k, \ldots, \mathbf{A}_n]$ and observe that $\det(A) = c\det(B)$. Now if we interchange the jth and kth columns of B, the matrix B remains the same, but the determinant changes sign (Theorem 2). This $[\det(B) = -\det(B)]$ can happen only if $\det(B) = 0$; and since $\det(A) = c\det(B)$, then $\det(A) = 0$.

Two special cases of Theorem 5 are particularly interesting. If A has two identical columns ($c = 1$ in the proof above), or if A has a zero column ($c = 0$ in the proof), then $\det(A) = 0$.

Theorems 4 and 5 can be used to analyze the effect of the last elementary column operation.

THEOREM 6 If A is an $(n \times n)$ matrix, and if a multiple of the kth column (or row) is added to the jth column (or row), then the determinant is not changed.

Proof Let $A = [\mathbf{A}_1, \mathbf{A}_2, \ldots, \mathbf{A}_j, \ldots, \mathbf{A}_k, \ldots, \mathbf{A}_n]$ and let $B = [\mathbf{A}_1, \mathbf{A}_2, \ldots, \mathbf{A}_j + c\mathbf{A}_k, \ldots, \mathbf{A}_k, \ldots, \mathbf{A}_n]$. By Theorem 4, $\det(B) = \det(A) + \det(Q)$, where $Q = [\mathbf{A}_1, \mathbf{A}_2, \ldots, c\mathbf{A}_k, \ldots, \mathbf{A}_k, \ldots, \mathbf{A}_n]$. By Theorem 5, $\det(Q) = 0$; so $\det(B) = \det(A)$, and the theorem is proved.

As shown in the examples that follow, we can use elementary column operations to introduce zero entries into the first row of a matrix A. The analysis of how these operations affect the determinant allows us to relate this effect back to $\det(A)$.

EXAMPLE 8 Use elementary column operations to simplify finding the determinant of the (4×4) matrix A:

$$A = \begin{bmatrix} 1 & 2 & 0 & 2 \\ -1 & 2 & 3 & 1 \\ -3 & 2 & -1 & 0 \\ 2 & -3 & -2 & 1 \end{bmatrix}.$$

Solution In Example 4 of Section 6.2, a laborious cofactor expansion showed that $\det(A) = -63$. In column form, $A = [\mathbf{A}_1, \mathbf{A}_2, \mathbf{A}_3, \mathbf{A}_4]$, and clearly we can introduce a zero into the $(1, 2)$ position by replacing $\mathbf{A}_2$ by $\mathbf{A}_2 - 2\mathbf{A}_1$. Similarly, replacing $\mathbf{A}_4$ by $\mathbf{A}_4 - 2\mathbf{A}_1$ creates a zero in the $(1, 4)$ entry. Moreover, by Theorem 6, the determinant is unchanged. The details are

$$\det(A) = \begin{vmatrix} 1 & 2 & 0 & 2 \\ -1 & 2 & 3 & 1 \\ -3 & 2 & -1 & 0 \\ 2 & -3 & -2 & 1 \end{vmatrix} = \begin{vmatrix} 1 & 0 & 0 & 2 \\ -1 & 4 & 3 & 1 \\ -3 & 8 & -1 & 0 \\ 2 & -7 & -2 & 1 \end{vmatrix}$$

$$= \begin{vmatrix} 1 & 0 & 0 & 0 \\ -1 & 4 & 3 & 3 \\ -3 & 8 & -1 & 6 \\ 2 & -7 & -2 & -3 \end{vmatrix}.$$

Thus it follows that $\det(A)$ is given by

$$\det(A) = \begin{vmatrix} 4 & 3 & 3 \\ 8 & -1 & 6 \\ -7 & -2 & -3 \end{vmatrix}.$$

We now wish to create zeros in the $(1, 2)$ and $(1, 3)$ positions of this (3×3) determinant. To avoid using fractions, we multiply the second and third columns by 4 (using Theorem 3), and then add a multiple of -3 times column 1 to columns 2 and 3:

$$\det(A) = \begin{vmatrix} 4 & 3 & 3 \\ 8 & -1 & 6 \\ -7 & -2 & -3 \end{vmatrix} = \frac{1}{16}\begin{vmatrix} 4 & 12 & 12 \\ 8 & -4 & 24 \\ -7 & -8 & -12 \end{vmatrix} = \frac{1}{16}\begin{vmatrix} 4 & 0 & 0 \\ 8 & -28 & 0 \\ -7 & 13 & 9 \end{vmatrix}.$$

Thus we again find $\det(A) = -63$. ■

EXAMPLE 9 Use column operations to find $\det(A)$, where

$$A = \begin{bmatrix} 0 & 1 & 3 & 1 \\ 1 & -2 & -2 & 2 \\ 3 & 4 & 2 & -2 \\ 4 & 3 & -1 & 1 \end{bmatrix}.$$

Solution As in Gaussian elimination, column interchanges are sometimes desirable and serve to keep order in the computations. Consider

$$\det(A) = \begin{vmatrix} 0 & 1 & 3 & 1 \\ 1 & -2 & -2 & 2 \\ 3 & 4 & 2 & -2 \\ 4 & 3 & -1 & 1 \end{vmatrix} = - \begin{vmatrix} 1 & 0 & 3 & 1 \\ -2 & 1 & -2 & 2 \\ 4 & 3 & 2 & -2 \\ 3 & 4 & -1 & 1 \end{vmatrix}.$$

Use column 1 to introduce zeros along the first row:

$$\det(A) = - \begin{vmatrix} 1 & 0 & 0 & 0 \\ -2 & 1 & 4 & 4 \\ 4 & 3 & -10 & -6 \\ 3 & 4 & -10 & -2 \end{vmatrix} = - \begin{vmatrix} 1 & 4 & 4 \\ 3 & -10 & -6 \\ 4 & -10 & -2 \end{vmatrix}.$$

Again column 1 can be used to introduce zeros:

$$\det(A) = - \begin{vmatrix} 1 & 0 & 0 \\ 3 & -22 & -18 \\ 4 & -26 & -18 \end{vmatrix} = - \begin{vmatrix} -22 & -18 \\ -26 & -18 \end{vmatrix} = 18 \begin{vmatrix} -22 & 1 \\ -26 & 1 \end{vmatrix},$$

and we calculate the (2×2) determinant to find $\det(A) = 72$. ■

Proof of Theorems 2, 3, and 4 (Optional)

We conclude this section with the proofs of Theorems 2, 3, and 4. Note that these proofs are very similar and fairly straightforward.

Proof of Theorem 2 The proof is by induction. The initial case ($k = 2$) was proved in Example 1.

Assuming the result is valid for any $(k \times k)$ matrix, $2 \le k \le n-1$, let B be obtained from A by interchanging the ith and jth columns. For $1 \le s \le n$, let M_{1s} and N_{1s} denote minor matrices of A and B, respectively.

If $s \neq i$ or j, then N_{1s} is the same as M_{1s} except for a single column interchange. Hence, by the induction hypotheses,

$$\det(N_{1s}) = -\det(M_{1s}), \quad s \neq i \quad \text{or} \quad j.$$

For definiteness let us suppose that $i > j$. Note that N_{1i} contains no entries from the original jth column. Furthermore, the columns of N_{1i} can be rearranged to be the same as the columns of M_{1j} by $i - j - 1$ successive interchanges of adjacent columns. By the induction hypotheses, each such interchange causes a sign change, and so

$$\det(N_{1i}) = (-1)^{(i-j-1)} \det(M_{1j}).$$

Therefore,

$$\det(B) = \left(\sum_{\substack{s=1 \\ s \neq i \text{ or } j}}^{n} a_{1s}(-1)^{1+s}\det(N_{1s}) \right) + a_{1j}(-1)^{i+1}\det(N_{1i})$$

$$+ \, a_{1i}(-1)^{1+j}\det(N_{1j})$$

$$= \left(\sum_{\substack{s=1 \\ s \neq i \text{ or } j}}^{n} a_{1s}(-1)^{1+s}[-\det(M_{1s})] \right) + a_{1j}(-1)^{1+i}(-1)^{i-j-1}\det(M_{1j})$$

$$+ \, a_{1i}(-1)^{1+j}(-1)^{i-j-1}\det(M_{1i})$$

$$= \sum_{s=1}^{n} a_{1s}(-1)^{2+s}\det(M_{1s}) = -\det(A). \qquad \blacksquare$$

Proof of Theorem 3   Again, the proof is by induction. The case $k = 2$ was proved in Example 3.

Assuming the result is valid for $(k \times k)$ matrices, $2 \leq k \leq n-1$, let B be the $(n \times n)$ matrix, where

$$B = [\mathbf{A}_1, \ldots, \mathbf{A}_{s-1}, c\mathbf{A}_s, \mathbf{A}_{s+1}, \ldots, \mathbf{A}_n].$$

Let M_{1j} and N_{1j} be minor matrices of A and B, respectively, for $1 \leq j \leq n$.

If $j \neq s$, then $N_{1j} = M_{1j}$ except that one column of N_{1j} is multiplied by c. By the induction hypothesis,

$$\det(N_{1j}) = c\det(M_{1j}), \quad 1 \leq j \leq n, \quad j \neq s.$$

Moreover, $N_{1s} = M_{1s}$. Hence

$$\det(B) = \left(\sum_{\substack{j=1 \\ j \neq s}}^{n} a_{1j}(-1)^{1+j}\det(N_{1j}) \right) + ca_{1s}(-1)^{1+s}\det(N_{1s})$$

$$= \left(\sum_{\substack{j=1 \\ j \neq s}}^{n} a_{1j}(-1)^{1+j}c\det(M_{1j}) \right) + ca_{1s}(-1)^{1+s}\det(M_{1s})$$

$$= c \sum_{j=1}^{n} a_{1j}(-1)^{1+j}\det(M_{1j}) = c\det(A). \qquad \blacksquare$$

Proof of Theorem 4   We use induction where the case $k = 2$ is done in Example 6. Assuming the result is true for $(k \times k)$ matrices for $2 \leq k \leq n-1$, let

$$A = [\mathbf{A}_1, \mathbf{A}_2, \ldots, \mathbf{A}_n], \; B = [\mathbf{A}_1, \ldots, \mathbf{A}_{s-1}, \mathbf{B}_s, \mathbf{A}_{s+1}, \ldots, \mathbf{A}_n], \quad \text{and}$$

$$C = [\mathbf{A}_1, \ldots, \mathbf{A}_{s-1}, \mathbf{C}_s, \mathbf{A}_{s+1}, \ldots, \mathbf{A}_n],$$

where $\mathbf{A}_s = \mathbf{B}_s + \mathbf{C}_s$, or

$$a_{is} = b_{is} + c_{is}, \quad \text{for } 1 \leq i \leq n.$$

Let M_{1j}, N_{1j}, and P_{1j} be minor matrices of A, B, and C, respectively, for $1 \leq j \leq n$. If $j \neq s$, then M_{1j}, N_{1j}, and P_{1j} are equal except in one column, which we designate as the rth column. Now the rth columns of N_{1j} and P_{1j} sum to the rth column of M_{1j}. Hence, by the induction hypothesis,

$$\det(M_{1j}) = \det(N_{1j}) + \det(P_{1j}), \quad 1 \leq j \leq n, \quad j \neq s.$$

Clearly, if $j = s$, then $M_{1s} = N_{1s} = P_{1s}$. Hence

$$\begin{aligned}
\det(B) + \det(C) &= \left(\sum_{\substack{j=1 \\ j \neq s}}^{n} a_{1j}(-1)^{1+j} \det(N_{1j}) \right) + b_{1s}(-1)^{1+s} \det(N_{1s}) \\
&\quad + \left(\sum_{\substack{j=1 \\ j \neq s}}^{n} a_{1j}(-1)^{1+j} \det(P_{1j}) \right) + c_{1s}(-1)^{1+s} \det(P_{1s}) \\
&= \left(\sum_{\substack{j=1 \\ j \neq s}}^{n} a_{1j}(-1)^{1+j} [\det(N_{1j}) + \det(P_{1j})] \right) \\
&\quad + (b_{1s} + c_{1s})(-1)^{1+s} \det(M_{1s}) \\
&= \sum_{j=1}^{n} a_{1j}(-1)^{1+j} \det(M_{1j}) = \det(A).
\end{aligned}$$

6.3 EXERCISES

In Exercises 1–6, use elementary column operations to create zeros in the last two entries in the first row and then calculate the determinant of the original matrix.

1. $\begin{bmatrix} 1 & 2 & 1 \\ 2 & 0 & 1 \\ 1 & -1 & 1 \end{bmatrix}$ **2.** $\begin{bmatrix} 2 & 4 & -2 \\ 0 & 2 & 3 \\ 1 & 1 & 2 \end{bmatrix}$

3. $\begin{bmatrix} 0 & 1 & 2 \\ 3 & 1 & 2 \\ 2 & 0 & 3 \end{bmatrix}$ **4.** $\begin{bmatrix} 2 & 2 & 4 \\ 1 & 0 & 1 \\ 2 & 1 & 2 \end{bmatrix}$

5. $\begin{bmatrix} 0 & 1 & 3 \\ 2 & 1 & 2 \\ 1 & 1 & 2 \end{bmatrix}$ **6.** $\begin{bmatrix} 1 & 1 & 1 \\ 2 & 1 & 2 \\ 3 & 0 & 2 \end{bmatrix}$

Suppose that $A = [\mathbf{A}_1, \mathbf{A}_2, \mathbf{A}_3, \mathbf{A}_4]$ is a (4×4) matrix, where $\det(A) = 3$. In Exercises 7–12, find $\det(B)$.

7. $B = [2\mathbf{A}_1, \mathbf{A}_2, \mathbf{A}_4, \mathbf{A}_3]$

8. $B = [\mathbf{A}_2, 3\mathbf{A}_3, \mathbf{A}_1, -2\mathbf{A}_4]$

9. $B = [\mathbf{A}_1 + 2\mathbf{A}_2, \mathbf{A}_2, \mathbf{A}_3, \mathbf{A}_4]$

10. $B = [\mathbf{A}_1, \mathbf{A}_1 + 2\mathbf{A}_2, \mathbf{A}_3, \mathbf{A}_4]$

11. $B = [\mathbf{A}_1 + 2\mathbf{A}_2, \mathbf{A}_2 + 3\mathbf{A}_3, \mathbf{A}_3, \mathbf{A}_4]$

12. $B = [2\mathbf{A}_1 - \mathbf{A}_2, 2\mathbf{A}_2 - \mathbf{A}_3, \mathbf{A}_3, \mathbf{A}_4]$

In Exercises 13–15, use only column interchanges to produce a triangular matrix and then give the determinant of the original matrix.

13. $\begin{bmatrix} 1 & 0 & 0 & 0 \\ 2 & 0 & 0 & 3 \\ 1 & 1 & 0 & 1 \\ 1 & 4 & 2 & 2 \end{bmatrix}$ **14.** $\begin{bmatrix} 0 & 0 & 2 & 0 \\ 0 & 0 & 1 & 3 \\ 0 & 4 & 1 & 3 \\ 2 & 1 & 5 & 6 \end{bmatrix}$

15. $\begin{bmatrix} 0 & 1 & 0 & 0 \\ 0 & 2 & 0 & 3 \\ 2 & 1 & 0 & 6 \\ 3 & 2 & 2 & 4 \end{bmatrix}$

In Exercises 16–18, use elementary column operations to create zeros in the (1, 2), (1, 3), (1, 4), (2, 3), and (2, 4) positions. Then evaluate the original determinant.

16. $\begin{vmatrix} 1 & 2 & 0 & 3 \\ 2 & 5 & 1 & 1 \\ 2 & 0 & 4 & 3 \\ 0 & 1 & 6 & 2 \end{vmatrix}$

17. $\begin{vmatrix} 2 & 4 & -2 & -2 \\ 1 & 3 & 1 & 2 \\ 1 & 3 & 1 & 3 \\ -1 & 2 & 1 & 2 \end{vmatrix}$

18. $\begin{vmatrix} 1 & 1 & 2 & 1 \\ 0 & 1 & 4 & 1 \\ 2 & 1 & 3 & 0 \\ 2 & 2 & 1 & 2 \end{vmatrix}$

19. Use elementary row operations on the determinant in Exercise 16 to create zeros in the (2, 1), (3, 1), (4, 1), (3, 2), and (4, 2) positions. Assuming the column results in this section also hold for rows, give the value of the original determinant to verify that it is the same as in Exercise 16.

20. Repeat Exercise 19, using the determinant in Exercise 17.

21. Repeat Exercise 19, using the determinant in Exercise 18.

22. Find a (2×2) matrix A and a (2×2) matrix B, where $\det(A + B)$ is not equal to $\det(A) + \det(B)$. Find a different A and B, both nonzero, such that $\det(A + B) = \det(A) + \det(B)$.

23. For any real number a, $a \neq 0$, show that

$$\begin{vmatrix} a+1 & a+4 & a+7 \\ a+2 & a+5 & a+8 \\ a+3 & a+6 & a+9 \end{vmatrix} = 0,$$

$$\begin{vmatrix} a & 4a & 7a \\ 2a & 5a & 8a \\ 3a & 6a & 9a \end{vmatrix} = 0,$$

and $$\begin{vmatrix} a & a^4 & a^7 \\ a^2 & a^5 & a^8 \\ a^3 & a^6 & a^9 \end{vmatrix} = 0.$$

24. Let $A = [\mathbf{A}_1, \mathbf{A}_2, \mathbf{A}_3]$ be a (3×3) matrix and set

$$B = \begin{bmatrix} 2 & 0 & 0 \\ 3 & -1 & 0 \\ 1 & 3 & 4 \end{bmatrix}.$$

a) Show that

$AB = [2\mathbf{A}_1 + 3\mathbf{A}_2 + \mathbf{A}_3, -\mathbf{A}_2 + 3\mathbf{A}_3, 4\mathbf{A}_3]$.

b) Use column operations to show that $\det(AB) = -8\det(A)$.

c) Conclude that $\det(AB) = \det(A)\det(B)$.

25. Let U be an $(n \times n)$ upper-triangular matrix and consider the cofactors U_{1j}, $2 \le j \le n$. Show that $U_{1j} = 0$, $2 \le j \le n$. [*Hint:* Some column in U_{1j} is always the zero column.]

26. Use the result of Exercise 25 to prove inductively that $\det(U) = u_{11}u_{22}\ldots u_{nn}$, where $U = (u_{ij})$ is an $(n \times n)$ upper-triangular matrix.

27. Let $y = mx + b$ be the equation of the line through the points (x_1, y_1) and (x_2, y_2) in the plane. Show that the equation is given also by

$$\begin{vmatrix} x & y & 1 \\ x_1 & y_1 & 1 \\ x_2 & y_2 & 1 \end{vmatrix} = 0.$$

28. Let (x_1, y_1), (x_2, y_2), and (x_3, y_3) be the vertices of a triangle in the plane where these vertices are numbered counterclockwise. Prove that the area of the triangle is given by

$$\text{Area} = \frac{1}{2}\begin{vmatrix} x_1 & y_1 & 1 \\ x_2 & y_2 & 1 \\ x_3 & y_3 & 1 \end{vmatrix}.$$

29. Let $\mathbf{x}$ and $\mathbf{y}$ be vectors in R^3, and let $A = I + \mathbf{x}\mathbf{y}^T$. Show that $\det(A) = 1 + \mathbf{y}^T\mathbf{x}$. [*Hint:* If $B = \mathbf{x}\mathbf{y}^T$, $B = [\mathbf{B}_1, \mathbf{B}_2, \mathbf{B}_3]$, then $A = [\mathbf{B}_1 + \mathbf{e}_1, \mathbf{B}_2 + \mathbf{e}_2, \mathbf{B}_3 + \mathbf{e}_3]$. Therefore, $\det(A) = \det[\mathbf{B}_1, \mathbf{B}_2 + \mathbf{e}_2, \mathbf{B}_3 + \mathbf{e}_3] + \det[\mathbf{e}_1, \mathbf{B}_2 + \mathbf{e}_2, \mathbf{B}_3 + \mathbf{e}_3]$. Use Theorems 4 and 5 to show that the first determinant is equal to $\det[\mathbf{B}_1, \mathbf{e}_2, \mathbf{B}_3 + \mathbf{e}_3]$, and so on.]

30. Use column operations to prove that

$$\begin{vmatrix} 1 & a & a^2 \\ 1 & b & b^2 \\ 1 & c & c^2 \end{vmatrix} = (b - a)(c - a)(c - b).$$

31. Evaluate the (4×4) determinant

$$\begin{vmatrix} 1 & a & a^2 & a^3 \\ 1 & b & b^2 & b^3 \\ 1 & c & c^2 & c^3 \\ 1 & d & d^2 & d^3 \end{vmatrix}.$$

[*Hint:* Proceed as in Exercise 30.]

32. Prove the corollary to Theorem 3.

6.4 CRAMER'S RULE

In Section 6.3, we saw how to calculate the effect that a column operation or a row operation has on a determinant. In this section, we use that information to analyze the relationships between determinants, nonsingular matrices, and solutions of systems $A\mathbf{x} = \mathbf{b}$. We begin with the following lemma, which will be helpful in the proof of the subsequent theorems.

LEMMA 1 Let $A = [\mathbf{A}_1, \mathbf{A}_2, \ldots, \mathbf{A}_n]$ be an $(n \times n)$ matrix, and let $\mathbf{b}$ be any vector in R^n. For each i, $1 \leq i \leq n$, let B_i be the $(n \times n)$ matrix:

$$B_i = [\mathbf{A}_1, \ldots, \mathbf{A}_{i-1}, \mathbf{b}, \mathbf{A}_{i+1}, \ldots, \mathbf{A}_n].$$

If the system of equations $A\mathbf{x} = \mathbf{b}$ is consistent and x_i is the ith component of a solution, then

$$x_i \det(A) = \det(B_i). \tag{1}$$

Proof To keep the notation simple, we give the proof of Eq. (1) only for $i = 1$. Since the system $A\mathbf{x} = \mathbf{b}$ is assumed to be consistent, there are values $x_1, x_2, \ldots, x_n$ such that

$$x_1\mathbf{A}_1 + x_2\mathbf{A}_2 + \cdots + x_n\mathbf{A}_n = \mathbf{b}.$$

Using the properties of determinants, we have

$$\begin{aligned} x_1 \det(A) &= \det[x_1\mathbf{A}_1, \mathbf{A}_2, \ldots, \mathbf{A}_n] \\ &= \det[\mathbf{b} - x_2\mathbf{A}_2 - \cdots - x_n\mathbf{A}_n, \mathbf{A}_2, \ldots, \mathbf{A}_n] \\ &= \det[\mathbf{b}, \mathbf{A}_2, \ldots, \mathbf{A}_n] - x_2 \det[\mathbf{A}_2, \mathbf{A}_2, \ldots, \mathbf{A}_n] \\ &\quad - \cdots - x_n \det[\mathbf{A}_n, \mathbf{A}_2, \ldots, \mathbf{A}_n]. \end{aligned}$$

By Theorem 5, the last $n - 1$ determinants are zero, so we have

$$x_1 \det(A) = \det[\mathbf{b}, \mathbf{A}_2, \ldots, \mathbf{A}_n];$$

and this equality verifies Eq. (1) for $i = 1$. Clearly, the same argument is valid for any i. ■

As the following theorem shows, one consequence of Lemma 1 is that a singular matrix has determinant zero.

THEOREM 7 If A is an $(n \times n)$ singular matrix, then $\det(A) = 0$.

Proof Since A is singular, $A\mathbf{x} = \boldsymbol{\theta}$ has a nontrivial solution. Let x_i be the ith component of a nontrivial solution, and choose i so that $x_i \neq 0$. By Lemma 1, $x_i \det(A) = \det(B_i)$, where $B_i = [\mathbf{A}_1, \ldots, \mathbf{A}_{i-1}, \boldsymbol{\theta}, \mathbf{A}_{i+1}, \ldots, \mathbf{A}_n]$. It follows from Theorem 3 that $\det(B_i) = 0$. Thus, $x_i \det(A) = 0$, and since $x_i \neq 0$, then $\det(A) = 0$. ■

Theorem 9, stated later, establishes the converse of Theorem 7: If $\det(A) = 0$, then A is a singular matrix. Theorem 9 will be an easy consequence of the product rule for determinants.

The Determinant of a Product

Theorem 8 states that if A and B are $(n \times n)$ matrices, then $\det(AB) = \det(A)\det(B)$. This result is somewhat surprising in view of the complexity of matrix multiplication. We also know, in general, that $\det(A + B)$ is distinct from $\det(A) + \det(B)$.

THEOREM 8 If A and B are $(n \times n)$ matrices, then

$$\det(AB) = \det(A)\det(B).$$

Before sketching a proof of Theorem 8, note that if A is an $(n \times n)$ matrix, and if B is obtained from A by a sequence of elementary column operations, then, by the properties of determinants given in Theorems 2, 3, and 6, $\det(A) = k\det(B)$, where the scalar k is completely determined by the elementary column operations. To illustrate, suppose that B is obtained by the following sequence of elementary column operations:

1. Interchange the first and third columns.
2. Multiply the second column by 3.
3. Add 2 times the second column to the first column.

It now follows from Theorems 2, 3, and 6 that $\det(B) = -3\det(A)$ or, equivalently, $\det(A) = (-1/3)\det(B)$. Moreover, the scalar $-1/3$ is completely determined by the operations; that is, the scalar is independent of the matrices involved.

The proof of Theorem 8 is based on the previous observation and on the following lemma.

LEMMA 2 Let A and B be $(n \times n)$ matrices and let $C = AB$. Let $\hat{C}$ denote the result of applying an elementary column operation to C and let $\hat{B}$ denote the result of applying the same column operation to B. Then $\hat{C} = A\hat{B}$.

The proof of Lemma 2 is left to the exercises. The intent of the lemma is given schematically in Fig. 6.1.

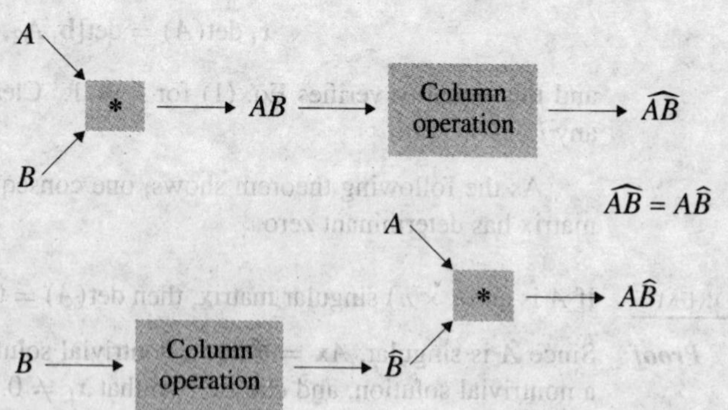

Figure 6.1 Schematic diagram of Lemma 2

Lemma 2 tells us that the same result is produced whether we apply a column operation to the product AB or whether we apply the operation to B first (producing $\hat{B}$)

and then form the product $A\hat{B}$. For example, suppose that A and B are (3×3) matrices. Consider the operation of interchanging column 1 and column 3:

$$B = [\mathbf{B}_1, \mathbf{B}_2, \mathbf{B}_3] \rightarrow \hat{B} = [\mathbf{B}_3, \mathbf{B}_2, \mathbf{B}_1]; \qquad A\hat{B} = [A\mathbf{B}_3, A\mathbf{B}_2, A\mathbf{B}_1]$$

$$AB = [A\mathbf{B}_1, A\mathbf{B}_2, A\mathbf{B}_3] \rightarrow \widehat{AB} = [A\mathbf{B}_3, A\mathbf{B}_2, A\mathbf{B}_1]; \qquad \widehat{AB} = A\hat{B}.$$

Proof of Theorem 8 Suppose that A and B are $(n \times n)$ matrices. If B is singular, then Theorem 8 is immediate, for in this case AB is also singular. Thus, by Theorem 7, $\det(B) = 0$ and $\det(AB) = 0$. Consequently, $\det(AB) = \det(A)\det(B)$.

Next, suppose that B is nonsingular. In this case, B can be transformed to the $(n \times n)$ identity matrix I by a sequence of elementary column operations. (To see this, note that B^T is nonsingular by Theorem 17, property 4, of Section 1.9. It now follows from Theorem 16 of Section 1.9 that B^T can be reduced to I by a sequence of elementary row operations. But performing row operations on B^T is equivalent to performing column operations on B.) Therefore, $\det(B) = k\det(I) = k$, where k is determined entirely by the sequence of elementary column operations. By Lemma 2, the same sequence of operations reduces the matrix AB to the matrix $AI = A$. Thus, $\det(AB) = k\det(A) = \det(B)\det(A) = \det(A)\det(B)$. ∎

EXAMPLE 1 Show by direct calculation that $\det(AB) = \det(A)\det(B)$ for the matrices

$$A = \begin{bmatrix} 2 & 1 \\ 1 & 3 \end{bmatrix} \quad \text{and} \quad B = \begin{bmatrix} -1 & 3 \\ 2 & -2 \end{bmatrix}.$$

Solution We have $\det(A) = 5$ and $\det(B) = -4$. Since AB is given by

$$AB = \begin{bmatrix} 0 & 4 \\ 5 & -3 \end{bmatrix},$$

it follows that $\det(AB) = -20 = (5)(-4) = \det(A)\det(B)$. ∎

The following theorem is now an easy consequence of Theorem 8.

THEOREM 9 If the $(n \times n)$ matrix A is nonsingular, then $\det(A) \neq 0$. Moreover, $\det(A^{-1}) = 1/\det(A)$.

Proof Since A is nonsingular, A^{-1} exists and $AA^{-1} = I$. By Theorem 8, $1 = \det(I) = \det(AA^{-1}) = \det(A)\det(A^{-1})$. In particular, $\det(A) \neq 0$ and $\det(A^{-1}) = 1/\det(A)$. ∎

Theorems 7 and 9 show that an $(n \times n)$ matrix A is singular if and only if $\det(A) = 0$. This characterization of singular matrices is especially useful when we want to examine matrices that depend on a parameter. The next example illustrates one such application.

EXAMPLE 2 Find all values λ such that the matrix $B(\lambda)$ is singular, where

$$B(\lambda) = \begin{bmatrix} 2-\lambda & 0 & 0 \\ 2 & 3-\lambda & 4 \\ 1 & 2 & 1-\lambda \end{bmatrix}.$$

Solution By Theorems 7 and 9, $B(\lambda)$ is singular if and only if $\det[B(\lambda)] = 0$. The equation $\det[B(\lambda)] = 0$ is determined by

$$\begin{aligned} 0 &= \det[B(\lambda)] \\ &= (2-\lambda)[(3-\lambda)(1-\lambda) - 8] \\ &= (2-\lambda)[\lambda^2 - 4\lambda - 5] \\ &= (2-\lambda)(\lambda-5)(\lambda+1). \end{aligned}$$

Thus, $B(\lambda)$ is singular if and only if λ is one of the values $\lambda = 2$, $\lambda = 5$, or $\lambda = -1$.

The three matrices discovered by solving $\det[B(\lambda)] = 0$ are listed next. As we can see, each of these matrices is singular:

$$B(2) = \begin{bmatrix} 0 & 0 & 0 \\ 2 & 1 & 4 \\ 1 & 2 & -1 \end{bmatrix}, \quad B(5) = \begin{bmatrix} -3 & 0 & 0 \\ 2 & -2 & 4 \\ 1 & 2 & -4 \end{bmatrix}, \quad B(-1) = \begin{bmatrix} 3 & 0 & 0 \\ 2 & 4 & 4 \\ 1 & 2 & 2 \end{bmatrix}.$$

Solving $A\mathbf{x} = \mathbf{b}$ with Cramer's Rule

A major result in determinant theory is Cramer's rule, which gives a formula for the solution of any system $A\mathbf{x} = \mathbf{b}$ when A is nonsingular.

THEOREM 10 **Cramer's Rule** Let $A = [\mathbf{A}_1, \mathbf{A}_2, \ldots, \mathbf{A}_n]$ be a nonsingular $(n \times n)$ matrix, and let $\mathbf{b}$ be any vector in R^n. For each i, $1 \le i \le n$, let B_i be the matrix $B_i = [\mathbf{A}_1, \ldots, \mathbf{A}_{i-1}, \mathbf{b}, \mathbf{A}_{i+1}, \ldots, \mathbf{A}_n]$. Then the ith component, x_i, of the solution of $A\mathbf{x} = \mathbf{b}$ is given by

$$x_i = \frac{\det(B_i)}{\det(A)}. \tag{2}$$

Proof Since A is nonsingular, $\det(A) \neq 0$. Formula (2) is now an immediate consequence of (1) in Lemma 1.

EXAMPLE 3 Use Cramer's rule to solve the system

$$\begin{aligned} 3x_1 + 2x_2 &= 4 \\ 5x_1 + 4x_2 &= 6. \end{aligned}$$

Solution To solve this system by Cramer's rule, we write the system as $A\mathbf{x} = \mathbf{b}$, and we form $B_1 = [\mathbf{b}, \mathbf{A}_2]$ and $B_2 = [\mathbf{A}_1, \mathbf{b}]$:

$$A = \begin{bmatrix} 3 & 2 \\ 5 & 4 \end{bmatrix}, \quad B_1 = \begin{bmatrix} 4 & 2 \\ 6 & 4 \end{bmatrix}, \quad B_2 = \begin{bmatrix} 3 & 4 \\ 5 & 6 \end{bmatrix}.$$

Note that $\det(A) = 2$, $\det(B_1) = 4$, and $\det(B_2) = -2$. Thus, from Eq. (2), the solution is

$$x_1 = \frac{4}{2} = 2 \quad \text{and} \quad x_2 = \frac{-2}{2} = -1.$$

EXAMPLE 4 Use Cramer's rule to solve the system

$$\begin{aligned} x_1 - x_2 + x_3 &= 0 \\ x_1 + x_2 - 2x_3 &= 1 \\ x_1 + 2x_2 + x_3 &= 6. \end{aligned}$$

Solution Writing the system as $A\mathbf{x} = \mathbf{b}$, we have

$$A = \begin{bmatrix} 1 & -1 & 1 \\ 1 & 1 & -2 \\ 1 & 2 & 1 \end{bmatrix}, \quad B_1 = \begin{bmatrix} 0 & -1 & 1 \\ 1 & 1 & -2 \\ 6 & 2 & 1 \end{bmatrix},$$

$$B_2 = \begin{bmatrix} 1 & 0 & 1 \\ 1 & 1 & -2 \\ 1 & 6 & 1 \end{bmatrix}, \quad B_3 = \begin{bmatrix} 1 & -1 & 0 \\ 1 & 1 & 1 \\ 1 & 2 & 6 \end{bmatrix}.$$

A calculation shows that $\det(A) = 9$, $\det(B_1) = 9$, $\det(B_2) = 18$, and $\det(B_3) = 9$. Thus, by Eq. (2), the solution is

$$x_1 = \frac{9}{9} = 1, \quad x_2 = \frac{18}{9} = 2, \quad \text{and} \quad x_3 = \frac{9}{9} = 1.$$

As a computational tool, Cramer's rule is rarely competitive with Gaussian elimination. It is, however, a valuable theoretical tool. Three specific examples illustrating the use of Cramer's rule in theoretical applications are as follows.

1. The method of variation of parameters (see W. E. Boyce and R. C. DiPrima, *Elementary Differential Equations and Boundary Value Problems*, p. 277. New York: John Wiley and Sons, 1986).
2. The theory of continued fractions (see Peter Henrici, *Applied and Computational Complex Analysis, Volume* 2, pp. 520–521. New York: John Wiley and Sons, 1977).
3. Characterization of best approximations (see E. W. Cheney, *Introduction to Approximation Theory*, p. 74. New York: McGraw-Hill, 1966).

CRAMER'S RULE In 1750, Gabriel Cramer (1704–1752) published a work in which, in the appendix, he stated the determinant procedure named after him for solving n linear equations in n unknowns. The first discoverer of this rule, however, was almost surely the Scottish mathematician Colin Maclaurin (1698–1746). It appeared in a paper of Maclaurin's in 1748, published two years after his death. This perhaps compensates for the fact that the famous series named after Maclaurin was not first discovered by him. (Ironically, the Maclaurin series is a special case of a Taylor series, named after the English mathematician Brook Taylor. However, as with the Maclaurin series, Taylor was not the first discoverer of the Taylor series!)

6.4 EXERCISES

In Exercises 1–3, use column operations to reduce the given matrix A to lower-triangular form. Find the determinant of A.

1. $A = \begin{bmatrix} 0 & 1 & 3 \\ 1 & 2 & 1 \\ 3 & 4 & 1 \end{bmatrix}$ **2.** $A = \begin{bmatrix} 1 & 2 & 1 \\ 2 & 4 & 3 \\ 2 & 1 & 3 \end{bmatrix}$

3. $A = \begin{bmatrix} 2 & 2 & 4 \\ 1 & 3 & 4 \\ -1 & 2 & 1 \end{bmatrix}$

In Exercises 4–6, use column operations to reduce the given matrix A to the identity matrix. Find the determinant of A.

4. $A = \begin{bmatrix} 1 & 0 & 1 \\ 2 & 1 & 1 \\ 1 & 2 & 1 \end{bmatrix}$ **5.** $A = \begin{bmatrix} 1 & 0 & -2 \\ 3 & 1 & 3 \\ 0 & 1 & 2 \end{bmatrix}$

6. $A = \begin{bmatrix} 2 & 2 & 2 \\ 4 & 3 & 4 \\ 2 & 1 & 2 \end{bmatrix}$

7. Let A and B be (3×3) matrices such that $\det(A) = 2$ and $\det(B) = 3$. Find the value of each of the following.

a) $\det(AB)$ **b)** $\det(AB^2)$
c) $\det(A^{-1}B)$ **d)** $\det(2A^{-1})$
e) $\det(2A)^{-1}$

8. Show that the matrices

$$\begin{bmatrix} \sin\theta & -\cos\theta \\ \cos\theta & \sin\theta \end{bmatrix} \text{ and } \begin{bmatrix} \sin\theta & -\cos\theta & 2 \\ \cos\theta & \sin\theta & 3 \\ 0 & 0 & 1 \end{bmatrix}$$

are nonsingular for all values of θ.

In Exercises 9–14, find all values λ such that the given matrix $B(\lambda)$ is singular.

9. $B(\lambda) = \begin{bmatrix} \lambda & 0 \\ 3 & 2-\lambda \end{bmatrix}$

10. $B(\lambda) = \begin{bmatrix} \lambda & 1 \\ 1 & \lambda \end{bmatrix}$ **11.** $B(\lambda) = \begin{bmatrix} 2 & \lambda \\ \lambda & 2 \end{bmatrix}$

12. $B(\lambda) = \begin{bmatrix} 1 & \lambda & \lambda^2 \\ 1 & 1 & 1 \\ 1 & 3 & 9 \end{bmatrix}$

13. $B(\lambda) = \begin{bmatrix} \lambda & 1 & 1 \\ 1 & \lambda & 1 \\ 1 & 1 & \lambda \end{bmatrix}$

14. $B(\lambda) = \begin{bmatrix} 2-\lambda & 0 & 3 \\ 2 & \lambda & 1 \\ 1 & 0 & -\lambda \end{bmatrix}$

In Exercises 15–21, use Cramer's rule to solve the given system.

15. $\begin{aligned} x_1 + x_2 &= 3 \\ x_1 - x_2 &= -1 \end{aligned}$ **16.** $\begin{aligned} x_1 + 3x_2 &= 4 \\ x_1 - x_2 &= 0 \end{aligned}$

17. $\begin{aligned} x_1 - 2x_2 + x_3 &= -1 \\ x_1 \quad\quad + x_3 &= 3 \\ x_1 - 2x_2 \quad\quad &= 0 \end{aligned}$

18. $\begin{aligned} x_1 + x_2 + x_3 &= 2 \\ x_1 + 2x_2 + x_3 &= 2 \\ x_1 + 3x_2 - x_3 &= -4 \end{aligned}$

19. $\begin{aligned} x_1 + x_2 + x_3 - x_4 &= 2 \\ x_2 - x_3 + x_4 &= 1 \\ x_3 - x_4 &= 0 \\ x_3 + 2x_4 &= 3 \end{aligned}$

20. $\begin{aligned} 2x_1 - x_2 + x_3 &= 3 \\ x_1 + x_2 \quad\quad &= 3 \\ x_2 - x_3 &= 1 \end{aligned}$

21. $\begin{aligned} x_1 + x_2 + x_3 &= a \\ x_2 + x_3 &= b \\ x_3 &= c \end{aligned}$

22. Suppose that A is an $(n \times n)$ matrix such that $A^2 = I$. Show that $|\det(A)| = 1$.

23. Prove Lemma 2. [*Hint:* Let

$$B = [\mathbf{B}_1, \mathbf{B}_2, \ldots, \mathbf{B}_i, \ldots, \mathbf{B}_j, \ldots, \mathbf{B}_n]$$

and consider the matrix $\hat{B}$ produced by interchanging column i and column j. Also consider the matrix $\hat{B}$ produced by replacing $\mathbf{B}_i$ by $\mathbf{B}_i + a\mathbf{B}_j$.]

24. We know that AB and BA are not usually equal. However, show that if A and B are $(n \times n)$, then $\det(AB) = \det(BA)$.

25. Suppose that S is a nonsingular $(n \times n)$ matrix, and suppose that A and B are $(n \times n)$ matrices such that $SAS^{-1} = B$. Prove that $\det(A) = \det(B)$.

26. Suppose that A is $(n \times n)$ and $A^2 = A$. What is $\det(A)$?

27. If $\det(A) = 3$, what is $\det(A^5)$?

28. Let A be a nonsingular matrix and suppose that all the entries of both A and A^{-1} are integers. Prove that $\det(A) = \pm 1$. [*Hint:* Use Theorem 9.]

29. Let A and C be square matrices, and let Q be a matrix of the form

$$Q = \begin{bmatrix} A & O \\ B & C \end{bmatrix}.$$

Convince yourself that $\det(Q) = \det(A)\det(C)$. [*Hint:* Reduce C to lower-triangular form with column operations; then reduce A.]

30. Verify the result in Exercise 29 for the matrix

$$Q = \begin{bmatrix} 1 & 2 & 0 & 0 & 0 \\ 2 & 1 & 0 & 0 & 0 \\ 3 & 5 & 1 & 2 & 2 \\ 7 & 2 & 3 & 5 & 1 \\ 1 & 8 & 1 & 4 & 1 \end{bmatrix}.$$

6.5 APPLICATIONS OF DETERMINANTS: INVERSES AND WRONSKIANS

Now that we have $\det(AB) = \det(A)\det(B)$, we are ready to prove that $\det(A^T) = \det(A)$ and to establish some other useful properties of determinants. First, however, we need the preliminary result stated in Theorem 11.

THEOREM 11 Let A be an $(n \times n)$ matrix. Then there is a nonsingular $(n \times n)$ matrix Q such that $AQ = L$, where L is lower triangular. Moreover, $\det(Q^T) = \det(Q)$.

The proof of Theorem 11 is based on the following fact: The result of any elementary column operation applied to A can be represented in matrix terms as AQ_i, where Q_i is an elementary matrix. We discuss this fact and give the proof of Theorem 11 at the end of this section.

Theorem 11 can be used to prove the following important result.

THEOREM 12 If A is an $(n \times n)$ matrix, then $\det(A^T) = \det(A)$.

Proof By Theorem 11, there is an $(n \times n)$ matrix Q such that $AQ = L$, where L is a lower-triangular matrix. Moreover, Q is nonsingular and $\det(Q^T) = \det(Q)$. Now, given $AQ = L$, it follows that

$$Q^T A^T = L^T.$$

Applying Theorem 8 to $AQ = L$ and to $Q^T A^T = L^T$, we obtain

$$\det(A)\det(Q) = \det(L)$$
$$\det(Q^T)\det(A^T) = \det(L^T).$$

Since L and L^T are triangular matrices with the same diagonal entries, it follows (see Theorem 1 of Section 6.2 and Exercise 26 of Section 6.3) that $\det(L) = \det(L^T)$. Hence, from the two equalities above, we have

$$\det(A)\det(Q) = \det(Q^T)\det(A^T).$$

Finally, since $\det(Q) = \det(Q^T)$ and $\det(Q) \neq 0$, we see that $\det(A) = \det(A^T)$. ■

At this point we know that Theorems 2–6 of Section 6.3 are valid for rows as well as for columns. In particular,we can use row operations to reduce a matrix A to a triangular matrix T and conclude that $\det(A) = \pm\det(T)$.

EXAMPLE 1 We return to the (4×4) matrix A in Example 8 of Section 6.3, where $\det(A) = -63$:

$$\det(A) = \begin{vmatrix} 1 & 2 & 0 & 2 \\ -1 & 2 & 3 & 1 \\ -3 & 2 & -1 & 0 \\ 2 & -3 & -2 & 1 \end{vmatrix}.$$

By using row operations, we can reduce $\det(A)$ to

$$\det(A) = \begin{vmatrix} 1 & 2 & 0 & 2 \\ 0 & 4 & 3 & 3 \\ 0 & 8 & -1 & 6 \\ 0 & -7 & -2 & -3 \end{vmatrix}.$$

Now we switch rows 2 and 3 and then switch columns 2 and 3 in order to get the number -1 into the pivot position. Following this switch, we create zeros in the (2, 3) and (2, 4) positions with row operations; and we find

$$\det(A) = \begin{vmatrix} 1 & 0 & 2 & 2 \\ 0 & -1 & 8 & 6 \\ 0 & 3 & 4 & 3 \\ 0 & -2 & -7 & -3 \end{vmatrix}$$

$$= \begin{vmatrix} 1 & 0 & 2 & 2 \\ 0 & -1 & 8 & 6 \\ 0 & 0 & 28 & 21 \\ 0 & 0 & -23 & -15 \end{vmatrix}.$$

(The sign of the first determinant above is the same as $\det(A)$ because the first determinant is the result of two interchanges.) A quick calculation shows that the last determinant has the value -63. ■

The next theorem shows that we can evaluate $\det(A)$ by using an expansion along any row or any column we choose. Computationally, this ability is useful when some row or column contains a number of zero entries.

THEOREM 13 Let $A = (a_{ij})$ be an $(n \times n)$ matrix. Then:

$$\det(A) = a_{i1}A_{i1} + a_{i2}A_{i2} + \cdots + a_{in}A_{in} \tag{1}$$

$$\det(A) = a_{1j}A_{1j} + a_{2j}A_{2j} + \cdots + a_{nj}A_{nj}. \tag{2}$$

Proof We establish only Eq. (1), which is an expansion of $\det(A)$ along the ith row. Expansion of $\det(A)$ along the jth column in Eq. (2) is proved the same way.

Form a matrix B from A in the following manner: Interchange row i first with row $i-1$ and then with row $i-2$; continue until row i is the top row of B. In other words, bring row i to the top and push the other rows down so that they retain their same relative ordering. This procedure requires $i-1$ interchanges; so $\det(A) = (-1)^{i-1}\det(B)$. An inspection shows that the cofactors $B_{11}, B_{12}, \ldots, B_{1n}$ are also related to the cofactors $A_{i1}, A_{i2}, \ldots, A_{in}$ by $B_{1k} = (-1)^{i-1}A_{ik}$. To see this relationship, one need only observe that if M is the minor of the $(1, k)$ entry of B, then M is the minor of the (i, k) entry of A. Therefore, $B_{1k} = (-1)^{k+1}M$ and $A_{ik} = (-1)^{i+k}M$, which shows that $B_{1k} = (-1)^{i-1}A_{ik}$. With this equality and Definition 2 of Section 6.2,

$$\begin{aligned}\det(B) &= b_{11}B_{11} + b_{12}B_{12} + \cdots + b_{1n}B_{1n}\\ &= a_{i1}B_{11} + a_{i2}B_{12} + \cdots + a_{in}B_{1n}\\ &= (-1)^{i-1}(a_{i1}A_{i1} + a_{i2}A_{i2} + \cdots + a_{in}A_{in}).\end{aligned}$$

Since $\det(A) = (-1)^{i-1}\det(B)$, formula (1) is proved. ∎

The Adjoint Matrix and the Inverse

We next show how determinants can be used to obtain a formula for the inverse of a nonsingular matrix. We first prove a lemma, which is similar in appearance to Theorem 13. In words, the lemma states that the sum of the products of entries from the ith row with cofactors from the kth row is zero when $i \neq k$ (and by Theorem 13 this sum is the determinant when $i = k$).

LEMMA If A is an $(n \times n)$ matrix and if $i \neq k$, then $a_{i1}A_{k1} + a_{i2}A_{k2} + \cdots + a_{in}A_{kn} = 0$.

Proof For i and k, given $i \neq k$, let B be the $(n \times n)$ matrix obtained from A by deleting the kth row of A and replacing it by the ith row of A; that is, B has two equal rows, the ith and kth, and B is the same as A for all rows but the kth.

In this event it is clear that $\det(B) = 0$, that the cofactor B_{kj} is equal to A_{kj}, and that the entry b_{kj} is equal to a_{ij}. Putting these together gives

$$\begin{aligned}0 = \det(B) &= b_{k1}B_{k1} + b_{k2}B_{k2} + \cdots + b_{kn}B_{kn}\\ &= a_{i1}A_{k1} + a_{i2}A_{k2} + \cdots + a_{in}A_{kn};\end{aligned}$$

thus the lemma is proved. ∎

This lemma can be used to derive a formula for A^{-1}. In particular, let A be an $(n \times n)$ matrix, and let C denote the matrix of cofactors; $C = (c_{ij})$ is $(n \times n)$, and $c_{ij} = A_{ij}$. The ***adjoint*** matrix of A, denoted $\text{Adj}(A)$, is equal to C^T. With these preliminaries, we prove Theorem 14.

THEOREM 14 If A is an $(n \times n)$ nonsingular matrix, then

$$A^{-1} = \frac{1}{\det(A)}\,\text{Adj}(A).$$

Proof Let $B = (b_{ij})$ be the matrix product of A and $\text{Adj}(A)$. Then the ijth entry of B is

$$b_{ij} = a_{i1}A_{j1} + a_{i2}A_{j2} + \cdots + a_{in}A_{jn},$$

and by the lemma and Theorem 13, $b_{ij} = 0$ when $i \neq j$, while $b_{ii} = \det(A)$. Therefore, B is equal to a multiple of $\det(A)$ times I, and the theorem is proved. ■

EXAMPLE 2 Let A be the matrix

$$A = \begin{bmatrix} 1 & -1 & 2 \\ 2 & 1 & -3 \\ 4 & 1 & 1 \end{bmatrix}.$$

We calculate the nine required cofactors and find

$$\begin{array}{lll} A_{11} = 4 & A_{12} = -14 & A_{13} = -2 \\ A_{21} = 3 & A_{22} = \;\;-7 & A_{23} = -5 \\ A_{31} = 1 & A_{32} = \;\;\;\;7 & A_{33} = \;\;3. \end{array}$$

The adjoint matrix (the transpose of the cofactor matrix) is

$$\text{Adj}(A) = \begin{bmatrix} 4 & 3 & 1 \\ -14 & -7 & 7 \\ -2 & -5 & 3 \end{bmatrix}.$$

A multiplication shows that the product of A and $\text{Adj}(A)$ is

$$\begin{bmatrix} 14 & 0 & 0 \\ 0 & 14 & 0 \\ 0 & 0 & 14 \end{bmatrix};$$

so $A^{-1} = (1/14)\text{Adj}(A)$, where of course $\det(A) = 14$. ■

Theorem 14 is especially useful when we need to calculate the inverse of a matrix that contains variables. For instance, consider the (3×3) matrix

$$A = \begin{bmatrix} a & 1 & b \\ 1 & 1 & 1 \\ b & 1 & a \end{bmatrix}. \qquad (3)$$

Although A has some variable entries, we can calculate $\det(A)$ and $\text{Adj}(A)$ and hence find A^{-1}.

EXAMPLE 3 Let A be the (3×3) matrix displayed in (3). Find A^{-1}.

Solution Although we can do this calculation by hand, it is more convenient to use a computer algebra system. We used Derive and found A^{-1} as shown in Fig. 6.2. ■

The Wronskian

As a final application of determinant theory, we develop a simple test for the linear independence of a set of functions. Suppose that $f_0(x), f_1(x), \ldots, f_n(x)$ are real-valued

$$7: \quad \begin{bmatrix} a & 1 & b \\ 1 & 1 & 1 \\ b & 1 & a \end{bmatrix}^{-1}$$

$$8: \quad \begin{bmatrix} \dfrac{a-1}{(a+b-2)(a-b)} & -\dfrac{1}{a+b-2} & \dfrac{1-b}{(a+b-2)(a-b)} \\ -\dfrac{1}{a+b-2} & \dfrac{a+b}{a+b-2} & -\dfrac{1}{a+b-2} \\ \dfrac{1-b}{(a+b-2)(a-b)} & -\dfrac{1}{a+b-2} & \dfrac{a-1}{(a+b-2)(a-b)} \end{bmatrix}$$

Figure 6.2 Using Derive to find the inverse of a matrix with variable entries, as in Example 3

functions defined on an interval $[a, b]$. If there exist scalars $a_0, a_1, \ldots, a_n$ (not all of which are zero) such that

$$a_0 f_0(x) + a_1 f_1(x) + \cdots + a_n f_n(x) = 0 \tag{4}$$

for all x in $[a, b]$, then $\{f_0(x), f_1(x), \ldots, f_n(x)\}$ is a linearly dependent set of functions (see Section 5.4). If the only scalars for which Eq. (4) holds for all x in $[a, b]$ are $a_0 = a_1 = \cdots = a_n = 0$, then the set is linearly independent.

A test for linear independence can be formulated from Eq. (4) as follows: If $a_0, a_1, \ldots, a_n$ are scalars satisfying Eq. (4) and if the functions $f_i(x)$ are sufficiently differentiable, then we can differentiate both sides of the identity (4) and have $a_0 f_0^{(i)}(x) + a_1 f_1^{(i)}(x) + \cdots + a_n f_n^{(i)}(x) = 0$, $1 \le i \le n$. In matrix terms, these equations are

$$\begin{bmatrix} f_0(x) & f_1(x) & \cdots & f_n(x) \\ f_0'(x) & f_1'(x) & \cdots & f_n'(x) \\ \vdots & & & \vdots \\ f_0^{(n)}(x) & f_1^{(n)}(x) & \cdots & f_n^{(n)}(x) \end{bmatrix} \begin{bmatrix} a_0 \\ a_1 \\ \vdots \\ a_n \end{bmatrix} = \begin{bmatrix} 0 \\ 0 \\ \vdots \\ 0 \end{bmatrix}.$$

If we denote the coefficient matrix above as $W(x)$, then $\det[W(x)]$ is called the ***Wronskian*** for $\{f_0(x), f_1(x), \ldots, f_n(x)\}$. If there is a point x_0 in $[a, b]$ such that $\det[W(x_0)] \neq 0$, then the matrix $W(x)$ is nonsingular at $x = x_0$, and the implication is that $a_0 = a_1 = \cdots = a_n = 0$. In summary, if the Wronskian is nonzero at any point in $[a, b]$, then $\{f_0(x), f_1(x), \ldots, f_n(x)\}$ is a linearly independent set of functions. Note, however, that $\det[W(x)] = 0$ for all x in $[a, b]$ does not imply linear dependence (see Example 4).

WRONSKIANS Wronskians are named after the Polish mathematician Josef Maria Hoëné-Wroński (1778–1853). Unfortunately, the violent character of his personal life often detracted from the respect he was due from his mathematical work. The Wronskian provides a partial test for linear independence. If the Wronskian is nonzero for some x_0 in $[a, b]$, then $f_0(x), f_1(x), \ldots, f_n(x)$ are linearly independent (see the first part of Example 4). If the Wronskian is zero for all x in $[a, b]$, then the test gives no information (see the second part of Example 4).

The Wronskian does provide a complete test for linear independence, however, when $f_0(x), f_1(x), \ldots, f_n(x)$ are solutions of an $(n + 1)$st-order linear differential equation of the form

$$y^{(n+1)} + g_n(x)y^{(n)} + \cdots + g_1(x)y' + g_0(x)y = 0,$$

where $g_0(x), g_1(x), \ldots, g_n(x)$ are all continuous on (a, b). In this case, $f_0(x), f_1(x), \ldots, f_n(x)$ are linearly independent if and only if the Wronskian is never zero for any x in (a, b).

EXAMPLE 4 Let $F_1 = \{x, \cos x, \sin x\}$ and $F_2 = \{\sin^2 x, |\sin x| \sin x\}$ for $-1 \le x \le 1$. The respective Wronskians are

$$w_1(x) = \begin{vmatrix} x & \cos x & \sin x \\ 1 & -\sin x & \cos x \\ 0 & -\cos x & -\sin x \end{vmatrix} = x$$

and

$$w_2(x) = \begin{vmatrix} \sin^2 x & |\sin x| \sin x \\ \sin 2x & |\sin 2x| \end{vmatrix} = 0.$$

Since $w_1(x) \neq 0$ for $x \neq 0$, F_1 is linearly independent. Even though $w_2(x) = 0$ for all x in $[-1, 1]$, F_2 is also linearly independent, for if $a_1 \sin^2 x + a_2 |\sin x| \sin x = 0$, then at $x = 1$, $a_1 + a_2 = 0$; and at $x = -1$, $a_1 - a_2 = 0$; so $a_1 = a_2 = 0$. ■

Elementary Matrices (Optional)

In this subsection, we observe that the result of applying a sequence of elementary column operations to a matrix A can be represented in matrix terms as multiplication of A by a sequence of elementary matrices. In particular, let I denote the $(n \times n)$ identity matrix, and let E be the matrix that results when an elementary column operation is applied to I. Such a matrix E is called an ***elementary matrix***.

For example, consider the (3×3) matrices

$$E_1 = \begin{bmatrix} 1 & 0 & 3 \\ 0 & 1 & 0 \\ 0 & 0 & 1 \end{bmatrix} \text{ and } E_2 = \begin{bmatrix} 0 & 1 & 0 \\ 1 & 0 & 0 \\ 0 & 0 & 1 \end{bmatrix}.$$

As we can see, E_1 is obtained from I by adding 3 times the first column of I to the third column of I. Similarly, E_2 is obtained from I by interchanging the first and second columns of I. Thus E_1 and E_2 are specific examples of (3×3) elementary matrices.

The next theorem shows how elementary matrices can be used to represent elementary column operations as matrix products.

THEOREM 15 Let E be the $(n \times n)$ elementary matrix that results from performing a certain column operation on the $(n \times n)$ identity. If A is any $(n \times n)$ matrix, then AE is the matrix that results when this same column operation is performed on A.

Proof We prove Theorem 15 only for the case in which the column operation is to add c times column i to column j. The rest of the proof is left to the exercises.

Let E denote the elementary matrix derived by adding c times the ith column of I to the jth column of I. Since I is given by $I = [\mathbf{e}_1, \mathbf{e}_2, \ldots, \mathbf{e}_i, \ldots, \mathbf{e}_j, \ldots, \mathbf{e}_n]$, we can represent the elementary matrix E in column form as

$$E = [\mathbf{e}_1, \mathbf{e}_2, \ldots, \mathbf{e}_i, \ldots, \mathbf{e}_j + c\mathbf{e}_i, \ldots, \mathbf{e}_n].$$

Consequently, in column form, AE is the matrix

$$AE = [A\mathbf{e}_1, A\mathbf{e}_2, \ldots, A\mathbf{e}_i, \ldots, A(\mathbf{e}_j + c\mathbf{e}_i), \ldots, A\mathbf{e}_n].$$

Next, if $A = [\mathbf{A}_1, \mathbf{A}_2, \ldots, \mathbf{A}_n]$, then $A\mathbf{e}_k = \mathbf{A}_k$, $1 \le k \le n$. Therefore, AE has the form

$$AE = [\mathbf{A}_1, \mathbf{A}_2, \ldots, \mathbf{A}_i, \ldots, \mathbf{A}_j + c\mathbf{A}_i, \ldots, \mathbf{A}_n].$$

From this column representation for AE, it follows that AE is the matrix that results when c times column i of A is added to column j. ■

We now use Theorem 15 to prove Theorem 11. Let A be an $(n \times n)$ matrix. Then A can be reduced to a lower-triangular matrix L by using a sequence of column operations. Equivalently, by Theorem 15, there is a sequence of elementary matrices $E_1, E_2, \ldots, E_r$ such that

$$AE_1E_2\cdots E_r = L. \tag{5}$$

In Eq. (5), an elementary matrix E_k represents either a column interchange or the addition of a multiple of one column to another. It can be shown that:

(a) If E_k represents a column interchange, then E_k is symmetric.

(b) If E_k represents the addition of a multiple of column i to column j, where $i < j$, then E_k is an upper-triangular matrix with all main diagonal entries equal to 1.

Now in Eq. (5), let Q denote the matrix $Q = E_1E_2\cdots E_r$ and observe that Q is nonsingular because each E_k is nonsingular. To complete the proof of Theorem 11, we need to verify that $\det(Q^T) = \det(Q)$.

From the remarks in (a) and (b) above, $\det(E_k^T) = \det(E_k)$, $1 \le k \le r$, since each matrix E_k is either symmetric or triangular. Thus

$$\begin{aligned}\det(Q^T) &= \det(E_r^T \cdots E_2^T E_1^T)\\ &= \det(E_r^T)\cdots\det(E_2^T)\det(E_1^T)\\ &= \det(E_r)\cdots\det(E_2)\det(E_1)\\ &= \det(Q).\end{aligned}$$

An illustration of the discussion above is provided by the next example.

EXAMPLE 5 Let A be the (3×3) matrix

$$A = \begin{bmatrix} 0 & 1 & 3 \\ 1 & 2 & 1 \\ 3 & 4 & 2 \end{bmatrix}.$$

Display elementary matrices E_1, E_2, and E_3 such that $AE_1E_2E_3 = L$, where L is lower triangular.

Solution Matrix A can be reduced to a lower-triangular matrix by the following sequence of column operations:

$$A = \begin{bmatrix} 0 & 1 & 3 \\ 1 & 2 & 1 \\ 3 & 4 & 2 \end{bmatrix} \xrightarrow{C_1 \leftrightarrow C_2} \begin{bmatrix} 1 & 0 & 3 \\ 2 & 1 & 1 \\ 4 & 3 & 2 \end{bmatrix}$$

$$\xrightarrow{C_3 - 3C_1} \begin{bmatrix} 1 & 0 & 0 \\ 2 & 1 & -5 \\ 4 & 3 & -10 \end{bmatrix} \xrightarrow{C_3 + 5C_2} \begin{bmatrix} 1 & 0 & 0 \\ 2 & 1 & 0 \\ 4 & 3 & 5 \end{bmatrix}.$$

Therefore, $AE_1E_2E_3 = L$, where

$$E_1 = \begin{bmatrix} 0 & 1 & 0 \\ 1 & 0 & 0 \\ 0 & 0 & 1 \end{bmatrix}, \quad E_2 = \begin{bmatrix} 1 & 0 & -3 \\ 0 & 1 & 0 \\ 0 & 0 & 1 \end{bmatrix}, \text{ and } E_3 = \begin{bmatrix} 1 & 0 & 0 \\ 0 & 1 & 5 \\ 0 & 0 & 1 \end{bmatrix}.$$

Note that E_1 is symmetric and E_2 and E_3 are upper triangular.

6.5 EXERCISES

In Exercises 1–4, use row operations to reduce the given determinant to upper-triangular form and determine the value of the original determinant.

1. $\begin{vmatrix} 1 & 2 & 1 \\ 2 & 3 & 2 \\ -1 & 4 & 1 \end{vmatrix}$ **2.** $\begin{vmatrix} 0 & 3 & 1 \\ 1 & 2 & 1 \\ 2 & -2 & 2 \end{vmatrix}$

3. $\begin{vmatrix} 0 & 1 & 3 \\ 1 & 2 & 2 \\ 3 & 1 & 0 \end{vmatrix}$ **4.** $\begin{vmatrix} 1 & 0 & 1 \\ 0 & 2 & 4 \\ 3 & 2 & 1 \end{vmatrix}$

In Exercises 5–10, find the adjoint matrix for the given matrix A. Next, use Theorem 14 to calculate the inverse of the given matrix.

5. $\begin{bmatrix} 1 & 2 \\ 3 & 4 \end{bmatrix}$ **6.** $\begin{bmatrix} a & b \\ c & d \end{bmatrix}$

7. $\begin{bmatrix} 1 & 0 & 1 \\ 2 & 1 & 2 \\ 1 & 1 & 2 \end{bmatrix}$ **8.** $\begin{bmatrix} 2 & 1 & 0 \\ 3 & 0 & 1 \\ 0 & 1 & 1 \end{bmatrix}$

9. $\begin{bmatrix} 1 & 1 & 1 \\ 1 & 2 & 2 \\ 1 & 3 & 1 \end{bmatrix}$ **10.** $\begin{bmatrix} 1 & 2 & 3 \\ 0 & 1 & 2 \\ 0 & 0 & 1 \end{bmatrix}$

In Exercises 11–16, calculate the Wronskian. Also, determine whether the given set of functions is linearly independent on the interval $[-1, 1]$.

11. $\{1, x, x^2\}$ **12.** $\{e^x, e^{2x}, e^{3x}\}$

13. $\{1, \cos^2 x, \sin^2 x\}$ **14.** $\{1, \cos x, \cos 2x\}$

15. $\{x^2, x|x|\}$ **16.** $\{x^2, 1 + x^2, 2 - x^2\}$

In Exercises 17–20, find elementary matrices E_1, E_2, and E_3 such that $AE_1E_2E_3 = L$, where L is lower triangular. Calculate the product $Q = E_1E_2E_3$ and verify that $AQ = L$ and $\det(Q) = \det(Q^T)$.

17. $A = \begin{bmatrix} 0 & 1 & 3 \\ 1 & 2 & 4 \\ 2 & 2 & 1 \end{bmatrix}$ **18.** $A = \begin{bmatrix} 0 & -1 & 2 \\ 1 & 3 & -1 \\ 1 & 2 & 1 \end{bmatrix}$

19. $A = \begin{bmatrix} 1 & 2 & -1 \\ 3 & 5 & 1 \\ 4 & 0 & 2 \end{bmatrix}$ **20.** $A = \begin{bmatrix} 2 & 4 & -6 \\ 1 & 1 & 1 \\ 3 & 2 & 1 \end{bmatrix}$

In Exercises 21–24, calculate $\det[A(x)]$ and show that the given matrix $A(x)$ is nonsingular for any real value of x. Use Theorem 14 to find an expression for the inverse of $A(x)$.

21. $A(x) = \begin{bmatrix} x & 1 \\ -1 & x \end{bmatrix}$ **22.** $A(x) = \begin{bmatrix} 1 & x \\ -x & 2 \end{bmatrix}$

23. $A(x) = \begin{bmatrix} 2 & x & 0 \\ -x & 2 & x \\ 0 & -x & 2 \end{bmatrix}$

24. $A(x) = \begin{bmatrix} \sin x & 0 & \cos x \\ 0 & 1 & 0 \\ -\cos x & 0 & \sin x \end{bmatrix}$

25. Let L and U be the (3×3) matrices

$$L = \begin{bmatrix} 1 & 0 & 0 \\ a & 1 & 0 \\ b & c & 1 \end{bmatrix} \text{ and } U = \begin{bmatrix} 1 & a & b \\ 0 & 1 & c \\ 0 & 0 & 1 \end{bmatrix}.$$

Use Theorem 14 to show that L^{-1} is lower triangular and U^{-1} is upper triangular.

26. Let L be a nonsingular (4×4) lower-triangular matrix. Show that L^{-1} is also a lower-triangular matrix. [*Hint:* Consider a variation of Exercise 25.]

27. Let A be an $(n \times n)$ matrix, where $\det(A) = 1$ and A contains only integer entries. Show that A^{-1} contains only integer entries.

28. Let E denote the $(n \times n)$ elementary matrix corresponding to an interchange of the ith and jth columns of I. Let A be any $(n \times n)$ matrix.

a) Show that matrix AE is equal to the result of interchanging columns i and j of A.

b) Show that matrix E is symmetric.

29. An $(n \times n)$ matrix A is called ***skew symmetric*** if $A^T = -A$. Show that if A is skew symmetric, then $\det(A) = (-1)^n \det(A)$. If n is odd, show that A must be singular.

30. An $(n \times n)$ real matrix is ***orthogonal*** provided that $A^T = A^{-1}$. If A is an orthogonal matrix, prove that $\det(A) = \pm 1$.

31. Let A be an $(n \times n)$ nonsingular matrix. Prove that $\det[\text{Adj}(A)] = [\det(A)]^{n-1}$. [*Hint:* Use Theorem 14.]

32. Let A be an $(n \times n)$ nonsingular matrix.

a) Show that

$$[\text{Adj}(A)]^{-1} = \frac{1}{\det(A)} A.$$

[*Hint:* Use Theorem 14.]

b) Show that

$$\text{Adj}(A^{-1}) = \frac{1}{\det(A)} A.$$

[*Hint:* Use Theorem 14 to obtain a formula for $(A^{-1})^{-1}$.]

SUPPLEMENTARY EXERCISES

1. Express

$$\begin{vmatrix} a_{11} + b_{11} & a_{12} + b_{12} \\ a_{21} + b_{21} & a_{22} + b_{22} \end{vmatrix}$$

as a sum of four determinants in which there are no sums in the entries.

2. Let $A = [\mathbf{A}_1, \mathbf{A}_2, \ldots, \mathbf{A}_n]$ be an $(n \times n)$ matrix and let $B = [\mathbf{A}_n, A_{n-1}, \ldots, \mathbf{A}_1]$. How are $\det(A)$ and $\det(B)$ related when n is odd? When n is even?

3. If A is an $(n \times n)$ matrix such that $A^3 = A$, then list all possible values for $\det(A)$.

4. If A is a nonsingular (2×2) matrix and c is a scalar such that $A^T = cA$, what are the possible values for c? If A is a nonsingular (3×3) matrix, what are the possible values for c?

5. Let $A = (a_{ij})$ be a (3×3) matrix such that $\det(A) = 2$, and let A_{ij} denote the ijth cofactor of A. If

$$B = \begin{bmatrix} A_{31} & A_{21} & A_{11} \\ A_{32} & A_{22} & A_{12} \\ A_{33} & A_{23} & A_{13} \end{bmatrix},$$

then calculate AB.

6. Let $A = (a_{ij})$ be a (3×3) matrix with $a_{11} = 1$, $a_{12} = 2$, and $a_{13} = -1$. Let

$$C = \begin{bmatrix} -7 & 5 & 4 \\ -4 & 3 & 2 \\ 9 & -7 & -5 \end{bmatrix}$$

be the matrix of cofactors for A. (That is, $A_{11} = -7$, $A_{12} = 5$, and so on.) Find A.

7. Let $\mathbf{b} = [b_1, b_2, \ldots, b_n]^T$.

a) For $1 \le i \le n$, let A_i be the $(n \times n)$ matrix $A_i = [\mathbf{e}_1, \ldots, \mathbf{e}_{i-1}, \mathbf{b}, \mathbf{e}_{i+1}, \ldots, \mathbf{e}_n]$. Apply Cramer's rule to the system $I_n\mathbf{x} = \mathbf{b}$ to show that $\det(A_i) = b_i$.

b) If B is the $(n \times n)$ matrix $B = [\mathbf{b}, \ldots, \mathbf{b}]$, then use part a) and Theorem 4 to determine a formula for $\det(B + I)$.

8. If the Wronskian for $\{f_0(x), f_1(x), f_2(x)\}$ is $(x^2 + 1)e^x$, then calculate the Wronskian for $\{xf_0(x), xf_1(x), xf_2(x)\}$.

CONCEPTUAL EXERCISES

In Exercises 1–8, answer true or false. Justify your answer by providing a counterexample if the statement is false or an outline of a proof if the statement is true.

1. If A, B, and C are $(n \times n)$ matrices such that $AB = AC$ and $\det(A) \neq 0$, then $B = C$.

2. If A and B are $(n \times n)$ matrices, then $\det(AB) = \det(BA)$.

3. If A is an $(n \times n)$ matrix and c is a scalar, then $\det(cI_n - A) = c^n - \det(A)$.

4. If A is an $(n \times n)$ matrix and c is a scalar, then $\det(cA) = c\det(A)$.

5. If A is an $(n \times n)$ matrix such that $A^k = \mathcal{O}$ for some positive integer k, then $\det(A) = 0$.

6. If $A_1, A_2, \ldots, A_m$ are $(n \times n)$ matrices such that $B = A_1A_2 \ldots A_m$ is nonsingular, then each A_i is nonsingular.

7. If the matrix A is symmetric, then so is $\mathrm{Adj}(A)$.

8. If A is an $(n \times n)$ matrix such that $\det(A) = 1$, then $\mathrm{Adj}[\mathrm{Adj}(A)] = A$.

In Exercises 9–15, give a brief answer.

9. Show that $A^2 + I = \mathcal{O}$ is not possible if A is an $(n \times n)$ matrix and n is odd.

10. Let A and B be $(n \times n)$ matrices such that $AB = I$. Prove that $BA = I$. [*Hint:* Show that $\det(A) \neq 0$ and conclude that A^{-1} exists.]

11. If A is an $(n \times n)$ matrix and c is a scalar, show that $\det(A^T - cI) = \det(A - cI)$.

12. Let A and B be $(n \times n)$ matrices such that B is nonsingular, and let c be a scalar.

a) Show that $\det(A - cI) = \det(B^{-1}AB - cI)$.

b) Show that $\det(AB - cI) = \det(BA - cI)$.

13. If A is a nonsingular $(n \times n)$ matrix, then prove that $\mathrm{Adj}(A)$ is also nonsingular. [*Hint:* Consider the product $A[\mathrm{Adj}(A)]$.]

14. a) If A and B are nonzero $(n \times n)$ matrices such that $AB = \mathcal{O}$, then prove that both A and B are singular. [*Hint:* What would you conclude if either A or B were nonsingular?]

b) Use part a) to prove that if A is a singular $(n \times n)$ matrix, then $\mathrm{Adj}(A)$ is also a singular matrix. [*Hint:* Consider the product $A[\mathrm{Adj}(A)]$.]

15. If $A = (a_{ij})$ is an $(n \times n)$ orthogonal matrix (that is, $A^T = A^{-1}$), then prove that $A_{ij} = a_{ij}\det(A)$, where A_{ij} is the ijth cofactor of A. [*Hint:* Express A^{-1} in terms of $\mathrm{Adj}(A)$.]

MATLAB EXERCISES

Exercises 1–6 will illustrate some properties of the determinant and help you sharpen your skills using MATLAB to manipulate matrices and perform matrix surgery. These exercises also reinforce the theoretical properties of the determinant that you learned in Chapter 6.

1. Use the `A = round(20*rand(5,5) - 10*ones(5,5))` command to generate a random (5×5) matrix A having integer entries selected from $[-10, 10]$. Use Definition 3 to calculate $\det(A)$, using the MATLAB `det` command to calculate the five cofactors $A_{11}, A_{12}, \ldots, A_{15}$. Use matrix surgery to create the five minor matrices M_{ij} (recall that the minor matrix is defined in Definition 2). Compare your result with the value of the determinant of A as calculated by the MATLAB command `det(A)`.

2. Use matrix A from Exercise 1 (or a similarly randomly generated matrix) to illustrate Theorems 2, 3, and the corollary to Theorem 3.

3. As in Exercise 2, use a randomly generated (5×5) matrix to illustrate Theorems 4, 5, and 6.

4. As in Exercise 2, use a randomly generated (5×5) matrix to illustrate Theorem 12.

5. As in Exercise 2, use a randomly generated (5×5) matrix and a randomly generated vector **b** to illustrate Cramer's Rule (Theorem 10).

6. As in Exercise 2, use a randomly generated (5×5) matrix A and a randomly generated (5×5) matrix B to illustrate Theorem 8.

7. How common are singular matrices? Because of the emphasis on singular matrices in matrix theory, it might seem that they are quite common. In this exercise, randomly generate 100 matrices, calculate the determinant of each, and then make a rough assessment as to how likely encountering a singular matrix would be.

The following MATLAB loop will generate the determinant values for 100 randomly chosen matrices:

```
determ = zeros(1,100);
for i = 1 : 100
  A = round(20*rand(5,5) - 10*ones(5,5));
 determ(1,i) = det(A);
end
```

After executing this loop, list the vector determinant to display the 100 determinant values calculated. Are any of the 100 matrices singular? Repeat the experiment using 1000 randomly generated matrices instead of 100. Rather than listing the vector determinant, use the `min(abs(determ))` command to find the smallest determinant in absolute value. Did you encounter any singular matrices?

8. Generating integer matrices with integer inverses For certain simulations, it is convenient to have a collection of randomly-generated matrices that have integer entries and whose inverses also have integer entries. Argue, using Theorem 14, that an integer matrix with determinant equal to 1 or -1 will have an integer inverse.

One easy way to create an integer matrix A with determinant equal to 1 or -1 is to set $A = LU$ where L is a lower-triangular integer matrix with 1's and -1's on its diagonal and where U is an upper-triangular integer matrix with 1's and -1's on its diagonal. Then, since $\det(A) = \det(L)\det(U)$, we see that both A and A^{-1} will be integer matrices.

Use these ideas to create a set of ten randomly generated (5×5) integer matrices with integer inverses. For each matrix A created, use the MATLAB `inv` command to generate the inverse for A. Note, because of roundoff error, that the MATLAB inverse for A is not always an integer matrix. To eliminate the roundoff error, you can use the command `round(inv(A))` in order to round the entries of A^{-1} to the nearest integer. Check, by direct multiplication, that this will produce the inverse.

7

Eigenvalues and Applications

Overview In this chapter we discuss a number of applications of eigenvalues. Sections 7.1 and 7.2 are independent and can be covered at any time. Section 7.3 is a prerequisite for Section 7.4 and Section 7.5 is a prerequisite for Section 7.6. Sections 7.3 and 7.5 are, however, independent. Sections 7.7 and 7.8 depend on Section 7.4.

Core Sections

7.1 Quadratic Forms
7.2 Systems of Differential Equations
7.3 Transformation to Hessenberg Form
7.4 Eigenvalues of Hessenberg Matrices
7.5 Householder Transformations
7.6 The QR Factorization and Least-Squares Solutions
7.7 Matrix Polynomials and the Cayley–Hamilton Theorem
7.8 Generalized Eigenvectors and Solutions of Systems of Differential Equations

7.1 QUADRATIC FORMS*

An expression of the sort

$$q(x, y) = ax^2 + bxy + cy^2$$

is called a ***quadratic form in x and y***. Similarly, the expression

$$q(x, y, z) = ax^2 + by^2 + cz^2 + dxy + exz + fyz$$

is a quadratic form in the variables x, y, and z.

In general, a ***quadratic form*** in the variables $x_1, x_2, \ldots, x_n$ is an expression of the form

$$q(\mathbf{x}) = q(x_1, x_2, \ldots, x_n) = \sum_{i=1}^{n}\sum_{j=1}^{n} b_{ij}x_i x_j. \tag{1}$$

In Eq. (1), the coefficients b_{ij} are given constants and, for simplicity, we assume that b_{ij} are *real* constants.

The term *form* means homogeneous polynomial; that is, $q(a\mathbf{x}) = a^k q(\mathbf{x})$. The adjective *quadratic* implies that the form is homogeneous of degrees 2; that is, $q(a\mathbf{x}) = a^2 q(\mathbf{x})$. Quadratic forms occur naturally in applications such as mechanics, vibrations, geometry, optimization, and so on.

Matrix Representations for Quadratic Forms

As we see in Eq. (1), a quadratic form is nothing more than a polynomial in several variables, where each term of the polynomial has degree 2 exactly. It turns out that such polynomials can be represented in the form $q(\mathbf{x}) = \mathbf{x}^T A\mathbf{x}$, where A is a uniquely determined symmetric matrix. For example, consider the quadratic form

$$q(x, y) = 2x^2 + 4xy - 3y^2.$$

Using the properties of matrix multiplication, we can verify that

$$q(x, y) = [x, y]\begin{bmatrix} 2 & 2 \\ 2 & -3 \end{bmatrix}\begin{bmatrix} x \\ y \end{bmatrix}.$$

There is a simple procedure for finding the symmetric matrix $A = (a_{ij})$ such that $q(\mathbf{x}) = \mathbf{x}^T A\mathbf{x}$. In particular, consider the general quadratic form given in Eq. (1). The procedure, as applied to (1), is simply:

1. Define $a_{ii} = b_{ii}, \quad 1 \le i \le n.$
2. Define $a_{ij} = (b_{ij} + b_{ij})/2, \quad 1 \le i, j \le n, \quad i \ne j.$

When these steps are followed, the $(n \times n)$ matrix $A = (a_{ij})$ will be symmetric and will satisfy the conditions $q(\mathbf{x}) = \mathbf{x}^T A\mathbf{x}$.

EXAMPLE 1 Represent the quadratic form in Eq. (2) as $q(\mathbf{x}) = \mathbf{x}^T A\mathbf{x}$:

$$q(\mathbf{x}) = x_1^2 + x_2^2 + 3x_3^2 + 6x_1x_2 + 4x_1x_3 - 10x_2x_3. \tag{2}$$

*The sections in this chapter need not be read in the order they are presented; see the Overview for details.

Solution In the context of Eq. (1), the constant b_{ij} is the coefficient of the term $x_i x_j$. With respect to Eq. (2), $b_{11} = b_{22} = 1, b_{33} = 3, b_{12} = 6, b_{13} = 4, b_{23} = -10$, and the other coefficients b_{ij} are zero. Following the simple two-step procedure, we obtain

$$A = \begin{bmatrix} 1 & 3 & 2 \\ 3 & 1 & -5 \\ 2 & -5 & 3 \end{bmatrix}.$$

A quick check shows that $\mathbf{x}^T A \mathbf{x} = q(\mathbf{x})$:

$$[x_1, x_2, x_3] \begin{bmatrix} 1 & 3 & 2 \\ 3 & 1 & -5 \\ 2 & -5 & 3 \end{bmatrix} \begin{bmatrix} x_1 \\ x_2 \\ x_3 \end{bmatrix}$$

$$= x_1^2 + x_2^2 + 3x_3^2 + 6x_1x_2 + 4x_1x_3 - 10x_2x_3.$$ ■

The procedure used in Example 1 is stated formally in the next theorem. Also, for brevity in Theorem 1, we have combined steps (1) and (2) using an equivalent formulation.

THEOREM 1 For $\mathbf{x}$ in R^n, let $q(\mathbf{x})$ denote the quadratic form

$$q(\mathbf{x}) = \sum_{i=1}^{n} \sum_{j=1}^{n} b_{ij} x_i x_j.$$

Let $A = (a_{ij})$ be the $(n \times n)$ matrix defined by

$$a_{ij} = (b_{ij} + b_{ij})/2, \quad 1 \le i, j \le n.$$

The matrix A is symmetric and, moreover, $q(\mathbf{x}) = \mathbf{x}^T A \mathbf{x}$. In addition, there is no other symmetric matrix B such that $\mathbf{x}^T B \mathbf{x} = q(\mathbf{x})$.

Proof The fact that A is symmetric comes from the expression that defines a_{ij}. In particular, observe that a_{ij} and a_{ji} are given, respectively, by

$$a_{ij} = \frac{b_{ij} + b_{ji}}{2} \quad \text{and} \quad a_{ji} = \frac{b_{ji} + b_{ij}}{2}.$$

Thus, $a_{ij} = a_{ji}$, which shows that A is symmetric. Also note that $a_{ii} = (b_{ii} + b_{ii})/2 = b_{ii}$, which agrees with step (1) of the previously given two-step procedure.

The rest of the proof is left to the exercises. ■

In Theorem 1, if we relax the condition that A be symmetric, then we no longer have uniqueness. That is, there are many nonsymmetric matrices B such that $\mathbf{x}^T B \mathbf{x} = q(\mathbf{x})$.

Diagonalizing Quadratic Forms

Theorem 1 shows that a quadratic form $q(\mathbf{x})$ can be represented as $q(\mathbf{x}) = \mathbf{x}^T A \mathbf{x}$, where A is a symmetric matrix. For many applications, however, it is useful to have the even simpler representation described in this subsection.

Recall that a real symmetric matrix A can be diagonalized with an orthogonal matrix. That is, there is a square matrix Q such that:

1. $Q^TQ = I$.
2. $Q^TAQ = D$, where D is diagonal.
3. The diagonal entries of D are the eigenvalues of A.

Now consider the quadratic form $q(\mathbf{x}) = \mathbf{x}^TA\mathbf{x}$, where A is $(n \times n)$ and symmetric. If we make the substitution $\mathbf{x} = Q\mathbf{y}$, we obtain

$$\begin{aligned} q(\mathbf{x}) &= q(Q\mathbf{y}) \\ &= (Q\mathbf{y})^TA(Q\mathbf{y}) \\ &= \mathbf{y}^TQ^TAQ\mathbf{y} \\ &= \mathbf{y}^TD\mathbf{y} \\ &= \lambda_1 y_1^2 + \lambda_2 y_2^2 + \cdots + \lambda_n y_n^2. \end{aligned} \tag{3}$$

The representation in Eq. (3) gives some qualitative information about $q(\mathbf{x})$. For instance, suppose that the matrix A has only positive eigenvalues. In this case, if $q(\mathbf{x})$ is evaluated at some specific vector $\mathbf{x}^*$ in R^n, $\mathbf{x}^* \neq \boldsymbol{\theta}$, then $q(\mathbf{x}^*)$ will always be a positive number.

EXAMPLE 2 Find the substitution $\mathbf{x} = Q\mathbf{y}$ that diagonalizes the quadratic form

$$q(\mathbf{x}) = q(r, s) = r^2 + 4rs - 2s^2.$$

Solution Following Theorem 1, we first represent $q(\mathbf{x})$ as $q(\mathbf{x}) = \mathbf{x}^TA\mathbf{x}$:

$$q(\mathbf{x}) = [r, s]\begin{bmatrix} 1 & 2 \\ 2 & -2 \end{bmatrix}\begin{bmatrix} r \\ s \end{bmatrix}.$$

For the preceding (2×2) matrix A, the eigenvalues and eigenvectors are (for a and b nonzero),

$$\lambda = 2, \quad \mathbf{w}_1 = a\begin{bmatrix} 2 \\ 1 \end{bmatrix} \quad \text{and} \quad \lambda = -3, \quad \mathbf{w}_2 = b\begin{bmatrix} 1 \\ -2 \end{bmatrix}.$$

An orthogonal matrix Q that diagonalizes A can be formed from normalized eigenvectors:

$$Q = \frac{1}{\sqrt{5}}\begin{bmatrix} 1 & 2 \\ -2 & 1 \end{bmatrix}.$$

The substitution $\mathbf{x} = Q\mathbf{y}$ is given by

$$\begin{bmatrix} r \\ s \end{bmatrix} = \frac{1}{\sqrt{5}}\begin{bmatrix} 1 & 2 \\ -2 & 1 \end{bmatrix}\begin{bmatrix} u \\ v \end{bmatrix},$$

or

$$r = \frac{1}{\sqrt{5}}(u + 2v), \qquad s = \frac{1}{\sqrt{5}}(-2u + v).$$

Using the substitution above in the quadratic form, we obtain

$$\begin{aligned} r^2 + 4rs - 2s^2 &= \frac{1}{5}(u + 2v)^2 + \frac{4}{5}(u + 2v)(-2u + v) - \frac{2}{5}(-2u + v)^2 \\ &= \frac{1}{5}[-15u^2 + 10v^2] = 2v^2 - 3u^2. \end{aligned}$$

Classifying Quadratic Forms

We can think of a quadratic form as defining a function form R^n to R. Specifically, if $q(\mathbf{x}) = \mathbf{x}^T A\mathbf{x}$, where A is a real $(n \times n)$ symmetric matrix, then we can define a real-valued function with domain R^n by the rule

$$y = q(\mathbf{x}) = \mathbf{x}^T A\mathbf{x}.$$

The quadratic form is classified as:

(a) ***Positive definite*** if $q(\mathbf{x}) > 0$ for all $\mathbf{x}$ in R^n, $\mathbf{x} \neq \boldsymbol{\theta}$.

(b) ***Positive semidefinite*** if $q(\mathbf{x}) \geq 0$ for all $\mathbf{x}$ in $\mathbf{R}^n$, $\mathbf{x} \neq \boldsymbol{\theta}$.

(c) ***Negative definite*** if $q(\mathbf{x}) < 0$ for all $\mathbf{x}$ in R^n, $\mathbf{x} \neq \boldsymbol{\theta}$.

(d) ***Negative semidefinite*** if $q(\mathbf{x}) \leq 0$ for all $\mathbf{x}$ in R^n, $\mathbf{x} \neq \boldsymbol{\theta}$.

(e) ***Indefinite*** if $q(\mathbf{x})$ assumes both positive and negative values.

The diagonalization process shown in Eq. (3) allows us to classify any specific quadratic form $q(\mathbf{x}) = \mathbf{x}^T A\mathbf{x}$ in terms of the eigenvalues of A. The details are given in the next theorem.

THEOREM 2 Let $q(\mathbf{x})$ be a quadratic form with representation $q(\mathbf{x}) = \mathbf{x}^T A\mathbf{x}$, where A is a symmetric $(n \times n)$ matrix. Let the eigenvalues of A be $\lambda_1, \lambda_2, \ldots, \lambda_n$. The quadratic form is:

(a) Positive definite if and only if $\lambda_i > 0$, for $1 \leq i \leq n$.

(b) Positive semidefinite if and only if $\lambda_i \geq 0$, for $1 \leq i \leq n$.

(c) Negative definite if and only if $\lambda_i < 0$, for $1 \leq i \leq n$.

(d) Negative semidefinite if and only if $\lambda_i \leq 0$, for $1 \leq i \leq n$.

(e) Indefinite if and only if A has both positive and negative eigenvalues. ■

The proof is based on the diagonalization shown in Eq. (3) and is left as an exercise.

EXAMPLE 3 Classify the quadratic form

$$q(r, s) = 3r^2 - 4rs + 3s^2.$$

Solution We first find the matrix representation for $q(\mathbf{x}) = q(r, s)$:

$$q(\mathbf{x}) = q(r, s) = [r, s]\begin{bmatrix} 3 & -2 \\ -2 & 3 \end{bmatrix}\begin{bmatrix} r \\ s \end{bmatrix} = \mathbf{x}^T A\mathbf{x}.$$

By Theorem 2, the quadratic form can be classified once we know the eigenvalues of A.

The characteristic polynomial is

$$\begin{aligned} p(t) = \det(A - tI) &= \begin{vmatrix} 3-t & -2 \\ -2 & 3-t \end{vmatrix} \\ &= t^2 - 6t + 5 \\ &= (t-5)(t-1). \end{aligned}$$

Thus, since all the eigenvalues of A are positive, $q(\mathbf{x})$ is a positive-definite quadratic form. ∎

Because the quadratic form in Example 3 is so simple, it is possible to show directly that the form is positive definite. In particular

$$\begin{aligned} q(r, s) &= 3r^2 - 4rs + 3s^2 \\ &= 2(r^2 - 2rs + s^2) + r^2 + s^2 \\ &= 2(r - s)^2 + r^2 + s^2. \end{aligned} \tag{4}$$

From Eq. (4), it follows that $q(\mathbf{x}) > 0$ for every nonzero $\mathbf{x} = [r, s]^T$.

EXAMPLE 4 Verify that the following quadratic form is indefinite:

$$q(\mathbf{x}) = q(r, s) = r^2 + 4rs - 2s^2.$$

Also, find vectors $\mathbf{x}_1$ and $\mathbf{x}_2$ such that $q(\mathbf{x}_1) > 0$ and $q(\mathbf{x}_2) < 0$.

Solution Example 2 showed that $q(\mathbf{x}) = \mathbf{x}^TA\mathbf{x}$, where A has eigenvalues $\lambda_1 = 2$ and $\lambda_2 = -3$. By Theorem 2, $q(\mathbf{x})$ is indefinite.

If $\mathbf{x}_1$ is an eigenvector corresponding to $\lambda_1 = 2$, then $q(\mathbf{x}_1)$ is given by

$$q(\mathbf{x}_1) = \mathbf{x}_1^TA\mathbf{x}_1 = \mathbf{x}_1^T(\lambda_1\mathbf{x}_1) = \mathbf{x}_1^T(2\mathbf{x}_1) = 2\mathbf{x}_1^T\mathbf{x}_1.$$

Thus, $q(\mathbf{x}_1) > 0$. Similarly, if $A\mathbf{x}_2 = \lambda_2\mathbf{x}_2$, where $\lambda_2 = -3$, then $q(\mathbf{x}_2)$ is negative since $q(\mathbf{x}_2) = -3\mathbf{x}_2^T\mathbf{x}_2$. ∎

Note that as in (4), the quadratic form in Example 4 can be seen to be indefinite by observing

$$\begin{aligned} q(r, s) &= r^2 + 4rs - 2s^2 \\ &= r^2 + 4rs + 4s^2 - 6s^2 \\ &= (r + 2s)^2 - 6s^2. \end{aligned} \tag{5}$$

From Eq. (5), if r and s are numbers such that $r + 2s = 0$ with s nonzero, then $q(r, s)$ is negative. On the other hand, $q(r, 0)$ is positive for any nonzero value of r. Therefore, Eq. (5) confirms that $q(r, s)$ takes on both positive and negative values. As specific instances, note that $q(2, -1) = -6$ and $q(2, 0) = 4$.

Conic Sections and Quadric Surfaces

The ideas associated with quadratic forms are useful when we want to describe the solution set of a quadratic equation in several variables. For example, consider this general quadratic equation in x and y:

$$ax^2 + bxy + cy^2 + dx + ey + f = 0. \tag{6}$$

(In Eq. (6) we assume that at least one of a, b, or c is nonzero.)

As we will see, the theory associated with quadratic forms allows us to make a special change of variables that will eliminate the cross-product term in Eq. (6). In particular, there is always a change of variables of the form

$$x = a_1u + a_2v, \qquad y = b_1u + b_2v,$$

which, when these expressions are substituted into Eq. (6), produces a new equation of the form

$$a'u^2 + b'v^2 + c'u + d'v + e' = 0. \tag{7}$$

If Eq. (7) has solutions, then the pairs (u, v) that satisfy Eq. (7) will define a curve in the uv-plane. Recall from analytic geometry that the solution set of Eq. (7) defines the following curves in the uv-plane:

(a) An ellipse when $a'b' > 0$.

(b) A hyperbola when $a'b' < 0$.

(c) A parabola when $a'b' = 0$ and one of a' or b' is nonzero.

In terms of the original variables x and y, the solution set for Eq. (6) is a curve in the xy-plane. Because of the special nature of the change of variables, the solution set for Eq. (6) can be obtained simply by rotating the curve defined by Eq. (7).

To begin a study of the general quadratic equation in Eq. (6), we first rewrite Eq. (6) in the form

$$\mathbf{x}^T A\mathbf{x} + \mathbf{a}^T\mathbf{x} + f = 0, \tag{8}$$

where

$$\mathbf{x} = \begin{bmatrix} x \\ y \end{bmatrix}, \quad A = \begin{bmatrix} a & b/2 \\ b/2 & c \end{bmatrix}, \quad \text{and} \quad \mathbf{a} = \begin{bmatrix} d \\ e \end{bmatrix}.$$

Now if Q is an orthogonal matrix that diagonalizes A, then the substitution $\mathbf{x} = Q\mathbf{y}$ will remove the cross-product term from Eq. (6). Specifically, suppose that $Q^TAQ = D$, where D is a diagonal matrix. In Eq. (8), the substitution $\mathbf{x} = Q\mathbf{y}$ leads to

$$\mathbf{y}^T D\mathbf{y} + \mathbf{a}^T Q\mathbf{y} + f = 0. \tag{9}$$

For $\mathbf{y} = [u, v]^T$, Eq. (9) has the simple form

$$\lambda_1 u^2 + \lambda_2 v^2 + c'u + d'v + f = 0. \tag{10}$$

In Eq. (10), λ_1 and λ_2 are the (1, 1) and (2, 2) entries of D, respectively. (Note that λ_1 and λ_2 are the eigenvalues of A.)

As we noted previously, if Eq. (10) has solutions, then the solution set will define an ellipse, a hyperbola, or a parabola in the uv-plane. Since the change of variables $\mathbf{x} = Q\mathbf{y}$ is defined by an orthogonal matrix Q, the pairs $\mathbf{x} = [x, y]^T$ that satisfy Eq. (6) are obtained simply by rotating pairs $\mathbf{y} = [u, v]^T$ that satisfy Eq. (7).

An example will illustrate these ideas.

EXAMPLE 5 Describe and graph the solution set of

$$x^2 + 4xy - 2y^2 + 2\sqrt{5}x + 4\sqrt{5}y - 1 = 0. \tag{11}$$

Solution The equation has the form $\mathbf{x}^T A\mathbf{x} + \mathbf{a}^T\mathbf{x} + f = 0$, where

$$\mathbf{x} = \begin{bmatrix} x \\ y \end{bmatrix}, \quad A = \begin{bmatrix} 1 & 2 \\ 2 & -2 \end{bmatrix}, \quad \mathbf{a} = \begin{bmatrix} 2\sqrt{5} \\ 4\sqrt{5} \end{bmatrix}, \quad \text{and} \quad f = -1.$$

From Example 2, we know that $Q^TAQ = D$, where

$$Q = \frac{1}{\sqrt{5}}\begin{bmatrix} 1 & 2 \\ -2 & 1 \end{bmatrix} \quad \text{and} \quad D = \begin{bmatrix} -3 & 0 \\ 0 & 2 \end{bmatrix}.$$

For $\mathbf{y} = [u, v]^T$, we make the substitution $\mathbf{x} = Q\mathbf{y}$ in Eq. (11), obtaining

$$2v^2 - 3u^2 - 6u + 8v - 1 = 0.$$

Completing the square, we can express the previous equation as

$$2(v^2 + 4v + 4) - 3(u^2 + 2u + 1) = 6,$$

or

$$\frac{(v+2)^2}{3} - \frac{(u+1)^2}{2} = 1. \tag{12}$$

From analytic geometry, Eq. (12) defines a hyperbola in the uv-plane, where the center of the hyperbola has coordinates $(-1, -2)$; Fig. 7.1 shows the hyperbola. (For reference, the vertices of the hyperbola have coordinates $(-1, -2 \pm \sqrt{3})$ and the foci have coordinates $(-1, -2 \pm \sqrt{13})$.)

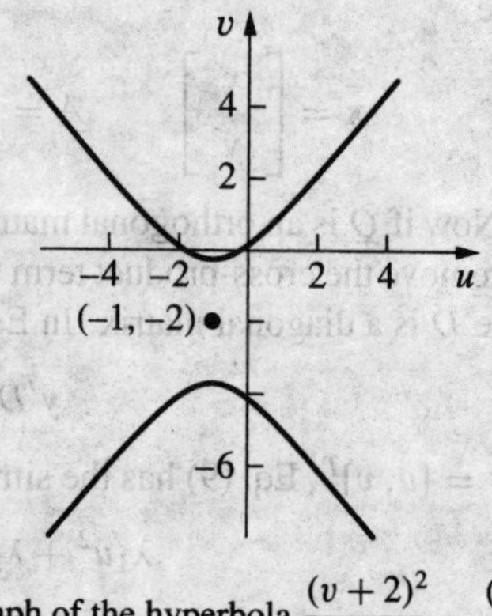

Figure 7.1 The graph of the hyperbola $\dfrac{(v+2)^2}{3} - \dfrac{(u+1)^2}{2} = 1$

Finally, Fig. 7.2 shows the solution set of Eq. (11), shown in the xy-plane. The hyperbola shown in Fig. 7.2 is a rotation of hyperbola (12) shown in Fig. 7.1. ■

Note that, as Example 5 illustrated, if Eq. (6) has real solutions, then the solution set is easy to plot when a change of variables is used to eliminate any cross-product terms. In some circumstances, however, the solution set of quadratic equation (6) might consist of a single point or there might be no real solutions at all. For instance, the solution set of $x^2 + y^2 = 0$ consists of the single pair $(0, 0)$, whereas the equation $x^2 + y^2 = -1$ has no real solutions.

For quadratic equations involving more than two variables, all the cross-product terms can be eliminated by using the same technique employed with Eq. (6). For instance, consider the general quadratic equation in the variables x, y, and z:

$$ax^2 + by^2 + cz^2 + dxy + exz + fyz + px + qy + rz + s = 0. \tag{13}$$

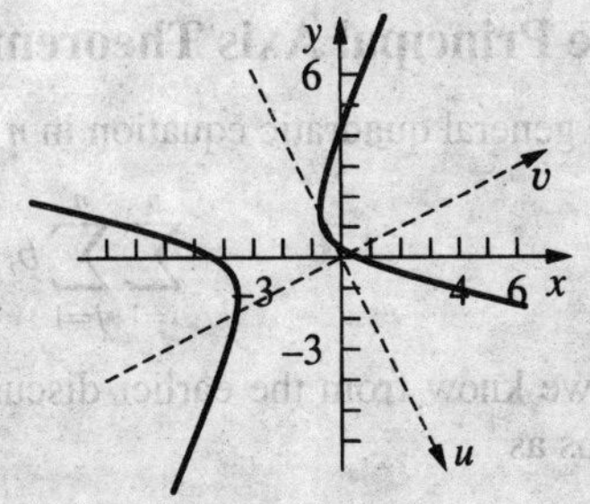

Figure 7.2 The graph of the hyperbola $x^2 + 4xy - 2y^2 + 2\sqrt{5}x + 4\sqrt{5}y - 1 = 0$

As with Eq. (6), we can express Eq. (13) in matrix-vector terms as

$$\mathbf{x}^T A\mathbf{x} + \mathbf{a}^T\mathbf{x} = s = 0, \tag{14}$$

where

$$\mathbf{x} = \begin{bmatrix} x \\ y \\ z \end{bmatrix}, \quad A = \begin{bmatrix} a & d/2 & e/2 \\ d/2 & b & f/2 \\ e/2 & f/2 & c \end{bmatrix}, \quad \text{and} \quad \mathbf{a} = \begin{bmatrix} p \\ q \\ r \end{bmatrix}.$$

If Q is an orthogonal matrix such that $Q^TAQ = D$, where D is diagonal, then the substitution $\mathbf{x} = Q\mathbf{y}$ will reduce Eq. (14) to

$$\mathbf{y}^T D\mathbf{y} + \mathbf{a}^T(Q\mathbf{y}) + s = 0. \tag{15}$$

For $\mathbf{y} = [u, v, w]^T$, Eq. (15) has no cross-product terms and will have the form

$$\lambda_1 u^2 + \lambda_2 v^2 + \lambda_3 w^2 + a'u + b'v + c'w + s = 0. \tag{16}$$

(Again, the scalars λ_1, λ_2, and λ_3 are the diagonal entries of D or, equivalently, the eigenvalues of A.)

If Eq. (16) has real solutions, then the triples (u, v, w) that satisfy (16) will define a surface in three-space. Such surfaces are called quadric surfaces, and detailed descriptions (along with graphs) can be found in most calculus books.

The geometric nature of a quadric surface depends on the λ_i and the scalars a', b', c', and s in Eq. (16). As a simple example, consider the equation

$$\lambda_1 u^2 + \lambda_2 v^2 + \lambda_3 w^2 = d, \quad d > 0. \tag{17}$$

If the λ_i are all positive, then the surface defined by Eq. (17) is an *ellipsoid*. If one of the λ_i is negative and the other two are positive, then the surface is a *hyperboloid of one sheet*. If two of the λ_i are negative and the other is positive, the surface is a *hyperboloid of two sheets*. If the λ_i are all negative, then Eq. (17) has no real solutions. The various other surfaces associated with solution sets of Eq. (16) can be found in a calculus book.

The Principal Axis Theorem

The general quadratic equation in n variables has the form

$$\sum_{i=1}^{n}\sum_{j=1}^{n} b_{ij}x_i x_j + \sum_{i=1}^{n} c_i x_i + e = 0. \tag{18}$$

As we know from the earlier discussions, Eq. (18) can be expressed in matrix-vector terms as

$$\mathbf{x}^T A\mathbf{x} + \mathbf{a}^T\mathbf{x} + e = 0,$$

where A is a real $(n \times n)$ symmetric matrix and $\mathbf{a} = [c_1, c_2, \ldots, c_n]^T$.

The following theorem tells us that it is always possible to make a change of variables that will eliminate the cross-product terms in Eq. (18).

THEOREM 3 **The Principal Axis Theorem** Let quadratic equation (18) be expressed as

$$\mathbf{x}^T A\mathbf{x} + \mathbf{a}^T\mathbf{x} + e = 0,$$

where A is real $(n \times n)$ symmetric matrix and $\mathbf{a} = [c_1, c_2, \ldots, c_n]^T$. Let Q be an orthogonal matrix such that $Q^TAQ = D$, where D is diagonal. For $\mathbf{y} = [y_1, y_2, \ldots, y_n]^T$, the substitution $\mathbf{x} = Q\mathbf{y}$ transforms Eq. (18) to an equation of the form

$$\lambda_1 y_1^2 + \lambda_2 y_2^2 + \cdots + \lambda_n y_n^2 + d_1 y_1 + d_2 y_2 + \cdots + d_n y_n + e = 0.$$

7.1 EXERCISES

In Exercises 1–6, find a symmetric matrix A such that $q(\mathbf{x}) = \mathbf{x}^T A\mathbf{x}$.

1. $q(\mathbf{x}) = 2x^2 + 4xy - 3y^2$

2. $q(\mathbf{x}) = -x^2 + 6xy + y^2$

3. $q(\mathbf{x}) = x^2 - 4y^2 + 3z^2 + 2xy - 6xz + 8yz$

4. $q(\mathbf{x}) = u^2 + 4w^2 - z^2 + 2uv + 10uw - 4uz + 4vw - 2vz + 6wz$

5. $q(\mathbf{x}) = [x, y]\begin{bmatrix} 2 & 0 \\ 4 & 1 \end{bmatrix}\begin{bmatrix} x \\ y \end{bmatrix}$

6. $q(\mathbf{x}) = [x, y, z]\begin{bmatrix} 1 & 3 & 1 \\ 5 & 2 & 4 \\ 3 & 2 & 1 \end{bmatrix}\begin{bmatrix} x \\ y \\ z \end{bmatrix}$

In Exercises 7–12, find a substitution $\mathbf{x} = Q\mathbf{y}$ that diagonalizes the given quadratic form, where Q is orthogonal. Also, use Theorem 2 to classify the form as positive definite, positive semidefinite, and so on.

7. $q(\mathbf{x}) = 2x^2 + 6xy + 2y^2$

8. $q(\mathbf{x}) = 5x^2 - 4xy + 5y^2$

9. $q(\mathbf{x}) = x^2 + y^2 + z^2 + 4(xy + xz + yz)$

10. $q(\mathbf{x}) = x^2 + y^2 + z^2 + 2(xy + xz + yz)$

11. $q(\mathbf{x}) = 3x^2 - 2xy + 3y^2$

12. $q(\mathbf{x}) = u^2 + v^2 + w^2 + z^2 - 2(uv + uw + uz + vw + vz + wz)$

In Exercises 13–20, find a substitution $\mathbf{x} = Q\mathbf{y}$ (where Q is orthogonal) that eliminates the cross-product term in the given equation. Sketch a graph of the transformed equation, where $\mathbf{y} = [u, v]^T$.

13. $2x^2 + \sqrt{3}xy + y^2 = 10$

14. $3x^2 + 2xy + 3y^2 = 8$

15. $x^2 + 6xy - 7y^2 = 8$

16. $3x^2 + 4xy + 5y^2 = 4$

17. $xy = 4$

18. $3x^2 + 2\sqrt{3}xy + y^2 + 4x = 4$

19. $3x^2 - 2xy + 3y^2 = 16$

20. $x^2 + 2xy + y^2 = -1$

21. Consider the quadratic form given by $q(\mathbf{x}) = \mathbf{x}^T A\mathbf{x}$, where A is an $(n \times n)$ symmetric matrix. Suppose that C is any $(n \times n)$ symmetric matrix such that $\mathbf{x}^TA\mathbf{x} = \mathbf{x}^TC\mathbf{x}$, for all $\mathbf{x}$ in R^n. Show that $C = A$. [*Hint:* Let $\mathbf{x} = \mathbf{e}_i$ and verify that $c_{ii} = a_{ii}$, $1 \le i \le n$. Next, consider $\mathbf{x} = \mathbf{e}_r + \mathbf{e}_s$, where $1 \le r, s \le n$.]

22. Consider the quadratic form $q(\mathbf{x}) = \mathbf{x}^TA\mathbf{x}$, where A is an $(n \times n)$ symmetric matrix. Let A have eigenvalues $\lambda_1, \lambda_2, \ldots, \lambda_n$.

a) Show that if the quadratic form is positive definite, then $\lambda_i > 0$ for $1 \le i \le n$. [*Hint:* Choose $\mathbf{x}$ to be an eigenvector of A.]

b) Show that if $\lambda_i > 0$ for $1 \le i \le n$, then the quadratic form is positive definite. [*Hint:* Recall Eq. 3.]

(*Note:* Exercise 22 proves property (a) of Theorem 2.)

23. Prove property (b) of Theorem 2.

24. Prove properties (c) and (d) of Theorem 2.

25. Prove property (e) of Theorem 2. [*Note:* The proof of property (e) is somewhat different from the proof of properties (a)–(d).]

26. Let A be an $(n \times n)$ symmetric matrix and consider the function R defined on R^n by

$$R(\mathbf{x}) = \frac{\mathbf{x}^TA\mathbf{x}}{\mathbf{x}^T\mathbf{x}}, \quad \mathbf{x} \ne \boldsymbol{\theta}.$$

The number $R(\mathbf{x})$ is called a ***Rayleigh quotient***. Let A have eigenvalues $\lambda_1, \lambda_2, \ldots, \lambda_n$, where $\lambda_1 \le \lambda_2 \le \lambda_3 \le \cdots \le \lambda_n$. Prove that for every $\mathbf{x}$ in R^n, $\lambda_1 \le R(\mathbf{x}) \le \lambda_n$. [*Hint:* By the corollary to Theorem 23 in Section 4.7, R^n has an orthonormal basis $\{\mathbf{u}_1, \mathbf{u}_2, \ldots, \mathbf{u}_n\}$, where $A\mathbf{u}_i = \lambda_i\mathbf{u}_i$, $1 \le i \le n$. For a given $\mathbf{x}$, $\mathbf{x} \ne \boldsymbol{\theta}$, we can express $\mathbf{x}$ as $\mathbf{x} = a_1\mathbf{u}_1 + a_2\mathbf{u}_2 + \cdots + a_n\mathbf{u}_n$. Using this expansion, calculate $\mathbf{x}^TA\mathbf{x}$ and $\mathbf{x}^T\mathbf{x}$.]

27. Let A be an $(n \times n)$ symmetric matrix, as in Exercise 26. Let D denote the set of all vectors $\mathbf{x}$ in R^n such that $\|\mathbf{x}\| = 1$ and consider the quadratic form $q(\mathbf{x}) = \mathbf{x}^TA\mathbf{x}$. Show that the maximum value of $q(\mathbf{x})$, $\mathbf{x}$ in D, is λ_n and the minimum value of $q(\mathbf{x})$, $\mathbf{x}$ in D, is λ_1. [*Hint:* Use the results of Exercise 26. Be sure to verify that the maximum and minimum values are attained.]

28. Let A be an $(n \times n)$ symmetric matrix, and let S be an $(n \times n)$ nonsingular matrix. Define the matrix B by $B = S^TAS$.

a) Verify that B is symmetric.

b) Consider the quadratic forms $q_1(\mathbf{x}) = \mathbf{x}^TA\mathbf{x}$ and $q_2(\mathbf{x}) = \mathbf{x}^TB\mathbf{x}$. Show that $q_1(\mathbf{x})$ is positive definite if and only if $q_2(\mathbf{x})$ is positive definite.

7.2 SYSTEMS OF DIFFERENTIAL EQUATIONS

In Section 4.8, we provided a brief introduction to the problem of solving a system of differential equations:

$$\begin{aligned} x_1'(t) &= a_{11}x_1(t) + a_{12}x_2(t) + \cdots + a_{1n}x_n(t) \\ x_2'(t) &= a_{21}x_1(t) + a_{22}x_2(t) + \cdots + a_{2n}x_n(t) \\ &\vdots \\ x_n'(t) &= a_{n1}x_1(t) + a_{n2}x_2(t) + \cdots + a_{nn}x_n(t). \end{aligned} \tag{1}$$

A solution to system (1) is a set of functions $x_1(t), x_2(t), \ldots, x_n(t)$ that simultaneously satisfy these equations.

In order to express system (1) in matrix terms, let us define the vector-valued function $\mathbf{x}(t)$ by

$$\mathbf{x}(t) = \begin{bmatrix} x_1(t) \\ x_2(t) \\ \vdots \\ x_n(t) \end{bmatrix}.$$

With $\mathbf{x}(t)$ defined in these terms, we can write system (1) as

$$\mathbf{x}'(t) = A\mathbf{x}(t), \tag{2}$$

where the vector $\mathbf{x}'(t)$ and the $(n \times n)$ matrix A are given by

$$\mathbf{x}'(t) = \begin{bmatrix} x_1'(t) \\ x_2'(t) \\ \vdots \\ x_n'(t) \end{bmatrix} \quad \text{and} \quad A = \begin{bmatrix} a_{11} & a_{12} & \cdots & a_{1n} \\ a_{21} & a_{22} & \cdots & a_{2n} \\ \vdots & & & \vdots \\ a_{n1} & a_{n2} & \cdots & a_{nn} \end{bmatrix}.$$

The General Solution of $\mathbf{x}' = A\mathbf{x}$

As in Section 4.8, let us assume that $\mathbf{x}' = A\mathbf{x}$ has a solution of the form

$$\mathbf{x}(t) = e^{\lambda t}\mathbf{u}. \tag{3}$$

For $\mathbf{x}(t) = e^{\lambda t}\mathbf{u}$, we have $\mathbf{x}'(t) = \lambda e^{\lambda t}\mathbf{u}$. Therefore, inserting the trial form (3) into $\mathbf{x}' = A\mathbf{x}$ leads to the condition

$$\lambda e^{\lambda t}\mathbf{u} = Ae^{\lambda t}\mathbf{u},$$

which can be rewritten as

$$e^{\lambda t}[A\mathbf{u} - \lambda\mathbf{u}] = \boldsymbol{\theta}. \tag{4}$$

Since $e^{\lambda t}$ is never zero, we see from Eq. (4) that $\mathbf{x}(t) = e^{\lambda t}\mathbf{u}$ will be a nontrivial solution of $\mathbf{x}' = A\mathbf{x}$ if and only if λ is an eigenvalue of A and $\mathbf{u}$ is a corresponding eigenvector.

In general, suppose that the $(n \times n)$ matrix A has eigenvalues $\lambda_1, \lambda_2, \ldots, \lambda_n$ and corresponding eigenvectors $\mathbf{u}_1, \mathbf{u}_2, \ldots, \mathbf{u}_n$. Then the vector-valued functions $\mathbf{x}_1(t) = e^{\lambda_1 t}\mathbf{u}_1, \mathbf{x}_2(t) = e^{\lambda_2 t}\mathbf{u}_2, \ldots, \mathbf{x}_n(t) = e^{\lambda_n t}\mathbf{u}_n$ are all solutions of $\mathbf{x}' = A\mathbf{x}$. It is easy to verify, moreover, that any linear combination of $\mathbf{x}_1(t), \mathbf{x}_2(t), \ldots, \mathbf{x}_n(t)$ is also a solution. That is,

$$\mathbf{x}(t) = a_1 e^{\lambda_1 t}\mathbf{u}_1 + a_2 e^{\lambda_2 t}\mathbf{u}_2 + \cdots + a_n e^{\lambda_n t}\mathbf{u}_n \tag{5}$$

will solve $\mathbf{x}' = A\mathbf{x}$ for any choice of scalars $a_1, a_2, \ldots, a_n$.

The question then arises: "Are there solutions to $\mathbf{x}' = A\mathbf{x}$ other than the ones listed in Eq. (5)?" The answer is: "If the eigenvectors $\mathbf{u}_1, \mathbf{u}_2, \ldots, \mathbf{u}_n$ are linearly independent, then every solution of $\mathbf{x}' = A\mathbf{x}$ has the form (5)." A proof of this fact can be found in a differential equations text. Equivalently, we can summarize the preceding discussion as follows:

> *Let A be an $(n \times n)$ nondefective matrix with linearly independent eigenvectors $\mathbf{u}_1, \mathbf{u}_2, \ldots, \mathbf{u}_n$. Then $\mathbf{x}(t)$ solves $\mathbf{x}' = A\mathbf{x}$ if and only if $\mathbf{x}(t)$ has the form (5).*

For A nondefective, the expression (5) is known as the ***general solution*** of $\mathbf{x}' = A\mathbf{x}$.

EXAMPLE 1 Write the following system of differential equations in the form $\mathbf{x}' = A\mathbf{x}$, and find the general solution:

$$\begin{aligned} u' &= 3u + v - w \\ v' &= 12u \qquad - 5w \\ w' &= 4u + 2v - w. \end{aligned}$$

Solution This system has the form $\mathbf{x}' = A\mathbf{x}$, where

$$\mathbf{x}(t) = \begin{bmatrix} u(t) \\ v(t) \\ w(t) \end{bmatrix} \quad \text{and} \quad A = \begin{bmatrix} 3 & 1 & -1 \\ 12 & 0 & -5 \\ 4 & 2 & -1 \end{bmatrix}.$$

The eigenvalues are $\lambda_1 = -1$, $\lambda_2 = 1$, and $\lambda_3 = 2$. Corresponding eigenvectors are

$$\mathbf{u}_1 = \begin{bmatrix} 1 \\ -2 \\ 2 \end{bmatrix}, \quad \mathbf{u}_2 = \begin{bmatrix} 3 \\ 1 \\ 7 \end{bmatrix}, \quad \text{and} \quad \mathbf{u}_3 = \begin{bmatrix} 1 \\ 1 \\ 2 \end{bmatrix}.$$

Therefore, the general solution is

$$\begin{aligned} \mathbf{x}(t) &= a_1 e^{-t}\mathbf{u}_1 + a_2 e^{t}\mathbf{u}_2 + a_3 e^{2t}\mathbf{u}_3 \\ &= a_1 e^{-t}\begin{bmatrix} 1 \\ -2 \\ 2 \end{bmatrix} + a_2 e^{t}\begin{bmatrix} 3 \\ 1 \\ 7 \end{bmatrix} + a_3 e^{2t}\begin{bmatrix} 1 \\ 1 \\ 2 \end{bmatrix}. \end{aligned}$$

In terms of the original variables, the general solution is $u(t) = a_1 e^{-t} + 3a_2 e^{t} + a_3 e^{2t}$, $v(t) = -2a_1 e^{-t} + a_2 e^{t} + a_3 e^{2t}$, $w(t) = 2a_1 e^{-t} + 7a_2 e^{t} + 2a_3 e^{2t}$, where a_1, a_2, and a_3 are arbitrary. ■

In practice, we are often presented with an initial condition as well as a differential equation. Such a problem,

$$\mathbf{x}'(t) = A\mathbf{x}(t), \qquad \mathbf{x}(0) = \mathbf{x}_0, \tag{6}$$

is called an ***initial-value problem***. That is, let $\mathbf{x}_0$ be a given initial vector. Then, among all solutions of $\mathbf{x}' = A\mathbf{x}$, we want to identify that special solution that satisfies the initial condition $\mathbf{x}(0) = \mathbf{x}_0$.

When A is nondefective, it is easy to solve the initial-value problem (6). In particular, every solution of $\mathbf{x}' = A\mathbf{x}$ has the form (5), and for $\mathbf{x}(t)$ as in (5) we have

$$\mathbf{x}(0) = a_1\mathbf{u}_1 + a_2\mathbf{u}_2 + \cdots + a_n\mathbf{u}_n.$$

Since the eigenvectors $\mathbf{u}_1, \mathbf{u}_2, \ldots, \mathbf{u}_n$ are linearly independent, we can always choose scalars $\alpha_1, \alpha_2, \ldots, \alpha_n$ such that $\mathbf{x}_0 = \alpha_1\mathbf{u}_1 + \alpha_2\mathbf{u}_2 + \cdots + \alpha_n\mathbf{u}_n$; therefore, $\mathbf{x}(t) = \alpha_1 e^{\lambda_1 t}\mathbf{u}_1 + \alpha_2 e^{\lambda_2 t}\mathbf{u}_2 + \cdots + \alpha_n e^{\lambda_n t}\mathbf{u}_n$ is the unique solution of $\mathbf{x}' = A\mathbf{x}$, $\mathbf{x}(0) = x_0$.

EXAMPLE 2 Solve the initial-value problem $\mathbf{x}' = A\mathbf{x}$, $\mathbf{x}(0) = \mathbf{x}_0$, where

$$A = \begin{bmatrix} 3 & 1 & -1 \\ 12 & 0 & -5 \\ 4 & 2 & -1 \end{bmatrix} \quad \text{and} \quad \mathbf{x}_0 = \begin{bmatrix} 7 \\ -3 \\ 16 \end{bmatrix}.$$

Solution From Example 1, the general solution of $\mathbf{x}' = A\mathbf{x}$ is $\mathbf{x}(t) = a_1 e^{-t}\mathbf{u}_1 + a_2 e^{t}\mathbf{u}_2 + a_3 e^{2t}\mathbf{u}_3$, where

$$\mathbf{u}_1 = \begin{bmatrix} 1 \\ -2 \\ 2 \end{bmatrix}, \quad \mathbf{u}_2 = \begin{bmatrix} 3 \\ 1 \\ 7 \end{bmatrix}, \quad \text{and} \quad \mathbf{u}_3 = \begin{bmatrix} 1 \\ 1 \\ 2 \end{bmatrix}.$$

Therefore, the condition $\mathbf{x}(0) = \mathbf{x}_0$ reduces to $a_1\mathbf{u}_1 + a_2\mathbf{u}_2 + a_2\mathbf{u}_3 = \mathbf{x}_0$, or

$$a_1\begin{bmatrix} 1 \\ -2 \\ 2 \end{bmatrix} + a_2\begin{bmatrix} 3 \\ 1 \\ 7 \end{bmatrix} + a_3\begin{bmatrix} 1 \\ 1 \\ 2 \end{bmatrix} = \begin{bmatrix} 7 \\ -3 \\ 16 \end{bmatrix}.$$

Solving, we find $a_1 = 2$, $a_2 = 2$, and $a_3 = -1$. Thus the solution of the initial-value problem is

$$\mathbf{x}(t) = 2e^{-t}\begin{bmatrix} 1 \\ -2 \\ 2 \end{bmatrix} + 2e^{t}\begin{bmatrix} 3 \\ 1 \\ 7 \end{bmatrix} - e^{2t}\begin{bmatrix} 1 \\ 1 \\ 2 \end{bmatrix}$$

$$= \begin{bmatrix} 2e^{-t} + 6e^{t} - e^{2t} \\ -4e^{-t} + 2e^{t} - e^{2t} \\ 4e^{-t} + 14e^{t} - 2e^{2t} \end{bmatrix}.$$

The problem of solving $\mathbf{x}' = A\mathbf{x}$ when A is defective is discussed in Section 7.8. Also, see Exercises 9 and 10 at the end of this section.

Solution by Diagonalization

As noted in Eq. (5), if an $(n \times n)$ matrix A has n linearly independent eigenvectors, then the general solution of $\mathbf{x}'(t) = A\mathbf{x}(t)$ is given by

$$\mathbf{x}(t) = b_1\mathbf{x}_1(t) + b_2\mathbf{x}_2(t) + \cdots + b_n\mathbf{x}_n(t)$$
$$= b_1e^{\lambda_1 t}\mathbf{u}_1 + b_2e^{\lambda_2 t}\mathbf{u}_2 + \cdots + b_ne^{\lambda_n t}\mathbf{u}_n.$$

Now, given that A has a set of n linearly independent eigenvectors, the solution of $\mathbf{x}'(t) = A\mathbf{x}(t)$ can also be described in terms of diagonalization. This alternative solution process has some advantages, especially for nonhomogeneous systems of the form $\mathbf{x}'(t) = A\mathbf{x}(t) + \mathbf{f}(t)$.

Suppose that A is an $(n \times n)$ matrix with n linearly independent eigenvectors. As we know, A is then diagonalizable. In particular, suppose that

$$S^{-1}AS = D, \quad D \text{ diagonal.}$$

Next, consider the equation $\mathbf{x}'(t) = A\mathbf{x}(t)$. Let us make the substitution

$$\mathbf{x}(t) = S\mathbf{y}(t).$$

With this substitution, the equation $\mathbf{x}'(t) = A\mathbf{x}(t)$ becomes

$$S\mathbf{y}'(t) = AS\mathbf{y}(t),$$

or

$$\mathbf{y}'(t) = S^{-1}AS\mathbf{y}(t),$$

or

$$\mathbf{y}'(t) = D\mathbf{y}(t). \tag{7}$$

Since D is diagonal, system (7) has the form

$$\begin{bmatrix} y_1'(t) \\ y_2'(t) \\ \vdots \\ y_n'(t) \end{bmatrix} = \begin{bmatrix} \lambda_1 & 0 & 0 & \cdots & 0 \\ 0 & \lambda_2 & 0 & \cdots & 0 \\ \vdots & & & & \\ 0 & 0 & 0 & \cdots & \lambda_n \end{bmatrix} \begin{bmatrix} y_1(t) \\ y_2(t) \\ \vdots \\ y_n(t) \end{bmatrix}.$$

Because D is diagonal, the equation above implies that the component functions, $y_i(t)$, are related by

$$y_i'(t) = \lambda_i y_i(t), \quad 1 \le i \le n.$$

Then, since the general solution of the scalar equation $w' = \lambda w$ is given by $w(t) = ce^{\lambda t}$, it follows that

$$y_i(t) = c_i e^{\lambda_i t}, \quad 1 \le i \le n.$$

Therefore, the general solution of $\mathbf{y}'(t) = D\mathbf{y}(t)$ in system (7) is given by

$$\mathbf{y}(t) = \begin{bmatrix} c_1 e^{\lambda_1 t} \\ c_2 e^{\lambda_2 t} \\ \vdots \\ c_n e^{\lambda_n t} \end{bmatrix}, \tag{8}$$

where $c_1, c_2, \ldots, c_n$ are arbitrary constants. In terms of $\mathbf{x}(t)$, we have $\mathbf{x}(t) = S\mathbf{y}(t)$ and $\mathbf{x}(0) = S\mathbf{y}(0)$, where $\mathbf{y}(0) = [c_1, c_2, \ldots, c_n]^T$. For an initial-value problem $\mathbf{x}'(t) = A\mathbf{x}(t)$, $\mathbf{x}(0) = \mathbf{x}_0$, we would choose $c_1, c_2, \ldots, c_n$ so that $S\mathbf{y}(0) = \mathbf{x}_0$ or $\mathbf{y}(0) = S^{-1}\mathbf{x}_0$.

EXAMPLE 3 Use the diagonalization procedure to solve the initial-value problem

$$\begin{aligned} u'(t) &= -2u(t) + v(t) + w(t), & u(0) &= 1 \\ v'(t) &= u(t) - 2v(t) + w(t), & v(0) &= 3 \\ w'(t) &= u(t) + v(t) - 2w(t), & w(0) &= -1. \end{aligned}$$

Solution First, we write the problem as $\mathbf{x}'(t) = A\mathbf{x}(t)$, $\mathbf{x}(0) = \mathbf{x}_0$, where

$$\mathbf{x}(t) = \begin{bmatrix} u(t) \\ v(t) \\ w(t) \end{bmatrix}, \quad A = \begin{bmatrix} -2 & 1 & 1 \\ 1 & -2 & 1 \\ 1 & 1 & -2 \end{bmatrix}, \quad \text{and} \quad \mathbf{x}_0 = \begin{bmatrix} 1 \\ 3 \\ -1 \end{bmatrix}.$$

The eigenvalues and eigenvectors of A are

$$\lambda_1 = 0, \quad \mathbf{u}_1 = \begin{bmatrix} 1 \\ 1 \\ 1 \end{bmatrix}; \quad \lambda_2 = -3, \quad \mathbf{u}_2 = \begin{bmatrix} 1 \\ 0 \\ -1 \end{bmatrix}; \quad \lambda_3 = -3, \quad \mathbf{u}_3 = \begin{bmatrix} 1 \\ -1 \\ 0 \end{bmatrix}.$$

Thus we can construct a diagonalizing matrix S such that $S^{-1}AS = D$ by choosing $S = [\mathbf{u}_1, \mathbf{u}_2, \mathbf{u}_3]$:

$$S = \begin{bmatrix} 1 & 1 & 1 \\ 1 & 0 & -1 \\ 1 & -1 & 0 \end{bmatrix}, \quad D = \begin{bmatrix} 0 & 0 & 0 \\ 0 & -3 & 0 \\ 0 & 0 & -3 \end{bmatrix}.$$

Next, solving $\mathbf{y}'(t) = D\mathbf{y}(t)$, we obtain

$$\mathbf{y}(t) = \begin{bmatrix} c_1 \\ c_2e^{-3t} \\ c_3e^{-3t} \end{bmatrix}.$$

From this, $\mathbf{x}(t) = S\mathbf{y}(t)$, or

$$\mathbf{x}(t) = \begin{bmatrix} c_1 + c_2e^{-3t} + c_3e^{-3t} \\ c_1 \qquad - c_3e^{-3t} \\ c_1 - c_2e^{-3t} \end{bmatrix}.$$

To satisfy the initial condition $\mathbf{x}(0) = \mathbf{x}_0 = [1, 3, -1]^T$, we choose $c_1 = 1$, $c_2 = 2$, and $c_3 = -2$. Thus, $\mathbf{x}(t)$ is given by

$$\mathbf{x}(t) = \begin{bmatrix} u(t) \\ v(t) \\ w(t) \end{bmatrix} = \begin{bmatrix} 1 \\ 1 + 2e^{-3t} \\ 1 - 2e^{-3t} \end{bmatrix}.$$

(*Note:* For large t, $\mathbf{x}(t) \approx [1, 1, 1]^T$.) ■

Complex Solutions

As we have seen, solutions to $\mathbf{x}'(t) = A\mathbf{x}(t)$ are built up from functions of the form

$$\mathbf{x}_i(t) = e^{\lambda_i t}\mathbf{u}_i. \tag{9}$$

In many applications, the function $\mathbf{x}_i(t)$ represents a particular state of the physical system modeled by $\mathbf{x}'(t) = A\mathbf{x}(t)$. Furthermore, for many applications, the state vector $\mathbf{x}_i(t)$ has component functions that are oscillatory in nature (for instance, see Example 5). Now, in general, a function of the form $y(t) = e^{\lambda t}$ has an oscillatory nature if and only if λ is a complex scalar. To explain this fact, we need to give the definition of $e^{\lambda t}$ when λ is complex. In advanced texts it is shown, for $\lambda = a + ib$, that

$$e^{\lambda t} = e^{(a+ib)t} = e^{at}(\cos bt + i \sin bt). \tag{10}$$

An example is presented below of a system $\mathbf{x}'(t) = A\mathbf{x}(t)$, where A has complex eigenvalues.

EXAMPLE 4 Solve the initial-value problem

$$u'(t) = 3u(t) + v(t), \quad u(0) = 2$$
$$v'(t) = -2u(t) + v(t), \quad v(0) = 8.$$

Solution The system can be written as $\mathbf{x}'(t) = A\mathbf{x}(t)$, $\mathbf{x}(0) = \mathbf{x}_0$, where

$$\mathbf{x}(t) = \begin{bmatrix} u(t) \\ v(t) \end{bmatrix}, \quad A = \begin{bmatrix} 3 & 1 \\ -2 & 1 \end{bmatrix}, \quad \text{and} \quad \mathbf{x}_0 = \begin{bmatrix} 2 \\ 8 \end{bmatrix}.$$

The eigenvalues are $\lambda_1 = 2 + i$ and $\lambda_2 = 2 - i$ with corresponding eigenvectors

$$\mathbf{u}_1 = \begin{bmatrix} 1+i \\ -2 \end{bmatrix} \quad \text{and} \quad \mathbf{u}_2 = \begin{bmatrix} 1-i \\ -2 \end{bmatrix}.$$

The general solution of $\mathbf{x}'(t) = A\mathbf{x}(t)$ is given by

$$\mathbf{x}(t) = a_1 e^{\lambda_1 t}\mathbf{u}_1 + a_2 e^{\lambda_2 t}\mathbf{u}_2. \tag{11}$$

From Eq. (10) it is clear that $e^{\lambda t}$ has the value 1 when $t = 0$, whether λ is complex or real. Thus to satisfy the condition $\mathbf{x}(0) = \mathbf{x}_0 = [2, 8]^T$, we need to choose a_1 and a_2 in Eq. (11) so that $a_1\mathbf{u}_1 + a_2\mathbf{u}_2 = \mathbf{x}_0$:

$$\begin{aligned} a_1(1+i) + a_2(1-i) &= 2 \\ a_1(-2) \quad + a_2(-2) \quad &= 8. \end{aligned}$$

Solving the preceding system by using Gaussian elimination, we obtain $a_1 = -2 - 3i$ and $a_2 = -2 + 3i$.

Having the coefficients a_1 and a_2 in Eq. (11), some complex arithmetic calculations will give the functions u and v that satisfy the given initial-value problem. In particular, since $\lambda_1 = 2 + i$, it follows that

$$e^{\lambda_1 t} = e^{(2+i)t} = e^{2t}(\cos t + i \sin t).$$

Similarly, from the fact that $\cos(-t) = \cos t$ and $\sin(-t) = -\sin t$,

$$e^{\lambda_2 t} = e^{(2-i)t} = e^{2t}(\cos t - i \sin t).$$

Thus, $\mathbf{x}(t)$ is given by

$$\begin{aligned} \mathbf{x}(t) &= e^{\lambda_1 t}(a_1\mathbf{u}_1) + e^{\lambda_2 t}(a_2\mathbf{u}_2) \\ &= e^{2t}(\cos t + i \sin t)\begin{bmatrix} 1-5i \\ 4+6i \end{bmatrix} + e^{2t}(\cos t - i \sin t)\begin{bmatrix} 1+5i \\ 4-6i \end{bmatrix} \\ &= \begin{bmatrix} e^{2t}(2\cos t + 10 \sin t) \\ e^{2t}(8\cos t - 12 \sin t) \end{bmatrix}. \end{aligned}$$

That is,

$$\begin{aligned} u(t) &= 2e^{2t}(\cos t + 5 \sin t) \\ v(t) &= 4e^{2t}(2\cos t - 3 \sin t). \end{aligned}$$

■

An example of a physical system that leads to a system of differential equations is illustrated in Fig. 7.3. This figure shows a spring–mass system, where $y_1 = 0$ and $y_2 = 0$ indicate the equilibrium position of the masses, and $y_1(t)$ and $y_2(t)$ denote the displacements at time t. For a single spring and mass as in Fig. 7.4, we can use Hooke's law and $F = ma$ to deduce $my''(t) = -ky(t)$; that is, the restoring force of the spring is proportional to the displacement, $y(t)$, of the mass from the equilibrium position, $y = 0$. The constant of proportionality is the spring constant k, and the minus sign indicates that the force is directed toward equilibrium.

In Fig. 7.3, the spring attached to m_2 is stretched (or compressed) by the amount $y_2(t) - y_1(t)$, so we can write $m_2 y_2''(t) = -k_2[y_2(t) - y_1(t)]$. The mass m_1 is being

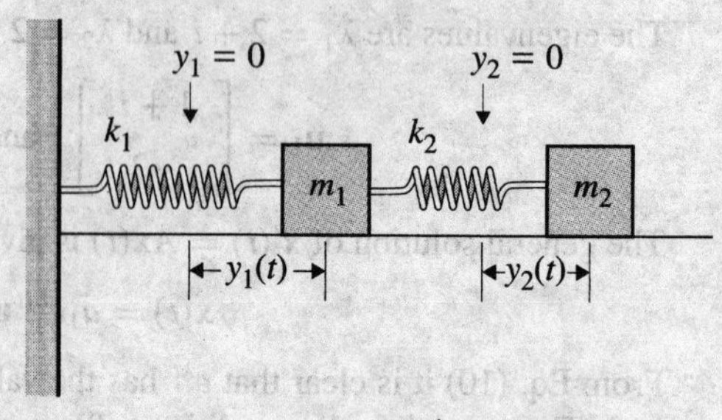

Figure 7.3 A coupled spring–mass system

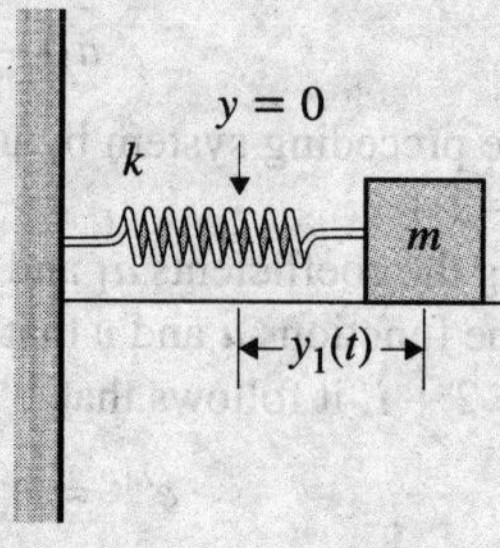

Figure 7.4 A single spring–mass system

pulled by two springs, so we have $m_1 y_1''(t) = -k_1 y_1(t) + k_2[y_2(t) - y_1(t)]$. Thus the motion of the physical system is governed by

$$\begin{aligned} y_1''(t) &= -\frac{k_1 + k_2}{m_1} y_1(t) + \frac{k_2}{m_1} y_2(t) \\ y_2''(t) &= \frac{k_2}{m_2} y_1(t) - \frac{k_2}{m_2} y_2(t). \end{aligned} \tag{12}$$

To solve these equations, we write them in matrix form as $\mathbf{y}''(t) = A\mathbf{y}(t)$, and we use a trial solution of the form $\mathbf{y}(t) = e^{\omega t}\mathbf{u}$, where $\mathbf{u}$ is a constant vector. Since $\mathbf{y}''(t) = \omega^2 e^{\omega t}\mathbf{u}$, we will have a solution if

$$\omega^2 e^{\omega t}\mathbf{u} - e^{\omega t} A\mathbf{u} = \boldsymbol{\theta} \tag{13}$$

or if $(A - \omega^2 I)\mathbf{u} = \boldsymbol{\theta}$. Thus to solve $\mathbf{y}''(t) = A\mathbf{y}(t)$, we solve $(A - \lambda I)\mathbf{u} = \boldsymbol{\theta}$ and then choose ω so that $\omega^2 = \lambda$. (It can be shown that λ will be negative and real, so ω must be a complex number.)

EXAMPLE 5 Consider the spring–mass system illustrated in Fig. 7.3 and described mathematically in system (12). Suppose that $m_1 = m_2 = 1$, $k_1 = 3$, and $k_2 = 2$. Find $y_1(t)$ and $y_2(t)$ if the initial conditions are

$$\begin{aligned} y_1(0) &= 0, \quad y_2(0) = 10 \\ y_1'(0) &= 0, \quad y_2'(0) = 0. \end{aligned}$$

Solution System (12) has the form $\mathbf{y}''(t) = A\mathbf{y}(t)$, where

$$\mathbf{y}(t) = \begin{bmatrix} y_1(t) \\ y_2(t) \end{bmatrix} \quad \text{and} \quad A = \begin{bmatrix} -5 & 2 \\ 2 & -2 \end{bmatrix}.$$

By Eq. (13), a function $\mathbf{x}$ of the form

$$\mathbf{x}(t) = e^{\beta t}\mathbf{u}$$

will satisfy $\mathbf{y}''(t) = A\mathbf{y}(t)$ if β^2 is an eigenvalue of A.

The eigenvalues of A are $\lambda_1 = -1$ and $\lambda_2 = -6$, with corresponding eigenvectors

$$\mathbf{u}_1 = \begin{bmatrix} 1 \\ 2 \end{bmatrix} \quad \text{and} \quad \mathbf{u}_2 = \begin{bmatrix} -2 \\ 1 \end{bmatrix}.$$

Thus four solutions of $\mathbf{y}''(t) = A\mathbf{y}(t)$ are

$$\mathbf{x}_1(t) = e^{it}\mathbf{u}_1, \qquad \mathbf{x}_2(t) = e^{-it}\mathbf{u}_1,$$
$$\mathbf{x}_3(t) = e^{\sqrt{6}it}\mathbf{u}_2, \qquad \mathbf{x}_4(t) = e^{-\sqrt{6}it}\mathbf{u}_2.$$

The general solution is

$$\mathbf{y}(t) = a_1\mathbf{x}_1(t) + a_2\mathbf{x}_2(t) + a_3\mathbf{x}_3(t) + a_4\mathbf{x}_4(t). \tag{14}$$

To satisfy the initial conditions, we need to choose the previous a_i so that

$$\mathbf{y}(0) = \begin{bmatrix} 0 \\ 10 \end{bmatrix} \quad \text{and} \quad \mathbf{y}'(0)\begin{bmatrix} 0 \\ 0 \end{bmatrix}.$$

An evaluation of Eq. (14) shows that

$$\mathbf{y}(0) = (a_1 + a_2)\mathbf{u}_1 + (a_3 + a_4)\mathbf{u}_2$$
$$\mathbf{y}'(0) = i(a_1 - a_2)\mathbf{u}_1 + i\sqrt{6}(a_3 - a_4)\mathbf{u}_2.$$

Since $\mathbf{y}'(0) = \boldsymbol{\theta}$, we see that $a_1 = a_2$ and $a_3 = a_4$. With this information in the condition $\mathbf{y}(0) = [0, 10]^T$, it follows that $a_1 = 2$ and $a_3 = 1$.

Finally, by Eq. (14), we obtain

$$\mathbf{y}(t) = 2[\mathbf{x}_1(t) + \mathbf{x}_2(t)] + [\mathbf{x}_3(t) + \mathbf{x}_4(t)]$$
$$= \begin{bmatrix} 4\cos t - 4\cos(\sqrt{6}t) \\ 8\cos t + 2\cos(\sqrt{6}t) \end{bmatrix}.$$

7.2 EXERCISES

In Exercises 1–8, write the given system of differential equations in the form $\mathbf{x}'(t) = A\mathbf{x}(t)$. Express the general solution in the form (5) and determine the particular solution that satisfies the given initial condition. (*Note:* Exercises 5 and 6 involve complex eigenvalues.)

1. $\begin{array}{l} u'(t) = 5u(t) - 2v(t) \\ v'(t) = 6u(t) - 2v(t) \end{array}, \quad \mathbf{x}_0 = \begin{bmatrix} 5 \\ 8 \end{bmatrix}$

2. $\begin{array}{l} u'(t) = 2u(t) - v(t) \\ v'(t) = -u(t) + 2v(t) \end{array}, \quad \mathbf{x}_0 = \begin{bmatrix} 2 \\ -1 \end{bmatrix}$

3. $u'(t) = u(t) + v(t)$
$v'(t) = 2u(t) + 2v(t)$, $\mathbf{x}_0 = \begin{bmatrix} 5 \\ 1 \end{bmatrix}$

4. $u'(t) = 5u(t) - 6v(t)$
$v'(t) = 3u(t) - 4v(t)$, $\mathbf{x}_0 = \begin{bmatrix} 3 \\ 2 \end{bmatrix}$

5. $u'(t) = .5u(t) + .5v(t)$
$v'(t) = -.5u(t) + .5v(t)$, $\mathbf{x}_0 = \begin{bmatrix} 4 \\ 4 \end{bmatrix}$

6. $u'(t) = 6u(t) + 8v(t)$
$v'(t) = -u(t) + 2v(t)$, $\mathbf{x}_0 = \begin{bmatrix} 8 \\ 0 \end{bmatrix}$

7. $u'(t) = 4u(t) + w(t)$
$v'(t) = -2u(t) + v(t)$, $\mathbf{x}_0 = \begin{bmatrix} -1 \\ 1 \\ 0 \end{bmatrix}$
$w'(t) = -2u(t) + w(t)$

8. $u'(t) = 3u(t) + v(t) - 2w(t)$
$v'(t) = -u(t) + 2v(t) + w(t)$, $\mathbf{x}_0 = \begin{bmatrix} -2 \\ 4 \\ -8 \end{bmatrix}$
$w'(t) = 4u(t) + v(t) - 3w(t)$

9. Consider the system

$$u'(t) = u(t) - v(t)$$
$$v'(t) = u(t) + 3v(t).$$

a) Write this system in the form $\mathbf{x}'(t) = A\mathbf{x}(t)$ and observe that there is only one solution of the form $\mathbf{x}_1(t) = e^{\lambda t}\mathbf{u}$. What is the solution?

b) Having λ and $\mathbf{u}$, find a vector $\mathbf{y}_0$ for which $\mathbf{x}_2(t) = te^{\lambda t}\mathbf{u} + e^{\lambda t}\mathbf{y}_0$ is a solution. [*Hint:* Substitute $\mathbf{x}_2(t)$ into $\mathbf{x}'(t) = A\mathbf{x}(t)$ to determine $\mathbf{y}_0$. The vector $\mathbf{y}_0$ is called a generalized eigenvector. See Section 7.8.]

c) Show that we can always choose constants c_1 and c_2 such that

$$\mathbf{y}(t) = c_1\mathbf{x}_1(t) + c_2\mathbf{x}_2(t)$$

satisfies $\mathbf{y}(0) = \mathbf{x}_0$ for any $\mathbf{x}_0$ in R^2.

10. Repeat Exercise 9 for the system

$$u'(t) = 2u(t) - v(t)$$
$$v'(t) = 4u(t) + 6v(t)$$

and find the solution that satisfies $u(0) = 1$, $v(0) = 1$.

7.3 TRANSFORMATION TO HESSENBERG FORM

In order to find the eigenvalues of an $(n \times n)$ matrix A, we would like to find a matrix H that has the same eigenvalues as A but in which the eigenvalues of H are relatively easy to determine. We already know from Section 4.7 that similar matrices have the same eigenvalues, so we shall look for a matrix H such that

$$H = S^{-1}AS$$

and such that H has some special sort of form that facilitates finding the characteristic polynomial for H.

We might hope that we could choose H to be a diagonal or triangular matrix since this choice would make the eigenvalue problem for H trivial. Unfortunately we cannot expect easily to reduce an arbitrary matrix A to a similar matrix H, where H is triangular or diagonal. To see why, recall that if $p(t)$ is any polynomial, then we can construct a matrix B for which $p(t)$ is the characteristic polynomial of B (see Exercise 27 of Section 4.4). If it were easy to reduce B to a similar matrix H that was triangular or diagonal, then we would have an easy means of finding the roots of $p(t) = 0$. But as we have commented, Abel showed that finding the roots of a polynomial equation cannot be an easy problem. Since we cannot expect to find an efficient procedure to transform an $(n \times n)$ matrix A into a similar matrix H that is triangular, we ask for the next best thing—a way to transform A into an almost triangular or Hessenberg matrix.

In this section, we establish the details of reduction to Hessenberg form, and in the next section, we state an algorithm that can be used to find the characteristic polynomial of a Hessenberg matrix.

We also prove that this algorithm is mathematically sound, and in the process we develop more of the theoretical foundation for the eigenvalue problem.

To begin, we say that an $(n \times n)$ matrix $H = (h_{ij})$ is a ***Hessenberg*** matrix if $h_{ij} = 0$ whenever $i > j+1$. Thus H is a Hessenberg matrix if all the entries below the subdiagonal of H are zero, where the ***subdiagonal*** of H means the entries $h_{21}, h_{32}, h_{43}, \ldots, h_{n,n-1}$. For example, a (6×6) Hessenberg matrix has the form

$$H = \begin{bmatrix} \times & \times & \times & \times & \times & \times \\ \times & \times & \times & \times & \times & \times \\ 0 & \times & \times & \times & \times & \times \\ 0 & 0 & \times & \times & \times & \times \\ 0 & 0 & 0 & \times & \times & \times \\ 0 & 0 & 0 & 0 & \times & \times \end{bmatrix}.$$

Note that the definition of a Hessenberg matrix insists only that the entries below the subdiagonal are zero; it is irrelevant whether the other entries are zero. Thus, for example, diagonal and upper-triangular matrices are in Hessenberg form; and as an extreme example, the $(n \times n)$ zero matrix is a Hessenberg matrix. Every (2×2) matrix is (trivially) a Hessenberg matrix since there are no entries below the subdiagonal. We will see shortly that Hessenberg form plays the same role for the eigenvalue problem as echelon form does for the problem of solving $A\mathbf{x} = \mathbf{b}$.

EXAMPLE 1 The following matrices are in Hessenberg form:

$$H_1 = \begin{bmatrix} 1 & 2 \\ 3 & 1 \end{bmatrix}, \quad H_2 = \begin{bmatrix} 1 & 2 & 1 \\ 2 & 3 & 1 \\ 0 & 4 & 2 \end{bmatrix}, \quad H_3 = \begin{bmatrix} 1 & 2 & 0 & 3 \\ 2 & 0 & 1 & 4 \\ 0 & 1 & 3 & 2 \\ 0 & 0 & 0 & 5 \end{bmatrix}.$$

Our approach to finding the eigenvalues of A has two parts:

1. Find a Hessenberg matrix H that is similar to A.
2. Calculate the characteristic polynomial for H.

As we show below, both of these steps are (relatively) easy. Transforming A to Hessenberg form is accomplished by simple row and column operations that resemble the operations used previously to reduce a matrix to echelon form. Next, the characteristic polynomial for a Hessenberg matrix can be found simply by solving a triangular system of equations. The main theoretical result of this section is Theorem 4, which asserts that every $(n \times n)$ matrix is similar to a Hessenberg matrix. The proof is constructive and shows how the similarity transformation is made.

In order to make the $(n \times n)$ case easier to understand, we begin by showing how a (4×4) matrix can be reduced to Hessenberg form. Let A be the (4×4) matrix

$$A = \begin{bmatrix} a_{11} & a_{12} & a_{13} & a_{14} \\ a_{21} & a_{22} & a_{23} & a_{24} \\ a_{31} & a_{32} & a_{33} & a_{34} \\ a_{41} & a_{42} & a_{43} & a_{44} \end{bmatrix}, \quad (1)$$

and suppose for the moment that $a_{21} \neq 0$. Define the matrix Q_1 by

$$Q_1 = \begin{bmatrix} 1 & 0 & 0 & 0 \\ 0 & 1 & 0 & 0 \\ 0 & \dfrac{-a_{31}}{a_{21}} & 1 & 0 \\ 0 & \dfrac{-a_{41}}{a_{21}} & 0 & 1 \end{bmatrix}, \quad (2a)$$

and observe that Q_1^{-1} is given by

$$Q_1^{-1} = \begin{bmatrix} 1 & 0 & 0 & 0 \\ 0 & 1 & 0 & 0 \\ 0 & \dfrac{a_{31}}{a_{21}} & 1 & 0 \\ 0 & \dfrac{a_{41}}{a_{21}} & 0 & 1 \end{bmatrix}. \quad (2b)$$

(That is, Q_1^{-1} is obtained from Q_1 by changing the sign of the off-diagonal entries of Q_1; equivalently, $Q_1 + Q_1^{-1} = 2I$.)

It is easy to see that forming the product $Q_1 A$ has the effect of adding a multiple of $-a_{31}/a_{21}$ times row 2 of A to row 3 and adding a multiple of $-a_{41}/a_{21}$ times row 2 of A to row 4 of A. Thus $Q_1 A$ has zeros in the (3, 1) and (4, 1) positions. The matrix $Q_1 A Q_1^{-1}$ is similar to A, and we note that the zeros in the (3, 1) and (4, 1) positions are not disturbed when the product $(Q_1 A) Q_1^{-1}$ is formed. (This fact is easy to see since Q_1^{-1} has the form $Q_1^{-1} = [\mathbf{e}_1, \mathbf{q}, \mathbf{e}_3, \mathbf{e}_4]$; so the first, third, and fourth columns of $Q_1 A$ are not disturbed when $(Q_1 A) Q_1^{-1}$ is formed.) In summary, when Q_1 and Q_1^{-1} are defined by (2), then $A_1 = Q_1 A Q_1^{-1}$ has the form

$$A_1 = \begin{bmatrix} b_{11} & b_{12} & b_{13} & b_{14} \\ b_{21} & b_{22} & b_{23} & b_{24} \\ 0 & b_{32} & b_{33} & b_{34} \\ 0 & b_{42} & b_{43} & b_{44} \end{bmatrix}. \quad (3)$$

Matrix A_1 is similar to A and represents the first step in Hessenberg reduction. As a point of interest, we note that there is an easy way to see how to construct Q_1. That is, if we wished to create zeros in the (3, 1) and (4, 1) entries of A by using elementary row operations, we could multiply row 2 by $-a_{31}/a_{21}$ and add the result to row 3, and next multiply row 2 by $-a_{41}/a_{21}$ and add the result to row 4. The matrix Q_1 is formed from the (4 × 4) identity I by performing these same row operations on I. (It is not usually possible to use row 1 to create zeros in the (2, 1), (3, 1), and (4, 1) positions and still produce a similar matrix.)

The next step in Hessenberg reduction is analogous to the first. We can introduce a zero into the (4, 2) position of A_1 if we multiply row 3 of A_1 by $-b_{42}/b_{32}$ and add the result to row 4. Following the discussion above, we define Q_2 to be the matrix

$$Q_2 = \begin{bmatrix} 1 & 0 & 0 & 0 \\ 0 & 1 & 0 & 0 \\ 0 & 0 & 1 & 0 \\ 0 & 0 & \dfrac{-b_{42}}{b_{32}} & 1 \end{bmatrix}, \tag{4a}$$

and we note as before that Q_2^{-1} is obtained from Q_2 by changing the sign of the off-diagonal entries:

$$Q_2^{-1} = \begin{bmatrix} 1 & 0 & 0 & 0 \\ 0 & 1 & 0 & 0 \\ 0 & 0 & 1 & 0 \\ 0 & 0 & \dfrac{b_{42}}{b_{32}} & 1 \end{bmatrix}. \tag{4b}$$

By a direct multiplication, it is easy to see that $H = Q_2A_1Q_2^{-1}$ is a Hessenberg matrix. Since H is similar to A_1 and A_1 is similar to A, we see that H is similar to A. In fact, $H = Q_2A_1Q_2^{-1} = Q_2(Q_1AQ_1^{-1})Q_2^{-1} = (Q_2Q_1)A(Q_2Q_1)^{-1}$.

Except for the possibility that $a_{21} = 0$ and/or $b_{32} = 0$, this discussion shows how to reduce an arbitrary (4 × 4) matrix to Hessenberg form. We will describe how to handle zero pivot elements after an example.

EXAMPLE 2 Reduce the (4 × 4) matrix A to Hessenberg form, where

$$A = \begin{bmatrix} 1 & -2 & 4 & 1 \\ 2 & 0 & 5 & 2 \\ 2 & -2 & 9 & 3 \\ -6 & -1 & -16 & -6 \end{bmatrix}.$$

Solution Following (2a) and (2b), we define Q_1 and Q_1^{-1} to be

$$Q_1 = \begin{bmatrix} 1 & 0 & 0 & 0 \\ 0 & 1 & 0 & 0 \\ 0 & -1 & 1 & 0 \\ 0 & 3 & 0 & 1 \end{bmatrix} \quad \text{and} \quad Q_1^{-1} = \begin{bmatrix} 1 & 0 & 0 & 0 \\ 0 & 1 & 0 & 0 \\ 0 & 1 & 1 & 0 \\ 0 & -3 & 0 & 1 \end{bmatrix}.$$

Given this definition,

$$Q_1A = \begin{bmatrix} 1 & -2 & 4 & 1 \\ 2 & 0 & 5 & 2 \\ 0 & -2 & 4 & 1 \\ 0 & -1 & -1 & 0 \end{bmatrix},$$

and

$$A_1 = Q_1AQ_1^{-1} = \begin{bmatrix} 1 & -1 & 4 & 1 \\ 2 & -1 & 5 & 2 \\ 0 & -1 & 4 & 1 \\ 0 & -2 & -1 & 0 \end{bmatrix}.$$

The final step of Hessenberg reduction is to use (4a) and (4b) to define Q_2 and Q_2^{-1}:

$$Q_2 = \begin{bmatrix} 1 & 0 & 0 & 0 \\ 0 & 1 & 0 & 0 \\ 0 & 0 & 1 & 0 \\ 0 & 0 & -2 & 1 \end{bmatrix}, \quad Q_2^{-1} = \begin{bmatrix} 1 & 0 & 0 & 0 \\ 0 & 1 & 0 & 0 \\ 0 & 0 & 1 & 0 \\ 0 & 0 & 2 & 1 \end{bmatrix}.$$

We obtain $H = Q_2A_1Q_2^{-1}$,

$$H = \begin{bmatrix} 1 & -1 & 6 & 1 \\ 2 & -1 & 9 & 2 \\ 0 & -1 & 6 & 1 \\ 0 & 0 & -13 & -2 \end{bmatrix};$$

and H is a Hessenberg matrix that is similar to A. ■

To complete our discussion of how to reduce a (4×4) matrix to Hessenberg form, we must show how to proceed when $a_{21} = 0$ in (1) or when $b_{32} = 0$ in (3). This situation is easily handled by using one of the permutation matrices (see Exercises 15–22 at the end of the section):

$$P_1 = \begin{bmatrix} 1 & 0 & 0 & 0 \\ 0 & 0 & 1 & 0 \\ 0 & 1 & 0 & 0 \\ 0 & 0 & 0 & 1 \end{bmatrix}, \quad P_2 = \begin{bmatrix} 1 & 0 & 0 & 0 \\ 0 & 0 & 0 & 1 \\ 0 & 0 & 1 & 0 \\ 0 & 1 & 0 & 0 \end{bmatrix}, \quad P_3 = \begin{bmatrix} 1 & 0 & 0 & 0 \\ 0 & 1 & 0 & 0 \\ 0 & 0 & 0 & 1 \\ 0 & 0 & 1 & 0 \end{bmatrix}.$$

Each of these matrices is its own inverse: $P_1P_1 = I$, $P_2P_2 = I$, $P_3P_3 = I$. Thus, P_1AP_1 is similar to A, as are P_2AP_2 and P_3AP_3. The action of these similarity transformations is easy to visualize; for example, forming P_1A has the effect of interchanging rows 2 and 3 of A, whereas forming $(P_1A)P_1$ switches columns 2 and 3 of P_1A. In detail, P_1AP_1

is given by

$$P_1AP_1 = \begin{bmatrix} a_{11} & a_{13} & a_{12} & a_{14} \\ a_{31} & a_{33} & a_{32} & a_{34} \\ a_{21} & a_{23} & a_{22} & a_{24} \\ a_{41} & a_{43} & a_{42} & a_{44} \end{bmatrix}.$$

If $a_{21} = 0$ in (1), but $a_{31} \neq 0$, then P_1AP_1 is a matrix similar to A with a nonzero entry in the (2, 1) position. We can clearly carry out the first stage of Hessenberg reduction on P_1AP_1. If $a_{21} = a_{31} = 0$ in (1), but $a_{41} \neq 0$, then P_2AP_2 has a nonzero entry in the (2, 1) position; and we can now carry out the first stage of Hessenberg reduction. Finally, if $a_{21} = a_{31} = a_{41} = 0$, the first stage is not necessary. In (3), if $b_{32} = 0$, but $b_{42} \neq 0$, then forming $P_3A_1P_3$ will produce a similar matrix with a nonzero entry in the (3, 2) position. Moreover, the first column of A_1 will be left unchanged, and so the second step of Hessenberg reduction can be executed. (In general, interchanging two rows of a matrix A and then interchanging the same two columns produces a matrix similar to A. Also note that the permutation matrices P_1, P_2, and P_3 are derived from the identity matrix I by performing the desired row-interchange operations on I.)

The discussion above proves that every (4×4) matrix is similar to a Hessenberg matrix H and also shows how to construct H. The situation with respect to $(n \times n)$ matrices is exactly analogous, and we can now state the main result of this section.

THEOREM 4 Let A be an $(n \times n)$ matrix. Then there is a nonsingular $(n \times n)$ matrix Q such that $QAQ^{-1} = H$, where H is a Hessenberg matrix.

A proof of Theorem 4 can be constructed along the lines of the discussion for the (4×4) case. Since no new ideas are involved, we omit the proof.

EXAMPLE 3 Reduce A to Hessenberg form, where

$$A = \begin{bmatrix} 1 & 1 & 8 & -2 \\ 0 & 3 & 5 & -1 \\ 1 & -1 & -3 & 2 \\ 3 & -1 & -4 & 9 \end{bmatrix}.$$

Solution In A, the entry a_{21} is zero, so we want to interchange rows 2 and 3. We construct the appropriate permutation matrix P by interchanging rows 2 and 3 of I, obtaining

$$P = \begin{bmatrix} 1 & 0 & 0 & 0 \\ 0 & 0 & 1 & 0 \\ 0 & 1 & 0 & 0 \\ 0 & 0 & 0 & 1 \end{bmatrix}.$$

Clearly, $PP = I$, so that $P^{-1} = P$.

With this, B is similar to A, where $B = PAP$:

$$B = PAP = \begin{bmatrix} 1 & 8 & 1 & -2 \\ 1 & -3 & -1 & 2 \\ 0 & 5 & 3 & -1 \\ 3 & -4 & -1 & 9 \end{bmatrix}.$$

Next, we define a matrix Q_1 and form $A_1 = Q_1BQ_1^{-1}$, where

$$Q_1 = \begin{bmatrix} 1 & 0 & 0 & 0 \\ 0 & 1 & 0 & 0 \\ 0 & 0 & 1 & 0 \\ 0 & -3 & 0 & 1 \end{bmatrix} \quad \text{and} \quad A_1 = Q_1BQ_1^{-1} = \begin{bmatrix} 1 & 2 & 1 & -2 \\ 1 & 3 & -1 & 2 \\ 0 & 2 & 3 & -1 \\ 0 & 14 & 2 & 3 \end{bmatrix}.$$

Finally, we form a matrix Q_2 and calculate $H = Q_2A_1Q_1^{-1}$:

$$Q_2 = \begin{bmatrix} 1 & 0 & 0 & 0 \\ 0 & 1 & 0 & 0 \\ 0 & 0 & 1 & 0 \\ 0 & 0 & -7 & 1 \end{bmatrix} \quad \text{and} \quad H = Q_2AQ_2^{-1} = \begin{bmatrix} 1 & 2 & -13 & -2 \\ 1 & 3 & 13 & 2 \\ 0 & 2 & -4 & -1 \\ 0 & 0 & 51 & 10 \end{bmatrix}.$$

Computational Considerations

A variety of similarity transformations, besides the elementary ones we have described, have been developed to reduce a matrix to Hessenberg form. Particularly effective are Householder transformations, a sequence of explicitly defined transformations involving orthogonal matrices (Section 7.5).

Although a reduction process like transformation to Hessenberg form may seem quite tedious, we show in the next section that it is easy to calculate the characteristic polynomial of a Hessenberg matrix. Also, however tedious Hessenberg reduction may seem, the alternative of calculating the characteristic polynomial from $p(t) = \det(A - tI)$ is worse. To illustrate this point, we note that in order to gauge the efficiency of an algorithm (particularly an algorithm that will be implemented on a computer), operations counts are frequently used as a first approximation. By an operations count, we mean a count of the number of multiplications and additions that must be performed in order to execute the algorithm. Given an $(n \times n)$ matrix A, it is not hard to see that a total of approximately n^3 multiplications and n^3 additions are needed to reduce A to Hessenberg form and then to find the characteristic polynomial. By contrast, if A is $(n \times n)$, calculating $p(t)$ from

$$p(t) = \det(A - tI)$$

requires on the order of $n!$ multiplications and $n!$ additions. In the language of computer science, reduction to Hessenberg form is a polynomial-time algorithm, whereas computing $\det(A - tI)$ is an exponential-time algorithm. In a polynomial-time algorithm, execution time grows at a rate proportional to n^k as n grows (where k is a constant); in an exponential time algorithm, execution time grows at least as fast as b^n (where b is

Table 7.1

n	n^3	$n!$
3	27	6
4	64	24
5	125	120
6	216	720
7	343	5,040
8	512	40,320
9	729	362,880
10	1,000	3,628,800
11	1,331	39,916,800
12	1,728	479,001,600

a constant larger than 1). The distinction is more than academic because exponential-time algorithms can be used on only the smallest problems, and the basic question is whether or not we can produce acceptable answers to practical problems in a reasonable amount of time. In fact, in some areas of application, the only known algorithms are exponential-time algorithms, and hence realistic problems cannot be solved except by an inspired guess. (An example of such a problem is the "traveling salesman's" problem, which arises in operations research.)

Table 7.1 should illustrate the difference between polynomial time and exponential time for the problem of calculating the characteristic polynomial. We can draw some rough conclusions from this table. For instance, if an algorithm requiring n^3 operations is used on a (12×12) matrix, and if the algorithm executes in 1 second, then we would expect any algorithm requiring $n!$ operations to take on the order of 77 hours to execute when applied to the same (12×12) matrix. For larger values of n, the comparison between polynomial-time and exponential-time algorithms borders on the absurd. For example, if an algorithm requiring n^3 operations executes in 1 second for $n = 20$, we would suspect that an algorithm requiring 20! operations would take something like 8×10^{10} hours, or approximately 9,000,000 years.

7.3 EXERCISES

In Exercises 1–10, reduce the given matrix to Hessenberg form by using similarity transformations. Display the matrices used in the similarity transformations.

1. $\begin{bmatrix} -7 & 4 & 3 \\ 8 & -3 & 3 \\ 32 & -15 & 13 \end{bmatrix}$

2. $\begin{bmatrix} -6 & 3 & -14 \\ -1 & 2 & -2 \\ 2 & 0 & 5 \end{bmatrix}$

3. $\begin{bmatrix} 1 & 3 & 1 \\ 0 & 2 & 4 \\ 1 & 1 & 3 \end{bmatrix}$

4. $\begin{bmatrix} 1 & 2 & -1 \\ 3 & 2 & 1 \\ -6 & 1 & 3 \end{bmatrix}$

5. $\begin{bmatrix} 3 & -1 & -1 \\ 4 & -1 & -2 \\ -12 & 5 & 0 \end{bmatrix}$

6. $\begin{bmatrix} 4 & 0 & 3 \\ 0 & 1 & 2 \\ 3 & 2 & 1 \end{bmatrix}$

7. $\begin{bmatrix} 1 & -1 & -1 & -1 \\ -1 & 1 & -1 & -1 \\ -1 & -1 & 1 & -1 \\ -1 & -1 & -1 & 1 \end{bmatrix}$ **8.** $\begin{bmatrix} 6 & 1 & 4 & 4 \\ 1 & 6 & 4 & 4 \\ 4 & 4 & 6 & 1 \\ 4 & 4 & 1 & 6 \end{bmatrix}$

9. $\begin{bmatrix} 1 & 2 & 1 & 3 \\ 0 & 1 & 1 & 2 \\ 0 & 3 & 1 & 1 \\ 1 & 2 & 0 & 2 \end{bmatrix}$ **10.** $\begin{bmatrix} 2 & -2 & 0 & -1 \\ -1 & -1 & -2 & 1 \\ 2 & 2 & 1 & 4 \\ 1 & 1 & -3 & 9 \end{bmatrix}$

11. Consider the general (4×4) Hessenberg matrix H, where a_2, b_3, and c_4 are nonzero:

$$H = \begin{bmatrix} a_1 & b_1 & c_1 & d_1 \\ a_2 & b_2 & c_2 & d_2 \\ 0 & b_3 & c_3 & d_3 \\ 0 & 0 & c_4 & d_4 \end{bmatrix}. \tag{5}$$

Suppose that λ is any eigenvalue of H, for simplicity, we assume λ is real. Show that the geometric multiplicity of λ must be equal to 1. [*Hint:* Consider the columns of $H - \lambda I$.]

12. Let H be a (4×4) Hessenberg matrix as in (5), but where a_2, b_3, and c_4 are not necessarily nonzero. Suppose that H is similar to a symmetric matrix A. Let λ be an eigenvalue of A, where λ has an algebraic multiplicity greater than 1. Use Exercise 11 to conclude that at least one of a_2, b_3, or c_4 must be zero.

13. Let A be the matrix in Exercise 7 and let H be the Hessenberg matrix found in Exercise 7. Determine the characteristic equation for H and solve the equation to find the eigenvalues of A. (Exercise 12 explains why some subdiagonal entry of H must be zero.)

14. Repeat Exercise 13 for the matrix in Exercise 8.

Exercises 15–22 deal with permutation matrices. Recall (Section 4.7) that an $(n \times n)$ matrix P is a ***permutation*** matrix if P is formed by rearranging the columns of the $(n \times n)$ identity matrix. For example, some (3×3) permutation matrices are $P = [\mathbf{e}_3, \mathbf{e}_2, \mathbf{e}_1]$, $P = [\mathbf{e}_2, \mathbf{e}_3, \mathbf{e}_1]$, and $P = [\mathbf{e}_1, \mathbf{e}_3, \mathbf{e}_2]$. By convention the identity matrix, $P = [\mathbf{e}_1, \mathbf{e}_2, \mathbf{e}_3]$, is also considered a permutation matrix.

15. List, in column form, all the possible (3×3) permutation matrices (there are six).

16. List, in column form, all the possible (4×4) permutation matrices (there are 24).

17. How many different $(n \times n)$ permutation matrices are there? [*Hint:* How many positions can $\mathbf{e}_1$ occupy? Once $\mathbf{e}_1$ is fixed, how many rearrangements of the remaining $n - 1$ columns are there?]

18. Let P be an $(n \times n)$ permutation matrix. Verify that P is an orthogonal matrix. [*Hint:* Recall (5) in Section 4.7.]

19. Let A be an $(n \times n)$ matrix and P an $(n \times n)$ permutation matrix, $P = [\mathbf{e}_i, \mathbf{e}_j, \mathbf{e}_k, \ldots, \mathbf{e}_r]$. Show that $AP = [\mathbf{A}_i, \mathbf{A}_j, \mathbf{A}_k, \ldots, \mathbf{A}_r]$; that is, forming AP rearranges the columns of A through the same rearrangement that produced P from I.

20. As in Exercise 19, show that P^TA rearranges the rows of A in the same pattern as the columns of P. [*Hint:* Consider A^TP.]

21. Let P and Q be two $(n \times n)$ permutation matrices. Show that PQ is also a permutation matrix.

22. Let P be an $(n \times n)$ permutation matrix. Show that there is a positive integer k such that $P^k = I$. [*Hint:* Consider the sequence, $P, P^2, P^3, \ldots$. Can there be infinitely many different matrices in this sequence?]

7.4 EIGENVALUES OF HESSENBERG MATRICES

In Section 7.3, we saw that an $(n \times n)$ matrix A is similar to a Hessenberg matrix H. In Section 7.7, we will prove a rather important result, the Cayley–Hamilton theorem (see the corollary to Theorem 15 in Section 7.7). In this section, we see that the Cayley–Hamilton theorem can be used as a tool for calculating the characteristic polynomial of Hessenberg matrices.

As we have noted, Hessenberg form plays somewhat the same role for the eigenvalue problem as echelon form plays with respect to solving $A\mathbf{x} = \mathbf{b}$. For instance, a square matrix A, whether invertible or not, can always be reduced to echelon form by using a sequence of simple row operations. Likewise, a square matrix A, whether diagonalizable or not, can always be reduced to Hessenberg form by using a sequence of simple similarity transformations.

For the problem $A\mathbf{x} = \mathbf{b}$, echelon form is easily achieved and reveals much about the possible solutions of $A\mathbf{x} = \mathbf{b}$, even when A is not invertible. Similarly (see Section 7.8), Hessenberg form provides a convenient framework for discussing generalized eigenvectors. We will need this concept in the event that A is not diagonalizable.

Finally, once the system $A\mathbf{x} = \mathbf{b}$ is made row equivalent to $U\mathbf{x} = \mathbf{c}$, where U is upper triangular (in echelon form), then it is fairly easy to complete the solution process. Likewise, if A is similar to H, where H is in Hessenberg form, then it is relatively easy to find the characteristic polynomial of H (recall that the similar matrices A and H have the same characteristic polynomial).

The Characteristic Polynomial of a Hessenberg Matrix

For hand calculations, an efficient method for determining the characteristic polynomial of a matrix A is as follows:

1. Reduce A to a Hessenberg matrix H, as in Section 7.3.
2. Find the characteristic polynomial for H according to the algorithm described in this subsection.

The algorithm referred to in step (2) is known as ***Krylov's method***. We outline the steps for Krylov's method in Eqs. (3)–(5). For a general $(n \times n)$ matrix A, we note that Krylov's method can fail. For an $(n \times n)$ Hessenberg matrix H, however, the procedure is always effective.

Let H be an $(n \times n)$ Hessenberg matrix. In Section 4.4, we defined the characteristic polynomial for H by $p(t) = \det(H - tI)$. In this section, it will be more convenient to define $p(t)$ by

$$p(t) = \det(tI - H). \tag{1}$$

Note that the properties of determinants show that

$$\begin{aligned}\det(tI - H) &= \det[(-1)(H - tI)]\\ &= (-1)^n \det(H - tI).\end{aligned}$$

Thus the zeros of $p(t)$ in Eq. (1) are the eigenvalues of H. We will call $p(t)$ the characteristic polynomial for H, even though it differs by a factor of $(-1)^n$ from our previous definition.

The algorithm described in Eqs. (3)–(5) is valid for Hessenberg matrices with *nonzero* subdiagonal elements. In this regard, a Hessenberg matrix, $H = (h_{ij})$, is said to be ***unreduced*** if

$$h_{k,k-1} \neq 0, \quad k = 2, 3, \ldots, n. \tag{2}$$

If H has at least one subdiagonal entry that is zero, then H will be called ***reduced***.

For example, the Hessenberg matrix H_1 is unreduced, whereas H_2 is reduced:

$$H_1 = \begin{bmatrix} 2 & 1 & 3 & 4 \\ 1 & 3 & 2 & 1 \\ 0 & 4 & 2 & 5 \\ 0 & 0 & 1 & 3 \end{bmatrix}, \quad H_2 = \begin{bmatrix} 4 & 2 & 5 & 1 \\ 3 & 6 & 4 & 2 \\ 0 & 0 & 1 & 3 \\ 0 & 0 & 4 & 7 \end{bmatrix}.$$

That is, H_2 is reduced since H_2 has a zero on the subdiagonal, in the (3, 2) position.

With these preliminaries, we can state the following algorithm for determining $p(t) = \det(tI - H)$.

ALGORITHM 1 Let H be an unreduced Hessenberg matrix, and let $\mathbf{w}_0$ denote the $(n \times 1)$ unit vector $\mathbf{e}_1$.

(a) Compute the vectors $\mathbf{w}_1, \mathbf{w}_2, \ldots, \mathbf{w}_n$ by

$$\mathbf{w}_k = H\mathbf{w}_{k-1}, \quad \text{for } k = 1, 2, \ldots, n. \tag{3}$$

(b) Solve the linear system

$$a_0\mathbf{w}_0 + a_1\mathbf{w}_1 + \cdots + a_{n-1}\mathbf{w}_{n-1} = -\mathbf{w}_n \tag{4}$$

for $a_0, a_1, \ldots, a_{n-1}$.

(c) Use the values from (b) as coefficients in $p(t)$:

$$p(t) = t^n + a_{n-1}t^{n-1} + \cdots + a_1 t + a_0. \tag{5}$$

It will be shown in Section 7.7 that $p(t)$ in Eq. (5) is the same as $p(t)$ in Eq. (1). The theoretical basis for Algorithm 1 is discussed in Exercise 23.

EXAMPLE 1 Use Algorithm 1 to find the eigenvalues of

$$H = \begin{bmatrix} 5 & -2 \\ 6 & -2 \end{bmatrix}.$$

Solution Note that $h_{21} = 6 \neq 0$, so H is unreduced. With $\mathbf{w}_0 = \mathbf{e}_1$, Eq. (3) yields

$$\mathbf{w}_0 = \begin{bmatrix} 1 \\ 0 \end{bmatrix}, \quad \mathbf{w}_1 = H\mathbf{w}_0 = \begin{bmatrix} 5 \\ 6 \end{bmatrix}, \quad \text{and} \quad \mathbf{w}_2 = H\mathbf{w}_1 = \begin{bmatrix} 13 \\ 18 \end{bmatrix}.$$

From Eq. (4), we have

$$a_0 \begin{bmatrix} 1 \\ 0 \end{bmatrix} + a_1 \begin{bmatrix} 5 \\ 6 \end{bmatrix} = -\begin{bmatrix} 13 \\ 18 \end{bmatrix},$$

or

$$\begin{aligned} a_0 + 5a_1 &= -13 \\ 6a_1 &= -18. \end{aligned}$$

The solution is $a_1 = -3$ and $a_0 = 2$. Thus, by Eq. (5),

$$p(t) = t^2 - 3t + 2 = (t - 2)(t - 1).$$

Hence $\lambda_1 = 2$ and $\lambda_2 = 1$ are the eigenvalues of H. For the simple example above, the reader can easily check that

$$\det(tI - H) = \begin{vmatrix} t - 5 & 2 \\ -6 & t + 2 \end{vmatrix} = t^2 - 3t + 2.$$

EXAMPLE 2 Use Algorithm 1 to find the eigenvalues of

$$H = \begin{bmatrix} 2 & 2 & -1 \\ -1 & -1 & 1 \\ 0 & 2 & 1 \end{bmatrix}.$$

Solution Note that h_{21} and h_{32} are nonzero, so H is unreduced. With $\mathbf{w}_0 = \mathbf{e}_1 = [1, 0, 0]^T$, Eq. (3) yields

$$\mathbf{w}_1 = H\mathbf{w}_0 = \begin{bmatrix} 2 \\ -1 \\ 0 \end{bmatrix}, \quad \mathbf{w}_2 = H\mathbf{w}_1 = \begin{bmatrix} 2 \\ -1 \\ -2 \end{bmatrix}, \quad \text{and} \quad \mathbf{w}_3 = H\mathbf{w}_2 = \begin{bmatrix} 4 \\ -3 \\ -4 \end{bmatrix}.$$

The system $a_0\mathbf{w}_0 + a_1\mathbf{w}_1 + a_2\mathbf{w}_2 = -\mathbf{w}_3$ is

$$\begin{aligned} a_0 + 2a_1 + 2a_2 &= -4 \\ -a_1 - a_2 &= 3 \\ -2a_2 &= 4. \end{aligned}$$

The solution is $a_2 = -2$, $a_1 = -1$, and $a_0 = 2$. So from Eq. (5),

$$p(t) = t^3 - 2t^2 - t + 2 = (t+1)(t-1)(t-2),$$

Thus the eigenvalues of H are $\lambda_1 = 2$, $\lambda_2 = 1$, and $\lambda_3 = -1$. ∎

EXAMPLE 3 Use Algorithm 1 to find the eigenvalues of

$$H = \begin{bmatrix} 1 & 1 & 1 & 1 \\ 2 & 0 & 1 & 1 \\ 0 & -1 & -2 & -2 \\ 0 & 0 & 2 & 2 \end{bmatrix}.$$

Solution Since h_{21}, h_{32}, and h_{43} are nonzero, H is unreduced. With $\mathbf{w}_0 = \mathbf{e}_1 = [1, 0, 0, 0]^T$, Eq. (3) yields

$$\mathbf{w}_1 = \begin{bmatrix} 1 \\ 2 \\ 0 \\ 0 \end{bmatrix}, \quad \mathbf{w}_2 = \begin{bmatrix} 3 \\ 2 \\ -2 \\ 0 \end{bmatrix}, \quad \mathbf{w}_3 = \begin{bmatrix} 3 \\ 4 \\ 2 \\ -4 \end{bmatrix}, \quad \text{and} \quad \mathbf{w}_4 = \begin{bmatrix} 5 \\ 4 \\ 0 \\ -4 \end{bmatrix}.$$

The system $a_0\mathbf{w}_0 + a_1\mathbf{w}_1 + a_2\mathbf{w}_2 + a_3\mathbf{w}_3 = -\mathbf{w}_4$ is

$$\begin{aligned} a_0 + a_1 + 3a_2 + 3a_3 &= -5 \\ 2a_1 + 2a_2 + 4a_3 &= -4 \\ -2a_2 + 2a_3 &= 0 \\ -4a_3 &= 4. \end{aligned}$$

Hence $a_3 = -1$, $a_2 = -1$, $a_1 = 1$, and $a_0 = 0$; so

$$p(t) = t^4 - t^3 - t^2 + t = t(t-1)^2(t+1).$$

Thus the eigenvalues are $\lambda_1 = \lambda_2 = 1$, $\lambda_3 = 0$, and $\lambda_4 = -1$. This example illustrates that Algorithm 1 is effective even when H is singular ($\lambda_3 = 0$). ■

As Examples 1–3 indicate, the system (4) that is solved to obtain the coefficients of $p(t)$ is both triangular and nonsingular. This fact is proved in Theorem 5. Knowing that system (4) is nonsingular tells us that Algorithm 1 cannot fail.

Of course, the characteristic polynomial $p(t)$ can also be obtained by expanding the determinant $\det(tI - H)$. Algorithm 1, however, is more efficient (requires fewer arithmetic operations) than a determinant expansion. Besides increased efficiency, we introduce this version of Krylov's method because the technique provides insight into matrix polynomials, generalized eigenvectors, and other important aspects of the eigenvalue problem.

THEOREM 5 Let H be an unreduced $(n \times n)$ Hessenberg matrix, and let $\mathbf{w}_0$ denote the $(n \times 1)$ unit vector e_1. Then the vectors $\mathbf{w}_0, \mathbf{w}_1, \ldots, \mathbf{w}_{n-1}$, defined by

$$\mathbf{w}_i = H\mathbf{w}_{i-1}, \quad i = 1, 2, \ldots, n-1$$

form a basis for R^n.

Proof Since any set of n linearly independent vectors in R^n is a basis for R^n, we can prove this theorem by showing that $\{\mathbf{w}_0, \mathbf{w}_1, \ldots, \mathbf{w}_{n-1}\}$ is a linearly independent set of vectors. To prove this, we observe first that $\mathbf{w}_0$ and $\mathbf{w}_1$ are given by

$$\mathbf{w}_0 = \begin{bmatrix} 1 \\ 0 \\ 0 \\ \vdots \\ 0 \end{bmatrix} \quad \text{and} \quad \mathbf{w}_1 = \begin{bmatrix} h_{11} \\ h_{21} \\ 0 \\ \vdots \\ 0 \end{bmatrix}.$$

Forming $\mathbf{w}_2 = H\mathbf{w}_1$, we find that

$$\mathbf{w}_2 = \begin{bmatrix} h_{11}h_{11} + h_{12}h_{21} \\ h_{21}h_{11} + h_{22}h_{21} \\ h_{32}h_{21} \\ 0 \\ \vdots \\ 0 \end{bmatrix}.$$

Since H was given as an unreduced Hessenberg matrix, the second component of $\mathbf{w}_1$ and the third component of $\mathbf{w}_2$ are nonzero.

In general (see Exercise 23) it can be shown that the ith component of $\mathbf{w}_{i-1}$ is the product $h_{i,i-1}h_{i-1,i-2}\cdots h_{32}h_{21}$, and the kth component of $\mathbf{w}_{i-1}$ is zero for $k = i+1, i+2, \ldots, n$. Thus the $(n \times n)$ matrix

$$W = [\mathbf{w}_0, \mathbf{w}_1, \ldots, \mathbf{w}_{n-1}]$$

is upper triangular, and the diagonal entries of W are all nonzero. In light of this, we conclude that $\{\mathbf{w}_0, \mathbf{w}_1, \ldots, \mathbf{w}_{n-1}\}$ is a set of n linearly independent vectors in R^n and hence is a basis for R^n. ■

Reduced Hessenberg Matrices

We now consider a reduced Hessenberg matrix H and illustrate that Algorithm 1 *cannot* be used on H.

EXAMPLE 4 Demonstrate why Algorithm 1 fails on the reduced Hessenberg matrix

$$H = \begin{bmatrix} 1 & 2 & 1 & 3 \\ 2 & 1 & 1 & 1 \\ 0 & 0 & 2 & 1 \\ 0 & 0 & 1 & 1 \end{bmatrix}.$$

Solution Since $h_{32} = 0$, H is reduced. From Eq. (3), with $\mathbf{w}_0 = \mathbf{e}_1$,

$$\mathbf{w}_1 = \begin{bmatrix} 1 \\ 2 \\ 0 \\ 0 \end{bmatrix}, \quad \mathbf{w}_2 = \begin{bmatrix} 5 \\ 4 \\ 0 \\ 0 \end{bmatrix}, \quad \mathbf{w}_3 = \begin{bmatrix} 13 \\ 14 \\ 0 \\ 0 \end{bmatrix}, \quad \text{and} \quad \mathbf{w}_4 = \begin{bmatrix} 41 \\ 40 \\ 0 \\ 0 \end{bmatrix}.$$

The vectors above are linearly dependent, and the solutions of $a_0\mathbf{w}_0 + a_1\mathbf{w}_1 + a_2\mathbf{w}_2 + a_3\mathbf{w}_3 = -\mathbf{w}_4$ are

$$\begin{aligned} a_0 &= -3a_2 - 6a_3 - 21 \\ a_1 &= -2a_2 - 7a_3 - 20, \end{aligned} \tag{6}$$

where a_2 and a_3 are arbitrary. The coefficients of the characteristic polynomial ($a_0 = -3, a_1 = 7, a_2 = 4, a_3 = -5$) are one of the solutions in (6), but in general it is impossible to discern this solution by inspection. ■

We now prove a result that shows how the eigenvalue problem for H uncouples into smaller problems when H is a reduced Hessenberg matrix. This theorem is based on the observation that a Hessenberg matrix that has a zero subdiagonal entry can be partitioned in a natural and useful way. To illustrate, we consider a (5×5) reduced Hessenberg matrix:

$$H = \begin{bmatrix} 2 & 1 & 3 & 5 & 7 \\ 6 & 2 & 1 & 3 & 8 \\ 0 & 1 & 2 & 1 & 3 \\ 0 & 0 & 0 & 4 & 1 \\ 0 & 0 & 0 & 1 & 6 \end{bmatrix}.$$

We can partition H into four submatrices, H_{11}, H_{12}, H_{22}, and $\mathcal{O}$, as indicated below:

$$H = \left[\begin{array}{ccc|cc} 2 & 1 & 3 & 5 & 7 \\ 6 & 2 & 1 & 3 & 8 \\ 0 & 1 & 2 & 1 & 3 \\ \hline 0 & 0 & 0 & 4 & 1 \\ 0 & 0 & 0 & 1 & 6 \end{array}\right] \tag{7}$$

$$= \begin{bmatrix} H_{11} & H_{12} \\ \mathcal{O} & H_{22} \end{bmatrix}.$$

For a matrix H partitioned as in Eq. (7), we can show that $\det(H) = \det(H_{11})\det(H_{22})$ and that $\det(tI - H) = \det(tI - H_{11})\det(tI - H_{22})$. This fact leads to Theorem 6, stated below. We provide a different proof of Theorem 6 in order to demonstrate how to find eigenvectors for a block matrix.

A matrix written in partitioned form, such as

$$H = \begin{bmatrix} H_{11} & H_{12} \\ \mathcal{O} & H_{22} \end{bmatrix},$$

is usually called a block matrix—the entries in H are blocks, or submatrices, of H. In fact, H is called block upper triangular since the only block below the diagonal blocks is a zero block.

When some care is exercised to see that all the products are defined, the blocks in a block matrix can be treated as though they were scalars when forming the product of two block matrices. For example, suppose Q is a (5×5) matrix partitioned in the same fashion as H in Eq. (7):

$$Q = \begin{bmatrix} Q_{11} & Q_{12} \\ Q_{21} & Q_{22} \end{bmatrix},$$

so that Q_{11} is (3×3), Q_{12} is (3×2), Q_{21} is (2×3), and Q_{22} is (2×2). Then it is not hard to show that the product HQ is also given in block form as

$$HQ = \begin{bmatrix} H_{11}Q_{11} + H_{12}Q_{21} & H_{11}Q_{12} + H_{12}Q_{22} \\ H_{22}Q_{21} & H_{22}Q_{22} \end{bmatrix}.$$

(Note that all the products make sense in the block representation of HQ.)

With these preliminaries, we now state an important theorem.

THEOREM 6 Let B be an $(n \times n)$ matrix of the form

$$B = \begin{bmatrix} B_{11} & B_{12} \\ \mathcal{O} & B_{22} \end{bmatrix},$$

where B_{11} is $(k \times k)$, B_{12} is $[k \times (n-k)]$, $\mathcal{O}$ is the $[(n-k) \times k]$ zero matrix, and B_{22} is $[(n-k) \times (n-k)]$. Then λ is an eigenvalue of B if and only if λ is an eigenvalue of B_{11} or B_{22}.

Proof Let **x** be any $(n \times 1)$ vector and write **x** in partitioned form as

$$\mathbf{x} = \begin{bmatrix} \mathbf{u} \\ \mathbf{v} \end{bmatrix}, \tag{8}$$

where **u** is $(k \times 1)$ and **v** is $[(n-k) \times 1]$. It is easy to see that the equation $B\mathbf{x} = \lambda\mathbf{x}$ is equivalent to

$$\begin{aligned} B_{11}\mathbf{u} + B_{12}\mathbf{v} &= \lambda\mathbf{u} \\ B_{22}\mathbf{v} &= \lambda\mathbf{v}. \end{aligned} \tag{9}$$

Suppose first that λ is an eigenvalue of B. Then there is a vector $\mathbf{x}$, $\mathbf{x} \neq \boldsymbol{\theta}$, such that $B\mathbf{x} = \lambda\mathbf{x}$. If $\mathbf{v} \neq \boldsymbol{\theta}$ in Eq. (8), then we see from (9) that λ is an eigenvalue of B_{22}. On the other hand, if $\mathbf{v} = \boldsymbol{\theta}$ in (8), then we must have $\mathbf{u} \neq \boldsymbol{\theta}$; and (9) guarantees that λ is an eigenvalue of B_{11}.

Conversely, if λ is an eigenvalue of B_{11}, then there is a nonzero vector $\mathbf{u}_1$ such that $B_{11}\mathbf{u}_1 = \lambda\mathbf{u}_1$. In (8) we set $\mathbf{u} = \mathbf{u}_1$ and $\mathbf{v} = \boldsymbol{\theta}$ to produce a solution of (9), and this result shows that any eigenvalue of B_{11} is also an eigenvalue of B. Finally, suppose that λ is not an eigenvalue of B_{11} but is an eigenvalue of B_{22}. Then there is a nonzero vector $\mathbf{v}_1$ such that $B_{22}\mathbf{v}_1 = \lambda\mathbf{v}_1$; and so $\mathbf{v}_1$ satisfies the last equation in (9). To satisfy the first equation in (9), we must solve

$$(B_{11} - \lambda I)\mathbf{u} = -B_{12}\mathbf{v}_1.$$

But since λ is not an eigenvalue of B_{11}, we know that $B_{11} - \lambda I$ is nonsingular, and so we can solve (9). Thus any eigenvalue of B_{22} is also an eigenvalue of B. ■

As another example, consider the (7×7) Hessenberg matrix

$$H = \begin{bmatrix} 2 & 3 & 1 & 6 & -1 & 3 & 8 \\ 5 & 7 & 2 & 8 & 2 & 2 & 1 \\ 0 & 0 & 4 & 1 & 3 & -5 & 2 \\ 0 & 0 & 6 & 1 & 2 & 4 & 3 \\ 0 & 0 & 0 & 4 & 1 & 2 & 1 \\ 0 & 0 & 0 & 0 & 0 & 6 & 5 \\ 0 & 0 & 0 & 0 & 0 & 7 & 3 \end{bmatrix}. \tag{10}$$

We first partition H as

$$H = \begin{bmatrix} H_{11} & H_{12} \\ \mathcal{O} & H_{22} \end{bmatrix},$$

where H_{11} is the upper (2×2) block

$$H_{11} = \begin{bmatrix} 2 & 3 \\ 5 & 7 \end{bmatrix}, \quad H_{22} = \begin{bmatrix} 4 & 1 & 3 & -5 & 2 \\ 6 & 1 & 2 & 4 & 3 \\ 0 & 4 & 1 & 2 & 1 \\ 0 & 0 & 0 & 6 & 5 \\ 0 & 0 & 0 & 7 & 3 \end{bmatrix}.$$

Now the eigenvalues of H are precisely the eigenvalues of H_{11} and H_{22}. The block H_{11} is unreduced, so we can apply the algorithm to find the characteristic polynomial for H_{11}. H_{22} is reduced, however, so we partition H_{22} as

$$H_{22} = \begin{bmatrix} C_{11} & C_{12} \\ \mathcal{O} & C_{22} \end{bmatrix},$$

where C_{11} and C_{22} are

$$C_{11} = \begin{bmatrix} 4 & 1 & 3 \\ 6 & 1 & 2 \\ 0 & 4 & 1 \end{bmatrix} \quad \text{and} \quad C_{22} = \begin{bmatrix} 6 & 5 \\ 7 & 3 \end{bmatrix}.$$

The eigenvalues of H_{22} are precisely the eigenvalues of C_{11} and C_{22}, and we can apply the algorithm to find the characteristic polynomial for C_{11} and C_{22}. In summary, the eigenvalue problem for H has uncoupled into three eigenvalue problems for the unreduced Hessenberg matrices H_{11}, C_{11}, and C_{22}.

7.4 EXERCISES

In Exercises 1–8, use Algorithm 1 to find the characteristic polynomial for the given matrix.

1. $\begin{bmatrix} 2 & 0 \\ 1 & 1 \end{bmatrix}$

2. $\begin{bmatrix} 0 & 0 \\ 3 & 0 \end{bmatrix}$

3. $\begin{bmatrix} 1 & 0 & 1 \\ 2 & 1 & 0 \\ 0 & 1 & 2 \end{bmatrix}$

4. $\begin{bmatrix} 1 & 2 & 1 \\ 1 & 3 & -1 \\ 0 & 1 & 2 \end{bmatrix}$

5. $\begin{bmatrix} 2 & 4 & 1 \\ 1 & 1 & 3 \\ 0 & 1 & 5 \end{bmatrix}$

6. $\begin{bmatrix} 0 & 0 & 1 \\ 1 & 0 & 0 \\ 0 & 1 & 0 \end{bmatrix}$

7. $\begin{bmatrix} 0 & 1 & 0 & 1 \\ 1 & 2 & 1 & 1 \\ 0 & 1 & 0 & 1 \\ 0 & 0 & 2 & 1 \end{bmatrix}$

8. $\begin{bmatrix} 0 & 2 & 1 & 2 \\ 1 & 0 & 1 & -1 \\ 0 & 2 & 0 & 2 \\ 0 & 0 & 1 & 1 \end{bmatrix}$

In Exercises 9–12, partition the given matrix H into blocks, as in the proof of Theorem 6. Find the eigenvalues of the diagonal blocks and for each distinct eigenvalue, find an eigenvector, as in Eq. (9).

9. $H = \begin{bmatrix} 1 & -1 & 1 & 4 \\ 1 & 3 & -2 & 1 \\ 0 & 0 & 2 & -1 \\ 0 & 0 & -1 & 2 \end{bmatrix}$

10. $H = \begin{bmatrix} 1 & 1 & 2 & 1 \\ 1 & 1 & 1 & 3 \\ 0 & 0 & 3 & 0 \\ 0 & 0 & 1 & 4 \end{bmatrix}$

11. $H = \begin{bmatrix} -2 & 0 & -2 & 1 \\ -1 & 1 & -2 & 3 \\ 0 & 1 & -1 & -2 \\ 0 & 0 & 0 & 2 \end{bmatrix}$

12. $H = \begin{bmatrix} 2 & 3 & 1 & 4 \\ 3 & 2 & 0 & 1 \\ 0 & 0 & 3 & 0 \\ 0 & 0 & 1 & 3 \end{bmatrix}$

13. Consider the block matrix B given by

$$B = \begin{bmatrix} a & b & c & d \\ e & f & g & h \\ 0 & 0 & w & x \\ 0 & 0 & y & z \end{bmatrix} = \begin{bmatrix} B_{11} & B_{12} \\ \mathcal{O} & B_{22} \end{bmatrix}.$$

Verify, by expanding $\det(B)$, that $\det(B) = \det(B_{11})\det(B_{22})$.

14. Use the result of Exercise 13 to calculate $\det(H)$, where H is the matrix in Exercise 9.

15. There is one (3×3) permutation matrix P such that P is an unreduced Hessenberg matrix. List this permutation matrix in column form.

16. As in Exercise 15, there is a unique (4×4) permutation matrix P that is both unreduced and Hessenberg. List P in column form.

17. Give the column form for the unique $(n \times n)$ permutation matrix P that is unreduced and Hessenberg.

18. Apply Algorithm 1 to determine the characteristic polynomial for the $(n \times n)$ matrix P in Exercise 17. [*Hint:* Consider $n = 3$ and $n = 4$ to see the nature of system (4).]

19. Let H be an unreduced $(n \times n)$ Hessenberg matrix and let λ be an eigenvalue of H. Show that the geometric multiplicity of λ is equal to 1. [*Hint:* See Exercise 11 of Section 6.3.]

20. Let H be an unreduced $(n \times n)$ Hessenberg matrix and let λ be an eigenvalue of H. Use Exercise 19 to show that if H is symmetric, then H has n distinct eigenvalues.

21. Consider the (2×2) matrix H, where

$$H = \begin{bmatrix} a & b \\ b & c \end{bmatrix}.$$

Calculate the characteristic polynomial for H and use the quadratic formula to show that H has two distinct eigenvalues if H is an unreduced matrix.

22. Let H be an unreduced $(n \times n)$ Hessenberg matrix and suppose $H\mathbf{u} = \lambda\mathbf{u}$, $\mathbf{u} \neq \boldsymbol{\theta}$. Show that the nth component of $\mathbf{u}$ is nonzero.

23. Complete the proof of Theorem 5 by using induction to show that the ith component of $\mathbf{w}_{i-1}$ is nonzero.

7.5 HOUSEHOLDER TRANSFORMATIONS

In this section, we consider another method for reducing a matrix A to Hessenberg form, using Householder transformations. A Householder transformation (or Householder matrix) is a symmetric orthogonal matrix that has an especially simple form. As we will see, one reason for wanting to use Householder matrices in a similarity transformation is that symmetry is preserved.

DEFINITION 1 Let $\mathbf{u}$ be a nonzero vector in R^n and let I be the $(n \times n)$ identity matrix. The $(n \times n)$ matrix Q given by

$$Q = I - \frac{2}{\mathbf{u}^T\mathbf{u}}\mathbf{u}\mathbf{u}^T \quad (1)$$

is called a ***Householder transformation*** or a ***Householder matrix***.

Householder matrices are a basic tool for applied linear algebra and are widely used even in applications not directly involving eigenvalues. For instance, we will see in the next section that Householder matrices can be used to good effect in least-squares problems.

The following theorem shows that a Householder matrix is both symmetric and orthogonal.

THEOREM 7 Let Q be a Householder matrix as in Eq. (1). Then:

(a) $Q^T = Q$.

(b) $Q^T Q = I$.

Proof We leave the proof of property (a) to the exercises. To prove property (b), it is sufficient to show that $QQ = I$, since $Q^T = Q$.

To simplify the notation, let b denote the scalar $2/(\mathbf{u}^T\mathbf{u})$ in Eq. (1). Thus

$$Q = I - b\mathbf{u}\mathbf{u}^T, \quad b = 2/(\mathbf{u}^T\mathbf{u}).$$

Forming QQ, we have

$$\begin{aligned} QQ &= (I - b\mathbf{u}\mathbf{u}^T)(I - b\mathbf{u}\mathbf{u}^T) \\ &= I - 2b\mathbf{u}\mathbf{u}^T + b^2(\mathbf{u}\mathbf{u}^T)(\mathbf{u}\mathbf{u}^T) \\ &= I - 2b\mathbf{u}\mathbf{u}^T + b^2\mathbf{u}(\mathbf{u}^T\mathbf{u})\mathbf{u}^T \\ &= I - 2b\mathbf{u}\mathbf{u}^T + b^2(\mathbf{u}^T\mathbf{u})(\mathbf{u}\mathbf{u}^T). \end{aligned} \tag{2}$$

(*Note:* We used the associativity of matrix multiplication to write $(\mathbf{u}\mathbf{u}^T)(\mathbf{u}\mathbf{u}^T) = \mathbf{u}(\mathbf{u}^T\mathbf{u})\mathbf{u}^T$.)

Next, observe that $\mathbf{u}^T\mathbf{u}$ is a scalar and that

$$b^2(\mathbf{u}^T\mathbf{u}) = \frac{4}{(\mathbf{u}^T\mathbf{u})^2}(\mathbf{u}^T\mathbf{u}) = \frac{4}{\mathbf{u}^T\mathbf{u}} = 2b.$$

Thus from Eq. (2) it follows that $QQ = I$. ∎

Operations with Householder Matrices

In practice it is neither necessary nor desirable to calculate explicitly the entries of a Householder matrix Q. In particular, if we need to form matrix products such as QA and AQ, or if we need to form a matrix–vector product $Q\mathbf{x}$, then the result can be found merely by exploiting the form of Q.

For instance, consider the problem of calculating $Q\mathbf{x}$, where Q is an $(n \times n)$ Householder matrix and $\mathbf{x}$ is in R^n. As in the proof of Theorem 7, we write Q as

$$Q = I - b\mathbf{u}\mathbf{u}^T, \quad b = 2/(\mathbf{u}^T\mathbf{u}).$$

Now $Q\mathbf{x}$ is given by

$$Q\mathbf{x} = (I - b\mathbf{u}\mathbf{u}^T)\mathbf{x} = \mathbf{x} - b(\mathbf{u}\mathbf{u}^T)\mathbf{x}. \tag{3}$$

In this expression, note that $b(\mathbf{u}\mathbf{u}^T)\mathbf{x} = b\mathbf{u}(\mathbf{u}^T\mathbf{x})$ and that $\mathbf{u}^T\mathbf{x}$ is a scalar. Thus, from Eq. (3), $Q\mathbf{x}$ has the form $\mathbf{x} - \gamma\mathbf{u}$, where γ is the scalar $b(\mathbf{u}^T\mathbf{x})$:

$$Q\mathbf{x} = \mathbf{x} - \gamma\mathbf{u}, \quad \gamma = 2\mathbf{u}^T\mathbf{x}/(\mathbf{u}^T\mathbf{u}). \tag{4}$$

Hence to form $Q\mathbf{x}$ we need only calculate the scalar γ and then perform the vector subtraction, $\mathbf{x} - \gamma\mathbf{u}$, as indicated by Eq. (4).

Similarly, if A is an $(n \times p)$ matrix, then we can form the product QA without actually having to calculate Q. Specifically, if $A = [\mathbf{A}_1, \mathbf{A}_2, \ldots, \mathbf{A}_p]$ is an $(n \times p)$ matrix, then

$$QA = [Q\mathbf{A}_1, Q\mathbf{A}_2, \ldots, Q\mathbf{A}_p].$$

As in Eq. (4), the columns of QA are found from

$$Q\mathbf{A}_k = \mathbf{A}_k - \gamma_k\mathbf{u}, \quad \gamma_k = 2\mathbf{u}^T\mathbf{A}_k/(\mathbf{u}^T\mathbf{u}).$$

EXAMPLE 1 Let Q denote the Householder matrix of the form (1), where $\mathbf{u} = [1, 2, 0, 1]^T$. Calculate $Q\mathbf{x}$ and QA, where

$$\mathbf{x} = \begin{bmatrix} 1 \\ 1 \\ 4 \\ 3 \end{bmatrix} \quad \text{and} \quad A = \begin{bmatrix} 1 & 6 \\ 2 & 0 \\ 1 & 5 \\ -2 & 3 \end{bmatrix}.$$

Solution By Eq. (1), Q is the (4×4) matrix $Q = I - b\mathbf{u}\mathbf{u}^T$, where $b = 2/(\mathbf{u}^T\mathbf{u}) = 2/6 = 1/3$. In detail, $Q\mathbf{x}$ is given by

$$Q\mathbf{x} = (I - (1/3)\mathbf{u}\mathbf{u}^T)\mathbf{x} = \mathbf{x} - \frac{\mathbf{u}^T\mathbf{x}}{3}\mathbf{u} = \mathbf{x} - \frac{6}{3}\mathbf{u} = \mathbf{x} - 2\mathbf{u}.$$

Thus $Q\mathbf{x}$ is the vector

$$Q\mathbf{x} = \mathbf{x} - 2\mathbf{u} = \begin{bmatrix} 1 \\ 1 \\ 4 \\ 3 \end{bmatrix} - 2\begin{bmatrix} 1 \\ 2 \\ 0 \\ 1 \end{bmatrix} = \begin{bmatrix} -1 \\ -3 \\ 4 \\ 1 \end{bmatrix}.$$

The matrix QA is found by forming $QA = [Q\mathbf{A}_1, Q\mathbf{A}_2]$. Briefly, the calculations are

$$Q\mathbf{A}_1 = \mathbf{A}_1 - \left(\frac{\mathbf{u}^T\mathbf{A}_1}{3}\right)\mathbf{u} = \mathbf{A}_1 - \mathbf{u}$$

$$Q\mathbf{A}_2 = \mathbf{A}_2 - \left(\frac{\mathbf{u}^T\mathbf{A}_2}{3}\right)\mathbf{u} = \mathbf{A}_2 - 3\mathbf{u}.$$

Thus QA is the (4×2) matrix given by

$$QA = \begin{bmatrix} 0 & 3 \\ 0 & -6 \\ 1 & 5 \\ -3 & 0 \end{bmatrix}.$$ ■

Householder Reduction to Hessenberg Form

In Section 7.3, we saw how an $(n \times n)$ matrix A could be reduced to Hessenberg form by using a sequence of similarity transformations

$$Q_{n-2} \cdots Q_2 Q_1 A Q_1^{-1} Q_2^{-1} \cdots Q_{n-2}^{-1} = H. \tag{5}$$

We will see that the matrices Q_i above can be chosen to be Householder matrices.

In the next subsection, we will give the details of how these Householder matrices are constructed. First, however, we want to comment on the significance of using orthogonal matrices in a similarity transformation.

Let us define a matrix Q by

$$Q = Q_{n-2} \cdots Q_2 Q_1,$$

where the Q_i are as in Eq. (5). Next, recall that Q^{-1} is given by

$$Q^{-1} = Q_1^{-1} Q_2^{-1} \cdots Q_{n-2}^{-1}.$$

Thus Eq. (5) can be written compactly as

$$QAQ^{-1} = H,$$

where H is a Hessenberg matrix.

THEOREM 8 Let A be an $(n \times n)$ matrix and let $Q = Q_{n-2} \cdots Q_2 Q_1$, where the Q_i are $(n \times n)$ and nonsingular. Also, suppose that $QAQ^{-1} = H$. If the matrices Q_i are orthogonal, $1 \le i \le n-2$, then:

(a) The product matrix Q is also orthogonal, so that

$$QAQ^{-1} = QAQ^T = H.$$

(b) If A is symmetric, then H is also symmetric.

We leave the proof of Theorem 8 to the exercises.

As Theorem 8 indicates, a sequence of similarity transformations of the form (5) will preserve symmetry when the matrices Q_i are orthogonal. So if the Q_i in (5) are orthogonal and A is symmetric, then the Hessenberg matrix H in (5) is also symmetric. A symmetric Hessenberg matrix has a special form—it is "tridiagonal." The form of a general (6×6) tridiagonal matrix T is given in Fig. 7.5.

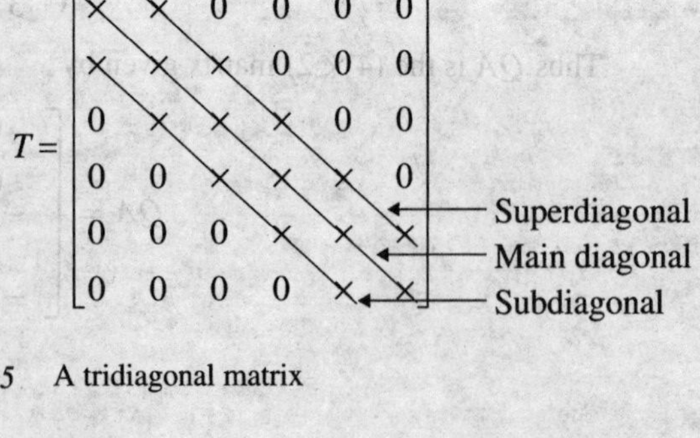

Figure 7.5 A tridiagonal matrix

As its name suggests, a tridiagonal matrix has three diagonals: a subdiagonal, the main diagonal, and a superdiagonal. Of course, every tridiagonal matrix is a Hessenberg matrix. Moreover, every symmetric Hessenberg matrix is necessarily tridiagonal.

Once we see how to design the orthogonal matrices Q_i in Eq. (5), we will have the following result.

> Let A be an $(n \times n)$ symmetric matrix. It is easy to construct an orthogonal matrix Q such that $QAQ^T = T$, where T is tridiagonal.

Although we cannot diagonalize a symmetric matrix A without knowing all the eigenvalues of A, we can always reduce A to tridiagonal form by using a sequence of Householder transformations. In this sense, tridiagonal form represents the closest we can get to diagonal form without actually finding the eigenvalues of A.

Constructing Householder Matrices

We now return to the main objective of this section. Given a general $(n \times n)$ matrix A, find orthogonal matrices $Q_1, Q_2, \ldots, Q_{n-2}$ such that

$$Q_{n-2} \cdots Q_2 Q_1 A Q_1^T Q_2^T \cdots Q_{n-2}^T = H,$$

where H is a Hessenberg matrix.

As with the procedure described in Section 7.3, the product $Q_1 A Q_1^T$ will have zeros in column 1, below the subdiagonal. Similarly, the product $Q_2(Q_1 A Q_1^T)Q_2^T$ will have zeros in columns 1 and 2, and so on. That is, we will be able to design Householder matrices $Q_1, Q_2, \ldots$ such that

$$Q_1 A Q_1^T = \begin{bmatrix} \times & \times & \times & \times & \cdots & \times \\ \times & \times & \times & \times & \cdots & \times \\ 0 & \times & \times & \times & \cdots & \times \\ 0 & \times & \times & \times & \cdots & \times \\ \vdots & & & & & \\ 0 & \times & \times & \times & \cdots & \times \end{bmatrix},$$

$$Q_2 Q_1 A Q_1^T Q_2^T = \begin{bmatrix} \times & \times & \times & \times & \cdots & \times \\ \times & \times & \times & \times & \cdots & \times \\ 0 & \times & \times & \times & \cdots & \times \\ 0 & 0 & \times & \times & \cdots & \times \\ \vdots & & & & & \\ 0 & 0 & \times & \times & \cdots & \times \end{bmatrix}.$$

To accomplish each of the individual steps of the previously described reduction process, we want to be able to design a Householder matrix that solves the following problem.

Problem

Let $\mathbf{v}$ be an $(n \times 1)$ vector,

$$\mathbf{v} = \begin{bmatrix} v_1 \\ v_2 \\ v_3 \\ \vdots \\ v_n \end{bmatrix}.$$

Given an integer k, $1 \le k \le n$, find a Householder matrix Q such that $Q\mathbf{v} = \mathbf{w}$ and that $\mathbf{w}$ has the form

$$\mathbf{w} = \begin{bmatrix} v_1 \\ v_2 \\ \vdots \\ v_{k-1} \\ s \\ 0 \\ 0 \\ \vdots \\ 0 \end{bmatrix} \qquad (6)$$

In words, the problem posed above is as follows: Given a vector $\mathbf{v}$ in R^n, find a Householder matrix Q so that forming the product $Q\mathbf{v}$ results in a vector $\mathbf{w} = Q\mathbf{v}$, where $\mathbf{w}$ has zeros in the $k+1, k+2, \ldots, n$ components. Furthermore, $\mathbf{w}$ and $\mathbf{v}$ should agree in the first $k-1$ components.

It is easy to form a Householder matrix Q such that the vector $\mathbf{w} = Q\mathbf{v}$ has the form (6). Specifically, suppose that $\mathbf{u}$ is a vector and $Q = I - b\mathbf{u}\mathbf{u}^T$, $b = 2/(\mathbf{u}^T\mathbf{u})$. Since $Q\mathbf{v}$ is given by

$$Q\mathbf{v} = \mathbf{v} - \gamma\mathbf{u},$$

we see that the form (6) can be achieved if $\mathbf{u}$ satisfies these conditions:

(a) $\gamma = 1$.

(b) $u_{k+1} = v_{k+1}, u_{k+2} = v_{k+2}, \ldots, u_n = v_n$.

(c) $u_1 = 0, u_2 = 0, \ldots, u_{k-1} = 0$.

The following algorithm will solve the problem posed above.

ALGORITHM 2

Given an integer k, $1 \le k \le n$, and a vector $\mathbf{v} = [v_1, v_2, \ldots, v_n]^T$, construct $\mathbf{u} = [u_1, u_2, \ldots, u_n]^T$ as follows:

1. $u_1 = u_2 = \cdots = u_{k-1} = 0$.

2. $u_k = v_k - s$, where

$$s = \pm\sqrt{v_k^2 + v_{k+1}^2 + \cdots + v_n^2}.$$

3. $u_i = v_i$ for $i = k+1, k+2, \ldots, n$.

In step (2), choose the sign of s so that $v_k s \le 0$. ■

For the vector $\mathbf{u}$ defined by Algorithm 2, the Householder matrix $Q = I - b\mathbf{u}\mathbf{u}^T$, $b = 2/(\mathbf{u}^T\mathbf{u})$, has the property that the product $Q\mathbf{v}$ is of the desired form (6). In detail, $Q\mathbf{v}$ is given by

$$Q\mathbf{v} = \mathbf{v} - \mathbf{u} = \begin{bmatrix} v_1 \\ v_2 \\ \vdots \\ v_{k-1} \\ v_k \\ v_{k+1} \\ \vdots \\ v_n \end{bmatrix} - \begin{bmatrix} 0 \\ 0 \\ \vdots \\ 0 \\ v_k - s \\ v_{k+1} \\ \vdots \\ v_n \end{bmatrix} = \begin{bmatrix} v_1 \\ v_2 \\ \vdots \\ v_{k-1} \\ s \\ 0 \\ \vdots \\ 0 \end{bmatrix}. \tag{7}$$

To verify Eq. (7), it is necessary only to calculate $Q\mathbf{v}$ according to Eq. (4). Thus

$$Q\mathbf{v} = \mathbf{v} - \gamma\mathbf{u}, \qquad \gamma = 2\mathbf{u}^T\mathbf{v}/(\mathbf{u}^T\mathbf{u}). \tag{8}$$

From the definition of $\mathbf{u}$, it is clear that

$$\begin{aligned} \mathbf{u}^T\mathbf{u} &= (v_k - s)^2 + (v_{k+1})^2 + \cdots + (v_n)^2 \\ &= v_k^2 - 2sv_k + s^2 + v_{k+1}^2 + \cdots + v_n^2 \\ &= 2s^2 - 2sv_k. \end{aligned}$$

Similarly,

$$\begin{aligned} \mathbf{u}^T\mathbf{v} &= (v_k - s)v_k + (v_{k+1})^2 + \cdots + (v_n)^2 \\ &= s^2 - sv_k. \end{aligned}$$

Therefore, from Eq. (8),

$$\gamma = \frac{2\mathbf{u}^T\mathbf{v}}{\mathbf{u}^T\mathbf{u}} = \frac{2(s^2 - sv_k)}{2s^2 - 2sv_k} = 1.$$

So, since $\gamma = 1$, the calculation in Eq. (7) follows from Eq. (8).

EXAMPLE 2 Let $\mathbf{v} = [1, 12, 3, 4]^T$. Use Algorithm 2 to determine Householder matrices Q_1 and Q_2, where:

(a) $$Q_1\mathbf{v} = \begin{bmatrix} 1 \\ s_1 \\ 0 \\ 0 \end{bmatrix};$$

(b) $$Q_2\mathbf{v} = \begin{bmatrix} 1 \\ 12 \\ s_2 \\ 0 \end{bmatrix}.$$

Solution

(a) Q is defined by selecting a vector $\mathbf{u}$ according to Algorithm 2. Since $k = 2$, we calculate

$$s = \pm\sqrt{v_2^2 + v_3^2 + v_4^2} = \pm\sqrt{144 + 9 + 16} = \pm 13.$$

Choosing the sign of s so that $sv_2 \leq 0$, we have $s = -13$. Thus Q_1 is defined by the vector $\mathbf{u} = [0, 25, 3, 4]^T$.

(b) $k = 3$, and we find

$$s = \pm\sqrt{v_3^2 + v_4^2} = \pm\sqrt{9 + 16} = \pm 5.$$

Choosing $s = -5$, the vector $\mathbf{u}$ that defines Q_2 is given by $\mathbf{u} = [0, 0, 8, 4]^T$. ■

EXAMPLE 3 Let $\mathbf{x} = [4, 2, 5, 5]^T$. Find the product $Q_2\mathbf{x}$, where Q_2 is the Householder matrix in Example 2.

Solution As we know from Eq. (4), the product $Q\mathbf{x}$ is given by

$$Q\mathbf{x} = \mathbf{x} - \gamma\mathbf{u}, \qquad \gamma = 2\mathbf{u}^T\mathbf{x}/(\mathbf{u}^T\mathbf{u}).$$

From Example 2, $\mathbf{u} = [0, 0, 8, 4]^T$. Thus

$$\gamma = \frac{2\mathbf{u}^T\mathbf{x}}{\mathbf{u}^T\mathbf{u}} = \frac{120}{80} = \frac{3}{2}.$$

Therefore,

$$Q\mathbf{x} = \mathbf{x} - \left(\frac{3}{2}\right)\mathbf{u} = \begin{bmatrix} 4 \\ 2 \\ 5 \\ 5 \end{bmatrix} - \begin{bmatrix} 0 \\ 0 \\ 12 \\ 6 \end{bmatrix} = \begin{bmatrix} 4 \\ 2 \\ -7 \\ -1 \end{bmatrix}.$$ ■

For a given vector $\mathbf{v}$ in R^n, Algorithm 2 tells us how to construct a Householder matrix Q so that $Q\mathbf{v}$ has zeros in its last $n - k$ components. We now indicate how the algorithm can be applied to reduce a matrix A to Hessenberg form. As in Section 7.3, we illustrate the process for a (4×4) matrix and merely note that the process extends to $(n \times n)$ matrices in an obvious fashion.

Let A be the (4×4) matrix $A = [\mathbf{A}_1, \mathbf{A}_2, \mathbf{A}_3, \mathbf{A}_4]$. Construct a Householder matrix Q so that the vector $Q\mathbf{A}_1$ has zeros in its last two components. Thus, forming $QA = [Q\mathbf{A}_1, Q\mathbf{A}_2, Q\mathbf{A}_3, Q\mathbf{A}_4]$ will produce a matrix of the form

$$QA = \begin{bmatrix} c_{11} & c_{12} & c_{13} & c_{14} \\ c_{21} & c_{22} & c_{23} & c_{24} \\ 0 & c_{32} & c_{33} & c_{34} \\ 0 & c_{42} & c_{43} & c_{44} \end{bmatrix}.$$

Next, form $B = QAQ$ and note that B is similar to A since Q is a Householder matrix. Also (see Exercise 25), it can be shown that forming $B = (QA)Q$ will not disturb the zero entries in the (3, 1) and (4, 1) positions. Thus, $B = QAQ$ has the form

$$B = \begin{bmatrix} b_{11} & b_{12} & b_{13} & b_{14} \\ b_{21} & b_{22} & b_{23} & b_{24} \\ 0 & b_{32} & b_{33} & b_{34} \\ 0 & b_{42} & b_{43} & b_{44} \end{bmatrix}. \qquad (9)$$

For the matrix above, $B = [\mathbf{B}_1, \mathbf{B}_2, \mathbf{B}_3, \mathbf{B}_4]$, choose a Householder matrix S such that the vector $S\mathbf{B}_2$ has a zero in its last component. It can be shown (see Exercise 25) that $S\mathbf{B}_1 = \mathbf{B}_1$. Thus, $SB = [S\mathbf{B}_1, S\mathbf{B}_2, S\mathbf{B}_3, S\mathbf{B}_4]$ has the form

$$SB = \begin{bmatrix} b_{11} & d_{12} & d_{13} & d_{14} \\ b_{21} & d_{22} & d_{23} & d_{24} \\ 0 & d_{32} & d_{33} & d_{34} \\ 0 & 0 & d_{43} & d_{44} \end{bmatrix}. \qquad (10)$$

Finally, the matrix SBS is similar to B and hence to A. Moreover (see Exercise 25), forming $(SB)S$ does not disturb the zero entries in (10). Therefore, $SBS = S(QAQ)S$ has the desired Hessenberg form

$$SBS = SQAQS = \begin{bmatrix} h_{11} & h_{12} & h_{13} & h_{14} \\ h_{21} & h_{22} & h_{23} & h_{24} \\ 0 & h_{32} & h_{33} & h_{34} \\ 0 & 0 & h_{43} & h_{44} \end{bmatrix}. \qquad (11)$$

The next example illustrates the final stage of reduction to Hessenberg form for a (4×4) matrix, the process of going from Eqs. (9) to (11) above.

EXAMPLE 4 Find a Householder matrix S such that $SBS = H$, where H is a Hessenberg matrix and where B is given by

$$B = \begin{bmatrix} 1 & 2 & 4 & 2 \\ 3 & 3 & -4 & 2 \\ 0 & 3 & 9 & -1 \\ 0 & -4 & -2 & 8 \end{bmatrix}.$$

Also, calculate the matrix SB.

Solution We seek a Householder matrix S such that the vector $S\mathbf{B}_2$ has a zero in the fourth component, where $\mathbf{B}_2 = [2, 3, 3, -4]^T$.

Using $k = 3$ in Algorithm 2, we define a vector $\mathbf{u}$, where

$$\mathbf{u} = \begin{bmatrix} 0 \\ 0 \\ 8 \\ -4 \end{bmatrix}.$$

The appropriate Householder matrix is $S = I - b\mathbf{u}\mathbf{u}^T$, $b = 2/(\mathbf{u}^T\mathbf{u}) = 1/40$.

Next, we calculate the matrix SB by using $SB = [S\mathbf{B}_1, S\mathbf{B}_2, S\mathbf{B}_3, S\mathbf{B}_4]$, where

$$S\mathbf{B}_i = \mathbf{B}_i - \gamma_i\mathbf{u}; \qquad \gamma_i = 2\mathbf{u}^T\mathbf{B}_i/(\mathbf{u}^T\mathbf{u}) = \mathbf{u}^T\mathbf{B}_i/40.$$

The details are:

(a) $\gamma_1 = \mathbf{u}^T\mathbf{B}_1/40 = 0,$ so $S\mathbf{B}_1 = \mathbf{B}_1 = [1, 3, 0, 0]^T$.

(b) $\gamma_2 = \mathbf{u}^T\mathbf{B}_2/40 = 1,$ so $S\mathbf{B}_2 = \mathbf{B}_2 - \mathbf{u} = [2, 3, -5, 0]^T$.

(c) $\gamma_3 = \mathbf{u}^T\mathbf{B}_3/40 = 2,$ so $S\mathbf{B}_3 = \mathbf{B}_3 - 2\mathbf{u} = [4, -4, -7, 6]^T$.

(d) $\gamma_4 = \mathbf{u}^T\mathbf{B}_4/40 = -1,$ so $S\mathbf{B}_4 = \mathbf{B}_4 + \mathbf{u} = [2, 2, 7, 4]^T$.

Thus the matrix SB is given by

$$SB = \begin{bmatrix} 1 & 2 & 4 & 2 \\ 3 & 3 & -4 & 2 \\ 0 & -5 & -7 & 7 \\ 0 & 0 & 6 & 4 \end{bmatrix}.$$

(*Note:* The Householder matrix S does not disturb the first column of B, since $\mathbf{u}^T\mathbf{B}_1 = 0$ and hence $\gamma_1 = 0$; see Exercise 25.)

In order to complete the similarity transformation begun in Example 4, we need to calculate the matrix $(SB)S$. Although we know how to form QA and $Q\mathbf{x}$ when Q is a Householder matrix, we have not yet discussed how to form the product AQ.

The easiest way to form AQ is to proceed as follows:

1. Calculate $M = QA^T$.

2. Form $M^T = (QA^T)^T = AQ^T = AQ$.

(*Note:* In step 2, $AQ^T = AQ$ since a Householder matrix Q is symmetric.)

EXAMPLE 5 For the matrix SB in Example 4, calculate H, where $H = SBS$.

Solution Following the two-step procedure above, we first calculate $S(SB)^T$. From Example 4 we have

$$(SB)^T = \begin{bmatrix} 1 & 3 & 0 & 0 \\ 2 & 3 & -5 & 0 \\ 4 & -4 & -7 & 6 \\ 2 & 2 & 7 & 4 \end{bmatrix}.$$

For notation, let the columns of $(SB)^T$ be denoted as $\mathbf{R}_i$, so $(SB)^T = [\mathbf{R}_1, \mathbf{R}_2, \mathbf{R}_3, \mathbf{R}_4]$. As in Example 4, the matrix $S(SB)^T$ has column vectors $S\mathbf{R}_i$, where

$$S\mathbf{R}_i = \mathbf{R}_i - \gamma_i \mathbf{u}, \qquad \gamma_i = \mathbf{u}^T\mathbf{R}_i/40, \quad 1 \le i \le 4.$$

With $\mathbf{u}$ from Example 4, the scalars are

$$\gamma_1 = 3/5, \qquad \gamma_2 = -1, \qquad \gamma_3 = -21/10, \quad \text{and} \quad \gamma_4 = 4/5.$$

Therefore, the matrix $S(SB)^T$ is given by

$$S(SB)^T = \begin{bmatrix} 1.0 & 3.0 & 0.0 & 0.0 \\ 2.0 & 3.0 & -5.0 & 0.0 \\ -.8 & 4.0 & 9.8 & -.4 \\ 4.4 & -2.0 & -1.4 & 7.2 \end{bmatrix}.$$

The transpose of the matrix above is the Hessenberg matrix H, where $H = SBS$. ■

7.5 EXERCISES

Let $Q = I - b\mathbf{u}\mathbf{u}^T$ be the Householder matrix defined by (1), where $\mathbf{u} = [1, -1, 1, -1]^T$. In Exercises 1–8, calculate the indicated product.

1. $Q\mathbf{x}$, for $\mathbf{x} = \begin{bmatrix} 3 \\ 2 \\ 5 \\ 8 \end{bmatrix}$ **2.** $Q\mathbf{x}$, for $\mathbf{x} = \begin{bmatrix} 0 \\ 1 \\ 1 \\ 8 \end{bmatrix}$

3. QA, for $A = \begin{bmatrix} 2 & 1 \\ 6 & 3 \\ 4 & 2 \\ 2 & 4 \end{bmatrix}$

4. QA, for $A = \begin{bmatrix} 0 & 1 & 2 \\ 2 & 2 & 1 \\ 1 & 4 & 3 \\ 3 & 7 & 2 \end{bmatrix}$

5. $\mathbf{x}^TQ$, for $\mathbf{x} = \begin{bmatrix} 3 \\ 2 \\ 2 \\ 5 \end{bmatrix}$

6. $\mathbf{x}^TQ$, for $\mathbf{x} = \begin{bmatrix} 1 \\ 3 \\ 2 \\ 2 \end{bmatrix}$

7. AQ, for $A = \begin{bmatrix} 2 & 1 & 2 & 1 \\ 1 & 0 & 1 & 4 \end{bmatrix}$

8. BQ, where B is the (4×4) matrix in Example 4.

For the given vectors **v** and **w** in Exercises 9–14, determine a vector **u** such that $(I - b\mathbf{u}\mathbf{u}^T)\mathbf{v} = \mathbf{w}$.

9. $\mathbf{v} = \begin{bmatrix} 1 \\ 2 \\ 2 \\ 1 \end{bmatrix}$, $\mathbf{w} = \begin{bmatrix} 1 \\ a \\ 0 \\ 0 \end{bmatrix}$

10. $\mathbf{v} = \begin{bmatrix} 1 \\ 1 \\ 1 \\ 1 \end{bmatrix}$, $\mathbf{w} = \begin{bmatrix} a \\ 0 \\ 0 \\ 0 \end{bmatrix}$

11. $\mathbf{v} = \begin{bmatrix} 2 \\ 1 \\ 4 \\ 3 \end{bmatrix}$, $\mathbf{w} = \begin{bmatrix} 2 \\ 1 \\ a \\ 0 \end{bmatrix}$

12. $\mathbf{v} = \begin{bmatrix} 2 \\ 0 \\ -2 \\ 2 \\ 1 \end{bmatrix}$, $\mathbf{w} = \begin{bmatrix} 2 \\ 0 \\ a \\ 0 \\ 0 \end{bmatrix}$

13. $\mathbf{v} = \begin{bmatrix} 0 \\ 0 \\ 0 \\ -3 \\ 4 \end{bmatrix}$, $\mathbf{w} = \begin{bmatrix} 0 \\ 0 \\ 0 \\ a \\ 0 \end{bmatrix}$

14. $\mathbf{v} = \begin{bmatrix} 1 \\ 1 \\ 4 \\ 0 \\ 0 \end{bmatrix}$, $\mathbf{w} = \begin{bmatrix} 1 \\ 1 \\ a \\ 0 \\ 0 \end{bmatrix}$

In Exercises 15–20, find a Householder matrix Q such that $QAQ = H$, with H a Hessenberg matrix. List the vector **u** that defines Q and gives the matrix H.

15. $A = \begin{bmatrix} 1 & 3 & 4 \\ 3 & 1 & 1 \\ 4 & 1 & 1 \end{bmatrix}$ **16.** $A = \begin{bmatrix} 1 & 0 & 5 \\ 0 & 2 & 1 \\ 5 & 1 & 2 \end{bmatrix}$

17. $A = \begin{bmatrix} 0 & -4 & 3 \\ -4 & 0 & 1 \\ 3 & 1 & 2 \end{bmatrix}$

18. $A = \begin{bmatrix} 1 & 2 & 0 & 0 \\ 2 & 1 & 3 & 4 \\ 0 & 3 & 1 & 1 \\ 0 & 4 & 1 & 1 \end{bmatrix}$

19. $A = \begin{bmatrix} 2 & 1 & 1 & 2 \\ 3 & 4 & 0 & 1 \\ 0 & -3 & 1 & 1 \\ 0 & 4 & 2 & 3 \end{bmatrix}$

20. $A = \begin{bmatrix} 1 & 2 & 3 & 0 \\ 4 & 1 & 2 & 3 \\ 0 & 0 & 2 & 1 \\ 0 & 1 & 3 & 2 \end{bmatrix}$

21. Let Q denote the Householder matrix defined by (1). Verify that Q is symmetric.

22. Let Q be the Householder matrix defined by (1) and calculate the product $Q\mathbf{u}$. If **v** is any vector orthogonal to **u**, what is the result of forming $Q\mathbf{v}$?

23. Consider the $(n \times n)$ Householder matrix $Q = I - b\mathbf{u}\mathbf{u}^T$, $b = 2/(\mathbf{u}^T\mathbf{u})$. Show that Q has eigenvalues $\lambda = -1$ and $\lambda = 1$. [*Hint:* Use the Gram–Schmidt process to argue that R^n has an orthogonal basis $\{\mathbf{u}, \mathbf{w}_2, \mathbf{w}_3, \ldots, \mathbf{w}_n\}$. Also, recall Exercise 22.]

24. Prove Theorem 8.

25. Consider a (4×4) matrix B of the form shown in (9), where $b_{31} = 0$ and $b_{41} = 0$. Let **u** be a vector of the form $\mathbf{u} = [0, a, b, c]^T$, and let $Q = I - b\mathbf{u}\mathbf{u}^T$ be the associated Householder matrix.

a) Show that forming the product BQ does not change the first column of B. [*Hint:* Form BQ by using the two-step procedure illustrated in Example 5.]

b) Let **u** be a vector of the form $\mathbf{u} = [0, 0, a, b]^T$, and let $Q = I - b\mathbf{u}\mathbf{u}^T$ be the associated Householder matrix. Show that forming QBQ does not alter the first column of B.

7.6 THE *QR* FACTORIZATION AND LEAST-SQUARES SOLUTIONS

The Householder transformations of Section 7.5 can be used effectively to construct an algorithm to find the least-squares solution of an overdetermined linear system, $A\mathbf{x} = \mathbf{b}$. This construction also yields a useful way of expressing A as a product of two other matrices, called the *QR* factorization. The *QR* factorization is a principal instrument in many of the software packages for numerical linear algebra.

Reduction to Trapezoidal Form

The following theorem is proved by construction, and hence its proof serves as an algorithm for the desired factorization.

THEOREM 9 Let A be an $(m \times n)$ matrix with $m \geq n$. There exists an $(m \times m)$ orthogonal matrix S such that

$$SA = \begin{bmatrix} R \\ \mathcal{O} \end{bmatrix},$$

where R is an $(n \times n)$ upper-triangular matrix and $\mathcal{O}$ is the $[(m-n) \times n]$ zero matrix. (If $m = n$, $SA = R$.)

Proof Let $A = [\mathbf{A}_1, \mathbf{A}_2, \ldots, \mathbf{A}_n]$, where the column vectors $\mathbf{A}_i$ are in R^m. Let S_1 be the $(m \times m)$ Householder matrix such that

$$S_1\mathbf{A}_1 = [s_1, 0, 0, \ldots, 0]^T.$$

Thus the product $S_1A = [S_1\mathbf{A}_1, S_1\mathbf{A}_2, \ldots, S_1\mathbf{A}_n]$ has the form

$$S_1A = \begin{bmatrix} s_1 & c_{12} & \cdots & c_{1n} \\ 0 & c_{22} & \cdots & c_{2n} \\ 0 & c_{32} & \cdots & c_{3n} \\ \vdots & \vdots & & \\ 0 & c_{m2} & \cdots & c_{mn} \end{bmatrix}.$$

For notation, let $B = S_1A$ and write B as $B = [\mathbf{B}_1, \mathbf{B}_2, \ldots, \mathbf{B}_n]$. Next, choose the Householder S_2 such that

$$S_2\mathbf{B}_2 = [c_{12}, s_2, 0, 0, \ldots, 0]^T.$$

As in reduction to Hessenberg form, notice that $S_2\mathbf{B}_1 = \mathbf{B}_1$. Thus the product $S_2B = S_2S_1A$ has the form

$$S_2S_1A = \begin{bmatrix} s_1 & c_{12} & d_{13} & \cdots & d_{1n} \\ 0 & s_2 & d_{23} & \cdots & d_{2n} \\ 0 & 0 & d_{33} & & d_{3n} \\ \vdots & \vdots & \vdots & & \vdots \\ 0 & 0 & d_{m3} & \cdots & d_{mn} \end{bmatrix}.$$

Continuing in this fashion, we ultimately find Householder matrices $S_1, S_2, \ldots, S_n$ such that the product $S_n \cdots S_2 S_1 A$ has the form

$$S_n \cdots S_2 S_1 A = \begin{bmatrix} \times & \times & \times & \times & \cdots & \times \\ 0 & \times & \times & \times & \cdots & \times \\ 0 & 0 & \times & \times & \cdots & \times \\ 0 & 0 & 0 & \times & \cdots & \times \\ \vdots & & & & & \\ 0 & 0 & 0 & 0 & \cdots & \times \\ 0 & 0 & 0 & 0 & \cdots & 0 \\ \vdots & & & & & \\ 0 & 0 & 0 & 0 & \cdots & 0 \end{bmatrix} \begin{matrix} \\ \\ \\ \\ \\ \leftarrow \text{row } n \\ \\ \\ \leftarrow \text{row } m. \end{matrix}$$

$$\uparrow \text{ column } n$$

Equivalently, with $S = S_n \cdots S_2 S_1$, we find that S is orthogonal and

$$SA = \begin{bmatrix} R \\ \mathcal{O} \end{bmatrix}, \quad \text{where} \quad \begin{cases} R \text{ is } (n \times n) \text{ upper triangular} \\ \mathcal{O} \text{ is the } [(m-n) \times n] \text{ zero matrix.} \end{cases}$$ ■

(*Note:* The block matrix $\begin{bmatrix} R \\ \mathcal{O} \end{bmatrix}$ in Theorem 9 is called an ***upper-trapezoidal*** matrix. Also note that we are not interested in preserving similarity in Theorem 9. Thus we do not form $S_1 A S_1$ or $S_2 S_1 A S_1 S_2$ in the construction described in the proof of Theorem 9.)

EXAMPLE 1 Following the proof of Theorem 9, find Householder matrices S_1 and S_2 such that $S_2 S_1 A$ is in trapezoidal form, where

$$A = \begin{bmatrix} 1 & -2/3 \\ -1 & 3 \\ 0 & -2 \\ -1 & 1 \\ 1 & 0 \end{bmatrix}.$$

Solution Following Algorithm 2 in Section 7.5, we define a vector $\mathbf{u}$ by

$$\mathbf{u} = \begin{bmatrix} 3 \\ -1 \\ 0 \\ -1 \\ 1 \end{bmatrix}.$$

The first Householder matrix S_1 is then $S_1 = I - b\mathbf{u}\mathbf{u}^T$, where $b = 2/(\mathbf{u}^T\mathbf{u}) = 1/6$.

We next calculate $S_1 A = [S_1\mathbf{A}_1, S_1\mathbf{A}_2]$, where $S_1\mathbf{A}_i = \mathbf{A}_i - \gamma_i\mathbf{u}$, $\gamma_i = \mathbf{u}^T\mathbf{A}_i/6$. The scalars γ_i are $\gamma_1 = 1$ and $\gamma_2 = -1$. Thus the matrix $S_1 A$ has columns $\mathbf{A}_1 - \mathbf{u}$

and $\mathbf{A}_2 + \mathbf{u}$:

$$S_1A = \begin{bmatrix} -2 & 7/3 \\ 0 & 2 \\ 0 & -2 \\ 0 & 0 \\ 0 & 1 \end{bmatrix}.$$

We now define the second Householder matrix S_2, where S_2 is designed so that $S_2(S_1A)$ has zeros in positions (3, 2), (4, 2), and (5, 2).

Following Algorithm 2, define a vector $\mathbf{v}$ by

$$\mathbf{v} = \begin{bmatrix} 0 \\ 5 \\ -2 \\ 0 \\ 1 \end{bmatrix}$$

and set $S_2 = I - b\mathbf{v}\mathbf{v}^T$, $b = 2/(\mathbf{v}^T\mathbf{v}) = 1/15$. Forming $S_2(S_1A)$, we obtain

$$S_2S_1A = \begin{bmatrix} -2 & 7/3 \\ 0 & -3 \\ 0 & 0 \\ 0 & 0 \\ 0 & 0 \end{bmatrix} = \begin{bmatrix} R \\ \mathcal{O} \end{bmatrix}; \qquad R = \begin{bmatrix} -2 & 7/3 \\ 0 & -3 \end{bmatrix}.$$ ■

Least-Squares Solutions

Suppose that $A\mathbf{x} = \mathbf{b}$ represents a system of m linear equations in n unknowns, where $m \geq n$. If the system is inconsistent, it is often necessary to find a "least-squares solution" to $A\mathbf{x} = \mathbf{b}$. By a least-squares solution (recall Section 3.8), we mean a vector $\mathbf{x}^*$ in R^n such that

$$\|A\mathbf{x}^* - \mathbf{b}\| \leq \|A\mathbf{x} - \mathbf{b}\|, \quad \text{for all } \mathbf{x} \text{ in } R^n. \tag{1}$$

In Section 3.8, we saw a simple procedure for solving Eq. (1). That is, $\mathbf{x}^*$ can be obtained by solving the normal equation:

$$A^TA\mathbf{x} = A^T\mathbf{b}.$$

In this subsection, we consider an alternative procedure. The alternative is not so efficient for hand calculations, but it is the preferred procedure for machine calculations. The reason is based on the observation that the matrix A^TA is often "ill-conditioned." Thus it is frequently difficult to compute numerically an accurate solution to $A^TA\mathbf{x} = A^T\mathbf{b}$.

Recall from Section 4.7 that orthogonal matrices preserve the length of a vector under multiplication. That is, if $\mathbf{y}$ is any vector in R^m and Q is an $(m \times m)$ orthogonal matrix, then

$$\|Q\mathbf{y}\| = \|\mathbf{y}\|.$$

In the context of (1), let Q be an $(m \times m)$ orthogonal matrix. Also, suppose that $\mathbf{x}^*$ is a vector in R^n such that

$$\|A\mathbf{x}^* - \mathbf{b}\| \leq \|A\mathbf{x} - \mathbf{b}\|, \quad \text{for all } \mathbf{x} \text{ in } R^n.$$

Then, since $\|A\mathbf{x}^* - \mathbf{b}\| = \|Q(A\mathbf{x}^* - \mathbf{b})\| = \|QA\mathbf{x}^* - Q\mathbf{b}\|$ and $\|A\mathbf{x} - \mathbf{b}\| = \|Q(A\mathbf{x} - \mathbf{b})\| = \|QA\mathbf{x} - Q\mathbf{b}\|$, we have

$$\|QA\mathbf{x}^* - Q\mathbf{b}\| \leq \|QA\mathbf{x} - Q\mathbf{b}\|, \quad \text{for all } \mathbf{x} \text{ in } R^n. \tag{2}$$

Similarly, if a vector $\mathbf{x}^*$ satisfies Eq. (2), then that same vector also satisfies Eq. (1).

In other words:

> If Q is an orthogonal matrix, then finding the least-squares solution of $AQ\mathbf{x} = Q\mathbf{b}$ is equivalent to finding the least-squares solution of $A\mathbf{x} = \mathbf{b}$.

Now, using the construction in Theorem 9, we can form an orthogonal matrix Q so that the least-squares solution of $QA\mathbf{x} = Q\mathbf{b}$ is easy to find.

In particular, for an $(m \times n)$ matrix A, let S be an orthogonal matrix such that SA is in trapezoid form. Consider the problem of finding the least-squares solution of $SA\mathbf{x} = S\mathbf{b}$, where

$$SA = \begin{bmatrix} R \\ \mathcal{O} \end{bmatrix}, \qquad S\mathbf{b} = \begin{bmatrix} \mathbf{c} \\ \mathbf{d} \end{bmatrix}, \qquad \text{where } \mathbf{c} \text{ is in } R^n \text{ and } \mathbf{d} \text{ is in } R^{m-n}.$$

For any vector $\mathbf{x}$ in R^n, we have

$$SA\mathbf{x} - S\mathbf{b} = \begin{bmatrix} R\mathbf{x} \\ \boldsymbol{\theta} \end{bmatrix} - \begin{bmatrix} \mathbf{c} \\ \mathbf{d} \end{bmatrix} = \begin{bmatrix} R\mathbf{x} - \mathbf{c} \\ -\mathbf{d} \end{bmatrix}.$$

Thus, $\|SA\mathbf{x} - S\mathbf{b}\|$ can be found from the relationship

$$\|SA\mathbf{x} - S\mathbf{b}\|^2 = \|R\mathbf{x} - \mathbf{c}\|^2 + \|\mathbf{d}\|^2. \tag{3}$$

By Eq. (3), a vector $\mathbf{x}^*$ in R^n minimizes $\|SA\mathbf{x} - S\mathbf{b}\|$ if and only if $\mathbf{x}^*$ minimizes $\|R\mathbf{x} - \mathbf{c}\|$.

As an example to illustrate these ideas, consider the (5×3) trapezoidal matrix SA, where

$$SA = \begin{bmatrix} 1 & 2 & 1 \\ 0 & 2 & 4 \\ 0 & 0 & 3 \\ 0 & 0 & 0 \\ 0 & 0 & 0 \end{bmatrix} = \begin{bmatrix} R \\ \mathcal{O} \end{bmatrix}. \tag{4}$$

In Eq. (4), R is the upper (3×3) block of SA and $\mathcal{O}$ is the (2×3) zero matrix.

Now for $\mathbf{x}$ in R^3 and SA given by Eq. (4), note that $SA\mathbf{x}$ has the form

$$SA\mathbf{x} = \begin{bmatrix} 1 & 2 & 1 \\ 0 & 2 & 4 \\ 0 & 0 & 3 \\ 0 & 0 & 0 \\ 0 & 0 & 0 \end{bmatrix} \begin{bmatrix} x_1 \\ x_2 \\ x_3 \end{bmatrix} = \begin{bmatrix} x_1 + 2x_2 + x_3 \\ 2x_2 + 4x_3 \\ 3x_3 \\ 0 \\ 0 \end{bmatrix} = \begin{bmatrix} R\mathbf{x} \\ \boldsymbol{\theta} \end{bmatrix}. \quad (5)$$

In Eq. (5) the vector $R\mathbf{x}$ is three-dimensional and $\boldsymbol{\theta}$ is the two-dimensional zero vector.

In general, as noted above, a vector $\mathbf{x}^*$ in R^n minimizes $\|SA\mathbf{x} - S\mathbf{b}\|$ if and only if $\mathbf{x}^*$ minimizes $\|R\mathbf{x} - \mathbf{c}\|$ in Eq. (3). Since R is upper triangular, the problem of minimizing $\|R\mathbf{x} - \mathbf{c}\|$ is fairly easy. In particular, if R is nonsingular, then there is a unique minimizer, $\mathbf{x}^*$, and $\mathbf{x}^*$ is the solution of $R\mathbf{x} = \mathbf{c}$. The nonsingular case is summarized in the next theorem.

THEOREM 10 Let A be an $(m \times n)$ matrix, and suppose that the column vectors of A are linearly independent. Let S be an orthogonal matrix such that SA is upper trapezoidal. Given a vector $\mathbf{b}$ in R^m, let SA and $S\mathbf{b}$ be denoted as

$$SA = \begin{bmatrix} R \\ \mathcal{O} \end{bmatrix} \quad \text{and} \quad S\mathbf{b} = \begin{bmatrix} \mathbf{c} \\ \mathbf{d} \end{bmatrix}.$$

Then:

(a) R is nonsingular.

(b) There is a unique least-squares solution of $A\mathbf{x} = \mathbf{b}$, $\mathbf{x}^*$.

(c) The vector $\mathbf{x}^*$ satisfies $R\mathbf{x}^* = \mathbf{c}$.

Proof In Exercise 19, the reader is asked to show that R is nonsingular when the columns of A are linearly independent. Then, since there is a unique vector $\mathbf{x}^*$ such that $R\mathbf{x}^* = \mathbf{c}$, the rest of the conclusions in Theorem 10 follow from Eq. (3). ■

EXAMPLE 2 Use Theorem 10 to find the least-squares solution of $A\mathbf{x} = \mathbf{b}$, where

$$A = \begin{bmatrix} 1 & -2/3 \\ -1 & 3 \\ 0 & -2 \\ -1 & 1 \\ 1 & 0 \end{bmatrix} \quad \text{and} \quad \mathbf{b} = \begin{bmatrix} 1 \\ 3 \\ -4 \\ -3 \\ 3 \end{bmatrix}.$$

Solution In Example 1, we found Householder matrices S_1 and S_2 such that S_2S_1A is in trapezoidal form. The matrices S_1 and S_2 were defined by vectors $\mathbf{u}$ and $\mathbf{v}$ (respectively), where

$$\mathbf{u} = \begin{bmatrix} 3 \\ -1 \\ 0 \\ -1 \\ 1 \end{bmatrix} \quad \text{and} \quad \mathbf{v} = \begin{bmatrix} 0 \\ 5 \\ -2 \\ 0 \\ 1 \end{bmatrix}.$$

The vector $S\mathbf{b} = S_2S_1\mathbf{b}$ is found from

$$S_1\mathbf{b} = \mathbf{b} - \mathbf{u} = \begin{bmatrix} -2 \\ 4 \\ -4 \\ -2 \\ 2 \end{bmatrix} \quad \text{and} \quad S_2(S_1\mathbf{b}) = S_1\mathbf{b} - 2\mathbf{v} = \begin{bmatrix} -2 \\ -6 \\ 0 \\ -2 \\ 0 \end{bmatrix} = \begin{bmatrix} \mathbf{c} \\ \mathbf{d} \end{bmatrix}.$$

By Example 1, the matrix SA is given by

$$SA = \begin{bmatrix} -2 & 7/3 \\ 0 & -3 \\ 0 & 0 \\ 0 & 0 \\ 0 & 0 \end{bmatrix} = \begin{bmatrix} R \\ \mathcal{O} \end{bmatrix}.$$

Thus the least-squares solution, $\mathbf{x}^*$, is found by solving $R\mathbf{x} = \mathbf{c}$, where $\mathbf{c} = [-2, -6]^T$:

$$\begin{aligned} -2x_1 + (7/3)x_2 &= -2 \\ -3x_2 &= -6. \end{aligned}$$

The solution of $R\mathbf{x} = \mathbf{c}$ is $\mathbf{x}^* = [10/3, 2]^T$. ■

The *QR* Factorization

The main result of this subsection is the following theorem.

THEOREM 11 Let A be an $(m \times n)$ matrix with $m \geq n$, where A has rank n. There is an $(m \times n)$ matrix Q with orthonormal column vectors such that

$$A = QR.$$

Moreover, in the factorization $A = QR$, the matrix R is upper triangular and nonsingular.

Proof From Theorem 9, we know there is an orthogonal matrix S such that

$$SA = \begin{bmatrix} R \\ \mathcal{O} \end{bmatrix},$$

where R is an $(n \times n)$ upper-triangular matrix and R is nonsingular.

Since S is orthogonal, the reduction displayed above is equivalent to

$$A = S^T \begin{bmatrix} R \\ \mathcal{O} \end{bmatrix}. \tag{6}$$

To simplify the notation, we let B denote the $(m \times m)$ matrix S^T so that Eq. (6) becomes

$$A = B \begin{bmatrix} R \\ \mathcal{O} \end{bmatrix} = [\mathbf{B}_1, \mathbf{B}_2, \ldots, \mathbf{B}_n, \ldots, \mathbf{B}_m] \begin{bmatrix} R \\ \mathcal{O} \end{bmatrix}.$$

Examination of this product on the right-hand side shows that

$$A = [\mathbf{B}_1, \mathbf{B}_2, \ldots, \mathbf{B}_n]R. \tag{7}$$

That is, the column vectors $\mathbf{B}_{n+1}, \ldots, \mathbf{B}_m$ are multiplied by the zero entries of $\mathcal{O}$. Hence, Eq. (7) yields a factorization of A that is different from Eq. (6) but is still valid.

The proof of Theorem 11 is complete once we define the $(m \times n)$ matrix Q to be given by

$$Q = [\mathbf{B}_1, \mathbf{B}_2, \ldots, \mathbf{B}_n].$$

That is, Q consists of the first n columns of the matrix S^T, where S is the $(m \times m)$ orthogonal matrix defined in Theorem 9. ∎

Note that if $m = n$ so that A is a square matrix, then the factors Q and R are also square, and Q is an orthogonal matrix. This feature is illustrated in the next example.

EXAMPLE 3 Find a QR factorization for the matrix A:

$$A = \begin{bmatrix} 3 & 1 & 2 \\ 0 & 3 & -1 \\ 4 & 8 & 6 \end{bmatrix}.$$

Solution Following the construction shown in the proof of Theorem 9, we use Householder matrices to reduce A to upper-triangular form.

First, define a Householder matrix S_1 from $S_1 = I - b\mathbf{u}\mathbf{u}^T$, where $\mathbf{u} = [8, 0, 4]^T$. Then we have

$$S_1 A = \begin{bmatrix} -5 & -7 & -6 \\ 0 & 3 & -1 \\ 0 & 4 & 2 \end{bmatrix}.$$

Next, define $S_2 = I - b\mathbf{u}\mathbf{u}^T$, where $\mathbf{u} = [0, 8, 4]^T$. Forming $S_2(S_1 A)$, we obtain

$$S_2 S_1 A = \begin{bmatrix} -5 & -7 & -6 \\ 0 & -5 & -1 \\ 0 & 0 & 2 \end{bmatrix} = R.$$

With the above, the desired QR factorization is given by

$$A = S_1 S_2 R = QR, \quad Q = S_1 S_2.$$ ∎

If we wished to do so, we could form the product S_1S_2 and list the matrix Q explicitly. For most applications, however, there is no need to know the individual entries of Q.

EXAMPLE 4 Use the QR factorization found in Example 3 to solve $A\mathbf{x} = \mathbf{b}_1$ and $A\mathbf{x} = \mathbf{b}_2$, where

$$\mathbf{b}_1 = \begin{bmatrix} 1 \\ 8 \\ 8 \end{bmatrix} \quad \text{and} \quad \mathbf{b}_2 = \begin{bmatrix} 10 \\ -4 \\ 10 \end{bmatrix}.$$

Solution The factorization found in Example 3 states that $A\mathbf{x} = \mathbf{b}_k$ can be written as $(QR)\mathbf{x} = \mathbf{b}_k$, $k = 1, 2$. Equivalently,

$$(S_1S_2R)\mathbf{x} = \mathbf{b}_k \quad \text{or} \quad R\mathbf{x} = S_2S_1\mathbf{b}_k, \quad k = 1, 2.$$

Since S_1 and S_2 are Householder matrices, it is easy to form the vectors $S_2S_1\mathbf{b}_k$, $k = 1, 2$. We find that

$$S_2S_1\mathbf{b}_1 = \begin{bmatrix} -7 \\ -8 \\ -4 \end{bmatrix} \quad \text{and} \quad S_2S_1\mathbf{b}_2 = \begin{bmatrix} -14 \\ 4 \\ 2 \end{bmatrix}.$$

Solving $R\mathbf{x} = S_2S_1\mathbf{b}_k$, we obtain the solutions to $A\mathbf{x} = \mathbf{b}_k$:

$$\mathbf{x} = \begin{bmatrix} 1 \\ 2 \\ -2 \end{bmatrix} \quad \text{and} \quad \mathbf{x} = \begin{bmatrix} 3 \\ -1 \\ 1 \end{bmatrix}.$$

The *QR* Algorithm

In practice, the eigenvalues of an $(n \times n)$ matrix A are usually found by transforming A to Hessenberg form H and then applying some version of the QR algorithm to H. The simplest and most basic version is given next.

The *QR* Algorithm

Given an $(n \times n)$ matrix B, let $B^{(1)} = B$. For each positive integer k, find the QR factorization of $B^{(k)}$. That is, $B^{(k)} = Q^{(k)}R^{(k)}$, where $Q^{(k)}$ is orthogonal and $R^{(k)}$ is upper triangular. Then set $B^{(k+1)} = R^{(k)}Q^{(k)}$ and repeat the process.

Since $R^{(k)} = [Q^{(k)}]^T B^{(k)}$, it follows that

$$B^{(k+1)} = [Q^{(k)}]^T B^{(k)} Q^{(k)}.$$

Hence each $B^{(k)}$ is similar to B. If all the eigenvalues of B have distinct absolute values, the QR iterates, $B^{(k)}$, converge to an upper-triangular matrix T with the eigenvalues of B on its diagonal. Under other conditions, the iterates converge to other forms whose eigenvalues are discernible.

EXAMPLE 5 Perform one step of the *QR* algorithm on matrix A in Example 3.

Solution Let $A^{(1)} = A$ and let $Q^{(1)}$ and $R^{(1)}$ be the orthogonal and upper-triangular matrices, respectively, that were computed in Example 3.

If we form the product $A^{(2)} = R^{(1)}Q^{(1)}$ by using the two-step method illustrated in Example 5 of Section 7.5, we find

$$A^{(2)} = R^{(1)}Q^{(1)} = \begin{bmatrix} 7.8 & 3.88 & 5.84 \\ .8 & 3.48 & 3.64 \\ -1.6 & -.96 & .72 \end{bmatrix}.$$

(*Note:* We can draw no conclusions from just one iteration, but already in $A^{(2)}$ we can see that the size of the (2, 1), (3, 1), and (3, 2) entries begins to diminish.)

7.6 EXERCISES

In Exercises 1–4, use Theorem 10 to find a vector $\mathbf{x}^*$ such that $\|A\mathbf{x}^* - \mathbf{b}\| \le \|A\mathbf{x} - \mathbf{b}\|$ for all $\mathbf{x}$.

1. $A = \begin{bmatrix} 1 & 2 \\ 0 & 1 \\ 0 & 0 \end{bmatrix}$, $\mathbf{b} = \begin{bmatrix} 3 \\ 1 \\ 3 \end{bmatrix}$

2. $A = \begin{bmatrix} 2 & 3 \\ 0 & 1 \\ 0 & 0 \end{bmatrix}$, $\mathbf{b} = \begin{bmatrix} 1 \\ -1 \\ 2 \end{bmatrix}$

3. $A = \begin{bmatrix} 1 & 2 & 1 \\ 0 & 1 & 3 \\ 0 & 0 & 2 \\ 0 & 0 & 0 \end{bmatrix}$, $\mathbf{b} = \begin{bmatrix} 6 \\ 7 \\ 4 \\ -1 \end{bmatrix}$

4. $A = \begin{bmatrix} 2 & 0 & 3 \\ 0 & 1 & 2 \\ 0 & 0 & 3 \\ 0 & 0 & 0 \end{bmatrix}$, $\mathbf{b} = \begin{bmatrix} 5 \\ 4 \\ 3 \\ 5 \end{bmatrix}$

In Exercises 5–10, find a Householder matrix S such that $SA = R$, with R upper triangular. List R and the vector $\mathbf{u}$ that defines $S = I - b\mathbf{u}\mathbf{u}^T$.

5. $A = \begin{bmatrix} 3 & 5 \\ 4 & 10 \end{bmatrix}$ **6.** $A = \begin{bmatrix} 0 & 3 \\ 1 & 5 \end{bmatrix}$

7. $A = \begin{bmatrix} 0 & 2 \\ 4 & 6 \end{bmatrix}$ **8.** $A = \begin{bmatrix} -4 & 20 \\ 3 & -10 \end{bmatrix}$

9. $A = \begin{bmatrix} 1 & 2 & 1 \\ 0 & 0 & 6 \\ 0 & 1 & 8 \end{bmatrix}$ **10.** $A = \begin{bmatrix} 3 & 1 & 2 \\ 0 & 3 & 5 \\ 0 & 4 & 10 \end{bmatrix}$

In Exercises 11–14, use Householder matrices to reduce the given matrix A to upper-trapezoidal form.

11. $A = \begin{bmatrix} 1 & -5/3 \\ 2 & 12 \\ 2 & 8 \\ 4 & 15 \end{bmatrix}$ **12.** $A = \begin{bmatrix} 1 & 2 \\ 1 & 3 \\ 1 & 3 \\ 1 & 6 \end{bmatrix}$

13. $A = \begin{bmatrix} 2 & 4 \\ 0 & 3 \\ 0 & 0 \\ 0 & 4 \end{bmatrix}$ **14.** $A = \begin{bmatrix} 3 & 5 \\ 0 & 2 \\ 0 & 1 \\ 0 & 2 \end{bmatrix}$

In Exercises 15–18, use Theorem 10 to find the least-squares solution to problem $A\mathbf{x} = \mathbf{b}$.

15. A in Exercise 11, $\mathbf{b} = \begin{bmatrix} 1 \\ 10 \\ 0 \\ 1 \end{bmatrix}$

16. A in Exercise 12, $\mathbf{b} = \begin{bmatrix} 5 \\ 0 \\ 2 \\ 1 \end{bmatrix}$

17. A in Exercise 13, $\mathbf{b} = \begin{bmatrix} 2 \\ 8 \\ 16 \\ 8 \end{bmatrix}$

18. A in Exercise 14, $\mathbf{b} = \begin{bmatrix} 5 \\ 3 \\ 0 \\ 2 \end{bmatrix}$

19. Prove property (a) of Theorem 10.

7.7 MATRIX POLYNOMIALS AND THE CAYLEY–HAMILTON THEOREM

The objective of this section is twofold. First, we wish to give a partial justification of the algorithm (presented in Section 7.4) for finding the characteristic polynomial of a Hessenberg matrix. Second, we want to lay some of the necessary foundation for the material in Section 7.8, which describes how a basis for R^n can be constructed by using eigenvectors and generalized eigenvectors. These ideas are indispensable if we want to solve a difference equation $\mathbf{x}_k = A\mathbf{x}_{k-1}$ or a differential equation $\mathbf{x}'(t) = A\mathbf{x}(t)$, where A is defective.

Matrix Polynomials

To complete our discussion of the algorithm presented in Section 7.4, it is convenient to introduce the idea of a matrix polynomial. By way of example, consider the polynomial

$$q(t) = t^2 + 3t - 2.$$

If A is an $(n \times n)$ matrix, then we can define a matrix expression corresponding to $q(t)$:

$$q(A) = A^2 + 3A - 2I,$$

where I is the $(n \times n)$ identity. In effect, we have inserted A for t in $q(t) = t^2 + 3t - 2$ and defined A^0 by $A^0 = I$. In general, if $q(t)$ is the kth-degree polynomial

$$q(t) = b_k t^k + \cdots + b_2 t^2 + b_1 t + b_0,$$

and if A is an $(n \times n)$ matrix, we define $q(A)$ by

$$q(A) = b_k A^k + \cdots + b_2 A^2 + b_1 A + b_0 I,$$

where I is the $(n \times n)$ identity matrix. Since $q(A)$ is obviously an $(n \times n)$ matrix, we might ask for the eigenvalues and eigenvectors of $q(A)$. It is easy to show that if λ is an eigenvalue of A, then $q(\lambda)$ is an eigenvalue of $q(A)$. (Note that $q(\lambda)$ is the scalar obtained by substituting the value $t = \lambda$ into $q(t)$.)

THEOREM 12 Suppose that $q(t)$ is a kth-degree polynomial and that A is an $(n \times n)$ matrix such that $A\mathbf{x} = \lambda\mathbf{x}$, where $\mathbf{x} \neq \boldsymbol{\theta}$. Then $q(A)\mathbf{x} = q(\lambda)\mathbf{x}$.

Proof Suppose that $A\mathbf{x} = \lambda\mathbf{x}$, where $\mathbf{x} \neq \boldsymbol{\theta}$. As we know, a consequence is that $A^2\mathbf{x} = \lambda^2\mathbf{x}$, and in general

$$A^i\mathbf{x} = \lambda^i\mathbf{x}, \quad i = 2, 3, \ldots.$$

Therefore, if $q(t) = b_k t^k + \cdots + b_2 t^2 + b_1 t + b_0$, then

$$\begin{aligned} q(A)\mathbf{x} &= (b_k A^k + \cdots + b_2 A^2 + b_1 A + b_0 I)\mathbf{x} \\ &= b_k A^k\mathbf{x} + \cdots + b_2 A^2\mathbf{x} + b_1 A\mathbf{x} + b_0\mathbf{x} \\ &= b_k \lambda^k\mathbf{x} + \cdots + b_2\lambda^2\mathbf{x} + b_1\lambda\mathbf{x} + b_0\mathbf{x} \\ &= q(\lambda)\mathbf{x}. \end{aligned}$$

Thus if λ is an eigenvalue of A, then $q(\lambda)$ is an eigenvalue of $q(A)$. ■

The next example provides an illustration of Theorem 12.

EXAMPLE 1 Let $q(t)$ denote the polynomial $q(t) = t^2 + 5t + 4$. Find the eigenvalues and eigenvectors for $q(A)$, where A is the matrix given by

$$A = \begin{bmatrix} 2 & 0 \\ 3 & 1 \end{bmatrix}.$$

Solution The eigenvalues of A are $\lambda = 2$ and $\lambda = 1$. Therefore, by Theorem 12, the eigenvalues of $q(A)$ are given by

$$q(2) = 18 \quad \text{and} \quad q(1) = 10.$$

By way of verification, we calculate $q(A)$:

$$q(A) = A^2 + 5A + 4I = \begin{bmatrix} 4 & 0 \\ 9 & 1 \end{bmatrix} + \begin{bmatrix} 10 & 0 \\ 15 & 5 \end{bmatrix} + \begin{bmatrix} 4 & 0 \\ 0 & 4 \end{bmatrix} = \begin{bmatrix} 18 & 0 \\ 24 & 10 \end{bmatrix}.$$

As the calculation above confirms, $q(A)$ has eigenvalues $\lambda = q(2) = 18$ and $\lambda = q(1) = 10$. ■

An interesting special case of Theorem 12 is provided when $q(t)$ is the characteristic polynomial for A. In particular, suppose that λ is an eigenvalue of A and that $p(t)$ is the characteristic polynomial for A so that $p(\lambda) = 0$. Since $p(\lambda)$ is an eigenvalue of $p(A)$ and $p(\lambda) = 0$, we conclude that zero is an eigenvalue for $p(A)$; that is, $p(A)$ is a singular matrix. In fact, we will be able to prove more than this; we will show that $p(A)$ is the zero matrix [$p(A) = \mathcal{O}$ is the conclusion of the Cayley–Hamilton theorem].

EXAMPLE 2 Calculate the matrix $p(A)$, where

$$A = \begin{bmatrix} 1 & -2 \\ 2 & 3 \end{bmatrix}$$

and where $p(t)$ is the characteristic polynomial for A.

Solution The characteristic polynomial for A is given by $p(t) = \det(A - tI) = t^2 - 4t + 7$. Therefore, the matrix $p(A)$ is given by

$$p(A) = A^2 - 4A + 7I = \begin{bmatrix} -3 & -8 \\ 8 & 5 \end{bmatrix} - \begin{bmatrix} 4 & -8 \\ 8 & 12 \end{bmatrix} + \begin{bmatrix} 7 & 0 \\ 0 & 7 \end{bmatrix} = \begin{bmatrix} 0 & 0 \\ 0 & 0 \end{bmatrix}.$$

Thus Example 4 provides a particular instance of the Cayley–Hamilton theorem: If $p(t) = \det(A - tI)$, then $p(A) = \mathcal{O}$.

The theorems that follow show that the algorithm given in Section 7.4 leads to a polynomial $p(t)$ whose zeros are the eigenvalues of H. In the process of verifying this, we will prove an interesting version of the Cayley–Hamilton theorem that is applicable to an unreduced Hessenberg matrix. Before beginning, we make an observation about the sequence of vectors $\mathbf{w}_0, \mathbf{w}_1, \mathbf{w}_2, \ldots$ defined in Algorithm 1:

$$\mathbf{w}_i = H\mathbf{w}_{i-1}, \quad i = 1, 2, \ldots.$$

Since $\mathbf{w}_0 = \mathbf{e}_1$, then $\mathbf{w}_1 = H\mathbf{w}_0 = H\mathbf{e}_1$. Given that $\mathbf{w}_1 = H\mathbf{e}_1$, we see that

$$\mathbf{w}_2 = H\mathbf{w}_1 = H(H\mathbf{e}_1) = H^2\mathbf{e}_1;$$

and in general $\mathbf{w}_k = H^k\mathbf{e}_1$. Thus we can interpret the sequence $\mathbf{w}_0, \mathbf{w}_1, \mathbf{w}_2, \ldots, \mathbf{w}_n$ as being given by $\mathbf{e}_1, H\mathbf{e}_1, H^2\mathbf{e}_1, \ldots, H^n\mathbf{e}_1$.

With this interpretation, we rewrite the equation $a_0\mathbf{w}_0 + a_1\mathbf{w}_1 + \cdots + a_{n-1}\mathbf{w}_{n-1} + \mathbf{w}_n = \boldsymbol{\theta}$ given in Algorithm 1 as

$$a_0\mathbf{e}_1 + a_1H\mathbf{e}_1 + a_2H^2\mathbf{e}_1 + \cdots + a_{n-1}H^{n-1}\mathbf{e}_1 + H^n\mathbf{e}_1 = \boldsymbol{\theta}; \tag{1}$$

or by regrouping, (1) is the same as

$$(a_0I + a_1H + a_2H^2 + \cdots + a_{n-1}H^{n-1} + H^n)\mathbf{e}_1 = \boldsymbol{\theta}. \tag{2}$$

Now Theorem 5 asserts that if H is an unreduced $(n \times n)$ Hessenberg matrix, then the vectors $\mathbf{e}_1, H\mathbf{e}_1, H^2\mathbf{e}_1, \ldots, H^{n-1}\mathbf{e}_1$ are linearly independent, and that there is a unique set of scalars $a_0, a_1, \ldots, a_{n-1}$ that satisfy (1). Defining $p(t)$ from (1) as

$$p(t) = a_0 + a_1t + a_2t^2 + \cdots + a_{n-1}t^{n-1} + t^n,$$

we see from Eq. (2) that $p(H)\mathbf{e}_1 = \boldsymbol{\theta}$. With these preliminaries, we prove the following result.

THEOREM 13 Let H be an $(n \times n)$ unreduced Hessenberg matrix; let $a_0, a_1, \ldots, a_{n-1}$ be the unique scalars satisfying

$$a_0\mathbf{e}_1 + a_1H\mathbf{e}_1 + a_2H^2\mathbf{e}_1 + \cdots + a_{n-1}H^{n-1}\mathbf{e}_1 + H^n\mathbf{e}_1 = \boldsymbol{\theta};$$

and let $p(t) = a_0 + a_1t + a_2t^2 + \cdots + a_{n-1}t^{n-1} + t^n$. Then:

(a) $p(H)$ is the zero matrix.

(b) If $q(t) = b_0 + b_1t + b_2t^2 + \cdots + b_{k-1}t^{k-1} + t^k$ is any monic kth-degree polynomial, and if $q(H)$ is the zero matrix, then $k \geq n$. Moreover, if $k = n$, then $q(t) \equiv p(t)$.

Proof For property (a), since $\{\mathbf{e}_1, H\mathbf{e}_1, H^2\mathbf{e}_1, \ldots, H^{n-1}\mathbf{e}_1\}$ is a basis for R^n, we can express any vector $\mathbf{y}$ in R^n as a linear combination:

$$\mathbf{y} = c_0\mathbf{e}_1 + c_1 H\mathbf{e}_1 + c_2 H^2\mathbf{e}_1 + \cdots + c_{n-1}H^{n-1}\mathbf{e}_1.$$

Therefore, $p(H)\mathbf{y}$ is the vector

$$p(H)\mathbf{y} = c_0 p(H)\mathbf{e}_1 + c_1 p(H)H\mathbf{e}_1 + \cdots + c_{n-1}p(H)H^{n-1}\mathbf{e}_1. \tag{3}$$

Now although matrix products do not normally commute, it is easy to see that $p(H)H^i = H^i p(H)$. Therefore, from Eq. (3), we can represent $p(H)\mathbf{y}$ as

$$p(H)\mathbf{y} = c_0 p(H)\mathbf{e}_1 + c_1 Hp(H)\mathbf{e}_1 + \cdots + c_{n-1}H^{n-1}p(H)\mathbf{e}_1;$$

and since $p(H)\mathbf{e}_1 = \boldsymbol{\theta}$ (see (1) and (2)), then $p(H)\mathbf{y} = \boldsymbol{\theta}$ for *any* $\mathbf{y}$ in R^n. In particular, $p(H)\mathbf{e}_j = \boldsymbol{\theta}$ for $j = 1, 2, \ldots, n$; and since $p(H)\mathbf{e}_j$ is the jth column of $p(H)$, it follows that $p(H) = \mathcal{O}$.

For the proof of property (b), suppose that $q(H)$ is the zero matrix, where

$$q(H) = b_0 + b_1 H + b_2 H^2 + \cdots + b_{k-1}H^{k-1} + H^k.$$

Then $q(H)\mathbf{y} = \boldsymbol{\theta}$ for every $\mathbf{y}$ in R^n, and in particular for $\mathbf{y} = \mathbf{e}_1$ we have $q(H)\mathbf{e}_1 = \boldsymbol{\theta}$, or

$$b_0\mathbf{e}_1 + b_1 H\mathbf{e}_1 + b_2 H^2\mathbf{e}_1 + \cdots + b_{k-1}H^{k-1}\mathbf{e}_1 + H^k\mathbf{e}_1 = \boldsymbol{\theta}. \tag{4}$$

However, the vectors $\mathbf{e}_1, H\mathbf{e}_1, \ldots, H^k\mathbf{e}_1$ are linearly independent when $k \le n - 1$; so Eq. (4) can hold only if $k \ge n$ (recall that the leading coefficient of $q(t)$ is 1; so we are excluding the possibility that $q(t)$ is the zero polynomial). Moreover, if $k = n$, we can satisfy Eq. (4) only with the choice $b_0 = a_0, b_1 = a_1, \ldots, b_{n-1} = a_{n-1}$ by Theorem 5; so if $k = n$, then $q(t) \equiv p(t)$. ■

Since it was shown above that $p(H)$ is the zero matrix whenever $p(t)$ is the polynomial defined by the algorithm of Section 7.4, it is now an easy matter to show that the zeros of $p(t)$ are precisely the eigenvalues of H.

THEOREM 14 Let H be an $(n \times n)$ unreduced Hessenberg matrix, and let $p(t)$ be the polynomial defined by Algorithm 1. Then λ is a root of $p(t) = 0$ if and only if λ is an eigenvalue of H.

Proof We show first that every eigenvalue of H is a zero of $p(t)$. Thus we suppose that $H\mathbf{x} = \lambda\mathbf{x}$, where $\mathbf{x} \ne \boldsymbol{\theta}$. By Theorem 12, we know that

$$p(H)\mathbf{x} = p(\lambda)\mathbf{x};$$

and since $p(H)$ is the zero matrix of Theorem 13, we must also conclude that

$$\boldsymbol{\theta} = p(\lambda)\mathbf{x}.$$

But since $\mathbf{x} \ne \boldsymbol{\theta}$, the equality $\boldsymbol{\theta} = p(\lambda)\mathbf{x}$ implies that $p(\lambda) = 0$. Thus every eigenvalue of H is a zero of $p(t)$.

Conversely, suppose that λ is a zero of $p(t)$. Then we can write $p(t)$ in the form

$$p(t) = (t - \lambda)q(t), \tag{5}$$

where $q(t)$ is a monic polynomial of degree $n-1$. Now equating coefficients of like powers shows that if $u(t) = r(t)s(t)$, where u, r, and s are polynomials, then we also have a corresponding matrix identity

$$u(A) = r(A)s(A)$$

for any square matrix A. Thus from Eq. (5) we can assert that

$$p(H) = (H - \lambda I)q(H). \tag{6}$$

If $H - \lambda I$ were nonsingular, we could rewrite Eq. (6) as

$$(H - \lambda I)^{-1}p(H) = q(H);$$

and since $p(H)$ is the zero matrix by property (a) of Theorem 13, then $q(H)$ would be the zero matrix also. However, $q(t)$ is a monic polynomial of degree $n-1$, so property (b) of Theorem 13 assures us that $q(H)$ is *not* the zero matrix. Thus, if λ is a root of $p(t) = 0$, we know that $H - \lambda I$ must be singular, and hence λ is an eigenvalue of H. ∎

We conclude this section by outlining a proof of the Cayley–Hamilton theorem for an arbitrary matrix. If H is a Hessenberg matrix of the form

$$H = \begin{bmatrix} H_{11} & H_{12} & \cdots & H_{1r} \\ \mathcal{O} & H_{22} & \cdots & H_{2r} \\ \vdots & & & \\ \mathcal{O} & \mathcal{O} & \cdots & H_{rr} \end{bmatrix}, \tag{7}$$

where $H_{11}, H_{22}, \ldots, H_{rr}$ are unreduced Hessenberg blocks, then we define $p(t)$ to be the characteristic polynomial for H, where

$$p(t) = p_1(t)p_2(t)\cdots p_r(t)$$

and where $p_i(t)$ is the characteristic polynomial for H_{ii}, $1 \le i \le r$.

THEOREM 15 If $p(t)$ is the characteristic polynomial for a Hessenberg matrix H, then $p(H)$ is the zero matrix.

Proof We sketch the proof for the case $r = 2$. If H has the form

$$H = \begin{bmatrix} H_{11} & H_{12} \\ \mathcal{O} & H_{22} \end{bmatrix},$$

where H_{11} and H_{22} are square blocks, then it can be shown that H^k is a block matrix of the form

$$H^k = \begin{bmatrix} H_{11}^k & V_k \\ \mathcal{O} & H_{22}^k \end{bmatrix}.$$

Given this, it follows that if $q(t)$ is any polynomial, then $q(H)$ is a block matrix of the form

$$q(H) = \begin{bmatrix} q(H_{11}) & W \\ \mathcal{O} & q(H_{22}) \end{bmatrix}.$$

From these preliminaries, if H_{11} and H_{22} are unreduced blocks, then

$$p(H) = p_1(H)p_2(H) = \begin{bmatrix} p_1(H_{11}) & R \\ \mathcal{O} & p_1(H_{22}) \end{bmatrix} \begin{bmatrix} p_2(H_{11}) & S \\ \mathcal{O} & p_2(H_{22}) \end{bmatrix};$$

and since $p_1(H_{11})$ and $p_2(H_{22})$ are zero blocks, it is easy to see that $p(H)$ is the zero matrix. This argument can be repeated inductively to show that $p(H)$ is the zero matrix when H has the form (7) for $r > 2$. ■

Finally, we note that the essential features of polynomial expressions are preserved by similarity transformations. For example, if $H = SAS^{-1}$ and if $q(t)$ is any polynomial, then (Exercise 5, Section 7.7)

$$q(H) = Sq(A)S^{-1}.$$

Thus if A is similar to H and if $p(H)$ is the zero matrix, then $p(A)$ is the zero matrix as well.

The remarks made above allow us to state the Cayley–Hamilton theorem as a corollary of Theorem 15.

COROLLARY **The Cayley–Hamilton Theorem** If $p(t)$ is the characteristic polynomial for an $(n \times n)$ matrix A, then $p(A)$ is the zero matrix. ■

7.7 EXERCISES

1. Let $q(t) = t^2 - 4t + 3$. Calculate the matrices $q(A)$, $q(B)$, and $q(C)$.

$$A = \begin{bmatrix} 1 & -1 \\ 1 & 3 \end{bmatrix}, \quad B = \begin{bmatrix} 2 & -1 \\ -1 & 2 \end{bmatrix},$$

$$C = \begin{bmatrix} -2 & 0 & -2 \\ -1 & 1 & -2 \\ 0 & 1 & -1 \end{bmatrix}$$

2. The polynomial $p(t) = (t-1)^3 = t^3 - 3t^2 + 3t - 1$ is the characteristic polynomial for A, B, C, and I.

$$A = \begin{bmatrix} 1 & 0 & 0 \\ 1 & 1 & 0 \\ 0 & 0 & 1 \end{bmatrix}, \quad B = \begin{bmatrix} 1 & 0 & 0 \\ 0 & 1 & 0 \\ 0 & 1 & 1 \end{bmatrix},$$

$$C = \begin{bmatrix} 1 & 0 & 0 \\ 1 & 1 & 0 \\ 0 & 1 & 1 \end{bmatrix}, \quad I = \begin{bmatrix} 1 & 0 & 0 \\ 0 & 1 & 0 \\ 0 & 0 & 1 \end{bmatrix}$$

a) Verify that $p(A)$, $p(B)$, $p(C)$, and $p(I)$ are each the zero matrix.

b) For A and B, find a quadratic polynomial $q(t)$ such that $q(A) = q(B) = \mathcal{O}$.

3. Suppose that $q(t)$ is any polynomial and $p(t)$ is the characteristic polynomial for a matrix A. If we divide $p(t)$ into $q(t)$, we obtain an identity

$$q(t) = s(t)p(t) + r(t),$$

where the degree of $r(t)$ is less than the degree of $p(t)$. From this result, it can be shown that $q(A) = s(A)p(A) + r(A)$; and since $p(A) = \mathcal{O}$, $q(A) = r(A)$.

a) Let $p(t) = t^2 - 4t + 3$ and $q(t) = t^5 - 4t^4 + 4t^3 - 5t^2 + 8t - 1$. Find $s(t)$ and $r(t)$ so that $q(t) = s(t)p(t) + r(t)$.

b) Observe that $p(t)$ is the characteristic polynomial for the matrix B in Exercise 1. Calculate the matrix $q(B)$ without forming the powers B^5, B^4, and so on.

4. Consider the (7×7) Hessenberg matrix H given in (10) of Section 7.4, where H is partitioned with three unreduced diagonal blocks, H_{11}, H_{22}, and H_{33}. Verify that $\det(H - tI) = -p_1(t)p_2(t)p_3(t)$, where $p_1(t)$, $p_2(t)$, and $p_3(t)$ are the characteristic polynomials for H_{11}, H_{22}, and H_{33} as given by Algorithm 1.

5. Suppose that $H = SAS^{-1}$ and $q(t)$ is any polynomial. Show that $q(H) = Sq(A)S^{-1}$. [*Hint:* Show that $H^k = SA^kS^{-1}$ by direct multiplication.]

Exercises 6–8 give another proof that a symmetric matrix is diagonalizable.

6. Let A be an $(n \times n)$ symmetric matrix. Let λ_1 and λ_2 be distinct eigenvalues of A with corresponding eigenvectors $\mathbf{u}_1$ and $\mathbf{u}_2$. Prove that $\mathbf{u}_1^T\mathbf{u}_2 = 0$. [*Hint:* Given that $A\mathbf{u}_1 = \lambda_1\mathbf{u}_1$ and $A\mathbf{u}_2 = \lambda_2\mathbf{u}_2$, show that $\mathbf{u}_1^TA\mathbf{u}_2 = \mathbf{u}_2^TA\mathbf{u}_1$.]

7. Let W be a subspace of R^n, where $\dim(W) = d$, $d \geq 1$. Let A be an $(n \times n)$ matrix, and suppose that $A\mathbf{x}$ is in W whenever $\mathbf{x}$ is in W.

a) Let $\mathbf{x}_0$ be any fixed vector in W. Prove that $A^j\mathbf{x}_0$ is in W for $j = 1, 2, \ldots$. There is a smallest value k for which the set of vectors $\{\mathbf{x}_0, A\mathbf{x}_0, A^2\mathbf{x}_0, \ldots, A^k\mathbf{x}_0\}$ is linearly dependent; and thus there are unique scalars $a_0, a_1, \ldots, a_{k-1}$ such that

$$a_0\mathbf{x}_0 + a_1A\mathbf{x}_0 + \cdots + a_{k-1}A^{k-1}\mathbf{x}_0 + A^k\mathbf{x}_0 = \boldsymbol{\theta}.$$

Use these scalars to define the polynomial $m(t)$, where $m(t) = t^k + a_{k-1}t^{k-1} + \cdots + a_1t + a_0$. Observe that $m(A)\mathbf{x}_0 = \boldsymbol{\theta}$; $m(t)$ is called the minimal annihilating polynomial for $\mathbf{x}_0$. By construction there is no monic polynomial $q(t)$, where $q(t)$ has degree less than k and $q(A)\mathbf{x}_0 = \boldsymbol{\theta}$.

b) Let r be a root of $m(t) = 0$ so that $m(t) = (t - r)s(t)$. Prove that r is an eigenvalue of A. [*Hint:* Is the vector $s(A)\mathbf{x}_0$ nonzero?] Note that part (b) shows that every root of $m(t) = 0$ is an eigenvalue of A. If A is symmetric, then $m(t) = 0$ has only real roots, so $s(A)\mathbf{x}_0$ is in W.

8. Exercise 6 shows that eigenvectors of a symmetric matrix belonging to distinct eigenvalues are orthogonal. We now show that if A is a symmetric $(n \times n)$ matrix, then A has a set of n orthogonal eigenvectors. Let $\{\mathbf{u}_1, \mathbf{u}_2, \ldots, \mathbf{u}_k\}$ be a set of k eigenvectors for A, $1 \leq k < n$, where $\mathbf{u}_i^T\mathbf{u}_j = 0$, $i \neq j$. Let W be the subset of R^n defined by

$$W = \{\mathbf{x}\colon \mathbf{x}^T\mathbf{u}_i = 0, \quad i = 1, 2, \ldots, k\}$$

From the Gram–Schmidt theorem, the subset W contains nonzero vectors.

a) Prove that W is a subspace of R^n.

b) Suppose that A is $(n \times n)$ and symmetric. Prove that $A\mathbf{x}$ is in W whenever $\mathbf{x}$ is in W. From Exercise 7, A has an eigenvector, $\mathbf{u}$, in W. If we label $\mathbf{u}$ as $\mathbf{u}_{k+1}$, then by construction $\{\mathbf{u}_1, \mathbf{u}_2, \ldots, \mathbf{u}_k, \mathbf{u}_{k+1}\}$ is a set of orthogonal eigenvectors for A. It follows that A has a set of n orthogonal eigenvectors, $\mathbf{u}_1, \mathbf{u}_2, \ldots, \mathbf{u}_n$. Using these, we can form Q so that $Q^TAQ = D$, where D is diagonal and $Q^TQ = I$.

7.8 GENERALIZED EIGENVECTORS AND SOLUTIONS OF SYSTEMS OF DIFFERENTIAL EQUATIONS

In this section, we develop the idea of a generalized eigenvector in order to give the complete solution to the system of differential equations $\mathbf{x}' = A\mathbf{x}$. When an $(n \times n)$ matrix A has real eigenvalues, the eigenvectors and generalized eigenvectors of A form a basis for R^n. We show how to construct the complete solution of $\mathbf{x}' = A\mathbf{x}$ from this special basis. (When some of the eigenvalues of A are complex, a few modifications are necessary to obtain the complete solution of $\mathbf{x}' = A\mathbf{x}$ in a real form. In any event, the eigenvectors and generalized eigenvectors of A form a basis for C^n, where C^n denotes the set of all n-dimensional vectors with real or complex components.)

To begin, let A be an $(n \times n)$ matrix. The problem we wish to solve is called an ***initial-value problem*** and is formulated as follows: Given a vector $\mathbf{x}_0$ in R^n, find a function $\mathbf{x}(t)$ such that

$$\begin{aligned}\mathbf{x}(0) &= \mathbf{x}_0 \\ \mathbf{x}'(t) &= A\mathbf{x}(t) \quad \text{for all } t.\end{aligned} \tag{1}$$

If we can find n functions $\mathbf{x}_1(t), \mathbf{x}_2(t), \ldots, \mathbf{x}_n(t)$ that satisfy

$$\mathbf{x}_1'(t) = A\mathbf{x}_1(t), \qquad \mathbf{x}_2'(t) = A\mathbf{x}_2(t), \ldots, \mathbf{x}_n'(t) = A\mathbf{x}_n(t)$$

and such that $\{\mathbf{x}_1(0), \mathbf{x}_2(0), \ldots, \mathbf{x}_n(0)\}$ is linearly independent, then we can always solve (1). To show why, we merely note that there must be constants $c_1, c_2, \ldots, c_n$ such that

$$\mathbf{x}_0 = c_1\mathbf{x}_1(0) + c_2\mathbf{x}_2(0) + \cdots + c_n\mathbf{x}_n(0)$$

and then note that the function

$$\mathbf{y}(t) = c_1\mathbf{x}_1(t) + c_2\mathbf{x}_2(t) + \cdots + c_n\mathbf{x}_n(t)$$

satisfies the requirements of (1). Thus to solve $\mathbf{x}' = A\mathbf{x}$, $\mathbf{x}(0) = \mathbf{x}_0$, we are led to search for n solutions $\mathbf{x}_1(t), \mathbf{x}_2(t), \ldots, \mathbf{x}_n(t)$ of $\mathbf{x}' = A\mathbf{x}$ for which $\{\mathbf{x}_1(0), \mathbf{x}_2(0), \ldots, \mathbf{x}_n(0)\}$ is linearly independent.

If A has a set of k linearly independent eigenvectors $\{\mathbf{u}_1, \mathbf{u}_2, \ldots, \mathbf{u}_k\}$, where

$$A\mathbf{u}_i = \lambda_i\mathbf{u}_i, \quad i = 1, 2, \ldots, k,$$

then, as in Section 7.2, we can immediately construct k solutions to $\mathbf{x}' = A\mathbf{x}$, namely,

$$\mathbf{x}_1(t) = e^{\lambda_1 t}\mathbf{u}_1, \qquad \mathbf{x}_2(t) = e^{\lambda_2 t}\mathbf{u}_2, \ldots, \mathbf{x}_k(t) = e^{\lambda_k t}\mathbf{u}_k.$$

Also, since $\mathbf{x}_i(0) = \mathbf{u}_i$, it follows that $\{\mathbf{x}_1(0), \mathbf{x}_2(0), \ldots, \mathbf{x}_k(0)\}$ is a linearly independent set. The difficulty arises when $k < n$, for then we must produce an additional set of $n - k$ solutions of $\mathbf{x}' = A\mathbf{x}$. In this connection, recall that an $(n \times n)$ matrix A is called ***defective*** if A has fewer than n linearly independent eigenvectors. (*Note:* Distinct eigenvalues give rise to linearly independent eigenvectors; so A can be defective only if the characteristic equation $p(t) = 0$ has fewer than n distinct roots.)

Generalized Eigenvectors

A complete analysis of the initial-value problem is simplified considerably if we assume A is a Hessenberg matrix. If A is not a Hessenberg matrix, then a simple change of variables can be used to convert $\mathbf{x}' = A\mathbf{x}$ to an equivalent problem $\mathbf{y}' = H\mathbf{y}$, where H is a Hessenberg matrix. In particular, suppose that $QAQ^{-1} = H$ and let $\mathbf{y}(t) = Q\mathbf{x}(t)$. Therefore, we see that $\mathbf{x}(t) = Q^{-1}\mathbf{y}(t)$ and $\mathbf{x}'(t) = Q^{-1}\mathbf{y}'(t)$. Thus, $\mathbf{x}'(t) = A\mathbf{x}(t)$ is the same as

$$Q^{-1}\mathbf{y}'(t) = AQ^{-1}\mathbf{y}(t).$$

Multiplying both sides by Q, we obtain the related equation $\mathbf{y}' = H\mathbf{y}$, where $H = QAQ^{-1}$ is a Hessenberg matrix. Given that we can always make this change of variables, we will focus for the remainder of this section on the problem of solving

$$\mathbf{x}'(t) = H\mathbf{x}(t), \quad \mathbf{x}(0) = \mathbf{x}_0. \tag{2}$$

As we know, if H is $(n \times n)$ and has n linearly independent eigenvectors, we can always solve (2). To see how to solve (2) when H is defective, let us suppose that $p(t)$ is the characteristic polynomial for H. If we write $p(t)$ in factored form as

$$p(t) = (t - \lambda_1)^{m_1}(t - \lambda_2)^{m_2} \cdots (t - \lambda_k)^{mk},$$

where $m_1 + m_2 + \cdots + m_k = n$, then we say that the eigenvalue λ_i has ***algebraic multiplicity*** m_i. Given λ_i, we want to construct m_i solutions of $\mathbf{x}' = H\mathbf{x}$ that are associated with λ_i. For example, suppose that λ is an eigenvalue of H of algebraic multiplicity 2. We have one solution of $\mathbf{x}' = H\mathbf{x}$, namely, $\mathbf{x}(t) = e^{\lambda t}\mathbf{u}$, where $H\mathbf{u} = \lambda\mathbf{u}$; and we would like another solution. To find this additional solution, we note that the theory from elementary differential equations suggests that we look for another solution to $\mathbf{x}' = H\mathbf{x}$ that is of the form $\mathbf{x}(t) = te^{\lambda t}\mathbf{a} + e^{\lambda t}\mathbf{b}$, where $\mathbf{a} \neq \boldsymbol{\theta}$, $\mathbf{b} \neq \boldsymbol{\theta}$. To see what conditions $\mathbf{a}$ and $\mathbf{b}$ must satisfy, we calculate

$$\begin{aligned} \mathbf{x}'(t) &= t\lambda e^{\lambda t}\mathbf{a} + e^{\lambda t}\mathbf{a} + \lambda e^{\lambda t}\mathbf{b} \\ H\mathbf{x}(t) &= te^{\lambda t}H\mathbf{a} + e^{\lambda t}H\mathbf{b}. \end{aligned}$$

After we equate $\mathbf{x}'(t)$ with $H\mathbf{x}(t)$ and group like powers of t, our guess leads to the conditions

$$\begin{aligned} t\lambda e^{\lambda t}\mathbf{a} &= te^{\lambda t}H\mathbf{a} \\ e^{\lambda t}(\mathbf{a} + \lambda\mathbf{b}) &= e^{\lambda t}H\mathbf{b}. \end{aligned} \tag{3}$$

If (3) is to hold for all t, we will need

$$\begin{aligned} \lambda\mathbf{a} &= H\mathbf{a} \\ \mathbf{a} + \lambda\mathbf{b} &= H\mathbf{b}, \end{aligned}$$

or equivalently,

$$\begin{aligned} (H - \lambda I)\mathbf{a} &= \boldsymbol{\theta} \\ (H - \lambda I)\mathbf{b} &= \mathbf{a}, \end{aligned} \tag{4}$$

where $\mathbf{a}$ and $\mathbf{b}$ are nonzero vectors. From (4) we see that $\mathbf{a}$ is an eigenvector and that $(H - \lambda I)^2\mathbf{b} = \boldsymbol{\theta}$, but $(H - \lambda I)\mathbf{b} \neq \boldsymbol{\theta}$. We will call $\mathbf{b}$ a generalized eigenvector of order 2. If we can find vectors $\mathbf{a}$ and $\mathbf{b}$ that satisfy (4), then we have two solutions of $\mathbf{x}' = H\mathbf{x}$ associated with λ, namely,

$$\begin{aligned} \mathbf{x}_1(t) &= e^{\lambda t}\mathbf{a} \\ \mathbf{x}_2(t) &= te^{\lambda t}\mathbf{a} + e^{\lambda t}\mathbf{b}. \end{aligned}$$

Moreover, $\mathbf{x}_1(0) = \mathbf{a}$, $\mathbf{x}_2(0) = \mathbf{b}$, and it is easy to see that $\mathbf{x}_1(0)$ and $\mathbf{x}_2(0)$ are linearly independent. (If $c_1\mathbf{a} + c_2\mathbf{b} = \boldsymbol{\theta}$, then $(H - \lambda I)(c_1\mathbf{a} + c_2\mathbf{b}) = \boldsymbol{\theta}$. Since $(H - \lambda I)\mathbf{a} = \boldsymbol{\theta}$, it follows that $c_2(H - \lambda I)\mathbf{b} = c_2\mathbf{a} = \boldsymbol{\theta}$, which shows that $c_2 = 0$. Finally, if $c_2 = 0$, then $c_1\mathbf{a} = \boldsymbol{\theta}$, which means that $c_1 = 0$.)

EXAMPLE 1 Solve the initial-value problem $\mathbf{x}'(t) = A\mathbf{x}(t)$, $\mathbf{x}(0) = \mathbf{x}_0$, where

$$A = \begin{bmatrix} 1 & -1 \\ 1 & 3 \end{bmatrix} \quad \text{and} \quad \mathbf{x}_0 = \begin{bmatrix} 5 \\ -7 \end{bmatrix}.$$

Solution For matrix A, the characteristic polynomial $p(t) = \det(A - tI)$ is given by

$$p(t) = (t - 2)^2.$$

Thus the only eigenvalue of A is $\lambda = 2$. The only eigenvectors for $\lambda = 2$ are those vectors $\mathbf{u}$ of the form

$$\mathbf{u} = a\begin{bmatrix} 1 \\ -1 \end{bmatrix}, \quad a \neq 0.$$

Since A is defective, we look for a generalized eigenvector associated with $\lambda = 2$. That is, as in (4) we look for a vector $\mathbf{v}$ such that

$$(A - 2I)\mathbf{v} = \mathbf{u}, \quad \mathbf{u} = \begin{bmatrix} 1 \\ -1 \end{bmatrix}.$$

In detail, the equation $(A - 2I)\mathbf{v} = \mathbf{u}$ is given by

$$\begin{bmatrix} -1 & -1 \\ 1 & 1 \end{bmatrix}\begin{bmatrix} v_1 \\ v_2 \end{bmatrix} = \begin{bmatrix} 1 \\ -1 \end{bmatrix}.$$

Now, although matrix $A - 2I$ is singular, the equation above does have a solution, namely, $v_1 = 1$, $v_2 = -2$.

Thus we have found two solutions to $\mathbf{x}'(t) = A\mathbf{x}(t)$, $\mathbf{x}_1(t)$ and $\mathbf{x}_2(t)$, where

$$\mathbf{x}_1(t) = e^{2t}\mathbf{u} \quad \text{and} \quad \mathbf{x}_2(t) = te^{2t}\mathbf{u} + e^{2t}\mathbf{v}.$$

The general solution of $\mathbf{x}'(t) = A\mathbf{x}(t)$ is

$$\mathbf{x}(t) = a_1 e^{2t}\mathbf{u} + a_2(te^{2t}\mathbf{u} + e^{2t}\mathbf{v}).$$

To satisfy the initial condition $\mathbf{x}(0) = \mathbf{x}_0 = [5, -7]^T$, we need a_1 and a_2 so that

$$\mathbf{x}(0) = a_1\mathbf{u} + a_2\mathbf{v} = \mathbf{x}_0.$$

Solving for a_1 and a_2, we find $a_1 = 3$ and $a_2 = 2$.

Therefore, the solution is

$$\mathbf{x}(t) = 3e^{2t}\mathbf{u} + 2(te^{2t}\mathbf{u} + e^{2t}\mathbf{v}) = \begin{bmatrix} 5e^{2t} + 2te^{2t} \\ -7e^{2t} - 2te^{2t} \end{bmatrix}.$$

In this section, we will see that the solution procedure illustrated in Example 1 can be applied to an unreduced Hessenberg matrix. To formalize the procedure, we need a definition.

DEFINITION 2 Let A be an $(n \times n)$ matrix. A nonzero vector $\mathbf{v}$ such that

$$(A - \lambda I)^j\mathbf{v} = \boldsymbol{\theta}$$

$$(A - \lambda I)^{j-1}\mathbf{v} \neq \boldsymbol{\theta}$$

is called a ***generalized eigenvector of order*** j corresponding to λ.

Note that an eigenvector can be regarded as a generalized eigenvector of order 1.

If a matrix H has a generalized eigenvector $\mathbf{v}_m$ of order m corresponding to λ, then the following sequence of vectors can be defined:

$$\begin{aligned}(H-\lambda I)\mathbf{v}_m &= \mathbf{v}_{m-1}\\ (H-\lambda I)\mathbf{v}_{m-1} &= \mathbf{v}_{m-2}\\ &\vdots\\ (H-\lambda I)\mathbf{v}_2 &= \mathbf{v}_1.\end{aligned} \tag{5}$$

It is easy to show that each vector $\mathbf{v}_r$ in (5) is a generalized eigenvector of order r and that $\{\mathbf{v}_1, \mathbf{v}_2, \ldots, \mathbf{v}_m\}$ is a linearly independent set (see Exercise 6). In addition, each generalized eigenvector $\mathbf{v}_r$ leads to a solution $\mathbf{x}_r(t)$ of $\mathbf{x}' = H\mathbf{x}$, where

$$\mathbf{x}_r(t) = e^{\lambda t}\left(\mathbf{v}_r + t\mathbf{v}_{r-1} + \cdots + \frac{t^{r-1}}{(r-1)!}\mathbf{v}_1\right) \tag{6}$$

(see Exercise 7).

We begin the analysis by proving two theorems that show that an $(n \times n)$ unreduced Hessenberg matrix H has a set of n linearly independent eigenvectors and generalized eigenvectors. Then, following several examples, we comment on the general case.

Theorem 16 Let H be an $(n \times n)$ unreduced Hessenberg matrix, and let λ be an eigenvalue of H, where λ has algebraic multiplicity m. Then H has a generalized eigenvector of order m corresponding to λ.

Proof Let $p(t) = (t-\lambda)^m q(t)$ be the characteristic polynomial for H, where $q(\lambda) \neq 0$. Let $\mathbf{v}_m$ be the vector $\mathbf{v}_m = q(H)\mathbf{e}_1$. By Theorem 13, $(H-\lambda I)^{m-1}q(H)\mathbf{e}_1 \neq \boldsymbol{\theta}$, so $(H-\lambda I)^{m-1}\mathbf{v}_m \neq \boldsymbol{\theta}$. Also by Theorem 13, $(H-\lambda I)^m\mathbf{v}_m = (H-\lambda I)^m q(H)\mathbf{e}_1 = p(H)\mathbf{e}_1 = \boldsymbol{\theta}$, so we see that $\mathbf{v}_m$ is a generalized eigenvector of order m. ∎

Theorem 16 is an existence result that is quite valuable. If we know that an unreduced Hessenberg matrix H has an eigenvalue of multiplicity m, then we know that the sequence of vectors in (5) is defined. Therefore, we can start with an eigenvector $\mathbf{v}_1$, then find $\mathbf{v}_2$, then find $\mathbf{v}_3$, and so on. (If H is a reduced Hessenberg matrix, the sequence (5) might not exist.)

Example 2 Consider the unreduced Hessenberg matrix H, where

$$H = \begin{bmatrix} 1 & 0 & 0\\ 1 & 1 & 0\\ 0 & 1 & 1\end{bmatrix}.$$

Note that the eigenvalue $\lambda = 1$ has algebraic multiplicity 3. Find generalized eigenvectors of orders 2 and 3.

Solution We work backward up the chain of vectors in (5), starting with an eigenvector $\mathbf{v}_1$. Now all eigenvectors corresponding to $\lambda = 1$ have the form $\mathbf{u} = a[0, 0, 1]^T$, $a \neq 0$. If we choose $\mathbf{v}_1 = [0, 0, 1]^T$, the equation $(H - I)\mathbf{v}_2 = \mathbf{v}_1$ has the form

$$\begin{bmatrix} 0 & 0 & 0\\ 1 & 0 & 0\\ 0 & 1 & 0\end{bmatrix}\begin{bmatrix} x_1\\ x_2\\ x_3\end{bmatrix} = \begin{bmatrix} 0\\ 0\\ 1\end{bmatrix}.$$

The solution to the equation above is $\mathbf{v}_2 = [0, 1, a]^T$, where a is arbitrary. For simplicity we choose $a = 0$ and obtain $\mathbf{v}_2 = [0, 1, 0]^T$.

Next, we need to solve $(H - I)\mathbf{v}_3 = \mathbf{v}_2$:

$$\begin{bmatrix} 0 & 0 & 0 \\ 1 & 0 & 0 \\ 0 & 1 & 0 \end{bmatrix} \begin{bmatrix} x_1 \\ x_2 \\ x_3 \end{bmatrix} = \begin{bmatrix} 0 \\ 1 \\ 0 \end{bmatrix}.$$

The solution to this equation is $\mathbf{v}_3 = [1, 0, a]^T$, where a is arbitrary. One solution is $\mathbf{v}_3 = [1, 0, 0]^T$.

To summarize, an eigenvector and two generalized eigenvectors for H are

$$\mathbf{v}_1 = \begin{bmatrix} 0 \\ 0 \\ 1 \end{bmatrix}, \quad \mathbf{v}_2 = \begin{bmatrix} 0 \\ 1 \\ 0 \end{bmatrix}, \quad \mathbf{v}_3 = \begin{bmatrix} 1 \\ 0 \\ 0 \end{bmatrix}.$$

(*Note:* For $i = 1, 2, 3$, $\mathbf{v}_i$ is a generalized eigenvector of order i.) ■

Example 2 illustrates a situation in which a (3×3) unreduced Hessenberg matrix has a set of eigenvalues and generalized eigenvectors that form a basis for R^3. As the next theorem demonstrates, Example 2 is typical.

THEOREM 17 Let H be an $(n \times n)$ unreduced Hessenberg matrix. There is a set $\{\mathbf{u}_1, \mathbf{u}_2, \ldots, \mathbf{u}_n\}$ of linearly independent vectors in which each $\mathbf{u}_i$ is an eigenvector or a generalized eigenvector of H.

Proof Suppose that H has eigenvalues $\lambda_1, \lambda_2, \ldots, \lambda_k$, where λ_i has multiplicity m_i. Thus the characteristic polynomial has the form

$$p(t) = (t - \lambda_1)^{m_1}(t - \lambda_2)^{m_2} \cdots (t - \lambda_k)^{m_k},$$

where $m_1 + m_2 + \cdots + m_k = n$. By Theorem 16, each eigenvalue λ_i has an associated generalized eigenvector of order m_i. For each eigenvalue λ_i, we can use (5) to generate a set of m_i generalized eigenvectors having order $1, 2, \ldots, m_i$. Let us denote this collection of n generalized eigenvectors as

$$\mathbf{v}_1, \mathbf{v}_2, \ldots, \mathbf{v}_{m_1}, \mathbf{w}_1, \mathbf{w}_2, \ldots, \mathbf{w}_r, \tag{7}$$

where $m_1 + r = n$. In (7), $\mathbf{v}_j$ is a generalized eigenvector of order j corresponding to the eigenvalue λ_i, whereas each of the vectors $\mathbf{w}_j$ is a generalized eigenvector for one of $\lambda_2, \lambda_3, \ldots, \lambda_k$.

To show that the vectors in (7) are linearly independent, consider

$$a_1\mathbf{v}_1 + a_2\mathbf{v}_2 + \cdots + a_{m1}\mathbf{v}_{m1} + b_1\mathbf{w}_1 + b_2\mathbf{w}_2 + \cdots + b_r\mathbf{w}_r = \boldsymbol{\theta}. \tag{8}$$

Now for $q(t) = (t - \lambda_2)^{m_2} \cdots (t - \lambda_k)^{m_k}$ and for $1 \le j \le r$, we note that

$$q(H)\mathbf{w}_j = \boldsymbol{\theta},$$

since $\mathbf{w}_j$ is a generalized eigenvector of order m_i or less corresponding to some λ_i. (That is, $(H - \lambda_i I)^{m_i}\mathbf{w}_j = \boldsymbol{\theta}$ for some λ_i and $(H - \lambda_i I)^{m_i}$ is one of the factors of $q(H)$. Thus, $q(H)\mathbf{w}_j = \boldsymbol{\theta}$ for any j, $1 \le j \le r$.)

Now multiplying both sides of (8) by $q(H)$, we obtain

$$a_1 q(H)\mathbf{v}_1 + a_2 q(H)\mathbf{v}_2 + \cdots + a_{m1} q(H)\mathbf{v}_{m1} = \boldsymbol{\theta}. \tag{9}$$

Finally, we can use (5) to show that $a_1, a_2, \ldots, a_{m_1}$ are all zero in Eq. (9) (see Exercise 8). Since we could have made this argument for any of the eigenvalues $\lambda_2, \lambda_3, \ldots, \lambda_k$, it follows that all the coefficients b_j in Eq. (8) are also zero. ■

EXAMPLE 3 Find the general solution of $\mathbf{x}' = H\mathbf{x}$, where

$$H = \begin{bmatrix} 1 & 0 & 0 \\ 1 & 3 & 0 \\ 0 & 1 & 1 \end{bmatrix}.$$

Solution The characteristic polynomial is $p(t) = (t-1)^2(t-3)$; so $\lambda = 1$ is an eigenvalue of multiplicity 2, whereas $\lambda = 3$ is an eigenvalue of multiplicity 1. Eigenvectors corresponding to $\lambda = 1$ and $\lambda = 3$ are (respectively)

$$\mathbf{v}_1 = \begin{bmatrix} 0 \\ 0 \\ 1 \end{bmatrix} \quad \text{and} \quad \mathbf{w}_1 = \begin{bmatrix} 0 \\ 2 \\ 1 \end{bmatrix}.$$

Thus we have two solutions of $\mathbf{x}' = H\mathbf{x}$, namely, $\mathbf{x}(t) = e^t\mathbf{v}_1$ and $\mathbf{x}(t) = e^{3t}\mathbf{w}_1$. We need one more solution to solve the initial-value problem for any $\mathbf{x}_0$ in R^3. To find a third solution, we need a vector $\mathbf{v}_2$ that is a generalized eigenvector of order 2 corresponding to $\lambda = 1$. According to the previous remarks, we solve $(H - I)\mathbf{x} = \mathbf{v}_1$ and obtain

$$\mathbf{v}_2 = \begin{bmatrix} -2 \\ 1 \\ 0 \end{bmatrix}.$$

By Eq. (6), a third solution to $\mathbf{x}' = H\mathbf{x}$ is given by $\mathbf{x}(t) = e^t(\mathbf{v}_2 + t\mathbf{v}_1)$. Clearly $\{\mathbf{v}_1, \mathbf{v}_2, \mathbf{w}_1\}$ is a basis for R^3; so if $\mathbf{x}_0 = c_1\mathbf{v}_1 + c_2\mathbf{v}_2 + c_3\mathbf{w}_1$, then

$$\mathbf{x}(t) = c_1 e^t\mathbf{v}_1 + c_2 e^t(\mathbf{v}_2 + t\mathbf{v}_1) + c_3 e^{3t}\mathbf{w}_1$$

will satisfy $\mathbf{x}' = H\mathbf{x}$, $\mathbf{x}(0) = \mathbf{x}_0$. ■

EXAMPLE 4 Find the general solution of $\mathbf{x}' = A\mathbf{x}$, where

$$A = \begin{bmatrix} -1 & -8 & 1 \\ -1 & -3 & 2 \\ -4 & -16 & 7 \end{bmatrix}.$$

Solution Reducing A to Hessenberg form, we have $H = QAQ^{-1}$, where H, Q, and Q^{-1} are

$$H = \begin{bmatrix} -1 & -4 & 1 \\ -1 & 5 & 2 \\ 0 & -8 & -1 \end{bmatrix}, \quad Q = \begin{bmatrix} 1 & 0 & 0 \\ 0 & 1 & 0 \\ 0 & -4 & 1 \end{bmatrix}, \quad \text{and} \quad Q^{-1} = \begin{bmatrix} 1 & 0 & 0 \\ 0 & 1 & 0 \\ 0 & 4 & 1 \end{bmatrix}.$$

The change of variables $\mathbf{y}(t) = Q\mathbf{x}(t)$ converts $\mathbf{x}' = A\mathbf{x}, \mathbf{x}(0) = \mathbf{x}_0$ to the problem $\mathbf{y}' = H\mathbf{y}, \mathbf{y}(0) = Q\mathbf{x}_0$.

The characteristic polynomial for H is $p(t) = (t-1)^3$, so $\lambda = 1$ is an eigenvalue of multiplicity 3 of H. Up to a scalar multiple, the only eigenvector of H is

$$\mathbf{v}_1 = \begin{bmatrix} 4 \\ -1 \\ 4 \end{bmatrix}.$$

We obtain two generalized eigenvectors for H by solving $(H - I)\mathbf{x} = \mathbf{v}_1$ to get $\mathbf{v}_2$, and $(H - I)\mathbf{x} = \mathbf{v}_2$ to get $\mathbf{v}_3$. These generalized eigenvectors are

$$\mathbf{v}_2 = \begin{bmatrix} 1 \\ -1 \\ 2 \end{bmatrix} \quad \text{and} \quad \mathbf{v}_3 = \begin{bmatrix} 3 \\ -1 \\ 3 \end{bmatrix}.$$

Thus the general solution of $\mathbf{y}' = H\mathbf{y}$ is

$$\mathbf{y}(t) = e^t \left[c_1\mathbf{v}_1 + c_2(\mathbf{v}_2 + t\mathbf{v}_1) + c_3\left(\mathbf{v}_3 + t\mathbf{v}_2 + \frac{t^2}{2}\mathbf{v}_1\right)\right],$$

and we can recover $\mathbf{x}(t)$ from $\mathbf{x}(t) = Q^{-1}\mathbf{y}(t)$.

If H is an $(n \times n)$ *reduced* Hessenberg matrix, it can be shown that R^n has a basis consisting of eigenvectors and generalized eigenvectors of H. This general result is fairly difficult to establish, however, and we do not do so here. ∎

7.8 EXERCISES

1. Find a full set of eigenvectors and generalized eigenvectors for each of the following.

a) $\begin{bmatrix} 1 & -1 \\ 1 & 3 \end{bmatrix}$ **b)** $\begin{bmatrix} -2 & 0 & -2 \\ -1 & 1 & -2 \\ 0 & 1 & -1 \end{bmatrix}$

c) $\begin{bmatrix} -6 & 31 & -14 \\ -1 & 6 & -2 \\ 0 & 2 & 1 \end{bmatrix}$

2. Find a full set of eigenvectors and generalized eigenvectors for the following. (*Note:* $\lambda = 2$ is the only eigenvalue of B.)

$$A = \begin{bmatrix} 1 & 0 & 0 & 0 \\ 1 & 1 & 0 & 0 \\ 0 & 1 & 1 & 0 \\ 0 & 0 & 1 & 1 \end{bmatrix}, \quad B = \begin{bmatrix} 2 & 3 & -21 & -3 \\ 2 & 7 & -41 & -5 \\ 0 & 1 & -5 & -1 \\ 0 & 0 & 4 & 4 \end{bmatrix}$$

3. Solve $\mathbf{x}' = A\mathbf{x}, \mathbf{x}(0) = \mathbf{x}_0$ by transforming A to Hessenberg form, where

$$\mathbf{x}_0 = \begin{bmatrix} -1 \\ -1 \\ 1 \end{bmatrix}, \quad \text{and}$$

a) $A = \begin{bmatrix} 8 & -6 & 21 \\ 1 & -1 & 3 \\ -3 & 2 & -8 \end{bmatrix}$,

b) $A = \begin{bmatrix} 2 & 1 & -1 \\ -3 & -1 & 1 \\ 9 & 3 & -4 \end{bmatrix}$

c) $A = \begin{bmatrix} 1 & 1 & -1 \\ -3 & -2 & 1 \\ 9 & 3 & -5 \end{bmatrix}$.

4. Give the general solution of $\mathbf{x}' = A\mathbf{x}$, where A is from Exercise 2.

5. Repeat Exercise 4, where A is in part (c) of Exercise 1.

6. Prove that each vector $\mathbf{v}_r$ in (5) is a generalized eigenvector of order r and that $\{\mathbf{v}_1, \mathbf{v}_2, \ldots, \mathbf{v}_m\}$ is linearly independent.

7. Prove that the functions $\mathbf{x}_r(t)$ defined in (6) are solutions of $\mathbf{x}' = H\mathbf{x}$.

8. Prove that the coefficients $a_1, a_2, \ldots$ in (9), are all zero. [*Hint:* Multiply (9) by $(H - \lambda_1 I)^{m_1-1}$.]

SUPPLEMENTARY EXERCISES

1. Consider the quadratic form $q(\mathbf{x}) = x_1^2 + 3x_1x_2 + x_2^2$. Describe all possible real (2×2) matrices A such that $q(\mathbf{x}) = \mathbf{x}^T A\mathbf{x}$.

2. Let

$$A = \begin{bmatrix} 2 & 6+a \\ a & 2 \end{bmatrix},$$

where a is a real constant. For what values a is A defective?

3. Let

$$B = \begin{bmatrix} 2 & 6 \\ 0 & 2 \end{bmatrix},$$

and consider the quadratic form defined by $q(\mathbf{x}) = \mathbf{x}^T B\mathbf{x}$.

a) Find a vector $\mathbf{x}$ such that $q(\mathbf{x}) < 0$.

b) Note that B has only positive eigenvalues. Why does this fact not contradict Theorem 2 in Section 7.1?

4. Let $q(t) = t^2 + 3t + 2$ and let A be a nonsingular $(n \times n)$ matrix. Show that $q(A)$ and $q(A^{-1})$ commute in the sense that $q(A)q(A^{-1}) = q(A^{-1})q(A)$.

5. A positive definite matrix A can be factored as $A = LL^T$, where L is a nonsingular lower-triangular matrix. (Such a factorization is called the ***Cholesky decomposition***.) Find the Cholesky decomposition for each of the following.

a) $A = \begin{bmatrix} 4 & 6 \\ 6 & 10 \end{bmatrix}$ b) $A = \begin{bmatrix} 1 & 3 & 1 \\ 3 & 13 & 7 \\ 1 & 7 & 6 \end{bmatrix}$

CONCEPTUAL EXERCISES

1. Let A be a (3×3) nonsingular matrix. Use the Cayley–Hamilton theorem to show that A^{-1} can be represented as $A^{-1} = aI + bA + cA^2$.

2. Let A and B be similar $(n \times n)$ matrices and let $p(t)$ denote a kth-degree polynomial. Show that $p(A)$ and $p(B)$ are also similar.

3. Let A be an $(n \times n)$ symmetric matrix and suppose that the quadratic form $q(\mathbf{x}) = \mathbf{x}^T A\mathbf{x}$ is positive definite. Show that the diagonal entries of A, a_{ii} for $1 \le i \le n$, are all positive.

4. Let A be a (3×3) matrix.

a) Use the Cayley–Hamilton theorem to show that A^4 can be represented as

$$A^4 = aI + bA + cA^2.$$

b) Make an informal argument that A^k can be represented as a quadratic polynomial in A for $k = 5, 6, \ldots$.

MATLAB EXERCISES

This exercise gives a concrete illustration of the Cayley–Hamilton theorem (the corollary to Theorem 15).

1. The Cayley–Hamilton theorem Begin by generating a randomly selected (4×4) matrix with integer entries. (As was shown in Chapter 6, the following simple MATLAB command will create such a matrix: `A = round(20*rand(4,4) - 10*ones(4, 4))`.) Next, use the MATLAB command `poly(A)` to obtain the coefficients of the characteristic polynomial for A; the vector produced by the `poly(A)` command gives the coefficients of $y = p(t)$, beginning with the coefficient of t^4 and ending with the constant term (the coefficient of t^0).

a) Calculate the matrix polynomial $p(A)$ and verify that it is indeed the (4×4) zero matrix.

b) The Cayley–Hamilton theorem can be used to find the inverse of a nonsingular matrix. To see how, suppose that $p(t) = t^4 + a_3t^3 + a_2t^2 + a_1t + a_0$. Then, as you illustrated in part a),

$$A^4 + a_3A^3 + a_2A^2 + a_1A + a_0I = 0. \tag{1}$$

If we now multiply Eq. (1) by A^{-1} and solve for A^{-1}, we will have a simple formula for A^{-1} in terms of powers of A. Carry out this idea using MATLAB and verify the matrix you form using powers of A is indeed the inverse of A.

c) Equation (1) can also be used to generate high powers of A without actually forming these high powers. For example, we can solve Eq. (1) for A^4 in terms of I, A, A^2, and A^3. Multiplying this equation by A, we obtain a formula for A^5 in terms of A, A^2, A^3, and A^4; but, since we already have A^4 represented in terms of I, A, A^2, and A^3, we can clearly represent A^5 in terms of I, A, A^2, and A^3. Use this idea to form the matrix A^6 as a linear combination of I, A, A^2, and A^3. Check your calculation by using MATLAB to form A^6 directly.

2. Krylov's method for finding the characteristic polynomial Algorithm 1 (Krylov's method) is presented in Section 7.4 where the method begins with an unreduced Hessenberg matrix. The original version of Krylov's method, however, does not insist on beginning with an unreduced Hessenberg matrix or with the starting vector $\mathbf{w}_0 = \mathbf{e}_1$. If we begin with an arbitrary square matrix A and with an arbitrary starting vector $\mathbf{w}_0$, however, we cannot guarantee that the algorithm will produce the characteristic polynomial (the algorithm will always produce a polynomial factor of the characteristic polynomial).

As in Example 1, choose a randomly generated (4×4) matrix with integer entries. Begin with the vector $\mathbf{w}_0 = [1, 1, 1]^T$ and generate vectors $\mathbf{w}_1$, $\mathbf{w}_2$, $\mathbf{w}_3$, and $\mathbf{w}_4$, as in Eq. (3) of Algorithm 1. Then solve the linear system (4) displayed in Algorithm 1. Verify that the coefficients you obtain are the coefficients of the characteristic polynomial for A. Note that the only way that the algorithm can fail is if the vectors $\mathbf{w}_0, \ldots, \mathbf{w}_4$ are linearly dependent.

$$A^4 + a_3A^3 + a_2A^2 + a_1A + a_0I = \mathcal{O}. \qquad (1)$$

APPENDIX: AN INTRODUCTION TO MATLAB

A

MATLAB is a powerful tool for scientific computing that can be used for both numerical and graphical purposes. MATLAB was designed to be especially user-friendly for calculations involving matrices and vectors.

In this appendix we introduce enough commands so that you can get started with MATLAB while restricting our discussion to those parts of MATLAB that are of particular value for linear algebra.

A.1 BASIC OPERATIONS

Open up MATLAB. The window you first see is referred to as the ***command window***. The ***command line*** is the input line next to the MATLAB prompt. You can use MATLAB for simple calculations, such as the following:

```
»8*17+49
ans =
   185
»alpha=sin(1.98)
alpha =
    0.9174
```

A semicolon at the end of a command will suppress screen output:

```
»beta=sqrt(1+0.7*alpha);
»
```

Note: If you type a MATLAB command incorrectly and get an error message, you do not need to retype the entire command. Hit the up arrow on the keyboard and you will see your last command repeated. Edit the last command and hit return. Your cursor need not be at the end of the command line when you hit return. Also, continuing to press the up arrow brings past commands back to the command line. This can save some typing when you want to repeat a command.

MATLAB has an extensive online help facility. Type `help` and a topic to get help on a specific topic. For example, `help plot` will give you help with the MATLAB plot command. The command `help help` will list what sort of online help is available.

A.1 EXERCISES

(Hint: `help elfun` describes the elementary mathematical functions.)

1. Evaluate $3.13^2 + |\cos\sqrt{7}|$

2. Evaluate $\tan^{-1} 4.32$

A.2 ENTERING MATRICES

Suppose we wish to enter the matrix

$$A = \begin{bmatrix} 1 & -1 & 0 \\ 1/2 & 3 & 1/3 \\ 0 & 10 & 1 \end{bmatrix}.$$

To enter A, type

```
»A=[1 -1 0; 1/2 3 1/3; 0 10 1]
```

The rows are separated by semicolons, but if it makes viewing a bit easier, the entries can be separated by commas. Notice that we gave the matrix the name A. This is not essential but it is good MATLAB form. If you do not name the matrix, MATLAB gives it the default name ***ans***. This will be overridden the next time you enter a matrix without naming it.

When the matrix A appears, you might be surprised that the fractions have become decimals. MATLAB's default format gives you a four-place decimal for any fraction it encounters. This format is called ***short*** format and if you want fractions displayed on the screen instead, you can type

```
»format rat
```

or from the ***Options*** menu, choose ***Numeric format*** and then choose ***Rat***. You can return to short format in the same way. Now enter the following matrix

$$B = \begin{bmatrix} 2 & 7 & 1/6 & .8 \\ 18/3 & 3/17 & .007 & 6 \\ 2 & -12 & 4 & 1 \end{bmatrix}$$

and notice the difference in output when using ***Short***, ***Rat***, and ***Long*** formats.

Suppose after entering the preceding matrix B you realize that b_{23} should have been 0.009 instead of 0.007. To correct the (2, 3) entry of B, type

```
»B(2,3)=0.009
```

A.2 EXERCISES

1. Change the (1, 3) entry of A from 0 to 3/7 and name the resulting matrix Q.

A.3 THE RREF COMMAND

The MATLAB command rref(A) uses elementary row operations to transform A to reduced row echelon form. The rref command is illustrated in Example 5, Section 1.2. As another example, consider the problem of solving the system

$$x_1 + 2x_2 + 2x_3 + x_4 = 3$$
$$2x_2 + 4x_2 + 3x_3 + 4x_4 = 6.$$

First, we create the augmented matrix, A:

```
»A=[1 2 2 1 3;2 4 3 4 6]
A =
      1   2   2   1   3
      2   4   3   4   6
```

Next, we row reduce A using the rref command:

```
»B=rref(A)
B =
      1   2   0   5   3
      0   0   1  -2   0
```

Interpreting B, we see that the original system is equivalent to

$$x_1 + 2x_2 \qquad + 5x_4 = 3$$
$$x_3 - 2x_4 = 0.$$

Therefore, the solution to the system is $x_1 = 3 - 2x_2 - 5x_4$, $x_3 = 2x_4$.

A.3 EXERCISES

1. Solve the systems in Exercises 30 and 31, Section 1.2.

A.4 SURGERY ON MATRICES

MATLAB makes it easy to manipulate matrices and construct new matrices by altering the rows and columns of existing matrices. Enter the (3×4) matrix

$$B = \begin{bmatrix} 1 & 3 & -5 & 0 \\ 9 & 6 & -2 & 1 \\ 0 & 4 & 4 & 1 \end{bmatrix}.$$

Suppose you wish to extract from B the (2×2) block B_1 where

$$B_1 = \begin{bmatrix} -5 & 0 \\ -2 & 1 \end{bmatrix}.$$

Type

```
»B1=B([1 2],[3 4])
```

The preceding command says to define a new matrix B_1 made from rows 1 and 2 of B and from columns 3 and 4 of B. Another way to accomplish the same result is by typing

```
»B1=B(1:2,3:4)
```

The colon notation 1 : 2 is shorthand and means take all rows, starting with row 1 and ending with row 2. Similarly, the command `Q = B(1:2, 2:4)` would define Q to be the upper-right (2×3) block of B. That is, Q would be made from rows 1 and 2 of B and from columns 2, 3, and 4 of B. (If you want to define P to consist of rows 1 and 2 along with columns 1, 3, and 4 you could enter `P = B[1:2, [1 3 4]]`. In particular, the colon notation could not be used to designate the nonconsecutive columns 1, 3, and 4.)

Now, suppose you want to extract the second row of B. In this case you would type

```
»B2=B(2,1:4)
```

or the shortcut

```
»B2=B(2,:)
```

Here, the colon means that *all* the columns are to be included.

Suppose you want the matrix C which is formed from two blocks of B:

$$C = \begin{bmatrix} 1 & 3 & -2 & 1 \\ 9 & 6 & 4 & 1 \end{bmatrix}$$

Type

```
»C1=B(1:2,1:2)
»C2=B(3:4,3:4)
»C=[C1 C2]
```

The last command treats $C1$ as one big entry and $C2$ as the next big entry. As long as the matrices have the same number of rows it will juxtapose them. On the other hand, if you want the matrix with $C1$ on top of $C2$, type

```
»C3=[C1;C2]
```

This treats $C1$ as the *first* row and $C2$ as the *second* row of the matrix. This command works provided $C1$ and $C2$ have the same number of columns. Finally, to extract the (2, 3) entry of the matrix B, simply type

```
»b=B(2,3)
```

A.4 EXERCISES

Consider the matrix

$$A = \begin{bmatrix} 1 & 3 & 4 & 2 & -8 \\ 0 & 0 & 8 & 5 & -6 \\ 2 & 3 & 4 & 3 & 7 \\ -1 & -1 & 0 & 6 & 4 \\ 4 & 4 & 3 & 3 & -7 \end{bmatrix}.$$

Create each of the following matrices by performing surgery on A.

1. $\begin{bmatrix} 1 & 3 \\ 0 & 0 \end{bmatrix}$

2. $\begin{bmatrix} 0 & 8 & -6 \\ 3 & 4 & 7 \\ 4 & 3 & -7 \end{bmatrix}$

3. $\begin{bmatrix} 1 & 3 & 4 \\ 0 & 0 & 8 \\ 4 & 3 & 7 \\ 0 & 6 & 4 \end{bmatrix}$

A.5 ELEMENTARY ROW OPERATIONS VIA SURGERY

One way to become proficient with matrix manipulations in MATLAB is by using matrix surgery to execute the elementary row operations required to transform a matrix to reduced echelon form. As an example, consider transforming A, where

$$A = \begin{bmatrix} 0 & 2 & 1 & 3 \\ 2 & 3 & 1 & 6 \\ 3 & 2 & 2 & 2 \end{bmatrix}.$$

First we need to interchange rows. Type

```
»A1=A;
»A1(1:2,:)=A(2:1,:)
```

Interpreting the preceding commands, we first let a new matrix $A1$ equal A. The next command changes the first and second rows of $A1$ to be the second and first row of A respectively. (Remember that the colon says to change *all* columns of the first and second rows; that is, change the *entire* row.) The result is

$$A1 = \begin{bmatrix} 2 & 3 & 1 & 6 \\ 0 & 2 & 1 & 3 \\ 3 & 2 & 2 & 2 \end{bmatrix}.$$

In general, to obtain a matrix $A1$ from A by interchanging the ith and jth rows of A, the commands are

```
»A1=A;
»A1([i,j],:)=A([j,i],:);
```

Now we need to divide the first row of $A1$ by 2. For clarity, let's choose rational format to display the results

```
»format rat
```

Then type

```
»A2=A1;
»A2(1,:)=(1/2)*A1(1,:)
```

You end up with

$$A2 = \begin{bmatrix} 1 & 3/2 & 1/2 & 3 \\ 0 & 2 & 1 & 3 \\ 3 & 2 & 2 & 2 \end{bmatrix}.$$

Next to eliminate the 3 in the third row, first column, type

```
»A3=A2;
```

To change the third row of $A3$ so that it is the result of adding -3 times the first row of $A2$ to the third row of $A2$, type

```
»A3(3,:)= -3*A2(1,:) + A2(3,:)
```

We obtain

$$A3 = \begin{bmatrix} 1 & 3/2 & 1/2 & 3 \\ 0 & 2 & 1 & 3 \\ 0 & -5/2 & 1/2 & -7 \end{bmatrix}.$$

You might wonder why we keep renaming the matrix at each step. This is so we don't override any previous steps. In this way we can backtrack to find an error if it occurs.

A.5 EXERCISES

1. Finish putting the matrix A into reduced row echelon form.

2. Use surgery to put the following matrix into reduced row echelon form

$$B = \begin{bmatrix} 0 & 1 & 2 & -1 \\ 1 & 1 & 1 & 1 \\ 3 & -2 & -6 & 0 \end{bmatrix}.$$

A.6 GRAPHING CURVES

First, we show you how to graph a curve in the plane. Type

```
»x=0:.1:10;
```

This command defines **x** to be a row vector consisting of all the numbers between 0 and 10 at 0.1 intervals. Thus **x** is made up of 101 points 0.0, 0.1, 0.2, . . . , 9.9, 10.0.

Suppose you want to graph the function $y = \cos(3x + 1) + \sin(2x - 3)$ for $0 \leq x \leq 10$. Type

```
»y=cos(3*x+1)+sin(2*x-3);
```

Note: MATLAB preserves data types. If **x** is a vector or even an $(m \times n)$ matrix, then so is $\mathbf{y} = \sin(\mathbf{x})$. If x is a scalar then so is $y = \sin(x)$. To see the **x** and **y** values that you will be graphing, type

```
»[x' y']
```

This gives you a (rather large) table of values of **x** and **y**. The $'$ notation puts **x** and **y** into columns rather than rows; MATLAB uses A' to denote A^T.

Now that the table of values has been generated, we are ready to graph the function $y = \cos(3x + 1) + \sin(2x - 3)$. To see the graph, type

```
»plot(x,y)
```

Suppose you wish to graph the function $y = \sin x$ in the same figure window. Click anywhere on the command window to bring it to the front. Type

```
»y1=sin(x);
```

If you had used `y` instead of `y1` above, then the old values of **y** would have been overridden and you would have lost them for good. Also, if you now type

```
»plot(x,y1)
```

the window will be cleared and the first graph lost. So, *before* you use the plot command, type the command

```
»hold on
```

This allows you to plot the new curve and keep the old one. (The `hold off` command releases the window when you are finished superimposing graphs.) If you now type the plot command, you will notice that the figure window does not come to the front. From the menu bar, choose ***Window***, and select the figure you want. A better way to keep the figure window in front is to type

```
»figure(gcf),plot(x,y1)
```

The first command brings the current figure to the foreground (gcf stands for get current figure). Note that both curves are colored yellow, which is the default color for a black background. If you want to distinguish between the two curves, type

```
»figure(gcf),plot(x,y1,'g')
```

This will color the second graph green. You may also use 'r', 'm', 'k', 'c', 'b', 'w', 'y' for red, magenta, black, cyan, blue, white, and yellow respectively. (If you want to erase a graph that already exists, just retype the plot command using black for the color. The curve will blend into the background.)

Suppose you want to identify a point of intersection of the two curves you have graphed. Type the command

```
»ginput(1)
```

Then, using your mouse, click on the point of intersection. The x and y coordinates of the point of intersection will appear in the command window. The number 1 in the `ginput` command allows you to click on one point. If you wish to identify and save, say, 5 points, type

```
»v=ginput(5)
```

You can click anywhere in the figure window to collect the five points.

A.6 EXERCISES

1. Consider the two functions

$$y = \cos 2x + \sin x$$

and

$$y = 0.01 \tan x,$$

where

$$0 \le x \le 9.$$

We want to estimate the points where the graphs of these two functions intersect. To that end, prepare an xy-table of values, where $x = 0.0, 0.1, 0.2, \ldots, 9.0$ and $y = \cos 2x + \sin x$.

a) Graph the curve you have just defined.

b) Superimpose the curve defined by $y = 0.01 \tan x$, coloring this latter curve red.

c) Note that there appear to be six places where these two curves intersect. Argue that, in reality, there can be only four points where the graphs of the two functions intersect. Can you give a reason for the two "extraneous" intersection points?

d) Estimate the (x, y) coordinates of the actual intersection points.

A.7 MATRIX OPERATIONS

Let A and B be matrices of the same size and let s be a scalar. The MATLAB command for addition is $A + B$ and the command for scalar multiplication is `s*A`. The command `A + s` adds the value s to each entry of A.

If A is $(m \times n)$ and B is $(n \times p)$, the command for multiplication is `A*B`. If A is a nonsingular $(n \times n)$ matrix and $\mathbf{b}$ is an $(n \times 1)$ vector, the command `A\b` will return the solution to the system $A\mathbf{x} = \mathbf{b}$. If A and B are the same size, the `.*` command, `A.*B`, multiplies each entry of A by the corresponding entry of B.

Note: The standard matrix operations of $+$ and $*$ are defined in MATLAB the same way as they are in linear algebra. The special MATLAB "dotted operations," .+, .−, .*, ./, and .^, are coordinate-wise operations used for matrices (and vectors) of the same size. As an example, suppose we want to prepare a table of values for the expression

$$y = \frac{(x^2 + 3x + 1)\cos(x)}{2 + \sin(x)}.$$

For this table, suppose we want the x values to be $x = 1.0, 1.2, 1.4, \ldots, 29.8, 30.0$. The following MATLAB statements will create the table:

```
»x=1:0.2:30;
»y=( (x.^2+3*x +1).*cos(x) )./(2+sin(x));
»table=[x', y'];
```

A.7 EXERCISES

1. Use MATLAB to do Exercises 31–41 from Section 1.5.
2. Use the MATLAB \ operation to solve the system in Exercise 27, Section 1.1.
3. Consider the x-values given by $x = 2.0, 2.1, \ldots, 4.9, 5.0$. Using these x-values, create a table for the expression

$$y = \frac{\tan^{-1}(1 + x^2)}{(1 + x^3)\sqrt{1 + x}}.$$

A.8 TRANSPOSE, NORM, AND INVERSE

To find the transpose of a matrix A, type `B = A'`. If $\mathbf{x}$ is a vector, the `norm` command calculates the norm of $\mathbf{x}$. If $\mathbf{x}$ is a column vector, then the MATLAB statements `norm(x)` and `sqrt(x'*x)` produce the same value.

To find the inverse of a square matrix A, use the command `inv(A)`. The inverse is calculated numerically, using Gaussian elimination. If the MATLAB Gaussian elimination routine suspects that the matrix A is nearly singular, then a warning message is issued.

A.8 EXERCISES

1. Use MATLAB to find the inverse of the matrix in Exercise 20, Section 1.9.
2. Use the MATLAB inv command to solve the system in Exercise 27, Section 1.1.

3. To illustrate the warnings given by MATLAB for singular and nearly singular matrices, consider A and B below

$$A = \begin{bmatrix} 3 & 6 \\ 1 & 2 \end{bmatrix}, \quad B = \begin{bmatrix} 2 & 4 \\ 1 & 2 \end{bmatrix}.$$

Execute the MATLAB commands `inv(A)` and `inv(B)` and note that MATLAB has actually calculated what it deems to be an inverse for A. In particular, MATLAB does not believe that A is singular but it does recognize A as being nearly singular. (Roundoff error causes MATLAB to think A has an inverse. That is, during the first step of reducing A, MATLAB multiplies row 1 by the scalar -0.3333333333333333 and adds the result to row 2. MATLAB has to use decimal numbers, not fractions. This fact produces a roundoff error since to have an exact result, we must multiply row 1 by $-1/3$, not -0.3333333333333333. For matrix B the same roundoff problem does not occur; this time, the first step is to multiply row 1 by $-1/2 = -0.5$ and add the result to row 2.)

A.9 ZEROS, ONES, EYE, AND RAND

MATLAB has commands that generate special matrices. Type the commands

```
»A=zeros(3)
»B=ones(5)
```

As you can see, A is the (3×3) zero matrix, while B is a (5×5) matrix of ones. In general, `zeros(n)` produces the $(n \times n)$ zero matrix and `zeros(m, n)` yields the $(m \times n)$ zero matrix. The `ones` command works the same way. These commands are especially useful when we want to initialize a matrix or vector. The statement `eye(m, n)` creates a matrix with ones on the main diagonal and zeros elsewhere. The command `eye(n)` is shorthand for `eye(n,n)`.

The `rand((m, n)-.5)` command can be used to generate matrices with random entries. This feature is useful, for example, if you want test a conjecture or simulate a series of random events such as traffic flow in a street network.

The `rand(m, n)` command produces a random $(m \times n)$ matrix with entries between 0 and 1. This basic command can then be used to generate other distributions of random matrices. For example, the command `10*rand(m, n)` puts the entries between 0 and 10. The command `rand(m, n)-.5)` puts them between $-.5$ and $.5$ and `10*(rand(m, n)-.5)` between -5 and 5. The command `round(10*rand(m, n))` gives you a matrix with integer entries between 0 and 10. The command `rand(n)` is shorthand for `rand(n, n)`.

A.9 EXERCISES

1. Create a (4×5) matrix consisting entirely of sevens.

2. Experiment with the random commands to generate 10 different homogeneous $(m \times n)$ systems with integer entries, the entries between -20 and 20. Make sure at least 6 of your systems have n larger than m. Solve the system by first using the `rref` command. Then use pencil and paper to find the form of the solutions. What can you conclude if n is larger than m? Compare to Theorem 4. (*Note:* You might notice that both you and a classmate get the same matrix when you type `rand(2,3)`. This is because MATLAB has a default system of selecting the seed for its random number generator. To personalize the `rand` command type

```
»rand('seed', 'yourfirstname
yourlastname')
```

You only need to type this once before you use the first `rand` command. Do not forget the single quotations. (Of course, in practice you can type anything between the second set of single quotations.)

A.10 NUMERICAL ROUTINES IN MATLAB

MATLAB has a variety of different routines that are designed for numerical purposes. Two examples are ***polyfit*** and ***polyval***. The routine polyfit gives the coefficients for a least-squares polynomial fit to data. The routine polyval evaluates a polynomial, given the coefficients and evaluation points. Type

```
»x=1:6
»y=[4, 12, 17, 33, 45, 52]
»a=polyfit(x,y,2)
»b=polyfit(x,y,5)
```

The vector **a** gives the coefficients of the best least-squares fit of degree 2 to the data defined by **x** and **y**. The vector **b** gives the coefficients of the best least-squares fit of degree 5 to the data (since we have 6 data points, this polynomial is the interpolating polynomial).

Type

```
»xe=1:.1:6;
»ye2=polyval(a,xe);
»ye5=polyval(b,xe);
```

The vector **xe** is the set of x-evaluation points and the vector **ye2** gives the values of the polynomial defined by **a** at the points in **xe** (the polynomial defined by **a** is the best least-squares fit of degree 2). Similarly, **ye5** gives the values of the interpolating polynomial at the points in **xe**.

You can plot the results in order to see the data and the two fits to the data:

```
»plot(x,y,'o',xe,ye2,'r',xe,ye5,'g')
```

Three other examples of numerical routines available in MATLAB are ***quad8***, a program that estimates integrals, ***fmins*** an optimization program for a real-valued function of several variables, ***ode45*** a differential-equation solver.

A.10 EXERCISES

Using the coordinates listed in the following two tables, find the best least-squares linear fit to the data and then find the polynomial interpolator for the data.. Plot the data points, the least-squares fit, and the interpolator on the same graph.

1.

x	1	2	3	4	5
y	3.3	5.2	6.7	9.0	10.8

2.

x	−3	−2	−1	0	1	2	3
y	3.3	7.8	10.5	12.2	10.9	8.2	3.1

A.11 M-FILES: SCRIPTS AND FUNCTIONS

If you are going to issue a certain sequence of MATLAB commands over and over again, then you should write a MATLAB program that executes this sequence whenever you type a keyword. Such a program is called an ***M-file***. These M-files are also a powerful tool when you begin writing long MATLAB programs—M-files are the MATLAB analogs of the subroutines and procedures used in other programming languages.

There are two types of M-files, ***scripts*** and ***functions***. A script is the easiest sort of M-file to visualize. As its name suggests, a script is nothing more than a set of MATLAB instructions that are executed whenever the name of the script is entered.

For example, suppose you are carrying out some data analysis and you want to try various least-squares polynomial fits to a given data set. You are not sure exactly which degree polynomial you want to use, nor are you sure how much of the data you want to fit with a given polynomial. To investigate this typical data analysis problem, you might write the following ***script***:

```
»a=polyfit(x,y,n);
»yval=polyval(a,xval);
»plot(x,y,'ro',xval,yval,'g');
```

As you can see, the first instruction takes a given set of xy-values (the vectors **x** and **y**) and a given value of n and then generates the coefficients **a** of the best least-squares fit of degree n. The second instruction takes a given set of evaluation points, **xval**, and evaluates the least-squares fit at those evaluation points. The last instruction plots the data points (as red circles) and superimposes the graph of the least-squares polynomial (as a green curve). On the basis of this graph, you might want to adjust the degree of the least-squares fit, or the range of data that you want the polynomial to approximate.

Now, place this list of instructions in a file named lsplot.m. Suppose that you enter a set of data points **x** and **y** and choose a polynomial degree, n. Also, define a set of evaluation points, **xval**. When you type the name of the script (`lsplot`) on the command line, the script will be executed and you will see the graph of the least-squares fit superimposed on a graph of the data points. If you want to change the degree of the fit, just change the value of n on the command line and type lsplot once again. Similarly, you can alter the data set (**x** and **y**) and the extent of the plot (**xval**) and type lspot to see the effects.

A MATLAB script can be produced with any editor, but MATLAB has a built-in editor that is easy to use. From the File menu select New. After creating the script, give it a name having the form filename.m and save it to a MATLAB folder, so that MATLAB can find the script when you type its name on the command line.

MATLAB ***functions*** are similar to scripts, except that the variables in the instructions in a function are local rather than global. In this sense, a MATLAB function resembles a function in BASIC or FORTRAN. Following is an example of a function that forms the scalar triple product $\mathbf{u} \cdot \mathbf{v} \times \mathbf{w}$:

```
function c=triple(u,v,w)
x=cross(v,w);
c=dot(u,x);
```

If we are in the MATLAB command window and have three vectors **a**, **b**, and **c**, then we can invoke the triple function to calculate $\mathbf{a} \cdot \mathbf{b} \times \mathbf{c}$:

```
»trip=triple(a,b,c)
```

Note that the function M-file triple used variables named u, v, w, x, and c, but the call to triple sent in variables named a, b, and c. The variables used in the two MATLAB instructions that define triple are all *local* to the function triple. Thus functions obey standard conventions of mathematical usage; if $f(x, y) = x^2+y$, then $f(u, v) = u^2 + v$. In other words, the order of the input variables *matter to the function*, but not the names of the input variables. By contrast, a script M-file has no input variables; when a script is invoked it uses the variables that are already in existence in the current MATLAB session. A MATLAB function M-file should be saved under the same file name as the function name, so when we created the function triple, we saved it as triple.m.

A.11 EXERCISES

1. Write a MATLAB function M-file that calculates the vector triple product $\mathbf{u} \times \mathbf{v} \times \mathbf{w}$. Test your function using the vectors $\mathbf{a} = [1, 1, 2]$, $\mathbf{b} = [2, -2, 1]$, and $\mathbf{c} = [0, 1, 4]$.

2. Use the script lsplot to choose an integer n so that the best least-squares polynomial approximation of degree n or less looks reasonable for the data $(x_i, y_i) = (i, \ln i)$, $i = 1, 2, \ldots, 10$. Restrict n to be between 1 and 5.

Answers to Selected Odd-Numbered Exercises*

CHAPTER 1

Exercises 1.1, p. 12

1. Linear

3. Linear

5. Nonlinear

7. $$\begin{aligned} x_1 + 3x_2 &= 7 \\ 4x_1 - x_2 &= 2 \end{aligned}$$

9. $$\begin{aligned} x_1 + x_2 &= 0 \\ 3x_1 + 4x_2 &= -1 \\ -x_1 + 2x_2 &= -3 \end{aligned}$$

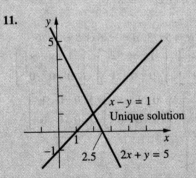

11.

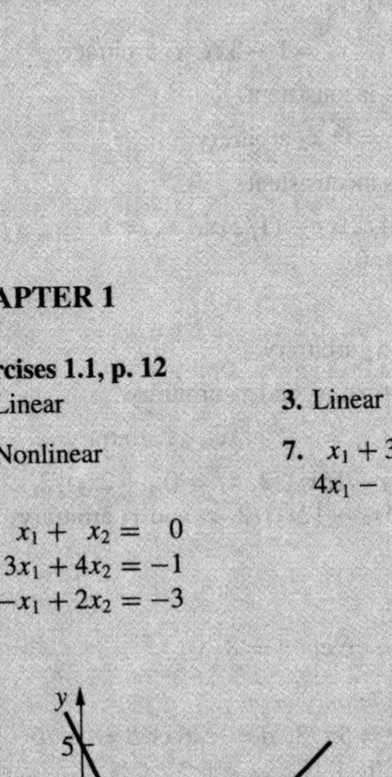

13.

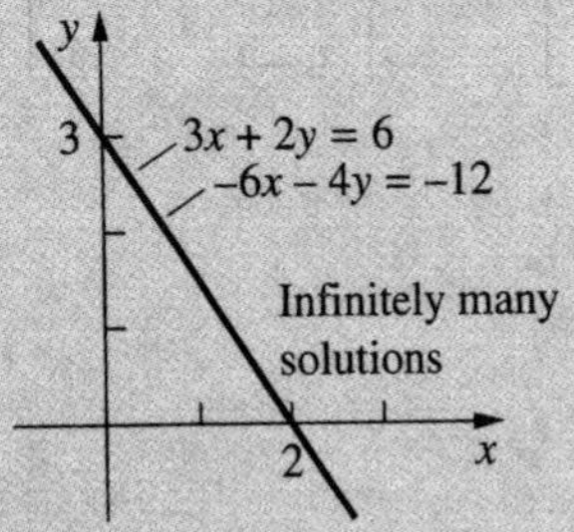

17. $$\begin{aligned} x_1 &= -3t + 4 \\ x_2 &= 2t - 1 \\ x_3 &= t \end{aligned}$$

19. $A = \begin{bmatrix} 2 & 1 & 6 \\ 4 & 3 & 8 \end{bmatrix}$

21. $Q = \begin{bmatrix} 1 & 4 & -3 \\ 2 & 1 & 1 \\ 3 & 2 & 1 \end{bmatrix}$

23. $\begin{aligned} 2x_1 + x_2 &= 6 \\ 4x_1 + 3x_2 &= 8 \end{aligned}$ and $\begin{aligned} x_1 + 4x_2 &= -3 \\ 2x_1 + x_2 &= 1 \\ 3x_1 + 2x_2 &= 1 \end{aligned}$

*Many of the problems have answers that contain parameters or answers that can be written in a variety of forms. For problems of this sort, we have presented one possible form of the answer. Your solution may have a different form and still be correct. You can frequently check your solution by inserting it in the original problem or by showing that two different forms for the answer are equivalent.

25. $A = \begin{bmatrix} 1 & 1 & -1 \\ 2 & 0 & -1 \end{bmatrix}$, $B = \begin{bmatrix} 1 & 1 & -1 & 2 \\ 2 & 0 & -1 & 1 \end{bmatrix}$

27. $A = \begin{bmatrix} 1 & 1 & 2 \\ 3 & 4 & -1 \\ -1 & 1 & 1 \end{bmatrix}$,

$B = \begin{bmatrix} 1 & 1 & 2 & 6 \\ 3 & 4 & -1 & 5 \\ -1 & 1 & 1 & 2 \end{bmatrix}$

29. $A = \begin{bmatrix} 1 & 1 & 1 \\ 2 & 3 & 1 \\ 1 & -1 & 3 \end{bmatrix}$, $B = \begin{bmatrix} 1 & 1 & 1 & 1 \\ 2 & 3 & 1 & 2 \\ 1 & -1 & 3 & 2 \end{bmatrix}$

31. $\begin{aligned} x_1 + 2x_2 - x_3 &= 1 \\ -x_2 + 3x_3 &= 1 \\ 5x_2 - 2x_3 &= 6 \end{aligned}$

33. $\begin{aligned} x_1 + x_2 &= 9 \\ -2x_2 &= -2 \\ -2x_2 &= -21 \end{aligned}$

35. $\begin{aligned} x_1 + 2x_2 - x_3 + x_4 &= 1 \\ x_2 + x_3 - x_4 &= 3 \\ 3x_2 + 6x_3 &= 1 \end{aligned}$

Exercises 1.2, p. 26

1. a) The matrix is in echelon form.

b) The operation $R_1 - 2R_2$ yields reduced echelon form $\begin{bmatrix} 1 & 0 \\ 0 & 1 \end{bmatrix}$.

3. a) The operations $R_2 - 2R_1$, $(1/2)R_1$, $R_2 - 4R_1$, $(1/5)R_2$ yield echelon form

$$\begin{bmatrix} 1 & 3/2 & 1/2 \\ 0 & 1 & 2/5 \end{bmatrix}.$$

5. a) The operations $R_1 \leftrightarrow R_2$, $(1/2)R_1$, $(1/2)R_2$ yield echelon form

$$\begin{bmatrix} 1 & 0 & 1/2 & 2 \\ 0 & 0 & 1 & 3/2 \end{bmatrix}.$$

7. a) The matrix is in echelon form.

b) The operations $R_1 - 2R_3$, $R_2 - 4R_3$, $R_1 - 3R_2$ yield reduced echelon form

$$\begin{bmatrix} 1 & 0 & 0 & 5 \\ 0 & 1 & 0 & -2 \\ 0 & 0 & 1 & 1 \end{bmatrix}.$$

9. a) The operation $(1/2)R_2$ yields echelon form

$$\begin{bmatrix} 1 & 2 & -1 & -2 \\ 0 & 1 & -1 & -3/2 \\ 0 & 0 & 0 & 1 \end{bmatrix}.$$

11. $x_1 = 0$, $x_2 = 0$

13. $x_1 = -2 + 5x_3$, $x_2 = 1 - 3x_3$, x_3 arbitrary

15. The system is inconsistent.

17. $x_1 = x_3 = x_4 = 0$; x_2 arbitrary

19. The system is inconsistent.

21. $x_1 = -1 - (1/2)x_2 + (1/2)x_4$, $x_3 = 1 - x_4$, x_2 and x_4 arbitrary, $x_5 = 0$

23. Inconsistent

25. $x_1 = 2 - x_2$, x_2 arbitrary

27. $x_1 = 2 - x_2 + x_3$, x_2 and x_3 arbitrary

29. $x_1 = 3 - 2x_3$, $x_2 = -2 + 3x_3$, x_3 arbitrary

31. $x_1 = 3 - (7x_4 - 16x_5)/2$, $x_2 = (x_4 + 2x_5)/2$, $x_3 = -2 + (5x_4 - 12x_5)/2$, x_4 and x_5 arbitrary

33. Inconsistent

35. Inconsistent

37. All values of a except $a = 8$

39. $a = 3$ or $a = -3$

41. $\alpha = \pi/3$ or $\alpha = 5\pi/3$; $\beta = \pi/6$ or $\beta = 5\pi/6$

45. $\begin{bmatrix} 1 & \times & \times \\ 0 & 1 & \times \end{bmatrix}$, $\begin{bmatrix} 1 & \times & \times \\ 0 & 0 & 1 \end{bmatrix}$, $\begin{bmatrix} 1 & \times & \times \\ 0 & 0 & 0 \end{bmatrix}$,

$\begin{bmatrix} 0 & 1 & \times \\ 0 & 0 & 1 \end{bmatrix}$, $\begin{bmatrix} 0 & 1 & \times \\ 0 & 0 & 0 \end{bmatrix}$, $\begin{bmatrix} 0 & 0 & 1 \\ 0 & 0 & 0 \end{bmatrix}$,

$\begin{bmatrix} 0 & 0 & 0 \\ 0 & 0 & 0 \end{bmatrix}$

47. The operations $R_2 - 2R_1$, $R_1 + 2R_2$, $-R_2$ transform B to I. The operations $R_2 - 3R_1$, $R_1 + R_2$, $(-1/2)R_2$ reduce C to I, so the operations $-2R_2$, $R_1 - R_2$, $R_2 + 3R_1$ transform I to C. Thus the operations $R_2 - 2R_1$, $R_1 + 2R_2$, $-R_2$, $-2R_2$, $R_1 - R_2$, $R_2 + 3R_1$ transform B to C.

49. $N = 135$

51. The amounts were \$39, \$21, and \$12.

53. Let A denote the number of adults, S the number of students, and C the number of children. Possible solutions are: $A = 5k$, $S = 67 - 11k$, $C = 12 + 6k$, where $k = 0, 1, \ldots, 6$.

55. $n(n+1)/2$

57. $n(n+1)(2n+1)(3n^2 + 3n - 1)/30$

Exercises 1.3, p. 37

1. $\begin{bmatrix} 1 & 1 & 0 & 5/6 \\ 0 & 0 & 1 & 2/3 \\ 0 & 0 & 0 & 0 \\ 0 & 0 & 0 & 0 \end{bmatrix}$ $n = 3$, $r = 2$, x_2

3. $\begin{bmatrix} 1 & 0 & 4 & 0 & 13/2 \\ 0 & 1 & -1 & 0 & -3/2 \\ 0 & 0 & 0 & 1 & 1/2 \end{bmatrix}$ $n = 4$, $r = 3$, x_3

5. $r = 2$, $r = 1$, $r = 0$

7. Infinitely many solutions

9. Infinitely many solutions, a unique solution, or no solution

11. A unique solution or infinitely many solutions

13. Infinitely many solutions

15. A unique solution or infinitely many solutions

17. Infinitely many solutions

19. There are nontrivial solutions.

21. There is only the trivial solution.

23. $a = 1$

25. a) $\begin{bmatrix} 1 & 0 & 0 \\ 0 & 1 & 0 \\ 0 & 0 & 1 \\ 0 & 0 & 0 \end{bmatrix}$

27. $7x + 2y - 30 = 0$

29. $-3x^2 + 3xy + y^2 - 54y + 113 = 0$

Exercises 1.4, p. 44

1. a)
$$\begin{aligned} x_1 \quad\quad + x_4 &= 1200 \\ x_1 + x_2 \quad\quad &= 1000 \\ x_3 + x_4 &= 600 \\ x_2 + x_3 \quad &= 400 \end{aligned}$$

b) $x_1 = 1100$, $x_2 = -100$, $x_3 = 500$;

c) The minimum value is $x_1 = 600$ and the maximum value is $x_1 = 1000$.

3. $x_2 = 800$, $x_3 = 400$, $x_4 = 200$

5. $I_1 = 0.05$, $I_2 = 0.6$, $I_3 = 0.55$

7. $I_1 = 35/13$, $I_2 = 20/13$, $I_3 = 15/13$

Exercises 1.5, p. 58

1. a) $\begin{bmatrix} 2 & 0 \\ 2 & 6 \end{bmatrix}$; **b)** $\begin{bmatrix} 0 & 4 \\ 2 & 4 \end{bmatrix}$; **c)** $\begin{bmatrix} 0 & -6 \\ 6 & 18 \end{bmatrix}$; **d)** $\begin{bmatrix} -6 & 8 \\ 4 & 6 \end{bmatrix}$

3. $\begin{bmatrix} -2 & -2 \\ 0 & 0 \end{bmatrix}$ **5.** $\begin{bmatrix} -1 & -1 \\ 0 & 0 \end{bmatrix}$

7. a) $\begin{bmatrix} 3 \\ -3 \end{bmatrix}$; **b)** $\begin{bmatrix} 3 \\ 4 \end{bmatrix}$; **c)** $\begin{bmatrix} 0 \\ 0 \end{bmatrix}$

9. a) $\begin{bmatrix} 2 \\ 1 \end{bmatrix}$; **b)** $\begin{bmatrix} 0 \\ 1 \end{bmatrix}$; **c)** $\begin{bmatrix} 17 \\ 14 \end{bmatrix}$

11. a) $\begin{bmatrix} 2 \\ 3 \end{bmatrix}$; **b)** $\begin{bmatrix} 20 \\ 16 \end{bmatrix}$

13. $a_1 = 11/3$, $a_2 = -4/3$

15. $a_1 = -2$, $a_2 = 0$ **17.** No solution

19. $a_1 = 4$, $a_2 = -3/2$ **21.** $\mathbf{w}_2 = \begin{bmatrix} 1 \\ 3 \end{bmatrix}$

23. $\mathbf{w}_3 = \begin{bmatrix} -1 \\ 2 \end{bmatrix}$ **25.** $\begin{bmatrix} -4 & 6 \\ 2 & 12 \end{bmatrix}$

27. $\begin{bmatrix} 4 & 12 \\ 4 & 10 \end{bmatrix}$ **29.** $\begin{bmatrix} 0 & 0 \\ 0 & 0 \end{bmatrix}$

31. $AB = \begin{bmatrix} 5 & 16 \\ 5 & 18 \end{bmatrix}$, $BA = \begin{bmatrix} 4 & 11 \\ 6 & 19 \end{bmatrix}$

33. $A\mathbf{u} = \begin{bmatrix} 11 \\ 13 \end{bmatrix}$, $\mathbf{v}A = [8, 22]$

35. 66 **37.** $\begin{bmatrix} 5 & 10 \\ 8 & 12 \\ 15 & 20 \\ 8 & 17 \end{bmatrix}$ **39.** $\begin{bmatrix} 27 \\ 28 \\ 43 \\ 47 \end{bmatrix}$

41. $(BA)\mathbf{u} = B(A\mathbf{u}) = \begin{bmatrix} 37 \\ 63 \end{bmatrix}$

43. $\mathbf{x} = \begin{bmatrix} x_1 \\ x_2 \\ x_3 \end{bmatrix} = \begin{bmatrix} -2 \\ 3 \\ 0 \end{bmatrix} + x_3 \begin{bmatrix} 1 \\ -2 \\ 1 \end{bmatrix}$

45. $\mathbf{x} = \begin{bmatrix} x_1 \\ x_2 \\ x_3 \\ x_4 \\ x_5 \end{bmatrix} = x_3 \begin{bmatrix} 1 \\ -2 \\ 1 \\ 0 \\ 0 \end{bmatrix} + x_5 \begin{bmatrix} 1 \\ -1 \\ 0 \\ -1 \\ 1 \end{bmatrix}$

47. $\mathbf{x}=\begin{bmatrix}x_1\\x_2\\x_3\\x_4\\x_5\end{bmatrix}=x_3\begin{bmatrix}1\\-2\\1\\0\\0\end{bmatrix}+x_4\begin{bmatrix}2\\-3\\0\\1\\0\end{bmatrix}+x_5\begin{bmatrix}3\\-4\\0\\0\\1\end{bmatrix}$

49. $\mathbf{x}=\begin{bmatrix}x_1\\x_2\\x_3\\x_4\\x_5\end{bmatrix}=x_2\begin{bmatrix}1\\1\\0\\0\\0\end{bmatrix}+x_4\begin{bmatrix}2\\0\\-2\\1\\0\end{bmatrix}$

51.

$C(A(B\mathbf{u}))$	$(CA)(B\mathbf{u})$	$(C(AB))\mathbf{u}$	$C((AB)\mathbf{u})$
12	16	20	16

53. **a)** AB is (2×4); BA is undefined.
b) Neither is defined.
c) AB is undefined; BA is (6×7).
d) AB is (2×2); BA is (3×3).
e) AB is (3×1); BA is undefined.
f) Both are (2×4).
g) AB is (4×4), BA is (1×1).

61. **a)** For (i), $A=\begin{bmatrix}2&-1\\1&1\end{bmatrix}$, $\mathbf{x}=\begin{bmatrix}x_1\\x_2\end{bmatrix}$,

$\mathbf{b}=\begin{bmatrix}3\\3\end{bmatrix}$; for (ii), $A=\begin{bmatrix}1&-3&1\\1&-2&1\\0&1&-1\end{bmatrix}$,

$\mathbf{x}=\begin{bmatrix}x_1\\x_2\\x_3\end{bmatrix}$, $\mathbf{b}=\begin{bmatrix}1\\2\\-1\end{bmatrix}$.

b) For (i), $x_1\begin{bmatrix}2\\1\end{bmatrix}+x_2\begin{bmatrix}-1\\1\end{bmatrix}=\begin{bmatrix}3\\3\end{bmatrix}$;

for (ii), $x_1\begin{bmatrix}1\\1\\0\end{bmatrix}+x_2\begin{bmatrix}-3\\-2\\1\end{bmatrix}+x_3\begin{bmatrix}1\\1\\-1\end{bmatrix}=\begin{bmatrix}1\\2\\-1\end{bmatrix}$.

c) For (i), $\mathbf{b}=2\mathbf{A}_1+\mathbf{A}_2$;
for (ii), $\mathbf{b}=2\mathbf{A}_1+\mathbf{A}_2+2\mathbf{A}_3$.

63. $B=\begin{bmatrix}2&-1\\-1&1\end{bmatrix}$

65. **a)** $B=\begin{bmatrix}-1&6\\1&0\end{bmatrix}$; **b)** Not possible;

c) $B=\begin{bmatrix}-2a&-2b\\a&b\end{bmatrix}$, a and b arbitrary

Exercises 1.6, p. 69

1. $(DE)F=D(EF)=\begin{bmatrix}23&23\\29&29\end{bmatrix}$

3. $DE=\begin{bmatrix}8&15\\11&18\end{bmatrix}$, $ED=\begin{bmatrix}12&27\\7&14\end{bmatrix}$

5. $F\mathbf{u}=F\mathbf{v}=\begin{bmatrix}0\\0\end{bmatrix}$ **7.** $\begin{bmatrix}3&4&2\\1&7&6\end{bmatrix}$

9. $\begin{bmatrix}5&5\\9&9\end{bmatrix}$ **11.** [0 0] **13.** −6

15. 36 **17.** 2 **19.** $\sqrt{2}$

21. $\sqrt{29}$ **23.** 0 **25.** $2\sqrt{5}$

29. D and F are symmetric.

31. AB is symmetric if and only if $AB=BA$.

33. $\mathbf{x}^T D\mathbf{x}=x_1^2+3x_2^2+(x_1+x_2)^2>0$

35. $\begin{bmatrix}-3&3\\3&-3\end{bmatrix}$ **37.** $\begin{bmatrix}-27&-9\\27&9\end{bmatrix}$

39. $\begin{bmatrix}-12&18&24\\18&-27&-36\\24&-36&-48\end{bmatrix}$

41. **a)** $\mathbf{x}=\begin{bmatrix}-10\\8\end{bmatrix}$; **b)** $\mathbf{x}=\begin{bmatrix}6\\-2\end{bmatrix}$

57. $n=5,\quad m=7$

59. $n = 4, \quad m = 6$

61. $n = 5, \quad m = 5$

Exercises 1.7, p. 78

1. Linearly independent

3. Linearly dependent, $\mathbf{v}_5 = 3\mathbf{v}_1$

5. Linearly dependent, $\mathbf{v}_3 = 2\mathbf{v}_1$

7. Linearly dependent, $\mathbf{u}_4 = 4\mathbf{u}_5$

9. Linearly independent

11. Linearly dependent, $\mathbf{u}_4 = 4\mathbf{u}_5$

13. Linearly dependent, $\mathbf{u}_4 = \frac{16}{5}\mathbf{u}_0 + \frac{12}{5}\mathbf{u}_1 - \frac{4}{5}\mathbf{u}_2$

15. Those in Exercises 5, 6, 13, and 14

17. Singular; $x_1 = -2x_2$ **19.** Singular; $x_1 = -2x_2$

21. Singular; $x_1 = x_2 = 0$, x_3 arbitrary

23. Nonsingular

25. Singular; $x_2 = x_3 = 0$, x_1 arbitrary

27. Nonsingular **29.** $a = 6$

31. $b(a-2) = 4$ **33.** $c - ab = 0$

35. $\mathbf{v}_3 = \mathbf{A}_2$ **37.** $\mathbf{v}_2 = (\mathbf{C}_1 + \mathbf{C}_2)/2$

39. $\mathbf{u}_3 = (-8\mathbf{F}_1 - 2\mathbf{F}_2 + 9\mathbf{F}_3)/3$

41. $\mathbf{b} = -11\mathbf{v}_1 + 7\mathbf{v}_2$ **43.** $\mathbf{b} = 0\mathbf{v}_1 + 0\mathbf{v}_2$

45. $\mathbf{b} = -3\mathbf{v}_1 + 2\mathbf{v}_2$

47. a) Any value a **b)** Any value a

Exercises 1.8, p. 90

1. $p(t) = (-1/2)t^2 + (9/2)t - 1$

3. $p(t) = 2t + 3$

5. $p(t) = 2t^3 - 2t^2 + 3t + 1$

7. $y = 2e^{2x} + e^{3x}$

9. $y = 3e^{-x} + 4e^{x} + e^{2x}$

11. $\int_0^{3h} f(t)\,dt \approx \frac{3h}{2}[f(h) + f(2h)]$

13. $\int_0^{3h} f(t)\,dt \approx \frac{3h}{8}[f(0) + 3f(h) + 3f(2h) + f(3h)]$

15. $\int_0^{h} f(t)\,dt \approx \frac{h}{2}[-f(-h) + 3f(0)]$

17. $f'(0) \approx [-f(0) + f(h)]/h$

19. $f'(0) \approx [-3f(0) + 4f(h) - f(2h)]/(2h)$

21. $f''(0) \approx [f(-h) - 2f(0) + f(h)]/h^2$

27. $p(t) = t^3 + 2t^2 + 3t + 2$

29. $p(t) = t^3 + t^2 + 4t + 3$

35. $f'(a) \approx \frac{1}{12h} \times [f(a-2h) - 8f(a-h) + 8f(a+h) - f(a+2h)]$

Exercises 1.9, p. 102

5. $x_1 = -3, \quad x_2 = 1.5$

7. $x_1 = 14, \quad x_2 = -20,\ x_3 = 8$

9. If $B = (b_{ij})$ is a (3×3) matrix such that $AB = I$, then $0b_{11} + 0b_{21} + 0b_{31} = 1$. Since this is impossible, no such matrix exists.

13. $\begin{bmatrix} 3 & -1 \\ -2 & 1 \end{bmatrix}$

15. $\begin{bmatrix} -1/3 & 2/3 \\ 2/3 & -1/3 \end{bmatrix}$ **17.** $\begin{bmatrix} 1 & 0 & 0 \\ -2 & 1 & 0 \\ 5 & -4 & 1 \end{bmatrix}$

19. $\begin{bmatrix} 1 & -2 & 0 \\ 3 & -3 & -1 \\ -6 & 7 & 2 \end{bmatrix}$

21. $\begin{bmatrix} -1/2 & -2/3 & -1/6 & 7/6 \\ 1 & 1/3 & 1/3 & -4/3 \\ 0 & -1/3 & -1/3 & 1/3 \\ -1/2 & 1 & 1/2 & 1/2 \end{bmatrix}$

23. $A^{-1} = (1/10)\begin{bmatrix} 3 & 2 \\ -2 & 2 \end{bmatrix}$

25. A has no inverse **27.** $\lambda = 2$ and $\lambda = -2$

29. $x_1 = 6, \quad x_2 = -8$ **31.** $x_1 = 18, \quad x_2 = 13$

33. $x_1 = 5/2, \quad x_2 = 5/2$

35. $Q^{-1} = C^{-1}A^{-1} = \begin{bmatrix} -3 & 1 \\ 3 & 5 \end{bmatrix}$

37. $Q^{-1} = (A^{-1})^T = \begin{bmatrix} 3 & 0 \\ 1 & 2 \end{bmatrix}$

39. $Q^{-1} = (A^{-1})^T(C^{-1})^T = \begin{bmatrix} -3 & 3 \\ 1 & 5 \end{bmatrix}$

41. $Q^{-1} = BC^{-1} = \begin{bmatrix} 1 & 5 \\ -1 & 4 \end{bmatrix}$

43. $Q^{-1} = (1/2)A^{-1} = \begin{bmatrix} 3/2 & 1/2 \\ 0 & 1 \end{bmatrix}$

45. $Q^{-1} = B(C^{-1}A^{-1}) = \begin{bmatrix} 3 & 11 \\ -3 & 7 \end{bmatrix}$

47. $B = \begin{bmatrix} 1 & 10 \\ 15 & 12 \\ 3 & 3 \end{bmatrix}$; $C = \begin{bmatrix} 13 & 12 & 8 \\ 2 & 3 & 5 \end{bmatrix}$

49. $(AB)^{-1} = B^{-1}A^{-1} = \begin{bmatrix} 2 & 35 & 1 \\ 14 & 35 & 34 \\ 23 & 12 & 70 \end{bmatrix}$,

$(3A)^{-1} = \dfrac{1}{3}A^{-1} = \begin{bmatrix} 1/3 & 2/3 & 5/3 \\ 1 & 1/3 & 2 \\ 2/3 & 8/3 & 1/3 \end{bmatrix}$,

$(A^T)^{-1} = (A^{-1})^T = \begin{bmatrix} 1 & 3 & 2 \\ 2 & 1 & 8 \\ 5 & 6 & 1 \end{bmatrix}$

63. $b_0 = -5, \quad b_1 = 2$

64. $b_0 = -7, \quad b_1 = 0$

CHAPTER 2

Exercises 2.1, p. 126

1.

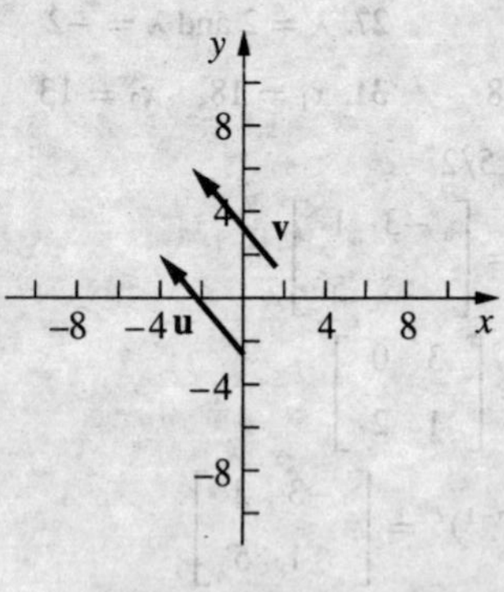

For vector AB the x-component is $-4 - 0 = 4$ and the y-component is $3 - (-2) = 5$. For vector CD the x-component is $1 - 5 = -4$ and the y-component is $4 - (-1) = 5$. The vectors are equal.

3.

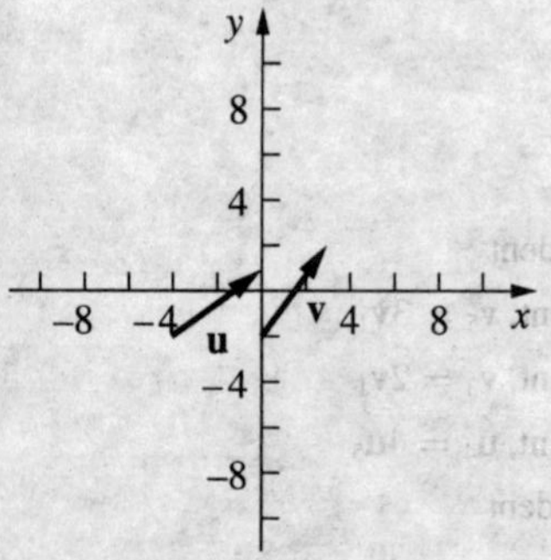

For vector AB the x-component is $0 - (-4) = 4$ and the y-component is $1 - (-2) = 3$. For vector CD the x-component is $3 - 0 = 3$ and the y-component is $2 - (-2) = 4$. The vectors are not equal.

5. a) For **u**: $\|\mathbf{u}\| = \sqrt{(2-(-3))^2 + (2-5)^2} = \sqrt{34}$.

For **v**: $\|\mathbf{v}\| = \sqrt{(-2-3)^2 + (7-4)^2} = \sqrt{34}$.

Therefore, $\|\mathbf{u}\| = \|\mathbf{v}\|$.

b) Segment AB has slope $(2-5)/(2-(-3)) = -3/5$. Segment CD has slope $(7-4)/(-2-3) = 3/(-5)$.

c) For vector AB the x-component is $2 - (-3) = 5$ and the y-component $2 - 5 = -3$. For vector CD the x-component is $-2 - 3 = -5$ and the y-component is $7 - 4 = 3$. The vectors are not equal.

d)

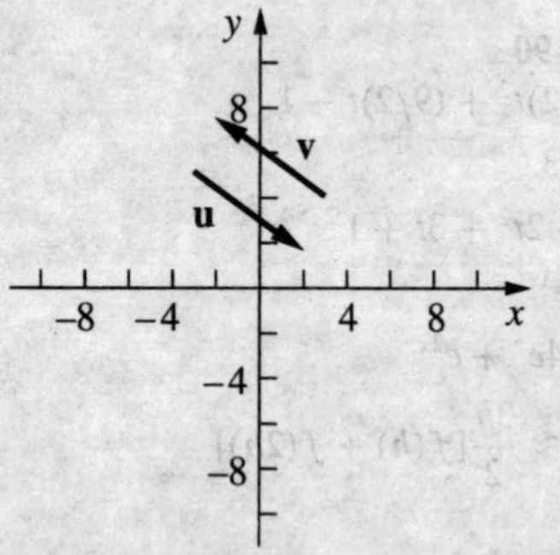

7. $D = (-2, 5)$

9. $D = (-1, 1)$

11. $v_1 = 5, v_2 = 3$

13. $v_1 = -6, v_2 = 5$

15. $B = (3, 3)$

17. $A = (2, 4)$

19. a) $B = (3, 2), \quad C = (5, 0)$

b)

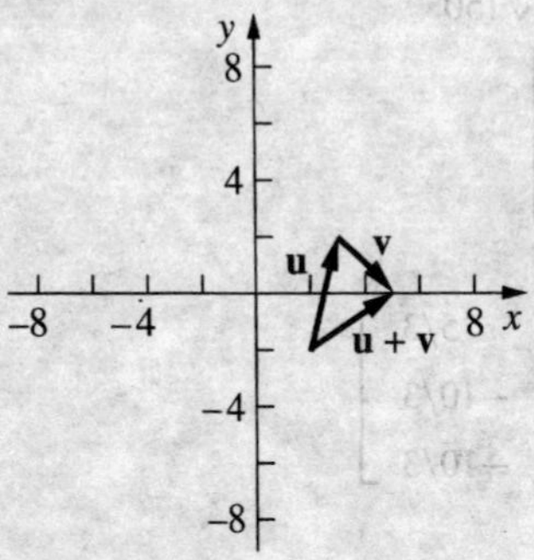

21. a) $Q = (7, 1)$

b)

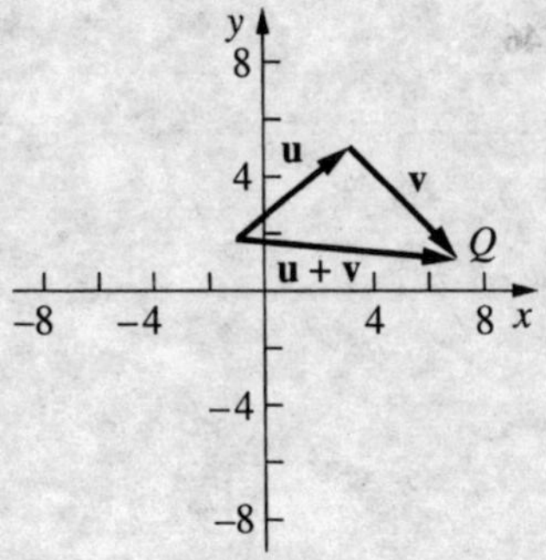

23. a) $B = (-1, 4), \quad C = (0, -1)$

b)

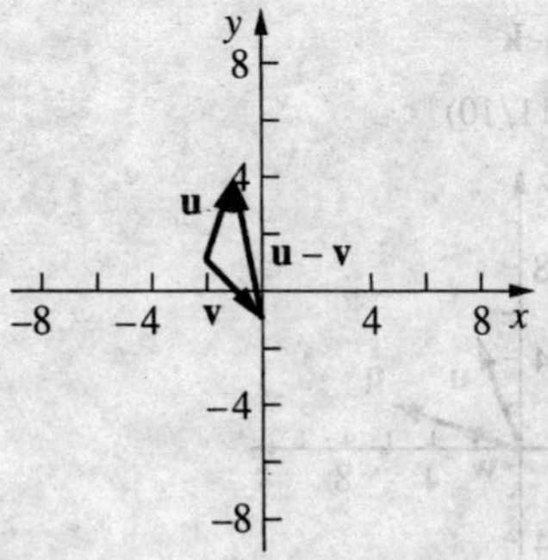

25. a) $B = (3, 3), \quad C = (6, 1)$

b)

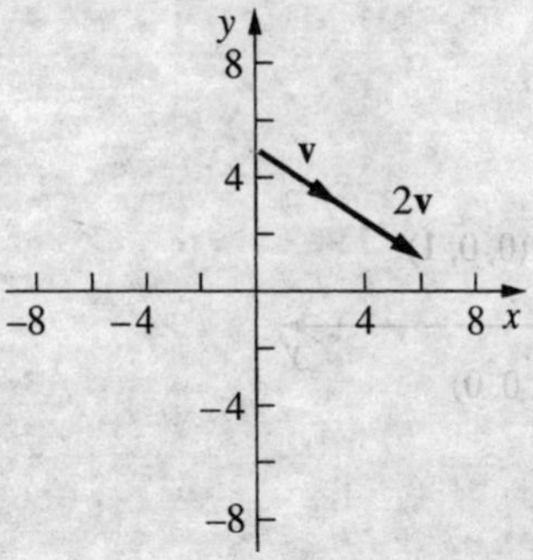

27. a) $D = (6, -3)$

b)

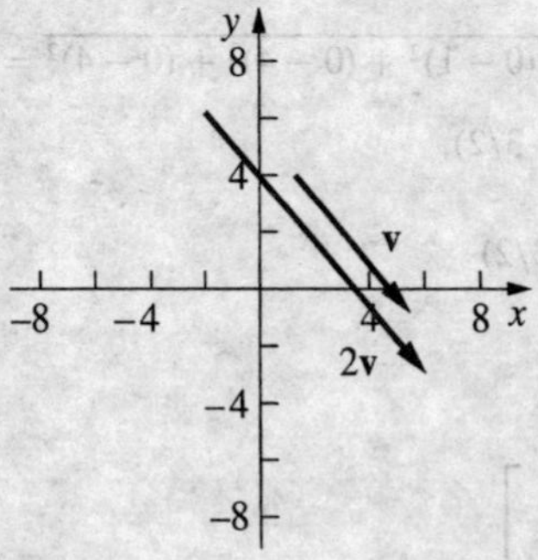

29. $\frac{1}{5}\begin{bmatrix} 3 \\ 4 \end{bmatrix}$

31. $\frac{3}{\sqrt{13}}\mathbf{i} - \frac{2}{\sqrt{13}}\mathbf{j}$

33. $B = (1, -2)$

35. $B = (1/3, -7)$

37. $\mathbf{u} + \mathbf{v} = \begin{bmatrix} 2 \\ 4 \end{bmatrix}, \quad \mathbf{u} - 3\mathbf{v} = \begin{bmatrix} -6 \\ 8 \end{bmatrix}$

39. $\mathbf{u} + \mathbf{v} = 4\mathbf{i} + \mathbf{j}, \quad \mathbf{u} - 3\mathbf{v} = -4\mathbf{i} - 7\mathbf{j}$

Exercises 2.2, p. 134

1.

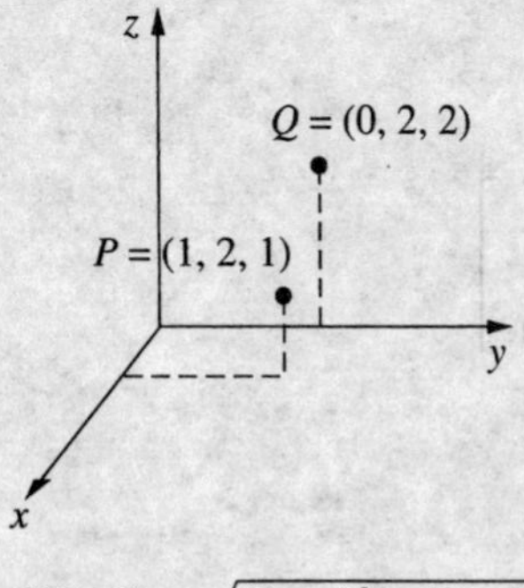

$$d(P, Q) = \sqrt{(0-1)^2 + (2-2)^2 + (2-1)^2} = \sqrt{2}$$

3.

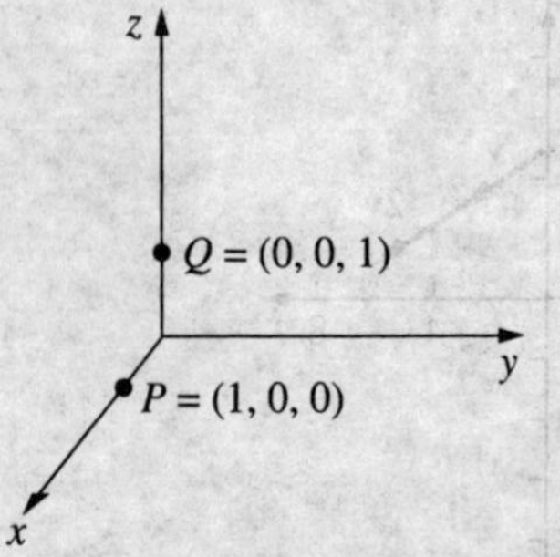

$d(P, Q) = \sqrt{(0-1)^2 + (0-0)^2 + (1-0)^2} = \sqrt{2}$

5. $M = (1, 4, 4)$;
$d(M, O) = \sqrt{(0-1)^2 + (0-4)^2 + (0-4)^2} = \sqrt{33}$

7. $B = (0, 3/2, -3/2)$,
$C = (1, 3, 0)$,
$D = (2, 9/2, 3/2)$

9. line

11. plane

19. a) $\mathbf{v} = \begin{bmatrix} 3 \\ 2 \\ -3 \end{bmatrix}$

b) $D = (2, 4, -2)$; $\mathbf{v} \begin{bmatrix} 3 \\ 2 \\ -3 \end{bmatrix}$

21. a) $\mathbf{v} = \begin{bmatrix} 0 \\ 5 \\ -7 \end{bmatrix}$

b) $D = (-1, 7, -6)$

23. $\lambda = 2$

25. $A = (-2, 3, -1)$

27. a) $\mathbf{u} + 2\mathbf{v} = \begin{bmatrix} 7 \\ 7 \\ 10 \end{bmatrix}$

b) $\|\mathbf{u} - \mathbf{v}\| = 3$

c) $\mathbf{w} \begin{bmatrix} -1 \\ 1/2 \\ -1 \end{bmatrix}$

29. a) $\mathbf{u} + 2\mathbf{v} = \begin{bmatrix} -1 \\ 1 \\ 2 \end{bmatrix}$

b) $\|\mathbf{u} - \mathbf{v}\| = \sqrt{150}$

c) $\mathbf{w} \begin{bmatrix} 7/2 \\ -5 \\ 1/2 \end{bmatrix}$

31. $\mathbf{u} = 2\mathbf{k}$

33. $\mathbf{u} = -\frac{5}{3}\mathbf{v} = \begin{bmatrix} 5/3 \\ -10/3 \\ -10/3 \end{bmatrix}$

35. $\mathbf{u} = \begin{bmatrix} -2 \\ -4 \\ -1 \end{bmatrix}$

Exercises 2.3, p. 146

1. -2

3. -1

5. $\cos\theta = \dfrac{11}{\sqrt{290}}$

7. $\cos\theta = \dfrac{1}{6}$

9. $\theta = \dfrac{\pi}{6}$

11. $\theta = \dfrac{\pi}{2}$

13. $\mathbf{u} = \mathbf{i} + 3\mathbf{j} + 4\mathbf{k}$

15. $\mathbf{u} = 3\mathbf{i} + 4\mathbf{k}$

17. $\mathbf{u} = -\mathbf{i} + 3\mathbf{j} + \mathbf{k}$

19. $R = (33/10, 11/10)$

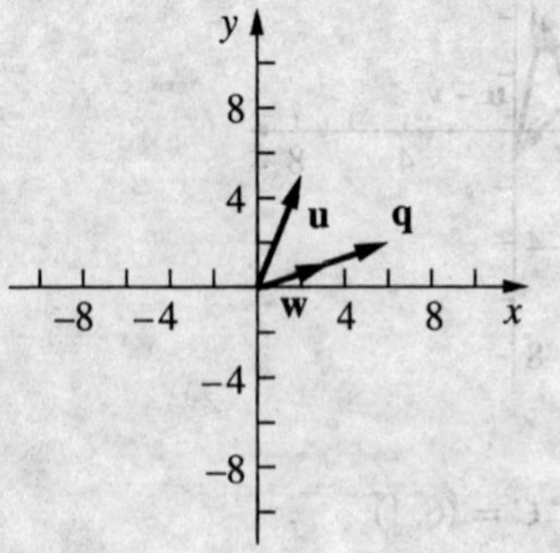

21. $R = (-3, -1)$

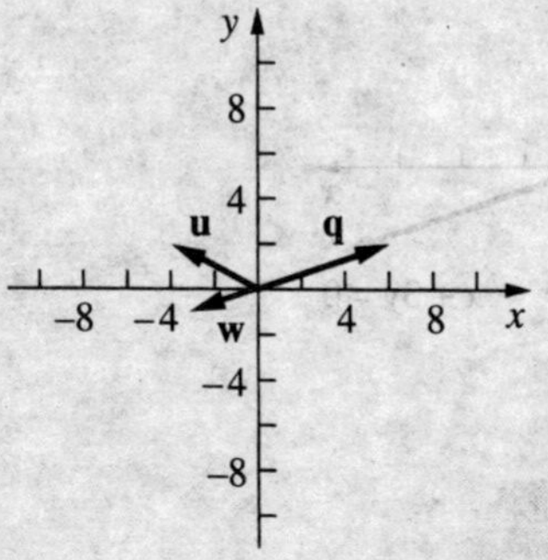

23. $\mathbf{u}_1 = \begin{bmatrix} 5 \\ 5 \end{bmatrix}$, $\mathbf{u}_2 = \begin{bmatrix} 2 \\ -2 \end{bmatrix}$

25. $\mathbf{u}_1 = \begin{bmatrix} 2 \\ 4 \\ 2 \end{bmatrix}$, $\mathbf{u}_2 = \begin{bmatrix} 4 \\ 0 \\ -4 \end{bmatrix}$

33. $\begin{bmatrix} -2 \\ 2 \\ 8 \end{bmatrix}$

35. $3\mathbf{i} - \mathbf{j} - 5\mathbf{k}$

37. $\begin{bmatrix} -2 \\ -5 \\ 4 \end{bmatrix}$

39. $\begin{bmatrix} 2 \\ -3 \\ 1 \end{bmatrix}$

41. $\begin{bmatrix} 1 \\ 1 \\ -4 \end{bmatrix}$

43. $4\sqrt{6}$ square units

45. $3\sqrt{11}$ square units

47. 24 cubic units

49. not coplanar

Exercises 2.4, p. 157

1. $x = 2 + 3t$, $y = 4 + 2t$,
$z = -3 + 4t$

3. $x = t$, $y = 4 - 2t$, $z = 1 + 3t$

5. The lines are parallel.

7. The lines are not parallel.

9. $x = 1 + 3t$, $y = 2 + 4t$, $z = 1 - t$

11. The line intersects the plane at $P = (-1, 4, 1)$.

13. The line intersects the plane at $P = (-8, -13, 36)$.

15. $6x + y - z = 16$

17. $-7x - y + 4z = 5$

19. $2x - 7y - 3z = 1$

21. $\mathbf{n} = \begin{bmatrix} 2/3 \\ 1/3 \\ -2/3 \end{bmatrix}$

23. $x + 2y - 2z = 17$

25. $x = 4 - t$, $y = 5 + t$, $z = t$

CHAPTER 3

Exercises 3.1, p. 166

1.

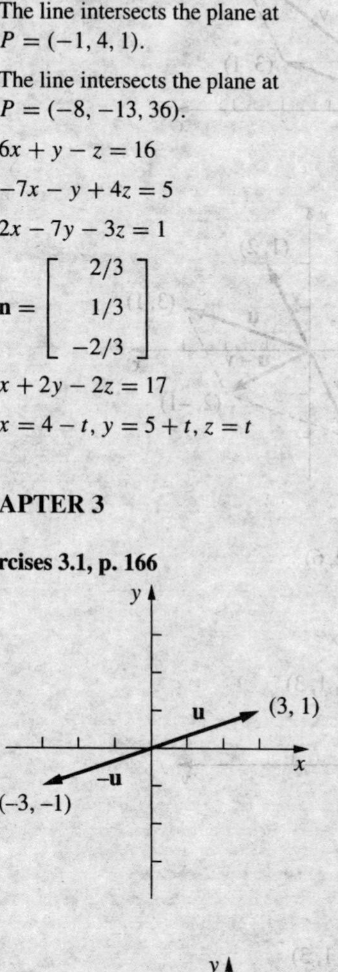

3.

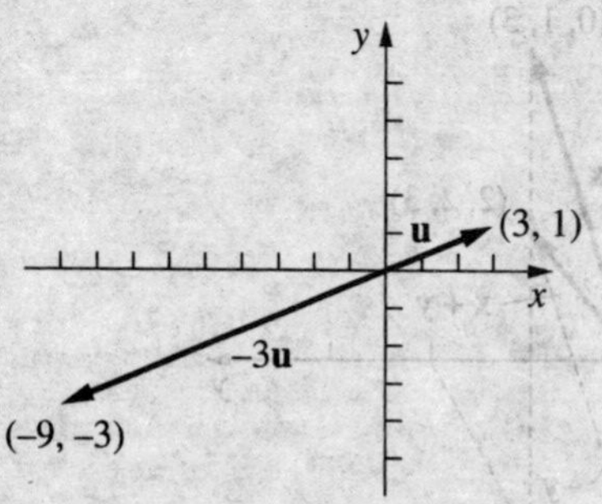

5.

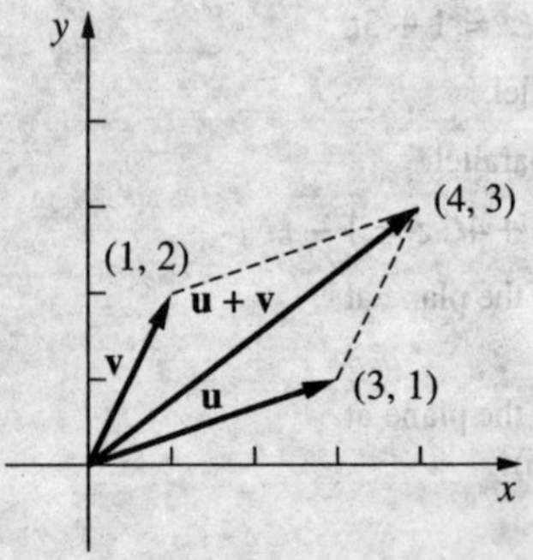

7.

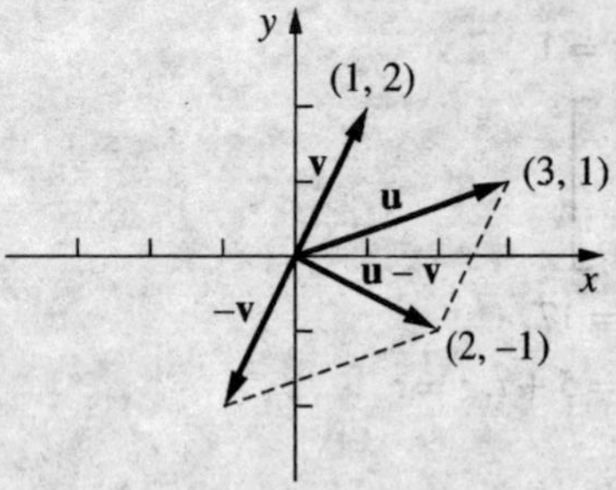

9.

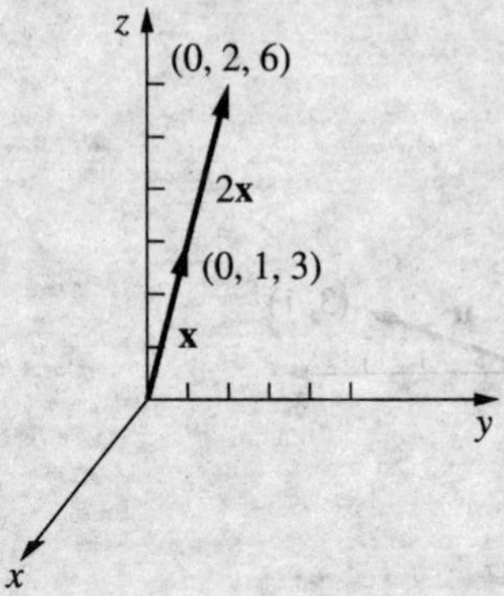

11.

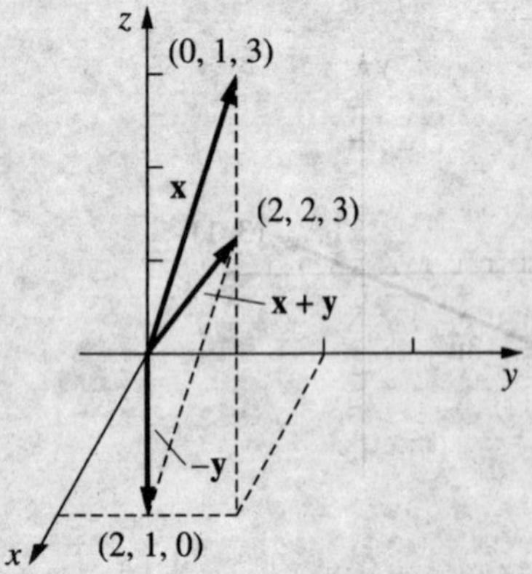

13.

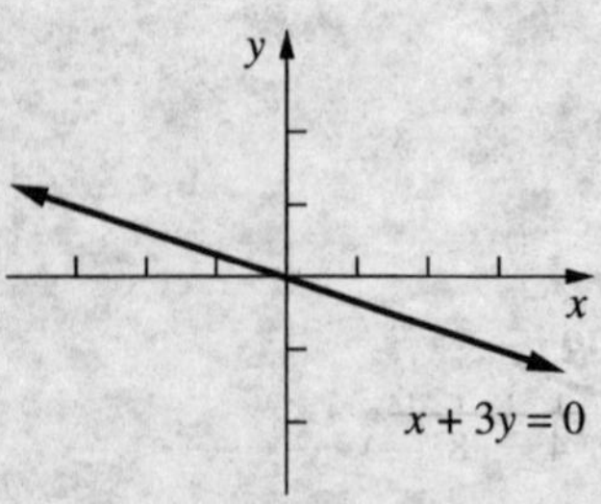

15.

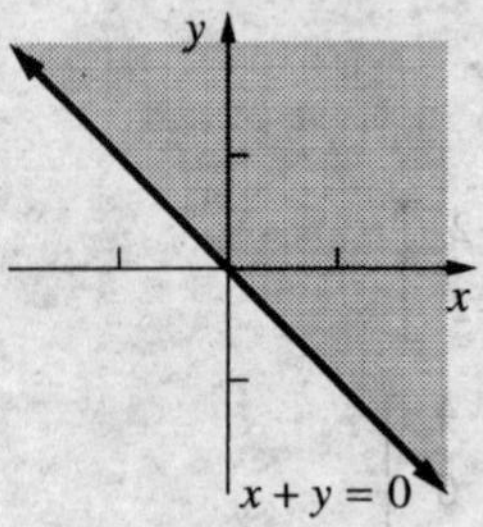

17.

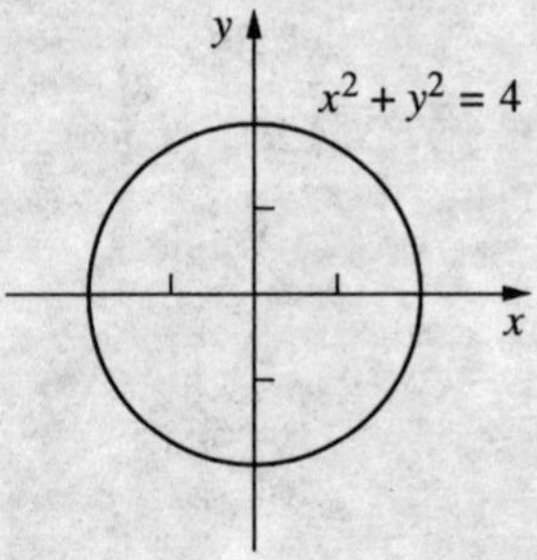

19. W is the plane with equation $x + y + 2z = 0$.

21. W is the set of points on the upper half of the sphere $x^2 + y^2 + z^2 = 1$.

23. $W = \left\{ \begin{bmatrix} a \\ 0 \end{bmatrix} : a \text{ any real number} \right\}$

25. $W = \left\{ \begin{bmatrix} a \\ 2 \end{bmatrix} : a \text{ any real number} \right\}$

27. $W = \left\{ \begin{bmatrix} x_1 \\ x_2 \\ x_3 \end{bmatrix} : x_1 + x_2 - 2x_3 = 0 \right\}$

29. $W = \left\{ \begin{bmatrix} 0 \\ x_2 \\ x_3 \end{bmatrix} : x_2, x_3 \text{ any real number} \right\}$

Exercises 3.2, p. 174

1. W is a subspace. W is the set of points on the line with equation $x = 2y$.

3. W is not a subspace.

5. W is the subspace consisting of the points on the y-axis.

7. W is not a subspace.

9. W is the subspace consisting of the points on the plane $2x - y - z = 0$.

11. W is not a subspace.

13. W is not a subspace.

15. W is the subspace consisting of the points on the line with parametric equations $x = 2t$, $y = -t$, $z = t$.

17. W is the subspace consisting of the points on the x-axis.

19. W is the set of points on the plane $x + 2y + 3z = 0$.

23. W is the line formed by the two intersecting planes $x+2y+2z = 0$ and $x+3y = 0$. The line has parametric equations $x = -6t$, $y = 2t$, $z = t$.

25. W is the set of points on the plane $x - z = 0$.

Exercises 3.3, p. 186

1. $\mathrm{Sp}(S) = \{\mathbf{x}\colon x_1 + x_2 = 0\}$; $\mathrm{Sp}(S)$ is the line with equation $x + y = 0$.

3. $\mathrm{Sp}(S) = \{\mathbf{e}\}$; $\mathrm{Sp}(S)$ is the point $(0, 0)$.

5. $\mathrm{Sp}(S) = R^2$

7. $\mathrm{Sp}(S) = \{\mathbf{x}\colon 3x_1 + 2x_2 = 0\}$; $\mathrm{Sp}(S)$ is the line with equation $3x + 2y = 0$.

9. $\mathrm{Sp}(S) = R^2$

11. $\mathrm{Sp}(S) = \{\mathbf{x}\colon x_1 + x_2 = 0\}$; $\mathrm{Sp}(S)$ is the line with equation $x + y = 0$.

13. $\mathrm{Sp}(S) = \{\mathbf{x}\colon x_2 + x_3 = 0 \text{ and } x_1 = 0\}$; $\mathrm{Sp}(S)$ is the line through $(0, 0, 0)$ and $(0, -1, 1)$. The parametric equations for the line are $x = 0$, $y = -t$, $z = t$.

15. $\mathrm{Sp}(S) = \{\mathbf{x}\colon 2x_1 - x_2 + x_3 = 0\}$; $\mathrm{Sp}(S)$ is the plane with equation $2x - y + z = 0$.

17. $\mathrm{Sp}(S) = R^3$

19. $\mathrm{Sp}(S) = \{\mathbf{x}\colon x_2 + x_3 = 0\}$; $\mathrm{Sp}(S)$ is the plane with equation $y + z = 0$.

21. The vectors $\mathbf{u}$ in b), c), and e) are in $\mathrm{Sp}(S)$; for b), $\mathbf{u} = \mathbf{x}$; for c), $\mathbf{u} = \mathbf{v}$; for e), $\mathbf{u} = 3\mathbf{v} - 4\mathbf{x}$.

23. **d** and **e**

25. **x** and **y**

27. $\mathcal{N}(A) = \{\mathbf{x} \text{ in } R^2\colon -x_1 + 3x_2 = 0\}$; $\mathcal{R}(A) = \{\mathbf{x} \text{ in } R^2\colon 2x_1 + x_2 = 0\}$

29. $\mathcal{N}(A) = \{\boldsymbol{\theta}\}$; $\mathcal{R}(A) = R^2$

31. $\mathcal{N}(A) = \{\mathbf{x} \text{ in } R^3\colon x_1 + 2x_2 = 0 \text{ and } x_3 = 0\}$; $\mathcal{R}(A) = R^2$

33. $\mathcal{N}(A) = \{\mathbf{x} \text{ in } R^2\colon x_2 = 0\}$; $\mathcal{R}(A) = \{\mathbf{x} \text{ in } R^3\colon x_2 = 2x_1 \text{ and } x_3 = 3x_1\}$

35. $\mathcal{N}(A) = \{\mathbf{x} \text{ in } R^3\colon x_1 = -7x_3 \text{ and } x_2 = 2x_3\}$; $\mathcal{R}(A) = \{\mathbf{x} \text{ in } R^3\colon -4x_1 + 2x_2 + x_3 = 0\}$

37. $\mathcal{N}(A) = \{\boldsymbol{\theta}\}$; $\mathcal{R}(A) = R^3$

39. **a)** The vectors **b** in ii), v), and vi) are in $\mathcal{R}(A)$.
b) For ii), $\mathbf{x} = [1, 0]^T$ is one choice; for v), $\mathbf{x} = [0, 1]^T$ is one choice; for vi), $\mathbf{x} = [0, 0]^T$ is one choice.
c) For ii), $\mathbf{b} = \mathbf{A}_1$; for v), $\mathbf{b} = \mathbf{A}_2$, for vi), $\mathbf{b} = 0\mathbf{A}_1 + 0\mathbf{A}_2$.

41. **a)** The vectors **b** in i), iii), v), and vi) are in $\mathcal{R}(A)$.
b) For i), $\mathbf{x} = [-1, 1, 0]^T$ is one choice; for iii), $\mathbf{x} = [-2, 3, 0]^T$ is one choice; for v), $\mathbf{x} = [-2, 1, 0]^T$ is one choice; for vi), $\mathbf{x} = [0, 0, 0]^T$ is one choice.
c) For i), $\mathbf{b} = -\mathbf{A}_1 + \mathbf{A}_2$; for iii), $\mathbf{b} = -2\mathbf{A}_1 + 3\mathbf{A}_2$; for v), $\mathbf{b} = -2\mathbf{A}_1 + \mathbf{A}_2$; for vi), $\mathbf{b} = 0\mathbf{A}_1 + 0\mathbf{A}_2 + 0\mathbf{A}_3$.

47. $\mathbf{w}_1 = [-2, 1, 3]^T$, $\mathbf{w}_2 = [0, 3, 2]^T$

49. $\mathbf{w}_1 = [1, 2, 2]^T$, $\mathbf{w}_2 = [0, 3, 1]^T$

Exercises 3.4, p. 200

1. $\{[1, 0, 1, 0]^T, [-1, 1, 0, 1]^T\}$

3. $\{[1, 1, 0, 0]^T, [-1, 0, 1, 0]^T, [3, 0, 0, 1]^T\}$

5. $\{[-1, 1, 0, 0]^T, [0, 0, 1, 0]^T, [0, 0, 0, 1]^T\}$

7. $\{[2, 1, -1, 0]^T, [-1, 0, 0, 1]^T\}$

9. **a)** $\mathbf{x} = 2\begin{bmatrix} 1 \\ 0 \\ 1 \\ 0 \end{bmatrix} + \begin{bmatrix} -1 \\ 1 \\ 0 \\ 1 \end{bmatrix}$; **b)** **x** is not in W.

c) $\mathbf{x} = -3\begin{bmatrix} -1 \\ 1 \\ 0 \\ 1 \end{bmatrix}$; **d)** $\mathbf{x} = 2\begin{bmatrix} 1 \\ 0 \\ 1 \\ 0 \end{bmatrix}$

11. **a)** $B = \begin{bmatrix} 1 & 0 & 1 & 1 \\ 0 & 1 & 1 & -1 \\ 0 & 0 & 0 & 0 \end{bmatrix}$
b) A basis for $\mathcal{N}(A)$ is $\{[-1, -1, 1, 0]^T, [-1, 1, 0, 1]^T\}$.
c) $\{\mathbf{A}_1, \mathbf{A}_2\}$ is a basis for the column space of A; $\mathbf{A}_3 = \mathbf{A}_1 + \mathbf{A}_2$ and $\mathbf{A}_4 = \mathbf{A}_1 - \mathbf{A}_2$.

d) {[1, 0, 1, 1], [0, 1, 1, −1]} is a basis for the row space of A.

13. a) $B = \begin{bmatrix} 1 & 0 & -1 & 2 \\ 0 & 1 & 1 & -1 \\ 0 & 0 & 0 & 0 \\ 0 & 0 & 0 & 0 \end{bmatrix}$

b) A basis for $\mathcal{N}(A)$ is $\{[1, -1, 1, 0]^T, [-2, 1, 0, 1]^T\}$.

c) $\{\mathbf{A}_1, \mathbf{A}_2\}$ is a basis for the column space of A; $\mathbf{A}_3 = -\mathbf{A}_1 + \mathbf{A}_2$ and $\mathbf{A}_4 = 2\mathbf{A}_1 - \mathbf{A}_2$.

d) {[1, 0, −1, 2], [0, 1, 1, −1]} is a basis for the row space of A.

15. a) $B = \begin{bmatrix} 1 & 2 & 0 \\ 0 & 0 & 1 \\ 0 & 0 & 0 \end{bmatrix}$

b) A basis for $\mathcal{N}(A)$ is $\{[-2, 1, 0]^T\}$.

c) $\{\mathbf{A}_1, \mathbf{A}_3\}$ is a basis for the column space of A; $\mathbf{A}_2 = 2\mathbf{A}_1$.

d) {[1, 2, 0], [0, 0, 1]} is a basis for the row space of A.

17. $\{[1, 3, 1]^T, [0, -1, -1]^T\}$ is a basis for $\mathcal{R}(A)$.

19. $\{[1, 2, 2, 0]^T, [0, 1, -2, 1]^T\}$ is a basis for $\mathcal{R}(A)$.

21. a) $\{[1, 2]^T\}$; **b)** $\{[1, 2]^T\}$

23. a) $\{[1, 2, 1]^T, [2, 5, 0]^T\}$;
b) $\{[1, 2, 1]^T, [0, 1, -2]^T\}$

25. a) $\{[0, 1, 0]^T\}$; **b)** $\{[-1, 1, 0]^T, [0, 0, 1]^T\}$
c) $\{[-1, 1, 0]^T\}$

27. $-2\mathbf{v}_1 - 3\mathbf{v}_2 + \mathbf{v}_3 = \boldsymbol{\theta}$, so S is linearly dependent. Since $\mathbf{v}_3 = 2\mathbf{v}_1 + 3\mathbf{v}_2$, if $\mathbf{v} = a_1\mathbf{v}_1 + a_2\mathbf{v}_2 + a_3\mathbf{v}_3$ is in Sp$\{\mathbf{v}_1, \mathbf{v}_2, \mathbf{v}_3\}$, then $\mathbf{v} = (a_1 + 2a_3)\mathbf{v}_1 + (a_2 + 3a_3)\mathbf{v}_2$. Therefore $\mathbf{v}$ is in Sp$\{\mathbf{v}_1, \mathbf{v}_2\}$.

29. The subsets are $\{\mathbf{v}_1, \mathbf{v}_2, \mathbf{v}_3\}$, $\{\mathbf{v}_1, \mathbf{v}_2, \mathbf{v}_4\}$, $\{\mathbf{v}_1, \mathbf{v}_3, \mathbf{v}_4\}$.

33. S is not a basis.

35. S is not a basis.

Exercises 3.5, p. 212

1. S does not span R^2.

3. S is linearly dependent.

5. S is linearly dependent and does not span R^2.

7. S does not span R^3.

9. S is linearly dependent.

11. S is a basis.

13. S is not a basis.

15. $\dim(W) = 3$

17. $\dim(W) = 2$

19. $\dim(W) = 1$

21. $\{[-2, 1]^T\}$ is a basis for $\mathcal{N}(A)$; nullity$(A) = 1$; rank$(A) = 1$.

23. $\{[-5, -2, 1]^T\}$ is a basis for $\mathcal{N}(A)$; nullity$(A) = 1$; rank$(A) = 2$.

25. $\{[1, -1, 1]^T, [0, 2, 3]^T\}$ is a basis for $\mathcal{R}(A)$; rank$(A) = 2$; nullity$(A) = 1$.

27. a) $\{[1, 1, -2], [0, -1, 1]^T, [0, 0, 1]^T\}$ is a basis for W; $\dim(W) = 3$.

b) $\{[1, 2, -1, 1]^T, [0, 1, -1, 1]^T, [0, 0, -1, 4]^T\}$ is a basis for W; $\dim(W) = 3$.

29. $\dim(W) = 2$

33. a) rank$(A) \le 3$ and nullity$(A) \ge 0$.
b) rank$(A) \le 3$ and nullity$(A) \ge 1$.
c) rank$(A) \le 4$ and nullity$(A) \ge 0$.

Exercises 3.6, p. 224

5. $\mathbf{u}_1^T\mathbf{u}_3 = 0$ requires $a + b + c = 0$; $\mathbf{u}_2^T\mathbf{u}_3 = 0$ requires $2a + 2b - 4c = 0$; therefore $c = 0$ and $a + b = 0$.

7. $\mathbf{u}_1^T\mathbf{u}_2 = 0$ forces $a = 3$; then $\mathbf{u}_2^T\mathbf{u}_3 = 0$ requires $-8 - b + 3c = 0$, while $\mathbf{u}_1^T\mathbf{u}_3 = 0$ requires $4 + b + c = 0$; therefore $b = -5$, $c = 1$.

9. $\mathbf{v} = (2/3)\mathbf{u}_1 - (1/2)\mathbf{u}_2 + (1/6)\mathbf{u}_3$

11. $\mathbf{v} = 3\mathbf{u}_1$

13. $\mathbf{u}_1 = \begin{bmatrix} 0 \\ 0 \\ 1 \\ 0 \end{bmatrix}, \quad \mathbf{u}_2 = \begin{bmatrix} 1 \\ 1 \\ 0 \\ 1 \end{bmatrix}, \quad \mathbf{u}_3 = \begin{bmatrix} 1/3 \\ -2/3 \\ 0 \\ 1/3 \end{bmatrix}$

15. $\mathbf{u}_1 = \begin{bmatrix} 1 \\ 1 \\ 0 \end{bmatrix}, \quad \mathbf{u}_2 = \begin{bmatrix} 1 \\ -1 \\ -1 \end{bmatrix}, \quad \mathbf{u}_3 = \begin{bmatrix} 2 \\ -2 \\ 4 \end{bmatrix}$

17. $\mathbf{u}_1 = \begin{bmatrix} 0 \\ 1 \\ 0 \\ 1 \end{bmatrix}, \quad \mathbf{u}_2 = \begin{bmatrix} -1 \\ -1 \\ 0 \\ 1 \end{bmatrix}, \quad \mathbf{u}_3 = \begin{bmatrix} -2/3 \\ 1/3 \\ 1 \\ -1/3 \end{bmatrix}$

19. For the null space: $\begin{bmatrix} -3 \\ -1 \\ 1 \\ 0 \end{bmatrix}, \begin{bmatrix} 7/11 \\ -27/11 \\ -6/11 \\ 1 \end{bmatrix}$;

for the range space: $\begin{bmatrix} 1 \\ 2 \\ 1 \end{bmatrix}, \begin{bmatrix} -11/6 \\ 8/6 \\ -5/6 \end{bmatrix}$

Exercises 3.7, p. 239

1. a) $\begin{bmatrix} 0 \\ 0 \end{bmatrix}$; **b)** $\begin{bmatrix} -1 \\ 0 \end{bmatrix}$; **c)** $\begin{bmatrix} 1 \\ -1 \end{bmatrix}$;

d) $\begin{bmatrix} -2 \\ 1 \end{bmatrix}$

3. c) is not but a), b), and d) are.

9. F is a linear transformation.

11. F is not a linear transformation.

13. F is a linear transformation.

15. F is a linear transformation.

17. F is not a linear transformation.

19. a) $\begin{bmatrix} 3 \\ 1 \\ -1 \end{bmatrix}$; **b)** $\begin{bmatrix} 0 \\ -1 \\ -2 \end{bmatrix}$; **c)** $\begin{bmatrix} 7 \\ 2 \\ -3 \end{bmatrix}$

21. $T\left(\begin{bmatrix} x_1 \\ x_2 \end{bmatrix}\right) = \begin{bmatrix} x_1 + x_2 \\ x_1 - 2x_2 \end{bmatrix}$

23. $T\left(\begin{bmatrix} x_1 \\ x_2 \\ x_3 \end{bmatrix}\right) = \begin{bmatrix} -\frac{1}{2}x_1 - \frac{1}{2}x_2 + \frac{1}{2}x_3 \\ \frac{1}{2}x_1 + \frac{1}{2}x_2 + \frac{1}{2}x_3 \end{bmatrix}$

25. $A = \begin{bmatrix} 1 & 3 \\ 2 & 1 \end{bmatrix}$; $\mathcal{N}(T) = \{\boldsymbol{\theta}\}$; $\mathcal{R}(T) = R^2$;

rank$(T) = 2$; nullity$(T) = 0$

27. $A = [3 \;\; 2]$; $\mathcal{N}(T) = \{\mathbf{x} \text{ in } R^2\text{: } 3x_1 + 2x_2 = 0\}$; $\mathcal{R}(T) = R^1$; rank$(T) = 1$; nullity$(T) = 1$

29. $A = \begin{bmatrix} 1 & -1 & 0 \\ 0 & 1 & -1 \end{bmatrix}$; $\mathcal{N}(T) = \{\mathbf{x} \text{ in } R^3\text{: } x_1 = x_3$ and $x_2 = x_3\}$; $\mathcal{R}(T) = R^2$; rank$(T) = 2$; nullity$(T) = 1$

Exercises 3.8, p. 254

1. $\mathbf{x}^* = \begin{bmatrix} -5/13 \\ 7/13 \end{bmatrix}$

3. $\mathbf{x}^* = \begin{bmatrix} (28/74) - 3x_3 \\ (27/74) + x_3 \\ x_3 \end{bmatrix}$, x_3 arbitrary

5. $\mathbf{x}^* = \begin{bmatrix} 2x_2 + 26/7 \\ -x_2 \end{bmatrix}$, x_2 arbitrary

7. $y = 1.3t + 1.1$ **9.** $y = 1.5t$

11. $y = 0.5t^2 + 0.1t$ **13.** $y = 0.25t^2 + 2.15t + 0.45$

Exercises 3.9, p. 266

1. $\mathbf{w}^* = \begin{bmatrix} 1/2 \\ 3 \\ 11/2 \end{bmatrix}$ **3.** $\mathbf{w}^* = \begin{bmatrix} 1 \\ 1 \\ 1 \end{bmatrix}$

5. $\mathbf{w}^* = \begin{bmatrix} 4 \\ 2 \\ 2 \end{bmatrix}$ **7.** $\mathbf{w}^* = \begin{bmatrix} 3 \\ -1 \\ 2 \end{bmatrix}$

9. $\mathbf{w}^* = \begin{bmatrix} 0 \\ 1 \\ -1 \end{bmatrix}$

11. $\mathbf{w}^* = \frac{4}{5}\begin{bmatrix} 2 \\ 1 \\ 0 \end{bmatrix} + \frac{11}{2}\begin{bmatrix} -1/5 \\ 2/5 \\ 1 \end{bmatrix}$

13. $\mathbf{w}^* = \begin{bmatrix} 1 \\ 1 \\ 0 \end{bmatrix} + 4\begin{bmatrix} 1/2 \\ -1/2 \\ 1 \end{bmatrix}$

15. $\mathbf{w}^* = 2\begin{bmatrix} 1 \\ -1 \\ 1 \end{bmatrix} + \begin{bmatrix} 1 \\ 1 \\ 0 \end{bmatrix}$

CHAPTER 4

Exercises 4.1, p. 279

1. $\lambda = 1$, $\mathbf{x} = a\begin{bmatrix} -1 \\ 1 \end{bmatrix}$, $a \neq 0$;

$\lambda = 3$, $\mathbf{x} = a\begin{bmatrix} 0 \\ 1 \end{bmatrix}$, $a \neq 0$

3. $\lambda = 1$, $\mathbf{x} = a\begin{bmatrix} 1 \\ 1 \end{bmatrix}$, $a \neq 0$;

$\lambda = 3$, $\mathbf{x} = a\begin{bmatrix} -1 \\ 1 \end{bmatrix}$, $a \neq 0$

5. $\lambda = 1, \mathbf{x} = a\begin{bmatrix} -1 \\ 1 \end{bmatrix}, \quad a \neq 0;$

$\lambda = 3, \mathbf{x} = a\begin{bmatrix} 1 \\ 1 \end{bmatrix}, \quad a \neq 0$

7. $\lambda = 1, \mathbf{x} = a\begin{bmatrix} 0 \\ 1 \end{bmatrix}, \quad a \neq 0$

9. $\lambda = 0, \mathbf{x} = a\begin{bmatrix} -1 \\ 1 \end{bmatrix}, \quad a \neq 0;$

$\lambda = 5, \mathbf{x} = a\begin{bmatrix} 2 \\ 3 \end{bmatrix}, \quad a \neq 0$

11. $\lambda = 2, \mathbf{x} = a\begin{bmatrix} -1 \\ 1 \end{bmatrix}, \quad a \neq 0$

Exercises 4.2, p. 288

1. $M_{11} = \begin{bmatrix} 1 & 3 & -1 \\ 2 & 4 & 1 \\ 2 & 0 & -2 \end{bmatrix}; \quad A_{11} = 18$

3. $M_{31} = \begin{bmatrix} -1 & 3 & 1 \\ 1 & 3 & -1 \\ 2 & 0 & -2 \end{bmatrix}; \quad A_{31} = 0$

5. $M_{34} = \begin{bmatrix} 2 & -1 & 3 \\ 4 & 1 & 3 \\ 2 & 2 & 0 \end{bmatrix}; \quad A_{34} = 0$

7. $\det(A) = 0$ **9.** $\det(A) = 0$; A is singular.

11. $\det(A) = -1$; A is nonsingular.

13. $\det(A) = 6$; A is nonsingular.

15. $\det(A) = 20$; A is nonsingular.

17. $\det(A) = 6$; A is nonsingular.

19. $\det(A) = 36$; A is nonsingular.

21. $y = 2x - 1$ **27.** 5 **29.** 3/5

Exercises 4.3, p. 296

1. $\det(A) = \begin{vmatrix} 1 & 2 & 1 \\ 3 & 0 & 2 \\ -1 & 1 & 3 \end{vmatrix} \overset{\substack{R_2 - 3R_1 \\ R_3 + R_1}}{=} \begin{vmatrix} 1 & 2 & 1 \\ 0 & -6 & -1 \\ 0 & 3 & 4 \end{vmatrix}$

$= \begin{vmatrix} -6 & -1 \\ 3 & 4 \end{vmatrix} = -21$

3. $\det(A) = \begin{vmatrix} 3 & 6 & 9 \\ 2 & 0 & 2 \\ 1 & 2 & 0 \end{vmatrix} = (3)(2)\begin{vmatrix} 1 & 2 & 3 \\ 1 & 0 & 1 \\ 1 & 2 & 0 \end{vmatrix}$

$\overset{\substack{R_2 - R_1 \\ R_3 - R_1}}{=} 6\begin{vmatrix} 1 & 2 & 3 \\ 0 & -2 & -2 \\ 0 & 0 & -3 \end{vmatrix} = 6\begin{vmatrix} -2 & -2 \\ 0 & -3 \end{vmatrix} = 36$

5. $\det(A) = \begin{vmatrix} 2 & 4 & -3 \\ 3 & 2 & 5 \\ 2 & 3 & 4 \end{vmatrix} = (\tfrac{1}{2})\begin{vmatrix} 2 & 4 & -3 \\ 6 & 4 & 10 \\ 2 & 3 & 4 \end{vmatrix}$

$\overset{\substack{R_2 - 3R_1 \\ R_3 - R_1}}{=} (\tfrac{1}{2})\begin{vmatrix} 2 & 4 & -3 \\ 0 & -8 & 19 \\ 0 & -1 & 7 \end{vmatrix}$

$= \begin{vmatrix} -8 & 19 \\ -1 & 7 \end{vmatrix} = -37$

7. $\begin{vmatrix} 1 & 0 & 0 & 0 \\ 2 & 0 & 0 & 3 \\ 1 & 1 & 0 & 1 \\ 1 & 4 & 2 & 2 \end{vmatrix} = (-1)\begin{vmatrix} 1 & 0 & 0 & 0 \\ 2 & 3 & 0 & 0 \\ 1 & 1 & 0 & 1 \\ 1 & 2 & 2 & 4 \end{vmatrix}$

$= \begin{vmatrix} 1 & 0 & 0 & 0 \\ 2 & 3 & 0 & 0 \\ 1 & 1 & 1 & 0 \\ 1 & 2 & 4 & 2 \end{vmatrix} = 6$

9. $\begin{vmatrix} 0 & 0 & 2 & 0 \\ 0 & 0 & 1 & 3 \\ 0 & 4 & 1 & 3 \\ 2 & 1 & 5 & 6 \end{vmatrix} = (-1)\begin{vmatrix} 2 & 0 & 0 & 0 \\ 1 & 0 & 0 & 3 \\ 1 & 4 & 0 & 3 \\ 5 & 1 & 2 & 6 \end{vmatrix}$

$= \begin{vmatrix} 2 & 0 & 0 & 0 \\ 1 & 3 & 0 & 0 \\ 1 & 3 & 0 & 4 \\ 5 & 6 & 2 & 1 \end{vmatrix}$

$= (-1)\begin{vmatrix} 2 & 0 & 0 & 0 \\ 1 & 3 & 0 & 0 \\ 1 & 3 & 4 & 0 \\ 5 & 6 & 1 & 2 \end{vmatrix} = -48$

11. $\begin{vmatrix} 0 & 0 & 1 & 0 \\ 0 & 2 & 6 & 3 \\ 2 & 4 & 1 & 5 \\ 0 & 0 & 0 & 4 \end{vmatrix} = (-1)\begin{vmatrix} 2 & 4 & 1 & 5 \\ 0 & 2 & 6 & 3 \\ 0 & 0 & 1 & 0 \\ 0 & 0 & 0 & 4 \end{vmatrix} = -16$

13. $\det(B) = 3\det(A) = 6$

15. $\det(B) = -\det(A) = -2$

17. $\det(B) = -2\det(A) = -4$

19. $R_4 - \frac{1}{2}R_1$ gives $\begin{vmatrix} 2 & 4 & 2 & 6 \\ 1 & 3 & 2 & 1 \\ 2 & 1 & 2 & 3 \\ 0 & 0 & 0 & -2 \end{vmatrix}$

$= (-2)\begin{vmatrix} 2 & 4 & 2 \\ 1 & 3 & 2 \\ 2 & 1 & 2 \end{vmatrix} = (-2)\begin{vmatrix} 2 & 4 & 2 \\ 0 & 1 & 1 \\ 0 & -3 & 0 \end{vmatrix}$

$= (-2)(2)\begin{vmatrix} 1 & 1 \\ -3 & 0 \end{vmatrix} = -12.$

21. $R_4 - 2R_3$ gives $\begin{vmatrix} 0 & 4 & 1 & 3 \\ 0 & 2 & 2 & 1 \\ 1 & 3 & 1 & 2 \\ 0 & -4 & -1 & 0 \end{vmatrix}$

$= \begin{vmatrix} 4 & 1 & 3 \\ 2 & 2 & 1 \\ -4 & -1 & 0 \end{vmatrix} = \begin{vmatrix} 4 & 1 & 3 \\ 2 & 2 & 1 \\ 0 & 0 & 3 \end{vmatrix}$

$= 3\begin{vmatrix} 4 & 1 \\ 2 & 2 \end{vmatrix} = 18.$

Exercises 4.4, p. 305

1. $p(t) = (1-t)(3-t)$; $\lambda = 1, \lambda = 3$

3. $p(t) = t^2 - 4t + 3 = (t-3)(t-1)$; $\lambda = 1, \lambda = 3$

5. $p(t) = t^2 - 4t + 4 = (t-2)^2$; $\lambda = 2$, algebraic multiplicity 2

7. $p(t) = -t^3 + t^2 + t - 1 = -(t-1)^2(t+1)$; $\lambda = 1$, algebraic multiplicity 2; $\lambda = -1$, algebraic multiplicity 1

9. $p(t) = -t^3 + 2t^2 + t - 2 = -(t-2)(t-1)(t+1)$; $\lambda = 2, \lambda = 1, \lambda = -1$

11. $p(t) = -t^3 + 6t^2 - 12t + 8 = -(t-2)^3$; $\lambda = 2$, algebraic multiplicity 3

13. $p(t) = t^4 - 18t^3 + 97t^2 - 180t + 100 = (t-1)(t-2)(t-5)(t-10)$; $\lambda = 1, \lambda = 2, \lambda = 5, \lambda = 10$

Exercises 4.5, p. 314

1. $\mathbf{x}$ is an eigenvector if and only if $\mathbf{x} = \begin{bmatrix} -x_2 \\ x_2 \end{bmatrix}$, $x_2 \neq 0$; basis consists of $\begin{bmatrix} -1 \\ 1 \end{bmatrix}$; algebraic and geometric multiplicities are 1.

3. $\mathbf{x}$ is an eigenvector if and only if $\mathbf{x} = \begin{bmatrix} -x_2 \\ x_2 \end{bmatrix}$, $x_2 \neq 0$; basis consists of $\begin{bmatrix} -1 \\ 1 \end{bmatrix}$; algebraic multiplicity is 2 and geometric multiplicity is 1.

5. $\mathbf{x}$ is an eigenvector if and only if $\mathbf{x} = \begin{bmatrix} a \\ -a \\ 2a \end{bmatrix}$, $a \neq 0$; basis consists of $\begin{bmatrix} 1 \\ -1 \\ 2 \end{bmatrix}$; algebraic and geometric multiplicities are 1.

7. $\mathbf{x}$ is an eigenvector if and only if $\mathbf{x} = \begin{bmatrix} x_4 \\ -x_4 \\ -x_4 \\ x_4 \end{bmatrix}$, $x_4 \neq 0$; basis consists of $\begin{bmatrix} 1 \\ -1 \\ -1 \\ 1 \end{bmatrix}$; algebraic and geometric multiplicities are 1.

9. $\mathbf{x}$ is an eigenvector if and only if $\mathbf{x} = \begin{bmatrix} x_4 \\ x_4 \\ x_4 \\ x_4 \end{bmatrix}$, $x_4 \neq 0$; basis consists of $\begin{bmatrix} 1 \\ 1 \\ 1 \\ 1 \end{bmatrix}$; algebraic and geometric multiplicities are 1.

11. **x** is an eigenvector if and only if

$$\mathbf{x} = \begin{bmatrix} -x_2 - x_3 - x_4 \\ x_2 \\ x_3 \\ x_4 \end{bmatrix};$$

basis consists of $\begin{bmatrix} -1 \\ 1 \\ 0 \\ 0 \end{bmatrix}, \begin{bmatrix} -1 \\ 0 \\ 1 \\ 0 \end{bmatrix},$

$\begin{bmatrix} -1 \\ 0 \\ 0 \\ 1 \end{bmatrix}$; algebraic and geometric multiplicities are 3.

13. For $\lambda = 2$, $\mathbf{x} = \begin{bmatrix} x_1 \\ -2x_3 \\ x_3 \end{bmatrix} = x_1 \begin{bmatrix} 1 \\ 0 \\ 0 \end{bmatrix} +$

$x_3 \begin{bmatrix} 0 \\ -2 \\ 1 \end{bmatrix}$; for $\lambda = 3$, $\mathbf{x} = \begin{bmatrix} x_2 \\ x_2 \\ 0 \end{bmatrix}$; the matrix is not defective.

15. For $\lambda = 2$, $\mathbf{x} = \begin{bmatrix} x_1 \\ x_2 \\ 0 \end{bmatrix} = x_1 \begin{bmatrix} 1 \\ 0 \\ 0 \end{bmatrix} + x_2 \begin{bmatrix} 0 \\ 1 \\ 0 \end{bmatrix}$;

for $\lambda = 1$, $\mathbf{x} = \begin{bmatrix} -3x_3 \\ -x_3 \\ x_3 \end{bmatrix}$; the matrix is not defective.

17. For $\lambda = 2$, $\mathbf{x} = \begin{bmatrix} x_1 \\ -x_1 \\ 2x_1 \end{bmatrix}$; for $\lambda = 1$, $\mathbf{x} =$

$\begin{bmatrix} -3x_2 \\ x_2 \\ -7x_2 \end{bmatrix}$; for $\lambda = -1$; $\mathbf{x} = \begin{bmatrix} x_1 \\ 2x_1 \\ 2x_1 \end{bmatrix}$; the matrix is not defective.

19. For $\lambda = 1$, eigenvectors are $\mathbf{u}_1 = \begin{bmatrix} 1 \\ 0 \\ 0 \end{bmatrix}$, $\mathbf{u}_2 =$

$\begin{bmatrix} 0 \\ 1 \\ 2 \end{bmatrix}$; for $\lambda = 2$, $\mathbf{u}_3 = \begin{bmatrix} 1 \\ 2 \\ 3 \end{bmatrix}$. Therefore $\mathbf{x} =$

$\mathbf{u}_1 + 2\mathbf{u}_2 + \mathbf{u}_3$, and thus $A^{10}\mathbf{x} = \mathbf{u}_1 + 2\mathbf{u}_2 + 2^{10}\mathbf{u}_3 =$

$\begin{bmatrix} 1025 \\ 2050 \\ 3076 \end{bmatrix}$.

Exercises 4.6, p. 324

1. $3 + 2i$

3. $7 - 3i$

5. 6

7. 17

9. $-5 + 5i$

11. $17 - 6i$

13. $(10 - 11i)/17$

15. $(3 + i)/2$

17. 1

19. $\lambda = 4 + 2i$, $\mathbf{x} = a \begin{bmatrix} 4 \\ -1 + i \end{bmatrix}$;

$\lambda = 4 - 2i$, $\mathbf{x} = a \begin{bmatrix} 4 \\ -1 - i \end{bmatrix}$

21. $\lambda = i$, $\mathbf{x} = a \begin{bmatrix} -2 + i \\ 5 \end{bmatrix}$;

$\lambda = -i$, $\mathbf{x} = a \begin{bmatrix} -2 - i \\ 5 \end{bmatrix}$

23. $\lambda = 2$, $\mathbf{x} = a \begin{bmatrix} -1 \\ 0 \\ 1 \end{bmatrix}$; $\lambda = 2 + 3i$,

$\mathbf{x} = a \begin{bmatrix} -5 + 3i \\ 3 + 3i \\ 2 \end{bmatrix}$; $\lambda = 2 - 3i$,

$\mathbf{x} = a \begin{bmatrix} -5 - 3i \\ 3 - 3i \\ 2 \end{bmatrix}$

25. $x = 2 - i$, $y = 3 - 2i$

27. $\sqrt{6}$

29. 4

Exercises 4.7, p. 336

1. A is symmetric, so A is diagonalizable. For $S = \begin{bmatrix} 1 & -1 \\ 1 & 1 \end{bmatrix}$, $S^{-1}AS = \begin{bmatrix} 1 & 0 \\ 0 & 3 \end{bmatrix}$ and $S^{-1}A^5S = \begin{bmatrix} 1 & 0 \\ 0 & 243 \end{bmatrix}$; therefore $A^5 = \begin{bmatrix} 122 & -121 \\ -121 & 122 \end{bmatrix}$.

3. A is not diagonalizable; $\lambda = -1$ is the only eigenvalue and $\mathbf{x} = a\begin{bmatrix} 1 \\ 1 \end{bmatrix}$, $a \neq 0$, are the only eigenvectors.

5. A is diagonalizable since A has distinct eigenvalues. For $S = \begin{bmatrix} -1 & 0 \\ 10 & 1 \end{bmatrix}$, $S^{-1}AS = \begin{bmatrix} 1 & 0 \\ 0 & 2 \end{bmatrix}$ and $S^{-1}A^5S = \begin{bmatrix} 1 & 0 \\ 0 & 32 \end{bmatrix}$; therefore $A^5 = \begin{bmatrix} 1 & 0 \\ 310 & 32 \end{bmatrix}$.

7. A is not diagonalizable; $\lambda = 1$ is the only eigenvalue and it has geometric multiplicity 2. A basis for the eigenspace consists of $[1, 1, 0]^T$ and $[2, 0, 1]^T$.

9. A is diagonalizable since A has distinct eigenvalues. For $S = \begin{bmatrix} -3 & -1 & 1 \\ 1 & 1 & 2 \\ -7 & -2 & 2 \end{bmatrix}$, $S^{-1}AS = \begin{bmatrix} 1 & 0 & 0 \\ 0 & 2 & 0 \\ 0 & 0 & -1 \end{bmatrix}$. Therefore $A^5 = \begin{bmatrix} 163 & -11 & -71 \\ -172 & 10 & 75 \\ 324 & -22 & -141 \end{bmatrix}$.

11. A is not diagonalizable; $\lambda = 1$ has algebraic multiplicity 2 and geometric multiplicity 1.

13. Q is orthogonal.

15. Q is not orthogonal since the columns are not orthonormal.

17. Q is orthogonal.

19. $\alpha = 1/\sqrt{2}$, $\beta = 1/\sqrt{6}$, $a = -1/\sqrt{3}$, $b = 1/\sqrt{3}$, $c = 1/\sqrt{3}$

33. $\lambda = 2$, $\mathbf{u} = \frac{1}{\sqrt{2}}\begin{bmatrix} 1 \\ -1 \end{bmatrix}$, $\mathbf{v} = \frac{1}{\sqrt{2}}\begin{bmatrix} 1 \\ 1 \end{bmatrix}$
$Q = [\mathbf{u}, \mathbf{v}]$, $Q^TAQ = \begin{bmatrix} 2 & -2 \\ 0 & 2 \end{bmatrix}$

35. $\lambda = 1$, $\mathbf{u} = \frac{1}{\sqrt{2}}\begin{bmatrix} 1 \\ 1 \end{bmatrix}$, $\mathbf{v} = \frac{1}{\sqrt{2}}\begin{bmatrix} 1 \\ -1 \end{bmatrix}$,
$Q = [\mathbf{u}, \mathbf{v}]$, $Q^TAQ = \begin{bmatrix} 1 & 0 \\ 0 & 3 \end{bmatrix}$.

Exercises 4.8, p. 349

1. $\mathbf{x}_1 = \begin{bmatrix} 4 \\ 2 \end{bmatrix}$, $\mathbf{x}_2 = \begin{bmatrix} 2 \\ 4 \end{bmatrix}$,
$\mathbf{x}_3 = \begin{bmatrix} 4 \\ 2 \end{bmatrix}$, $\mathbf{x}_4 = \begin{bmatrix} 2 \\ 4 \end{bmatrix}$

3. $\mathbf{x}_1 = \begin{bmatrix} 80 \\ 112 \end{bmatrix}$, $\mathbf{x}_2 = \begin{bmatrix} 68 \\ 124 \end{bmatrix}$,
$\mathbf{x}_3 = \begin{bmatrix} 65 \\ 127 \end{bmatrix}$, $\mathbf{x}_4 = \begin{bmatrix} 64.25 \\ 127.75 \end{bmatrix}$

5. $\mathbf{x}_1 = \begin{bmatrix} 7 \\ 1 \end{bmatrix}$, $\mathbf{x}_2 = \begin{bmatrix} 11 \\ 8 \end{bmatrix}$,
$\mathbf{x}_3 = \begin{bmatrix} 43 \\ 19 \end{bmatrix}$, $\mathbf{x}_4 = \begin{bmatrix} 119 \\ 62 \end{bmatrix}$

7. $\mathbf{x}_k = 3(1)^k\begin{bmatrix} 1 \\ 1 \end{bmatrix} + (-1)^k\begin{bmatrix} -1 \\ 1 \end{bmatrix} = \begin{bmatrix} 3+(-1)^{k+1} \\ 3+(-1)^k \end{bmatrix}$; $\mathbf{x}_4 = \begin{bmatrix} 2 \\ 4 \end{bmatrix}$,
$\mathbf{x}_{10} = \begin{bmatrix} 2 \\ 4 \end{bmatrix}$; the sequence $\{\mathbf{x}_k\}$ has no limit, but $\|\mathbf{x}_k\| \leq \sqrt{20}$.

9. $\mathbf{x}_k = 64(1)^k\begin{bmatrix} 1 \\ 2 \end{bmatrix} - 64(1/4)^k\begin{bmatrix} -1 \\ 1 \end{bmatrix} = 64\begin{bmatrix} 1+(1/4)^k \\ 2-(1/4)^k \end{bmatrix}$; $\mathbf{x}_4 = \begin{bmatrix} 64.25 \\ 127.75 \end{bmatrix}$,
$\mathbf{x}_{10} = \begin{bmatrix} 64.00006 \\ 127.99994 \end{bmatrix}$; the sequence $\{\mathbf{x}_k\}$ converges to $[64, 128]^T$.

11. $\mathbf{x}_k = (3/4)(3)^k \begin{bmatrix} 2 \\ 1 \end{bmatrix} + (5/4)(-1)^k \begin{bmatrix} -2 \\ 1 \end{bmatrix} = \frac{1}{4}\begin{bmatrix} 6(3)^k - 10(-1)^k \\ 3(3)^k + 5(-1)^k \end{bmatrix}$; $\mathbf{x}_4 = \begin{bmatrix} 119 \\ 62 \end{bmatrix}$; $\mathbf{x}_{10} = \begin{bmatrix} 88571 \\ 44288 \end{bmatrix}$; the sequence $\{\mathbf{x}_k\}$ has no limit and $\|\mathbf{x}_k\| \to \infty$.

13. $\mathbf{x}_k = -2(1)^k \begin{bmatrix} -3 \\ 1 \\ -7 \end{bmatrix} - 2(2)^k \begin{bmatrix} -1 \\ 1 \\ -2 \end{bmatrix} - 5(-1)^k \begin{bmatrix} 1 \\ 2 \\ 2 \end{bmatrix} = \begin{bmatrix} 6 + 2(2)^k - 5(-1)^k \\ -2 - 2(2)^k - 10(-1)^k \\ 14 + 4(2)^k - 10(-1)^k \end{bmatrix}$; $\mathbf{x}_4 = \begin{bmatrix} 33 \\ -44 \\ 68 \end{bmatrix}$; $\mathbf{x}_{10} = \begin{bmatrix} 2049 \\ -2060 \\ 4100 \end{bmatrix}$; the sequence $\{\mathbf{x}_k\}$ has no limit and $\|\mathbf{x}_k\| \to \infty$.

15. $\mathbf{x}(t) = 3e^{2t}\begin{bmatrix} 2 \\ 1 \end{bmatrix} - 2e^{-t}\begin{bmatrix} 1 \\ 1 \end{bmatrix}$

17. $\mathbf{x}(t) = \begin{bmatrix} 0 \\ -2 \\ 2 \end{bmatrix} - e^{2t}\begin{bmatrix} -2 \\ -3 \\ 1 \end{bmatrix} + e^{3t}\begin{bmatrix} 1 \\ 2 \\ 0 \end{bmatrix}$

21. $\alpha = -.18$; $\mathbf{x}_k = \frac{16}{118}(1)^k \begin{bmatrix} 3 \\ 10 \end{bmatrix} + \frac{7}{118}(-.18)^k \begin{bmatrix} 10 \\ -6 \end{bmatrix}$; the limit is $\frac{16}{118}\begin{bmatrix} 3 \\ 10 \end{bmatrix}$.

CHAPTER 5

Exercises 5.2, p. 366

1. $\begin{bmatrix} 0 & -7 & 5 \\ -11 & -3 & -12 \end{bmatrix}, \begin{bmatrix} 12 & -22 & 38 \\ -50 & -6 & -15 \end{bmatrix}, \begin{bmatrix} 7 & -21 & 28 \\ -42 & -7 & -14 \end{bmatrix}$

3. $e^x - 2\sin x$, $e^x - 2\sin x + 3\sqrt{x^2+1}$, $-2e^x - \sin x + 3\sqrt{x^2+1}$

5. $c_1 = -2 + c_3$, $c_2 = 3 - c_3$, c_3 arbitrary

7. Not a vector space **9.** Not a vector space

11. Not a vector space **13.** A vector space

15. Not a vector space **25.** A vector space

27. Not a vector space **29.** A vector space

Exercises 5.3, p. 373

1. Not a subspace **3.** A subspace

5. A subspace **7.** Not a subspace

9. A subspace **11.** Not a subspace

13. A subspace **15.** Not a subspace

17. $p(x) = -p_1(x) + 3p_2(x) - 2p_3(x)$

19. $A = (-1 - 2x)B_1 + (2 + 3x)B_2 + xB_3 - 3B_4$, x arbitrary

21. $\cos 2x = -\sin^2 x + \cos^2 x$

23. $W = \text{Sp}\{1, x^2\}$

25. In Exercise 2, $W = \text{Sp}\left\{\begin{bmatrix} 1 & 1 & 0 \\ 0 & 0 & 0 \end{bmatrix}, \begin{bmatrix} -2 & 0 & 1 \\ 0 & 0 & 0 \end{bmatrix}, \begin{bmatrix} 0 & 0 & 0 \\ 1 & 0 & 0 \end{bmatrix}, \begin{bmatrix} 0 & 0 & 0 \\ 0 & 1 & 0 \end{bmatrix}, \begin{bmatrix} 0 & 0 & 0 \\ 0 & 0 & 1 \end{bmatrix}\right\}$; in Exercise 3, $W = \text{Sp}\left\{\begin{bmatrix} -1 & -1 & 1 \\ 0 & 0 & 0 \end{bmatrix}, \begin{bmatrix} 0 & 0 & 0 \\ 1 & 0 & 0 \end{bmatrix}, \begin{bmatrix} 0 & 0 & 0 \\ 0 & 1 & 0 \end{bmatrix}\right\}$; in Exercise 5, $W = \text{Sp}\{-1 + x, -2 + x^2\}$; in Exercise 6, $W = \text{Sp}\{1, -4x + x^2\}$; in Exercise 8, $W = \text{Sp}\{1 - x^2, x\}$

27. $W = \text{Sp}\{B_1, B_2, E_{12}, E_{13}, E_{21}, E_{23}, E_{31}, E_{32}\}$, where $B_1 = \begin{bmatrix} -1 & 0 & 0 \\ 0 & 1 & 0 \\ 0 & 0 & 0 \end{bmatrix}$ and $B_2 = \begin{bmatrix} -1 & 0 & 0 \\ 0 & 0 & 0 \\ 0 & 0 & 1 \end{bmatrix}$

29. $A = B + C$ where $B = (A + A^T)/2$ and $C = (A - A^T)/2$

31. a) $W = \mathrm{Sp}\{E_{12}, E_{13}, E_{23}\}$;

b) $W = \mathrm{Sp}\left\{\begin{bmatrix} -1 & 0 & 0 \\ 0 & 1 & 0 \\ 0 & 0 & 0 \end{bmatrix}, \begin{bmatrix} -1 & 0 & 0 \\ 0 & 0 & 0 \\ 0 & 0 & 1 \end{bmatrix}, \begin{bmatrix} 0 & -1 & 0 \\ 0 & 0 & 1 \\ 0 & 0 & 0 \end{bmatrix}, \begin{bmatrix} 0 & 0 & 1 \\ 0 & 0 & 0 \\ 0 & 0 & 0 \end{bmatrix}\right\}$;

c) $W = \mathrm{Sp}\left\{\begin{bmatrix} 1 & 1 & 0 \\ 0 & 0 & 0 \\ 0 & 0 & 0 \end{bmatrix}, \begin{bmatrix} 0 & 0 & 1 \\ 0 & 0 & 1 \\ 0 & 0 & 0 \end{bmatrix}, \begin{bmatrix} 0 & 0 & 0 \\ 0 & 1 & 0 \\ 0 & 0 & 1 \end{bmatrix}\right\}$;

d) $W = \mathrm{Sp}\left\{\begin{bmatrix} 1 & 0 & 0 \\ 0 & 1 & 0 \\ 0 & 0 & 1 \end{bmatrix}, \begin{bmatrix} 0 & -1 & 1 \\ 0 & 0 & 1 \\ 0 & 0 & 0 \end{bmatrix}, \begin{bmatrix} 0 & 0 & 1 \\ 0 & 0 & 0 \\ 0 & 0 & 0 \end{bmatrix}\right\}$

33. $x_1 = -6a + 5b + 37c + 15d$;
$x_2 = 3a - 2b - 17c - 7d$;
$x_3 = -a + b + 5c + 2d$; $x_4 = 2c + d$;
$C = -12B_1 + 6B_2 - B_3 - B_4$;
$D = 8B_1 - 3B_2 + B_3 + B_4$

Exercises 5.4, p. 386

1. $\left\{\begin{bmatrix} -1 & 1 \\ 0 & 0 \end{bmatrix}, \begin{bmatrix} -1 & 0 \\ 1 & 0 \end{bmatrix}, \begin{bmatrix} -1 & 0 \\ 0 & 1 \end{bmatrix}\right\}$

3. $\{E_{12}, E_{21}, E_{22}\}$ **5.** $\{1 + x^2, x - 2x^2\}$

7. $\{x, x^2\}$

9. $\{-9x + 3x^2 + x^3, 8x - 6x^2 + x^4\}$

13. a) $[2 \ \ -1 \ \ 3 \ \ 2]^T$; **b)** $[1 \ \ 0 \ \ -1 \ \ 1]^T$;
c) $[2 \ \ 3 \ \ 0 \ \ 0]^T$

15. Linearly independent

17. Linearly dependent

19. Linearly dependent

21. Linearly independent

23. $\{p_1(x), p_2(x)\}$ **25.** $\{A_1, A_2, A_3\}$

27. $[-4 \ \ 11 \ \ -3]^T$

31. $[a + b - 2c + 7d, -b + 2c - 4d, c - 2d, d]^T$

38. The set $\{\mathbf{u}, \mathbf{v}\}$ is linearly dependent if and only if one of the vectors is a scalar multiple of the other.
a) Linearly independent;
b) Linearly independent; **c)** Linearly dependent;
d) Linearly dependent; **e)** Linearly dependent

Exercises 5.5, p. 390

1. b) $\{E_{11}, E_{21}, E_{22}, E_{31}, E_{32}, E_{33}\}$ is a basis for V_1. $\{E_{11}, E_{12}, E_{13}, E_{22}, E_{23}, E_{33}\}$ is a basis for V_2.
c) $\dim(V) = 9$, $\dim(V_1) = 6$, $\dim(V_2) = 6$

3. $V_1 \cap V_2 = \left\{\begin{bmatrix} a_{11} & 0 & 0 \\ 0 & a_{22} & 0 \\ 0 & 0 & a_{33} \end{bmatrix} : a_{11}, a_{22}, a_{33}\right.$ arbitrary real numbers$\}$; $\dim(V_1 \cap V_2) = 3$

5. $\dim(W) = 3$ **7.** $\dim(W) = 3$

9. iii) The set S is linearly dependent.

11. ii) The set S does not span V.

13. iii) The set S is linearly dependent.

21. a) $A = \begin{bmatrix} 1 & -1 & 1 \\ 0 & 1 & -2 \\ 0 & 0 & 1 \end{bmatrix}$; **b)** $[5 \ \ 2 \ \ 1]^T$

23. $A^{-1} = \begin{bmatrix} 1 & 1 & 1 \\ 0 & 1 & 2 \\ 0 & 0 & 1 \end{bmatrix}$; **a)** $p(x) = 6 + 11x + 7x^2$;
b) $p(x) = 4 + 2x - x^2$; **c)** $p(x) = 5 + x$;
d) $p(x) = 8 - 2x - x^2$

Exercises 5.6, p. 401

9. $\langle \mathbf{x}, \mathbf{y} \rangle = -3$, $\|\mathbf{x}\| = \sqrt{5}$, $\|\mathbf{y}\| = \sqrt{2}$, $\|\mathbf{x} - \mathbf{y}\| = \sqrt{13}$

11. $\langle p, q \rangle = 52$, $\|p\| = 3\sqrt{6}$, $\|q\| = 3\sqrt{6}$, $\|p - q\| = 2$

13. For $\langle \mathbf{x}, \mathbf{y} \rangle = \mathbf{x}^T\mathbf{y}$, the graph of S is the circle with equation $x^2 + y^2 = 1$. For $\langle \mathbf{x}, \mathbf{y} \rangle = 4x_1y_1 + x_2y_2$, the graph of S is the ellipse with equation $4x^2 + y^2 = 1$.

15. $a_1 = 7$, $a_2 = 4$

17. $q = (-5/3)p_0 - 5p_1 - 4p_2$

19. $p_0 = 1$, $p_1 = x$, $p_2 = x^2 - 2$, $p_3 = x^3 - (17/5)x$, $p_4 = x^4 - (31/7)x^2 + 72/35$

25. $p^*(x) = (3/2)x^2 - (3/5)x + 1/20$

27. $p^*(x) \cong 0.841471p_0(x) - 0.467544p_1(x) - 0.430920p_2(x) + 0.07882p_3(x)$

29. d) $T_2(x) = 2x^2 - 1$, $T_3(x) = 4x^3 - 3x$, $T_4(x) = 8x^4 - 8x^2 + 1$, $T_5(x) = 16x^5 - 20x^3 + 5x$

Exercises 5.7, p. 410

1. Not a linear transformation

3. A linear transformation

5. A linear transformation

7. Not a linear transformation

9. a) $11 + x^2 + 6x^3$;
b) $T(a_0 + a_1x + a_2x^2) = (a_0 + 2a_2) + (a_0 + a_1)x^2 + (-a_1 + a_2)x^3$

11. a) $8 + 14x - 9x^2$;
b) $T\left(\begin{bmatrix} a & b \\ c & d \end{bmatrix}\right) = (a + b + 2d) + (-a + b + 2c + d)x + (b - c - 2d)x^2$

13. a) $\{2, 6x, 12x^2\}$ is a basis for $\mathcal{R}(T)$.
b) $\text{Nullity}(T) = 2$
c) $T[(a_0/2)x^2 + (a_1/6)x^3 + (a_2/12)x^4] = a_0 + a_1x + a_2x^2$

15. $\mathcal{N}(T) = \{a_0 + a_1x + a_2x^2\colon\ a_0 + 2a_1 + 4a_2 = 0\}$; $\mathcal{R}(T) = R^1$

17. b) $\mathcal{N}(I) = \{\boldsymbol{\theta}\}$; $\mathcal{R}(I) = V$

19.

rank(T)	3	2	1	0
nullity(T)	2	3	4	5

T cannot be one-to-one.

21.

rank(T)	3	2	1	0
nullity(T)	0	1	2	3

$\mathcal{R}(T) = \mathcal{P}_3$ is not possible.

27. b) $\text{Nullity}(T) = 0$; $\text{rank}(T) = 4$

Exercises 5.8, p. 418

1. $(S + T)(p) = p'(0) + (x + 2)p(x)$;
$(S + T)(x) = 1 + 2x + x^2$; $(S + T)(x^2) = 2x^2 + x^3$

3. $(H \circ T)(p) = p(x) + (x + 2)p'(x) + 2p(0)$;
$(H \circ T)(x) = 2x + 2$

5. b) There is no polynomial p in $\mathcal{P}_3$ such that $T(p) = x$, so $T^{-1}(x)$ is not defined.

7. $T^{-1}(e^x) = e^x$; $T^{-1}(e^{2x}) = (1/2)e^{2x}$;
$T^{-1}(e^{3x}) = (1/3)e^{3x}$;
$T^{-1}(ae^x + be^{2x} + ce^{3x}) = ae^x + (b/2)e^{2x} + (c/3)e^{3x}$

9. $T^{-1}(A) = A^T$

11. c) $T\left(\begin{bmatrix} a & b \\ c & d \end{bmatrix}\right) = a + bx + cx^2 + dx^3$

Exercises 5.9, p. 429

1. $\begin{bmatrix} 0 & 1 & 0 & 0 \\ 0 & 0 & 0 & 0 \\ 0 & 0 & 0 & 0 \\ 0 & 0 & 0 & 0 \\ 0 & 0 & 0 & 0 \end{bmatrix}$ **3.** $\begin{bmatrix} 2 & 1 & 0 & 0 \\ 1 & 2 & 0 & 0 \\ 0 & 1 & 2 & 0 \\ 0 & 0 & 1 & 2 \\ 0 & 0 & 0 & 1 \end{bmatrix}$

5. $\begin{bmatrix} 1 & 1 & 0 & 0 & 0 \\ 0 & 0 & 2 & 0 & 0 \\ 0 & 0 & 0 & 3 & 0 \\ 0 & 0 & 0 & 0 & 4 \end{bmatrix}$ **7.** $\begin{bmatrix} 2 & 2 & 0 & 0 & 0 \\ 1 & 1 & 4 & 0 & 0 \\ 0 & 0 & 2 & 6 & 0 \\ 0 & 0 & 0 & 3 & 8 \\ 0 & 0 & 0 & 0 & 4 \end{bmatrix}$

9. a) $[p]_B = \begin{bmatrix} a_0 \\ a_1 \\ a_2 \\ a_3 \end{bmatrix}$, $[T(p)]_C = \begin{bmatrix} 2a_0 \\ a_0 + 2a_1 \\ a_1 + 2a_2 \\ a_2 + 2a_3 \\ a_3 \end{bmatrix}$

11. a) $Q = \begin{bmatrix} 1 & 0 & 0 \\ 0 & 2 & 0 \\ 0 & 0 & 3 \end{bmatrix}$;
b) $P = \begin{bmatrix} 1 & 0 & 0 \\ 0 & 1/2 & 0 \\ 0 & 0 & 1/3 \end{bmatrix}$

13. a) $Q = \begin{bmatrix} 1 & 0 & 0 & 0 \\ 0 & 0 & 1 & 0 \\ 0 & 1 & 0 & 0 \\ 0 & 0 & 0 & 1 \end{bmatrix}$

15. $\begin{bmatrix} 3 & 6 & 0 \\ 3 & 3 & 0 \\ -1 & -1 & 3 \\ 0 & 0 & 0 \end{bmatrix}$ **17.** $\begin{bmatrix} 1 & 0 & 0 \\ 0 & 3 & 6 \\ 0 & 1 & 4 \end{bmatrix}$

19. $\begin{bmatrix} 0 & 0 & 1 & 1 \\ 1 & 0 & 1 & 0 \\ 0 & 1 & 0 & 0 \\ 0 & 0 & 0 & 3 \end{bmatrix}$ **21.** $\begin{bmatrix} -4 & -2 & 0 \\ 3 & 3 & 0 \\ -1 & 2 & 3 \end{bmatrix}$

23. $\begin{bmatrix} 2 & 0 & 0 \\ 0 & -3 & 0 \\ 0 & 0 & 3 \end{bmatrix}$

31. $T(a_0 + a_1x + a_2x^2 + a_3x^3) = (a_0 + 2a_2) + (a_1 + a_3)x + (-a_0 + a_1 - a_3)x^2$

Exercises 5.10, p. 438

1. $T(\mathbf{u}_1) = \mathbf{u}_1,\quad T(\mathbf{u}_2) = 3\mathbf{u}_2, \begin{bmatrix} 1 & 0 \\ 0 & 3 \end{bmatrix}$

3. $T(A_1) = 2A_1, T(A_2) = -2A_2, T(A_3) = 3A_3,$

$T(A_4) = -3A_4, \begin{bmatrix} 2 & 0 & 0 & 0 \\ 0 & -2 & 0 & 0 \\ 0 & 0 & 3 & 0 \\ 0 & 0 & 0 & -3 \end{bmatrix}$

5. $\begin{bmatrix} 1 & -1 & -1 \\ 1 & -1 & 0 \\ -1 & 2 & 1 \end{bmatrix}$;

$p(x) = (1 + x - x^2) + (1 + x^2);$
$q(x) = -5(1 + x - x^2) - 3(1 + x^2) + 7(1 + x);$
$s(x) = -2(1 + x - x^2) - (1 + x^2) + 2(1 + x);$
$r(x) = (a_0 - a_1 - a_2)(1 + x - x^2) + (a_0 - a_1)(1 + x^2) + (-a_0 + 2a_1 + a_2)(1 + x)$

7. $\begin{bmatrix} 1/3 & 5/3 \\ 1/3 & -1/3 \end{bmatrix}$

9. $\begin{bmatrix} -1 & 1 & 2 & 3 \\ 1 & 0 & 0 & -3 \\ 0 & 0 & 1 & 0 \\ 0 & 0 & 0 & 1 \end{bmatrix}$

$p(x) = -7x + 2(x + 1) + (x^2 - 2x);$
$q(x) = 13x - 4(x + 1) + (x^3 + 3);$
$r(x) = -7x + 3(x + 1) - 2(x^2 - 2x) + (x^3 + 3)$

11. The matrix of T with respect to B is $Q_1 = \begin{bmatrix} 2 & 1 \\ 1 & 2 \end{bmatrix}$. The transition matrix from C to B is $P = \begin{bmatrix} -1 & 1 \\ 1 & 1 \end{bmatrix}$. The matrix of T with respect to C is Q_2, where $Q_2 = P^{-1}Q_1P = \begin{bmatrix} 1 & 0 \\ 0 & 3 \end{bmatrix}$.

13. The matrix of T with respect to B is $Q_1 = \begin{bmatrix} -3 & 0 & 0 & 5 \\ 0 & 3 & -5 & 0 \\ 0 & 0 & -2 & 0 \\ 0 & 0 & 0 & 2 \end{bmatrix}$. This transition matrix from C to B is $P = \begin{bmatrix} 1 & 0 & 0 & 1 \\ 0 & 1 & 1 & 0 \\ 0 & 1 & 0 & 0 \\ 1 & 0 & 0 & 0 \end{bmatrix}$. The matrix of T with respect to C is Q_2, where $Q_2 = P^{-1}Q_1P = \begin{bmatrix} 2 & 0 & 0 & 0 \\ 0 & -2 & 0 & 0 \\ 0 & 0 & 3 & 0 \\ 0 & 0 & 0 & -3 \end{bmatrix}$.

15. a) $Q = \begin{bmatrix} 1 & 1 & 0 \\ 0 & 2 & 4 \\ 0 & 0 & 3 \end{bmatrix}$;

b) $S = \begin{bmatrix} 1 & 1 & 2 \\ 0 & 1 & 4 \\ 0 & 0 & 1 \end{bmatrix}$; $R = \begin{bmatrix} 1 & 0 & 0 \\ 0 & 2 & 0 \\ 0 & 0 & 3 \end{bmatrix}$;

c) $C = \{1, 1 + x, 2 + 4x + x^2\}$;

d) $P = \begin{bmatrix} 1 & -1 & 2 \\ 0 & 1 & -4 \\ 0 & 0 & 1 \end{bmatrix}$;

e) $T(\mathbf{w}_1) = -1 + 18x + 3x^2;$
$T(\mathbf{w}_2) = 5 + 4x + 3x^2;$
$T(\mathbf{w}_3) = 1 + 2x + 6x^2$

CHAPTER 6

Exercises 6.2, p. 453

1. -5

3. $0, \mathbf{x} = \begin{bmatrix} -2 \\ 1 \end{bmatrix}$

5. 25

7. 6

9. $A_{11} = -2, A_{12} = 6, A_{13} = -2, A_{33} = 1$

11. $A_{11} = -2, A_{12} = 7, A_{13} = -8, A_{33} = 3$

13. $A_{11} = 3, A_{12} = -6, A_{13} = 2, A_{33} = -3$

15. 8

17. −35

19. −11

21. −9

23. 22

29. $C = \begin{bmatrix} 10 & 5 & -10 \\ -5 & -1 & 4 \\ -5 & -3 & 7 \end{bmatrix}$

35. a) $H(n) = n!/2$;

b) 3 seconds for $n = 2$; 180 seconds for $n = 5$; 5,443,200 seconds for $n = 10$

Exercises 6.3, p. 463

1. $$\begin{vmatrix} 1 & 2 & 1 \\ 2 & 0 & 1 \\ 1 & -1 & 1 \end{vmatrix} = \begin{vmatrix} 1 & 0 & 0 \\ 2 & -4 & -1 \\ 1 & -3 & 0 \end{vmatrix} = \begin{vmatrix} -4 & -1 \\ -3 & 0 \end{vmatrix}$$
$$= -3$$

3. $$\begin{vmatrix} 0 & 1 & 2 \\ 3 & 1 & 2 \\ 2 & 0 & 3 \end{vmatrix} = -\begin{vmatrix} 1 & 0 & 2 \\ 1 & 3 & 2 \\ 0 & 2 & 3 \end{vmatrix} = -\begin{vmatrix} 1 & 0 & 0 \\ 1 & 3 & 0 \\ 0 & 2 & 3 \end{vmatrix}$$
$$= -\begin{vmatrix} 3 & 0 \\ 2 & 3 \end{vmatrix} = -9$$

5. $$\begin{vmatrix} 0 & 1 & 3 \\ 2 & 1 & 2 \\ 1 & 1 & 2 \end{vmatrix} = -\begin{vmatrix} 1 & 0 & 3 \\ 1 & 2 & 2 \\ 1 & 1 & 2 \end{vmatrix} = -\begin{vmatrix} 1 & 0 & 0 \\ 1 & 2 & -1 \\ 1 & 1 & -1 \end{vmatrix}$$
$$= -\begin{vmatrix} 2 & -1 \\ 1 & -1 \end{vmatrix} = 1$$

7. −6

9. 3

11. 3

13. Use the column interchanges: $[C_1, C_2, C_3, C_4] \rightarrow [C_1, C_4, C_3, C_2] \rightarrow [C_1, C_4, C_2, C_3]$; the determinant is 6.

15. Use the column interchanges: $[C_1, C_2, C_3, C_4] \rightarrow [C_2, C_1, C_3, C_4] \rightarrow [C_2, C_4, C_3, C_1] \rightarrow [C_2, C_4, C_1, C_3]$; the determinant is −12.

17. $$\begin{vmatrix} 2 & 4 & -2 & -2 \\ 1 & 3 & 1 & 2 \\ 1 & 3 & 1 & 3 \\ -1 & 2 & 1 & 2 \end{vmatrix} = \begin{vmatrix} 2 & 0 & 0 & 0 \\ 1 & 1 & 2 & 3 \\ 1 & 1 & 2 & 4 \\ -1 & 4 & 0 & 1 \end{vmatrix}$$
$$= 2\begin{vmatrix} 1 & 2 & 3 \\ 1 & 2 & 4 \\ 4 & 0 & 1 \end{vmatrix} = 2\begin{vmatrix} 1 & 0 & 0 \\ 1 & 0 & 1 \\ 4 & -8 & -11 \end{vmatrix}$$
$$= 2\begin{vmatrix} 0 & 1 \\ -8 & -11 \end{vmatrix} = 16$$

19. $$\begin{vmatrix} 1 & 2 & 0 & 3 \\ 2 & 5 & 1 & 1 \\ 2 & 0 & 4 & 3 \\ 0 & 1 & 6 & 2 \end{vmatrix} = \begin{vmatrix} 1 & 2 & 0 & 3 \\ 0 & 1 & 1 & -5 \\ 0 & -4 & 4 & -3 \\ 0 & 1 & 6 & 2 \end{vmatrix}$$
$$= \begin{vmatrix} 1 & 1 & -5 \\ -4 & 4 & -3 \\ 1 & 6 & 2 \end{vmatrix} = \begin{vmatrix} 1 & 1 & -5 \\ 0 & 8 & -23 \\ 0 & 5 & 7 \end{vmatrix}$$
$$= \begin{vmatrix} 8 & -23 \\ 5 & 7 \end{vmatrix} = 171$$

21. $$\begin{vmatrix} 1 & 1 & 2 & 1 \\ 0 & 1 & 4 & 1 \\ 2 & 1 & 3 & 0 \\ 2 & 2 & 1 & 2 \end{vmatrix} = \begin{vmatrix} 1 & 1 & 2 & 1 \\ 0 & 1 & 4 & 1 \\ 0 & -1 & -1 & -2 \\ 0 & 0 & -3 & 0 \end{vmatrix}$$
$$= \begin{vmatrix} 1 & 4 & 1 \\ -1 & -1 & -2 \\ 0 & -3 & 0 \end{vmatrix} = \begin{vmatrix} 1 & 4 & 1 \\ 0 & 3 & -1 \\ 0 & -3 & 0 \end{vmatrix}$$
$$= \begin{vmatrix} 3 & -1 \\ -3 & 0 \end{vmatrix} = -3$$

Exercises 6.4, p. 470

1. $$A \rightarrow \begin{bmatrix} 1 & 0 & 3 \\ 2 & 1 & 1 \\ 4 & 3 & 1 \end{bmatrix} \rightarrow \begin{bmatrix} 1 & 0 & 0 \\ 2 & 1 & -5 \\ 4 & 3 & -11 \end{bmatrix} \rightarrow$$
$$\begin{bmatrix} 1 & 0 & 0 \\ 2 & 1 & 0 \\ 4 & 3 & 4 \end{bmatrix}; \ \det(A) = -4.$$

3. $A \to \begin{bmatrix} 2 & 0 & 0 \\ 1 & 2 & 2 \\ -1 & 3 & 3 \end{bmatrix} \to \begin{bmatrix} 2 & 0 & 0 \\ 1 & 2 & 0 \\ -1 & 3 & 0 \end{bmatrix}$;

$\det(A) = 0$.

5. $A \to \begin{bmatrix} 1 & 0 & 0 \\ 3 & 1 & 9 \\ 0 & 1 & 2 \end{bmatrix} \to \begin{bmatrix} 1 & 0 & 0 \\ 3 & 1 & 0 \\ 0 & 1 & -7 \end{bmatrix} \to$

$\begin{bmatrix} 1 & 0 & 0 \\ 0 & 1 & 0 \\ 0 & 0 & -7 \end{bmatrix} \to I$; $\det(A) = -7$.

7. a) 6; **b)** 18; **c)** 3/2; **d)** 4; **e)** 1/16

9. $\det[B(\lambda)] = -\lambda^2 + 2\lambda$; $\lambda = 0$ and $\lambda = 2$

11. $\det[B(\lambda)] = 4 - \lambda^2$; $\lambda = 2$ and $\lambda = -2$

13. $\det[B(\lambda)] = (\lambda + 2)(\lambda - 1)^2$; $\lambda = -2$ and $\lambda = 1$

15. $\det(A) = -2$, $\det(B_1) = -2$, $\det(B_2) = -4$; $x_1 = 1, x_2 = 2$

17. $\det(A) = -2$, $\det(B_1) = -8$, $\det(B_2) = -4$, $\det(B_3) = 2$; $x_1 = 4, x_2 = 2, x_3 = -1$

19. $\det(A) = \det(B_1) = \det(B_2) = \det(B_3) = \det(B_4) = 3$; $x_1 = x_2 = x_3 = x_4 = 1$

21. $\det(A) = 1$, $\det(B_1) = a - b$, $\det(B_2) = b - c$, $\det(B_3) = c$; $x_1 = a - b$, $x_2 = b - c$, $x_3 = c$

27. $\det(A^5) = [\det(A)]^5 = 3^5 = 243$

Exercises 6.5, p. 478

1. $\begin{vmatrix} 1 & 2 & 1 \\ 2 & 3 & 2 \\ -1 & 4 & 1 \end{vmatrix} = \begin{vmatrix} 1 & 2 & 1 \\ 0 & -1 & 0 \\ 0 & 6 & 2 \end{vmatrix} = \begin{vmatrix} 1 & 2 & 1 \\ 0 & -1 & 0 \\ 0 & 0 & 2 \end{vmatrix} = -2$

3. $\begin{vmatrix} 0 & 1 & 3 \\ 1 & 2 & 2 \\ 3 & 1 & 0 \end{vmatrix} = -\begin{vmatrix} 1 & 2 & 2 \\ 0 & 1 & 3 \\ 3 & 1 & 0 \end{vmatrix} = -\begin{vmatrix} 1 & 2 & 2 \\ 0 & 1 & 3 \\ 0 & -5 & -6 \end{vmatrix} = -\begin{vmatrix} 1 & 2 & 2 \\ 0 & 1 & 3 \\ 0 & 0 & 9 \end{vmatrix} = -9$

5. $\text{Adj}(A) = \begin{bmatrix} 4 & -2 \\ -3 & 1 \end{bmatrix}$; $A^{-1} = -\frac{1}{2}\text{Adj}(A)$

7. $\text{Adj}(A) = \begin{bmatrix} 0 & 1 & -1 \\ -2 & 1 & 0 \\ 1 & -1 & 1 \end{bmatrix}$; $A^{-1} = \text{Adj}(A)$

9. $\text{Adj}(A) = \begin{bmatrix} -4 & 2 & 0 \\ 1 & 0 & -1 \\ 1 & -2 & 1 \end{bmatrix}$; $A^{-1} = -\frac{1}{2}\text{Adj}(A)$

11. For all x, $w(x) = 2$; therefore, the set is linearly independent.

13. For all x, $w(x) = 0$; the Wronskian gives no information; the set is linearly dependent since $\cos^2 x + \sin^2 x = 1$.

15. For all x, $w(x) = 0$; the Wronskian gives no information; the set is linearly independent.

17. $L = \begin{bmatrix} 1 & 0 & 0 \\ 2 & 1 & 0 \\ 2 & 2 & -1 \end{bmatrix}$, $E_1 = \begin{bmatrix} 0 & 1 & 0 \\ 1 & 0 & 0 \\ 0 & 0 & 1 \end{bmatrix}$,

$E_2 = \begin{bmatrix} 1 & 0 & -3 \\ 0 & 1 & 0 \\ 0 & 0 & 1 \end{bmatrix}$, $E_3 = \begin{bmatrix} 1 & 0 & 0 \\ 0 & 1 & 2 \\ 0 & 0 & 1 \end{bmatrix}$

19. $L = \begin{bmatrix} 1 & 0 & 0 \\ 3 & -1 & 0 \\ 4 & -8 & -26 \end{bmatrix}$, $E_1 = \begin{bmatrix} 1 & -2 & 0 \\ 0 & 1 & 0 \\ 0 & 0 & 1 \end{bmatrix}$,

$E_2 = \begin{bmatrix} 1 & 0 & 1 \\ 0 & 1 & 0 \\ 0 & 0 & 1 \end{bmatrix}$, $E_3 = \begin{bmatrix} 1 & 0 & 0 \\ 0 & 1 & 4 \\ 0 & 0 & 1 \end{bmatrix}$,

21. $\det[A(x)] = x^2 + 1$; $[A(x)]^{-1} = \dfrac{1}{x^2+1}\begin{bmatrix} x & -1 \\ 1 & x \end{bmatrix}$

23. $\det[A(x)] = 4(2 + x^2)$;

$[A(x)]^{-1} = \dfrac{1}{4(2+x^2)}\begin{bmatrix} 4+x^2 & -2x & x^2 \\ 2x & 4 & -2x \\ x^2 & 2x & 4+x^2 \end{bmatrix}$

CHAPTER 7

Exercises 7.1, p. 492

1. $A = \begin{bmatrix} 2 & 2 \\ 2 & -3 \end{bmatrix}$

3. $A = \begin{bmatrix} 1 & 1 & -3 \\ 1 & -4 & 4 \\ -3 & 4 & 3 \end{bmatrix}$ **5.** $A = \begin{bmatrix} 2 & 2 \\ 2 & 1 \end{bmatrix}$

7. $Q = \frac{1}{\sqrt{2}}\begin{bmatrix} 1 & 1 \\ 1 & -1 \end{bmatrix}$; the form is indefinite with eigenvalues $\lambda = 5$ and $\lambda = -1$.

9. $Q = \frac{1}{\sqrt{6}}\begin{bmatrix} \sqrt{2} & \sqrt{3} & -1 \\ \sqrt{2} & -\sqrt{3} & -1 \\ \sqrt{2} & 0 & 2 \end{bmatrix}$; the form is indefinite with eigenvalues $\lambda = 5$ and $\lambda = -1$.

11. $Q = \frac{1}{\sqrt{2}}\begin{bmatrix} 1 & 1 \\ 1 & -1 \end{bmatrix}$; the form is positive definite with eigenvalues $\lambda = 2$ and $\lambda = 4$.

13. $Q = \begin{bmatrix} 1/2 & \sqrt{3}/2 \\ -\sqrt{3}/2 & 1/2 \end{bmatrix}$; the graph corresponds to the ellipse $\frac{u^2}{20} + \frac{v^2}{4} = 1$.

15. $Q = \frac{1}{\sqrt{10}}\begin{bmatrix} -1 & 3 \\ 3 & 1 \end{bmatrix}$; the graph corresponds to the hyperbola $\frac{v^2}{4} - u^2 = 1$.

17. $Q = \frac{1}{\sqrt{2}}\begin{bmatrix} 1 & -1 \\ 1 & 1 \end{bmatrix}$; the graph corresponds to the hyperbola $\frac{u^2}{4} - \frac{v^2}{4} = 1$.

19. $Q = \frac{1}{\sqrt{2}}\begin{bmatrix} 1 & 1 \\ -1 & 1 \end{bmatrix}$; the graph corresponds to the ellipse $\frac{u^2}{4} + \frac{v^2}{8} = 1$.

Exercises 7.2, p. 501

1. $\mathbf{x}'(t) = A\mathbf{x}(t)$, $A = \begin{bmatrix} 5 & -2 \\ 6 & -2 \end{bmatrix}$, $\mathbf{x}(t) = \begin{bmatrix} u(t) \\ v(t) \end{bmatrix}$;

$\mathbf{x}(t) = b_1 e^t \begin{bmatrix} 1 \\ 2 \end{bmatrix} + b_2 e^{2t} \begin{bmatrix} 2 \\ 3 \end{bmatrix}$;

$\mathbf{x}(t) = e^t \begin{bmatrix} 1 \\ 2 \end{bmatrix} + 2e^{2t} \begin{bmatrix} 2 \\ 3 \end{bmatrix} = \begin{bmatrix} e^t + 4e^{2t} \\ 2e^t + 6e^{2t} \end{bmatrix}$

3. $\mathbf{x}'(t) = A\mathbf{x}(t)$, $A = \begin{bmatrix} 1 & 1 \\ 2 & 2 \end{bmatrix}$, $\mathbf{x}(t) = \begin{bmatrix} u(t) \\ v(t) \end{bmatrix}$;

$\mathbf{x}(t) = b_1 \begin{bmatrix} 1 \\ -1 \end{bmatrix} + b_2 e^{3t} \begin{bmatrix} 1 \\ 2 \end{bmatrix}$;

$\mathbf{x}(t) = 3 \begin{bmatrix} 1 \\ -1 \end{bmatrix} + 2e^{3t} \begin{bmatrix} 1 \\ 2 \end{bmatrix} = \begin{bmatrix} 3 + 2e^{3t} \\ -3 + 4e^{3t} \end{bmatrix}$

5. $\mathbf{x}'(t) = A\mathbf{x}(t)$, $A = \begin{bmatrix} .5 & .5 \\ -.5 & .5 \end{bmatrix}$, $\mathbf{x}(t) = \begin{bmatrix} u(t) \\ v(t) \end{bmatrix}$;

$\mathbf{x}(t) = b_1 e^{(1+i)t/2} \begin{bmatrix} 1 \\ i \end{bmatrix} + b_2 e^{(1-i)t/2} \begin{bmatrix} 1 \\ -i \end{bmatrix}$;

$b_1 = 2 - 2i$ and $b_2 = 2 + 2i$, or $\mathbf{x}(t) = 4e^{t/2} \begin{bmatrix} \cos(t/2) + \sin(t/2) \\ \cos(t/2) - \sin(t/2) \end{bmatrix}$

7. $\mathbf{x}'(t) = A\mathbf{x}(t)$, $A = \begin{bmatrix} 4 & 0 & 1 \\ -2 & 1 & 0 \\ -2 & 0 & 1 \end{bmatrix}$,

$\mathbf{x}(t) = \begin{bmatrix} u(t) \\ v(t) \\ w(t) \end{bmatrix}$;

$\mathbf{x}(t) = b_1 e^t \begin{bmatrix} 0 \\ 1 \\ 0 \end{bmatrix} + b_2 e^{2t} \begin{bmatrix} -1 \\ 2 \\ 2 \end{bmatrix} + b_3 e^{3t} \begin{bmatrix} -1 \\ 1 \\ 1 \end{bmatrix}$;

$\mathbf{x}(t) = e^t \begin{bmatrix} 1 \\ 1 \\ 0 \end{bmatrix} - e^{2t} \begin{bmatrix} -1 \\ 2 \\ 2 \end{bmatrix} + 2e^{3t} \begin{bmatrix} -1 \\ 1 \\ 1 \end{bmatrix}$

$= \begin{bmatrix} & e^{2t} - 2e^{3t} \\ e^t - & 2e^{2t} + 2e^{3t} \\ & -2e^{2t} + 2e^{3t} \end{bmatrix}$

9. a) $\mathbf{x}'(t) = A\mathbf{x}(t)$, $A = \begin{bmatrix} 1 & -1 \\ 1 & 3 \end{bmatrix}$,

$\mathbf{x}(t) = \begin{bmatrix} u(t) \\ v(t) \end{bmatrix}$; $x_1(t) = b_1 e^{2t} \begin{bmatrix} 1 \\ -1 \end{bmatrix}$

b) The vector $\mathbf{y}_0$ is determined by the equation $(A - 2I)\mathbf{y} = \mathbf{u}$, where $\mathbf{u} = \begin{bmatrix} 1 \\ -1 \end{bmatrix}$. One choice is $\mathbf{y}_0 = \begin{bmatrix} -2 \\ 1 \end{bmatrix}$. Thus,

$\mathbf{x}_2(t) = te^{2t} \begin{bmatrix} 1 \\ -1 \end{bmatrix} + e^{2t} \begin{bmatrix} -2 \\ 1 \end{bmatrix}$ is another solution of $\mathbf{x}'(t) = A\mathbf{x}(t)$.

c) Note that $\mathbf{x}_1(0) = \begin{bmatrix} 1 \\ -1 \end{bmatrix}$ and $\mathbf{x}_2(0) = \begin{bmatrix} -2 \\ 1 \end{bmatrix}$. Thus, $\{\mathbf{x}_1(0), \mathbf{x}_2(0)\}$ is a basis for R^2.

Exercises 7.3, p. 509

1. $H = Q_1 A Q_1^{-1} = \begin{bmatrix} -7 & 16 & 3 \\ 8 & 9 & 3 \\ 0 & 1 & 1 \end{bmatrix}$;

$Q_1 = \begin{bmatrix} 1 & 0 & 0 \\ 0 & 1 & 0 \\ 0 & -4 & 1 \end{bmatrix}$

3. $H = Q_1 A Q_1^{-1} = \begin{bmatrix} 1 & 1 & 3 \\ 1 & 3 & 1 \\ 0 & 4 & 2 \end{bmatrix}$;

$Q_1 = \begin{bmatrix} 1 & 0 & 0 \\ 0 & 0 & 1 \\ 0 & 1 & 0 \end{bmatrix}$

5. $H = Q_1 A Q_1^{-1} = \begin{bmatrix} 3 & 2 & -1 \\ 4 & 5 & -2 \\ 0 & 20 & -6 \end{bmatrix}$;

$Q_1 = \begin{bmatrix} 1 & 0 & 0 \\ 0 & 1 & 0 \\ 0 & 3 & 1 \end{bmatrix}$

7. $H = Q_1 A Q_1^{-1} = \begin{bmatrix} 1 & -3 & -1 & -1 \\ -1 & -1 & -1 & -1 \\ 0 & 0 & 2 & 0 \\ 0 & 0 & 0 & 2 \end{bmatrix}$;

$Q_1 = \begin{bmatrix} 1 & 0 & 0 & 0 \\ 0 & 1 & 0 & 0 \\ 0 & -1 & 1 & 0 \\ 0 & -1 & 0 & 1 \end{bmatrix}$

9. $H = Q_2 Q_1 A Q_1^{-1} Q_2^{-1} = \begin{bmatrix} 1 & 3 & 5 & 2 \\ 1 & 2 & 4 & 2 \\ 0 & 1 & 7 & 3 \\ 0 & 0 & -11 & -5 \end{bmatrix}$;

$Q_1 = \begin{bmatrix} 1 & 0 & 0 & 0 \\ 0 & 0 & 0 & 1 \\ 0 & 0 & 1 & 0 \\ 0 & 1 & 0 & 0 \end{bmatrix}$,

$Q_2 = \begin{bmatrix} 1 & 0 & 0 & 0 \\ 0 & 1 & 0 & 0 \\ 0 & 0 & 1 & 0 \\ 0 & 0 & -2 & 1 \end{bmatrix}$

13. The characteristic polynomial is $p(t) = (t+2)(t-2)^3$.

15. $[\mathbf{e}_1, \mathbf{e}_2, \mathbf{e}_3]$, $[\mathbf{e}_1, \mathbf{e}_3, \mathbf{e}_2]$, $[\mathbf{e}_2, \mathbf{e}_1, \mathbf{e}_3]$, $[\mathbf{e}_2, \mathbf{e}_3, \mathbf{e}_1]$, $[\mathbf{e}_3, \mathbf{e}_1, \mathbf{e}_2]$, $[\mathbf{e}_3, \mathbf{e}_2, \mathbf{e}_1]$

17. $n!$

Exercises 7.4, p. 518

1. The system (4) is

$$\begin{aligned} a_0 + 2a_1 &= -4 \\ a_1 &= -3 \end{aligned}; \quad p(t) = t^2 - 3t + 2$$

3. The system (4) is

$$\begin{aligned} a_0 + a_1 + a_2 &= -3 \\ 2a_1 + 4a_2 &= -6; \quad p(t) = t^3 - 4t^2 + 5t - 4 \\ 2a_2 &= -8 \end{aligned}$$

5. The system (4) is

$$\begin{aligned} a_0 + 2a_1 + 8a_2 &= -29 \\ a_1 + 3a_2 &= -14; \\ a_2 &= -8 \end{aligned}$$

$p(t) = t^3 - 8t^2 + 10t + 15$

7. The system (4) is

$$\begin{aligned} a_0 \quad + a_2 + 2a_3 &= -8 \\ a_1 + 2a_2 + 6a_3 &= -18 \\ a_2 + 2a_3 &= -8 \\ 2a_3 &= -6 \end{aligned}$$

$p(t) = t^4 - 3t^3 - 2t^2 + 4t$

9. The blocks are $B_{11} = \begin{bmatrix} 1 & -1 \\ 1 & 3 \end{bmatrix}$ and $B_{22} = \begin{bmatrix} 2 & -1 \\ -1 & 2 \end{bmatrix}$. The only eigenvalue of B_{11} is $\lambda = 2$; the eigenvalues of B_{22} are $\lambda = 1$ and $\lambda = 3$. The eigenvectors are $\lambda = 2$, $\mathbf{u} = [1, -1, 0, 0]^T$; $\lambda = 1$, $\mathbf{u} = [-9, 5, 1, 1]^T$; and $\lambda = 3$, $\mathbf{u} = [3, -9, 1, -1]^T$.

11. The blocks are $B_{11} = \begin{bmatrix} -2 & 0 & -2 \\ -1 & 1 & -2 \\ 0 & 1 & -1 \end{bmatrix}$ and $B_{22} =$ [2]. The eigenvalues of B_{11} are $\lambda = 0$ and $\lambda = -1$; the eigenvalue of B_{22} is $\lambda = 2$. The eigenvectors are $\lambda = 0$, $\mathbf{u} = [-1, 1, 1, 0]^T$; $\lambda = -1$, $\mathbf{u} = [2, 0, -1.0]^T$; and $\lambda = 2$, $\mathbf{u} = [1, 15, 1, 6]^T$.

15. $P = [\mathbf{e}_2, \mathbf{e}_3, \mathbf{e}_1]$

Exercises 7.5, p. 529

1. $Q\mathbf{x} = \mathbf{x} + \mathbf{u} = [4, 1, 6, 7]^T$

3. $Q\mathbf{A}_1 = \mathbf{A}_1 + \mathbf{u}$, $Q\mathbf{A}_2 = \mathbf{A}_2 + 2\mathbf{u}$; therefore,

$$QA = \begin{bmatrix} 3 & 3 \\ 5 & 1 \\ 5 & 4 \\ 1 & 2 \end{bmatrix}$$

5. $\mathbf{x}^T Q = \mathbf{x}^T + \mathbf{u}^T = [4, 1, 3, 4]$

7. $AQ = \begin{bmatrix} 1 & 2 & 1 & 2 \\ 2 & -1 & 2 & 3 \end{bmatrix}$

9. $\mathbf{u} = \begin{bmatrix} 0 \\ 5 \\ 2 \\ 1 \end{bmatrix}$ **11.** $\mathbf{u} = \begin{bmatrix} 0 \\ 0 \\ 9 \\ 3 \end{bmatrix}$

13. $\mathbf{u} = \begin{bmatrix} 0 \\ 0 \\ 0 \\ -8 \\ 4 \end{bmatrix}$ **15.** $\mathbf{u} = \begin{bmatrix} 0 \\ 8 \\ 4 \end{bmatrix}$

17. $\mathbf{u} = \begin{bmatrix} 0 \\ -9 \\ 3 \end{bmatrix}$ **19.** $\mathbf{u} = \begin{bmatrix} 0 \\ 0 \\ -8 \\ 4 \end{bmatrix}$

Exercises 7.6, p. 539

1. $\mathbf{x}^* = \begin{bmatrix} 1 \\ 1 \end{bmatrix}$

3. $\mathbf{x}^* = \begin{bmatrix} 2 \\ 1 \\ 2 \end{bmatrix}$

5. $R = \begin{bmatrix} -5 & -11 \\ 0 & 2 \end{bmatrix}$, $\mathbf{u} = \begin{bmatrix} 8 \\ 4 \end{bmatrix}$

7. $R = \begin{bmatrix} -4 & -6 \\ 0 & -2 \end{bmatrix}$, $\mathbf{u} = \begin{bmatrix} 4 \\ 4 \end{bmatrix}$

9. $R = \begin{bmatrix} 1 & 2 & 1 \\ 0 & -1 & -8 \\ 0 & 0 & -6 \end{bmatrix}$, $\mathbf{u} = \begin{bmatrix} 0 \\ 1 \\ 1 \end{bmatrix}$

11. $Q_2 Q_1 A = \begin{bmatrix} -5 & -59/3 \\ 0 & -7 \\ 0 & 0 \\ 0 & 0 \end{bmatrix}$,

where $\mathbf{u}_1 = \begin{bmatrix} 6 \\ 2 \\ 2 \\ 4 \end{bmatrix}$, $\mathbf{u}_2 = \begin{bmatrix} 0 \\ 13 \\ 2 \\ 3 \end{bmatrix}$

13. $Q_1 A = \begin{bmatrix} 2 & 4 \\ 0 & -5 \\ 0 & 0 \\ 0 & 0 \end{bmatrix}$, where $\mathbf{u}_1 = \begin{bmatrix} 0 \\ 8 \\ 0 \\ 4 \end{bmatrix}$

15. $\mathbf{x}^* = \begin{bmatrix} -38/21 \\ 15/21 \end{bmatrix}$

17. $\mathbf{x}^* = \begin{bmatrix} -87/25 \\ 56/25 \end{bmatrix}$

Exercises 7.7, p. 545

1. $q(A) = \begin{bmatrix} -1 & 0 \\ 0 & -1 \end{bmatrix}$; $q(B) = \begin{bmatrix} 0 & 0 \\ 0 & 0 \end{bmatrix}$;

$$q(C) = \begin{bmatrix} 15 & -2 & 14 \\ 5 & -2 & 10 \\ -1 & -4 & 6 \end{bmatrix}$$

3. a) $q(t) = (t^3 + t - 1)p(t) + t + 2$;

b) $q(B) = B + 2I = \begin{bmatrix} 4 & -1 \\ -1 & 4 \end{bmatrix}$

Exercises 7.8, p. 553

1. a) $p(t) = (t-2)^2$; $\mathbf{v}_1 = \begin{bmatrix} 1 \\ -1 \end{bmatrix}$, $\mathbf{v}_2 = \begin{bmatrix} 1 \\ -2 \end{bmatrix}$

b) $p(t) = t(t+1)^2$; for $\lambda = -1$,

$$\mathbf{v}_1 = \begin{bmatrix} -2 \\ 0 \\ 1 \end{bmatrix}, \quad \mathbf{v}_2 = \begin{bmatrix} 0 \\ 1 \\ 1 \end{bmatrix}; \quad \text{for } \lambda = 0,$$

$$\mathbf{v}_1 = \begin{bmatrix} -1 \\ 1 \\ 1 \end{bmatrix}$$

c) $p(t) = t(t-1)^2(t+1)$; for $\lambda = 1$,

$$\mathbf{v}_1 = \begin{bmatrix} -2 \\ 0 \\ 1 \end{bmatrix}, \quad \mathbf{v}_2 = \begin{bmatrix} 5/2 \\ 1/2 \\ 0 \end{bmatrix};$$

for $\lambda = -1$, $\mathbf{v}_1 = \begin{bmatrix} -9 \\ -1 \\ 1 \end{bmatrix}$

3. a) $QAQ^{-1} = H$, where $Q = \begin{bmatrix} 1 & 0 & 0 \\ 0 & 1 & 0 \\ 0 & 3 & 1 \end{bmatrix}$,

$$H = \begin{bmatrix} 8 & -69 & 21 \\ 1 & -10 & 3 \\ 0 & -4 & 1 \end{bmatrix},$$

$$Q^{-1} = \begin{bmatrix} 1 & 0 & 0 \\ 0 & 1 & 0 \\ 0 & -3 & 1 \end{bmatrix}$$

The characteristic polynomial for H is $p(t) = (t+1)^2(t-1)$; and the eigenvectors and generalized eigenvectors are

$$\lambda = -1, \quad \mathbf{v}_1 = \begin{bmatrix} 3 \\ 1 \\ 2 \end{bmatrix}, \quad \mathbf{v}_2 = \begin{bmatrix} -7/2 \\ -1/2 \\ 0 \end{bmatrix};$$

$$\lambda = 1, \quad \mathbf{w}_1 = \begin{bmatrix} -3 \\ 0 \\ 1 \end{bmatrix}.$$

The general solution of $\mathbf{y}' = H\mathbf{y}$ is $\mathbf{y}(t) = c_1e^{-t}\mathbf{v}_1 + c_2e^{-t}(\mathbf{v}_2 + t\mathbf{v}_1) + c_3e^t\mathbf{w}_1$; and the initial condition $\mathbf{y}(0) = Q\mathbf{x}_0$ can be met by choosing $c_1 = 0$, $c_2 = 2$, $c_3 = -2$.

Finally $\mathbf{x}(t) = Q^{-1}\mathbf{y}(t)$, or

$$\mathbf{x}(t) = \begin{bmatrix} e^{-t}(6t-7) + 6e^t \\ e^{-t}(2t-1) \\ e^{-t}(-2t+3) - 2e^t \end{bmatrix}.$$

b) $QAQ^{-1} = H$, where

$$Q = \begin{bmatrix} 1 & 0 & 0 \\ 0 & 1 & 0 \\ 0 & 3 & 1 \end{bmatrix}, H = \begin{bmatrix} 2 & 4 & -1 \\ -3 & -4 & 1 \\ 0 & 3 & -1 \end{bmatrix},$$

$$Q^{-1} = \begin{bmatrix} 1 & 0 & 0 \\ 0 & 1 & 0 \\ 0 & -3 & 1 \end{bmatrix}.$$

The characteristic polynomial is $p(t) = (t+1)^3$; and

$$\mathbf{v}_1 = \begin{bmatrix} 1 \\ 0 \\ 3 \end{bmatrix}, \quad \mathbf{v}_2 = \begin{bmatrix} 0 \\ 1 \\ 3 \end{bmatrix}, \quad \mathbf{v}_3 = \begin{bmatrix} 0 \\ 1 \\ 4 \end{bmatrix}.$$

The general solution of $\mathbf{y}' = H\mathbf{y}$ is

$$\mathbf{y}(t) = e^{-t}\left[c_1\mathbf{v}_1 + c_2(\mathbf{v}_2 + t\mathbf{v}_1) + c_3\left(\mathbf{v}_3 + t\mathbf{v}_2 + \frac{t^2}{2}\mathbf{v}_1\right)\right];$$

and the initial condition $\mathbf{y}(0) = Q\mathbf{x}_0$ is met with $c_1 = -1$, $c_2 = -5$, $c_3 = 4$. Finally $Q^{-1}\mathbf{y}(t)$ solves $\mathbf{x}' = A\mathbf{x}$, $\mathbf{x}(0) = \mathbf{x}_0$.

c) $QAQ^{-1} = H$, where

$$Q = \begin{bmatrix} 1 & 0 & 0 \\ 0 & 1 & 0 \\ 0 & 3 & 1 \end{bmatrix}, H = \begin{bmatrix} 1 & 4 & -1 \\ -3 & -5 & 1 \\ 0 & 3 & -2 \end{bmatrix},$$

$$Q^{-1} = \begin{bmatrix} 1 & 0 & 0 \\ 0 & 1 & 0 \\ 0 & -3 & 1 \end{bmatrix}.$$

The characteristic polynomial is $p(t) = (t+2)^3$; and

$$\mathbf{v}_1 = \begin{bmatrix} 1 \\ 0 \\ 3 \end{bmatrix}, \quad \mathbf{v}_2 = \begin{bmatrix} 0 \\ 1 \\ 3 \end{bmatrix}, \quad \mathbf{v}_3 = \begin{bmatrix} 0 \\ 1 \\ 4 \end{bmatrix}.$$

The general solution of $\mathbf{y}' = H\mathbf{y}$ is

$$\mathbf{y}(t) = e^{-2t}\left[c_1\mathbf{v}_1 + c_2(\mathbf{v}_2 + t\mathbf{v}_1) + c_3\left(\mathbf{v}_3 + t\mathbf{v}_2 + \frac{t^2}{2}\mathbf{v}_1\right)\right];$$

and the initial condition $\mathbf{y}(0) = Q\mathbf{x}_0$ is met with $c_1 = -1$, $c_2 = -5$, $c_3 = 4$. Finally $Q^{-1}\mathbf{y}(t)$ solves $\mathbf{x}' = A\mathbf{x}$, $\mathbf{x}(0) = \mathbf{x}_0$.

5. $$\mathbf{x}(t) = c_1e^t\begin{bmatrix} -2 \\ 0 \\ 1 \end{bmatrix} + c_2e^t\left(\begin{bmatrix} 5/2 \\ 1/2 \\ 0 \end{bmatrix} + t\begin{bmatrix} -2 \\ 0 \\ 1 \end{bmatrix}\right) + c_3e^{-t}\begin{bmatrix} -9 \\ -1 \\ 1 \end{bmatrix}$$

INDEX

Addition,
of linear transformations, 411
of matrices, 47
Additive identity, 363
Additive inverse, 363
Adjoint matrix, 473
Algebraic multiplicity, 300, 548
Algebraic vector(s), 114, 118, 131
Augmented matrix, 7

Basis, 189, 195, 378
change of, 431
coordinate vectors, 379
natural, 189
ordered, 380
orthogonal, 214, 395
orthonormal, 216
unique representation, 195
Block matrix, 109, 353
eigenvalues and, 353
upper-triangular, 353

$C[a, b]$, 364
Cancellation laws for
vector addition, 365
Cartesian coordinate system, 128
Cauchy–Schwarz inequality, 225
Cayley–Hamilton Theorem, 306, 540, 555
Change of basis, 431
matrix representation and, 435
transition matrix, 434
Characteristic equation, 300
Characteristic polynomial, 300
Chebyshev polynomials, 402
Cholesky decomposition, 554
Closure properties, 168
Coefficient matrix, 7
Cofactor expansions, 283, 288, 448
Collinearity, tests for, 145
Column form of a matrix, 55–56
Column space of a matrix, 182
Companion matrix, 306
Complex arithmetic, 316
Complex Eigenvalues, 315
Complex Eigenvectors, 315
Complex Gaussian elimination, 320
Complex numbers, 316
imaginary part, 316
magnitude, 317
real part, 316
Complex plane, 317
Complex vectors, 316
conjugate, 318
magnitude (norm), 318
Components, vector, 117, 131
Composition
of linear transformation, 412
Condition number, 110
Conjugate vector, 318
Consistent system, 6
solution set, 28
Contraction, 230
Coordinate vector, 379
Coordinates, 217, 375
of a vector, 195, 379
Coplanarity, tests for, 145
Cramer's rule, 281, 465
Cross product, 135, 141
algebraic properties of, 143
definition of, 141
determinants and, 142
finding normals with, 155
geometric properties of, 144

Data fitting, 80
Defective matrix, 310
Determinants, 285, 450
block matrices, 353
cofactor, 283, 449
cofactor expansion, 284, 448
Cramer's rule, 468
eigenvalue problems and, 300
elementary operations and, 290, 455
of matrix inverses, 471
of nonsingular matrices, 287, 467
of products, 287, 466
singular matrices, 287, 465
three-by-three, 282
of triangular matrices, 453
two-by-two, 278, 448
Vandermonde, 297
Wronskian, 471
Diagonalizable,
linear transformation, 431
matrix, 327
symmetric matrices, 333
Difference equations, 338
solution to, 340
Differential equations, 347, 493
Dilation, 230
Dimension, 202, 388
Distance formula, 256
Dot product, 50, 135
algebraic properties of, 137
definition of, 136
two vectors, 135

Echelon form, 14
Eigenspace, 307
Eigenvalues, 276, 298, 432
algebraic multiplicity, 300
characteristic equation, 300
characteristic polynomial, 300
complex, 315
computational considerations, 304, 508
conjugate pairs, 319
determinants and, 280
dominant, 354
eigenspace, 307
geometric multiplicity, 309
Hessenberg matrices and, 510
initial value problems, 495
MATLAB, 324
Rayleigh quotient, 352, 493
similar matrix, 327
singular matrix, 303

Eigenvalues (*Continued*)
symmetric matrices, 319
triangular matrix, 303
Eigenvectors, 276, 298, 307, 432
complex, 315
dominant, 354
eigenspace and, 307
generalized, 350, 546
linearly independent, 306, 312
symmetric matrices, 333
Electronic aids, 23
Elementary matrices, 476
Elementary operations
determinants and, 290, 455
effects of, 291
for linear systems, 8
for matrices, 10
notation, 10
Elementary row operations, 9
Ellipsoid, 491
Equal matrices, 46
Equality test
for geometric vectors, 117
Equations
consistent/inconsistent, 6
Equivalent systems, 8
Error function, 446
Euclidean n-space, 48

Fresnel integral, 446
Frobenius norm, 262
Full rank, 252

Gauss–Jordan elimination, 9, 12, 14
General solution, 23
Generalized eigenvectors, 350, 547
Geometric multiplicity, 309
Geometric vector(s), 114, 131
adding, 120, 132
angle between, 135, 137
calculating algebraic vectors for, 121
components, 117, 131
cross product, 135
dot product, 135
equality of, 115, 117
initial point, 115
initial/terminal point, 131
length of, 124, 132
magnitude of, 129
norm of **u**, 124
position, 116
scalar multiplication, 122, 132
subtracting, 123
terminal point, 115
unit, 124
zero, 72
Gram matrix, 444
Gram–Schmidt process, 219, 395

Hermite interpolation, 91
Hermitian matrix, 325
Hessenberg form, 502
characteristic polynomial, 511, 542
computational considerations, 508
eigenvalues and, 510
Householder reduction, 522
matrix, 503
reduced, 511
reduction to, 503
subdiagonal, 503
unreduced, 511
Hilbert matrix, 101
Homogeneous systems, 31
nontrivial, 31
trivial, 31
zero solution, 31
Householder matrix, 519
construction of, 523
multiplication by, 520
Hyperboloid, 491

Idempotent matrix, 108, 314
Identity matrix, 65
Identity transformation, 230, 405
Ill-conditioned matrix, 101
Imaginary numbers, 316
Inconsistent systems, 6, 19
Indefinite quadratic form, 487
Initial point, 115
Initial value problems, 83, 495
Inner product, 393
Inner product space, 392
Integer inverses, 481
Integer matrices, 481
Integers, 26
Interpolating polynomial, 81, 272
Inverse
calculating, 95
existence of, 94
matrix, 92
properties of matrix, 99
Inverse,
linear transformations, 414
matrix representation, 419
Invertible linear transformations, 413
Isomorphic, 416

Kernel
linear transformation and, 405
of a matrix, 179
Krylov's method, 511

Law of Cosines, 135
Least–squares
approximation, 256, 397, 531
criterion, 246
general fits and, 250
inconsistent systems and, 260, 531
linear fit, 247
normal equations, 245
polynomial fit, 272
solution, 531
theory and practice of, 255
using MATLAB to find, 248
Legendre polynomials, 402
Length of a vector, 67, 124
Linear combination, 49, 71, 370
Linear
equation, 2
solution, 2
Linear independence and dependence, 73
Linear transformations, 225, 403
composition, 412
contraction, 230
definition of, 226
diagonalization, 431
dilation, 230
eigenvalue, 432
examples of, 227
identity, 230, 405
inverse, 414
invertible, 413
isomorphism, 416
matrix of, 230
matrix representation, 419
null space (kernel), 233, 405
nullity, 234, 406
one to one, 406
onto, 413
orthogonal, 235
range, 233, 405
rank, 234, 406
reflection, 237
rotation, 236
scalar multiplication, 411
sum, 411
zero, 230, 405
Lines
equation of, 149
parametric equations for, 149
segments, 151
in space, 148
vector form of, 149

Markov chains, 338, 345, 354
MATLAB, 24
basic operations, AP1
command window/line, AP1
elementary row operations, matrix surgery, AP5
entering matrices, AP2
graphing in two dimensions, AP6
matrix operations, AP8
M-files, scripts and functions, AP10
numerical routines in, AP10
RREF command, AP3

short/rat/long/numeric formats, AP2
transpose, norm, and inverse, AP8
zeros, ones, eye, and Rand, AP9
Matrix, 6
addition, 47
adjoint, 473
augmented, 7
block, 353
coefficient, 7
column form, 54–56
column space, 182
defective, 310, 547
diagonalizable, 327
echelon form, 14
elementary, 476
equality, 46
Gram, 444
Hermitian, 325
Hessenberg, 503
Hilbert, 101
Householder, 519
idempotent, 108, 314
identity, 65
ill-conditioned, 101
integer, 481
inverse, 92
kernel, 179
main diagonal, 65
minor, 449
nonsingular, 76
null space of, 179
nullity, 208
orthogonal, 108, 239, 325
partitioned (block), 109
permutation, 331, 510
positive definite, 325, 401
product, 52
range, 181
rank, 208
rank deficient, 252
reduced echelon form, 15, 17
row space, 183
scalar multiplication, 47
similar, 326
singular, 76
skew symmetric, 297, 372, 479
square, 65
stochastic, 350
sum, 47
symmetric, 64
transition, 108, 346, 434
tridiagonal, 522
transpose, 63
unitary, 325
upper-trapezoidal, 532
upper-triangular, 60
Vandermonde matrix, 82
zero, 61
Matrix inverse,
computation, 97
definition, 92
determinants, 473
eigenvalues, 302
properties of, 99
in terms of adjoint, 473
two-by-two, 98
Matrix multiplication,
definition, 50
other formulations, 55
Matrix of a transformation, 230
Matrix polynomials, 540
Matrix representation of linear transformation, 419
Midpoint formula, 130
Minor matrix, 283, 449

Negative definite quadratic form, 487
Negative semidefinite quadratic form, 487
Nonsingular matrix, 76
Norm of a vector, 67, 394
Normal equations, 245, 444
Normal to a plane, 151
Normalized vector, 216
Null space, of a linear transformation, 233, 405
Nullity, of a linear transformation, 234, 406
of a matrix, 208
Numerical differentiation, 88
Numerical integration, 84

Octants, 128
Operator, 404
Ordered basis, 380
Orthogonal, basis, 214, 392, 395
constructing an, 219
linear transformation, 235
matrix, 108, 239, 325, 330
projections, 397
set, 395
vectors, 138, 140
Orthonormal basis, 216
Outer product, 69
Overdetermined systems
least-square solution, 243

Parallel planes, 156
Parallel vector, 124, 132
Parametric equations, 150
Partitioned matrix, 109
Permutation matrix, 331
Physical vector(s), 114
adding, 120
resultant force and, 120
Plane(s)
coordinate, 128
equation of, 153
normal vectors, 152
parallel, 156
scalar form for equation of, 154
vector form for equation of, 154
Polyfit, AP10
Polynomial interpolation, 80
Polyval, AP10
Population dynamics, 108
steady state, 109
transition matrix, 108
Position vector, 116, 131
Positive definite, matrix, 325, 401
Positive semidefinite quadratic form, 487
Power method, 306, 354
Principle Axis Theorem, 492
Projection of a vector, 139, 397
calculating, 139
Pseudoinverse, 262

QR Algorithm, 538
QR factorization, 531
Quadratic forms, 484
conic sections, 488
diagonalizing, 485
indefinite, 487
matrix representation, 484
negative definite (semi), 487
positive definite (semi), 487
quadric surfaces, 488
Quadric surface, 36, 488

Range,
of a linear transformation, 181, 233, 405
of a matrix, 181
Rank,
of a linear transformation, 234, 406
of a matrix, 208
Rank deficient, 252, 262
Rational function, 273
Rayleigh quotient, 352, 493
Real vector space, 362
Reduced echelon form, 16, 19
Reflection, 237
Relative error, 111
Residual vector, 243
Right-hand rule, 128, 143
Rotation, 236
Row equivalent matrices, 10
Row space of a matrix, 183

Same direction vector, 124
Scalar, 8, 46, 361
form for equation of plane, 154

Scalar multiplication
linear transformation and, 411
of a matrix, 47
of a vector, 122
Scalar product, 50
Scalar quantities, 114
Schur decomposition
(factorization), 333
Sherman–Woodberry formula, 104
Similar matrices, 326
Sine integral, 446
Singular matrix, 76
determinants, 287, 481
eigenvalues of, 303
Skew symmetric matrix, 297, 372, 479
Solution sets
geometric interpretations of, 4
Solution sets for consistent linear
systems, 28
Spanning set, 176, 189, 370
Spectral decomposition, symmetric
matrix, 336
Square matrix, 65
main diagonal, 65
State vectors, 60, 108
Stochastic matrix, 350
Subspace, 168, 368
bases for, 185, 195
column space of a matrix, 182
dimension, 202
kernel of transformation, 405
null space of a matrix, 179
null space of a transformation,
233, 405
orthogonal bases for, 216
properties of p-dimensional, 207
of R^n, 168
range of a matrix, 181
range of a transformation, 233, 405
row space of a matrix, 183
spanning set, 176, 190
verifying subsets as, 171
Symmetric matrix, 64
diagonalizable, 333
Systems of differential equations,
347, 546
complex solutions, 498
diagonalization and, 496
Systems of linear equations, 2
consistent, 6, 28
Cramer's rule, 281, 469
equivalent, 8
homogeneous, 31
inconsistent, 6, 19
least-squares solution, 243, 533
matrix equation, 54
solution, 2

Terminal point, 115
Transition matrix, 108, 346, 434
Transpose of a matrix, 63
determinant, 290, 471
eigenvalue, 305
properties, 63
Trapezoidal form
reduction to, 531
Triangular matrix
determinant, 287, 453
eigenvalues, 303
upper, 60
Tridiagonal matrix, 522
Triple products, 145
scalar, 145
vector, 145

Unit vector, 74, 125, 132
Unitary matrix, 325
Upper-trapezoidal matrix, 532

Vandermonde matrix, 82, 297
Vector. *See also* algebraic vectors
Vector. *See also* geometric vectors
Vector. *See also* physical vectors
Vector space, 164, 360
additive identity, 362
additive inverse, 362
basis, 377
$C[a, b]$, 364
cancellation laws, 365
dimension, 388
infinite dimensional, 388
inner product, 392–393
isomorphic, 416
ordered basis, 380
p-dimensional, 389
properties, 365
properties of R^n, 167
real, 362
zero, 366
Vector(s)
basic i and j, 125
complex, 316
conjugate, 318
coordinate, 379
distance between, 256
Euclidean length (norm), 68
form for general solution, 48
form for plane equation, 153
length, 124
linear combination of, 370
linear independence and
dependence, 73, 375
magnitude, 124
n-dimensional, 48
norm, 68
normal, 152
normalized, 216
opposite direction, 124
parallel, 124
projections of, 138, 397
quantity, 114
residual, 243
same direction, 124
state, 60, 108
unit, 74
zero, 72, 362

Weight functions, 444
Weighted sum, 449
Wheatstone bridge, 46
Wronskian, 471

Zero matrix, 61
Zero transformation, 230, 405
Zero vector, 72, 362
Zero vector space, 362, 366